Business Cycles and Depressions

GARLAND REFERENCE LIBRARY OF SOCIAL SCIENCE (VOL. 505)

Business Cycles and Depressions
An Encyclopedia

Editor

David Glasner
Federal Trade Commission

Consulting Editors

Thomas F. Cooley
University of Rochester

Barry Eichengreen
University of California at Berkeley

Harald Hagemann
University of Hohenheim

Philip A. Klein
Pennsylvania State University

Roger Kormendi
University of Michigan

David Laidler
University of Western Ontario

Phillip Mirowski
University of Notre Dame

Edward Nell
New School for Social Research

Lionello F. Punzo
University of Siena

Anna J. Schwartz
National Bureau of Economic Research

Alesandro Vercelli
University of Siena

Victor Zarnowitz
Center for International Business-Cycle Research, Columbia University

GARLAND PUBLISHING, INC.
New York & London
1997

Library of Congress Cataloging-in-Publication Data

Business cycles and depressions : an encyclopedia / editor, David Glasner ;
     consulting editors, Thomas F. Cooley . . . [et al.].
             p.   cm. — (Garland reference library of social science ;
     vol. 505)
     Includes bibliographical references and index.
     ISBN 0-8240-0944-4 (acid-free paper)
     1. Business cycles—Encyclopedias.   2. Depressions—Encyclopedias.
I. Glasner, David.   II. Cooley, Thomas F.   III. Series: Garland reference
library of social science ; v. 505.
     HB3711.B936   1997
     338.5'42'03—dc20   96-18457
                                                                                    CIP

Cover art supplied by Tony Stone. Photographer, Lonnie Duka.
Cover design: Lawrence Wolfson Design, New York.

Printed on acid-free, 250-year-life paper
Manufactured in the United States of America

Contents

vii   Introduction

ix   Contributors

3   The Encyclopedia

729   Appendix

739   Author Index

757   Subject Index

Introduction

This volume has been designed to aid students, scholars, and laymen interested in learning about a range of topics related to business cycles and depressions. It includes articles on theories of business cycles, recessions, depressions, financial panics, and crises as well as on the theoretical concepts related to those phenomena, on statistical techniques used to study them, and on specific historical events or episodes such as the Great Depression or the crisis of 1873. It also contains biographical articles on important contributors to the study of business cycles and related phenomena.

The study of business cycles and financial panics and crises is not a field of study clearly demarcated from others in economics. Historically, the development of business-cycle theory or, more generally, of theories of aggregate economic fluctuations, was closely related to the development of monetary theory. More recently, the study of business cycles was largely eclipsed by the development of macroeconomics during the Keynesian Revolution and its aftermath. Whereas business-cycle theories involved, at least implicitly, some sort of dynamic model, early macroeconomic models and many formal monetary models were models of static equilibrium. Although it was possible to introduce dynamic elements into macroeconomic models, much of macroeconomic theory was formulated in a static or a comparative-statics framework. Given the lack of any precise boundaries between the domain of business-cycle analysis and those of monetary analysis and macroeconomic analysis and the overlap between analytical and statistical tools used in business-cycle research and in other branches of economics, the choice of topics to include or exclude may appear arbitrary in certain instances. In any event, when discussing topics that may not be generically related to business-cycle research, contributors have endeavored to draw out the relationships between those topics and the concerns of those engaged in business-cycle research, broadly understood.

Although static macroeconomic or static monetary models are not necessarily uninteresting from the perspective of business-cycle theory, this volume is generally not concerned with such models. Similarly, the choice of theoreticians or researchers to be included in this volume has been dictated largely by whether the individual made substantial contributions to the study of cyclical or dynamic phenomena as opposed to static theory. These decisions often depended on subjective assessments of the importance and relevance of a given individual's contributions to the general study of business cycles and economic fluctuations. But obviously the absence of entries in this volume on such figures as Léon Walras, Carl Menger, P. H. Wicksteed, and James Meade reflects no judgment about their contributions to economics in general. A second, more formal, criterion for the choice of researchers about whom to write articles was that they not be born after 1920.

A few words about the citation practices adopted in this volume may be in order. To make the articles more accessible, I have tried to discourage excessive citations to the literature. Thus, many assertions for which a citation might be provided in a journal article have been left without citation in the articles in this volume. However, sources for any significant quotations, important facts, or controversial propositions are provided. This is usually done, in accord with current practice, by citing the author and the year of publication of the work cited. When the work cited is otherwise unrelated to the topic of the article, the full source of the quotation may be given in the text rather than in the bibliography.

I have tried to make the citations as uniform as possible throughout the volume, so that where multiple editions of a particular work appear, the same edition is cited across all articles, e.g., the fourth edition of Haberler's *Prosperity and Depression* (1962) is generally cited whenever that work is referred to. When reprints, modern editions, or translations are cited, the date of original publication (in brackets) and the date of the particular edition cited are included within the parentheses following the author's name, e.g., Smith's *Wealth of Nations* is cited as Smith ([1776] 1976) and Wicksell's *Interest and Prices* is cited as Wicksell ([1898] 1936). I have also tried, where possible, to provide references to more recent republications of older journal articles that often may no longer be easily accessible. For example, the reference to Samuelson's famous 1939 article on multiplier-accelerator interaction is to volume 2 of his *Collected Scientific Writings* rather than to the *Review of Economic Statistics* and is cited as Samuelson ([1939] 1966).

Finally, I have asked contributors to include in their bibliographies not only works actually cited within their articles but also other works that a reader interested in doing further research on the topic would want to consult. The bibliographies make no distinction between works referred to in the text and works included simply for their interest to one wishing to do further research on the topic. But the distinction will be clear to any careful reader.

I was assisted from the very outset by a group of contributing editors who provided wise advice and counsel to me, particularly in the early process of selecting topics to be included and in finding authors to contribute articles. The process has been long and arduous, and without the generous assistance of my editors at crucial stages, the project would never have been completed. I particularly would like to thank Anna Schwartz, David Laidler, Tom Cooley, Phil Mirowski, Edward Nell, and Victor Zarnowitz for allowing me to make inordinate demands on their time during the long process of planning and editing this volume. Finally, my deepest thanks go to Tovi, Chaya, and Shifra without whose love and patience this project would not have been possible.

Contributors

Jalal Uddin Ahmad
American Express

Alain Alcouffe
University of Toulouse

Gerhard Michael Ambrosi
University of Trier

Arie Arnon
Ben-Gurion University
of the Negev

Athanasios Asimakopulos
(deceased)
McGill University

Nahid Aslanbeigui
Monmouth College

Martin J. Bailey
Emory University

Daniel Barbezat
Amherst College

William A. Barnett
Washington University

James R. Barth
Auburn University

Lisa Barrow
Princeton University

William J. Baumol
Princeton University

Jess Benhabib
New York University

Dianne C. Betts
Southern Methodist University

Mark Bils
University of Rochester

Ronald G. Bodkin
University of Ottawa

Michael D. Bordo
Rutgers University

John F. Boschen
College of William and Mary

Michael D. Bradley
George Washington University

Hans Brems
University of Illinois at Urbana-Champaign

E. Carey Brown
Massachusetts Institute of Technology

James Bullard
Federal Reserve Bank of St. Louis

Forrest H. Capie
City University Business School

Julia Campos
University of Salamanca

Thomas F. Cargill
University of Nevada at Reno

John A. Carlson
Purdue University

Dennis W. Carlton
University of Chicago

Will J. Carrington
Johns Hopkins University

Stephen G. Cecchetti
Ohio State University

Alpha C. Chiang
University of Connecticut

Attila Chikán
Budapest University of Economics

K. Alec Chrystal
City University Business School

David Colander
Middlebury College

Tyler Cowen
George Mason University

Roger Craine
University of California at Berkeley

William Darrity Jr.
University of North Carolina

Pierre Dehez
Erasmus University

Patrick Deutscher
Department of Treasury,
Government of Ontario

David G. Dickinson
University of Birmingham

Patricia Dillon
Scripps College

Robert W. Dimand
Brock University

John B. Donaldson
Columbia University

Mohammed I. H. Dore
Brock University

Michael Dotsey
Federal Reserve Bank
of Richmond

Kevin Dowd
Sheffield Hallam University

Gilbert Ducos
University of Toulouse

Andrzej Dudzinski
University of Toulouse

Jacob J. van Duijn
Robeco Group

Robert Eisner
Northwestern University

Neil R. Ericsson
Federal Reserve Board

Jon Faust
Federal Reserve Board

Steven M. Fazzari
Washington University

John F. Feid
Federal Housing Finance Board

G.R. Feiwel
University of Tennessee

Piero Ferri
University of Bergamo

Mark D. Flood
Concordia University

Evelyn L. Forget
University of Manitoba

Günter Gabisch
University of Göttingen

Giancarlo Gandolfo
University of Rome

James H. Gapinski
Florida State University

Peter M. Garber
Brown University

Roger W. Garrison
Auburn University

Frank C. Genovese
Babson College

David Glasner
Federal Trade Commission

C. A. E. Goodhart
London School of Economics

Gary Gorton
University of Pennsylvania

Jo Anna Gray
University of Oregon

Richard S. Grossman
Wesleyan University

Harald Hagemann
University of Hohenheim

Joseph Halevi
University of Sydney

Thomas E. Hall
Miami University

David Hamilton
University of New Mexico

James D. Hamilton
University of California at San Diego

Omar F. Hamouda
York University

Gikas A. Hardouvelis
Rutgers University

Peter R. Hartley
Rice University

Andrew Harvey
London School of Economics

Michael Haupert
University of Wisconsin
at La Crosse

Pierre-Cyrille Hautcoeur
Ecole Normal Superieure

Thomas Havrilesky
(deceased)
Duke University

Gunnar Heinsohn
University of Bremen

David F. Hendry
Nuffield College, Oxford

Rolf G. H. Henriksson
University of Stockholm

Robert Stanley Herren
North Dakota State University

Philip M. Holleran
Hampden-Sydney College

Kevin D. Hoover
University of California at Davis

George Horwich
Purdue University

M. C. Howard
University of Waterloo

Peter Howitt
University of Western Ontario

Michael Hudson
University of Leeds

Thomas M. Humphrey
Federal Reserve Bank of Richmond

Harold James
Princeton University

Bob Jessop
Lancaster University

Andrew John
University of Virginia

Lars Jonung
Stockholm School of Economics

Vibha Kapuria-Foreman
Colorado College

Heejoon Kang
Indiana University

Robert E. Keleher
G7 Council

J. E. King
La Trobe University

Arjo Klamer
George Washington
University

Allan W. Kleidon
Stanford University

Judy L. Klein
Mary Baldwin College

Philip A. Klein
Pennsylvania State University

Thomas J. Kniesner
Indiana University

Meir Kohn
Dartmouth College

Manfred Kraft
University of Paderborn

Randall Kroszner
University of Chicago

Heinz D. Kurz
University of Graz

David Laibman
Brooklyn College

David Laidler
University of Western Ontario

Michael Syron Lawlor
Wake Forest University

Richard G. Lipsey
Simon Fraser University

Hans-Walter Lorenz
University of Göttingen

Thomas A. McGahagan
University of Pittsburgh
at Johnstown

Jaime Marquez
Federal Reserve Board

Kanta Marwah
Carlton University

Massimo Di Matteo
University of Siena

Alfredo Medio
University of Venice

Rajnish Mehra
University of California
at Santa Barbara

Perry Mehrling
Barnard College

Ghanshyam Mehta
University of Queensland

Michael Melvin
Arizona State University

Piero V. Mini
Bryant College

Jeffrey A. Miron
Boston University

Philip M. Mirowski
University of Notre Dame

Frederic S. Mishkin
Columbia University

Geoffrey H. Moore
Center for International Business-Cycle
Research, Columbia University

Fred Moseley
Mt. Holyoke College

Laurence S. Moss
Babson College

Tracy Mott
University of Denver

Andrew Mullineux
University of Birmingham

Antoin E. Murphy
University of Dublin

Michele I. Naples
Trenton State College

James M. Nason
University of British Columbia

Philippe Nataf
University of Paris

Clark Nardinelli
U.S. Food and Drug Administration

Larry Neal
University of Illinois
at Urbana-Champaign

Michael P. Niemira
Mitsubishi Bank

Anthony Patrick O'Brien
Lehigh University

D. P. O'Brien
University of Durham

Sandra J. Peart
Baldwin-Wallace College

Mark Perlman
University of Pittsburgh

George L. Perry
Brookings Institution

Thomas A. Peters
Brock University

Wolfgang Pollan
Austrian Institute for Economic Research

Georges Prat
University of Paris

Maurizio Pugno
University of Trento

Douglas D. Purvis
(deceased)
Queens University

James B. Ramsey
New York University

Yngve Ramstad
University of Rhode Island

Hugh Rockoff
Rutgers University

Charles E. Rockwood
Florida State University

Sherwin Rosen
University of Chicago

Philip Rothman
Eastern Carolina University

Randal R. Rucker
Montana State University

Christof Rühl
University of California
at Los Angeles

Pascal Salin
University of Paris

Gary J. Santoni
Ball State University

Chera L. Sayers
University of Houston

Michael Schneider
La Trobe University

Aurel Schubert
Austrian National Bank

Eric S. Schubert
Research and Planning Consultants

Anna J. Schwartz
National Bureau
of Economic Research

Ernesto Screpanti
University of Florence

John J. Seater
North Carolina State University

Janet A. Seiz
Grinnel College

Richard T. Selden
University of Virginia

George A. Selgin
University of Georgia

Willi Semmler
New School for Social Research

Apostolos Serlitis
University of Calgary

Steven M. Sheffrin
University of California at Davis

Robert J. Shiller
Yale University

Allen Sinai
Lehman Brothers

Claes-Henric Siven
University of Stockholm

Neal T. Skaggs
Illinois State University

W. Gene Smiley
Marquette University

Vernon L. Smith
University of Arizona

Alan L. Sorkin
University of Maryland,
Baltimore County

Aris Spanos
University of Cyprus

Wolfgang F. Stolper
University of Michigan

Otto Steiger
University of Bremen

Daniel A. Sumner
University of California at Davis

Vincent J. Tarascio
University of North Carolina

John A. Tatom
Union Banque Suisse

Bjorn Thalberg
Lund University

A. P. Thirlwall
University of Kent

Earl A. Thompson
University of California at Los Angeles

Richard H. Timberlake Jr.
University of Georgia

Hong-Anh Tran
Tillike and Gibbins Consultants, Ltd.

Paul B. Trescott
Southern Illinois University

Marjorie S. Turner
San Diego State University

William Veloce
Brock University

Carl E. Walsh
University of California at Santa Cruz

Vivian Walsh
Muhlenberg College

Peter Weise
University of Kassel

Andrew Weiss
Boston University

Kenneth D. West
University of Wisconsin at Madison

David C. Wheelock
Federal Reserve Bank of St. Louis

Eugene N. White
Rutgers University

Lawrence H. White
University of Georgia

Elmus Wicker
Indiana University

David W. Wilcox
Federal Reserve Board

Thomas D. Willett
Claremont Graduate School

Arlington W. Williams
Indiana University

Thomas Wilson
(retired)
University of Glasgow

Geoffrey E. Wood
City University Business School

Nancy J. Wulwick
State University of New York
at Binghamton

Linus Yamane
Pitzer College

Leland B. Yeager
Auburn University

Victor Zarnowitz
Center for International Business Cycle
Research, Columbia University

Robert B. Zevin
United States Trust Company

Business Cycles and Depressions

A

Abramovitz, Moses (1912–)

Born in New York City, Moses Abramovitz received a B.A. from Harvard in 1932 and a Ph.D. from Columbia in 1939. His main work encompasses price theory, business cycles, and the economic growth of industrialized countries.

His first major empirical effort involved the analysis of the movement of inventories and their components during changes in business activity. Abramovitz discovered that shifts in inventory investment were a significant (as well as the most volatile) element of cyclical changes in output, especially in shorter business cycles. He also found an approximate synchronism between business cycles and inventory investment, with the latter tending to lag behind the rate of change in output. Abramovitz ascribed this lag to the disparate responses of various components of inventories: goods in process, raw materials, and stocks of finished goods. He concluded that the existence of this lag between inventory investment and the rate of change of manufactured output moderated the pace and extended the duration of both expansions and contractions.

While working at the National Bureau of Economic Research, Abramovitz (1959b) charted 18–20 year swings in output, additions to labor force and capital stock, their rates of utilization, and their productivity. Building on earlier work by Kuznets, Abramovitz's explanation of these long swings, which he called "Kuznets cycles," departed from the model advanced by Kuznets himself while incorporating the efforts of numerous economists. He maintained that waves in economic growth resulted from oscillations in the supplies of labor and capital and most probably in their productivity. These waves reflect variations in the intensity of resource use and thereby cause swings in employment, investment, and the use of capital. Shifts in rates of unemployment lead to subsequent variations in population, either through immigration or through changes in marriage and birth rates. Both produce waves in the demand for housing and thereby affect the composition of capital formation.

The long-term changes in employment also cause waves in labor-force participation and systematically affect the productivity of capital and the marginal efficiency of investment. These factors could, in turn, explain patterns in the composition of capital formation and changes in demand for various types of financial assets. Further, each Kuznets cycle is accompanied by an inverse movement in the balance of payments which results from the need, under a specie standard, for gold exports or capital imports during an expansion. These flows, in turn, affect the money supply and, hence, prices.

In this schema, upward trends were prolonged by lags and backlogs. A wave of expansion would be brought to a close through the tightening of financial markets as well as by changes in input productivity. In addition, Abramovitz attributed the intermittent character of upward movements to their dependence on developments in the transport sector. He emphasized the need to finance expansions through the import of capital raised by the sale of transport bonds. Such sales were subject to the uneven increase in the potential profitability of railroads and canals (Abramovitz [1961] 1989). However, due to restrictions on migration and the expansion of government, Abramovitz ([1968] 1989) concluded that Kuznets cycles had ceased to exist after World War II in the forms known in the period from the 1830s to the Great Depression.

Abramovitz's concurrent and later work on economic growth emphasized the roles of capital formation and productivity changes in the economic growth of industrialized countries (Abramovitz [1956] 1989, [1979] 1989, [1986] 1989; Abramovitz and David 1973) as well as the relationship between economic growth and changes in welfare (Abramovitz 1959a).

Vibha Kapuria-Foreman

See also INVESTMENT; KONDRATIEFF CYCLES; KITCHIN CYCLE; KUZNETS, SIMON SMITH; LONG-WAVE THEORIES; MITCHELL, WESLEY CLAIR; THOMAS, BRINLEY

Bibliography

Abramovitz, M. 1950. *Inventories and Business Cycles.* New York: NBER.
———. [1956] 1989. "Resource and Output Trends in the U.S. since 1870." Chap. 3 in *Thinking About Growth and Other Essays.* Cambridge: Cambridge Univ. Press.
———. 1959a. "The Welfare Interpretation of Secular Trends in National Income and Product." In *The Allocation of Economic Resources,* 1–22. Stanford: Stanford Univ. Press.
———. 1959b. Statement in *Hearings on Employment, Growth and Price Levels,* 411–66. United States Congress, Joint Economic Committee. 86th Cong. 1st sess., part 2.
———. [1961] 1989. "The Nature and Significance of Kuznets Cycles." Chap. 8 in *Thinking About Growth and Other Essays.* Cambridge: Cambridge Univ. Press.
———. [1968] 1989. "The Passing of Kuznets Cycles." Chap. 9 in *Thinking About Growth and Other Essays.* Cambridge: Cambridge Univ. Press.
———. [1979] 1989. "Rapid Growth Potential and its Realization: The Experience of Capitalist Economies in the Postwar Period." Chap. 6 in *Thinking About Growth and Other Essays.* Cambridge: Cambridge Univ. Press.
———. [1986] 1989. "Catching Up, Forging Ahead, and Falling Behind." Chap. 7 in *Thinking About Growth and Other Essays.* Cambridge: Cambridge Univ. Press.
———. 1989. *Thinking About Growth and Other Essays.* Cambridge: Cambridge Univ. Press.
Abramovitz, M. and P. A. David. 1973. "Reinterpreting Economic Growth: Parables and Realities." *American Economic Review Papers and Proceedings* 63:428–39.

Acceleration Principle

The acceleration principle is a hypothesis that says that net investment, the change in the stock of capital, depends positively on the change in output. Often expressed as a linear relation, it implies that investment likely displays instability, and hence it can be both a destabilizing force in a macroeconomic system and a cause of business cycles. Nevertheless, it can be viewed as a forerunner of a more general and temperate investment schedule called the flexible accelerator or the capital-stock-adjustment principle.

Development of the acceleration principle dates back at least to the 1903 work of T. N. Carver, who, in searching for a theory of industrial depressions, noted an inherently unstable relationship between producers' goods and consumers' goods. In his view "the value of producers' goods tends to fluctuate more violently than the value of consumers' goods" (498) although he added the qualification that what counts in the relationship is the extent to which the changed valuation of consumers' goods is regarded as permanent.

In 1917, J. M. Clark advanced the discussion by asserting that "the demand for new construction or enlargement of stocks depends upon whether or not the sales of the finished product are growing" (238). That is, net investment "varies, not with the volume of the demand for the finished product, but rather with the acceleration of that demand" (253). Like Carver, Clark identified circumstances that might alter the relationship, referring to an asymmetry in the investment response. More precisely, he held that investment would rise faster than it would fall.

On theoretical grounds the acceleration principle appears to be well founded. For instance, microeconomic theory suggests that a profit-maximizing competitive firm selects capital stock K in proportion to output Q; that is,

$$K = vQ, \qquad (1)$$

where the nonnegative proportionality coefficient v may be influenced by, say, factor prices. Appealing to the calculus, but afterward retreating behind some approximations, one obtains

$$I = v\Delta Q + Q\Delta v, \qquad (2)$$

with Δ denoting change and I denoting net investment, ΔK. According to theory, therefore, investment has an acceleration component, $v\Delta Q$. It also has a substitution component, $Q\Delta v$, which captures how firms modify their input mix if factor prices change. If factor prices remain unchanged, then investment has *only* an acceleration component characterized by a constant coefficient:

$$I = v\Delta Q, \qquad (3)$$

where v is constant. This special version of the acceleration principle is known as the simple accelerator, and v is known as the *acceleration coefficient* or the *accelerator*.

Because of its mathematical convenience, the simple accelerator found its way into a number of important business-cycle models. Among the most notable is the 1939 paradigm of Paul Samuelson. Combining the simple accelerator with the multiplier process, Samuelson showed that the temporal behavior of a macrosystem depends crucially on the value of the acceleration coefficient. In particular, larger values of v induce more volatile patterns. For instance, if the marginal propensity to consume equals 0.8, a v of zero leads to unidirectional convergence, wherein the system approaches a new equilibrium without cyclical fluctuation. By contrast, a v of one produces oscillations that dampen through time while a v of 1.25 yields oscillations that exactly repeat themselves, without shrinking or growing as time advances. Furthermore, a v of three produces exploding oscillations; a v of six, nonoscillating explosion. In short, the more powerful the acceleration effect, the more unstable the system and the more pronounced the cyclical motion.

Behind the simple accelerator lies the presumption that capital is destroyed as readily as it is created—equal increments or decrements in output cause equal expansions or contractions in the capital stock. In his 1950 treatment, J. R. Hicks joined Clark in challenging that proposition and instead argued that the investment schedule takes two different forms. On an upswing of a cycle, it manifests a simple accelerator format, but on most of the downswing, it follows a nonacceleration decay sequence. In this setup cycles still occur, but the asymmetry sets a floor to the level of output.

The simple accelerator entered other cycle theories, on one occasion through the back door. In 1941 Lloyd Metzler, postulating models to explain inventory cycles, made use of a quantity called the coefficient of expectation. Relating the expected change in sales to the previous actual change, the coefficient becomes equivalent to the acceleration coefficient under select conditions. Correspondingly, Metzler's framework becomes an expanded version of Samuelson's wherein the "accelerator" can be negative. Negative values create the possibility of cobweb cycles (i.e., alternating highs and lows with nothing in between).

In 1954, A. W. Phillips considered the possibility of controlling macromovements through policy rules and in so doing threw additional light on the destabilizing nature of acceleration. Phillips introduced among other rules a proportional feedback control that may be written as

$$D = -a\Delta Q, \qquad (4)$$

where D represents some policy stimulus such as the budget deficit. Coefficient a is nonnegative, so that an increase in economy-wide output typically reduces the stimulus and conversely. Control [equation (4)], which helps to smooth business cycles, can be seen as the negative of equation (3). In other words, the simple accelerator is a negative stabilizer—a destabilizer.

A simple accelerator is naive not only because it supposes symmetry, but also because it supposes that entrepreneurs adjust the capital stock fully to any change in product demand, even one expected to be temporary. Yet in practice, temporary upswings in demand are probably met by working the existing capital stock more intensively, not by expanding the stock. What really matters for investment is not actual output, but output that entrepreneurs regard as normal, or, in Carver's terms, permanent.

The notion of permanent output leads to a generalization of the simple accelerator. Signified by Q^*, permanent output might be quantified in accordance with the 1954 contribution of L. M. Koyck as a linear function of current and past actual outputs, whose weights decline geometrically by output chronology:

$$Q^* = (1 - b)(Q + bQ_{-1} + b^2 Q_{-2} + ...). \qquad (5)$$

Constant b lies between zero and one, and Q_{-1} indicates actual output of the previous period. Q_{-2} has a similar interpretation. Restating formulation (1) as

$$K = vQ^* \qquad (6)$$

and inserting expression (5) into it yield

$$I = (1 - b)(vQ - K_{-1}), \qquad (7)$$

K_{-1} representing the capital stock at the end of the last period.

Equation (7) is called the *flexible accelerator*. That it involves flexible acceleration and that it contains the simple accelerator as a special case can be established by adding to its right-hand side zero disguised as $(1 - b)vQ_{-1} - (1 - b)vQ_{-1}$. Rearrangement soon leaves

$$I = Av\Delta Q, \qquad (8)$$

with $A = (1 - b)[1 - (K_{-1} - vQ_{-1})]/(v\Delta Q)$. Coefficient A varies over the course of a cycle, so that a given change in output has a flexible effect on investment. However, when b equals zero, Q^* reduces to Q by equation (5), K_{-1} reduces to vQ_{-1} by equation (6), and A reduces to unity. In that case, the flexible accelerator (equation 8) reduces to the simple accelerator (equation 3).

Since the flexible accelerator presumes that entrepreneurs adjust capital gradually to changing economic conditions, it implies less instability for investment and for the macrosystem than does the simple accelerator. Such diminished instability can be inferred from the coefficients of Q in equations (3) and (7). Formal consideration of that diminution appears in the 1959 work by R. C. O. Matthews.

James H. Gapinski

See also AFTALION, ALBERT; CAPITAL GOODS; CASSEL, CARL GUSTAV; INVESTMENT; METZLER, LLOYD APPLETON; PHILLIPS, ALBAN WILLIAM HOUSEGO; SAMUELSON, PAUL ANTHONY

Bibliography

Carver, T. N. 1903. "A Suggestion for a Theory of Industrial Depressions." *Quarterly Journal of Economics* 17:497–500.

Clark, J. M. [1917] 1951. "Business Acceleration and the Law of Demand: A Technical Factor in Economic Cycles." In *Readings in Business Cycle Theory*, 235–60. Philadelphia: Blakiston.

Gapinski, J. H. 1982. *Macroeconomic Theory: Statics, Dynamics, and Policy.* New York: McGraw-Hill.

Haberler, G. 1962. *Prosperity and Depression: A Theoretical Analysis of Cyclical Movements.* 4th rev. ed. Cambridge: Harvard Univ. Press.

Hicks, J. R. 1950. *A Contribution to the Theory of the Trade Cycle.* Oxford: Clarendon.

Koyck, L. M. 1954. *Distributed Lags in Investment Analysis.* Contributions to Economic Analysis, no. 4. Amsterdam: North-Holland.

Matthews, R. C. O. 1959. *The Business Cycle.* Cambridge: Cambridge Univ. Press.

Metzler, L. A. 1941. "The Nature and Stability of Inventory Cycles." *Review of Economic Statistics* 23:113–29.

Phillips, A. W. H. 1954. "Stabilisation Policy in a Closed Economy." *Economic Journal* 64:290–305.

Samuelson, P. A. [1939] 1966. "Interactions Between the Multiplier Analysis and the Principle of Acceleration." Chap. 82 in *The Collected Scientific Papers of Paul A. Samuelson.* Vol. 2. Cambridge: MIT Press.

Aftalion, Albert (1874–1956)

Albert Aftalion is best known for his discovery of the acceleration principle (1913). His analysis of the impact of a slowdown in final demand growth on capital-goods industries stressed that producers were obliged to anticipate demand due to the need to allow for time to build. His stress on the real causes of the business cycle gives his version of the accelerator a strikingly modern resonance (Henin 1989, 540).

Aftalion's *Les crises périodiques de la surproduction* shows his discomfort with both the underconsumptionism of Rodbertus and Tugan-Baranovsky and the classical interpretation of Say's Law. Aftalion's own interpretation of the cycle minimized the role of money, though admitting that rising prices tempt entrepreneurs to lengthen the period of production. He also allowed for declining national income to prolong a crisis through its impact on effective demand, though he insisted that "the cyclic fluctuations of supply remain the decisive factor" (1913, 2:351).

His works on international economics (1927b, 1937) questioned the quantity theory and purchasing-power-parity doctrines, and offered in their place two complementary alternatives: an income theory and a psychological theory.

His income theory (1927b, 164–76) stressed the dependence of aggregate demand on incomes and noted the cumulative impact of an initial increase in demand. He clearly recognized that income adjustments are more likely than price changes to reestablish international equilibrium (1937, 150–70). His failure to quantify the income theory or the multiplier effect he associated with it was in part due to his stress on psychological factors: expected income is more important than actual, the propensity to save is not subject to quantification because it is an essentially qualitative judgment by the individual of the marginal utility of money balances and consumption expenditure, and tight money policy has its prime impact not through interest rates but through its impact on the spirit of the entrepreneur (1927b, 193, 210, 245).

His work was reviewed by, and clearly influenced, Dennis Robertson; Ralph Hawtrey found the income theory of *Monnaie, prix et change* a potentially valuable tool for the analysis of short-run economic fluctuations; and Alvin Hansen felt that Keynes's *Treatise on Money* provided the desired extension of Aftalion's income theory. Michal Kalecki acknowledged a parallel to Aftalion's income theory in his formulation of a multiplier model of income determination.

Thomas A. McGahagan

See also ACCELERATION PRINCIPLE; INVESTMENT; REAL BUSINESS-CYCLE THEORIES

Bibliography

Aftalion, A. 1913. *Les crises périodiques de surproduction.* 2 vols. Paris: Rivière.
———. 1927a. "The Theory of Economic Cycles Based on the Capitalist Technique of Production." *Review of Economic Statistics* 9:165–70.
———. 1927b. *Monnaie, prix et change. Expériences récents et théorie.* Paris: Sirey.
———. 1933. "Les variations cycliques irrégulières dans les relations internationales." *Revue d'économie politique* 43:273–91.
———. 1937. *L'équilibre dans les relations économiques internationales.* Paris: Montchrestien.
Hansen, A. H. and H. Tout. 1933. "Annual Survey of Business Cycle Theory." *Econometrica* 1:119–47.
Hawtrey, R. G. 1928. Review of *Monnaie, prix et change,* by A. Aftalion. *Weltwirtschaftliches Archiv* 28:99–102.
Henin, P.-Y. 1989. "Une macroéconomie sans monnaie pour les années 90?" *Revue d'économie politique* 99:531–96.
Kalecki, M. 1935. "Essai d'une theorie du mouvement cyclique des affaires." *Revue d'économie politique* 45:1320–24.
Lhomme, J., et al. 1969. *Contributions théoriques à la memoire d'Albert Aftalion.* Paris: Cujas.
Perroux, F., et al. 1945. *L'oeuvre scientifique d'Albert Aftalion.* Paris: Montchrestien.
Robertson, D. H. 1914. Review of *Les crises périodiques de surproduction,* by A. Aftalion. *Economic Journal* 24:81–89.
Wicharz, M. 1935. *Albert Aftalions Tatsachenbild und Lehre der Wirtschaftlichen Wechsellagen.* Jena: Fischer.

A

Aggregate Supply and Demand

Aggregate supply, *AS*, and aggregate demand, *AD*, are functional relations between the general price level, *P*, and total real income or product, *y*. They constitute the standard framework of short- and intermediate-run macrotheory, as developed in most macroeconomics texts. When related graphically to underlying component markets, they are a convenient way to show the net impact on *P* and *y* of shifts in various expenditure functions and monetary, labor-market, and production variables under alternative assumptions about form and structure. Although *AD* and *AS* were originally designed for comparative-static analysis, they are readily applied to dynamic problems, including cyclical phenomena.

The schedules, usually drawn with the price level on the vertical axis, bear a superficial resemblance to the supply and demand curves of microeconomics. But the aggregate schedules are not summations of the individual microschedules. The latter depend on relative prices, whereas the former are functions of the *general* price level. The aggregate-supply schedule is derived from an aggregate production function and labor-market equilibrium and the aggregate-demand schedule is derived from the introduction of real-balance effects into the Hicksian *IS-LM* system (Hicks [1937] 1967).

IS-LM was John Hicks's brilliant generalization of the Keynesian-cross demand model in which the interest rate and price level are held constant. Constancy of these variables is plausible, however, only if the supply of or demand for money is infinitely elastic at the prevailing interest rate and the supply of output is infinitely elastic at the prevailing price level. This might be true of an economy in a deep depression in which interest rates were so low that, for given transactions costs, money (or bank reserves) and securities were perfect substitutes and, additionally, underemployment of both labor and the capital stock were so widespread that additional output would be forthcoming at constant marginal costs, but not otherwise.

Relaxing the assumption of a fixed interest rate, Hicks showed how consumption (or saving) and investment, on the one hand, and the stock of and demand for real money balances, on the other, imply independent functional relations between the rate of interest and real income. Since saving depends positively on income while investment varies inversely with the rate of interest, the interest-income relationship, IS, implied by saving-investment equilibrium, is negative. Since the demand for real balances varies positively with income and negatively with the rate of interest, a positive interest-income function, LM, results from money-market equilibrium for a given stock of real balances. The intersection of IS and LM thus determines a level of income and interest compatible simultaneously with equilibrium in both saving-investment and the money market.

The next step in deriving aggregate supply and demand was taken by Jacob Marschak (1951), who relaxed the assumption of a fixed price level. A rise in P reduces the real value of a given nominal stock of money, which, for a given demand schedule for real balances, raises the interest rate at which the money market is in equilibrium. As a result, LM, a rising schedule, shifts up and to the left (interest is on the vertical axis and income on the horizontal), intersecting IS, a declining function, at a reduced equilibrium income. The negative market-equilibrium relation between P and y so derived constitutes the AD schedule.

The relation between AD and P can be interpreted as the result of a real-balance effect in the money market: the loss of real balances due to the higher price level reduces wealth and the stock demand for securities (which is the wealth complement of the demand for money).

The attempt to unload securities raises the rate of interest and reduces the income necessary to reestablish IS-LM equilibrium. A real-balance effect in the expenditure stream, the so-called (negative) wealth-saving relation, would augment that in the money market. The rise in prices and fall in the real-balance portion of wealth reduce consumption and increase saving out of any given income. This shifts IS down and to the left, reducing the income at which IS intersects the positively sloped LM schedule. AD, with P on the vertical axis and y on the horizontal, is thus flatter than it would be if real balances affected only the money market.

AD can be extended to include government and foreign sectors. Government spending G is added to private investment I, and tax revenues T to saving S (all are real magnitudes). The equilibrium condition is now $I + G = S + T$, where S depends on disposable income $y - T$, and T itself is a positive function of y. A foreign sector can be accommodated by the model by adding exports Ex to $I + G$, and imports Im (a positive function of income) and the net capital outflow F (a negative function of r) to $S + T$. Equilibrium is defined by $I + G + Ex = S + T + Im + F$.

Aggregate supply is related to P via a labor market in which money wages are fixed or adapt less than fully to changes in the price level. An increase in P reduces the real wage and increases the quantity of labor demanded and employed. Given the production function, output also rises. The stickiness of money wages may result either from "money illusion" or from a willingness of labor to allow inflation to reduce real wages and raise employment to the full-employment level.

AD shifts to the right in response to an increase in the stock of money or in any of the expenditure functions or to a decrease in the demand for money. AS shifts to the right in response to a fall in the money wage rate or an increase in labor productivity or capacity output.

The schedules, connected diagrammatically to all of their component markets, are useful for showing the broad macroeffects of a shock, such as the oil disruptions of the 1970s (Horwich 1982). The sharply reduced world supply and increased price of oil raised the marginal cost of producing almost every component good and service of the GDP. These increased costs shifted AS up and to the left along AD. The resulting increase in P and reduction in y reduced real balances, shifted the saving schedule to the left and reduced investment, raised the real rate of interest, reduced tax revenues and increased government expenditures and the government deficit, reduced the demand for labor, and reduced the level of employment and real wages.

If only one country in the world were affected by an oil price shock, its reduced income and increased interest rate would raise its real exchange rate and, depending on underlying elasticities, its net exports and net outflow of capital or its net imports and net inflow of capital. But an oil disruption is, of course, worldwide in its effects. The impact on any country's exchange rate and balance of payments can be positive, negative, or even nil depending on international linkages, including disposition of the new oil revenue.

The stability of aggregate supply/demand can be established by analyzing the behavior of the supply of and the effective demand for output in nonequilibrium situations. The early literature tended to analyze macrostability without explicitly deriving dynamic adjustment paths or considering the behavior of the price level and aggregate supply. A typical approach was to assert that if IS were upward-sloping owing to $I_y > S_y$ (where y might serve as a surrogate for the effect of expected future business conditions on investment), and if the slope of IS exceeded that of LM, the system was ipso facto unstable (Modigliani [1944] 1980, Chang and Smyth 1972). An increase in investment, for example, would raise IS and establish a lower equilibrium output with LM while simultaneously generating $I > S$ and an expansion of demand. In fact, all that can confidently be said about this model is that it is based on very special assumptions: $(IS)_y > (LM)_y$ implies that AD is upward-sloping; the failure to refer to the movement of the price level implies that P is constant at a level determined by an AS schedule that is horizontal.

A general analysis considers the whole range of possible AS schedules while explicitly deriving dynamic adjustment paths for both output and effective demand. This was done by Horwich and Hu (1981), who assumed that AS was the locus of output during adjustment periods. Since effective demand in disequilibrium tends to involve unequal levels of S and I, AD, along which $S = I$, cannot be the locus of out-of-equilibrium demand paths. Instead, effective demand reflects transfers of cash balances between portfolios and the expenditures stream in response to differences between the levels of intended saving and investment. Within this framework, the necessary condition for stability is that AD, whether rising or falling, have a smaller slope than AS—a requirement that is obviously not met when AD is rising and AS is horizontal. This stability condition holds under alternative assumptions about the nature of the supply response. The sufficiency condition entails minimum speeds of adjustment in the securities market.

The aggregate schedules can also be expressed dynamically as functions and determinants of the rate of inflation. Dornbusch and Fischer (1990), for example, derive a dynamic aggregate-demand schedule by adding a term for expected inflation to the nominal interest rate in the investment function and expressing the change in real balances in the money market as the difference between the rate of growth of nominal balances and the de facto rate of inflation. In a simplified version in which the terms for expected inflation and autonomous expenditures are dropped, the dynamic curve shifts upward in response to an increased growth of the money stock (the rate of inflation is on the vertical axis, output is on the horizontal). The curve will continue to shift upward in every period in which output rises since demand is a positive function of past output.

A dynamic aggregate supply is based on A.W. Phillips's (1958) negative relation between the rate of unemployment and the rate of change of money wages. These variables are transformed into corresponding changes in employment and prices and a term for expected inflation is added as a determinant of wages and hence prices. The result is an aggregate supply that depends positively on expected inflation and the difference between current and full-employment output. The entire schedule shifts upward or downward when current output exceeds or falls below the full-employment level.

The intersections of the shifting schedules trace dynamic paths in response to supply-side or demand-side shocks. Disinflationary monetary policy, for example, shifts both the dynamic demand and dynamic supply curves downward, but supply by a lesser amount. The resulting path is initially southwest toward both lower (but positive) inflation and lower output. Eventually, as supply-side inflationary expectations subside, the recession ends and the path veers southeast toward still lower inflation and full-employment output.

Thus extending the fundamental Keynesian relationships to an open economy and dynamic expectations, aggregate supply and demand continue to provide a useful framework for macroanalysis in general and for the analysis of business cycles and economic crises in particular.

George Horwich

See also HICKS, JOHN RICHARD; KEYNES, JOHN MAYNARD; LANGE, OSKAR; LOANABLE-FUNDS DOCTRINE; PIGOU EFFECT; ROBERTSON, DENNIS HOLME; SUPPLY SHOCKS

Bibliography

Chang, W. W. and D. J. Smyth. 1972. "The Stability and Instability of *IS-LM* Equilibrium." *Oxford Economic Papers* 24:372–84.

Dornbusch, R. and S. Fischer. 1990. *Macroeconomics*, 5th ed. New York: McGraw-Hill.

Hicks, J. R. [1937] 1967. "Mr. Keynes and the 'Classics': A Suggested Interpretation." Chap. 7 in *Critical Essays in Monetary Theory.* Oxford: Clarendon Press.

Horwich, G. 1982. "Government Contingency Planning for Petroleum-Supply Interruptions: A Macroperspective." In *Policies for Coping with Oil-Supply Disruptions,* edited by G. Horwich and E. J. Mitchell, 53–65. Washington: American Enterprise Institute.

Horwich, G. and S. C. Hu. 1981. "The Stability of Macro Models." In *Essays in Contemporary Fields of Economics,* edited by G. Horwich and J. P. Quirk, 242–73. West Lafayette, Ind.: Purdue Univ. Press.

Marschak, J. 1951. *Income, Employment, and the Price Level.* New York: A. M. Kelley.

Modigliani, F. [1944] 1980. "Liquidity Preference and the Theory of Interest and Money." Chap. 2 in *The Collected Papers of Franco Modigliani.* Vol. 1. Cambridge: MIT Press.

Phillips, A.W. 1958. "The Relation between Unemployment and the Rate of Change of Money Wage Rates in the United Kingdom, 1861–1957." *Economica* 25: 283–99.

Agriculture and Business Cycles

The study of how events in the agricultural sector affect business cycles has a long history in economics, dating from times when the agricultural sector was large enough to make impossible any analysis of aggregate economic activity that ignored the role of agriculture. Those days are long past in developed countries. Recent studies typically consider how aggregate economic variables affect economic conditions in agriculture and ignore the influences of agriculture on the macroeconomy.

The relative size of the agricultural sector largely determines how much fluctuations in this sector affect general business conditions. In 1990, farm output comprised just under 2 percent of gross national product (GNP) and less than 3 percent of employment in the United States. This compares to 24 percent of GNP and 39 percent of employment in 1890. If one includes as part of the agricultural sector the food and fiber processing and marketing system and the agricultural input industry then "agriculture" now accounts for up to 15 percent of GNP and employment. In the past, farms supplied most of their own inputs and processed and marketed much of their own output.

Whereas it may once have been reasonable to view the U.S. agricultural sector as separate from the general economy, farming is now highly integrated with the rest of the economy. Half of all farmers work off the farm. Most of these farm on a strictly part-time basis, purchasing most of their inputs and marketing most of their output off the farm. Thus, not only is the farm sector too small to have much effect on the general business cycle, it is too fully integrated with the rest of the economy to be treated as a special factor in causing business cycles.

In the nineteenth century, the British economy experienced commercial crises in 1810–12, 1816, 1825, 1836–39, 1847, 1857, 1866, and 1878. The American economy endured substantial downturns in 1818–19, 1839–43, 1857, 1873, 1884, and 1893. Given the importance of agriculture during that period, hard times on the farm often coincided with hard times in the U.S. economy as a whole. There is agreement, for example, that an important cause of the collapse of 1818–19, the depression of 1839, and the panic of 1857 was adverse conditions in agriculture.

Nineteenth-century analysts searched for regularities in general business fluctuations and pondered their causes. Several considered the relationships among meteorological factors, agricultural output, prices, and general business fluctuations. W. S. Jevons, a leading figure in this group, advanced a theory of business cycles running from sunspots to agricultural output levels to general business activity. Theories attributing business cycles to fluctuations in agricultural output and prices continued to be developed until the early 1930s (e.g., by Moore and Anderson). Moore (1914, 135) claimed to have discovered the law and cause of economic cycles: "The law of the cycles of rainfall is the law of the cycles of the crops and the law of Economic Cycles."

After the Great Depression of the 1930s—a depression that was not attributed to agricultural fluctuations—most business-cycle theorists either ignored or gave limited consideration to the role of the agricultural sector. J. M. Clark (1935) and W. C. Mitchell (1927), for example, suggested that although agricultural factors doubtless played an important role in some general business cycles, these factors were not an important cause in all crises. Examining the relationship between business fluctuations and agriculture, T. W. Schultz (1945) argued that macroeconomic conditions are a key determinant of conditions in the agricultural economy and ignored the effects of agriculture on the general economy.

In the two decades following the wartime agricultural boom, the farm sector underwent widespread adjustment as steadily rising productivity and declining prices forced the farm labor force to contract. The general business cycle did not have major impacts on the farm sector in either the 1950s or the 1960s.

The last twenty years have been turbulent in agriculture, but the periods of boom and bust have, if anything, run counter to the business cycle in the rest of the economy. The 1970s were characterized by expanding trade, high real commodity prices and rising real land prices. The farm economy prospered during the severe recession of 1981 and 1982. Shortly afterwards, however, farm exports dropped, market prices for major crops fell dramatically, and severe financial distress became widespread. Prices for farmland stopped rising and began their only sustained decline in recent history. These problems persisted during a long economic expansion. It was not until the drought of 1988 that this agricultural recession ended. The worldwide recession of 1981–82, with its increased dollar exchange rates and real interest rates and sluggish growth in less developed countries, may have initiated this farm recession. But the general business cycle was not a central factor in its continuation. Further, due to agriculture's small share of total GNP, severe problems in agriculture had only minor or local effects on the rest of the economy.

A significant recent literature examines how macroeconomic factors affect agriculture. Although this literature typically does not examine the effects of the general business cycle per se on the agricultural sector, it does examine the effects on agriculture of particular macroeconomic factors that doubtless play important roles in general business cycles. Important contributions have been made by Feldstein (1980), Frankel (1984, 1986), and Rausser et al. (1986). A major issue in this literature is how flexible are agricultural commodity prices compared to other prices in the economy—if agricultural prices are more flexible, then business-cycle shocks (changes in exchange rates, inflation, and the level of aggregate demand) may cause relatively severe reactions in the farm economy because of overshooting in commodity prices.

Although the farm economy currently constitutes a very small share of aggregate economic activity, the drought of 1988 demonstrated that shocks in farm output may still cause significant perturbations in measured economic growth. The 1988 drought reduced the aggregate crop output of the farm sector by 15 percent from the previous year. This reduction caused the measured rate of aggregate real economic growth for all of 1988 to fall 0.25 percentage points below what would otherwise have obtained. For the fourth quarter of 1988, the drought caused a 1.1 percentage point reduction in aggregate growth (from 3.5 to 2.4 percent). Under current accounting methods for measuring seasonally adjusted national income, all of the lost output growth attributed to the drought was recovered in the first quarter of 1989. The Commerce Department attributed 2.2 percentage points of the measured 3.7 percent increase in GNP growth in the first quarter of 1989 to return to normal crop conditions. The underlying real growth therefore was only a weak 1.5 percent. It is noteworthy that reports from the Department of Commerce in 1988 and 1989 attempted to isolate the direct effects of the drought from other factors affecting GNP movements to avoid confusion between the temporary weather shocks and longer term movements in economic growth or general business-cycle patterns.

Randal R. Rucker
Daniel A. Sumner

See also DEMAND FOR CURRENCY; JEVONS, WILLIAM STANLEY; MITCHELL, WESLEY CLAIR; MOORE, HENRY LUDWELL; SEASONAL FLUCTUATIONS AND FINANCIAL CRISES; SUNSPOT THEORIES OF FLUCTUATIONS; SUPPLY SHOCKS

Bibliography

Anderson, M. D. 1931. "An Agricultural Theory of Business Cycles." *American Economic Review* 16:427–49.

Clark, J. M. 1935. *Strategic Factors in Business Cycles*. New York: NBER.

Feldstein, M. 1980. "Inflation, Portfolio Choice, and the Prices of Land and Corporate Stock." *American Journal of Agricultural Economics* 62:910–16.

Frankel, J. A. 1984. "Commodity Prices and Money: Lessons from International Finance." *American Journal of Agricultural Economics* 66:560–66.

———. 1986. "Expectations and Commodity Price Dynamics: The Overshooting Model." *American Journal of Agricultural Economics* 68:344–48.

Jevons, W. S. 1884. *Investigations in Currency and Finance*. London: Macmillan.

Mitchell, W. C. 1927. *Business Cycles: The Problem and Its Setting*. New York: NBER.

Moore, H. L. 1914. *Economic Cycles: Their Law and Cause*. New York: Macmillan.

———. 1923. *Generating Economic Cycles*. New York: Macmillan.

Rausser, G. C., J. A. Chalfant, H. A. Love, and K. G. Stamoulis. 1986. "Macroeconomic Linkages, Taxes, and Subsidies in the U.S. Agricultural Sector." *American Journal of Agricultural Economics* 68:399–412.

Schultz, T. W. 1945. *Agriculture in an Unstable Economy*. New York: McGraw-Hill.

Akerman, Johan Henrik (1896–1982)

Johan Henrik Akerman, Professor of Economics at the University of Lund (1943–61), studied at Stockholm, Harvard, and Lund. His dissertation (1928) at Lund was a comprehensive study of business cycles. In this study, Akerman, after an examination of earlier cycle theories, sought to develop an original contribution to cycle theory. His approach was ambitious, as he aimed at a general and simultaneous explanation of the main characteristics of both the short cycle (three to four years) and the (two or three times longer) secondary cycles. He also made great efforts to support his arguments by utilizing available statistical data.

Akerman (1928) referred to Wicksell's famous rocking-horse analogy, that if you hit a rocking-horse with a stick, the movement of the horse will be very different from that of the stick. According to Wicksell's idea, the shape and length of the observed cycles (and what Akerman described as the typical "rhythm" of economic life), are more or less strictly determined by the intrinsic structure of the economy, while irregular erratic "shocks" (i.e., technological inventions, sudden political events, etc.) which impinge on the system keep the cycles alive (and can therefore be considered the ultimate cause of the cycles). Akerman, however, attempted to modify the general Wicksellian cycle theory. He searched for a regular and repetitive factor that could explain the striking regularity of the observed cycles. He concluded that this factor or mechanism is to be found in yearly seasonal fluctuations (98, 173).

Analyzing such time series as pig-iron production with Fourier's harmonic analysis, Akerman argued that upturns and downturns of observed cycles typically start with the seasonal ups or downs. The psychological effects of the turning of a seasonal curve often precipitate a cyclical upturn or downturn, and therefore can constitute an impulse for economic agents. Thus, in addition to the stream of irregular stochastic impulses imagined by Wicksell, Akerman added impulses of a very regular kind, impulses which help to increase the regularity of cycles. A central hypothesis of Akerman's theory was, accordingly, that, as a rule, an exact number of seasonal fluctuations correspond to each primary cycle and an exact number of primary cycles to each secondary cycle.

Akerman's theory was criticized by Ragnar Frisch (1931). While finding both Akerman's approach and his efforts to build arguments on statistical data stimulating and important, Frisch criticized Akerman's modification of Wicksell's general cycle theory. The idea of a strict synchronism between shorter and longer cycles was not, Frisch maintained, convincingly established, and presented a distorted picture of economic reality directly contrary to Wicksell's rocking-horse analogy.

In the 1930s, Akerman turned to analyses of structural changes by means of fairly disaggregated models. But he retained a keen interest in business cycles, and in the 1940s he did original work on political business cycles. Struck by the apparent correlation between business cycles and the duration of different cabinets, Akerman (1947a) studied cycles in England (1855–1945), the United States (1865–1945), Germany (1871–1945), and Sweden (1866–1945). Particularly for England and the United States, he found a close relationship between economic conditions and the outcome of elections (1947a, 108). Akerman also considered the opposite question, examining, with U.S. data, the possible impact of political events on economic conditions. He concluded that between 1896 and 1944, distinct regular political short-wave cycles of four years' duration (i.e., the Presidential period) could be observed. This 48-month political-economic cycle had, he argued, been earlier mischaracterized as a 40 to 42-month Kitchin cycle. A "Kitchin wave" of this length could not be connected with seasonal variations (1947a, 115).

Akerman identified the following U.S. cycles: seasonal variations of one year, a two-year agricultural cycle, a short industrial cycle of four years (the political-economic cycle), the Juglar cycle with an average of eight years, and the final building cycle of 16–18 years. The geometric series stops at this period, according to Akerman, although there may be a secular wave connected with the length of a generation (1947a, 116).

Akerman's cardinal ideas about the significance of seasonal variations in the formation of cycles and the strict synchronization of cycles of various lengths may not have gained strong support. However, he did seminal work on the subject of political business cycles, and his lifelong writings in the area of business cycles were on the whole met with great interest.

Bjorn Thalberg

See also ELECTORAL CYCLE IN MONETARY POLICY; FRISCH, RAGNAR ANTON KITTEL; KITCHIN CYCLE; POLITICAL BUSINESS CYCLE; SEASONAL CYCLES; WICKSELL, JOHAN GUSTAV KNUT

Bibliography
Akerman, J. H. 1928. *Om det ekonomiska livets rytmik*. Stockholm: Nordiska Bokhandeln.
———. 1946. *Ekonomist skeende och politiska förändringar*. Lund: C.W.K. Gleerup.
———. 1947a. "Political Economic Cycles." *Kyklos* 1:107–17.
———. 1947b. "Ekonomi och politik. Ekonomiska konjunktur och politiska val i USA 1868–1944." *Ekonomisk Tidskrift* 40:239–54.
Frisch, R. 1931. Review of *Om det ekonomiska livets rytmik* by J. H. Akerman. *Statsvet. Tidskrift* 34:281–300.

Allais, Maurice (1911–)

Although the 1988 Nobel Memorial Prize awarded to Maurice Allais singled out Allais's work on the allocation of scarce resources, Allais has also intensively studied monetary phenomena because he believes that monetary disturbances are a source of inefficient fluctuations in economic activity. Thus, Allais's monetary theory of economic cycles is embedded in his work on economic efficiency. Allais's 1956 paper presented the fundamental hypotheses of his theory of cycles, which he has since extended in several important ways (see Allais 1989, 1992 and Drèze and Grandmont 1989 for information on Allais's contributions, life and career).

Foundations of the Theory: The General Monetary Framework

Allais's 1956 paper develops a monetary theory of cycles based on a nonlinear model. Allais considered successive periods of duration T, where T represents the "reaction time" (i.e., the average lag separating expenditure decisions). At time t, the preceding and following periods are $(t - T, t)$ and $(t, t + T)$. Economic agents are assumed to make all expenditure decisions at times $t, t + T, t + 2T, \ldots$. At time t, agents receive payments of the previous period and decide their expenditure for the following period. Receipts at time t are denoted by $TR(t)$ and expenditures planned at time t are denoted by $TD(t + T)$. By definition of desired cash balances at time t, we have:

$$TD(t + T) = TR(t) + [M(t) - M_d(t)], \qquad (1)$$

$M(t)$ and $M_d(t)$ being, respectively, the total money supply and the total desired cash balances at time t. Since the expenditure of one agent is the receipt of another, $R(t) = D(t)$, and consequently,

$$D(t + T) - D(t) = (1/T)[M(t) - M_d(t)]. \qquad (2)$$

Equation (2), the Fundamental Equation of Monetary Dynamics (FEMD), defines the change of nominal global expenditure per period as a function of actual and desired cash balances.

The FEMD depends on the money demand and supply functions. For money demand, it is assumed that

$$M_d(t) = D(t)f[u(t)], \qquad (3)$$

where f is a positive monotonically decreasing function and $u(t)$ (the "psychological rate of economic expansion") is an index of economic conditions as perceived on average by economic agents.

For the supply of money, it is assumed that

$$M(t) = g[v(t)], \qquad (4)$$

where g is a positive monotonically increasing function and $v(t)$ (the "banking psychological rate of economic expansion") is an index of economic conditions as perceived on average by the managers of the banking system.

As a first approximation, it is assumed that $u(t) = v(t) = z(t)$ and that

$$z(t) = \chi \int_{-\infty}^{t} \frac{1}{D(\Theta)} \frac{dD(\Theta)}{d\Theta} e^{-\chi(t-\Theta)} d\Theta \qquad (5)$$

where χ represents the "rate of forgetfulness" and $z(t)$ (the "rate of psychological expansion") is a weighted average of past values of the rate of change of D.

If we denote by D_e and M_e the values of D and M in a stationary equilibrium and by V_e the corresponding value of the money velocity $V = D/M$; we have $M_e = g(0)$, $D_e = g(0)/f(0)$ and $V_e = 1/f(0)$. Then, define

$$\phi(z) = \frac{f(z)}{f(0)}, \gamma(z) = \frac{g(z)}{g(0)}, d(t) = \frac{D(t)}{D_e} \qquad (6)$$

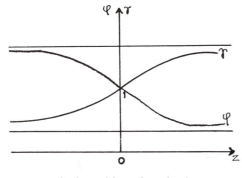

Figure 1. The demand for and supply of money functions.

where $\phi(0) = \gamma(0) = 1$. Substituting into equation (2), we obtain:

$$d(t+T) - d(t) = \frac{1}{V_e T}\big[\gamma(z(t)) - d(t)\phi(z(t))\big] \qquad (7)$$

which is an autoregressive equation, determining d at time t from previous periods. We note that the solution of equation (7) depends on the shapes of ϕ and γ (graphed in Figure 1) and on the values of T and V_e.

According to this theory, the essential variable is the global expenditure D and not the price level, because it is rising aggregate expenditure (and not the price level) which occasions profits, and thus gives rise to an optimistic appraisal of economic prospects. Thus, what is important is relative desired cash balances M_d/D, which depend on the cumulative hereditary effects of past rates of growth of D (i.e., the rate z).

Illustrations

For applied work, Allais assumes that d is proportional to national income r, so that the FEMD is unchanged if d is replaced by r. Allais illustrates the general model where t takes only integer values $(1,2,...,n,...)$. One such version is defined by the following equations:

$$r(n+1) - r(n) = \frac{1}{V_e T}\big\{\gamma[z(n)] - r(n)\phi[z(n)]\big\} \qquad (8)$$

$$z(n) = (1-k)\Big[x(n) + kx(n-2) + k^2 x(n-2) + ...\Big],$$
$$k = e^{-\chi T} \qquad (9)$$

$$x(n) = \frac{r(n) - r(n-1)}{Tr(n-1)} \qquad (10)$$

After simplifying, Allais showed that, depending on the slopes of the ϕ and γ curves, the model implies solutions in r which could be stable, unstable (tending to collapse or hyperinflation), or cyclical (tending to a stable limit cycle, as graphed in Figure 2 in the r, n space). Allais also showed that the larger T and V_e are and the smaller χ is, the larger is the period Θ of the limit cycle ($\Theta = 0$ for $T = 0$, and $\Theta = \infty$ for $\chi = 0$). Thus, the stronger is the memory of the past, the more stable is the economy.

Theory and Evidence

Using data for the United States between 1909 and 1952, Allais estimated the parameters of the ϕ and γ curves. He found that given these estimates, a necessary and sufficient condition for a limit cycle to exist is for T to be between 0.6 and 4.7 months, which seems plausible. If this con-

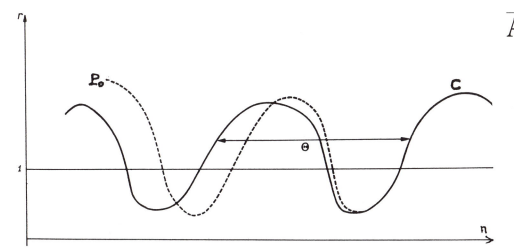

Figure 2. One limit cycle.

dition is satisfied, Θ is between 25 and 120 months, which corresponds to the empirical evidence. Furthermore, for the calculated limit cycle, changes in M lead changes in D by three months, and changes in D are twice the changes in M, which is also consistent with the empirical data.

Consequences for Economic Analysis and Political Economy

According to Allais's model, the underlying cause of the limit cycle is a dynamic relation between actual and past values of D. Indeed, the model implies that changes in global expenditure that characterize economic cycles result from the difference between the money supply M and desired cash balances M_d [equation (2)], these two variables depending in turn on past values of D [equations (3) and (4)]. Thus, in any period, D is determined by its past values.

It should be noted that if M were constant, no cycle would be possible, so economic cycles must have a monetary source. This result contradicts real-business-cycle theories based on productivity shocks or other real disturbances, and Allais's theory of cycles implies that economic policy should seek to stabilize global expenditure by stabilizing the money supply.

Generalization of the Model

At the end of his 1956 article, Allais presented new hypotheses to generalize the model: (1) the reaction-time T is a decreasing function of z; (2) the rate of forgetfulness χ is an increasing function of z; (3) the money supply may take into account the increase of the monetary base generated by the government deficit (as shown

strikingly during hyperinflations); and (4) exogenous perturbations (either random or periodic) should be introduced into equation 2.

Under these additional and less restrictive hypotheses, Allais has built unpublished models characterized by three limit cycles, one stable and two unstable. This last result is important, because it suggested the existence of a stability zone for small values of z, of a stable limit cycle when z is somewhat larger, and of an explosive trend (hyperinflation or collapse) if z exceeds some critical value, as shown by Figure 3 in the r, z space. Shifts in the nature of the dynamic path could result from exogenous disturbances affecting the rate of change of total expenditure. Thus, Allais's theory of cycles seems to have anticipated Thom's catastrophe theory.

Improvements in the Endogenous Framework of the Theory

Since 1956, Allais has improved the specification of the theory by introducing new concepts which have been presented in successive publications. First, Allais (1965, 1974, 1986) derived

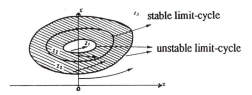

Figure 3. Three limit cycles. z_1: zone of stable equilibrium, z_2: zone of stable limit-cycle, z_3: zone of hyperinflation.

new functions for money demand and supply. These functions result from a single theory that simultaneously determines the money demand and supply and the "psychological rate of interest," which expresses the collective trade-off between the present and the future and thereby determines the general level of market interest rates. This theory (the "hereditary and relativistic formulation") is based on two new concepts without precedent in the economic literature: (1) the analogy between forgetfulness and discounting and (2) the invariance of the laws of monetary dynamics when considered in the metric of psychological time instead of physical time. Hence, money demand (f) and supply (g) functions became respectively decreasing and increasing logistic functions, the rate of forgetfulness χ became a positive function of z, and the function g now stands for the ratio M/B where B is the monetary base. Finally, specifying the psychological rate of interest (which equals χ in this new formulation) allowed Allais (1947, 1969) to link his theories of the capitalistic optimum and monetary dynamics. These further theoretical developments have yielded impressive empirical results (Allais 1965, 1969, 1974).

Second, Allais (1968, 1986) revised the FEMD to take into account the variations of the money supply M and of nonbanking debt E through a continuous-time formulation:

$$\frac{1}{D}\frac{dD}{dt} = \frac{1}{VT^2}\frac{M-M_d}{M} + \frac{1}{VT}\frac{1}{M}\frac{dM}{dT} + \frac{1}{T}\frac{E}{D}\frac{1}{E}\frac{dE}{dT} \qquad (11)$$

where V is the velocity of money. This equation is more general than equation (2) and its properties are consistent with dynamic equilibrium (i.e., the rate of change of D equals the rate of change in M). It also implies that the purchasing power created *ex nihilo* through the credit mechanism is an important cause of economic cycles (Allais 1985).

Third, Allais supposed that the reaction time T is inversely related to the rate of forgetfulness χ: T is small when economic agents forget past events quickly and large when they forget slowly (Allais 1982, 1986).

Using these new formulations, Allais (1982) showed that global expenditure may be characterized by periodic fluctuations around its trend, thus confirming and generalizing the main results of his original model.

Introduction and Specification of Exogenous Disturbances: The X-Factor and the T-Theorem

Because the purely endogenous model may only explain one period (from 35 to 55 months) but cannot reproduce the numerous quasi-periodic components of actual time series, Allais (1982, 1983, 1992) introduced exogenous effects, which he called the X-factor. Allais suggested that fluctuations in economic time series are affected by innumerable vibrations scattered through space and whose existence is nowadays obvious (atoms, light, quanta, planetary rotations, sunspots, etc.). These vibrations affect economic behavior through human psychology apart from the endogenous economic structure, but this endogenous structure modifies the exogenous vibrations to generate economic cycles through resonance effects.

Thus, after some analyses of time series, Allais (1983) described the X-factor as an almost-periodic function defined as the sum of numerous sinusoidal components whose periods are incommensurable. As a result of the Central Limit Theorem, Allais's T-Theorem shows that under very general conditions, the successive values of an almost-periodic function are asymptotically normally distributed. In addition, Allais showed that a given number of observations of an almost-periodic function may be indistinguishable from a sequence of independent terms. It follows that the deterministic vibratory structure of the universe can also generate the seemingly random effects that are observed in the world.

Simulations in the Improved Model

Incorporating the X-factor in the FEMD [equation (11)] through the improved money demand and supply functions and taking into account the potential variability of the reaction time, Allais (1982) found that the X-factor tends to impose its own periods. Moreover, even if the magnitude of a vibratory component of X is small, its influence may be significant through a resonance effect. Hence, the X-factor provides a new framework to explain the very complex temporal structures of money and expenditure.

Finally, assuming reciprocal hereditary influences between economic variables and exogenous perturbations, Allais (1986) suggests a new general interpretation of the numerous dynamic interdependencies observed in the world, and particularly of leads and lags between economic indicators.

According to Allais, purely endogenous theories of business cycles are inadequate, because they cannot explain within a general framework the magnitudes of the fluctuations, the leads and lags, and the multiplicity of the observed quasi-periodic components characterizing each variable. The search for fundamental causes of fluctuations in time series led Allais to combine an endogenous model with the X-factor which represents a set of latent variables reflecting exogeneous physical influence on time series. Only further empirical research can determine the validity of the X-factor hypothesis. But, like other elements of Allais's theory of cycles, it provides a rich agenda for further research.

Georges Prat

See also MONETARY DISEQUILIBRIUM THEORIES OF THE BUSINESS CYCLE; NONLINEAR BUSINESS-CYCLE THEORIES

Bibliography

Allais, M. 1947. *"Intérêt et monnaie."* Chap. 8 in *Economie et Intérêt.* 2 vols. Paris: Imprimerie nationale.

———. 1954. "Illustration de la théorie monétaire des cycles économiques par des modèles non linéaires." (Illustration of the monetary theory of business cycles by non-linear models.) Abstract. *Econometrica* 22:116–20.

———. 1956. "Explication des cycles économiques par un modèle non linéaire à régulation retardée." (Explanation of economic cycles by a non-linear model with lagged adjustment.) *Metroeconomica* 8:4–83 (English summary).

———. 1965. "A Restatement of the Quantity Theory." *American Economic Review* 56:1125–57

———. 1968. "Equation Fondamentale de la Dynamique Monétaire." Appendix 1 of *Monnaie et Développement.* Vol. 1. Paris: Ecole Normal Supérieur des Mines.

———. 1969. "Growth and Inflation." *Journal of Money, Credit and Banking* 1:355–426.

———. 1974. "The Psychological Rate of Interest." *Journal of Money, Credit and Banking* 6:285–331.

———. 1982. "Génération de fluctuations conjoncturelles endogènes à partir de l'équation fondamentale de la dynamique monétaire." And "Analyse des séries temporelles et facteur x—tests de périodicité." Rapport d'Activité du Centre d'Analyse Economique, Centre National de la Recherche Scientifique. Document no. C-4081, Part IV, 21–27, 31–35.

———. 1983. "Frequency, Probability, and Chance." In *Foundations of Utility and Risk Theory with Applications,* edited by B. Stigum and F. Wynstøp, 35–86. Doderecht, Netherlands: Reidel.

———. 1985. "The Credit Mechanism and its Implications." In *Arrow and the Foundations of the Theory of Economic Policy,* edited by G. R. Feiwel, 491–561. London: Macmillan.

———. 1986. "The Empirical Approaches of the Hereditary and Relativistic Theory of the Demand for Money." *Economia della Scelte Publiche* 3–83.

———. 1989. "My Life Philosophy." *The American Economist* 33:3–17.

———. 1992. "An Outline of My Main Contributions to Economic Science." In *Nobel Lectures: Economic Science,* edited by K. Göran-Mäller, 233–52. Singapore: World Scientific.

Drèze, J. H., and J. M. Grandmont. 1989. "The Nobel Memorial Prize in Economics 1988: Maurice Allais and the French Marginal School; Report on Maurice Allais' Scientific Work." *Scandinavian Journal of Economics* 91:1–46.

Amoroso, Luigi (1886–1965)

Luigi Amoroso was born in Naples in 1886. Trained as a mathematician, he began his academic career in 1908 as an assistant professor of mathematics in Rome, where he taught until 1913. In 1914 he won a chair in financial mathematics at the University of Bari; but a few years later he turned to economics, teaching at the Universities of Naples and Rome. He was a member of the Academia Nazionale dei Lincei and a fellow of the Econometric Society.

Amoroso's mathematical background led him quite naturally to analyze dynamic economic phenomena using differential and other functional equations. It is interesting to note that Amoroso's writings contain both microeconomic and macroeconomic theories of business cycles.

Amoroso's macroeconomic theory of business cycles can be found in several papers published in the late 1920s and, more systematically, in Amoroso (1932, sects. 2–3, 1935, 1949, chap. 57). He divided the economic system into three sectors: production, commerce, and banking, represented by the index of industrial and agricultural production, T, the general price level, P, and the interest rate, i. Each sector reacts to what is happening both inside itself ("own reaction") and in the other sectors ("induced reactions"). The own reactions always resist any change, as expressions of the forces (vested interests, etc.) that would be harmed by the change itself. The induced reactions are more complicated. For example, the induced reaction from the production to the commerce sector involves expectations: more precisely, the market tends to cause an increase or a decrease in prices according to whether it expects a slowing down or an acceleration in the future flow of production. Thus the reaction occurs while the action that determines it (the change in the rate of change of output) is still *in fieri*: this behavior "is the expression of an intelligent action, directed to foresee and mould the future" (1949, 373). The important thing to note is that Amoroso used what we would now call deterministic rational expectations (perfect foresight). In fact, in his mathematical formulations of his theory, if $P(t)$ is the current price level and $T(t + w)$ actual output at time $t + w$ (w a positive constant), then the induced reaction described above is given by $P(t) = -aT'(t + w)$, where a is a positive constant and T' denotes the time derivative.

By similarly describing the other reactions, Amoroso derived a set of three functional equations, which he analyzed in detail, whose solutions give rise to cycles. Amoroso showed how these equations can provide a theoretical foundation for the economic barometer, which, according to Amoroso (1949, 338) was originally conceived by Maffeo Pantaleoni, and was later reconstructed at Harvard University.

Amoroso's microeconomic theory of cycles and trend (1933, 1942, chap. 16) is based on a general-equilibrium model of supply and demand as functions of prices (including the rate of interest). Here Amoroso introduced inventories to account for the possibility of demand and supply in a period being different (reflected in the change in inventories). The change in inventories then feeds back to prices. Suppose, for example, that in the previous phase there was a huge increase in the stock of inventories that caused an output contraction. Now, if the movement of inventories reverses,

this does not cause an *immediate* increase in prices: this increase occurs after a certain amount of time, when the decrease in inventories has reached a certain level. It follows that the change in inventories does not influence the *velocity*, but the *acceleration* of prices. By formalizing these concepts, Amoroso obtained a set of integral-differential equations which he reduced to a system of n second-order differential equations. He then showed that the solution of this system gives rise to both cycles and trends. "Thus these equations contain an explanation both of the *cyclical* movement (namely of *economic crises*) and of the *secular process of depreciation of money*" (1942, 176).

In all instances Amoroso stressed that—contrary to the opinion of many authors—business cycles and crises are not due to exogenous factors, but are endogenous phenomena due to the workings of the economic system itself. And, as a believer in the free-market economy, he concluded that "economic crises constitute the price of such freedom" (1949, 385).

Although the theory of business cycles was not the main theme of Amoroso's research—thus, he did not integrate his macroeconomic and microeconomic theories of cycles into a unified whole—his contributions to the subject are worthy of consideration because of their analytical rigor and their interesting, and in some respects, pioneering, results.

Giancarlo Gandolfo

See also EXPECTATIONS; SNYDER, CARL

Bibliography
Amoroso, L. 1932. "Contributo all teoria matematica della dinamica economica." In *Nuova collana di economisti*. Vol. 5. *Dinamica economica*. Edited by G. Demaria, 421–40. Turin: UTET.
———. 1933. *La dinamica dei prezzi*. Rome: Castellani.
———. 1935. "La dynamique de la circulation." *Econometrica* 3:400–10.
———. 1942. *Meccanica economica*. Bari: Macri.
———. 1949. *Economia di mercato*. Bologna: Zuffi.
Gandolfo, G. 1987. "Luigi Amoroso." In *The New Palgrave: A Dictionary of Economics*. Vol. 1. Edited by J. Eatwell, M. Milgate, and P. Newman. London: Macmillan.

Angell, James Waterhouse (1898–1986)

James W. Angell was one of the first economists to publish historical time-series estimates of the quantity of money, to relate them to national money income, *NI*, and to focus attention on the ratio of national money income to the stock of money, *NI/M*, which he designated as the circuit velocity of money, *C*. After publication of Keynes's *General Theory*, Angell repeatedly reminded the profession that any change in the national money income could come about only through a change in money or its circuit velocity.

In *The Recovery of Germany*, Angell cited many of the elements of cyclical vulnerability that were reaching crisis proportions. He warned of painful deflation should Germany attempt to maintain the gold value of the mark even if the inflow of foreign funds were to decline.

Angell's main contributions to the literature on business fluctuations came between 1933 and 1941. In these works he consistently maintained the importance of the flow of national money income and its relation to the stock of money and its circuit velocity. He repeatedly relied on an equation in the form $MC = NI$, which improved on Irving Fisher's version of the equation in two important ways.

1. Fisher's equation, $MV + M'V' = PT$, assigned separate velocities to currency, M, and deposits, M'. Angell was one of the first economists to assemble estimates of the money supply as a combination of currency and deposits, with appropriate adjustments to eliminate double counting.
2. Fisher's equation utilized the unwieldy aggregate PT, the money value of all transactions using money, which was dominated by stock-market volume and bore little relation to the size of national income. Angell stressed the value of national-income data as measures of the demand for goods and services, using the primitive national-income estimates for the United States which began to appear in the 1920s.

In two important articles, Angell (1933a, b) presented data for the money stock, national income, and circuit velocity for the period 1909–28, which showed a remarkable stability of circuit velocity—the annual values all lying between 1.50 and 1.58. Angell was later able to extend this series back to 1899, finding even more impressive stability. He referred to this series repeatedly, but was not always consistent about its causal implications or its relevance for the 1930s.

Whatever the causality, he never wavered in recommending that over the long run, the money stock should be kept relatively stable, perhaps growing in proportion to population (provided that the economy's initial income level was satisfactory).

Angell's 1933 articles identified changes in the money supply as a major source of change in the flow of national income and expressed confidence that Federal Reserve monetary control could keep monetary changes within reasonable limits. However, as data for the 1930s became available, it was evident that the 1929–33 decline in national income involved a large drop in velocity as well as a decrease in money. Furthermore, the assumed close control by the Federal Reserve over the money supply dissolved in the face of increased excess reserves held by the banking system.

In 1935, Angell responded to the deterioration in monetary linkage by supporting the proposal to require banks to maintain 100-percent reserves for deposits. He felt that this requirement would have prevented the 1930–33 collapse of the money multiplier that occurred in response to bank failures and currency outflow and would enable the Federal Reserve to stabilize or gradually increase the money stock.

In *The Behavior of Money*, Angell examined time-series data to find patterns that would explain the ratio of currency to deposits and the impact of money on spending, output, and prices. He was not very successful, admitting that he had failed to find "a clearly defined and closely knit system of monetary and general relations" (1936, 165). He expressed doubt that monetary policy could be used to manage the macroeconomy.

In 1937, Angell argued with uncharacteristic boldness that the decline in velocity after 1929 could have been a reaction to the decrease in the money supply, suggesting that "preventing the wide declines . . . in the quantity of money, with their accompaniments of self-feeding waves of liquidation and fear, would also have checked the struggle for increased cash liquidity itself" (1937b, 57–58).

Angell thus appeared inconsistent, sometimes attributing great importance to the money supply and at other times doubting its macroeconomic influence. While he continued to monitor the relation between money and national income, and, indeed, was the first economist to estimate the regression relationship (1941a, 150–52), his emphasis increasingly shifted from monetary policy toward fiscal policy, following the trend among American economists generally.

Beginning in 1937, Angell (1937c) began to develop a theory of self-generating cyclical behavior in which investment played a central role. He believed the expected profitability of investment would tend to change in proportion to the recent rate of growth of national money income, a relationship resembling that between the multiplier and the acceleration principle. "Anticipations" of profitability would not only raise investment demand but would also tend to reduce hoarding and perhaps elicit an increase in the stock of money (implicitly assumed to have an elastic supply). Angell outlined such a model largely in verbal form in his *Investment and Business Cycles*, but it added little to the succinct and quantified multiplier-accelerator models which Samuelson ([1939] 1966) had already presented.

Angell's writings after 1936 contained numerous criticisms and extensions of Keynes's *General Theory*. He consistently pointed out that, for changes in the marginal efficiency of capital, the propensity to consume, or liquidity preference to affect aggregate demand, they must alter either the quantity of money or its velocity. By 1941, Angell's data set enabled him to observe that the circuit velocity of money, although lower than in the pre-1929 period, was relatively stable from 1933 to 1939. Thus, using the estimated marginal velocity (about 1.75), Angell (1941b) estimated the impact on national money income of a fiscal deficit financed by creating new money. He correctly noted that Keynes's multiplier analysis implied that a change in income would not induce a change in investment. The relevant magnitude was not the marginal propensity to consume, but the marginal propensity to spend, taking account of all types of spending, which, he recognized, could equal one. Angell's analysis showed that the method of financing a fiscal deficit would significantly affect its impact on national income. He was also probably the first American economist to show the relationship between monetary policy and the inflationary potential of the defense buildup.

Angell's work was marred by inconsistencies and by a verbose and turgid style. His mon-etary analysis was incomplete, notably in the lack of systematic attention to the determinants of the demand for money or the behavior of interest rates. His most notable achievement was his dogged attention to the quantity of money, even as Keynesian economics was completely disregarding it. Many of his best ideas were revived and extended in later work by Warburton and Friedman. The stable circuit velocity of broadly defined money, which Angell first identified for the period before 1929, reappeared in U.S. data beginning in the 1950s.

Angell served on the faculty of Columbia University for forty years. He was an adviser to the United States delegation to the Bretton Woods conference in 1944 and participated in drafting the charter for the World Bank.

Paul B. Trescott

See also FISHER, IRVING; FRIEDMAN, MILTON; MONETARY DISEQUILIBRIUM THEORIES OF THE BUSINESS CYCLE; MONETARY POLICY; SAMUELSON, PAUL ANTHONY

Bibliography

Angell, J. W. 1929. *The Recovery of Germany*. New Haven: Yale Univ. Press.

———. 1933a. "Monetary Prerequisites for Employment Stabilization." In *Stabilization of Employment*, edited by C. F. Roos, 206–26. Bloomington, Ind.: Principia Press.

———. 1933b. "Money, Prices and Production, Some Fundamental Concepts." *Quarterly Journal of Economics* 48:39–76.

———. 1935. "The 100 Per Cent Reserve Plan." *Quarterly Journal of Economics* 50:1–35.

———. 1936. *The Behavior of Money*. New York: McGraw-Hill.

———. 1937a. "The Components of the Circular Velocity of Money." *Quarterly Journal of Economics* 51:224–72.

———. 1937b. "The General Objectives of Monetary Policy." In *The Lessons of Monetary Experience*, edited by A. G. Gayer, 50–88. New York: Farrar and Rinehart.

———. 1937c. "The General Dynamics of Money." *Journal of Political Economy* 45:289–346.

———. 1941a. *Investment and Business Cycles*. New York: McGraw-Hill.

———. 1941b. "Taxation, Inflation, and the

Defense Programs." *Review of Economic Statistics* 23:78–82.

Lee, J. K. and D. C. Wellington. 1984. "Angell and the Stable Money Rule." *Journal of Political Economy* 92:972–78.

Samuelson, P. A. [1939] 1966. "Interactions Between the Multiplier Analysis and the Principle of Acceleration." Chap. 82 in *The Collected Scientific Papers of Paul A. Samuelson.* Vol. 2. Cambridge: MIT Press.

Trescott, P. B. 1982. "Discovery of the Money-Income Relationship in the United States, 1921–1944." *History of Political Economy* 14:65–88.

Asymmetry

Asymmetry refers to the shape of the cyclical path traced by economic time-series data. Sine and cosine waves, for example, display smooth, symmetrical upswings and downswings. Not only are business cycles much less regular than those functions, they appear to be asymmetric, inasmuch as the average upswing is longer than the average downswing.

The irregularity of the series could indicate that they are generated by a stochastic process or by the presence of nonlinearities giving rise to chaotic behavior. Asymmetry is evidence that nonlinearities are present and that linear deterministic or stochastic modeling of the business cycle is inadequate.

In the tradition of linear statistical time-series analysis, economic time series are often decomposed into seasonal, cyclical, and trend components. The combination of a positive trend and a cycle would tend to elongate the upswing relative to the downswing. In fact the rate of growth could always be positive, exceeding the trend rate in the upswing and falling below it in the downswing. Such cycles are called growth cycles. Until the major recession or depression of the early 1980s, when negative growth was recorded in a number of countries, growth cycles broadly represented the postwar experience of the major industrialized countries.

To remove the bias toward asymmetry created by the trend, which is traditionally assumed to be linear, tests for asymmetry are normally performed on deviations from an estimated trend or "detrended" data. The importance of testing for asymmetry stems from the inability of simulations with linear deterministic or stochastic models to generate systematic asymmetry. Following Ragnar Frisch,

many researchers employ stochastic linear models to represent the business cycle (Blatt 1980). Two types of cyclical paths typically emanate from such models. If they imply an explosive path, then a cycle can only occur if ceilings and floors, as postulated by Hicks (1950), are imposed. This amounts to imposing nonlinearities on an otherwise linear model. If they imply a damped path, then as Frisch assumed, the energy dissipated over time is replaced by ongoing random shocks, so that a damped process is converted into a cycle displaying considerable irregularity. In the latter case, however, no systematic asymmetry, in the sense of expansions being longer, on average, than contractions, is displayed.

Marked asymmetry in detrended data (for example, in the form of differences in the average lengths of upswings and downswings) therefore suggests the presence of nonlinearities and implies that upswings are essentially different from downswings. The presence or absence of asymmetry is, therefore, an important qualitative feature of business cycles and has major conceptual implications for modeling business cycles.

The degree of asymmetry may change over time, according to the position of the business cycle in a long wave or cycle. The ratio of the length of business-cycle upswings, measured perhaps in quarters of a year or months, to downswings might be expected to increase as the upswing of a long wave progresses and to decline during the downswing of a long wave. Therefore, systematic changes over time in the degree of asymmetry, particularly in non-detrended data, may indicate the existence of long waves. If long waves really do exist, however, then the trend is itself changing over time, and it may be inappropriate to derive "detrended" data using a linear trend.

There has been a lively empirical debate, which has come to no firm conclusion, about testing the asymmetry hypothesis. Some contributions to this debate appear in the bibliography. However, the issue has been clouded by the presumption that tests for asymmetry must use detrended data while the meaning of the trend remains ambiguous (Nelson and Plosser 1982, Neftci 1984, 1986, DeLong and Summers 1986).

Marked asymmetry between upswings and downswings indicates the presence of nonlinearity. It is not clear, however, whether the nonlinearity should be regarded as a feature of the business-cycle-generating mechanism or of the "trend" process itself. The business cycle could, in other words, be occurring around a nonlinear longer-term path, rather than, as traditionally assumed, a linear trend. The "trend" may perhaps be a long wave or its slope, perhaps in response to major technological innovations or shocks (such as world wars), and may change abruptly.

A. W. Mullineux

See also GROWTH CYCLES; TRENDS AND RANDOM WALKS; UNIT ROOT TESTS

Bibliography

Blatt, J. M. 1978. "On the Econometric Approach to Business-Cycle Analysis." *Oxford Economic Papers* 30:292–300.
———. 1980. "On the Frisch Model of Business Cycles." *Oxford Economic Papers* 32:467–79.
DeLong, J. B. and L. H. Summers. 1986. "Are Business Cycles Symmetrical?" In *The American Business Cycle: Continuity and Change,* edited by R. J. Gordon, 679–734. Chicago: Univ. of Chicago Press.
Frisch, R. [1933] 1965. "Propagation and Impulse Problems in Dynamic Economics." In *A.E.A. Readings in Business-Cycles,* 155–85. Homewood, Ill.: Irwin.
Hicks, J. R. 1950. *A Contribution to the Theory of the Trade Cycle.* Oxford: Clarendon Press.
Mullineux, A. W. 1990. *Business Cycles and Financial Crises.* Hemel Hempstead: Harvester-Wheatsheaf.
Neftci, S. N. 1984. "Are Economic Time Series Asymmetric over Business Cycles?" *Journal of Political Economy* 92:307–28.
———. 1986. "Is There a Cyclical Time Unit?" In *The National Bureau Method, International Capital Mobility and Other Essays. Carnegie-Rochester Conference Series on Public Policy.* Spring, 11–48.
Nelson, C. R. and C. I. Plosser. 1982. "Trends and Random Results in Macroeconomic Time Series: Some Evidence and Implications." *Journal of Monetary Economics* 10:139–62.

Attwood, Thomas (1783–1856)

Banker, Member of Parliament, and spokesman for the depressed industrial areas of the West-Midlands after the Napoleonic Wars, Thomas Attwood was a leading advocate of an inconvertible paper currency and critic of the gold standard. He and his associates, notably his brother Mathias—also a banker, Member of Parliament, and prolific writer on currency matters—formed what became known as the Birmingham School.

The convertibility of Bank of England notes had been suspended during the Napoleonic Wars. With Napoleon's final defeat, a deflation began in anticipation of the promised resumption of convertibility at the prewar parity. Attwood opposed resumption. In *A Letter to the Right Honourable Nicholas Vansittart,* he argued that a "scarcity of money" was causing glutted markets and general depression. He therefore proposed unlimited issues of new money until all who wished to work could find employment. Thus, Attwood explicitly elevated full employment over convertibility, and even over a more general concept of price stability, as the primary goal of economic policy.

Attwood and his associates continued to agitate against the gold standard and in favor of some sort of managed monetary system, whose precise nature they never spelled out. Though vague on specific proposals, Attwood suggested that monetary policy could be conducted through open-market operations.

On a theoretical level, Attwood argued for inflation by denying the Ricardian proposition that changes in the quantity of money would be fully offset by corresponding changes in all wages and prices. Instead, believing that inflation would promote capital formation and economic growth by transferring wealth from the unproductive to the productive classes, he articulated an early form of the forced-saving doctrine. However, he was ambiguous about the impact inflation would have on real wages.

Although his theoretical arguments, acknowledging a close relation between prices and the quantity of money, were broadly within the quantity-theory tradition, some of his writings also contained formulations of an income-expenditure approach and a multiplier effect. It is interesting that J. M. Keynes, who cited Malthus as a precursor, never even mentioned Attwood in his writings.

Attwood also proposed an activist role for the Bank of England in combating depressions. Several weeks before the crisis of December 1825, Attwood warned of the impending crisis in a letter to Lord Liverpool and advised the Bank of England to provide itself with a stock of one-pound notes—an expedient that was crucial to stemming the crisis. And in a memorandum to Sir Robert Peel, Attwood then argued that the exclusive powers the Bank of England had to issue paper currency were akin to the King's control over the mint. The Bank of England therefore had a public duty to provide an adequate supply of currency, even if it had to lend on security that its directors, from their narrow perspective as private bankers, considered inadequate.

His contemporaries and later commentators in the nineteenth and early twentieth centuries viewed Attwood as a crude inflationist and something of a monetary crank. Such condescension is evident in J. S. Mill's references to Attwood and in F. Y. Edgeworth's article on Attwood and the Birmingham School in *Palgrave's Dictionary* (1919). But subsequently, Attwood's reputation has steadily risen. Even the recent consensus among economists that there is no long-run trade-off between inflation and unemployment and the growing acceptance of some form of rational expectations is unlikely to diminish Attwood's standing as an important early contributor to the theory of economic and monetary policy.

David Glasner

See also BULLIONIST CONTROVERSIES; FORCED SAVING; MONETARY POLICY; PANIC OF 1825

Bibliography
Attwood, T. [1817] 1964. *A Letter to the Right Honourable Nicholas Vansittart, On the Creation of Money, and on its Action on National Prosperity.* Reprinted in T. Attwood, *Selected Economic Writings of Thomas Attwood.* London: London School of Economics.
———. 1964. *Selected Economic Writings of Thomas Attwood.* Edited with an introduction by F. W. Fetter. London: London School of Economics.
Checkland, S. G. 1948. "The Birmingham Economists." *Economic History Review* 2:1–19.
Corry, B. A. 1962. *Money, Saving, and Investment in English Economics 1815–1850.* London: St. Martin's.
Edgeworth, F. Y. 1919. "Thomas Attwood and the Birmingham School." In *Dictionary of Political Economy.* Vol. 1. Edited by R. H. I. Palgrave. London: Macmillan.
Wakefield, C. M. 1885. *A Life of Thomas Attwood.* London.

A

Austrian Theory of Business Cycles

Grounded in the economic theory set out in Carl Menger's *Principles of Economics* and built on the vision of a capital-using production process developed in Eugen von Böhm-Bawerk's *Capital and Interest,* the Austrian theory of business cycles remains sufficiently distinct to justify its national identification. But even in its earliest rendition in Ludwig von Mises's *Theory of Money and Credit* and in subsequent exposition and extension in F. A. Hayek's *Prices and Production,* the theory incorporated important elements from Swedish and British economics. Knut Wicksell's *Interest and Prices,* which showed how prices respond to a discrepancy between the bank rate and the real (natural) rate of interest, provided the basis for the Austrian account of the misallocation of capital during the boom. The market process that eventually reveals the intertemporal misallocation and turns the boom into bust resembles an analogous process described by the British Currency School, in which international misallocations induced by credit expansion are subsequently eliminated by changes in the terms of trade and hence in specie flows.

The Austrian theory of the business cycle emerges directly from a simple comparison of a savings-induced expansion, which is sustainable, with a credit-induced expansion, which is not. An increase in saving by households and a credit expansion orchestrated by the central bank set into motion market processes whose initial allocational effects on the economy's capital structure are similar but whose ultimate consequences are sharply different.

The general thrust of the theory, though not the full argument, can be stated in terms of the conventional macroeconomic aggregates of saving and investment. The level of investment is determined by the supply of and demand for loanable funds, as shown in Figures 1a and 1b. Supply reflects the willingness of households to save at various rates of interest; demand reflects the willingness of businesses to borrow in order to finance investment projects. Each figure represents a state of equilibrium in the loan market: the market-clearing rate of interest is i; the

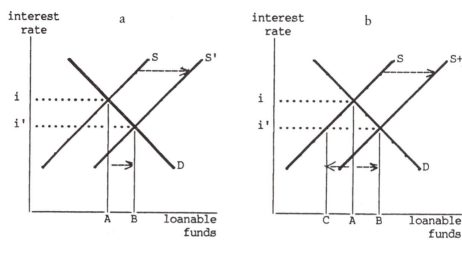

Figure 1. The supply of and demand for loanable funds; (a) increased thrift, (b) credit expansion.

amount of income saved and borrowed for investment purposes is *A*.

An increase in the supply of loanable funds, as shown in both figures, has obvious initial effects on the interest rate and on the level of investment borrowing. But the ultimate consequences differ importantly depending on whether the increased supply of loanable funds derives from increased saving by households or from increased credit creation by the central bank.

Figure 1a shows the market's reaction to increased thriftiness by households, as represented by a shift of the supply curve from *S* to *S'*. Households have become more future-oriented; they prefer to shift consumption from the present to the future. As a result of the increased availability of loanable funds, the rate of interest falls from *i* to *i'*, enticing businesses to undertake investment projects previously considered unprofitable. At the new lower market-clearing rate of interest, both saving and investment increase by the amount *AB*. This increase in the economy's productive capacity constitutes genuine growth.

Figure 1b shows the effect of an increase in credit creation brought about by the central bank, as represented by a shift of the supply curve from *S* to *S + ΔM*. Households have *not* become more thrifty or future-oriented; the central bank has simply inflated the supply of loanable funds by injecting new money into credit markets. As the market-clearing rate of interest falls from *i* to *i'*, businesses are enticed to increase investment by the amount *AB*, while genuine saving actually falls by the amount *AC*.

Padding the supply of loanable funds with new money holds the interest rate artificially low and drives a wedge between saving and investment. The low bank rate of interest has stimulated temporary—rather than sustainable—growth. The credit-induced artificial boom is inherently unsustainable and is followed inevitably by a bust, as investment falls back into line with saving.

Even in this simple loanable-funds framework, many aspects of the Austrian theory of the business cycle are evident. The *natural rate* of interest is the rate that equates saving and investment. The bank rate diverges from the natural rate as a result of credit expansion. When new money is injected into credit markets, the injection effects, which the Austrian theorists emphasize over price-level effects, take the form of too much investment. And actual investment in excess of desired saving, *CB*, constitutes what Austrian theorists call *forced saving*.

Other significant aspects of the Austrian theory of the business cycle can be identified only after the simple concept of investment reflected in Figures 1a and 1b is replaced by the Austrian vision of a multi-stage, time-consuming production process. The rate of interest governs not only the level of investment, but also the allocation of resources within the investment sector. The economy's intertemporal structure of production consists of investment sub-aggregates, which are defined in terms of their temporal relationship to the consumer goods they help to produce. Some stages of production, such as research and development and resource extraction, are temporally distant from the output of consumer goods. Other stages, such as wholesale and retail operations, are temporally close to final goods in the hands of consumers. As implied by standard calculations of discounted factor values, interest-rate sensitivity increases with the temporal distance of the investment sub-aggregate, or stage of production, from final consumption.

The interest rate governs the intertemporal pattern of resource allocation. For an economy to exhibit equilibrating tendencies over time, the intertemporal pattern of resource allocation must adjust to changes in the intertemporal pattern of consumption preferences. An increase in the rate of saving implies a change in the preferred consumption pattern such that planned consumption is shifted from the near future to the remote future. A savings-induced decrease in the rate of interest favors investment over current consumption, as shown in Figures 1a and 1b. Further—and more significant in the Austrian theory—it favors investment in more durable over less durable capital and in capital suited for temporally more remote rather than less remote stages of production. Such changes within the capital structure are necessary to shift output from the near future to the more remote future in conformity with changing intertemporal consumption preferences.

The shift of capital away from final output—and hence the shift of output towards the more remote future—can also be induced by credit creation. However, the credit-induced decrease in the rate of interest engenders a *dis*conformity between intertemporal resource usage and intertemporal consumption preferences. Market mechanisms that allocate resources within the capital structure are imperfect enough to permit substantial intertemporal disequilibria, but the market process that shifts output away from the near future when savings preferences have not changed is bound to be ill-fated. The spending pattern of income earners clashes with the production decisions that generated their income. The intertemporal mismatch between earning and spending patterns eventually turns boom into bust. More specifically, the artificially low rate of interest that triggered the boom eventually gives way to a high real rate of interest as overcommitted investors bid against one another for increasingly scarce resources. The bust, which is simply the market's recognition of the unsustainability of the boom, is followed by liquidation and capital restructuring through which production ac-

tivities are brought back into conformity with consumption preferences.

Mainstream macroeconomics bypasses all issues involving intertemporal capital structure by positing a simple inverse relationship between aggregate (net) investment and the interest rate. The investment aggregate is typically taken to be interest-inelastic in the context of short-run macroeconomic theory and interest-elastic in the context of long-run growth. Further, the very simplicity of this formulation suggests that expectations—which are formulated in the light of current and anticipated policy prescriptions—can make or break policy effectiveness. The Austrian theory recognizes that whatever the interest elasticity of the conventionally defined investment aggregate, the impact of interest-rate movements on the structure of capital is crucial to the maintenance of intertemporal equilibrium. Changes within the capital structure may be significant even when the change in net investment is not. And those structural changes can be equilibrating or disequilibrating, depending on whether they are savings-induced or credit-induced, or—more generally—depending on whether they are preference-induced or policy-induced. Further, the very complexity of the interplay between preferences and policy within a multi-stage intertemporal capital structure suggests that market participants cannot fully sort out and hedge against the effects of policy on product and factor prices.

In mainstream theory, a change in the conventionally defined investment aggregate not accommodated by an increase in saving, commonly identified as *over*-investment and represented as *CB* in Figure 1b, is often downplayed on both theoretical and empirical grounds. In Austrian theory, the possibility of over-investment is recognized, but the central concern is with the more complex and insidious *mal*investment (not represented at all in Figure 1b) which involves the intertemporal misallocation of resources within the capital structure.

Conventionally, reference cycles are marked by changes in employment and in total output. The Austrian theory suggests that the boom and bust are more meaningfully identified with intertemporal misallocations of resources within the economy's capital structure followed by liquidation and capital restructuring. Under extreme assumptions about labor mobility, an economy could undergo a policy-induced intertemporal distortion and its subsequent elimination with no change in total employment. Actual market processes, however, involve adjustments in both capital and labor markets that translate capital-market distortions into labor-market fluctuations. During the artificial boom, when workers are bid away from late stages of production into earlier stages, unemployment is low; when the boom ends, workers are simply being released, and unemployment rises.

Mainstream theory distinguishes between broadly conceived structural unemployment (a mismatch of job openings and job applicants) and cyclical unemployment (a decrease in job openings). In the Austrian view, cyclical unemployment is, at least initially, a particular kind of structural unemployment: the credit-induced restructuring of capital has created too many jobs in the early stages of production. A relatively high level of unemployment ushered in by the bust involves workers whose subsequent employment prospects depend on reversing the credit-induced capital restructuring.

The Austrian theory allows for the possibility that while malinvested capital is being liquidated and reabsorbed elsewhere in the economy's intertemporal capital structure, unemployment can increase dramatically as reduced incomes and reduced spending feed on one another. The self-aggravating contraction of economic activity was designated as a *secondary deflation* by the Austrians to distinguish it from the structural maladjustment that, in their view, is the primary problem. By contrast, mainstream theories, which ignore the intertemporal capital structure, deal exclusively with the downward spiral.

Questions of policy and institutional reform are answered differently by Austrian and mainstream economists because of the difference in focus as between intertemporal distortions and downward spirals. The Austrians, who see the intertemporal distortions as the more fundamental problem, recommend monetary reform aimed at avoiding credit-induced booms. Hard money and decentralized banking are key elements of the Austrian reform agenda. Mainstream macroeconomists take structural problems (intertemporal or otherwise) to be completely separate from the general problem of demand deficiency and the periodic problem of downward spirals of demand and income. Their policy prescriptions, which include fiscal and monetary stimulants aimed at maintaining economic expansion, are seen by the Austrians

as the primary source of intertemporal distortions of the capital structure.

Although the purging in the 1930s of capital theory from macroeconomics consigned the Austrian theory of the business cycle to a minority view, a number of economists working within the Austrian tradition continue the development of capital-based macroeconomics.

Roger W. Garrison

See also BANKING SCHOOL, CURRENCY SCHOOL, AND FREE BANKING SCHOOL; BÖHM-BAWERK, EUGEN RITTER VON; BURCHARDT, FRITZ (FRANK) ADOLPH; CAPITAL GOODS; FORCED SAVING; HAYEK, FRIEDRICH AUGUST [VON]; KALDOR, NICHOLAS; LACHMANN, LUDWIG MAURITS; LOANABLE FUNDS DOCTRINE; MISES, LUDWIG EDLER VON; MONETARY POLICY; NATURAL RATE OF INTEREST; PERIOD OF PRODUCTION; SRAFFA, PIERO; WICKSELL, JOHAN GUSTAV KNUT

Bibliography
Bellante, D. and R. W. Garrison. 1988. "Phillips Curves and Hayekian Triangles: Two Perspectives on Monetary Dynamics." *History of Political Economy* 20:207–34.
Garrison, R. W. 1984. "Time and Money: The Universals of Macroeconomic Theorizing." *Journal of Macroeconomics* 6:197–213.
———. 1986. "Hayekian Trade Cycle Theory: A Reappraisal." *Cato Journal* 6:437–53.
———. 1989. "The Austrian Theory of the Business Cycle in the Light of Modern Macroeconomics." *Review of Austrian Economics* 3:3–29.
———. 1991. "Austrian Capital Theory and the Future of Economics." In *Austrian Economics: Perspectives on the Past and Prospects for the Future,* edited by R. M. Ebeling, 303–24. Hillsdale, Mich.: Hillsdale College Press.
Hayek, F. A. 1931. *Prices and Production.* London: Routledge and Sons.
Mises, L. von. [1912] 1953. *The Theory of Money and Credit.* 2d ed. Translation. New Haven: Yale Univ. Press.
Mises, L. von et al. 1983. *The Austrian Theory of the Trade Cycle and Other Essays.* Auburn, Ala.: The Ludwig von Mises Institute.
O'Driscoll, G. P., Jr. 1977. *Economics as a Coordination Problem: The Contribu-*

tion of *Friedrich A. Hayek*. Kansas City: Sheed Andrews and McMeel.

Robbins, L. 1934. *The Great Depression.* London: Macmillan.

Rothbard, M. N. 1975. *America's Great Depression.* 3d ed. Kansas City: Sheed and Ward.

Skousen, M. 1990. *The Structure of Production.* New York: New York Univ. Press.

Ayres, Clarence Edwin (1891–1972)

C. E. Ayres was the major figure in Institutional economics, if not just before, certainly immediately after, World War II. His work in the business-cycle arena spans the pre- and post-World War II period. He was not primarily concerned with the business cycle, but saw it as one manifestation of nineteenth- and twentieth-century capitalism. His treatment was incidental to a larger cultural analysis of the industrial economy and of capitalism. And although he most certainly was highly influenced by Veblen, that influence was from Veblen's general theory of cultural economics rather than his more limited business-cycle theory.

In rejecting any rhythmical movement to economic fluctuations, Ayres contended that the notion that such a rhythm exists sprang from the preconception of more conventional theories that the economic system tended toward equilibrium. Thus, a depression was an aberration that would be offset by recovery and that the course of the economy was "gravitating" about equilibrium. Booms followed busts sequentially.

As with other Institutional analyses of economic phenomena, Ayres did not treat the business cycle as a matter of simple dislocations in an otherwise flawless market. In fact, the source of rises and collapses is an integral part of that market system. Ayres resorted to an analysis drawn in institutional, technological, and cultural processes that have a historical derivation.

His analysis of the business cycle is found in four volumes written over the period 1938–52: *The Problem of Economic Order, The Theory of Economic Progress, The Divine Right of Capital,* and *The Industrial Economy.* Only the third of these is devoted exclusively to the business cycle and even in that volume the problem is treated within a larger capitalist cultural context.

Like Veblen, Ayres contended that a tendency to deflation is endemic within capitalism.

However, his reasoning is slightly different from, though not antithetical to, Veblen's. The critical concept in Ayres's analysis is the confused meaning of capital. As has been frequently observed, the term has at least two distinct meanings: one is money capital and the other is physical instruments devoted to production. The confusion arises because it is easy from the individual standpoint to confuse the process by virtue of which ownership of the instruments of production is acquired with the creation of that which is owned. And since it is money that is essential to ownership, the saving of money is considered to be essential to technological progress. However, as in Veblen, the latter is an autochthonous process which may be affected negatively by "investment for profit" and may be permitted by it, but cannot be caused by it.

Within capitalism, savings—being held to be the source of progress—is viewed as a virtue. Hence, no matter how seemingly gross and inequitable the division of the "social dividend," it all works out to a good end for both the beneficiaries as well as those left out. Economic progress is assured and a growth in the social dividend is an automatic outcome.

However, Ayres contends that this distribution results in a surfeit of funds as well as of goods. Capitalism suffers endemically from anemic consumption expenditure. Of course, he rejects Say's Law and emphasizes that, of what we call investment, much may be bogus inflation of securities and the creation of paper unrelated to any new creation of physical assets. In doing so, he cites the Brookings Institution study of the American economy in the 1920s, and especially the volume in that study by Harold Moulton.

The lack of consumer purchasing power may be offset by military expenditure, which is almost 100-percent consumption, as well as by an excess of exports funded by the surfeit of funds by way of foreign investments, but which can never be paid off by the recipients of the largesse. He drew much from John Hobson who argued that imperialism can be understood as a by-product of efforts to enlarge a domestic market suffering from insufficient consumption expenditures.

At some length in his *Divine Right of Capital,* Ayres urged the development of a third source of income in addition to the already existing sources, labor and the ownership of property. He argued that we had, in fact, already gone some distance through welfare measures toward establishing what he referred to as independent income, meaning independent of ownership of means of production or of direct participation in the work force. In this he was making much the same argument made by William Beveridge in England, and less directly, by Alvin Hansen in this country. In Ayres the stream of independent income would be regulated in its flow on the basis of what was needed to maintain economic stability and to remedy what he saw as a basic flaw in capitalism—inadequate consumption expenditures.

David Hamilton

See also HOBSON, JOHN ATKINSON; VEBLEN, THORSTEIN

Bibliography

Ayres, C. E. 1938. *The Problem of Economic Order.* New York: Farrar and Rinehart.

———. 1944. *The Theory of Economic Progress.* Chapel Hill: Univ. of North Carolina Press.

———. 1946. *The Divine Right of Capital.* Boston: Houghton Mifflin.

———. 1952. *The Industrial Economy.* Boston: Houghton Mifflin.

Breit, W. 1979. "Clarence E. Ayres." In *International Encyclopedia of the Social Sciences.* Vol. 18. New York: Free Press.

Breit, W. and W. P. Culbertson. 1976. *Science and Ceremony: The Institutional Economics of C. E. Ayres.* Austin: Univ. of Texas Press.

Walker, D. A. 1978. "The Economic Policy Proposals of Clarence Ayres." *Southern Economic Journal* 44:616–28.

———. 1979. "The Institutionalist Economic Theories of Clarence Ayres." *Economic Inquiry* 17:519–38.

B

Bagehot, Walter (1826–1877)

The premier financial journalist of his, and perhaps any, time, Walter Bagehot was educated as a lawyer. He succeeded his father-in-law, James Wilson, the founder of *The Economist,* as editor. In this post he exercised enormous influence at home and abroad. Although unsuccessful in securing a Parliamentary seat, he was called by Gladstone "the permanent Chancellor of the Exchequer."

Representing his family's banking firm in London, Bagehot was both a participant in business and finance, and an acute observer of contemporary affairs. While concern for the popularity and finances of *The Economist* inhibited emphasis on theory, Bagehot acknowledged that theory guided him in his selections of historical criteria on which he based his opinions. His cogent and detailed descriptions of unique events reveal a coherent and well-developed theory of the trade cycle.

In his "Postulates of English Political Economy" (a part of *Economic Studies* in either collection of his works listed below) he described English political economy "as the science of business, such as business is in large productive and trading communities" (1889, 5:243). He noted its two difficulties: stating abstractions to be applicable everywhere, and looking at "one part only" of human nature. Also it bore "a special hardship: those who are conversant with its abstractions are usually without a true contact with its facts; those who are in contact with its facts have usually little sympathy with and little cognizance of its abstractions" (1889, 5:245). Particularly telling is his observation that statistics are read differently by persons in the trade to which they pertain, and by others who wrongly take them as "facts."

Malthus was "a poor hand at a dry argument" (1889, 5:359) and thus Bagehot rejected what is now considered an anticipation of the trade-cycle views of Keynes. Jevons fared better. "Some," Bagehot wrote, "hold—and I think, hold justly—that, extraordinary as it may seem . . . regular changes in the sun have much to do with the regular recurrence of difficult times in the money market" (1889, 5:248).

Bagehot questioned the assumption of the easy and ready transferability of labor. He pointed out that capital might transfer quickly in search of high profits but that this can be overdone. Profits might then languish in the field for many years. Movement may not cause an averaging of profits everywhere.

Important to Bagehot's thinking was his view of capital. He envisaged capital as "an aggregate" of two different kinds of "artificial commodities, co-operative things which help labour, and remunerative things which pay for it" (1889, 5:291). In the paper, "Cost of Production" (included in *Economic Studies*), he explicitly identified materials, land use, and power, as well as advertising, as things the capitalist must buy.

Much of his explanation of the alternation of good and bad times can be found in the famous chapter six in *Lombard Street,* "Why Lombard Street Is Often Very Dull and Sometimes Extremely Excited." But the main focus of the book was on the critical role that the Bank of England had come to occupy, how its actions affected the whole economy, particularly the solvency of the country and its financial institutions. This amounted to a delineation of the responsibilities of a central bank, its purposes, means of operation, and the need for expert management.

The Bank was to be the knowledgeable and conservative guardian and sole holder of the nation's metallic reserve. It was to issue all currency, and in any amounts needed to stave off panics and thus prevent wholesale collapses of the nation's banks. It was to vary its interest rates on accommodations to the financial system (through the bill market), sometimes to encourage expansion and, on occasion, contraction of credit. It was to be the lender of the last resort when necessary. Its interest rate, in times of crises, should be high enough to penalize the firms seeking help, encouraging them to avoid often having to seek the Bank's accommodation. Their more careful operation would lessen fluctuations in economic activity. All doubt about the Bank's capacity to issue as much currency as needed should be removed by changing the Bank Charter Act.

His discussion of business fluctuations in chapter six allowed for the exogenous events, which suddenly increased the demand for cash. Past panics had been triggered by "bad harvest," and "threat of invasion," and the "sudden failure of a great firm which everybody trusts." But he could see little point in classifying crises by such precipitating causes. "But . . . our industrial organization is liable . . . to regular internal changes . . ." (1889, 5:82). Books on political economy did not clearly explain the flows of good and bad times, of high and low profits, because they did not sufficiently consider time as a factor in an economy in which capitalists, anticipating future buyers' desires, produce things they wish to sell as quickly as possible. Much later, Marshall mentioned time as a matter of particular difficulty for economic analysis.

When savings get into bankers' hands they increase lending and sales of commodities and prices rise. Wholesale prices are first affected and bills to finance them rise in volume also affecting economic conditions. While cycles could happen in a non-money-using economy, the use of money amplifies the phenomenon.

When the price of corn falls, there are more funds for buying other things and the economy expands. The expansion of loans, because of increasing confidence, aids the "common process." Cheap money, cheap corn, and improved credit cause prices to rise. In bad times, even if the supply of precious metals increases because foreign debts are called, or the savings in the country increase faster than the outlet for them, "a new channel of demand is required to take off the new money or the new money will not raise prices. It will lie idle in the banks . . ." Bagehot noted "the common phenomenon of dull trade and cheap money existing side by side" (1889, 5:95).

In a depression, credit is bad, industry is unemployed and, frequently, provisions are dear. Their dearness may have contributed to bringing on the bad times. But then their prices weaken, or some great industry makes, for some temporary cause, a quick step forward. During depressions savings accumulate, new securities are lacking, then credit begins to improve as memory and fear fade. Labor and capital begin to find better use. "The certain result is a bound of national prosperity" and "a buoyant cheerfulness overflows the mercantile world" (1889, 5:99). But while the real increase in output is a solid basis for the prosperity, the rise in prices (which might follow an increase in the nation's holdings of precious metals) is an "imaginary" one. Then misfortunes will appear in particular industries, or, because of bad harvests, food prices rise, and this decreases the demand for other goods.

Since an unusual plentifulness of loanable capital causes rising prices and an apparent prosperity, a reaction will set in. "The same causes which generated prosperity will . . . generate an equivalent adversity" (1889, 5:100). As trade increases, and as prices rise, more and more money is needed to finance trade. Interest rates will rise at first slowly and then rapidly. Credit shortages constrain some firms and excessive speculations are revealed along with frauds. The deficiency in loanable funds causes activity and profits to decrease. Fears, even for the currency, may then develop.

In sum, Bagehot believed that expansions and contractions of credit (currency) occurred naturally and regularly, and were aided by shifts in optimism and pessimism. These, and chance events, wars, gold discoveries, variations in harvests and investment opportunities, and even in laws (e.g., the Corn laws) and institutions, affected the course of the economy. "The history of a panic is the history of a confused conflict of many causes; and unless you know what sort of effect each cause is likely to produce, you cannot explain any part of what happens . . ." (1889, 5:253).

Frank C. Genovese

See also BANK CHARTER ACT; BANK OF ENGLAND; BANKING PANICS; BARING CRISIS; CENTRAL BANKING; JEVONS, WILLIAM STANLEY; LENDER OF LAST RESORT; MONETARY POLICY

Bibliography

Bagehot, W. [1873] 1962. *Lombard Street: A Description of The Money Market.* Homewood, Ill.: Irwin.

———. 1889. *The Works of Walter Bagehot, with Memoirs by R. H. Hutton.* 5 vols. Edited by F. Morgan. Hartford: The Travellers Insurance Company.

———. 1978–86. *The Collected Works of Walter Bagehot.* 15 vols. Edited by N. St. John-Stevas. London: *The Economist.*

Fetter, F. W. 1965. *The Evolution of British Monetary Orthodoxy: 1797–1873.* Cambridge: Harvard Univ. Press.

Laidler, D. 1988. "British Monetary Orthodoxy in the 1870s." *Oxford Economic Papers* 40:74–109.

Rostow, W. W. 1948. "Bagehot and the Trade Cycle." Chap. 8 in *The British Economy of The Nineteenth Century.* Oxford: Clarendon Press.

Bank Charter Act of 1844

The Bank of England was created as the first, and for a long time the only, joint-stock bank in England by Parliament in 1694. William of Orange was at war with the French and could neither persuade Parliament to raise taxes nor borrow funds at reasonable interest rates. William was forced to resort to a more creative means of raising revenue. His plan was for Parliament to grant a charter creating the Bank of England as the sole joint-stock bank in England and extending limited liability to its shareholders. Although the 1694 Act created no formal monopoly privileges, Parliament quickly granted the Bank a de facto monopoly by prohibiting any establishment owned by more than six partners from engaging in banking, which was then understood to mean issuing banknotes. Thus, in London and vicinity, the notes of no other bank were thereafter able to circulate. This article is specifically concerned with the Act of 1844 that renewed the Bank's charter and, in so doing, altered the structure of both the Bank and the British banking system.

The original charter, in effect, exchanged monopoly privileges in banking for a loan to the government at a reduced interest rate. From its inception, therefore, the intimate involvement of the Bank with government finance and its monopoly privileges were thought to impose on it responsibilities besides advancing the interests of its shareholders.

But the Bank's public responsibilities were never enumerated. Only in 1797, during another war with France, was the nature of those responsibilities explicitly addressed owing to the suspension of convertibility of Bank of England notes. But the only conclusion of those discussions was a consensus that convertibility be restored after the war.

However, the monetary instability in the 1820s after the resumption of convertibility led to further controversy about the role of the Bank of England. Two issues were particularly controversial. One was whether the Bank's monopoly over joint-stock banking throughout England should be retained. The other was whether some form of the Currency Principle should be imposed on the entire banking system. That principle, in its most general form, called for the total quantity of a mixed currency consisting of notes and precious metals to fluctuate by exactly as much as a purely metallic currency would fluctuate.

Attempting to implement the Currency Principle, the Bank adopted the Palmer rule—so called after the Bank's governor, J. Horsley Palmer. Under the rule, the Bank kept its holding of securities constant, thereby allowing the quantity of its liabilities to correspond exactly to its gold reserves. Then, in 1833, responding to objections to the extent of the Bank's monopoly privileges, Parliament renewed the Bank's charter and withdrew its monopoly over joint-stock banking and for the first time granted the Bank an explicit monopoly over note issue within a sixty-five-mile radius of London.

Monetary difficulties continued despite these steps, and monetary reform remained an issue. Supporters of the Currency Principle thought that monetary disturbances were caused by country banks that expanded their note issue irrespective of the state of the foreign exchanges. Moreover, they held the Palmer rule to be inadequate, since it did not affect the country banks and made no distinction between deposits and banknotes. In the teachings of the Currency School, only the latter were considered to be part of the circulating medium, and, consequently only the latter were required to fluctuate with the quantity of gold.

Persuaded by this analysis, Sir Robert Peel introduced legislation in 1844 designed to control the note issue of the country banks and to reform the internal structure of the Bank of England. Peel's Act accomplished the first by capping the note issues of the country banks at their current levels and providing for their eventual replacement by notes issued by the Bank of England. It accomplished the second by dividing the Bank into two independent departments: a banking department and an issue department. The banking department was to operate as a profit-maximizing bank, but the issue department was to be governed by a simple principle: beyond a fiduciary issue of £14 million, no notes could be issued without an equal amount of gold reserves.

Under the Act, except as country bank notes were retired and replaced by Bank of England notes, the note issue of the country banks and the fiduciary issue of the Bank of England would remain constant. Thus, the total quantity of banknotes would supposedly vary, as the Currency School wished, only in response to changes in the gold reserves held by the Bank of England.

But, in practice, the correspondence between the total quantity of banknotes and the gold reserves of the Bank of England did not have to be as tight as supporters of the Bank Charter Act had anticipated. First, the Act only set a ceiling on the note issues of the country banks. Their note issue could fall even without gold exports, and, having fallen, it could again rise to its ceiling without gold imports. Moreover, the Bank of England could sterilize gold inflows thereby enabling it to avoid reducing its note issue in case of an efflux of gold.

Aside from this technical problem, the Bank Charter Act suffered from serious conceptual difficulties. First, in accord with the Currency School doctrine that deposits were not part of the circulating medium, the Act left the quantity of deposits unconstrained. Such a distinction, which opponents of the Act disputed at the time, is now understood to be untenable.

Second, even if it were true that monetary disturbances were caused by fluctuations in the quantity of banknotes that did not correspond to inflows and outflows of gold, it might still be possible for an increased demand to hold money to be most easily met by an increase in the quantity of banknotes. But the Bank Charter Act ruled out that response whenever the note issue of the banking system was at its legal maximum. Moreover, just the apprehension that the legal barrier to an increase in the quantity of notes could cause a shortage of money could itself precipitate a precautionary demand for additional cash that, under the terms of the Act, would cause a financial crisis.

Although the Bank Charter Act is sometimes viewed in hindsight as the first official recognition that the Bank of England had the responsibilities of a central bank, its supporters never intended to impose such responsibilities on the Bank. Their aim was to eliminate any exercise of discretion by the Bank of England over its note issue, while allowing the rest of the Bank's activities to be conducted strictly to maximize the Bank's profits. They did not envision for the Bank anything like the role that Henry Thornton had laid out for it in his *Paper Credit of Great Britain*.

Yet, indirectly, the Bank Charter Act did help to create a recognition of the special responsibilities the Bank had to act as a lender of last resort for the rest of the financial system. That understanding evolved gradually, particularly as a result of the financial crises that subsequently occurred in 1847, 1857, and 1866. In these instances, financial panics were created by a fear that, owing to the constraints of the Bank Charter Act, the Bank of England would be unable to lend to the market. Each time the panic was eased when the government made it known that the Bank would be subject to no legal sanction if it exceeded the ceiling the Act placed on its fiduciary issue. As Bagehot ([1873] 1962) pointed out, just the assurance that the accommodation would be forthcoming if needed was enough to calm the market with the Bank required to overstep the limits of the Bank Charter Act only during the panic of 1857.

Those precedents made it clear that the Bank Charter Act would not be allowed to prevent the Bank of England from coming to the aid of the market in a crisis. Thus, the Bank's role as lender of last resort was confirmed not by the terms of the Act but by the periodic violation of those terms.

After the crisis of 1866, Britain did not undergo another financial panic requiring suspension of the Bank Charter Act until the outbreak of World War I. In 1890, the Bank of England took quick action to prevent the failure of the Baring Brothers firm in 1890 from developing into a panic. Thus, in a curious and typically British way, central banking and the doctrine of a lender of last result evolved in the second half of the nineteenth century from the process of adapting the terms of the Act of 1844 to the requirements of the British financial system.

David Glasner

See also BANK OF ENGLAND; BANKING SCHOOL, CURRENCY SCHOOL, AND FREE BANKING SCHOOL; BARING CRISIS; CENTRAL BANKING; CRISIS OF 1847; CRISIS OF 1857; GOLD STANDARD: CAUSES AND CONSEQUENCES; LENDER OF LAST RESORT; OVEREND GURNEY CRISIS

Bibliography

Bagehot, W. [1873] 1962. *Lombard Street.* Homewood, Ill.: Irwin.

Fetter, F. W. 1965. *The Evolution of British Monetary Orthodoxy, 1797–1875.* Cambridge: Harvard Univ. Press.

Hawtrey, R. G. 1932. "The Art of Central Banking." Chap. 4 in *The Art of Central Banking.* London: Longmans.

Thornton, H. [1802] 1939. *An Inquiry into the Nature and Causes of the Paper Credit of Great Britain.* Edited with an introduction by F. A. von Hayek. London: Allen and Unwin.

Viner, J. 1937. *Studies in the Theory of International Trade.* New York: Harper Bros.

Whale, P. B. 1944. "A Retrospective View of the Bank Charter Act of 1844." *Economica,* n.s., 11:109–11.

White, L. H. 1984. *Free Banking in Britain: Theory, Debate, and Experience, 1800–1844.* New York: Cambridge Univ. Press.

Bank of England
1694–1821

The Bank of England was established for the purpose of financing the War of the Grand Alliance. When a war chest was required in 1694, a proposal that had twice previously been put forward by William Paterson was adopted in the Ways and Means Act of that year. The Act provided that those who subscribed for and towards the raising and paying into the receipt of the Exchequer (the sum of £1,200,000, or part of the sum of £1,500,000) were to constitute jointly the Company of the Bank of England.

The loan was a perpetuity, paying interest at the rate of 8 percent. This was considerably below the interest rates that previously had been charged the Crown. However, the subscribers received additional rights to (1) form a joint-stock banking company, (2) deal in bills of exchange, gold, and silver, (3) grant advances on security, and (4) issue promissory notes transferable by endorsement in an amount not exceeding the Bank's capital.

These terms apparently were very attractive. The entire loan was subscribed within twelve days. Every subscriber became a shareholder of the Bank to the extent of his subscription, and all or any fraction of his share could be sold to others. The Bank opened for business on 27 July 1694 in Mercers' Chappell. From its inception, every effort was made by the Governor and Court of Directors (board of directors of the bank) to attract depositors and to promote the circulation of its "running cash notes." These notes were convertible at the Bank into legal tender money, gold coins, at a fixed exchange rate on demand.

Subsequent legislation strengthened the bank's position. The Bank was granted a monopoly in joint-stock banking in early 1697. In 1708, the Bank obtained a monopoly in the issue of joint-stock banknotes. Later, in 1742, Act 10 and 11 George II., C. 13 (par. 5), reaffirmed the earlier rights granted to the Bank. Each of these pieces of legislation was accompanied by an additional bank loan to the government. The Bank subscribed an additional £1,001,017 for loan to the government at 8 percent in 1697. In 1707, it extended a £1,500,000 loan at 4.5 percent and, in 1742, another £1,600,000 at 3 percent.

No further significant legislative changes regarding the Bank's position occurred until 1826. In that year, the Bank's monopoly on joint-stock banking was limited to a sixty-five-mile radius of London. Subsequently, in 1833, its monopoly of joint-stock banknote issue was also limited to the same area. However, Bank of England notes were made legal tender at this time. This legislation provided legal force to the practice that had already been adopted by other banks of holding their reserves in the form of Bank of England notes.

Despite its status as a privately owned profit-seeking bank, the Bank of England on at least two occasions in the eighteenth century did serve, in a limited way, as a lender of last resort during the financial crises of 1763 and 1772–73. In the former episode, the Bank of England, along with other London bankers, sent emergency shipments of specie to Amsterdam to prevent the collapse of the Amsterdam money market with which London was closely connected in the eighteenth century. In the latter episode, the Bank of England again eased a crisis in Amsterdam by allowing the ready withdrawal of specie for shipment by London merchants to their correspondents in Amsterdam.

The Napoleonic Wars began in 1793 and continued until 1815. Government demands from the Bank for financing rose substantially during this period. Of course, the Bank's contract with its depositors to redeem its notes at a fixed price in terms of gold conflicted with the government's interest and, on 26 February 1797, the King and Privy Council ordered the Bank to suspend specie payments.

During the suspension, control of the money supply, which had rested with the Bank's owners, was largely usurped by the government. Clapham (1958, 2:33) notes that

> The minutes of the Court and those of the Committee of Treasury are full of . . . requests for help from Perceval, and of the Bank's reluctant but invariable acquiescence.

The Bank apparently acquiesced because of an "understanding, a gentleman's understanding . . . to do this business and to do it in the way most convenient to the Treasury."

This situation was to persist for more than twenty years. Control of the money supply was not fully restored to the owners of the Bank until convertibility into gold was formally reestablished on 1 May 1821.

The reluctance of the Bank's owners to do this business for the Treasury is not surprising. Real dividend payments, inclusive of bonuses, did not increase and the real price of bank shares fell sharply during the suspension. This led to trouble between the Bank's shareholders, the Court of Directors, and the government. In 1801, Alexander Allardyce, spokesman for the shareholders, moved that a complete accounting of the Bank's financial condition be presented to the stockholders. The shareholders viewed the "Treasury's business" as a thinly veiled expropriation of their wealth.

In October 1797, six months after it was ordered to suspend payments, the Bank indicated that it could "with safety resume its accustomed functions (payment of specie), if the political circumstances of the country do not render it inexpedient" (Clayham 1958, 1:272). The Bank's report was virtually ignored by government. In June 1810, the "Report from the Select Committee on the High Price of Bullion" (Cannan 1919) recommended to Parliament that the resumption of specie payments (at the old par) begin within two years. The issue was not even taken up for discussion until the following July. A vote on the recommendation was taken in the House of Commons in 1811. The House voted 180 to 45 against the issue.

On its own initiative, the Bank began partial resumption of specie payments for notes of five pounds or less in January of 1817. Early in 1819, however, Parliament required the Bank to discontinue the practice. Parliament had promised on five different occasions eventually to resume specie payments, but continued to drag its feet on fixing a date. Finally, on 2 July 1819, the House of Commons passed an act permitting the resumption of cash payments (bullion and coin) after 1 May 1822. At the request of the Bank, this date eventually was moved forward to 1 May 1821.

The Bank of England presents an interesting case in studying the effect of different incentives on the behavior of central bankers. The reason is that the original organization of the bank differed from its modern counterparts in one fundamental respect: the Bank of England was a privately owned, profit-seeking bank from its inception in 1694 until the early 1930s. Further, the Bank was operating within a set of institutional arrangements that related the wealth of its owners inversely to the rate of inflation. Consequently, the costs and benefits of monetary expansion as viewed by the directors of the Bank of England were different from the costs and benefits typically perceived by modern central bankers.

An interesting piece of evidence concerning the effect of private versus government control of the money supply is England's history of inflation before, during and after the Napoleonic Wars. From the establishment of the Bank in 1694 until the beginning of the Napoleonic Wars in 1793, the annual average rate of inflation in England was 0.01 percent. In contrast, the price level rose at an average annual rate of 4.85 percent (t-score = 2.67) during the years 1793–1813 (see Figure 1). This was associated with a significant increase in the monetary growth rate during this period (see Figure 2).

The Bank resumed control of the money supply in 1821. Private control continued until 1913. Between 1822 and 1913, England's annual average rate of inflation was 0.42 percent which, again, is statistically indistinguishable from zero.

Finally, the Bank was nationalized in 1931 and, since then, the annual average rate of inflation in Britain has been significantly positive at about 6.5 percent.

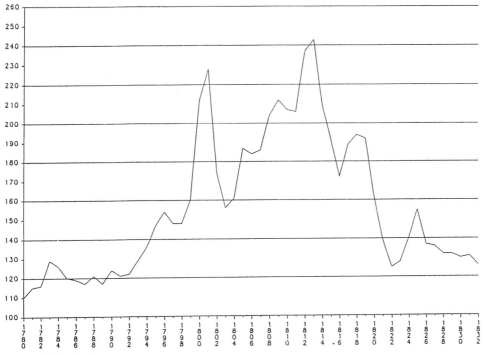

Figure 1. Price level.

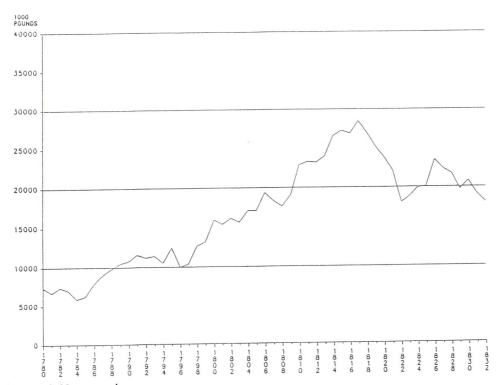

Figure 2. Money supply.

There are a number of conclusions to draw from the previous discussion concerning the incentives faced by England's central bankers. First, given the one exception noted, the right to control the money supply was held privately. This right, in the form of ownership shares in the Bank, was traded in an organized market. Any expected changes in the future profits of the Bank would be reflected by changes in the price of bank shares and would immediately affect the wealth of bank owners.

Second, the owners of the Bank lent considerable sums to the government in perpetuity at fixed rates of interest. By 1743, the sum was well in excess of £9 million, a sum which represented the vast bulk of the Bank's capital. These loans are particularly important in assessing the incentives of the Bank's Court of Directors. For example, an inflationary monetary policy raises the nominal interest rate as inflationary expectations are revised upward and this reduces the present value of the fixed-rate government perpetuities held by the Bank. In other words, inflating the quantity of Bank notes tended to reduce the Bank's capital and the wealth of its owners.

For similar reasons, the government would prefer a higher rate of inflation to a lower rate once the terms of the loan were fixed. A rate of inflation above that expected at the time the loan was negotiated would transfer wealth from the Bank's owners to the government.

The early history of the Bank of England suggests that decisions regarding the control of money depend more on the incentives individuals face in making choices than on the particular individuals who make the choice. Various methods of organizing monetary control produce distinct policy outcomes insofar as they confront policymakers with different incentives.

1821–73

After the resumption of convertibility in 1821, England enjoyed a rapid economic expansion that was supported by an expansion of credit by the Bank of England and the banking system at large. In late 1825, a severe financial panic nearly caused a collapse of the British financial system. A contagion of bank failures hit the country banks, causing an acute shortage of currency in parts of England. The demand for currency was such that demands on the Bank of England itself nearly forced it to suspend convertibility in December 1825. The fortuitous discovery of a stock of one-pound notes enabled the bank to satisfy demands for hand-to-hand currency without depleting its gold reserves and avoided a suspension of convertibility.

Many observers attributed the severity of the banking panic to the fragmented and undercapitalized country banks, which, by law, could be owned by a maximum of six partners. As a result, legislation was enacted in 1826 to permit the formation of joint-stock banks. Until then, the Bank of England had been the only such bank chartered in England. The 1826 legislation did not allow new joint-stock banks to issue circulating banknotes, but legislation in 1833 renewing the charter of the Bank of England allowed joint-stock banks to issue banknotes outside a sixty-five-mile radius of London.

Another crisis in 1837, followed by an uneven recovery in 1838–40 and a deep depression in 1841–42 occasioned further debates about reform of the banking system. Parliament created a Select Committee on Banks of Issue in 1840 to investigate the issue of banking reform. And a historic three-sided debate between members of the Banking, Currency, and Free Banking Schools ensued over the proper role of the Bank of England and its relation to the rest of the banking system.

The position of the Currency School largely prevailed when the prime minister, Sir Robert Peel, proposed his Bank Charter Act in 1844. The act separated the Bank of England into a department of issue and a department of banking which were to operate independently of each other. The department of issue was permitted a fixed fiduciary issue of £14,000,000 with any additional banknotes subject to a 100-percent marginal reserve requirement. The banking department, meanwhile, was free to extend credit and take deposits under the same conditions as any other private banking institution.

The Bank Charter Act was supposed to prevent, or at least moderate, financial crises, by forcing the note issue of the Bank of England to fluctuate exactly as a purely metallic currency would have in response to inflows and outflows of gold. According to the Currency School, financial crises occurred because a fractional-reserve banking system did not immediately respond to the contractionary impulse of an outflow of gold. The delay in contracting the note issue simply aggravated the impact of the inevitable contraction in response to the efflux.

Despite the expectations of its supporters, a serious financial crisis occurred in 1847, just three years after the enactment of the Bank Charter Act. Not only did the Act fail to prevent the occurrence of the crisis, the realization that the Act would prohibit the Bank of England from accommodating a demand for liquidity was itself an important factor in precipitating the crisis. In the event, the crisis was finally dispelled when the government issued a letter to the Bank of England advising it to extend credit at a high interest rate without reference to the legal constraints of the 1844 Act and promising to introduce a bill of indemnity to prevent any sanctions from being applied against the bank or its officers for violating the provisions of the Act. Publication of the letter calmed the panic that had seized the financial community. The precautionary demand for liquidity largely evaporated and, in the end, the constraints of the 1844 Act did not have to be breached.

Similar financial crises occurred in 1857 and 1866. In both instances, the crises were dispelled only upon publication of a similar letter to the Bank of England by the government, in effect, suspending the terms of the Bank Charter Act. After the precedents of 1847, 1857, and 1866, no financial crisis was ever again precipitated by the fear that the provisions of the Bank Charter Act would prohibit the Bank of England from accommodating a demand for liquidity.

1873 to the Present

In 1873, Walter Bagehot published his famous book *Lombard Street,* in which he proposed, based on the precedents of 1847, 1857, and 1866, that a central bank facing a contagious crisis in financial markets should lend freely, but at high interest rates, to borrowers (from within the financial system) who had good collateral and could reasonably be expected to remain solvent (or to regain solvency) under normal conditions. Although the Bank of England had already received similar advice on how to cope with crises, notably from Thornton ([1802] 1939), its attitude toward its putative responsibilities had varied over time, partly out of concern with moral-hazard problems, but more probably because the incentives of the Bank as an ordinary profit-seeking, competitive bank in these earlier years conflicted with its duties as a central bank.

Indeed, the Bank Charter Act of 1844 had separated Bank of England into two independent issue and banking departments. In principle, the latter was supposed to operate just as any other commercial bank. Although operating as a commercial bank soon proved unworkable, the attempt to do so perpetuated for some years both the commercial rivalry between the Bank of England and its competitors (a rivalry that played a considerable role in the Overend, Gurney crash of 1866) and a confusion among the Bank's directors about its real duties in a crisis. Thus, the role of the Bank in crises before 1873 was complex and changing, depending on the shifting view of the directors of the Bank's responsibilities and on their response to a particular set of historical circumstances. Besides Thornton's early contribution, the theoretical issues have been surveyed by Fetter (1965) while the historical events have been described by Matthews (1954).

However, since 1873, the Bank of England has accepted that it has a duty to sustain the health of the banking system and to prevent the onset of a contagious crisis. Its position in this respect was strengthened both by withdrawing from commercial operations and from rivalry with the London joint-stock banks, and by the central role that it came to assume in the conduct of macroeconomic monetary policy. Before 1914, monetary policy was virtually synonymous with maintaining the gold standard. Indeed, Bagehot's advice to lend at a high rate of interest was largely conditioned on the likelihood that a financial crisis would be accompanied by both external and internal drains of specie from the bank, which could only be counteracted by high rates of interest. In more modern terms, this part of his advice could be restated as a proposition that the instruments of monetary policy, notably interest rates, should be targeted at *macro*-targets, e.g., the maintenance of the external or internal value of the currency, from which they should not be deflected by strains and stresses within the financial system.

While the macro/monetary policy of the Bank of England over the years has been criticized, there have been virtually no complaints that it has ever eased policy unduly out of concern with the solvency of the financial system. Although monetary policy was tightened enough or in time in 1972–73, the emergence of the Fringe Banking Crisis in 1973–74 (Reid 1982) did not deter eventual tightening. Indeed, before the 1970s, criticism of the macro/monetary policy of the Bank was that it had been too tight in the 1930s (Pollard 1962).

Bagehot had advised the Bank to lend freely to deserving (solvent) borrowers requiring additional liquidity. In due course the Bank had to face several problems in carrying out this function. First, the Bank of England, which had been the largest English bank in the early nineteenth century, was outgrown by the private-sector institutions, especially the massive, and increasingly oligopolistic, London clearing banks. So, when faced with distress in any but the smallest private houses, the Bank found itself too small to take all such lending onto its own books. From the Baring Crisis in 1890 onwards (Pressnell 1968), the Bank of England invariably sought to orchestrate collective support from the banking system to forestall a crisis. Its ability to do so, and the comparative infrequency of crises, both stemmed in part from the oligopolistic, club-like structure of the U.K. banking system. As competition from new domestic and foreign entrants and from non-bank intermediaries became fiercer, the ability of the Bank to organize a whip-round of guarantees and collective support form the commercial banks has diminished, as evidenced by the Johnson-Matthey bank crash in 1984. The growing disinclination of the core British banks to support a competitor in difficulties leaves the form and financing of future support operations in doubt.

The second major problem that the Bank of England, like all other central banks, had to face was how to distinguish between those deserving support, and those that should be let go. Laissez-faire purists argue that only those who are clearly solvent, or could reasonably expect to be once the worst of the crisis was over, deserve assistance. That this position is too extreme, and cannot be generalized, is evidenced by the crisis at the outset of World War I, when the unanticipated outbreak of war disrupted payments between the combatants, and left much, possibly most, of the London money market effectively insolvent. Fortunately, after some uncertain moments, the authorities saved the day by buying up the claims on the enemy countries at face value. More frequently, a financial crisis breaks so suddenly that an initial response, which often constrains subsequent decisions, must be made before the true balance-sheet position of the endangered banks can be ascertained (e.g., as was true in the Johnson-Matthey episode). Such comparative ignorance biases the response of the Bank of England towards supportive intervention, even though nowadays, given liability management through the wholesale money markets, liquidity problems almost always foreshadow solvency problems, as was also demonstrated in the 1973–74 Fringe Banking crisis. But the danger of contagious panic, if a bank should fail, is immediate, whereas the shortfall of capital if the bank were closed usually remains hypothetical when a decision whether to render assistance must be made.

The resulting proclivity for the Bank of England to protect all depositors, *ex post facto*, represents implicit insurance protection for all depositors. This contributes to moral hazard, especially as the financial system emerges from its previous structure, with restricted ranges of specialist business under oligopolistic control. Consequently, increasing competition has led the bank to move toward much more formal and extensive regulation of the banking system. The Banking Acts of 1979 (a reaction to the earlier Fringe Banking Crisis) and of 1987 (a reaction to the Johnson-Matthey affair) have codified that regulatory shift. The shift has been further reinforced by the Financial Services Act (1986), the Bank of International Settlements Capital Adequacy provisions, and the European Community's two Banking Directives.

David Glasner
C. A. E. Goodhart
Gary J. Santoni

See also BAGEHOT, WALTER; BANK CHARTER ACT OF 1844; BANK OF FRANCE; BANKING AND FINANCIAL REGULATION; BANKING PANICS; BANKING SCHOOL, CURRENCY SCHOOL, AND FREE BANKING SCHOOL; BARING CRISIS; BULLIONIST CONTROVERSIES; CENTRAL BANKING; CRISES OF 1763 AND 1772–1773; CRISIS OF 1847; CRISIS OF 1857; CRISIS OF 1914; FEDERAL RESERVE SYSTEM: 1914–1941; FEDERAL RESERVE SYSTEM: 1941–1993; GOLD STANDARD; GOLD STANDARD: CAUSES AND CONSEQUENCES; INTERNATIONAL LENDER OF LAST RESORT; LENDER OF LAST RESORT; MONETARY POLICY; NAPOLEONIC WARS; OVEREND GURNEY CRISIS; PANIC OF 1825; PANIC OF 1837; THORNTON, HENRY

Bibliography

Andreades, A. [1909] 1924. *History of the Bank of England*. 2d ed. Translation. London: P. S. King.

Bagehot, W. [1873] 1962. *Lombard Street*. Homewood, Ill.: Irwin.

Bank of England. 1985. "The Bank of England and Johnson Matthey Bankers

Ltd." In Bank of England *Report and Accounts 1985*, 33–42.

Bisschop, W. R. [1896] 1968. *The Rise of the London Money Market: 1640–1826.* Translation. London: Frank Cass.

Cannan, E. 1919. *The Paper Pound of 1797–1821: The Bullion Report.* London: P. S. King.

Clapham, J. 1958. *The Bank of England: A History.* 2 vols. Cambridge: Cambridge Univ. Press.

Fetter, F. W. 1965. *The Evolution of British Monetary Orthodoxy, 1797–1875.* Cambridge: Harvard Univ. Press.

Goodhart, C. A. E. 1989. *The Evolution of Central Banks.* Cambridge: MIT Press.

Hawtrey, R. G. 1932. "The Art of Central Banking." Chap. 4 in *The Art of Central Banking.* London: Longmans.

Macleod, M. A. 1897. *The Theory of Credit.* 2d ed. London: Longmans.

Martin, F. 1865. *Stories of Banks and Bankers.* London: Macmillan.

Matthews, R. C. O. 1954. *A Study in Trade-Cycle History: Economic Fluctuations in Great Britain, 1833–1842.* Cambridge: Cambridge Univ. Press.

Pollard, S. 1962. *The Development of the British Economy, 1914–1950.* London: Arnold.

Pressnell, L. 1968. "Gold Reserves, Banking Reserves, and the Banking Crisis of 1890." In *Essays in Money and Banking in Honour of R. S. Sayers,* edited by C. R. Whittlesey and J. S. G. Wilson, 167–228. Oxford: Clarendon Press.

Reid, M. 1982. *The Secondary Banking Crisis, 1973–75.* London: Macmillan.

Rogers, T. 1887. *The First Nine Years of the Bank of England.* Oxford: Clarendon Press.

Santoni, G. J. 1984. "A Private Central Bank: Some Olde English Lessons." Federal Reserve Bank of St. Louis *Review,* July/August, 12–22.

Seabourne, T. 1986. "The Summer of 1914." In *Financial Crisis and the World Banking System,* edited by F. Capie and G. E. Wood, 77–116. London: Macmillan.

Thornton, H. [1802] 1939. *And Enquiry into the Nature and Effects of the Paper Credit of Great Britain.* Reprint. Edited with an introduction by F. A. von Hayek. London: Allen and Unwin.

White, L. H. 1984. *Free Banking in Britain: Theory, Debate, and Experience, 1800–1844.* New York: Cambridge Univ. Press.

B

Bank of France

The Bank of France was founded in 1800 by a group of Parisian banks as a discount bank with a local monopoly on note issue. It subsequently acquired the central-banking responsibility of protecting the country against domestic as well as international crises, having a special role in providing the Bank of England access to its gold reserves. In the nineteenth century, the Bank of France enjoyed a high degree of autonomy, but its intransigent anti-inflationary stance during the Great Depression caused the government to limit its independence after 1935.

Domestic Lender of Last Resort

As early as 1810, 1818, and 1826, the Bank of France responded to the shortage of money by generously discounting commercial paper. In 1830, it accepted almost any paper, although doing so violated its statute.

The Bank was accused of having acted primarily in its own interest in many crises. In 1848, it allowed all the provincial banks of issue to fail in a successful attempt to transform them into branches (Gille 1970). Moreover, some attribute the fall of the Pereires' Credit Mobilier in 1868 to the rivalry between the Currency School ideas of the Bank and the Banking School or "Saint-Simonian" ideas of the Pereires who had intended to compete with the Bank of France and its Rothschild allies by taking over the bank of issue of the annexed Kingdom of Savoy (Cameron 1961). Similar charges have been made about the Union Générale crash in 1882. But a close analysis of both episodes shows that the Credit Mobilier and the Union Générale were deeply involved in industrial speculations and that the Bank of France did not cause their failure (Levy-Leboyer 1976b).

The Bank did save many other banks in difficulty, or organized their liquidation to avoid a general panic, as in the cases of the Laffitte (1831), the Comptoir d'Escompte (1889), and the Banque Nationale de Crédit (1931). The 1931 bank crisis was not very serious, because of the conservatism of major French banks in the cover of all sight obligations and in their attitude toward industrial operations. The Bank of France intervened in favor of many provincial banks with limited industrial commitments. However, the Bank was criticized for only intervening to aid large and medium-size banks, never to aid commerce or industry, and for asking the large banks and the government to share in the cost of rescue operations. In the Great Depression, the banks protested against competition by the Bank of France through "direct discount" (maintained by the government since the founding of the Bank although the growth of the banking sector had made it unnecessary). But the principal reason for hostility against the Bank—its very conservative posture in supplying money for normal economic activity—was only indirectly related to the crisis.

Macroeconomic Policy

The Bank never publicly accepted responsibility for economic fluctuations. "The Bank," wrote the Conseil Général of the Bank in 1857, "does not regulate the price of money, it only records it officially" (Plessis 1985, 215). Throughout the nineteenth century, "the only service the Bank has to offer is to moderate business activity" (Plessis 1985, 165), by raising its discount rate, thus signaling the beginning of a crisis as well as dampening its impact. However, its practice was different, and for the entire century the Bank tried to keep its discount rate at a low level. Its method was also different from that of the Bank of England (even if the result was exactly the same mean rate in the long run). The Bank of France kept its discount rate stable at a "normal" rather than at the lowest level possible. The 4-percent rate did not change from 1820 to 1847 and the rate was never more than one point above or below 3 percent from 1882 to 1914. Such a policy was possible before 1870 because of the strict limitation of the money supply and of the liabilities of the Bank. It was facilitated thereafter by a balance-of-payments surplus.

The Bank of France opposed the founding of many banks (particularly provincial banks of issue before the Bank's monopoly privilege was extended to the entire country in 1848) until the liberty to incorporate was granted in 1863. Before the new joint-stock banks started competing in the 1870s, the Bank's discount was strictly limited to a small number of Parisian banks. Its reluctance to issue notes of medium or small amount (because of fears of panic dating back to the 1720 Law experience and the Revolutionary Assignats) and the late (1865) legal recognition of the check by the govern-

ment resulted in a low degree of monetization of the French economy and the continued use of gold coins (Cameron 1967).

A flexible rate policy like that of the Bank of England from the 1840s was adopted only between 1857 and 1882, and did not match the frequency of the English variations. This was the only period in which a determined countercyclical macroeconomic policy was practiced.

The Bank's influence on the money market declined between 1880 and 1940 because its share of total discounts diminished, because the great deposit banks (that never needed to rediscount at the Bank) had excess liquidity, and because it refused to engage in open-market operations. After 1918, the Bank increased the supply of money, not because of a change in its discount policy, but because it could not limit the advances it made to the state budget. The belated resistance of Governor Robineau during the resulting franc crisis of 1925 was continued by his successors Moreau and Moret. But after January 1935, the Bank, increasingly subordinated to the finance minister, was obliged to discount Treasury bills and to make advances to the state. These inflationary practices combined with an increasing discount rate and a policy of strictly restricting lending to private business, which reflect the lack of a coherent macroeconomic policy, were continued after 1935, partly explaining the duration of the Great Depression in France.

Defense of the Franc

Guaranteeing the franc was always said to be the principal aim of the Bank of France. From 1800 to 1914, the convertibility of the notes it issued was guaranteed at an invariable rate, except in two cases of political origin, from 1848 to 1852 and from 1870 to 1878. Despite the preoccupation with convertibility, exchange-rate crises rarely required a high interest rate. In 1836, the Bank lost 55 percent of its reserves without raising its discount rate, preventing the international crisis from affecting France. In 1855, 1857, and 1864, the solvency of the Bank was imperiled by the high London rates, and its rate reached 10 percent in 1857—the highest level of the century. But after 1866, high English interest rates did not attract enough gold to force the Bank of France to raise its rate.

The reason for the relative insulation of France from world crises was the very high reserve/liability ratio (often more than 80 percent) that the Bank maintained until the 1930s, a consequence of its strict Currency School principles and of the resulting low degree of monetization of the French economy.

After 1918, the Bank was unable to prevent the fall of the franc, except briefly in 1924, with the help of the Morgan bank. But it assisted the Poincaré government in stabilizing the franc in 1926. During the Great Depression, its preoccupation with the franc led the Bank to pursue a deflationary policy. However, after 1935, the Bank could not prevent the growth of advances to the state and the subsequent recurrence of speculation, inflation, and devaluations.

International Policy

The Bank of France played an important international role in the nineteenth century, mainly because it was the only bank with enough gold reserves and international influence to help the Bank of England, providing assistance in 1825, in 1836–39, in the Baring crisis of 1890, in 1906–07, and in 1931 (by forbearing to convert its Sterling holdings and arranging large credit for the Bank of England). The Bank of France may be considered as the second center of the international monetary system between 1840 and 1914.

During the 1930s, the Bank of France was widely held responsible for the Great Depression and the devaluation of the pound in 1931. The Bank of England accused it of sterilizing gold inflows to monopolize the world's supply of gold. In fact, the Bank tried to return to its old Currency School principles that required a large gold reserve. From 1924 to 1926, the gold flows had been purely speculative, unrelated to differences in discount rates, which explains the reluctance of the Bank to let the money supply reflect those flows. But the inflows of 1926–32 were consistent with the French economy's traditional wide use of notes issued by the Bank of France in preference to deposits and with a Currency School approach that rejected the use of open-market operations as inflationary. But sterilization was not a cause of the Great Depression since the sterilization of gold inflows did not continue after the formal resumption of convertibility in June 1928. Thereafter, the ratio of gold plus foreign-exchange reserves to the Bank's liabilities stopped rising (Hautcoeur 1990). A more likely cause is that the extent of exchange-rate speculation in the 1920s was too great for central-bank cooperation to cope with, undermining the nineteenth-century equilibrium in which gold reserves were largely concentrated in the Bank of France. Credits organized by the Banks of France and England and the Federal Reserve Bank of New York could not halt the crisis, because speculators soon suspected that disagreements between the main countries would limit their responses to speculation and that no one could act as the international lender of last resort.

After 1945, the Bank of France was called on to finance the postwar reconstruction and to prevent crises, while exchange control was used to protect the franc's stability. From then on, the Bank was simply the principal agent of the government in implementing the government's monetary policy.

Pierre-Cyrille Hautcoeur

See also BANK OF ENGLAND; CENTRAL BANKING; GOLD STANDARD; GOLD STANDARD: CAUSES AND CONSEQUENCES; GREAT DEPRESSION IN FRANCE (1929–1938); HAWTREY, RALPH GEORGE; INTERNATIONAL LENDER OF LAST RESORT; LAW, JOHN; LENDER OF LAST RESORT

Bibliography

Cameron, R. 1961. *France and the Economic Development of Europe, 1800–1914.* Princeton: Princeton Univ. Press.

———. 1967. *Banking in the Early Stages of Industrialization.* New York: Oxford Univ. Press.

Eichengreen, B. [1986] 1990. "The Bank of France and the Sterilization of Gold, 1926–1932." Chap. 5 in *Elusive Stability: Essays in the History of International Finance, 1919–1939.* Cambridge: Cambridge Univ. Press.

Gille, B. 1970. *La banque en France au XIXème siècle.* Genève: Droz.

Hautcoeur, P.-C. 1990. "La Banque de France et la crise bancaire, 1930–1932." *Etudes et documents* 2:295–315.

———. 1993. "Surevaluation ou crise de confiance? Hausse des taux d'interêt et duree de la grande depression en France." In *Du Franc Poincaré à l'Ecu,* edited by M. Levy-Leboyer, 97–123. Paris: Imprimerie Nationale.

Kindleberger, C. P. 1989. *Manias, Panics, and Crashes.* 2d ed. New York: Basic Books.

Kindleberger, C. P. and J. P. Laffargue, eds. 1977. *Financial Crises: Theory, History and Policy.* Cambridge: Cambridge Univ. Press.

B

Levy-Leboyer, M. 1964. *Les banques européennes et l'industrialisation internationale*. Paris: Presses Universitaires de France.

———. 1976a. "Le crédit et la monnaie." In *Histoire économique et sociale de la France*. Vol. 3. Edited by F. Braudel and E. Labrousse, 347–429. Paris: Presses Universitaires de France.

———. 1976b. "La spécialisation des établissements bancaires." In *Histoire économique et sociale de la France*. Vol. 3. Edited by F. Braudel and E. Labrousse, 431–71. Paris: Presses Universitaires de France.

Plessis, A. 1985. *La politique de la Banque de France de 1851 à 1870*. Genève: Droz.

Bank of United States

The largest and most famous failure of the 1930 banking crisis occurred when the Bank of United States closed its doors on 11 December 1930. The demise of this bank worsened the panic. As deposits were withdrawn, banks contracted credit, driving the economy deeper into recession.

The Bank of United States was founded in 1913 by Joseph S. Marcus. It was a small Manhattan bank, whose clientele was predominantly Jewish. When Marcus died in 1927, the bank had a capital of $6 million. His son, Bernard K. Marcus, succeeded him and began to expand the bank quickly by merger and acquisition. By mid-1929 the bank had merged with four other banks, raising its capital to $25 million.

As the bank grew, Marcus assembled a risky portfolio full of mortgages and low-grade securities. While New York City banks had on average 12 percent of their assets in mortgages, the Bank of United States had 45 percent. This excessive and illegal investment in real estate did not appear on the bank's balance sheet. The mortgages were hidden by selling them to the bank's many securities and investment affiliates. To complete these transactions, the bank gave its affiliates short-term unsecured loans to pay for the mortgages.

Mortgages were not the bank's only problem. In arranging its mergers, the bank had promised to buy back any stock whose price fell below the negotiated value used to purchase other banks. The bank gave the same commitment to depositors who bought stock. Lastly, the bank made unsecured loans of $16 million to bank officers and their relatives to buy stocks.

Marcus's house of cards began to collapse in 1929. Real-estate values declined and mortgages turned into bad investments. When the bull stock market collapsed in October 1929, stockholders exercised their option to sell back their shares, creating a liquidity drain on the bank. The bank became insolvent, and two years after closing only sixty cents on each dollar of deposits were paid out, 20 percent of which were offsets. For his part in this fraudulent operation, Marcus was eventually sentenced to three to six years in prison.

At the same time as the Bank of United States was faltering, the United States economy entered a recession, prompted in part by the contractionary policy of the Federal Reserve. Beginning in October 1930, the number of bank failures rose sharply. These were located primarily in agricultural areas. In November, 256 banks with $180 million of deposits failed, followed by another 352 banks with $370 million of deposits in December. The fear of failure drove the public to convert deposits into currency, exacerbating the monetary contraction.

The Bank of United States was a large urban bank, and both state and federal regulators feared that its failure would worsen the banking crisis. The state banking authorities were aware of the bank's weak condition, but allowed it to carry assets at inflated values. In the two months before its closure, the New York State Superintendent of Banks, Joseph Broderick, sponsored various merger plans. When a slow run began on the Bank of United States, the Federal Reserve provided substantial assistance. Out of $26 million in loans to member banks made by the Federal Reserve Bank of New York in December 1930, $19 million were to the Bank of United States.

In the fall of 1930, the Federal Reserve Bank of New York led the negotiations to rescue the bank by merging it with three larger banks. This plan would have created the fourth largest institution in the city with an infusion of $30 million of capital by the Clearing House banks. This plan ultimately failed, because the proposed merger partners and Clearing House banks saw it as a dangerous deal with unknown future real-estate losses and an open commitment to honor the stock-repurchase agreements. Nor did they trust Marcus and his associates.

When the merger talks collapsed, the authorities were forced to close the bank. The

Bank of United States was the largest failure up to that date in American history with $200 million of deposits. A state-chartered bank and member of the Federal Reserve System, its closure was a blow to the Federal Reserve and the banking system. There were further complications as some foreigners erroneously assumed it was connected with the government. The loss of confidence put pressure on other banks. The public's continued conversion of deposits to currency forced banks to reduce their credit, pushing the economy further into a depression.

The problems of the Bank of United States highlight the dilemma faced by a central bank during a banking crisis. All the banking authorities knew that the condition of the Bank of United States was extremely weak. In normal times, the bank should have been allowed to fail. However, the authorities feared that a failure of this magnitude could worsen the crisis. Their attempts to keep the bank open to calm the public would have imposed a high cost on other banks. But when the bank did fail, it increased the severity of the banking crisis, which was also costly to other banks.

Eugene N. White

See also BANKING PANICS; FEDERAL RESERVE SYSTEM: 1914–1941; GREAT DEPRESSION IN THE UNITED STATES (1929–1938); LENDER OF LAST RESORT

Bibliography
Friedman, M. and A. J. Schwartz. 1963. *A Monetary History of the United States, 1867–1960.* Princeton: Princeton Univ. Press.

———. 1986. "The Failure of the Bank of United States: A Reappraisal. A Reply." *Explorations in Economic History* 23:199–204.

Lucia, J. L. 1985. "The Failure of the Bank of United States: A Reappraisal." *Explorations in Economic History* 22:402–16.

Temin, Peter. 1976. *Did Monetary Forces Cause the Great Depression?* New York: Norton.

Banking and Financial Regulation

No consensus exists about the role that banking and financial systems play in business cycles. Business-cycle theories that highlight crises, panics, and crashes tend to emphasize the importance of the financial, and particularly the banking, sectors as sources of instability. An alternative view is that the source of instability is the "real" sector of the economy and that the role of the financial sector may be to transmit and amplify effects of real shocks, from the markets in which they occur to other markets. If the financial sector is itself prone to instability or, as a conduit for speculative excess, amplifies real shocks, then there is a strong rationale for regulating the financial sector as a means of moderating the business cycle.

The analysis of financial panics, crises, and fragility clearly indicates that it is the financial sector that generates asset-price inflation and speculative bubbles. The banking system is usually given special attention because of its importance as a supplier of money and a provider of money-transaction services, such as check clearing. The heavy reliance of advanced economies on credit relationships implies that their breakdown could disrupt commercial relationships in general and, if a credit crunch results, even precipitate a recession or depression.

Some contributions to the theory of banking stress the monitoring function performed by banks. As suppliers of debt finance, they obtain information not normally published in compliance with stock-exchange regulations. Therefore, to signal financial soundness to the financial markets and gain access to alternative sources of debt finance and capital, even the most liquid companies commonly negotiate credit lines. Given this crucial monitoring role, the question arises: who should monitor the monitors? This problem suggests that an alternative rationale for bank regulation may be found in possible market failures caused by deficient information in the market for bank loans. This deficiency may have been reduced recently with the emergence of secondary markets for some types of bank loans.

Other contributions to monetary and banking theory stress the roles of money and banks as buffers. One reason that economic agents hold bank deposits is to be able to cope with unforeseen expenditures. Rather than attempt to maintain optimal stocks of deposits on a daily, weekly, or even monthly basis, they allow their balances to fluctuate until certain thresholds are reached indicating that they are too high or too low. Banks also hold liquid balances, and the combined effect of liquidity held by depositors in banks and by banks themselves is to provide a buffer against real or financial shocks. As the ability of the banking sector to absorb shocks declines, financial fragility increases and financial crises become more likely. This approach also provides a rationale for regulation to safeguard the banking sector's buffer function. Moreover, even if the business cycle is primarily a real phenomenon, because the financial sector transmits shocks from one sector of the economy to another, preventing the amplification of these shocks by speculative reactions or financial fragility is also important.

Instability in the banking sector is the result of depositors placing cash in bank accounts which they have a legal right to withdraw on demand. Since depositors ordinarily only demand to withdraw a small amount of cash during any short period of time, banks try to assure their ability to meet such demands while earning profits for shareholders by acquiring portfolios of assets, including loans, whose riskiness is difficult to assess due to the aforementioned information deficiency. The asymmetry of information between banks and depositors requires that depositors trust in the ability and intentions of the banks' management. Greater disclosure of information concerning bank balance sheets might help to reduce reliance on trust, but, without active secondary markets for bank loans, the riskiness of banks' portfolios remains difficult to assess. This suggests that the service of assessing and publicizing the riskiness of bank portfolios should be provided by a government agency, as a public good.

The existence of an information deficiency makes contagion more likely, because if one bank gets into difficulties, depositors tend to lose confidence in other banks, either because other banks may have portfolios similar to the troubled bank's or because they may have lent to the troubled bank or invested in its securities. To reduce the risk of systemic failures and assure depositor confidence, it is therefore essential to curb excessive risk taking, especially by large banks.

Short of imposing 100-percent reserve requirements for demand deposits, underwriting is normally achieved by the provision of lender-of-last-resort cover by the central bank, or, in the United States, by a comprehensive deposit-insurance scheme. Once protected, depositors have little incentive to place deposits with the safest banks and instead place deposits with the banks paying the highest interest rates. If the banks offering the highest returns to depositors are the most aggressive and risk prone, then

adverse selection occurs and total risk in the system increases.

To cope with the moral-hazard and adverse-selection problems, bank regulation used to impose restraints on bank-portfolio composition to restrict risk taking and to limit interest rates charged for loans and paid on deposits. But this approach inhibited portfolio diversification, which tends to reduce risk, and restricted competition at the expense of consumers. The financial liberalization and deregulation that took place in the major financial markets in the 1970s and 1980s swept away many of these restrictions. New forms of regulation were therefore required.

The approach adopted by the monetary authorities of the major member countries of the Organization for Economic Cooperation and Development is a result of the 1988 Basle Agreement. It establishes a common definition of bank capital and sets common capital-adequacy requirements for the international banks whose head offices are located in the countries of the participating authorities. Weights reflecting the riskiness of various on- and off-balance-sheet exposures are used to assess the riskiness of a bank's portfolio. The greater the risk, the more capital the bank has to hold, so that risk taking is discouraged. In addition, since the Mexican debt crisis in 1982, central banks have required a general increase in capital holdings. Banking systems should be better able to withstand shocks as a result. Publication of the capital requirements set by the authorities on individual banks would increase market discipline, since a bank's cost of capital would reflect the assessment of riskiness implicit in the requirement.

Despite the Basle Agreement and the chastening experience with Latin American loans in the 1980s, the major international banks seem prone to build up large exposures to markets while underestimating their riskiness, as has happened in the United States in the property and the highly leveraged debt markets. This could be because some banks believe that they are too large to be allowed to fail, since their failure could interrupt commercial credit relationships, leading to bankruptcies and unemployment, and possibly a general financial crisis. The behavior of the monetary authorities in the United States and elsewhere confirms that big banks enjoy more protection than small ones.

The shortcomings of U.S. federal deposit-insurance schemes were the result of providing insurance at non-risk-related premia. The approach adopted following the Basle Agreement is potentially wasteful in requiring banks to hold large in-house insurance funds, in the form of capital, with no opportunity for pooling. Deposit-insurance schemes with risk-related premia and other asset and liability insurance contributions would facilitate pooling and may in the future be encouraged by regulators. This approach would allow capital-adequacy requirements to be reduced if risk can be shown to be covered through insurance contracts.

To the extent that it has a role to play in anticyclical or disinflationary policy, monetary restraint can be effectively applied only in the absence of financial fragility. Liquid reserve requirements are often imposed to facilitate monetary control and to ensure that the banking system can absorb fluctuations in the demand for liquidity. There is a case for requiring big banks to pay for the privilege of having automatic access to support from the lender of last resort. This objective could be achieved by applying higher percentage reserve requirements to big banks than to small ones. If the insurance package for the banking system is to include liquid reserve requirements, as well as deposit insurance, capital-adequacy requirements and lender-of-last-resort cover, then an international agreement may be required to complement the Basle Agreement on capital-adequacy requirements.

The advantage of increased reliance on appropriately funded insurance schemes or capital (and perhaps reserve) requirements is that they induce banks to reduce their reliance on the lender of last resort, and ultimately the taxpayer, which limits the moral-hazard problem.

In conclusion, the regulation and supervision of banks and other financial institutions can be regarded as an essential component of anticyclical policy, because it aims to reduce the risk of a financial crisis which may lead to recession or depression. Moreover, unless financial fragility is counteracted, monetary restraint for disinflationary or anticyclical purposes cannot be safely applied.

A. W. Mullineux

See also BANKING PANICS; CENTRAL BANKING; CLEARINGHOUSES; FEDERAL DEPOSIT INSURANCE; FINANCIAL INTERMEDIATION; LENDER OF LAST RESORT; MINSKY, HYMAN PHILLIP; MONETARY POLICY

Bibliography
Bank for International Settlements. 1988. *International Convergence of Capital Measurement and Capital Standards.* Committee on Banking Regulation and Supervisory Practices. Basle: Bank for International Settlements.
Benston, G. J., ed. 1986. *Perspectives in Safe and Sound Banking: Past, Present and Future.* Cambridge: MIT Press.
Gardener, E. P. M., ed. 1986. *U.K. Banking Supervision: Evolution, Practice and Issues.* London: Allen and Unwin.
Karaken, J. H. 1986. "Federal Reserve Bank Regulatory Policy: A Description and Some Observations." *Journal of Business* 59:3–48.
Kindleberger, C. P. 1978. *Manias, Panics and Crashes.* New York: Basic Books.
Laidler, D. 1984. "The 'Buffer Stock' Notion in Monetary Economics." *Economic Journal* 94(Supplement):17–34.
Minsky, H. P. 1986. *Stabilizing an Unstable Economy.* New Haven: Yale Univ. Press.
Portes, R. P. and K. S. Swoboda. 1987. *Threats to International Financial Stability.* Cambridge: Cambridge Univ. Press.

B

Banking Panics

"On extraordinary occasions," wrote Ricardo, "a general panic may seize the country, when everyone becomes desirous of possessing himself of the precious metals as the most convenient mode of realizing or concealing his property—against such panic banks have no security [under] . . . any system." At the onset of such a panic, holders of bank debt (demand deposits or banknotes) decide en masse to redeem the debt for cash or precious metals. The demand for redemption is so great and so sudden that the system cannot satisfy them.

A panic is a sudden scramble out of bank money into currency. The Panic of 1825 in England, according to Bagehot ([1873] 1962, 98), "was a period of frantic and almost inconceivable violence; scarcely any one knew whom to trust; credit was almost suspended; the country was . . . within twenty-four hours . . . [reduced to] . . . a state of barter." With no market in which to quickly sell their assets, banks cannot possibly honor their contractual liabilities during a panic. Banks must default on their debt obligations, and the banking system becomes insolvent. Generally, banks suspend convertibility in unison, that is, they temporarily refuse to honor their contractual obligations to redeem their debt for cash on demand.

Though unusual now, banking panics were not uncommon in the past. In the United States, banking panics occurred in 1837, 1857, 1873, 1884, 1890, 1893, 1907, and 1914. Panics occurred subsequently in the 1930s, and in Maryland and Ohio savings and loans in 1985. In England, panics date back to the seventeenth century. The most famous are the collapses associated with Overend, Gurney & Co. Ltd. in 1866, the liquidation of Baring Brothers in 1890, and those of 1825 and 1857. Typically, banking panics occur at the onset of economic downturns, and consequently, are associated with crises and depressions.

Consider the Panic of 1907 in the United States, which began in October when the liabilities of non-financial business failures, a leading indicator of recession, rose sharply. The panic also coincided with the collapse of the Knickerbocker Trust Company, the third largest trust company in New York City. On Tuesday morning, 15 October, a line of depositors seeking to withdraw currency from Knickerbocker stretched for two blocks. In the few hours before it went bankrupt Knickerbocker paid out more than $8 million of its $62 million of deposits. A suspension by all New York City banks on 26 October was soon followed by a nationwide suspension, which lasted until early January 1908. The peak of the business cycle had been the previous May, and the trough was to be June 1908. As with many, though not all, panics, this one coincided with a steep decline in stock prices. The deposit-currency ratio declined from 6.0 to 5.0 as a result of the panic. The ratio of bank deposits to bank reserves fell from 8.2 to 7.0. The money stock declined by nearly 14 percent.

In the U.S., it is the panic of the Great Depression, when about a third of U.S. banks went bankrupt, which shapes the popular image of a banking panic. But the panics before the Federal Reserve System was formed differed significantly from the subsequent episodes. The average loss per dollar of deposits caused by the panic and recession of 1907 was only one-tenth of a cent. And despite some spectacular bank failures, less than 0.5 percent of all National Banks were declared insolvent in the aftermath. The losses on deposits, and the number of banks failing in the Panic of 1907 were typical of the pre-Fed panics.

Why do bank depositors suddenly demand currency from their banks? Two fundamentally different types of theories have been advanced to explain banking panics. In one, panics are seen as random events, perhaps manifestations of "mob psychology" or "mass hysteria." It is argued that the debt contract itself can create panics. Since bank debt can be returned to the bank and exchanged for cash at any time according to a first-come-first-served rule, depositors of an insolvent bank who withdraw first gain at the expense of those at the end of the line. Thus, any time depositors think other depositors are going to withdraw, they will all withdraw—a panic. In this view panics are fundamentally inexplicable, since no theory explains why depositors suddenly conjecture that other depositors will withdraw.

In the second view, panics result from reassessments of the riskiness of the banking system. If depositors cannot tell the value of bank assets, because bank loans are unmarketable, and perhaps because bank equity is not traded, then they cannot distinguish the riskiness of one bank from that of another. In such a setting, a rational reevaluation of the riskiness of banks may provoke withdrawals of cash. What information can cause such a reevaluation of risk? Recalling the Panic of 1907, notice that the panic occurred during the fall harvesting season, coincident with a sharp rise in business failures, and occurred when the Knickerbocker Trust failed. Thus, the three candidates for the relevant information are: (1) seasonal factors, (2) the news of an imminent recession, (3) the failure of a particular corporation.

During spring and fall, rural areas used proportionately more cash than during summer and winter. Unexpectedly large demands for cash, it is argued, could cause a panic. The failure of a single company might start a panic if the company seemed to have important links to the banking system. If so, some banks might fail, but which ones cannot be predicted, so all become suspect. This is known as a contagion effect. Finally, if depositors believe that a recession is looming, they might withdraw to avoid bank failures which are expected to occur during a recession. It is difficult to discriminate among these hypotheses since the number of panics is small. However, many large seasonal movements in interest rates in the U.S. have not lead to panics. Similarly, many failures of firms have not caused panics. But every panic did coincide with a threshold level of business failures.

Panics are not inherent in the activity of banking. Not all banking systems have experienced panics. Superficially similar banking systems have had widely varying records in this regard. A crucial necessary condition for the possibility of panics appears to be a highly decentralized banking system. Banking systems with many banks appear prone to panics, while systems with a few banks, perhaps heavily branched, are not susceptible to panics, because banks in the latter type of system are well diversified. Depositors understand that if their bank is well diversified, it is very unlikely to fail. Thus, they do not revise their evaluation of the riskiness of their bank when receiving new information or when conjecturing that other depositors are about to withdraw funds from the bank. Consequently, Canada, with a small number of heavily branched banks (roughly thirty banks for most of the nineteenth century), does not have a history of panics. Nor did the Scottish banking system (which also had unlimited liability for bank-equity holders) experience any panics. However, the United States and England, with many small banks, did experience panics. It is also notable that England had a central bank and experienced panics, while most panics in the U.S. occurred without a central bank.

Because of the potiential real effects of an insolvent banking system, panics, and the possibility of panics, have played a central role in the evolution of the banking industry of every country. Even before governments became involved, banks were organizing their own responses to panics. Such responses have usually been directed by private bank clearinghouses. Originally formed to help clear bank liabilities by centralizing the operation, clearinghouses in some countries quickly evolved unique ways of responding to panics. In the U.S., clearinghouses introduced coinsurance to prevent depositors from bearing the loss of an individual bank's failure during a panic. Like systems with a small number of well-diversified banks, a system with many small banks may be well diversified as a whole. Clearinghouses took advantage of this fact during panics.

Banks were willing to bear risks of other clearinghouse members' losses because, by doing so, they could credibly convince depositors that the system was not insolvent. By coinsuring, banks created incentives for mutual monitoring by clearinghouse members. For example, clearinghouses set reserve requirements, required quarterly reports, audited member banks, and, in general, limited the risk taking of members. These restrictions later evolved into the government's regulatory system. Similar arrangements existed in England, Scotland, Canada, Japan, and so on.

The threat of panic continues to govern central-bank policies and bank regulation throughout the world. Indeed, the classic work on central banking, Bagehot's *Lombard Street,* was mainly concerned with the central bank's response to panics. Bagehot's advice was for the central bank to lend freely at high interest rates. But central banks in England and the United States were never successful at preventing panics. The continuing possibility of panic led some countries to adopt deposit insurance. To date, credible deposit-insurance systems have prevented banking panics. But, recent experience in the U.S. has raised concerns about the design and cost of such systems.

Gary Gorton

See also BANK CHARTER ACT; BANK OF UNITED STATES; BARING CRISIS; CENTRAL BANKING; CLEARINGHOUSES; CREDIT-ANSTALT; CRISIS OF 1857; CRISIS OF 1907; FEDERAL DEPOSIT INSURANCE; GREAT DEPRESSION IN THE UNITED STATES (1929–1938); LENDER OF LAST RESORT; OPTION CLAUSE; OVEREND, GURNEY CRISIS; PANIC OF 1825

Bibliography

Bagehot, W. [1873] 1962. *Lombard Street: A Description of the Money Market.* Homewood, Ill.: Irwin.

Gorton, G. 1988. "Banking Panics and Business Cycles." *Oxford Economic Papers* 40:751–81.

Gorton, G. and C. Calomiris. 1991. "The Origins of Banking Panics: Models, Facts, and Bank Regulation." In *Financial Markets and Financial Crises,* edited by R. G. Hubbard, 109–73 . Chicago: Univ. of Chicago Press.

Sprague, O. M. W. 1910. *History of Crises Under the National Banking System.* Washington, D.C.: Government Printing Office.

Banking School, Currency School, and Free Banking School

After the Bullionist controversies dissipated in 1819 with the decision to restore gold redeemability for Bank of England notes, British monetary economists turned their attention to the causes of and potential cures for business cycles. The crises of 1825, 1836–37, and 1839 especially fueled a large pamphlet literature and volumes of Parliamentary testimony. Three major schools of thought emerged in a classic debate whose influence was felt around the world and continues to be felt today. The Banking School advanced a non-monetary, wave-of-speculation theory of the cycle. Members of the Currency School charged the Bank of England, but especially the country banks, with exacerbating speculative cycles by procyclical note-issuing policies. The Free Banking School held that the Bank of England was driving the cycle from start to finish, but absolved the country banks from responsibility, because their note issues were constrained by competition.

Thomas Tooke, chief theorist of the Banking School, inferred from historical studies of price movements that British cycles arose from non-monetary causes. Speculative booms could be financed entirely by trade credit, extended in a spirit of over-confidence, though "over-banking" (lending to unsafe borrowers, or operating with too low a reserve ratio) could also contribute.

The Currency School mainstream, as represented by J. R. McCulloch and Samuel Loyd Jones (later Lord Overstone), also attributed the upswing in the cycle to nonmonetary sources. A wave of optimism (whose origin was unexplained) sparked increased demand for loanable funds, leading to increased note issue. Rising nominal income and monetary expansion fed one another until high domestic commodity prices eventually (in two years or so) led to an external drain of gold (the price-specie-flow mechanism came into play). The crisis came when reserve losses forced the Bank of England to contract. In McCulloch's view, an external drain did not mean that the Bank had overexpanded, but the drain affected it as the sole holder of gold in London. Prices fell and bankruptcies followed.

Robert Mushet and James William Gilbart did most to develop the Free Banking School's analysis of the cycle. Those members of the Currency School who were most critical of the Bank of England, particularly Robert Torrens, shared the theory. A cycle began with an overissue of notes by the Bank of England (expansion of the stock of banknotes beyond the quantity demanded at the price level given by the international gold standard).

The Bank's expansion created an excess supply of money, generating excess demands for commodities and financial assets, thereby bidding up commodity and asset prices and reducing the rate of interest. The country banks, treating Bank of England liabilities as high-powered money, were swept along. Both the monetary expansion and the subsequent business boom were unsustainable, because high domestic commodity prices and low domestic interest rates promoted an external drain of gold from the Bank of England. As above, reserve losses forced the Bank to reverse course to protect its reserves. The sudden curtailment of its circulation reduced the supply of bank credit, pulling interest rates back up and precipitating a crisis.

The reform proposals of the schools followed from their diagnoses of the cycle. All were committed to maintaining the gold standard, and saw the self-regulating character of a purely metallic currency (via the Humean price-specie-flow mechanism) as an ideal to be emulated in a mixed currency of coin and notes. However, the Banking School thought that the English currency already was self-regulating. Structural reform of the monetary system would be pointless at best. They did advise that the Bank of England increase its gold reserve. The Currency School advocated centralizing the issue of notes, and imposing a rule on the issuer designed to simulate the price-specie-flow mechanism and prevent procyclical behavior. The "Currency Principle" held that changes in the currency stock should correspond one-for-one with international gold flows. Peel's Bank Charter Act of 1844 implemented this program by creating a national monopoly issuer, and imposing on it a 100-percent marginal reserve requirement. The Free Banking School proposed to make the English currency self-regulating by eliminating the monopoly of the Bank of England over the London circulation. All issuers would then be subject to competitive constraints that would make their circulation demand determined even in the short run.

Debate among the schools likewise followed their differences regarding the cycle. Tooke and John Fullarton of the Banking School rejected the other schools' shared view that variations in the circulation of the Bank of England influenced prices and thereby international gold flows. Fullarton's *law of reflux* denied that the Bank could create an excess stock of money lasting long enough to have cyclical effects. The price level varied from nonmonetary causes, and the stock of notes, including Bank of England notes, passively responded. The Free Banking School affirmed that the country banks passively responded to the "needs of trade" (demand to hold notes), rejecting the Currency School view that they were a disequilibrating force. But the monopolistic Bank of England was not passive and could overissue, contrary to the Banking School view, because it was not similarly constrained by interbank clearings. The Free Banking School rejected the Currency School's view that the national currency stock should be governed by an artificial mechanism. Only under competitive arrangements would the currency be self-regulating.

The Currency School disputed the contention of the Free Banking School that interbank clearings effectively restrained a competitive banking system as a whole from overissuing, arguing instead (implausibly, in their opponents' view) that banks would overexpand in concert. McCulloch even denied that interbank clearings would restrain a single bank from relative overissue. If competition made banks respond to the needs of trade, rather than to international specie flows as the Currency Principle required, so much the worse for competition. Loyd incisively probed a weak point in both Banking School and Free Banking School arguments, the erroneous tendency to identify the demand to hold money with the demand for credit (i.e., the "real-bills doctrine" that banks discounting commercial paper of the right sort cannot issue too much currency).

The debate between the Currency Banking and Free Banking Schools was the first sophisticated debate among economists over the causes of business cycles, and as such was a great seedbed for ideas developed later. The Currency and Free Banking Schools are important as precursors of business-cycle theories that focus on the real effects of monetary disturbances, most immediately Wicksellian theories (like the Austrian theory) that revolve around discrepancies between market and natural rates of interest. The Currency School attributed the upswing to a rise in loan demand; bank expansion then kept the market rate of interest from rising appropriately, and fueled an artificial boom. The Free Banking School attributed the upswing to central-bank overexpansion that pushed the market rate below an unchanged natural rate.

Banking-School doctrine is important as a precursor of real business-cycle theories.

Lawrence H. White

See also Austrian Theory of Business Cycles; Bank Charter Act of 1844; Bank of England; Free Banking; Fullarton, John; Gilbart, James William; Joplin, Thomas; Loyd, Samuel Jones; Mushet, Robert; Parnell, Henry Brooke; Tooke, Thomas; Torrens, Robert

Bibliography

Arnon, A. 1991. *Thomas Tooke: Pioneer of Monetary Theory.* Ann Arbor: Univ. of Michigan Press.

Fetter, F. W. 1965. *The Development of British Monetary Orthodoxy, 1797–1875.* Cambridge: Harvard Univ. Press.

Fullarton, J. 1845. *On the Regulation of Currencies.* 2d ed. London: John Murray.

Gilbart, J. W. 1841. *Currency and Banking: A Review. . . .* London: H. Hooper.

Gregory, T. E., ed. 1929. *Select Statutes, Documents and Reports Relating to British Banking, 1832–1928.* Vol. 1. London: Humphrey Milford.

McCulloch, J. R. 1837. "The Bank of England and the Country Banks." *Edinburgh Review* 65:61–84.

Mushet, R. 1826. *An Attempt to Explain from Facts the Effect of the Issues of the Bank of England upon Its Own Interests, Public Credit, and the Country Banks.* London: Baldwin, Cradock, and Joy.

Overstone, Lord (S. J. Loyd). [1857] 1972. *Tracts and Other Publications on Metallic and Paper Currency.* Edited by J. R. McCulloch. Englewood Cliffs, N.J.: A. M. Kelley.

Schwartz, A. J. 1987. "Banking School, Currency School, Free Banking School." In *The New Palgrave: The Dictionary of Economics.* Vol. 1. Edited by J. Eatwell, M. Milgate, and P. Newman. London: Macmillan.

Smith, V. C. 1936. *The Rationale of Central Banking.* London: P. S. King.

Tooke, T. 1840. *A History of Prices.* Vol. 3. London: Longmans.

Torrens, R. 1840. *A Letter to Thomas Tooke, . . .* London: Longmans.

White, L. H. 1984. *Free Banking in Britain: Theory, Experience, and Debate, 1800–1845.* Cambridge: Cambridge Univ. Press.

Baring Crisis (1890)

During the first three-quarters of the nineteenth century, Britain regularly experienced financial crises, at a rate of about one per decade. Following the failure of Overend, Gurney and Company in 1866, however, Britain was not threatened with a major crisis until November 1890, when the firm of Baring Brothers and Company neared failure (note, however, the City of Glasgow Bank crisis in 1878). By engineering an orderly liquidation of Baring, the Bank of England spared the City from what contemporary observers believed would have been the most severe financial crisis of the century. The Baring episode marked the acceptance of Bagehot's view, expressed in *Lombard Street,* that the Bank of England had both the resources and responsibility to act as lender of last resort.

Like its predecessors of 1847, 1857, and 1866, the Baring crisis followed on the heels of an investment boom. While the object of speculation in previous crises had been grain (1847), railroads (1847 and 1857), and limited-liability companies (1866), the 1890 crisis was preceded by increased investment in Latin American securities. Spurred by low interest rates at home in the 1880s (aided by Chancellor of the Exchequer George Goschen's debt conversion scheme of 1888), British investors looked increasingly overseas for more substantial returns. Foreign investment rose from a trough of less than 1 percent of GNP in 1877 to over 7 percent in 1890.

A favorite destination for British investment in the 1880s was Argentina, where £65 million of British capital found its way in 1888–89. The most prominent South American specialist in the city of London was the firm of Baring Brothers and Company, which had made its first Latin American loan—to Argentina—in 1824. Baring became deeply committed to issuing and underwriting loans on behalf of South American governments and public works projects in the second half of the nineteenth century. By 1890 loans to Argentina and Uruguay made up about three-quarters of Baring's portfolio.

The booming conditions that made investment in Argentina attractive were accompanied by rising land prices, an expansion of development projects, and a substantial increase in external debt. By 1890, Argentina's external debt was approximately £200 million, and its annual debt service of £12 million was equal to about 60 percent of total exports. The growing external debt, combined with civil disturbances, a change in government, the collapse of the land boom, a run on the banking system, and an abortive attempt to arrange a moratorium led to a fall in the value of Argentina's inconvertible paper currency and discouraged European investors from taking more Argentine securities. With the demand for its large block of Argentine securities drying up, Baring's position became desperate in late October.

News of Baring's difficulties reached William Lidderdale, the Governor of the Bank of England, on Saturday, 8 November. In the rough statement of accounts Baring presented to the Governor on Monday—confirmed by a more detailed audit carried out under the Bank's supervision several days later—it appeared that the firm was solvent but, because the demand for South American securities had dried up, illiquid. Baring convinced the Governor that the demand for these securities would eventually recover and, therefore, that Baring's liquidity problem was temporary.

Lidderdale felt that the failure of Baring would have far more serious consequences for the Bank and the City than the failure of Overend, Gurney had had almost a quarter of a century earlier. Overend had been almost exclusively a domestic concern, and its failure had provoked an internal drain. As the creator of domestic liquidity, the Bank of England had been able, with the suspension of the Bank Charter Act, to supply enough liquidity to meet the internal drain. Baring, however, was an international financial house, and its failure would have provoked an external drain of specie from the Bank which might well have resulted in the suspension of the gold standard.

Given the international nature of the threat, it is not surprising that Lidderdale refused the government's offer to suspend the fiduciary limit set in the Bank Charter Act (an offer which his predecessors at the Bank had accepted—though not always willingly—in the crises of 1847, 1857, and 1866), since such assistance would have afforded the Bank little protection against an external drain. Instead, Lidderdale buttressed the Bank's gold reserve by mid-week with loans of £1.5 million from the Russian government and £3 million from the Bank of France.

In addition to bolstering the Bank's reserve, Lidderdale, on Friday, set about assembling subscriptions towards a guarantee fund. Subscribers were not required to advance any money and, in fact, would only be called on in the event that the Bank-supervised liquidation of Baring's assets was not sufficient to cover its liabilities. Lidderdale placed the Bank's name at the top of the list of subscribers for £1 million and began coaxing, cajoling, and in some cases even threatening potential subscribers. By 4 PM on Saturday he had commitments for approximately £10 million, equal to nearly half of Baring's liabilities.

The success of Lidderdale's bold action, as evidenced by the equanimity with which the City reacted to the news of Baring's difficulties, can be attributed in large part to the speed with which it was carried out. The Governor arranged both the loans and the guarantee fund within a week of hearing of Baring's position— just hours before news of Baring's difficulties became public.

Unlike its predecessors of 1847, 1857, and 1866, which were accompanied by widespread commercial and financial failures, the Baring crisis made barely a ripple in London's financial markets. While Governors during the previous episodes had spoken vaguely of the Bank's "duty" in the wake of crises, it was not until Bagehot's *Lombard Street* that the Bank's duty was defined. Bagehot's lucid exposition, combined with Lidderdale's determination, permanently changed the way the Bank and the City viewed the Bank's role as lender of last resort.

Richard S. Grossman

See also BANK CHARTER ACT OF 1844; BANK OF ENGLAND; CENTRAL BANKING; CRISIS OF 1847; CRISIS OF 1857; INTERNATIONAL LENDER OF LAST RESORT; LENDER OF LAST RESORT; OVEREND, GURNEY CRISIS

Bibliography
Bagehot, W. [1873] 1962. *Lombard Street.* Homewood, Ill.: Irwin.
Batchelor, R. 1986. "The Avoidance of Catastrophe: Two Nineteenth-Century Banking Crises." In *Financial Crises and the World Banking System,* edited by F. Capie and G. Wood, 41–73. New York: St. Martin's Press.
Clapham, J. 1945. *The Bank of England: A History.* 2 vols. New York: Macmillan.
Gregory, T. E., ed. 1929. *Select Statutes, Documents and Reports Relating to British Banking, 1832–1928.* 2 vols. London: Humphrey Milford.
Humphrey, T. 1975. "The Classical Concept of the Lender of Last Resort." Federal Reserve Bank of Richmond, *Economic Review,* January/February, 2–9.
Kindleberger, C. 1978. *Manias, Panics, and Crashes.* New York: Basic Books.
Pressnell, L. S. 1986. "Comment on Batchelor Paper." In *Financial Crises and the World Banking System,* edited by F. Capie and G. Wood, 74–76. New York: St. Martin's Press.
Sayers, R. S. 1957. *Central Banking After Bagehot.* Oxford: Clarendon Press.
Schwartz, A. J. 1986. "Real and Pseudo-Financial Crises." In *Financial Crises and the World Banking System,* edited by F. Capie and G. Wood, 11–31. New York: St. Martin's Press.
Thornton, H. [1802] 1939. *An Enquiry into the Nature and Effects of the Paper Credit of Great Britain.* Reprint. Edited with an introduction by F. A. von Hayek. London: Allen and Unwin.

Bauer, Otto (1881–1938)

Along with Rudolf Hilferding, Otto Bauer was the most prominent economic thinker among the so-called "Austro-Marxists." In 1913 he published a trenchant critique of Rosa Luxemburg's theory of imperialism, setting out an alternative model of economic crises in which fluctuations in real wages played a central role. In 1936 Bauer produced the first formal Marxian model of underconsumption.

A native of Vienna, Bauer studied economics under Eugen von Böhm-Bawerk. In 1907 he became secretary of the Austrian Social-Democratic Party (SPÖ), and in the same year published a major book on the problem of nationalism in Marxian theory. Bauer served as Austrian Foreign Minister in the Republican government of 1918–19, and until the Dollfuss coup in 1934 was the principal theoretician and effective leader of the SPÖ. His final years were spent in exile in Czechoslovakia and in Paris, where he died.

Bauer's early writings on crisis theory included a lengthy but unoriginal exposition of Marx's analysis in volume two of *Capital,* stressing the difficulty of securing proportionality between the two departments of the economy in the face of technical progress and an increasing organic composition of capital. He also defended Marx's analysis of the falling rate of profit in volume three against the objections of Mikhail Tugan-Baranovsky.

Despite a lengthy discussion on the economics of imperialism in his *Die Nationalitätenfrage und die Sozialdemokratie* (1907), Bauer failed to establish any links between militarism and the export of capital, on the one hand, and the trade cycle on the other. This omission was partially rectified in 1913 when, in his review of Luxemburg's *Accumulation of Capital,* Bauer ([1913] 1986) attributed economic crises to the "over-accumulation" of capital. By this he meant the tendency, at the peak of the cycle, for the demand for labor power to grow faster than the available supply. The consequent reduction in the reserve army of the unemployed, Bauer argued, allowed real wages to rise. This reduced both the rate of exploitation and the rate of profit, inducing capitalists to cut back on the accumulation of capital. In the ensuing depression, unemployment rose again, real wages fell, and profits were restored, leading to renewed prosperity. Marx had hinted at a similar theory of crises in volume one of *Capital,* but Bauer seems to have been the first to take it seriously.

In *Zwischen Zwei Weltkriegen?*, Bauer took a quite different line. He began by maintaining, like Marx in volume three, that technical progress in the upswing could be expected to increase the organic composition of capital. This meant that capitalist economies were on a knife-edge. If the rate of exploitation were to rise rapidly enough to prevent the rate of profit from declining, demand from wage-earners would be insufficient to permit the full realization of surplus value, and an underconsumption crisis would result. If, however, the rate of exploitation were to rise more slowly than this, the rate of profit would decline owing to the rising organic composition. In addition to these arguments (55–57) *Zwischen Zwei Weltkriegen?* is notable for containing the first mathematical model of underconsumption by a Marxian economist (351–53).

Although somewhat eclectic in his ideas, Bauer was one of the most influential of all Marxian crisis theorists. His critique of Rosa Luxemburg won widespread acceptance, before being itself severely criticized by Henryk Grossman in 1929. Bauer's "over-accumulation" interpretation of Marxian crisis theory was taken over in the 1930s and 1940s by such writers as Paul Sweezy and Maurice Dobb, resurfacing several decades later in a number of important accounts of the post-1973 crisis, such as that of Armstrong, Glyn, and Harrison (1984). His underconsumption model, too, was adopted by Sweezy and through the latter's *Theory of Capitalist Development* (186–89) became incorporated in one major strand of Marxist thought.

M. C. Howard
J. E. King

See also FALLING RATE OF PROFIT; HILFERDING, RUDOLF; LUXEMBURG, ROSA; MARX, KARL HEINRICH; OVERSAVING THEORIES OF BUSINESS CYCLES; SWEEZY, PAUL MARLOR; TUGAN-BARANOVSKY, MIKHAIL IVANOVICH

Bibliography
Armstrong, P., A. Glyn, and J. Harrison. 1984. *Capitalism Since World War II.* London: Fontana.
Bauer, O. 1904–05. "Marx' Theorie der Wirtschaftskrisen." *Die Neue Zeit* 23:133–8, 164–70.
———. 1906–07. "Mathematische Formeln Gegen Tugan-Baranovsky." *Die Neue Zeit* 25:822–23.
———. [1913] 1986. "Otto Bauer's 'Accumulation of Capital.'" Translated by J. E. King. *History of Political Economy* 18:87–110.
———. 1936. *Zwischen Zwei Weltkriegen?* Bratislava: Eugen Prager.
Blum, M. E. 1985. *The Austro-Marxists 1890–1918: A Psychobiographical Study.* Lexington: Univ. Press of Kentucky.
Braunthal, J. 1961. "Otto Bauer: Ein Lebensbild." In *Otto Bauer, Eine Auswahl aus seinem Lebenswerk. Mit einem Lebensbild Otto Bauers,* edited by J. Braunthal, 9–101. Vienna: Verlag der Wiener Volksbuchhandlung.
Bronfenbrenner, M. and M. Wolfson. 1984. "Marxian Macrodynamics and the Harrod Growth Model." *History of Political Economy* 16:174–86.
Howard, M. C. and J. E. King. 1989. *A History of Marxian Economics.* Vol. 1, *1883–1929.* Princeton: Princeton Univ. Press.
Orzech, Z. and S. Groll. 1983. "Otto Bauer's Scheme of Expanded Reproduction: An Early Harrodian Growth Model." *History of Political Economy* 15:529–48.
Sweezy, P. M. 1942. *The Theory of Capitalist Development.* New York: Oxford Univ. Press.

Bernstein, Eduard (1850–1932)

Eduard Bernstein was the most prominent writer in the revisionist movement in German Social Democracy before 1914. He rejected the claims of many orthodox Marxists that capitalism would necessarily break down because of the increasing severity of economic crises, arguing instead that planning and liberal reform would allow the trade cycle to be tamed.

The son of a Jewish locomotive driver from Berlin, Bernstein worked in a bank before becoming a journalist and lecturer for the Social Democratic Party (SDP). He spent more than two decades in exile in Switzerland and London before returning to Germany in 1901, shortly after the publication of his wide-ranging criticisms of mainstream Marxist thinking. Bernstein served as a deputy in the Reichstag from 1902 until 1928.

Drawing upon the ideas of the British Fabians and "New Liberals," Bernstein argued that Marx's interpretation of capitalism was inconsistent with contemporary reality. Real wages were growing, and the distribution of income and property was becoming more (not less) equal. Hence there was no basis for the underconsumptionist theory of crisis supported by Karl Kautsky and other SDP luminaries. Bernstein also denied the second principal strand in Marxian crisis theory, which centered on the disproportionalities between the various industries resulting from the anarchy of capitalist production. He maintained that the development of cartels had made the planned expansion of capacity possible, and that the growth of credit mechanisms and the world market had allowed overproduction in particular branches to be eliminated without precipitating a general crisis. Capitalism, Bernstein concluded, would not break down under its own internal contradictions. Nor, as many of his opponents asserted, was intensified imperialist rivalry an inescapable consequence of uncontrollable economic instability.

Bernstein's rejection of Marxian orthodoxy was comprehensive. In addition to his views on crisis theory, it involved a critique of the materialist conception of history, the labor theory of value, and the notion that proletarian revolution was both welcome and inevitable. He was vigorously attacked by Rosa Luxemburg, Karl Kautsky, and (by implication) Rudolf Hilferding, all of whom defended the majority position that crises could be eliminated only under socialism. Bernstein's ideas were more favorably received by Russian revisionists like Tugan-Baranovsky, and by the 1920s his former adversaries in the SDP had come to accept the validity of his criticisms. Hilferding's model of a crisis-free "organized capitalism" owed much to Bernstein's earlier work.

Although he was not a major economic theorist, Eduard Bernstein played an important role in undermining the dominance of Marxian crisis theory in the Western labor movement. He prepared the ground for the rapid and general acceptance of Keynesian ideas after 1936.

M. C. Howard
J. E. King

See also HILFERDING, RUDOLF; KAUTSKY, KARL; LUXEMBURG, ROSA; OVERSAVING THEORIES OF BUSINESS CYCLES; TUGAN-BARANOVSKY, MIKHAIL IVANOVICH

Bibliography

Angel, P. 1961. *Eduard Bernstein et l'evolution du socialisme allemande.* Paris: Marcel Didier.

Bernstein, E. 1901. *Zur Geschichte und Theorie des Socialismus.* Berlin: Akademischer Verlag für Sociale Wissenschaft Dr. John Edelheim.

———. [1899] 1961. *Evolutionary Socialism: a Criticism and an Affirmation.* Translation. New York: Schocken.

Gay, P. 1962. *The Dilemma of Democratic Socialism: Eduard Bernstein's Challenge to Marx.* London: Collier-Macmillan.

Howard, M. C. and J. E. King. 1989. *A History of Marxian Economics.* Vol. 1, *1883–1929.* Princeton: Princeton Univ. Press.

Kautsky, K. 1899. *Bernstein und das Sozialdemokratische Program: Eine Antikritik.* Stuttgart: Dietz.

Luxemburg, R. 1970. *Reform or Revolution.* New York: Pathfinder Press.

Böhm-Bawerk, Eugen Ritter von (1851–1914)

A founder, along with Carl Menger and Friedrich von Wieser, of the Austrian School of economics, Böhm-Bawerk is best known for his theory of capital and interest. Böhm-Bawerk himself made no direct contribution to business-cycle analysis. Indeed, his student Joseph Schumpeter records (*History of Economic*

Analysis, 1134) that Böhm-Bawerk denied that business cycles were a uniform phenomenon susceptible to a single theoretical explanation. However, the next generation of Austrian economists, notably F. A. Hayek (1931) sought to merge Böhm-Bawerk's theory of capital and roundabout production with the monetary theory of the business cycle that had been developed by the Swedish economist Knut Wicksell and by another student of Böhm-Bawerk's, Ludwig von Mises.

Böhm-Bawerk advanced a theory of roundabout, capital-using production in which producers could increase output by using capital, but only with a delay. The more capital applied and the longer the delay, the more roundabout the process.

In the Wicksell-Mises paradigm, the expansion phase of the business cycle was the consequence of credit expansion financed by banks' lending at less than the *natural rate* of interest (i.e., the rate at which real savings and investment would be equal). The reduced rate of interest, in the Böhm-Bawerkian scheme, lengthened the period of production since entrepreneurs would find it profitable to adopt increasingly roundabout processes. Since the shift to more roundabout production processes was not induced by an increase in the public's desire to save, the free capital needed to sustain the elongated period of production would only be forthcoming if banks continued lending at less than the natural rate of interest. But an internal or external drain would eventually force the banking system lending at less than the natural rate to curtail its lending. When that happened, entrepreneurs would face a capital shortage and would be unable to maintain such roundabout production processes. This period of capital shortage with the implied abandonment of some of the most durable and long-lived investment projects characterizes the upper-turning point of the cycle.

While Böhm-Bawerk's theory of capital and interest could thus find direct application in the Austrian theory of the business cycle, Böhm-Bawerk's analysis also had a more subtle, but perhaps even more far-reaching impact on the dynamic analysis of economic problems in general and the analysis of business cycles in particular. Böhm-Bawerk viewed the problem of capital and interest as a problem inherent in the analysis of a complex web of economic relationships of production and consumption extending through time. Capital was the means by which

decisions about future production and consumption could be made in the present, while the rate of interest was an intertemporal exchange rate reflecting the opportunities for intertemporal transformations in production or consumption.

In trying to make sensible the notion of an equilibrium interest rate, Böhm-Bawerk had to introduce a notion of the intertemporal consistency of plans to produce and to consume. Within the highly aggregated model of capital that Böhm-Bawerk used, an equilibrium rate of interest sufficed to achieve that intertemporal consistency.

But when Hayek ([1928] 1984, [1937] 1948) and Hicks (1939) tried to generalize the concept of intertemporal equilibrium for a multi-commodity general-equilibrium model with incomplete markets, they were led to introduce the concept of price expectations and to define intertemporal equilibrium in terms of correct future price expectations. The origin of that line of theoretical development, which eventually led to the rational-expectations hypothesis, was Böhm-Bawerk's theory of capital and interest.

David Glasner

See also AUSTRIAN THEORY OF BUSINESS CYCLES; BURCHARDT, FRITZ (FRANK) ADOLPH; CAPITAL GOODS; EXPECTATIONS; HAYEK, FRIEDRICH AUGUST [VON]; LACHMANN, LUDWIG MAURITS; MISES, LUDWIG EDLER VON; PERIOD OF PRODUCTION

Bibliography

Böhm-Bawerk, E. [1889] 1959. *Capital and Interest.* 3 vols. Translation. South Holland, Ill.: Libertarian Press.

Hayek, F. A. [1928] 1984. "Intertemporal Price Equilibrium and Movements in the Value of Money." In *Money, Capital, and Fluctuations: Early Essays,* edited by R. McCloughry, 71–117. Chicago: Univ. of Chicago Press.

———. 1931. *Prices and Production.* London: Routledge and Sons.

———. [1937] 1948. "Economics and Knowledge." Chap. 2 in *Individualism and Economic Order.* Chicago: Univ. of Chicago Press.

Hicks, J. R. 1939. *Value and Capital.* Oxford: Clarendon Press.

Milgate, M. 1979. "On the Origin of the Notion of 'Intertemporal Equilibrium.'" *Economica* 46:1–10.

Brunner, Karl (1916–1989)

Karl Brunner is best known as a major figure in the development of Monetarism during the 1960s and 1970s. Indeed, it was he who first used the label for this body of doctrine, and his contributions to it in collaboration with Allan Meltzer rank second only to those of Milton Friedman. As the label suggests, Monetarist theory stresses the importance of the monetary system in general, and the quantity of money in particular, to economic activity. Its claims to relevance, usually supported by empirical evidence, range more widely than the area of business cycles, and impinge also on such phenomena as inflation and the balance of payments.

A distinguishing characteristic of Brunner's Monetarism is the particular care which he gave to analyzing the way in which the quantity of money is generated in a sophisticated financial system. There is little disagreement among economists that, if the monetary authorities can control the quantity of money, then that variable may have important effects. The Monetarist proposition that those effects are essentially the same in a modern monetary system as they would be under an old-fashioned commodity-money system are more controversial. Brunner and Meltzer (1976) argued that in the modern world, money gets into and out of circulation as a by-product of the borrowing and lending activities of banks and their customers; and that because money is created and destroyed without completely offsetting changes in the planned money holdings of private-sector agents, the effects of such changes are in important respects similar to those that would arise if money were to be injected into the system (to use Friedman's analogy) by being dropped from a helicopter.

According to Brunner, then, in a modern banking system, changes in the quantity of money disturb the nonbank sector and have consequences for expenditure. They do not represent a merely passive response of the banking system to changes in the public's demand for money. Though the ultimate effects of changes in the quantity of money are on the price level, Brunner paid careful attention to the mechanisms which linked the cause in question with its ultimate effects. Here he stressed the short-term, but nevertheless empirically important effects of monetary changes on interest rates, output, and employment. This naturally led him to link up a monetary theory of inflation with a monetary explanation of fluctuations in these intermediate variables, and to produce a monetary theory of cyclical fluctuations in economic activity. Thus, and again in the company of Friedman, he became a leading exponent of a tradition in business-cycle theory that can be traced back to such writers as Henry Thornton and Irving Fisher, among others.

In the 1970s, Brunner initiated and supervised empirical studies of a number of countries which utilized a common structural econometric framework to provide empirical support for the view that then recent fluctuations had been driven by what he termed a "dominant impulse" originating in the monetary sector. The main results of this endeavor were published in Brunner and Meltzer (1978). At that time, the evidence seemed largely to support this dominant-impulse hypothesis; shortly before his death, however, he explicitly repudiated it (Brunner and Meltzer 1993). His later position was that, though money remained dominant in determining nominal variables such as the price level, cyclical fluctuations in real variables such as output and employment could arise from a variety of shocks, some monetary and some real.

Though it is common to regard so-called "New-Classical" theory as a more theoretically refined version of Monetarism, Brunner (1989) was adamant that it was not. He regarded the reliance of New Classical theory on a Walrasian system of markets which clear continuously as rendering it irrelevant to the analysis of an economy in which monetary exchange is the essential characteristic of economic activity. Money, Brunner argued, draws its very existence from a pervasive uncertainty in economic life; the monetary system allows agents to cope with that uncertainty, but does not eliminate it. Hence, the informational assumptions made by New Classical business-cycle theory, whether in its original "monetary surprise" form, or its later "real shocks" version, were not just unrealistic, but unrealistic in a fundamentally misleading way.

In the 1990s, the style of business-cycle theory to which Karl Brunner contributed has become unfashionable, but it belongs to a tradition in economic thought of nearly two centuries' standing. It seems likely, then, that the passage of time will deal kindly with his contributions as that tradition remains an important element of our understanding of economic life.

David Laidler

See also FRIEDMAN, MILTON; MONETARY DISARRAY THEORIES OF THE BUSINESS CYCLE; MONETARY EQUILIBRIUM THEORIES OF THE BUSINESS CYCLE; REAL BUSINESS-CYCLE THEORIES

Bibliography

Brunner, K. 1989. "The Disarray in Macroeconomics." In *Monetary Economics in the 1980s: The Henry Thornton Lectures,* edited by F. Capie and G. Wood, 1–8. London: Macmillan.

Brunner, K. and A. H. Meltzer. 1976. "An Aggregative Theory for a Closed Economy." In *Monetarism*, edited by J. Stein, 69–103. Amsterdam: North Holland.

———, eds. 1978. *The Problem of Inflation.* Vol. 8 in *Carnegie-Rochester Conference Series.*

———. 1993. *Money and the Economy: Issues in Monetary Analysis.* Cambridge: Cambridge Univ. Press.

Laidler, D. 1991. "Karl Brunner's Monetary Economics: An Appreciation." *Journal of Money, Credit, and Banking* 23:633–58.

Bullionist Controversies

The Bullionist Controversies constitute an important milestone in the development of monetary theory and policy. Although an explicit theory of the business cycle was not one of the achievements that this set of diverse and wide-ranging controversies produced, many of the essential ingredients that went into later cycle theories—particularly monetary ones—can be found in them.

The controversies began within a year or two after the government, responding to a request from the Bank of England, prohibited the Bank in 1797 from converting any of its notes into gold. The immediate cause of the suspension (which was at first supposed to last only a few months, but was reinstated by subsequent legislation) was a rumor of a French invasion that started a run on the banks. The suspension was soon followed by a depreciation of pound sterling on the foreign exchanges and a premium on bullion.

The depreciation of sterling and the premium on bullion that emerged subsequently led to the first round of the controversies. It was set off by Walter Boyd's *Letter to Mr. Pitt* (1800) in which he attributed the depreciation to excess issues by the Bank of England.

Defenders of the bank denied that the depreciation had been caused by excess issues and instead blamed the depreciation on the unfavorable impact war-related foreign remittances had on the balance of payments. In his *Remarks on Currency and Commerce* (1802) John Wheatley replied by insisting that any depreciation was ipso facto evidence of overissue. This extreme Bullionist position would be joined in only by Ricardo when he entered the controversies in their next phase between 1809 and 1811.

The initial stage of the controversies was marked by the most outstanding contribution of the period, Thornton's *Enquiry into the Nature and Causes of the Paper Credit of Great Britain.* Thornton, on the one hand, defended the bank against the charge that the depreciation of sterling was conclusive proof of overissue by noting that heavy foreign remittances could turn the exchange against a country even if its internal price level did not change. On the other hand, he refuted the argument of the Bank's directors that by limiting themselves to lending on real bills they could not possibly have engaged in an overissue.

Whatever its merits as a practical guide for an individual bank in a competitive system constrained by convertibility, the real-bills doctrine, Thornton pointed out, was fatally in error as a policy for, what would now be termed, a central bank, unconstrained by convertibility. The amount of lending and hence the quantity of paper it could issue depended on the relationship between the rate of profit anticipated by borrowers and the rate of interest charged by the bank. If the latter was below the former, there could be an indefinite demand for loans from the bank and simply by confining itself to lending on real bills, the bank would not prevent inflation from occurring.

With the exception of Thomas Joplin, no one until Knut Wicksell gave as cogent an analysis of the implications of bank lending at less than the *natural rate* of interest. Although Thornton did not use the distinction between the natural and the market rates of interest to develop an explicit theory of the business cycle, in the hands of Wicksell and his diverse followers, it became the critical mechanism for explaining business cycles.

After Thornton's great performance, only one other contribution of note, *Thoughts on the Effects of the Bank Restrictions* by Lord King (1804), was written over the next several years as the premium on bullion stayed low. But in

1809, a rapid increase of the premium elicited a condemnation of the Bank of England from David Ricardo ([1810] 1952). Ricardo straightforwardly assigned blame to the Bank for overissue using the depreciation of sterling as a proxy for the price level and an index of the extent of overissue.

Concern about the growing depreciation of the pound and Ricardo's powerful attacks on the Bank's policy led to the creation of a Parliamentary Committee to study the cause of the high price of bullion. The Committee, which included Thornton among its members, issued a report in 1811 advocating the resumption of convertibility within two years. The Report of the Bullion Committee, written by Thornton, Francis Horner, and William Huskisson, contained a compelling indictment of the Bank's policy for allowing a persistent depreciation of the pound. But it did not go as far as Ricardo and Wheatley in identifying any depreciation, even a temporary one, with an overissue. For the Bullion Committee it was the persistent nature of the depreciation that was crucial. Parliament, however, refused to adopt the Committee's recommendations, voting down a resolution to implement the Committee's recommendations. Nevertheless, the desirability of eventually restoring convertibility at the old parity was widely accepted.

In the event, the improving military situation led to a decline in the premium on gold. The appreciation of the pound created deflationary pressures that produced serious financial pressure in 1815 and 1816. When peace finally came in 1816, Parliament committed itself to ultimate restoration of convertibility by defining the pound as a fixed weight of gold.

While suspension, inflation, and depreciation were the main topics at issue until publication of the Bullion Report, resumption and deflation were the main topics at issue after the Bullion Report. Many critics blamed the falling prices and depressed business conditions on the resumption. Much of the discussion was of low quality, but it did produce some work of high quality. In particular, the work of Thomas Attwood and his brother Mathias, from the depressed manufacturing areas around Birmingham, cogently analyzed the evils of deflation and recommended monetary expansion and even outright inflation as a cure for business depression. Such a policy was impossible as long as resumption was the chief goal of economic policy, so the Attwoods and the Birmingham School that formed around them became the chief spokesmen for an inconvertible paper currency that could be expanded until a state of full employment was achieved.

Another notable achievement on the anti-Bullionist side was that of John Rooke ([1824] 1969) who opposed resumption at the old or any fixed parity and instead advocated a constantly adjusting gold price designed to achieve a stable price level. This proposal anticipated Irving Fisher's famous compensated-dollar plan by almost a full century.

Contrary to widespread impression, Ricardo was not insensitive to the deflationary implications of the resumption. His *Proposal for an Economical and Secure Currency* was designed to minimize the impact of the resumption on the world supply of gold and thus to minimize any deflationary pressure beyond that implied by restoring the pound to its prewar parity. Although Ricardo's plan for withdrawing the gold circulation and creating an ingot standard was approved by Parliament in 1819, the Bank of England accumulated such a large gold reserve that Ricardo felt it had defeated the purpose of the plan by forcing an appreciation in the international value of gold that exacerbated the deflation.

Oddly enough, although the precedent of the 1819–21 restoration was frequently cited when restoration was contemplated after World War I, many of the qualifications Ricardo expressed about restoring a depreciated currency to its old parity and the rapid accumulation of large gold reserves were largely ignored in the 1920s.

Thus, by the end of the Bullionist Controversies, all the ingredients necessary for a well-reasoned monetary theory of the business cycle were in place and familiar to contemporary economists. The continuing fluctuations of business activity following the resumption led to the synthesis of these elements into the first explicit theories of a recurrent business cycle in the 1820s and 1830s largely, but not entirely, associated with the next great series of monetary debates—that between the Currency and the Banking Schools.

David Glasner

See also ATTWOOD, THOMAS; BANKING SCHOOL, CURRENCY SCHOOL, AND FREE BANKING SCHOOL; GOLD STANDARD; GOLD STANDARD: CAUSES AND CONSEQUENCES; NAPOLEONIC WARS; REAL BILLS DOCTRINE; RICARDO, DAVID; SMITH, ADAM; THORNTON, HENRY

Bibliography

Attwood, T. 1964. *Selected Economic Writings of Thomas Attwood*. Edited with an introduction by F. W. Fetter. London: London School of Economics.

Cannan, E., ed. 1919. *The Paper Pound*. London: P. S. King.

Fetter, F. W. 1965. *The Evolution of British Monetary Orthodoxy, 1797–1875*. Cambridge: Harvard Univ. Press.

King, Lord. 1804. *Thoughts on the Effects of the Bank Restriction*. 2d ed. London.

Ricardo, D. [1810] 1952. *The High Price of Bullion*. In *The Works and Correspondence of David Ricardo*. Vol. 3. Edited by P. Sraffa, 47–127. Cambridge: Cambridge Univ. Press.

———. [1816] 1952. *Proposal for an Economical and Secure Currency*. In *The Works and Correspondence of David Ricardo*. Vol. 4. Edited by P. Sraffa, 43–141. Cambridge: Cambridge Univ. Press.

Thornton, H. [1802] 1939. *An Enquiry into the Nature and Effects of the Paper Credit of Great Britain*. Reprint. London. Edited with an introduction by F. A. von Hayek. London: Allen and Unwin.

Rooke, J. [1824] 1969. *An Inquiry into the Principles of National Wealth*. New York: A. M. Kelley.

Bullock, Charles Jesse (1869–1941)

As Director of the Harvard University Committee on Economic Research, Charles J. Bullock presided over the development of the "three-curve barometer," an indicator of turning points in the business cycle. During the 1920s, the three-curve barometer was highly respected as a forecasting device and its methods widely copied. Bullock's Committee began publishing *The Review of Economic Statistics* (later *Review of Economics and Statistics*) in 1919 as a forum for statistical and historical examination of the timing and magnitude of business cycles.

Bullock received his undergraduate degree from Boston University in 1892 and his Ph.D. from the University of Wisconsin in 1895. He taught at Cornell (1895–99), Williams (1899–1903), and Harvard (1903–35), where he directed the Harvard Committee on Economic Research from 1917 to 1929. Bullock served as an advisor to the governments of several states on matters of taxation; he was president of the National Tax Association from 1917 to 1919, and a Fellow of the American Academy of Arts and Sciences.

Bullock and his colleagues on the Harvard Committee constructed the three-curve barometer from monthly time series of economic data dating from 1903 onward. They corrected their data for trend and for seasonal variations; cycles in each series were thus left as residuals. Bullock's committee then grouped series with similar timing of cyclical fluctuations and from these groupings constructed composite indices reflecting the average of the component series.

In this fashion, Bullock and his colleagues obtained three composite series, which gave rise to the "three-curve" appellation. The so-called "A curve" reflected speculative conditions and was based on series on stock prices and New York City bank debits. The "B curve" reflected business conditions and was based on series on wholesale prices and bank debits outside New York. The "C curve" reflected money and banking conditions and was based on short-term interest rates. This A-B-C grouping was based solely on statistical criteria; the researchers assumed that cycles were deviations from linear trends. Bullock and his colleagues admitted—indeed, boasted—that "no theory as to the interrelations of various aspects of the economic movement" underlay their empirical investigations. They simply found statistical correlations among time series, which common sense told them were especially relevant. Only after the groupings were complete did the Committee realize that the series in each group were related economically as well as statistically.

Bullock and his committee were able to date turning points of business cycles and make forecasts by inspecting the three curves in relation to one another. They paid particular attention to lags between the movements of the curves. Bullock gave special emphasis to the index of money and banking conditions. Despite lacking theoretical underpinnings, the three-curve barometer performed quite well. For example, the barometer forecast clearly the 1920 crisis and depression and the 1922 recovery. A "mechanical" interpretation of the barometer also clearly revealed the coming downturn in 1929, though Bullock chose to ignore that interpretation. A series of overly optimistic forecasts in the early stages of the Great Depression led to the dissolution of the Committee's forecasting effort.

Bullock also conducted empirical research into Colonial monetary practices. In *Essays on* the *Monetary History of the United States*, Bullock developed series, since superseded, on the stock of Colonial paper money. In examining the relation between inflation and the issue of paper currency, Bullock was an early quantity theorist, sharply criticizing what he saw as monetary mismanagement by the Colonial authorities.

Bullock directed the development of a tool of empirical business-cycle research, the three-curve barometer, whose methods were widely discussed and copied. For example, the Berlin Institute for Business Cycle Research founded its work on the statistical methods of measurement and interpretation developed by Bullock's Harvard Committee. Though the statistical methods of the three-curve barometer were soon enough superseded, under Bullock's direction the Harvard Committee on Economic Research was highly regarded as a leader in empirical business-cycle research.

Philip M. Holleran

See also LEADING INDICATORS: HISTORICAL RECORD; PERSONS, WARREN MILTON; SNYDER, CARL

Bibliography

Bullock, C. J. 1900. *Essays on the Monetary History of the United States*. New York: Macmillan.

Bullock, C. J. and W. L. Crum. 1932. "The Harvard Index of Economic Conditions: Interpretations and Performance, 1919–1931." *Review of Economic Statistics* 14:132–48.

Bullock, C. J., J. B. Fox, and A. R. Eckler. 1931. "Postal Revenues and the Business Cycle." *Review of Economic Statistics* 13:47–58.

Bullock, C. J. and H. L. Micoleau. 1931. "Foreign Trade and the Business Cycle." *Review of Economic Statistics* 13:138–59.

Bullock, C. J., W. M. Persons, and W. L. Crum. 1927. "The Construction and Interpretation of the Harvard Index of Business Conditions." *Review of Economic Statistics* 9:74–92.

Burchardt, Fritz (Frank) Adolph (1902–1958)

Fritz (later Frank) Burchardt was a leading critic of monetary trade-cycle theories in Weimar, Germany. He wrote an excellent survey of the history of monetary explanations of the business cycle (1928). In two influential papers, Burchardt (1931–32) also provided the first synthesis of the sector model and the stage model which Adolph Lowe later applied to the analysis of real capital formation and transitions between equilibrium growth paths.

Burchardt was born in Barneberg, Germany, in 1902. He earned his doctorate at the University of Kiel in 1925 with a dissertation on Schumpeter's contributions to the static analysis in which he challenged Schumpeter's assertion that dynamics, understood as a theory of development, was necessarily less precise than, and unrelated to, the theory of stationary equilibrium. Burchardt became Lowe's closest collaborator between 1926 and 1933. He had already submitted his habilitation thesis at the University of Frankfurt when the Nazis came to power and ended his university career. Burchardt emigrated to England in 1935, joining the Oxford Institute of Statistics and becoming its director in 1949. He built up the Institute's *Bulletin* and was also the editor of the famous cooperative 1944 study on *The Economics of Full Employment*. Burchardt died on 21 December 1958.

In his 1928 paper on the history of monetary trade-cycle theory, Burchardt showed how structural changes in economic history altered the character of theory. During the nineteenth century, crisis theory mutated to trade-cycle theory. Credit expansion and interest-rate movements became increasingly important as symptoms of the cycle. Recognizing that monetary influences, in particular, manifested themselves through changes in the price level, Burchardt concluded that monetary factors alone could not explain cyclical phenomena. In his view non-monetary factors, especially technical progress, play a central role in the cycle. Concerning Wicksell's influential theory, for example, Burchardt emphasized that, although changes in the bank's market rate of interest may cause movements of the price level, the equilibrium of an economy is disturbed by technical progress which causes the natural rate to rise above the market rate.

Burchardt's greatest research achievement was to compare, contrast, and combine the two most important alternative ways of modeling the production system: the schemes of the stationary circular flow in Böhm-Bawerk and in Marx. Burchardt thus provided the first synthesis of the vertical-integration approach and the interindustry approach. (For its significance for modern theory of structure and change see the contributions in Baranzini and Scazzieri 1990.) Burchardt did not question the ability of Austrian analysis to deal with working capital, but he criticized the problematical role of fixed capital in the model of production as it was devised by Böhm-Bawerk (which later underlay Hayek's *Prices and Production*). In the Austrian representation of the structure of production, a sequence of original inputs is transformed into a single output of consumable commodities. There is no distinction between fixed and circulating capital. Both types of capital are intermediate products or working capital. The production process is treated as *unidirectional,* i.e., causal, rather than *circular.* Each stage or circle of Böhm-Bawerk's "*Ringschema*" represents intermediate products, with the highest stage, or innermost circle, where original factors (labor and natural resources) continuously produce the first intermediate products of the synchronized production process without the aid of intermediate products (capital goods) and the lowest stage, or outermost circle, passing each year into consumption. But tracing back the production process to some original combination of labor and land leaves the reproduction and expansion requirements of the stock of fixed capital unexplained.

Böhm-Bawerk's scheme of production thus proves deficient mainly in two respects. First, Böhm-Bawerk confused two entirely different problems, namely the *historical* conditions for the original construction of capital and the *present* conditions for reproducing the existing capital stock. Second, the physical *self-reproduction* of some fixed capital goods is an important technological property of an industrial system. Thus, a particular group of fixed capital goods, which Lowe later called *machine tools,* can be maintained and increased only through a circular process in which these machine tools are themselves inputs. The role of these goods in industrial production is thus analogous to that of seed-corn in agricultural production. It is therefore impossible to trace, as the Austrians suggested, all finished goods back to nothing but labor and land and to treat fixed capital goods as the output of some intermediate stages in the vertical model. The downward flow to the lowest or final stage of finished output properly describes the structure of working capital if a stock of fixed capital goods is added to the original inputs of labor and natural resources on the highest stage. In other words, to account for the reproduction, expansion, and structural change of an industrial economy, the vertical model must be supplemented by a classical model of the circular flow which clearly depicts the self-reproduction of certain fixed capital goods.

The seminal character of Burchardt's work was recognized immediately in the Anglo-Saxon literature (Nurkse 1935). And it was applied by Kähler in his study (1933) of the displacement of workers by machinery and, especially, by Lowe (1976) in his pioneering traverse analysis which relied on a model of production that synthesized classical circularity and Austrian sequentiality.

Harald Hagemann

See also AUSTRIAN THEORY OF BUSINESS CYCLES; BÖHM-BAWERK, EUGEN RITTER VON; CAPITAL GOODS; HAYEK, FRIEDRICH AUGUST [VON]; LOWE, ADOLPH

Bibliography

Baranzini, M. and R. Scazzieri. 1990. *The Economic Theory of Structure and Change.* Cambridge: Cambridge Univ. Press.

Burchardt, F. A. 1928. "Entwicklungsgeschichte der monetären Konjunkturtheorie." *Weltwirtschaftliches Archiv* 28:78–143.

———. 1931–32. "Die Schemata des stationären Kreislaufs bei Böhm-Bawerk und Marx." *Weltwirtschaftliches Archiv* 34:525–64 and 35:116–76.

Burchardt, F. A., et al. 1944. *The Economics of Full Employment.* Oxford: Basil Blackwell.

Hayek, F. A. 1931. *Prices and Production.* London: Routledge.

Kähler, A. 1933. *Die Theorie der Arbeiterfreisetzung durch die Maschine.* Greifswald: Julius Abel.

Lowe, A. 1959. "F. A. Burchardt, Part I: Recollections of his Work in Germany." *Bulletin of the Oxford University Institute of Statistics* 21:59–65.

———. 1976. *The Path of Economic Growth.* Cambridge: Cambridge Univ. Press.

Nurkse, R. 1935. "The Schematic Representation of the Structure of Production." *Review of Economic Studies* 2:232–44.

Worswick, G. D. N. 1959. "F. A. Burchardt, Part II: Burchardt's Work in Oxford." *Bulletin of the Oxford University Institute of Statistics* 21:66–71.

Burns, Arthur Frank (1904–1987)

It is illuminating to consider Arthur Burns, along with Wesley Clair Mitchell and economists such as Geoffrey H. Moore, as engaged in a massive intellectual crusade to describe, with quantitative measurements, what happens during a business cycle. Under the auspices of the National Bureau of Economic Research, Burns invented a variety of graphical techniques and simple statistical artifacts for comparing historical business expansions and contractions within as well as between nations.

Born in Austria in 1904, Burns emigrated with his family to New York City when he was a boy. After graduating from Columbia College, Burns pursued graduate studies at Columbia under Mitchell. Like Mitchell, Burns dedicated himself to the research program of the National Bureau of Economic Research, where he remained for nearly two decades, becoming the Bureau's president in 1957. Burns also taught at Rutgers University (1927–44) and later at Columbia University.

From 1953 to 1956, Burns took an academic leave to serve as Chairman of the Council of Economic Advisers. Subsequently, Burns became a well-known policymaker, advising presidents and lecturing around the world about economic policy. Burns served as Chairman of the Board of Governors of the Federal Reserve from 1970 to 1978. His final official post was U.S. Ambassador to the Federal Republic of Germany (1981–85).

In their classic study *Measuring Business Cycles* Burns and Mitchell (1946, 3) defined a business cycle as:

> a type of fluctuation found in the aggregate economic activity of nations that organize their work mainly in business enterprises: a cycle consists of expansions occurring at about the same time in many economic activities, followed by similarly general recessions, contractions, and revivals which merge into the expansion phase of the next cycle, and this sequence of changes is recurrent but not periodic, in duration business cycles vary from more than one year to ten or twelve years, and they are not divisible into shorter cycles of similar character with amplitudes approximating their own.

Because the periods and amplitudes of historical business cycles vary, Burns and Mitchell argued that business cycles cannot be reduced to the wave movements observed in the natural sciences. Unlike those wave phenomena, business cycles cannot be described by simple, mathematical equations.

The regularities that Burns and Mitchell observed reflect what they call *co-movements* among different aggregate time series. Thus, the study of "what happens during a business cycle" becomes a study of these co-movements. To study these co-movements, Burns and Mitchell studied more than one thousand economic series in four countries.

The approach presupposes what are called *reference dates*. Reference dates are benchmarks in historical time when experts agree that *aggregate* economic activity has stopped rising (falling) and started to decline (rise)—so-called *peaks* (*troughs*). After these reference dates are agreed upon, all other time series are sliced into segments corresponding precisely to those reference dates.

For example, consider the monthly totals for a particular economic variable, say, U.S. housing starts. The first step is to examine the behavior of housing starts between the reference dates of two consecutive troughs by comparing each monthly value and its average value between the reference dates. The next step is to observe when this *reference cycle relative* for housing starts peaks in relation to aggregate economic activity. If housing starts peak earlier than the peak in aggregate economic activity, housing starts would be a *leading indicator.* If they peak later, they would be a *lagging indicator* of the business cycle.

Much more is done with these data. The amplitude of the fluctuation in the reference cycle relatives can be compared with the amplitude in the fluctuations in aggregate economic activity and so on. The ultimate goal is to show "how the wavelike movements in a given series conform to the waves in general business activity" (Burns and Mitchell 1946, 31). The practical result of such investigations is to help forecast the next expansion or contraction.

The Burns and Mitchell approach to the study of business cycles was criticized by the econometrician T. C. Koopmans for pretending to be "measurement without theory." Koopmans complained that the calculations were "in almost complete detachment from any knowledge . . . of the motives of such actions" and pointed to the "pedestrian character of the statistical devices employed" ([1947] 1965, 195, 203).

Not all econometricians have been so harsh. For example, Robert E. Lucas ([1976]

1981, 236n) harked back to the "basic technical reference," *Measuring Business Cycles,* as providing the first excellent description of certain features of the business cycle that must be accounted for by any general theory.

During the 1960s and 1970s, Burns remained a critic of "quick and dirty" theorizing associated with Keynesianism. Burns described his work as stressing "the importance of breaking down aggregates because this matter, [is] so slighted by the Keynesian economists, [and] is a central feature of [my] work on business cycles" (1954, 23). In principle, Burns was not opposed to government stabilization policies. Indeed, in his lectures, Burns approved of the Employment Act of 1946, in which Congress mandated that the executive branch actively manage aggregate economic activity. The question for Burns was not whether, but how, the economy should be stabilized.

In a rich monograph published posthumously in 1988, Burns documented the massive changes then underway in banking practice and reflected on his years as Fed Chairman. Burns blamed the inflation of the 1970s on an ominous, ideological change sweeping the United States. Social Consciousness had moved away from the creed of individualism and balanced budgets toward pressure-group politics, expensive government programs, and the inflationary financing of those programs. Burns favored increased attention to fundamentals—even a balanced-budget amendment to the U.S. Constitution to restore fiscal restraint.

These reforms would restore business confidence and encourage business investment, the lifeblood of continued prosperity. According to Burns, it is not clear what role economists can play in stabilizing the economy when ideology has become more important than sober analysis and more valued than wisdom steeped in historical understanding. Unfortunately, Burns did not resume his studies of the business cycle during the closing decades of his life. He never investigated, for example, whether the ideological changes he detected could have changed the character of the business cycle itself.

Laurence S. Moss

See also BUSINESS CYCLES; FEDERAL RESERVE SYSTEM: 1941–1993; KOOPMANS, TJALLINGS CHARLES; LEADING INDICATORS: HISTORICAL RECORD; MITCHELL, WESLEY CLAIR; MOORE, GEOFFREY HOYT

Bibliography

Burns, A. F. 1934. *Production Trends in the United States since 1870.* New York: NBER.

———. 1954. *The Frontiers of Economic Knowledge.* New York: Wiley.

———. 1969. *The Business Cycle in a Changing World.* Columbia Univ. Press.

———. 1988. *The Ongoing Revolution in American Banking.* Washington: American Enterprise Institute.

Burns, A. F. and W. C. Mitchell. 1946. *Measuring Business Cycles.* New York: NBER.

Koopmans, T. C. [1947] 1965. "Measurement without Theory." *Review of Economic Statistics.* In *A.E.A. Readings in Business Cycles,* 186–203. Homewood, Ill.: Irwin.

Lucas, R. E. Jr. [1976] 1981. "Understanding Business Cycles." In *Studies in Business-Cycle Theory,* 215–39. Cambridge: MIT Press.

Moore, G. H. 1983. *Business Cycles, Inflation, and Forecasting.* Cambridge, Mass.: Ballinger.

Business Cycles

This article considers the sources and characteristics of business cycles as studied in economic history and theory. The subject is vast and is treated here only in broad outline, with emphasis on the evolution of the concepts and phenomena under inquiry and on methods of analysis.

History
Crises

Since indefinitely ancient times, natural and man-made disasters have caused suffering by destroying or wasting resources. More recently, speculative excesses have repeatedly caused "overtrading" and sharp rises in the prices of some real or financial assets, followed by panics, i.e., distress selling at rapidly falling prices (e.g., the Tulip Mania of 1625–37).

The disruptive economic effects of noneconomic disasters are easier to understand than the reasons for and consequences of financial crises. Both sets of phenomena had been observed long before the concept of a business cycle (or, as called in England, trade cycle) was introduced, sometime in the mid-nineteenth century.

According to W. R. Scott (1912), thirty crises, half of them "serious," occurred in England between 1558 and 1720. Scott attributed most of them to noneconomic causes such as wars, plagues, bad harvests, and civil disorders. Ashton (1959) dated twenty-two "economic fluctuations" in England between 1700 and 1802, and related them to seventeen financial crises, eleven incidents of poor harvest or short supplies of grain, and several wars. Thus, frequent alternations of good and bad trade have a long history. Explanations of the early fluctuations were unsystematic, relying mainly on external disturbances and financial crises.

Recurrent Fluctuations

Throughout the nineteenth century, from Sismondi and Malthus to Marx and Hobson, Say's Law that supply creates its own demand was a source of intense controversy. The denial of the possibility of a "general glut" by classical theorists seemed to be inconsistent with widespread, recurrent, and unexplained declines in sales, production, and profits.

Lord Overstone was among the first to speak of a multi-stage "cycle of trade." Juglar, in the earliest major work on the history of commercial crises (1862), assembled annual statistical series to show the recurrence of interrelated fluctuations in discounts, deposits, bullion reserves, and prices. Crises were no longer seen in isolation but as stages in the motion of the market economy.

Historians, like contemporary observers, paid foremost attention to the diverse disturbances, from bad weather to political upheavals and financial panics, which seemed to account for crises and downturns. Concentrating on separate episodes and outside shocks, they mostly ignored the entire "cycle" as an economic phenomenon and analytical entity.

By contrast, economists who accepted that the economy as a whole may be subject to recurrent fluctuations naturally sought reasons for what would cause the downturns and contractions, the upturns and expansions. Some theorists stressed the transitory nature of cyclical movements and their dependence on a few variables, but most early scholars saw business cycles as complex and varied phenomena with multiple causes and effects.

Defining Business Cycles

The literature contains few systematic attempts to define business cycles. And the definitions that were proposed often reflected the narrowly formulated theories of certain writers.

In contrast, Wesley Mitchell, first alone (1927) and then with Arthur Burns (1946) and associates at the National Bureau of Economic Research (NBER), proceeded by identifying the principal "stylized facts" about business cycles. According to a working definition by Burns and Mitchell, business cycles occur in market-oriented economies; they involve recurrent but not periodic sequences of expansions, downturns, contractions, and upturns occurring at about the same time in many economic activities. Their duration ranges from one to twelve years.

Although the NBER definition refers to fluctuations in "aggregate economic activity," its main point is the roughly synchronous (allowing for moderate leads and lags) co-movement of many economic variables or processes in any cycle. The diverse activities that tend to expand and contract together cannot be reduced to any single aggregate. The question of what precisely constitutes "aggregate economic activity" is therefore properly left open. The essence of business cycles lies in their pervasiveness, not in the fluctuations of a single variable, however comprehensive. The definition is uniquely accommodative, admitting equally vigorous and weak expansions, severe and mild contractions, major and minor, short and long cycles. It proved to be highly durable and influential, but was meant to be a point of departure for historical, statistical, and theoretical study, not a conclusion.

Links to Modern Capitalism

Before the great technological innovations and industrial revolutions beginning in the second half of the eighteenth century, production involved mostly processing raw materials by labor and household provision of goods and services for consumption and sale. Consumption was probably stable for most people most of the time, apart from wars and other disasters. Fluctuations in inventory investment and trade, which tend to be short and random, may then have accounted for much of the economic instability. Investment in plant, machinery, and equipment displays longer and more systematic fluctuations, reflecting gestation lags and adjustments of capital stocks to flows of demand, output, and technical change. But only after the first strides of industrialization did this investment in fixed capital begin to expand rapidly.

B

The great waves of industrialization coincided with large advances in economic organization: monetization of exchange, legal protection of property rights, and modern accounting. The scale and diversity of business enterprise increased greatly as did the interdependence of prices and production within and beyond the national frontiers. The technological and organizational progress reduced the vulnerability of market-oriented economies to exogenous disasters, but it also increased the role of endogenous dynamic forces. All this received early recognition in business-cycle studies that stressed the interplay of the institutional framework and the creation of money and credit, changes in saving, and investment in real capital. Pioneers in this field, otherwise holding very different views, largely agreed that business cycles belong to the age of modern capitalism.

The Wrong Forecast of Crippling Crises

Marx and other radical critics repeatedly predicted that increasingly frequent and severe crises would eventually cause capitalism to collapse, because of several underlying long-run tendencies: a growing centralization of capital; technological, labor-saving progress; a falling rate of profit; growing pauperization and class consciousness of workers; and finally an inevitable "expropriation of the expropriators."

Clearly, this composite prophecy failed in the developed capitalist countries. Business contractions or crises continued to occur but did not get worse. Firms grew in size, but competition did not degenerate into monopoly. Workers began to share in middle-class prosperity and did not become an impoverished and militant proletariat.

Capitalism survived the Great Depression of the 1930s, but with important alterations and reforms. Governments grew in size and capacity to spend, tax, and regulate; they also became more activist, attempting to reduce unemployment and inflation. Communism came to power in backward rather than advanced capitalist countries, and after decades of oppressive, inefficient, and corrupt rule, it, not capitalism, collapsed.

The Moderation of Business Cycles

Prices as well as quantities of industrial products tended to increase in expansions and decrease in contractions before World War II, so nominal aggregates must have then had larger average procyclical movements than the corresponding real aggregates. In contrast, prices in general continued rising during more recent contractions, albeit often at a slow pace. Business expansions were on the whole longer after World War II, and contractions were weaker. The first half of the post-1945 era, which witnessed the reconstruction of the market economies in Europe and the Far East, was particularly favored by rapid technological progress and economic growth and low cyclical instability. New problems of persistent and rising inflation, oil-price hikes, slowing productivity growth, deepening recessions, and growing monetary and financial instability appeared in the last quarter-century. Still, the postwar cycles in general have been distinctly more moderate than in earlier times. No major depression has occurred in the United States since 1938.

The reasons are several (Zarnowitz 1992, 92–124). (1) Employment in service industries and government, which is weakly procyclical or acyclical, expanded rapidly; employment in manufacturing industries, which is strongly procyclical, did not. (2) Procyclical income taxes and countercyclical transfer payments acted as automatic stabilizers, particularly before the impact of rising inflation and its distortionary tax effects. (3) Deposit insurance and last-resort lending prevented banking panics, although lately at high cost to the taxpayers. (4) Changes in money supply were more volatile before than after World War II. (5) Discretionary policies, though uneven in their effects, probably on balance shortened periods of high unemployment. (6) The gradual recognition that recessions have become shorter and milder strengthened consumer and business confidence through much of the postwar era.

Stylized Facts and Dynamics

Regularities and Theories of Cyclical Behavior
Business cycles vary greatly in duration and intensity, less in diffusion. They are both diverse and evolving. What they have in common is mainly the interaction of their constituent processes. Thus, production, employment, real incomes, and real sales tend to expand and contract together, though unevenly, across many industries and regions. Hours worked per week, real contracts and orders for plant and equipment, housing starts, changes in money, credit, and sensitive prices, among others, tend to lead at both peaks and troughs with variable leads. Interest rates, inventories, loans outstanding, and changes in unit labor costs also move

procyclically but tend to lag. These sequential movements are usually recurrent, persistent, and pervasive.

Cyclical movements in different processes vary systematically in timing, relative size, and conformity to the business-cycle chronology. Activities relating to durable goods have particularly large and well-conforming cyclical fluctuations. Business profits, investment in plant and equipment, inventory investment, and cost and volume of credit used to finance such investments are also highly cyclical. These variables figure prominently in the predominantly endogenous theories of business cycles. Thus, some of these theories stress the instability or temporal disproportionality of fixed investment; some rely mainly on maladjustments of inventory investment; some focus on cost-price imbalances and volatile expectations affecting business profits; and some emphasize variations in the supply of and demand for money and credit, and the role of nominal and real interest rates.

The cyclical variables are endogenous—generated by the set of relationships within which they interact. To produce business cycles, these interrelations must contain important nonlinearities or leads and lags. But given our meager knowledge of how these dynamic elements work, we still do not understand how well endogenous models can explain business cycles.

Investment Imbalances

Most of the rich early writings on business cycles reviewed by Haberler (1962) proposed theories of fluctuations driven by internal dynamics rather than external forces. In the process, imbalances arise and are eliminated over time. Exogenous factors may contribute disturbances, affecting the movement of the economy, but they have a secondary role.

The dominant type of imbalance in the early literature was *vertical maladjustment*. Plans to invest outrun decisions to save in a boom, causing overproduction in capital-goods industries; in a slump, investment lags behind savings. Investment fluctuations reflect spurts of innovation: new techniques, new products, new markets, new forms of organization. Innovations open new opportunities for profitable investment, which are identified first by pioneering entrepreneurs, then followed up and exhausted by imitators. Meanwhile, the rate of saving from income proceeds

at a fairly steady rate (Tugan-Baranovsky [1894] 1913, Schumpeter 1939).

Monetary imbalances amplify and help explain the real ones. The market rate of interest on bank loans is sticky, lagging behind changes in the natural or equilibrium rate. At below-equilibrium market rates, excessive bank lending produces a cumulative inflation in addition to financing overinvestment. This imposes *forced saving* on those whose incomes lag behind inflation. But banks are constrained by available reserves (particularly under the gold standard) and cannot expand credit indefinitely; also, people seek to restore their former consumption levels. As demand and resources shift to consumer-goods industries, capital-goods producers sustain losses. A deflationary contraction begins, which runs its course by gradually diminishing the real and monetary imbalances, opening the way for a new expansion (Wicksell [1898] 1936; Hayek [1929] 1933).

Overinvestment may be limited to one or a few sectors and still significantly depress aggregate activity. Such *horizontal maladjustments* may matter because detecting and correcting errors is very costly, particularly where fixed capital is long-lived, indivisible, and specific to a particular sector.

Not surprisingly, some elements in the old theories are unsatisfactory or out-of-date. For example, some writings overstate the role of bank credit: business cycles did not die out with the gold standard, or with the more recent decline in the importance of commercial banks as credit suppliers. But much of the older literature retains great theoretical and empirical interest.

A good example is the acceleration principle, which posits a relation between the desired capital stock and expected output, and has strong dynamic implications (Aftalion 1913). It is most plausible and useful as a *flexible accelerator*, where current investment equals some fraction of the gap between the desired and the actual capital stocks. Allowing for interaction of the investment accelerator and the consumption multiplier, with applications to inventories and feedback effects on income (Samuelson [1939] 1966; Metzler 1941), expands the range of dynamic possibilities.

Cost-Price and Expectational Imbalances

Another important type of imbalance is that between changes in input costs and output prices. When costs rise faster than prices, profit margins and expectations fall, depressing investment and output; when costs rise more slowly (or fall faster) than prices, profitability and business activity rise. Mitchell (1913) hypothesized that the former condition tends to precede the business-cycle downturns, and the latter the upturns.

Economic prospects are uncertain, particularly so concerning projects involving capital goods with long gestation periods. When many such undertakings are under way and are financed by credit, money growth tends to exceed output growth, causing prices to rise; and when many projects are completed at about the same time, the reverse tends to be true. Business expectations of profits under such conditions are strongly interdependent, generating waves of optimistic error in expansions and of pessimistic error in contractions (Pigou 1927).

During long periods of prosperity, debt is often overaccumulated relative to equity and income. If for any reason the rise of output prices falters, heavy and rising real burdens of debt service fall on businesses and individuals with high propensities to borrow, invest, and spend. Credit lines are cut, and debtors, finding themselves in a crisis of illiquidity, curtail their activities drastically, selling off assets and triggering a downward spiral of asset prices (Fisher 1933).

Formal Endogenous Models
Some mathematical models which are either strictly nonlinear or piecewise-linear need no outside shocks to produce self-sustaining fluctuations. Some use constraints and regime switches, e.g., ceilings and floors on the movement of output, or a high value of the accelerator which is suspended in downswings (Hicks 1950). Another mechanism relies on shifts in, and interaction of, nonlinear investment and savings functions, which depend on the flow of output and the stock of capital (Kaldor [1940] 1960). Still another involves a nonlinear wage/employment Phillips curve as well as cyclical shifts in the relative growth rates of employment, labor supply, and the stock of capital (Rose 1967). The motion of the economy, unlike that of heavenly bodies, conforms to no immutable mathematical laws and follows no repetitive patterns. The advantage of nonlinear models is that they can handle asymmetries, irreversibilities, and discontinuities which may characterize cyclical behavior (Goodwin [1951] 1982). Nonlinearities certainly deserve continued attention, particularly in view of recent improvements in analytical and computational techniques. But many nonlinear endogenous models imply limit cycles that, unlike the observed business fluctuations, are periodic and much too regular. What is lacking and much needed is good empirical work to complement the abstract mathematical modeling which now dominates this field.

Chaotic Movement and Cyclical Dynamics
A new development in the theory of nonlinear dynamics was the discovery that certain dynamic mechanisms called *chaos,* although purely deterministic and in principle simple, can generate time series that are very diversified, complex, and often indistinguishable from purely random numbers by conventional tests (Baumol and Benhabib 1989). Even small differences between certain parameter values can produce highly irregular trajectories that vary greatly from each other. Some cases include sudden qualitative breaks in the time path, e.g., from sharp oscillations to nearly steady behavior or vice versa. Results seem to be highly sensitive to initial conditions and measurement errors.

For profit-maximizing firms, profit is a hill-shaped function of output, which implies that total profits are strongly pro-cyclical and lead other variables. High profits may stimulate investment and output, with lags. Perhaps these processes can together produce such hill-shaped dynamic relationships as would be needed to make the chaos approach useful for the study of business cycles.

Proposed examples of chaotic dynamics are ingenious constructs but based on heroic assumptions. The movements produced so far by these models look much less persistent and more volatile than those observed in economic aggregates during business cycles.

Impulse and Propagation
Exogenous Factors and Random Noise
A comprehensive explanation of business cycles can be neither purely endogenous nor purely exogenous. Outside changes (in technology, tastes, politics, weather) always influence the economy, but they cannot by themselves produce the pervasive, persistent, and recurrent observed fluctuations. What is required theoretically is a dynamic model of a system of interdependent markets, representative of an industrialized and growing competitive economy.

In the recently dominant class of models, cyclical variables, although still important as propagators of business cycles, are no longer the central part of a system that can produce self-sustaining fluctuations. Rather it is changes in observable exogenous factors or unobservable random shocks that drive the business cycle.

The various "imbalance" theories summarized above were, as noted, *mainly* endogenous. Most of the newer theories assign greater weights to the outside factors, and some are *mainly* exogenous. They are also more explicitly stochastic. The shift reflects several trends in the literature: the convenience and popularity of linear models; the rise of modern econometrics; the growing belief in the stability of the market economy and concomitant opposition to Keynesian "depression" economics; and the increased influence of general-equilibrium theory.

It is widely accepted in contemporary thought that business cycles result from the way the economy transmits (*propagates*) exogenous random disturbances (*impulses*). The economy is assumed to be dynamically stable, so that a single shock would produce only a damped oscillation; but impulses are sufficiently frequent to keep the system fluctuating. The propagation mechanism converts a stream of highly erratic impulses into considerably more regular, recurrent movements of alternating expansion and contraction. This notion, traceable to Wicksell, Slutsky, and Pigou, was formalized in an influential paper by Frisch ([1933] 1965).

One reason why business cycles are diverse is that they are influenced not only by frequent and small discontinuous and unidentified random shocks but also by large changes in, or shocks to, identifiable exogenous factors. The small white-noise shocks produce fluctuations with common characteristics that may be excessively regular. The large shocks, which are often but not always serially correlated, produce more irregular fluctuations.

Types of Shock and Estimates of their Effects
Shocks come in great variety. They can be small or large, unidentified or specific, random or correlated, temporary or permanent in effect, adverse or benign. Some shocks affect real variables, others affect nominal variables. Both real and nominal shocks can affect aggregate demand (e.g., the former move the *IS* curve, the latter the *LM* curve in the familiar *IS-LM*

model). Shocks to the production function and relative input prices directly affect aggregate supply. Shifts in macroeconomic policy fall mainly on the demand side; micropolicy shocks (e.g., changes in tariffs, regulations) primarily affect the supply side. In practice, however, most shocks influence directly or indirectly both demand and supply, so their effects on output and the price level are difficult to disentangle.

Empirically implemented stochastic models suggest that the U.S. economy is exposed to a mixture of shocks, mostly small but occasionally large, with no source predominating. In small "structural" models using *vector autoregressions* (VAR), aggregate-demand disturbances account for the largest proportion of the variance of total output; aggregate supply, fiscal, and money disturbances exert smaller effects. As the horizon of forecasts or simulations lengthens, the relative importance of demand shocks tends to decrease, that of supply shocks tends to increase.

Econometric Model Simulations
Studies of several macroeconomic models have shown them to be noncyclical in the sense of not generating movements with the cyclical properties observed in the data (Hickman 1972). This contradicts the familiar charge that econometric evidence refutes the endogenous-cycle theories and favors the random-shock theories of business cycles. The inadequate cyclicality of the stochastically simulated trajectories could well reflect misspecification errors in the existing very large and difficult-to-evaluate macroeconometric models. In particular, the models probably fail to capture important nonlinearities and lag structures, and thus attribute too much dampening to the propagation mechanism.

However, at least some of the present macroeconometric forecasting models have considerably reduced their reliance on the random noise in the equation errors and increased the role of internal dynamics, though they also show strong effects of exogenous changes and ad hoc devices such as dummy variables (Eckstein and Sinai 1986). Such models generally assign the largest effects to demand disturbances, mainly those in durables consumption, housing, and business fixed and inventory investment; fiscal, monetary, and supply shocks taken together explain statistically less than half of the variance of output in the near future.

Recent Currents of Thought

The Role of Monetary Changes and Expectations

Policy variables such as the monetary base, tax rates, and government spending influence the economy and are influenced by it. Nevertheless, they have been traditionally treated as exogenous; only recently have some of them been endogenized in some models through the device of *reaction functions* describing government behavior.

In the Monetarist theory, changes in the stock of money are the main exogenous cause of changes in total nominal income. The demand for money is a relatively stable function linking real balances to wealth or permanent income and to expected rates of return on money and alternative assets. Since wages and prices adjust only with significant lags, sequences of alternating phases of high and low monetary growth tend to produce business slowdowns or recessions; sufficiently long periods of negative money growth, which are quite rare, produce depressions or stagnations (Friedman and Schwartz 1963).

Under the present standard, monetary authorities can influence the money supply only indirectly and over time. Money growth rates tend to lead at business-cycle peaks and troughs, but by highly variable intervals. Cyclical changes in the deposit-reserve and the deposit-currency ratios, which reflect the chain of influence that runs from business activity to money, contribute strongly to the observed patterns of monetary movement during business cycles, but the stability of these patterns is subject to much doubt and debate (Cagan 1965; Friedman 1986).

The Monetarist theory explains the duration of cyclical movements with *adaptive expectations,* which often imply long adjustment lags and the persistence of apparently systematic errors. But the more recent *rational expectations hypothesis* (REH) requires expectations to be consistent with the given model. Such expectations are, by assumption, free of bias and subject to random errors only. Hence, all persistent monetary changes are taken to be correctly anticipated and reflected in proportional price changes. Only random monetary shocks can have important real effects, causing price surprises and misperceptions which, in this view, are necessary and sufficient to explain cyclical movements in employment and output (Lucas [1977] 1981). But monetary changes are now promptly documented in the data, and tests of their effects on the whole do not confirm these conclusions.

The REH is attractive on general theoretical grounds, since market incentives and penalties should favor the most efficient use of information. But it does not follow at all that the available data and models provide sufficient knowledge about the future for expectations to be free from systematic errors and consistent with *continuous* aggregate equilibrium. Individual rationality does not necessarily imply the collective consistency of individual plans needed to assure a unique and stable equilibrium path along which prices always clear all markets. The REH dominates recent modeling efforts and proved fruitful for work on endogenous expectations and their policy implications in various market settings. But the weight of evidence so far, both from direct observations from surveys and from indirect statistical tests, appears to be unfavorable to the REH (Zarnowitz 1992, 60–65, 489–91).

Productivity Shifts in New Equilibrium Models

Because of the implausibility of its informational assumptions, the hypothesis of recurrent misperceptions of absolute for relative price changes no longer attracts strong research interest. But business cycles continue to be modeled as consistent with the maintained general equilibrium of an economy with complete information, rational expectations, flexible prices, and competitive markets. The currently active class of such models is represented by the theory of *real business cycles* (RBC).

In the aggregate RBC model, mixed transitory/permanent shocks to technology cause stochastic oscillations in real economic growth (Kydland and Prescott 1982). A long gestation lag in producing capital goods imparts persistence to output movements. As productivity gains fluctuate, so do real returns to work effort, and labor supply responds pro-cyclically. But most estimates show the cyclical sensitivities of real wages and real interest rates to be quite low. Nor do tests lend much support to the implied hypothesis of highly elastic intertemporal substitution of labor for leisure.

The overall shifts in productivity in either direction must be large to cause general expansions and contractions. But technical innovations tend to be local, not global, and to be gradually, not immediately, diffused throughout the economy. Such changes seem more relevant to long waves in the rate of economic growth than to business cycles of relatively short duration and high frequency. Between the Industrial Revolution and World War II, there have been several deep depressions but no corresponding episodes of large-scale technological *regress*. When interpreted as productivity shocks, the procyclical movement of the *Solow residual* (Solow 1957) supports the RBC hypothesis, but much of this movement probably reflects labor hoarding and measurement errors.

The aggregative RBC model concentrates on supply shocks, which suggests countercyclical changes in prices. But the predominant relationship over the business cycle between output and prices is positive, not negative. In the 1970s, actions of the OPEC cartel caused explosive increases in the price of oil that resulted in unique inflationary recessions. The RBC model can help explain these episodes but no other similar examples have been identified.

Other Real Factors and Disaggregation
Several originating factors other than shifts in technology and productivity are in principle consistent with the RBC theory, e.g., temporary changes in defense and other government purchases, income-tax rates, preferences for consumption, relative input prices, etc. Keynesian, Monetarist, and New Classical economists would largely agree on the directional effects of these factors, and some have stressed their role as sources of outside shocks. But so far these factors have not been integrated into the existing RBC models.

In the disaggregated versions of the RBC theory, random local shocks to technology and tastes are propagated across markets. Although prices are flexible, complex lags may arise because sectoral shifts are not recognized promptly and correctly, and specialized labor and capital require time to be reallocated. But the shifts benefit some sectors and harm others, and their net macroeconomic effects may not be strong or persistent. There is as yet little evidence either to support or to refute the sectoral-shifts hypothesis convincingly.

Financial Instability
Speculative excesses and financial crises marked by large business and bank failures occurred before or during a number of severe economic contractions, notably in 1818–19, 1836–37, 1856–57, 1872–73, 1892–93, 1907, 1929–33.

Some of them were associated with stock-exchange panics or banking crises and panics, in several cases on an international scale. However, no systematic timing relationship exists between these events and the chronology of business-cycle peaks and troughs.

No significant financial disruptions occurred between 1934 and 1965 despite the tumultuous events of this period. Federal insurance of bank deposits prevented bank panics by radically reducing both bank failures and depositors' fears for the safety of their money. The depression of the 1930s led to a large reduction in private debt and a temporary rise in financial conservatism.

Financial disorders became more frequent and serious in the next quarter-century as real growth slowed, inflation accelerated, and interest rates fluctuated widely and reached very high levels. But it was only in the 1980s that total nonfinancial debt, and mainly the federal government's debt, increased sharply relative to GNP. Concurrently, a massive deterioration occurred in the liabilities of the financial sector, particularly the loans to less-developed countries and real-estate developers. A new wave of failures followed, involving some large banks and many savings-and-loan associations that suffered huge losses on their fixed-interest mortgages. The federal deposit-insurance system greatly reduced the incentives for bankers to be careful with other people's money and those of depositors to be watchful.

Financial disturbances range from minor credit crunches to major banking and market panics, and their sources and effects vary greatly. Some are consistent with the hypothesis of speculative bubbles in selected asset prices driven by contagious and temporarily self-fulfilling expectations. The bubbles may or may not have important macroeconomic causes or consequences. Some financial disorders can be linked to deflationary shocks and disruptions in the availability and cost of credit (Bernanke 1983).

Monetarists link banking panics to prior monetary disturbances, whose real effects they aggravate (Friedman and Schwartz 1963).

According to Minsky (1982), long periods of prosperity breed overconfidence, excessive short-term financing of long-term investments, growing indebtedness, and illiquidity. Such predominantly expansionary times are terminated by rising uncertainty about real investment prospects, cutbacks in credit supply, steep increases in interest rates, forced liquidation of debts by asset sales, and asset deflation. In this view, which combines an interpretation of Keynes ([1936] 1973) and the debt-deflation theory of Fisher (1933), financial and economic crises are interrelated and basically endogenous processes.

A related possibility is that financial speculation at times may be encouraged by low prospective returns on real assets. This is particularly likely after long investment booms in which some types of physical capital are overbuilt.

Rigidities and Imperfections

Much of the recently burgeoning literature on the "microfoundations" of macroeconomics attempts to explain why wages and prices do not adjust promptly to changes in the demand for labor and output. The last half-century has seen almost uninterrupted inflation and increasing downward rigidity of prices. In earlier times, the price level often decreased during contractions, but more recently only the rate of inflation decreased. Major deflations exacerbated demand contractions in some past depressions, and their nonoccurrence in recent times was salutary. But in the postwar period, monetary growth tilted upward, resulting in a long and persistent inflation, which could not remain moderate or unanticipated. Inflation itself became a source of instability as it accelerated and decelerated, causing much uncertainty, discontent, and ill-timed or ill-proportioned policy interventions.

Several factors may be responsible for the reduced cyclicality (or increased "rigidity") of wages and prices: the structural shift toward services whose prices are less sensitive to shifts in demand; the spread of long and staggered union contracts with partial indexation; the growth of long-term implicit contracts for career employment in the corporate sector, professions, and government. Some new hypotheses invoke monopolistic competition or oligopoly: one assumes that labor productivity is a rising function of real or relative wages that are therefore kept high (*efficiency wages*), another posits that small deviations from the equilibrium price reduce profits only slightly and are therefore not worth correcting from the individual firm's point of view (*menu costs*). Though intriguing, these ideas remain underdeveloped. The reduced risk and cost borne by long-term transaction partners may favor nonprice market-clearing devices even under conditions of intense competition (Zarnowitz 1973; Carlton 1979).

Depending on their sources, departures from price flexibility may or may not be destabilizing. The main contrast is between the stabilizing potential of flexible relative prices and the destabilizing potential of large movements in the general price level (Zarnowitz 1992, 125–63).

Some General Observations

Growth in the developed market-oriented economies has long proceeded through recurrent (but nonperiodic) sequences of business expansions and contractions. These movements vary greatly in length, size, and spread. But since the 1930s industrial economies have suffered no major depression, while expansions have become longer and recessions milder. The reasons include some profound structural, institutional, and policy changes, but the conditions in the early post-World War II period were especially favorable and continued moderation of business cycles cannot be taken for granted.

Business cycles are characteristically persistent and pervasive, interact with longer growth trends, and show many important regularities of comovement, relative timing, and relative amplitude of economic variables. The economy is always exposed to and affected by numerous external disturbances, but its major fluctuations are not simply aberrations due to random shocks; instead, they are to a large extent endogenous.

Although they have important common elements, business cycles are not all alike and cannot be ascribed to any single factor or mechanism. Real, financial, and expectational variables all interact. No monocausal theory has explained these movements or is likely to do so.

Major economic contractions are not necessarily inevitable. In periods and countries with strong growth trends, recessions have generally been short, mild, and infrequent. Thus, market economies can achieve both higher and more stable growth, an obviously desirable result. Some economists *assume* that business cycles are caused by external disturbances about which little can be done. This not only neglects the role of internal imbalances, but may prejudice the consideration of any pro-growth stabilization policies.

Victor Zarnowitz

See also ACCELERATION PRINCIPLE; BURNS, ARTHUR FRANK; CEILINGS AND FLOORS; CHAOS AND BIFURCATION; CONSUMPTION EXPENDITURES; DEBT-DEFLATION THEORY; EFFICIENCY WAGES; EXPECTATIONS; FALLING RATE OF PROFIT; FINANCIAL INTERMEDIA-

TION; FISCAL POLICY; FRIEDMAN, MILTON; FRISCH, RAGNAR ANTON KITTEL; GREAT DEPRESSION IN THE UNITED STATES (1929–1938); HAYEK, FRIEDRICH AUGUST [VON]; IMPLICIT CONTRACTS; INVESTMENT; KEYNES, JOHN MAYNARD; LEADS AND LAGS; MACROECONOMETRIC MODELS, HISTORICAL DEVELOPMENT; MACROECONOMETRIC MODELS, USE OF; MARX, KARL HEINRICH; MINSKY, HYMAN PHILLIP; MITCHELL, WESLEY CLAIR; MONETARY DISEQUILIBRIUM THEORIES OF THE BUSINESS CYCLE; MONETARY EQUILIBRIUM THEORIES OF THE BUSINESS CYCLE; MONETARY POLICY; NEW KEYNESIAN ECONOMICS; NONLINEAR BUSINESS-CYCLE THEORIES; PHILLIPS CURVE; PRICE RIGIDITY; REAL BUSINESS-CYCLE THEORIES; SAMUELSON, PAUL ANTHONY; SAY, JEAN-BAPTISTE; SAY'S LAW; SECTORAL SHIFTS; STYLIZED FACTS; SUNSPOT THEORIES OF FLUCTUATIONS; WAGE RIGIDITY; WICKSELL, JOHAN GUSTAV KNUT

Bibliography

Aftalion, A. 1913. *Les crises périodiques de surproduction.* 2 vols. Paris: Rivière.

Ashton, T. S. 1959. *Economic Fluctuations in England, 1700–1800.* Oxford: Clarendon Press.

Baumol, W. J. and J. Benhabib. 1989. "Chaos: Significance, Mechanism, and Economic Applications." *Journal of Economic Perspectives,* Winter, 77–105.

Bernanke, B. S. 1983. "Nonmonetary Effects of the Financial Crisis in the Propagation of the Great Depression." *American Economic Review* 73:257–76.

Burns, A. F. and W. C. Mitchell. 1946. *Measuring Business Cycles.* New York: NBER.

Cagan, P. 1965. *Determinants and Effects of Changes in the Stock of Money, 1875–1960.* New York: NBER.

Carlton, D. W. 1979. "Contracts, Price Rigidity, and Market Equilibrium." *Journal of Political Economy* 87:1034–62.

Eckstein, O. and A. Sinai. 1986. "The Mechanisms of the Business Cycle in the Postwar ·Era." In *The American Business Cycle: Change and Continuity,* edited by R. J. Gordon, 39–122. Chicago: Univ. of Chicago Press.

Fisher, I. 1933. "The Debt-Deflation Theory of Great Depressions." *Econometrica* 1:337–57.

Friedman, B. M. 1986. "Money, Credit, and Interest Rates in the Business Cycle." In *The American Business Cycle: Continuity and Change,* edited by R. J. Gordon, 395–458. Chicago: Univ. of Chicago Press.

Friedman, M. and A. J. Schwartz. 1963. *A Monetary History of the United States, 1867–1960.* Princeton: Princeton Univ. Press.

Frisch, R. [1933] 1965. "Propagation Problems and Impulse Problems in Dynamic Economics." In *A.E.A. Readings in Business Cycles,* 155–85. Homewood, Ill.: Irwin.

Goodwin, R. M. [1951] 1982. "The Non-Linear Accelerator and the Persistence of Business Cycles." Chap. 6 in *Essays in Economic Dynamics.* London: Macmillan.

Gordon, R. J., ed. 1986. *The American Business Cycle: Change and Continuity.* Chicago: Univ. of Chicago Press.

Haberler, G. 1962. *Prosperity and Depression.* 4th rev. ed. Cambridge: Harvard Univ. Press.

Hayek, F. A. [1929] 1933. *Monetary Theory and the Trade Cycle.* Translation. London: Jonathan Cape.

Hickman, B. G., ed. 1972. *Econometric Models of Cyclical Behavior.* 2 vols. NBER Studies in Income and Wealth, no. 36. New York: Columbia Univ. Press.

Hicks, J. R. 1950. *A Contribution to the Theory of the Trade Cycle.* Oxford: Clarendon Press.

Juglar, C. 1889. *Des crises commerciales et leur retour périodique, en France, en Angleterre, et aux Etats-Unis.* 2d ed. Paris: Guillaumin. Partially translated as *A Brief History of Panics and Their Periodical Occurrence in the United States.* New York: Putnam, 1916.

Kaldor, N. [1940] 1960. "A Model of the Trade Cycle." Chap. 8 in *Essays on Economic Stability and Growth.* Glencoe, Ill.: Free Press.

Keynes, J. M. [1936] 1973. *The General Theory of Employment, Interest, and Money.* Vol. 7 of *The Collected Writings of John Maynard Keynes.* London: Macmillan.

Kydland, F. and E. C. Prescott. 1982. "Time to Build and Aggregate Fluctuations." *Econometrica* 50:1345–70.

Lucas, R. E., Jr. [1977] 1981. "Understanding Business Cycles." In *Studies in Business Cycle Theory,* 215–39. Cambridge: MIT Press.

Metzler, L. A. 1941. "The Nature and Stability of Inventory Cycles." *Review of*

B

Economic Statistics 23:113–29.

Minsky, H. P. 1982. *Can "It" Happen Again? Essays on Instability and Finance.* New York: M. E. Sharpe.

Mitchell, W. C. 1913. *Business Cycles.* Berkeley: Univ. of California Press.

———. 1927. *Business Cycles: The Problem and Its Setting.* New York: NBER.

Pigou, A. C. 1927. *Industrial Fluctuations.* London: Macmillan.

Rose, H. 1967. "On the Non-Linear Theory of the Employment Cycle." *Review of Economic Studies* 34:153–73.

Samuelson, P. A. [1939] 1966. "Interactions between the Multiplier Analysis and the Principle of Acceleration." Chap. 82 in *The Collected Scientific Papers of Paul A. Samuelson.* Vol. 2. Cambridge: MIT Press.

Schumpeter, J. A. 1939. *Business Cycles: A Theoretical, Historical, and Statistical Analysis of the Capitalist Process.* 2 vols. New York: McGraw-Hill.

Scott, W. R. 1912. *The Constitution and Finance of English, Scottish, and Irish Joint-Stock Companies to 1720.* Cambridge: The University Press.

Solow, R. M. 1957. "Technical Change and the Aggregate Production Function." *Review of Economics and Statistics* 39:312–20.

Tugan-Baranovsky, M. I. [1894] 1913. *Les crises industrielles en Angleterre.* 2d ed. Translated from Russian. Paris: Giard & Brière.

Wicksell, K. [1898] 1936. *Interest and Prices: A Study of the Causes Regulating the Value of Money.* Translation. London: Macmillan.

Zarnowitz, V. 1973. *Orders, Production, and Investments: A Cyclical and Structural Analysis.* New York: NBER.

———. 1985. "Recent Work on Business Cycles in Historical Perspective: A Review of Theories and Evidence." *Journal of Economic Literature* 23:523–80.

———. 1992. *Business Cycles: Theory, History, Indicators, and Forecasting.* Chicago: Univ. of Chicago Press.

Business Cycles in Russia (1700–1914)

As the Russian Empire gradually became integrated into the world economy in the eighteenth and nineteenth centuries, the business cycles that punctuated the economic history of Europe strongly affected Russian commerce and industry, especially in the port cities of St. Petersburg, Riga, and Odessa. However, as Russian agriculture became commercialized, especially in the two decades before World War I, cycles in the peasant economy increasingly affected Russian businesses, independently of European cyclical patterns. Russian business cycles also reflected such unique events as the Crimean War (1853–56), the "cotton famine" caused by the U.S. Civil War (1861–65), the famine of 1891, the Russo-Japanese War of 1904–05, and the Revolution of 1905.

These general conclusions rest on a meager scholarly foundation. Research on Russian business cycles is inadequate largely because of the devastation suffered by Soviet social science from the late 1920s to the mid-1950s. The secret trial of Professor Nikolai D. Kondratieff, his fatal incarceration, and the abolition of his institute for the study of economic cycles typified Stalin's repression of independent economic thought. Although the monograph of A. F. Iakovlev (1955) contained some statistical data on business crises in Tsarist Russia (in 1839, 1847, 1857–58, 1873, 1882, 1890, 1900–03, and 1908–09), it exhibited the characteristic flaws of Soviet scholarship in this period: fragmentary time series, inadequate documentation, and polemical rhetoric. Ideological constraints persisted well into the 1980s. Fortunately, the Tsarist government published a variety of economic data, some of which underwent sophisticated statistical analysis by Russian economists in the 1920s. Soviet and American scholars have added new insights in recent years.

Both national and regional fluctuations in grain prices from 1700 to 1914 have been analyzed by the Leningrad historian Boris N. Mironov (1985). His major finding was that Russian grain prices (in constant gold currency) rose to European levels during the eighteenth century and fluctuated in clearly defined patterns. In *Annales* (1986), he described the cyclical movements as follows: rising prices in 1707–30, 1761–1818, 1831–80, and 1901–14; and falling prices in 1731–60, 1819–30, and 1881–90. In his 1985 monograph, a nine-year moving average fluctuated in slightly different cycles: falling prices in 1663–1710, 1723–57, 1805–28, and 1871–98; and rising prices in 1710–23, 1757–1805, 1828–71, and 1898–1914. In 32 cases between 1662 and 1911, unusually small harvests (as in 1710, 1833, and 1891) occurred one year before unusually high grain prices (as in 1711, 1834, and 1892). The principal shortcoming of Mironov's study for business-cycle research is that high and low grain prices do not necessarily indicate high and low points in the business cycle.

Relatively abundant data published by the imperial ministries indicated periodic fluctuations in Russian commerce and industry at the end of the Tsarist period. Substantial economic data for the period from 1890 to 1914 suggested the influence of both foreign business cycles and domestic agricultural trends on the Russian business cycle. The diagram of annual shifts in business activity in Mitchell's 1927 study of business cycles included Russia from 1890 onward. Depression years in Russia were 1891–92, 1900–03, 1905–06, and 1908–09. Mitchell drew these data from the monograph on Russian economic cycles in 1870–1920 by

the Soviet scholar Sergei A. Pervushin, as summarized by the young Simon Kuznets. Pervushin's 1928 *Quarterly Journal of Economics* article reiterated his methods and findings.

Pervushin's many time series contain annual figures for such diverse indicators as the length of track added to the rail network, the value of goods brought to the Nizhnii Novgorod fair, and the discount operations of commercial banks. From his series, Pervushin created two "general indices," one for commerce and industry, the other for agricultural production (1870 = 1.000).

Pervushin's monumental monograph has been supplemented by a 1982 study of Russian national income between 1885 and 1913 by the American economic historian Paul R. Gregory, who compiled various time series for all components of national income, including totals

TABLE 1 Business Cycles in Russia, 1885–1914

Year	Mitchell	Pervushin		Gregory	
		Agr.	Com.-ind.	NNP	PCI
1885	———	1.035	1.403	7904	72.5
1886	———	1.014	1.445	7732	69.2
1887	———	1.291	1.384	9210	81.5
1888	———	1.524	1.637	9012	78.4
1889	———	1.213	1.409	8527	72.9
1890	Mild prosperity	1.236	1.472	8572	72.6
1891	Recession, depression	1.089	0.918	7917	66.5
1892	Depression	0.813	1.330	8739	72.8
1893	Revival	1.339	1.795	10069	82.5
1894	Prosperity	1.524	2.382	11533	93.8
1895	Prosperity	1.409	2.312	10766	86.8
1896	Prosperity	1.426	2.655	11950	95.6
1897	Prosperity	1.390	2.571	11842	94.0
1898	Prosperity	1.542	2.773	12356	96.5
1899	Prosperity	1.380	3.342	13312	102.4
1900	Prosperity; depression	1.455	3.236	13327	100.2
1901	Depression	1.445	3.304	13869	102.7
1902	Depression	1.888	2.576	15293	111.6
1903	Depression; revival	1.936	2.254	14438	103.9
1904	Recession; depression	2.239	2.704	16196	114.9
1905	Depression	2.218	2.667	14646	101.7
1906	Depression; slight revival	1.879	3.548	14184	97.2
1907	Revival	1.919	2.951	13915	93.4
1908	Recession; depression	1.820	2.037	15452	101.0
1909	Depression; revival	2.845	2.032	16623	105.9
1910	Prosperity	2.891	2.089	18194	113.0
1911	Prosperity	2.523	2.931	17126	104.4
1912	Prosperity	2.471	2.158	18953	112.8
1913	Prosperity on bourse	2.710	2.296	20266	118.5
1914	Panic; depression	———	———	———	———

Sources: Mitchell, pp. 429–35; Pervushin, 1925, p. 159; Gregory, pp. 56–57.

TABLE 2 Agricultural and Commercial-Industrial Indices, 1870–1884

Year	Agriculture	Commerce and Industry
1870	1.000	1.000
1871	0.766	1.035
1872	0.692	0.760
1873	0.766	1.001
1874	0.935	1.119
1875	0.759	0.984
1876	0.847	0.997
1877	1.042	1.222
1878	1.256	1.349
1879	1.145	0.975
1880	0.861	0.824
1881	0.933	0.972
1882	1.122	1.074
1883	1.219	1.349
1884	1.199	1.374

Source: Pervushin, 1925, p. 159.

and per-capita income, in both current and 1913 prices. In addition to revising upward the estimates of economic performance, especially in agriculture, made by Goldsmith in 1961, Gregory stressed the close relationship between prices and levels of capital investment in the major European countries and in Russia.

The findings of Mitchell, Pervushin, and Gregory for the period from 1885 to 1914 are presented in Table 1. (Gregory's figures for millions of rubles of net national product and for per-capita income, based on the Moscow-Petersburg retail price index, are expressed in 1913 rubles.)

Pervushin's study has remained important because he extended his indices of agricultural and industrial production back to 1870; and some of his time series begin as early as 1866. Table 2 presents Pervushin's agricultural and commercial-industrial indices for this earlier period, which show the influence of such events as the Panic of 1873.

In 1972, the Soviet historian A. S. Nifontov examined economic cycles in Russia in 1850–1900 in light of various times series. Like Pervushin, Nifontov stressed the congruence between industrial and agricultural cycles. However, he implicitly contradicted Pervushin by asserting that the connection between the two sectors began long before the 1890s, as shown in Table 3. His failure to prove this causal relationship by statistical correlations demonstrated the inability of recent Soviet scholarship to surpass the achievements of Pervushin and his fellow researchers in the 1920s.

The most recent contribution to the study of business cycles in Russia is a database of corporations, called RUSCORP, compiled by Thomas C. Owen (1992). For the half-century examined by Nifontov, a linear regression of Nifontov's annual series of new corporate

TABLE 3 Cycles in Russian Industry and Agriculture, 1851–1900

Years	Industrial Cycles	Harvests	General Economic Conditions
1851–1853	Recovery	Good	Good
1854–1855	Decline	Inadequate	Poor
1856–1858	Prosperity	Good	Good
1859–1860	Prosperity	Inadequate	Deteriorating
1861–1865	Depression	Irregular	Mediocre
1866–1869	Partial recovery	Irregular	Improving
1870–1873	Prosperity	Good	Good
1874–1877	Crisis, depression	Fluctuating	Poor
1878–1880	Recovery	Fluctuating	Good, but at low level
1881–1886	Crisis, depression	Fluctuating	Poor
1887–1890	Recovery	Good	Good
1891–1892	Crisis	Inadequate	Poor
1893–1896	Prosperity	Abundant	Very good
1897–1898	Prosperity	Inadequate	Mediocre
1899–1900	Crisis	Good	Mediocre

Source: Nifontov, p. 63.

capital and Owen's series of new corporations founded in each year yielded a very high coefficient of correlation (0.9594) and high R-squared (92.05 percent). The major advantage of the new RUSCORP database consists in extending back to 1700 the record of corporate entrepreneurship, including data on the proposed basic capital accounts of all new corporations chartered by the imperial government, their function, location of operations, names and social status of founders, and other indicators. (The richly documented monograph on Russian corporations by the Leningrad historian and archivist Leonid E. Shepelev, published in 1973, presents mostly empire-wide totals because the Tsarist statistics available to him lack consistent regional and sectoral disaggregations.) Fluctuations in the number of new charters confirmed by the Tsarist government annually between 1830 and 1913 closely correspond to world business cycles. High points (generally followed by a sharp decline in the following year) occurred as follows: 6 charters in 1830; 15 in 1838; 6 in 1844; 36 in 1858; 15 in 1866; 114 in 1873; 45 in 1881; 46 in 1890; 331 in 1899; and 357 in 1913, the last year of the series.

Although the outlines of Russian business cycles have been discerned, the precise role of international and domestic factors in each instance remains unclear. The pioneering statistical studies of Kondratieff and Pervushin have languished in obscurity for six decades. Russian business history scarcely existed as a scholarly discipline in the Soviet Union. The research agenda in this field therefore remains long and varied.

Thomas C. Owen

See also KONDRATIEFF, NIKOLAI DMITRIYEVICH; PERVUSHIN, SERGEI ALEKSEEVICH; SLUTSKY, EUGEN

Bibliography
Goldsmith, R. 1961. "The Economic Growth of Tsarist Russia, 1860–1913." *Economic Development and Cultural Change* 9:441–75.
Gregory, P. R. 1982. *Russian National Income, 1885–1913*. Cambridge: Cambridge Univ. Press.
Iakovlev, A. F. 1955. *Ekonomicheskie krizisy v Rossii* (Economic crises in Russia). Moscow: Gosudarstvennoe izdatel'stvo politicheskoi literatury.
Lyashchenko, P. I. 1949. *History of the National Economy of Russia to the 1917 Revolution*. Translated by L. M. Herman. New York: Macmillan.
Mironov, B. N. 1985. *Khlebnye tseny v Rossii za dva stoletii (XVIII–XIX vv)*. [Grain prices in Russia in the course of two hundred years (eighteenth and nineteenth centuries)]. Leningrad: Nauka.
———. 1986. "Le mouvement des prix des céréales en Russie du XVIIIe siècle au début du XXe siècle." *Annales: économies, sociétés, civilisations* 41:217–51.
Mitchell, W. C. 1927. *Business Cycles: The Problem and Its Setting*. New York: NBER.
Nifontov, A. S. 1972. "Khoziaistvennaia kon"iunktura v Rossii vtoroi poloviny XIX veka" (The Economic Cycle in Russia in the Second Half of the Nineteenth Century). *Istoriia SSSR*, May–June, 42–64.
Owen, T. C. 1992. *RUSCORP: A Database of Corporations in the Russian Empire, 1700–1914* [machine-readable data file]. Rev. ed. Baton Rouge: Louisiana State University [producer]. Distributed by the Inter-University Consortium for Political and Social Research, Ann Arbor, Mich.
———. 1995. *Russian Corporate Capitalism from Peter the Great to Perestroika*. New York: Oxford Univ. Press.
Pervushin, S. A. 1925. *Khoziaistvennaia kon"iunktura: vvedenie v izuchenie dinamiki russkogo narodnogo khoziaistva za polveka* (The economic cycle: An introduction to the study of the dynamics of the Russian economy in the past fifty years). Moscow: Ekonomicheskaia zhizn'.
———. 1928. "Cyclical Fluctuations in Agriculture and Industry in Russia, 1869–1926." Translated by S. Kuznets. *Quarterly Journal of Economics* 42:564–92.
Shepelev, L. E. 1973. *Aktsionernye kompanii v Rossii* (Joint-stock companies in Russia). Leningrad: Nauka.

Business Cycles in Socialist Economies
Even though the collapse of the Eastern European economies at the end of the 1980s has shown that the centrally planned (socialist, soviet-type) economies (CPEs) as they existed and operated were not viable, their fundamental features remain of interest. As of this writing, several CPEs remain in Asia and in Cuba. Moreover, a number of market economies dis-

play phenomena similar to those observed in the CPEs. Finally, understanding the basic character of these economies may help to avoid misunderstandings about the potential for reforming market economies.

Among the most interesting phenomena observed in the CPEs was that, notwithstanding early theoretical expectations and the hopes of the central planners, growth was uneven and cyclical rather than smooth. It also became quickly apparent that, owing to the predominance of institutional forces rather than market forces in CPEs, cyclical growth in CPEs required explanations substantially different from those relevant to market economies.

Traditional views of the socialist economy denied that cycles would exist in socialist society. The orthodox view held that socialism eliminates those antagonistic contradictions, which (under capitalism) give birth to crises and cause the reproduction process to be cyclical. (For references see Bauer 1978 and Sabov 1983.) This was the "official" ideology in the Soviet Union and in the Eastern European countries until as late as the 1970s, even though theorists had demonstrated decades before that cycles could occur and even though the observed facts contradicted the ideology. Then, in the relatively more tolerant atmosphere of the 1970s, several important and theoretically wellfounded studies appeared, which generated a rapidly growing literature on the topic.

Early contributions have been summarized by Ickes (1986) and Sabov (1983). As early as 1909, years before the first socialist state was established, Albert Aftalion concluded that central planning would not eliminate periodic tensions and disturbances in the economy. His reasoning rested on the modern distribution of labor and the gestation period necessary for investments. In the famous debates of the 1920s in the Soviet Union, several scholars argued that the socialist economy would manifest cyclical fluctuations. Their argument relied on the transitory character of socialist society, which would retain elements of the capitalist economy. In addition, they mentioned linkages to the world market, the importance of agriculture, and the spasmodic character of technical development as reasons for the continuing cycles under socialism.

When the first Stalinist five-year plan was instituted in 1928–29, debates were forcibly terminated and discussions about economic cycles practically disappeared from the litera-

ture in the socialist countries during the next three decades. It should be noted that many Western economists (e.g., such theorists as Schumpeter and Haberler and such specialists on Eastern Europe as A. Nove and P. Wiles) also accepted that a soviet-type economy is immune to growth cycles.

The idea of growth cycles under socialism was reintroduced into the literature by the Argentine economist J. H. A. Olivera. In an often cited article, Olivera (1960) attributed the cycle to the difference between the time-preference schedules of the planning authority and of the consumers: planners are more willing than consumers to postpone present consumption till the future. The upswing (characterized by increasing investments) lasts until the tensions created by this difference become grave enough to force the planners to modify their priorities. This narrows the gap between preferences, investments drop, and the decrease of tensions gives way to those permanent forces that recreate high investments and leads again to the buildup of tensions.

In an analysis of the economic development of Czechoslovakia, East Germany, Hungary, and Poland, Goldman (1964) found that forced rapid growth in these countries created disproportions (foreign-trade deficits, raw-materials and capacity shortages, organizational and other bottlenecks) which required reduction of investment. In the subsequent breathing period, these disproportions are eliminated, preparing the way for a new "investment drive." "The fluctuations in the rate of growth . . . obviously differ in principle from cyclical development under capitalism . . . [they] are not inherent to the socialist order, but ensue from insufficient knowledge of the economic laws of socialism and from shortcomings in their application" (Goldman 1964, 94). This was a typical interpretation of the time. However, Bajt (1971), while accepting that the upswing was the result of ambitious investment projects, followed Olivera in questioning the realism of the assumption of "infinite social patience."

After some further contributions (summarized in Bajt 1971, Bauer 1978, Ickes 1986), the appearance of the so-called Hungarian School in the late 1970s offered further insight into the nature of the cycles under socialism. The basic difference between this school and its predecessors is that its representatives (mainly Kornai and Bauer) considered centrally planned economies to be inherently cyclical despite any reforms. Kornai provided the general theoretical background while Bauer described the cyclical mechanism. Though many analysts dispute the Kornai-Bauer theory, it remains the most complete and most widely accepted description of cycles under central planning.

The theoretical approaches to analyze cycles in planned economies differ significantly from those to analyze cycles in market economies. While in market economies pressures and tensions are automatically reflected in price adjustments, in planned economies the authorities have some control over how such tensions are manifested. Institutional considerations are therefore crucial in analyzing cycles under socialism.

Kornai emphasized the paternalistic relationship between the state and its enterprises. Unlike their counterparts in a market economy, socialist enterprises are not subject to bankruptcy. The absence of bankruptcy leads to a permanent overdemand for investment resources—the so-called "investment hunger"— as managers seek to increase their prestige and power through the growth of their companies. Efforts to increase capacity and production in normal times are also supported by the governmental authorities, since fast growth was a major success criterion under socialism.

This institutional perspective provided the starting point for Bauer's theory. He showed that in the postwar economic history of Eastern Europe and the Soviet Union, investment cycles were the main driving force of economic dynamics. Bauer distinguished four phases of cycles under socialism. In the first or "run-up" phase, authorities accommodate investment hunger. Many projects are started, and investment costs remain relatively low. However, investment engagement (i.e., the future demand for investment funds to finance projects already in progress) rises rapidly.

In the second ("rush") phase, new projects are still being approved, but the heavy commitments of the first phase start to affect general economic conditions. Since the actual costs of the projects usually turn out to be higher than the expected costs (upon which approval was based), actual investment rises as a proportion of national income. Either the growth of consumption must be postponed or the balance of payments must be allowed to deteriorate.

Facing these tensions in the third ("halt") phase, central authorities approve few new projects while previously approved projects are

allowed to continue. Costs continue to be driven higher because of the shortages in investment capacities, and tensions in the allocation of national income (balance-of-payments deficits versus slow consumption growth) are aggravated.

Finally, in the fourth ("slowdown") phase, the authorities try to ease tensions not only by approving fewer new projects, but also reducing outlays on old ones. Some projects are temporarily or permanently discontinued to reallocate funds to finish others that the authorities consider more important. Thus, more projects are completed than started, so that the stock of unfinished investments decreases, and the efficiency of the investment sector increases. This adjustment enables the ever-present "investment hunger" to push the economy into the first phase again.

It should be observed that it is not the investment aspirations of enterprises that change in the successive phases of the cycle, but the possibility of realizing those aspirations. The upper turning point occurs when the central authorities decide to interrupt the "natural" tendency of increasing investments, while the lower turning point occurs when eased pressure by the authorities allows the "natural" tendency to be restored.

A key decision facing the authorities in any socialist economy is whether to use consumption or foreign trade to ease tensions caused by overinvestment. In the early stages of all socialist economies and in some cases even at later stages, the increasing share of investment is accompanied by decreasing consumption (consumption-symmetric cycles), while in other cases (e.g., Hungary and Poland in the 1970s) money borrowed from abroad finances the increased investments (foreign-trade-symmetric cycles).

Bauer's theory is supported by other theoretical analyses and empirical evidence (Chavance 1987, Imai 1994, Simonovits 1986). Still many questions remain open, for example, the features that cycles in the various socialist economies had in common and the role of money in those cycles, and whether cycles in socialist economies differed in any essential way from those in market economies (Chavance 1987). The continuing transformation of Eastern Europe has diverted attention from these questions.

However, it should be noted that the occurrence of cycles played an important role in making the crisis in CPEs apparent and in causing their failure. The mechanism was the following: by the end of the 1970s it was becoming evident in most CPEs that neither consumption-symmetric nor foreign-trade symmetric cycles could be continued. The main reason was the inefficient use of capacities created by the investment projects (which was the consequence of inherent characteristics of socialist systems). More and more resources were required to maintain growth, i.e., to ensure that there would be an upturn in the cycle. Both foreign indebtedness and public unrest started to rise dangerously. Treating one meant exacerbating the other. Under the particular circumstances of the individual countries, this dilemma led to the downfall of the socialist systems in Eastern Europe.

Attila Chikán

See also CREATIVE DESTRUCTION; RÖPKE, WILHELM; SCHUMPETER, JOSEPH ALOIS

Bibliography

Bajt, A. 1971. "Investment Cycles in European Socialist Economies: A Review Article." *Journal of Economic Literature* 9:53–63.

Bauer, T. 1978. "Investment Cycles in Planned Economies." *Acta Oeconomica* 21:243–60.

Chavance, B., ed. 1987. *Regulation, cycles et crises dans les économies socialistes.* Paris: EHESS.

Goldman, J. 1964. "Fluctuations and Trends in the Rate of Growth in Some Socialist Countries." *Economics of Planning* 4:88–98.

Ickes, B. W. 1986. "Cyclical Fluctuations in Centrally Planned Economies." *Soviet Studies* 38:36–52.

———. 1988. "Do Socialist Countries Suffer a Common Business Cycle?" *Review of Economics and Statistics* 72:397–405.

Imai, H. 1994. "China's Endogenous Investment Cycle." *Journal of Comparative Economics* 19:188–216.

Kornai, J. 1980. *The Economics of Shortage.* Amsterdam: North-Holland.

Olivera, J. H. G. 1960. "Cyclical Economic Growth under Collectivism." *Kyklos* 13:229–55.

Sabov, Z. 1983. *Zykische Wirtschaftliche Aktivitätsschwankungen in sozialistichen Planwirtschaften.* Berlin: Dunker und Humblot.

Simonovits, A. 1986. "Growth, Control and Tensions in an Open Socialist Economy." *Economics of Planning* 20:145–61.

C

Cantillon, Richard (1680/90–1734/36)

Richard Cantillon, international banker and foreign-exchange dealer who led a mysterious life, and suffered an even more mysterious death, was the author of one of the most celebrated, and certainly one of the most important works in the history of economics, *Essai sur la Nature du Commerce en Général,* probably written between 1728 and 1730.

The *Essai* sets forth a general-equilibrium system with both national and international aspects, with which to analyze monetary disequilibrium. The system involved equilibrium in the markets for goods; equilibrium in the relative prices in different parts of a state (so that if town prices exceeded country prices by more than a competitive allowance for carriage and risk, metal would flow to the country and adjust the relative prices); and equilibrium in the international distribution of the precious metals. Cantillon then used this basic framework to analyze the effects of monetary changes. He distinguished between the money supply and its velocity of circulation, estimating that with the velocity then ruling, the required cash in France was around one half to two-thirds of agricultural gross output. However, the velocity was determined by institutional factors, especially the frequency of cash payments, and could be altered by a change in these institutional factors. There was some interdependence between money supply and velocity, velocity rising where money was in short supply. Money was also economized by commercial credit and by banks.

Cantillon devoted a good deal of attention to the size of the reserves required by banks under different circumstances. Banknotes, the main form of credit in his time, were particularly useful in economizing on metallic money for security purchases. However, the wealth effects produced by a speculative bubble would increase demand for metallic money for making consumer purchases, causing financial collapse as there was insufficient metal in the system to support the level of planned expenditure.

State-induced variations in the money supply, whether through depreciation of coinage or through excess issue of paper, were uniformly harmful and caused a flight from money, a rise in velocity, a rise in the price level, which then produced an adverse balance of payments, a metallic outflow, a shortage of loans for working capital, bankruptcy, distress sales, a falling price level, and a significant worsening of the terms of trade.

Cantillon believed that money-supply changes produced significant *relative*-price effects. In tracing these effects, he distinguished three possible sources of an increase in the money supply. First, an increase in the output of mines would raise employment (the economy had a natural rate of unemployment which he estimated to be as high as 25 percent) and the consumption of those newly employed would impose forced saving on other sections of the community as market prices rose with demand. It would also raise farm income and (after a lag) output, and reduce the real incomes of those whose incomes did not adjust to inflation, causing them to emigrate, thus raising income per head both because GNP had risen and because population had fallen.

Second, the money supply could rise because of a balance-of-payments surplus on visible account, the new money coming, in the first instance, into the hands of merchants. This would raise employment in the manufacturing sector since the merchants would demand manufactures to export, increasing consumption of the manufacturing classes and the prices of inputs.

Third, a balance-of-payments surplus on invisible account and on capital account could raise the money supply. Cantillon analyzed the financial flows through the different sectors which might be affected, emphasizing that the effect on relative prices depended on three factors: the preferred commodities of the newly rich, the elasticity of demand for those commodities on the part of other consumers, and the elasticity of supply.

A country gaining metal enjoyed the advantage not only of increased employment and income but also of improved terms of trade. However, Cantillon believed that, over a long period, the process was self-reversing. As prosperity spread through the system, both rents and the prices of manufactures rose, and imports increased. Citing the case of Spain, Cantillon argued that the long-run effect of this would be deindustrialization and a depressed economy. Once a population had, through prosperity, acquired a taste for luxuries (and here the example he cited was the Roman Empire), the days of prosperity were strictly numbered.

Cantillon's analysis of the effect of an increase in the money supply on the rate of interest is, not surprisingly, in view of the general level of sophistication of his work, particularly interesting. If new money came into the hands of merchants, their demand for loans would be reduced and the rate of interest, which is a market value, would *fall*. (Actual interest paid was pure interest—the mortgage rate—plus a risk premium.) If new money came into the hands of rich consumers, demand for manufactured goods would increase as would the demand from entrepreneurs for loans, raising the rate of interest. If moneylenders received the increase in the money supply, the interest rate would *fall*.

Cantillon's work is remarkably sophisticated in its analysis of the disequilibrating effects of monetary flows within a general-equilibrium system with particular institutional characteristics. As an achievement of a man busily amassing an enormous fortune and beset by every kind of personal problem, it is a truly astonishing achievement.

D. P. O'Brien

See also HUME, DAVID

Bibliography

Bordo, M. D. 1983. "Some Aspects of the Monetary Economics of Richard Cantillon." *Journal of Monetary Economics* 12:235–58.

Cantillon, R. [1755] 1931. *Essai sur la Nature du Commerce en Général*. Edited and translated by H. Higgs. London: Macmillan.

Murphy, A. 1986. *Richard Cantillon: Entrepreneur and Economist*. Oxford: Clarendon Press.

Capital Goods

Capital goods are produced means of production. They may be short-lived *circulating,* or long-lasting *fixed* capital goods. In the latter case, their high initial cost, durability, and immobility have long been seen as important sources of inflexibility which accentuate and contribute to cycles and crises. Recent work has confirmed the role of capital goods in making smooth adjustment problematic, once steady-state conditions are no longer assumed.

Consider an economy so simple that capital goods as yet play no part: an island on which some wild wheat appears each "year." Laborers increase the production of wheat by clearing weeds from the land, but assume that wheat cannot be *stored* from year to year. A fixed supply of "land services" and "labor services" is available in each year. Land is neither improved (beyond a given year) by cultivation nor allowed to deteriorate by excessive use. The laborers weed and then gather the wheat by hand, using no equipment. Finally, no money or paper assets exist. This is perhaps the nearest one can come to a model without capital goods.

The island story is obviously strained in several respects. If, for example, we assumed that islanders could store wheat into the following year, to be planted as seed, then a capital good would make its appearance. Despite their highly unreal nature, single-good models in which the good itself serves as an input in its production have preoccupied a number of theorists. Their attraction is that input and output are measured in identical units, so that a rate of return can be calculated without resort to a theory of valuation (or of prices). "Corn," for example, can be measured in bushels, whatever its price, and this unit applies equally to input and output.

Sometimes, the capital good in what are in fact single-capital-good models (though this is not always stressed by their authors) is an industrial good like "steel." If the islanders had manufactured a single agricultural implement—say, a hoe—but continued to depend on wheat growing wild, the model would be of this kind. If corn can be stored, however, there is a source of subsistence for the work force, plus a vital produced input into the further production of corn. But, if "hoes" are the only capital good, then the survival of the population must (whether or not the model makes the point explicitly) depend on seed blowing in the wind.

Deep questions concerning the nature of capital, which haunt sophisticated models, begin to appear in a simple circulating-capital model with more than one capital good. If hoes as well as corn saved from last year's harvest are used, the question arises: in what units can a "quantity of capital" be measured? Various expedients have been employed in attempts to aggregate, or measure (or avoid having to measure), heterogeneous capital goods. In particular, three approaches are worth mentioning. The first seeks to *aggregate* heterogeneous capital goods, the second seeks to arrive at a *value* sum representing a "quantity of capital," the third seeks to bypass the capital goods used in production to consider the *roundaboutness* of capital-using processes and thus to measure the time embodied in capital.

Physical aggregation would be possible if we found that wherever certain capital goods were used as inputs into production they were always used in the same proportions. One could then define a unit of "capital" as a basket containing the heterogeneous inputs in the exact proportions needed. And, if two capital goods, despite possessing different physical properties, were nevertheless perfect substitutes as inputs into the relevant processes, one could call either a unit of "capital." After a careful investigation of these matters, C. J. Bliss (1975, 155) concluded that the conditions for aggregation are so stringent "that it might be deemed a waste of time to detail the further niceties of the theory." A model that depended on a general capital aggregation would be confined "to instances so special that it would be hard to find parallels elsewhere in economic theory for such a constrained theory" (1975, 162).

Knut Wicksell tried out the second alternative—the attempt to find a value sum, but had the insight (as well as the honesty) to abandon it.

The productive contribution of a piece of technical capital, such as a steam engine, is determined not by its cost but by the horse power which it develops, and by the excess or scarcity of similar machines. If capital were also to be measured in technical units, the defect would be remedied and the correspondence [with other factors of production] would be complete. ([1901] 1934, 149)

If on the contrary, one measures the "quantity of capital" corresponding to a set of capital goods in terms of their exchange value, one must accept that this collection of capital goods is to count as a different "quantity of capital" if a change in prices alters its value. As Wicksell saw, the *value* of these capital goods will change with changes in the rate of interest. So, if one treats capital (construed as a sum of values) as if it were a factor of production (whose "price" is the rate of interest) with physically measured units, one is arguing in a circle.

These problems lay smoldering for many years. They finally exploded in controversy, in which a distinction between *price* "Wicksell effects" and *real* "Wicksell effects" was a central issue between Cambridge, England and Cambridge, Massachusetts. An important symposium in which both sides were well represented was published in the *Quarterly Journal of Economics* (Burmeister et al., 1966). Surveys of the debate are available, that of Harcourt (1972) being the best known. A more recent, more specialized treatment is offered by Kurz ([1985] 1988). General surveys of capital theory in the mainstream tradition of neoclassical theory include those of Bliss (1975) and Burmeister (1980).

Even Wicksell did not escape criticism in this controversy, notably from P. Garegnani (1970). Wicksell had tried (despite his own insights) to explain interest in terms of the "scarcity" of capital. But Sraffa (1960) and Robinson (1953, 1956) showed that in general no inverse monotonic relationship exists between the interest rate (interpreted as the "price" of capital) and the aggregate capital-labor ratio. Hence the rate of interest could not be used, as Wicksell had wanted, as a general index of the relative scarcity of "capital" in any capital-goods model. This phenomenon, known as "capital reversal," was taken seriously by general-equilibrium theorists in the non-Walrasian tradition, where it had in any case been the practice to distinguish each individual capital good (as well as each individual kind of labor, type of land, etc.). In such "activity-analysis" models, the marginal product of each separate input is reflected in a shadow price, thus avoiding the problem of aggregate capital. But, as has been noted by E. J. Nell (1989, 382), "for that very reason activity analysis cannot easily analyze the forces that bear on capital as a whole—for instance, saving and investment and their relation to the rate of interest."

Various expedients have been resorted to in the effort to escape these problems. One expedient involves ruling out so-called "real Wicksell effects" by *assumption,* thereby restoring many standard neoclassical results (Burmeister 1980, 205–07). Thus, the problems are "solved" by assuming them away.

Wicksell had worked with circulating capital, and the problems so far noted concerning heterogeneous capital goods do not *require* that these capital goods be "long-lasting" or "fixed." It is time now, however, to consider fixed capital and, more broadly, the role of time in the analysis of capital goods. Among the classical economists, capital was often seen as a fund needed for "advances," the wherewithal to buy raw materials, equipment, and to pay wages to productive workers, while output is being produced. However, this view sees time as simply an *aspect* of capital. But for W. S. Jevons (1871) and above all for E. Böhm-Bawerk ([1889] 1959), time was so far the essence of capital that capital could be measured by time.

This Austrian theory of capital has seemed incapable either of victory or of final defeat. It never converted the overwhelming majority of those who should have been its natural allies: those seeking to reduce the heterogeneity of capital goods to a single measure, a "quantity" of something scarce, whose "price" could be related to the interest rate of interest. Yet it has kept reappearing, evanescent as a woodland mist, haunting and perplexing some of the most brilliant minds in economic theory, C. C. von Weizsäker (1971) and Sir John Hicks (1973), among others. However, G. O. Orosel (1979) found that no formulation of the concept of a period of production could measure aggregate capital, because the period of production fell foul of the problems with the aggregate capital already familiar. Moreover, Orosel argues that (aside from aggregate capital problems) the Austrian

approach is at best only suitable for steady states, rather than for transition between such states involving disequilibrium or cycles. Since it is mainly in states of transition that the specific characteristics of *particular* capital goods become most important, there may still be senses in which *time* (despite the failure of repeated attempts to treat it as the essence of capital) is still important for capital theory: particularly in light of the problems posed for analysis by the character of fixed capital goods.

Capital theory has always been primarily concerned with the steady state. Models of a capital-using economy that is *not* always in a steady state are now, however, increasingly being developed. Pioneering work was done by A. Lowe, J. R. Hicks, and L. Pasinetti. The occurrence of *cycles* in models of the reproduction of capital, studied in early works of R. Goodwin, is being investigated by younger theorists like P. Flaschel and W. Semmler.

It has been argued that neither Hicks in his analysis of "traverse," nor Pasinetti in his analysis of "vertically integrated" sectors, fully confront some of the unique and specific properties of fixed capital goods. Again, Lowe has evidently felt that some of the implications of long-lasting capital goods for non-steady-state dynamic analysis have not been captured in two-sector models, and therefore added a third sector to his models: producing machines *to produce machines.* This contrasts with the normal assumption that fixed capital goods can be transferred from the capital-goods sector to the consumer-goods sector.

The standard treatment of the problem of *aging* fixed capital goods takes on a somewhat new light as a result of these developments. At least since Robert Torrens it has been usual to treat used machines as a "joint product" of a production process. In Lowe's work, however, where there is excess demand in a particular sector and underutilization in another, changing from period to period, "it becomes difficult to specify the quantity of equipment appearing in each period as joint product with (varying) output. If equipment is underutilized will more of it appear as the joint product, or products?" (Nell 1976, 292). Thus, some recent developments of theory suggest that the disequilibrating effects of fixed capital goods may well be greater than could be shown in the models used until recently. This clearly should concern theorists of cycles and crises.

Vivian Walsh

See also AUSTRIAN THEORY OF BUSINESS CYCLES; BÖHM-BAWERK, EUGEN RITTER VON; BURCHARDT, FRITZ (FRANK) ADOLPH; HAYEK, FRIEDRICH AUGUST [VON]; INVESTMENT; LOWE, ADOLPH; OVERINVESTMENT THEORIES OF THE BUSINESS CYCLE; PERIOD OF PRODUCTION; WICKSELL, JOHAN GUSTAV KNUT

Bibliography

Bliss, C. J. 1975. *Capital Theory and the Distribution of Income.* New York: American Elsevier.

Böhm-Bawerk, E. von. [1889] 1959. *Capital and Interest.* Vol. 2. *The Positive Theory of Capital.* South Holland, Ill.: Libertarian Press.

Burmeister, E. 1980. *Capital Theory and Dynamics.* Cambridge: Cambridge Univ. Press.

Burmeister, E., E. Sheshinski, P. Garegnani, D. Levhari, and P. A. Samuelson. 1966. *Paradoxes in Capital Theory: A Symposium. Quarterly Journal of Economics* 80:503–83.

Champernowne, D. G. 1953. "The Production Function and the Theory of Capital: A Comment." *Review of Economic Studies* 21:112–35.

Flaschel, P. and W. Semmler. 1989. "On the Integration of Dual and Cross-Dual Adjustment Processes in Leontief Systems." *Richerche Economiche* 42:403–32.

Garegnani, P. 1970. "Heterogeneous Capital, the Production Function and the Theory of Distribution." *Review of Economic Studies* 37:407–36.

Goodwin, R. M. 1983. *Essays in Linear Economic Structures.* London: Macmillan.

Harcourt, G. C. 1972. *Some Cambridge Controversies in the Theory of Capital.* Cambridge: Cambridge Univ. Press.

Hicks, J. R. 1965. *Capital and Growth.* Oxford: Clarendon Press.

———. 1973. *Capital and Time: A Neo-Austrian Theory.* Oxford: Clarendon Press.

Jevons, W. S. 1871. *The Theory of Political Economy.* London: Macmillan.

Kurz, H. D. [1985] 1988. "Sraffa's Contribution to the Debate in Capital Theory." In *Sraffian Economics,* edited by I. Steedman. Vol. 1, 42–63. Aldershott, U.K.: Elgar.

———. 1986. "Classical and Early Neoclassical Economists on Joint Production." *Metroeconomica* 38:1–38.

Lowe, A. 1955. "Structural Analysis of Real Capital Formation." In *Capital Formation and Economic Growth,* edited by M. Abramovitz, 581–634. Princeton: Princeton Univ. Press.

———. 1976. *The Path of Economic Growth.* Cambridge: Cambridge Univ. Press.

Nell, E. G. 1976. "Appendix: An Alternative Presentation of Lowe's Basic Model." In A. Lowe, *The Path of Economic Growth.* Cambridge: Cambridge Univ. Press.

———. 1989. "Accumulation and Capital Theory." In *Joan Robinson and Modern Economic Theory,* edited by G. R. Feiwel, 377–412. New York: New York Univ. Press.

Orosel, G. O. 1979. "A Reformulation of the Austrian Theory of Capital and its Application to the Debate on Reswitching and Related Paradoxes." *Zeitschrift für Nationalökonomie* 39:1–31.

Pasinetti, L. L., ed. 1980. *Essays on the Theory of Joint Production.* London: Macmillan.

———. 1981. *Structural Change and Economic Growth: A Theoretical Essay on the Dynamics of the Wealth of Nations.* Cambridge: Cambridge Univ. Press.

Robinson, J. 1953. "The Production Function and the Theory of Capital." *Review of Economic Studies* 21:81–106.

———. 1956. *The Accumulation of Capital.* London: Macmillan.

Salvadori, N. and I. Steedman. 1988. "Joint Production Analysis in a Sraffian Framework." *Bulletin of Economic Research* 40:165–95.

Sraffa, P. 1960. *The Production of Commodities by Means of Commodities: Prelude to a Critique of Economic Theory.* Cambridge: Cambridge Univ. Press.

Weizsäker, C. C. von. 1971. *Steady State Capital Theory.* Berlin: Springer-Verlag.

Wicksell, K. [1901] 1934. *Lectures on Political Economy.* Vol. 1. *General Theory.* Translation. London: Routledge.

Cassel, Carl Gustav (1866–1945)

Gustav Cassel was born in Stockholm on 20 October 1866, earned a doctorate in mathematics at the University of Uppsala in 1895, turned to economics, taught at the University of Stockholm (1904–33), and was a highly influential international consultant. His

Theoretische Sozialökonomie (1918) appeared in five German editions, two English translations, a French, a Japanese, and a Swedish translation. Book four of this work contained Cassel's business-cycle analysis. Cassel died in Stockholm on 14 January 1945.

Scope and Method
Cassel saw a regular business cycle only for the period 1870–1914. Before 1870 a fully monetized industrial economy based on an international division of labor had not yet developed. After 1914, World War I and its aftermath destroyed both the monetary system and the international division of labor. The dust had settled at the time of neither the last English translation (1932) nor the ultimate Swedish edition (1934), so Cassel left his analysis of the business cycle essentially as it had appeared in the first edition. It may be summarized as follows:

Physical Output
A bit of algebra will facilitate a restatement of Cassel's output analysis, so let us begin by writing a rigid accelerator model using the following notation:

$b \equiv$ accelerator
$C \equiv$ physical consumption
$G \equiv$ physical gross investment
$I \equiv$ physical net investment
$R \equiv$ physical replacement
$S \equiv$ physical capital stock
$u \equiv$ useful life of durable producers' goods

Write the three definitions:

$$G \equiv I + R \qquad (1)$$

$$I \equiv dS/dt \qquad (2)$$

$$R(t) \equiv G(t - u) \qquad (3)$$

and the assumption of a rigid accelerator:

$$S = bC. \qquad (4)$$

Insert equation (4) into (2), (2) and (3) into (1), and write physical gross investment

$$G(t) = b\frac{dC(t)}{dt} + G(t - u) \qquad (5)$$

A quarter-century before modern national income accounting, how did Cassel measure his physical gross investment G and his consumption C?

With the Bessemer, Siemens-Martin, and Thomas processes, iron became the most important material embodied in plant and equipment, so Cassel (1932, 548–49) used world output of pig iron in millions of tons from 1865 to 1910 to represent physical gross investment G and found it peaking in 1873, 1882, 1890, 1900, and 1907.

Before World War I, coal fueled heating, powered lighting, powered manufacturing processes, and propelled ships, trains, and trolleys, so Cassel (550–51) used world output of coal in millions of tons from 1865 to 1910 to represent physical output of consumers' goods C and found it much more steady than pig-iron output: coal output displayed no peaks. With the exception of 1907 in the United States it never declined.

Equation (5) simulates Cassel's facts: $G(t)$ could decline without any decline in $C(t)$; a decline in $dC(t)/dt$ would do. While declining, $G(t)$ would always remain positive: $dC(t)/dt$ might briefly decline to zero, but there was always a positive physical replacement $R(t) \equiv G(t-u)$.

J. M. Clark ([1917] 1951) applied the acceleration principle to transportation on land and contrasted United States railroad traffic with orders for new railroad cars. Independently, Cassel (597–98) applied the same principle to transportation at sea and contrasted tonnage of British freight with tonnage of new ships launched in British yards. A slight dip or even no change in freight could reduce launchings sharply.

Cassel saw two reasons why reality would be less rigid than a strict accelerator model. First he offered blast-furnace data showing that in the depression, durable producers' goods might be replaced *before* reaching their uth birthday, but in the boom, *after* reaching it. Second, Cassel (589–91) offered railroad data that overtime and extra shifts might enable industry to produce more output C without installing more capital stock S—thus softening equation (4).

Unemployment
For unemployment rates, Cassel (576–77) used British Board of Trade data for five groups of industries. The overall average rate had minima in 1872, 1882, 1890, 1899, and 1906, i.e., at or within a year of the peaks of world pig-iron output. Fully as interesting were the years of maxima. Singling out the unemployment rate in

engineering, shipbuilding, and metal industries, Cassel found it to be much higher in such years than the unemployment rates of other industries.

Prices, Income, and Saving

For prices, Cassel (600–602) used Sauerbeck index numbers. Singling out the price index for minerals, Cassel found it to have peaked in 1873, 1882, 1890, 1900, and 1907—just as had world pig-iron output—and to be much more cyclically sensitive than the indices for other commodities.

For income, Cassel (610–16) used Prussian, Saxon,and Swedish income-tax data and found nonwage income to be more cyclically sensitive than wage income. The nonwage share peaked in the early upswing when excess capacity was disappearing. Cassel speculated that the propensity to save was higher for nonwage income, especially corporate and proprietor's income. If so, saving would also peak in the early upswing.

Saving and Investment

Saving and investment would meet in a capital market whose equilibrating variable was the rate of interest, and here is where Cassel (622–38) found the heart of the business cycle.

Let the present gross worth of another physical unit of durable producers' good be the sum of its future revenue *minus* operating costs discounted at the market rate of interest. Let its present net worth be its present gross worth *minus* its market price.

In the depression, widespread excess capacity would make present gross worth zero even at the prevailing low rate of interest and would make present net worth negative even at the prevailing low market price of durable producers' goods. Investment would drop below its previous peak.

But consumption displayed no peaks, so in the early upswing, excess capacity would be disappearing, and the accelerator would gather momentum. Saving would be at its peak, and consequently the rate of interest would still be low. Discounted at such a low rate of interest, future revenues *minus* operating costs would be looking very favorable: present gross worth would be at its maximum. Furthermore, in the early upswing, the market price of durable producers' goods would still be low. As a result, present net worth would be at its maximum, too.

In the late upswing, no excess capacity would be left, and the accelerator would have reached its full force. But saving would have passed its peak and now be driving up the rate of interest. Discounted at such a higher rate of interest, future revenues *minus* operating costs would now be looking less favorable: present gross worth would be waning. Furthermore, in the late upswing the market price of durable producers' goods would be higher. As a result, present net worth would be sharply reduced. But once started, long-term investment projects could be salvaged only by completing them despite worsening conditions. Cassel (539–40 compared with 594) found that money market rates in Berlin and London and world output of pig iron had peaked in the same years (1873, 1882, 1890, 1900, and 1907) as investment.

Conclusion

Cassel's business-cycle analysis was surprisingly modern.

First, it was a macrodynamic theory confronting the composition of physical output between consumers' goods and durable producers' goods with the disposition of income between consumption and saving. By using not only prices but also unemployment as a variable, Cassel's model was superior to Hayek's model advanced thirteen years later. By using not only unemployment but also prices as a variable, it was also superior to Keynes's model advanced eighteen years later. By using the accelerator, Cassel's model was superior to both.

Second, wherever possible, Cassel confronted his macrodynamic theory with statistical measurement. Of such measurement Keynes made little use and Hayek none at all.

Hans Brems

See also ACCELERATION PRINCIPLE; INVESTMENT

Bibliography

Cassel, C. G. [1918] 1932. *The Theory of Social Economy.* 5th ed. Translation. New York: Harcourt, Brace.

Clark, J. M. [1917] 1951. "Business Acceleration and the Law of Demand: A Technical Factor in Economic Cycles." In *Readings in Business Cycle Theory,* 235–60. Philadelphia: Blakiston.

Wicksell, K. [1919] 1934. "Professor Cassel's System of Economics." Appendix 1 in *Lectures on Political Economy.* Vol. 1. *General Theory.* Translation. London: Routledge.

C

Catchings, Waddill (1879–1968)

See FOSTER, WILLIAM TRUFANT

Ceilings and Floors

Ceilings and floors are theoretical constructs postulated to check explosive patterns that are otherwise implied by linear difference equations. Because ceilings and floors introduce nonlinearities, they imply a richer menu of dynamic paths than do simple linear models. These paths are more consistent with historical experiences than are those implied by linear models in which instability necessarily implies an explosive dynamic path. This view of business cycles is in contrast with that which attributes cycles to exogenous (stochastic) shocks. The apparently greater econometric support for the latter view discouraged the development of endogenous explanations of economic fluctuations. However, enough contrary evidence has been presented recently to revive interest in nonlinear models, including those with ceilings and floors.

Ceilings and floors were introduced by Hicks in a slightly altered version of Samuelson's accelerator-multiplier model. Hicks's version of this model postulates an investment, I, accelerator function of the difference of lagged output, Y, together with a consumption, C, function of lagged output. Combining these two equations with the material-balance equation yields a second-order linear difference equation:

$$Y_t = C(Y_{t-1}) + I(Y_{t-1} - Y_{t-2}). \qquad (1)$$

This equation, like those obtained in continuous time by combining the value of a variable with its velocity and its acceleration, can typically generate either stationarity, damped monotonic behavior, monotonic increase, damped oscillations, increasing oscillations, or harmonic oscillations. Which pattern occurs depends on the values of the parameters. In fact, the solution to equation (1) is given by:

$$Y_t = A_1\mu^{t_1} + A_2\mu^{t_2} + k, \qquad (2)$$

where k represents the particular solution and the roots μ, which govern the dynamic pattern, depend on the parameter values. In particular, real roots imply one of the first three patterns, while complex roots imply one of the others. Harmonic oscillation can be obtained only for unrealistic parameter values.

To obtain more robust cyclical patterns than those implied by linear difference equations, equation (1) must be turned into a piecewise linear equation to capture the effects of floors and ceilings. The ceiling, or upper bound, was originally defined as the maximal growth path that is sustainable with available resources. The floor, or lower bound, reflects the fact that gross investment in fixed capital cannot be negative. Thus, this model implies an unstable endogenous dynamic path that is constrained by the existence of ceilings and floors. It is then possible to distinguish between an endogenous behavior and a constrained one, when ceilings and floors become binding. Minsky (1959) interpreted such floors and ceilings as imposing new initial conditions, so that the dynamic process could start anew whenever they became effective. In fact, one has to consider that the solution to equation (2) is a transformation of a second-order difference equation of the form:

$$Y_t = f(Y_{t-1}, Y_{t-2}). \qquad (3)$$

This recursive process is changed whenever initial conditions are changed, which happens when ceilings or floors are hit.

The relevance of ceilings and floors has been questioned on several grounds (for example, by Matthews 1959). On empirical grounds, ceilings have been questioned, because upper cyclical turning points often occur before full employment is reached. The floor concept is even more debatable, both empirically and theoretically.

Such criticisms have led to two different research strategies. One alternative mentioned above, which became the dominant paradigm in business-cycle theory, introduced stochastic disturbances into linear models. Consequently, interest in the endogenous approach waned after the 1950s. Pronounced business cycles did not appear and the persistence of rather steady growth made it plausible to assume that the observed fluctuations could best be interpreted as transformations of stochastically determined deviations from a growth path. The other was to seek to develop nonlinear models whose parameters vary with system behavior. Goodwin, for instance, developed models which could generate closed orbits and, under certain more restrictive hypotheses, limit cycles towards which all possible paths of the variable converge.

The validity of the macroeconometric evidence supporting the random-shock theory is open to question, however, and the results are less definitive than was once believed (Brock 1986). Furthermore, new developments in the theory of nonlinearity and chaos can imply complex behavior that is indistinguishable from stochastic time series (Baumol and Benhabib 1989). Nevertheless, it is not clear that renewed interest in nonlinear systems warrants reconsideration of piecewise models based on ceilings or floors, since cyclical behavior can be derived from either one of the two. One difficulty lies in the definition of the concepts themselves. A ceiling is not necessarily determined by full employment or by the capacity of the investment-goods industry. It could also be determined by a quantity-of-money constraint on money income, resulting from the limited variability of velocity. Integration of dynamics in real and monetary terms may thereby be achieved. However, as Hicks observed in his final contribution, a monetary constraint could operate only in the old style of a financial cycle when the gold standard provided a firm check on expansion, a monetary ceiling.

Ceilings and floors, however, can be reinterpreted and given a more general meaning, as has long been recognized. Goodwin (1950) suggested the term "threshold" which corresponds to the terminology used in systems-control theory. Matthews talked about "buffers." One can generalize further and consider ceilings and floors as thresholds that depend on the institutional context. The simple accelerator-multiplier models with ceilings that reflect endogenously determined economic relations should be understood as primitive examples valid only as illustrations or "metaphors" of the behavior of a complex dynamic system in which new initial conditions are provided by new institutional set-ups (Ferri and Minsky 1989) or by regime switching (Ferri and Greenberg 1989), which intervene discontinuously when certain quantity or value thresholds are overcome or when policy changes are introduced. In such a system stability can be achieved by appropriate interventions that can be interpreted mathematically as imposing new initial conditions or as changing parameters. Stabilizers and multipliers interact to produce complex results that mimic economic fluctuations more closely than they do periodic business cycles, which are too regular to be empirically satisfactory.

Viewing the economy as potentially unstable while recognizing that institutional structures and interventions may help to stabilize is an approach that in some respects resembles Leijonhufvud's concept of a "corridor." In an economy subject to two kinds of forces (i.e., deviation-counteracting and the deviation-amplifying feedback effects), Leijonhufvud ([1973] 1981) argues, the stabilizing price-effects usually dominate the destabilizing multiplier-effects for small exogenous displacements of the equilibrium. The basic notion of the corridor is that although the economic system usually exhibits desirable stability properties, it can handle shocks only of a certain maximum size.

Like ceiling-and-floor models, the corridor implies nonlinearities. However, two differences are worth noting. Leijonhufvud's model is locally stable but globally unstable, while models with ceilings and floors are locally unstable but globally stable. Moreover, in a model with ceilings, instability is endogenous and is not necessarily created by large shocks.

Finally, it should be noted that ascertaining whether models are truly deterministic is not important. They may have both stochastic and deterministic elements. What matters is identifying particular kinds of nonlinearities capable of generating cycles. Moreover, both stochastic and nonlinear models suggest that apt intervention and appropriate institutions are necessary for market economies to avoid severe fluctuations.

Piero Ferri

See also DIFFERENTIAL AND DIFFERENCE EQUATIONS; HICKS, JOHN RICHARD; NONLINEAR BUSINESS-CYCLE THEORIES; SAMUELSON, PAUL ANTHONY

Bibliography
Baumol, W. J. and J. Benhabib. 1989. "Chaos: Significance, Mechanism, and Economic Applications." *Journal of Economic Perspectives,* Winter, 77–105.
Brock, W. A. 1986. "Distinguishing Random and Deterministic Systems: Abridged Version." *Journal of Economic Theory* 40:168–95.
Ferri, P. and E. Greenberg. 1989. *The Labor Market and Business Cycles.* New York: Springer-Verlag.
Ferri, P. and H. P. Minsky. 1989. "The Breakdown of the IS-LM Synthesis: Implications for Post-Keynesian Economic Theory." *Review of Political Economy* 1:125–43.

C

Goodwin, R. M. 1950. "Non-Linear Theory of the Cycle." *Review of Economics and Statistics* 32:316–20.

———. [1967] 1983. "A Growth Cycle." Chap. 14 in *Essays in Economic Dynamics*. London: Macmillan.

Hicks, J. R. 1950. *A Contribution to the Theory of Trade Cycle*. Oxford: Clarendon Press.

Leijonhufvud, A. [1973] 1981. "Effective Demand Failures." Chap. 6 of *Information and Coordination*. New York: Oxford Univ. Press.

Matthews, R. C. O. 1959. *The Trade Cycle*. Cambridge: Cambridge Univ. Press.

Medio, A. 1979. *Teoria Non-Lineare del Ciclo*. Bologna: Il Mulino.

Minsky, H. P. 1959. "A Linear Model of Cyclical Growth." *Review of Economics and Statistics* 41:137–45.

Samuelson, P. A. [1939] 1966. "Interaction Between the Multiplier Analysis and the Principle of Acceleration." Chap. 82 in *The Collected Scientific Papers of Paul A. Samuelson*. Vol. 2. Cambridge: MIT Press.

Central Banking

A central bank is a national institution whose primary function is to control the quantity of money in circulation. It may also perform other functions, but these vary from one country to another, depending on the local financial structure and history.

The name "central bank" signifies that the institution occupies a central position within a country's financial system. Central banks are also known as banks of issue, since they have usually enjoyed either a monopoly of note issue or a power of issue surpassing that of other banks.

Origins and Spread of Central Banking

Institutions that eventually became central banks were initially established for reasons other than the exercise of central-banking functions. The Bank of England, for example, was chartered in 1694 as a private corporation with a capital of £1.2 million—the amount that it lent to the government and in return for which it was authorized to issue an equal sum in notes. Nearly two centuries elapsed before it willingly assumed the responsibilities of a central bank. The same was true of the Riksbank, which was established as a private bank in Sweden twenty-six years before the Bank of England. It failed in 1664 and was reorganized in 1668 under the ownership and supervision of the Swedish Parliament, operating thereafter as a commercial bank until the close of the nineteenth century.

The use of the term "central banking" dates from the beginning of this century. By that time the larger European countries had well-established central banks as did also Japan. Some countries—Australia and Brazil—had embryonic central banks. In the United States, however, central banking did not exist. Nor were there any genuine central banks south of its borders.

The Federal Reserve System, organized in 1914, became the central bank of the United States. In Europe in the 1920s central banks were established in each of the countries created by the Treaty of Versailles and in this hemisphere in Chile and Mexico. In the 1930s central banks were introduced in Argentina, Colombia, and Mexico, Canada, and India. After World War II the former colonial countries of Asia and Africa created central banks as membership in the international financial bodies presupposed that a central bank represented each country, big or small.

Central Banking Under a Specie Standard

Historically, central banking developed under a metallic standard. The specie standard required the central bank to convert into coin on demand the notes it issued. The central bank's paramount responsibility was to buy and sell the metallic commodity—gold or silver or both—at a fixed price and to maintain the country's ultimate reserves. That is why the word "reserve" appears in the title of some central banks that were established when a specie standard was in operation (for example, the Reserve Bank of India, the Federal Reserve System). The country's ultimate reserves were specie, lodged either wholly at the central bank or in part at other banks in the financial system, the national Treasury, or exchange-stabilization fund.

The gold standard prevailed during the late nineteenth and early twentieth century until 1914. It was briefly revived after World War I and again broke down during the later interwar years. Under the Bretton Woods system after World War II, central banks undertook to buy or sell dollars in the foreign-exchange market to keep their currencies from appreciating or depreciating more than one percent from their par values. The United States as the reserve-currency country in turn undertook to convert dollars into gold or the reverse at the fixed price of $35 an ounce.

The Bretton Woods system collapsed in 1973 and gold has since essentially been demonetized although countries continue to hold gold reserves.

Central Banking in a Fiat Money World

Since the convertibility requirement no longer limits central-bank issues of money, in a fiat-money world each institution chooses the quantity it makes available. That choice has been influenced by domestic as well as external considerations. Central banks in recent decades have increased monetary growth to reduce unemployment and stimulate real growth, and have reduced monetary growth to offset inflation and depreciation of their currencies in foreign-exchange markets. The net effect has been a worldwide drift to higher inflation.

How do central banks influence the rate of growth of the quantity of money? They do so by controlling the provision of reserves to the banking system. Historically, bank notes were an important component of the money supply (since overshadowed by deposits). Ordinary banks met their reserve requirements—a fraction of the deposits on their books—by holding as vault cash the notes of the central bank or maintaining reserve balances with the central bank.

The volume of reserves available to banks, a primary influence on the size of the deposit component, reflects mainly the use of two central bank instruments—open-market operations and discount policy. A central bank controls the pace at which it supplies reserves to the banking system by determining how much it will lend banks at the discount window and the size of its securities portfolio.

A central bank pays for an open-market purchase of securities by a check drawn on itself. The deposit of the check in a bank by a nonbank seller increases the seller's deposit. The bank in turn deposits the check at the central bank, which credits the bank's reserve account. The opposite sequence occurs when the central bank sells securities in the open market, the sale leading to a decrease in the bank deposits of a nonbank purchaser and a debit of the bank's reserve account.

A central bank relies mainly on changes in the discount rate to control the volume of reserves the banks obtain by borrowing. Central banks may also rely on moral suasion to deter borrowing by banks or to restrict bank lending deemed to be speculative, however ineffective such action.

In a system with fractional reserve requirements, an increase in bank reserves can support a multiple expansion of deposits and a decrease can cause a multiple contraction of deposits. Central banks supply banks with the currency their customers demand and, when their demand falls, accept a return flow from the banks. The central bank debits the reserves of the banks when it provides currency and credits their reserves when they return currency.

Bank reserves and currency are components of the monetary base, sometimes known as high-powered money. Central banks have the power to control the issue of both components. They also may have the power to alter reserve requirements, changing the percentage of deposit liabilities the banks must set aside as reserves.

Central Banks as Lenders of Last Resort

During the nineteenth century, bank failures periodically led to runs on solvent banks as depositors, fearing for the safety of their deposits, attempted to withdraw them as cash. Panic conditions ensued when banks exhausted their reserves and convertibility was threatened. Central banks had to learn the role of lender of last resort, initially providing the banks with additional reserves to cut short a panic once it had begun, but eventually acting in advance to avert its occurrence.

According to at least one modern student of central banking, the lender of last resort should provide reserves not only to solvent institutions facing a temporary liquidity problem—the classical position—but also to insolvent ones. Failures per se on this view are disruptive of financial stability.

Many countries do not depend solely on a lender of last resort to maintain public confidence in the banking system. They also provide government insurance of bank deposits. Bank failures then may not provoke runs.

Business Cycles and Central Banks

Some monetary theories associate business cycles with central-bank actions, attributing business expansions to expansionary monetary policy and business contractions to contractionary monetary policy. Other theories assume that business cycles are initiated by nonmonetary forces but that central banks can act as a stabilizing influence by raising interest rates when the real economy is at full capacity and reducing interest rates when the real economy is depressed.

Other Functions Central Banks Exercise

Central banks may perform fiscal services for their governments including management of the public debt, and they may have authority to supervise and regulate the banks, manage exchange rates, and provide elements of the payments system by which checks are cleared.

Constraints on Central Banks

All countries impose a franchise tax on the interest earnings of the central bank's portfolio as well as on the profits of its monopoly note issue. The tax is not an important influence on central-bank operations, since, to the extent that they are independent of government, their budgets are not appropriated by governments. Examples of relatively independent central banks are the Bundesbank and the Federal Reserve System. Many central banks are not, however, independent policymakers. Finance ministers, not central bank governors, may be in charge of monetary policy.

The real constraints on central-bank operations are market driven. In a fiat-money system, if monetary policy is inflationary, the market will impose higher interest costs on government debt and the country's currency will depreciate in foreign-exchange markets.

Dissenting Views on Central Banks

In recent years, inflationary outcomes of central-bank actions have occasioned debate on various aspects of their operation. Among the issues raised, the following may be noted:

1. In democratic countries, why should central banks be secretive and insist on delays in reporting their decisions?
2. Should central banks be permitted discretion or required to operate under rules; for example, a rule limiting monetary growth or a rule freezing the monetary base?
3. Should central banks be permitted to retain a monopoly of note issue?
4. Should the central banks that are independent instead operate as a government bureau?
5. Did central banks evolve naturally in response to a market need for them or were they artificial creations of needy governments?
6. Could a private banking system operate successfully without a central bank?

Epilogue

Existing central banks are national institutions. In the European Economic Community they may be superseded by a single European central bank if the move to achieve monetary union at some early future date is realized. Existing national monies would disappear, replaced by a new currency that the single European central bank would issue.

Anna J. Schwartz

See also BANKING AND FINANCIAL REGULATION; BANK OF ENGLAND; BANK OF FRANCE; CLEARINGHOUSES; DEMAND FOR CURRENCY; DEUTSCHE BUNDESBANK; FEDERAL RESERVE SYSTEM: 1914–1941; FEDERAL RESERVE SYSTEM: 1941–1993; FREE BANKING; GOLD STANDARD; GOLD STANDARD: CAUSES AND CONSEQUENCES; INTERNATIONAL LENDER OF LAST RESORT; LENDER OF LAST RESORT; MONETARY DISEQUILIBRIUM THEORIES OF THE BUSINESS CYCLE; MONETARY EQUILIBRIUM THEORIES OF THE BUSINESS CYCLE; MONETARY POLICY; REICHSBANK; SUPPLY OF MONEY

Bibliography

Bagehot, W. [1873] 1962. *Lombard Street.* Homewood, Ill.: Irwin.

Friedman, M. and A. J. Schwartz. 1986. "Has Government Any Role in Money?" *Journal of Monetary Economics* 17:37–62.

Glasner, D. 1989. *Free Banking and Monetary Reform.* New York: Cambridge Univ. Press.

Goodfriend, M. and R. G. King. 1988. "Financial Deregulation, Monetary Policy, and Central Banking." In *Restructuring Banking and Financial Services in America,* edited by W. S. Haraf and R. M. Kushmeider, 216–53. Washington, D.C.: American Enterprise Institute.

Goodhart, C. A. E. 1987. "Why Do Banks Need a Central Bank?" *Oxford Economic Papers* 39:75–89.

———. 1989. *The Evolution of Central Banks.* Cambridge: MIT Press.

Hawtrey, R. G. 1932. *The Art of Central Banking.* London: Longmans.

Humphrey, T. M. 1975. "The Classical Concept of the Lender of Last Resort." Federal Reserve Bank of Richmond *Economic Review*, January/February, 2–9.

Sayers, R. S. 1957. *Central Banking After Bagehot*. Oxford: Clarendon Press.

Smith, V. C. 1936. *The Rationale of Central Banking*. London: P. S. King.

Wood, G. E. 1989. *Banking and Monetary Control After 1992: A Central Bank for Europe?* London: Institute of Economic Affairs.

Chaos and Bifurcations

One traditional approach to explaining the business cycle has been to use a deterministic model that generates endogenous oscillations. The Hicks-Samuelson multiplier-accelerator model and the Metzler cycle model follow this route. Another approach, associated with E. Slutsky and R. Frisch, has stressed stochastic disturbances as the driving force of the business cycle. Modern real business-cycle theory is certainly in this tradition.

Recently, various authors have shown that standard equilibrium models with complete price flexibility and with no frictions or barriers to trade can generate cyclic or chaotic dynamics. This was somewhat surprising, because, with the introduction of perfect-foresight (or rational expectations) models with flexible prices, it had been presumed that intertemporal arbitrage would eliminate the possibility of systematically and predictably oscillating prices. Furthermore, the capacity of deterministic chaotic dynamics to generate time series that can look random offered the promise of explaining real-world data that typically also appear stochastic.

We can usually describe a dynamical system in discrete time as *chaotic* if it can generate cycles of every periodicity, where a sequence $\{x_i\}$ is of period n if $x_j = x_{j+n}$ but $x_j \neq x_i$ for $j < i < n-1$. In addition, this simple definition of chaos requires the existence of an uncountable number of initial conditions which give rise to bounded but aperiodic (not even asymptotically) sequences. For example the well-known hump-shaped function, $4x(1-x)$, when iterated, generates such chaotic dynamics. The kind of chaotic dynamics described above is usually referred to as *topological* chaos. If in addition we require that the set of initial conditions giving rise to aperiodic sequences are not simply uncountable but also have a positive (Lebesgue) measure, then we also have *ergodic* chaos. A useful sufficient condition to obtain topological chaos with a simple difference equation $x_{t+1} = f(x_t)$, with f continuous and mapping a closed interval into itself, is the existence of some x such that $f(f(f(x))) \leq x \leq f(x) < f(f(x))$. A particularly interesting feature of some dynamic systems that are chaotic is *sensitive dependence* on *initial conditions:* initial conditions that are arbitrarily close can generate sequences that tend to diverge over time. Thus, small measurement errors in initial conditions may cause large forecasting errors, which may explain some of the difficulties associated with business-cycle forecasting.

Bifurcations describe the qualitative changes of the dynamical systems which depend on a parameter, as the parameter crosses critical values which induce a change in the stability of a stationary point, a periodic cycle, or another invariant set. For example we may consider two intersecting offer curves that determine the equilibrium terms of trade, which under the usual excess-demand dynamics will be stable. As we vary a preference parameter we may begin to bend the offer curves so that beyond some point they intersect three times rather than only once. The terms of trade in the middle become unstable, but we also obtain two additional equilibrium terms of trade that are stable. The two additional equilibrium terms of trade will have bifurcated from the original equilibrium terms of trade at the critical point at which it loses its stability as we vary the preference parameter. However, loss of stability may also cause the bifurcation not of new stationary equilibria but also of periodic orbits and of more complicated invariant and possibly attracting sets. In fact one route to chaotic dynamics is through successive bifurcations, as the value of a parameter that controls the dynamical system is moved across critical points at which a change of stability occurs.

Chaotic dynamics and the bifurcation of cycles can occur in both of the standard equilibrium paradigms that are used in modern business-cycle theories: the overlapping-generations model and the optimal-growth model with an infinitely lived agent. In the simple overlapping-generations model strong income effects (although without the requirements of inferior goods) can give rise to periodic cycles and chaos. In addition, when investments are financed out of the wage income of the young, an elastic labor supply coupled with a low elasticity of substitution in production can generate an aggregate savings function of capital that is hump-shaped, as for example in $4x(1-x)$, and give rise to cycles, and chaos. Similar results also obtain when investment is mostly financed out of profits. In the multi-sector optimal-growth model, cycles and even chaos can arise from the structure of technology. If a capital good is more intensively used in the production of other goods than in its own production, an expansion in its supply will shift the production possibility curve in favor of other goods and at the expense of its own production. This will tend to reverse the original expansion of the capital good and will tend to generate oscillations, sustained equilibrium cycles, and possibly chaos. There are many other models and equilibrium "generating mechanisms" that result in cyclic and chaotic dynamics without violating the modern theoretical requirements of rational expectations and market equilibrium. Some of the important papers in this mold are collected in Benhabib (1992). Also the surveys by Baumol and Benhabib (1989) and Boldrin and Woodford (1990) provide an overview and a more technical discussion of this literature.

Determining the empirical relevance of chaotic and cyclic dynamics for business cycles remains a difficult subject. Some of the early papers describing the methodologies for discovering whether a particular time series has been generated by a deterministic but chaotic system, rather than a stochastic one, can be found in Benhabib (1992). The basic difficulty is that at the present time, the most interesting time series, like GNP, only contain, at most, a few hundred observations. However, the properties that distinguish random motions from deterministic chaos are identifiable, if at all, only with much longer time series, which may also be plagued by non-stationarities. This suggests that estimating theoretical models and then checking to see whether the estimated parameters fall within the range that can generate chaotic dynamics may be a more fruitful approach. Finally, the sharp distinction between deterministic chaotic dynamics and stochastic dynamics seems misplaced. More likely, stochastic components may be superimposed on, and interact with, the deterministic (autoregressive) part of a dynamical system to generate cyclic or chaotic dynamics, which would make their detection even more difficult. At the present time, solid empirical evidence for the presence of chaotic dynamics in business-cycle fluctuations has not yet been established.

Jess Benhabib

See also BUSINESS CYCLES; CEILINGS AND FLOORS; CHAOS, CONTINUOUS-TIME MODELS OF; DIFFERENTIAL AND DIFFERENCE EQUATIONS; FRISCH, RAGNER KITTEL; HICKS, JOHN RICHARD; NONLINEAR BUSINESS-CYCLE THEORIES; NONLINEAR STATISTICAL INFERENCE; SAMUELSON, PAUL ANTHONY; SLUTSKY, EUGEN

Bibliography

Baumol, W. J. and J. Benhabib. 1989. "Chaos: Significance, Mechanism and Economic Applications." *Journal of Economic Perspectives,* Winter, 77–105.

Benhabib, J., ed. 1992. *Cycles and Chaos in Economic Equilibrium.* Princeton: Princeton Univ. Press.

Boldrin, M. and M. Woodford. 1990. "Equilibrium Models Displaying Endogenous Fluctuations and Chaos: A Survey." *Journal of Monetary Economics* 25:189–222.

Chaos, Continuous-Time Models of

In recent years, the economics profession has shown a growing interest in those new concepts and methods of analyzing the stochastic behavior of deterministic dynamical systems, which are often referred to as chaos theory. Such behavior seems to be associated with the presence of *attractors* that are *chaotic*, in the sense that they are characterized by the so-called *sensitive dependence on initial conditions* (SDIC). Roughly speaking, by attractor we mean a state towards which a dynamic system tends as time goes by, e.g., a stable equilibrium point, a stable limit cycle, or a more complicated attracting set. The presence of SDIC implies that, no matter how close to one another two initial states of the system may be, the trajectories originating from them diverge exponentially within a finite length of time.

The presence of SDIC has deep consequences, which are relevant to applications in the physical as well as the social sciences. It suffices here to say that, given *any* finite error in observation, SDIC implies that the observed position of a system will be causally disconnected from its initial conditions in finite time. Thus, inevitable errors in measurement imply that the long-run evolution of the system is inherently unpredictable.

However, if a chaotic attractor is bounded, the separation of trajectories cannot continue forever, so that some mechanism in the system must "bend" them back. It is precisely this double action of "stretching" trajectories locally, and "folding" them globally, which determines the complex behavior of a system, as well as the special geometric property of strange attractors which has been labeled *fractal*. The latter term refers to a structure more complex than those of familiar geometrical objects, such as points, circles, squares, and spheres, and is characterized by a non-integer dimension.

SDIC and fractal dimension are interrelated, and they can be subjected to rigorous estimates. The most important tool to perform those estimates is based on the so-called *Lyapunov Characteristic Exponents* (LCEs). Roughly speaking, for a continuous-time dynamical system, one may say that the LCE of a trajectory measures the (exponential) rate at which the trajectory diverges from one nearby, under the action of the flow generated by the system, this rate being calculated in the limit for $t \to +\infty$. In general, there will be as many different LCEs as there are degrees of freedom in the system.

If at least one of the LCEs is positive, then SDIC is present and the flow is chaotic. Moreover, the fractal dimension of a chaotic attractor can be estimated by methods based on the knowledge of the LCE spectrum.

Our discussion so far explains why chaos theory has been of such interest to the economics profession. The evolution of the main indicators of real economies, such as output, employment, and the price level, has over the last two centuries been characterized by persistent and irregular fluctuations with or without a trend. Indeed, the branch of economics broadly defined as business-cycle theory was developed to explain precisely those irregularities. In this field of research, mathematical economists have long been divided into two schools. Some maintain that economic laws would lead the economy to an equilibrium position, if their operation were not continuously disturbed by more or less random shocks that rekindle the oscillations, which, if unperturbed, would be damped and, therefore, only transitory. Consequently, deviations from equilibrium are best studied by means of probabilistic instruments while anti-cyclical policies should aim at eliminating the sources of shocks when possible, or at cushioning the economy from their impact.

Other economists, however, believe that cycles are endogenous to economic systems, and have endeavored to develop theories that give simple, but rigorous, representations of those mechanisms that, in their view, keep economic variables oscillating. Their analyses imply that anti-cyclical policies should mainly seek to counteract the intrinsic instability of the economic system, by reforming its structure or counteracting the adverse consequences of its spontaneous mode of operation.

Little wonder that the recent developments in the field of dynamical system theories were greeted with enthusiasm by the advocates of endogenous theories of business cycles, who realized that the new ideas and results offer great potentialities for their approach.

It must be observed, however, that the applications of chaos theory to economics so far consist almost exclusively of variations of the celebrated one-dimensional difference equation so brilliantly illustrated by the biologist R. May (1976) and whose mathematical properties have been widely investigated. In economics, continuous-time models of chaos are indeed rare.

Discussions about the use of continuous or discrete time models of chaos have renewed the old controversy on the superiority, in general, of a continuous versus a discrete representation of reality. This often leads to arguments about the "true" nature of time, or the continuity (or lack of it) of reality, whatever the latter concept may mean.

Undoubtedly, these are very profound and unsettled philosophical questions. But for economics, the argument is, in most cases of practical interest, unnecessary. The essential questions are what mechanisms account for dynamic complexity, are these mechanisms present in certain specific economic circumstances, and how can they be more effectively represented. The answers to these questions, especially the last one, cannot be given *a priori*, once and for all. As examples from other disciplines show, the same mechanism may often be investigated by both a continuous and a discrete dynamical system, and a number of illuminating relations can often be established between the two representations.

For example, the basic dynamical properties of the Lorenz and the Rössler attractors, two of the classic examples of "continuous chaos," can be (and have been) investigated by means of auxiliary one-dimensional maps. The latter can be defined by a method which, together with so many others in this field, is due to Poincaré, and the discrete-time system associated with the original, continuous-time one is usually referred to as a *Poincaré map*.

The method consists in constructing a surface *transverse* to the attractor (i.e., such that no trajectory belonging to the attractor is tangent or inflected to the surface) and then studying the sequence of points at which the flow generated by the original set of differential equations intersects the surface. This procedure offers several advantages, of which the most important are perhaps the following: (1) it reduces the dimensionality of the problem; (2) in low-dimensional problems, it provides powerful insights, and very suggestive displays, of the global dynamics of the system; (3) it allows one to redefine more simply and clearly certain problems that would be cumbersome to state

for the original differential equations, e.g., the stability of periodic orbits.

To understand the advantage of the method in applications, consider that the original set of differential equations define a flow, supposedly describing the action of a physical (economic) mechanism that takes the system from one state to the next. In low-dimensional chaotic systems, this action is characterized by a certain "stretching" and "folding" of trajectories, which produces the complex behavior of the system. The map resulting from the Poincaré method preserves much of the behavior of the full flow on which it is based. In particular, certain crucial overall features of the system (e.g., its periodicity, or its chaoticity) may be detected.

On the other hand, when a system is represented *directly* by means of a map, a certain amount of information on its dynamics is lost, e.g., we are not told what happens between two

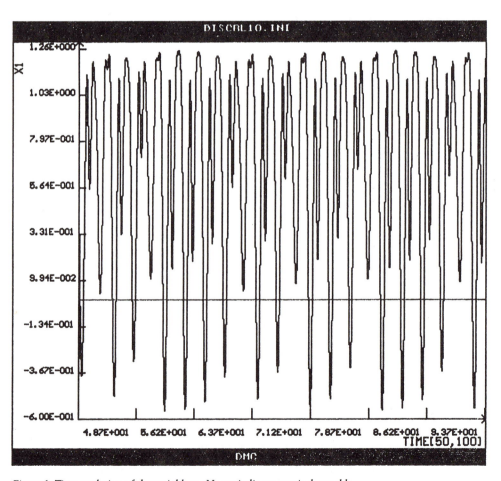

Figure 1. Time-evolution of the variable x_1. No periodic pattern is detectable.

intersections of the Poincaré plane. The loss of information may or may not be important, depending on the specific problem we are analyzing. At any rate, the crucial point is not whether the system is "really" discrete or continuous, but whether its idealized representation (and its dynamic implications) lead to conclusions that accurately portray the workings of the real system.

The best way of clarifying this point is to consider an economic application of the May equation. The general form of the latter is:

$$x_{t+T} = f(x_t), \qquad (1)$$

where x is a real number, t is time, and the function $f(.)$ belongs to a class broadly defined as "generally quadratic" or, more colloquially, "one-hump," and describes a mechanism by which a variable affects another positively up to some point, and negatively afterwards.

Equation (1) may be thought of as a highly aggregate mechanism consisting of two parts: a nonlinear functional relationship and a lag, the latter being a delay of fixed length T.

The nonlinearity in question is common in economics and several instances of it have been discussed in the literature (Benhabib and Day 1982, Grandmont 1985, Stutzer 1980). Let us consider the following specification of f:

$$f(x) = rx(1 - x)$$

where r is a constant parameter.

The weak point of the model described by equation (1), when applied to economics, is the lag structure that it implicitly assumes. Even though economic transitions do not take place continuously and are therefore discrete, in general they are not perfectly synchronized, but overlap in time in some stochastic manner. Only in very rare circumstances (e.g., for an agricul-

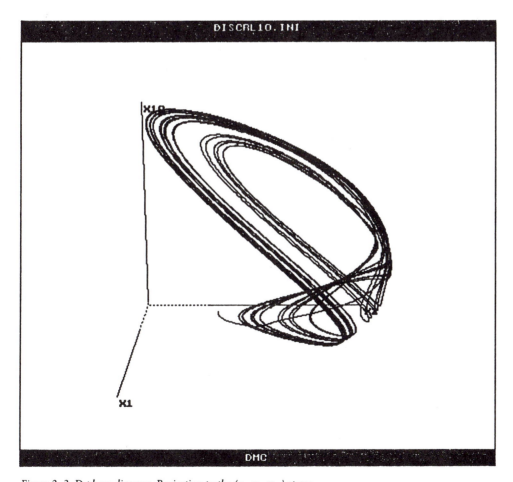

Figure 2. 3–D phase diagram. Projection to the (x_1, x_2, x_{10}) space.

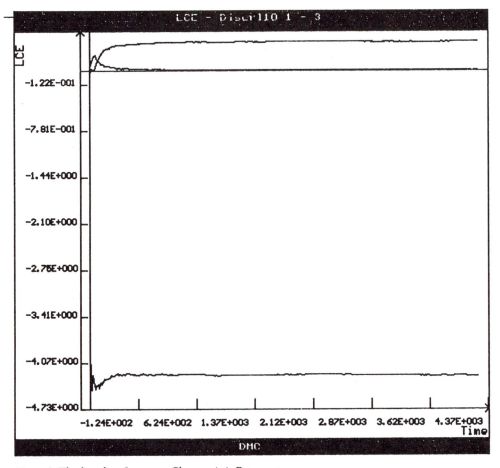

Figure 3. The first three Lyapunov Characteristic Exponents.

tural, single-crop economy) could one define a "natural period" for economic states. Whenever this is not possible, there is a danger that the implicit assumption underlying the fixed-delay hypothesis may yield misleading conclusions.

To overcome this danger, and to show that chaotic dynamics may indeed exist in a more realistic setting, a continuous-time generalization of the May model may be formulated as follows (Medio 1991, Invernizzi and Medio 1992).

Consider the following system of differential equations:

$$\left(\frac{DT}{n}+1\right)x_j = x_{j-1}, \qquad j = 2, \dots, n,$$

$$\left(\frac{DT}{n}+1\right)x_1 = f(x_n), \qquad (2)$$

where $D \equiv d/dt$, t being time. By iterative substitution, (2) can be easily transformed into:

$$x_n = \left(\frac{DT}{n}+1\right)^{-n} f(x_n). \qquad (3)$$

Equation (3) is a continuous-time generalization of equation (1). Instead of a fixed delay of length T, in equation (3) we have a multiple exponential lag of order n and time-constant T. In fact, it can be shown that, in the limit for $n \to +\infty$, the two mechanisms coincide. It can also be shown that a multiple exponential lag is equivalent to assuming that the number of agents is indefinitely large and that each of them reacts to inputs with a *discrete* lag of length τ_i, $i = 1, 2, \dots$ so that the (positive) quantities τ_i are randomly distributed and the overall lag T is a random, gamma-distributed variable with shape parameter n and expectation τ. Finally, the variance of this distribution is inversely related to the parameter n.

These are interesting results and they show that exponential lags allow one to describe eco-

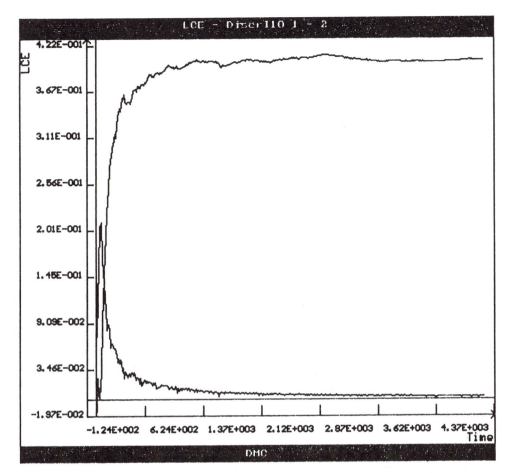

Figure 4. Enlargement of the dominant LCE.

nomically relevant situations in a more realistic and flexible manner than the fixed-delay hypothesis does. For example, by changing the parameter n, i.e., the order of the lag, one can study the behavior of economies with lag structures of varying degrees of homogeneity.

It must also be shown that some values of the "homogeneity parameter" n and the "steepness parameter" r will reproduce the most interesting result derived from the study of equation (1) (the occurrence of chaotic dynamics) in the continuous version of the model.

At present, complete global information on the structure of trajectories of continuous dynamical systems of dimension greater than two can only be obtained by integrating numerically the differential equations of the systems, studying their geometry and computing the values of certain crucial quantities. Although theoretical knowledge cannot completely characterize the dynamics of the system, it is nevertheless indis-pensable to guide and interpret numerical computations.

The numerical investigation of system (3) indicates that, if the system is rather dishomogeneous (i.e., n is small and the variance of the lag distribution is large), however steep the hump, the system converges either to a fixed point, or to a limit cycle. However, when n becomes sufficiently large (i.e., the lags with which different agents respond to inputs cluster closely around their expected value), for a certain interval of the "steepness parameter" r, chaos may occur. For example, for $n = 10$ and $r \approx 5$, the evolution of the variables of the system shows no apparent regularities (Figure 1). Moreover, the 3-D phase diagram (Figure 2) indicates that the system converges to an (almost) two-dimensional attractor, whose geometrical properties closely resemble those of the chaotic Rössler attractor.

Further and more decisive information can be obtained by estimating the Lyapunov char-

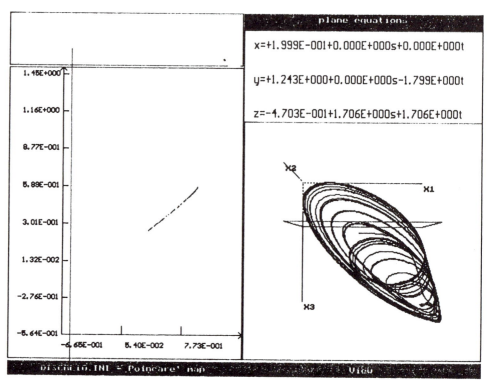

Figure 5. The first return map.

acteristic exponents of trajectories on the attractor, and thereby establishing its SDIC.

The essential results are shown by Figures 3 and 4. The latter diagram shows the first three LCEs (the other seven are all strongly negative). The diagram of Figure 3 shows an enlargement of the picture of the dominant LCE. One will notice that the convergence is strong and the exponent (≈ 0.35) is distinctly positive. This indicates that the attractor possesses SDIC, i.e., is chaotic.

LCEs can also be used to estimate the fractal dimension of the attractor. By making use of the Kaplan and Yorke procedure, we can calculate the dimension to be approximately 2.08, which is in full accord with the visual inspection of the attractor.

Recalling our discussion of the Poincaré map, one may wonder whether this essential feature of the (continuous multidimensional) system represented by equation (3) could be captured by means of a one-dimensional map. The answer is yes. It is possible, by conveniently positioning a plane across the attractor and computing the resulting Poincaré map, to obtain an (approximately) one-dimensional representation like the one shown in Figure 5, cor-

responding to the same values of the parameters as above. It can be shown that the (discrete) dynamics of the map preserve the essential properties of the continuous flow. In particular, interpolating by cubic splines the set of intersection points generated by the map, and calculating the corresponding (unique) LCE, one obtains a value of approximately 0.68, which indicates that the map possesses SDIC and therefore is chaotic.

Alfredo Medio

See also BUSINESS CYCLES; CHAOS AND BIFURCATIONS; DIFFERENTIAL AND DIFFERENCE EQUATIONS

Bibliography

Benhabib, J. and R. H. Day. 1981. "Rational Choice and Erratic Behavior." *Review of Economic Studies* 48:459–71.
———. 1982. "A Characterization of Erratic Dynamics in the Overlapping Generations Model." *Journal of Economic Dynamics and Control* 4:37–55.
Day, R. H. 1982. "Irregular Growth Cycles." *American Economic Review* 72:406–14.

Deneckere, R. and S. Pelikan. 1986. "Competitive Chaos." *Journal of Economic Theory* 40:13–25.

Grandmont, J. M. 1985. "On Endogenous Competitive Business Cycles." *Econometrica* 53:995–1045.

Invernizzi, S. and A. Medio. 1992. "On Lags and Chaos in Dynamic Models." *Journal of Mathematical Economics* 20:521–50.

May, R. M. 1976. "Simple Mathematical Models with Very Complicated Dynamics." *Nature* 261:459–67.

Medio, A. 1991. "Discrete and Continuous Models of Chaotic Dynamics in Economics." *Structural Change and Economic Dynamics* 2:99–118.

Strutzer, M. J. 1980. "Chaotic Dynamics and Bifurcation in a Macro-Model." *Journal of Economic Dynamics and Control* 2:353–76.

Clearinghouses

A *clearinghouse* is a private association of banks which is "a device to simplify and facilitate the daily exchanges of items and settlements of balances among banks, and a medium for united action upon questions affecting their mutual welfare" (Cannon 1908). Today, clearinghouses continue to serve the rather mundane function of overseeing the netting-out, or clearing, of interbank liabilities. But, historically, this activity was coupled with regulating risk-taking by individual banks for the mutual welfare of the members. In this latter role the clearinghouse assumed a unique importance. In the United States, clearinghouses provided deposit insurance, and issued currency during banking panics when they acted as lenders of last resort.

Private associations of banks with enormous power over members are found repeatedly in banking history. The first formal clearinghouse was established in London in the mid-eighteenth century. The Scottish clearing system of the eighteenth century became a model for later systems. Clearinghouses were subsequently established in the United States, Canada, Japan, and European countries. Other associations of banks have behaved like clearinghouses. The Suffolk System of early nineteenth-century New England is an example of one of these less formal systems. In all these cases, organizations of banks were involved in clearing liabilities and in regulating risk-taking by members.

In 1853 the first private bank clearinghouse in the U.S., the New York Clearinghouse Association, was founded. By the end of the nineteenth century, many other clearinghouses had been formed in the U.S. Between 1863 and 1914, the National Banking Era, seven banking panics occurred in the U.S. During a panic, depositors demand redemption of their bank debt, because they fear that the banks will fail. The problem is that depositors cannot tell whether individual banks are solvent. Asymmetric information between banks and their depositors prevents banks from credibly announcing to depositors the state of their balance sheets. Nor can banks sell their loans, because there are no markets for loans.

Clearinghouses gradually evolved a response to panics during these episodes. During a panic, clearinghouses created a market for bank assets in a special way. The clearinghouse would declare a suspension of convertibility of demand deposits into currency. Then the banks in the association would, as a group, buy individual bank assets by exchanging the assets for newly created liabilities of the clearinghouse, called clearinghouse loan certificates. Depositors could then exchange deposits for these certificates and use them as hand-to-hand currency.

From a bank depositor's point of view, a loan certificate, being a claim on the group of banks jointly, rather than on an individual bank, was a form of deposit insurance. A depositor would suffer a loss only if the banks were jointly insolvent. In the Panic of 1893 clearinghouses issued $100 million of loan certificates, about 2.5 percent of the money stock. In the Panic of 1907 they issued about $500 million, equal to 4.5 percent of the money stock.

For loan certificates to be effective, member-bank risk-taking had to be jointly monitored by the member banks. Otherwise, individual banks would free ride on the co-insurance arrangement. In the U.S., self-regulation meant regular audits and accounting reports, reserve requirements, and portfolio restrictions. Regulation was enforced by the credible threat of denying members access to the clearing facilities of the clearinghouse. In other countries, many of the same regulatory activities took place, even though not all other countries experienced panics. Asymmetric information apparently creates an incentive for banks to self-regulate, even without panics.

Gary Gorton

See also BANKING PANICS; BANKING AND FINANCIAL REGULATION; CENTRAL BANKING; CRISIS OF 1857; CRISIS OF 1873; CRISIS OF 1907; LENDER OF LAST RESORT

Bibliography

Cannon, J. 1908. *Clearing Houses.* New York: D. Appleton and Company.

Gibbons, J. S. 1859. *The Banks of New York, Their Dealers, The Clearinghouse, and the Panic of 1857.* New York: D. Appleton.

Gorton, G. and D. Mullineaux. 1987. "The Joint Production of Confidence: Endogenous Regulation and Nineteenth Century Commercial Bank Clearinghouses." *Journal of Money, Credit and Banking* 19:457–68.

Cobweb Cycle

The prices of several goods, particularly in the agricultural sector, display strong cyclic patterns with periods between several months and a few years. The first empirical inquiry into this cyclic behavior was by A. Hanau. Original theoretical treatments of the subject were offered by W. W. Leontief and by M. Ezekiel who attributed the onset of oscillations in the equilibrium prices of these goods to time lags in their production.

Let x_t^d denote the demand for a specific good in period t and assume that it reacts immediately to the price p_t in that period, i.e., $x_t^d = f(p_t)$. However, production takes time. When the length of the period t is identical with the gestation time, a good whose production starts in period t will be available only in period $t + 1$. The decision of how much to produce in t and supply in $t + 1$ is assumed to depend on the equilibrium price in t, implying that producers' expectations about next period's price are static. Thus, the supply function is $x_{t+1}^s = g(p_t)$ or $x_t^s = g(p_{t-1})$. In period t, the supply is obviously price-inelastic with respect to p_t.

For simplicity, let $x_t^d = f(p_t) = a - bp_t$, a linear function. The supply of goods, x_t^s, available at the beginning of period t, depends on the realized equilibrium price p_{t-1} in the previous period, e.g., $x_t^s = g(p_{t-1}) = c + ep_{t-1}$. With $x_t^d = x_t^s$ as the equilibrium condition it follows that

$$a - bp_t = c + ep_{t-1}$$

or

$$p_t = h(p_{t-1}) = \frac{a-c}{b} - \frac{e}{b} p_{t-1}.$$

The solution of this nonhomogeneous, first-order, difference equation is

$$p_t = p^* + \left(p_0 - p^*\right)\left(-\frac{e}{b}\right)^t$$

with p^* as the stationary price at which $p_t = p^*$ for all t. The sequence of equilibrium prices p_t oscillates because $-e/b < 0$. It converges to (diverges from) p^* if $|-e/b| < 1$ (> 1).

Figure 1.a demonstrates how the model works in the more general case of nonlinear but monotonically increasing or decreasing supply and demand functions. For a given initial price p_0, the supply of goods in $t = 1$ is x_1^s. The equilibrium price in $t = 1$ is determined by the intersection of inelastic supply x_1^s with the demand curve. The subsequent supply quantities x_2^s, x_3^s,

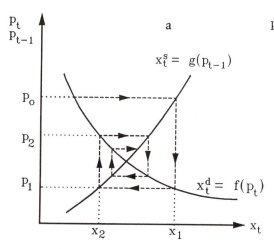

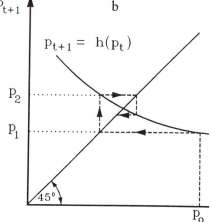

Figure 1. The cobweb cycle.

etc. and the corresponding equilibrium prices p_2, p_3, etc., can be determined in the same manner. The dashed line in Figure 1.a resembles a cobweb and explains why N. Kaldor applied the term to this model. Figure 1.b depicts the solution of the model in a p_t vs. p_{t+1} diagram. It can be seen that an oscillating behavior can be observed only for negative slopes of the function $h(p_t)$ (i.e., if $-e/b < 0$ in the linear case). The slope at the stationary value p^* determines whether the trajectory converges toward p^*. A converging, oscillating behavior can be observed in the model if the price elasticity of demand is larger than the price elasticity of supply (with respect to prices in the previous period).

The simplest cobweb model has been extended in several directions. M. Nerlove replaced the naive static-expectations hypothesis with the assumption of adaptive expectations. Producers adjust their expectations about next period's price when they experience expectational errors in the current period. This version of the cobweb model was also compatible with the common assumption that the demand for agricultural goods is more or less inelastic. In recent work on the model it has been demonstrated that the sequence of prices p_t may display complicated and even irregular patterns when particular kinds of nonlinearity are involved in the demand or supply curves.

Most versions of the cobweb model rely on the assumption of non-forward-looking expectations, i.e., the expected prices in the future depend exclusively on current and/or past prices. When forward-looking expectations are assumed, the generation of oscillations in the style of a cobweb cycle requires the assumption of strong nonlinearities or other modifications.

Hans-Walter Lorenz

See also EXPECTATIONS; RATIONAL EXPECTATIONS

Bibliography
Allen, R. G. D. 1964. *Mathematical Economics*. 3d ed. London: Macmillan.
Chiarella, C. 1990. *The Elements of a Nonlinear Theory of Economic Dynamics*. Berlin: Springer-Verlag.
Ezekiel, M. [1938] 1951. "The Cobweb Theorem." In A.E.A. *Readings in Business Cycles Theory*, 422–42. Philadelphia: Blakiston.
Sheffrin, S. M. 1983. *Rational Expectations*. Cambridge: Cambridge Univ. Press.

Cointegration

C

Cointegration expresses statistically the presence of a long-run relationship between a group of nonstationary economic time series. In so doing, the concept of cointegration ties together several apparently disparate topics, including economic theories of the long run and agent optimization, unit-root processes, spurious regressions, error correction models, and forecasting.

First, cointegration embeds the economic notion of a long-run relationship between economic variables in a statistical model of those variables. If a long-run relationship exists, the variables are "cointegrated." Often, market forces or optimizing behavior provide the economic rationale for cointegration. For instance, gold prices in New York and London may be cointegrated if, when they drift far enough apart, arbitrage opportunities arise that bring those prices back in line with each other. Likewise, consumers' expenditure and income may be cointegrated because of a budget constraint or intertemporal optimization.

Second, statistical theory on unit-root processes aids inference about the empirical existence of cointegration. Via that theory, cointegration also clarifies the "spurious regressions" or "nonsense correlations" problem associated with trending time-series data. Econometric theory has historically relied on the assumption of stationary data, even though many economic time series are trending and nonstationary. The concept of cointegration explicitly allows for nonstationary data, thus providing a sounder footing for empirical inference.

Third, cointegration implies and is implied by the existence of an error correction representation of the relevant variables. Thus, cointegration solidifies the statistical and economic basis for the empirically successful error correction models. Fourth, via error correction models, cointegration provides a systematic framework for jointly analyzing short-run (e.g., cyclical) and long-run properties. This framework resolves the debate on whether to model data in levels or differences, with Box-Jenkins-type time-series models and classical "structural" models both being special cases of error correction models. Finally, optimal forecasts of cointegrated variables are themselves cointegrated.

The concepts *integration* and *cointegration* apply to individual time series and sets of time series respectively. Loosely speaking, a variable is integrated if its level is nonstationary but its difference is stationary. Empirically, nonstationarity is often reflected in the series drifting upward or downward over time. A set of integrated time series is cointegrated if some linear combination of those (nonstationary) series is stationary. Thus, cointegration formalizes in statistical terms the property of a long-run relation between integrated economic variables.

This article illustrates the nature of integration by first-order and finite-order scalar autoregressions, and cointegration by the equivalent vector autoregressions (VARs). The first-order bivariate VAR is examined in detail to show the relationship between cointegration and error correction models. Then, several techniques for testing the order of integration and the existence of cointegration are summarized.

For the initial development of cointegration, see Granger (1981) and Engle and Granger (1987). For recent summaries and extensions, see Engle and Granger (1991), Johansen (1991), P. C. B. Phillips (1991), Ericsson (1992), Banerjee, Dolado, Galbraith, and Hendry (1993), and Hendry (1995). For the initial development of error correction models, see A. W. Phillips (1954). Important subsequent empirical and analytical contributions include Sargan ([1964] 1984), Davidson, Hendry, Srba, and Yeo (1978), Salmon (1982), and Hendry, Pagan, and Sargan (1984). Also, several journals have published special issues on integration, cointegration, and error correction, including the *Oxford Bulletin of Economics and Statistics* (1986, 1992), the *Journal of Economic Dynamics and Control* (1988), *Advances in Econometrics: A Research Annual* (1990), and the *Journal of Policy Modeling* (1992).

Integration

Consider a scalar variable x_t following a first-order autoregression:

$$x_t = \pi_1 x_{t-1} + \varepsilon_t \quad \varepsilon_t \sim IN(0, \Omega)$$
$$t = 1, \ldots, T, \tag{1}$$

where π_1 is the first-order autoregressive coefficient, ε_t is the disturbance (which for simplicity is assumed to be independent and normally distributed with zero mean and variance Ω), t is the time subscript, there are T observations, and the initial condition is (e.g.) $x_0 = 0$. By sub-

tracting x_{t-1} from both sides of equation (1), that equation may be rewritten as:

$$\Delta x_t = \pi x_{t-1} + \varepsilon_t, \tag{2}$$

where $\pi = \pi_1 - 1$ and Δ is the difference operator (so $\Delta x_t = x_t - x_{t-1}$). If $\pi_1 = 1$ (or equivalently $\pi = 0$), then x_t has a unit root and is said to be integrated of order one, denoted $I(1)$. Being $I(1)$ means that x_t must be differenced once to achieve stationarity. For the first-order process in equation (1), x_t is a random walk if it has a unit root ($\pi_1 = 1$). If $|\pi_1| < 1$, then x_t is stationary (ignoring the asymptotically negligible effects of the initial condition x_0).

More generally, x_t could be a finite-order autoregressive process, in which case equation (1) includes additional lags of x_t:

$$x_t = \sum_{i=1}^{\ell} \pi_i x_{t-i} + \varepsilon_t, \tag{3}$$

where π_i is the autoregressive coefficient on x_{t-i}, ℓ is the maximum lag, and the initial condition is (e.g.) $\{x_0, x_{-1}, \ldots, x_{1-\ell}\} = 0$. By adding and subtracting lags of x_t in equation (3), the generalization of equation (2) includes lags of Δx_t:

$$\Delta x_t = \pi x_{t-1} + \sum_{i=1}^{\ell-1} \Gamma_i \Delta x_{t-i} + \varepsilon_t, \tag{4}$$

where the $\{\Gamma_i\}$ are

$$\Gamma_i = -\left(\pi_{i+1} + \cdots + \pi_\ell\right) \quad i = 1, \ldots, \ell-1 \tag{5}$$

and π is

$$\pi = \left(\sum_{i=1}^{\ell} \pi_i\right) - 1. \tag{6}$$

The variable x_t is at least $I(1)$ if $\pi = 0$ in equation (4), and it may be of a higher order of integration, depending upon the coefficients $\{\Gamma_i\}$. Below, x_t is always assumed to be $I(0)$ or $I(1)$.

Empirically, many macroeconomic time series appear $I(1)$ (Granger 1969, Nelson and Plosser 1982). Market-efficiency theories in economics and finance also suggest that asset and commodity prices generally follow a random walk, which is the simplest $I(1)$ process. Thus, models with integrated variables are highly appealing in economics.

Cointegration

Cointegration concerns relationships between integrated variables, so it is convenient to generalize equations (1)–(4) to represent a vector of variables. Now, x_t and ε_t are interpreted as $p \times 1$ vectors (say); the $\{\pi_i\}$, $\{\Gamma_i\}$, and Ω and π are $p \times p$ matrices; and the "1" in equation (6) is the identity matrix I_p. The matrix polynomial

$$\left(\textstyle\sum_{i=1}^{\ell} \pi_i z^i\right) - I_p$$

will be useful, and is denoted $\pi(z)$ where z is the argument of the polynomial. [Note that $\pi = \pi(1)$.]

The rank of π (denoted r) determines the presence and nature of cointegration, as follows:

(i) $r = 0$. The matrix π is a zero matrix for $I(1)$ x, as in the scalar case with a unit root. Δx_t in equation (4) depends on ε_t and lags of Δx_t alone, all of which are $I(0)$; so x_t is $I(1)$. $|\pi(z^{-1})| = 0$ has p unit roots.

(ii) $r = p$. For π to have full rank, none of the roots of $|\pi(z^{-1})| = 0$ can be unity. Provided $|\pi(z^{-1})| = 0$ has all its ℓp roots strictly inside the unit circle, x_t is stationary. This parallels $|\pi| < 1$ in the univariate model.

(iii) $0 < r < p$. Because π is a matrix rather than a scalar, π may be of less than full rank, but of rank greater than zero. Under this condition, π can be expressed as the outer product of two $p \times r$ matrices α and β, both of full column rank:

$$\pi = \alpha\beta'. \qquad (7)$$

There are $p - r$ unit roots in $|\pi(z^{-1})| = 0$. Thus, each of the variables in x_t could be $I(1)$, but with some linear combinations of those variables (i.e., $\beta'x_t$) being $I(0)$. The variables in x_t are then said to be cointegrated. Univariate $I(1)$ models have $p = 1$ and so have no comparable condition.

In equation (7), β' is the matrix of cointegrating vectors, and α is the matrix of "weighting elements." Substituting equation (7) into equation (4) gives:

$$\Delta x_t = \alpha\beta'x_{t-1} + \sum_{i=1}^{\ell-1} \Gamma_i \Delta x_{t-i} + \varepsilon_t. \qquad (8)$$

Each $1 \times p$ row β_i' in β' is an individual cointegrating vector, as is required for "balance" to make each cointegrating relation $\beta_i'x_{t-1}$ an $I(0)$ process in equation (8). Each $1 \times r$ row α_j of α is the set of weights for the r cointegrating relations appearing in the jth equation. Thus, the rank r is also the number of cointegrating vec-

tors in the system. While α and β themselves are not unique, β uniquely defines the cointegration space, and suitable normalizations for α and β are available.

In essence, $\alpha\beta'x_{t-1}$ in equation (8) contains all the long-run (levels) information on the process for x_t: the only other observables in equation (8) are current and lagged Δx_t. The vector $\beta'x_{t-1}$ measures the extent to which actual data deviate from the long-run relationship(s) among the variables in x_{t-1}.

Granger (1986) and Engle and Yoo (1987) have shown that cointegration has important implications for economic forecasting. For cointegrated economic time series with cointegrating vector β, their optimal forecasts also are cointegrated with cointegrating vector β. Thus, modeling cointegration may improve the long-term forecasting of economic time series.

Error Correction Models
Cointegration can be helpful in model specification. Engle and Granger (1987) establish an isomorphism between cointegration and error correction models (ECMs): ECMs entail and are entailed by cointegration. ECMs explicitly incorporate the notion of a steady state into a dynamic model by embedding a steady-state solution for the variables, while allowing them to deviate from the steady state in the short run.

To illustrate these and related issues, consider cases (i)–(iii) for equation (3) as a first-order ($\ell = 1$) bivariate ($p = 2$) VAR, expressed as equation (4):

$$\Delta y_t = \pi_{(11)} y_{t-1} + \pi_{(12)} z_{t-1} + \varepsilon_{1t}$$
$$\varepsilon_{1t} \sim IN(0, \omega_{11}) \qquad (9a)$$

$$\Delta z_t = \pi_{(21)} y_{t-1} + \pi_{(22)} z_{t-1} + \varepsilon_{2t}$$
$$\varepsilon_{2t} \sim IN(0, \omega_{22}), \qquad (9b)$$

where $x_t = (y_t, z_t)'$, $\pi = \{\pi_{(ij)}\}$, and $\Omega = \{\omega_{ij}\}$. If $r = 0$ [case (i): no cointegrating vectors], all the $\pi_{(ij)}$ are zero, and y_t, z_t, and all linear combinations of y_t and z_t are random walks. If $r = p$ [$= 2$; case (ii): two cointegrating vectors], then π is nonsingular, implying that (y, z) has a unique solution in nonstochastic steady state (and so is stationary). If $r = 1$ [case (iii): one cointegrating vector], then α and β' are 2×1 and 1×2 vectors, denoted $(\alpha_1, \alpha_2)'$ and (β_1, β_2). Without loss of generality, β may be normalized with $\beta_1 = 1$. For convenience, denote the normalized β' vector as $(1, -\delta)$. Thus, equation (9) may be rewritten as:

$$\Delta y_t = \alpha_1\left(y_{t-1} - \delta z_{t-1}\right) + \varepsilon_{1t} \qquad (10a)$$

$$\Delta z_t = \alpha_2\left(y_{t-1} - \delta z_{t-1}\right) + \varepsilon_{2t}, \qquad (10b)$$

where $\alpha_1 = \pi_{(11)}$, $\alpha_2 = \pi_{(21)}$, and $\delta = -\pi_{(12)}/\pi_{(11)} = -\pi_{(22)}/\pi_{(21)}$. If lags of Δx_t appear in equation (9) (i.e., $\ell > 1$), then lagged values of Δy_t and Δz_t will be present in equations (10a) and (10b).

The cointegrating relation $\beta' x_{t-1}$ is $(y_{t-1} - \delta z_{t-1})$. In a nonstochastic steady state, the equilibrium relation between y and z is:

$$y - \delta z = constant,$$

and would typically be motivated by economic theory. Conversely, economic hypotheses about δ are testable in this framework. For example, when y and z are logarithms of the underlying economic data Y and Z (say), then δ is a long-run elasticity of Y with respect to Z. Theory often implies values about such elasticities: for instance, one-half for the transactions elasticity in a Baumol-Tobin money demand function, and unity for the income elasticity in most models of consumption.

Equations (10a) and (10b) express the growth rate of each variable in terms of a past disequilibrium $(y_{t-1} - \delta z_{t-1})$ and a random error. Specifically, $\alpha_1(y_{t-1} - \delta z_{t-1})$ reflects the impact on Δy_t of having y_{t-1} out of line with δz_{t-1}. Such discrepancies could arise from errors in economic agents' past decisions, with the presence of $\alpha_1(y_{t-1} - \delta z_{t-1})$ reflecting their attempts to correct such errors in the next period: hence the term *error correction* model. Equally, $(y_{t-1} - \delta z_{t-1})$ measures the extent of disequilibrium in the last period. For equation (10) to be an error correction representation and for y and z to be cointegrated, α_1 and/or α_2 must be nonzero. Thus, ECMs imply and are implied by cointegration. [Strictly speaking, $(y_{t-1} - \delta z_{t-1})$ is an *equilibrium* correction mechanism rather than an error correction mechanism. It would adjust inappropriately if the equilibrium altered—e.g., if δ changed to δ^*—and hence need not error-correct in such a setting; see Hendry (1995) for details.]

Because equation (10a) explicitly omits Δz_t, equation (10a) is a *marginal* ECM. In empirical practice, the primary focus has been on *conditional* ECMs, in part because many empirical conditional ECMs have been constant over extended samples, and they may be interpretable

as agents' contingent plans. Conditional ECMs are obtained as follows.

Cointegration and Conditional Error Correction Models

Together, equations (10a) and (10b) correspond to the joint distribution of x_t conditional on its past. Without loss of generality, equations (10a)–(10b) may be rewritten as the conditional distribution of y_t given (current) z_t and lags of both variables, and the marginal distribution of z_t (also given lags of both variables):

$$\Delta y_t = \gamma_1\Delta z_t + \gamma_2\left(y_{t-1} - \delta z_{t-1}\right) + v_{1t}$$
$$v_{1t} \sim IN\left(0, \sigma^2\right) \qquad (11a)$$

$$\Delta z_t = \alpha_2\left(y_{t-1} - \delta z_{t-1}\right) + \varepsilon_{2t}, \qquad (11b)$$

where

$$\gamma_1 = \omega_{12}/\omega_{22}, \gamma_2 = \alpha_1 - (\omega_{12}/\omega_{22})\alpha_2,$$
$$v_{1t} = \varepsilon_{1t} - \gamma_1\varepsilon_{2t},$$

and so $\sigma^2 = \omega_{11} - \omega_{12}^2 / \omega_{22}$.

The coefficient γ_1 measures the immediate, short-run effect of a change in z on y, whereas δ measures the long-run effect. Equation (11a) is a conditional ECM because Δy_t is conditional on Δz_t as well as on the lags y_{t-1} and z_{t-1}. Equation (11a) is also a reparameterization of the first-order autoregressive distributed lag of y on z; and it generalizes the conventional partial-adjustment model, allowing more flexible adjustment of y to z over time.

Conditional ECMs have been highly successful empirically in many applications, including wages and prices, consumers' expenditure, money demand, and exchange rates: see *inter alia* Sargan ([1964] 1984), Davidson, Hendry, Srba, and Yeo (1978), and the 1992 special issues of the *Journal of Policy Modeling*. Also, if $\alpha_2 = 0$, the variable z_t is weakly exogenous for the parameter δ, and so the conditional model (11a) can be estimated efficiently by itself. Specifically, there are no cross-equation restrictions involving the cointegrating vector. See Engle, Hendry, and Richard (1983) on exogeneity, and Ericsson (1992) on the relationships between cointegration and exogeneity.

Testing for Integration and Cointegration

Cointegration makes the economic concept of equilibrium operational by incorporating the long-run relation directly into the model, so that the researcher can use the data to test whether the long-run relation holds. Economic theory is generally silent about the order of integration of variables, so the practitioner must analyze the data for both integration and cointegration. While the presence of unit roots complicates inference because some associated limiting distributions are nonstandard, critical values have been tabulated for many common cases.

Dickey and Fuller (1979) have calculated critical values of the least-squares estimator of π and its t-ratio for the univariate process, equation (2). The presence of lagged Δx_t does not affect their limiting distributions under the null hypothesis of one unit root (Dickey and Fuller 1981). More "robust" unit-root tests have been developed recently.

Numerous cointegration tests have been proposed. The conceptually most straightforward is Johansen's (1991) system-based approach, in which r, β, and α in equation (8) are estimated via maximum likelihood. Test statistics for the value of r generalize the Dickey-Fuller statistic to the multivariate context, and critical values are tabulated in Osterwald-Lenum (1992) *inter alia*.

An alternative, earlier approach is due to Engle and Granger (1987), who proposed testing whether an error u_t (defined as $\beta' x_t$) is $I(0)$ by testing whether an autoregression in u_t had its roots within the unit circle. Test statistics include the Dickey-Fuller statistic, with β estimated by least squares in a static regression of the variables in x_t. While computationally simple, the Engle-Granger technique suffers from several problems, including nuisance parameters in inference about β, biases in estimating β, and lack of power relative to Johansen's procedure. See the *Oxford Bulletin of Economics and Statistics* (1986, 1992) special issues.

In Johansen's framework, hypotheses on α and β are also testable, providing statistical and economic theory information. Hypotheses on β are related to testing economic theories about long-run relationships. As a simple example, assume that y_t and z_t in equations (11a) and (11b) are logarithms of money and prices. Testing $\delta = 1$ is equivalent to testing long-run homogeneity of money with respect to prices. As a further example, consider a trivariate cointegration analysis involving the exchange rate and domestic and foreign prices. Testing whether $\beta' = (1:-1:1)$ provides information on whether purchasing-power parity holds in the long run.

Zero restriction hypotheses on α are related to testing for weak exogeneity of the conditioning variables for the parameters α and β. Weak exogeneity is satisfied if the cointegrating vector entering the conditional model does not appear in the marginal model of the conditioning variables. If $\alpha_2 = 0$ in equation (11b), then Δz_t is weakly exogenous for $(\gamma_1, \gamma_2, \delta)$. Hence, inference on those parameters from the conditional model (11a) alone is without loss of information relative to the complete system.

Cointegration analysis also can help avoid spurious regressions. Standard regression analysis of integrated variables can lead to misleading inference (Granger and Newbold 1974, P. C. B. Phillips 1986). By testing for cointegration, asymptotically correct inferences can be obtained; and "unbalanced" regressions involving variables of different orders of integration can be detected and avoided.

Summary

Cointegration and error correction help model short- and long-run properties of economic data. In doing so, they provide a framework for testing economic hypotheses and understanding the nature of economic fluctuations. In practice, the integration and cointegration properties of economic time-series data should be established at the outset of an empirical investigation, using readily available tests. Such analysis can aid in the interpretation of subsequent results, and may suggest possible modeling strategies and specifications that are consistent with the data while reducing the risk of spurious regressions.

Lisa Barrow
Julia Campos
Neil R. Ericsson
David F. Hendry
Hong-Anh Tran
William Veloce

See also DISTRIBUTED LAGS; MODEL EVALUATION AND DESIGN; TRENDS AND RANDOM WALKS; UNIT ROOT TESTS; VECTOR AUTOREGRESSIONS

Bibliography

Banerjee, A., J. J. Dolado, J. W. Galbraith, and D. F. Hendry. 1993. *Co-integration, Error Correction, and the Econometric Analysis of Non-stationary Data*. Oxford: Oxford Univ. Press.

Davidson, J. E. H., D. F. Hendry, F. Srba, and S. Yeo. 1978. "Econometric Modelling of the Aggregate Time-series Relationship between Consumers' Expenditure and Income in the United Kingdom." *Economic Journal* 88:661–92.

Dickey, D. A. and W. A. Fuller. 1979. "Distribution of the Estimators for Autoregressive Time Series with a Unit Root." *Journal of the American Statistical Association* 74:427–31.

———. 1981. "Likelihood Ratio Statistics for Autoregressive Time Series with a Unit Root." *Econometrica* 49:1057–72.

Engle, R. F. and C. W. J. Granger. 1987. "Co-integration and Error Correction: Representation, Estimation, and Testing." *Econometrica* 55:251–76.

———, eds. 1991. *Long-run Economic Relationships: Readings in Cointegration.* Oxford: Oxford Univ. Press.

Engle, R. F., D. F. Hendry, and J.-F. Richard. 1983. "Exogeneity." *Econometrica* 51:277–304.

Engle, R. F. and B. S. Yoo. 1987. "Forecasting and Testing in Co-integrated Systems." *Journal of Econometrics* 35:143–59.

Ericsson, N. R. 1992. "Cointegration, Exogeneity, and Policy Analysis: An Overview." *Journal of Policy Modeling* 14:251–80.

Granger, C. W. J. 1969. "Investigating Causal Relations by Econometric Models and Cross-spectral Methods." *Econometrica* 37:424–38.

———. 1981. "Some Properties of Time Series Data and Their Use in Econometric Model Specification." *Journal of Econometrics* 16:121–30.

———. 1986. "Developments in the Study of Cointegrated Economic Variables." *Oxford Bulletin of Economics and Statistics* 48:213–28.

Granger, C. W. J. and P. Newbold. 1974. "Spurious Regressions in Econometrics." *Journal of Econometrics* 2:111–20.

Hendry, D. F. 1995. *Dynamic Econometrics.* Oxford: Oxford Univ. Press.

Hendry, D. F., A. R. Pagan, and J. D. Sargan. 1984. "Dynamic Specification." In *Handbook of Econometrics*, vol. 2. Edited by Z. Griliches and M. D. Intriligator, 1023–1100. Amsterdam: North-Holland.

Johansen, S. 1991. "Estimation and Hypothesis Testing of Cointegration Vectors in Gaussian Vector Autoregressive Models." *Econometrica* 59:1551–80.

Nelson, C. R. and C. I. Plosser. 1982. "Trends and Random Walks in Macroeconomic Time Series: Some Evidence and Implications." *Journal of Monetary Economics* 10:139–62.

Osterwald-Lenum, M. 1992. "A Note with Quantiles of the Asymptotic Distribution of the Maximum Likelihood Cointegration Rank Test Statistics." *Oxford Bulletin of Economics and Statistics* 54:461–72.

Phillips, A. W. 1954. "Stabilisation Policy in a Closed Economy." *Economic Journal* 64:290–323.

Phillips, P. C. B. 1986. "Understanding Spurious Regressions in Econometrics." *Journal of Econometrics* 33:311–40.

———. 1991. "Optimal Inference in Cointegrated Systems." *Econometrica* 59:283–306.

Salmon, M. 1982. "Error Correction Mechanisms." *Economic Journal* 92:615–29.

Sargan, J. D. [1964] 1984. "Wages and Prices in the United Kingdom: A Study in Econometric Methodology." In *Econometrics and Quantitative Economics*, edited by D. F. Hendry and K. F. Wallis, 275–314. Oxford: Basil Blackwell.

Commons, John Rogers (1862–1945)

John R. Commons is mainly known as the founder of the pro-labor "Wisconsin School" of economists and as the originator of a complex "institutional" theory of economic life. He sought over his long career to identify actions that would provide wage workers with "a larger and more just legal share in government and industry" (Commons 1900, 65) and thereby "save Capitalism by making it good" (Commons 1934b, 143). Foremost among the "evils" to be corrected was unemployment occasioned by the business cycle (Commons 1934b, 67). Early in his career, Commons (1904, 21) perceived that the business cycle originates in a widening profit margin brought about by rising prices, but only after the severe downturn following the inflation of 1919 did Commons turn his attention to the problem of dampening the business cycle (Commons, McCracken, and Zeuch 1922).

Drawing in part on the theories of Knut Wicksell and Irving Fisher, Commons expanded his earlier "insight" into a full-fledged credit-

and expectations-based "profit margin" explanation of the business cycle. Commons maintained that business depressions were wholly an aftermath of price inflation. Hence if only the upswing in prices could be prevented, cyclical unemployment would disappear. Guided by his "theory," Commons drafted a bill in 1927 requiring the Federal Reserve to stabilize the wholesale price level.

Unfortunately, there is no straightforward statement in Commons's writings of his theory of the business cycle. Commons always adhered to a "holistic" mode of reasoning and hence never presented his "theories" as abstract logical structures; instead he grounded his explanations in concepts as close as possible to actual observations. Interpretation is further complicated by Commons's convoluted and idiosyncratic writing style, his use of unconventional terminology, his penchant for classification and reclassification, as well as his tendency to embed his own ideas in "corrections" or "extensions" of theories developed by others without stating them directly. However, based on Commons's discussion of the relevant issues in his magnum opus (1934a, 506–612), his profit-margin theory may be summarized as follows.

Capitalist businesses produce solely to earn profit. Since production takes time, business activity is inherently forward-looking; inputs are purchased only on the expectation that the expenditures will be recouped, with a surplus, in the future. Based on its forecast of the future, a business assesses the advisability of a given production decision by calculating its impact on the profit margin—the ratio of net profit to sales revenue—expected to obtain in the future. Since the profit margin for the typical capitalist firm is often no more than one or two percent, business behavior is highly responsive to cost and revenue changes that seem small compared to total costs.

Private profit-seeking banks advance businesses the money required to purchase inputs with which to produce outputs. Loan transactions, however, are entered into only with the expectation by both parties that the debtor will be able to repay the loan on time from the revenues generated by sale of the output, or, stated differently, that the business will be able to maintain a "financial margin" (from which interest and profit disbursements must be made) at least equal to the discount rate. Clearly, risk is a major factor in forecasting whether a sufficient financial margin will be maintained and hence in determining the willingness of businesses to obtain and of banks to extend credit. Since credit is a prerequisite for production, a business's ability to employ wage workers and commence production depends on a correspondence between its own risk-adjusted forecast of the price at which it will be able to sell in the future and the forecast made by the lender.

A downward adjustment of the "risk discount" widens, often substantially, the forecasted risk-adjusted profit margin and hence induces businesses to expand production. Accordingly, given the loan discount rate, firms react to a reduced risk discount by increasing their borrowing to purchase additional inputs. However, the credit expansion *parri passu* increases the money chasing the existing stock of productive inputs (including raw materials and intermediate goods), thereby raising their prices, and, ultimately, the wholesale price level.

Paradoxically, the induced expectation that input prices will continue to increase leads businesses to purchase additional inputs speculatively (in advance of even higher prices), thereby further expanding production and employment. However, some debtors, eventually finding that they have borrowed too much, resort to "distress selling" to pay their debts and maintain solvency. Some prices start to fall, thereby increasing all risk-discounts and triggering a sequence of actions opposite to that outlined above. When distress selling ends, the price level stabilizes, thereby reducing risk discounts and initiating the upward swing already discussed.

Commons's interpretation of contraction and expansion rests on a presumption that, due to very narrow profit margins, small changes in the risk premium or in expected input prices can induce large changes in expected profit margins and hence large changes in desired levels of production. For the changes to take place, however, banks must extend additional credit. Thus, to stabilize employment, Commons wanted the Federal Reserve to regulate the volume of bank lending to maintain a stable price level and hence to eliminate the "monetary" source of the business cycle. This requires that when the risk discount is falling and the expected "financial margin" rising, the bank discount rate be raised to maintain a constant profit margin, and vice versa.

Commons was thus an early advocate of activist monetary policy to promote economic stabilization and anticipated the central role of expectations would come to have in economic theory. However, his writings about the business cycle have had little influence on the work of subsequent theorists.

Yngve Ramstad

Bibliography

Biddle, J. 1991. "The Ideas of the Past as Tools for the Present: The Instrumental Presentism of John R. Commons." In *The Estate of Social Knowledge,* edited by J. Browne and D. K. van Keuran, 84–105. Baltimore: Johns Hopkins Univ. Press.

Commons, J. R. 1900. "Discussion of the President's [Hadley] Address." *Publications of the American Economic Association.* 3rd ser. 1:62–80.

———. 1904. "Social and Industrial Problems." *The Chautauquan* 39:13–22.

———. 1934a. *Institutional Economics: Its Place in Political Economy.* New York: Macmillan.

———. 1934b. *Myself.* New York: Macmillan.

Commons, J. R., H. L. McCracken, and W. E. Zeuch. 1922. "Secular Trends and Business Cycles." *Review of Economic Statistics* 4:244–63.

Harter, L. G., Jr. 1962. *J. R. Commons: His Assault on Laissez-Faire.* Corvallis: Oregon State Univ. Press.

Ramstad, Y. 1986. "A Pragmatist's Quest for Holistic Knowledge: The Scientific Methodology of John R. Commons." *Journal of Economic Issues* 20:1067–1105.

Composite and Diffusion Indexes

Composite and diffusion indexes are special cases of a general form of an index model (Sargent and Sims 1977). While the rationale for forming these indexes is based on a mathematical theory, the economic interpretation of these "baskets of indicators" generally is based on an eclectic economic theory and empirical findings (de Leeuw 1991). The most notable application of the index model is the traditional National Bureau of Economic Research (NBER) formulation of the composite cyclical indexes, which are updated by the United States Department of Commerce.

Composite indexes, in their simplest form, are weighted averages of other economic indicators drawn together because of a common feature such as a tendency to lead the reference business cycle. Three key issues in the use and formulation of composite indexes are: (1) what is being measured by the composite, (2) what is gained by forming a composite index instead of using the individual components, and (3) how the composite index is used.

Unlike a statistical regression model, most composite indexes attempt to measure an unobservable economic phenomenon—such as a turning point in the business cycle. Although the phenomenon may be unobservable, it still may be measurable. For example, it has been argued that the composite index of leading indicators compiled by the Department of Commerce attempts to forecast turning points in an unobservable reference business cycle. To make the leading indicators more useful, Stock and Watson (1989) have formulated a composite leading indicator using modern time-series techniques that produces a six-month ahead forecast of economic growth.

A second issue is whether a composite index contains any information not already contained in the components. A study of the Commerce Department's composite index of leading indicators by Niemira and Fredman (1991) confirms that composite indexes are superior to the individual components alone for forecasting business-cycle turning points. The logic for a composite indicator is simple but general: since no individual indicator is always reliable, diversification reduces the risk of an incorrect signal.

Another important reason for using a composite index is that it summarizes what is happening in a way that is easy to understand and to communicate. That is one reason why many governments, such as the United Kingdom and Canada, or multi-governmental agencies, such as the Organization for Economic Cooperation and Development, compile and publish composite cyclical indicators. Regional composite leading indicators also have been developed for similar reasons.

As an aid to interpreting changes in composite indicators, Neftci (1982) has proposed a nonlinear model to determine statistically when a turning point has occurred. Successive observations are used to calculate a "probability of a turning point" based on the Neftci formula. This technique, which is also known as sequential analysis, has been generalized by Hamilton (1989) and provides a real-time monitoring scheme for predicting or identifying a turning point.

A diffusion index, on the other hand, measures the percentage of components rising (or falling) relative to the total number of components. Lovell (1975, 397) showed the relationship between a diffusion index and the underlying time series. In the special case, when every component changes by the same amount, the change in the underlying series will be strictly proportional to the diffusion index. A well-known example of this technique is the National Association of Purchasing Management's composite diffusion index of U.S. manufacturing activity.

Several business-cycle observations have been developed around the diffusion concept. For example, Arthur Burns (1969) described an "unseen" cycle in economic development as the percentage of expanding (or contracting) sectors within the aggregate economy. Burns noted that this unseen cycle led changes in business activity. The one exception to Burns's observation is with the broadening of inflationary pressures; inflation is often more narrowly based in the early stages of accelerating and decelerating inflation. For example, bouts of high/low inflation are often triggered by a single commodity such as an oil-price shock or from weather-induced food price impacts. As a result, a price diffusion index generally lags overall inflation since it reflects the unfolding and collapse of a price-wage spiral. Another business-cycle theory tied to diffusion is William Fellner's "law of diminishing offsets," which was developed further by Bert Hickman (1959).

Because diffusion indexes can be very erratic, numerous smoothing techniques have been suggested by Shohan (1963) and Alexander (1958). Anderson (1966) proposed using discriminant analysis to interpret changes in diffusion indexes. Discriminant analysis is similar to the Neftci technique, although Neftci's method allows for a dynamic component whereas discriminant analysis is static.

Michael P. Niemira

See also BURNS, ARTHUR FRANK; INDICATORS, QUALITATIVE; LEADS AND LAGS; LEADING INDICATORS: HISTORICAL RECORD; MITCHELL, WESLEY CLAIR; MOORE, GEOFFREY HOYT

Bibliography

Alexander, S. S. 1958. "Rate of Change Approaches to Forecasting—Diffusion Indexes and First Differences." *Economic Journal* 68:288–301.

Anderson, L. C. 1966. "A Method of Using Diffusion Indexes and First Differences to Indicate the Direction of National Economic Activity." *Proceedings of the Business and Economics Section, American Statistical Association* 12:424–34.

Burns, A. F. 1969. *The Business Cycle in a Changing World.* New York: NBER.

de Leeuw, F. 1991. "Toward a Theory of Leading Indicators." In *Leading Economic Indicators: New Approaches and Forecasting Methods,* edited by K. Lahiri and G. H. Moore, 15–56. Cambridge: Cambridge Univ. Press.

Hamilton, J. D. 1989. "A New Approach to the Economic Analysis of Nonstationary Time Series and the Business Cycle." *Econometrica* 57:357–84.

Hertzberg, M. P. and B. A. Beckman. 1989. "Business Cycle Indicators: Revised Composite Indexes." *Survey of Current Business* 69:23–28.

Hickman, B. 1959. "Diffusion, Acceleration, and Business Cycles." *American Economic Review* 49:535–65.

Kozlowski, P. J. 1987. "Regional Indexes of Leading Indicators: An Evaluation of Forecasting Performance." *Growth and Change* 18:62–73.

Lovell, M. C. 1975. *Macroeconomics: Measurement, Theory and Policy.* New York: Wiley.

Neftci, S. 1982. "Optimal Prediction of Cyclical Downturns." *Journal of Economic Dynamics and Control* 4:225–41.

Niemira, M. P. and G. T. Fredman. 1991. "An Evaluation of the Composite Index of Leading Economic Indicators for Signalling Turning Points in Business and Growth Cycles." *Business Economics* 26:49–55.

Nilsson, R. 1987. "OECD Leading Indicators." *OECD Economic Studies,* Autumn, 105–45.

Phillips, K. R. 1990. "The Texas Index of Leading Economic Indicators: A Revision and Further Evaluation." Federal Reserve Bank of Dallas *Economic Review,* July, 17–25.

Sargent, T. J. and C. A. Sims. 1977. "Business Cycle Modeling Without Pretending to Have Too Much A Priori Economic Theory." In *New Methods in Business Cycle Research: Proceedings from a Conference,* 45–109. Minneapolis: Federal Reserve Bank of Minneapolis.

C

Shohan, L. B. 1963. *The Conference Board's New Diffusion Indexes.* New York: Conference Board.

Stock, J. H. and M. W. Watson. 1989. "Indexes of Coincident and Leading Indicators. In *NBER Macroeconomics Annual 1989*, edited by O. J. Blanchard and S. Fischer, 351–94. Cambridge: MIT Press.

Rufolo, A. M. 1979. "An Index of Leading Indicators for the Philadelphia Region." Federal Reserve Bank of Philadelphia *Business Review*, March/April, 13–23.

Composite Trends

One of the most important aspects of empirical studies of economic fluctuations and the business cycle is to detect the long-run tendency in the data. When a time series depends on a linear time trend, the series is said to have a *deterministic trend*, whereas if a time series is (homogeneous) nonstationary, the series is said to have a *stochastic trend*. When a time series contains both deterministic and stochastic trends, it will be here defined to have *composite trends*. A simple example of a series, Y_t, with a deterministic trend can be described by

$$Y_t = \alpha + \beta T_t + \varepsilon_t, \tag{1}$$

and a time series with a simple stochastic trend can be modeled by

$$Y_t = \delta + Y_{t-1} + u_t. \tag{2}$$

In equations (1) and (2), ε_t and u_t are white-noise series which are independently and identically distributed, and T_t is a linear time-trend variable. A *homogeneous nonstationary series* becomes *stationary*, by definition, when one or more differences are taken of the given series. Though no consensus exists, many economic (and certainly most macroeconomic) variables are believed to contain stochastic trends. The importance of the distinction between the two trends is discussed by Nelson and Plosser (1982) and by Stock and Watson (1988).

In the simple examples above, ε_t and u_t were assumed to be white-noise series. Those disturbance (or error) terms can take a more complex process. In general, they may contain an *autoregressive* and *moving average process* of order p and q—ARMA(p, q)—without changing central arguments that follow.

Recently, a number of researchers have discovered that some, if not many, macroeconomic time series may in fact contain both stochastic and deterministic trends. Stock and Watson (1989) show that the money supply in the United States is best modeled with composite trends, and Said (1991) similarly shows the possibility that both trends are present. Kang (1990) shows, more extensively, that most of the fourteen key macroeconomic variables in the U.S. contain composite trends. That is, those fourteen variables—including gross national product, GNP deflator, civilian labor force—were best represented by a composite model. A composite model, which predicted the given series better than either stochastic or deterministic trend models, explicitly includes both deterministic and stochastic trends.

A simple composite model is given by

$$Y_t = \delta + \beta T_t + Y_{t-1} + v_t, \tag{3}$$

where v_t is a white-noise error series. A more general form of composite model can be expressed as a transfer function of T_t as in equation (4):

$$(1-B)^d Y_t = \alpha + (\varpi(B)/\delta(B))T_t + (\theta(B)/\phi(B))\varepsilon_t,$$

where $\varpi(B) = \varpi_0 - \varpi_1 B - \varpi_2 B^2 - ... - \varpi_m B^m$;

$\delta(B) = 1 - \delta_1 B - \delta_2 B^2 - ... - \delta_n B^n$;

$\theta(B) = \theta_0 - \theta_1 B - \theta_2 B^2 - ... - \theta_q B^q;$ $\qquad$ (4)

and $\phi(B) = 1 - \phi_1 B - \phi_2 B^2 - ... - \phi_p B^p$.

By definition, B is the lag operator or backward-shift operator and $B^i X_t = X_{t-i}$, and d is the number of differencing operations. Those four polynomials in B above are called, respectively, numerator, denominator, moving average, and autoregressive parameter polynomials. All the roots of these polynomials are assumed to lie outside the unit circle to satisfy the conditions of invertibility and stationarity.

Kang (1990) has identified and estimated composite models which produce more accurate *ex post* forecasts than a time-series ARMA model based either on the detrended series or differenced series. That is, the detrending analysis does not extract fully the information contained in the stochastic trend and the differencing analysis does not adequately model the information contained in the deterministic trend. Since the composite model includes both trends, it is not surprising that it produces better forecasts than a model in which either one of two trends is assumed to be present. It is not trivial, however, to show this seemingly obvious result: it has generally been believed (Box and Jenkins 1976, 92) and is commonly practiced that time series are typically differenced *in order to* remove the deterministic trend. Detrending has also been widely used in tests for unit roots or for cointegration under the assumption (Schwert 1989) that it removes the stochastic trend. However, both prescriptions are inadequate.

A composite model is called for when the variable in question contains (or may contain) both types of trends. Detrending such a series will distort the detrended series as Nelson and Kang (1981) have shown. The detrending introduces spurious periodicity into the series. Likewise, differencing a series that contains a deterministic trend will produce an inappropriate series as it does not fully remove the trend. The differenced series still contains a deterministic trend. To avoid such spurious periodicity or trend, researchers have to model the series by assuming that both types of trends may be present in forecasting as well as in hypothesis testing. In tests for unit roots or in the investigation of cointegration, composite-trend models should be used unless researchers can make a stronger assumption that at least one type of trend is not present in the series.

Heejoon Kang

See also ASYMMETRY; COINTEGRATION; TRENDS AND RANDOM WALKS; UNIT ROOT TESTS

Bibliography
Box, G. E. P. and G. M. Jenkins. 1976. *Time Series Analysis: Forecasting and Control.* Rev. ed. San Francisco: Holden-Day.
Kang, H. 1990. "A Composite Model for Deterministic and Stochastic Trends." *International Journal of Forecasting* 6:175–86.
Nelson, C. R. and H. Kang. 1981. "Spurious Periodicity in Inappropriate Detrended Time Series." *Econometrica* 49:741–51.
Nelson, C. R. and C. I. Plosser. 1982. "Trends and Random Walks in Macroeconomic Time Series." *Journal of Monetary Economics* 10:139–62.
Said, S. E. 1991. "Unit-Roots Test for Time-Series Data with Linear Time Trend." *Journal of Econometrics* 47:285–303.
Schwert, G. W. 1989. "Tests for Unit Roots: A Monte Carlo Investigation." *Journal of Business and Economic Statistics* 7:147–59.
Stock, J. H. and M. W. Watson. 1988. "Variable Trends in Economic Time Series." *Journal of Economic Perspectives,* Summer, 147–74.
———. 1989. "Interpreting the Evidence on Money-Income Causality." *Journal of Econometrics* 40:161–81.

Consumer Durables

Durable goods are goods that provide useful services over an extended period of time. In the United States, spending on durable goods by consumers averages only about 14 percent of total personal consumption expenditures (PCE). However, purchases of durable goods fluctuate proportionally much more than do other consumer outlays. Spending on durables, therefore, accounts for nearly half the variability of total PCE. Consumer durables play an important role in determining the course of the business cycle.

Goods differ widely in their durability. Food provides services to the eater for only a few hours before more consumption is needed, but shoes may be worn for a year or two, and an automobile may remain in service for a decade or more. In the national-income accounts of the United States, a good is classified as "durable" if it is expected to remain in service for three years or more.

In 1990, outlays for consumer-durable goods in the United States totalled $480 billion—about 9 percent of gross national product. Of total spending on durable goods in 1990, nearly half was outlays for motor vehicles—a category that includes spending on cars and light trucks as well as tires, accessories, and parts. About one-third of spending on durable goods in 1990 was outlays for furniture and household equipment, including kitchen appliances and home electronics, and the remainder was spending on such items as jewelry, books, bicycles, and boats.

Spending on durable goods must be distinguished from consumption of the services provided by those goods. In the case of a new car which is paid for in cash and driven off the dealer's lot immediately, the two concepts are easy to distinguish: expenditure occurs when the purchaser turns the cash over to the dealer.

Consumption of services continues as long as the car remains in operation. The national-income accounts tabulate expenditures on durable goods, entering the entire purchase amounts as "personal consumption expenditures" regardless of whether the purchases were financed or paid for in cash. If the purchases were financed, then the interest payments over the life of the finance contract are recorded in the national-income accounts as "personal outlays"—a slightly wider aggregate than PCE. This method of accounting keeps personal saving, as computed in the national-income accounts, invariant to consumers' decisions about whether to finance or to pay up front.

A long-standing controversy in the literature on durable goods is whether spending on durable goods should be considered a form of saving. Proponents of this view note that purchasing a durable good does not reduce a consumer's net worth by the full amount of the purchase price: the durable good itself becomes part of the consumer's portfolio of assets. Thus, durable goods—like financial instruments—represent claims on future consumption. However, there is a crucial distinction between purchasing a durable good and acquiring a financial asset. As noted by Mankiw (1987), "the 'durables as savings' model implies that transitory income should affect spending on durables"; in contrast, traditional formulations predict that durable-goods spending should be unaffected by transitory fluctuations in income. Mankiw (1987, 55) concludes that "the decision to save and the decision to buy durables are conceptually distinct."

Simple theoretical models predict that spending on durables should be more sensitive to news about income than should outlays for nondurables. Consider the following accelerator model, in which the desired stock of the durable good is proportional to income:

$$K_t = \alpha Y_t, \qquad (1)$$

where K_t denotes the stock of the durable good held at the end of period t and Y_t is labor income earned in period t. If depreciation is proportional to the stock of the good held at the end of the previous period, then the durable good will accumulate according to:

$$K_t = (1 - \delta)K_{t-1} + X_t, \qquad (2)$$

where X_t denotes gross purchases of the durable good in period t and δ is the depreciation rate. Equations (1) and (2) can be used to derive an expression for the percentage variation in spending on the durable good as a function of the percentage variation in income. (A first-order Taylor expansion underlies this derivation.) In the special case where logarithmic changes in income are uncorrelated over time,

$$\sigma^2_{\Delta \log x} = [1 + (1 - \delta)^2]\left(\frac{1}{\delta}\right)^2 \sigma^2_{\Delta \log y} \qquad (3)$$

where $\Delta \log X$ denotes the logarithmic difference (and thus, approximately, the percentage change) of X, and $\sigma^2_{\Delta \log x}$ denotes the variance of that quantity; $\Delta \log Y$ and $\sigma^2_{\Delta \log y}$ are defined similarly. Equation (3) states that the variability of spending should be an increasing function of the durability of the good (that is, a decreasing function of δ). The model predicts that spending on a good that is 90-percent depreciated after four years ($\delta = .438$) would be nearly seven times as variable as spending on a completely nondurable good ($\delta = 1$).

Figure 1 compares the behavior of outlays for durables, nondurables, and services over the period 1959–90. The figure uses quarterly data for the United States, and shows percent changes from four quarters earlier. Clearly, the model's prediction that spending on durable goods should be more variable than spending on nondurable goods is consistent with the data.

A second implication of standard theoretical models is that durable goods purchases should be more sensitive to changes in the real interest rate than should outlays for nondurable goods. Mankiw (1987) derives the following expression for the semi-elasticity of the durable goods stock with respect to the real interest rate:

$$\frac{d \log(K_t)}{dr} = \frac{d \log(C_t)}{dr} - \varepsilon \frac{(1 - \delta)}{(r + \delta)(1 + r)}, \qquad (4)$$

where C_t measures spending on the nondurable good, and ε measures the elasticity of substitution between the durable good and the nondurable good. According to equation (4), the stock of durables—and hence purchases of durables—can be quite sensitive to changes in the real interest rate even if consumption of nondurables is completely insensitive to changes in the real interest rate. For example, suppose that the semi-elasticity of nondurables expenditure with respect to the real interest rate is zero, that the real interest rate is 5 percent, and that

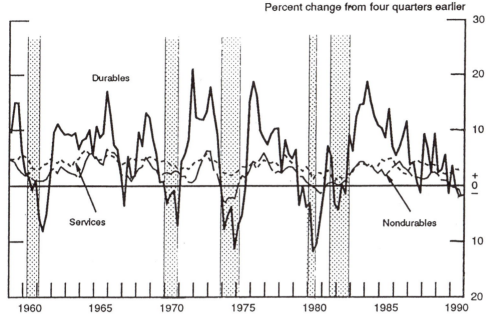

Percent change from four quarters earlier

* The shaded areas denote recessions as defined by the National Bureau of Economic Research.

Figure 1. Growth in real spending on durables, nondurables and services.

the depreciation rate is 40 percent. Also suppose that ε equals one, in line with the evidence presented by Mankiw. Then a one-percentage-point increase in the real interest rate would reduce the stock of durable goods by 1.27 percent; given that the stock of durable goods in the United States in 1990 was an estimated $1.775 trillion (measured in 1982 dollars), a 1.27 percent reduction would have amounted to $22.5 billion (again in 1982 dollars), or a bit more than 5 percent of total PCE for durable goods in 1990. Mankiw (1985) presents statistical evidence strongly supporting the hypothesis that changes in real interest rates have significantly affected purchases of durable goods in the United States.

On a third issue, however, the prediction of the model outlined above is strongly contradicted by the data. The model predicts that an increase in purchases of durable goods in one period should, on average, be partially offset by a decrease in the following period. Similarly, a decrease in one period should, on average, be followed by an increase in the following period. The intuition for this prediction is that a consumer receiving positive news about her permanent income will want to increase her holdings of durable goods. Doing so will require a one-time burst of expenditure suffi-

cient to raise the stock of durable goods to the new desired level. In the new steady state, spending will be lower than during the burst, because the stock of the durable good will no longer be increasing, but higher than in the old steady state, because replacement demand will have increased given the larger stock of the durable good. Importantly, the model predicts that the size of the reversal in spending will be related to the durability of the consumption good: the more durable the good, the larger the burst of spending in response to positive news about permanent income and the greater the reversal in the next period. At the other extreme, if the good is entirely nondurable, then spending will adjust immediately to its new steady-state level upon receipt of news about permanent income, with no overshooting or subsequent reversal. Mankiw (1982) tested this prediction of the model using postwar data for the United States, and found no evidence of such reversals in durable-goods purchases. That is, the behavior of durable-goods purchases appeared more consistent, in this respect, with the model's prediction for nondurable-goods purchases than for durable-goods purchases.

One possible reason for the simple model's failure along this dimension might be its assumption that adjusting the durable goods stock is costless, and so should be complete and instantaneous upon receipt of news about permanent income. Costs of adjustment could, in principle, damp the runup in spending after good news about income, and so reduce or eliminate the subsequent reversal. Analytically, the simplest way to introduce adjustment costs into a theoretical model is to assume that those costs are quadratic. Stone and Rowe performed an early test of such a model. Using British data on durable goods purchases during the interwar and early postwar periods, they found—in results strikingly similar to Mankiw's—that the implied depreciation rates are still implausibly high. Stone and Rowe (1960, 415) attributed their results "to both the defects of the data and the limitations of the model."

Aside from failing to solve the durability puzzle, the model studied by Stone and Rowe (and many others) also has some unappealing implications about the characteristics of adjustments. In particular, the model predicts that adjustments to news about permanent income will be stretched out over time and occur only bit by bit. In reality, adjustments do not conform to this description. Most households transact in markets for durable goods only infrequently, and they appear to be aiming for full adjustment. The challenge for theorists is to derive a model that predicts sluggish aggregate adjustments while allowing for rapid and complete adjustment by individuals.

Bertola and Caballero (1990) posit that costs of transacting in durable goods have a fixed component (or, more generally, are nonconvex). Facing such costs, a consumer generally will choose to adjust her holdings of durable goods only infrequently; however, the adjustment will be complete when it occurs. Bertola and Caballero work out the implications of nonconvex adjustment costs for aggregate spending on durable goods, and report considerable success in accounting for the apparently sluggish adjustment of the stock of durable goods, while preserving attractive properties at the individual level. Eberly (1993) applies the Bertola-Caballero analytical framework to household data on automobile purchases, and also finds strong support for nonconvex adjustment costs.

Further work will be required before a more complete assessment of the empirical success of such models can be provided.

David W. Wilcox

See also CONSUMPTION EXPENDITURES; MODIGLIANI, FRANCO

Bibliography
Bar-Ilan, A. and A. S. Blinder. 1992. "Consumer Durables: Evidence on the Optimality of Usually Doing Nothing." *Journal of Money, Credit and Banking* 24:258–72.
Bernanke, B. S. 1985. "Adjustment Costs, Durables, and Aggregate Consumption." *Journal of Monetary Economics* 15:41–68.
———. 1984. "Permanent Income, Liquidity, and Expenditure on Automobiles: Evidence from Panel Data." *Quarterly Journal of Economics* 99:587–614.
Bertola, G. and R. J. Caballero. 1990. "Kinked Adjustment Costs and Aggregate Dynamics." *NBER Macroeconomics Annual,* edited by O. J. Blanchard and S. Fischer, 237–88. Cambridge: MIT Press.
Diewert, W. E. 1974. "Intertemporal Consumer Theory and the Demand for Durables." *Econometrica* 42:497–516.
Eberly, J. C. 1993. "Adjustment of Consumers' Durables Stocks: Evidence from Automobile Purchases." *Journal of Political Economy* 102:403–36.
Hymans, S. 1970. "Consumer Durable Spending: Explanation and Prediction." *Brookings Papers on Economic Activity,* Number Two, 173–99.
Mankiw, N. G. 1982. "Hall's Consumption Hypothesis and Durable Goods." *Journal of Monetary Economics* 10:417–25.
———. 1985. "Consumer Durables and the Real Interest Rate." *Review of Economics and Statistics* 67:353–62.
———. 1987. "Consumer Spending and the After-Tax Real Interest Rate." In *The Effects of Taxation on Capital Accumulation,* edited by M. S. Feldstein, 53–67. Chicago: Univ. of Chicago Press.
Stone, R. and D. A. Rowe. 1960. "The Durability of Consumers' Durable Goods." *Econometrica* 28:407–16.
Williams, R. A. 1972. "Demand for Consumer Durables: Stock Adjustment Models and Alternative Specifications of Stock Depletion." *Review of Economic Studies* 39:281–96.

Consumption Expenditures

Household expenditures on consumption goods and services constitute about two-thirds of

GNP. Goods, which have tangible substance, are separated into nondurables and durables based on the length of economic life. Nondurables (e.g., food and clothing) are arbitrarily assumed to have economic lives of less than three years, while durables (e.g., automobiles and appliances) have economic lives of three years or longer. Services, which typically have no tangible substance, include housing, electricity, transportation, and medical care.

It is important to distinguish between consumption expenditures and consumption. Aggregate consumption spending is household spending per period on consumption goods and services, while consumption describes their actual usage. This distinction is important because consumption spending and consumption take place at roughly the same time for services and nondurable goods, but at quite different times for durable goods.

Since consumption spending is by far the dominant component of aggregate demand, economists have long been interested in modeling its behavior. Apparently the first to do so explicitly was Keynes ([1936] 1973), who contended that current consumption expenditures consist of a positive autonomous amount plus an induced component that depends largely on current disposable income. This implies that if current income is unstable then both consumption and consumption expenditures will be unstable. And because of the positive autonomous component and Keynes's assumption that the marginal propensity to consume is less than one, as disposable income rises the proportion of disposable income allocated to consumption expenditures (the average propensity to consume) declines.

Kuznets's (1946) investigation of consumption expenditures noted that Keynes's theory was consistent with cross-section data by household income bracket, but not with aggregate time-series data. The time-series data suggested constant average propensities to save and consume over time and a marginal propensity to consume greater than that implied by the cross-section data. With this discovery, Kuznets identified what became known as the time-series/cross-section conflict in consumption data. Attempts to reconcile the data along with the realization that consumption expenditures vary less than income inspired the development of modern consumption theory which marked a major advance in our understanding of business cycles.

The two most widely accepted theories are Friedman's (1957) permanent-income hypothesis (PIH) and Modigliani and Brumberg's ([1954] 1980) life-cycle hypothesis (LCH) which are together sometimes referred to as the forward-looking theory of consumption. Both theories assert that households consume a constant proportion of their expected long-run resources (permanent income in the PIH and lifetime resources in the LCH). The long-run (time-series) marginal propensity to consume is the marginal propensity to consume out of expected long-run income.

Current measured income is broken down into permanent and transitory components. The permanent component (e.g., expected labor income) is expected to recur over the long run, while the transitory component (e.g., prize winnings or an inheritance) is not. The forward-looking view contends that the marginal propensity to consume out of transitory income is much smaller than the marginal propensity to consume out of permanent income. The PIH with an infinite time horizon asserts that an additional dollar of transitory income, which raises permanent income by the interest rate times the dollar, is entirely devoted to saving, while the LCH contends that the marginal propensity to consume is the fraction of the dollar that an individual would spend annually for the remainder of his life, so that the entire dollar plus accrued interest would be spent by the time of his expected death. Thus, the forward-looking view contends that income shocks that are perceived as transitory primarily affect saving. Shocks to permanent income primarily affect consumption.

The forward-looking view implies that consumption of goods and services is stable, because the permanent component of lifetime resources is stable. When transitory income is positive (measured income exceeds permanent income) saving rises, and when transitory income is negative (permanent income exceeds measured income), households deplete their assets to maintain their long-run level of consumption. Since the widely accepted natural-rate hypothesis views business cycles as temporary deviations of output from a trend, this predicted consumption-smoothing pattern tends to reduce the amplitude of economic fluctuations.

Consumption smoothing is consistent with the observed stability of spending on services and nondurables, but not with spending on durables. Expenditures on durables are more unstable than income, so they contribute to economic instability which raises questions about the ability of the forward-looking model to explain this component of spending.

There are apparently two reasons for the instability of spending on durables. First, households consider the acquisition of a durable good to be similar to saving. In both cases, households acquire assets that will provide benefits for a long period of time. Since consumption smoothing implies saving instability, if durables are treated as saving then both measured saving and purchases of durables will exhibit instability. Second, if, as Friedman assumed, households form their expectations of permanent income adaptively based on past actual income, then even temporary deviations of output around a relatively stable trend will cause perceived permanent income to change. During expansions some of the increased income is viewed as permanent, which causes households to desire a higher level of consumption. Since a permanently higher level of consumption requires the acquisition of new goods, households tend to acquire their new desired level of durable goods according to a stock-adjustment model. Household spending on durables rises to a level necessary to build up the stock to the new desired level, and, once that level is achieved, spending falls back to the long-run level. During recessions if part of the decline in measured income is viewed as permanent, households move to their new lower level of durables consumption by reducing their spending in this category and running down their stock of durables. Even though all categories of consumption may respond in the same way to the change in perceived permanent income, the spending pattern of durables is quite different from that of services and nondurables, because in the case of durables the spending on and actual consumption of durables do not occur contemporaneously.

Thus, spending on services and nondurables is stable over time and do not appear to be an important source of business cycles—in fact these spending categories tend to smooth economic fluctuations. Spending on consumer durables, on the other hand, is relatively unstable and is sometimes cited as a source of business cycles or, at least, contributing to an increased amplitude. Keynesians contend that spending on durables is heavily influenced by household expectations of the future which can be quite erratic. They believe that a change in household expectations can significantly affect spending on durables and actually initiate an

economic cycle. In fact Temin (1976) contends that an unexplained shift in consumption spending triggered the Great Depression. Monetarists tend to argue that monetary-induced changes in aggregate-demand growth cause changes in economic output, which are amplified by the pattern of spending on consumer durable goods described above.

Some have questioned Friedman's assumption that expectations of permanent income are formed adaptively, not rationally. Applying this notion to the forward-looking theory of consumption, Hall (1978) argued that if expectations are rational, consumption spending should follow a random walk, because the best forecast of next period's permanent income is this period's permanent income. Empirical tests generally do not support the random-walk model of consumption spending, because consumption spending is too sensitive to transitory income, perhaps because imperfect capital markets do not allow households to borrow against their expected permanent income during recessions. In such cases, they are said to be liquidity-constrained.

In summary, household expenditures on services and nondurables tend to reduce the amplitude of economic fluctuations. Consumption smoothing in these categories of spending occurs because consumption and consumption spending take place at roughly the same time and consumption is a function of stable permanent income. Household expenditures on durables, however, vary more than income, so that this category of spending tends to be destabilizing. Here instability results in part from the fact that consumption and consumption spending do not occur at the same time.

Thomas E. Hall

See also CONSUMER DURABLES; FRIEDMAN, MILTON; GREAT DEPRESSION IN THE UNITED STATES (1929–1938); KEYNES, JOHN MAYNARD; MODIGLIANI, FRANCO; NATURAL RATE OF UNEMPLOYMENT

Bibliography

Blinder, A. S. and A. Deaton. 1985. "The Time Series Consumption Function Revisited." *Brookings Papers on Economic Activity*, Number Two, 465–511.

Friedman, M. 1957. *A Theory of the Consumption Function*. Princeton: Princeton Univ. Press.

Hall, R. E. 1978. "Stochastic Implications of the Life Cycle-Permanent Income Hypothesis: Theory and Evidence." *Journal of Political Economy* 86:971–88.

Hayashi, F. 1987. "Tests for Liquidity Constraints: A Critical Survey and Some New Observations." In *Advances in Econometrics, 5th World Congress,* edited by T. F. Bewley, 91–120. New York: Cambridge Univ. Press.

Keynes, J. M. [1936] 1973. *The General Theory of Employment, Interest and Money.* Vol. 7 of *The Collected Writings of John Maynard Keynes.* London: Macmillan.

Kuznets, S. S. 1946. *National Income: A Summary of Findings.* New York: NBER.

Modigliani, F. and R. Brumberg. [1954] 1980. "Utility Analysis and the Consumption Function: An Interpretation of Cross-Section Data." Chap. 3 in F. Modigliani, *The Collected Papers of Franco Modigliani.* Vol. 2. Cambridge: MIT Press.

Temin, Peter. 1976. *Did Monetary Forces Cause the Great Depression?* New York: Norton.

Coquelin, Charles (1802–1852)

Charles Coquelin, known for his famous *Dictionnaire de l'Economie Politique* (1854), made lasting contributions to the understanding of money, credit, banking, and business cycles. After completing his undergraduate education, Coquelin moved to Paris in 1821 to study law. Upon graduation, he began his career as an economic writer and as a lawyer.

In 1827 and 1828, in the newspaper *Les Annales du Commerce,* he published several articles analyzing the economic and financial problems of the times. Noting a connection between credit fluctuations and the business cycle, he advocated increasing banking freedom, because this would permit increased capital investment in a larger number of banks while promoting prosperity and minimizing fluctuations. Coquelin's particularly original contribution coherently and clearly linked business-cycle analysis to restrictions on banks' freedom.

Although only fifty years old when he died, Coquelin's economic contributions were unusually numerous. His writings have been compiled in Nataf (1987). Coquelin's works range from books and articles on the linen industry to free-banking theory and free-trade advocacy.

His interest in economic depressions, triggered by the crisis of 1825, led him to study the British inquiries and debates. He closely followed the debates of the Currency School, the Banking School, and the Free Banking School, becoming familiar with the writings of Henry Parnell, Robert Mushet, James Wilson, W. F. Lloyd, Robert Torrens, Lord Overstone (S. J. Loyd), Thomas Tooke, John Fullarton, and, apparently his favorite British economist, James William Gilbart. Though accepting the Currency School's bank-credit-expansion theory of the business cycle, Coquelin opposed its views on the origin of this artificial increase in credit, arguing that this credit was mainly financed by deposits and not by an overissue of notes. On this important point he analyzed bank balance sheets along lines closer to the Banking School. Consequently and consistently, he opposed Peel's Bank Charter Act of 1844 on the grounds that the restriction of notes could not stop banks' credit expansion. But he did not espouse the Banking School theories either, believing that economists like Tooke failed to understand the artificial nature of deposit fluctuations.

Borrowing from J. B. Say, Gilbart, and even more from Henry Charles Carey, Coquelin developed an original theory of the business cycle. Largely accepted by later French economists for decades, Coquelin's views reappeared in the work of the Austrian economists Ludwig von Mises and F. A. Hayek in the 1920s.

Analyzing the "periodical crises" (he apparently coined the term) in nineteenth-century France, England, and the United States, Coquelin identified the banking systems of these countries as the origin of recurring depressions. He found that whenever banks decreased their interest rate and increased the credit supply, an economic boom followed along with inflation, feverish business activity, and an increase in speculative stock creation and valuation. Once credit expansion eased, a collapse became inevitable. But while panics occurred regularly in Paris, London, and New York, some areas were surprisingly depression-proof. Scotland and the New England states enjoyed numerous prosperous and stable banking institutions and, consequently, prosperity and monetary stability. Borrowing largely from Carey's works, Coquelin observed that freedom for banks on the one hand, and economic progress and banking stability on the other, appeared paradoxically correlated. Coquelin showed that when bank competition was severely restricted, as in mid-nineteenth century France, credit was scarce, economic backwardness was widespread, and banks were unstable. When banking regulations did not prevent bank creation, numerous credit institutions were opened in England and New York state. Industrialization or agricultural progress became possible, but at the same time bank instability generated recurring panics and crises. When freedom of banks was almost complete, as in Scotland or in New England, competition increased the cost of banks' funds to their maximum. The result, Coquelin argued, was that banks could not artificially decrease the interest charged on loans. With artificial credit expansion precluded, depressions were avoided for half a century in New England, and more than a century in Scotland.

Philippe Nataf

See also BANK OF FRANCE; BANKING SCHOOL, CURRENCY SCHOOL, AND FREE BANKING SCHOOL; FREE BANKING

Bibliography

Coquelin, C. 1848. "Les Crises commerciales et la liberté des banques." *La Revue des Deux Mondes,* 1 November, 445–70.
———. 1850. "Notice sur les banques de l'Etat de New York." *Journal des Economistes,* 15 October, 235–42.
———. 1854. *Dictionnaire de l'Economie Politique.* 2d ed. Paris: Guillaumin.
———. 1876. *Le Crédit et les banques.* 3d ed. Paris: Guillaumin.
Dowd, K., ed. 1992. *The Experience of Free Banking.* London: Routledge.
Mises, L. von. 1966. *Human Action.* 3d rev. ed. Chicago: Regnery.
Molinari, G. de. 1852. "Notice biographique sur Charles Coquelin." *Journal des Economistes,* September–October.
Nataf, P. 1987. *An Inquiry into the Free Banking Movement in Nineteenth Century France, with Particular Emphasis on Charles Coquelin's Writings.* San Diego: William Lyon Univ.
Nouvion, G. de. 1908. *Charles Coquelin: Sa Vie et ses Travaux.* Paris: Felix Alcan et Guillaumin réunis.
Smith, V. C. 1936. *The Rationale of Central Banking.* London: P. S. King.

Creative Destruction

"Creative destruction" is the somewhat dramatic name for an adjustment process in the course of the business cycle which Joseph A. Schumpeter called an *Einordnungzprozess,* a process of integration, in the original German edition of his *Theory of Economic Development.* The technical meaning of the term must be understood in the context of Schumpeter's business-cycle theory.

All development, not only capitalist development, occurs in a wave-like manner. The characteristic of development is growth with an irreversible change in the parameters of the production functions. The entrepreneur changes parameters, perhaps even the form of the function and possibly even the type of good, to satisfy existing or newly created wants.

There are always adaptive processes, which are discussed adequately by general-equilibrium theory, at work in an economy. In adaptive processes at most very small changes in the parameters occur. Standard equilibrium theory (or mathematically speaking, differential calculus) can easily handle such changes. In fact, standard equilibrium theory assumes no changes in parameters; the notion of "very small changes of parameters" is a Schumpeterian addendum. The changes in parameters are brought about by entrepreneurs ("Entrepreneur" is itself also a technical term for the agent who, against the resistance of the environment, brings changes about). Since in equilibrium all factors of production are (more or less) optimally employed, the entrepreneur must direct them into the new channels envisaged by him, as a rule (though this is not strictly necessary logically) using newly created money. In a capitalistic economy, as defined by Schumpeter, the entrepreneur must get hold of the resources with borrowed money. In other developing economies, e.g., in a developing socialist economy, he may have direct command over the necessary resources.

Time lags result, because the new processes cannot replace the traditional ones immediately and smoothly. The new processes are developed while the old ones continue to operate, perhaps even more profitably than in equilibrium (in which economic profits strictly defined are zero). The trouble starts when the new processes begin to spew out new goods which compete with existing ones, either in price, quality, in better ways of satisfying existing wants, or—and this is perhaps the most characteristically Schumpeterian idea—in satisfying wants that the new processes have created. In this moment begins a struggle of the new with the old that, if the original entrepreneurial decisions turn out to be ratified by the future decisions of consumers, must lead to the elimination of the old.

It is this elimination of production processes and goods that development has rendered obsolete and uneconomic that Schumpeter called creative destruction. It is essentially an adaptive process toward a new equilibrium that, while possessing the same general characteristics as any equilibrium, has changed parameters—an equilibrium that once (approximately) achieved opens new possibilities for further development.

The following points need to be stressed. Development necessarily proceeds discontinuously and in waves. The basic cause of waves in economic life is changing production functions coming from *within* the economic system. The dynamic nature of any economy—in the technical sense of time subscripts referring to different periods—requires that the new appear side-by-side with the old. The actually observed course of a developing economy need not be as violent as faulty monetary policies, speculation, or other avoidable mistakes, frequently make it. But no matter how effective stabilization policies may be, a process of creative destruction must from time to time slow down development and would also do so under socialism or any other kind of developing economy. Where there is development, nature does proceed by fits and starts as Schumpeter remarked already in 1912 on Alfred Marshall's motto *natura non facit saltum!*

Wolfgang F. Stolper

See also BUSINESS CYCLES IN SOCIALIST ECONOMIES; SCHUMPETER, JOSEPH ALOIS

Bibliography

Scherer, F. M. 1988. "Schumpeter's Mikroökonomie." In *Über Schumpeter's Theorie der wirtschaftlichen Entwicklung*, 75–87. Düsseldorf: Verlag Wirtschaft und Finanzen Gmbh.

Schumpeter, J. A. [1926] 1934. *The Theory of Economic Development*. 2d ed. Translation. Cambridge: Harvard Univ. Press.

———. 1939. *Business Cycles: A Theoretical, Historical and Statistical Analysis of the Capitalist Process*. 2 vols. New York: McGraw-Hill.

———. 1942. *Capitalism, Socialism and Democracy*. New York: Harper and Brothers.

Shionoya, Y. 1990. "The Origin of the Schumpeterian Research Program: A Chapter Omitted from Schumpeter's *Theory of Economic Development*." *Journal of Institutional and Theoretical Economics* 146:314–27.

Stolper, W. F. 1988. "Schumpeter's Theories der wirtschaftlichen Entwicklung—Eine kritische Exegese." In *Über Schumpeters Theorie der Wirtschaftlichen Entwicklung*, 35–74. Düsseldorf: Verlag Wirtschaft und Finanzen Gmbh.

———. 1994. *Joseph Alois Schumpeter: The Public Life of a Private Man*. Princeton: Princeton Univ. Press.

Credit-Anstalt

Revealing to the world the fragility of the international financial system, the failure of the Credit-Anstalt (Österreichische Credit-Anstalt für Handel und Gewerbe) in May 1931 started a series of bank collapses and foreign-exchange crises throughout Europe and the United States which culminated in the abandonment of the gold standard by England in September 1931. The crisis also had far-reaching consequences for economic activity in Central Europe, prolonging and deepening the Great Depression.

On 8 May 1931, the Credit-Anstalt informed the Austrian government and the Austrian National Bank that its 1930 balance sheet showed a loss of 140 million schillings, amounting to about 85 percent of its equity. The information shocked even the Austrian authorities, who were used to crises.

The Credit-Anstalt was not a "normal" bank. Established in 1855 by a financial group led by the Viennese Rothschild bank, its main goal was to promote industry and long-term credit. By 1931 it was not only the largest bank in Austria, with a balance sheet the size of the state's expenditures, accounting for more than 50 percent of the balance-sheet totals of all Austrian joint-stock banks, but also the largest European bank east of Germany. Almost 70 percent of all Austrian limited companies did their business through the Credit-Anstalt. Moreover, it had an excellent international reputation, with a member of the Rothschild family as its president. Its stocks were quoted on twelve foreign stock exchanges, including New York, and more than half its shares were in foreign hands. A number of prominent foreigners sat on its board of directors. Its business interests extended into eleven banks and forty industrial enterprises in the states of the former

Austro-Hungarian Empire and its creditors included the most important foreign—especially British and American—banks.

Because of its international ties and because a bankruptcy of the bank could cause numerous business failures, the otherwise noninterventionist Austrian government decided to accept a socialization of the losses. Within only three days a reconstruction plan was put together to cover the bank's losses and to raise new capital from the Austrian state, the shareholders, the Rothschilds, and the Austrian National Bank. The outstanding feature of the plan was the generous treatment of shareholders while the state was to absorb the largest share of the losses. The share capital was to be devalued by only 25 percent.

On 11 May 1931, the problems of the bank and the reconstruction plan were announced to the public. It was thought that this strategy would preserve confidence in the troubled institution by preventing any interruption of its business and by securing it on a new capital base.

The news of the problems of the largest and most respected Austrian bank surprised and shocked the public. The reconstruction plan could not dispel the doubts. For four days the Credit-Anstalt and other Viennese banks witnessed runs. In only two days the Credit-Anstalt lost about 16 percent of its deposits, and within two weeks about 30 percent, mainly due to withdrawals by domestic creditors. These large withdrawals would have rendered it illiquid had not the Austrian National Bank rediscounted freely all bills presented. It even violated its charter by accepting financial bills instead of trade bills. But the withdrawals from the Credit-Anstalt continued.

To obtain a short-term loan from the Bank for International Settlements the Austrian government had to pass a state guarantee for the credits to the Credit-Anstalt. But when the loan finally arrived it was too late and too small. The distrust of the public had already targeted the Austrian schilling. To avoid foreign repercussions of a possible Austrian moratorium, the Bank of England extended an emergency short-term credit.

The announcement of this failure shocked other financial centers, especially—but not exclusively—those in the neighboring countries. While there had been bank collapses occurring at that time in Europe, none of them matched the Credit-Anstalt either in size or importance. In particular, the already strained situation in Germany became even more critical as German banks were in many respects very similar to their Austrian counterparts. Problems in Germany culminated in the collapse of the Danatbank on 13 July and a subsequent bank holiday. From there the shock waves swept to London, which had been heavily exposed to Austria and Germany, leading to the suspension of the gold standard in late September, and subsequently reached New York.

In mid-June 1931 negotiations with the foreign creditor banks of the Credit-Anstalt led to a standstill agreement under which foreign credits would be renewed for two years in exchange for an extension of the governmental guarantee to all foreign liabilities of the bank. Two weeks later the guarantee was extended to virtually all liabilities of the Credit-Anstalt. From then on, the Austrian state, with a budget of 1,800 million schillings, stood as guarantor for 1,200 million schillings of bank liabilities.

Nevertheless, withdrawals continued and the Credit-Anstalt kept on rediscounting financial bills at the Austrian National Bank which the central bank accepted to keep the ailing institution afloat. Large increases in the discount rate in June and July had no significant effect on withdrawals.

As the government was unable to raise long-term foreign loans, the Austrian reserves continued declining and the schilling was increasingly backed only by financial bills of the Credit-Anstalt. Finally, on 9 October 1931, after the Austrian National Bank had lost the majority of its foreign reserves, the government decided to introduce exchange controls.

Not until January 1933 was a permanent settlement reached with the foreign creditors of the bank and the reconstruction of the Credit-Anstalt finally started. The losses, initially reported as 140 million schillings, turned out to be around one billion schillings, 90 percent of which were borne by the Austrian state.

Aurel Schubert

See also BANKING PANICS; INTERNATIONAL LENDER OF LAST RESORT; LENDER OF LAST RESORT

Bibliography

Schubert, A. 1991. *The Credit-Anstalt Crisis of 1931.* New York: Cambridge Univ. Press.

Stiefel, D. 1989. *Finanzdiplomatie und Weltwirtschaftskrise.* Frankfurt am Main: Fritz Knapp Verlag.

Credit Cycle

The phenomenon of a credit cycle was first described by the nineteenth-century British economist John Mills. This phenomenon involves a tendency toward increasing indebtedness by businesses and individuals until a peak level of indebtedness is reached. Debt is then reduced to more manageable levels until, at some point, the level of indebtedness begins increasing again. Mills and others observed that the credit cycle seems to coincide with the business cycle with levels of indebtedness increasing during expansions and declining during recessions. Indebtedness reaches its peak near the upper turning point of the cycle and reaches a trough near the lower turning point of the cycle.

It was natural for theorists to seek some causal relationship between the credit cycle and the overall business cycle. The creation of debt seems to be closely related to the process of economic expansion. The issuance of debt helps finance business expansion and increased consumer spending, particularly on durable assets, so that the creation of increasing amounts of debt can be viewed as integral to the process of economic expansion. On the other hand, over-indebtedness can cause consumers and businesses to retrench their spending plans, thereby causing economic activity to begin to decline.

At an extreme, the debt burden may become so heavy that the process of retrenchment cannot be undertaken smoothly, but degenerates into a process of widespread bankruptcy which can feed on itself, resulting in a system-wide deflation of asset values. The best-known articulation of this view is Irving Fisher's debt-deflation theory of great depressions.

In principle, theories which causally relate the credit cycle to a general business cycle need not involve a monetary mechanism. However, those monetary theories that emphasize the role of a divergence between the market and the natural rates of interest imply a corresponding credit cycle which results from the same monetary disturbance that generates the overall business cycle. In such natural-rate theories, the artificial stimulus of a market interest rate below the natural rate stimulates borrowing by businesses to finance investment projects. Given the opportunity to borrow at low interest rates, businesses become overindebted in the sense that the cash flows generated by the associated investment projects will ultimately not suffice to retire the debt incurred to finance the investment. In Hawtrey's version of this theory, the stimulus of low rates mainly affects inventory accumulation, while in other versions (notably the Austrian one), the stimulus of low rates operates on business investment in fixed assets.

Although there is a clear causal link between the credit cycle and the business cycle in those monetary business-cycle theories that emphasize the divergence between the market and the natural rates of interest, business-cycle theories that stress changes in expectations can also account for a credit cycle that roughly coincides with the business cycle. In periods of optimism or periods when the expected profitability of investment is high, businesses are more willing to issue debt than when expected profits are low. If economic expansions are driven by expectations of rising profits, expansions ought to be associated with increasing indebtedness. If expectations become too optimistic, the level of indebtedness may become unsustainable and will at least be greater than is desired. The process of reducing indebtedness will then coincide with a period of economic contraction (or in extreme cases, a process of debt deflation). Similarly, real business-cycle theories, whether of the New Classical or of the Schumpeterian varieties, that emphasize the role of investment in generating the business cycle, may also account for a credit cycle that roughly coincides with the business cycle.

Despite the compatibility of a wide range of business-cycle theories with the phenomenon of a credit cycle, it is only in those theories that emphasize what Hawtrey termed "the inherent instability of credit," that the credit cycle has been singled out as a key component of the business cycle. This difference in approach is well exemplified by Keynes's attention to the credit cycle in his *Treatise on Money* and his comparative indifference to the phenomenon in the *General Theory*.

David Glasner

See also AUSTRIAN THEORY OF BUSINESS CYCLES; DEBT-DEFLATION THEORY; FISHER, IRVING; HAWTREY, RALPH GEORGE; HAYEK, FRIEDRICH AUGUST [VON]; KEYNES, JOHN MAYNARD; MILLS, JOHN; MINSKY, HYMAN PHILLIP; NATURAL RATE OF INTEREST; WICKSELL, JOHAN GUSTAV KNUT

Bibliography
Fisher, I. 1933. "The Debt-Deflation Theory of Great Depressions." *Econometrica* 1:337–57.

Haberler, G. 1962. *Prosperity and Depression.* 4th rev. ed. Cambridge: Harvard Univ. Press.

Hawtrey, R. G. 1913. *Good and Bad Trade: An Inquiry into the Causes of Trade Fluctuations.* London: Constable and Co.

———. 1919. *Currency and Credit.* London: Longmans, Green and Co.

Hayek, F. A. 1935. *Price and Production.* 2d ed. London: Routledge.

Keynes, J. M. [1930] 1971. *A Treatise on Money.* 2 vols. Vols. 5 and 6 of *The Collected Writings of John Maynard Keynes.* London: Macmillan.

Minsky, H. P. 1986. *Stabilizing an Unstable Economy.* New Haven: Yale Univ. Press.

Crises of 1763 and 1772–1773

The financial crises of 1763 and 1772–73 were the most serious international financial crises between the Mississippi and South Sea Bubbles in 1720 and the crises associated with the Wars of the French Revolution. The bankruptcies of Dutch financial houses caused by these crises increased the power of London in Western European financial markets at the expense of Amsterdam. The crises also further secured a role for a lender of last resort in British financial markets.

European Finance in the Eighteenth Century

For much of the eighteenth century, London and Amsterdam were the two dominant financial centers of Western Europe. A tight financial link between the cities arose in the early eighteenth century when England modernized its financial structure and encouraged Dutch lenders to enter its financial markets. The process culminated in 1720 during the Mississippi and South Sea Bubbles, and the link between the London and Amsterdam markets held firm until the Fourth Anglo-Dutch War (1780–84).

During those sixty years, the London-Amsterdam axis anchored a tight network of financial markets in Western Europe. The strong financial ties linking the network allowed traders to draw funds promptly from business correspondents in other cities with which to invest and speculate in volatile securities markets. Quick transfers of funds in the form of sight bills of exchange required centralized banking facilities to guarantee the redemption of bills into specie at short notice with little or no risk. The Bank of England, created in 1694, provided these vital services for the London stock market, while the Bank of Amsterdam and the Bank of Hamburg provided the same services in those cities.

The creation of fractional-reserve banking on a large scale expanded and destabilized credit in a way that transformed the character of financial crises. The ability to finance extensive leveraged positions in equities and commodities gave financial crises after 1715 their modern features still seen today. At the same time, this elasticity allowed the Bank of England, in particular, to play the role of lender of last resort for markets in London and abroad.

Crisis of 1763

During the Seven Years' War (1756–63), England had been forced to advance large sums to support Prussia, as well as to pay for the maintenance of her own troops in Hanover. These payments were made by bills payable in Amsterdam or Hamburg, and the opportunity to expand the normal volume of drawing credit tempted many dealers in Amsterdam to grant credits without requiring a parallel security in commodities. This led to credit inflation in the form of unsecured finance bills as many inexperienced dealers failed to keep adequate cash reserves at the Bank of Amsterdam when they entered the market. The resulting chain of accommodation bills became known as *wisselruiterij* ("kite flying").

The exaggerated expansion of credit during the Seven Years' War reached its limit in 1763 when peace came. When the *wisselruiterij* finally broke in the summer of 1763, bankers and merchants who had borrowed from each other became insolvent, causing bankruptcies in Amsterdam and Hamburg in July 1763. London bankers (including the Bank of England) intervened to ease the liquidity squeeze in Amsterdam in August and September by shipping specie to desperate financial houses.

Crisis of 1772–73

The Crisis of 1772–73 began in London in the summer of 1772, then, after a pause, continued six months later in Amsterdam in the winter of 1773. The English portion of the crisis resulted from speculation in English East India Company stock by Alexander Fordyce, a Scottish banker. Using his poorly capitalized financial institution, the Ayr Bank, for highly leveraged loans, Fordyce financed a substantial short position in English East India stock. When the prices of English East India stock failed to fall as expected, Fordyce went bankrupt and fled Great Britain for France on 9 June 1772. The departure of Fordyce caused the collapse of his over-extended bank, in turn causing severe stress on his large network of financial connections in London. A number of important firms went bankrupt in late June as a result of the crisis.

The Dutch portion of the crisis also resulted from speculation in English East India stock. By the fall of 1772, major Dutch financial houses had highly leveraged long positions in the stock. The Amsterdam financial house of Cliffords lost substantial sums, and in the first week of January 1773, the lines of credit among Amsterdam financiers and merchants snapped, halting both trade and finance between London and Amsterdam. The Bank of England came to the rescue on 10 January, allowing anyone who wished to withdraw specie from the bank to do so. Many British merchants quickly sent money to their ailing Dutch correspondents.

Conclusion

The crises of 1763 and 1772–73 had an evolutionary, rather than revolutionary, impact on trends in European finance: they furthered the role of a lender of last resort in European finance and made London the center of international finance just as the Industrial Revolution was beginning to make Great Britain the leading economy in Europe. These trends were to make the British economy the focus of business cycles and financial crises for the next 150 years.

Eric S. Schubert

See also BANK OF ENGLAND; INDUSTRIAL REVOLUTION; INTERNATIONAL LENDER OF LAST RESORT; LENDER OF LAST RESORT

Bibliography

Kindleberger, C. P. 1989. *Manias, Panics, and Crashes.* Rev. ed. New York: Basic Books.

Neal, L. 1990. *The Rise of Financial Capitalism.* Cambridge: Cambridge Univ. Press.

Schubert, E. S. 1986. "The Ties That Bound: Market Behavior in Foreign Exchange in Western Europe During the Eighteenth Century." Ph.D. diss., University of Illinois, Urbana-Champaign.

———. 1988. "Innovations, Debts, and Bubbles: International Integration of Financial Markets in Western Europe, 1688–1720." *Journal of Economic History* 48:299–306.

Wilson, C. H. 1941. *Anglo-Dutch Commerce and Finance in the Eighteenth Century.* Cambridge: Cambridge Univ. Press.

C

Crisis of The 1780s

The new American nation suffered a severe economic crisis during its first decade of existence. The crisis was characterized by a general decline of prices of approximately 25 percent and the widespread bankruptcies of merchants, farmers, and manufacturers. The crisis was one of the important precipitating events leading to the Constitutional Convention of 1787 and to the adoption of the new constitution.

The American economy at the end of the colonial period was still overwhelmingly agricultural, with approximately 90 percent of the labor force engaged in agriculture. The remainder were divided roughly equally between trade and manufacturing. During the Revolutionary War, many nascent manufacturing industries expanded rapidly because of government spending on war-related supplies and because imports from England were largely cut off.

The Northern agricultural sector consisted mainly of small farmers who produced primarily for their own subsistence and only secondarily for the market. These small farmers typically purchased their supplies of household goods, tools, and equipment from small retail merchants, usually on credit until the next harvest. The retail merchants in turn purchased their goods mostly on credit from large wholesale merchants, who in turn imported most of their goods on credit from England. Credit transactions predominated because of a general shortage of money, which in turn was primarily caused by a balance-of-trade deficit with England.

The economic crisis of the 1780s was a fairly typical "postwar depression," produced by disturbances associated with the cessation of the war and, in this case, from the resulting severance of colonial ties with England. The most important of these disturbances were a shift to very restrictive fiscal policy, excessive imports from England, and the restrictions on United States exports and shipping imposed by England. After the war, the central government drastically reduced its spending, which primarily affected the producers of war supplies (armaments, ships, clothing, boots and shoes, etc.). In addition, fiscal policy was made even more restrictive by tax increases that many states enacted to pay off their war debts. At the same time, imports from England quickly returned to prewar levels, providing stiff competition for and threatening the continued existence of many new American manufacturing enterprises. Exports remained significantly below prewar levels because of the war-inflicted destruction of Southern staples (mainly tobacco and rice) and because of English restrictions on exports to the British West Indies (mainly foodstuffs, lumber, and naval stores) and on American shipping to and from England (Bjork 1964).

It soon became obvious that the large increase of imports following the war would not find a sufficient market because of the contracting American economy. The onset of the crisis in 1784 was evidenced by large inventories of unsold goods and falling prices. Many merchants, both wholesale and retail, were forced into bankruptcy.

The crisis adversely affected small farmers by reducing the prices of their agricultural goods and hence their incomes and by raising their taxes. The double squeeze of reduced incomes and increased taxes made it impossible for many farmers to repay their debts to merchants. The merchants often responded to the farmers' defaults by suing them for their land and household possessions. Some farmers were even imprisoned for their inability to repay their debts (which were often quite small sums of money). The farmers responded to such threats to their livelihoods by trying to shut down the bankruptcy courts and by demanding that state governments change the bankruptcy laws, reduce taxes, and increase the money supply. Eventually, when peaceful means failed to achieve these goals, many farmers resorted to armed rebellion. The participants in Shay's Rebellion in central Massachusetts in the winter of 1786–87 (and other smaller uprisings in other Northern states) were primarily such small farmers.

These rebellions increased the desire, especially among the wealthy, for a central government strong enough to protect private property, enforce contracts, limit the increase in the money supply, and suppress revolts. Soon after Shay's Rebellion was defeated, the Congress called for a constitutional convention to revise the Articles of Confederation. James Madison wrote at the time: "Among the ripening events (of the new constitution) was the insurrection of Shay in Massachusetts" (Madison 1895, 45). Many of his contemporaries echoed Madison's views. Thus the eco-nomic crisis of the 1780s was an important factor in the movement for the new constitution, which eventually bestowed new powers on the central government.

Fred Moseley

Bibliography
Bjork, G. 1964. "The Weaning of the American Economy." *Journal of Economic History* 24:541–60.
Madison, J. 1895. *Journal of the Constitutional Convention.* Chicago: Albert, Scott, and Company.
Morris, R. 1952. "Insurrection in Massachusetts." In *America in Crisis,* edited by D. Aaron, 21–49. New York: Knopf.
———. 1987. "The New Nation's First Depression." Chap. 6 in *The Forging of the Union, 1781–89.* New York: Harper and Row.
Nettels, C. 1962. *The Emergence of a National Economy.* New York: Holt, Rinehart and Winston.
Smith, J. 1948. "The Depression of 1785 and Shay's Rebellion." *William and Mary Quarterly,* 3d Ser., 5:77–94.

Crisis of 1819

The Crisis of 1819 was the first great economic crisis in United States history. It ushered in a depression that lasted until 1821. The panic had many features of modern monetary business-cycle downturns, since the driving force behind the panic was a sharp contraction of money and credit. The credit contraction was accompanied by numerous bank failures, which caused people of all political views to place much of the blame for the panic on "speculative lending" by banks.

The seeds of the panic were sown during the War of 1812. The federal government, finding its largest source of revenue—import duties—greatly diminished, was forced to rely heavily on borrowing to finance the war. When the government found itself unable to sell an adequate quantity of ordinary bonds, it turned to the issue of treasury notes. These notes were interest-bearing securities with one-year maturities that also could be used to discharge liabilities to the federal government. This legal-tender status for government transactions conferred on the notes a quasi-legal tender status for all transactions. However, because treasury notes were issued only in denominations of $100 or more (until 1815), they did not serve as an ordinary medium of exchange. Instead, they became an extremely popular reserve asset for banks (Timberlake 1978, 13–18).

The U.S. economy boomed during the War of 1812. Manufacturing grew especially rapidly after the curtailment of European imports. The federal government fed the boom both through its debt-financed war spending and, following the war, through its sales of public lands. High commodity export prices and liberal government credit for the vast tracts of land put up for sale sustained the strong growth of credit initiated by the war. The expansion of money and credit pushed prices above the level compatible with the gold standard. Accordingly, in August 1814 all banks outside New England suspended convertibility (Rothbard 1962, 3–9).

In 1817, the newly chartered second Bank of the United States began operations. The Bank was required to redeem its notes in specie and was expected to require state banks to redeem their notes as well. However, the inability of state banks to redeem their notes, together with the Bank's desire to maximize its profits, led the Bank to forbear requiring the conversion of state bank notes and to extend over $41 million in loans in its first year. The economy boomed in 1818, but the convertibility of paper dollars into specie was everywhere (except New England) more nominal than real. A growing trade deficit caused an outflow of specie from the Bank of the United States. Large purchases of specie from abroad failed to stanch the specie outflow. Thus, in the summer of 1818, the Bank of the United States began contracting. The Bank's demand liabilities fell from $22 million in the fall of 1818 to only $12 million in January 1819.

The contraction of Bank lending followed the redemption of virtually all of the treasury notes issued from 1812 to 1815. State banks no longer had enough reserves to maintain convertibility of their expanded note and deposit issues. Consequently, state banks began to contract rapidly. The results were predictable: an inability to acquire customary financing led to a wave of bankruptcies. Prices fell sharply, increasing the real burden of debtors. Borrowers defaulted on bank loans, pushing many banks into insolvency. Despite a significant decline in wages, large-scale urban unemployment emerged for the first time in U.S. history.

The severity of the depression led to widespread agitation for government action. Several states enacted laws providing direct relief to debtors. Others chartered new state-owned banks or permitted privately owned state banks to suspend convertibility. All such banking schemes caused the inconvertible bank notes to depreciate rapidly. None of the plans put forth for an inconvertible national currency—issued either by the Bank of the United States or by the Treasury—received serious consideration by Congress. In 1821, European economies began to emerge from their own depressions, and the demand for U.S. commodities rose correspondingly. Commodity prices began to rise, credit availability increased, and manufacturing and trade gradually recovered.

Neil T. Skaggs

See also BANKING PANICS

Bibliography

Hammond, B. 1957. *Banks and Politics in America: From the Revolution to the Civil War.* Princeton: Princeton Univ. Press.

Rothbard, M. 1962. *The Panic of 1819: Reactions and Policies.* New York: Columbia Univ. Press.

Schur, L. M. 1960. "The Second Bank of the United States and the Inflation After the War of 1812." *Journal of Political Economy* 68:118–34.

Taus, E. R. 1943. *Central Banking Functions of the United States Treasury, 1789–1941.* New York: Columbia Univ. Press.

Timberlake, R. H., Jr. 1978. *The Origins of Central Banking in the United States.* Cambridge: Harvard Univ. Press.

Wright, D. M. 1953. "Langdon Cheves and Nicholas Biddle: New Data for a New Interpretation." *Journal of Economic History* 13:305–19.

Crisis of 1825
See PANIC OF 1825

Crisis of 1837
See PANIC OF 1837

Crisis of 1847
The crisis of 1847 occurred just three years after the enactment of the Bank Charter Act. Codifying proposals advocated by the Currency School, the Act separated the Bank of England into independent Banking and Issue Departments and imposed a 100-percent marginal gold reserve requirement on any banknotes

exceeding the £14 million fiduciary issue allowed the Bank.

The theory behind the Bank Charter Act was that crises resulted from a failure of the "circulating medium" (i.e., gold coin and convertible banknotes) to fluctuate as a purely gold currency would, on a one-to-one basis, with inflows and outflows of gold. Since banknotes could be issued without matching gold reserves, the circulating medium did not automatically respond to metallic inflows and outflows. But banks would eventually act to protect their reserves, so commercial crises would occur when the banking system belatedly reacted (or overreacted) to a persistent loss of gold reserves. A ceiling on the fiduciary issue of the Bank of England, coupled with a 100-percent gold reserve requirement on notes issued beyond the ceiling, were supposed to ensure that the currency in circulation would behave exactly as an ideal gold currency would have. Supporters of the Act expected enforcement of the Currency Principle to prevent a sustained overissue of convertible banknotes such as had, in their view, caused the panics of 1825 and 1837.

Not only did the Bank Charter Act fail to prevent the crisis of 1847, disappointing the expectations of its supporters, but the government's suspension of the act in October 1847 to forestall a financial collapse suggests that the act may in fact have been one of the causes of the crisis. An examination of the events surrounding the crisis confirms that the act, if not the direct cause of the crisis, at least exacerbated its impact on the financial system.

Background

After the panic of 1837, the British economy entered a period of recession and stagnation from which it did not begin to emerge until 1843. The recovery was marked by increases in almost all manufacturing sectors. Although interest rates were at historically low levels, investment spending was not a leading element in the recovery.

The recovery helped revive interest in railway construction, which had been depressed since the late 1830s. Private Parliamentary acts were required for each new railway construction project, so that actual railway construction lagged behind the general economic recovery. By 1845, when economic activity seems to have peaked in most sectors, the boom in railway construction was just getting underway.

Many contemporary and subsequent observers have maintained that the railway boom drove up interest rates after 1845, diverting funds that could have financed investment in other sectors into railway construction. The subsequent crisis and downturn were therefore widely attributed to a speculative railway boom that first discouraged investment in other sectors and then triggered a financial crisis when it finally collapsed. However, evidence compiled by Boot (1984) shows that railway investment in 1846–47, when the railway boom was cresting, helped maintain overall economic activity when output in other sectors was already declining. Moreover, even after the peak of the railway boom in 1847, railway investment remained strong in 1848–49, thereby cushioning a recession which deepened after the crisis of 1847 until a recovery began in 1849. From this perspective, railway investment, far from being a destabilizing force in the 1840s, appears to have exerted a fortuitous countercyclical impact on the British economy in that decade.

The April Crisis

Although railway construction appears to have moderated the British business cycle of the 1840s, poor harvests in England and the Continent and the destruction of the potato crops in Ireland and Scotland had a severely adverse impact in 1846 and 1847. High grain prices and a high demand for imports led to a balance-of-payments deficit and an outflow of gold in 1846. In the first four months of 1847, the situation worsened and the Bank of England lost over £6 million in gold reserves, largely to pay for imported grain.

After raising its rate twice by half a percent in January (to 4 percent), the Bank of England kept the rate fixed at that level even as it continued to lose gold and market interest rates continued rising. Finally, on 8 April 1847, the Bank of England responded to the external drain by raising its rate to 5 percent and restricting the range of bills it would accept for discount. Market rates rose as high as 10 percent for those unable to draw on the Bank of England.

Opinions about the performance of the Bank of England in early 1847 are conflicting. Most contemporary and subsequent observers have held that by tolerating the gold outflow until April without taking countermeasures, the Bank ultimately had to apply excessive pressure when it did act. However, Boot (1984, 49–50) contends that the Bank's policy from January to March does not merit this criticism, because the Bank did twice increase its interest rate and notes in the hands of the public did fall by £1.5 million while gold reserves fell by £2.2 million. The situation began to deteriorate badly only in March, when the Bank's losses of gold reserves continued while its liabilities were allowed to increase. Though it recognized the need to raise rates, the Bank was then reluctant to do so, because the government was seeking to raise a loan for famine relief in Ireland. This delay was critical, because the differential between rates in New York and London became so great in March that the Bank lost over £2 million in gold between 6 March and 17 April (Dornbusch and Frenkel 1984, 261). The sudden tightening by the Bank initially increased distress by restricting access to credit, but the increase in interest rates soon dispelled the crisis, halting and reversing the outflow of gold which had been its principal cause. In any event, the events leading up to the April crisis indicate that Bank of England notes held by the Banking Department as a reserve against deposit liabilities acted as a buffer between the Bank of England notes held by the public and the gold reserves held by the Issue Department. That buffer prevented the Currency Principle from operating as supporters of the Bank Charter Act had intended.

The October Crisis

However, a more serious problem was brewing. In the spring of 1847, fears of another bad harvest were leading to a speculative rise in grain prices in London. Importers financed their purchases on credit extended by the London financial houses. By the summer of 1847 it was becoming clear that supplies of grain would be plentiful, and prices fell steadily from the speculative peaks reached in May. Having bought on credit at the peak of the market, grain merchants took severe losses as they liquidated their positions. Many merchants failed, as did several financial houses from which they had borrowed. The difficulties of the financial houses also affected merchants in other branches of foreign trade. Deprived of normal credit facilities, many of these merchants also had to liquidate their stocks, forcing down the prices of numerous internationally traded commodities.

Conditions deteriorated steadily in the late summer and early fall, as bankruptcies mounted. The outflow of gold resumed, and the Bank of England responded by raising interest rates. But by September, the problem was more fundamental than a misalignment of interest rates between New York and London; it was a loss of confidence, which made lenders unwilling to extend credit and creditors unwilling to accept the liabilities of formerly reputable financial institutions. The public recognized only two safe assets, gold and Bank of England notes. Unlike the April crisis, the Bank was threatened with an internal, not an external, drain.

In these circumstances, the Bank Charter Act, if and when it became binding, would force the Bank to respond in precisely the wrong way. The demand of the public (including the commercial banks) for liquidity was reflected in an increased desire to hold Bank of England notes. But the Bank of England was required by the Bank Charter Act to respond to a loss of gold reserves by restricting its note issue even as the public demand for notes was increasing. As long as the Banking Department's reserves of Bank of England notes were sufficient, the perverse impact of the Bank Charter Act could be avoided. The Banking Department could accommodate the demand for liquidity by allowing its holdings of Bank of England notes to run down.

But the reduction in the note reserves of the Banking Department could go only so far. In October, with the gold reserve of the Issue Department rapidly dwindling, the Bank of England seemed to be in danger of insolvency. Yet, it is clear that there was no loss of confidence in the Bank of England, since there was no demand to convert Bank of England notes into gold. The threat to the Bank's solvency was solely the result of the legal limit on the Bank's ability to satisfy demands to hold Bank of England notes. Fearing that the Bank of England could no longer accommodate its demand for liquidity, the financial community panicked as traders and financial institutions scrambled to obtain Bank of England notes.

Finally, on 25 October, the government issued a letter signed by the Chancellor of the Exchequer and his deputy to the Bank of England suggesting that the Bank of England increase its lending to the market on sound security at an interest rate of at least 8 percent, even if in so doing, the Bank would have to exceed the limits on note issue set by the Bank Charter Act. The government promised to introduce a bill of indemnity to prevent any sanctions from being applied to the Bank's officials for violating the terms of the Act.

Almost immediately after the letter was published, the panic came to an end as the financial community no longer had to fear that the Bank of England would be prevented from meeting demands for liquidity. Once that fear was dispelled, the precautionary demand for liquidity largely abated. And in the end, it was not even necessary for the Bank of England to exceed the limits on note issue set by the Bank Charter Act.

This fact was cited by defenders of the Act to show that the Act had not caused the panic. However, contemporary accounts demonstrate that the panic was itself precipitated by the understanding that no accommodation from the Bank of England was possible because the Issue Department was approaching its ceiling on the issue of banknotes. Once the legal constraint on the power of the Bank of England to meet a demand for liquidity was lifted, the panic evaporated. Very similar scenarios were replayed in the crises of 1857 and 1866, when the government wrote letters to the Bank of England suspending the terms of the Bank Charter Act to dispel crises caused by the fear that the Bank Charter Act would prevent the Bank of England from accommodating demands for liquidity.

Conclusion

In the aftermath of the October crisis, even with a restoration of financial stability, Britain remained in a relatively mild recession, partly cushioned by the last stages of the railway boom, until 1849. The rapid growth of the middle 1840s and the subsequent downturn presaged the rapid and sustained growth that Britain enjoyed in the 1850s and the 1860s.

David Glasner

See also BANK CHARTER ACT OF 1844; BANK OF ENGLAND; BANKING SCHOOL, CURRENCY SCHOOL, AND FREE BANKING SCHOOL; CRISIS OF 1857; LENDER OF LAST RESORT; OVEREND, GURNEY CRISIS; PANIC OF 1825; PANIC OF 1837

Bibliography

Bagehot, W. [1873] 1962. *Lombard Street.* Homewood, Ill.: Irwin.
Boot, H. M. 1984. *The Commercial Crisis of 1847.* Occasional Papers in Economic and Social History, no. 11. Hull, U.K.: Hull Univ. Press.
Clapham, J. 1944. *The Bank of England: A History.* Cambridge: Cambridge Univ. Press.
Dornbusch, R. and J. Frenkel. 1984. "The Bank of England in the Crisis of 1847." In *A Retrospective on the Classical Gold Standard, 1821–1931,* edited by M. D. Bordo and A. J. Schwartz, 233–64. Chicago: Univ. of Chicago Press.
Fetter, F. W. 1965. *The Evolution of British Monetary Orthodoxy, 1797–1875.* Cambridge: Harvard Univ. Press.
Ward-Perkins, C. N. 1950. "The Commercial Crisis of 1847." *Oxford Economic Papers,* n.s. 2:75–94.

Crisis of 1857

Financial markets in the United States were generally calm during the first half of 1857, but signs of an impending crisis were visible in the summer. The prices of Western land and Western railroad stocks were the first to decline. Calomiris and Schweikart (1991) have suggested that the decline in these prices may have been linked to the Dred Scott decision and the resulting political and institutional uncertainty in the territories. But in any case, the decline in asset prices soon became general. Stock prices fell, commercial-paper rates and call-loan rates rose, and the spread between the returns on risky and safe railroad bonds increased. According to Mishkin (1991, 78–80), the increase in interest rates may have made it harder for banks to distinguish between good and bad loans (because the pool of loans offered the banks contained fewer safe projects), so that banks reduced their lending and economic activity declined. But there can be little doubt that the decline in economic activity was greatly exacerbated by the banking panic that followed in the fall of 1857. The panic was centered on the East Coast and especially on New York City, but it eventually spread around the world.

In the United States the key events were the failure of the Ohio Life Insurance and Trust Company on 24 August 1857; the decision by banks in Philadelphia, Baltimore, and Washington, after major bank failures, to suspend convertibility of deposits and bank notes into gold on 26 September; and finally the suspension by banks in New York City on 13 October. The Ohio Life did a considerable business in receiving deposits and making long-term investments in New York as well as in Ohio. The New York office had invested heavily in railroads—the extent to which fraud by the director of the New York office was involved is still uncertain—and the souring of these investments brought down the bank. Confidence in the banking system as a whole seems to have been shaken by this one failure, precisely because the Ohio Life had enjoyed a reputation for sound and cautious banking until the moment it failed. The failure of an institution with a reputation for sailing close to the wind might not have been so damaging.

It is tempting to see the crisis as the inevitable result of the excesses of the long boom that came before: morality demands it. Certainly the boom did touch off considerable speculative activity. Asset prices—prices of land, financial instruments, and (in the South) of slaves—rose, and certain features of the crisis do appear to have been linked with the speculative boom. The failure of the Ohio Life, for example, was linked to speculation in railroad stocks. Nevertheless, it is still not clear why on this occasion, and not others, the end of a speculative boom triggered a complete breakdown of the payments mechanism.

A concerted expansion by the New York City banks following the fall of the Ohio Life, perhaps operating through their clearinghouse formed in 1853, might have averted a panic. An injection of new funds was needed to calm the market. Instead, in the months after the Ohio Life failed, the New York City banks ran for cover, refusing to renew loans. By not lending, they strengthened their cash positions for a time, but in the end they caused just what they thought they were avoiding, a growing panic, a run on banks, a loss of reserves, and a general suspension. The United States Treasury, it is true, tried to compensate by purchasing government bonds, but its actions were insufficient to make a difference.

Temin (1975) has carefully reanalyzed the events in New York City. He divides the crisis into three phases: first, the months before the failure of the Ohio Life, when the banks were losing deposits and specie, but continued to increase lending; second, the three weeks after the failure when the banks cut lending substantially in a successful effort to build up their reserves; and third, the next three weeks when runs on the banks drastically reduced their reserves, despite further cuts in lending.

Temin argues that the Ohio Life failed because of the forces producing the earlier decline in specie, and therefore could not have caused the crisis. But this is debatable. First, it is not clear that the failure of the Ohio Life was re-lated to the previous fall of reserves in New York City, since total lending, supported by an increase in bank capital, was increasing. The failure of the Ohio Life, moreover, seems to have created a sense of betrayal in the public, which undermined confidence in the banks generally.

Another question Temin raises is why in the second phase the New York City banks reacted so violently to the previous fall in reserves. Several factors aside from the failure of the Ohio Life may have played a role. The flow of gold from California was interrupted. One boat was delayed in August and a second was lost in early September. The gold lost was small relative to the total loss of reserves of the New York City banks, but interruption of gold shipments may have aggravated the public's fears of a banking crisis. The international situation was also unsettling, since the Bank of England was tightening credit to bolster its own unsatisfactory reserve position. The New York City banks may have feared pressures on their reserves as gold flowed toward London. But Temin shows that the New York financial press did not report any such fears, so the potential role of this factor remains conjectural.

The New York City banks were also suffering heavy withdrawals because they acted as correspondents for New York country banks. Paradoxically, a regulation intended to make the market for banknotes more efficient, which went into effect in June 1857, may have increased the potential threat to the reserves of the banks in New York City. Each bank in New York state was required to have an agent in New York City or Albany to redeem its notes. The redemption agents could charge for redeeming notes, but the maximum was 0.25 percent. Normally, this regulation caused little difficulty. But when country banknotes fell to a discount of about 1 percent because of the decline in confidence in the banking system, arbitragers had a powerful incentive to bring notes to New York City for redemption. The redemption agents could send these notes back to their banks of issue, but since the redemption agents were often paid with checks on other New York City banks, sending the notes home did not build up specie reserves in New York City.

Another factor that has often been cited to explain the reaction by the New York City banks is an (alleged) history of unsound banking. Increased lending by banks in New York City in the mid-1850s had been supported not only by increased deposits and note issue, but also by increased capital. Much of this was supposedly "fictitious" capital financed by loans to investors from banks issuing shares. What was gained by these transactions? One advantage would be to secure loans greater than the amounts of stock purchased; but the evidence for this is ambiguous. It is also possible that the aim was to acquire the stock, in transactions akin to leveraged buyouts. Investors would do this if they expected the dividends on the shares purchased to exceed the interest payments. Banks would do it because additional capital would help attract deposits.

But everything depends on who is purchasing the stock. A sale to a wealthy physician might be a prudent step. The loan would be well secured by future earnings and would increase the protection afforded note holders and depositors; it would be a genuine addition to capital. But a sale to an impecunious insider or speculator, even if secured by some collateral securities, would only add "fictitious capital" designed to fool the public. No direct evidence to distinguish between these possibilities is available. And a comparison of banks adding capital in the year before the crisis with banks that did not reveals no sharp differences in performance during the crisis. The question merits further study.

Thus, despite a number of careful studies of the crisis, we come to the less than fully satisfying conclusion that some combination of negative developments, including prominently the decline in the value of Western lands and railroads and the associated failure of the Ohio Life, caused a collapse of confidence in the banking system, a downward spiral of withdrawals and credit contraction, and, ultimately, a suspension of specie payments.

The suspension, although an important sign of the extent of the crisis, was not an unmitigated disaster. While it undoubtedly increased caution on the part of business and the public, thereby reducing spending, it was also therapeutic. After the suspension, banks no longer were forced into the self-destructive game of trying to reduce loans and build up reserves. Fortunately, the continuing influx of gold from California assured banks and the public that reserves eventually would be rebuilt sufficiently to allow lifting the suspension without further liquidation of credit.

The impact of the crisis on the banking system varied from state to state. The crisis hit with gale force where small, independent, and rural banks predominated. But the result was often very different, as Calomiris and Schweikart have stressed, where the structure of the banking system permitted coordinated responses. In New York City, the clearinghouse, which had not distinguished itself during the onset of the crisis, facilitated recovery by setting a date for country banks to resume specie payments while requiring the city banks to present country notes for redemption gradually. The country banks were thus given time to prepare for resumption. The clearinghouse also set a date for resumption by all banks in New York City, which was accomplished without incident on 11 December.

In Ohio there existed a system of mutually insured banks (it was one system among several), coordinated by a Board of Control. During the crisis, the Board forced member banks to aid troubled banks. As a result, the insured banks did not suspend, and only one bank in Ohio failed. In Indiana a similar system, the State Bank of Indiana, was also able to avoid suspension, although numerous other banks in Indiana failed. In the South, the branch-banking system of Virginia was noticeably successful in meeting the crisis. And New Orleans, which had only about ten banks and large specie reserves, met the crisis without suspending. Canadian banks, few in number because of branch banking, also avoided any panic. In this respect the panic of 1857 clearly illustrates what banking historians have inferred from later crises in the United States: the absence of branch banking left the banking system unusually vulnerable to panics.

Although short-lived, the crisis had substantial effects on the real economy. It brought to a close the long economic expansion of the 1850s. The expansion, fueled by the discovery of gold in California and Australia, is among the longest business-cycle expansions in the reference-cycle chronology of the National Bureau of Economic Research. The stock of money fell by about 20 percent from the end of 1856 to the end of 1857. At the end of 1858 the money stock was still lower than it had been two years earlier. Prices also fell. The GNP deflator is estimated to have fallen 12.7 percent from 1857 to 1858, before recovering in 1859. The monthly wholesale commodity price index compiled by Smith and Cole (1935, 167) peaked at 133 in June 1857 and bottomed out at 95 in February 1858. The 1857 levels were not surpassed until 1862. Real GNP fell 9.8 percent from 1857 to 1858.

Commercial failures were numerous, and the railroads were especially hard hit. Overall statistics on unemployment are unavailable, but some estimates suggest that the unemployment rate reached 6–8 percent. This was not high compared to later depressions (in part because of the large share of the labor force employed in agriculture), but in the major Northern cities the distress was acute. The South, however, seems to have survived the crisis unscathed, partly because of the strong market for cotton, and partly because of the structure of Southern banking systems and the high specie reserve in New Orleans, the financial center of the South.

The crisis was not confined to the United States. Indeed, it has been called the first worldwide commercial crisis. Although earlier crises had international dimensions, this one spread throughout the commercial world with unprecedented speed and violence. A month after the suspension of the New York City banks, a series of bank and commercial failures, and resulting drains on the Bank of England, nearly emptied its coffers, and forced the government to suspend the Bank Charter Act of 1844 (which limited the amount of notes the Bank could issue in excess of its bullion reserves). The panic in London, the financial center of the world, touched off a panic in Paris, and the effects were soon felt elsewhere in Europe, Central and South America, the Caribbean, South Africa, India, and the Far East. Despite recent talk about a new age of world economic integration, the diffusion of the 1857 crisis proves that the close-knit structure of world financial markets was already an established fact before the Civil War.

Britain, as J. R. T. Hughes (1956) has shown, was ripe for a crisis. Industry was depressed after the long expansion of the 1850s, prices of industrial products had fallen since 1854, and inventories were rising. Stock-market prices had fallen steadily throughout the summer of 1857, as these difficulties became evident, and news of the Indian Mutiny, which reached London in July, was also unsettling.

The Bank of England, moreover, was ill-prepared: its stock of bullion had been falling steadily after reaching a peak in 1852, despite the continuing increase in the world's gold stock. On 8 October, bank rate was raised from 5.5 to 6 percent in response to losses of bullion. It was subsequently raised in stages, finally to 10 percent after the failure of the Western Bank of Scotland. But even this rate did not stop the demands on the Bank of England, and the Bank Charter Act was suspended. Suspension permitted the Bank of England to issue additional notes and ended the panic.

Handling of the crisis by the Bank of England has been criticized. A more timely suspension of the Bank Charter Act (which would probably have been granted had the Bank pressed for it) might have restored confidence. Moreover, the failure of the Bank to build a bullion reserve in the 1850s consistent with its role as lender of last resort has also been criticized. But we cannot be sure that either measure would have sufficed to prevent a crisis. Efforts to build up the reserve might have depressed the economy, and the suspension of the Bank Charter Act might itself have shaken confidence. Under a gold standard, the lender of last resort cannot create the ultimate form of liquidity, and its attempt to increase its store of liquidity may actually undermine confidence.

The crisis of 1857 did not usher in a great depression, and so it has faded somewhat from historical memory. Yet it illustrates the fragility of a fractional-reserve banking system (especially when combined with a gold standard), the relationship between monetary and real sectors of the economy, and the integration, even a century ago, of world financial markets. It is in some ways the classic example of a financial crisis.

Hugh Rockoff

See also BANK CHARTER ACT OF 1844; BANK OF ENGLAND; BANKING PANICS; CLEARINGHOUSES

Bibliography

Calomiris, C. W. and L. Schweikart. 1991. "The Panic of 1857: Origins, Transmission, and Containment." *Journal of Economic History* 51:807–34.

Evans, D. M. [1859] 1960. *The History of the Commercial Crises, 1857–58, and the Stock Exchange Panic of 1859.* New York: Burt Franklin.

Gibbons, J. S. 1859. *The Banks of New York, Their Dealers, the Clearing House, and the Panic of 1859.* New York: D. Appleton.

Hammond, B. 1957. *Banks and Politics in America, from the Revolution to the Civil War.* Princeton: Princeton Univ. Press.

Hughes, J. R. T. 1956. "The Commercial Crisis of 1857." *Oxford Economic Papers* 8:194–222.

———. 1960. *Fluctuations in Trade, Industry and Finance: A Study of British Economic Development, 1850–1860.* Oxford: Clarendon Press.

Huston, J. L. 1987. *The Panic of 1857 and the Coming of the Civil War.* Baton Rouge: Louisiana State Univ. Press.

Kindleberger, C. P. 1978. *Manias, Panics, and Crashes.* New York: Basic Books.

Mishkin, F. S. 1991. "Asymmetric Information and Financial Crises: A Historical Perspective." In *Financial Markets and Financial Crises,* edited by R. G. Hubbard, 69–108. Chicago: Univ. of Chicago Press.

Smith, W. B. and A. H. Cole. 1935. *Fluctuations in American Business, 1790–1860.* Cambridge: Harvard Univ. Press.

Temin, P. 1975. "The Panic of 1857." *Intermountain Economic Review* 6:1–12.

Van Vleck, G. W. 1943. *The Panic of 1857: An Analytical Study.* New York: Columbia Univ. Press.

Crisis of 1866

See OVEREND GURNEY CRISIS

Crisis of 1873

The crisis of 1873 has been described as the first truly international crisis (McCartney 1935, Kindleberger 1993). The crisis began in May with a panic and stock market crash in Vienna. In early fall the crisis recurred in New York, resulting in a ten-day closure of the New York Stock Exchange and a suspension of cash payments by the banking system. From New York, the crisis was transmitted back to Europe with the recurrence of another panic in Vienna and widespread failures in Germany and much of the Continent. The panic in the fall signalled a severe downturn in business activity that lasted for most of the decade in both America and Europe. The severity and international extent of the crisis mark it as perhaps the most severe of the nineteenth century. Nevertheless, although the Bank of England raised the bank rate as high as 9 percent, London itself was spared from the sort of crisis that had occurred in every decade since the 1820s.

The origins of the crisis are generally thought to reside in the investment boom of the late 1860s and early 1870s, which had been especially intense in both the United States and in Central Europe. The boom in Central Europe was coupled in its later stages with a burst of inflation and financial speculation fueled by the Franco-Prussian War of 1870 and the subsequent indemnity of £200 million that France was required to pay the newly formed German empire. To finance the transfer, France adopted a policy of deliberate deflation. By contrast, payment of the indemnity to Germany initiated a major inflationary boom that extended well beyond Germany to much of Central Europe.

The 1850s and 1860s were decades of rapid technological progress and economic growth in both Europe and particularly the United States. Those decades saw the rapid rise of emerging new industries and the increasing mechanization and transformation of old ones. Despite the enormous costs of the Civil War in America between 1861 and 1865, the war stimulated further investment in new plants and equipment. After a not very serious post-war recession in 1865–67, an investment boom of unprecedented magnitude began in the late 1860s, lasting well into the 1870s. Stimulated by large grants of public lands and other governmental subsidies, much of the investment involved the construction of new railroads, particularly in the West. Investment in U.S. railroads was financed largely by the sale of securities to foreign investors, including many from Germany and Central Europe. Massive railroad construction and the introduction of the new Bessemer steel-making process led to an enormous expansion of steel-producing capacity around the Great Lakes to take advantage of the Lake Superior ores best suited for the Bessemer process.

The investment boom in Germany and Central Europe was in many ways similar to that in the United States. In both cases relatively underdeveloped economic areas were integrated into the industrialized international economy on either side of the North Atlantic. And in both cases, rapid economic growth engendered unrealistic expectations that became the basis for new investment projects that proved to be unsustainable. Railroad investment in the West, in particular, was based on unrealistic expectations of profitability. Population in the West was too sparse to support the number of roads under construction. The failure of numerous projects based on unfounded hopes necessarily had grave repercussions that caused expectations of profitability generally to be revised (perhaps excessively) downward.

By early 1873, the optimism that had been driving the investment boom was beginning to recede. At the end of April, the Vienna stock market was showing signs of panic. The market crashed on 8 May; the crash continued until 10 May when the market was closed. When the stock market was reopened on 13 May, the panic had abated. However, business conditions in Austria-Hungary were gravely affected by the panic.

The spring panic did not have immediate repercussions outside Austria-Hungary, and the remainder of the spring and most of the summer passed with no major disturbance. For example the NBER does not date the cyclical peak for the United States until October. Nevertheless, the financial consequences of the crisis and the disappointment of optimistic expectations were immediately transmitted to the United States as European investors sought to liquidate their holdings of American securities that no longer seemed attractive. Monetary conditions in the United States were highly seasonal in the nineteenth century, with the demand for money dropping during the winter and summer and rising during the spring and fall in step with seasonal agricultural activity. The declining demand for money during the summer temporarily insulated United States banks from the immediate effects of the collapsing market for railroad securities. But in September, when the monetary demands of an early harvest season were superadded to the liquidity demands of banks and businesses resulting from the rapidly deteriorating financial situation, the strain was too great for the fragmented U.S. financial system to withstand.

The heaviest blow was the failure of Jay Cooke and Company on 18 September, which helped trigger a panic in New York. The most ambitious of the Western railroad projects was the Northern Pacific Railroad, which had received a land grant of 40 million acres and was supposed to connect Lake Superior with a Pacific Coast seaport. In 1870 Jay Cooke, who had marketed $500,000,000 of U.S. Treasury bonds during the Civil War, undertook to raise $100,000,000 to finance construction of the Northern Pacific. The railroad having reached only the North Dakota territory and the largely European market for new American railroad issues having dried up, Cooke's bank collapsed under the weight of the unsalable bond issue, whereupon the Northern Pacific went bankrupt. Several other major financial houses failed over the next two days. On 20 September, the New York Stock Exchange was closed and did not reopen until 30 September.

The reversal of investor psychology was now truly international. On 1 November, the Vienna stock market crashed again, and panic spread throughout most of the major business centers of Europe. Among these, Paris, having already endured deflation during 1871 and 1872, was notably absent. London, too, was spared. By that time, perhaps, the financial community had come to expect that, in the event of a crisis, the provisions of the Bank Charter Act that constrained ability of the Bank of England to meet the liquidity demands of the public would be suspended, as they had in the crises of 1847, 1857, and 1866. The expectation that liquidity would be available if needed forestalled a preemptive precautionary demand for liquidity that had characterized the earlier crises in London.

In the United States the financial panic was quickly dispelled by the effective action of the New York clearinghouse association, which partially suspended cash payments, causing a suspension of payments throughout the country. In their place, clearinghouses issued clearinghouse certificates that began to circulate as an ersatz currency during the suspension period. Although a temporary expedient, the issue of clearinghouse certificates helped prevent the contagion of bank failure from engulfing the entire banking system, as nearly happened in the Great Depression of 1929–33 when the authority of the Federal Reserve System preempted the resort to this remedy.

Although the financial disorder created by the crisis was largely overcome by the end of 1873, business conditions, under severe deflationary pressure, generally remained stagnant for most of the 1870s. However, in contrast to the 1930s, to which the 1870s are sometimes compared, the deflation of the 1870s was not associated with a corresponding decline in aggregate real output.

David Glasner

See also BANK CHARTER ACT OF 1844; CLEARINGHOUSES; CRISIS OF 1847; DEMAND FOR CURRENCY; DEPRESSION OF THE 1870S; GREAT DEPRESSION OF 1873–1896; SEASONAL FLUCTUATIONS AND FINANCIAL CRISES

Bibliography

Fels, R. 1959. *American Business Cycles*. Chapel Hill: Univ. of North Carolina Press.

Hyndemann, H. M. 1897. *Commercial Crises of the Nineteenth Century.* London: S. Sonnenschein.

Kindleberger, C. P. 1993. *A Financial History of Western Europe.* 2d ed. New York: Oxford Univ. Press.

McCartney, R. R. 1935. *The Crisis of 1873.* Minneapolis: Burgess.

Schumpeter, J. A. 1939. *Business Cycles: A Theoretical, Historical and Statistical Analysis of the Capitalist Process.* 2 vols. New York: McGraw-Hill.

Crisis of 1893

See PANIC OF 1893

Crisis of 1907

The crisis of 1907 precipitated one of the sharpest downturns in economic activity in the history of the United States. This experience convinced contemporaries of the deficiencies of the existing National Banking system, notably the absence of a central bank that could provide an *elastic currency.* As a direct consequence, the National Monetary Commission was established in 1909 to report on possible monetary reforms. The deliberations of the commission, which became subject to intensive political/economic debate and lobbying, led Congress to establish the Federal Reserve System in 1913.

Before 1914 the United States was still largely an agricultural society, subject to a natural seasonal cycle. At harvest time, when agricultural activity was high and produce was being shipped to the ports, the interior agricultural areas withdrew funds from New York. In turn, New York ran a (seasonal) current account surplus with Europe, especially the United Kingdom. But the seasonal pattern also caused the dollar to strengthen in winter and weaken in summer, leading United States exporters in the autumn to hold their proceeds in London to take advantage of the expected seasonal movement of the exchange rate between the gold-point limits. As a result, gold flows were insufficient to offset the internal drain of cash, hence causing interest rates to firm in the autumn. Such monetary pressures were focused in the New York money market, though the seasonal tightening was felt throughout the international monetary (gold standard) system. Nor was the requirement that collateral, in the form of (scarce) United States Treasury bonds, be deposited when National Bank notes were issued conducive to accommodation of the seasonal rhythm of activity. Thus, shocks to the system in the autumn were potentially more serious than at other times, because seasonal stress was superimposed on cyclical pressures.

However, the crisis in October 1907 struck *after* the cyclical peak had been passed in the summer (Mitchell 1913), and the downturn initially seemed mild. The cyclical peak followed earlier periods of financial pressure in autumn 1906 (partly alleviated by measures taken by the independent U.S. Treasury which were opposed by laissez-faire economists such as Andrew [1907, 1908a]) and a shakeout on the New York stock exchange in March 1907. While the combination of seasonal and residual cyclical pressure was keeping the New York money market quite tight in the early autumn of 1907, the actual onset of the crisis was brought about by a series of chance events.

A group of shady New York businessmen had gained control over some (small) New York banks and had (or so it was alleged) illegally used bank funds to speculate on a rise in copper prices. Instead, copper prices fell, ruining the businessmen. Facing a run, banks involved in the speculation applied to the New York clearinghouse for aid; the aid was granted (after the speculating businessmen had been sacked), and by 20 October a minor disturbance was thought to be over. However, one of the speculators was believed to have business connections with the president of the third largest trust company in New York, the Knickerbocker. On 21 October, the National Bank of Commerce publicly refused to clear for it.

This was an extraordinary step, since the Knickerbocker had not suffered a severe run, and subsequently proved to be solvent. It is possible that commercial rivalries between the National Banks, which ran the clearinghouse, and the trust companies, which were growing more rapidly than the National Banks owing to less burdensome regulatory constraints, had some bearing on this refusal.

Whatever its motivation, the refusal provoked an immediate run first on the Knickerbocker, and, within a day, on all the trust companies. Once the trust companies closed, a contagious panic spread; in cities throughout the Unites States, not just in New York, the public sought to shift out of deposits into cash from national banks as well as from state banks and trust companies. The Treasury tried to help by increasing public deposits in New York banks; J. P. Morgan sought to organize a coordinated response by the main New York banks. The clearinghouse authorized the (formally illegal) issue of emergency substitute for currency in the guise of clearinghouse loan certificates. But the contagious panic spread so rapidly that none of these palliatives prevented a widespread restriction by banks of the convertibility of their deposits into currency.

A premium on currency, ranging as high as 4 percent, then ensued. A large variety of cash substitutes appeared, some provided by the clearinghouses (Andrew 1908b, Timberlake 1984). Even so, the restriction of payments thoroughly disrupted normal commerce, generating fear and uncertainty. Meanwhile, the sky-high interest rates, and the premium on currency, provided an enormous incentive for gold imports. But even though orders could be transmitted by telegraph to London, it took over a week to arrange the physical shipment, so gold, which started to leave London late in October, did not reach New York till November. The influx of gold in November was massive ($53 million). Although it was too late to prevent the restriction of payments, the gold imports provided the reserves needed to restore convertibility. But by then, the shock to the economy was severely depressing activity in the United States. Moreover, the drain of gold from London and the subsequent rise in interest rates in Europe ensured that the shock, though reduced in intensity, was transmitted throughout the Western world.

The best contemporary account of this episode was provided by Sprague (1910). The moral that was drawn by Sprague and most contemporary observers was that the United States needed a central bank to prevent such crises from recurring. However, the experience of subsequent episodes of financial and monetary difficulties since the founding of the Federal Reserve System has led some economists in recent years to query whether that conclusion was wholly justified.

C. A. E. Goodhart

See also BANKING PANICS; CENTRAL BANKING; CLEARINGHOUSES; DEMAND FOR CURRENCY; FEDERAL RESERVE SYSTEM 1914–1941; LENDER OF LAST RESORT; SPRAGUE, OLIVER MITCHELL WENTWORTH

Bibliography
Andrew, A. P. 1907. "The Treasury and the Banks under Secretary Shaw." *Quarterly Journal of Economics* 21:519–66.
———. 1908a. "The United States Treasury and the Money Market." *American Economic Association Quarterly: Papers and Discussions of the Twentieth Annual Meeting of the American Economic Association* 9:218–31.
———. 1908b. "Substitutes for Cash in the Crisis of 1907." *Quarterly Journal of Economics* 22:497–516.
Friedman, M. and A. J. Schwartz. 1963. *A Monetary History of the United States, 1867–1960*. Princeton: Princeton Univ. Press.
Goodhart, C. A. E. 1969. *The New York Money Market and the Finance of Trade, 1900–13*. Cambridge: Harvard Univ. Press.
Kemmerer, E. W. 1910. *Seasonal Variations in the Relative Demand for Money and Capital in the United States*. National Monetary Commission. S. Doc. 588, 61st Cong., 2d sess.
Mitchell, W. C. 1913. *Business Cycles*. Berkeley: Univ. of Calif. Press.
Sprague, O. M. W. 1910. *History of Crises under the National Banking System*. Washington, D.C.: Government Printing Office.
Timberlake, R. H., Jr. 1978. *The Origins of Central Banking in the United States*. Cambridge: Harvard Univ. Press.
———. 1984. "The Central Banking Role of Clearinghouse Associations." *Journal of Money, Credit and Banking* 16:1–15.

Crisis of 1914

In 1914, London suffered its first financial crisis in a very long time—possibly for as long as half a century. Precisely how long depends on how the events of 1878 and the Baring Crisis of 1890 are viewed. The former (1878) was certainly a period of considerable general pressure on liquidity. The balance of evidence suggests that the latter was essentially a firm in distress; it might have turned into a crisis, but the Bank of England organized an operation that kept Baring afloat until its problems were over, and strain on the market at large was thus avoided. Working with Anna Schwartz's (1986) distinction between real and pseudo-crises, we prefer to dismiss both as crises. There were well known and undisputed crises earlier in the century—in the 1840s, 1850s, and 1860s, but 1914 was different from these. The earlier crises were all surmounted by raising bank rate and agreeing to suspend the 1844 Bank Charter Act. The 1914 crisis was different, for it arose as a direct result of the war, and required different remedies.

The Main Events

The crisis was comparatively short-lived. At the end of June 1914, alarm spread across Europe when the heir to the Austrian throne was assassinated. War between Austria and Serbia was inevitable by late July and was declared on 28 July. In the second half of July, fears of a European war grew and anticipation of the war provoked the financial crisis. The crisis broke quickly and ferociously in the last week of July. Intense efforts by all the interested parties resolved it by the end of the first week in August, but its repercussions were long-lasting.

As soon as a European war became likely in late July, selling speeded up on the Stock Exchange, exchange rates became volatile, and foreigners could not make remittances to the London acceptance houses. There was, unlike the crises of the previous century, no preceding boom. The 1914 crisis was a collapse from a modest base. On 28 July, banks in London started calling in loans that they had made to the stock market. Brokers sold and the resulting collapse in prices caused the Stock Exchange to close on 31 July—the first time that it had closed on a normal business day since its founding in 1773. Bank rate which had been eased up from 3 to 4 percent on 31 July was raised to 8 percent on 1 August and then to 10 percent on 2 August. The one-day bank holiday of that week was extended by three days and a moratorium placed on bills of exchange. Britain declared war on Germany on 5 August. On 7 August, the banks reopened with bank rate down to 5 percent. There had been some failures in the City, but the system remained sound.

Interestingly, aside from the dangers of war, there had for a long time been concern in various quarters in London over the adequacy of the country's gold reserves. That concern clearly intensified in the immediate run-up to the war. A hostile nation could easily exploit any such weakness by using its holdings of bills to deplete gold reserves and precipitate a financial crisis. However, the discussions on this subject had been carried on with no thought of war. They constitute the only discussion that might have led to preparation for the crisis. But the occurrence of these discussions was pure coincidence. That a crisis would occur when it did was totally unexpected until just before its outbreak.

The Cause

The root cause of the crisis was a failure of remittance. London was a massive creditor to most of the world, including the enemy. British stockbrokers were owed money by foreigners, but in late July, foreign stock exchanges were closing, moratoria were being declared, and debts became irrecoverable at least for the foreseeable future. The London banks had lent money to the brokers "on the margin." That is, they had called for securities as collateral for the loans to an amount 10 to 20 percent greater in value than the loan. When security prices fell, that margin was eroded and the banks, not unreasonably, began to call in the loans. The brokers sold more securities to repay the loans, but, in the process, drove security prices down further, and so on. This is a familiar pattern in such circumstances.

The public picked up the mood and began to queue for gold at the Bank of England. Bank rate moved up. In the three days after 29 July, the Bank advanced £18 million (this when the money stock was £1198 million and the monetary base was £247 million). Reserves, which included high-quality bills and gold reserves, fell precipitously. The London *clearing* banks have often been heavily criticized for calling in these loans to brokers, but some have argued that *foreign* banks in London were most culpable (Seabourne 1986).

Responses

A variety of responses was made to these events, and, taken together, they must be judged largely successful in containing the crisis. At the beginning of August, a conference was called at the Treasury. All the concerned parties from the City and Whitehall were represented. The conference lasted from the second to the sixth of the month. All manner of suggestions were considered, but the principal ones were: suspending the 1844 Act (this had taken place on 1 August, but had served no useful purpose as the drain was external); suspending specie payments; a general moratorium; the issue of Treasury Notes of £1 and 10-shilling denominations.

All these proposals were adopted, though the details of the arrangements were the subject of lengthy discussion, and some modification. For example, the Treasury notes were issued up to a specific percentage of bank liabilities and carried a rate of interest tied to bank rate. The issue of the notes solved the internal currency problem. On 3 August there was a partial moratorium on bills of exchange; that enabled the acceptance houses to postpone, for one month, payment of all bills accepted before 3 August. The bill market needed reviving. The Bank of England was authorized to discount any bill accepted before 4 August. The Bank also offered to lend sufficient funds to meet bills at 2 per cent above bank rate.

After the moratoria, the authorities had to assume the bad debts comprising the bills and acceptances that were unlikely to be recovered from the various payers in the hostile countries and from others whose circumstances were irrevocably altered by the war. The extent of this operation and the means whereby the costs were absorbed have never been assessed accurately.

The response to the crisis injected base money on a scale that raised the monetary base by 29 percent in the first few months of the war. This was an entirely appropriate response to the needs of the time. The continued injection of base money was not appropriate. What is needed to allay a panic is to provide sufficient cash, or at least to promise to do so. But once the crisis is over, some plan for withdrawing the extra cash should be implemented; otherwise, inflation results. That there was no such plan, in 1914 or thereafter, partly explains the extent of the war-time inflation.

It would be accurate to say that the 1914 crisis was without precedent; not in its symptoms, but in its causes. Nonetheless, appropriate remedies were found, and the financial system survived. The price was the war-time inflation, because the initial injection of base money was allowed to remain in the economy. Why that price was paid is unclear; nothing in the currently available evidence indicates that it was necessary.

Forrest H. Capie
Geoffrey E. Wood

Bibliography

Clapham, J. C. 1940. "Account of the Financial Crisis in August 1914." Appendix 3 in *The Bank of England, 1891–1944.* Vol. 3. Edited by R. S. Sayers. Cambridge: Cambridge Univ. Press.

Schwartz, A. J. 1986. "Real and Pseudo Financial Crises." In *Financial Crises and the World Banking System,* edited by F. H. Capie and G. E. Wood, 11–40. London: Macmillan.

Seabourne, T. 1986. "The Summer of 1914." In *Financial Crises and the World Banking System,* edited by F. H. Capie and G. E. Wood, 77–116. London: Macmillan.

D

Davis, Harold Thayer (1892–1974)

Harold T. Davis, a mathematician and statistician, was associate editor at *Econometrica* for the first twenty-six years after its founding. He served continuously as research consultant to the Cowles Commission for Research in Economics from 1931 to the 1960s. His book, *The Analysis of Economic Time Series,* originally published in 1941 as a Cowles Commission monograph, is a classic in statistical time-series research.

Although much of his book is devoted to the statistical analysis of time series and the testing of theories of business cycles, his most important contribution to business-cycle research was his discussion of a fifty-year cycle in which he related war cycles to economic cycles. His analysis begins with a definition of major and minor wars. Since wars place demands on a nation's resources, he classified wars according to how much price inflation they were associated with. He developed an index of wholesale price changes ("a war-intensity ratio") for this purpose. He found that "major" wars occur about every fifty years, during the expansion phase of the long cycle. The economic impact of major wars persists beyond their duration through the economic long cycle. The latter can be examined in terms of six main phases, following the termination of the conflict.

1. A drop in prices commencing as long as several years after peace is declared. In the United States, this has been mainly associated with a decline in farm-commodity prices and farm values, frequently referred to as the "farm problem."
2. A "price shelf" during which the precipitous decline in prices is halted. This period, during which business prospers even as problems in the agricultural sector persist, lasts two to eight years.
3. A second price decline nearly as long and as severe as the first. Business suffers its worst depression, and this is generally a period of bank failures, unemployment, and business restructuring.
4. A price reaction, accompanied by a relative prosperity; this trend reversal is usually caused by monetary inflation.
5. A final collapse in prices, which carries the price index to the bottom of the war cycle; this is a period of major financial distress. Business completely stagnates, the credit of government is impaired, banks fail, and unemployment is widespread. Debt is annihilated; dead capital is eliminated, and institutions are restructured.
6. A period of steady increase in trade, accompanied by approximately 20 years of moderately advancing prices. Prosperity returns, profits rise and unemployment falls. Unfortunately, during this period nations build huge credit reserves and competition for markets increases, leading to international conflicts. War begins at the slightest pretext.

According to Davis, most wars are caused by national rivalries brought about by slackening trade, and, in turn, major wars have economic consequences that last many years after the hostilities end. Although World War II is an anomaly, since it began during an economic depression, the Vietnam War, which followed World War I by approximately 50 years, and its aftermath, seem to follow the pattern described by Davis.

Vincent J. Tarascio

See also Spectral Analysis

Bibliography
Davis, H. T. 1941. *The Analysis of Economic Time Series*. Cowles Commission Monograph, No. 6. Chicago: Cowles Commission.

Debt-Deflation Theory

The debt-deflation theory of depressions emphasizes the crucial destabilizing influence of outstanding nominal debt when price-level changes occur that were not anticipated when the debt was issued. The institution of bankruptcy introduces an asymmetry in the effect of unexpected changes in the real value of inside debt. This theory differs from the widespread view that changes in the real value of inside debt merely transfer wealth between debtors and creditors without affecting net wealth or aggregate demand.

Partially anticipated by Thorstein Veblen (1904, chap. 7), Irving Fisher (1933) made the debt-deflation process central to his explanation of the Great Depression. John Maynard Keynes discussed the real value of inside debt in his 1931 Harris Foundation lectures, when he cited the effect of bankruptcy and asset liquidation on the financial system as grounds for avoiding deflation. Subsequently, Fisher's debt-deflation analysis was joined with Keynes's ([1931] 1973) analysis of uncertainty and volatile investment in Hyman Minsky's (1982a) theory of financial-system fragility, which has been applied to financial history by Charles Kindleberger (1989).

Fisher held a monetary theory of economic fluctuations, viewing the "so-called business cycle" as largely a "dance of the dollar." In the early 1930s, he identified excessive nominal indebtedness as the reason why business contractions sometimes became deep depressions: "if debt and deflation are absent, other disturbances are powerless to bring on crises comparable in severity to those of 1837, 1873, or 1929–33 (1933, 341)." In the wake of some negative shock to price expectations, fear of bankruptcy and default would increase risk premia on loans, and lead to liquidation of assets, repayment of loans, and withdrawal of uninsured deposits from banks with loan portfolios considered in danger of default. This would depress asset prices and contract the money supply. The attempt to restore liquidity by selling assets to repay loans and increase bank reserves, while individually rational, would be collectively self-defeating. Fisher calculated that while liquidation reduced nominal private debt by 20 percent from October 1929 to March 1933, real debt rose by 40 percent because of deflation. Increased desire for liquidity by both banks and the public during the debt-deflation process would reduce the money supply even if there were no reduction in the monetary base, as happened in the United States during the Great Depression. As a remedy, Fisher proposed reflation—monetary expansion to raise prices and reduce the real value of existing nominal debt. He praised President Roosevelt's increase of the dollar price of gold.

Although the deflation of 1921 was more rapid than that beginning in 1929, only the latter was followed by a deep depression. Fisher explained this by the much higher value of nominal debt outstanding in 1929, noting the tripling of the nominal value of urban mortgages in the United States from 1920 to 1929 and substantial increases in margin loans and other debts, not reflecting any rise in commodity prices. The vulnerability of the economy to unanticipated deflation would depend on the volume of outstanding debt of fixed nominal value, a concern which motivated the empirical investigation by A. G. Hart (1938) for the Twentieth Century Fund.

Fisher's debt-deflation theory held that, given sufficient outstanding debt of fixed nominal value and a large enough initial shock, a price deflation could become cumulative, reducing real aggregate demand and leading to a deep depression. This channel for deflation to reduce real demand is important for the debate whether wage and price flexibility ensures the return of a monetary economy to full employment equilibrium after a negative demand shock. The so-called Keynes effect of a lower price level, reducing interest rates and stimulating investment by reducing liquidity preference (in Hicks's diagram, shifting the LM curve to the right), will not work if nominal interest rates are bound from below (as in the United States in the 1930s, when the Treasury bill rate was 0.375 percent). A reduced price level would stimulate demand even in a liquidity trap through the Pigou-Haberler effect of the increased real value of outside money on net wealth and hence on consumption. Kalecki and Keynes noted as early as 1944 that this effect depended only on the amount of outside money, not on bank deposits backed by inside debt and, Keynes argued, not on government debt.

James Tobin (1980) argues that the Pigou-Haberler stimulus from an increased value of outside money due to price deflation must be balanced against Fisher's contractionary debt-deflation effect. Tobin extends the debt-deflation effect to the influence on spending of a wealth transfer from debtors to creditors, who presumably became debtors and creditors because of differing propensities to spend. He points out that "the gross amount of these 'inside' assets was and is orders of magnitude larger than the net amount of the base . . . if the spending propensity were systematically greater for debtors, even by a small amount, the Pigou effect would be swamped by this Fisher effect (1980, 10)." Models such as that of Tobin (1975), incorporating both the Fisher effect of more rapid deflation reducing demand and the real-balance effect of a lower price level stimulating demand, can display the property of a stable return to potential output after shocks of less than some critical value, but not for larger shocks, with the critical value depending on the volume of inside debt fixed in nominal value. This fits in with the argument of chapter nineteen of Keynes's *General Theory* that wage and price flexibility does not guarantee return to full employment.

Interest in Fisher's debt-deflation theory of depressions was revived both by the controversy whether increased price flexibility is stabilizing and by the growth of nominal debt in the 1980s, notably junk bonds (corporate debt rated below investment grade) issued to finance mergers and acquisitions, which drew post-Keynesian attention to Hyman Minsky's work on financial-system fragility. Minsky draws on the insights of both Fisher and Keynes to argue that monetary economies are subject to fluctuations because of the fragility of nominally indebted agents and institutions, and stresses the stabilizing role of the central bank.

Robert W. Dimand

See also FISHER, IRVING; MINSKY, HYMAN PHILLIP; PIGOU-HABERLER EFFECT

Bibliography

Dimand, R. W. 1994. "Irving Fisher's Debt-Deflation Theory of Great Depressions." *Review of Social Economy* 52:92–107.

Federal Reserve Bank of Kansas City. 1986. *Debt, Financial Stability, and Public Policy.* Kansas City, Mo.: Federal Reserve Bank of Kansas City.

Fisher, I. 1932. *Booms and Depressions.* New York: Adelphi.

———. 1933. "The Debt-Deflation Theory of Great Depressions." *Econometrica* 1:337–57.

Hart, A. G. 1938. *Debts and Recovery.* New York: Twentieth Century Fund.

Keynes, J. M. [1931] 1973. "An Economic Analysis of Unemployment." In *The Collected Writings of John Maynard Keynes.* Vol. 13, edited by D. M. Moggeridge, 343–67. London: Macmillan.

Kindleberger, C. P. 1989. *Manias, Panics, and Crashes.* Rev. ed. New York: Basic Books.

King, M. 1994. "Debt Deflation: Theory and Evidence." *European Economic Review* 38:419–45.

Minsky, H. P. 1982a. *Can "It" Happen Again?* Armonk, N.Y.: M. E. Sharpe.

———. 1982b. "Debt Deflation Processes in Today's Institutional Environment." *Banca Nazionale del Lavoro Quarterly Review,* December, 375–93.

———. 1986. *Stabilizing an Unstable Economy.* New Haven: Yale Univ. Press.

Tobin, J. 1975. "Keynesian Models of Recession and Depression." *American Economic Review* 65:195–202.

———. 1980. *Asset Accumulation and Economic Activity.* Chicago: Univ. of Chicago Press.

Veblen, T. B. 1904. *The Theory of Business Enterprise.* New York: Scribner.

Wojnilower, A. 1980. "The Central Role of Credit Crunches in Recent Financial History." *Brookings Papers on Economic Activity,* Number Two, 277–326.

De Foville, Alfred (1842–1913)

Despite an engineering diploma from the Ecole Polytechnique, Alfred de Foville abandoned the public-sector appointment to which his qualifications entitled him to continue his studies in law, history, and architecture. Eventually appointed to the Conseil d'Etat and the upper reaches of the civil service, he became head of the Bureau des Statistiques in 1877 where he began the development of economic statistics in France. His work led him to an interest in the growth and fluctuation of national wealth over time. In 1892, as a member of the French delegation, he took part in the International

Monetary Conference in Brussels, also attending the Latin Union Conference in the following year.

De Foville attached great importance to monetary questions. Thus, in *La France Economique*, he explored how currencies evolved in France and abroad, calculating the currency stocks of the main trading nations. This information was important since the currency of each country comprising the Latin Union (Belgium, Italy, France, Switzerland, Greece) could be used in the others. When France and other countries were still maintaining bimetallic standards, it was not without interest to know the quantities of coins struck by the different countries. De Foville found that in 1884, foreign coins accounted for 10.4 percent of the gold coins and 28.8 percent of the silver coins circulating in France. Silver was then depreciating in terms of gold, so that, in accord with Gresham's Law, silver tended to enter and gold to leave the country.

De Foville's interests in statistics can be traced to his "Essai sur les variations de prix au XIXème siècle" which won the prize of the Académie des Sciences Morales et Politiques in 1873. The essay was not published, but its substance can be found in numerous articles on the topic that the weekly *L'Economiste Français* published between 1874 and 1878. De Foville scrutinized the evolution of prices in France between 1820 and 1870. He distinguished eleven groups of prices and searched for the major causes of their variations. Moreover, he used a general index number which weighted the relative importance of the groups of prices. This index number allowed him to estimate the evolution of the purchasing power of money. This general index number resembled the Laspeyres index. In subsequent works, he employed a Paasche index as well. In 1879, he estimated the prices of imports and exports, using customs statistics with a Paasche index. His conception of price evolution and his calculations are contained in his article "Prix" for the *Nouveau Dictionnaire d'Economie Politique* (1892).

However important de Foville's role in establishing a modern statistical office in France, his most original contribution lies in the study of business cycles, particularly his graphical representation of cyclical fluctuations. In an 1888 essay, de Foville attempted to depict business cycles despite "the apparent independence of economic factors" (1888, 244). In so doing, he enlarged and systematized a notion suggested previously by Neumann-Spallart (1887). The idea was to take into account all social phenomena that might affect "the general prosperity of the country." De Foville chose a double-entry system to represent conditions in the time period 1877–87. The years were in columns and the "social phenomena" in rows. The intersections of any given column and row represent the condition of economic and social variables in a given year. "When it is a good year, the corresponding square is red. The square is pink when the year is only fairly good. It is grey, (*demi-deuil*) when the year is mediocre, rather poor than good. Finally black shows the years that are really bad."

Among the large number of quantifiable indicators chosen by de Foville, some grew (declined) during the periods of prosperity (depression), or conversely. But, as de Foville's aim was to show the general evolution of economic activity, he assumed that the direction (positive or negative) of the correlation is reflected in the choice of colors attributed to each square (thus an increase of bankruptcies associated with depressions is shown by a darker color on the relevant square). Betraying the traditional reluctance of French liberals to use mathematical statistics, de Foville justified his presentation in terms of his conception of statistics as a means to communicate information in a convenient synthetic form "that even the masses could understand" (1888, 245). For an author widely versed in mathematics with a professional interest in developing statistics as a tool, this reluctance is surprising to say the least.

The originality of his work lies in his attempt to remedy the absence of general statistics on business cycles by observing variables that could play the role of warning signals (e.g., postal traffic) as well as variables less certainly linked with economic activity (e.g., suicides or the excess of births over deaths). Despite its inadequacies, de Foville's attempt is a landmark in the history of the development of economic barometers.

Alain Alcouffe
Gilbert Ducos

See also INDICATORS, QUALITATIVE

Bibliography

de Foville, A. 1872. "Essai sur les variations de prix au XIXe siècle." Manuscript in the archives of l'Académie des Sciences Morales et Politiques.

———. 1875. "Les variations de prix en France depuis un demi-siècle." *L'Economiste français* 9 janvier 35–37.

———. 1879. "Le mouvement des prix dans le commerce extérieur de la France." *L'Economiste français* 5 juillet 3–5, 19 juillet 64–65, 1 novembre 533–34.

———. 1888. "Essai de Météorologie Economique et Sociale." *Journal de la Société de Statistique de Paris* July, 243–49.

———. 1887–90. *La France Economique.* 2d ed. Paris: A. Colin et cie.

———. 1892. "Prix." *Nouveau Dictionnaire d'Economie Politique.* Vol. 2. Edited by L. Say, 591–617. Paris: Berger-Levrault.

Laspeyres, E. 1871. "Die Berechnung einer mittleren Waarenpreissteigerung." *Jahrbücher für Nationalökonomie und Statistik* 16:296–314.

Neumann-Spallart, F. X. von. 1887. "Mesure des variations de l'état économique et social des peuples." *Bulletin de l'Institut International de Statistique* 2:150–59.

Paasche, H. 1874. "Über die Preisentwicklung der letzten Jahre nach der Hamburger Börsennotirungen." *Jahrbücher für Nationalökonomie und Statistik* 23:168–78.

Demand for Currency

The term "currency" generally refers to circulating media of exchange or "hand-to-hand" money. It may thus include private banknotes and redeemable or irredeemable government paper money as well as token and full-bodied coins.

The public demands currency because checks—the most widely used final-payment medium—are less convenient than currency for small purchases and because sellers fear that unknown customers will draw checks on accounts lacking sufficient funds. The relative demand for currency, measured by the ratio of the public's holdings of currency to its holdings of demand deposits, has in recent years been slightly over one-third in the United States. This ratio varies from one-fifth to one-half in other countries, higher values being typical of poorer countries.

Before World War II, the relative demand for currency in the U.S. fell steadily, owing to the growing popularity of checks and checking accounts. This trend seems to have reversed itself subsequently. In part this may reflect a rise in "underground" economic activity, for which currency is preferred because it offers greater anonymity than checks. However, the reversal probably occurred because demand shifted from demand deposits to other financial instruments (such as NOW accounts and money market mutual funds) that now offer check-writing privileges.

Seasonal and cyclical changes also affect the relative demand for currency. In fractional-reserve banking systems, fluctuations in currency demand owing to seasonal and cyclical factors are an important cause of changes in the total money stock. Phillip Cagan (1965) found that such fluctuations accounted for approximately half of all cyclical fluctuations in the U.S. money stock between 1875 and 1960. This effect arises because conventional central-banking arrangements confine the public's currency holdings to paper money issued by the central bank. These holdings are thus part of the stock of high-powered money (the remainder is held by banks as reserves against outstanding deposits). With a constant base, a change in the demand for currency shifts base money into or out of bank reserves. This in turn causes a multiple change in the quantity of deposits, as each unit of reserves supports several units of deposits.

Fluctuations in the money stock linked to changes in currency demand have been an important cause of financial crises. Before 1914, harvest-time increases in the demand for currency in the U.S. often led to financial disturbances. The disturbances were caused primarily by restrictive bond-collateral requirements on the notes of national banks that prevented those banks from issuing more of their own notes to meet customers' demands, forcing the banks instead to draw down their reserves. The worst of these episodes, in 1893 and 1907, were marked by a lack of currency for the conduct of everyday business. Banks, bank-clearinghouse associations, and nonbank business firms were led to issue currency substitutes illegally.

World War I also caused a large increase in the relative demand for currency, which the newly established Federal Reserve System accommodated by increasing its discounts. After the war the return of currency to the commercial banks was not offset by an equivalent contraction of their Federal Reserve credits. An inflationary boom resulted, which led to a financial crisis and deflation in 1920–21.

By far the most serious U.S. crisis in which currency demand played a part was the monetary contraction of 1930–33. Expectations of falling interest rates and real income following the stock-market crash prompted the initial increase in currency demand. Higher postal rates and a federal tax on checks, both imposed in mid-1932, reinforced this increase. The Federal Reserve System failed to accommodate the currency drain, which, together with a deepening agricultural crisis, led to an unprecedented number of bank closings. Then, beginning in October 1932, Nevada and several other states responded to bank closings by declaring bank holidays. These holidays—combined with depositors' fears that President Roosevelt would devalue the dollar—provoked even more massive currency withdrawals from still-open banks and led Roosevelt to declare a national bank holiday.

The conventional solution to fluctuating currency demand is for the monetary authority to use open-market operations to accommodate shifts in currency demand. A shortcoming of this approach is that changes in the demand for currency are often unpredictable, so that compensatory adjustments to the monetary base can only be made imperfectly and belatedly. Another problem is that increasing the monetary base through open-market purchases may not increase the reserves of the banks immediately affected by shifts in the demand for currency. Interbank lending mitigates, but cannot entirely eliminate, these mismatches.

More radical suggestions for avoiding the destabilizing effects of changes in currency demand include proposals for 100-percent-reserve banking and for the competitive, unregulated issue of private banknotes. The former solution was first suggested by Irving Fisher and by Chicago School economists during the 1930s. Its principal disadvantage is that it would prevent commercial banks from using deposits as a source of loanable funds. Monetary savings could no longer finance bank-intermediated investments.

Free note issue, in contrast, would preserve the intermediary role of commercial banks by allowing banks to replace high-powered reserve media with their own liabilities in supplying the public with currency. Given the power to issue their own notes, banks could alter the mix of their outstanding liabilities to accommodate routine changes in the currency requirements of their customers. Because it would not change banks' holdings of high-powered reserves, such a swapping of liabilities would not change,

other things equal, the volume of deposits. Thus, adjusting the stock of base money to achieve reserve compensation would be unnecessary. This solution is effective, however, only when currency demand does not increase because of a loss of confidence in the banking system.

Although interest in competitive note issue has grown substantially in recent years, the idea still lacks popular support owing to fears that free note issue would be inflationary and that it would lead to a confusing and unmanageable mixture of currency instruments, introducing new sources of financial instability.

George A. Selgin

See also AGRICULTURE AND BUSINESS CYCLES; BANKING PANICS; CENTRAL BANKING; CLEARINGHOUSES; CRISIS OF 1907; DEMAND FOR MONEY; FEDERAL RESERVE SYSTEM: 1914–1941; FINANCIAL INTERMEDIATION; FREE BANKING; GREAT DEPRESSION IN UNITED STATES; PANIC OF 1893; SEASONAL FLUCTUATIONS AND FINANCIAL CRISES; SUPPLY OF MONEY

Bibliography

Becker, W. E., Jr. 1975. "Determinants of the United States Currency-Demand Deposit Ratio." *Journal of Finance* 30:57–79.

Boughton, J. M. and E. R. Wicker. 1979. "The Behavior of the Currency-Deposit Ratio during the Great Depression." *Journal of Money, Credit and Banking* 11:405–18.

Cagan, P. 1958. "The Demand for Currency Relative to Total Money Supply." National Bureau of Economic Research Occasional Paper No. 62. New York: NBER.

———. 1965. *Determinants and Effects of Changes in the Stock of Money, 1870–1960.* New York: NBER.

Dotsey, M. 1988. "The Demand for Currency in the United States." *Journal of Money, Credit and Banking* 20:22–40.

Hart, A. G. 1935. "The Chicago Plan of Banking Reform." *Review of Economic Studies* 2:104–16.

Khazzoom, J. D. 1966. *The Currency Ratio in Developing Countries.* New York: Praeger.

McDonald, S. L. 1956. "Some Factors Influencing the Increased Relative Use of Currency Since 1939." *Journal of Finance* 11:313–27.

Selgin, G. 1988. "Accommodating Changes in the Relative Demand for Currency: Free Banking versus Central Banking." *Cato Journal* 7:621–41.

Demand for Money

Money consists of financial instruments that have particular qualities desirable to individual holders. Explaining the demand for money means identifying these qualities and comparing them with those of nonmonetary assets.

Classical works on money (e.g., Fisher 1913, Wicksell [1906] 1935) emphasized three functions that money performs: medium of exchange, store of value, and unit of account. However, until Keynes ([1936] 1973) discussed why individuals hold money in terms of the transactions, precautionary, and speculative motives, little attempt was made to analyze the form of the money-demand function. At about the same time, Hicks ([1935] 1967) proposed that the demand for money (and for other financial assets) should be analyzed using the same marginalist approach as other goods. Later work on the demand for money can be seen to flow from this proposal.

A discussion of the demand for money requires clarity about which assets are classified as money. Under the classical definition of money in terms of its functions, only those assets which are media of exchange can be classified as money. In the light of later work, this seems to be an unduly narrow classification. Thus, if the store-of-value function of money is emphasized, there are assets that are equally good stores of value and could thus also be classified as money. The concept of *liquidity* is important in this respect. Assets are liquid insofar as they can be sold at short notice with no significant loss. As the medium of exchange, money is normally considered the most liquid of all assets. We may, therefore, classify financial assets as money if they are highly liquid. The form of the demand function is obviously very sensitive to how money is defined.

The transactions motive for holding money is the one closest in spirit to the medium-of-exchange function of money, and therefore to the quantity theory of money. Keynes, working in the Cambridge tradition, viewed income as an important variable influencing the desire of individuals to hold transaction balances. Baumol (1952) and Tobin (1956) subsequently formulated the decision problem within an inventory model. They considered an individual who receives income at the start of a period and spends at a constant rate through the period. Such an individual would be sacrificing interest payments by holding non-interest-bearing (narrow) money for the whole period, but would incur a lump-sum cost of converting interest-bearing bonds into money. If interest rates increased, the average amount of money held would decline as individuals arranged more conversions of smaller amounts. Alternatively, if conversion costs increased, the incentive to economize on conversion of bonds to money by adding to money balances would increase. A further implication of this model is that there are economies of scale in holding transaction balances. However, this result applies only to narrow money, since the real-world interpretation of bonds would include assets within the definition of broad money.

The development of the inventory-theoretic approach to the transactions demand for money established that the ratio of (narrow) money balances to income (the income velocity of money defined by the classical quantity theory) could no longer be treated as constant, determined by institutional arrangements, but would vary with the rate of interest. Since it is well established that velocity and short-term interest rates vary over the course of the cycle (Friedman and Schwartz 1982), this is an important result. In particular, the income velocity of money and short-term interest rates are both found to vary procyclically with velocity coincident and short-term interest rates lagging the cycle. Such behavior is consistent with a demand-for-money function derived from an inventory-theoretic foundation. The model also explains how changes in institutional arrangements lead to secular changes in the demand for narrow money. This results from changes in the conversion cost between money and bonds, and through the economies of scale which the inventory-theoretic approach establishes. However, as has been pointed out by Akerlof and Milbourne (1980), the inventory-theoretic approach must be interpreted with care, because of the integer constraint on the number of conversions between bonds and money. This means that there may be very little incentive to respond immediately to changes in interest rates or income-expenditure patterns.

Introducing stochastic features into the transactions demand for money is an obvious extension of the Baumol-Tobin model and leads in two directions. One is a modeling of the transactions demand for money where both payments and income can be stochastic. This has been considered by Miller and Orr (1966). More recently, Frenkel and Jovanovic (1980) have demonstrated that the results obtained by Baumol and Tobin hold qualitatively in a stochastic environment.

An implication of stochastic cash flows, which generates an additional motive for holding money, is that assets may have to be liquidated unexpectedly at a substantial loss. Tsiang (1969) introduced a stochastic rate of expenditure into a Baumol-Tobin model. If unexpected conversions of bonds into money occasion penalties, individuals have an incentive to reduce the expected costs of cash management by holding additional money balances. Such analysis accounts for the precautionary demand. This demand depends on the rate of interest, the size of the expected liquidation cost, and the subjectively perceived uncertainty concerning income or expenditure. In a stable economic environment, precautionary holdings of cash balances may be small compared to transaction holdings. However, it would be reasonable to suppose that, in periods of significant turmoil, the precautionary demand for money would account for a substantial part of the holding of narrow money balances. Once again, note that these results hold for narrow money balances only, since the bonds which are the alternative, interest-bearing assets, are included in broader definitions of money.

The third motive for holding money is the speculative motive which is related to the store-of-value function and the desire of individuals to hold their wealth in the most suitable mix (portfolio) of financial assets. Keynes ([1936] 1973) analyzed this motive by considering how expectations of future interest rates affect the choice between holding money or bonds. Agents hold (narrow) money if the expected return on bonds (interest earnings plus capital gain) is less than zero and hold bonds if it is greater than zero. If expectations of future interest rates are static and distributed smoothly across individuals, the aggregate speculative demand for money responds gradually to changes in the current interest rate. Tobin (1958) regarded the expectations approach as too restrictive, because it neglected the risk that expectations are incorrect. He developed a mean-variance portfolio-selection model of the demand for money in which risk-averse individuals would normally hold both money and bonds. In his model the speculative demand for money depends on the mean and variance of the probability distribution of returns on interest-earning assets, individuals' attitudes to risk, and total wealth. It has been widely recognized that the speculative motive applies to a broad definition of money. In particular, there are interest-earning assets that are not susceptible to capital-value fluctuations (for example, bank savings accounts), and for which the return (net of any transaction costs), over the holding period, is positive. In this case, money is dominated as a speculative asset and hence a speculative demand for money function should relate to a broad definition of money only.

Introducing rate-of-return uncertainty into the demand for money also provides further insight into the behavior of money holdings during financial panics and crises. Periods of financial turmoil are characterized by high variances of asset returns and, thus, an increased desire of individuals to hold safe assets. The previous discussion suggests that this would mean a shift into assets like bank savings deposits. However, if a financial crisis threatens the safety of the banking system, then a shift into narrow money may result. In very severe panics, confidence in the central bank may be shaken, in which case the only safe haven will be foreign currencies or physical assets, as occurs in episodes of hyperinflation.

These ideas lead to the demand-for-money function proposed by Friedman (1956) who maintains that individuals do not consider just financial assets when deciding on their holdings of money. This implies that inflation, and its effect on the return to holding real assets, affect the demand for money. If the only relevant choice is between money and financial instruments (assets), the rate of price inflation affects the demand for money through the nominal rate of return on assets. If individuals can also hold real assets, the rate of inflation affects money demand directly through the average return on these real assets. The idea was used by Cagan (1956) in studying the demand for money under hyperinflation. Assuming a very simple demand-for-money function whose only argument was expected inflation, Cagan analyzed the dynamics of the price level conditional on the assumed dynamics of monetary growth. The basic behavioral hypothesis underpinning Cagan's formulation was that the demand for money would go to zero as the inflation rate approached infinity. This accorded well with the experience of Central and Eastern Europe during the 1920s when money was abandoned as hyperinflation took hold. This formulation clearly applies to any financial instrument whose rate of interest does not rise in line with the rate of inflation. Note that since inflationary expectations determine the demand for money, even if monetary growth is still at reasonable levels but is expected to rise to the very high levels associated with hyperinflation, money would no longer be held.

Empirical work on the demand for money has shown that the basic functional forms implied by the three motives for holding money cannot adequately explain short-run changes in the demand for money, over the course of the business cycle. This has led to the use of a partial-adjustment specification within a speculative model, which has been justified by the possible impact of transactions costs and the resulting lags in adjustment to the desired portfolio. However, the order of magnitude of transactions costs required for the partial-adjustment model to work seems unacceptably high. An alternative approach is the buffer-stock idea which concentrates on the transactions motive, utilizing an (s,S) inventory model (Laidler 1984), familiar to analysts of optimal stock-holding behavior. The idea is that, faced with stochastic cash flow, individuals will set upper and lower bounds for cash balances and only undertake adjustment if the actual holdings move outside of these limits. However, a theory of the short-run demand for money, that can adequately explain the observed fluctuations in money holdings, does not yet seem to be available.

David G. Dickinson

See also AGGREGATE SUPPLY AND DEMAND; DEMAND FOR CURRENCY; LIQUIDITY PREMIUM; MONETARY DISEQUILIBRIUM THEORIES OF THE BUSINESS CYCLE; MONETARY EQUILIBRIUM THEORIES OF THE BUSINESS CYCLE; SUPPLY OF MONEY; TOBIN, JAMES

Bibliography
Akerlof, G. A. and Milbourne, R. M. 1980. "The Short Run Demand for Money." *Economic Journal* 90:885–900.
Baumol, W. J. 1952. "The Transactions Demand for Money: An Inventory Theoretic Approach." *Quarterly Journal of Economics* 66:545–56.
Cagan, P. 1956. "The Monetary Dynamics of Hyperinflation." In *Studies in the Quantity Theory of Money,* edited by M. Friedman, 25–117. Chicago: Univ. of Chicago Press.
Fisher, I. 1913. *The Purchasing Power of Money.* 2d ed. New York: Macmillan.
Frenkel, J. A. and Jovanovic, B. 1980. "On Transactions and Precautionary Demand for Money." *Quarterly Journal of Economics* 94:25–43.
Friedman, M. 1956. "The Quantity Theory of Money: A Restatement." In *Studies in the Quantity Theory of Money,* edited by M. Friedman, 3–21. Chicago: Univ. of Chicago Press.
Friedman, M. and Schwartz, A. J. 1982. *Monetary Trends in the U.S. and the U.K.: Their Relation to Income, Prices and Interest Rates.* Chicago: Univ. of Chicago Press.
Hicks, J. R. [1935] 1967. "A Suggestion for Simplifying the Theory of Money." Chap. 4 in *Critical Essays in Monetary Theory.* Oxford: Clarendon Press.
Keynes, J. M. [1930] 1971. *A Treatise on Money.* 2 vols. Vols. 5–6 of *The Collected Writings of John Maynard Keynes.* London: Macmillan.
———. [1936] 1973. *The General Theory of Employment, Interest, and Money.* Vol. 7 of *The Collected Writings of John Maynard Keynes.* London: Macmillan.
Laidler, D. 1984. "The 'Buffer Stock' Notion in Monetary Economics." *Economic Journal* 94(Supplement):17–34.
———. 1985. *The Demand for Money: Theories, Evidence, and Problems.* 3d ed. New York: Harper and Row.
Miller, M. H. and Orr, D. 1966. "A Model of the Demand for Money by Firms." *Quarterly Journal of Economics* 80:413–35.
Tobin, J. 1956. "The Interest Elasticity of the Transactions Demand for Cash." *Review of Economics and Statistics* 38:241–47.
———. 1958. "Liquidity Preference as Behaviour Towards Risk." *Review of Economic Studies* 25:65–86.
Tsiang, S. C. 1969. "The Precautionary Demand for Money: An Inventory Theoretic Analysis." *Journal of Political Economy* 77:99–117.
Wicksell, K. [1906] 1935. *Lectures on Political Economy.* Vol. 2, *Prices.* London: Routledge and Kegan Paul.

D

Depression of 1873–1879

The depression of the 1870s was the longest cyclical contraction in United States history, lasting from 1873 to 1879, as measured by the National Bureau of Economic Research. Unfortunately, the scholarly literature on this depression is very limited. Rendigs Fels (1959) provides the only extensive analysis of the causes of this depression, which he attributes to the deterioration of investment opportunities, especially in railroad and building construction.

It appears from the meager available data that the contraction was primarily a monetary phenomenon. Prices fell by about 25 percent, but the decline in real output was probably no greater than 5 percent. The decline in output was concentrated in railroad construction, building construction, and manufacturing industries that produced raw materials for these two. Most other manufacturing industries did not contract and some even continued to expand modestly during the depression. Frickey's (1947) general index of manufacturing production shows a 10-percent decline from 1872 to 1876. The decline in durable goods was approximately 30 percent, with the biggest decline in iron and steel (45 percent). Long's (1940) index of building construction declined by over 50 percent and remained at this low level throughout the 1870s. On the other hand, agriculture continued to expand fairly rapidly.

The railroad industry was by far the most important in generating the depression of the 1870s. The mileage of railroads in operation increased by 50 percent from 1867 to 1873, and then hardly increased at all until 1878. Some lines, such as the Northern Pacific, were left uncompleted until the 1880s. Railroad construction absorbed 15–20 percent of the total capital investment in the economy during the boom and was financed almost entirely by bonds, which were sold primarily to foreign, especially English, investors. Railroad construction also had important direct and indirect effects on other industries that produced its inputs: iron and steel, locomotives, cars, mining, etc. Thus the primary questions to be answered for an understanding of the causes of the depression of the 1870s are why the railroad boom of the late 1860s and early 1870s collapsed so completely and why railroad building remained depressed for so long.

The collapse of the railroad boom was initiated by the widespread default on loans by railroad companies in the fall of 1873. Railroad companies could not service their debt because the actual profits of new railroads turned out to be far below expectations. The insufficiency of profits was caused by over-optimistic expectations of the demand for railroads and by increased construction costs (wages, raw materials, and interest rates) during the boom. Fraud also played a role: the financing device of subsidiary construction companies enabled developers to reap large profits by overcharging costs to the parent companies, but exacerbated the financial crisis of the latter. Railroad investment remained depressed until 1878 because of continued pessimism about profit prospects (Fels 1959). Long also attributes the depression in building construction to a sharp decline in profit expectations, due primarily to psychological factors (excessive swings from optimism to pessimism).

The collapse of the railroad boom also created a banking crisis in October 1873 because many large New York banks were engaged in the dubious practice of making long-term loans to the railroads. The banking crisis was intensified by structural weaknesses in the banking system: primarily the absence of a central bank that could act as the "lender of last resort," and secondarily the pyramiding of reserves in New York banks (Sprague 1910). The banking crisis in turn exacerbated the depression by creating a shortage of capital and credit, as the banks reduced their lending and foreign investors stopped buying American bonds.

Fels argues that the depression of the 1870s was also prolonged by the U.S. monetary system, which was based on inconvertible paper with flexible exchange rates (the U.S. went off the gold standard during the Civil War and did not return to it until 1879). Under the paper system, the depression caused the dollar to appreciate, rather than induce a balance-of-trade surplus which would have mitigated the contraction. Fels also attributes the relative mildness of the decline in output to the high degree of price flexibility during this period.

The prolonged depression of the 1870s resulted in a significant increase of social unrest among farmers and workers. The decline in agricultural prices forced many small farmers into bankruptcy. Farmers responded to these difficult times by agitating for "easy money" (both greenbacks and silver) and against railroads, which were seen as a major contributor to their problems. These movements achieved the passage of the Silver Purchase Act of 1878 and of laws regulating the railroads in a few states. The most important organizational form of these farmers' movements, the Grange, grew rapidly during the 1870s.

The depression of the 1870s also meant hard times for workers, especially railroad workers, who were forced to accept a series of wage cuts and labor-cutting retrenchments. In July 1877, another attempted wage cut provoked the nation's first nationwide strike, which effectively stopped most railroad traffic for a week or so. In a few cities, such as Pittsburgh, Buffalo, and St. Louis, the railroad strike spread into a general strike of all workers. The railroad strike was eventually ended when President Hayes assigned the U.S. Army to get the trains running again.

Recovery finally began in 1878. During the depression, railroad companies were reorganized on sounder financial footing and railroad construction was again the main impetus in the upswing. The number of railroad miles built rose spectacularly from 2,665 in 1878 to 11,569 in 1882. Especially good agricultural crops also contributed to the recovery.

Fred Moseley

See also CRISIS OF 1873; GOLD STANDARD; GOLD STANDARD: CAUSES AND CONSEQUENCES; GREAT DEPRESSION OF 1873–1896; LENDER OF LAST RESORT

Bibliography
Fels, R. 1959. "The Cycle of 1865–79." Chap. 6 in *American Business Cycles, 1865–97*. Chapel Hill: Univ. of North Carolina Press.

Frickey, E. 1947. *Production in the U.S., 1860–1914*. Cambridge: Harvard Univ. Press.

Long, C. 1940. *Building Cycles and the Theory of Investment*. Princeton: Princeton Univ. Press.

Partington, J. 1929. *Railroad Purchasing and the Business Cycle*. Washington, D.C.: Brookings Institution.

Rezneck, S. [1950] 1968. "Distress, Relief, and Discontent in the United States during the Depression of 1873–78." Chap. 6 in *Business Depressions and Financial Panics*. New York: Greenwood Press.

Shannon, F. 1945. *The Farmers' Last Frontier*. Armonk, N.Y.: M. E. Sharpe.

Sprague, O. 1910. *History of Crises Under the National Banking System*. Washington, D.C.: Government Printing Office.

Depression of 1882–1885

D

The downturn of 1882–85 was a serious depression which was attended by a banking panic in New York and also had a significant impact on financial institutions outside New York.

After the long depression of the middle and late 1870s, business prospects began to improve in early 1879. The United States had successfully returned to the gold standard, and a bountiful harvest, combined with low agricultural production in Europe, provided business in the United States with a decisive stimulus.

Railroad construction was the principal impetus for the 1879–82 upswing. The number of railroad miles built rose from 2,665 in 1878 to 11,569 in 1882. According to Walton and Rockoff (1990), the expansion of the American railroad system accounted for 15 percent of U.S. capital formation in the 1880s.

Much of the railroad building aimed at completing the main lines of roads that had been left unfinished after the panic of 1873 and the subsequent depression. Even more important was the construction of feeders and branches for parent lines. Repairs and improvements postponed in the depression were also initiated.

Another impetus for the upswing was building construction. The value of construction permits rose two and a half times between 1879 and 1883. Roofing slate production rose by more than 50 percent over the same period.

The favorable balance of trade increased gold supplies, allowing the money supply to expand as needed to support increased economic activity. Interest rates remained relatively low during the expansion, and capital, particularly domestic capital, was plentiful.

The early 1880s were characterized by full employment despite increased immigration. Unemployment rates are estimated to have been under 2.5 percent.

The 1882–85 Business Decline

The cyclical decline of the early 1880s began gradually. Profits declined sharply in 1882 and business deteriorated steadily in 1883. However, not until 1884 did a rapid contraction begin.

Railroad prospects worsened in 1882. Rate wars and mismanagement undermined public confidence in rail stocks and bonds. Businessmen grew less willing to invest in railroads because expected profits had declined. Railroad construction fell from its peak of 11,569 miles in 1882 to 6741 miles in 1883 and 2866 miles in 1885.

The railroad decline not only eliminated the jobs of many workers employed in railroad building, but also transmitted the depression to other industries. For example, the price of steel rails fell from $71 per ton in January 1880 to $20 per ton in January 1884. In 1884, blast furnaces and rail mills were shut down. Workers were laid off and wages were cut. Production and wages also fell in other branches of mining and manufacturing. Poor crops in 1883 reduced the demand for rail freight cars. Although the money supply did not contract during 1883, banks became reluctant to make new loans.

In 1884, a bank panic occurred in New York. On 8 May the brokerage firm Grant and Ward failed, dragging down the Marine National Bank which had "overcertified" a Grant and Ward check for $750,000. Five days later the Second National Bank had to close its doors, because the president had stolen $3 million. A run forced the Metropolitan Bank to close the next day and financial panic ensued. Stock prices fell rapidly as attempts were made to raise cash and recall loans. At one point interest rates rose to 4 percent for a twenty-four-hour period.

Under an act of 1878, the Secretary of the Treasury had to buy and coin $2–4 million dollars of silver every month. During the depression, the banks retained their gold and made payments to the Treasury in silver. According to Friedman and Schwartz (1973) and Fels (1959), this led to fears that the United States would go off the gold standard. Foreigners started selling American securities and gold was exported in the amount of $32 million in 1882 and $41 million in 1884.

The stringency in the money market was occasioned not only by the displacement of gold by newly coined silver, but by the loss of bank reserves due to railroad and other construction loans. It was practically impossible for banks to collect their call loans as the borrowers could obtain money by selling their securities only at severely depressed prices. The New York clearinghouse issued certificates (as it had done during the panic of 1873) which found ready acceptance among the business community, thereby calming fears and greatly reducing the heavy withdrawals. According to Lightner (1922), eleven New York banks went into receivership during 1884 and more than 100 state banks and banking firms throughout the country with liabilities exceeding $32 million failed.

Smaller institutions failed in every state, but gold and currency payments were never suspended. The issue of loan certificates was confined to the New York City banks, which soon were able to collect their loans and make good their reserves.

In 1883, the rapid repayment of the national debt also had a major impact on the money supply. From November 1882 to November 1883, more than $105 million of the public debt was redeemed.

The Severity and Consequences of the Depression of 1882–85

The downswing of the early 1880s was severe enough for most investigators to rate it a major depression. Using an index comprising six series (railway revenues, pig-iron production, coal production, domestic cotton consumption, bank clearings, and merchandise imports), Rezneck ([1956] 1968) found that business activity fell by almost a fourth. The decline in durable-goods output alone was also nearly 25 percent. New York City bank clearings dropped from more than $46 billion in 1882 to $25 billion in 1885. According to Carroll Wright (1886) (the first U.S. Commissioner of Labor), nearly one million persons were out of work in 1884–85 or about 7.5 percent of the labor force. By October 1884, the unemployment rate in the Northeast was 13 percent. This compared to an estimated unemployment rate of 2.5 percent at full employment. Rising unemployment caused immigration to fall from 750,000 in 1882 to 400,000 in 1885.

During the depression, wheat fell to $.64 a bushel, one-half its normal price at the time. Farmers suffered enormous losses and would not repay their loans to banks and Eastern creditors. Kansas farmers burned corn instead of coal or wood in 1885, because corn was the cheaper fuel. Agricultural conditions were barely improved in the ensuing period of recovery and prosperity between 1885 and 1890.

Business failures, which totaled 6,738 in 1883, rose to nearly 10,000 in 1884 and 1885. The liabilities of bankrupt firms, amounting to $65 million in 1880, rose to $226 million in 1884.

The Revival

By May 1885, the contraction was over. The cyclical decline came to an end partly because of the severe depletion of inventories and because consumption tends to fall less than income. The improvement of general business was one of the causes of railroad revival. The upswing continued to be sluggish during the first part of 1886, but with good crop prospects and expanded investment in railroad and building construction, the revival became vigorous in the second half of the year.

Even during the depression of 1882–85, investors maintained confidence in the long-term earnings of the railroads. However, the decline in dividends on railroad stocks during 1883–85 caused railroad investors to be cautious even after the crisis had passed. By the close of 1885, however, the railroad companies had found it both practical and necessary to divide the traffic among themselves to maintain rates and stabilize profits. During 1886, confidence in the railroad industry was fully restored, and capital once more was invested in new railway construction.

International Dimensions

Great Britain, France, Belgium, and Germany each experienced severe business depressions which began in 1882 and lasted until 1885 or 1886. Studies by Hull (1911) and Lightner (1922) indicate that analysts in each country believed a major cause of the depression was overproduction in manufactures and the impact of foreign competition from the other industrial nations. Moreover, the growth of manufacturing industries in the U.S. greatly reduced the level of manufactured imports, particularly from England.

The failure of the *Union Générale,* a French banking institution, in early 1882 had important consequences for the European financial sector. Nearly £3 million were withdrawn from the Bank of England for France between 30 January 1882 and 15 February 1882. Stock prices fell dramatically, affecting not only France but other neighboring countries.

Alan L. Sorkin

See also BANKING PANICS; CLEARINGHOUSES; GOLD STANDARD; GOLD STANDARD: CAUSES AND CONSEQUENCES; GREAT DEPRESSION OF 1873–1896

Bibliography

Fels, R. 1959. *American Business Cycles, 1865–1897.* Chapel Hill: Univ. of North Carolina Press.

Friedman, M. and A. J. Schwartz. 1963. *A Monetary History of the United States, 1867–1960.* Princeton: Princeton Univ. Press.

Hull, G. 1911. *Industrial Depressions.* New York: Frederick A. Stokes Co.

Lightner, O. 1922. *The History of Business Depressions.* New York: Northeastern Press.

Rezneck, S. [1956] 1968. "Patterns of Thought and Action in an American Depression." Chap. 7 in *Business Depressions and Financial Panics.* New York: Greenwood Press.

U.S. Department of Labor. 1886. *The First Annual Report of the Commissioner of Labor.* Washington, D.C.: Government Printing Office.

Walton, G. and H. Rockoff. 1990. "Transportation, Government Assistance, and Regulation." Chap. 19 in *History of the American Economy.* 6th ed. New York: Harcourt Brace Jovanovich.

D

Depression of 1920–1921

The macroeconomic experiences of the major Western countries differed more sharply during the early 1920s than during any other period in the last hundred years. Although the American economy during these years was affected by the economic consequences of World War I, the depression of 1920–21 and the subsequent recovery were similar in a number of important respects to cycles of more normal times. The situation in Europe, however, was much more strongly influenced by the political and economic repercussions of the war.

At the end of the war, businessmen in the United States were generally expecting the 90 percent increase in the price level that had occurred since 1914 would be largely reversed, just as the price increases of 1861–65 had been substantially reversed. In fact, very little deflation occurred after the war ended. The lack of deflation is attributable to the maintenance of a high level of federal spending well into 1919 and to the continuation of an easy-money policy by the Federal Reserve. A brief recession did begin in August 1918, most likely as an inevitable consequence of the industrial adjustments necessary for a conversion back to peacetime production, but it lasted only seven months. During this brief downturn, pig-iron production fell about 8 percent and automobile production declined about 4 percent. Wages and prices overall declined about 5 percent.

The mildness of the 1918–19 downturn and the failure of a mild deflation to trigger the expected downward spiral towards 1914 price levels increased business and consumer optimism. This optimism combined with the pent-up demand for producer and consumer durables led to a boom in spending on residential construction, business fixed investment, and automobiles. High levels of spending on these goods continued through the beginning of 1920. Compared to the first six months of 1919, residential construction in the first six months of 1920 increased by 40 percent, nonresidential construction increased by 8 percent, the production of producers' durable equipment increased by 30 percent, and the production of automobiles increased by 50 percent.

In other industries, however, the first months of 1920 saw declines in sales. Output of most textile products peaked in December 1919 or January 1920. New orders for most iron and steel products peaked in January 1920. Deflationary forces were beginning to affect the economy. Government purchases declined by 35 percent in real terms between the first quarter of 1919 and the first quarter of 1920. They declined another 15 percent between the first and second quarters of 1920. Exports, which had been surprisingly strong throughout 1919 and in the first quarter of 1920, declined by 20 percent between the first and second quarters of 1920.

Meanwhile, the price level recovered from its mild decline of late 1918–early 1919 and by December 1919 the wholesale price index was 10 percent higher than it had been in December 1918. The Federal Reserve responded by raising discount rates from 4 to 4.75 percent in late 1919 and then to 6 percent in early 1920. When inflation did not appear to be abating, the New York Federal Reserve Bank raised its discount rate to 7 percent on 1 June (a level not reached again until the 1970s). This increase caused a sharp contraction in member-bank borrowing from the Federal Reserve and, consequently, a reduction in member-bank lending to businesses and consumers.

The price level peaked in May and then, under the impact of these contractionary forces, began its most precipitous decline in history. Between May 1920 and January 1922, the wholesale price index declined by 45 percent. Many businesses that had gambled on continued inflation by accumulating inventories of raw materials and intermediate goods sustained heavy losses. To quickly reduce inventories, firms sharply curtailed production. In the automobile industry, production declined by 60 percent between May 1920 and July 1921. Total industrial production declined by 30 percent during the same period.

The downturn, while severe and marked by an unprecedented deflation, was short. The National Bureau of Economic Research dates the trough of the cycle as July 1921. The subsequent recovery was quite rapid, with industrial production recovering its May 1920 level by October 1922.

The depression of 1920–21 had a lasting impact on American business, as well it might, given the extraordinary losses and numbers of bankruptcies that occurred. The failure rate per 10,000 of commercial and industrial firms rose from 37 in 1919 to 120 in 1922. The average liability per failure was greater in 1921 than in any year of the Great Depression. Among firms that avoided bankruptcy, declines in profit of 75 percent between 1920 and 1921 were not uncommon. Businesses responded to the disasters of 1920–21 with wholesale changes in their methods of operation. Among other things, they adopted new methods of controlling inventories, placed much less reliance on bank loans for short-run financing, and stopped cutting money wages as an initial response to declining sales.

The salient features of the depression in Canada resembled those in the United States. Both countries experienced roughly the same levels of inflation during 1919–20: about 15 percent as measured by the GNP implicit price deflator. In both countries, real GNP declined by about nine percent during 1920–21, but the Canadian price deflator declined only about 11 percent, while the U.S. price deflator declined about 17 percent. As the money stock in the two countries declined by roughly the same amount, the reasons for the differing movements in prices are unclear.

The experiences of the major European economies varied greatly during the early 1920s. Britain went through an inflationary boom during 1919–20 similar to the one in the United States. In part, the boom was based on the mistaken expectation that the war would give several important British industries a durable advantage over their German counterparts. An increase in bank rate to 7 percent in April 1920 and a decline in government spending helped bring the boom to an end. The ensuing downturn was similar in magnitude to that in the United States; industrial production declined by 32 percent between 1920 and 1921. The deflation in Britain was also quite sharp; wholesale prices fell by 35 percent between 1920 and 1921. While wholesale prices in the United States remained at their 1921 level, with only minor fluctuations, through 1929, wholesale prices in Britain declined by another 20 percent between 1921 and 1922 and then drifted downward to end the decade about 14 percent below their 1922 level. Industrial production lagged through the decade, not regaining its 1920 level until 1929. The return to the gold standard in 1925 at the prewar parity overvalued the pound and contributed to Britain's weak economic performance in the late 1920s.

France did not participate in the 1919–20 boom in production and experienced only a relatively mild decline of about 7.5 percent in industrial production between 1920 and 1921. By the end of 1922, industrial production was already nearly 20 percent above its 1920 level. Despite the relative mildness of the decline in production, wholesale prices fell by more than 30 percent between 1920 and 1921. They declined again slightly between 1921 and 1922 before increasing at an average annual rate of better than 20 percent per year between 1922 and 1926. Inflation was brought to an end late in 1926 and the franc was returned to the gold standard at a rate that left it undervalued. Although the immediate sequel to the return to gold was the recession of 1926–27, the undervaluation of the franc improved the competitive position of French products in international trade. This helped industrial production increase by 20 percent between 1927 and 1929.

While Germany experienced little expansion in output during 1919–20, it avoided the 1920–21 decline altogether. German industrial production expanded by more than 40 percent between 1920 and 1922, while wholesale prices fell by 23 percent between March 1920 and May 1921. The disruptions caused by the French occupation of the Ruhr in January 1923 and by hyperinflation (by December 1923, wholesale prices were several million percent higher than they had been in January) caused production to fall sharply. German manufacturing production at the end of 1923 was barely half its 1913 level. However, a strong recovery, beginning in early 1924, helped by an influx of foreign loans, restored industrial production to its 1922 level by 1925. The German economy continued to perform relatively well into 1928,

when a sharp fall off in foreign lending, principally from the United States, caused a decline in output late in the year.

The macroeconomic events of the early 1920s exhibited such extremes of inflation and deflation and of rapid production declines and equally rapid recoveries, and the experiences of the major Western countries differed so markedly, that the period will remain one of considerable interest to researchers. Perhaps the most puzzling aspect of the American experience during these years is that an economy capable of the rapid recovery of 1921–22 proved incapable of a similar recovery following the downturn of 1929–30.

Anthony Patrick O'Brien

See also FEDERAL RESERVE SYSTEM: 1914–1941; GOLD STANDARD; GOLD STANDARD: CAUSES AND CONSEQUENCES; GREAT DEPRESSION IN THE UNITED STATES (1929–1938)

Bibliography

Aldcroft, D. H. 1970. *The Inter-War Economy: Britain, 1919–1939.* New York: Columbia Univ. Press.

Friedman, M. and A. J. Schwartz. 1963. *A Monetary History of the United States, 1867–1960.* Princeton: Princeton Univ. Press.

Gordon, R. A. 1974. *Economic Instability and Growth: The American Record.* New York: Harper and Row.

Gordon, R. J. and N. S. Balke. 1986. "Appendix B: Historical Data." In *The American Business Cycle: Continuity and Change,* edited by R. J. Gordon, 781–850. Chicago: Univ. of Chicago Press.

Graham, F. 1930. *Exchange, Prices, and Production in Hyper-Inflation: Germany, 1920–1923.* Princeton: Princeton Univ. Press.

Kindleberger, C. P. 1986. *The World in Depression, 1929–1939.* Rev. ed. Berkeley and Los Angeles: Univ. of California Press.

Lewis, W. A. 1949. *Economic Survey: 1919–1939.* London: Allen and Unwin.

Saint-Etienne, C. 1984. *The Great Depression, 1929–1938: Lessons for the 1980s.* Stanford: Hoover Inst. Press.

Urquhart, M. C. 1986. "New Estimates of Gross National Product, Canada, 1870–1926: Some Implications for Canadian Development." In *Long-Term Factors in*

D

American Economic Growth, edited by S. L. Engerman and R. E. Gallman, 9–88. Chicago: Univ. of Chicago Press.

U.S. Bureau of the Census. 1975. *Historical Statistics of the United States, Colonial Times to 1970.* Bicent. ed. Washington, D.C.: Government Printing Office.

Depression of 1937–1938

The recovery from the Great Depression of 1929–33 is usually characterized as weak and uneven. But after the United States Supreme Court ruled in 1935 that the National Industrial Recovery Act (NIRA) was unconstitutional, economic activity expanded at an increasing pace. The expansion ended in May 1937 when a slow decline began, lasting till the end of August 1937. From August 1937 through May 1938, production, income, and employment plummeted. Between August 1937 and April 1938, the Standard and Poor's Common Stock Price Index fell 50.9 percent or by 6.4 percent a month, one of the sharpest declines on record. The index of total industrial production fell 37.7 percent between August 1937 and May 1938, a steeper drop than in the depression of 1920–21 or the similar downturn at the beginning of the 1929–33 depression. According to one estimate, the number of unemployed increased from 5.1 million in August and September of 1937 to 10.8 million in May 1938.

The 1937–38 depression brought a change in federal policies to restore economic activity. Like his predecessor, President Roosevelt desired a balanced budget. This was his campaign pledge in 1932 and 1936, but the weak economy led him to accept budget deficits and raise many taxes. He also vetoed an early payment of World War I veterans' bonuses only to have Congress override the veto. In November 1936, the Treasury Secretary announced that the federal budget in fiscal 1938 would be balanced. The depression shattered this vision and the administration turned to compensatory spending to revive the economy. Though probably not a conscious application of Keynes's new theory, the policy was consistent with it. Finally, amid charges that powerful monopolies had arbitrarily raised prices and initiated the recession, the administration called for a study of the concentration of economic power and the decline of competition, which resulted in the creation of the Temporary National Economic Committee.

The depression also shook public confidence in the administration's New Deal. The first test of the New Deal's fiscal, monetary, and social measures to manage the economy seemed to indicate that they were a failure. From May 1938 through December 1939, the index of total industrial production rose 43.1 percent. Real GNP per capita rose 7.4 percent from 1938 to 1939, but unemployment fell only from 19.0 to 17.2 percent. How long the recovery might have lasted is unknown as World War II intervened to provide the stimulus for a quick return to full employment.

Virtually all studies agree that sources of the 1937–38 depression in the United States were domestic. No similar recession occurred in other countries. Some early explanations for the American contraction, such as secular stagnation, falling consumption as prices rose faster than wages, increased income and capital-gains taxes, and monopoly pricing, were quickly discarded.

One widely accepted explanation holds that a shift to a restrictive fiscal policy initiated the contraction as the full-employment deficit of 1936 was transformed into a full-employment surplus in 1937. The $1.7 billion of veterans' bonus payments, approved in 1935, began in June 1936. In 1937, this source of spending disappeared. Moreover, social security taxes on employers rose from 1 percent in 1936 to 3 percent in 1937.

Another explanation focuses on the impact of tightened monetary policy. During the preceding recovery, banks had accumulated large excess reserves, and there had been a dramatic shift in bank portfolios from loans to securities. Federal Reserve authorities believed that the large excess reserves reflected a lack of qualified borrowers and an insufficient supply of qualified securities. Thus, the excess reserves were viewed as an inflation waiting to happen. To reduce the risk of inflation the Fed used its new policy tool of variable reserve requirements. In July 1936, the Fed announced that reserve requirements for member banks would increase by 50 percent in August 1936. Inflows of gold offset part of the reduction in excess reserves, so in December 1936 the Treasury began sterilizing the inflows. On 30 January 1937, the Fed announced that member-bank reserve requirements would increase on 1 March 1937 and 1 May 1937 to the legal maximum, a doubling of the requirements in effect in July 1936.

In the fall of 1936, member banks had sold some securities and used the added reserves from the gold inflow to satisfy increasing loan demand and replenish some of the excess reserves. The gold sterilization and the further increases in reserve requirements induced member banks to sell securities to obtain reserves to support additional loans. Most studies agree that the banks then desired to hold substantial excess reserves as a precaution against renewed banking panics, after the Fed had failed to provide the support during banking panics of the early 1930s. The prices of short-term government securities began to fall in December 1936. In January 1937, prices of municipal bonds began to decline, followed soon thereafter by the prices of long-term corporate bonds, long-term government bonds, and common stocks.

The increase in reserve requirements caused the money stock to contract and securities yields to rise. It was suggested that rising borrowing costs reduced business borrowing for capital expansion, particularly for the small risky firms. Large firms, whose borrowing carried lower default risks, borrowed less due to a combination of relatively larger retained profits for investment and more excess capacity. Small firms without the excess capacity and with relatively less retained profits found it more difficult to borrow because of higher risks. This fall in capital spending contributed to the downturn that began in May 1937.

A third explanation holds that the contraction occurred because diminished profits depressed investment. Profits, both current and expected, fell because the costs of commodities, raw materials, and labor rose faster than output prices. The prices of commodities and raw materials increased sharply in the fall of 1936 and early 1937. Price increases slowed down in the second quarter as inventories were drawn down. Following the elections of 1936, union organizers used the new National Labor Relations Act to gain union recognition. From February through June, most of the automobile industry, except Ford, was unionized, as were U.S. Steel, other smaller steel firms, and other major industries. Average hourly wage rates rose 11 percent between December 1936 and June 1937. The portion of the social security tax paid by employers rose to 3 percent in 1937 from 1 percent in 1936. These cost increases were not accompanied by productivity increases and outraced product price increases. The resulting profit decline was expected to continue, so firms cut back their plans for capital investment.

A further cause of reduced investment spending was the excess-profits tax imposed in June 1936, but repealed early in 1938. Though the disbursement of undistributed corporate profits in December 1936 initially stimulated consumption spending, the resulting lack of internal funds, combined with depressed profits, forced firms to resort to external financing. Larger firms that could have obtained external funds generally did not, while the smaller firms with marginal credit ratings, which would have used the funds, could not obtain funds.

While most observers regard monetary policy as the chief cause of the 1937–38 depression, there are many who argue that the other two factors were the primary causes. No general agreement on this question has yet emerged.

W. Gene Smiley

See also FEDERAL RESERVE SYSTEM: 1914–1941; GREAT DEPRESSION IN THE UNITED STATES (1929–1938)

Bibliography

Anderson, B. M. [1949] 1979. *Economics and the Public Welfare: A Financial and Economic History of the United States, 1914–1946.* Indianapolis: Liberty Press.

Brockie, M. D. 1950. "Theories of the 1937–1938 Depression." *Economic Journal* 60:292–310.

Brown, E. C. 1956. "Fiscal Policy in the Thirties: A Reappraisal." *American Economic Review* 46:857–79.

Campagna, A. S. 1987. *U.S. National Economic Policy, 1917–1985.* New York: Praeger.

Friedman, M. and A. J. Schwartz. 1963. *A Monetary History of the United States, 1867–1960.* Princeton: Princeton Univ. Press.

Hansen, A. H. 1938. *Full Recovery or Stagnation?* New York: Norton.

Hayes, D. A. 1951. *Business Confidence and Business Activity: A Case Study of the Recession of 1937.* Michigan Business Studies, vol. 10, no. 5. Ann Arbor: Univ. of Michigan Press.

Peppers, L. 1973. "Full-Employment Surplus Analysis and Structural Change: The 1930s." *Explorations in Economic History* 10:197–210.

Roose, K. D. 1954. *The Economics of Recession and Revival: An Interpretation of 1937–38.* New Haven: Yale Univ. Press.

Schumpeter, J. A. 1939. *Business Cycles: A Theoretical, Historical, and Statistical Analysis of the Capitalist Process*. 2 vols. New York: McGraw-Hill.

Slichter, S. H. 1938. "The Downturn of 1937." *Review of Economic Statistics* 20:97–110.

Stein, H. 1969. *The Fiscal Revolution in America*. Chicago: Univ. of Chicago Press.

Deutsche Bundesbank

The Deutsche Bundesbank (the West German Central Bank) was established by law in 1957, but inherited the traditions both of the bank Deutscher Länder (a system based in part on the model of the Federal Reserve System), which supervised the currency reform introducing the deutsch mark of 1948, and of the central bank of prewar Germany, the Reichsbank. The Bundesbank Act defines (Para. 3) the duty of the Bank as regulation of the currency in circulation and the supply of credit in order to "safeguard the currency." The importance of this objective derives from Germany's two severe and politically damaging inflations in the twentieth century. The Bank is also obligated to support the government's economic policy, but Para. 12 of the Act specifically subordinates this duty to its primary obligation. Many politicians, including Chancellor Konrad Adenauer, who once described the Bank's discount policy as a guillotine for the economy, have expressed dismay at the Bundesbank's insulation from political pressures. Policy is determined by a Central Bank Council, composed of the Directorate and the eleven Länder Central Bank presidents, who may outvote the Directorate and on occasion have done so.

In setting monetary policy, the Bundesbank can use the following policy instruments: the discount rate for rediscounting bills presented by banks (usually below the market rate), changes in the rediscount quotas allocated to banks in accordance with their capital and reserve state, the Lombard rate for loans against securities (usually above the market rate), banks' minimum reserve requirements, open-market transactions with short-term and (since 1967) long-term securities, currency-swap business, and most recently, "repo" business (the buying of bills on the open market with an agreement to repurchase after a fixed period).

The Bundesbank's monetary policy may be considered in two phases. First, in the period of fixed-exchange rates between the liberalization of international capital transactions at the end of 1958 and the collapse of the Bretton Woods system in 1971, monetary policy was subordinate to the external exchange rate. Policies desirable from the point of view of domestic stability were often counter-indicated by the exchange position.

The Bundesbank's first boom cycle illustrates the dilemma. From the spring of 1959, demand rose in conditions of full employment. The Bundesbank raised discount rates (in September and October 1959), and increased banks' minimum reserves, but failed to slow monetary and credit expansion as foreign funds flowed in. In 1960, further measures—a ban on interest on non-residents' accounts and massive open-market sales—also had little impact and were described in the Bank's 1960 report as "completely ineffective." In November 1960, the Bank spectacularly reversed policy and took rates down, but the inflow of foreign funds continued. The goal of the exercise was to show that only a revaluation of the Deutschmark (actually carried out in March 1961) could create more room for maneuver in monetary policy. A similar situation occurred in 1969, when currency inflows again frustrated monetary attempts to counter threats to price stability, so that revaluation (in October 1969) again offered the only way out. On both occasions, the Bundesbank was criticized for allowing an investment boom to continue too long.

The converse of this inability to cope with excessive aggregate demand was a reluctance to respond to signs of recession. Although the pace of increases in wages and prices faltered by mid-1966, no action was taken until the end of the year. Instead, the increases in discount rates, which started in 1965, continued in 1966. The failure of the Bundesbank to undertake countercyclical action either in upswings or recessions resulted in the enactment in 1967 of the Law on Stability and Growth, which made the government responsible for macroeconomic management, and specifically for maintaining high employment with "steady and appropriate" economic growth. The 1967 law created a peculiar division of labor, assigning the government responsibility for macroeconomic policy while leaving responsibility for monetary policy with the autonomous Bundesbank. By the early 1970s, the old problem of monetary management was handled differently, and large exchange inflows in 1970 and 1971 were met by a relaxed monetary policy instead of revaluation, which meant importing world inflation.

The abandonment of the fixed-exchange-rate regime allowed a new approach to monetary policy. Since 1974, the Bundesbank has been the most consistent follower of monetary targeting, criticized by opponents as the application of Monetarist theory. Until 1988, these targets referred to the Central Bank Money Stock (CBMS): currency in circulation and minimum reserves for domestic liabilities calculated at the constant reserve requirement for January 1974 (to avoid the impact of changes in minimum reserves). There are thus different ratios corresponding to sight, time, and savings deposits in banks. Between 1979 and 1988, the targets defined a range (or "corridor"). After 1988, M_3 replaced CBMS as the target. Since M_3 includes bank deposits, the relative weight of currency in M_3 is much less than in the CBMS measure. The targets are based on a calculation of the average growth of productive potential and an allowance for "necessary" price increases. After 1985, the concept of an unavoidable price increase was abandoned, and the target reflected solely an assessment of the potential for growth.

Targeting meant a new way of achieving price stability. It was based in part on the observation that price movements and CBMS lagged by nine quarters are highly correlated. It also depended on the assumption that velocity stays relatively constant, so that there is a steady relationship between monetary aggregates and nominal GNP. Finally, it reflected the view that stable and predictable monetary growth forms the best environment for business decisions. The Monetarist assumption about the neutrality of money is thus built into the Bundesbank's view of the world, though this view did not dominate discussions at the beginning of the era of targeting.

In fact, the Bundesbank's targeting responded to the major international shocks of the 1970s in very different ways. After the first oil-price increase, the Bundesbank allowed a substantial rise in the monetary base from the middle of 1973 to the first quarter of 1975, abandoning an anti-inflationary strategy in an attempt to bring GNP back to its potential path. From 1979 to 1981, despite the second great oil-price rise, the actual path of CBMS was at the lowest end of the target range in each year,

slowing economic growth and inducing recession by the fourth quarter of 1980. This response broke inflationary expectations, so that the increase in the consumer price index reached a maximum of 6.3 percent in 1981, before falling rapidly to negative values by 1986.

The Bundesbank was less successful in meeting its monetary targets from 1975 to 1978 and again from 1986 to 1988. In both periods, the major obstacle was attempted international collaboration over exchange rates. In the first instance, the Bundesbank intervened to support other European currencies in the European Currency Union or "snake." In the second, the major action was driving the dollar down after the Plaza Agreement of September 1985. This required a reduction in U.S. and international interest rates, thus inducing German expansion beyond the target range.

Even after 1974, therefore, the Bundesbank could not conduct policy solely with regard to its monetary targets or ignore international considerations. In addition, definitional problems of money have played an increasingly important role, and even the new indicator M_3 does not take Euro-deposits into account. Once European markets have been completely deregulated, national monetary aggregates such as M_3 will lose predictive value. Recent work suggests that the long-term relationship between nominal GNP and monetary aggregates is now steadier on the European level than in the national economies. The appropriate institutional response to these problems is an unresolved question. In the longer term, the Bundesbank's commitment to a policy objective is threatened by proposals to create a common European currency and European Central Bank, which could be subject to greater political control than the Bundesbank.

The Bundesbank has never conceived its task as being primarily to conduct countercyclical policy. Its concern with price stability antedated the theoretical advance of Monetarism in the 1970s. Despite the international complications that arise from the growing significance of the Deutschmark as a reserve currency since 1974, the history of the Bundesbank stands out as the most successful application of Monetarist principles for an anti-inflationary strategy.

Harold James

See also CENTRAL BANKING; MONETARY POLICY; REICHSBANK; RECESSIONS (SUPPLY-SIDE) OF THE 1970S

Bibliography

Deutsche Bundesbank. 1976. *Währung und Wirtschaft in Deutschland 1876–1975*. Frankfurt: Deutsche Bundesbank.

Düwendag, D. 1970. *Macht und Ohnmacht der Deutschen Bundesbank*. Frankfurt: Athenäum.

Issing, O. 1990. *Einführung in die Geldpolitik*. Munich: Fritz Vahlen.

Rohwer, B. 1988. *Konjunktur und Wachstum*. Berlin: Duncker and Humblot.

Schlesinger, H. and H. Bockelmann. 1973. "Monetary Policy in the Federal Republic of Germany." In *Monetary Policy in Twelve Industrial Countries,* edited by K. Holbik, 161–213. Boston: Federal Reserve Bank of Boston.

Sherman, H. C. 1990. "Central Banking in Germany and the Process of European Monetary Integration." In *Tokyo Club Papers,* no. 3, 147–78.

Differential and Difference Equations

Introduction

Differential equations and difference equations are frequently used in models of business cycles because their solutions often take the form of time paths that fluctuate cyclically.

Differential Equation

A *differential equation* is an equation with differential or derivative expressions in it, such as $dy/dt + 5y = 10$ where t, usually denoting time, is a continuous variable. A derivative would enter into an economic model, for instance, when one uses the adaptive-expectations hypothesis

$$\frac{dp^e}{dt} = j(p - p^e), \qquad (0 \le j \le 1)$$

where p^e and p denote, respectively, the expected and the actual rates of inflation.

The solution of a differential equation is a time path—a function $y(t)$—which, along with its derivative $y'(t)$, satisfies the given equation. For example, the time path $y(t) = Ae^{-5t} + 2$ (where A = an arbitrary constant), and its derivative $dy/dt = -5Ae^{-5t}$, together satisfy the linear differential equation $dy/dt + 5y = 10$. Hence that path represents a family of solutions (since A can take arbitrary values) of the latter differential equation.

The above example illustrates several common traits of a solution path. In general the solution is the sum of two components, one of which involves a natural exponential expression of the form Ae^{rt}, and the other, a constant or nonconstant function of t. The latter, referred to as the *particular integral*, gives the intertemporal equilibrium value of y at every point of time. And the other term which involves the Ae^{rt} expression, referred to as the *complementary function*, reflects the deviation from the equilibrium at each moment. Note, however, that this example does *not* illustrate cyclical movements, since Ae^{-5t} traces a monotonic path over time. To generate a cyclical path, the differential equation in the model must possess certain special features.

Difference Equation

A *difference equation* is an equation that contains difference expressions, such as $\Delta y_t = y_t + 5$, or equivalently, $y_{t+1} - 2y_t = 5$ (since by definition $\Delta y_t \equiv y_{t+1} - y_t$). Here, the time variable t is a discrete variable, admitting integer values only. In other words, the time subscripts refer to time *periods*. A simple example of a difference entering an economic model is the accelerator,

$$I_{t+1} = \alpha(Y_{t+1} - Y_t), \qquad (\alpha > 0),$$

where I and Y denote, respectively, investment and national income.

The solution of a difference equation, like that of a differential equation, is also a time path. For instance, the time path $y_t = A(2)^t - 5$ (where A is an arbitrary constant), and the implied expression for the next period, $y_{t+1} = A(2)^{t+1} - 5$, together satisfy the difference equation $y_{t+1} - 2y_t = 5$. Thus, that time path represents a family of solutions (since A can take arbitrary values) of the latter difference equation.

Again, the solution of a difference equation is seen to be the sum of two components: a complementary function (deviations from equilibrium) and a particular solution (stationary or moving intertemporal equilibrium). While the complementary function appears again as an exponential, this time it takes the form of Ab^t, with t admitting integer values only. Since $A(2)^t$ yields a monotonically increasing step function of t, this example also fails to illustrate cyclical movements. To produce cycles, a difference equation must possess certain special features.

Cycles from Differential Equations

For simplicity, attention will be focused here on linear differential equations, in which the variable y and its derivatives all appear in the first degree, and they are not multiplied together. To have a cyclical solution path, a linear differential equation must be of the second (or higher) order, i.e., it must contain a second- (or higher-) order derivative. Moreover, its "characteristic roots" must be complex numbers, such as $3 \pm 2i$, where i (for *imaginary* number) is defined by $i \equiv \sqrt{-1}$.

Characteristic Roots

To understand these concepts, consider the second-order liner differential equation

$$y''(t) + a_1 y'(t) + a_2 y(t) = 0, \qquad (1)$$

where $y''(t) \equiv d^2 - y/dt^2$, $y'(t) \equiv dy/dt$, and a_1 and a_2 are constants. Because of the zero constants on the right-hand side of equation (1), the equation is said to be *homogeneous*. For such an equation, the particular integral is zero, so its solution is identical with its complementary function. This enables us to concentrate first on the complementary function.

Taking a hint from the earlier differential-equation example, we expect the complementary function to take the form $y(t) = Ae^{rt}$, which automatically implies that $y'(t) = rAe^{rt}$ and $y''(t) = r^2 Ae^{rt}$. With these expressions for y, y' and y'', equation (1) can be written as

$$\left(r^2 + a_1 r + a_2\right) Ae^{rt} = 0. \qquad (2)$$

If the constant A happens to be zero, equation (2) becomes an uninteresting identity, because then $y(t) = Ae^{rt} = 0$ for all t, and y displays no dynamic features. If $A \neq 0$, however, then equation (2) can be satisfied if and only if

$$r^2 + a_1 r + a_2 = 0. \qquad (3)$$

This quadratic equation is called the *characteristic equation* of equation (1), and its roots

$$r_1, r_2 = \frac{1}{2}\left(-a_1 \pm \sqrt{a_1^2 - 4a_2}\right), \qquad (4)$$

which are called the *characteristic roots* of equation (1), give the only values of r that are consistent with the complementary function form $y(t) = Ae^{rt}$. In fact, both r_1 and r_2 should be used in the complementary func-

tion. Thus the solution of equation (1) can be written as

$$y(t) = A_1 e^{r_1 t} + A_2 e^{r_2 t}, \qquad (5)$$

where A_1 and A_2 are arbitrary constants whose definite values are to be determined by two given initial conditions.

Complex Roots

If r_1 and r_2 are real numbers, no cyclical movements can arise in equation (5); such would be the outcome if $a_1^2 > 4a_2$ under the square-root sign in equation (4). But if $a_1^2 < 4a_2$, then equation (4) requires taking the square roots of a negative number, which is not possible in the real-number system. The only way to make this possible is to go beyond real numbers.

Using $i \equiv \sqrt{-1}$, we may rewrite equation (4) as

$$r_1, r_2 = \frac{1}{2}\left(-a_1 \pm \sqrt{4a_2 - a_1^2}\,i\right), \qquad (6)$$

or, using the shorthand symbols

$$h = -\frac{1}{2} a_1, \text{ and } v = \frac{1}{2}\left(\sqrt{4a_2 - a_1^2}\right),$$

$$r_1, r_2 = h \pm vi, \qquad (6')$$

The two numbers $h \pm vi$, consisting of a real part h and an imaginary part $\pm vi$, are called *complex numbers*; accordingly, the two roots in equation (6′) are referred to as *complex roots*. Complex roots always come in pairs owing to the square-root origin of the imaginary part, one with $+vi$ and the other with $-vi$.

Periodic Fluctuations

With complex roots, equation (5) emerges—after factoring out e^{ht}—as

$$y(t) = e^{ht}\left(A_1 e^{vit} + A_2 e^{-vit}\right). \qquad (7)$$

While the real exponential e^{ht} is readily understandable, it is not easy to interpret the imaginary exponentials in the parentheses. Fortunately, by using the Euler relations, which state that

$$e^{\pm vit} \equiv \cos vt \pm i \sin vt,$$

we can convert equation (7) into the more easily interpretable form

$$y(t) = e^{ht}\left(B_1 \cos vt + B_2 \sin vt\right) \qquad (7')$$

where B_1 and B_2 are arbitrary constants that are to be determined by two initial conditions.

Given the periodic nature of sine and cosine functions equation (7′) yields a cyclical path. Specifically, the $B_1 \cos vt$ term produces perpetual fluctuations with an amplitude of B_1 and a period of $2\pi/v$ (completing a cycle every time the variable t goes a distance of $2\pi/v$). Similarly, the $B_2 \sin vt$ term produces perpetual fluctuations with an amplitude of B_2 and a period of $2\pi/v$. Since these two terms share a common period, their sum produces a cyclical pattern with the same period. Finally, the multiplicative factor e^{ht} either continually increases the original amplitude of $(B_1 \cos vt + B_2 \sin vt)$ over time (if $h > 0$), or continually decreases it (if $h < 0$). In the special case of $h = 0$, however, the $y(t)$ path in equation (7′) maintains a constant amplitude forever, since $e^0 = 1$.

The three possible cases of h are illustrated in Figure 1. Panel (a) illustrates a divergent time path, and a dynamically unstable intertemporal equilibrium (here, equilibrium value = 0). Panel (b) illustrates a convergent time path and a dynamically stable equilibrium. And panel (c) shows uniform fluctuations with the variable overshooting and undershooting the equilibrium target in turn but never converging to it.

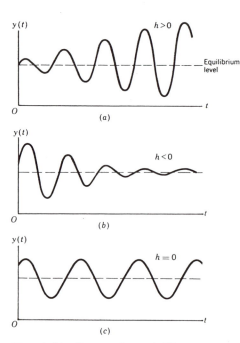

Figure 1. (a) a divergent time path, (b) a convergent time path, (c) a time path with uniform fluctuations around the equilibrium target.

The Intertemporal Equilibrium

Being homogenous, equation (1) yields an equilibrium value of zero, which generally has no meaningful economic application. To have a nonzero equilibrium, the differential equation must be nonhomogeneous, e.g.:

$$y''(t) + a_1 y'(t) + a_2 y(t) = c, \quad (c \neq 0). \quad (8)$$

From equation (8), the particular integral is found to be

$$\bar{y} = \frac{c}{a_2}, \quad (a_2 \neq 0). \quad (9)$$

To derive this result, assume that a stationary equilibrium $\bar{y}$ exists, so that y' and y'' are both zero in that equilibrium. Then equation (8) reduces to $a_2 \bar{y} = c$, which leads directly to equation (9). Note, however, that if $a_2 = 0$, then equation (9) is undefined, and no stationary equilibrium exists; in that case, the equilibrium of y would be a moving equilibrium (provided a_1 is nonzero):

$$\bar{y}(t) = \frac{c}{a_1} t, \quad (a_1 \neq 0). \quad (10)$$

This result can be derived by assuming a moving equilibrium $\bar{y}(t) = kt$ (where $k =$ a constant), which implies that $y' = k$ but $y'' = 0$. On the basis of equation (8), with $a_2 = 0$, k must equal c/a_1, which establishes equation (10).

Moving equilibria can also arise if the right-hand side of equation (8) is a nonconstant function of time. Indeed, a moving equilibrium may itself contain cyclical patterns.

With nonzero equilibrium values of y, Figure 1 needs to be modified. For a stationary equilibrium such as equation (9), the horizontal axis in Figure 1 should be relabelled to represent $\bar{y} = c/a_2$. For a moving equilibrium such as equation (10), the curves in Figure 1 must be replotted as the vertical deviations from the $\bar{y}(t)$ path rather than from a horizontal straight line.

The above discussion shows how a second-order differential equation may generate cycles. But fluctuating paths can also be derived from higher-order differential equations so long as complex roots are present.

Cycles from Difference Equations

One remarkable feature of difference equations is that, unlike differential equations, even simple first-order difference equations can generate cycles.

A first-order difference equation is one that contains only the first-order difference $\Delta y_t \equiv$

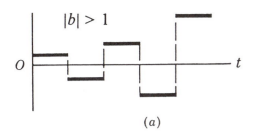

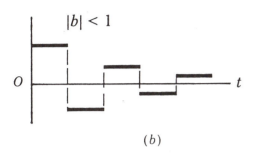

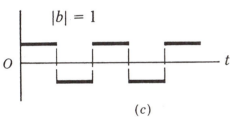

Figure 2. (a) a time path with explosive oscillation, (b) a time path with damped oscillation, (c) a time path with uniform oscillation.

$y_{t+1} - y_t$. Such a difference equation would involve two consecutive time periods (period t and period $t + 1$), or a one-period lag, such as

$$y_{t+1} + ay_t = 0. \tag{11}$$

In view of the zero constant, equation (11) is a homogeneous difference equation, with a zero particular solution.

The Complementary Function

As suggested by the earlier difference-equation example, the complementary function of a difference equation involves the exponential expression Ab^t. If $y_t = Ab^t$, it follows that $y_{t+1} = Ab^{t+1}$, and equation (11) becomes

$$(b+a)Ab^t = 0. \tag{12}$$

This equation holds only if $(b + a) = 0$ or $Ab^t = 0$. The latter possibility, however, would mean

$y_t = 0$ for all t, a case devoid of dynamic interest. The former possibility, on the other hand, implies that

$$b + a = 0 \tag{13}$$

which means that the only value of b consistent with the complementary-function form Ab^t is

$$b = -a. \tag{14}$$

Equation (13) is the characteristic equation of equation (11), and equation (14) gives the characteristic root b. Thus the complementary function (in this case also the solution) is

$$y_t = A(-a)^t, \tag{15}$$

where A is an arbitrary constant to be determined by an initial condition.

Oscillations

Since t is a discrete variable here, the time path equation (15) is a step function, with the value of y constant over any one period. The configuration of the successive steps in the path depends on the constant A and the characteristic root b, the base of the exponential (here, $-a$). The generation of cycles, however, requires that the algebraic sign of b be negative. The illustrative numerical examples in Table 1 make this clear. In each of the cases shown there, with $b < 0$, the values of y alternate in sign from one period to the next, forming an oscillating pattern. The oscillation is explosive if $|b| > 1$, damped if $|b| < 1$, and uniform if $|b| = 1$. These types of paths are illustrated in Figure 2.

TABLE 1

Value of y_t	if b = -2	if b = $-\frac{1}{2}$	if b = -1
$y_0 = Ab^0$	A	A	A
$y_1 = Ab^1$	$-2A$	$-\frac{1}{2}A$	$-A$
$y_2 = Ab^2$	$4A$	$\frac{1}{4}A$	A
$y_3 = Ab^3$	$-8A$	$-\frac{1}{8}A$	$-A$
$y_4 = Ab^4$	$16A$	$\frac{1}{16}A$	A

The Intertemporal Equilibrium

The paths in Figure 2 are based on a zero equilibrium value from the homogeneous equation (11). For the nonhomogeneous difference equation

$$y_{t+1} + ay_t = c, \quad (c \neq 0), \tag{16}$$

the particular solution gives a nonzero equilibrium:

$$\bar{y} = \frac{c}{1+a}, \quad (a \neq -1). \quad (17)$$

This result can be verified by setting $y_{t+1} = y_t = \bar{y}$ in equation (16), and solving for $\bar{y}$.

Note that in case $a = -1$, equation (17) is undefined; if so, there will be a moving equilibrium. Let $\bar{y}_t = kt$, so that $\bar{y}_{t+1} = k(t+1)$. Then equation (16) becomes (with $a = -1$):

$$k(t+1) - kt = c, \quad \text{so that} \quad k = c.$$

Thus, if $a = -1$, the moving equilibrium is

$$\bar{y}_t = ct. \quad (18)$$

Moving equilibria can also emerge when the right-hand side of equation (16) is a nonconstant function of t.

When the particular solution yields a nonzero equilibrium, Figure 2 must be duly modified. In particular, for a moving equilibrium, the oscillatory paths in Figure 2 must be replotted as vertical deviations from the moving equilibrium rather than from a horizontal line.

Second-Order Difference Equation

If an economic model involves a second-order difference equation, then the solution may have not only the oscillatory patterns associated with negative characteristic roots, but also the fluctuating patterns originating from complex roots.

To see this, consider the second-order linear equation

$$y_{t+2} + a_1 y_{t+1} + a_2 y_t = c, \quad (19)$$

which, being of the second-order, has a two-period lag with three consecutive time periods. If the particular solution is a stationary equilibrium, it can be found—by setting $y_{t+2} = y_{t+1} = y_t = \bar{y}$ in equation (19)—to be

$$\bar{y} = \frac{c}{1 + a_1 + a_2}, \quad (a_1 + a_2 \neq -1). \quad (20)$$

If $a_1 + a_2 = -1$, then a moving equilibrium must be sought, for example $\bar{y}_t = kt$.

The complementary function is to be found, as before, from the homogeneous version of equation (19), i.e., with c set equal to

zero in equation (19). By substituting into such a homogeneous equation the solution form $y_t = Ab^t$ (which implies $y_{t+1} = Ab^{t+1}$ and $y_{t+2} = Ab^{t+2}$), we obtain

$$(b^2 + a_1 b + a_2) Ab^t = 0. \quad (21)$$

And if the uninteresting case of $Ab^t = 0$ is ruled out, equation (21) leads immediately to the characteristic equation

$$b^2 + a_1 b + a_2 = 0, \quad (22)$$

with the characteristic roots

$$b_1, b_2 = \frac{1}{2}\left(-a_1 \pm \sqrt{a_1^2 - 4a_2}\right). \quad (23)$$

Depending on whether the expression $(a_1^2 - 4a_2)$ is positive, zero, or negative, the characteristic roots can be either (i) real and distinct ($b_1 \neq b_2$) or (ii) real and repeated ($b_1 = b_2 = b$), or (iii) complex ($h \pm vi$). For case (i), the complementary function is simply

$$y_t = A_1 b_1^{\;t} + A_2 b_2^{\;t}, \quad (b_1 \neq b_2). \quad (24)$$

For case (ii), since the two roots share the same value, the complementary function must be written as

$$y_t = A_1 b^t + A_2 t b^t, \quad (b_1 = b_2 = b), \quad (25)$$

where a multiplicative t has been inserted into the second term on the right to prevent the two terms from collapsing into one. Finally, for case (iii), the complementary function is

$$y_t = A_1(h + vi)^t + A_2(h - vi)^t, \quad (26)$$

where

$$h = -\frac{1}{2}a_1, \quad \text{and} \quad v = \frac{1}{2}\sqrt{4a_2 - a_1^2}.$$

Exponentials with complex bases are difficult to interpret, but by DeMoivre's Theorem, equation (26) can be transformed into terms of sine and cosine functions again:

$$y_t = R^t(B_1 \cos \theta t + B_2 \sin \theta t). \quad (26')$$

In equation (26'), $R = \sqrt{a_2}$; θ is the radian measure of an angle in the interval $[0, 2\pi)$ that satisfies the conditions $\cos \theta = h/R$ and $\sin \theta = v/R$;

and B_1 and B_2 are arbitrary constants to be determined by two given initial conditions.

The general solution of equation (19) is the sum of the particular solution (20) and the complementary function in either equations (24), (25), or (26′). Whenever one or both of the roots in equations (24) and (25) are negative, oscillation will appear in the solution path—either explosive, damped, or a mixture thereof. And whenever the roots are complex, the type of fluctuation associated with sine and cosine functions will emerge, except that, inasmuch as t is a discrete variable in the difference-equation framework, only those points on the sine and cosine curves corresponding to integer values of t would matter in constructing the step-function path. In this latter case, it is the R^t term in (26′) that will determine whether the original sine and cosine cycles are made explosive ($R > 1$) or damped ($R < 1$).

Mathematical Cycles vs. Real Cycles

The mathematical generation of cycles, as presented above, pertains only to models that reduce to a single dynamic (differential or difference) equation. If an economic model involves a system of simultaneous dynamic equations, the methods of solution would be somewhat more complicated. But the underlying procedure closely parallels what has been presented above (Chiang 1984, chap. 18). Some dynamic economic models also make use of mixed difference–differential equations (Allen 1964, chap. 8).

While mathematically generated cycles have obvious applicability to business-cycle models, certain problems arise in actual applications. For one thing, only three types of paths are portrayed in Figures 1 and 2: explosive, damped, and uniform. But actual cyclical movements do not appear to be characterized by either ever-increasing, ever-decreasing, or constant amplitude. How, then, can the use of differential and difference equations be reconciled with economic reality?

One device, appropriated for models with inherently explosive cyclical tendencies, is to impose a *ceiling* and a *floor* to bound the path, thereby taming the explosiveness of the model. This device was employed, for example, by Hicks (1950). What ceiling and floor boundaries do is, in essence, to make the model nonlinear. Another device, relevant to models with inherently damped cyclical fluctuations, is to allow for *exogenous shocks* to revitalize the waning endogenous cyclical movements at random intervals. Such exogenous shocks constitute what Frisch ([1933] 1965) referred to as "impulses" that could prevent the "propagation" process of cycles from coming to an end.

Another problem with the cyclical patterns in Figures 1 and 2 is their rigid periodicity, i.e., the length of successive cycles does not vary, as real cycles tend to do. Here, too, introducing an element of nonlinearity can be of help. One especially noteworthy recent development in this regard is known as *chaos theory*. Its subject matter concerns the ways in which a nonlinear dynamic equation can produce time paths displaying successive cycles of diverse lengths and amplitudes, and even cycles interspersed with periods of noncyclical behavior. The pattern of such time paths can appear to be irregular and disorderly enough to resemble something brought about by random exogenous shocks; hence the name "chaos theory." Chaotic paths can result even from a relatively simple nonlinear first-order difference equation.

Another interesting recent development in mathematics with potential applications to business cycles is *catastrophe theory*. Catastrophe theory employs a system of differential equations in which the variables adjust quickly to attain some equilibrium in the short run, whereas certain parameters adjust slowly in the long run. The interactions between the "fast variables" and the "slow variables" trace out the movements of successive short-run equilibria as the parameters (slow variables) undergo changes. Under certain circumstances, as the long-run forces evolve, a short-run equilibrium could jump abruptly from one region of the state space to another, much as a ball might roll over a cliff and fall to the ground below. This type of precipitous movement, which suggests the name "catastrophe theory," may be a useful tool for explaining sharp crises that occur in the real economic world, including stock-market crashes.

Although the words "chaos" and "catastrophe" do not in themselves impart a feeling of comfort and joy, chaos theory and catastrophe theory do hold promise as tools for business-cycle modelling. Much that is valuable and powerful may well be forthcoming from these two developments in the future.

Alpha C. Chiang

See also ACCELERATION PRINCIPLE; CEILINGS AND FLOORS; CHAOS AND BIFURCATIONS; GOODWIN, RICHARD MURPHEY; HICKS,

John Richard; Lundburg, Erik Filip; Nonlinear Business-Cycle Theories; Samuelson, Paul Anthony

Bibliography
Allen, R. G. D. 1964. *Mathematical Economics.* 3d ed. London: Macmillan.

Baumol, W. J. and J. Benhabib. 1989. "Chaos: Significance, Mechanism, and Economic Applications." *Journal of Economic Perspectives,* Winter, 77–105.

Chiang, A. C. 1984. *Fundamental Methods of Mathematical Economics.* 3d ed. New York: McGraw-Hill.

Frisch, R. [1933] 1965. "Propagation Problems and Impulse Problems in Dynamic Economics." In A.E.A. *Readings in Business Cycles,* 155–85. Homewood, Ill.: Irwin.

Hicks, J. R. 1950. *A Contribution to the Theory of the Trade Cycle.* Oxford: Clarendon Press.

Varian, H. 1979. "Catastrophe Theory and the Business Cycle." *Economic Inquiry* 17:14–28.

Disintermediation

Disintermediation occurs when funds are shifted from financial institutions to direct money-market instruments to take advantage of higher open-market interest rates that more than compensate for the cost of transferring the funds. Such transfers generated considerable instability from the mid-1960s to the early 1980s by disrupting financial markets, contributing to business fluctuations, and complicating monetary policy.

Disintermediation can be understood by considering five aspects of the process as it evolved in the United States: (1) the source of disintermediation, (2) its impact on financial institutions, (3) its contribution to business fluctuations, (4) its implications for monetary policy, and (5) the solution of the disintermediation problem.

The Source of Disintermediation

Transfers of funds from financial institutions to money markets occur in a competitive environment whenever money-market interest rates rise above those offered by depository institutions; however, the shifting of funds soon brings direct and indirect interest rates into balance and disintermediation ceases.

The disintermediation that occurred in the U.S. during the 1960s and 1970s would not have been possible without binding interest-rate ceilings (Regulation Q) covering the savings and time deposits of banks and thrift institutions. As a result, there was no market mechanism to end disintermediation. Originally established in 1933 and imposed only on bank deposits, Regulation Q was extended to federally insured thrift institutions in 1966. Demand deposits were subject to a zero-interest-rate ceiling by the 1933 Banking Act, though the ceiling was not administered by Regulation Q, and could not be changed without Congressional action. Credit unions were also subject to deposit-rate ceilings, which were administered by the National Credit Union Administration. Thus, after 1966, the savings and time deposits of the majority of depository institutions (banks, thrifts, and credit unions) were subject to government imposed ceilings.

Impact on Financial Institutions and Other Micro Effects

The Regulation-Q ceilings constrained the interest rates that depository institutions could pay on deposits, which, in turn, restricted the income of depositors. The constraint became increasingly tight after 1966 as money-market interest rates, which were unregulated, rose well above the Regulation-Q ceilings. Whenever money-market rates rose above the ceilings, depositors withdrew funds from depository institutions to purchase money-market instruments such as Treasury bills, commercial paper, large certificates of deposit (CDs), etc. The purchase of large CDs recycled some of the disintermediated funds back to the banking system; however, the funds were returned only to the larger banks that regularly issued CDs while the funds had been withdrawn from banks and thrifts of all sizes.

Disintermediation was very disruptive in 1966, 1969, 1974–75, and 1979–82 when money-market interest rates rose well above the Regulation-Q ceilings. At such times, disintermediation threatened the viability of depository institutions, because their reduced liquidity prevented them from satisfying consumer- and mortgage-credit demand. Institutions also sought out unregulated sources of funds, such as Eurodollars that exposed them to new and higher levels of risk.

In addition, large deposits were easiest to transfer; thus, small depositors were frequently forced to earn a deposit rate considerably less than the market rate. Studies indicated that the lost income to depositors was substantial.

Impact on Credit Flows and Business Fluctuations

Depository institutions were the primary suppliers of consumer and mortgage credit, and, as a result, Regulation Q severely limited the quantity of consumer and mortgage credit whenever market rates rose above the Regulation-Q ceilings. This disrupted the flow of funds in financial markets and amplified cyclical swings. As the economy expanded and interest rates rose above the Regulation-Q ceilings, the reduced flow of consumer and mortgage credit ensured a sharp contraction. Not all observers regarded credit crunches as a problem, however. Some argued that regulatory-induced credit crunches brought an earlier end to an expansion that might have ended with even more severe impacts on the financial system.

The term "credit crunch" was used to characterize periods of intense disintermediation, indicating that consumer and mortgage credit were available only at very high interest rates.

Impact on Monetary Policy

The gap between regulated interest rates (Regulation-Q ceilings) and unregulated interest rates (Treasury-bill rates, etc.) had additional implications for the financial system, which in turn, changed the environment for conducting monetary policy. Binding Regulation-Q ceilings provided strong incentives for *financial innovation*, i.e., the creation of new financial services and instruments designed to circumvent regulations that limited profit. Many of these innovations facilitated disintermediation by reducing the transactions costs of transferring funds.

Money-market mutual funds offered by securities companies were the most notable innovation of the 1970s. Securities companies sold fund shares in minimum amounts of as little as $100 and reinvested those funds in money-market instruments. Thus, money-market funds earned a market interest rate (less a management fee) and frequently offered limited transactions services as well. Virtually nonexistent in 1971, by year-end 1982, money-market funds totaled $206.6 billion.

Disintermediation and rapid financial innovation greatly complicated the conduct of monetary policy. Regulation-Q ceilings ensured that any major variation in market interest rates induced by Federal Reserve actions would induce fund transfers between indirect and direct financial markets. The adverse effects of these transfers thus tempered Federal Reserve resolve to control inflation. The innovation process that emerged from disintermediation also complicated monetary policy by making it more difficult to define the money supply and increasing the role of nonbanks (which were not subject to bank-like reserve requirements) in the money-supply process.

Solution to Disintermediation

The 1980 Deregulation and Monetary Control Act and the 1982 Garn-St. Germain Depository Institutions Act brought an end to disintermediation by phasing in market-determined deposit rates to enable depository institutions to compete with direct markets. As of 31 March 1986, all deposit ceilings except the zero ceiling on demand deposits had been removed. Depository institutions now determine the rate they offer on all savings, time, and checking deposits (except demand deposits). Thus, by 1986, the primary source of the disruptive disintermediation in the 1960s, 1970s, and early 1980s had largely been removed.

Thomas F. Cargill

See also BANKING AND FINANCIAL REGULATION; FEDERAL RESERVE SYSTEM: 1941–1993; FINANCIAL INTERMEDIATION; MONETARY POLICY; RECESSION OF 1969–1970; THRIFT CRISIS

Bibliography

Cargill, T. F. and G. G. Garcia. 1985. *Financial Reform in the 1980s.* Stanford: Hoover Institution Press.

Kane, E. J. 1970. "Short-Changing the Small Saver During the Vietnam War." *Journal of Money, Credit and Banking* 2:507–20.

Mayer, T. 1982. "A Case Study of Federal Reserve Policymaking: Regulation Q in 1966." *Journal of Monetary Economics* 10:259–71.

Pyle, D. H. 1974. "The Losses on Savings Deposits from Interest Rate Regulation." *Bell Journal of Economics and Management Science* 5:614–22.

Wojnilower, A. M. 1980. "The Central Role of Credit Crunches in Recent Financial History." *Brookings Papers on Economic Activity,* Number Two, 277–339.

Disproportionality Theory

Disproportionalities, or imbalances, between different sectors of production appear in Marx as symptoms of breakdowns in investment activity. At the beginning of the twentieth century, this issue became a major aspect of the Marxian debate over the sources of economic crises. The emphasis on sectoral proportions stemmed from the impact on European socialists of the reproduction schemes—where output is divided between capital-goods and consumption-goods sectors—presented in volume two of *Capital*. The schemes establish a specific relation in the exchange flows between the two departments of production: the value of capital goods sold to the consumption-goods sector must equal the value of consumables purchased by workers and capitalists in the capital-goods sector. In terms of Keynesian aggregates we have:

$$I - I_i = I_c = wL_i + Z_i, \qquad (1)$$

where I is the value of total gross investment, I_i and I_c are the corresponding values in the investment-goods and in the consumption-goods sectors, w is money wage rate which is entirely spent, L_i is the labor force in the investment-goods sector, Z_i is that sector's capitalist consumption.

Equation (1) expresses the condition for smooth accumulation. Rosa Luxemburg ([1912] 1951) used this relation to argue that not all the surplus would be invested or consumed, so that the availability of markets was crucial for the validation of Marx's condition. By contrast, others [Bulgakov (1897), Tugan-Baranovsky (1905), Hilferding ([1910] 1981), Preobrazhensky ([1931] 1985)] stressed the equilibrium, or proportionality aspect of the relation.

Marx himself never built a theory of business cycles on the reproduction schemes, because he believed that cycles were generated by the interaction between accumulation and the *reserve army* of labor. Accumulation, by reducing unemployment, raises real wages and lowers profits, setting the stage for a recession: "one could remark that crises are always prepared by precisely a period in which wages rise generally and the working class actually gets a larger share of that part of the annual product which is intended for consumption" (Marx [1867–94] 1967, 2:411). For Marx, sectoral flows highlight the monetary aspect of investment. His analysis starts from the observation that even

under a simple reproduction (i.e., with no growth and investment equal to depreciation), the proportions between expiring fixed capital and circulating capital are not constant in every single period.

For Marx—given the rate of total investment—nonuniformity implies that in some periods too many or too few capital goods are produced. He observed that nothing would necessarily prevent the absorption of the extra machinery as a buffer against the periods in which the replacement of fixed capital rises. Yet, under capitalism, investment is primarily a monetary decision. Hence, whenever replacement requirements are low, the monetary demand for investment will also be low as amortization funds are held in liquid form. Thus, the excess machinery will not be sold, which disrupts the smoothness of the intersectoral flows. Marx concluded that fluctuations are inherent in the material structure of the economy. Such movements, however, are not the focus of a general theory of cycles which, instead, is centered on the relationship between accumulation and the reserve army of labor.

The disproportionality approach was developed mostly by Tugan-Baranovsky just when Marxian thought was gradually rejecting the theses of falling profit rates and underconsumption. Tugan viewed accumulation as unhindered by falling consumption and falling employment, provided that the correct sectoral proportions were maintained, so that growth was deemed possible even with just one worker operating all the machines. This polar case captures the essence and the limits of Tugan's analysis.

According to equation (1), the single worker would be employed in the capital-goods sector, the other sector being fully automated. Accumulation and the real wage are independent of the reserve army of labor. Only the proportions in which capital goods are distributed between the two sectors affect the real wage. Neglecting capitalists' consumption and setting $L_i = 1$, equation (1) becomes:

$$(I - I_i)^* = x, \qquad (2)$$

where x is the real wage rate, and the asterisk denotes the value of investments in terms of the consumption good. The greater the difference $(I - I_i)^*$, the higher the real wage.

The relation of proportionality equation (2) can be read in two ways.

Consider what happens if $(I - I_i)^*$ turns out to be different from x. Equality could be restored through variations in market prices, thereby establishing the correct proportions in terms of Marxian values. Now, if all the variables in equation (2) are read in constant prices, overproduction can emerge as an excess of capital goods relative to the availability of labor. An increase in the difference $(I - I_i)^*$ means that the consumption-goods sector can obtain proportionately more machines than the capital-goods sector. If no labor is available, the additional machines will remain idle with a depressing effect on investment—a case discussed by Kaldor ([1938] 1960).

Therefore, the crucial factor that can trigger the type of crisis envisaged by Tugan is an imbalance between capital formation and the supply of labor. However, the function of the labor market—so important in Marx's business cycle—is completely disregarded by Tugan-Baranovsky, for whom accumulation is unconnected to the supply of workers. This means that, with a fully automated consumption-goods sector, the capital-labor ratio in the investment sector would automatically ensure that the single worker operated all the machines. Clearly, disproportionalities would not occur under these circumstances. The distribution of capital goods between the two sectors can, in fact, always change—$(I - I_i)^*$ varies—with the real wage adapting as market prices change. Tugan's procedure does not allow for an unambiguous identification of what the correct proportions should be. Instead, it describes a form of growth in which the labor market has no role at all.

Rudolf Hilferding's concern was not with whether accumulation was immune to underconsumption or to the falling rate of profit, but with the impact of the rise of cartels and of monopolies. He therefore accepted the disproportionality approach, though not mechanically, as he understood clearly how market prices ensure Marx's equilibrium condition. In his *Finance Capital* he wrote: "If one considers the complicated relations of proportionality which must exist in production . . . one is led to pose the question as to where the responsibility for maintaining these relations lies. Clearly, it is the price mechanism which performs this function, since prices regulate capitalist production . . ." (Hilferding [1910] 1981, 257). It follows that, for Hilferding, prices in a cartelized economy no longer function as reliable indicators of production allocation, thereby causing sectoral disproportions.

According to Hilferding, price fluctuations occur largely in the competitive branches of the economy, so that in a crisis small producers will suffer the largest number of bankruptcies. By contrast, cartelized industries will maintain prices by cutting production. The ensuing asymmetric price structure prevents the restoration of proportionality conditions which, for Hilferding, are essential for economic recovery. Thus, the possibility of restoring proportionalities and the degree of competition are clearly linked. This implies that cartelization greatly weakens the endogenous forces for recovery, increasing the dependence of the upswing on an exogenous expansion of demand and of innovations.

Analytically, the disproportionality approach has severe shortcomings. It failed to identify the conditions of proportionality, chiefly because the concept of balanced growth was not rendered explicit. Had it been made so, the difference between the instability of growth paths and a crisis would have become apparent. Understanding the latter requires a theory of how the system behaves once it leaves the steady state. A major reason for such a lack of clarity was, perhaps, the absence of an analysis of the labor market. Having produced no alternative view to Marx's reserve army of labor, disproportionality theorists studied only how sectoral outputs ought to change to stay in balance. Yet, the dynamic path of the economy depends also on how the labor market operates.

Nevertheless, disproportionality theorists raised two crucial issues: the stability of growth paths and the impact of monopolies on accumulation. The first issue has been tackled successfully by postwar growth theory: we now know that growth models, whether Marxian, Keynesian, or neoclassical are unlikely to imply a stable equilibrium. The second is still an open research area as the results of the major works on the subject (Kalecki 1971) are not fully convincing. Thus, the limitations of the disproportionality approach do not make it inferior to subsequent developments. In particular, the assumption that disproportions cause a crisis is no more suspect than the assumption of an exogenous shock made in most post-Keynesian/Kaleckian theories of the business cycle.

Moreover, the disproportionality question enabled Marxian thought to grasp the relevance of monopoly for the process of capital accumulation well in advance of its "bourgeois" counterpart. Nowhere is this more evident than in Preobrazhensky's *The Decline of Capitalism,* the last book of the early twentieth century Marxist tradition. Using numerical examples of Marx's schemes of reproduction, the author attempted to show the different impact of a disproportionality crisis under "monopolism" as opposed to a competitive system.

The numerical examples are confused, because Preobrazhensky dealt with unused capacity, fixed capital, and differential profit rates; whereas Marx's schemes involved circulating capital, uniform profit rates, and full capacity. Yet, his approach allowed him to reach very profound insights: "In free competition the reduced demand for heavy industrial production brought about a decline of prices, as a result of which the stronger enterprises, by maintaining demand attempted to acquire more means of production from heavy industry . . ." (Preobrazhensky [1931] 1985, 34). The impact on prices was therefore greater than the impact on production. Thanks to the flexibility of prices, the disproportion was overcome by a transfer of capital from one branch of the economy to another. By contrast, under a monopolistic regime the impediments to the mobility of capital imply that a part of the productive forces—equipment as well as labor—is paralyzed, preventing the transition to a new phase of expanded reproduction.

Unlike Hilferding, Preobrazhensky realized that the excess capacity prevailing under monopolistic conditions altered the Marxian link between accumulation and the reserve army of labor. In his view, monopoly caused a "thrombosis in the process of expanded reproduction" ([1931] 1985, 67), so that unused capacity tended to become endemic, hampering the absorption of the redundant workers. It was the only attempt to explore the implications of monopolies on the labor market.

The themes stemming from the disproportionality school end up converging towards those developed by the American Institutionalists and by the Post-Keynesian literature. This convergence should make it easier to evaluate their merit on the basis of the analytical and historical strength of the arguments.

Joseph Halevi

See also HILFERDING, RUDOLF; LUXEMBURG, ROSA; MARX, KARL HEINRICH; PREOBRAZHENSKY, EVGENII ALEXEYEVICH; TUGAN-BARANOVSKY, MIKHAIL IVANOVICH

Bibliography

Bulgakov, S. 1897. *On the Question of the Markets in the Capitalist Mode of Production* (in Russian). Moscow.

Hilferding, R. [1910] 1981. *Finance Capital: A Study of the Latest Phase of Capitalist Development.* London: Routledge and Kegan Paul.

Kaldor, N. [1938] 1960. "Stability and Full Employment." Chap. 5 in *Essays in Economic Stability and Growth.* Glencoe, Ill.: Free Press.

Kalecki, M. 1971. *Selected Essays on the Dynamics of the Capitalist Economy.* Cambridge: Cambridge Univ. Press.

Luxemburg, R. [1912] 1951. *The Accumulation of Capital.* London: Routledge and Kegan Paul.

Marx, K. [1867–94] 1967. *Capital.* 3 vols. New York: International Publishers.

Preobrazhensky, E. [1931] 1985. *The Decline of Capitalism.* Armonk, N.Y.: M. E. Sharpe.

Tugan-Baranovsky, M. 1905. *The Theoretical Foundations of Marxism* (in German). Leipzig.

Distributed Lags

Distributed-lag analysis is a standard empirical technique for determining how one variable affects another over time. Short- and long-run responses can be estimated, and they are often interpreted as the temporary and permanent effects of a specified change. Such distinctions are central to business-cycle analysis, which distinguishes between cycle and trend. Sims (1974), Dhrymes (1981), and Hendry, Pagan, and Sargan (1984) are central references on distributed lags and discuss both their economic and statistical aspects. Two issues are key to distributed-lag analysis: the general choice of lag length and, conditional on that choice, parametric restrictions on the lag distribution.

Choice of Lag Length
Consider the linear autoregressive distributed-lag (ADL) model:

$$a(L)y_t = \alpha + b(L)z_t + v_t$$
$$v_t \sim IN(0, \sigma_v^2), \tag{1}$$

where y_t and z_t are the endogenous and weakly exogenous variables at time t; α is the constant term; $a(L)$ and $b(L)$ are pth- and qth-order (finite) polynomials in the lag operator L, with

$a(L) = 1 - a_1L - a_2L^2 - \cdots - a_pL^p$ and $b(L) = b_0 + b_1L + b_2L^2 + \cdots + b_qL^q$; and the error v_t is assumed independent, normally distributed with mean zero and variance σ_v^2. Equation (1) is called an autoregressive distributed lag because y_t depends on its own lags and on current and lagged z_t.

For given maximal lag lengths p and q, the determination of actual lag length requires checking whether shorter lags are feasible. For the pure autoregression, i.e., $b(L) = 0$, Anderson (1971, chap. 6) proposes testing $a_p = 0$, then $a_p = a_{p-1} = 0$, and so on in a sequence of nested hypothesis tests, thereby extending the Neyman-Pearson framework for hypothesis testing. For pure distributed lags, i.e., $a(L) = 1$, Sargan (1980a) proposes a parallel framework. When both $a(L)$ and $b(L)$ are unrestricted, numerous routes (rather than just one) exist for shortening lag length, with the Neyman-Pearson framework still applying for each route from equation (1).

Proper choice of lag length also entails ensuring that p and q are large enough. Sargan (1980a) and Hendry, Pagan, and Sargan (1984) propose Lagrange multiplier statistics for testing whether a longer lag length is required. However, the specific to general nature of the procedure underscores the practical importance of selecting long enough lags initially.

Restrictions on Lag Polynomial Shape: Nine Model Classes

From the autoregressive distributed-lag relationship in equation (1), nine distinct model classes are derivable, each corresponding to a different parametric restriction on the coefficients ($\{a_i\}, \{b_i\}$). For expositional simplicity, only current and one-period lags of y_t and z_t as scalar variables in (1) are considered. Generalizations to longer lags and more variables follow immediately and appear in Hendry, Pagan, and Sargan (1984). Thus, with a slight change of notation, equation (1) in its simplified form is:

$$y_t = \alpha + \beta_0 z_t + \beta_1 z_{t-1} + \beta_2 y_{t-1} + v_t$$
$$v_t \sim IN(0, \sigma_v^2), \tag{2}$$

where the ADL coefficients are $\beta_0 = b_0$, $\beta_1 = b_1$, and $\beta_2 = a_1$.

As summarized in Table 1, parametric restrictions on ($\beta_0, \beta_1, \beta_2$) imply the following models: static regression, univariate time series, differenced data (i.e., growth rate), leading indicator, distributed lag, partial adjustment, common factor (i.e., models with autoregressive errors), homogeneous error correction, and reduced form (i.e., dead start). Volumes have been written on the properties of these models, with summaries in Hendry, Pagan, and Sargan

TABLE 1. Model Classes for the Autoregressive Distributed Lag[a]

Model type	Equation	Restrictions
Autoregressive distributed lag	$y_t = \beta_0 z_t + \beta_1 z_{t-1} + \beta_2 y_{t-1} + v_t$	None
General error correction	$\Delta y_t = \beta_0 \Delta z_t + (\beta_2 - 1)(y - \delta z)_{t-1} + v_t$	None[b]
Static regression	$y_t = \beta_0 z_t + v_t$	$\beta_1 = \beta_2 = 0$
Univariate time series	$y_t = \beta_2 y_{t-1} + v_t$	$\beta_0 = \beta_1 = 0$
Differenced data (growth rate)	$\Delta y_t = \beta_0 \Delta z_t + v_t$	$\beta_2 = 1, \beta_1 = -\beta_0$
Leading indicator	$y_t = \beta_1 z_{t-1} + v_t$	$\beta_0 = \beta_2 = 0$
Distributed lag	$y_t = \beta_0 z_t + \beta_1 z_{t-1} + v_t$	$\beta_2 = 0$
Partial adjustment	$y_t = \beta_0 z_t + \beta_2 y_{t-1} + v_t$	$\beta_1 = 0$
Common factor (AR error)	$y_t = \beta_0 z_t + u_t \quad u_t = \beta_2 u_{t-1} + v_t$	$\beta_1 = -\beta_0 \beta_2$
Homogeneous error correction	$\Delta y_t = \beta_0 \Delta z_t + (\beta_2 - 1)(y - z)_{t-1} + v_t$	$\beta_0 + \beta_1 + \beta_2 = 1$
Reduced form (dead start)	$y_t = \beta_1 z_{t-1} + \beta_2 y_{t-1} + v_t$	$\beta_0 = 0$

Notes: [a]The typology is illustrated here with equation (2), a first-order autoregressive distributed lag; and the constant term α (in (2)) is ignored throughout for ease of exposition. For generalizations, see Hendry, Pagan, and Sargan (1984, 1042).
[b]The general error correction model is isomorphic to the autoregressive distributed lag, with the parameter δ being $-(\beta_0 + \beta_1)/(\beta_2 - 1)$ (assuming $\beta_2 \neq 1$).

(1984, 1040–49) and Hendry (1995). First, all of these models impose testable restrictions relative to the unrestricted ADL in equation (2). In practice, these restrictions are frequently not tested, thereby quite possibly excluding important variables and resulting in biases. Even so, the autoregressive distributed-lag model is almost invariably trivial to estimate, so there is little justification for omitting the corresponding test. Second, the Neyman-Pearson framework is a natural basis for simplifying the ADL model to each of these model types.

Data Transformations and Associated Reparameterizations

Data transformations and the resulting reparameterizations aid understanding the properties of ADLs. For illustration and because of their importance, four model classes are examined in detail: error correction, common factor, differenced data, and (pure) distributed lag.

Two data transformations are particularly useful for interpreting dynamic multivariate models: differences and differentials. Specifically, the isomorphic transformation of equation (2) into the general error correction model (ECM) illustrates both transformations and provides a clearer understanding of each. The steps are as follows.

Beginning with differences, consider the distributed lag of z_t in equation (2): $\beta_0 z_t + \beta_1 z_{t-1}$. Estimates of β_0 and β_1 may be quite imprecise if z_t and z_{t-1} are highly correlated (which is common empirically). However, the distributed lag for z_t is equivalent to $\beta_0 \Delta z_t + (\beta_0 + \beta_1) z_{t-1}$, where Δ is the difference operator $1 - L$. So, equation (2) is also:

$$y_t = \alpha + \beta \Delta z_t + \delta^* z_{t-1} + \beta_2 y_{t-1} + v_t, \quad (3)$$

where $\beta = \beta_0$ and $\delta^* = \beta_0 + \beta_1$. For highly positively autocorrelated z_t, the growth rate Δz_t and the (lagged) level z_{t-1} are nearly *un*correlated, with β (or δ^*) being possibly quite precisely estimated. Further, β and δ^* are economically appealing coefficients to estimate: β is the immediate, short-run response of y to a change in z, whereas δ^* measures the long-run response, which is the sum of coefficients in the original distributed lag in levels. (This ignores the effect of y_{t-1} on the long-run response.) By an equivalent transformation of y_t and y_{t-1}, equation (3) becomes:

$$\Delta y_t = \alpha + \beta \Delta z_t + \delta^* z_{t-1} + \gamma y_{t-1} + v_t, \quad (4)$$

where $\gamma = \beta_2 - 1$.

Differentials are similar to differences, but with the subtraction operator being applied to different variables rather than to different lags of the same variable. In equation (4), $\delta^* z_{t-1} + \gamma y_{t-1}$ can be rewritten as γ times the "quasi-differential" $(y_{t-1} - \delta z_{t-1})$, where $\delta = -\delta^*/\gamma = -(\beta_0 + \beta_1)/(\beta_2 - 1)$ (provided $\beta_2 \neq 1$). The parameter δ measures the long-run effect of z on y: if $\delta = 1$, y is long-run homogeneous in z. Parameterization of equation (4) in terms of the quasi-differential $(y_{t-1} - \delta z_{t-1})$ results in the general error correction model:

$$\Delta y_t = \alpha + \beta \Delta z_t + \gamma \left(y_{t-1} - \delta z_{t-1} \right) + v_t. \quad (5)$$

The transformation from equation (2) through (3) and (4) to (5) involves no loss of generality.

As with differences, differentials often transform highly correlated data into less correlated data. Economically, the differential transformation is appealing. In equation (5), it generates the cointegrating relationship $y_{t-1} - \delta z_{t-1}$. More generally, economic agents might themselves transform their information set into relatively orthogonal pieces of information, using data transformations such as those just described.

Error Correction Models

A. W. Phillips and J. D. Sargan developed ECMs in the 1950s and 1960s. ECMs were brought into the limelight of the profession by numerous empirically successful implementations (notably Davidson, Hendry, Srba, and Yeo's 1978 study of U.K. consumers' expenditure) and by C. W. J. Granger and R. F. Engle's discovery that cointegration and error correction are isomorphic.

Consider the relationship between ECMs, economic theory, and distributed lags. Specifically, consider a non-stochastic steady-state theory that implies homogeneity of degree δ between two variables Y and Z (e.g., consumption and income, money and nominal income, or wages and prices), so that $Y = KZ^\delta$, where K is constant for a given growth rate of Z (and so of Y). In logarithms, that theory becomes

$$y = \kappa + \delta z, \quad (6)$$

with $y = \ln(Y)$, $\kappa = \ln(K)$, and $z = \ln(Z)$. Without a precise, real-time economic theory of the dynamic relationship between the variables y_t and z_t, a general autoregressive distributed-lag relationship is postulated, with the parameters satisfying the restriction entailed by the steady-state solution: that ADL is an ECM. (Alternatively, Nickell [1985] justifies ECMs as arising from the optimal response of economic agents in certain dynamic environments.)

For example, the first-order ADL in equation (2) is the ECM in equation (5), which satisfies the steady-state solution in equation (6). The ECM has numerous important properties. First, equation (5) is representative of a large class of models belonging to equation (1): that class satisfies steady-state economic-theoretic restrictions and allows for general dynamic responses. ECMs contrast with other model types, which typically restrict dynamic responses.

Second, equation (5) has a straightforward economic interpretation. The term $\beta \Delta z_t$ reflects the immediate impact that a change in z_t has on y_t. The term $\gamma(y_{t-1} - \delta z_{t-1})$ (with γ negative for dynamic stability) is statistically equivalent to having $\gamma(y_{t-1} - \kappa - \delta z_{t-1})$ in equation (5) instead, and hence reflects the impact on Δy_t of having y_{t-1} out of line with $\kappa + \delta z_{t-1}$. Such discrepancies could arise from errors in agents' past decisions, with the presence of $\gamma(y_{t-1} - \delta z_{t-1})$ reflecting their attempts to correct such errors: hence the name *error correction* model.

Third, for a steady-state growth rate of Z_t equal to g (i.e., $\Delta z_t = g$ and $\Delta y_t = \delta g$) and $v_t = 0$, solving equation (5) yields:

$$Y_t = Z_t^\delta \cdot \exp\left\{\left[-\alpha + g(\delta - \beta)\right]/\gamma\right\}. \tag{7}$$

This reproduces the assumption of δ-homogeneity between Y_t and Z_t entailed by the nonstochastic steady-state theory in equation (6), with $K = \exp\{[-\alpha + g(\delta - \beta)]/\gamma\}$.

Fourth, the ECM class arises naturally from considering the time-series properties of economic data, as is apparent from the related concept cointegration.

Common Factors and Autoregressive Errors
This model type is particularly important because of its ubiquity in the empirical literature, its relation to the Engle-Granger two-step procedure (for cointegrated processes), and the confusion over its logical status. Specifically, on the last issue, models with autoregressive (AR) errors imply a restriction on a more general model, rather than a generalization from a more specific model. See Hendry and Mizon (1978) and Sargan (1980b) for detailed analyses.

Consider the model:

$$y_t = bz_t + u_t \tag{8}$$

with an autoregressive error:

$$u_t = \rho u_{t-1} + v_t. \tag{9}$$

Substituting equation (9) into (8) and noting the definition of u_{t-1} from lagging equation (8) yields:

$$\begin{aligned}
y_t &= bz_t + \rho u_{t-1} + v_t \\
&= bz_t + \rho(y_{t-1} - bz_{t-1}) + v_t \\
&= bz_t - \rho bz_{t-1} + \rho y_{t-1} + v_t.
\end{aligned} \tag{10}$$

Thus, relative to equation (2), this model imposes the restriction that $\beta_0 \beta_2 = -\beta_1$. It is referred to as the "common factor" or "comfac" restriction because equation (10) can be rewritten with y_t and z_t being pre-multiplied by the common factor $(1 - \rho L)$:

$$(1 - \rho L)y_t = (1 - \rho L)bz_t + v_t. \tag{11}$$

To paraphrase Hendry and Mizon's (1978) title, autoregressive errors are a testable and possibly convenient restriction [on equation (2)], not a nuisance.

The comfac restriction is testable by Lagrange-multiplier, likelihood-ratio, and Wald procedures. The Wald statistic is the easiest to calculate, being based on the unrestricted (e.g., OLS) estimates of $(\beta_0, \beta_1, \beta_2)$ in equation (2). The likelihood-ratio statistic can be calculated from the likelihoods (or, often equivalently, the residual sums of squares) from equations (8)–(9) and (2). Although feasible, the Lagrange-multiplier statistic is rarely used in this context because of the necessarily iterative techniques for estimating equations (8)–(9). See Sargan (1980b) and Sargan ([1964] 1984) on testing for comfac restrictions with Wald and likelihood-ratio statistics, and Engle (1984) on testing in general.

Equations (8)–(9) are also the basis for Engle and Granger's test of cointegration, with $\rho = 1$ being the null hypothesis of no cointegration and $|\rho| < 1$ being the alternative hypothesis of cointegration. The restriction $\rho = 1$ also implies that y_t and z_t are related to each other through their differences only, leading to the next model class.

Models in Differenced Data
In the ECM examples above, differencing and differentials have been applied *without* loss of generality, because a suitable term in levels has always been retained, e.g., z_{t-1} in equation (3).

This contrasts with a common approach, wherein an entire equation is differenced. That latter procedure is *with* loss of generality and imposes restrictions on the lag structure. For instance, differencing equation (8) implies a common-factor restriction with the root of that common factor being unity ($\rho = 1$). Equivalently, such differencing can be interpreted as excluding both z_{t-1} and y_{t-1} from equation (4), or as excluding the error correction $(y_{t-1} - \delta z_{t-1})$ from equation (5). These exclusion restrictions are testable. Further, the restricted coefficients are interpreted quite differently when viewed as arising from a special case of equation (4) [or of (5)] rather than as a filter applied to equation (8).

"Pure" Distributed-Lag Models

ADLs without lagged dependent variables have been given two interpretations. First, they imply $a(L) = 1$, which is a testable restriction (see table 1) that is often rejected empirically. Second, they can be viewed as "solved" infinite-order (rational) distributed lags, where equation (1) has been pre-multiplied by $a(L)^{-1}$ (assuming that $a(1) \neq 0$). That is,

$$
\begin{aligned}
y_t &= \frac{\alpha}{\alpha(1)} + \frac{b(L)}{a(L)} z_t + \frac{v_t}{a(L)} \\
&= \alpha^* + c(L) z_t + e_t,
\end{aligned}
\tag{12}
$$

where $\alpha^* = \alpha/a(1)$, $c(L) = b(L)/a(L)$ and $e_t = v_t/a(L)$. In practice, $c(L)$ is approximated by a finite-order distributed-lag polynomial. Because the lags of z_t in equation (12) may be multicollinear, $c(L)$ is often restricted to be a smooth function, perhaps with end-point constraints. Almon (1965) polynomials are the most common form for imposing such restrictions; see Cooper (1972), Shiller (1973), and Trivedi (1984) for development and expositions.

While equation (12) may be a convenient interpretation of pure distributed-lag models, its estimation is problematic. Empirically, e_t is often highly autocorrelated, even for long lags in $c(L)$; and unless z_t is strongly exogenous, biases can arise in estimating $c(L)$.

Summary

Distributed-lag analysis helps sort out the short- and long-run effects of one variable on another. Relatedly, dynamic specification influences model design because of the economic and statistical importance of white-noise, innovation disturbances. Dynamics may appear in empiri-

cal models because agent optimization explicitly dictates its presence, because agent behavior implies cointegrated variables and hence dynamics, because *ceteris paribus* conditions of the theory-model may not hold in fact, or because of any combination of the above. As a rule, dynamic *mis*specification invalidates inference, so dynamics cannot be safely ignored, and a general specification (at the outset, at least) often is advisable.

Neil R. Ericsson

See also COINTEGRATION; EXPECTATIONS; FISHER, IRVING; LEADS AND LAGS; MODEL EVALUATION AND DESIGN

Bibliography

Almon, S. 1965. "The Distributed Lag Between Capital Appropriations and Expenditures." *Econometrica* 33:178–96.

Anderson, T. W. 1971. *The Statistical Analysis of Time Series.* New York: Wiley.

Cooper, J. P. 1972. "Two Approaches to Polynomial Distributed Lags Estimation: An Expository Note and Comment." *American Statistician* 26:32–35.

Davidson, J. E. H., D. F. Hendry, F. Srba, and S. Yeo. 1978. "Econometric Modelling of the Aggregate Time-series Relationship between Consumers' Expenditure and Income in the United Kingdom." *Economic Journal* 88:661–92.

Dhrymes, P. J. 1981. *Distributed Lags: Problems of Estimation and Formulation.* 2d rev. ed. Amsterdam: North-Holland.

Engle, R. F. 1984. "Wald, Likelihood Ratio, and Lagrange Multiplier Tests in Econometrics." In *Handbook of Econometrics,* edited by Z. Griliches and M. D. Intriligator. Vol. 2, 775–826. Amsterdam: North-Holland.

Engle, R. F. and C. W. J. Granger. 1987. "Cointegration and Error Correction: Representation, Estimation, and Testing." *Econometrica* 55:251–76.

Hendry, D. F. 1995. *Dynamic Econometrics.* Oxford: Oxford Univ. Press.

Hendry, D. F. and G. E. Mizon. 1978. "Serial Correlation as a Convenient Simplification, Not a Nuisance: A Comment on a Study of the Demand for Money by the Bank of England." *Economic Journal* 88:549–63.

Hendry, D. F., A. R. Pagan, and J. D. Sargan. 1984. "Dynamic Specification." In *Handbook of Econometrics,* edited by

Z. Griliches and M. D. Intriligator. Vol. 2, 1023–1100. Amsterdam: North-Holland.

Nickell, S. 1985. "Error Correction, Partial Adjustment and All That: An Expository Note." *Oxford Bulletin of Economics and Statistics* 47:119–29.

Phillips, A. W. 1954. "Stabilisation Policy in a Closed Economy." *Economic Journal* 64:290–323.

Sargan, J. D. [1964] 1984. "Wages and Prices in the United Kingdom: A Study in Econometric Methodology." In *Econometrics and Quantitative Economics*, edited by D. F. Hendry and K. F. Wallis, 275–314. Oxford: Basil Blackwell.

———. 1980a. "The Consumer Price Equation in the Post War British Economy: An Exercise in Equation Specification Testing." *Review of Economic Studies* 47:113–35.

———. 1980b. "Some Tests of Dynamic Specification for a Single Equation." *Econometrica* 48:879–97.

Shiller, R. J. 1973. "A Distributed Lag Estimator Derived from Smoothness Priors." *Econometrica* 41:775–88.

Sims, C. A. 1974. "Distributed Lags." In *Frontiers of Quantitative Economics*, edited by M. D. Intriligator and D. A. Kendrick. Vol. 2, 289–338. Amsterdam: North-Holland.

Trivedi, P. K. 1984. "Uncertain Prior Information and Distributed Lag Analysis." In *Econometrics and Quantitative Economics*, edited by D. F. Hendry and K. F. Wallis, 173–210. Oxford: Basil Blackwell.

Divisia Monetary Aggregates

Aggregation theory and index-number theory both have histories dating back to the turn of the century. The use of the techniques from those fields to generate official government data began in the 1920s, and nearly all economic data have subsequently been generated by methods developed in those literatures.

Nevertheless, one conspicuous exception remains. The monetary quantity aggregates supplied by nearly every central bank in the world are not based on index-number or aggregation theory, but are rather the simple sums of the components. The Divisia monetary aggregates, originated by Barnett (1980), remedy this problem by applying economic index-number theory.

The problem with using the exact aggregates of aggregation theory for constructing official data is that they depend on unknown aggregator functions, which typically are utility, production, cost, or distance functions. Such functions must first be econometrically estimated. Hence the resulting exact quantity and price indexes become estimator- and specification-dependent. This dependency is troublesome to governmental agencies, which therefore view aggregation theory as strictly a research tool.

Statistical index-number theory, on the other hand, provides quantity and price indexes which are computable from quantity and price data, without first estimating unknown functions. Such index numbers, whether price or quantity indexes, always depend jointly on all prices and all quantities, but not on any unknown parameters. The exact aggregates of aggregation theory, however, depend on unknown parameters, and either solely on quantity data (if a quantity aggregate) or solely on price data (if a price aggregate). In a sense, index-number theory trades joint dependency on prices and quantities for independence of unknown parameters. Examples of such statistical index numbers are the Laspeyres, Paasche, Divisia, and Törnqvist indexes. Despite their obvious usefulness, these statistical index numbers could not be derived until recently from aggregation-theoretic microeconomic theory. As a result, statistical index numbers were judged primarily by their known "good" and "bad" properties, none of which were their order of approximation to the exact aggregates of aggregation theory.

The absence of a direct link between aggregation theory and index-number theory caused some aggregation theorists to view index-number theory as ad hoc and lacking solid theoretical foundations, and also caused a tremendous proliferation of index-number formulas in index-number theory. Although most reputable index numbers usually move closely together, the multitude of index numbers reinforced the impression that index-number theory was ad hoc.

Until recently, the link between statistical index-number theory and microeconomic aggregation theory was even weaker for aggregating monetary quantities than for aggregating other quantities. The problem (only recently solved when Barnett (1978, 1980) derived formulas for the user cost for demanded monetary services and in 1987 for supplied monetary services) was that quantity indexes depend on prices as well as quantities, and the "price" of a monetary asset's services is not clearly defined. An early implicit attempt to apply index-number theory to monetary aggregation was Hutt (1963, 92n), and his index is noteworthy since recently a similar index has been advocated by Rotemberg (1991).

The loose link between index-number theory and aggregation theory was reinforced when Diewert (1976) defined the class of "superlative" index numbers. Statistical index-number theory became part of microeconomic theory, as aggregation theory had been for decades. Barnett's results on the user cost of the services of monetary assets set the stage for introducing index-number theory into monetary economics.

The Economic Decision

Consider a decision problem over monetary assets that illustrates the capability of the Divisia monetary aggregates in theory. The decision problem will be defined so that the relevant literature on economic aggregation over goods is immediately applicable.

Let m_t be the vector of real balances of monetary assets during period t, r_t be the vector of nominal holding-period yields for monetary assets during period t, A_t be the planned holdings of the benchmark asset during period t, and R_t be the expected one-period holding yield on the benchmark asset during period t. The benchmark asset is defined to provide no services other than its yield, R_t, so that the asset is held solely to accumulate wealth. Thus, R_t is the maximum expected holding-period yield in the economy in period t.

In practice, the benchmark yield is computed by maximizing over the yield-curve-adjusted holding-period yields on all of the monetary assets on which the central bank has data. Usually, some other yields are also included within the set of rates of return over which that upper envelope is computed. Since this maximization is repeated each period, the asset that serves the role of the benchmark asset can change each period.

Let y_t be the real value of total budgeted expenditure on monetary services during period t. The optimal portfolio allocation decision is:

$$\text{maximize } u(m_t)$$
$$\text{subject to } \pi_t' m_t = y_t, \tag{1}$$

where $\pi_t = (\pi_{1t}, \ldots, \pi_{nt})'$ is the vector of monetary asset real user costs, and

$$\pi_{it} = \frac{R_t - r_{it}}{1 + R_t} \tag{2}$$

The function u is the decision-maker's utility function, assumed to be monotonically increasing and strictly concave. The decision problem [equation (1)] is a constrained-optimization problem, so that results from the literature on aggregation theory and index-number theory for consumers are immediately applicable. The user-cost formula [equation (2)], derived by Barnett (1978), measures the foregone interest or opportunity cost of holding monetary asset i, when the higher yielding benchmark asset could have been held.

The exact monetary aggregate of economic theory is the utility level associated with holding the portfolio and hence is the optimized value of the objective function of the decision:

$$M_t = u(m_t) \tag{3}$$

The Divisia Index

Although equation (3) is exactly correct, it depends upon the unknown utility function, u. Nevertheless, statistical index-number theory enables us to track M_t exactly, without estimating the unknown function u.

If m_t^* is derived by solving equation (3), then $u(m_t^*)$ is the exact monetary aggregate M_t. In continuous time, $M_t = u(m_t^*)$ can be tracked exactly (Barnett 1983) by the Divisia index, which solves the differential equation

$$d \log M_t^c / dt = \sum_i s_{it} \, d \log m_{it}^* / dt, \tag{4}$$

for M_t^c, where $s_{it} = \pi_{it} m_{it}^*/y_t$ is the i'th asset's share in expenditure on the total portfolio's service flow. As a formula for aggregating over quantities of perishable consumer goods, that index was first proposed by Francois Divisia (1925) with market prices of those goods in place of the user costs in equation (4).

In continuous time, the Divisia index, under conventional neoclassical assumptions, is perfect. However, in discrete time, many different approximations to equation (4) are possible. The most popular is the Törnqvist-Theil approximation (often called the Törnqvist index), which is just the Simpson's rule approximation:

$$\log M_t - \log M_{t-1} =$$
$$\sum_1 \bar{s}_{it}\left(\log m_{it}^* - \log m_{i,t-1}^*\right), \qquad (5)$$

where $\bar{s}_{it} = (1/2)(s_{it} + s_{i,t-1})$. In discrete time we shall call equation (5) simply the Divisia index.

A compelling reason for using equation (5) as the discrete-time approximation to the Divisia index is that Diewert (1976) has defined a class of *superlative* index numbers, which have particular appeal in producing discrete-time approximations to $M_t^c = u(m_t^*)$. Diewert defines a superlative index number to be one that is exactly correct for some quadratic approximation to u. The discrete Divisia index equation (5) is superlative. With weekly or monthly monetary data, the Divisia index equation (5) is accurate to within three decimal places, which typically is smaller than the data's round-off error of the data (Barnett 1980).

Applications

A number of important extensions and applications recently have appeared. Serletis (1991), Belongia and Chalfant (1989), Swofford and Whitney (1987), and Hancock (1985) have produced some high-quality applications of this literature. Hancock's work deals with supply-side aggregation, while the work by the others is on the demand side. Ewis and Fisher (1985) introduced foreign-currency substitution into monetary aggregation theory and applied the resulting microeconomic foundations empirically. Hancock (1985) introduced transaction costs into the supply-side user costs, and Barnett, Hinich, and Weber (1986) tested the statistical significance of the regulatory wedge, produced by the nonpayment of interest on required reserves. Poterba and Rotemberg (1987) and Barnett, Hinich, and Yue (1991) have extended the theory to the case of risk aversion.

Ishida (1984) investigated the performance of the Divisia monetary aggregates as a substitute for the Bank of Japan's official simple-sum monetary aggregates. The dynamic behavior of the Divisia monetary aggregates has been studied by Barnett and Chen (1988), and Barnett, Hinich, and Yue (1991). Barnett, Offenbacher, and Spindt (1984) used Granger-causality testing and other conventional comparisons of monetary assets to compare the Divisia with the simple-sum monetary aggregates.

In some applications, monetary wealth rather than the monetary service flow is relevant. It is necessary to compute the expected dis-

counted present value of the service flow. The expected service flow in a future period is measured by its expected Divisia index. The simple-sum aggregates can be derived from discounting only if the investment yield is discounted to present value along with nominal expenditure on the service flow. However, the interest yield on an asset has never been viewed as a monetary service in macroeconomic theory. For the formula for the discounted service flow (net of the investment yield), see Barnett, Hinich, and Yue (1991).

Barnett, Fisher, and Serletis (1992) have surveyed the voluminous available empirical results, which now are available from many countries and using many empirical criteria. However, certain of these empirical criteria (structural change, regulation, and controllability) seem to be particularly relevant to the objectives of this survey.

Structural Change

A major issue in monetary economics recently has been whether structural change affects the stability of the demand-for- and supply-of-money functions. The weight of the evidence is that using Divisia monetary aggregates instead of simple-sum aggregates produces functions that are much more stable than the functions produced from the simple-sum aggregates, but at the cost of greater interest elasticity. When Divisia monetary data are used, the economic variables in the models explain the demand for and supply of monetary services adequately, and tests for structural change reject the hypothesis of shifts in the economy's structure. When simple-sum monetary data are used, the interest elasticities of the demand and supply functions are usually lower than those found with the Divisia data, but the functions estimated with simple-sum monetary-aggregate data are subject to recurring unexplained structural shifts.

It is perhaps not surprising that greater explanatory power of economic variables tends to increase elasticities to variations in those variables and conclusions about structure based on the simple-sum aggregates are probably untenable. The structural innovations usually observed in money markets are widely viewed to have been triggered by spikes in nominal interest rates caused by surges in inflationary expectations. However, nominal interest rates already are variables in the equations purported to have shifted. Since, by definition, structural shifts are produced by omitted variables, to attribute a functional shift to a shift in an included variable is self-contradictory. Divisia data do not involve this inconsistency.

Regulation

There are circumstances under which simple-sum aggregation is justifiable over certain subsets of monetary aggregates, although never over an aggregate that includes currency as a component. Paradoxically, the breadth of the span of assets over which simple-sum aggregation is justified increases as regulation either becomes very tight or is totally abandoned.

Simple-sum aggregation can be justified only over those assets which have nearly equal user costs, since the Divisia index converges to the simple-sum index as the user costs approach each other. Under severe regulation of all monetary assets, the benchmark asset's yield may be very large relative to the own rates of return on monetary assets. If so, even though the own rates of the monetary components may differ, their user costs nevertheless may be nearly equal. The Divisia index can then be approximated by the simple-sum index. The considerable evidence that demand deposits have always yielded a substantial implicit rate of return to corporate depositors makes it doubtful this was ever true in the United States. Even if once true, that time is now long past.

Under total deregulation, the rates of return on many monetary assets converged, since rate differentials and the corresponding differentiation of the competing monetary products have to some degree been produced by regulation. Similar yielding, closely substitutable, deregulated assets may be aggregated by simple summation. But since currency's yield is zero, the user cost of currency is much greater than that of such deregulated monetary assets. Hence, no subgrouping of monetary assets that can be aggregated by simple summation under deregulation can include currency.

Controllability

Procedures for controlling the Divisia monetary aggregates are necessarily fundamentally different from those for controlling the simple-sum aggregates. The simple-sum aggregates do not enter into the decisions of any economic agents, and hence are not variables within the structure of the economy. The Divisia monetary aggregates, on the other hand, track exact aggregation-theoretic monetary aggregates [which are separable functions, $M_t = u(m_t)$, of the component asset quantities, as in equation (3) above]

and hence measure variables that satisfy the existence condition for a structural variable. Only when the component assets in m_t are perfect substitutes, so that $u(m_t)$ is a simple sum, does the simple-sum aggregate appear within the structure of the economy as a separable subfunction, and hence only then does the simple sum index satisfy the existence condition for an economic aggregate.

The only possible way to control the sum of imperfect substitutes is to control each individual component asset. The imposition of reserve requirements on component assets—a tendency which has been growing in recent years in the U.S.—is intended precisely to allow such direct controllability of each component asset. While the same method is equally as applicable to controlling the Divisia aggregates, direct control over components is not necessary. Any procedure that alters the economy's general equilibrium will alter the economic variables being equilibrated. Since the Divisia monetary aggregates do indeed measure such separable structural variables, control of the Divisia monetary aggregates can operate on the aggregate itself, as if it were an elementary asset. In fact, in economic aggregation theory, an aggregate is defined to be exact, if and only if economic agents act as if the aggregate were an elementary variable.

Whether the money supply should be controlled is a separate issue requiring consideration of the properties of the entire macroeconomy. The theory and empirical evidence above demonstrate only that a control procedure operating directly on the monetary aggregate is available with the Divisia aggregates, but not with the simple-sum aggregates.

Whether or not the money supply is deliberately controlled by the central bank, the Divisia monetary aggregates can serve as indicators. Since the simple-sum aggregates do not measure service-flow variables within the economy's structure, the simple-sum aggregates cannot serve as indicators. The simple-sum aggregates discount to present value both expenditure on the monetary service flow and also the investment yield from interest-yielding monetary components. The confounding of fundamentally different motives explains why the simple-sum aggregates have no counterpart in the structure of the economy.

Conclusion

Much progress in monetary aggregation theory has recently been made. Much remains to be done. The basic issue is that only economic aggregates measure structural variables within the economy. The simple-sum monetary aggregates are just accounting identities, not economic aggregates. The Divisia monetary aggregates are economic aggregates, and hence are relevant to understanding the behavior of economic time series. In fact, the only economic data in which deterministic chaos has yet been detected are the Divisia monetary aggregates, which are sufficiently free from noise to permit detection of the underlying nonlinear determinism below the noise (Barnett and Chen 1988). Links to national and international sources of data on Divisia monetary aggregates can be found on the World Wide Web at URL location: http://econwpa.wustl.edu:80/~barnett/.

William A. Barnett

See also CHAOS AND BIFURCATIONS; DEMAND FOR MONEY; SUPPLY OF MONEY

Bibliography

Barnett, W. A. 1978. "The User Cost of Money." *Economic Letters* 1:145–49.

———. 1980. "Economic Monetary Aggregates: An Application of Index Number and Aggregation Theory." *Journal of Econometrics* 14:11–48.

———. 1983. "Understanding the New Divisia Monetary Aggregates." *Review of Public Data Use* 11:349–55.

———. 1987. "The Microeconomic Theory of Monetary Aggregation." In *New Approaches to Monetary Economics*, edited by W. A. Barnett and K. J. Singleton, 115–68. Cambridge: Cambridge Univ. Press.

Barnett, W. A. and P. Chen. 1988. "The Aggregation-Theoretic Monetary Aggregates are Chaotic and Have Strange Attractors." In *Dynamic Econometric Modeling*, edited by W. A. Barnett, E. R. Berndt, and H. White, 199–245. Cambridge: Cambridge Univ. Press.

Barnett, W. A., D. Fisher, and A. Serletis. 1992. "Consumer Theory and the Demand for Money." *Journal of Economic Literature* 30:2086–2119.

Barnett, W. A., M. J. Hinich, and W. Weber. 1986. "The Regulatory Wedge between the Demand-Side and Supply-Side Aggregation-Theoretic Monetary Aggregates." *Journal of Econometrics* 33:165–85.

Barnett, W. A., M. J. Hinich, and P. Yue. 1991. "Monitoring Monetary Aggregates Under Risk Aversion." In *Monetary Policy on the 75th Anniversary of the Federal Reserve System*, edited by M. T. Belongia, 189–222. Boston: Kluwer Academic Publishers.

Barnett, W. A., E. K. Offenbacher, and P. A. Spindt. 1984. "The New Divisia Monetary Aggregates." *Journal of Political Economy* 92:1049–85.

Belongia, M. T. and J. Chalfant. 1989. "The Changing Empirical Definition of Money: Some Estimates from a Model of the Demand for Money Substitutes." *Journal of Political Economy* 97:387–97.

Diewert, W. E. 1976. "Exact and Superlative Index Numbers." *Journal of Econometrics* 4:115–45.

Divisia, F. 1925. "L'indice monétaire et la théorie de la monnaie." *Revue d'Economie Politique* 29:980–1008.

Ewis, N. A. and D. Fisher. 1985. "Toward a Consistent Estimate of the Demand for Monies: An Application of the Fourier Flexible Form." *Journal of Macroeconomics* 7:151–74.

Hancock, D. 1985. "The Financial Firm: Production with Monetary and Nonmonetary Goods." *Journal of Political Economy* 93:859–80.

Hutt, W. H. 1963. *Keynesianism—Retrospect and Prospect*. Chicago: Regnery.

Ishida, K. 1984. "Divisia Monetary Aggregates and Demand for Money: A Japanese Case." *Bank of Japan Monetary Studies* 2:49–80.

Poterba, J. M. and J. J. Rotemberg. 1987. "Money in the Utility Function: An Empirical Implementation." In *New Approaches to Monetary Economics*, edited by W. A. Barnett and K. Singleton, 219–40. Cambridge: Cambridge Univ. Press.

Rotemberg, J. 1991. "Commentary: Monetary Aggregates and Their Uses." In *Monetary Policy on the 75th Anniversary of the Federal Reserve System*, edited by M. T. Belongia, 223–31. Boston: Kluwer Academic Publishers.

Serletis, A. 1991. "The Demand for Divisia Money in the United States: A Dynamic Flexible Demand System." *Journal of Money, Credit, and Banking* 23:35–52.

Swofford, J. L. and G. A. Whitney. 1987. "Nonparametric Tests of Utility Maximization and Weak Separability for Consumption, Leisure, and Money." *Review of Economics and Statistics* 69:458–64.

Douglas, Clifford Hugh (1879–1952)

Major Douglas offered academic economists of the 1930s a convenient name to attach to the doctrine of underconsumption in its simplest form, and offered less orthodox economists an opportunity to distinguish their ideas from so crude a doctrine, while claiming that orthodoxy had "no valid reply to much of his destructive criticism" (Keynes [1936] 1973, 370–71). Dennis Robertson and Ralph Hawtrey appeared at debates with Douglas in 1933 (Dutton and King 1986, 274–75); E. F. M. Durbin (1934) and H. T. N. Gaitskell (1933) provided systematic critiques, with Gaitskell's being notable for its attempt at sympathetic understanding.

Douglas had great appeal outside the ranks of professional economists (Ezra Pound, T. S. Eliot, Archbishop William Temple, and Lewis Mumford were all sympathetic). His appeal rested on his ability to embrace modern technology and its promise of abundance, while simultaneously delivering a populist critique of modern finance. Both the technocrat and the guild socialist were interested in *Social Credit;* and it is hardly surprising that it proved impossible to build a coherent political movement on such a basis.

Douglas discovered in early life that perfectly sensible engineering projects could not be begun or had to be abandoned for lack of credit; he attributed the necessity for credit to the lack of purchasing power in the general community and to the bank monopoly of credit creation. Conspiratorial theories of bank monopoly were the common coin of libertarian advocates of free banking and populists, of O. E. Wesslau and Arthur Kitson. Douglas added to their doctrines his own great discovery, the "A + B theorem" which became the test of Social Credit orthodoxy and the favorite target of the academic economists. While conducting an audit of the operations of the aircraft plant at Farnsworth for the Royal Air Force, Douglas looked at wage and salary data until he dreamed of Hollerith cards, and came to the realization that the wages and salaries would not buy the output. In his terms, the "A payments" (which included dividends as well as wages and salaries) would not suffice to buy output, and the financial system failed to fully return to circulation the "B payments" (interest and depreciation charges).

Douglas understood more clearly than orthodox economists often realized that such things as intermediate and capital goods exist and that expenditures on them generate incomes; he insisted, however, that in the context of an expanding economy those incomes would raise the prices of consumption goods which could not be reversed later without a crash. The financial conspiracy, by refusing to increase the money supply in proportion to the increased productive power of society, was ultimately responsible for the crash. Restoring purchasing power to the public by a National Dividend was the central proposal by which Douglas meant to break that conspiracy. Although Douglas was often accused of being an inflationist, he took particular care to hedge against that danger: attempts to evade work at a suggested 25-percent wage cut, or attempts to charge more than the just price defined by the appropriate authorities, would result in cancellation of the National Dividend payments to violators. Douglas defined the "just price" as a fraction of the cost of production— the fraction being determined by the ratio of consumption to total production, so that at the "just price," the A payments would suffice to purchase all output.

Douglas's economic ideas had little practical impact in Britain, where the "Green Shirt" organization lacked the skill and the ruthlessness needed to become an effective fascist party; and only slightly more in Canada, where Douglas's distinctive propositions were less influential than agrarian populism in shaping the Social Credit governments of Alberta in the 1930s and 1940s. Despite a brief resurgence in the 1960s in Quebec, the Social Credit party has remained influential only in British Columbia, where it led most governments since the 1950s.

Thomas A. McGahagan

See also GESELL, SILVIO; OVERSAVING THEORIES OF BUSINESS CYCLES

Bibliography

Douglas, C. H. 1921. *Credit Power and Democracy*. London: Palmer.

———. 1933. *Social Credit*. New York: Norton.

Durbin, E. F. M. 1934. *Purchasing Power and Trade Depression: A Critique of Underconsumption Theories*. London: J. Cape.

Dutton, H. I. and J. E. King. 1986. "'A Private, Perhaps, but not a Major': The Reception of C. H. Douglas's Social Credit

Ideas in Britain, 1919–1939." *History of Political Economy* 18:259–79.

Finlay, J. L. 1972. *Social Credit: The English Origins*. Montreal: McGill/Queens Univ. Press.

Gaitskell, H. T. N. 1933. "Four Monetary Heretics." In *What Everybody Wants to Know About Money*, edited by G. D. H. Cole, 280–335. New York: Knopf.

Keynes, J. M. [1936] 1973. *The General Theory of Employment, Interest and Money*. Vol. 7 in *The Collected Writings of John Maynard Keynes*. London: Macmillan.

Macpherson, C. B. 1953. *Democracy in Alberta: Social Credit and the Party System*. Toronto: Univ. of Toronto Press.

Pinard, M. 1971. *The Rise of a Third Party: A Study in Crisis Politics*. Englewood Cliffs, N.J.: Prentice-Hall.

Duesenberry, James Stemble (1918–)

For most of his scholarly career, James Duesenberry has concentrated on understanding the causes of the recurring yet always changing phenomenon of the business cycle. Organizing his work around the Keynesian *IS-LM* framework, he has helped to elaborate and develop each of its various components. It is ironic that he is best known for his early work on consumption behavior in *Income, Saving, and the Theory of Consumer Behavior*, since business cycles play a rather minor role in that work. In later work, by contrast, business cycles take center stage. His writings on wage and price formation, investment behavior, and financial flows are all dedicated to developing a model of business cycles simple enough to understand but complicated enough to capture the sectoral and dynamic effects which he considered central. As the culmination of this research program, Duesenberry took a leadership role in the project of constructing the first large-scale econometric model, *The Brookings Quarterly Econometric Model of the United States*, and its natural sequel, the first large-scale model of financial flows, "A Flow of Funds Model."

It is in *Business Cycles and Economic Growth* that Duesenberry formulates the conception of business cycles that guides his later work. In his view, business cycles can be understood as the outcomes of shocks to a system of damped differential equations. These equations capture the characteristic institutional features of the economy, "the forms of business organization, the structure of capital markets, the character of competition, to mention only a few" (1958, ix). Because there is a wide variety of shocks and each one works its way through the system differently, no business cycle is ever quite the same as any other. Moreover, in the longer run, institutional change alters the system of equations, so that even identical shocks will generally affect the economy quite differently at different stages in its development.

This vision of the business cycle led Duesenberry to seek in his early research to identify the institutional regularities of particular sectors, paying special attention to the sources of dynamic impulse to the system. In his work on price formation (1950b, 1959), Duesenberry characterizes price-setting institutions in different sectors and shows how a wage-price spiral can readily occur even with considerable unemployment. His work on investment (1958, chap. 5) emphasizes the importance of internal funds as a source of finance for investment, an institutional regularity which helps rationalize the accelerator model of investment (since profits are procyclical) while also explaining why investment is not more destabilizing (since profits turn down at the end of expansions). His work on financial flows (1962, Bosworth and Duesenberry 1973) focuses on how different sectors respond to financial shocks with a view to understanding why different shocks have such different aggregate effects.

Turning this institutional detail into a full-fledged theory of the business cycle involves understanding the dynamic interaction of all sectors. In Duesenberry's view, large-scale econometric models offer an approach specially suited to studying the complex dynamical system which is the macroeconomy. Numerical simulation, using equations estimated with actual data to capture the regularities of particular sectors, allows the dynamical properties of very detailed and complex models to be studied. For Duesenberry, the principal purpose of econometric modeling is to develop an economic theory of business cycles, a mathematical picture of the economy which would render comprehensible the complexity of macroeconomic fluctuations. As these modeling techniques came to be used by others for forecasting rather than research, Duesenberry lost interest in the project. His vision of the character of economic fluctuations led him to have strong reservations about the possibility of precise quantitative prediction. Moreover, he anticipated the need to constantly re-estimate econometric models in line with the constantly changing dynamical properties of economic institutions.

Duesenberry doubted the efficacy of pump-priming and fine-tuning using fiscal and monetary policy. In his view, the central focus of macroeconomic policy should instead be to identify and correct structural weaknesses in the economy which render it vulnerable to shocks. Fiscal and monetary policy cannot prevent the cycle, in Duesenberry's schema, since they cannot prevent the shocks that are its proximate cause. However, government actions can decrease the vulnerability of the economy to those shocks by promoting stabilizing institutions. As a policy advisor—he served on the Council of Economic Advisers (1966–68) and was Chairman of the Board of Directors of the Federal Reserve Bank of Boston (1969–74)—Duesenberry urged taking the long view by improving economic institutions rather than simply seeking a quick fix of current crises. For example, his doubts about using monetary policy as a stabilizing tool led him to propose differential taxes on borrowing and direct credit controls as alternatives to monetary policy (1974).

In a career devoted largely to the study of business cycles, Duesenberry contributed much to understanding the economic events of his day. But his enduring contribution to the understanding of business cycles lies in showing how to adapt methods of economic analysis to the study of complex macroeconomic phenomena. His vision of each business cycle as the unique product of slowly changing institutional structures adapting to diverse shocks posed a genuine challenge for scientific research. Emphasizing the institutional regularity of dynamic response to shocks, he analyzed business cycles without the usual analytically attractive but misleading assumptions that all business cycles are the same, that aggregative behavior is similar to the behavior of a representative agent, that the economy is always close to a Walrasian market-clearing equilibrium, and so forth. Developing methods for quantitative study of these institutional regularities using numerical simulation, he demonstrated that his preferred institutional approach is a progressive research program for the economic analysis of business cycles.

Perry Mehrling

See also CONSUMPTION EXPENDITURES; ECKSTEIN, OTTO; EXPENDITURES; FISCAL POLICY; MACROECONOMETRIC MODELS, HISTORICAL DEVELOPMENT OF; MACRO-ECONOMETRIC MODELS, USE OF; MONETARY POLICY; SMITHIES, ARTHUR

Bibliography

Bosworth, B. and J. S. Duesenberry. 1973. "A Flow of Funds Model and its Implications." In *Issues in Federal Debt Management*, 39–149. Conference Series No. 10. Boston: Federal Reserve Bank of Boston.

Duesenberry, J. S. 1950a. *Income, Saving and the Theory of Consumer Behavior*. Cambridge: Harvard Univ. Press.

———. 1950b. "The Mechanics of Inflation." *Review of Economic Statistics* 32:144–49.

———. 1954. "The Methodological Basis of Economic Theory." *Review of Economic Statistics* 36:361–63.

———. 1958. *Business Cycles and Economic Growth*. New York: McGraw-Hill.

———. 1959. "Underlying Factors in the Post-War Inflation." In *Wages, Prices, Profits, and Productivity*, edited by C. A. Myers, 61–89. New York: American Assembly.

———. 1962. "A Process Approach to Flow-of-Funds Analysis." In *The Flow-of-Funds Approach to Social Accounting: Appraisal, Analysis and Applications*, 173–89. NBER Studies in Income and Wealth. Vol. 25. Princeton: Princeton Univ. Press.

———. 1974. "Alternatives to Monetary Policy." *American Economic Review* 64:105–11.

Duesenberry, J. S., O. Eckstein, and G. Fromm. 1960. "A Simulation of the United States Economy in Recession." *Econometrica* 28:749–809.

Duesenberry, J. S., G. Fromm, L. R. Klein, and E. Kuh. 1965. *The Brookings Quarterly Econometric Model of the United States*. Chicago: Rand-McNally.

Dynamic Decentralization

The underlying structure of most dynamic business-cycle and consumption-based asset-pricing models is a variant of the neoclassical stochastic growth model. Such models have been analyzed by, among others, Cass (1965), Brock and

Mirman (1972), and Donaldson and Mehra (1983), and focus on how an omniscient central planner, attempting to maximize the utility of a representative agent, would optimally allocate resources over an infinite time horizon.

Production is limited by an aggregate production function subject to technological shocks. The solution to the planning problem is characterized by time-invariant decision rules of the state variables (capital stock and technology) which determine optimal consumption and investment each period.

However, business cycles are not predicated on the actions of a central planner but arise from interactions among economic agents. Given the desirable features of the stochastic growth paradigm—the solution methods are well known and the model generates well-defined proxies for all the major macroaggregates: consumption, investment, output, etc.—it is natural to ask if the allocations arising in that model can be viewed as competitive equilibria. That is, do price sequences exist such that economic agents, optimizing at these prices and interacting through competitive markets, would achieve the allocations in question as competitive equilibria? This is the essential question of dynamic-decentralization theory.

There are two notions of a decentralized equilibrium that can be used to support the above central-planning allocation: (1) the stationary Recursive Competitive Equilibrium concept of Prescott and Mehra (1980) and the closely related Decentralized Equilibrium Paradigm concept of Brock (1979, 1982); and (2) the Valuation Equilibrium concept of Debreu (1954) as developed by Bewley (1972) and Prescott and Lucas (1972). As in the planning problem, both formulations are cast in discrete time. An overview of each, beginning with the Valuation Equilibrium concept, the more general of the two, follows. For a more thorough treatment, see Harris (1987) or Stokey, Lucas, and Prescott (1989).

Valuation Equilibrium
The notion of a valuation equilibrium extends the standard finite-dimensional equilibrium theory to the infinite-dimensional commodity space presumed by the infinite-horizon planning problem. Under this interpretation, all trading takes place in the first period. The commodities traded are *contingent claims*—promises to deliver goods (e.g., consumption and capital goods) at a future date, contingent on a particular realization of uncertainty. Markets are assumed to be complete, so that for any possible future realization of uncertainty (sequence of technology shocks) up to and including some future period, a market exists for promises to deliver each good at that date contingent on that realization (event). This requires a very rich set of markets. Consumer preferences are the same as those assumed for the representative agent in the planning problem; consumers undertake all investment decisions. In the first period, consumers contract to receive consumption and investment goods and to deliver capital goods in future periods contingent on future states so as to maximize the expected present value of the utility of consumption over their infinite lifetimes. Firms maximize the present value of discounted profits. Given current prices, they contract to deliver consumption and investment goods to and to receive capital goods from the consumer-investors.

In its most general formulation, the Valuation Equilibrium is characterized simply as a continuous linear function that assigns a value to each bundle of contingent commodities. Only under more restrictive assumptions can this function be represented as a series of prices (Prescott and Lucas 1972, Mehra 1988). The basic result is that for any solution to the planner's problem—that is, sequences of consumption, investment and capital goods—a set of state-contingent prices exists such that these sequences coincide with the contracted quantities in the Valuation Equilibrium given the corresponding realization of productivity shocks.

This decentralization concept is quite general and applies to central-planning formulations much more general than the neoclassical growth paradigm. Nevertheless, it is a somewhat unnatural perspective for macroeconomists, and it presumes a set of markets much richer than any observed. These shortcomings led to the development of the concept of a recursive competitive equilibrium.

Recursive Competitive Equilibrium Concepts
This abstraction postulates a continuum of identical economic agents indexed on the unit interval (again with preferences identical to those of the representative agent in the planning formulation), and a finite number of firms. As in the Valuation Equilibrium approach, consumers undertake all consumption and saving decisions. Firms, which have equal access to a single constant-returns-to-scale technology,

D

maximize their profits each period and are assumed to produce two goods, a consumption good and a capital good. Unlike the Valuation Equilibrium approach, trading between agents and firms occurs every period. At the start of each period, firms observe the technological shock to productivity and purchase capital and labor services, which are supplied inelastically at competitive prices. The capital and labor are used to produce the capital and consumption goods. At the close of the period, individuals, acting competitively, use their wages and the proceeds from the sale of capital to buy the consumption and capital goods produced by the firms. The capital good is then carried into the next period when it again becomes available to firms and the process repeats itself. Note that firms are liquidated at the end of each period (retaining no capital assets while technology is freely available) and that no trades between firms and consumer-investors extend over more than one time period. Capital goods carried over from one period to the next are the only link between periods, and period prices depend only on the state variables in that period.

Brock's (1979, 1982) formulation closely resembles that of Prescott and Mehra (1980)—trading takes place period-by-period for instance—except for two noteworthy technical differences: the production technology need not exhibit constant returns to scale and the capital-stock sequence need not be bounded. The first of these distinctions allows firms to earn a positive profit stream which Brock capitalizes in a manner similar to that suggested by Lucas (1978). The possibility of an unbounded capital-stock sequence means that Brock's setting can accommodate certain types of non-stationary equilibria precluded by the Recursive Competitive Equilibrium (RCE) formulation. But if constant returns to scale and a bounded production-possibility set are imposed on Brock's setting, it can be mapped into the RCE structure and its pricing functions reduce to those of Prescott and Mehra. While the restrictive structure of markets and trades makes both concepts less general than the Valuation Equilibrium Approach, they do provide an interpretation of decentralization that is better suited to macro-analysis than the Valuation Equilibrium Approach. Since an RCE is Pareto-optimal and its allocation coincides with that of the planning problem, the solution to the central-planning stochastic-growth problem may be regarded as the aggregate investment and consumption functions that would arise from a decentralized homogeneous consumer economy.

Researchers have recently begun to formulate models that can be cast in the customary recursive setting, yet whose equilibria are not Pareto-optimal. As a consequence, model equilibrium can no longer be obtained as the solution to a central-planning-optimum formulation. These models incorporate such features as monetary phenomena, distortionary taxes, externalities, and borrowing-lending constraints. Besides increasing general model realism, such features not only enable the models to better replicate the stylized facts of the business cycle, but also provide a rationale for interventionist government policies. Monetary models of this sort include those of Lucas and Stokey (1987, a monetary exchange model) and Coleman (1996, a monetary production model). Bizer and Judd (1989) and Coleman (1991) present models in which non-optimality is induced by tax distortions while Danthine and Donaldson (1990) present a model in which non-optimality results from efficiency-wage externalities. For this class of models, equilibrium is characterized as an aggregate-consumption and an aggregate-investment function which jointly solve a system of first-order optimality equations on which market-clearing conditions have been imposed. To date, Coleman (1991) provides the most widely applicable set of conditions under which these suboptimal equilibrium functions exist. However, these optimality conditions cannot, in general, be derived as the characterization of an optimum problem.

In another context, Cox, Ingersoll, and Ross (1985) propose a notion of decentralized equilibrium appropriate to a continuous time-setting. In the interest of brevity we have not considered this concept, as it has not yet been employed in business-cycle studies.

John B. Donaldson
Rajnish Mehra

See also INCOMPLETE MARKETS; REAL BUSINESS-CYCLE THEORIES

Bibliography

Bewley, T. 1972. "Existence of Equilibria in Economies with Infinitely Many Commodities." *Journal of Economic Theory* 4:514–40.

Bizer, D. and K. Judd. 1989. "Taxation and Uncertainty." *American Economic Review Papers and Proceedings* 19:331–36.

Brock, W. A. 1979. "An Integration of Stochastic Growth Theory and the Theory of Finance, Part I: The Growth Model." In *General Equilibrium, Growth and Trade: Essays in Honor of Lionel McKenzie,* edited by J. Green and J. Scheinkman, 65–92. New York: Academic Press.

———. 1982. "Asset Prices in a Production Economy." In *The Economics of Information and Uncertainty,* edited by J. J. McCall, 1–43. Chicago: Univ. of Chicago Press.

Brock, W. A. and L. J. Mirman. 1972. "Optimal Economic Growth and Uncertainty: The Discounted Case." *Journal of Economic Theory* 4:497–513.

Cass, D. 1965. "Optimal Growth in an Aggregative Model of Capital Accumulation." *Review of Economic Studies* 32:233–40.

Coleman, W. J. 1991. "Equilibrium in a Production Economy with an Income Tax." *Econometrica* 59:1091–1104.

———. 1996. "Money and Output: A Test of Reverse Causation." *American Economic Review* 86:90–111.

Cox, J., J. Ingersoll, and S. Ross. 1985. "An Intertemporal General Equilibrium Model of Asset Pricing." *Econometrica* 53:363–84.

Danthine, J. P. and J. B. Donaldson. 1990. "Efficiency Wages and the Business Cycle Puzzle." *European Economic Review* 34:1275–1301.

Debreu, G. 1954. "Valuation Equilibrium and Pareto Optimum." *Proceedings of the National Academy of Sciences* 40:588–92.

Donaldson, J. B. and R. Mehra. 1983. "Stochastic Growth with Correlated Production Shock." *Journal of Economic Theory* 29:282–312.

Harris, M. 1987. *Dynamic Economic Analysis.* New York: Oxford Univ. Press.

Lucas, R. E., Jr. 1978. "Asset Prices in an Exchange Economy." *Econometrica* 46:659–81.

Lucas, R. E., Jr. and N. Stokey. 1987. "Money and Interest in a Cash Advance Economy." *Econometrica* 55:491–513.

Mehra, R. 1988. "On the Existence and Representation of Equilibrium in an Economy with Growth and Non-Stationary Consumption." *International Economic Review* 29:131–35.

Prescott, E. C. and R. E. Lucas, Jr. 1972. "A Note on Price Systems in Infinite Dimensional Space." *International Economic Review* 13:416–22.

Prescott, E. C. and R. Mehra. 1980. "Recursive Competitive Equilibria: The Case of Homogeneous Households." *Econometrica* 48:1365–79.

Stokey, N., R. E. Lucas, and E. C. Prescott. 1989. *Recursive Methods in Economic Dynamics.* Cambridge: Harvard Univ. Press.

D

E

Eckstein, Otto (1927–1984)

Otto Eckstein was a pioneer in developing and applying large-scale macroeconometric models, economic and financial databases, interactive computer technology, and economic information systems for business-cycle analysis and forecasting. He was Founder, President, and Chairman of Data Resources, Inc. (DRI) and Professor of Economics at Harvard University. Through DRI, econometrics-based analyses of the economy and financial markets became widespread.

Eckstein developed a National Economic Information Systems Approach to economic forecasting and the analysis of business conditions. The approach integrated scientific economic analysis and computerized econometric models with the monitoring of the economic, financial, and policy environment to track, chronicle, and forecast business conditions.

The centerpiece of the system was a large-scale macroeconometric model, developed by Eckstein in collaboration with colleagues at DRI. He described the model in *The DRI Model of the U.S. Economy*, "The Mechanisms of the Business Cycle in the Postwar Era" (co-authored with A. Sinai), and "The Data Resources Model: Uses, Structure, and Analysis of the U.S. Economy" (co-authored with E. W. Green and A. Sinai).

Eckstein was unusual in that his professional work and contributions spanned academia, business, and government. He was the author, co-author, or editor of six books, twenty-one articles, and two major public reports on business cycles and the econometric approach to forecasting and analysis. He also was the principal author and editor of a monthly publication, *The DRI Review of the Economy*. A frequent witness before Congress, he served on the Council of Economic Advisers in the Johnson administration, and consulted with federal government agencies and Congressional committees. Under his direction, DRI grew to be the largest economic-information company in the world. DRI pioneered distributed-process computing through remote terminal access to models, databases, and forecasts which became widely used by practitioners. DRI was a major educator of business and financial economists in applying econometric models to the analysis of business conditions, thereby helping to link academic economic research to the business world.

Eckstein's work on business cycles can be divided into four areas: (1) the inflation process and its dynamics; (2) large-scale macroeconometric model development, testing, and simulation; (3) applications of the DRI Model to forecasting, policy analysis, and business cycles; and (4) recording, analyzing, and forecasting business conditions.

Eckstein's studies of inflation, a key element of the business cycle, were largely empirical, including early studies on cost-markup inflation, industry price models, wage-price interactions, and the effects of supply shocks on the inflationary process, as well as a seminal book, *Core Inflation*.

In *Core Inflation*, Eckstein brought together all elements of his work on inflation. Within a pricing framework in which prices are marked up over costs at each processing stage, Eckstein focused on the level of demand relative to cost as the major determinant of inflation. Costs included unit labor costs, unit capital costs, and unit materials costs. Since they directly and indirectly affected all three types of business costs, Eckstein concluded that oil and energy costs were important factors in both the inflationary spiral and the cyclical fluctuations of the 1970s and 1980s.

Eckstein's work on large-scale macroeconometric models was principally concerned with elaborating and understanding the structural processes of the U.S. economy, how it might behave under certain "what if" conditions, and its response to various macroeconomic policies. The models were used as efficient, consistent generators of macroeconomic and financial-market forecasts. Links between the macroeconomy and specific industries, sectors, or markets also were developed through the econometric approach.

Ongoing testing and simulation, involving standard econometric regression analysis and full system performance of the model, were critical elements in the progressive development and improvement of the DRI model. The DRI Model was used extensively to determine the structure of the business cycle, to analyze the potential effects on the economy of various economic policies, and to forecast future economic conditions. Eckstein (1981b, 1983) described the structure and underlying theory of the DRI Model and provided some underlying theory and policy experiments. Eckstein (1978) used the DRI Model to examine the recession of the 1970s, its causes, determinants, and behavioral characteristics through counterfactual analysis.

Finally, Eckstein provided regular forecasts and analyses of the economy and its major sectors in *The DRI Monthly Review*. The *Review* was a chronicle of the business cycle and its prospects. Eckstein (1976b, 1977) discussed the forecasting approach and its use in business decisions.

Otto Eckstein played a major role in developing econometric-model-based simulation techniques to understand, analyze, and forecast business cycles. A further contribution was to translate difficult macroeconomic theory and applied econometrics into usable and understandable terms for economists in industry, financial institutions, and government. Eckstein's contributions to the analysis of inflation and to large-scale macroeconometric modeling continue to inform the work of most economists in these two areas.

Allen Sinai

See also INFLATION; KLEIN, LAWRENCE ROBERT; MACROECONOMETRIC MODELS, HIS-TORICAL DEVELOPMENT; MACROECONOMETRIC MODELS, USE OF; RECESSIONS (SUPPLY-SIDE) IN THE 1970S; SUPPLY SHOCKS

Bibliography
Eckstein, O. 1958. "Inflation, the Wage-Price Spiral and Economic Growth." In *The Relationship of Prices to Economic Stability and Growth*, 361–74. Joint Economic Committee, U.S. Congress.
———, ed. 1976a. *Parameters and Policies in the U.S. Economy*. Amsterdam: North-Holland.
———. 1976b. "Econometric Models and the Formation of Business Expectations." *Challenge*, March/April, 12–19.
———. 1977. "National Economic Information Systems for Developed Countries." In *The Organization and Retrieval of Economic Knowledge*, edited by M. Perlman, 67–76. New York: Macmillan.
———. 1978. *The Great Recession*. Amsterdam: North-Holland.
———. 1981a. *Core Inflation*. New York: Prentice-Hall.
———. 1981b. "Econometric Models for Forecasting and Policy Analysis: The Present State of the Art." In *Large-Scale Macroeconometric Models*, edited by J. Kmenta, 155–76. Amsterdam: North-Holland.
———. 1983. *The DRI Model of the U.S. Economy*. New York: McGraw-Hill.
Eckstein, O. and R. Brinner. [1972] 1976. "The Inflation Process in the United States." In *Parameters and Policies in the U.S. Economy*, edited by O. Eckstein, 99–158. Amsterdam: North-Holland.
Eckstein, O., J. S. Duesenberry, and G. Fromm. 1960. "Simulation of the United States Economy in Recession." *Econometrica* 28:749–809.
Eckstein, O. and G. Fromm. 1968. "The Price Equation." *American Economic Review* 58:1159–83.
Eckstein, O. and J. Girola. 1978. "Long-Term Properties of the Price-Wage Mechanism in the United States, 1891 to 1977." *Review of Economics and Statistics* 60:323–33.
Eckstein, O., E. W. Green, and A. Sinai. 1974. "The Data Resources Model: Uses, Structure, and the Analysis of the U.S. Economy." In *Econometric Model Performance*, edited by L. R. Klein and

E. Burmeister, 211–31. Philadelphia:
Univ. of Pennsylvania Press.

Eckstein, O. and A. Sinai. 1986. "The
Mechanisms of the Business Cycle in the
Postwar Era." In *The American Business
Cycle: Continuity and Change,* edited by
R. J. Gordon, 39–120. Chicago: Univ. of
Chicago Press.

Eckstein, O. and D. Wyss. 1972. "Industry
Price Equations." In *The Econometrics
of Price Determination,* edited by O.
Eckstein, 133–65. Washington, D.C.:
Federal Reserve System.

Effective Demand

Effective demand is demand that actually results in spending on output as a whole. According to some business-cycle theories, recessions
and inflations are the result respectively of deficient and of excessive effective demand. The
term was first used in recent times by Keynes in
the *General Theory.*

To make sense of effective demand, one
must first distinguish between two types of economic theory—real analysis and monetary
analysis. Real analysis begins with the assumption that money is a veil: all essential aspects of
an economy may be understood purely in real
terms—in terms of the quantities of commodities and services traded and the exchange ratios
between them. The use of money in actual
transactions is of no fundamental significance:
the economy may be analyzed as if trading took
place under frictionless barter.

Monetary analysis rejects this view. It considers money to be essential: the economic process, particularly at the aggregate level, cannot
be understood without taking into account the
monetary nature of actual transactions. In the
context of real analysis, effective demand can be
neither deficient nor excessive. Under barter,
Say's Law must hold: the supply of one good is
the demand for another. Hence, the total value
of goods offered for sale is identically equal to
the total value of desired purchases. Of course,
if prices are wrong there may be imbalances of
supply and demand for individual goods, but
there can be no general imbalance with respect
to output as a whole.

In the context of monetary analysis, on
the other hand, effective demand can be deficient or excessive. In a monetary economy, the
supply of one good is no longer per se the demand for another. Goods are sold for money,
and money is used to buy goods. In the circular flow of money payments, money earned
from the sale of goods is distributed as money
income, and this money income is then used to
purchase goods. Because the act of supply and
the act of demand are separate and distinct, the
total value of all goods offered for sale need
not equal the total value of desired purchases.
In a monetary economy, Say's Law does not
hold.

If effective demand is deficient, desired
expenditure falls short of money income. This
may be the result either of hoarding (an increase
in the quantity of money held as an asset) or of
a decrease in the quantity of money. Deficient
effective demand puts deflationary pressure on
the economy. The outcome will depend on the
flexibility of prices. If prices are flexible, they
will fall, with little change in output or employment. If prices are not flexible, then output and
employment will fall.

If effective demand is excessive, desired
expenditure exceeds money income. This may
be the result either of dishoarding (a decrease
in the quantity of money held as an asset) or of
an increase in the quantity of money. Excessive
effective demand puts inflationary pressure on
the economy. If prices are flexible, they will rise.
If not, output and employment will increase or
there will be shortages.

Different theories suggest different causes
of deficient or excessive effective demand. The
two favorite culprits are failures of intertemporal coordination—coordination of saving
and investment—and failures of monetary
control. The Physiocrats were the first to
worry about deficient effective demand, fearing that saving or taxation might interfere with
the circular flow of payments. Malthus and
Sismondi raised the issue again, arguing that
there could be a general glut (a deficiency of
effective demand). The refutation of their arguments by Ricardo and Say, reasoning from
real analysis, was generally accepted, and the
issue was considered closed for almost a century. Then, a growing concern with business
cycles stimulated renewed interest in the
theory of effective demand and gave birth to
a rich literature on the subject. Major contributors included Mises and Hayek in Austria;
Wicksell, Myrdal, Lindahl, Ohlin and Lundberg in Sweden; and Robertson, Hawtrey, and
Keynes in England.

Modern understanding of effective demand, perhaps regrettably, is completely domi-

nated by Keynes's treatment in the *General Theory*. That treatment shared many features with those of his contemporaries, but also differed from them in some important respects. Like the others, it had its origins in monetary analysis, seeing the problem as inherent in a monetary economy. And, like the others, it, too, saw the cause of imbalance as a coordination failure involving saving and investment.

Where the *General Theory* differed from all previous treatments of effective demand was in its theoretical method. While others had relied on some form of sequence analysis of the circular flow, Keynes relied instead on a new concept of static equilibrium. Previous writers, from Malthus on, had seen the problem of effective demand as being one of stability. They had generally accepted the real-analysis characterization of long-run equilibrium, but thought that problems of effective demand could lead to temporary deviations from that equilibrium. Keynes instead substituted his own concept of long-run equilibrium, positing the existence of an unemployment equilibrium that could persist indefinitely.

One unintended consequence of Keynes's shift in method was the waning of interest in effective demand and in monetary analysis in general. Discussion of Keynes's unemployment equilibrium revealed that wage rigidity was a necessary and sufficient condition for its existence. Given wage rigidity, an identical unemployment equilibrium could be derived from real analysis: money proved inessential. Consequently, professional attention largely switched to price and wage rigidity (e.g., Malinvaud 1985).

In recent years, monetary analysis and effective demand have enjoyed some renewed interest. A new literature has developed around the concept of the finance constraint. Current demand is constrained not only by the real intertemporal budget constraint, but also by the need to finance that demand. In Clower's terminology, demand without the necessary finance is only *notional*; finance is required to make demand effective.

Meir Kohn

See also HUTT, WILLIAM HAROLD; KEYNES, JOHN MAYNARD; LAVINGTON, FREDERICK; MALTHUS, THOMAS ROBERT; RICARDO, DAVID; SAY, JEAN-BAPTISTE; SAY'S LAW; SISMONDI, JEAN CHARLES LEONARD SIMONDE DE

Bibliography

Clower, R. W. 1965. "The Keynesian Counter-Revolution: A Theoretical Appraisal." In *The Theory of Interest Rates,* edited by F. H. Hahn and F. P. R. Brechling, 103–25. London: Macmillan.

———. 1967. "A Reconsideration of the Microfoundations of Monetary Theory." *Western Economic Journal* 6:1–8.

Gertler, M. 1988. "Financial Structure and Aggregate Economic Activity." *Journal of Money, Credit, and Banking* 20:559–88.

Haberler, G. 1962. *Prosperity and Depression.* 4th rev. ed. Cambridge: Harvard Univ. Press.

Keynes, J. M. [1936] 1973. *The General Theory of Employment, Interest, and Money.* Vol. 7 of *The Collected Writings of John Maynard Keynes.* London: Macmillan.

Kohn, M. 1981. "A Loanable Funds Theory of Unemployment and Monetary Disequilibrium." *American Economic Review* 71:859–79.

———. 1986. "Monetary Analysis, the Equilibrium Method, and Keynes's 'General Theory.'" *Journal of Political Economy* 94:1191–1224.

———. 1988. "The Finance Constraint Theory of Money: A Progress Report." Dartmouth College, October.

Leijonhufvud, A. 1981. *Information and Coordination.* New York: Oxford Univ. Press.

Lundberg, E. [1937] 1955. *Studies in the Theory of Economic Expansion.* Reprinted with an additional preface by the author. Oxford: Basil Blackwell.

Malinvaud, E. 1985. *The Theory of Unemployment Reconsidered.* Oxford: Basil Blackwell.

Efficiency Wages

Efficiency-wage models show that wage cuts may be unprofitable, because the productivity of a firm's labor force depends on the wages it pays. The key assumption of efficiency-wage models is that the effects of wages on productivity can be sufficient for wage cuts to reduce firm profits. Consequently, efficiency-wage theory explains why profit-maximizing firms do not cut wages when facing an excess supply of labor. In contrast, in traditional labor-market models, which assume that workers are identical and that effort is exogenous, firms would always cut wages if they could attract workers at the reduced wages.

Downward wage rigidity is a necessary condition for involuntary unemployment in equilibrium. By rationalizing downward wage rigidity in equilibrium models with profit-maximizing firms, efficiency-wage theories provide a microeconomic foundation for theories of involuntary unemployment.

Efficiency-wage theories suggest that wage cuts may be unprofitable for the following reasons:

1. The better workers would quit or would not apply to the firm (adverse selection).
2. Workers would be more likely to shirk or quit (incentive effects).
3. Workers would be more likely to get sick (nutrition effects).
4. Workers would be less cooperative (gift-exchange effects).
5. Replacing high-wage workers with low-wage workers makes the remaining high-wage workers unwilling to cooperate with the new workers (insider-outsider theory).
6. Vacancies take longer to fill (vacancy effects).

Each of these explanations is associated with a distinct group of efficiency-wage models.

Adverse-Selection Models

Adverse-selection models assume that unrewarded productivity differences are positively correlated with the alternative opportunities available to workers. Since firms are either unable or unwilling to set wage differentials that fully reflect productivity differences, a firm that cuts wage offers to new workers will degrade the quality of new applicants. Similarly, wage cuts for the firm's current employees would cause its better employees to quit. If these adverse-selection effects outweigh the gains to a firm from cutting wages, it will not cut wages when facing an excess supply of workers.

Adverse-selection models also explain why unemployment rates differ markedly among different groups in the labor force, and why changes in labor demand affect some groups far more than others. In a standard model, the workers with the lowest reservation wages are the most likely (i.e., first) to be hired. In adverse-selection models, the groups of workers with the lowest cost per efficiency unit of labor (at their efficiency wage) are the most likely (i.e., first) to be hired. We can call these the lowest-cost types. Firms hiring this group at their efficiency wage minimize their cost per efficiency unit of labor. If labor supply by this group at its efficiency wage exceeds labor demand, then only workers from this group are hired and some of them will be unemployed. No workers from other groups are hired, because they would be more expensive to the firm than the lowest-cost types regardless of the wage they were paid.

If demand for the lowest-cost group exceeds the supply of that group at its efficiency wage, the wage for that group is bid up until either supply equals demand, or until that group's wage rises enough to make another group equally cheap. In the latter case, members of the next-lowest cost group are hired at their efficiency wage. Such a labor-market equilibrium is characterized by market-clearing wages for the lowest-cost types, and (possibly) by an excess supply of labor for the next lowest-cost types. Other, more expensive types are not employed unless labor demand is sufficient to bid up the wages of the lower-cost types.

In general, only one type of worker is paid its efficiency wage and faces job queues. However, some types may be excluded from the labor market. If labor demand falls sufficiently, the types that previously faced job queues will be excluded from the market, and other types will find that their wages fall, perhaps also facing job queues. While in equilibrium, all types of employed workers are equally costly; increases in unemployment will be concentrated on those workers whose cost per efficiency unit cannot be reduced sufficiently by wage reductions.

Because all workers of the same group are paid the same wage, the more homogeneous groups of workers tend to have lower costs. These types of workers are the first hired and the last fired during business cycles. Of course, partitioning workers into "types" depends on how well employers can differentiate between workers. Workers whose ability is more readily discernable are more likely to be employed, because their adverse-selection effects are less costly to the firms hiring them.

Workers whose backgrounds are familiar to employers (such as middle-class white males) appear to be more likely to be hired than workers with unfamiliar backgrounds. This may be because employers can more accurately predict the productivity of members of familiar groups.

Incentive Models

High wages deter workers from quitting, shirking, or stealing. The first efficiency-wage incentive models, developed by Salop (1979), focused on quits. Higher-wage firms incur lower turnover costs than lower-wage firms. If there is a continuum of firms, then, in equilibrium, the difference in turnover costs roughly offsets the difference in wages (Stiglitz 1985). High-wage firms face an excess supply of labor, but cannot increase profits by cutting wages, because their turnover costs would increase by more than their savings in wages.

These models can generate aggregate unemployment. Suppose many firms are offering a wage at which there is an excess supply of labor. A small wage cut by any firm would cause a discontinuous increase in its quit rate. If the initial wage was sufficiently near the reservation wage of workers, no firm could profitably cut its wage offer. Thus, for given parameter values, a wide range of single-wage equilibria is possible. Because labor demand is downward-sloping, each equilibrium corresponds to a different level of unemployment. The higher the wage, the higher level of unemployment. A similar line of reasoning could be used to analyze multiple-wage equilibria.

Subsequent efficiency-wage incentive models (e.g., Shapiro and Stiglitz 1984) have focused on how wages affect effort. In those models, firms prevent shirking (or stealing) by paying relatively high wages, so that workers lose something if they are fired. The higher the unemployment rate, the lower the wage needed to deter shirking. Consequently, a fall in aggregate demand generally causes wages to fall and unemployment to rise. In both quit and effort models, unemployment is involuntary. The unemployed would be strictly better off if they were employed at the current wage.

Carmichael (1990) has criticized these models on the grounds that firms could sell their jobs, or equivalently require workers to post bonds which would be lost if they were to quit or were caught shirking. Either of these arrangements could eliminate involuntary unemployment. One shortcoming of the Carmichael critique is that workers typically lack sufficient capital or access to capital markets to post significant bonds. However, if workers are suffi-

ciently risk-averse, even small bonds would eliminate job queues. In a pure incentive model, firms would demand bonds that exhausted all the capital resources of job applicants. However, these transactions, while profit-maximizing, generate large deadweight losses, reflecting the risk imposed on workers. We rarely see contracts that impose large deadweight losses. This may be because firms are not simple profit maximizers and therefore may not adopt grossly inefficient policies even if they did maximize short-run profits. Another explanation hinges on the risk aversion of some workers. Worker heterogeneity would keep risk-averse workers (who might be particularly productive) from applying to firms that required bonds.

It has also been argued that firms could require workers to accept low wages initially and raise wages later if the workers did not quit and were not caught shirking. Such upward-sloping wage contracts, in effect, would seem to require workers to buy their jobs and thereby eliminate unemployment. But this would only be true if firms could costlessly monitor effort on the initial low-wage entry jobs, and therefore were unconcerned about shirking on those jobs. Akerlof and Katz (1990) have shown that if firms must deter shirking in every period and if workers have higher discount rates than firms, the profit-maximizing contract always pays workers more than the wage needed to attract them to the firm.

Nutrition Models

At very low wages, a wage cut can harm the health and stamina of workers. As in the adverse-selection and incentive models, this effect of wages on productivity can lead firms to offer wages that are above the market-clearing level. The main difference between nutrition models and the previous efficiency-wage models is that the aggregate unemployment rate and the wages paid by other firms do not affect firms' wage offers in the nutritional models. Macroeconomic conditions may play an indirect role insofar as they affect the nonwage income of workers and the incomes of spouses and other relatives from whom workers may get support. Because outside income contributes to the nutrition of workers, increases in outside income increase labor demand and employment at each wage.

The effect of increases in outside income on wages depends on whether the labor-supply constraint is binding. If it is binding at the efficiency wage, wages will rise; if it is not binding, wages will fall because the efficiency wage falls.

Gift-Exchange Models
Akerlof ([1982] 1986) has stressed the gift-exchange nature of employment relationships. He argues that when firms pay "high" wages they are in effect making a gift to workers, which they in turn reciprocate by acting for the firm's benefit even when not otherwise rewarded for their actions. The gift-exchange model superficially resembles the incentive models discussed above. However, in incentive models, only anticipated future wages and termination probabilities affect the current behavior of workers. In the gift-exchange model, past and current wages affect current behavior by changing their preferences.

Insider-Outsider Models
Lindbeck and Snower (1988a, b) have developed insider-outsider models to explain why firms do not cut the wages of newly hired workers when there is an excess supply of workers. Lindbeck and Snower stress the morale problems caused by replacing experienced workers with lower-wage newly hired workers. In insider-outsider models, firms commit to lifetime wages when they hire workers; experienced and inexperienced workers are complements; and if a firm replaced any of its experienced workers with less-experienced, lower-paid workers, the remaining experienced workers would refuse to cooperate with the lower-paid ones. Taken together, these assumptions reduce the responsiveness of wages to macroeconomic shocks.

Vacancy Models
In any plausible model in which workers are matched with jobs, low-wage firms have more difficulty filling vacancies than do high-wage firms. Montgomery (1991) has shown that the costs of vacancies can give rise to an equilibrium wage distribution with both vacancies and involuntary unemployment. Firms would not reduce their wages, because the increase in vacancy costs offsets the savings from reduced wages.

Evidence
The recent interest in efficiency-wage models has been accompanied by research showing significant wage differentials across industries and firms. Industry wage differentials seem to persist over time and across countries. High-wage industries in a given country and time period tend to be high-wage industries in other countries and time periods. These differentials persist after correcting for all observed characteristics of the workers. In addition, the characteristics that are associated with high wages *within* industries tend also to be possessed by the average worker in high-wage industries. For example, high-wage industries tend to have workers with better than average education.

It has been suggested that industry and firm wage differentials provide support for the efficiency-wage models, and that by examining the factors correlated with high industry wages, we can distinguish between the various efficiency-wage models. The principal factors associated with high-wage industries are high capital-labor ratios, high profit rates, large firm size, and a highly qualified work force. In the fast-food industry, company-owned stores pay higher wages than do franchises.

Unfortunately, these data do not allow us to reject any of the efficiency-wage models. For instance, the costs of shirking, absenteeism, quits, vacancies, and low ability are all likely to be positively correlated with capital-labor ratios or operating profits per worker. Consequently, the incentive, sorting, and gift-exchange models all predict high wages in such industries.

One observation that almost all models of the labor market have difficulty explaining is that industry wage differentials are highly correlated across occupations. At first blush, it seems unlikely that firms in one industry pay high wages to machinists for the same reasons that they pay high wages to janitors, or to cooks in the company cafeteria.

These correlations can be explained by a combination of efficiency-wage considerations and psychological explanations. For efficiency-wage reasons, some workers receive both compensation and amenities that provide high levels of satisfaction. One such amenity is to have highly competent support personnel. By offering higher wages to support personnel than they are offered elsewhere, a firm can attract harder-working support personnel. Moreover, larger wage differentials across jobs than is customary could hurt morale, reducing the amenity level for the highly paid workers as well as the productivity of support personnel.

Policy Implications
Typically the market equilibria implied by efficiency-wage models are not Pareto-optimal.

The adverse-selection model can be used to illustrate the nature of these market imperfections and how government policies may be able to remedy these imperfections, thereby increasing aggregate output.

In the adverse-selection model, workers are likely to be mismatched with jobs. Workers in the industrial sector may have a comparative *disadvantage* in industrial employment. Because observationally identical workers are paid the same wage, firms tend to favor types of workers for whom adverse-selection considerations are not too important. The desire of firms to hire from relatively homogeneous labor pools generally prevents the efficient allocation of workers. Also, within a given labor pool, the allocation of labor can generally be improved by either a wage increase or decrease.

In an efficiency-wage setting, a subsidy per worker financed by a payroll tax reduces the efficiency wage. Firms will add workers to take advantage of the subsidy. Thus, if wages exceed the output-maximizing level, the government could increase output by subsidizing employment.

There are several problems with using efficiency-wage models to formulate policy. First, as the example above shows, the correct policy may depend on variables such as the distribution of unobserved abilities which policy makers are unlikely to know. Second, the different efficiency-wage models do not always imply the same policy. Third, problems caused by the entry and exit of firms, by vacancies, and by labor-market dynamics have been ignored. Finally, efficiency-wage models (in common with more traditional labor-market models) typically assume that labor inputs can be aggregated in terms of efficiency units. But if the production process worked at the pace of the slowest worker as in an assembly line, or if production required some highly skilled workers, that assumption would not be valid.

Andrew Weiss

See also IMPLICIT CONTRACTS; NATURAL RATE OF UNEMPLOYMENT; NEW KEYNESIAN ECONOMICS; UNEMPLOYMENT; WAGE RIGIDITY; WORKER AND JOB TURNOVER

Bibliography

Akerlof, G. A. [1982] 1986. "Labor Contracts as Partial Gift Exchanges." In *Efficiency-Wage Models of the Labor Market,* edited by G. A. Akerlof and J. L. Yellen, 66–92. Cambridge: Cambridge Univ. Press.

Akerlof, G. A. and L. F. Katz. 1990. "Do Deferred Wages Eliminate the Need for Involuntary Unemployment as a Worker Discipline Device?" In *Advances in the Theory and Measurement of Unemployment,* edited by Y. Weiss and G. Fishelson, 172–203. New York: St. Martin's Press.

Bowles, S. 1985. "The Production Process in a Competitive Economy: Walrasian, Neo-Hobbesian, and Marxian Models." *American Economic Review* 75:16–36.

Bulow, J. I. and L. H. Summers. 1986. "A Theory of Dual Labor Markets with Application to Industrial Policy, Discrimination, and Keynesian Unemployment." *Journal of Labor Economics* 4:376–414.

Calvo, G. A. 1979. "Quasi-Walrasian Theories of Unemployment." *American Economic Review Papers and Proceedings* 69:102–07.

Cappelli, P. and K. Chauvin. 1991. "An Interplant Test of the Efficiency Wage Hypothesis." *Quarterly Journal of Economics* 106:769–87.

Carmichael, H. L. 1990. "Efficiency-Wage Models of Unemployment—One View." *Economic Inquiry* 28:269–95.

Dasgupta, P. and D. Ray. 1986. "Inequality as a Determinant of Malnutrition and Unemployment: Theory." *Economic Journal* 96:1011–34.

———. 1987. "Inequality as a Determinant of Malnutrition and Unemployment: Policy." *Economic Journal* 97:177–88.

Guasch, J. L. and A. Weiss. 1980a. "Wages as Sorting Mechanisms in Competitive Markets with Asymmetric Information: A Theory of Testing." *Review of Economic Studies* 47:653–64.

———. 1980b. "Adverse Selection by Markets and the Advantage of Being Late." *Quarterly Journal of Economics* 94:453–66.

———. 1981. "Self-Selection in the Labor Market." *American Economic Review* 71:275–84.

———. 1982. "An Equilibrium Analysis of Wage Productivity Gaps." *Review of Economic Studies* 49:485–97.

Holzer, H. J., L. F. Katz, and A. B. Krueger. 1991. "Job Queues and Wages." *Quarterly Journal of Economics* 106:739–68.

Lang, K. 1991. "Persistent Wage Dispersion and Involuntary Unemployment." *Quarterly Journal of Economics* 106:181–202.

Lazear, E. P. and R. L. Moore. 1984. "Incentives, Productivity, and Labor Contracts." *Quarterly Journal of Economics* 99:275–96.

Leonard, J. S. 1987. "Carrots and Sticks: Pay, Supervision, and Turnover." *Journal of Labor Economics* 5(October Supplement):S136–52.

Levine, D. J. 1992. "Can Wage Increases Pay for Themselves? Tests with a Production Function." *Economic Journal* 102:1102–15.

———. 1993. "What Do Wages Buy?" *Administrative Science Quarterly* 38:462–83.

Lindbeck, A. and D. Snower. 1988a. "Cooperation, Harassment and Involuntary Unemployment." *American Economic Review* 78:167–88.

———. 1988b. "Job Security, Work Incentives and Unemployment." *Scandinavian Journal of Economics* 90:454–74.

Montgomery, J. D. 1991. "Equilibrium Wage Dispersion and Interindustry Wage Differentials." *Quarterly Journal of Economics* 106:163–79.

Okuno-Fujiwara, M. 1987. "Monitoring Cost, Agency Relationship, and Equilibrium Mode of Labor Contract." *Journal of Japanese and International Economics* 1:147–67.

Salop, S. C. 1979. "A Model of the Natural Rate of Unemployment." *American Economic Review* 69:117–25.

Shapiro, C. and J. E. Stiglitz. 1984. "Equilibrium Unemployment as a Worker Discipline Device." *American Economic Review* 74:433–44.

Solow, R. 1979. "Another Possible Source of Wage Stickiness." *Journal of Macroeconomics* 1:79–82.

Stiglitz, J. E. 1985. "Equilibrium Wage Distributions." *Economic Journal* 95:575–98.

Weitzman, M. 1989. "A Theory of Wage Dispersion and Job Market Segmentation." *Quarterly Journal of Economics* 104:121–37.

Electoral Cycle in Monetary Policy

Nordhaus's original theory of the political business cycle proved inconsistent with both rational-expectations reasoning and the data. Recently emerging from the underground of business-cycle research, two theories of the interelection behavior of the monetary aggregates offer new insights and suggest a broad research agenda. While the theories are somewhat complementary, one purports to explain more of the interelection behavior of the money supply across, as well as within, policy regimes than the other.

The POT

Much of the literature explains interelection money growth in terms of the different targets for output, or unemployment, and inflation desired by the political parties (Alesina and Sachs 1988). We call this the *Political/Macroeconomic Outcomes Theory*, or POT.

The POT maintains that expected, postelection, output and inflation outcomes influence the voting behavior of each party's constituencies in different ways. Support for this view comes from three sources. First, the conventional wisdom, fortified by public-opinion surveys, holds that changes in output affect Democratic constituencies more than Republican ones, while opposite effects are ascribed to changes in inflation. Second, output is positively correlated with Democratic tenure in the Oval Office. Third, portions of the reaction-function literature report stronger monetary-policy responses to output or unemployment under Democratic administrations than under Republican ones.

Because election results are not fully predictable, the POT conjectures that money growth increases unexpectedly immediately after a Democratic president is elected and decreases unexpectedly immediately after a Republican is elected. Following these surprises, the POT predicts a higher, time-consistent, money-growth path during the interelection period under Democratic than under Republican administrations.

The PIT

An alternative explanation of interelection money growth is that monetary surprises are intended to compensate for the sectoral burdens (and hence the adverse electoral consequences) that redistributive policy imposes by affecting interest rates, exchange rates, effective tax rates, and output. In every administration in the past quarter century (the caretaker interregnum of Gerald Ford excepted), redistributive policy has produced sectoral dissonances which then induced monetary ease and, ultimately, politically telling inflation. According to this theory, monetary policy does not systematically respond to targets for output or inflation, but instead reacts to political signals that reflect sectoral dissonance. Only when inflation reaches intolerable heights does monetary policy respond. Such responses are unique to neither political party. We call this the *Political/Income Redistribution Theory,* or PIT. The PIT regards the partisanship correlations and reaction-function results on which the POT is premised as epiphenomena, reflecting the response of monetary policy to anterior redistributive causes.

Inasmuch as it sees political rent-seeking as the dominant motivation for monetary surprises, the PIT is a proper public-choice theory of monetary policy which purports to explain the behavior of the money supply across a variety of political arrangements. It is not conditional on the proximity or even the existence of free elections.

The PIT is motivated by two fundamental observations. First, rather than converging on a time-consistent path, money growth is highly erratic, largely because it responds to political pressures. Second, promises to redistribute income not only to dominate formal election campaigns, they are always and everywhere the bread and butter of politicians. This approach to monetary policy is thus consonant with the voluminous literature on monetary accommodation as well as with the public-choice view of macroeconomic policymaking in general. Moreover, the cycle in monetary regimes, marked by oscillation between prolonged periods of ever-rising inflation (that are propelled by political rent-seeking) and shorter periods of monetary restraint (that are intended to restore the economic health eroded by inflation) can also be explained by the PIT.

The PIT distinguishes between two kinds of surprises. The first is the immediate, post-election surprise, timed similarly to that of the POT, but intended to offset the disincentive effects on output of an administration's redistributive program. The second is intended to counteract the adverse electoral consequences of dissonances caused by the sectoral burdens imposed by an administration's redistributive programs. Thus, the money supply responds periodically to sectoral flak generated by changes in output, interest rates, exchange rates, etc. This would account for the unstable

reaction-function estimates of responses of monetary aggregates to such variables.

Choosing between the Theories

The POT is driven by voter demands and is consistent with median-voter models of the political process that are most relevant during election periods when politicians respond to voter concerns. In contrast, the PIT is driven by rent-seeking specialized interest groups. As a public-choice theory, it suggests that politicians respond to organized pressures throughout the interelection period.

Both theories are consistent with the assumption of forward-looking agent behavior. Under the POT, monetary policy can have real effects because voters know politicians' preferences, but election outcomes are uncertain and thus entail a post-election surprise. PIT surprises have real effects because politicians disguise their preferences for allocating the redistributive burdens while the economic and political mechanisms that determine which sectors bear the burden are unclear. Moreover, the magnitude and timing of monetary surprises cannot be foreseen, because private agents cannot easily filter credible signals from the barrage of pressures on monetary policymakers.

Within regimes, the POT focuses on purported partisan differences in desired outcomes for output and inflation whereas the PIT emphasizes political pressures arising from the sectoral unrest associated with changes in output, interest rates, exchange rates, etc. Therefore, under either theory, modeling how political preferences and pressures are transformed into actual policies should be on the agenda for future research.

Across regimes, the PIT should have much broader applicability than the POT. As pointed out by Alesina and Sachs, POT surprises hinge on particular institutional arrangements, namely monetary-policy activism, periodic elections, and competing parties whose macroeconomic goals differ. (The POT research agenda should include modeling changes in government that occur without periodic elections.) In contrast, the PIT is compatible with a wide array of historical arrangements. Redistributive promises, from the bread and circuses of ancient times to Reagan's supply-side tax cuts, seem to have consistently provoked monetary surprises, from the ancient sovereign's debasing the coinage to the Reagan administration's outburst of monetary growth in 1985–86. Because it is far less specific than the POT about the timing of monetary surprises, the PIT is more difficult to reject by statistical testing. Despite differences in their breadth of applicability and ease of rejection, the prospects for further historical testing of the PIT and the POT are inviting.

Consider, for example, the income-redistribution/money-supply linkage in the late nineteenth century. Republican administrations effected politically favorable redistributions by raising tariffs. Dissonance from the aggrieved agricultural sector was tempered first by issuing greenbacks and later by silver-purchase legislation intended to provide monetary ease. But doubts that the United States would remain on the gold standard led to gold outflows, which inhibited monetary expansion. The 1867–1914 period may thus be a fertile area for testing the PIT.

Money-growth increases immediately after new Democratic presidents were elected in 1961, 1965, and 1977 support both the PIT and the POT. Anti-inflationary money-growth slowdowns after the ascendancy of Republican presidents in 1969 and 1981 favor the POT over the PIT, but the absence of a money-growth slowdown in 1989 does not. The PIT does not associate dips in money growth with post-election years or with either political party, arguing instead that such slowdowns occur when inflation seems excessive, as in 1974 and 1979. An item for future POT research would be to measure the strength of the post-election surprise by the difference between election results and pre-election polls. Post-election surprises should be small whenever pre-election polls correctly forecast a lopsided outcome.

The money-growth explosion under Nixon in 1972 and the money-growth slowdown under Kennedy-Johnson in 1963 and 1964 are inconsistent with POT predictions. Nor can the POT account for the 1985–86 money-growth explosion in Reagan's second term. This suggests that extending the data set might significantly weaken support for the POT prediction that Republican administrations generate lower time-consistent money growth than Democratic ones.

In contrast, the PIT explains the money-growth peaks under Johnson in 1967–68, Nixon in 1972, Carter in 1980 and Reagan in 1985–86 as attempts to quell the sectoral dissonance associated with interest-rate increases (1967–68, 1972, and 1980), the rise in the value of the dollar (1985–86), price controls (1972), and credit controls (1980). It adds interesting dimensions to historical accounts of modern activist macroeconomic policy. Given the financial regulatory environment of the time, redistributive programs of the 1960s and 1970s imposed formidable burdens on new homebuyers, and on the home-financing and home-construction industries. Bouts of monetary ease during the Johnson, Nixon, and Carter administrations reflect the tilting of the political balance of power toward baby-boom, first-time homebuyers and toward the home-financing and home-construction industries.

Ronald Reagan's inegalitarian reversal enriches the public-choice approach to monetary policy, the PIT. By the 1980s, the political balance of power had tilted in favor of creditor senior citizens. In the deregulated financial environment of the 1980s, real interest rates could be permitted to rise far more than they did in the 1960s and 1970s without risking resounding sectoral dissonance. Because of the repeal of the withholding tax on interest paid to foreigners and liberalized Japanese foreign-exchange laws, foreign saving flows responded to increased real interest rates. As a result the dollar soared and Reagan's *status quo ante* redistribution harmed important constituencies in the tradable-goods and import-sensitive sectors. The money-growth explosion of 1985–86 was an obvious reaction to deafening dissonance from these sectors.

Thomas Havrilesky

See also AKERMAN, JOHAN HENRIK; FEDERAL RESERVE SYSTEM: 1941–1993; POLITICAL BUSINESS CYCLE

Bibliography

Alesina, A. and J. Sachs. 1988. "Political Parties and the Business Cycle in the United States, 1948–1984." *Journal of Money, Credit and Banking* 20:63–82.

Friedlaender, A. F. 1973. "Macro Policy Goals in the Postwar Period: A Study in Revealed Preferences." *Quarterly Journal of Economics* 87:25–43.

Havrilesky, T. 1987. "A Partisanship Theory of Fiscal and Monetary Regimes." *Journal of Money, Credit and Banking* 19:308–25.

———. 1988. "The Electoral Cycle in Fiscal and Monetary Policy." *Challenge*, July-August, 14–21.

———. 1989. "Monetary Activism as an Addiction." *Challenge*, May/June, 55–57.

Hetzel, R. 1990. "The Political Economy of Monetary Policy." In *The Political Economy of American Monetary Policy*, edited by T. Mayer, 99–114. Cambridge: Cambridge Univ. Press.

Hibbs, D. 1987. *The American Political Economy: Macroeconomics and Electoral Politics*. Cambridge: Harvard Univ. Press.

Nordhaus, W. 1975. "The Political Business Cycle." *Review of Economic Studies* 42:169–90.

Streissler, E. 1976. "Personal Income Distribution and Inflation." In *Inflation in Small Countries*, edited by H. Frisch, 343–56. Berlin: Springer-Verlag.

Wagner, R. E. 1986. "Central Banking and the Fed: A Public Choice Perspective." *Cato Journal* 6:519–38.

Ellis, Howard Sylvester (1898–1992)

A distinguished theorist, Howard S. Ellis made valuable contributions in several fields including economic development, international economics, and macroeconomics. His most important contribution to business-cycle theory is his book, *German Monetary Theory: 1905–1933*, which grew out of his doctoral dissertation at Harvard.

Born in Denver, Ellis studied at the University of Iowa (B.A., 1920), the University of Michigan (M.A., 1922), the University of Heidelberg (1924–25), Harvard University (Ph.D., 1929), and the University of Vienna (1933–35). After teaching at the University of Michigan (1925–38), Ellis joined the economics department at the University of California, Berkeley (1938–43, 1946–65). He was an economic analyst at the Federal Reserve between 1943 and 1946.

German Monetary Theory: 1905–1933 was a comprehensive review of the German literature on monetary theory; it remains the standard secondary source in any language on that subject. The first two-thirds of the book deals with static issues while the last third reviews the fertile output of business-cycle theories by German-speaking authors in the first part of this century. Aside from the many important German and Austrian writers on business cycles, Ellis also surveyed the contributions of the Swedes Knut Wicksell and Gustav Cassel, much of whose work was written in German. Ellis went beyond a mere survey of theories and provided an incisive commentary on them, showing their strengths and weaknesses and comparing them with the work of their non-German speaking contemporaries, particularly Keynes, Hawtrey, and Robertson.

Although he never advanced his own theory of the cycle, Ellis leaned toward both the Schumpeter-Hahn theory of a cyclical process propelled by technical progress and innovation and the Mises-Hayek theory of a cycle driven by unsustainable credit expansion and overinvestment, which he did not regard as mutually incompatible. He reiterated his sympathy for the Schumpeterian paradigm in his 1949 Presidential Address to the American Economic Association.

Ellis never accepted Keynesian nostrums even at the height of their popularity. In "Some Fundamentals in the Theory of Velocity," he published an early criticism of the Keynesian assertion that liquidity preference affected interest rates rather than the price level. He contended that the concept of velocity, properly analyzed, could not be eliminated from business-cycle theory.

Furthermore, he strongly disputed Alvin Hansen's claim that secular stagnation imminently threatened the United States. His 1940 work outlined his belief that ultimately low long-term interest rates would stimulate investment spending sufficiently to maintain full employment. He argued, moreover, that technological progress had previously tended to increase the demand for labor, thereby reducing unemployment, and had provided new goods and services that maintained adequate levels of consumption. He saw no evidence that this situation would change.

Although not a modern-day Monetarist, Ellis believed that monetary policy could significantly affect aggregate demand. In various publications Ellis argued (1940, 1951) that Keynesians underestimated the potency of monetary policy, particularly that of tight money. He stressed credit rationing as another way, along with higher real interest rates, that tight monetary policy could contract spending (1951). Moreover, Ellis vigorously argued that monetary policy often should be the preferred stabilization policy as it was more impersonal and less discriminatory than either fiscal policy or direct wage-price controls.

In order to achieve full employment, the government needed to adopt the appropriate fiscal and monetary policies. Ellis argued (1945, 1946) that by utilizing pro-competitive and free trade policies the government could increase output and reduce unemployment at full employment; in other words, the institutional structure affected the level of full-employment output. He attributed a stagnant economy to an inappropriate institutional structure and too much governmental interference rather than to oversaving.

Ellis's articles were often reprinted, particularly during the 1940s, 1950s, and 1960s. After 1950, he increasingly devoted his creative energies to analyzing issues of economic development, particularly of Latin America and of the Middle East.

Ellis's writings display a clarity of thought and expression. He was an influential and insightful critic of early Keynesian economics. His important contribution to business-cycle analysis was primarily to clarify important concepts and to disseminate German ideas to English-speaking economists, particularly before the original works of those economists became accessible in English.

David Glasner
Robert Stanley Herren

Bibliography
Ellis, H. S. 1934. *German Monetary Theory: 1905–1933.* Cambridge: Harvard Univ. Press.
———. 1938a. "Some Fundamentals in the Theory of Velocity." *Quarterly Journal of Economics* 52:431–72.
———. 1938b. "Notes on Recent Business-Cycle Literature." *Review of Economic Statistics* 20:111–19.
———. 1940. "Monetary Policy and Investment." *American Economic Review* 30:27–38.
———. 1945. "Economic Expansion Through Competitive Markets." In *Financing American Prosperity: A Symposium of Economists,* edited by P. T. Homan and F. Machlup, 126–98. New York: Twentieth Century Fund.
———. 1946. "Monopoly and Unemployment." In *Prices, Wages and Employment,* edited by C. O. Hardy, K. B. Williams, and H. S. Ellis, 67–94. Washington: Federal Reserve System.
———. 1950. "The Economic Way of Thinking." *American Economic Review* 40:1–12.
———. 1951. "The Rediscovery of Money." In *Money, Trade, and Economic Growth: Essays in Honor of John Henry Williams,* 253–69. New York: Macmillan.
———. [1955] 1987. "Monetary Policy as an Instrument of Progress." In *Economic Progress,* edited by L. H. Dupriez, 327–40. New York: St. Martin's Press.

E

Endogenous and Exogenous Money

From the perspective of business-cycle analysis, the endogeneity or exogeneity of money depends on the relation between money and the basic set of endogenous variables that are the center of attention in most macroeconomic models. Briefly, money is endogenous if the money stock is determined in conjunction with any of the principal endogenous variables in macroeconomics; the price level, the interest rate, aggregate output, and the exchange rate. Money is exogenous if these variables play no role in the determination of the money stock. In the case where money is endogenous, the money supply may also be influenced by variables that are ordinarily considered exogenous in macroeconomic models. Exogenous influences on the money supply would include seasonal movements in the money multiplier, changes in the preferences of policymakers or the public for inflation, technological innovations in the banking sector, and changes in bank regulations, such as reserve requirements, that affect the money multiplier.

The issue of monetary endogeneity and exogeneity arises in such business-cycle controversies as the role of money in causing business cycles, whether the money stock can be controlled, the role of money in price-level determination, and the efficacy of fixed-exchange-rate schemes. In some of these controversies, the potential endogeneity of money makes it difficult to trace the interaction between money and other macroeconomic variables, thereby contributing to continuing uncertainty about the role of money in the economy.

Inside money is often treated as an endogenous aggregate because the volume of transactions deposits depends on the response of deposit holders and the financial sector to interest rates and expected real income. Several models illustrate how private agents and banks cause fluctuations in inside money. In the popular model of King and Plosser (1984), transaction services produced in the financial sector are demanded by producers of goods and services as an intermediate input in an intertemporal production process. In this setup, an increased return to production leads to an increase in demand for transactions services and an accompanying increase in deposits. A related set of models identifies the variation in real returns to bank-intermediated loans as a source of endogenous fluctuations in deposits. Individuals lend capital by holding bank deposits. If inside-money deposits, D, are related to loans, L, through the balance-sheet condition $D = \alpha L$, then loan expansion induced by a rise in anticipated returns to investment projects will also increase deposits.

Models of endogenous inside money are often designed to explain why money growth temporally leads aggregate output, or why money Granger-causes aggregate output, as Sims (1972) has found. The apparent fact that money growth leads output is often taken as evidence that money is nonneutral in the short-run. However, in the theoretical models described above, money is both endogenous and neutral, yet monetary fluctuations lead output movements. Sims's findings were consistent with the exogeneity of money with respect to GNP, but depend on defining exogeneity in terms of a temporal ordering in which current money growth is statistically associated with future output. However, the relation between temporal exogeneity and the theoretical exogeneity of money discussed above is problematic. The results of time-series tests of monetary exogeneity must be evaluated in the light of endogenous money models that also predict that money growth precedes GNP movements.

The operating procedures and the objectives of monetary policy can make outside money endogenous. The description by Lombra and Moran (1988) of how the Federal Reserve formulates policy shows that monetary policy is in fact sensitive to the perceived state of the economy, and particularly to interest rates. Monetarists, such as Poole, have pointed out that the Federal Reserve's traditional policy of smoothing movements in short-term interest rates involves accommodating fluctuations in money demand, which imparts to money a degree of automatic responsiveness to endogenous variables. Monetarists argue that the central bank can choose the degree to which money growth is endogenous. In principle, the monetary authority could choose a policy that

makes money growth exogenous, at least in the medium or long run. Friedman's constant money-growth rule is one such policy. Monetarists also argue that, historically, money growth, while partly endogenous, has been a major cause of price-level changes and business cycles.

The endogeneity of money due to interest-rate-smoothing figures prominently in the Post-Keynesian literature. Post-Keynesians such as Kaldor (1982) assert that the monetary authority's role as the lender of last resort to the banking system requires it to be completely accommodative, standing ready to supply reserves on demand within a given interest-rate band. Post-Keynesians differ from Monetarists in denying that the degree of monetary endogeneity is a choice of the central bank.

Sargent and Wallace (1975) and McCallum (1981) have evaluated the price-level implications of interest-rate-feedback monetary policies under rational expectations. Sargent and Wallace showed that a pure interest-rate peg (that is, a commitment to buy and sell bonds at a fixed interest rate) means that monetary policy does not determine the price level. McCallum showed that interest-rate-smoothing monetary rules with sufficient information on the values of future nominal variables can ensure determination and control of the contemporaneous values of nominal variables.

A historically important example of an endogenous monetary policy is a fixed-exchange-rate regime. In such a regime, the central bank stands ready to buy and sell foreign exchange at the official exchange rate, thereby letting relative demands for national currencies determine the size of the monetary base. Under this system any exogenous monetary-policy shock that increases central-bank domestic credit ultimately causes an offsetting loss of foreign-exchange reserves by the central bank. The fixed-exchange-rate system is often considered desirable because it reduces the scope for discretionary inflation policy as the monetary authority must subordinate its inflation target to maintaining the exchange-rate parity. However, allowing the domestic inflation rate to be partially determined by foreign monetary authorities is often difficult to sustain in practice. Domestic monetary-policy considerations, including the incentive to use monetary growth for government finance, and the degree of domestic tolerance of inflation, may imply a desired domestic inflation rate above or below the world inflation rate.

An important work by Barro and Gordon (1983) suggests that endogenous monetary growth is an implication of policy arrangements in which the monetary authority has competing objectives concerning inflation and unemployment. The monetary authority can reduce unemployment by creating unanticipated inflation. Monetary policy is viewed as the outcome of a game involving the ongoing interaction of the monetary authority and private agents. The monetary authority optimizes its objective function each period, treating the rational expectations of private agents as given, and in light of current endogenous variables. Private agents form expectations about the behavior of the monetary authority using knowledge of the monetary authority's objectives for inflation and unemployment. Depending on reputation effects and other considerations, the analysis suggests that the monetary authority varies money growth as the benefits of inflating vary with changes in the current state of the economy. Monetary growth is more rapid when the benefits of inflation appear to be high, such as when unemployment is high, and less rapid when the benefits appear to be low.

Current models of monetary determination indicate that money is likely to be determined, at least in part, by the endogenous variables that appear in business-cycle models. Consequently money is properly considered an endogenous variable, indeed it is hard to argue otherwise. However, this conclusion does not imply that exogenous monetary disturbances do not occur, or that these disturbances have not had important effects. The endogeneity of money confronts researchers with a potentially severe problem in identifying passive movements in money from episodes in which monetary policy was a major causal factor. In considering monetary endogeneity and exogeneity, one should recognize that the proposition that monetary growth is endogenous does not imply that monetary fluctuations are neutral, or that the money supply is unimportant in the determination of nominal magnitudes.

John F. Boschen

See also MONETARY POLICY; MONEY-INCOME CAUSALITY; ROSTOW, WALT WHITMAN; SUPPLY OF MONEY

Bibliography

Barro, R. J. and D. B. Gordon. 1983. "Rules, Discretion and Reputation in a Model of Monetary Policy." *Journal of Monetary Economics* 12:101–21.

Goldfeld, S. M. and A. S. Blinder. 1972. "Some Implications of Endogenous Stabilization Policy." *Brookings Papers on Economic Activity,* Number Three, 585–640.

Kaldor, N. 1982. *The Scourge of Monetarism.* Oxford: Oxford Univ. Press.

King, R. G. and C. I. Plosser. 1984. "Money, Credit, and Prices in a Real Business Cycle." *American Economic Review* 74:363–80.

Lombra, R. and M. Moran. 1980. "Policy Advice and Policymaking at the Federal Reserve." *Journal of Monetary Economics* 13:9–68.

McCallum, B. T. 1981. "Price Level Determinacy with an Interest Rate Rule and Rational Expectations." *Journal of Monetary Economics* 8:319–29.

Poole, W. 1982. "Federal Reserve Operating Procedures: A Survey and Evaluation of the Historical Record Since October 1979." *Journal of Money, Credit and Banking* 14:575–96.

Sargent, T. J. and N. Wallace. 1975. "Rational Expectations, the Optimal Money Supply Instrument, and the Optimal Money Supply Rule." *Journal of Political Economy* 83:241–54.

Sims, C. A. 1972. "Money, Income and Causality." *American Economic Review* 62:540–52.

Williamson, S. D. 1987. "Financial Intermediation, Business Failures, and Real Business Cycles." *Journal of Political Economy* 95:1196–1216.

E

Engels, Friedrich (1820–1895)

Friedrich Engels was Karl Marx's lifelong collaborator and intellectual partner. After Marx's death in 1883, Engels was responsible for editing his papers, including the second and third volumes of *Capital,* and for applying Marx's ideas on economic crises to changing contemporary conditions.

Engels was born into a German textile manufacturing family with interests in Manchester, where he moved in 1842. After spending the middle and late 1840s with Marx, in theoretical work and revolutionary activity on the Continent, he returned to Manchester in 1850 to manage the family cotton mill. Over the next two decades Engels corresponded prolifically with Marx, who had settled in London, sending him money and acting as a sounding-board in the development of Marx's political economy. After Marx's death, he became the unchallenged ultimate source of authority in the international socialist movement.

In his *Outlines of a Critique of Political Economy* (or *Umrisse*), written in 1843, Engels approached the analysis of economic fluctuations from an Owenite perspective, under the particular influence of John Watts. For the young Engels, periodic industrial crises were the inevitable result of unbridled competition, in which

> supply always follows close on demand without ever quite covering it. It is either too big or too small, never corresponding to demand; because in this unconscious condition of mankind no one knows how big supply or demand is. . . . But as long as you continue to produce in the present unconscious, thoughtless manner, at the mercy of chance—for just so long trade crises will remain; and each successive crisis is bound to become more universal and therefore worse than the preceding one . . . (433–34).

Engels argued that competition between workers had forced wages down to "the very barest necessities, the mere means of subsistence" (441), and that this itself was a major cause of depression. "Here a new contradiction in economics comes to light. The economist's 'demand' is not the real demand; his 'consumption' is an artificial consumption. For the economist, only that person really demands, only that person is a real consumer, who has an equivalent to offer for what he receives" (438). This emphasis on effective demand, with its underconsumptionist implications, was also a feature of Marx's early writings on economic crises, most notably in his 1847 lecture notes on *Wages*.

The Condition of the Working Class in England, written by Engels in 1844–45, contained a brief and largely descriptive passage on crises. Engels did, however, stress that intense competition served to generalize partial depressions in trade. Competition "has gradually brought the single minor crises nearer together and united them into one periodically recurring crisis" which broke out about every five years (382). This, too, was a theme that recurred in Marx's mature writings on cyclical fluctuations.

After 1845 there was a hiatus in Engels's economic writings which lasted for almost four decades. He and Marx agreed on an informal division of labor in which Engels concentrated on philosophy, politics, and military affairs, leaving political economy to Marx. But Marx's death forced Engels to pay attention to economic issues once more. As editor of Marx's unpublished papers, he was responsible for bringing volumes two and three of *Capital* to press. The relevant manuscripts contain much of Marx's later analysis of economic crises. They were organized, annotated and in certain places augmented by Engels, to whom we owe the form, if not the content, of the two volumes.

As the principal interpreter of Marx's writings, and the last court of appeal in theoretical disputes inside European social democracy, Engels's own ideas on crises—if not especially profound—were extremely influential. He argued that after 1876, constant depression had replaced the five-to-ten-year trade cycle identified by Marx. Chronic overproduction, resulting from a lack of markets, was preparing the ground for a crisis of major proportions in which England (having lost her industrial monopoly) would fare worst. Engels maintained that the growth of monopoly and the re-imposition of protective tariffs had given the world economy a precarious stability; but these developments contained the seeds of a far more powerful future crisis.

In his early writings Engels had foreshadowed certain key elements of the Marxian theory of crises. His later thinking was, however, less incisive. Significantly, he proved unable to trace any connection between imperialist expansion, the rise of militarism, and the susceptibility of capitalism to crises. Engels also failed to elaborate a cogent theory of the trade cycle, or to convince those within the socialist movement, like Eduard Bernstein, who were becoming increasingly dissatisfied with the teachings of orthodox Marxism.

M. C. Howard
J. E. King

See also MARX, KARL HEINRICH

Bibliography
Carver, T. 1977. *Marx and Engels: The Intellectual Relationship*. Hassocks: Harvester.

Claeys, G. 1984. "Engels's *Outlines of a Critique of Political Economy* (1843) and the Origins of the Marxist Critique of the Capitalism." *History of Political Economy* 16:207–32.

Engels, F. [1843] 1975. *Outlines of a Critique of Political Economy*. In *The Collected Works of Karl Marx and Friederich Engels*. Vol. 3, 418–43. London: Lawrence and Wishart.

———. [1845] 1958. *The Condition of the Working Class in England*. Translation. Standford: Standford Univ. Press.

———. [1885] 1962. "England 1845 and 1885." In K. Marx and F. Engels, *Werke*. Vol. 21, 191–97. Berlin: Dietz.

———. [1892] 1963. "Über Einige Besonderheiten der Ökonomischen und Politischen Entwicklungen Englands." In K. Marx and F. Engels, *Werke*. Vol. 22, 331. Berlin: Dietz.

———. [1893] 1976. "Can Europe Disarm?" In *The Life Of Friedrich Engels* by W. O. Henderson. Vol. 2, 810–32. London: Cass.

Howard, M. C. and J. E. King, 1989. *A History of Marxian Economics*. Vol. 1, *1883–1929*. Princeton: Princeton Univ. Press.

Marx, K. [1847] 1976. "Wages." In K. Marx and F. Engels, *Collected Works*. Vol. 6, 415–37. London: Lawrence and Wishart.

———. [1885–94] 1967. *Capital*. Vols. 2–3. New York: International Publishers.

McLellan, D. 1979. *Engels*. Hassocks: Harvester.

Stedman, J. G. 1982. "Engels and the History of Marxism." *The History of Marxism,* edited by E. J. Hobsbawm. Vol. 1, *Marxism in Marx's Day,* 290–326. Hassocks: Harvester.

Equity Premium

The most general asset-pricing models developed to date are essentially decentralized versions of the one-good, representative-agent, stochastic growth model. Built on the same theoretical foundations is the stream of macroeconomic research referred to as real-business-cycle theory. Unfortunately, empirical tests of asset-pricing models have led, unequivocally, to their rejection. Perhaps the most striking of these rejections is contained in a study by Mehra and Prescott (1985). Since the two paradigms are predicated on the same theoretical constructs, the inability of the neoclassical growth model to explain financial data poses a major challenge to real-business-cycle theorists to reformulate basic models of decision-making under uncertainty.

Historically, the average return on equity has far exceeded the average return on short-term virtually default-free debt. From 1889 to 1978, the average real annual yield on the Standard and Poor 500 Index was 7 percent, while the average yield on short-term debt was less than 1 percent. In 1985, Mehra and Prescott addressed the question whether this large differential in average yields could be accounted for by models that abstract from transaction costs, liquidity constraints, and other frictions absent in the Arrow-Debreu set-up. They found that standard competitive theory, sensibly restricted, could not rationalize this observation.

They studied a class of competitive pure-exchange economies for which the equilibrium growth-rate process on consumption and equilibrium asset returns is stationary. Attention was restricted to economies for which the elasticity of substitution for the composite consumption good between the year t and year $t+1$ is consistent with findings in micro, macro, and international economics. In addition, the economies were constructed to display equilibrium consumption growth rates with the same mean, variance, and serial correlation as those observed for the United States between 1889 and 1978. They concluded that for such economies, the average real annual yield on equity is at most .4 percent higher than that on short-term debt, in sharp contrast to the 6 percent observed. Further, their results were robust to nonstationarities in the means and variances of the economies' growth process. This anomaly and repeated unsuccessful attempts to explain it have caused it to be dubbed the "Equity Premium Puzzle."

Recent examples of attempts to resolve the puzzle have ranged from a disaster scenario proposed by Rietz (1988) to the introduction of alternative preference structures. These include dropping the expected-utility assumption (Epstein and Zin 1990, Weil 1989) and introducing habit formation (Abel 1990, Constantinides 1990). For such efforts to be successful, however, they must convince the profession that the proposed alternative preference structure is more useful than the now standard one for organizing and interpreting observations not only of average asset returns but also other observations in growth theory, business-cycle theory, labor-market behavior and so on. For a further discussion see Mehra and Prescott (1988).

Rajnish Mehra

See also STOCK-MARKET PRICES; TASTE SHOCKS

Bibliography

Abel, A. 1990. "Asset Prices Under Habit-Formation and Catching Up with the Joneses." *American Economic Review Papers and Proceedings* 80:38–42.

Constantinides, M. 1990. "Habit Formation: A Resolution of the Equity Premium Puzzle." *Journal of Political Economy* 98:519–43.

Epstein, L. G. and S. E. Zin. 1991. "Substitution, Risk Aversion and the Temporal Behavior of Consumption and Asset Returns: An Empirical Analysis." *Journal of Political Economy* 99:263–86.

Mehra, R. and E. C. Prescott. 1985. "The Equity Premium: A Puzzle." *Journal of Monetary Economics* 15:145–61.

———. 1988. "The Equity Premium: A Solution?" *Journal of Monetary Economics* 22:133–36.

Rietz, T. A. 1988. "The Equity Risk Premium: A Solution." *Journal of Monetary Economics* 22:117–31.

Weil, P. 1990. "The Equity Premium Puzzle and the Risk-Free Rate Puzzle." *Journal of Monetary Economics* 24:401–21.

Error Correction

See COINTEGRATION

Excess Volatility

Asset prices are said to show excess volatility if they vary through time more than is consistent with efficient markets, given the variability through time of the dividends of earnings that represent the source of value of the assets. S. F. LeRoy and R. D. Porter (1981) and R. J. Shiller (1981) have independently claimed to find evidence of excess volatility in United States common-stock prices. Their claims have provoked a debate about the validity of efficient-markets models and a reassessment of the evidence for such models.

Let p_t be the real (inflation-corrected) price of an asset, say, a share of common stock. Effi-cient-markets models assert that this price is the optimal forecast of the *ex post* value p of the asset, or formally that:

$$p_t = E_t p \tag{1}$$

where E_t denotes the mathematical expectation given the information available at time t. The *ex post* value p is defined as a present discounted value at time t of real dividends (per share) actually paid after time t.

Ex post value at time t is usually not known at time t. If it *were* known at time t, then by equation (1) price p_t would equal *ex post* value p; that is why the *ex post* value has been referred to as the *ex post* rational price or the perfect-foresight price. *Ex post* value p gradually becomes known after time t as dividends subsequent to time t are revealed. We now know fairly well the *ex post* value of twenty or more years ago, if the rate of discount is high enough to make dividends more than twenty years after time t negligible.

Figure 1 (from Shiller 1981) shows a plot for 1871 to 1979 of p_t defined as the real Standard and Poor Composite Stock Price Index detrended by dividing by an exponential growth factor. Also shown in the plot is the corresponding *ex post* value p computed as the present value (discount rate equals 6.363 percent per year) of real subsequent dividends, detrended by dividing by the same exponential growth factor. In computing p, we assume that dividends after 1979 follow the estimated trend line.

Note that p_t is much more variable around its mean than is p in Figure 1, apparently contrary to the efficient markets model (equation 1).

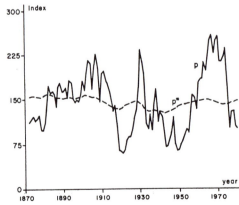

Figure 1. Plot for real Standard and Poor Composite Stock Price Index.

Equation (1) implies that p equals p_t plus a forecast error u_t, and since a forecast error must be unforecastable, u_t must be uncorrelated with p_t which is known as time t. Therefore the efficient-markets hypothesis requires:

$$\text{var}(p) = \text{var}(p_t) + \text{var}(u_t). \qquad (2)$$

Since variances cannot be negative, it follows that $\text{var}(p) \geq \text{var}(p_t)$. Under efficient markets, the variance of p thus puts an upper bound on the variance of p_t, a bound that can be attained only if information about p is perfect at time t. In Figure 1 the variance of p_t is 31.234 times that of p.

Excess volatility has been disputed by a number of authors. One criticism concerned how detrending was performed in the original papers. When, to avoid using any information after time t to produce detrended values at time t, the data are detrended instead by dividing by a 30-year moving average of lagged real earnings, the ratio of the variance of p_t to that of p falls, according to calculations for 1901 to 1988, to 17.331 (Shiller 1989); the variance bound is still grossly violated. Another concern of the critics was that since p tends to be a smoother time series than is p_t, ordinary estimates of variance will tend to be downward-biased more for p than for p_t. Monte Carlo experiments for a variety of dividend processes show that this downward bias may indeed produce substantial spurious violation of the variance bound under efficient markets, but generally not as large as actually observed (Shiller 1989).

Subsequent research has also confirmed another implication of excess volatility: returns to investing measured over long time intervals are substantially predictable (Fama and French 1988, Poterba and Summers 1988).

While the issue remains controversial, an acceptable summary of our state of knowledge is that although evidence presented in Figure 1 may give an exaggerated impression of excess volatility, the evidence for excess volatility is still substantial.

Prices of Different Assets Appear to Move Together Too Much

The above analysis can be generalized by redefining p_t as a k-element vector whose ith element is the price at time t of asset i and p as a k-element vector whose ith element is the ex post value at time t of asset i. Then the variances in equation (2) are $k \times k$ matrices, and the i,jth element of equation (2) is:

$$\text{cov}(p_i, p_j) = \text{cov}(p_{it}, p_{jt}) + \text{cov}(u_{it}, u_{jt}). \qquad (2')$$

Since the covariance between u_{it} and u_{jt} can be negative, it is possible under efficient markets that the covariance between prices of two assets can exceed the covariance between their ex post values. It is in fact even possible that there could be a perfect correlation between the prices when there is no correlation at all between ex post values. This would happen if the only information available at time t consisted of pooled ex post values: the information is the sum of the two ex post values. Such information pooling implies a negative covariance between forecast errors u_{it} and u_{jt}. In an analysis (where ex post values were computed and detrending essentially as above) of British and American stock-price data between 1919 and 1987, the covariance of prices was found to exceed that of ex post values by a wide margin, but the covariance of forecast errors was not negative (Shiller 1989). Thus, comovement of stock prices between the two countries appears to be excessive.

The violation of the variance bound for stock price indexes for the individual countries (as described in the preceding section) may be characterized as excess co-movement among prices of individual stocks, since the variance of p_t is approximately equal to a weighted average of the covariances between all pairs of stocks.

Time-Varying Discount Rates

It was assumed above that the rate of discount in the present-value formula was constant through time. One may instead assume time-varying real interest rates to compute ex post value. If rates of discount are assumed to vary with real short-term interest rates, then the variability of ex post value with U.S. or U.K. data increases dramatically, so that $\text{var}(p_t)$ and $\text{var}(p)$ are of about equal magnitudes. But, the correlation between p_t and p is negligible, which contradicts the implication of the efficient-markets theory that $\text{var}(p_t)$ can be as high as $\text{var}(p)$ only if there is no forecast error.

Another alternative is to compute ex post value using as discount factors marginal rates of substitution between real consumption at time t and at the time of future dividend payments, using an assumed utility function and data on aggregate real consumption (Grossman and Shiller 1981). Ex post value so computed may also be much more volatile than it is with a constant discount rate, but the model cannot be sustained for moderate levels of risk aversion in the assumed utility function (Campbell and Shiller 1988).

Significance of Excess Volatility
Whether there is substantial proof of excess volatility in speculative markets remains controversial, and there is even less agreement on what it means. However, the alleged excess volatility is commonly thought to support theories of stock prices that involve changing investor fashions, fads, or overreaction to news. Such theories are related to theories of the business cycle deriving at least in part from changing public confidence or attitudes.

Robert J. Shiller

See also EXPECTATIONS; EXPERIMENTAL PRICE BUBBLES; RATIONAL EXPECTATIONS; STOCK-MARKET PRICES; STOCK-MARKET CRASH OF 1929; STOCK-MARKET CRASHES OF 1987 AND 1989; SUNSPOT THEORIES OF FLUCTUATIONS; TULIPMANIA

Bibliography
Campbell, J. Y. and R. J. Shiller. 1988. "The Dividend-Price Ratio and Expectations of Future Dividends and Discount Factors." *Review of Financial Studies* 1:195–228.

Fama, E. F. and K. R. French. 1988. "Dividend Yields and Expected Stock Returns." *Journal of Financial Economics* 22:3–25.

Flavin, M. A. 1983. "Excess Volatility in the Financial Markets: A Reassessment of the Empirical Evidence." *Journal of Political Economy* 91:929–56.

Grossman, S. J. and R. J. Shiller. 1981. "The Determinants of the Variability of Stock Market Prices." *American Economic Review Papers and Proceedings* 71:222–27.

Kleidon, A. W. 1986. "Variance Bounds Tests and Stock Price Valuation Models." *Journal of Political Economy* 94:953–1001.

LeRoy, S. F. and R. D. Porter. 1981. "The Present-Value Relation: Tests Based on Implied Variance Bounds." *Econometrica* 49:555–74.

Marsh, T. A. and R. C. Merton. 1986. "Dividend Variability and Variance Bounds Tests for the Rationality of Stock Market Prices." *American Economic Review* 76:483–98.

Poterba, J. M. and L. H. Summers. 1988. "Mean Reversion in Stock Prices." *Journal of Financial Economics* 22:27–59.

Shiller, R. J. 1981. "Do Stock Prices Move Too Much to be Justified by Subsequent Changes in Dividends?" *American Economic Review* 71:421–36.

———. 1989. *Market Volatility*. Cambridge: MIT Press.

Expectations
When economic agents are uncertain about future conditions that bear on their decisions they must form expectations about those conditions. Because of their potential fickleness, expectations are identified by a number of business-cycle theories as a major cause of economic instability. Economists have attempted to measure actual expectations and have advanced various theories (models) of their formation.

Expectations in the History of Economic Thought
In thinking about economic decisions, one cannot easily overlook the importance of expectations. Someone who buys a stock in a company does so expecting that the company will do well and that the price of the stock (or the dividend) will rise. Managers of that company decide to expand, contract, or maintain its production facilities based on their expectations about future sales and returns. Only homebuyers who are expected by lenders to be able to meet the monthly payments get mortgages. Even the simplest economic acts involve expectations. Buyers of lottery tickets expect to win. Buyers of coffee expect to use it. If they expect the price of coffee to decline sharply, they will delay their purchase.

However obvious the importance of expectations in economic decisions may be, expectations were not considered systematically in the economic literature until late in the nineteenth century. Expectations did not weigh on the classical economic mind. This is not to say that expectations were ignored altogether. Henry Thornton, for example, argued that expectations about the future course of prices affect the interest rate, and Walter Bagehot considered changes in expectations an important factor in business cycles. The discussion of expectations, however, did not go beyond the mere mentioning of the subject; expectations played a minor role in the analysis. Towards the end of the nineteenth century, economists had become seriously interested in individual decision making and could no longer avoid a serious analysis of expectations. During the twentieth century, expectations came to play a major role in economic theorizing. That role became especially prominent in the business-cycle literature of the 1920s and 1930s.

When, in the 1920s, economists considered the phenomenon of economic instability, they questioned the rationality that the then dominant theory ascribed to economic agents. In attempting to account for booms and depressions, they leaned heavily, instead, on psychological factors. Wesley Mitchell, for example, postulated that a boom is fueled by an "epidemic of optimism" which generates unrealistic profit expectations. A depression starts, he maintained, when people realize that their expectations will not be realized; they panic, their optimism turns into gloom, and expectations become unrealistically pessimistic. His argument was typical of the time.

Expectations also began to penetrate the more theoretical discussion. They underlie, for example, the distinction between *ex ante* and *ex post* magnitudes that the Stockholm School introduced. *Ex ante* demand was defined as the demand that consumers expect to extend during a given period and the demand *ex post* as the realized demand at the end of the period. Expectations also figured prominently in Hicks's period analysis in *Value and Capital*. Even so, the nature and formation of expectations were still left out of the investigation.

In his *General Theory*, Keynes advanced the claim that "changing views about the future are capable of influencing the quantity of employment and not merely its direction" ([1936] 1973, ii). This claim is reflected in the three major theoretical concepts that Keynes introduced, all of which incorporate expectations in a critical way. The marginal propensity to consume is partly determined by expectations of future income and consumption, liquidity preference by expectations of future interest rates, and the marginal efficiency of capital by expectations of future returns to investments. Keynes suspected that the marginal efficiency of capital, in particular, would be subject to sudden changes because the implied expectations relate to a long period into the future. In chapter 22 entitled "Notes on the Trade Cycle," Keynes attributed the instability of the overall economic system to the instability of the marginal efficiency of capital.

The subsequent neo-Keynesian interpretations of Keynes's theory downplayed the role of expectations. Whenever Paul Samuelson, Abba Lerner, Robert Solow, James Tobin explicitly introduced expectations into their models, they assumed them to be exogenous and thus constant. The practice changed in the late 1950s when the formation of expectations became a serious issue on the theoretical agenda of mainstream economics. A major impetus for this change came from the challenge that Milton Friedman ([1968] 1969) posed to the Keynesian orthodoxy of the time. Expectations became an integral part of economic analysis first in the form of adaptive expectations and in the early 1970s in the form of rational expectations. In either case the hypothesis is that individuals are bound to make mistakes in forming their expectations and that macroeconomic fluctuations may result.

Theories of Expectations

Mitchell appealed to psychological factors to account for excessively optimistic or pessimistic expectations because he did not believe that a rational explanation of expectations was possible. Neither did Keynes. In the *General Theory*, he invoked "animal spirits" to account for decisions with consequences for an extended future and scoffed at the idea that those decisions are "the outcome of a weighted average of quantitative benefits multiplied by quantitative probabilities" ([1936] 1973, 161).

Keynes characterized a situation which precludes the formation of "mathematical expectations" as one of fundamental uncertainty. Frank Knight (1921) advanced a similar definition of uncertainty. Both Post-Keynesian and Austrian economists consider situations of fundamental uncertainty sufficiently relevant to reject theories of expectations based on mathematical calculations with quantitative probabilities. But they do not offer a theory that accounts for the expectations that people hold. George Katona (1951), a psychological economist, proposed to measure expectations directly by asking people. Various studies, some of which seek to test theories of mathematical expectations, have followed his lead. Even though mathematical expectations often do not stand up to such empirical scrutiny, they have dominated mainstream economics.

Irving Fisher (1913) was among the first to suggest a theoretical treatment of the formation of expectations. He hypothesized that the expected future value of a variable such as the price level is determined by a distributed lag of past price levels with coefficients that decline linearly with time into the past. A variant on Fisher's formula is the adaptive-expectations hypothesis, which was first introduced by Philip Cagan (1956) in a study of hyperinflation and subsequently applied more broadly by Milton Friedman.

The adaptive-expectations hypothesis states that people adjust their current expectations of a variable, such as the price level, to correct expectational errors made previously. The hypothesis can be formalized as follows:

$$P_t^* - P_{t-1}^* = (1-\lambda)(P_{t-1} - P_{t-1}^*) \qquad (1)$$

where P_t is the price at time t, λ is a parameter between one and zero and an asterisk denotes the expected value of a variable. This equation says that individuals revise their expectations by a fraction $(1-\lambda)$ of the expectational error $(P_{t-1} - P_{t-1}^*)$. Equation (1) can be transformed into:

$$P_t^* = (1-\lambda)P_{t-1} + \lambda P_{t-1}^* =$$
$$(1-\lambda)(P_t + \lambda P_{t-1} + \lambda^2 P_{t-2} + ...) \qquad (2)$$

which says that the expected price level for time t is determined by a distributed lag of past observations of the price level. This formulation differs from Fisher's in two ways: the coefficients decline exponentially and they add up to one. The latter condition guarantees that if the price level has been constant, the expected price level will remain constant.

A major objection to the adaptive-expectations hypothesis is that it lacks theoretical justification. For why would people consider only previous values of a variable when trying to estimate its future value? If they are rational, they will use whatever other relevant information is available (e.g., changes in policy) as well as the best available economic theory. An alternative approach to modeling expectations that could meet these objections is the rational-expectations hypothesis, which was first formalized by John Muth in 1961.

Muth's rational-expectations hypothesis is represented by:

$$P_t^* = E_{t-1}(P_t | I_{t-1}) \qquad (3)$$

which reads: the expected price for period t, P_t^*, equals the optimal expectation of P_t at time $t-1$, $E_{t-1}(P_t)$, given all available information at $t-1$, I_{t-1}. The commonsense interpretation of this expression is that people use all available information including announced changes in economic policies in addition to their knowledge of the economy to form their expectations of, say, next year's price level.

In the practice of economic theorizing, Muth's hypothesis implies that the expected price must equal the prediction of the economic model in use. Accordingly, the rational-expectations hypothesis is a device to endogenize the expected price, that is, to let the economic model determine it.

After Robert Lucas ([1972] 1981) showed how the assumption of rational expectations could be applied in macroeconomic models, adaptive expectations fell into disuse. Although a minority of economists continue to question the unrealism of any mathematical theory of expectations and prefer the use of psychological theories or direct measurements, the assumption of rational expectations has become routine in macroeconomic and business-cycle models. The implication is that expectations are assigned a role in the explanation of economic instability only insofar as people make rational mistakes.

Arjo Klamer

See also EXCESS VOLATILITY; EXPERIMENTAL PRICE BUBBLES; FISHER, IRVING; FRIEDMAN, MILTON; HABERLER, GOTTFRIED; HICKS, JOHN RICHARD; KEYNES, JOHN MAYNARD; LINDAHL, ERIK ROBERT; MITCHELL, WESLEY CLAIR; MYRDAL, GUNNAR; NATURAL RATE OF UNEMPLOYMENT; OHLIN, BERTIL GOTTHARD; PHILLIPS CURVE; RATIONAL EXPECTATIONS; STOCKHOLM SCHOOL; SUNSPOT THEORIES OF FLUCTUATIONS

Bibliography

Cagan, P. 1956. "The Monetary Dynamics of Hyperinflation." In *Studies in the Quantity Theory of Money,* edited by M. Friedman, 25–117. Chicago: Univ. of Chicago Press.

Fisher, I. 1913. *The Purchasing Power of Money.* 2d ed. New York: Macmillan.

Friedman, M. [1968] 1969. "The Role of Monetary Policy." Chap. 5 in *The Optimum Quantity of Money and Other Essays.* Chicago: Aldine.

Hicks, J. R. 1939. *Value and Capital.* Oxford: Clarendon Press.

Katona, G. 1951. *Psychological Aspects of Economic Behavior.* New York: McGraw-Hill.

Keynes, J. M. [1936] 1973. *The General Theory of Employment, Interest and Money.* Vol. 7 in *The Collected Writings* of *John Maynard Keynes*. London: Macmillan.

Knight, F. H. 1921. *Risk, Uncertainty and Profit*. Boston: Houghton Mifflin.

Lucas, R. E., Jr. [1972] 1981. "Expectations and the Neutrality of Money." In *Studies in Business-Cycle Theory*, 66–89. Cambridge: MIT Press.

Mitchell, W. C. 1913. *Business Cycles*. Berkeley: Univ. of Calif. Press.

Muth, J. F. 1961. "Rational Expectations and the Theory of Price Movements." *Econometrica* 29:315–35.

Experimental Price Bubbles

Rational-expectations models predict that if people have common expectations (or priors) about the value of an asset, and this common value is equal to its intrinsic or fundamental value, then if trades occur at all, they will occur at prices near intrinsic value. In a naturally occurring economy, studying the validity of rational-expectations models and the general role of expectations in asset valuation is extremely difficult, because researchers lack knowledge of intrinsic value, the information set of investors, and an explicit theory of the price expectations of investors. In experimental laboratory stock markets, a researcher can control the intrinsic value of asset shares by limiting the only external source of value to a series of per-share dividends drawn from a predetermined probability distribution.

In experimental laboratory markets, a per-share dividend can be awarded at the end of each trading period, so that the intrinsic value of a share is the expected one-period dividend value times the number of trading periods remaining in the experiment. All traders in the experimental stock market are fully informed about the exact structure of the probability distribution of per-share dividends (including an explicit statement of expected value) and the final trading period. Consequently, they have common information about the intrinsic value of asset shares.

Studies by Smith, Suchanek, and Williams (1988) and by King, Smith, Williams, and Van Boening (1993) have reported results from a series of laboratory stock markets with an initial time horizon of fifteen trading periods. Before the initial period, each trader received an endowment of initial shares and money. At the end of the experiment (after the period-15 divi-

dend is awarded), a sum equal to all dividends received on shares, plus the initial money endowment, plus capital gains minus capital losses was paid to each trader according to the trader's actual transactions and accumulated dividends. All trading was via a computerized version of the double-auction rules used on the New York Stock Exchange. Subjects earned an average of about \$16–17 each from dividends and initial endowments in experiments lasting about two hours.

The results of these experimental studies can be summarized in the form of responses to six questions that partially motivated the research.

1. *Is common information sufficient to induce common expectations and trading prices near intrinsic dividend value?* Almost without exception, inexperienced traders (participating in their first stock-market experiment) appear to have heterogeneous "home-grown" expectations of capital gains despite having common information on the structure of dividends. The result is large price bubbles that diverge from intrinsic dividend value on high trading volume—up to five or six times the total number of shares outstanding. Common information on intrinsic dividend value is not sufficient to induce common expectations among traders and dividend-value pricing.

2. *Given that price bubbles are commonplace with inexperienced subjects, will subsequent market bubbles be dampened or eliminated with increased subject experience?* Once-experienced traders continue to produce price bubbles, but the bubbles are typically on smaller trading volume, of shorter duration, and of smaller amplitude than with inexperienced traders. The tendency for volume to decline and for prices to approach intrinsic value continues when traders are twice-experienced traders. Furthermore, it appears that increasing experience levels *with the same group of traders* decreases the likelihood of a price bubble by more than does increasing experience levels while the composition of the group changes. The data suggest that common experience may do more than independent experience to create common expectations. In the former case, each trader sees that all other traders had the same experience. The rational-expectations pricing model is supported in markets with common information only after traders' actual experience teaches them that sustainable profits are unlikely if one buys above dividend value or sells below dividend value.

3. *By asking traders at the end of each market period to forecast the mean price next period, what can be learned about the relationship between price expectations and subsequent price realizations?* The results from laboratory markets in which forecasting data were collected suggest that the mean forecast predicts the period-two price to be greater than the period-one mean realized price. Thus, traders' consensus forecast tends to reveal bullish capital-gains expectations. In markets in which a price bubble ensues, the mean forecast fails to predict the turning point, or crash, in prices, and also fails to predict sharp jumps in prices in the boom phase of the cycle. In general, the mean forecast is a good predictor only in those intervals when mean prices are stable or changing gradually from period to period. Ordinary least squares regressions indicate that mean forecasts are highly adaptive; i.e., jumps in the mean price as well as turning points yielded next-period forecasts reflecting such unanticipated price changes. The accuracy and lagged adaptation of traders' forecasts parallels that of professional forecasters whose forecasts also have a strong tendency to miss turning points and to be highly adaptive.

4. *Does the opportunity to short sell diminish the amplitude and duration of the speculative price bubbles observed in laboratory stock markets?* The hypothesis that bubbles are moderated if traders can sell short rests on the argument that those traders who expect the bubble to burst can leverage their sales by taking a short position. Consequently, a small number of traders who have countercyclical expectations would be able to offset the ebullient expectations of others. The data fail to support this hypothesis. The duration and amplitude of bubbles remain about the same, but the volume of trading rises significantly above those of experiments in which short selling is not allowed.

5. *Will the presence of "informed insiders"— subjects who are knowledgeable about the behavior of previous laboratory stock markets—eliminate or moderate bubbles?* Rational-expectations theory predicts that if irrational trading patterns create profitable arbitrage, then knowledgeable traders will exploit these opportunities, thereby eliminating the irrational trading patterns. This hypothesis has been tested by having three graduate students read the Smith, Suchanek, and Williams paper, which is the source for much of the material summarized here. Each period the informed insiders were provided with a count of the total bids and total offers in the previous period, since the excess of bids over offers was found in that paper to be a leading indicator of average price changes. These three informed traders then participated in a market with six or nine uninformed traders. The results supported the predictions of the theory when the informed traders were endowed with a capacity to sell short, and the uninformed subjects were not inexperienced. The insiders need the short-selling capacity to dominate the market; when the other traders were inexperienced the bubble forces were so strong that informed traders were swamped by the boom.

6. *Is the existence of speculative price bubbles a phenomenon that is unique to the use of college students as traders in the market? Will bubbles vanish when business professionals or over-the-counter stock traders are used as subjects in laboratory stock markets?* In any set of market experiments it is always appropriate to ask whether the results are sensitive to characteristics of the subject pool. One reported experiment used small-business men and women from the Tucson community as traders. This group recorded one of the most severe bubbles observed among the experiments reported by Smith, Suchanek, and Williams.

Another stock-market experiment used fifteen corporate executives as traders. This experimental design raised the reward level more than 60 percent above that of student subjects, and, since the subjects were thought to be more sophisticated than undergraduate students (although inexperienced), each trader was endowed with the capacity both to sell short and to buy on margin. The results show an inordinately large discrepancy between share prices and intrinsic dividend value. Heavy buying, including some margin purchases, kept prices well above dividend value; furthermore the inevitable crash at the end failed to decline to dividend value. Individual earnings ranged from a loss of $17 to a profit of $60.

Finally, one experiment was conducted using six over-the-counter dealers and the higher reward levels utilized in the above experiment. These subjects were accustomed to using computer stock quotation screens. An additional three "subjects" (the experimenters) traded as informed insiders. However, the latter were not endowed with any short-selling capacity. By period eight, the insiders had exhausted their inventory of shares. This selling pressure moderated price increases relative to intrinsic value, but when that selling pressure was removed, market prices rose and did not crash until the final period.

The general results observed for inexperienced student subjects are robust with respect to the use of small-business persons, corporate executives, and stock-market traders. For all subject populations utilized in the stock-market experiments summarized here, traders required not only common information on an unchanging trading environment, but also market experience, for their price expectations to converge on the intrinsic dividend value of asset shares.

Vernon L. Smith
Arlington W. Williams

See also EXCESS VOLATILITY; EXPECTATIONS; RATIONAL EXPECTATIONS; SUNSPOT THEORIES OF FLUCTUATIONS; TULIPMANIA

Bibliography
King, R. R., V. L. Smith, A. W. Williams, and M. Van Boening. 1993. "The Robustness of Bubbles and Crashes in Experimental Stock Markets." In *Evolutionary Dynamics and Nonlinear Economics—A Transdisciplinary Dialogue,* edited by R. Day and P. Chen, 183–200. New York: Oxford Univ. Press.

Smith, V. L., G. L. Suchanek, and A. W. Williams. 1988. "Bubbles, Crashes and Endogenous Expectations in Experimental Spot Asset Markets." *Econometrica* 56:1119–51.

E

Falling Rate of Profit

Declines in the rate of return on capital are central to Marxian theories of the business cycle and of long-term trends in the capitalist economy. While similar concepts can be found outside the Marxian tradition, this article focuses on views developed within the Marxian and Marxian-influenced literature.

To sort out these views, we use a canonical equation of the sort developed by Weisskopf (1979). Define:

r_i ≡ private-sector realized inside rate of profit

P_i ≡ private-sector realized inside profit

K_i ≡ private-sector inside capital stock

K_o ≡ private-sector outside capital stock

P ≡ private-sector realized total (inside plus outside) profit

Y ≡ private-sector realized total output (net of raw materials consumption and depreciation)

X ≡ gross (including public-sector) realized total output

Z ≡ full-capacity gross total output

K ≡ total private-sector capital stock

D ≡ outside/inside capital ratio, K_o/K_i ($1 + D \equiv K/K_i$)

The terms "inside" and "outside" correspond roughly to Marx's distinction between entrepreneurial (industrial) capital and interest-bearing capital. Realized output and profits are goods produced and sold; the unrealized portion is unproduced, and represents the gap between actual production, X, and capacity, Z.

We now define the strategic behavioral variable r_i:

$$r_i \equiv \frac{P_i}{K_i} \equiv \frac{P_i}{P}\frac{P}{Y}\frac{Y}{X}\frac{X}{Z}\frac{Z}{K}\frac{K}{K_i}$$
$$\equiv \left[\frac{P_i}{P}\frac{P}{Y}\frac{X}{Z}\right]\left[(1+D)\frac{Y}{X}\frac{Z}{K}\right] \tag{1}$$

In the second line of equation (1), r_i is decomposed into six items, which are arranged in two groups: the first predominantly cyclical, the second secular (i.e., shaping the underlying trend). The cyclical group contains an inside-to-total profits ratio, P_i/P, which is thought to move cyclically, and in particular to fall rapidly at the peak of a boom when money is tight and interest rates rise (Itoh 1978); and an output-to-capacity ratio, X/Z, reflecting the effective-demand constraint. This latter ratio may contribute independently to profit-rate cycles via swings in investment demand caused by changing expectations over the cycle; these may of course be pro- or countercyclical, depending on how they are specified.

However, the primary role in Marxian cycle theory goes to the profit share, P/Y. The classic argument is in Marx ([1867–94] 1967, vol. 3). See also Sweezy (1942). A particularly fruitful modern formulation using simultaneous nonlinear differential equations has been provided by Goodwin ([1967] 1983). In this application to economics of the Volterra-Lotka, predator-prey paradigm, tight labor markets force wages to rise. This encroachment on profits reduces the profit and growth rates, causing the employment rate (the ratio of employed workers to the total labor force) to turn down. This, in turn, produces a peak and fall in the wage (which thus, like the fox preying on the rabbit, gobbles up its prey and induces its own decline). Falling wages restore profits and growth, and employment subsequently hits bottom and begins to rise, returning the cycle to its starting point. The falling rate of profit, then, is what limits periodic wage increases; rising wages, in turn, follow profit booms and prevent them from exceeding the bounds of systemic reproduction. The cycle therefore reflects the shifting balance of class forces between capitalists and workers.

The Goodwin cycle is a smooth, closed limit cycle; once started, it persists. Its explanatory power therefore exceeds that of cycles based on multiplier-accelerator interactions which, barring unbelievable accident, either disappear or explode over time. The Marxian cycle, however, is not smooth; periodic crises followed by rapid decline are essential moments, and a falling rate of profit is invoked to explain their onset. One classical argument holds that the existing profit rate is regarded as customary, with a threshold of perception of variations around that rate. When r falls outside that threshold, a *liquidation crisis* ensues, in which capitalists seek to protect their assets by rushing into liquidity, triggering a collapse of demand and reinforcing the original panic. This story, while evocative, is vague and hard to formalize.

A similar approach refers to the problem of effective demand. If the profit share is rising in a boom, the supply of consumer goods will progressively outrun the demand. When this gap crosses a threshold of perception, the market for investment goods will collapse as well. While investment could conceivably fill the gap between consumption demand and production, in this conjuncture it cannot do so, and a sudden and general collapse ensues. This argument, however, rests on a *rising* profit share, and thus seems incompatible with the "profit-squeeze" conception of the boom found in the Goodwin cycle approach. A possible reconciliation (Laibman 1992, chap. 10) sees the profit rate and share falling as employment rises; even though the wage share is rising, the *growth rate* of demand falls suddenly when the employment rate stabilizes at its cyclical peak, and this causes a collapse in the investment rate and an ensuing crisis initiating the depression phase. Finally, the financial sector [represented by the term P_f/P in equation (1)] is subject to sudden swings in mood and catastrophes induced by bankruptcies and breaks in the chains to credit relations, and is therefore another potential source of crisis (Itoh 1978).

The predator-prey cycle incorporates these and other complexities, and explains the persistence of cycles, as noted. But does it adequately explain their *necessity*, or their *amplitude* and *evolution* over time? Marx's industrial reserve army of unemployed is, in fact, a dynamic concept (Marx [1867–94] 1967, vol. 1; Boddy and Crotty 1974). If the unemployment rate were constant over time—the economy happened to be at the stable point of the Goodwin cycle—the working class would learn to cope with the known burden of the threat of joblessness. For the threat to be real, employed workers must periodically experience *rising* rates of unemployment, and the reserve army must therefore ebb and flow. A similar point holds for the rate of profit. If it is constant, its expectation becomes less and less uncertain over time, undermining the rationale for differing inside and outside rates of return. To keep r_i from eventual precipitous collapse, cyclicality is necessary. All this suggests that the amplitude of the cycle is more than mere historical accident. Marx expected cyclical crises of increasing intensity as capitalism's inner contradictions became more severe. This raises the issue of the long-term trend of the profit rate.

In canonical equation (1), the second set of terms relates directly to this issue. The rise of government spending and production (the public sector) is represented by the term Y/X; a massive literature (e.g., Foster 1986) points to an inexorable rise in state activity and corresponding decline in Y/X, a proximate cause of a falling r_i. Recent experience in the United States suggests a rising trend in the outside-to-inside (or debt-equity) ratio, D, which may counteract the falling-r tendency. Attention, however, has mainly been focused on the last term, Z/X, representing Marx's *organic composition of capital*, the expression of the capital-intensity of output and thus in some sense of the level of the production forces.

Marx's law of the rising organic composition of capital corresponds in our notation to a law of falling Z/K, clearly a factor depressing r over time. Since $Z/K \equiv (Z/L)/(K/L)$ (where L represents current labor input), the postulated law requires the degree of mechanization, K/L, to rise more rapidly than labor productivity, Z/L. Marx ([1867–94] 1967, 1:chaps. 24–25) asserted (but notoriously failed to demonstrate) that this would be the case (Sweezy 1942, Robinson 1942). Subsequent Marxian work has either avoided the issue altogether, rejected the theory and built on other aspects of Marx's thought, defended the orthodox view by reproducing its assumptions while failing to address the problems raised in the critical literature (Weeks 1981), or proposed novel formulations to surmount the objections. Along with the problem of indeterminacy of the trend in Z/K, the most salient point has been that capitalists would avoid any technical change that reduced the profit rate, making it necessary for falling-r theory to come to terms with "micro-rational" behavior (Okishio 1961).

Novel formulations are too numerous to summarize here. Three categories stand out, however: theories that assume rising unproductive expenditures or waste; those that rest on diminishing returns to non-renewable resources; and one that posits that, in the competitive struggle for survival, capitalists will sacrifice their profit rate for a higher profit *margin* (the amount or mass of profit). (The latter theory rescues the falling rate of profit by depriving it of relevance.)

Is a rigorous formulation of a falling-r theory possible? Given atomistically competitive firms, acting independently for momentary advantage, technical changes would be chosen to maximize the momentary (innovator's) rate of profit. These changes are constrained by a function relating obtainable increases in productivity to the associated increases in the capital-to-labor ratios. It can be shown (Laibman 1992) that reasonable conditions *may* obtain in which optimally chosen technical change results in increasing capital intensity (falling Z/K), after the innovator's advantage is lost and the new technique generalized. This, in turn, and with the other elements in equation (1) unchanged, entails either a falling r_i or a rising profit share, P/Y, either of which may lead to structural crisis. While far from an iron-clad law of falling r, this approach preserves the falling Z/K-falling r path as a potentially important component in the analysis of capitalist growth. (The other trend factors—D, Y/X, and possibly some aspects of X/Z as well—deserve further study.)

What unifies the diverse Marxian literature is an emphasis on the rate of profit as the central strategic-behavioral variable: the ever-present target of capitalist accumulation, the barometer of the capitalist economy's health and capacity for reproduction, and the trigger of periodic cyclical crises. The Marxian view of the cycle as inherently *critical* has been a fruitful source of theoretical insight and empirical

research. The trend analysis, in turn, may illuminate structural transformations, provided all of the determinants of r and r_i trends are brought into the analytical picture.

David Laibman

See also BAUER, OTTO; BUSINESS CYCLES; DISPROPORTIONALITY THEORY; FALLING RATE OF PROFIT, EMPIRICAL TESTS; MARX, KARL HEINRICH; PROFIT SQUEEZE

Bibliography

Boddy, R. and J. Crotty. 1974. "Class Conflict, Keynesian Policies, and the Business Cycle." *Monthly Review* 26:1–17.

Foster, J. B. 1986. *The Theory of Monopoly Capitalism*. New York: Monthly Review Press.

Goodwin, R. M. [1967] 1983. "A Growth Cycle." Chap. 14 in *Essays in Economic Dynamics*. London: Macmillan.

Itoh, M. 1978. "The Formation of Marx's Theory of Crisis." *Science and Society* 42:129–55.

Laibman, D. 1992. *Technical Change, Profit and Growth: Explorations in Marxist Economic Theory.* Armonk, N.Y.: M. E. Sharpe.

Marx, K. [1867–94] 1967. *Capital*. 3 vols. New York: International Publishers.

Okishio, N. 1961. "Technical Change and the Rate of Profit." *Kobe University Economic Review* 7:86–99.

Robinson, J. 1942. *An Essay on Marxian Economics*. New York: St. Martin's Press.

Sweezy, P. M. 1942. *The Theory of Capitalist Development*. New York: Monthly Review Press.

Weeks, J. 1981. *Capital and Exploitation*. Princeton: Princeton Univ. Press.

Weisskopf, T. E. 1979. "Marxian Crisis Theory and the Rate of Profit in the Postwar U.S. Economy." *Cambridge Journal of Economics* 3:341–78.

Falling Rate of Profit, Empirical Tests

The most important prediction of Marx's theory of crises and depressions is that the rate of profit tends to decline over time because technological change increases the composition of capital faster than the rate of surplus-value. This article summarizes the main empirical evidence related to Marx's theory of the falling rate of profit, discussing various estimates of the rate of profit in the American economy from 1880 to the present. There have been a few studies of Marx's rate of profit for other countries (see bibliography), but they are only for the post-World War II period, and resemble Weisskopf's estimates discussed below.

The appropriate time period for an empirical test of Marx's theory of the falling rate of profit is generally considered to be either a long-wave expansion (30–40 years, including several short-run cycles) or an even longer secular period that includes more than one long wave. Short-run cycles are considered to be too short for the Marxian dynamics to operate.

Conceptual Issues

Marx's theory of the rate of profit depends on three key ratios involving three fundamental magnitudes: constant capital, variable capital, and surplus-value. The composition of capital is defined as the ratio of the stock of constant capital to the annual flow of variable capital; the rate of surplus-value is defined as the ratio of the annual flow of surplus-value to the annual flow of variable capital; and the rate of profit is defined as the ratio of the annual flow of surplus-value to the stock of constant capital (the stock of variable capital is usually assumed to be negligibly small).

Four major conceptual issues are involved in the precise definition of Marx's concepts of constant capital, variable capital, and surplus-value, and thus in the estimation of the three

key Marxian ratios: (1) Do Marx's concepts refer to observable quantities of money (or prices) or to observable quantities of labor-time? (2) Do the concepts of constant capital and variable capital apply only to capitalist production, or also to noncapitalist (mainly government) production? (3) Do the concepts of constant and variable capital refer only to capital invested in production activities or also to capital invested in nonproduction (circulation and supervision) activities? (4) Are the taxes paid by workers part of variable capital or surplus-value?

Table 1 summarizes how the studies to be discussed below interpret these conceptual issues. Different interpretations of one or more of these issues account for the differences in the trends of the composition of capital and the rate of surplus-value estimated by these studies.

Early Studies

Gillman (1958) was the first to attempt to estimate the three key Marxian variables, for the period 1880–1952. One shortcoming of his estimates is that they are for only the manufacturing sector, rather than for the total capitalist economy, to which Marx's theory most rigorously applies. Gillman found that until about 1920 the trends of the three Marxian variables behaved closely to Marx's predictions: the composition of capital increased much faster than the rate of surplus-value, so that the rate of profit fell by more than 50 percent. However, after 1920, all three variables show essentially

TABLE 1: Interpretations of Conceptual Issues

	Gillman	Mage	Weisskopf	Wolff	Moseley
Labor or money?	money	both[1]	money[2]	labor	money
Include noncapitalist production?	no	no	no	yes	no
Distinguish nonproduction capital?	yes[3]	yes[4]	no	no	yes
Taxes on wages?	variable capital	neither	variable capital	surplus value	variable capital

1. Mage presents two sets of estimates, one in units of current prices and one in units of labor-hours, but argues that the latter are more rigorously correct.

2. Weisskopf's interpretation is that Marx's concepts most rigorously refer to observable quantities of labor, but that estimates in terms of money are nonetheless reliable approximations; thus his estimates are in terms of money.

3. Gillman distinguishes between productive and unproductive capital invested in labor-power, but not in means of production.

4. Mage also distinguishes between productive and unproductive capital invested in labor-power, but not in means of production. In addition, Mage considers the wages of unproductive labor to be a part of constant capital, rather than surplus value.

no trend (apart from cyclical fluctuations), contradicting Marx's predictions.

The second important attempt to estimate the Marxian variables was by Mage (1963). Mage's estimates, covering the period 1900–60, were based on the total non-farm private economy, and thus correspond more closely to the Marxian concepts than do Gillman's estimates. Mage estimated that the rate of profit declined by 50–60 percent over the entire period. However, only about one-third of this decline was due to an increase in the composition of capital; the remaining two-thirds was due to a sharply falling rate of surplus-value, contrary to Marx's prediction of a rising rate of surplus-value. Mage observed that his estimates of the rate of profit and the rate of surplus-value are sensitive to his exclusion of taxes on profits from his estimates of surplus-value. If taxes on profits are included in Mage's estimates of surplus-value, the rate of profit declined by only about 30 percent, with the increase in the composition of capital and the decline in the rate of surplus-value each accounting for about half of the total decline.

Recent Contributions

The first major Marxian empirical study of the postwar period was by Weisskopf (1979). Weisskopf's estimates, covering the period 1949–75, are based on the nonfinancial corporate business sector (approximately 60 percent of the private capitalist economy). Weisskopf's estimates show that the rate of profit declined, as predicted by Marx, but for the opposite reason: a major decline in the rate of surplus-value, with a roughly constant composition of capital.

Wolff (1986) was the first to attempt to estimate the Marxian variables in units of labor-time, rather than in monetary units, covering the period 1947–76 and based on capitalist and noncapitalist sectors. Wolff's estimates show roughly the same trends as Weisskopf's: the rate of profit declined, but because the rate of surplus-value declined, not because the composition of capital increased.

Weisskopf's and Wolff's studies lend empirical support to the "profit-squeeze" interpretation of Marx's theory, according to which a falling rate of profit is caused primarily by a falling rate of surplus-value.

However, Moseley (1985) argues that Weisskopf's and Wolff's estimates for the U.S. are unreliable, because they are derived from conventional data categories that differ significantly from the corresponding Marxian concepts. According to Moseley, the most important discrepancy between the Marxian variables and these conventional data categories is that the latter do not take into account Marx's distinction between productive labor (employed in production activities that produce value and surplus-value) and unproductive labor (employed in circulation and supervision activities that does not produce value and surplus-value). Moseley presents alternative estimates of the Marxian variables for the postwar U.S. economy, which do take into account this distinction in Marx's theory (following Gillman and Mage in many respects). His estimates show that, as predicted by Marx, the rate of profit declined because the composition of capital increased faster than the rate of surplus-value.

An important (1987) contribution by Dumenil, Glick, and Rangel (DGR hereafter) examines the long-run secular trends of the Marxian variables in the U.S. from 1900 to 1982. Their estimates are conceptually similar to Weisskopf's in Table 1 (and thus subject to Moseley's criticism). DGR conclude that the rate of profit fell significantly during two periods: from 1900 to 1930 and from World War II to the present. However, they emphasize that these periods of decline were interrupted by the Great Depression and World War II, during which the rate of profit rose sharply. They estimate the rate of profit in 1945 at about the same level it was in 1900, whereas Gillman and Mage estimate the rate of profit in 1945 at about 20 percent below its level in 1900. DGR's estimates also show that the decline of the rate of profit in the postwar period was about twice as great as in the predepression period. They identify the main cause of the decline in both periods as a decline in the rate of surplus-value (or in the share of profit).

To summarize, there is general consensus that the rate of profit in the U.S. economy declined significantly over most of the twentieth century (except for 1930–45), as Marx predicted. However, the evidence about whether the main cause of this decline was an increase in the composition of capital, as Marx predicted, or contrary to Marx, a decline in the rate of surplus-value, is mixed. For the postwar period, the relative significance of these two possible causes of the falling rate of profit is sensitive to how one interprets Marx's distinction between productive and unproductive labor. For the predepression period, Gillman's and

F

Mage's estimates suggest differing causes of the declining rate of profit, and it remains to be seen which of their conceptual differences can account for their differing estimates of the trends in the composition of capital and especially the rate of surplus-value. A thorough reexamination of this earlier period would be an important contribution to the study of the secular trends of the rate of profit and its determinants.

Fred Moseley

See also FALLING RATE OF PROFIT; PROFIT SQUEEZE

Bibliography

Dumenil, G., M. Glick, and J. Rangel. 1987. "The Rate of Profit in the United States: From the Turn of the Century to the 1980s." *Cambridge Journal of Economics* 11:331–59.

Gillman, J. 1958. *The Falling Rate of Profit.* New York: Carmen Associates.

Glyn, A. and B. Sutcliffe. 1972. *Capitalism in Crisis.* New York: Pantheon.

Lipietz, A. 1986. "Behind the Crisis: The Exhaustion of a Regime of Accumulation." *Review of Radical Political Economics* 18:1–2.

Mage, S. 1963. "The Law of the Falling Tendency of the Rate of Profit." Ph.D. diss., Columbia University.

Moseley, F. 1985. "The Rate of Surplus-Value in the Postwar U.S. Economy: A Critique of Weisskopf's Estimates." *Cambridge Journal of Economics* 9:57–79.

———. 1988. "The Rate of Surplus Value, the Organic Composition, and the General Rate of Profit in the U.S. Economy, 1947–67: A Critique and Update of Wolff's Estimates." *American Economic Review* 78:298–304.

Reati, A. 1986. "The Rate of Profit and the Organic Composition of Capital in West German Industry from 1960 to 1981." *Review of Radical Political Economy* 18:56–86.

———. 1989. "The Rate of Profit and the Organic Composition of Capital Over the Long Postwar Cycle: The Case of French Industry from 1959 to 1981." *International Journal of Political Economy* 19:10–32.

Weisskopf, T. E. 1979. "Marxian Crisis Theory and the Rate of Profit in the Postwar U.S. Economy." *Cambridge Journal of Economics* 3:341–78.

Wolff, E. N. 1979. "The Rate of Surplus Value, the Organic Composition, and the General Rate of Profit in the U.S. Economy, 1947–67." *American Economic Review* 69:329–41.

———. 1986. "The Productivity Slowdown and the Fall in the U.S. Rate of Profit, 1947–76." *Review of Radical Political Economy* 18:87–109.

Fanno, Marco (1878–1965)

Marco Fanno was born at Conegliano Veneto, Italy. A disciple of Achille Loria, he taught at the universities of Sassari, Cagliari, Messina, Parma, and Padua. In 1932 he became a member of the Accademia dei Lincei. His scholarly output spans the period from before the First to after the Second World War, leaving its mark on the fields of economic history and colonial expansion ("Il regime e le concessioni delle terre nelle colonie moderne," 1905; "L'espansione commerciale degli Stati moderni," 1906); pure economics ("Contributo alla teoria dell'offerta a costi congiunti," 1914; "Contributo alla teoria economica dei beni succedanei," 1926; "Della identità di alcuni teoremi di economia pura," 1934); and, above all, business-cycle theory ("Cicli di produzione, cicli di credito e fluttuazioni industriali," 1931; and *La teoria delle fluttuazioni economiche,* 1947).

His 1931 article marks him as a business-cycle theorist of distinction. He made two innovations. First, he pointed out that a change in consumption affects investment in direct proportion to the length of the industrial process. Second, he introduced the notion of *"errori di tempo"* (time lags), which magnify exogenous changes.

La teoria builds on these insights, presenting an eclectic theory of business fluctuations around a trend of long-run growth caused by rising population, increasing savings, and technological progress. Some of the relations examined in the book are those between profits, prices, and the volume of credit; between output and the velocity of money; between stock prices, issues of new shares, and capital investment; between costs, profits, and output. Considering the interaction of all these factors, Fanno described significant fluctuations and turning points.

Fanno's method was primarily descriptive and statistical, using English, German, and United States data. The work was broad-based and related to that of many other economists: his statistical approach shows debt to W. C. Mitchell and Simon Kuznets; his emphasis on the role of debt relates him to Irving Fisher's *Booms and Depressions*. Schumpeter might have inspired his vision of an unstable capitalism. With Robertson and Pigou he shared the notion of periodic spurts of capital-equipment spending for replacement purposes. Like Cassel and Wicksell, he believed that "abnormal" expansion of bank credit keeps an upswing going beyond its natural limits. Very modern were his use of lags, his emphasis on *"fiducia nell'avvenire"* (business confidence), and his belief that involuntary unemployment is normal in a market system. The *Teoria* makes reference to the work of Aftalion, Angell, Cassel, Bowley, Tarshis, Hansen, Samuelson, Kahn, Marshall, Haberler, J. M. Clark and others. There are forty-two references to J. M. Keynes, mostly to *A Treatise on Money*.

The second, expanded edition of the *Teoria* (1956) shows Fanno abreast of economic-theoretical developments, if somewhat critical of the stylized cycles produced by Hicks, Harrod, and Domar because of their lack of attention to the institutional characteristics of the economic system.

Inductive, statistical, and historical, Fanno's study did not readily produce "laws" and immutable relations between variables. His work is *sub specie temporis*, specific to its times and institutions. What it lost in generality it gained in realism, but in the long run the realism can be maintained only by continually updating the material. This has not happened to Fanno's work, which was superseded by the econometric approach.

The rise of the econometric approach and the ignorance of foreign languages by English-speaking economists are the main reasons for the comparative neglect of his work outside Italy.

Piero V. Mini

Bibliography
Bagiotti, T., ed. 1966. *Studies in Honour of Marco Fanno: Investigations in Economic Theory and Methodology*. 2 vols. Padua: CEDAM.
Fanno, M. 1928. "Credit Expansion, Savings and Gold Exports." *Economic Journal* 38:126–31.
———. 1931. "Cicle di produzione, cicle di credito e fluttuazioni industriali." *Giornale degli Economisti* 27:98–128.
———. 1939. *Normal and Abnormal International Capital Transfers*. Minneapolis: Univ. of Minnesota Press.
———. 1947. *La teoria delle fluttuazioni economiche*. Torino: Mondadori.

F

Federal Deposit Insurance

Thousands of commercial banks and thrift institutions failed during the Great Depression in the United States. The failures resulted from contagious runs that—given the failure of the Federal Reserve to act as a lender of last resort—even many healthy institutions could not survive. As a result, the money stock fell sharply and bank lending was severely curtailed. The breakdown in financial intermediation contributed to a general economic collapse. In 1933, federal deposit insurance was instituted to prevent such panic-induced runs from recurring and to protect small depositors. Congress established two separate insurance funds: the Federal Deposit Insurance Corporation (FDIC) for commercial banks in 1933 and the Federal Savings and Loan Insurance Corporation (FSLIC) for thrift institutions in 1934.

Federal deposit insurance seemed to work well until the 1980s. There were few failures, which were not very costly, so that federal insurers always had sufficient funds to close down troubled institutions. But conditions deteriorated in the 1980s as interest rates rose to unexpectedly high levels and became unusually volatile. Banks and thrifts failed in numbers not seen since the 1930s. The costs of resolving these failures reached record levels, forcing the insurance fund for thrifts into insolvency. Although public confidence in the financial system remained intact, these developments highlighted the *moral-hazard* problem inherent in all insurance schemes, especially federal deposit insurance.

Moral hazard refers to the diminished incentive of the insured to prevent losses from occurring. Federal deposit insurance removes the incentive for bank runs by assuring depositors that they can redeem their deposits no matter what happens to the assets acquired with those funds. Yet, it is this very confidence that eliminates depositors' incentives to monitor and discipline the activities of their depository institutions. At the same time, the owners or managers of banks and thrifts operating with insured deposits on which they pay a flat insurance fee have an incentive to engage in riskier activities than they otherwise would, because they receive all the gain and bear only a portion of any loss. The federal insurer, on the other hand, is responsible for protecting depositors but shares only in losses. Furthermore, the less equity owners have at risk, the greater their incentive to "gamble" with insured funds. Investors may even be attracted to weak financial institutions, which offer a large potential gain and limited risk. People buy lottery tickets for a similar reason. This is just what happened in the 1980s when hundreds of thrift institutions were permitted to remain open and compete for funds long after becoming insolvent. It was not, however, the intent of the federal insurer to let moral hazard go unchecked. Federal insurers have simply never adopted the kinds of practices private insurers use to control excessive risk-taking.

In fact, federal deposit insurance was not designed to operate like private insurance. The initial premiums were set not to cover the average loss experience of depository institutions, but only losses in non-crisis periods. Regulation, supervision, and examination were supposed to prevent abnormal losses and federal insurance per se was supposed to prevent catastrophic losses resulting from economy-wide bank runs. Not only were the premiums set below the levels dictated by the average loss experience, they were also uniform, regardless of differences in portfolio risk at individual institutions.

The devastating events of the 1980s prompted a reassessment of these and other aspects of federal deposit insurance. Indeed, the Financial Institutions Reform, Recovery, and Enforcement Act of 1989 actually mandated some changes in the system, including increased deposit-insurance premiums for both banks and thrifts and placing both the Bank Insurance Fund (BIF) and the Savings Association Insurance Fund (SAIF) under the sole administration of the Federal Deposit Insurance Corporation (FDIC). The Act also mandated a study of risk-adjusted deposit premiums and, more generally, the entire federal deposit-insurance system.

Many proposals to reform federal deposit insurance have been made. All involve adopting some private-insurance practices by the federal insurer. The most radical proposals would abolish federal insurance altogether, in the expectation that private insurers would fill the void left by the withdrawal of federal insurers. But short of this proposal which, in the view of many, raises the specter of widespread bank runs, other proposals would require the retention of federal regulation, supervision, and examination, and limit moral hazard by inducing depositors, creditors, and owners to discipline banks and thrifts. This would be accomplished through such proposals as co-insurance, risk-based insurance premiums, increased capital requirements, risk-based capital requirements, and reduced deposit-insurance limits. Moreover, adoption of market-value accounting techniques would improve the monitoring of depository institutions and allow more timely intervention to close troubled institutions. However, nobody has yet determined the optimal *combination* of such practices.

The evidence is overwhelming that the major cause of the thrift debacle of the 1980s was the design and operation of federal deposit insurance—not fraud and mismanagement, deregulation of deposit rates by the Depository Institutions Deregulation and Monetary Control Act of 1980, or the granting of broader asset powers by the Garn–St. Germain Depository Institutions Act of 1982. These factors certainly contributed to failures and failure costs, but were not the major causes. To prevent the financial problems of the 1980s from recurring, reforming federal deposit insurance seems necessary. Reform will involve making federal insurance practices resemble private insurance practices more closely.

James R. Barth
John F. Feid

See also BANKING AND FINANCIAL REGULATION; BANKING PANICS; GREAT DEPRESSION IN THE UNITED STATES (1929–1938); LENDER OF LAST RESORT

Bibliography

Baer, H. 1985. "Private Prices, Public Insurance: The Pricing of Federal Deposit Insurance." Federal Reserve Bank of Chicago, *Economic Perspectives,* September/October, 45–57.

Barth, J. R. 1991. *The Great Savings and Loan Debacle.* Washington, D.C.: American Enterprise Institute.

Barth, J. R., P. F. Bartholomew, and M. G. Bradley. 1991. "Reforming Federal Deposit Insurance: What Can Be Learned From Private Insurance Practices?" *Consumer Finance Law Quarterly Report,* 45:140–47.

Barth, J. R., P. F. Bartholomew, and C. J. Labich. 1989. "Moral Hazard and the Thrift Crisis: An Analysis of 1988 Resolutions." In *The 25th Annual Conference on Bank Structure and Competition*, 344–84. Chicago: Federal Reserve Bank of Chicago.

Barth, J. R., J. J. Feid, G. Riedel, and M. H. Tunis. 1989. "Alternative Federal Deposit Insurance Regimes." In *Problems of the Federal Savings and Loan Insurance Corporation (FSLIC)*. Hearings before the Senate Committee on Banking, Housing, and Urban Affairs, part 2. 100th Cong., 1st Sess.

Benston, G. and G. Kaufman. 1988. "Regulating Bank Safety and Performance." In *Restructuring Banking and Financial Services in America*, edited by W. S. Haraf and R. M. Kushmeider, 63–99. Washington, D.C.: American Enterprise Institute.

Bernanke, B. S. 1983. "Nonmonetary Effects of the Financial Crisis in the Propagation of the Great Depression." *American Economic Review* 73:257–76.

Brumbaugh, R. D., Jr. 1988. *Thrifts Under Siege: Restoring Order to American Banking*. Cambridge, Mass.: Ballinger.

Kane, E. J. 1989. *The S&L Insurance Mess: How Did It Happen?* Washington, D.C.: Urban Institute.

Scott, K. E. 1989. "Deposit Insurance and Bank Regulation: The Policy Choices." *Business Lawyer* 44:907–33.

Short, E. D. and G. P. O'Driscoll, Jr. 1983. "Deregulation and Deposit Insurance." Federal Reserve Bank of Dallas *Economic Review*, Sept., 11–23.

Federal Reserve System: 1914–1941

Two issues are important in analyzing the relationship between Federal Reserve policy and the business cycle: (1) how policymakers respond to the business cycle, and (2) how much monetary policy affected the business cycle. Milton Friedman and Anna J. Schwartz (1963) have studied the Fed's behavior and the effect of monetary policy on economic activity between 1914 and 1941. Their work has spawned extensive research into the conduct of monetary policy and its impact on the business cycle.

Friedman and Schwartz conclude that monetary forces powerfully affected economic activity during the interwar period. They argue that economic downturns resulted directly from contractionary monetary policy in 1920–21, 1929–33, and 1936–37. They contend also that the Fed stabilized output effectively between 1924 and 1929. While their views are not accepted universally, few would deny that specific episodes of contractionary policy, such as the Fed's increases of the discount rate in October 1931, contributed directly to economic decline. What remains controversial, however, is whether the Fed really tried to limit fluctuations in economic activity, and whether it did indeed stabilize output during the 1920s. If the Fed did attempt successfully to limit economic fluctuations during the 1920s, then the question arises why the Great Depression was so unlike the preceding period.

American monetary policy in the early years of the Reserve System was shaped largely by World War I. The outbreak of hostilities coincided with the Fed's creation. The war caused a sharp increase in American exports, which led to large gold inflows. The Fed allowed these inflows to expand the money stock—in fact, it could do little else—and inflation resulted. The inflows ceased once the United States entered the war, but the money stock continued to grow, because the Fed used credit expansion to help finance government deficits. Throughout the war the Fed maintained a low discount rate, encouraging member banks to borrow reserves and invest in government securities.

The Fed kept its discount rate low through 1919, but the expansion of Federal Reserve credit, coupled with gold outflows, began to reduce the Fed's reserves. This reduction, along with concern over inflation and speculation, led the Fed to raise the discount rate three times from December 1919 to June 1920. And, despite a sharp downturn in economic activity, the Fed maintained a high rate until May 1921, when officials believed system reserves had risen sufficiently.

The discount rate increases in 1919–20 constrained bank borrowing and produced a contraction of the money stock. Undoubtedly, Fed policies worsened the 1920–21 recession. The criticism of its policies in these years may have prompted the Fed to seek to limit fluctuations in economic activity throughout the rest of the 1920s.

According to Friedman and Schwartz, the Fed, under the leadership of Benjamin Strong,

F

Governor of the Federal Reserve Bank of New York, had, by 1924, developed a countercyclical policy. But this policy was short-lived. They contend that Strong's death in 1928 and a subsequent reorganization of the Open Market Committee significantly reduced the Fed's sensitivity to economic fluctuations. The officials gaining authority, Friedman and Schwartz contend, lacked the capacity or interest to pursue a vigorous countercyclical policy. Thus, in sharp contrast to its behavior during relatively minor recessions in 1924 and 1927, the Fed failed to pursue expansionary policies to counter the Great Depression.

Others have questioned whether Fed behavior changed with the onset of the depression. For example, Wicker (1966) argues that the Fed had not intended to stabilize economic activity during the 1920s, but rather had tried to help Great Britain return to and then remain on the gold standard. The Fed did make open-market purchases during recessions in 1924 and 1927, but Wicker argues that the Fed's principal objective was to reduce U.S. interest rates in relation to those in London, so that gold would flow to Britain. The weak Fed response to the depression did not reflect a change in policy, because the Fed had not previously responded to fluctuations in economic activity.

Brunner and Meltzer (1968) also conclude that Fed behavior did not change, but disagree that the Fed was motivated primarily by international goals. They argue that the Fed failed to pursue expansionary policies during the depression because officials believed that low nominal interest rates indicated that monetary conditions were already exceptionally easy, so that large open-market purchases were unnecessary. Brunner and Meltzer contend that the Fed was guided similarly by interest rates during the recessions of 1924 and 1927, and thus Fed behavior remained consistent.

Wheelock (1989) has analyzed econometrically the Fed's responses to various policy goals during the 1920s. He finds that the Fed did respond to fluctuations in economic activity, and that its response was indeed much less vigorous during the depression than it had been from 1924 to 1929. However, like Brunner and Meltzer, he found little change in Fed behavior over time.

Wheelock attributes the apparent inconsistency in the Fed's responsiveness to economic activity between the 1920s and early 1930s to differences in the levels of the Fed's policy guides: bank borrowing and interest rates. During the 1920s, the Fed developed a strategy of using open-market operations to influence the level of discount-window borrowing. During recessions, open-market operations supplied reserves, which allowed banks to reduce their borrowing. Once bank borrowing had declined to near zero, the Fed suspended its operations. Following the stock-market crash of 1929, bank borrowing and market interest rates fell to historically low levels. Fed officials therefore believed that money was already easy and that open-market operations were unnecessary. It does not seem that Fed performance changed dramatically with the onset of the depression.

If policy was consistent over the 1920s and early 1930s, what explains the apparently greater success of policy in limiting economic fluctuations in the 1920s than in the 1930s? Recent research suggests that in fact monetary policy was really not particularly stabilizing during the 1920s. Miron (1989) shows that output was less stable after the Fed's founding in 1914 than it had been before, even when the depression years (1929–33) are ignored. And Toma (1989) finds that the Fed's open-market operations during the 1920s had no discernable effect on the supply of money.

Monetary policy was ineffective during the 1920s partly because the policy strategy employed by the Reserve System did not effectively control the money stock. Indeed, the Fed did not seek to control the stock of money. During recessions, the money stock tends to fall since loan demand declines as does the number of profitable investments available to banks. Consequently, banks reduce borrowings from the Federal Reserve, and bank reserves and the money stock contract (or their rates of increase decline). Although the Fed did buy securities during recessions, it purchased too few to offset these declines. Further, because the Fed viewed a low level of borrowing by banks as a sign of monetary ease, it tended to buy fewer securities as borrowing fell. Thus, the Fed bought fewer securities during the severe recession of 1930–31, when bank borrowing fell sharply, than it did during the minor recessions of 1924 and 1927, when bank borrowing fell little. Hence the Fed allowed a greater decline in the money stock during the early 1930s than during 1924 or 1927.

A similar misinterpretation of bank-reserve positions led Fed officials to increase reserve requirements in 1936 and 1937, which contributed to the recession of 1937–38. Policymakers mistook large holdings by banks of excess reserves for a sign of exceptional ease. Fearing inflation, the Fed undertook contractionary policies, despite continued economic weakness. Friedman and Schwartz argue persuasively that banks held substantial excess reserves as a precaution against deposit outflows, because bank runs in the early 1930s had forced the closure of numerous illiquid, but solvent, institutions. Thus, the buildup of excess reserves in later years did not reflect monetary ease, only increased demand for liquidity by banks.

In sum, Federal Reserve actions significantly affected the business cycle from 1914 to 1941. The most dramatic effects of policy were negative. While some of the Fed's mistakes undoubtedly were caused by institutional flaws, the Fed's policy strategy failed to control the money stock. The Fed allowed greater declines in money during severe economic downturns than during minor recessions, and its misinterpretation of bank borrowing, interest rates, and excess reserves prevented it from taking steps to stabilize economic activity.

David C. Wheelock

See also BANKING PANICS; CENTRAL BANKING; CRISIS OF 1907; DEPRESSION OF 1920–1921; DEPRESSION OF 1937–1938; FEDERAL RESERVE SYSTEM: 1941–1993; GREAT DEPRESSION IN THE UNITED STATES (1929–1938); MONETARY POLICY

Bibliography

Brunner, K. and A. H. Meltzer. 1968. "What Did We Learn from the Monetary Experience of the United States in the Great Depression?" *Canadian Journal of Economics* 1:334–48.

Chandler, L. V. 1958. *Benjamin Strong, Central Banker.* Washington, D.C.: Brookings Institution.

———. 1971. *American Monetary Policy, 1928–1941.* New York: Harper and Row.

Epstein, G. and T. Ferguson. 1984. "Monetary Policy, Loan Liquidation, and Industrial Conflict: The Federal Reserve and the Open-Market Operations of 1932." *Journal of Economic History* 44:957–83.

Friedman, M. and A. J. Schwartz. 1963. *A Monetary History of the United States, 1867–1960.* Princeton: Princeton Univ. Press.

Miron, J. A. 1989. "The Founding of the Fed and the Destabilization of the Post-1914 Economy." In *A European Central Bank? Perspectives on Monetary Unification after Ten Years of the EMS,* edited by M. de Cecco and A. Giovannini, 290–328. Cambridge: Cambridge Univ. Press.

Temin, P. 1976. *Did Monetary Forces Cause the Great Depression?* New York: Norton.

Toma, M. 1989. "The Policy Effectiveness of Open Market Operations in the 1920s." *Explorations in Economic History* 26:99–116.

Wheelock, D. C. 1989. "The Strategy, Effectiveness, and Consistency of Federal Reserve Monetary Policy, 1924–1933." *Explorations in Economic History* 26:453–76.

Wicker, E. 1966. *Federal Reserve Monetary Policy, 1917–33.* New York: Random House.

Federal Reserve System: 1941–1993

Political pressures on monetary policy play a fundamental role in the political economy of monetary policy and therefore in related theories of the political business cycle. Monetary shocks regularly precipitate cyclical swings in the economy. These shocks often occur when politicians pressure the monetary authority to effect monetary expansions to disguise the adverse impacts on interest, exchange, and unemployment rates of their redistributive (fiscal) policies. Systematic overt political pressures only began in the 1960s, and for two extended subperiods of the entire timespan, 1970–74 and 1977–78, the Federal Reserve failed to resist these pressures.

The Role of Congress in Liberating the Fed

During and immediately after World War II, the Federal Reserve was the handmaiden to Treasury financing. The Federal Reserve committed itself to pegging interest rates while the war lasted, causing a huge injection of liquidity into private portfolios. Because of Congressional reluctance to raise taxes, the United States borrowed more heavily than its allies. The resulting increase in the money supply had tremendous inflationary potential. In addition, the contemporary concern that mature capitalist economies were most vulnerable, not to inflation, but to chronic stagnation, was belied by the unexpected postwar boom. Thus, a few years after the war ended, Marriner Eccles, the Fed Chairman, and other Fed officials recommended terminating the peg. In 1948, President Truman replaced Eccles with Thomas McCabe, partly because Eccles's authority within the system was in decline and partly because Truman and Treasury Secretary Snyder no longer trusted Eccles to support the peg.

While legally independent of the executive branch, the Federal Reserve, acting alone, could not oppose both the Treasury and the president. In the late 1940s, the Federal Reserve position was particularly weak, because of divisions in its leadership. For example, in 1947, Eccles wanted the board to control consumer credit and secondary reserve requirements, but was opposed by Allan Sproul, president of the New York Reserve Bank. In 1949, Sproul, in turn, wanted the Federal Open Market Committee (FOMC) rather than the board to control reserve requirements and the discount rate and favored placing the Treasury Secretary on the board to hasten an end to the peg. Chairman McCabe disagreed, arguing, instead, that two board positions should go to Reserve Bank presidents. Not surprisingly, a disunited Fed could not free itself from Treasury domination. Yet, complying with Treasury demands threatened its legitimacy as a bulwark against inflationary excesses.

The arguments of the executive branch for reining in the Fed were increasingly unpersuasive to Congress. As inflationary concerns mounted in 1950–51, Congress seemed ready to shelve its traditional obsession with the issue of private representatives versus political appointees in the system and to assume responsibility for monetary policy. A key figure was Senator Paul Douglas of Illinois, a renowned economist formerly at the University of Chicago. Douglas wrote a report in 1950 defending the Federal Reserve's prerogative to raise interest rates for stabilization purposes.

In fall 1950, Fed moves to tighten policy in the face of rising inflation conflicted with Treasury refunding operations. A public feud erupted. Federal Reserve and Treasury officials made contradictory statements about monetary policy. The showdown came in January 1951. In an unheralded personal meeting with the entire FOMC, Truman invoked the financing needs of the Korean War to gain support for the peg. In a letter to the press he prematurely announced that he had won FOMC support. Surprised by the letter, the committee members agreed to confront Truman. The startled Truman ended the dispute by forming an interagency study group to resolve the problem. In February, Douglas threatened to introduce a resolution to subordinate Treasury financing operations to Federal Reserve monetary policy. Truman headed off Congressional action by appointing a special committee to settle the dispute. This proved to be unnecessary. When McCabe resigned as chairman in March, because he was trapped between Fed and Administration hard-liners, Truman replaced him with William McChesney Martin, just six days after the accord between the Treasury and the Fed ending the peg was announced.

The pivotal support of Congress for the Fed was made clear in the Joint Economic Committee hearings in 1952. Many legislators voiced concern over the Treasury's domination of the Federal Reserve as well as over Congress's exclusion from making monetary policy.

The New Monetary Order

For forty years, with the exceptions of periodic hearings in the 1920s, its promotion of inflationism in 1933, and its enactment of the Banking Act of 1935, Congress had avoided involvement in monetary policy. The 1952 hearings reestablished its authority to intervene, periodically becoming the Fed's ally in resisting executive-branch pressure. At the same time Congress refused to give the Fed its marching orders. It prescribed no specific policy objectives for the monetary authority and established no continuing oversight over Federal Reserve policy, leaving the Fed only with the ambiguous and contradictory directives of the Employment Act of 1946.

During its first two decades, Federal Reserve independence was secured by balance between the authority of the Reserve Banks and the power of administration appointees to the board. Uncertainty about this balance contributed directly to the policy deadlock of 1929–32, but the Banking Act of 1935 resolved the issue in favor of the board. This had both a good and a bad side. On the one hand, the centralization of control resolved the disputes over authority that created the policy deadlock of 1929–32; on the other hand, it enhanced the influence of the executive branch. Thus, after 1935, Federal Reserve "independence" required a balance between cooperation with and subservience to the executive branch. After the accord, lacking specific direction from Congress, the Fed would have to discover the terms that would maintain that balance.

The 1951 accord set the stage for consolidating Federal Reserve power and for developing the symbiosis between executive branch, legislative branch, private financial sector, and autonomous Federal Reserve interests that would permeate monetary policymaking for the next forty years. Most important, by failing to impose constraints on Fed policy goals and operating strategies and by failing to participate in monetary-policy management, Congress gave the executive branch *carte blanche* to influence monetary policy. Moreover, Congress laid the groundwork for selective Federal Reserve responses to these and other pressures. Thus, both the uncertainty surrounding monetary policy since the accord and the suboptimal inflation performance over the same period (because of periodic Fed capitulation to outside pressures) result ultimately from Congressional default.

Since 1952, Congress has occasionally shown concern about the powers that it conferred on the Federal Reserve. Few other public agencies have been investigated as often by Congress as has the Federal Reserve. Thus, while Congress has occasionally tried to protect the central bank from excessive executive branch influence, it has itself sometimes been a source of pressure.

Congressional Pressures on Monetary Policy: 1952–93

Between 1952 and 1993, Congress rarely resisted executive-branch efforts to influence monetary policy. For the first twenty of these forty years, Representative Wright Patman, scourge of the Federal Reserve, warned against private-banking, rather than administration, leverage over the system. However, his extremism alienated his colleagues. Patman's populist obsession with private-banking influence deterred members of Congress who might have wished to police monetary policy from criticizing the monetary authority for fear of association with Patman. Patman repeatedly proposed disclosure of FOMC minutes, an annual GAO audit, an annual request for budgetary appropriations from Congress, and terms of the chairman and vice chairman that would coincide with the president's. Except for a limited annual audit enacted in 1977, none of these measures was ever passed.

During the 1960s, Congress continued its passive role in monetary policymaking. But, distressed by executive-branch victories in confrontations with Fed officials and alarmed by rising real interest rates and rising unemployment rates, Congress began to assert itself in the early 1970s. Patman gained new allies in his incessant battle with the Federal Reserve.

Partisan cleavages added to the potential for Congressional confrontation. Few doubt that political considerations were important in the appointment and reappointment of Arthur Burns, a Nixon loyalist, as chairman of the Fed. Moreover, key Congressional leaders Henry Reuss and William Proxmire found Burns irascible and secretive and his remarks in Congressional hearings offensive.

By the mid-1970s, a barrage of legislation had been proposed to hobble the central bank. Never before had Fed powers come under such serious and sustained Congressional attack. Nevertheless, the Federal Reserve successfully blocked each element of that package, exempting the Fed from disclosing FOMC minutes, limiting GAO audits to certain expense items and stymieing any change in the chairman's term. The Fed's institutional self-preservation can be attributed partly to the prestige it gained under Martin's aegis, partly to its traditional ties with the financial community, and, despite repeated charges of intransigence, partly to Arthur Burns for his pliability in responding to Congressional and administration demands from 1970 to 1973 for monetary ease.

Perhaps the only lasting result of the Congressional activity of the 1970s was the biannual oversight hearings at which the Fed chairman testifies to the House and Senate Banking Committees on the conduct of monetary policy. For the first time, Congress opted to exercise continual oversight over monetary policy. At first, students of monetary policy welcomed the prospect of a more open monetary policy. Later this enthusiasm waned, as Federal Reserve officials skillfully obfuscated their policy intentions.

Executive Branch Pressures on Monetary Policy: 1951–93

For the first nine years after the accord, the executive branch exerted little pressure on monetary policy, despite the three recessions of that decade. President Eisenhower maintained a hands-off posture toward monetary policy. In this placid setting, William McChesney Martin easily managed the pressures on monetary policy, building up the prestige of the system.

All this changed in the 1960s. The Kennedy administration applied systematic pressure on the monetary authority, which was continued by Lyndon Johnson, and raised to an extreme intensity by the Nixon regime. Most of these pressures directed the Fed to hold down interest rates, which were continually driven upward by the expansionary side-effects of redistributive (fiscal) policy. Arrangements that functioned smoothly during the 1950s came under increasing stress during the economic expansions and political upheavals of the late 1960s and 1970s. In the early 1960s, the Kennedy team seemed to pride itself in wringing concessions from chairman Martin in head-on confrontations. In the mid-1960s, until the Vietnam War absorbed its energies, the Johnson administration employed similar tactics to extract concessions from Martin. Despite episodic concessions, Martin usually resisted such pressures. Nevertheless, by 1967–68, inflation had become a problem and in 1969, the Nixon administration came to power pledging to stop it.

Despite his reputation as a conservative and his life-long homage to anti-inflationism, Burns's tenure at the central bank was marked by consistent acquiescence to monetary expansionism, especially from 1970 to 1974 (Havrilesky 1993). Each concession was justified by Burns as necessitated by new or extraordinary circumstances. In 1970, Burns endorsed the Nixon administration's *new* policy of gradualism in reducing inflation, thereby enabling it to combat the recession. Thus, in 1970 and 1971, money growth was high by historical standards. To try to suppress the inflation that was sure to follow, Nixon imposed comprehensive wage and price controls. In 1971, Burns headed Nixon's Committee on Interest and Dividends (created under those controls) which was instructed to hold down interest rates, an injunction that led to rapid monetary expansion in 1972–73. In 1973, Burns attributed the rising rate of inflation to *extraordinary* nonmonetary (supply) shocks. Ironically, when the Federal Reserve finally did tighten in 1974, and recession again ensued, Burns's reputation as an inflation fighter was rehabilitated. From the advent of the Carter presidency until his term ended in January 1978, Burns only mildly resisted administration remonstrances for monetary ease.

Burns justified his role in monetary expansion in his 1979 Per Jacobsson Lecture at the International Monetary Fund, "The Anguish of Central Banking." He argued that the Federal Reserve could have contained money growth, but was prevented from doing so by a political climate that demanded monetary accommodation.

Because Burns appeared reluctant to yield unconditionally to pressures for monetary expansion, Carter replaced him with an easy-money loyalist, G. William Miller. At least initially, Carter got exactly what he wanted. Before his appointment, Miller stated publicly that he did not consider inflation a serious threat to the national welfare, and questioned whether monetary policy could control inflation.

During the next year and a half, chairman Miller clung stubbornly to his views. Despite accelerating inflation he resisted suggestions to tighten monetary policy. At first these suggestions arose within the Federal Reserve, but later they emanated from the Carter administration itself. For example, in October 1978 when the discount rate was raised by one-fourth percent, Miller dissented, and in November 1978, Treasury Secretary Blumenthal, not Miller, announced a full percentage point hike in the discount rate. Apparently the soft-on-inflation imprint that helped him win his job made Miller unresponsive to suggestions for sound monetary policy. As part of Carter's cabinet shakeup in July 1979, Miller resigned to become Treasury secretary.

With inflation in double digits and international confidence in the dollar plummeting, Carter replaced Miller with the conservative Paul Volcker. Soon thereafter in October 1979, Volcker, boldly allowing interest rates to soar to stop inflation, adopted a strategy of targeting monetary growth rather than interest rates.

In 1980, the Oval Office reasserted itself in a replay of Nixon's 1971–72 game plan, imposing controls on credit instead of prices and wages. The administration continued signaling for a restrictive policy until early 1980 when, with recession threatening, it suddenly switched to ease. In October, Carter publicly attacked Volcker for monetary stringency. After the election, signaling for restraint resumed.

The stop-and-go pressure on the Fed in the last year of the Carter administration continued in the first three years of the Reagan administration. However, switches in signaling were now motivated, not by changes in policy objectives as under Carter, but rather by whether money-supply growth was on target. As had Nixon before him, Reagan campaigned on a promise to stop inflation. When the recession followed, Reagan, unlike Nixon (and Carter), did not flag in his determination to stop inflation.

By 1984 with the recession over and inflation under control, the administration abandoned money-supply-growth targeting, shifting to an easy-money stance. Supply-side arguments for easier monetary policy emanated from the Treasury. Volcker was under attack both from supply-siders in the administration and in Congress and from Congressional Democrats. In the early 1980s, as in the early 1970s, a wave of legislation was introduced in Congress to restructure the Federal Reserve and limit its powers. After 1983, virtually all the new appointees to the Federal Reserve Board, at the Council of Economic Advisers, and at Treasury supported monetary expansion. The primary objective of monetary ease was to reduce interest rates and the value of the dollar in the foreign-exchange markets. By 1987, the dollar having fallen, tightness signaling was resumed, largely because of mounting inflationary pressures.

Throughout the 1981–83 period, the Fed under Volcker responded only to signals for tightness from the administration (Havrilesky 1993). Throughout the 1984–86 period of incessant signaling for monetary ease, Volcker advocated moderation and the Fed did not systematically respond to this signaling. These pressures, coupled with administration resentment at the anti-inflationary accolades bestowed on him by the press, led Volcker to announce that he would not serve as chairman beyond the end of his term in 1987. Alan Greenspan was appointed to succeed him.

During the Bush administration, most signals reflected concern over Federal Reserve attempts to raise interest rates, and after July 1990, ease signaling increased because of the administration's recession fears. Ironically, in 1991, with the economy mired in recession, signaling fell. The decline in signaling over Bush's first term may reflect reduced need for signaling as Bush appointees joined the board, but it should be noted that under Greenspan the evidence (Havrilesky 1993) suggests that the Federal Reserve was not systematically responsive to these signals.

Thomas Havrilesky

See also BURNS, ARTHUR FRANK; CENTRAL BANKING; ELECTORAL CYCLE IN MONETARY POLICY; FEDERAL RESERVE SYSTEM, 1914–1941; MONETARY POLICY; RECESSION OF 1969–70; RECESSIONS AFTER WORLD WAR II; RECESSIONS (SUPPLY-SIDE) IN THE 1970S

Bibliography

Bach, G. L. 1971. *Making Monetary and Fiscal Policy*. Washington, D.C.: Brookings Institution.

Buchanan, J. M. and R. E. Wagner. 1977. *Democracy in Deficit*. New York: Academic Press.

Burns, A. F. 1965. "Wages and Prices by Guideline." *Harvard Business Review,* March/April, 55–64.

———. 1973. "The Role of the Money Supply in the Conduct of Monetary Policy." Federal Reserve Bank of Dallas *Business Review,* December, 1–7.

Canterbury, E. R. 1968. *Economics on a New Frontier*. Belmont, Calif.: Wadsworth.

Chandler, L. 1958. *Benjamin Strong: Central Banker*. Washington, D.C.: Brookings Institution.

Clifford, A. J. 1965. *The Independence of the Federal Reserve System*. Philadelphia: Univ. of Pennsylvania Press.

Friedman, M. and A. J. Schwartz. 1963. *A Monetary History of the United States*. Princeton: Princeton Univ. Press.

Greider, W. 1988. *Secrets of the Temple*. New York: Random House.

Havrilesky, T. 1988. "Monetary Policy Signaling from the Administration to the Federal Reserve." *Journal of Money, Credit and Banking* 19:83–101.

———. 1990. "The Influence of the Federal Advisory Council on Monetary Policy." *Journal of Money, Credit and Banking* 22:431–51.

———. 1991a. "The Frequency of Monetary Policy Signaling from the Administration to the Federal Reserve." *Journal of Money, Credit and Banking* 23:423–30.

———. 1991b. "The Chairman as Hero: Our Defense Against Monetary Excess?" *Cato Journal* 11:134–49.

———. 1993. *The Pressures on American Monetary Policy*. Boston: Kluwer.

Havrilesky, T. and J. A. Gildea. 1992. "Reliable and Unreliable Partisan Appointees to the Board of Governors." *Public Choice* 73:397–417.

Havrilesky, T. and R. L. Schweitzer. 1990. "A Theory of FOMC Dissent Voting with Evidence from Time Series." In *The Political Economy of American Monetary Policy,* edited by T. Mayer 192–210. New York: Cambridge Univ. Press.

Katz, B. S., ed. 1991. *Biographical Dictionary of Federal Reserve Governors.* New York: Greenwood Press.

Kettl, D. 1986. *Leadership at the Fed.* New Haven: Yale Univ. Press.

Maisel, S. 1973. *Managing the Dollar.* New York: Norton.

Woolley, J. T. 1984. *Monetary Politics: The Federal Reserve and the Politics of Monetary Policy.* New York: Cambridge Univ. Press.

Fellner, William John (1905–1983)

Born in Budapest, Hungary, Fellner received his Ph.D. from the University of Berlin in 1929. After emigrating to the United States in 1938, he taught at the University of California at Berkeley and at Yale University. He served on the President's Council of Economic Advisors from 1973 to 1975, and thereafter was resident scholar with the American Enterprise Institute where his main concern was with the effects of government policies on business cycles and economic growth.

In his first book, *Monetary Policies and Full Employment,* Fellner noted that while economic theory assumed that the macroeconomy followed a dynamic path toward a long-run equilibrium, experience suggested that a combination of unstable equilibria and chronic disturbances meant that the economy was instead typically in disequilibrium. The fluctuations of the business cycle were a manifestation of this disequilibrium.

He continued this theme in a later book, *Trends and Cycles in Economic Activity,* which emphasized the application of the "acceleration principle" to the problem of cyclical disturbances. His analysis interpreted cyclical disturbances as violations of certain growth requirements relating to technological and organizational progress, the mobility of resources, and the proper degree of flexibility in monetary management. In particular, these growth requirements called for innovation to offset any diminishing returns to investors that a rapidly growing capital stock might cause and for enough mobility of resources to compensate for shifts in the structure of demand. If, for example, temporary violations of the growth requirements of the economy cause economic growth to slow appreciably, then a further contraction becomes likely. Production would be reduced in those sectors geared to growth elsewhere in the economy. Only if the economy possessed a very high degree of flexibility and mobility could sectors not dependent on growth elsewhere expand promptly. He also argued that monetary disturbances could cause a downturn even when structural problems were minor. This could occur under a metallic standard, for example, if the money supply could not expand quickly enough to finance the rapid rate of growth characterizing a cyclical upswing.

Fellner's interest in the disequilibrium associated with economic growth and business cycles led him to seek ways to temper the effects of this inherent disequilibrium by carefully applying government policy. However, he discouraged attempts to precisely "stabilize" output along a full-employment growth path since this would deprive the economy of the flexibility to make adjustments. Instead, he advocated intervention with anti-deflationary policies when existing cyclical contractionary pressures presented a serious threat of deflation, and intervention with boom-moderating measures when it became evident that the current rate of expansion could not continue for long. In either case, the price level had to be stabilized in order to move toward a short-run or long-run equilibrium. While Fellner supported demand-management policies in general, he urged policymakers to avoid excessive intervention, which would invariably conflict with more judiciously implemented monetary and fiscal policy. In short, the studies Fellner conducted for the American Enterprise Institute reflected his desire for a cautious, yet significant, governmental role in minimizing the amplitude of cyclical fluctuations and their impact on the economy.

Dianne C. Betts

See also FISCAL POLICY; MONETARY POLICY

Bibliography

Fellner, W. J. 1949. *Monetary Policies and Full Employment.* Berkeley and Los Angeles: Univ. of California Press.

———. 1956. *Trends and Cycles in Economic Activity*. New York: Holt.

———. 1960. *Modern Economic Analysis*. New York: McGraw-Hill.

———. 1971a. *Aiming for a Sustainable Second Best During the Recovery from the 1970 Recession*. Washington, D.C.: American Enterprise Institute.

———. 1971b. *The Case for Moderation in the Economic Recovery of 1971*. Washington, D.C.: American Enterprise Institute.

———. 1972a. *Economic Policy in the Sixties*. Washington, D.C.: American Enterprise Institute.

———. 1972b. *Employment Policy at the Crossroads: An Interim Look at Pressures to be Resisted*. Washington, D.C.: American Enterprise Institute.

———. 1976a. "Lessons from the Failure of Demand-Management Policies: A Look at the Theoretical Foundations." *Journal of Economic Literature* 14:34–53.

———. 1976b. *The High-Employment Budget and Potential Output: A Critique Focusing on Two Recent Contributions*. Washington, D.C.: American Enterprise Institute.

———. 1976c. *Towards a Reconstruction of Macroeconomics: Problems of Theory and Policy*. Washington, D.C.: American Enterprise Institute.

———. 1977. *Problems to Keep in Mind When It Comes to Tax Reform*. Washington, D.C.: American Enterprise Institute.

———. 1982. "Economic Theory Amidst Political Currents: The Spreading Interest in Monetarism and the Theory of Market Expectations." *Weltwirtschalftliches Archiv* 118:409–29.

Henderson, J. P. 1957. "Contemporary Growth Economics." *Science and Society*. 21:135–53.

Perlo, V. 1958. "A Current View of the Business Cycle." *Science and Society* 22:239–49.

Filters

Filters are operations applied to time series to estimate or remove certain components. In studying business cycles, we may be tempted to apply seasonal-adjustment and detrending filters first. The question then is whether such filters achieve their intended effect or introduce unwanted distortions into the series. One particularly disturbing possibility is that they might create spurious cyclical movements that have no relation to the real economy. This phenomenon has been recognized for many years and is called the *Yule-Slutsky effect*.

A filter is a function of the observations, y_t, $t = 1, \ldots T$, computed for each time period. A *linear* filter has the form

$$y_t^* = \sum_{j=-r}^{s} w_{tj} y_{t+j} \qquad (1)$$

where the w_{tj}'s are weights. The filter is said to be *one-sided* if $s = 0$, or, less commonly, if $r = 0$, and *time-invariant* if the weights do not depend on t.

Many filters, especially simpler ones, are applied with no particular statistical model in mind. This contrasts with the approach in which a model is formulated in terms of *components* that the series is thought to contain. Given such a model, an optimal filter can be constructed to estimate those components of interest. The classical formulae for such filters are worked out under the assumption of an infinite sample, and their appeal lies in their easy application and the insight they give into the nature of the weighting in equation (1). More generally, optimal filters may be computed by casting the model in *state-space* form (Harvey 1989, chap. 3). The *Kalman filter* is a one-sided filter which can be used to compute the optimal estimates of components from past and current observations; the associated *smoother* is a two-sided filter that computes optimal estimates based on all the observations. These filters are not normally time-invariant, which is why they are able to produce optimal estimates at the beginning and end of a finite sample. Indeed the algorithms apply even if the model itself is time-varying and in some cases they work even when the time-variation is such that the model is non-linear.

The simpler filters are normally time-invariant over most of the sample and their effects on different frequencies can be determined analytically. Moreover, if a series is assumed to be generated by a particular statistical model, the properties of the filtered series may be derived. An unobserved-components model is particularly useful in this respect, since the effect of filtering on different components may be analyzed. If the filter has a particular objective, such as detrending, it can be compared with the corresponding optimal filter.

Analysis of Linear Filters

The effect of a linear, time-invariant filter can be derived using spectral analysis (Fishman 1969). Let L denote a lag operator, so that $Ly_t = y_{t-1}$, and write equation (1) as

$$y_t^* = W(L)y_t \qquad (2)$$

where

$$W(L) = \sum_{j=-r}^{s} w_j L^j \qquad (3)$$

Replacing L by $\exp(-i\lambda)$, where λ denotes frequency in radians and i is the square root of minus one, gives the frequency-response function, $W(e^{-i\lambda})$. This tells us the extent to which different frequencies are shifted backwards or forwards in time and whether they are increased or diminished in importance. This latter effect is captured by the transfer function, $|W(e^{-i\lambda})|^2$. If y_t is stationary, the spectrum of the filtered series is obtained by multiplying the spectrum of y_t by the transfer function. When y_t is non-stationary, it may still be possible to define a pseudo-spectrum. However, such a spectrum will go to infinity at certain frequencies, so the effect of a filter may not be clear from the transfer function. If y_t can be made stationary by certain operations, such as differencing, a better approach may be to determine the effect of the filter on the spectrum of the stationary series.

When an unobserved-components model has been formulated, the classical Kolmogorov-Wiener approach to signal extraction is applicable (Whittle 1983). The formulae developed are applicable to the optimal estimation of stationary components embedded in a stationary observed process. Each component may be expressed as an autoregressive-integrated-moving average process, so that

$$y_t = \sum_{m=1}^{M} \frac{\theta_m(L)}{\phi_m(L)} \xi_{mt}, \qquad (4)$$

where the ξ_{mt}'s are mutually uncorrelated white-noise processes, and $\phi_m(L)$ and $\theta_m(L)$ are polynomials in the lag operator for $m = 1$ to M. (White-noise processes are serially uncorrelated with mean zero and constant variance.) The results extend to cases where the autoregressive polynomials, $\phi_m(L)$, may have unit roots, thereby allowing components to be nonstationary (Bell 1984). Suppose, without loss in generality, that the component to be extracted is the one corresponding to $m = 1$. The optimal esti-

mator is given by a filter of the form equation (2) in which

$$W(L) = \frac{|\theta_1(L)|^2 \sigma_1^2}{|\phi_1(L)|^2} \bigg/ \sum_{m=1}^{M} \frac{|\theta_m(L)|^2 \sigma_m^2}{|\phi_m(L)|^2} \qquad (5)$$

where $|\theta_m(L)|^2 = \theta_m(L)\theta_m(L^{-1})$.

The classical results may be used to analyze the weighting implicit in smoothing filters for points that are not too close to the beginning or end of a series. For example, suppose that a model consists of a random-walk component plus white noise. Applying equation (5) shows that the optimal estimator of the random walk is formed by giving the observations on either side of y_t exponentially declining weights.

Structural Time-Series Models

Structural time-series models are set up explicitly in terms of unobserved components that have a direct interpretation (Harvey 1989). A useful model to consider is

$$y_t = \mu_t + \psi_t + \varepsilon_t, \qquad t = 1, \dots, T, \qquad (6)$$

where μ_t is the trend, ψ_t is the cycle and ε_t is the irregular component. The trend is defined as

$$\mu_t = \mu_{t-1} + \beta_{t-1} + \eta_t \qquad (7a)$$

$$\beta_t = \beta_{t-1} + \zeta_t, \qquad (7b)$$

where β_t is the slope and η_t and ζ_t, are mutually uncorrelated white-noise processes. The trend is therefore stochastic with the level and slope changing over time, but in the special case when the variances of η_t and ζ_t are both zero it becomes deterministic. The cycle is also stochastic, being specified as

$$\psi_t = \rho\cos\lambda_c.\psi_{t-1} + \rho\sin\lambda_c.\psi_{t-1}^* + \kappa_t \qquad (8a)$$

$$\psi_t^* = -\rho\sin\lambda_c.\psi_{t-1} + \rho\cos\lambda_c.\psi_{t-1}^* + \kappa_t^*, \qquad (8b)$$

where λ_c is frequency in radians, ρ is a damping factor between zero and one, and κ_t and κ_t^* are mutually uncorrelated white-noise processes with a common variance σ_κ^2. A series generated by the stochastic-cycle model has the sort of characteristics that one reasonably might expect of an economic cycle. The cyclical movements are irregular with the amplitude and period varying over time. The spectrum has a peak around λ_c. This peak becomes progressively more sharply defined as ρ tends to one (Harvey 1989, 60–62). When ρ is equal to one the process is no longer stationary and if σ_κ^2 is zero it reduces to a deterministic sine-cosine wave.

If the observations are assumed to be normally distributed, the parameters ρ, λ_c, and the variances of η_t, ζ_t, ε_t, and κ_t, can be estimated by maximum likelihood. The Kalman filter and the associated smoothing algorithms then provide estimates of the trend, cycle, and irregular components. Figure 1 shows the estimated cycle in quarterly postwar United States GNP obtained in this way; see Harvey and Jaeger (1993) for details of a similar exercise. The essential point to stress about this approach is that the cycle and the other components in the series are estimated simultaneously. This contrasts with approaches in which detrending is performed before an analysis of the cycle. Further examples of fitting structural time-series models with cyclical components can be found in Clark (1987), Crafts et al. (1989), and Watson (1986). In a completely different context, Harvey and Souza (1987) used a stochastic cycle to model rainfall in northeast Brazil.

Other components may be included in a structural time-series model. If the observations are quarterly or monthly, a seasonal component is usually appropriate. Again there is a contrast to working with a seasonally adjusted series, where the seasonal-adjustment filter may take no account of the properties of the series and the possible presence of other components. Finally, the model may contain more than one cycle; thus a twenty-year, long-swing cycle may be included along with a business cycle.

Detrending and Spurious Cycles

Series are often detrended before analysis. One possibility is to fit a linear or polynomial time trend, but, as Nelson and Kang (1981) have observed, this can cause severe distortion. Another approach is to smooth the series by means of a simple moving average and then to subtract from the original observations. Detrending by this method can be analyzed quite easily by noting that

$$W(L) = 1 - \left[S(L)/(2r+1) \right] \qquad (9)$$

where $S(L) = (L^r + L^{r-1} + \ldots + L + 1 + L^{-1} + \ldots + L^{-r})$. Different weighting patterns can be handled in a similar way. A slightly different approach is to detrend by combining moving

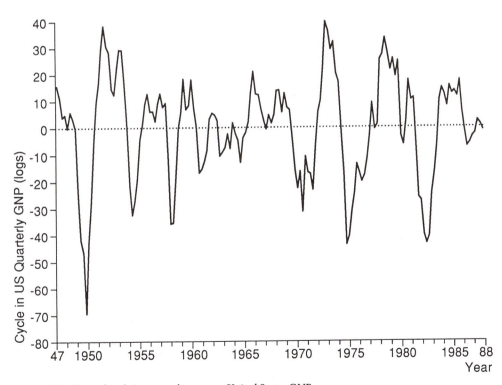

Figure 1. Estimated cycle in quarterly postwar United States GNP.

averages with differences. The study by Kuznets ([1958] 1965) of the long-swing hypothesis, which postulates the existence of a cycle of around twenty years, is a classic example of the pitfalls of such an approach. Kuznets applied two filters: a simple five-year moving average to remove the trade cycle, and an eleven-year differencing operation to remove the trend. The result, as shown by Fishman (1969, 45–49), is a transfer function with a peak at 20.3 years. The evidence for long swings could therefore be a statistical artifact.

A certain detrending procedure that fits a smooth curve through the data and identifies this with the trend has gained some popularity in recent years. The trend estimated in this way is a cubic spline. The approach was used by Hodrick and Prescott in an unpublished paper and is sometimes known as the *Hodrick-Prescott filter* (Kydland and Prescott 1990). For an infinite series the detrended series is given by the filter

$$W^*(L) = \left|1 - L\right|^4 \Big/ \left(q + \left|1 - L\right|^4\right) \qquad (10)$$

where q is a prespecified constant. It is interesting to note that equation (10) is, from equation (5), the optimal filter for estimating the noise, ε_t, in a model of the form equation (6) with no cycle and the variance of η_t set to zero; the constant q is then equal to the ratio of the variance of ζ_t to that of ε_t. However, the prime reason for applying the filter is a belief that something other than white noise remains after the trend has been removed. This is why q is prespecified rather than estimated.

The transfer function of equation (10) is roughly constant for the middle and higher frequencies but close to zero for the very low frequencies. Thus, it removes long-run movements in the series without affecting short-run movements. This would seem to be an ideal property for a detrending filter. However, this analysis is misleading for a nonstationary process where the power of the spectrum at frequency zero goes to infinity. Thus suppose the process generating the observations is stationary in first differences and the spectrum of the stationary process is $f(\lambda)$. The spectrum of the detrended series is then

$$f^*(\lambda) = \left(\left|W^*\left(e^{-i\lambda}\right)\right|^2 \Big/ \left|1 - e^{i\lambda}\right|^2\right) f(\lambda) \qquad (11)$$

Dividing the original transfer function by $|1 - e^{-i\lambda}|^2$ results in a pronounced peak at moderate frequencies; for the value of $q = 1/1600$ fa-

vored by Hodrick and Prescott, this peak corresponds to a period of around thirty. Thus for quarterly data, applying the filter to a random walk is likely to create a spurious cycle with a period of about seven or eight years which could easily be identified as a business cycle (see Cogley and Nason 1995 and Jaeger 1994). Of course the application of the Hodrick-Prescott filter yields quite sensible results in some cases, but everything depends on the properties of the series in question.

Conclusion

Detrending and seasonal-adjustment filters can seriously distort the properties of a series. In particular, detrending can create spurious cycles. A better approach is to apply a filter appropriate for a statistical model which explicitly contains all the components thought to be present in the series. This requires the researcher to have some idea of the kind of components that may be present and to estimate a model consistent with the data. The problem is that in small samples more than one model may be consistent with the data, so different estimates of components may be obtained (Harvey and Jaeger 1993). A possible solution is a multivariate approach in which a cycle or trend is estimated with a model fitted to several series at the same time.

Andrew Harvey

See also ASYMMETRY; COMPOSITE TRENDS; KUZNETS, SIMON SMITH; MOVING AVERAGES; PERSONS, WARREN MILTON; PHASE AVERAGING; SEASONAL ADJUSTMENT; SLUTSKY, EUGEN; SPECTRAL ANALYSIS; TRENDS AND RANDOM WALKS; UNIT ROOT TESTS

Bibliography

Bell, W. R. 1984. "Signal Extraction for Nonstationary Time Series." *Annals of Statistics* 13:646–64.

Clark, P. 1987. "The Cyclical Component of U.S. Economic Activity." *Quarterly Journal of Economics* 102:797–814.

Cogley, T. and J. H. Nason. 1995. "Effects of the Hodrick-Prescott Filter on Trend and Difference Stationary Time Series: Implications for Business Cycle Research." *Journal of Economic Dynamics and Control* 19:253–78.

Crafts, N. F. R., S. J. Leybourne, and T. C. Mills. 1989. "Trends and Cycles in British Industrial Production." *Journal of the Royal Statistical Society* 152:43–60.

Fishman, G. S. 1969. *Spectral Methods in Econometrics*. Cambridge: Harvard Univ. Press.

Harvey, A. C. 1989. *Forecasting, Structural Time Series Models and the Kalman Filter*. Cambridge: Cambridge Univ. Press.

Harvey, A. C. and A. Jaeger. 1993. "Detrending, Stylized Facts and the Business Cycle." *Journal of Applied Econometrics* 8:231–47.

Harvey, A. C. and R. C. Souza. 1987. "Assessing and Modelling the Cyclical Behavior of Rainfall in Northeast Brazil." *Journal of Climate and Applied Meteorology* 26:1317–22.

Jaeger, A. 1994. "Mechanical Detrending by Hodrick-Prescott Filtering: A Note." *Empirical Economics* 19:493–500.

Kuznets, S. S. [1958] 1965. "Long Swings in Population Growth and Related Economic Variables." In *Economic Growth and Structure: Selected Essays*, 328–78. New York: Norton.

Kydland, F. E. and E. C. Prescott. 1990. "Business Cycles: Real Facts and a Monetary Myth." Federal Reserve Bank of Minneapolis *Quarterly Review*, Spring, 3–18.

Nelson, C. R. and H. Kang. 1981. "Spurious Periodicity in Inappropriately Detrended Time Series." *Econometrica* 49:741–51.

Watson, M. W. 1986. "Univariate Detrending Methods with Stochastic Trends." *Journal of Monetary Economics* 18:44–75.

Whittle, P. 1983. *Prediction and Regulation*. 2d rev. ed. Oxford: Basil Blackwell.

Financial Intermediation

Economists have long disagreed on the role played by financial intermediaries both in affecting the accumulation of capital and in influencing or contributing to business cycles. While some models view intermediaries as veils whose presence has little or no effect on the allocation of real resources in the economy, a long tradition in macroeconomics has emphasized the impact of the economy's financial structure on real economic decisions. Intermediaries can matter for business cycles either because they serve as a key channel in the transmission of monetary shocks to the real economy or because financial-sector instability is an important source of macroeconomic disturbances. Both the asset and liability sides of intermediaries' balance sheets influence the role intermediaries play in business cycles.

Microeconomic Foundations of Intermediaries

A number of authors recently have extended our understanding of the microfoundations of financial intermediaries, showing how they arise in response to imperfect information and transactions costs. Asymmetric information and increasing returns to scale appear to be sufficient conditions for the presence of intermediaries. For example, Diamond (1984) develops a model in which entrepreneurs have access to a technology that requires a fixed investment and yields a random real return of known expected value. The random return is observed (*ex post*) by the entrepreneur, but other individuals can observe the realized return only by incurring a fixed cost to monitor the project. Fixed monitoring costs make it costly for individual investors to diversify by lending to many different investors.

This rudimentary framework is sufficient to generate a role for intermediaries whose loans take the form of debt contracts. Since only the entrepreneur knows the actual return from any project, his incentive, in the absence of monitoring, is to report a low realized return and retain the profits. To prevent underreporting, each of the individuals who finances a project must incur the monitoring cost. An intermediary, on the other hand, can finance many projects and incur the fixed monitoring cost only once for each project. The intermediary thereby exploits the increasing returns to scale implicit in the fixed-cost monitoring technology. In addition, the intermediary's ability to finance many projects permits diversification of nonsystematic risk. Financial intermediation improves aggregate efficiency, and, in circumstances in which credit rationing can occur, increases the availability of credit.

Banks are distinguished from other intermediaries such as mutual funds and insurance firms by the fact that only bank liabilities are accepted as media of exchange. This acceptance results from the commitment of banks to make their liabilities convertible on demand into base money at a fixed rate of exchange. To support this commitment, banks hold inventories of base money.

The demand for bank liabilities is primarily a demand for a medium of exchange and not an indirect demand for bank assets. If bank liabilities could not be used to finance transactions, individuals would have to hold an increased fraction of their wealth in the form of inventories of base money. Banks thus transform the public's demand for a medium of exchange into a means of financing real investment. While this transformation adds to the economy's real stock of capital, it makes real investment sensitive to disruptions in the demand for and supply of alternative media of exchange.

Intermediaries and the Transmission of Monetary Disturbances

Standard macromodels today typically allow intermediaries to influence the economy only by affecting the stock of money. Banks are accorded a more critical role than other intermediaries, because their liabilities (inside money) constitute part of the transactions balances of the economy. Nevertheless, banks have often been treated summarily in the form of a money multiplier tightly linking high-powered (outside) money and broader measures of money. That a part of the economy's transactions balances consists of inside money tends to amplify the impact of variations in outside money due to the multiple expansion of credit under fractional-reserve banking, but does not fundamentally alter the properties of the model.

The 1960s saw a movement away from a mechanical money-multiplier analysis towards a view that the multiplier depends on the portfolio decisions of banks. (Much of this work on intermediaries was associated with Tobin and the Yale School.) The availability of close substitutes for outside money was thought to reduce the real effects of variations in the stock of money. For example, a fall in outside money would drive up market interest rates thereby raising banks' opportunity costs of holding reserves. In response, banks would exchange non-interest-bearing reserves for interest-earning assets, thereby expanding the stock of inside money, and partially offsetting the original movement in outside money. The work of Tobin and Brainard (1963) applied portfolio theory to understand the determination of the size of intermediaries, focusing on the pecuniary rate of return of the liabilities of intermediaries relative to the return on real capital.

An alternative view (Hartley 1988) emphasizes that intermediary liabilities are close substitutes for outside money as transactions balances. While the elasticity of substitution between intermediary liabilities and real physical assets is probably quite small, the elasticity of substitution between outside money and intermediary liabilities that provide transaction services is likely to be large. Thus, interest-rate variations can induce large shifts in the demand for outside money relative to the demand for interest-earning inside transactions balances. As a result, variations in monetary policy affect the size of the banking sector even in equilibrium models of the business cycle that assume all markets constantly clear.

Variations in the demand for currency and bank deposits may affect the total volume of bank liabilities and, thus, the volume of bank lending. But while banks are distinguished by the transaction accounts they offer, banks are not the only intermediaries supplying credit. How a reduction in bank lending affects the total supply of credit depends on how easily borrowers can replace bank loans with credit from nonbank sources. Changes in the volume of bank loans will have the greatest impact on economic activity if there is something "special" about bank credit, or more generally, if direct credit is an imperfect substitute for intermediated credit.

Banks have informational advantages over other intermediaries, because they simultaneously lend to and maintain the transaction accounts of borrowers. A borrower's transaction account provides the bank with low-cost information about the borrower. A nonbank intermediary lacking such information must incur additional costs to monitor its borrowers. Consequently, if monetary policy affects the size of the banking sector, it also will affect the amount of lending and thus real economic activity.

This discussion has shown that intermediaries can amplify the real effects of monetary disturbances in an equilibrium macroeconomic model. The same is true in a disequilibrium model in which imperfectly flexible nominal prices or wages result in unemployed resources. And, if the presence of financial intermediaries adds to the instability of the demand for base money, it also adds to the instability of equilibrium nominal prices. In a disequilibrium model, banks might magnify deviations between actual and equilibrium nominal prices and thereby increase the real effects of money disturbances.

Intermediaries as the Source of Business-Cycle Disturbances

The transaction services provided by intermediary liabilities (particularly those of banks) are an important element of the exchange process of the economy. Any disturbance to the intermediation sector of the economy can have real effects by altering the level of transaction services. Thus, a major disruption of the payments system, such as occurred during the massive bank failures of the 1930s in the United States, would reduce real output by diminishing the quantity of an important input into production. Real economic activity would fall even if prices are perfectly flexible and goods markets clear. For example, in recent real-business-cycle models that assume markets continuously clear, money is neutral, but because transaction services produced by banks are inputs into the production of other goods and services, a real shock to the banking sector can affect production in other sectors (King and Plosser 1984). Consistent with this stress on the aggregate stock of money and the liabilities of banks has been the emphasis on the role of bank runs in the banking crises of the prewar period in the United States.

Compared to direct lending, intermediaries increase the availability and reduce the cost of credit to borrowers. Thus, disruptions to the financial sector can also affect the real economy through the asset sides of intermediaries' balance sheets. This is the basis for Bernanke's (1983) alternative interpretation of the bank runs of the 1930s that, by reducing the size of the banking sector, they reduced real economic activity by restricting the availability and raising the cost of credit.

Peter R. Hartley
Carl E. Walsh

See also DEMAND FOR CURRENCY; DEMAND FOR MONEY; DISINTERMEDIATION; MONETARY DISEQUILIBRIUM THEORIES OF THE BUSINESS CYCLE; MONETARY EQUILIBRIUM THEORIES OF THE BUSINESS CYCLE; MONETARY POLICY; NEW MONETARY ECONOMICS; REAL BUSINESS-CYCLE THEORIES; SUPPLY OF MONEY

Bibliography

Bernanke, B. S. 1983. "Non-Monetary Effects of the Financial Crisis in the Propagation of the Great Depression." *American Economic Review* 73:257–76.

Diamond, D. W. 1984. "Financial Intermediation and Delegated Monitoring." *Review of Economic Studies* 51:393–414.

Friedman, M. and A. J. Schwartz. 1963. *A Monetary History of the United States, 1867–1960.* Princeton: Princeton Univ. Press.

Gertler, M. 1988. "Financial Structure and Aggregate Economic Activity." *Journal of Money, Credit and Banking* 20:559–88.

Gertler, M. and R. G. Hubbard. 1988. "Financial Factors in Business Fluctuations." In *Financial Markets and Volatility: Causes, Consequences and Policy Recommendations,* 33–71. Kansas City, Mo.: Federal Reserve Bank of Kansas City.

Gurley, J. G. and E. S. Shaw. 1960. *Money in a Theory of Finance.* Washington, D.C.: Brookings Institution.

Hartley, P. R. 1988. "The Liquidity Services of Money." *International Economic Review* 29:1–24.

King, R. G. and C. I. Plosser. 1984. "Money, Credit, and Prices in a Real Business Cycle." *American Economic Review* 74:363–80.

Stiglitz, J. E. 1988. "Money, Credit, and Business Fluctuations." *Economic Record* 64:307–22.

Tobin, J. "Commercial Banks as Creators of Money." In *Banking and Monetary Studies,* edited by D. Carson, 408–19. Homewood, Ill.: Irwin.

Tobin, J. and W. C. Brainard. 1963. "Financial Institutions and Monetary Policy." *American Economic Review* 53:383–400.

Walsh, C. E. and P. R. Hartley. 1988. "Financial Intermediation, Monetary Policy, and Equilibrium Business Cycles." Federal Reserve Bank of San Francisco *Economic Review,* Fall, 19–28.

Williamson, S. D. 1986. "Increasing Returns to Scale in Financial Intermediation and the Non-Neutrality of Government Policy." *Review of Economic Studies* 53:863–75.

Wojnilower, A. M. 1980. "The Central Role of Credit Crunches in Recent Financial History." *Brookings Papers on Economic Activity,* Number Two, 277–326.

F

Fiscal Policy

Fiscal policy relates to government expenditures and taxes. It is to be distinguished from monetary policy, which relates to the supply of money and credit. Fiscal policy at the national level in the United States, then, is essentially the province of the Congress and the president, as they determine expenditures for goods and services and transfer payments (such as for social security) and tax rates. Monetary policy is the province of the Federal Reserve. The Fed, however, as it buys and sells Treasury securities, affects interest rates and the amount of government expenditures for the payment of interest on its debt. Thus, the Fed also affects fiscal policy, if indirectly.

The major importance attributed to fiscal policy dates from the Keynesian Revolution in the 1930s. Along with the recognition that a free-market economy might suffer persistent unemployment due to lack of demand or purchasing power for all that a fully employed labor force could produce, came the notion that government might compensate for that shortage. It could do this by buying goods and services itself, by giving people income in the form of transfer payments which they could use to buy goods and services, or by cutting taxes to increase the after-tax income out of which economic agents could spend.

Fiscal policy was viewed as particularly potent because of the *multiplier*. An initial increase in production and employment brought on, say, by increased government expenditures on highway construction, would generate further increases in demand, output, and employment as the initial recipients of government payments spent at least some part of their additional income.

Just as the fiscal stimulus of increased government expenditures and decreased taxes could increase demand and thus combat the unemployment of a recession or depression, fiscal restraint could be applied to combat an excess-demand inflation. The tools of fiscal policy would merely be pointed in the opposite direction.

One simple, obvious measure of fiscal policy is the budget deficit, the difference between the total of government outlays—for goods and services, transfer payments, and interest on the debt—and tax receipts. A larger deficit might be seen as stimulative and a smaller deficit, or a surplus, as depressing. Changes in the actual budget deficit, however, may occur with no change in government policy, in the sense that no new expenditures are made or taxes levied. Rather, changes in the economy itself may alter the deficit. A recession increases the deficit as businesses and individuals with reduced incomes pay less in taxes and the government pays more to the newly unemployed collecting unemployment compensation. Similarly, in a boom, the deficit is reduced or may even turn into a surplus, with no change in government policy, as higher incomes swell tax revenues and government transfer payments decline. These automatic or endogenous reactions of government spending and taxes to economic fluctuations are known as "built-in stabilizers."

As an overall measure of fiscal policy or fiscal stance, that is, of the likely impact of the budget on the economy independent of the impact of the economy on the budget, economists have devised what has been variously called the full-employment, high-employment, cyclically adjusted, or structural deficit or surplus. This is defined as the deficit or surplus that the government *would* have if employment or economic activity were at some specified level. Changes in actual employment or real income or output affect the actual deficit but not the structural one. (Changes in prices or interest rates, however, affect both deficits.) Larger structural deficits indicate more stimulative fiscal policies and lesser ones (or greater surpluses) less stimulative or more constraining or depressing policies.

Of course, the deficit is not a complete measure of fiscal policy. For one thing, the composition of government expenditures and taxes matters. Expenditures for goods and services have an immediate, direct effect. Changes in transfer payments and taxes affect the economy only insofar as they in turn affect spending. Thus, increases in government purchases of goods and services, even if fully matched by increases in taxes, can be expected to increase aggregate demand. Indeed, under one set of assumptions, essentially that all private spending depends only on after-tax income, we can derive a *balanced-budget multiplier* of unity; a change in government spending for goods and services matched by an equal ultimate change in taxes, hence with no change in the deficit, will generate an equal change, in the same direction, in output.

Other major qualifications about the impact of fiscal policy must be raised. Much may depend on the associated monetary policy. If an increase in government spending and the deficit is met, for example, by a constant supply of money and credit, the increased income and output resulting from the fiscal stimulus is likely to raise the demand for money and thus interest rates. Increased interest rates in turn constrain private (and perhaps, in the United States, state- and local-government) spending, particularly investment in housing, plant and equipment, and durable goods. The fiscal stimulus may then be considerably damped. If the money supply is allowed to grow with the demand for it, as might be expected if the Fed aims at stabilizing interest rates, the fiscal stimulus will have a fuller effect.

Further complications arise in an open economy, since fiscal stimulus, rather than exclusively affecting domestic sales, output, and employment, may be dissipated in increased purchases of foreign goods. If there is no matching increase in exports (or gifts from foreigners), the increased imports must imply payment from the sale of foreign assets or foreigners' accumulation of increased claims to domestic assets. In either event, the domestic burden of future net payments of interest or earnings to foreigners will increase.

The increases in imports—hence in the supply of domestic currency to foreigners—may be expected, though, to reduce the value of the currency, thus raising prices by making imports more expensive, but also stimulating exports. If the monetary authority strives to maintain the value of its currency by tightening monetary policy (reducing the supply of money and raising interest rates and international demand for financial instruments denominated in its currency) the fiscal stimulus may again, at least in part, be choked off.

Much also depends upon expectations of future fiscal policy. A deficit occasioned by an increase in transfer payments or a cut in income taxes expected to be temporary will have much less effect than one viewed as long-lasting or relatively permanent. A $100 billion budget deficit over one year, for example, adds $100 billion to private wealth holdings in government debt. If the deficit is not expected to recur, however, those with increased wealth may be expected to try to conserve a major part of it for future needs. Current spending, except by those who had great current needs but were previously constrained by lack of liquidity, may thus be little affected.

These considerations weigh heavily against many tools of fiscal policy for stabilization or countercyclical purposes. People may respond only modestly to changes in after-tax income that are viewed as short-run and even reversible consequences of countercyclical policy.

The difficulties are compounded by the problem of lags in the initiation, implementation, and effects of changes in fiscal policies. Thus, by the time a cut in taxes to combat a recession is perceived to be necessary, is requested, is enacted, and generates more private spending and finally greater output and employment, the recession may already have ended

on its own. The economy may by then be so much in boom that fiscal restraint would be in order, but may yet suffer the effects of the stimulus initiated previously. Conversely, fiscal restraint initiated in the face of excess-demand inflation may aggravate fluctuations by finally having its effect when the economy has already on its own lapsed into recession.

The force of this concern may be reduced somewhat, however, if the objective of stabilization is, as Keynes urged, to fill in the troughs in business cycles but not lop off the booms. If one is then willing to accept the risk of greater average inflation, one may aim for a generally stimulative fiscal policy that would minimize errors in a downward direction and thus tend to stabilize real output around a higher level.

More potent and timely fiscal tools may still be found in direct purchases of goods and services by government and in temporary changes in taxes directly related to private purchases. For example, removing the excise tax on automobiles for six months may well generate automobile sales during that period if the tax is expected to be restored, or even increased, later. Similarly, taxes or tax credits relating to business purchases of new equipment can be varied to promote sales when agents view the taxes as relatively low or the credits as relatively high. And if planned adequately in advance, government public works or other expenditures might be initiated and curtailed promptly in response to varying cyclical conditions.

Fiscal policy has important effects not merely on current aggregates but on the distribution of income and output, both to individuals and between current consumption and investment for the future. As the government pays individuals and business with its expenditures and takes from them in taxes, some receive more than they give and some less. Both expenditures and taxes are likely to affect others than those directly involved. And since neither expenditures nor taxes are "lump sum," but rather depend on some activity (or lack of it), they both affect economic behavior.

Stimulative fiscal policy and budget deficits are seen by some as encouraging consumption—private or collective—at the expense of investment. In a sometimes simplistic confusion of accounting identities with economic behavior, it is pointed out that national saving is the sum of public saving—taken to be the excess of government tax receipts over government outlays or the government budget surplus—

F

and private saving. The less, then, the government surplus or the greater the deficit, which is negative public saving, the less, it is argued, must be the total of public and private saving.

But surely this is necessarily true only as an accounting identity, or if private saving can be assumed to be unaffected by public saving or dissaving. If deficits affect private income and output, they must also affect private saving and investment. We cannot therefore conclude that bigger budget deficits must mean less total saving.

A potentially sounder line of reasoning is that increased private wealth in the form of government securities reduces the need for private saving and hence increases consumption. If we assume that the economy is generally in a state of full employment, we can argue that output cannot be increased. With more labor devoted to producing consumer goods, less labor will be left to produce capital goods, and investment must decline. The same result follows if the government spends for noninvestment purposes—bread and circuses, maintaining camp sites in national parks, or allocating part of the labor force to military service. Again, less resources are left to produce capital goods.

The first critical point here is the assumption of full employment and the consequent impossibility of short-run variation of output. That assumption makes much of the discussion thus far irrelevant. Fiscal policy then, by assumption, cannot affect aggregate output and employment. It can only change the mix of output and, possibly, the level of prices or the rate of inflation. If, however, employment varies, as it does generally in market economies, more consumption may well mean more employment, output, *and* private investment. That has clearly generally been the case in the United States. Whether it will prove true in the future depends on whether output can and does increase enough to permit more investment as well as more consumption. That in turn depends on how close the economy is to full employment and full utilization of its resources. If it is close and if, as explained immediately below, the monetary authority is not fully accommodative, the result depends on whether the stimulative effects on investment demand produced by increases in output that do occur outweigh the depressing effects of higher interest rates.

Secondly, even with full employment, fiscal stimulus need not crowd out private invest-

ment. For one thing, the stimulus may be focused on investment, as by offering accelerated tax depreciation or direct tax credits or subsidies for the acquisition of new buildings, structures, or equipment. And if the stimulus is a general cut in income taxes, the initial increase in private wealth of interest-bearing government debt would cause households to try to increase current and future consumption. Rational business firms would then try to invest more to provide capacity to meet the increased future consumer demand. With no resources available currently for more production, all of the increased demand will merely raise prices.

If the monetary authority is accommodative, there is then no reason why the fiscal stimulus, aside from the consequences of any non-lump-sum components, will have other than proportional nominal effects—on prices, income, money, and debt—with no change in real magnitudes. If the monetary authority does not accommodate but rather permits interest rates to rise, investment will be crowded out, but then the responsibility may be attributed to monetary policy or the fiscal-monetary mix, not to the fiscal stimulus itself.

One can argue that repeated fiscal stimuli—the effort to maintain a persistently higher nominal budget deficit—will, with monetary accommodation, only generate more rapid inflation. This, as explained below, will keep the real value of the government debt from growing, despite the nominal deficit. The increased inflation and expected inflation would then generate a substitution of real assets for money, a lower real rate of interest and actually more investment in tangible capital, but less investment in real cash balances.

Thirdly, though, the argument that stimulative fiscal policy or structural budget deficits must reduce investment ignores the fact that much of government expenditure is in fact investment—the accumulation of capital in roads, bridges, harbors, and airports, in the preservation of public land, water, and air, in vast amounts of investment in research and, most important, in the human capital of the health, education, and training of the work force. Increased expenditures in these directions increase total investment; cutting deficits by measures that reduce such expenditures reduces investment.

An argument that deficits affect neither aggregate demand and output nor total saving and investment is that of so-called "Ricardian

Equivalence." It asserts that there is no difference between the effects of government expenditures financed by borrowing (a deficit) and those financed by taxes. Economic agents recognize that the government must pay interest on its debt or pay it off; any deficit now must be balanced by future taxes for that debt service. Hence agents save an amount equal to the deficit to pay future taxes; spending and the total of public and private saving are not affected.

While this argument has had a considerable run among New Classical macroeconomic theorists, it has been largely rejected by other theorists and most policymakers. Initial objections were that many would be unconcerned about tax liabilities after their death. To the counter-argument that they would be worried about the taxes to be paid by their children and grandchildren, it was pointed out that some would have no descendants, some would not care about their descendants, and some would expect their children and grandchildren to be so much better off as to need no bequests to compensate for higher taxes. Further, with the infinite chain of connections by marriage, current taxpayers would not provide fully for extra tax liabilities of their grandchildren, because their other grandparents might be expected to meet the burden. Indeed, along these lines the argument is reduced to an absurdity in that all effects of any kind on the distribution of income, from any source, are negated by private transfers of related individuals.

Another argument against Ricardian Equivalence or the irrelevance of deficits and public debt (except to permit the smoothing of tax rates over time) is that current deficits will increase employment, income, and investment, so that current taxpayers, anticipating higher future incomes, will see no need to save more for the future. Further, since some are liquidity-constrained and government and private borrowing costs differ, deficits may serve as low-interest loans, which might not otherwise be available at all, that permit current taxpayers to increase current spending.

It may be added finally that events of the 1980s in the United States are difficult if not impossible to square with Ricardian Equivalence. Conventionally measured private saving, at least as a proportion of income, far from increasing to balance the public dissaving constituted by the large deficits, generally declined.

Proper conclusions about the impact of fiscal policy, though, require dispelling of major confusions relating to the implications of both real economic growth and inflation. Budget deficits, it must be recalled, add to debt—interest-bearing or, if financed by money creation, non-interest-bearing. In an economy in balanced growth we might expect the ratio of debt to income or GNP to remain constant. This implies that the debt must grow at the same rate as GNP. In the United States currently, with the federal debt held by the public just about 52 percent of GNP and nominal GNP growing at about 5 percent a year, an equivalent growth in that debt would entail a deficit equal to 2.5 percent of GNP, more than the $164 billion deficit reported for the 1995 fiscal year, which came to only 2.3 percent of GNP. In a meaningful sense, the United States, despite all the rhetoric about the deficit, is now in fiscal balance.

Inflation itself, even without real growth, plays major tricks in conventional accounting. The significance of government deficits, we have noted, is that they add to government debt, which is in turn an asset of the private sector. But what is relevant is surely the real value of that debt. With inflation even at a modest 2–3 percent, the some $3.6 trillion of federal debt now held by the public loses over $75–100 billion in real value in a year. Because of this "inflation tax" on the holders of government securities, we can run a nominal deficit of over $75–100 billion with no increase in the real value of the debt owed by the government or owned by the public, and hence no fiscal stimulus.

Failure to recognize this inflation tax in the period of rapid inflation in the late 1970s and early 1980s meant a failure to recognize that the nominal budget deficits of that time were *real* budget surpluses. The declining real public holdings of government debt were the manifestation of a really tight fiscal policy which, combined with tight money, brought the U.S. by 1982 the worst recession since the Great Depression of the 1930s. The subsequent very large nominal deficits combined with a lower rate of inflation then produced large real budget deficits and a highly stimulative fiscal policy. There ensued the longest peacetime economic expansion in recent U.S. history, cutting unemployment by more than half from its 1982 high of 10.7 percent.

One may conclude that, for better or for worse, fiscal policy matters, and can make a big difference in the overall rate of economic activity.

Robert Eisner

See also FUNCTIONAL FINANCE; HANSEN,
ALVIN HARVEY; HAWTREY, RALPH GEORGE;
KEYNES, JOHN MAYNARD; MINSKY, HYMAN
PHILLIP; MONETARY POLICY; PUMP-PRIMING;
RICARDIAN EQUIVALENCE

Bibliography

Barro, R. J. 1974. "Are Government Bonds
    Net Wealth?" *Journal of Political
    Economy* 82:1095–1117.
Eisner, R. 1986. *How Real Is the Federal
    Deficit?* New York: The Free Press.
Eisner, R. and P. J. Pieper. 1984. "A New
    View of the Federal Debt and Budget
    Deficits." *American Economic Review*
    74:11–29.
Friedman, M. [1948] 1953. "A Monetary
    and Fiscal Framework for Economic Sta-
    bility." In *Essays in Positive Economics,*
    133–56. Chicago: Univ. of Chicago Press.
Lerner, A. 1943. "Functional Finance and the
    Federal Debt." *Social Research* 10:38–58.
Lucas, R. E., Jr. and T. J. Sargent. 1981. "Af-
    ter Keynesian Economics." In *Rational
    Expectations and Economic Practice,*
    edited by R. E. Lucas, Jr. and T. J.
    Sargent, 295–313. Minneapolis: Univ. of
    Minnesota Press.
Tobin, J. and W. Buiter. 1980. "Fiscal and
    Monetary Policies, Capital Formation,
    and Economic Activity." In *The Govern-
    ment and Capital Formation,* edited by
    G. M. von Furstenberg, 73–151. Cam-
    bridge, Mass.: Ballinger.

Fisher, Irving (1867–1947)

Among the most prolific and creative American
economists of the twentieth century, Fisher did
pathbreaking work on general-equilibrium
theory, index numbers, social accounting, econometrics, monetary theory, and the theory of
capital and interest. He argued in many books
and articles that economic fluctuations were
primarily caused by avoidable monetary disturbances, and in the early 1930s presented a
debt-deflation theory of great depressions
which emphasized the interaction of real and
monetary-financial phenomena.

Fisher studied mathematics and economics
at Yale, receiving his Ph.D. in 1891. His dissertation, a formulation of general-equilibrium
theory, was published in 1892 as *Mathematical
Investigations in the Theory of Value and
Prices.* He taught at Yale (at first mathematics,

then economics) from 1892 until his retirement
in 1935. He was president of the American
Economic Association in 1918, and in 1930
was a cofounder and first president of the
Econometric Society.

Fisher's writings on business cycles fall into
three groups. First, there are discussions of fluctuations in his books on interest theory (*The
Rate of Interest* and *The Theory of Interest*) and
on the quantity theory of money (*The Purchasing Power of Money*). In these discussions, fluctuations are attributed to monetary disturbances, chiefly because interest rates fail to
adjust quickly and adequately to inflation. Second, several articles published in the 1920s reported the results of his econometric studies of
fluctuations. Finally, in 1932–33 he developed
his debt-deflation theory in which both real and
monetary factors played important roles.

Fisher never integrated these fragmentary
treatments, with their very different emphases,
into a comprehensive theory of economic fluctuations. But his central message concerned
policy, and he may have considered that message to be adequately supported by any of his
presentations, however different their theoretical particulars. Briefly put, his message was (1)
fluctuations in output and employment are
caused by fluctuations in price levels; (2) these
fluctuations are undesirable, because price
changes tend to be imperfectly foreseen, so that
decisions are based on incorrect expectations
and resources are misallocated; and (3) these
fluctuations could be prevented if monetary
institutions and practices were reformed.

Fisher liked to assert that "*the* business
cycle" was "a myth." In contrast to Wesley
Mitchell and others, he saw fluctuations as
"oscillatory" responses to irregular "external"
disturbances; there was no self-generating, recurrent cycle. The shocks most likely to be
harmful are those affecting the supply of money.
As Fisher put it in a 1923 article, "Business
dances attendance on the dollar."

In his books on interest, Fisher explained
that when price levels are rising or falling, the
optimal real interest rate can be maintained
only if the nominal rate is adjusted appropriately; but since price-level changes are imperfectly foreseen, nominal rates tend to adjust
only slowly and partially. Real interest rates,
then, fall during inflations (encouraging investment, if borrowers perceive the decline) and rise
during deflations (discouraging investment).
Thus price-level fluctuations are accompanied

by fluctuations in output and employment. In *The Purchasing Power of Money,* Fisher presented essentially the same account in a quantity-theoretic framework: changes in price levels are shown to result from changes in the quantity of money. Although in the "long run" a change in the money supply should affect only nominal variables, during a "transition period" real variables fluctuate as well, due to the interest-adjustment lag and perhaps to other nominal rigidities.

In three articles published in 1923, 1925, and 1926, Fisher presented what he regarded as overwhelming empirical evidence that it is price-level fluctuations that cause fluctuations in output and employment. For these studies Fisher invented the distributed lag, and found high correlations between the rate of change of a price index and (with a distributed lag) both an index of "trade" (in the 1923 and 1925 articles) and an index of employment (in the 1926 piece, reprinted in 1973 with the title "I Discovered the Phillips Curve"). Fisher acknowledged that correlation didn't prove causation, but he stated his conclusion emphatically: "The ups and downs of employment are the effects, in large measure, of the rises and falls of prices, due in turn to the inflation and deflation of money and credit" ([1926] 1973, 502).

The depth and duration of the Great Depression came as a shock to Fisher. Shortly before the stock-market crash of 1929, he was widely quoted as predicting that stock prices would remain high. In 1930 he wrote a book (*The Stock Market Crash—And After*) which argued that American industry was basically healthy and that recovery should not be long in coming. When the recovery failed to materialize, Fisher went back to the theoretical drawing board, and the result was his debt-deflation theory of depressions.

The debt-deflation theory was presented to the general public in a book (*Booms and Depressions: Some First Principles*) and to the economics profession in a 1933 article in *Econometrica.* Fisher apparently still believed that his monetary-disturbance theory explained most fluctuations, and he offered the debt-deflation theory as a separate explanation of *great* booms and depressions.

The theory departed sharply from Fisher's earlier work in focusing on "real" causes of fluctuations. In this account, the economy reaches a state of *overindebtedness* due to heavy investments (financed by debt) spurred by inventions, new industries, the development of new resources, or the opening of new markets. Some weak debtors find themselves unable to meet their obligations. Threatened with insolvency, they resort to distress selling of their assets, and they put pressure on their own debtors. A chain reaction follows: more and more creditors press for immediate payment, and panic withdrawals force banks to call loans and to curtail new lending. The distress selling of products and the slackening of expenditure cause the price level to fall; many business costs lag, and so profitability and output and employment decline.

Fisher recognized that these phenomena occur to some degree in any financial panic, and that such panics do not always cause prolonged deep depressions. His explanation of when great depressions would occur was, in his view, the most valuable and original part of his new theory: the decline in the price level may outpace the shrinkage of the volume of nominal debt, increasing the "real burden of debt." Unless the monetary authorities intervened to stabilize or raise the price level, the result could be "almost universal bankruptcy" (1933, 346).

Fisher campaigned avidly for two major schemes of monetary reform. The first was the "compensated dollar plan," a reform of the gold standard which would have sacrificed exchange-rate stability in favor of domestic price-level stability. The second, which he began to promote in the mid-1930s, was the "100-percent reserves plan," which would have required banks to hold reserves equal to their demand-deposit liabilities. During the depression, Fisher argued adamantly against the idea that the economy should be left to recover on its own; in addition to his books and articles of that period, he wrote many letters to members of the Roosevelt administration urging expansionary monetary action (Allen 1977). And to boost velocity he proposed a "dated stamp scrip" plan, the issuance of a currency that would be accepted as legal tender only if it had a special stamp (one cent per dollar) affixed each week.

Fisher was a key forerunner of modern Monetarist thought, and his monetary theory of fluctuations differs little from that of Milton Friedman (Tobin 1987). On the other hand, his debt-deflation theory provided important insights into financial phenomena which have only recently begun to receive the attention they deserve.

Janet A. Seiz

See also DEBT-DEFLATION THEORY; EXPECTATIONS; FRIEDMAN, MILTON; GESELL, SILVIO; INDEX NUMBERS; MACROECONOMETRIC MODELS, HISTORICAL DEVELOPMENT; MINSKY, HYMAN PHILLIP; MONETARY DISEQUILIBRIUM THEORIES OF THE BUSINESS CYCLE; PHILLIPS CURVE

Bibliography

Allen, W. R. 1977. "Irving Fisher, FDR, and the Great Depression." *History of Political Economy* 9:560–87.

Fisher, I. 1907. *The Rate of Interest*. New York: Macmillan.

———. 1913. *The Purchasing Power of Money*. 2d ed. New York: Macmillan.

———. 1923. "The Business Cycle Largely a 'Dance of the Dollar.'" *Journal of the American Statistical Association* 18:1024–28.

———. 1925. "The Unstable Dollar and the So-Called Business Cycle." *Journal of the American Statistical Association* 20:179–202.

———. [1926] 1973. "A Statistical Relation Between Unemployment and Price Changes." Reprinted as "I Discovered the Phillips Curve." *Journal of Political Economy* 81:496–502.

———. 1930a. *The Theory of Interest*. New York: Macmillan.

———. 1930b. *The Stock Market Crash—And After*. New York: Macmillan.

———. 1932. *Booms and Depressions: Some First Principles*. New York: Adelphi.

———. 1933. "The Debt-Deflation Theory of Great Depressions." *Econometrica* 1:337–57.

Fisher, I. N. 1956. *My Father, Irving Fisher*. New York: Comet Press.

Tobin, J. 1987. "Irving Fisher." In *The New Palgrave: A Dictionary of Economics*. Vol 2. Edited by J. Eatwell, M. Milgate, and P. Newman. London: Macmillan.

Föhl, Carl (1901–1973)

Carl Föhl was one of the pioneers of modern macroeconomic analysis in Germany. An engineer by training and early profession, he turned to economics at the age of twenty-four. Stressing the circular-flow analysis of economic activity, he anticipated in the 1930s and 1960s important aspects of Keynesian and Post-Keynesian economics. His most important publication was his Ph.D. thesis, written in 1935, before (!) enrolling at the Berlin Economic College (Wirtschaftshochschule) and thus predating Keynes's *General Theory*. Published two years later as *Geldschöpfung und Wirtschaftskreislauf* (Creation of money and economic circular flow) (*GuW*), it was favorably reviewed. Schumpeter, in his *History of Economic Analysis* (1954, 1174), recommended it as "extremely instructive to American economists." Further praise came from the director of the Kiel Institute of World Economics, Erich Schneider (1966, 1).

Since Schumpeter praised its "apparently un-Keynesian approach," modern readers might turn to this work in search of a macroeconomic alternative to Keynes. But, in fact, Föhl independently stated important elements of the *General Theory*. He treated the rate of interest as a monetary phenomenon; he assumed that consumption is a function of income; and he viewed investment expenditure as dependent on profit expectations and—at a second remove—on the rate of interest. Föhl drew *IS*-curves for alternative levels of profits, and he extensively discussed alternative levels of equilibrium in the income/interest-rate plane (1937, 274), and described what later became known as the Keynes Effect—the expansionary effect of nominal wage reductions on the real quantity of money and of the resulting reduction in the rate of interest (1937, 159–60). And many of the analytical differences between *GuW* and the *General Theory* are more apparent than real (Hohn 1970). Thus, Föhl's early work already contained much of what later became Keynesian *LM* (money market) and *IS* (goods market) analysis.

Despite these similarities, the analytical flavor of *GuW* is quite different from that of the *General Theory*. It contains a particularly strong element of circular-flow analysis, foreshadowing later "hydraulic" macroeconomic developments, which are now sometimes denounced as not being "authentically" Keynesian. But whatever their genealogy, such analyses were important for the development of modern national-income accounting.

The predominant analytical method in *GuW* is comparative statics, but it also contains truly dynamic sequential period analyses of money-supply processes. Föhl employed a two-sector economic model and assumed that the consumption sector always operated at full capacity. Föhl was dissatisfied with this aspect of his early work and later tried to incorporate a cost-returns calculus of macroeconomic quasi-rents to provide an endogenous explanation of economic activity in all sectors.

Bolle et al. (1966, 184)—a group of Föhl's assistants—trace this part of his work to Enrico Barone's *Principi*. But the strongest influences on Föhl were Keynes's *Treatise on Money,* Schumpeter, and the period analysis of Knut Wicksell.

It is noteworthy that for most of his life Föhl did not pursue an academic career. In 1939–40 he held a minor position in the Ministry of Economics in Berlin. From 1940 to 1945 he was director of a chemical firm in Cracow. But in 1941 he was guest lecturer at the University of Aarhus, Denmark. These lectures were published and were later praised by Kalecki and Schumacher (1946).

After World War II he continued to work in business, but in 1963 he became Full Professor at the Free University Berlin where he held the chair for the Theory of Economic Policy. He won several honorary positions and academic honors, serving as president of the German Association of Economists (BDVB) from 1961 to 1967. From then on he was honorary president of that body. In 1967 the Economic College of St. Gallen (Switzerland) awarded him an honorary Ph.D. degree in economics.

In his later academic life, Föhl became known to a wider public for two main new contributions to contemporary economic debates. One was a monograph on a Circular Flow Analytic Inquiry into the Creation of Wealth in the Federal Republic of Germany and into the Possibilities of its Redistribution (1964). In this work Föhl applied his previously cultivated circular-flow approach to a political-economic analysis of wealth redistribution and taxation in the Federal Republic of Germany. In these inquiries he followed a theoretical line which in many respects was not dissimilar to the Cambridge Post-Keynesian theory of distribution associated with the name of Nicholas Kaldor.

A further contribution to German macroeconomic debates of his time became known as the Föhl Theorem (Jürgensen 1966, 84), which asserts that under certain conditions taxes on profits will be passed on entirely to consumers (Föhl 1953, 1956).

Gerhard Michael Ambrosi

See also POST-KEYNESIAN BUSINESS-CYCLE THEORY

Bibliography

Bolle, M., H. Brekenfeld, M. Dittmar, K. Engelke, and M. Hennies. 1966. "Zum Erlös-Kosten-Diagramm." In *Wirtschaftskreislauf und Wirtschaftswachstum: Carl Föhl zum 65 Geburtstag,* edited by E. Schneider, 183–222. Tübingen: Mohr.

Föhl, C. [1937] 1955. *Geldschöpfung und Wirtschaftskreislauf.* 2d ed. Berlin: Duncker und Humblot.

———. 1941. "Kinematik und Dynamik des Wirtschaftskreislaufs." *Nordisk Tidskrift for Teknisk Ökonomi* 7:121–46.

———. [1941] 1955. "Die Erhaltung der Vollbeschäftigung." In Föhl, *Geldschöpfung und Wirtschaftskreislauf.* 2d ed., 409–36. Berlin: Duncker und Humblot.

———. 1953. "Kritik der progressiven Einkommensbesteuerung." *Finanzarchiv,* n.s., 14:88–109.

———. 1956. "Das Steuerparadoxon." *Finanzarchiv,* n.s., 17:1–3.

———. 1957. "Volkswirtschaftliche Regelkreise höherer Ordnung in Modelldarstellung." In *Volkswirtschaftliche Regelungsvorgänge im Vergleich zu Regelungsvorgängen der Technik, Beihefte [4] zur Regelungstechnik,* 49–75. Munchen: Oldenbourg.

———. 1964. *Kreislaufanalytische Untersuchung der Vermögensbildung in der Bundesrepublik und der Beeinflußbarkeit ihrer Verteilung.* Tübingen: Mohr.

Hohn, H.-W. 1970. "John Maynard Keynes und Carl Föhl: Eine vergleichende Darstellung ihres Beitrags zur Entwicklung der modernen Beschäftigungstheorie." Ph.D. diss., Department of Political Economy, Ludwig-Maximilians University, Munich.

Jürgensen, H. 1966. "Bemerkungen zu Wachstums- und Verteilungseffekten privater und öffentlicher Investitionen." In *Wirtschaftskreislauf und Wirtschaftswachstum: Carl Föhl zum 65 Geburtstag,* edited by E. Schneider, 75–99. Tübingen: Mohr.

Kalecki, M. and E. F. Schumacher. 1946. *The Economics of Full Employment.* Oxford: Basil Blackwell.

Pedersen, J. 1957. "Remarks to Carl Föhl's 'Geldschöpfung und Wirtschaftskreislauf.'" *Weltwirtschaftliches Archiv.* 78:1*–10*.

Schneider, E., ed. 1966. *Wirtschaftskreislauf und Wirtschaftswachstum: Carl Föhl zum 65 Geburtstag.* Tübingen: Mohr.

F

Forced Saving

Forced saving may arise in any dynamic process in which *ex ante* investment, *I*, exceeds *ex ante* or voluntary saving, *S*. At any given interest rate, forced saving corresponds to the amount by which *ex post* investment exceeds *ex ante* saving. As such, it is a familiar element of traditional monetary and overinvestment theories of the business cycle. However, its practical significance today pertains less to mainline cycle theory than to the role of wealth in economic models.

In the following discussion, investment is assumed to be a positive function of the difference between the marginal product of capital and the cost of capital, where the latter includes the relative price of capital goods and the real rates of interest and depreciation. Saving is a positive function of income and may or may not be positive in interest. It also depends on the distribution of income and negatively on the level of wealth.

The possibility of forced saving has long been recognized in both the literature on credit expansion and investment (Haberler 1962, Hansson 1987). It can occur whether investment exceeds saving because of a reduction in the market rate of interest below the natural rate (at which saving equals investment) or because of a spontaneous increase in the natural rate, as postulated by Wicksell. In either case, the analysis of real, as opposed to purely monetary, outcomes is incomplete without consideration of the magnitude of saving and investment *ex post*.

The market rate can remain below the natural rate only as long as investment is being financed by bank credit or by dishoarded balances from portfolios outside the circular flow of income. Thus, if investment exceeds saving, then total expenditures in the economy exceed the existing value of output. In the ensuing competition for resources between suppliers of consumer goods and suppliers of producer goods, the initial advantage would appear to lie with the latter, since, at the lower market rate of interest, investing firms are the first to acquire the excess funding. Their expenditures raise the prices of producer goods and of resources used by those industries. The degree to which they increase capital-goods production varies directly with the elasticities of the resource supply functions and the technological substitutability between consumer- and capital-goods output. The elasticities will tend to be greater the higher the level of resource unemployment in the economy at large.

The funds are subsequently paid as income to resources, including labor, whose additional outlays are directed primarily to consumption goods, raising those prices. Since money is being created or dishoarded, the process raises the absolute price level while bringing about a level and distribution of real income and relative prices that yield an *ex post* division of the output. *Ex post* investment and hence forced saving are greater the greater and the more rapid is the rise in the prices of capital goods relative to those of consumer goods, the greater is the supply elasticity of capital goods relative to that of consumer goods, and the more slowly do wages and thus the income of labor rise in the adjustment process.

In overinvestment theories of the business cycle, writers such as Hayek (1931) argued that capital and more roundabout methods of production secured through forced saving were unsustainable. When the forces maintaining the market rate below the natural rate ceased to operate, not only would investment decline, but the structure of production, including some of the capital stock, created through inflationary means at the lower rate would be abandoned, ushering in a depression. An unexpected reduction in the rate of monetary increase may indeed trigger a downturn. This can occur if inflationary supply-side pricing throughout the economy continues despite the overall deceleration in expenditures. A downturn can also occur as aggregate activity declines while resources shift from producer-back to consumer-goods industries.

Hayek's insistence on the need to liquidate already completed (and partially completed) capital and capitalistic methods was not widely accepted (Haberler 1962, Hansen 1951). To the modern reader, his analysis of the investment process seems asymmetric. On the one hand, firms are assumed to calculate carefully the expected future revenues of each project. But somehow they fail to recognize that interest rates and the cost of capital may later rise and require prompt disinvestment in existing methods and projects. Inexplicably, firms ignore the future cyclical behavior of interest rates and relative prices. They fail to lock into debt at cyclically low yields or secure a high enough real return on additions to the capital stock and on the restructuring of production to justify maintaining them beyond the current upswing.

Discussion of forced saving peaked during the flowering of monetary literature in the 1930s and early 1940s and disappeared. It did not arise again until the great postwar debates on the role of wealth, particularly real balances, in achieving full employment. Pigou (1943) and others pointed out that consumption is a positive function of real wealth. Hence, an economy in which aggregate demand was less than output at full employment ("Keynes's Day of Judgment" in which saving exceeds investment at all attainable interest rates) could achieve a full-employment equilibrium at a sufficiently low price level and correspondingly high level of real balances. Metzler (1951) responded that one consequence of the Pigou effect was to introduce an uncharacteristic monetary influence on the full-employment-equilibrium rate of interest. [Patinkin (1965), who came to a similar conclusion, did not regard this result as unusual, particularly because of the widely acknowledged influence on interest of distributional changes due to forced saving.] An open-market purchase by the central bank, for example, would, at a lower market rate of interest, remove securities from private portfolios in exchange for cash balances. But the lower rate would cause investment to exceed saving and the price level to rise, reducing real balances and thus privately perceived wealth. At the given full-employment income, a new equilibrium would result in which wealth was lower, consumption lower, saving higher, and the rate of interest lower than before the purchase.

What Metzler overlooked was forced saving as an incremental source of wealth during the inflationary adjustment process (Horwich 1962). Depending on the interest elasticities of saving and investment, the adjustment could generate a wide range of *ex post* investment levels and corresponding values of privately issued securities. At one extreme, with saving a positive function of interest but investment completely interest-inelastic, an adjustment that produced no forced saving (*ex post* investment lies along the S schedule) would magnify the wealth loss due to the open-market operation: the capital stock would increase less rapidly than its previous trend in saving-investment equilibrium, as would the derived value of securities issued to finance that investment level. At the other extreme, with saving completely interest-inelastic but investment a negative function of interest, complete forced saving (*ex post* investment lies along the I schedule) would

compensate more or less for the loss of securities to the central bank: the capital stock and the value of corresponding securities would increase more rapidly than along their previous trend.

Taking account of forced saving in monetary adjustment can thus yield widely differing wealth outcomes, where wealth includes both real balances and the value of securities backed by the capital stock. Even Pigou's analysis must be qualified by the time path of *ex post* investment (Horwich 1964, chap. 10). For the deflationary process he described, one in which saving exceeds investment at full employment, will change the growth rate of capital, either reinforcing or offsetting the wealth gains due to the simultaneous increase in real balances. This can be seen by first establishing a pre-disturbance reference for capital growth, which is done by specifying whether saving exceeds investment at full employment because investment declined or because saving increased. If (not implausibly) the former, then relative to the predisturbance trend in which saving was equal to investment, the growth of capital as determined by *ex ante* investment during the deflationary process will be reduced. Relative to trend, wealth, including both real balances and securities backed by the capital stock, may fail to increase, leaving saving and the saving-investment gap intact.

The only way wealth might be increased sufficiently to end the deflationary spiral would be if the *ex post* investment level were greater than *ex ante* investment. That phenomenon would be "forced investment"—the deflationary analogue of forced saving and the outcome of a process opposite to the inflationary adjustment: at a market rate above the natural rate, consumers reduce their outlays and attempt to reduce consumption by more than investing firms curtail their outlays and seek to curtail investment. Forced investment occurs when, because of relative price movements, relative supply elasticities, and changes in the distribution of income, investing firms are not wholly successful in reducing investment *ex post*.

Forced saving (or investment) thus continues to play a critical role in the analysis of any dynamic process in which wealth is a relevant variable. Although cyclical or transitional changes in the capital stock may be small compared to the existing stock of capital, they are not small compared to, and may even dominate, simultaneous changes in other wealth components such as real balances.

George Horwich

See also Austrian Theory of Business Cycles; Business Cycles; Hayek, Friedrich August [von]; Metzler, Lloyd Appleton; Mises, Ludwig Edler von; Natural Rate of Interest; Overinvestment Theories of Business Cycles; Period of Production; Pigou-Haberler Effect; Robertson, Dennis Holme; Wicksell, Johan Gustav Knut

Bibliography

Haberler, G. 1962. *Prosperity and Depression.* 4th rev. ed. Cambridge: Harvard Univ. Press.

Hansen, A. H. 1951. *Business Cycles and National Income.* New York: Norton.

Hansson, B. A. 1987. "Forced Saving." *The New Palgrave: A Dictionary of Economics.* Vol. 2. Edited by J. Eatwell, M. Milgate, and P. Newman. London: Macmillan.

Hayek, F. A. 1931. *Prices and Production.* London: Routledge.

Horwich, G. 1962. "Real Assets and the Theory of Interest." *Journal of Political Economy* 70:157–69.

———. 1964. *Money, Capital, and Prices.* Homewood, Ill.: Irwin.

Metzler, L. A. 1951. "Wealth, Saving, and the Rate of Interest." *Journal of Political Economy* 59:93–116.

Patinkin, D. 1965. *Money, Interest, and Prices.* 2d ed. New York: Harper and Row.

Pigou, A. C. 1943. "The Classical Stationary State." *Economic Journal* 53:342–51.

Wicksell, K. [1901] 1935. *Lectures on Political Economy.* Vol. 2. *Money.* London: Routledge.

Foster, William Trufant (1879–1950)

W. T. Foster and Waddill Catchings were popular writers on the business cycle in the 1920s. Although disparaged by professional economists at the time, their work anticipated significant aspects of Keynesian macroeconomics and of modern growth theory. While Roosevelt's New Deal is often seen as the first example of a Keynesian stabilization policy, it may have derived its inspiration more from Foster and Catchings than from Keynes.

Foster and Catchings believed the business cycle to be the result of insufficient effective demand attributable to a savings-investment problem. As incomes rose, consumption would inevitably fall short of money income. To make up this deficiency in demand, the resultant saving would have to be transformed into investment. However, additional investment would mean additional income in the future, requiring yet more investment to prevent a deficiency of demand. Although the required investment might be forthcoming, there was no guarantee of it. If it were not, Foster and Catchings suggested that the slack be taken up by a program of public works.

The theory of Foster and Catchings resembles in certain respects the earlier underconsumptionist theory of J. A. Hobson, and the subsequent theory of Keynes. Unlike Hobson, Foster and Catchings realized that the act of saving did not necessarily entail an equivalent amount of investment. But they failed to develop the insight that *ex ante* savings and investment are not identical into a theory of equilibrium income and output, as Keynes succeeded in doing via his multiplier analysis.

Foster, a former president of Reed College, and Catchings, a business executive, founded the Pollak Foundation for Economic Research. The foundation published works by Irving Fisher and by Paul Douglas as well as by Foster and Catchings themselves. Following the publication of their *Profits,* setting out their views on the business cycle, the foundation offered a prize of $5,000 for the best adverse criticism of the book. The 400 entrants numbered among them such distinguished economists as J. R. Commons, E. Durbin, A. H. Hansen, F. A. Hayek, and D. H. Robertson.

Meir Kohn

See also Hobson, John Atkinson; Oversaving Theories of Business Cycles; Say, Jean-Baptiste; Say's Law; Saving Equals Investment

Bibliography

Foster, W. T. and W. Catchings. 1925. *Profits.* Boston: Houghton Mifflin.

———. 1927. *Money.* 3d rev. ed. Boston: Houghton Mifflin.

———. 1928a. *Business Without a Buyer.* Boston: Houghton Mifflin.

———. 1928b. *The Road to Plenty.* Boston: Houghton Mifflin.

Gleason, A. H. 1959. "Foster and Catchings: A Reappraisal." *Journal of Political Economy* 67:156–72.

Hayek, F. A. [1926] 1939. "The Paradox of Saving." Translation. Appendix to *Prof-*

its, Interest, and Investment. London: Routledge.

Pollak Foundation for Economic Research. 1927. *Pollak Prize Essays: Criticism of Profits, A Book by W. T. Foster and W. Catchings.* Newton, Mass.: Pollak Foundation for Economic Research.

Free Banking

Free banking, a term used in Europe and America for over two centuries, means free trade in banking. "Free competition . . . obliges all bankers to be more liberal in their dealings with their customers, lest their rivals should carry them away," wrote Adam Smith ([1776] 1976, 1:329) when free banking had been working successfully and contributing to economic progress in Scotland for several decades. Free banking flourished there for more than a century until terminated by Peel's Bank Charter Act of 1844. It performed well, albeit briefly, in France between 1796 and 1803, and in the six New England states for at least half a century before the Civil War.

For such nineteenth-century advocates of free banking as H. C. Carey, J. W. Gilbart, and Charles Coquelin, seven main features characterized free banking. First, it requires free entry into banking. Second, bank shareholders should have the right to raise or increase bank capital (net worth, in modern terms). Third, customers and bank management should have an unrestricted right to contract interest-bearing deposit accounts. Fourth, banks should be allowed to issue redeemable notes. Fifth, asset management, including the reserve ratio, should be left to the discretion of banks. Sixth, bank bylaws should be freely contracted without government intervention. Finally, banks should not be subject to legal bond-deposit requirements.

The impressive growth of banking activities in Scotland, where free banking first evolved, was studied by several economists and became a model for other countries. Jacques Turgot tried unsuccessfully as a member of the French government (1774–76) to introduce such a system in France. Du Pont de Nemours and Camille Saint-Aubin later helped bring down the old restrictive regime for credit institutions, launching the brief French free-banking period. Despite the troubled times, free banking promoted economic prosperity and monetary stability and was terminated by the authoritarian regime of Napoleon I to increase the power of the state and its access to credit.

At about the same time, the first modern banks were being formed in the United States. Pre-Civil War America had no uniform banking system. Each state retained the power to allow new banks to begin operations. The New England states granted unrestricted authorization for the operation of banks, but such authorization was less liberally granted elsewhere.

The American economists H. C. Carey and Richard Hildreth admired the free-banking institutions of New England. Noting the relation between greater competition in Massachusetts and Rhode Island with more efficient and stronger banks, they advocated free banking throughout the Union. In his *History of Banks* (1837), Hildreth noted the spectacular performance of New England free banks and in his *Banks, Banking and Paper Currencies* (1840), he relied on the success of free banking in New England to advocate its adoption elsewhere. With considerable statistical data, Carey, in his *The Credit System of France, Great Britain and the United States* (1838), compared New England's free banking with the more restrictive credit systems in other states. He also argued that free banking, which was almost as complete in Scotland as in New England, provided monetary stability in Scotland, while England and France underwent recurring depressions.

In the considerable free-banking literature of the time, the *Democratick Editorials* ([1838] 1984) of William Leggett, recently compiled and edited by L. H. White, is worthy of note. Leggett pleaded for abolishing the privileged monopolies chartered by most state administrations. In the third part of the nineteenth century, Michel Chevalier noted that with only one exception (Louis Wolowski), French economists favored free banking. Among them, Charles Coquelin, Jean Gustave Courcelle-Seneuil, and Edouard Horn are still important. In *Le Crédit et les banques*, Coquelin integrated Carey's and Gilbart's historical data into a broader business-cycle theory. In his "Notice sur les Banques de l'Etat de New York" (*Journal des Economistes*, 15 October 1850, 235–42), Coquelin showed that the banking legislation enacted by New York state in 1838 was erroneously labelled a free-banking act. On the contrary, he argued, the law imposed severe and dangerous restrictions on banks. Credit became more scarce and more unstable, leading the state to a financial crisis. The depression of 1857–58 caused numerous bank failures in New York, but was absorbed with astonishing ease in Boston.

Free banking promotes prosperity through increased capital investments in banks, industry, and commerce. It strengthens bank balance sheets, thereby stabilizing the monetary system. Artificial credit expansion is discouraged under such a system, because such expansion would require banks to reduce interest rates on loans while competition would raise the cost of the funds needed to finance those loans. Thus, credit expansion is unprofitable under free banking because the spread, i.e., the difference between the revenues from and costs of bank funds, would become negative. Scottish banks funded their business loans from interest-bearing deposits and from equity funds yielding dividends to the stockholders. Only a small percentage of credit was funded by inexpensive demand deposits or notes.

In New England, particularly in Massachusetts and Rhode Island, banks engaged in especially low leverage financing. In Massachusetts, banks financed their loans with more than 60 percent equity and only 11 percent interest-yielding deposits. In Rhode Island, equity-funded credits averaged 72 percent. Under such conditions it is understandable that New England free banks (like their Scottish counterparts) absorbed panics coming from outside with remarkable ease. Banks with such financial strength could scarcely fail. Paradoxically, Karl Marx viewed the Scottish banking system positively. "Scotland," he wrote ([1859] 1973, 133) "never experienced a real monetary crisis: no depreciation of notes, no complaints and no inquiries into the sufficiency or the insufficiency of the currency in circulation."

But despite the impressive performance of free banking wherever it was tried and the support of many leading nineteenth-century economists, by the end of the century, discussion of free banking had virtually disappeared from economic debates. In the twentieth century, free banking was ignored by most monetary theorists, with the exception of Ludwig von Mises and Vera C. Smith, until F. A. Hayek, responding to the accelerating inflation of the 1970s, published a short, but influential work, *The Denationalisation of Money*.

Building on the work of Hayek, Mises, and Smith, others have pursued the topic further both theoretically and empirically. White (1984) showed that the British monetary debates of the early nineteenth century involved not two but three schools of thought. Besides the well-known Currency and Banking Schools, there was a distinct Free Banking School which proposed the Scottish system as a remedy for English banking instability. White's contribution considerably enlarged our understanding of history and the theoretical debates on monetary issues in Great Britain. Following White, G. A. Selgin (1988) has shown that central-bank-monopoly note issue could be advantageously replaced by an unregulated system more efficiently supplying bank notes as well as deposits. It is noteworthy that, partly in response to the developing free-banking literature, two leading Monetarists, Milton Friedman and Anna J. Schwartz (1986) have revised their earlier position and concluded that "leaving monetary and banking arrangements to the market would have produced a more satisfactory outcome" (59).

In fact, recent historical research shows free banking to have been more widespread than generally recognized. Studies in Dowd (1992) provide important insights into free-banking experiences in Australia, Canada, Colombia, China, Ireland, and Switzerland. Thus free banking is not only a theoretical model defended for more than two centuries by renowned economists; it has also worked successfully in several parts of the world for significant periods of time.

Philippe Nataf

See also BANKING SCHOOL, CURRENCY SCHOOL, AND FREE BANKING SCHOOL; CENTRAL BANKING; COQUELIN, CHARLES; DEMAND FOR CURRENCY; FINANCIAL INTERMEDIATION; GILBART, JAMES WILLIAM; HAYEK, FRIEDRICH AUGUST [VON]; JUGLAR, CLÉMENT; LENDER OF LAST RESORT; MUSHET, ROBERT; NEW MONETARY ECONOMICS; OPTION CLAUSE; PARNELL, HENRY BROOKE; SMITH, ADAM; TOOKE, THOMAS

Bibliography

Carey, H. C. 1838. *The Credit System of France, Great Britain and the United States*. Philadelphia: Carey, Lea and Blanchard.

———. 1840. *Answers to the Questions: What Constitutes Currency? What Are the Causes of Unsteadiness of the Currency? And What Is the Remedy?* Philadelphia: Lea and Blanchard.

———. 1865. *Principles of Social Science*. Vol. 2. Philadelphia: J. B. Lippincott and Co.

Coquelin, C. 1876. *Le Crédit et les banques.* 3d ed. Paris: Guillaumin.

Dowd, K., ed. 1992. *The Experience of Free Banking.* London: Routledge.

Friedman, M. and A. J. Schwartz. 1986. "Has Government Any Role in Money?" *Journal of Monetary Economics* 17:37–62.

Gilbart, J. W. 1865. *A Practical Treatise on Banking.* London: Bell and Daley.

Hayek, F. A. 1978. *The Denationalisation of Money: The Argument Refined.* 2d ed. London: Institute of Economic Affairs.

Leggett, W. [1838] 1984. *Democratick Editorials.* Edited with an introduction by L. H. White. Indianapolis: Liberty Press.

Marx, Karl H. [1859] 1973. Gundrisse: Introduction to the Critique of Political Economy. Translated with an introduction by M. Nicolaus. New York: Vintage.

Mises, L. von. 1966. *Human Action.* 3d rev. ed. Chicago: Henry Regnery.

Nataf, P. 1987. *An Inquiry into the Free Banking Movement in Nineteenth Century France, with Particular Emphasis on Charles Coquelin's Writings.* San Diego: William Lyon University.

Salin, P. 1984. *Currency Competition and Monetary Union.* The Hague: Martinus Nijhoff.

Schwartz, A. J. 1987. "Banking School, Currency School and Free Banking School." In *The New Palgrave: A Dictionary of Economics.* Vol. 1. Edited by J. Eatwell, M. Milgate, and P. Newman. London: Macmillan.

Selgin, G. A. 1988. *The Theory of Free Banking: Money Supply under Competitive Note Issue.* Totowa, N.J.: Rowman and Littlefield.

Selgin, G. A. and L. H. White. 1994. "How Would the Invisible Hand Handle Money?" *Journal of Economic Literature* 32:1718–49.

Smith, A. [1776] 1976. *An Inquiry into the Nature and Causes of the Wealth of Nations.* 2 vols. Oxford: Clarendon Press.

Smith, V. C. 1936. *The Rationale of Central Banking.* London: P. S. King.

White, L. H. 1984. *Free Banking in Britain: Theory, Experience, and Debate, 1800–1845.* New York: Cambridge Univ. Press.

Friedman, Milton (1912–)

The son of immigrants, Milton Friedman spent his early years in Rahway, New Jersey, where he attended the public schools. After graduating from Rutgers University in 1932, he studied at the University of Chicago under Jacob Viner, Frank Knight, and Henry Simons. His Chicago classmates included George Stigler and W. Allen Wallis. He continued his graduate studies in economics and statistics at Columbia University, working closely with Harold Hotelling, Wesley C. Mitchell, and Arthur Burns. In 1976, Friedman received the Nobel Memorial Prize in Economic Science.

Friedman is probably best known among economists as the founding father of Monetarism, or perhaps as the leader of the Chicago School of economics. Yet Friedman's contributions to economic knowledge range far beyond his monetary research and his policy polemics. Included in this vast scholarly output are important studies of business cycles, along with major works on the consumption function, labor, price theory, statistics, and methodology. Unfortunately, Friedman has not summarized his work on cycles in a single publication, making it difficult to examine his views on the subject. However, his major contributions are available in two books: *A Monetary History of the United States, 1867–1960,* coauthored with Anna Schwartz, and *The Optimum Quantity of Money and Other Essays.* Especially noteworthy in the latter collection are Friedman and Schwartz ([1963] 1969) and Friedman ([1964] 1969)].

One way to characterize a body of research is in terms of its empirical orientation. We can arrange business-cycle studies along a continuum, with one pole representing abstract models unsupported by empirical data, and the other representing compilations of data unsupported by economic theory. On such a continuum Friedman stands near the center. Virtually all of his cycle studies have been done in association with the National Bureau of Economic Research, which—under the leadership of Mitchell and Burns—was famous for the assembly and refinement of economic time series, but was often criticized for slighting the theoretical modeling of cycles. While it is true that Friedman has always relied on a solid empirical base (in fact, spent years *creating* that base), and has shown little interest in abstract models of the cycle, he has not neglected economic theory. Friedman's work on business cycles shows his deep concern with extracting broad implications from the data, carefully blending data analysis and theorizing.

Data analysis can take many forms. Friedman's work on business cycles has used the National Bureau's stylized framework, as set forth in Burns and Mitchell (1946). In this approach, each business (or "reference") cycle is divided into nine stages, extending from one trough to the next. Stage averages are calculated for the variables under study, expressed relative to mean values for each whole cycle to minimize the effects of secular trends that are found in many economic time series. Comparisons are then made across cycles—e.g., the mean monetary growth rate in (say) Stage II of a given cycle is compared with the same statistic in other cycles. The aim is to investigate the typical behavior, stage by stage, of the variables selected for study. Standard econometrics is largely absent from this type of analysis.

We can sharpen our understanding of Friedman's substantive views on business cycles by comparing him with J. M. Keynes. Like Keynes, Friedman views cycles not as the outcome of a self-generating process but as the result of exogenous shocks. Given the variability in the timing and magnitude of these shocks, one should not expect to find that historical "business cycles" are highly regular from one episode to the next.

Both Keynes and Friedman attribute business cycles primarily to demand shocks. For Keynes these shocks usually reflect fluctuations in expected returns on investment projects (the marginal efficiency of capital), while Friedman attributes them to unevenness in the rate of monetary growth due to erratic monetary policies, rather than to unstable investment demand.

Still another similarity between Friedman and Keynes is that neither assumes that a recession is inevitable every few years. Keynes clung to the notion that governments could prevent slumps by adopting active fiscal policies. While Friedman has been a vigorous critic of activist macropolicies—monetary as well as fiscal—he has argued that cycles could be greatly moderated, perhaps avoided altogether, if shocks stemming from erratic monetary policies were eliminated.

The principal findings on which Friedman bases these views can be summarized briefly. Although the trend of the U.S. money stock is strongly upward, rising not only in cyclical expansions but also in most recessions, the monetary growth rate follows an irregular but unmistakably cyclical path, reaching peaks an average of fourteen months before reference cycle peaks and troughs an average of eight months before reference troughs.

The role of monetary shocks in generating economic fluctuations is especially clear, in Friedman's view, for "deep depression cycles." Since the middle of the nineteenth century there have been six trough-to-trough cycles in the United States that ended with unusually severe recessions: 1870–79, 1891–94, 1904–08, 1919–21, 1927–33, and 1933–38. According to Friedman and Schwartz ([1963] 1969), each of these episodes involved severe monetary disturbances. For example, during the 1929–33 downswing, the stock of broad money outstanding fell by 35.2 percent. In contrast, during mild depression cycles in the United States, broad money has actually *risen* during recessions (with two minor exceptions). Moreover, Friedman contends that no monetary shocks occurred during any of the mild depression cycles. In his view, then, the evidence is as conclusive as one ever finds in economics: severe depressions are very unlikely to occur in the absence of monetary shocks.

Critics were quick to challenge Friedman's conclusions on the role of money in business cycles, especially deep depression cycles (Temin 1976, Tobin 1970). Perhaps the most significant criticism has been the reverse-causality argument: that changes in monetary growth merely reflect changes in business conditions, while the cycle is driven by entirely different forces. Friedman ([1964] 1969) presents his fullest response to the reverse-causality argument, drawing not only on his work with Anna Schwartz (1963, [1963] 1969) but on the important related study by Cagan (1965). Cagan analyzed the proximate determinants of the money stock over essentially the same period studied by Friedman and Schwartz. He found that during deep depression cycles the dominant determinant of the money stock was the stock of high-powered money (i.e., the monetary base) in existence. Cagan searched for feedback mechanisms that could explain how a change in business conditions might influence the stock of high-powered money, and thus the money stock itself. He concluded that with trivial exceptions such feedback mechanisms were not important during this period of American history. Hence he rejected the reverse-causality argument in relation to severe recessions.

It should be noted that Cagan's findings concerning mild cycles were considerably more ambiguous. In Friedman's summary ([1964]

severe contractions, Cagan finds clear evidence of the influence of business on money." Both the deposit-currency ratio and the reserve-deposit ratio, especially the former, contribute significantly to changes in monetary growth rates during mild cycles, and Cagan interprets these as feedback mechanisms running from business activity to monetary growth.

Milton Friedman is often portrayed as an extreme Monetarist for whom "only money matters." Possibly in some sense this is true, but clearly it does not accurately describe his views on the nature of business cycles. On the contrary, the explicit statement of Friedman and Schwartz (1963, 687) on this point is clear: "Mutual interaction, but with money rather clearly the senior partner in longer-run movements and in major cyclical movements, and more nearly an equal partner with money income and prices in shorter-run and milder movements—this is the generalization suggested by our evidence."

In summary, Milton Friedman's contributions to our understanding of business cycles consist mainly of empirical analyses of monetary processes, focusing on American experience extending back to the last third of the nineteenth century. These contributions show that monetary disturbances are intimately linked to business fluctuations, including those that we call "business cycles," even though the precise nature of this linkage remains unresolved. Finally, it is worth noting that Friedman's views on the role of money in business cycles leave room for a variety of "nonmonetary" approaches to cycle studies, including the real-business-cycle theories that have received so much attention since the 1980s.

Richard T. Selden

See also ANGELL, JAMES WATERHOUSE; BURNS, ARTHUR FRANK; CENTRAL BANKING; CONSUMPTION EXPENDITURES; DEMAND FOR MONEY; EXPECTATIONS; FEDERAL RESERVE SYSTEM: 1914–1941; FEDERAL RESERVE SYSTEM: 1941–1993; FISHER, IRVING; GREAT DEPRESSION IN THE UNITED STATES (1929–1938); MONETARY DISEQUILIBRIUM THEORIES OF THE BUSINESS CYCLE; MONETARY EQUILIBRIUM THEORIES OF THE BUSINESS CYCLE; MITCHELL, WESLEY CLAIR; MONETARY POLICY; MONEY-INCOME CAUSALITY; NATURAL RATE OF UNEMPLOYMENT; PERSONS, WARREN MILTON; PHILLIPS CURVE; ROBERTSON, DENNIS HOLME; SCHWARTZ, ANNA JACOBSON; SUPPLY OF MONEY; WARBURTON, CLARK

Bibliography

Burns, A. F. and W. C. Mitchell. 1946. *Measuring Business Cycles*. New York: NBER.

Cagan, P. D. 1965. *Determinants and Effects of Changes in the Stock of Money 1875–1960*. New York: Columbia Univ. Press.

Frazer, W. 1988. *Power and Ideas: Milton Friedman and the Big U-Turn*. 2 vols. Gainesville: Gulf/Atlantic Publishing.

Friedman, M. 1953. *Essays in Positive Economics*. Chicago: Univ. of Chicago Press.

———. [1954] 1968. "Why the American Economy is Depression-Proof." Chap. 2 in *Dollars and Deficits*. Englewood Cliffs, N.J.: Prentice-Hall.

———. 1957. *A Theory of the Consumption Function*. Princeton: Princeton Univ. Press.

———. 1958. "The Supply of Money and Changes in Prices and Output." In *The Relationship of Prices to Economic Stability and Growth*. 85th Congress, 2d Session, Joint Economic Committee. Washington, D.C.: Government Printing Office.

———. [1959] 1969. "The Demand for Money: Some Theoretical and Empirical Results." Chap. 6 in *The Optimum Quantity of Money and Other Essays*. Chicago: Aldine.

———. 1960. *A Program for Monetary Stability*. New York: Fordham Univ. Press.

———. [1964] 1969. "The Monetary Studies of the National Bureau." Chap. 12 in *The Optimum Quantity of Money and Other Essays*. Chicago: Aldine.

———. [1967] 1969. "The Monetary Theory and Policy of Henry Simons." Chap. 4 in *The Optimum Quantity of Money and Other Essays*. Chicago: Aldine.

———. 1968. "The Lessons of U.S. Monetary History and Their Bearing on Current Policy." Chap. 4 in *Dollars and Deficits*. Englewood Cliffs, N.J.: Prentice-Hall.

———. 1969. *The Optimum Quantity of Money and Other Essays*. Chicago: Aldine.

Friedman, M. and A. J. Schwartz. [1963] 1969. "Money and Business Cycles." Chap. 10 in M. Friedman, *The Optimum Quantity of Money and Other Essays*. Chicago: Aldine.

———. 1963. *A Monetary History of the United States, 1867–1960*. Princeton: Princeton Univ. Press.

———. 1982. *Monetary Trends in the United States and the United Kingdom: Their*

F

Relations to Income, Prices, and Interest Rates. Chicago: Univ. of Chicago Press.

Gordon, R. J., ed. 1970. *Milton Friedman's Monetary Framework: A Debate with His Critics.* Chicago: Univ. of Chicago Press.

Temin, P. 1976. *Did Monetary Forces Cause the Great Depression?* New York: Norton.

Tobin, J. 1965. "The Monetary Interpretation of History." *American Economic Review* 55:646–85.

————. 1970. "Post Hoc Ergo Propter Hoc?" *Quarterly Journal of Economics* 84:301–17.

Walters, A. W. 1987. "Milton Friedman." In *The New Palgrave: A Dictionary of Economics.* Vol. 2. Edited by J. Eatwell, M. Milgate, and P. Newman. London: Macmillan.

Frisch, Ragnar Anton Kittel (1896–1973)

Ragnar Frisch was professor of economics at University of Oslo (1931–65). He was a founder of the Econometric Society and the first editor of *Econometrica* (1933–55). In 1969, he was awarded along with Jan Tinbergen the first Nobel Memorial Prize in economics.

In the late 1920s and early 1930s, Frisch concentrated on the analysis of cyclical phenomena and the development of economic dynamic methods. His first works in the field were within the Mitchell-Persons tradition of empirical business-cycle analysis, decomposing time series by statistical tools and harmonic analysis. He worked out a modified decomposing method which, he claimed, did not require a fixed time length for each component nor a closed data set or an extremely large number of observations (Frisch 1931).

However, a few years later Frisch turned to a more genuinely theoretical approach in his study of the cycle. In 1933 he published his famous essay on propagation problems and impulse in dynamic economics, which was followed the next year by his *Lectures in Macrodynamics,* mimeographed in Norwegian, where he extended his analysis. The main idea of the essay goes back to Wicksell (1918, 70–71) who had observed that business-cycle analysis must consider, besides what may be regarded as the literal "causes" of cycles, the intrinsic structure of the economic system itself. Wicksell offered an admirable analogy. If a rocking horse is hit with a stick, the movement of the horse will be different from that of the stick. The hits are the cause of the movement, but the system's own equilibrium laws condition the form of the movement.

Frisch ([1933] 1965, 178–79) quoted Wicksell (and Johann Akerman), but noted that neither of them "had taken up to a closer mathematical study the *mechanism* by which such irregular fluctuations may be transformed into cycles." While observing that Slutsky ([1927] 1937) and Yule had established that some sort of swings will be produced by the accumulation of erratic influences, Frisch concluded that the main problem concerning the form of the propagation mechanism, and its economic interpretation, remained.

Frisch offered a model of the propagation mechanism which included only three variables: the production of capital goods, z; the production of consumption goods, x; and the inflow of new orders of capital goods, y. His model contained the acceleration principle, as y depended on x and its time derivative dx/dt. The construction of capital goods was supposed to be very time-consuming, hence x depended on an integral of y. The last equation explained the time derivative of x as a function of x and z. The multiplier was missing, as there was no (Keynesian) consumption function.

The dynamic structure of the model was complicated (being a mixed differential-difference type of system). But Frisch was able to work out the general form of the solution. He also made great and pioneering efforts to illustrate the properties of his model by simulating numerical examples. With plausible values of parameters, the model was found to generate a primary cycle with a period of about 8.5 years, and secondary and tertiary cycles with periods of 3.5 and 2.2 years. All cycles were heavily damped. The result, Frisch claimed, was of "considerable interest," because he strongly believed that economic systems (or the "rocking horse") were stable (implying that to explain recurrent cycles one had to account for erratic shocks providing the needed "energy" to keep fluctuations alive). Moreover, the lengths of the primary and secondary cycles corresponded nearly exactly to actual observations. In his *Lectures* he was able to demonstrate how his model produced recurrent cycles when hit by a series of erratic shocks; i.e., adding additive stochastic terms to his equations, he displayed a single computed time path of consumption x (as deviation from its average)

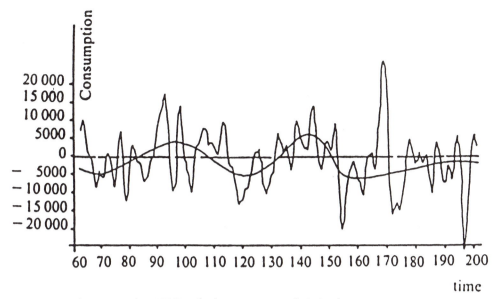

Figure 1. Frisch's computed (in 1934) path of consumption as deviation from mean.

which is reproduced above as Figure 1. (The figure also shows a moving-average curve which has a periodicity of about fifty years.) In this computed time path, Frisch claimed, without substantiation, to be able to distinguish an 8.5-year component as well as a less distinct 3.5-year component.

Thus, Frisch was able to demonstrate that erratic shocks can keep fluctuations alive even when the degree of dampening of the propagation mechanism is strong, and, moreover, that while the amplitude of the fluctuations may depend heavily on the size of the shocks, the length of the cycles is tied to the propagation mechanism. This result, preliminary in the 1930s as Frisch's mathematical analysis was in many ways rudimentary, was reinforced by Irma and Frank Adelman's simulation experiments with the Klein-Goldberger model of the United States. Frisch's cycle theory also suggested that, owing to the role of erratic shocks, fluctuations tend to be highly irregular and unpredictable. Thus, his model confirmed the well-known inability of forecasters to predict the phase of the cycle more than five or six quarters into the future.

Frisch himself felt that he had in principle solved the problem of how to account for cyclical fluctuations. He of course agreed that both his quite small model of the propagation mechanism and his short analysis of the nature of the impulses or shocks could be substantially elaborated and improved on. But he strongly believed in the stability axiom, and hence that the solution must rest on a "synthesis between the stochastical point of view, and the point of view of rigidly determined dynamic laws" (i.e., his deterministic model of the propagation mechanism)([1933] 1965, 178). He also believed that the periodicity of the cyclical fluctuations should be explained by the propagation mechanism, i.e., as a "free swing," and not linked to any periodic or quasi-periodic variable. His quite simple model was appropriate, he seems to have claimed, to give a first-approximation explanation of the cycle phenomenon.

Much modern analysis, such as that of Kydland and Prescott (1982), accords with Frisch in the sense that the discussion focuses on the nature of the impulses or shocks causing macroeconomic fluctuations studied within some impulse-propagating framework. Among the criticisms against this sort of analysis, one may mention that of Blatt (1980) who contends that all Frisch-type econometric models contradict the facts. This must be so, Blatt argues, because a linear model cannot explain the asserted important fact that downswings are as a rule shorter and more abrupt than upturns. Certainly, not all stylized facts associated with business cycles can be explained by a linear model. However, Frisch did not in principle assume a linear model of the propagation system. The linearity of his specified model is assumed a first approximation (Frisch [1933] 1965) to make the model manageable. In fact, the last section of Frisch's 1933 essay contains some suggestions which in an extended version of his model may help to explain dissimilarities between upturns and downturns.

Bjorn Thalberg

See also AKERMAN, JOHAN; ASYMMETRY; BUSINESS CYCLES; HAAVELMO, TRYGVE; KOOPMANS, TJALLINGS CHARLES; MACRO-ECONOMETRIC MODELS, HISTORICAL DEVELOPMENT; NONLINEAR THEORIES OF THE BUSINESS CYCLE; SLUTSKY, EUGEN; TINBERGEN, JAN; WICKSELL, JOHAN GUSTAV KNUT

Bibliography

Adelman, I. 1960. "Business Cycles—Endogenous or Exogenous?" *Economic Journal* 70:783–96.

Adelman, I. and F. L. Adelman. 1959. "The Dynamic Properties of the Klein-Goldberger Model." *Econometrica* 27:596–625.

Blatt, J. M. 1980. "On the Frisch Model of Business Cycles." *Oxford Economic Papers* 32:467–79.

Frisch, R. 1931. "A Method of Decomposing an Empirical Series into Its Cyclical and Progressive Components." *Journal of the American Statistical Association* 26(March Supplement): 73–78.

———. [1933] 1965. "Propagation Problems and Impulse Problems in Dynamic Economics." In *AEA Readings in Business-Cycle Theory*, 155–85. Homewood, Ill.: Irwin.

Kydland, F. and E. C. Prescott. 1982. "Time to Build and Aggregate Fluctuations." *Econometrica* 50:1345–70.

Slutsky, E. [1927] 1937. "The Summation of Random Causes as the Source of Cyclic Processes." *Econometrica* 5:105–46.

Thalberg, B. 1990. "A Reconsideration of Frisch's Original Cycle Model." In *Nonlinear and Multisectoral Macrodynamics: Essays in Honour of Richard Goodwin*, edited by K. Velupillai, 96–117. London: Macmillan.

Wicksell, K. 1918. "Karl Petander: Goda och dårliga tider." *Economic Tidskrift* 19:66–75.

Fullarton, John (1780–1849)

The reputation of John Fullarton, a surgeon and later banker in India, who retired to England after making his fortune, rests entirely on a single work, *On the Regulation of Currencies*. The work was a detailed criticism of the Currency Principle and its legislative embodiment, the Bank Charter Act of 1844. It established Fullarton as one of the leaders, along with Thomas Tooke, of the Banking School.

Fullarton's principal contribution to monetary analysis was his exposition of the law of reflux, which he applied to both country banks and to the Bank of England. The law of reflux as applied to the country banks stated that any excess issues of the banking system would be rapidly returned to the banking system before they could affect prices. The banking system, therefore, could not create an inflationary excess supply of money or cause an outflow of gold. A quantitative limit on the creation of liabilities by the banking system, such as that proposed by the Currency School, was neither necessary nor desirable.

The Law of Reflux has been mistakenly confused with the real-bills doctrine which, in one of its formulations, states that, so long as the banking system lends only the security of real bills of exchange, the banking system cannot create too much money. But, despite their superficial similarity, the two propositions are fundamentally distinct. The law of reflux asserts that there is a market mechanism by which the public can directly dispose of an excess supply of bank money without an inflationary increase in spending on goods, whereas the real-bills doctrine asserts that by limiting itself to the acceptance of certain kinds of liabilities the banking system will avoid creating an excess supply of money in the first place (Glasner 1992). In fact, the classical doctrine to which the law of reflux is logically related is Say's Law which, according to certain interpretations, says that an excess demand for money is directly satisfied by an increased quantity of bank money without a deflationary decrease in spending on goods (Glasner 1985, 1989).

Despite J. S. Mill's qualified support for the Banking School in general and the law of reflux in particular, the law of reflux never gained general acceptance among economists. Support was lacking, because Fullarton did not offer a convincing explanation of why an over-issue necessarily had to be returned to the banking system before stimulating an inflationary increase in spending. However, modern attempts to model a competitive banking system by Tobin (1963), Black (1970), Klein (1974), and Thompson (1974) have shown that the impossibility of overissue asserted by Fullarton is implicit in the profit-maximizing behavior of unregulated banks. Banks are limited in issuing their liabilities by the same considerations of marginal cost and marginal revenue that limit the expansion of every other business firm. An incentive for expansion at the margin could exist only if banks were effectively precluded from paying interest on their liabilities. Interestingly, Fullarton (1845, 92–93) cites the payment of interest on deposits as one reason that overissue is impossible.

Fullarton's application of the law of reflux to the Bank of England took account of the Bank's monopoly power. Fullarton recognized that by allowing its bill-discounting business to dwindle and by aggressively purchasing securities on the open market, the Bank could flood the market with its notes, putting upward pressure on prices (1845, 198–99). However, he also recognized that if the Bank followed an appropriate bank rate policy and maintained an active bill-discounting business, excess Bank notes would return via the reflux mechanism. His theory of the reflux of Bank of England notes was worked out in two examples, both of which assume that the Bank maintains bank rate at a level somewhat above the market rate on bills (1845, 78–80, 95–97).

Because Fullarton believed that the supply of money produced by the banking system adjusted automatically to the demand, he denied that the banking system was responsible for disturbances in the balance of payments. In the absence of monetary disturbances, only real disturbances could cause balance-of-payments deficits. Unlike monetary disturbances, real disturbances are necessarily self-limiting and temporary. All that was required of the Bank of England was to hold enough gold to be able to sustain any temporary outflow. Since a gold outflow did not signify an excess quantity of money, trying to halt the outflow by adopting a more restrictive credit stance might well trigger a financial panic.

Fullarton also outlined a theory of financial panics based on a credit cycle in which generally optimistic expectations about prices induce borrowing by speculators. If the expectations are disappointed, the borrowers may become insolvent, leading to a general liquidation and a collapse of prices. The banking system, in Fullarton's view, simply responded to such expectations and it was futile to try to suppress this cycle by restrictive regulations on the banking system.

Although his treatment of expectations was not in the spirit of the rational-expectations hypothesis, Fullarton's treatment of the money supply as a purely endogenous variable may be viewed as an anticipation of recent attempts by New Classical economists such as King and Plosser (1984) to model real business cycles in which money plays a purely passive role. As recent scholarship (e.g., Laidler [1972] 1975 and Glasner 1985, 1989, 1992) has begun to take a more favorable view of the Banking School than did earlier commentators such as Viner (1937) and Fetter (1965), Fullarton's stature as a monetary theorist is likely to become more widely acknowledged than it has been in the past.

David Glasner
Neil T. Skaggs

See also BANK CHARTER ACT OF 1844; BANKING SCHOOL, CURRENCY SCHOOL, AND FREE BANKING SCHOOL; CREDIT CYCLE; REAL-BILLS DOCTRINE; REAL BUSINESS-CYCLE THEORIES; SAY, JEAN-BAPTISTE; SAY'S LAW; SCHUMPETER, JOSEPH ALOIS; TOOKE, THOMAS

Bibliography
Black, F. 1970. "Banking and Interest Rates in a World Without Money: The Effects of Uncontrolled Banking." *Journal of Bank Research* 1:9–20.
Fetter, F. W. 1965. *The Evolution of British Monetary Orthodoxy, 1797–1875.* Cambridge: Harvard Univ. Press.
Fullarton, J. 1845. *On the Regulation of Currencies.* 2d ed. London: John Murray.
Glasner, D. 1985. "A Reinterpretation of Classical Monetary Theory." *Southern Economic Journal* 52:46–67.
———. 1989. "On Some Classical Monetary Controversies." *History of Political Economy* 21:201–29.
———. 1992. "The Real-Bills Doctrine in the Light of the Law of Reflux." *History of Political Economy* 24:201–28.
King, R. G. and C. I. Plosser. 1984. "Money, Credit, and Prices in a Real Business Cycle." *American Economic Review* 74:363–80.
Klein, B. 1974. "The Competitive Supply of Money." *Journal of Money, Credit and Banking* 6:423–53.

F

Laidler, D. [1972] 1975. "Thomas Tooke on Monetary Reform." Chap. 11 in *Essays on Money and Inflation*. Chicago: Univ. of Chicago Press.

Skaggs, N. T. 1991. "John Fullarton's Law of Reflux and Central Bank Policy." *History of Political Economy* 23:457–80.

Thompson, E. A. 1974. "The Theory of Money and Income Consistent with Orthodox Value Theory." In *Trade, Stability, and Macroeconomics*, edited by G. Horwich and P. A. Samuelson, 427–53. New York: Academic Press.

Tobin, J. 1963. "Banks as Creators of Money." In *Banking and Monetary Studies*, edited by D. Carson, 408–19. Homewood, Ill.: Irwin.

Viner, J. 1937. *Studies in the Theory of International Trade*. New York: Harper.

Full Information Maximum Likelihood

The likelihood principle provides a well-known method for estimating the parameters of an econometric model. Under suitable conditions, full information maximum-likelihood estimates are consistent and asymptotically efficient, and provide a convenient framework for testing economic and statistical hypotheses.

The role of maximum likelihood in modeling arises from the stochastic nature of economic phenomena. Economic variables may be viewed as the outcome of a complex unknown stochastic mechanism, often called the data generation process (DGP). The functional form of the DGP, the relevant set of economic variables, and the values of the associated parameters are all unknown. To draw inferences from the observed data about how the economy works, econometricians represent the DGP by a model. In doing so, they choose a particular function (often linear or log-linear) relating a specified set of economic variables over some sample period and postulate a family of distributions (usually the normal distribution), from which the unknown parameters in the postulated relationship may be estimated. These choices imply that operations such as marginalization (i.e., excluding variables) and conditioning (upon realized values of other variables) are performed on the DGP, so that the econometric model is implicitly a reduction of the DGP. Parameter estimates for the model can be obtained by the maximum-likelihood method using all or part of the information available,

leading to full or limited information maximum-likelihood estimates. Key issues include the relationship between density functions and likelihood, the representation of econometric models in a likelihood framework, the implications of parametric restrictions, and the properties of the resulting maximum-likelihood estimates.

Density Functions and Likelihood

Formally, an econometric model is expressed as a probabilistic distribution with a vector of random variables, denoted X (say). X includes variables such as consumption, income, the interest rate, and inflation, whose unknown generating mechanism we are seeking to specify. One way to solve this problem is to obtain a set of realizations $(x_1,...,x_T)$ on those random variables (i.e., a sample of T observations on X), choose a family of probability density functions $\mathcal{D}(x,\theta)$, and select from the family $\mathcal{D}$ the density that is most likely to have generated the sample. This may be accomplished by defining the likelihood function and maximizing it with respect to the unknown parameters θ.

The likelihood function is simply an alternative interpretation of the density. If θ were known, we would have a particular density out of the family $\mathcal{D}$, providing us with information on how the density varies with realized values of X. We will denote a specific density from $\mathcal{D}$ by $D(x; \theta)$. For unknown θ, D shows how the density changes with θ for a particular set of observed values of the random variables. This latter interpretation of D is known as the likelihood function, and we denote it by $L(\theta; x_1, x_2,...,x_T)$.

Density functions can be joint, marginal, or conditional: likewise with likelihoods. For instance, we may consider the (joint) likelihood of a whole set of variables (e.g., of consumption, income, the interest rate, and inflation), the (marginal) likelihood of a subset of variables (e.g., of consumption and income), and the likelihood of a subset of variables conditional upon realizations of another subset of variables (e.g., of consumption conditional on income, the interest rate, and inflation). All three types of likelihood are useful in econometrics.

Maximum Likelihood in Econometrics

Full information maximum likelihood (FIML) is a method for estimating systems of econometric equations with as many jointly determined variables as equations. To implement FIML, the likelihood function is specified in terms of observable variables via the econometric system and is maximized with respect to the system's unknown parameters. FIML's implementation depends upon whether the system is just identified or over-identified, as described below.

Econometric systems are inexact mathematical representations of relationships between observable economic variables, which are treated as endogenous or exogenous, with the former being conditioned upon the latter. Depending upon beliefs about the economic phenomena and the desired degree of approximation, systems may be formulated as linear or nonlinear, static or dynamic, simultaneous or recursive, and with white noise or autocorrelated disturbances. The disturbances are a set of unobservable variables reflecting the inexactness of the relationships, and they capture the effects of any factors that are actually involved in the DGP but are not explicitly included in the system.

FIML requires specifying both the system of econometric relationships and the distribution of the disturbances. Doing so implies a family of joint densities for the endogenous variables and thereby the corresponding likelihood function conditional upon the exogenous variables. For expositional convenience, we consider linear systems with normal disturbances.

Following Koopmans, Rubin, and Leipnik (1950), we write the system as:

$$By_t + Cz_t = u_t, \qquad (1)$$

where B and C are $n \times n$ and $n \times k$ matrices of unknown coefficients (i.e., parameters); y_t, z_t, and u_t are $n \times 1$, $k \times 1$, and $n \times 1$ vectors of the endogenous variables, strongly exogenous variables, and disturbances, all at time t; and $(y_t' z_t')'$ is the x_t from above. Equation (1) is known as the structural form of the system. Generalizations on equation (1) include dynamics (Hendry 1976), weakly rather than strongly exogenous z's (Engle, Hendry, and Richard 1983), and autoregressive or autoregressive moving-average error processes (Hendry 1976, Reinsel 1979). FIML requires a somewhat different derivation in these instances, so we restrict ourselves to equation (1).

The distribution of the disturbances,

$$D_u(u_1, u_2, ..., u_T; \theta), \qquad (2)$$

can be transformed into the joint density of the y's conditional upon the z's:

$$D_y(y_1, y_2, ..., y_T; \alpha \mid Z) = \\ |\det J| \cdot D_u(u_1, u_2, ..., u_T; \theta)|_y. \qquad (3)$$

The vector α contains the parameters resulting from the transformation and involves functions of B, C, and the parameter vector θ specifying the distribution of the u's. Z is the matrix of T observations on z_t; $|_y$ means that the u's in D_u are replaced by their expressions in terms of the y's (and z's); and $|\det J|$ is the absolute value of the determinant of the Jacobian matrix for that transformation, where the Jacobian matrix J is given by:

$$J = \frac{\partial\left((u_1' ... u_T')'\right)}{\partial(y_1' ... y_T')} = \begin{bmatrix} \dfrac{\partial u_1}{\partial y_1'} & \cdots & \dfrac{\partial u_1}{\partial y_T'} \\ \vdots & \ddots & \vdots \\ \dfrac{\partial u_T}{\partial y_1'} & \cdots & \dfrac{\partial u_T}{\partial y_T'} \end{bmatrix}. \qquad (4)$$

The function D_y in equation (3) shows how the density varies for all feasible values of the y's conditional on values of the z's, or alternatively how the density changes as α changes for a given sample of the y's. The latter interpretation can be emphasized by writing D_y in equation (3) as follows:

$$L(\alpha; y_1, ..., y_T \mid Z). \qquad (5)$$

L in equation (5) is called the likelihood function of the y's.

By maximizing L with respect to α, we obtain the maximum-likelihood estimate of α. Difficulties arise if more than one estimate is associated with the maximum of the likelihood function: the data do not distinguish between these estimates. A model with such estimates is said to be unidentified, i.e., different mathematical representations of the model are observationally equivalent. The identification problem may be solved by using additional information on the parameters in B and C and on the distribution of the disturbances, since alternative mathematical representations may be affected differently by such information. This information may entail that the system in equation (1) is underidentified, just-identified, or overidentified. That is, too little, just enough, or too much information exists to identify the system. Because underidentified equations cannot be estimated uniquely, we consider FIML estimation of just-identified and overidentified systems only.

FIML for a Just-Identified System

Premultiplying equation (1) by B^{-1} yields the reduced form of the system, i.e.,

$$Y' = \Pi Z' + V', \qquad (6)$$

where $\Pi = -B^{-1}C$; $V' = B^{-1}U'$; and Y', Z', and U' are the matrices of T observations on the endogenous variables, exogenous variables, and disturbances in system (1). In the just-identified case, $\Pi = -B^{-1}C$ defines a unique mapping between the reduced form and structural form parameters. Thus, FIML in the just-identified case can be derived from equation (6) because the estimates of the parameters in the structural form [equation (1)] can be uniquely obtained from the estimates of the parameters in equation (6).

To obtain the maximum-likelihood estimator of the parameters Π and Ω (and so of B, C, and Σ), the precise distribution of u_t must be specified. As is common in practice, we assume that u_t is independently and identically distributed as a multivariate normal variable with zero mean and covariance Σ. Because V is a linear transformation of U, V is also normally distributed, having a density:

$$D_v\left(v_1, \ldots, v_T; \Omega\right) =$$
$$(2\pi)^{-nT/2}(\det \Omega)^{-T/2} \exp\left\{-\frac{1}{2}\operatorname{tr}\Omega^{-1}V'V\right\}, \quad (7)$$

where Ω $(=B^{-1}\Sigma(B')^{-1})$ is the variance covariance matrix of the v_t's. From equation (7), we can transform the v's into the y's and obtain the latter's density as in equation (3). We will interpret the resulting density as a likelihood function, as in equation (5):

$$L\left(\Pi, \Omega; y_1, \ldots, y_T \mid z_1, \ldots, z_T\right)$$
$$= (2\pi)^{-nT/2}(\det \Omega)^{-T/2}$$
$$\cdot \exp\left\{-\frac{1}{2}\operatorname{tr}\Omega^{-1}(Y' - \Pi Z')(Y - Z\Pi')\right\}. \quad (8)$$

For mathematical convenience, FIML estimates of Π and Ω are obtained by maximizing the logarithm of L in equation (8) rather than L itself; and parameters are stacked using the row-vectoring operator vec, which transforms a matrix into a vector by stacking the transposed rows of the matrix, one below the other.

To obtain the maximum-likelihood estimate (MLE) $\hat{\Pi}$ of Π, we differentiate $\ln L$ with respect to vec Π and equate this derivative to zero. That obtains:

$$\hat{\Pi} = Y'Z(Z'Z)^{-1}. \qquad (9)$$

We obtain the maximum-likelihood estimate of Ω by concentrating the log-likelihood of equation (8) with respect to Π [i.e., replacing Π with $\hat{\Pi}$ from equation (9)] and differentiating that concentrated log-likelihood with respect to vec Ω^{-1}. The resulting MLE $\hat{\Omega}$ of Ω is:

$$\hat{\Omega} = T^{-1}(Y'M_Z Y) = T^{-1}(\hat{V}'\hat{V}), \qquad (10)$$

where $M_Z = I - Z(Z'Z)^{-1}Z'$ and $\hat{V}$ is the matrix of residuals $Y - Z\hat{\Pi}'$. Equations (9) and (10) parallel the standard least-squares estimates in the regression framework, where least squares is in fact maximum likelihood. Because maximum likelihood is invariant to one-to-one transformations, the MLEs of B, C, and Σ can be obtained by solving:

$$\hat{B}\hat{\Pi} + \hat{C} = 0 \qquad (11)$$

$$\hat{\Omega} = \hat{B}^{-1}\hat{\Sigma}\left(\hat{B}^{-1}\right)'. \qquad (12)$$

FIML for an Overidentified System

FIML for overidentified equations must be obtained directly from the structural form because the unrestricted reduced form estimates of Π and Ω in equations (9)–(10) do not map uniquely to the restricted estimates for the structural parameters B, C, and Σ. We start by setting up the density of U:

$$D_u\left(u_1, \ldots, u_T; \Sigma\right) =$$
$$(2\pi)^{-nT/2}(\det \Sigma)^{-T/2} \exp\left\{-\frac{1}{2}\operatorname{tr}\Sigma^{-1}U'U\right\}. \quad (13)$$

We transform the u's into the y's [as in equation (3)], expressed as a likelihood [equivalent to (5)]:

$$L\left(B, C, \Sigma; y_1, \ldots, y_T \mid z_1, \ldots, z_T\right)$$
$$= |\det B|^T (2\pi)^{-nT/2}(\det \Sigma)^{-T/2}$$
$$\cdot \exp\left\{-\frac{1}{2}\operatorname{tr}\Sigma^{-1}(BY' + CZ')(YB' + ZC')\right\}. \quad (14)$$

The FIML estimates of B, C, and Σ are obtained in two stages: maximize $\ln L$ with respect to vec Σ^{-1}; and maximize ln L with respect to vec B' and vec C', having concentrated ln L with respect to Σ via the latter's solution in the first stage. Without concentration, the first-order conditions (in reverse order) are:

$$\frac{\partial \ln L}{\partial \operatorname{vec} A'} = -\operatorname{vec} Q\, Z'XA'\Sigma^{-1} = 0 \qquad (15)$$

$$\Sigma = T^{-1}(AX'XA'), \qquad (16)$$

where $A = (B\ C)$, $X = (Y\ Z)$, $Q' = (\Pi'\ I_k)$, and I_k is a $k \times k$ identity matrix.

FIML estimates solve equations (15)–(16) and require specifying the restrictions on A and Σ. For instance, with linear restrictions on A alone, we have:

$$\operatorname{vec} A' = S\psi + s, \qquad (17)$$

where S is a selection matrix of known constants, s is a vector of known constants, and ψ is the vector of the unrestricted coefficients from A. Hence, from equations (15) and (17):

$$\frac{\partial \ln L}{\partial \psi'} = \left[\frac{\partial \ln L}{\partial \operatorname{vec} A'}\right]' \frac{\partial \operatorname{vec} A'}{\partial \psi'} =$$

$$-\left(\operatorname{vec} Q Z'XA'\Sigma^{-1}\right)' S. \qquad (18)$$

Finally, by solving:

$$S'\operatorname{vec}\hat{Q}Z'X\hat{A}'\hat{\Sigma}^{-1} = 0, \qquad (19)$$

we find the FIML estimates $\hat{\psi}$ of ψ, i.e., of the unrestricted coefficients in A. The restricted estimates of B and C are obtained from equation (17) evaluated at $\hat{\psi}$. To solve equation (19), we require iterative procedures such as those developed in Powell (1964) or Gill, Murray, and Pitfield (1972).

Equation (19) has an econometric as well as numerical interpretation. Hendry (1976) derived it, calling it the "estimator generating equation" because almost all known econometric estimators for linear systems can be obtained by solving this equation for particular values of Σ, A, and Q. For instance, three-stage least squares can be obtained by setting Σ to its two-stage least-squares value and defining the Π in Q as the ordinary least-squares estimator of the unrestricted reduced form Π matrix. Hausman (1977) provides an instrumental variables representation akin to equation (19).

Properties of FIML

Under suitable regularity conditions, $\hat{\psi}$ approaches ψ as the sample size increases, $\hat{\psi}$ is normally distributed in large samples after suitable rescaling, and $\hat{\psi}$ is asymptotically efficient. Formally,

$$\hat{\psi} \overset{a.s.}{\to} \psi \qquad (20)$$

and

$$\sqrt{T}\left(\hat{\psi} - \psi\right) \underset{a}{\sim}$$

$$N\left(0, \left[\operatorname{plim} T^{-1}S'\left(QZ'X \otimes \Sigma^{-1}\right)S\right]^{-1}\right), \qquad (21)$$

where $\overset{a.s.}{\to}$ denotes almost sure convergence, $\underset{a}{\sim}$ stands for "is asymptotically distributed as," and plim denotes "the probability limit as $T \to \infty$."

The likelihood also provides the basis for testing economic and statistical hypotheses. For instance, after FIML estimation, we can test the validity of the overidentifying restrictions with the likelihood-ratio statistic, defined as:

$$-2\ln\left(\frac{L_2}{L_1}\right) \underset{a}{\sim} \chi_p^2, \qquad (22)$$

where L_1 and L_2 are values of the likelihood function evaluated at their just-identified and overidentified maximum-likelihood estimates, and there are p overidentifying restrictions, corresponding to p degrees of freedom in the χ^2 distribution. We can also test for cointegration within a set of economic variables after FIML estimation of a vector autoregressive (VAR) system. In this case, the likelihood-ratio statistic is not asymptotically distributed as a χ^2, but Johansen (1988), Johansen and Juselius (1990), and Osterwald-Lenum (1992) provide suitable critical values.

Advantages and Disadvantages of FIML Estimates

FIML estimates may benefit or suffer from using all information in the system. Except in special situations, full information methods are more efficient than limited information techniques. However, FIML may be inconsistent if some part of the system is misspecified. Also, FIML estimation may be infeasible if the sample size is too small relative to the number of parameters being estimated. Under weak conditions, the FIML estimator described above is consistent and asymptotically normally distributed in linear models, even if the disturbances are nonnormal (Mann and Wald 1943, Anderson and Rubin 1950, Chernoff and Rubin 1953). However, for nonlinear models, correct specification of the error distribution may be required to ensure consistency (Amemiya 1977, Phillips 1982).

Julia Campos
Neil R. Ericsson

See also COINTEGRATION; DISTRIBUTED LAGS; LUCAS CRITIQUE; MACROECONOMETRIC MODELS, HISTORICAL DEVELOPMENT; VECTOR AUTOREGRESSIONS

Bibliography

Amemiya, T. 1977. "The Maximum Likelihood and the Nonlinear Three-stage Least Squares Estimator in the General Nonlinear Simultaneous Equation Model." *Econometrica* 45:955–68.

Anderson, T. W. and H. Rubin. 1950. "The Asymptotic Properties of Estimates of the Parameters of a Single Equation in a Complete System of Stochastic Equations." *Annals of Mathematical Statistics* 21:570–82.

Chernoff, H. and H. Rubin. 1953. "Asymptotic Properties of Limited-information Estimates under Generalized Conditions." In *Studies in Econometric Method*, Cowles Foundation Monograph 14. Edited by W. C. Hood and T. C. Koopmans, 200–12. New Haven: Yale Univ. Press.

Engle, R. F., D. F. Hendry, and J.-F. Richard. 1983. "Exogeneity." *Econometrica* 51:277–304.

Gill, P. E., W. Murray, and R. A. Pitfield. 1972. "The Implementation of Two Revised Quasi-Newton Algorithms for Unconstrained Optimization." *National Physical Laboratory Report*, NAC 11.

Hausman, J. A. 1977. "Errors in Variables in Simultaneous Equation Models." *Journal of Econometrics* 5:389–401.

Hendry, D. F. 1976. "The Structure of Simultaneous Equations Estimators." *Journal of Econometrics* 4:51–88.

Johansen, S. 1988. "Statistical Analysis of Cointegration Vectors." *Journal of Economic Dynamics and Control* 12:231–54.

Johansen, S. and K. Juselius. 1990. "Maximum Likelihood Estimation and Inference on Cointegration—With Applications to the Demand for Money." *Oxford Bulletin of Economics and Statistics* 52:169–210.

Koopmans, T. C., H. Rubin, and R. B. Leipnik. 1950. "Measuring the Equation Systems of Dynamic Economics." In *Statistical Inference in Dynamic Economic Models*, Cowles Foundation Monograph 10. Edited by T. C. Koopmans, 53–237. New York: Wiley.

Mann, H. B. and A. Wald. 1943. "On the Statistical Treatment of Linear Stochastic Difference Equations." *Econometrica* 11:173–220.

Osterwald-Lenum, M. 1992. "A Note with Quantiles of the Asymptotic Distribution of the Maximum Likelihood Cointegration Rank Test Statistics." *Oxford Bulletin of Economics and Statistics* 54:461–72.

Phillips, P. C. B. 1982. "On the Consistency of Nonlinear FIML." *Econometrica* 50:1307–24.

Powell, M. J. D. 1964. "An Efficient Method for Finding the Minimum of a Function of Several Variables without Calculating Derivatives." *Computer Journal* 7:155–62.

Reinsel, G. 1979. "FIML Estimation of the Dynamic Simultaneous Equations Model with ARMA Disturbances." *Journal of Econometrics* 9:263–81.

Functional Finance

Functional finance is a policy in which government fiscal policy, its spending and taxing, its borrowing and repayment of loans, its issue of new money and its withdrawal of money, shall all be taken with an eye only to the results of these actions on the economy. This policy consists of three rules (Lerner 1941, 4–5):

1. The government shall maintain a reasonable level of demand at all times. If there is not enough spending so that there is excessive unemployment, the government shall reduce taxes or increase its own spending. If there is too much spending the government shall prevent inflation by reducing its own expenditures or by increasing taxes.

2. By borrowing money when it wishes to raise the rate of interest and by lending money or repaying debt when it wishes to lower the rate of interest, the government shall maintain that rate of interest which induces the optimum amount of investment.

3. If either of the first two rules conflict with the principles of "sound finance" or of balancing the budget or of limiting the national debt, so much the worse for these principles. The government press shall print any money that may be needed in carrying out these rules.

While the rules seem simple, in 1941, when Abba Lerner first published them, they were revolutionary, because they broke with the political timidity of most Keynesians, stating clearly that, in Keynesian economics, deficits and debt do not matter; what matters is the deficit's effect on the level of employment and inflation. The rules of functional finance became synonymous with the Keynesian policies that were taught in the textbooks: monetary and fiscal policy should be conducted to achieve the desired level of employment and inflation.

By the late 1960s, Lerner recognized that these three rules were insufficient to deal with simultaneous unemployment and inflation and began trying to remedy that insufficiency. In the 1970s, he concurred with a colleague's addition of a fourth rule of functional finance (Colander 1979):

4. The government must establish policies which stabilize the price level and coordinate both the money supply rule and the aggregate total spending rule with this stable price level.

The policy Lerner was working on at the time of his death was designed to supplement monetary and fiscal policy to implement this rule. That policy was the market anti-inflation plan (MAP), which would establish property rights in prices, so that in order to change their price, individuals would have to buy the right from other individuals who would change their price by an offsetting amount. This policy would directly control the aggregate price level while allowing individuals to set whatever relative price they desired, as long as they adhered to the rules. Lerner held that MAP would internalize the inflation externality and permit the first three rules of functional finance to be devoted to maintaining high employment.

David Colander

See also Fiscal Policy; Lerner, Abba

Bibliography

Colander, D. 1979. "Rationality, Expectations and Functional Finance." In *Essays in Post Keynesian Inflation,* edited by J. Gapinski and C. Rockwood, 197–215. Cambridge, Mass.: Ballinger.

Lerner, A. 1941. "The Economic Steering Wheel." *The University Review* 7:2–8.

———. 1944. *The Economics of Control.* New York: Macmillan.

———. 1983. *Selected Writings of Abba Lerner.* Edited by D. Colander. New York: New York Univ. Press.

G

Gesell, Silvio (1862–1930)

The monetary heretic Silvio Gesell was described by J. M. Keynes ([1936] 1973, 353) as a "strange, unduly neglected prophet . . . whose work contains flashes of deep insight and who only just failed to reach down to the essence of the matter." His proposal for stamped scrip attracted the favorable notice of Keynes and Irving Fisher.

Born in Rhenish Prussia, in an area later ceded to Belgium, of a German father and a French mother, Gesell emigrated to Argentina in 1886, where he was successful enough as an importer and as a manufacturer of cardboard boxes to be able to retire to Switzerland in 1900. His first two works on currency reform were published in German in Buenos Aires in 1891, and were influenced by the Argentine monetary disorder of the period. Although opposed to socialism (except of land), Gesell served as Minister of Finance in the short-lived Bavarian Soviet Republic in April 1919. He was subsequently tried and acquitted by court-martial for high treason.

Gesell's major work, *The Natural Economic Order,* was published in two parts in 1906 and 1911. Dedicated to the memory of Henry George (and Moses and Spartacus), this book proposed a system of rent-free land and interest-free money. Gesell's plan for land nationalization, using state bonds to compensate the owners, was similar to other, contemporaneous plans for land nationalization, such as that advanced by Leon Walras, and to George's proposal for taxing away the unearned increment of land value. Gesell's innovation was the idea to allow money to remain current only if a stamp purchased from the government was regularly affixed. Money would lose 0.1 percent of its value per week unless stamped, and the price of the stamp was to equal the amount of depreciation that would be avoided by stamping. Hoarding would thus be discouraged by being taxed without inflationary overissue of notes, and money rates of interest would be driven to zero by reducing the nominal rate of return on money below zero.

Although, as Keynes noted, Gesell's scheme had theoretical flaws, notably his assumption that money is the only asset with a liquidity premium, Gesell for a time attracted a significant following, and several "free money" experiments were tried on a local level, such as the one reported by Gaitskell ([1929] 1934) in Worgl in the Austrian Tyrol. Both Fisher and Keynes acknowledged Gesell as a precursor of some of their own proposals for reducing money rates of interest during periods of inadequate effective demand.

Robert W. Dimand

See also DOUGLAS, CLIFFORD HUGH; FISHER, IRVING; KEYNES, JOHN MAYNARD; LIQUIDITY PREMIUM

Bibliography

Darrity, W. 1995. "Keynes' Political Philosophy: The Gesell Connection." *Eastern Economic Journal* 21:27–41.

Dillard, D. 1942. "Gesell's Monetary Theory of Social Reform." *American Economic Review* 32:348–52.

Fisher, I. 1932a. *Booms and Depressions.* Appendix VII. New York: Adelphi.

———. 1932b. *Stamp Scrip.* New York: Adelphi.

Gaitskell, H. T. N. 1933. "Four Monetary Heretics." In *What Everybody Wants to*

Know About Money, edited by G. D. H. Cole, 280–335. London: Gollancz.

Gesell, S. [1929] 1934. *The Natural Economic Order.* 6th ed. Translation. With a biographical note by H. R. Fack. San Antonio, Texas: Free-Economy Publishing Co.

Keynes, J. M. [1936] 1973. "Notes on Mercantilism, the Usury Laws, Stamped Money and Theories of Under-Consumption." Chap. 23 in *The General Theory of Employment, Interest and Money.* Vol. 7 of *The Collected Writings of John Maynard Keynes.* London: Macmillan.

Gilbert, James William (1794–1863)

The leading theorist of the Free Banking School in the British monetary controversies of the 1830s and 1840s, J. W. Gilbart helped to develop a monetary theory of the origin and transmission of the business cycle that blamed the crises of 1825, 1836, and 1839 on the overexpansions and subsequent contractions of the Bank of England. He contributed to the theory of free banking as a self-regulatory monetary order in several works in the 1830s and 1840s. He also gave important testimony before the 1841 Select Committee on Banks of Issues.

As manager of the London and Westminster Bank from its founding in 1833 to his retirement in 1859, Gilbart was a spokesman for the interests of the joint-stock banks. These banks had come on the English scene after legal barriers were lowered, in accord with the Scottish free-banking model, in 1826 and 1833. In contrast to representatives of the Currency School (e.g., Lord Overstone) and spokesmen for the Bank of England who considered the joint-stock banks a source of monetary disturbance, Gilbart argued that the note circulation of competitive banks were necessarily governed by the "needs of trade" (i.e., were demand-determined). He provided statistical evidence on the seasonality of the demand for currency.

In contrast to the Banking School (e.g., Thomas Tooke and John Fullarton), Gilbart found the Bank of England *not* similarly constrained, and in fact guilty of having initiated unsustainable booms by unwarranted expansions of its issues. Like the Banking School, however, he was influenced by the real-bills doctrine. He suggested that the Bank could avoid overissue by ceasing to issue notes through purchases of bullion and government securities, and instead discounting only commercial paper. Here he confused the demand for discounts with the demand to hold banknotes.

Because the circulation of the joint-stock banks in England and Scotland was constrained by competition, it required no political control. The Bank of England should be subject to similar constraint by repealing its legal monopoly on note issue within sixty-five miles of London. Gilbart thus opposed the program of the Currency School to place the issue of notes entirely in the hands of one institution, and to regulate that institution by an artificial rule. However, Peel's Bank Charter Act of 1844 coopted his opposition by freezing both entry into note issue and existing banks' shares of the circulation, relieving competitive pressures on the joint-stock banks. Gilbart published a series of letters under a pseudonym (1845) pointing out to his fellow joint-stock bankers that the cartelizing provisions of Peel's Act favored their interests, however defective was its rule for regulating the note issue.

Despite his co-option, and despite his acceptance of the real-bills doctrine, Gilbart was an articulate spokesman for the free-banking position, and an important early developer and publicizer of the theory that business cycles are principally caused by monetary shocks emanating from the central bank.

Lawrence H. White

See also BANK CHARTER ACT OF 1844; BANKING SCHOOL, CURRENCY SCHOOL, AND FREE BANKING SCHOOL; FULLARTON, JOHN; LOYD, SAMUEL JONES; MUSHET, ROBERT; PARNELL, HENRY BROOKE; TOOKE, THOMAS; TORRENS, ROBERT

Bibliography

Gilbart, J. W. 1834. *The History and Principles of Banking.* London: Longmans.

———. 1837. *The History of Banking in America: with . . . a Review of the Causes of the Recent Pressure on the Money Market.* London: Longmans.

———. 1840. *An Inquiry into the Causes of the Pressure on the Money Market during the Year 1839.* London: Longmans.

———. 1841. *Currency and Banking: A Review.* London: H. Hooper.

———. 1844. "The Laws of Currency." *Foreign and Colonial Quarterly Review* 3:592–622.

———. 1845. *The Letters of Nehemiah; Re-*

lating to the Laws of Joint Stock Banks. London, n.p.

———. 1865–66. *The Works of James William Gilbart.* London: Bell and Paldy.

Gregory, T. E., ed. 1964. *Select Statutes Documents and Reports Relating to British Banking 1832–1928.* Vol. 1. London: Frank Cass.

White, L. H. 1984. *Free Banking in Britain: Theory, Experience, and Debate, 1800–1845.* Cambridge: Cambridge Univ. Press.

Wood, E. 1939. *English Theories of Central Banking Control, 1819–1858.* Cambridge: Harvard Univ. Press.

Glass-Steagall Act

The Banking Act of 1933, generally known as the Glass-Steagall Act, responded to the banking crises of the 1930s and restructured the American banking system. This act regulated interest rates, created deposit insurance, and increased the powers of the Federal Reserve System. It is of continuing importance because it separated commercial and investment banking, by forbidding Federal Reserve member banks from affiliating with firms engaged in the issue, floatation, underwriting, public sale, or distribution at wholesale or retail of securities.

The Glass-Steagall Act ended the growing penetration of investment banking by commercial banks. In the late nineteenth century, commercial banks began to enter the securities business by offering brokerage services through their bond departments. Legally barred from handling stocks, banks could directly offer only a limited number of services. The need to compete with investment banks by providing a wider range of financial services led a few banks to establish securities affiliates before the First World War. Unlike their parent commercial banks, these subsidiaries could engage in all aspects of investment banking.

The movement into investment banking accelerated in World War I, when banks were pressed into selling government bonds. After the war, new opportunities arose in the securities business. The market for foreign bonds grew as the United States became a creditor nation, and the market for domestic stocks and bonds swelled as firms began to switch their financing from commercial loans. Commercial banks were able to compete successfully with investment banks, because strong complementarities between the supply of the two types of financial services reduced the costs of supplying each one by a single entity. These advantages and the growth of the securities markets rapidly allowed them to acquire a large share of the business.

After the stock market crashed in October 1929, Congress, the press, and the public looked for scapegoats. The coincidence of the stock-market boom and commercial banks' entry into the securities markets led some observers to blame the securities affiliates. The affiliates were criticized for undermining the soundness of parent banks and for conflicts of interest in serving both their depositors and buyers of securities.

There is, however, very little evidence to suggest that the affiliates contributed to the banking crises of the 1930s. Very few banks with affiliates failed, and their liquidity and solvency were not impaired. Banks with affiliates were large and diversified, characteristics that helped to protect them during the banking crises. Although there were abuses in the sales and manipulation of securities, investment banks were also involved. These problems were generally solved by the New Deal regulation of the securities markets, which could have simply been extended to the affiliates, without divorcing commercial and investment banking.

Federal supervision of affiliates would have satisfied almost all legislators, but Senator Carter Glass, who insisted that commercial banks must be excluded from the securities business for banking to be safe and sound. A fervent believer in the real-bills doctrine, Glass wanted banks to provide only short-term credit to finance the production or exchange of goods. As chairman of the Senate's Banking Committee and an influential member of the Democratic Party, he was able to have his views adopted in the 1932 party platform and put into the Banking Act of 1933.

Senator Glass successfully eliminated the securities affiliates, but commercial banks still retained a few investment-banking functions. They were permitted to underwrite securities of the federal government and general-obligation municipal bonds, because these were believed to be low-risk activities. This exception implicitly recognized a cost-benefit test for allowing banks into some parts of the securities business. Commercial-bank subsidiaries were allowed to engage in some investment banking, as long as it was not their principal activity. This loophole has led to long legal battles over the Glass-Steagall Act. Commercial banks have constantly tested its limits, but with only modest success. Although blocked domestically, they have entered investment banking overseas. Many American banks have overseas affiliates that underwrite and deal in the Eurosecurities markets.

In spite of the regulations in place, there was a trend in the 1980s towards reintegrating commercial and investment banking, raising the possibility of an eventual repeal of the Glass-Steagall Act. However, these developments were halted by the 1987 stock-market crash that made investment banking less attractive to commercial banks and Congress more cautious. A further impediment to any change in the law has been the deposit-insurance debacle, which has made deposit-insurance reform a precondition for allowing commercial banks to engage in new forms of risk taking.

Eugene N. White

See also BANKING AND FINANCIAL REGULATION; GREAT DEPRESSION IN THE UNITED STATES (1929–1938); REAL-BILLS DOCTRINE; STOCK MARKET CRASH OF 1929

Bibliography

Huertas, T. F. 1984. "The Economic Brief Against Glass-Steagall." *Journal of Bank Research* 15:148–59.
Perkins, E. J. 1971. "The Divorce of Commercial and Investment Banking: A History." *Banking Law Journal* 88:483–529.
White, E. N. 1986. "Before the Glass-Steagall Act: An Analysis of the Investment Banking Activities of National Banks." *Explorations in Economic History* 23:33–55.

Gold Standard

The essence of the gold standard is the definition of the monetary unit as a fixed weight of gold and free conversion of currency (all forms of money) into gold at the fixed price. Thus, the Coinage Act of 1792 defined a dollar as 24.74 grains of gold with 480 grains to the ounce. This was equivalent to $19.39 per ounce. The mint price was raised in 1834 to $20.67 per ounce and remained there until 1933.

The gold standard can operate as both a domestic standard—the arrangements regulating the quantity and growth rate of the internal money supply, and as an international standard—the arrangements by which the external value of the currency is determined. Domesti-

cally, because new production would add a small fraction to the accumulated stock and because of the guarantee of the authorities of free convertibility of nongold money into gold, the gold standard assured that the money supply, and hence, the price level would not fluctuate excessively. Internationally, fixing the price of gold ensured fixed exchange rates among countries adhering to the gold standard and closely linked national price levels either by the operation of the price-specie-flow mechanism (aided by capital flows) or by commodity arbitrage. A fixed exchange rate also ensured that both monetary and nonmonetary shocks would be transmitted via gold and capital flows between countries. Central banks, where they existed, held national gold reserves and were supposed to play by the "rules of the game"— raising their discount rates in case of a gold outflow, lowering their discount rates in case of a gold inflow. Long-run world price stability would be ensured in accordance with the commodity theory of money. Falling (rising) price levels would encourage (discourage) gold production and the substitution of monetary for nonmonetary stocks.

The gold standard evolved in the eighteenth century from gold-silver bimetallism. England adopted a de facto gold standard in 1717 after the Master of the Mint, Sir Isaac Newton, overvalued the silver guinea. Gold became the de jure standard in 1819. The United States, though formally on a bimetallic standard, switched to gold de facto in 1834 and de jure in 1900. Other major countries joined the gold standard in the 1870s. The period 1880 to 1914 was the era of the classical gold standard when the majority of countries adhered (in varying degrees) to gold. The period was one of unprecedented prosperity with relatively free trade in goods, labor, and capital.

The classical gold standard broke down during World War I, and a period of "managed fiduciary money" followed. The gold standard was briefly reinstated from 1925 to 1931 as a *gold exchange standard*, under which gold was generally withdrawn from circulation and foreign exchange as well as gold were held as monetary reserves. The Bretton Woods system, instituted in 1944, was an attempt to adopt an attenuated gold exchange standard (without free conversion). The United States pegged the price of gold at $35 an ounce and other currencies pegged their exchange rates to the dollar.

When the United States in 1971 ceased pegging the price of gold, the gradual demise of the gold standard was completed.

The gold standard, as it operated in its heyday, was characterized by long-term, but not short-term, price stability; exchange-rate stability; the international transmission of nominal and real shocks; and synchronous movements in national price levels.

Long-term price stability may be explained in accordance with the commodity theory of money—gold supplies responded (through lengthy lags) to movements in its real price (Bordo 1981). However, periodic surges in the world's gold stock were a significant source of short-term price instability (Rockoff 1984).

Recent evidence suggests that although exchange rates in principal countries frequently deviated from par, violations of the gold points were rare (Officer 1986) as were devaluations by major countries. Suspension of convertibility in England (1797–1821, 1914–25) and the United States (1862–78) occurred in wartime emergencies, but resumption at the original parity, as promised, after the emergency fortified the credibility of the gold standard.

Under the gold standard, both monetary and real shocks were transmitted through the balance of payments, thereby affecting domestic money supplies, expenditures, price levels, and real income. The price-specie-flow mechanism worked through the current account supplemented by the capital account (Bordo and Schwartz 1988).

An example of monetary disturbance was a gold discovery in a large country. To the extent that the new gold was monetized, the increase in the money stock raised domestic expenditure, nominal income, and, ultimately, the price level. The rise in the domestic price level improved the terms of trade, but a balance-of-payments deficit resulted. The same forces produced balance-of-trade surpluses in the country's trading partners.

The deficit was financed by a specie outflow from the inflating country to its trading partners, reducing the monetary gold stock in the former and raising it in the latter. As a consequence, money supplies increased in countries trading with the inflating country, raising domestic expenditure, nominal income, and ultimately, price levels. Depending on the share of the inflating country's monetary gold stock in the world total, world prices and income rose. Monetary change initially affected real output, reflecting possible rigidities, but eventually its full effect was on the price level.

Since the initial effects of increases in the money supply tend to reduce interest rates, capital flows abroad were also a channel of transmission. Short-term capital inflows, however, provided temporary financing of current-account deficits.

An alternative channel was price arbitrage. Insofar as the law of one price held, the prices of traded goods were continuously equated across the world without relative prices of exports and imports having to adjust. However, relative prices of traded and nontraded goods domestically would be altered. Fixed exchange rates and traded-goods arbitrage entailed parallel national price-level movements (McCloskey and Zecher 1976).

Monetary induced business cycles were transmitted through the specie standard from Great Britain to the United States before the Civil War, and in the reverse direction thereafter (Huffman and Lothian 1984). In addition, financial crises including stock-market crashes and bank runs occurred nearly simultaneously in numerous countries linked together under the classical gold standard (Bordo 1986).

Real shocks, such as harvest failures in England, affected numerous other countries closely linked to gold. The shocks were transmitted through the current account and the Bank of England reaction to an external drain (Dornbusch and Frenkel 1984). An important real disturbance was the transfer of long-term capital from the developed to the developing world. Long-term capital movements to Canada, Australia, and Argentina were effected through gold flows and the price-specie-flow mechanism, changes in real income, and short-term capital flows (Ford 1962, Rich 1989).

Central banks from 1880 to 1914 did not systematically follow the rules of the game, but periodically sterilized gold flows to shield domestic money supplies from external disequilibrium (Bloomfield 1959). In the face of a financial crisis with both an external and an internal drain, Bagehot's rule "to lend freely but at a penalty rate" was a temporary violation of the rules, which, in the long run, helped preserve the system. In any case, before 1914, intervention was rarely extensive enough to threaten convertibility.

The classical gold standard has often been viewed as a standard managed by the Bank of England. Because the world's principal gold, commodities, and capital markets were located in London, because of the magnitude of outstanding sterling-dominated assets, and because sterling was the primary international reserve currency (as a substitute for gold), the Bank of England could supposedly attract whatever gold it needed by manipulating its bank rate, inducing other central banks to adjust their discount rates accordingly. Thus, the Bank of England could exert powerful influences on money supplies and price levels of other gold-standard countries. The evidence suggests that the Bank of England did have some, though limited, influence on other European central banks (Lindert 1969, Eichengreen 1987).

The interwar gold exchange standard was far less successful that its pre-World-War-I predecessor. The system suffered from several basic flaws: asymmetric adjustment between deficit countries such as Britain (with an overvalued parity) which was forced to deflate and surplus countries such as France (with an undervalued currency) and the United States, whose absorption and sterilization of gold inflows put deflationary pressure on the international monetary system; the inadequacy of international reserves; and a lack of confidence which led foreign-exchange balances to be shifted from weak (London) to strong (New York) reserve centers and ultimately precipitated the collapse of the system when a massive attempt to convert sterling into gold occurred in September 1931. Before it completely disintegrated in the mid-1930s, the gold standard helped transmit deflation and depression between countries (Friedman and Schwartz 1963, Bernanke and James 1991). Once countries cut the link with gold, devalued their currencies and followed expansionary monetary policies, recovery began quickly (Eichengreen and Sachs [1985] 1990).

Although the last vestiges of the gold standard disappeared in 1971, its appeal remains strong. Opponents of discretion are attracted by the simplicity of its basic rule, others view it as an effective anchor to the world price level, while still others look back to the fixity of exchange rates. However, despite its appeal, many of the conditions that made the gold standard so successful vanished in 1914; and the political importance of internal aggregate stability makes its restoration unlikely.

Michael D. Bordo

See also BANK OF ENGLAND; CENTRAL BANKING; GOLD STANDARD: CAUSES AND CONSE-

QUENCES; GREAT DEPRESSION IN BRITAIN (1929–1932); GREAT DEPRESSION IN FRANCE (1929–1938); GREAT DEPRESSION IN THE UNITED STATES (1929–1938); HAWTREY, RALPH GEORGE; MONETARY POLICY; PANIC OF 1893

Bibliography

Bernanke, B. and H. James. 1991. "The Gold Standard, Deflation and Financial Crisis in the Great Depression: An International Comparison." In *Financial Markets and Financial Crisis,* edited by R. G. Hubbard, 33–68. Chicago: Univ. of Chicago Press.

Bloomfield, A. I. 1959. *Monetary Policy Under the International Gold Standard.* New York: Federal Reserve Bank of New York.

Bordo, M. D. 1981. "The Classical Gold Standard—Some Lessons for Today." Federal Reserve Bank of St. Louis *Review,* May, 2–17.

———. 1986. "Financial Crises, Banking Crises, Stock Market Crashes, and the Money Supply: Some International Evidence, 1870–1933." In *Financial Crises and the World Banking System,* edited by F. H. Capie and G. E. Wood, 190–248. London: Macmillan.

Bordo, M. D. and A. J. Schwartz. 1988. "Transmission of Real and Monetary Disturbances Under Fixed and Floating Rates." *Cato Journal* 8:451–72.

Brown, W. A. 1940. *The International Gold Standard Reinterpreted, 1914–1934.* New York: NBER.

Dornbusch, R. and J. A. Frenkel. 1984. "The Gold Standard and the Bank of England in the Crisis of 1847." In *A Retrospective on the Classical Gold Standard, 1821–1931,* edited by M. D. Bordo and A. J. Schwartz, 233–64. Chicago: Univ. of Chicago Press.

Eichengreen, B. 1987. "Conducting the International Orchestra: Bank of England Leadership Under the Classical Gold Standard." *Journal of International Money and Finance* 6:5–29.

Eichengreen, B. and J. D. Sachs. [1985] 1990. "Exchange Rates and Economic Recovery in the 1930s." Chap. 9 in B. Eichengreen, *Elusive Stability: Essays in the History of International Finance, 1919–1939.* Cambridge: Cambridge Univ. Press.

Ford, A. G. 1962. *The Gold Standard, 1880–1914: Britain and Argentina*. Oxford: Clarendon Press.

Friedman, M. and A. J. Schwartz. 1963. *A Monetary History of the United States: 1867–1960*. Princeton: Princeton Univ. Press.

Huffman, W. E. and J. R. Lothian. 1984. "The Gold Standard and the Transmission of Business Cycles, 1873–1932." In *A Retrospective on the Classical Gold Standard, 1821–1931*, edited by M. D. Bordo and A. J. Schwartz, 455–507. Chicago: Univ. of Chicago Press.

Lindert, P. 1969. *Key Currencies and Gold, 1900–1913*. Princeton Studies in International Finances, no. 24. Princeton: International Finance Section, Princeton Univ.

McCloskey, D. N. and J. R. Zecher. 1976. "How the Gold Standard Worked, 1880–1913." In *The Monetary Approach to the Balance of Payments*, edited by J. Frenkel and H. G. Johnson, 357–85. Toronto: Univ. of Toronto Press.

Officer, L. H. 1986. "The Efficiency of the Dollar-Sterling Gold Standard (1890–1908)." *Journal of Political Economy* 94:1038–73.

Rich, G. 1989. *The Cross of Gold: Money and the Canadian Business Cycle, 1867–1913*. Ottawa: Carleton Univ. Press.

Rockoff, H. 1984. "Some Evidence on the Real Price of Gold, Its Cost of Production, and Commodity Prices." In *A Retrospective on the Classical Gold Standard, 1821–1931*, edited by M. D. Bordo and A. J. Schwartz, 613–44. Chicago: Univ. of Chicago Press.

Gold Standard: Causes and Consequences

A *gold standard* (or more generally any *convertible monetary system*) signifies a paper-money system in which the government is contractually bound to convert a unit of its paper money into a prespecified amount of gold (or some other valuable commodity). Whether or not a country is on a gold standard has important effects on the welfare of its people.

The gold standard first appeared in China in the early ninth century renaissance in ancient Chinese religion and effective democracy. It was consistently maintained there in some form throughout China's lengthy golden age of technological and economic progress until the

standard, and the extended renaissance, were brought to an end in 1620 with China's unfortunately durable reversion to philosopher-authoritarianism. Although the idea of the gold standard was introduced to the West at the end of the thirteenth century by Marco Polo, who was greatly impressed by the convertible certificates of the initially silver-rich Mongol emperors, not until four centuries later did the gold standard begin an independent life-cycle of its own in the West

Rise and Fall of the Gold Standard in the West

Economic folklore attributes the evolution of the gold standard in the West to the development of a fractional gold-reserve system by seventeenth-century English goldsmiths who lent out a fraction of their idle gold reserves in exchange for promissory notes that they used to back private issues of negotiable paper debt (paper money). But similar private banking institutions had already developed much earlier without special notice in Medieval Florence and Venice.

The true innovators were the governmental leaders of England's new democracy following the "Glorious Revolution" of 1688. This pathbreaking democratic revolution, while providing a legal and philosophical ("rights-of-man") commitment to compensate the citizen-soldiers of the huge new armies of rifle-equipped Englishmen for their large wartime personal sacrifices, did nothing to prevent the new democracy from subsequently repealing its debts to those who had made large wartime *financial* sacrifices. Yet such financial sacrifices had been necessary for the survival of the fledgling democracy, because, as we shall see, military leaders cannot defend a democracy unless they can override the self-destructive—but narrowly rational—appeasement response to potential aggressors that characterizes any democratic legislature. The *governmental* invention of the gold standard, by solving this critical problem in defense-finance for the newly forming democracies of the West, cleared the path to modernity.

The evolution of the gold standard in the West was thus begun by the newly established Bank of England during the early years of what was to become our first successful national democracy. Then, almost a century later, after a failed Swedish attempt to establish a national democracy supported by a cumbersome copper standard (1719–72), a second viable precious-

G

metal standard was adopted in 1791 by the newly formed Bank of the United States in what was to become our second successful national democracy. Due largely to the remarkable success of these two nations relative to their neighbors, the standard—usually accompanied by substantial democratization—gradually spread to Continental Europe, Latin America, and Japan during the nineteenth century. The restructured countries similarly enjoyed eras of remarkably successful national defense and exceptionally high, albeit fitful, economic growth well into the twentieth century.

Then, during the Great Depression, every European country, beginning with England in September 1931, successively abandoned the gold standard to increase the power of its central bank to fight unemployment in line with the new macroeconomic doctrines of the increasingly influential John Maynard Keynes.

Only the U.S. remained on a gold standard, albeit one with harsh curbs on the export and possession of gold. And only the U.S. could finance the military defense of the democracies during World War II.

After World War II, an *international gold exchange standard* was set up in 1946. This was achieved by executing the 1944 agreement reached in an international monetary conference at Bretton Woods, New Hampshire, in which financial representatives of the democratic countries of Europe all agreed to work to make their countries' paper currencies convertible into the U.S. dollar as long as the U.S. maintained a fixed conversion rate of the dollar into gold in official transactions. Such international cooperation helped meet the emergency military requirements of the recovering European democracies, but in a recession-producing way similar to that of the earlier, noncooperative "classical" gold standard. Then, upon the completion of a nuclear defense system for all the Western democracies in the late 1960s, this last remnant of the gold standard was rapidly phased out and finally eliminated when the U.S. closed the gold window on 15 August 1971.

Business Cycles and the Gold Standard

Because the free convertibility of paper money into a real commodity implies that the public is free to exchange idle real commodity stocks for paper money, or vice versa, the total demand for this money at the fixed conversion price determines its supply. The correspondingly passive money supply has, since the writings of Adam Smith, been generally understood by political economists to be a property of the classical gold standard, an understanding reflected in the policy-oriented writings of the English Banking School in the 1840s, of J. Laurence Laughlin and the U.S. "sound money school" of the 1890s, and of the early supporters of the Federal Reserve Act. All these authors saw great benefits in the system's ability to expand and contract the peacetime paper-money supply automatically in response to "the needs of trade" without significantly affecting prices.

Such benefits are absent when convertibility does not obtain. At such times, governments are free to fix the supply of paper money *exogenously*, i.e., without regard to prior legal commitments. Thus, with governmental authorities unwilling to surrender their discretionary control to an automatic mechanism such as a gold standard, sudden expansions or contractions in the demand for inconvertible paper money have regularly depressed or raised commodity prices and correspondingly generated avoidable business cycles. This pattern has been well recognized since the early days of classical economics, as reflected in Henry Thornton's famous analysis of the effects of a monetary shock on prices and interest rates during periods of suspended gold payments. In the late 1930s, this analysis was restated for permanently inconvertible (*fiat*) money economies in a simplified general-equilibrium setting by Keynes and J. R. Hicks, and survives today in what is commonly called neo-Keynesian macroeconomics.

However, a gold standard produces its own unique brand of business cycle. In particular, gold-standard depressions occur when, and only when, there are shocks that increase the equilibrium value of the conversion commodity relative to other commodities, thereby decreasing the general price level by the same percentage. A correspondingly severe gold-standard depression induces a percentage reduction in the passive money supply roughly equal to the percentage reduction in this price level. In sharp contrast, the same relative-demand shock would occasion no systematic change in the overall price level or aggregate output if there were an exogenously fixed money supply. The government's inability to control the money supply under the gold standard, and thereby avoid the severe depressions caused by shocks that substantially raise the total demand for the conversion commodity relative to other commodities, is by far the main disadvantage of the gold standard.

Such business cycles (including the Great Depression) occurred regularly under the gold standard. And, despite the relative ease with which they could be—and actually were—predicted by financial experts, the cycles in real output under the gold standard were of much greater amplitude and duration than those under more recent, inconvertible, governmentally managed, monetary systems. Viewed *solely* from the standpoint of the economic costs of the business cycle, the gold standard was, therefore, probably, on net, socially disadvantageous.

Emergency Finance and the Gold Standard

However, as already noted, by far the main advantage of a gold standard to an adopting country was its historically unique ability to facilitate the financing of large-scale military emergencies. The basis for this ability was a general belief that a wartime suspension of a governmental conversion promise was a temporary *force majeure,* an excusable but temporary abrogation of an otherwise inviolable contract between a powerful government and an innocent individual citizen entitled to the substantial protection of the law. Postemergency law courts and legislatures therefore typically enforced depression-producing resumptions of prewar gold conversion payments on their paper monies, although usually only after several years of legislative debate during which alternative measures for financing the retirement of the large issues of wartime debt could be devised.

Before the nuclear age, when emergency national defense was a prolonged and expensive affair, such a financial advantage had been necessary for the survival of national democracies. Theoretically, this financial *sine qua non* arises because there is a time-inconsistent, overly appeasing, response of any narrowly rational collection of voters to each in a series of broadly rational threats of all-out war by external aggressors demanding individually small concessions. A democracy whose leaders were unable to overcome this legislative appeasement problem by *independently* financing their country's defense would, sooner or later, be subjugated by external aggressors.

The late seventeenth-century founders of the Bank of England were acutely aware both of the historical reluctance of parliaments to supply funds necessary for emergency military defense and of the recent military failure of neighboring Holland's pioneering, but short-lived, national democracy. These perceptive British bankers, along with their new Dutch king, William III, saw that Holland's failure was due to the disastrous legal inability of the Bank of Amsterdam to expand her innovative paper money supply in a defensive emergency (the War of 1672). This unfortunate inflexibility was due to a rule in the bank's constitution limiting its issue of paper to its effective gold reserve.

In any case, the war-troubled William III, his pragmatic English bankers, and a Scottish banking promoter, William Patterson, worked to create a national paper currency that would flexibly expand during military emergencies, but without a proportionate increase in the price level. Under a gold standard, extra paper money could be created and spent during the defensive emergencies, although convertibility would have to be temporarily suspended to prevent a *reflux* of the paper money back to the Bank. (The first formal suspension of gold payments occurred barely one year after the new money was issued; and the suspension lasted only the two years that William required to defeat the formidable France of Louis XIV.) The suspension-induced expansion of the paper money supply would in turn cause some wartime inflation. But since the new paper money represented a durable contract between the individual money-holder and the government, English judges would likely attempt to enforce an eventual resumption of gold payments at the original conversion rate as a matter of common law. Parliament, unwilling to risk yet another constitutional crisis and civil war, predictably ordered the resumption of gold payments at the old conversion rate—and continued to do so until 1931—despite the need for both a real postwar tax increase to finance the payments and a depressionary return to the prewar price trend. The rational expectation of this postwar depression by the financial community allowed the wartime expansion in governmental purchasing power that was in turn required for the survival of the democracy.

Early in the eighteenth century, after a couple of such wars, widespread parliamentary support arose for large wartime issues of long-term national debt. Such borrowing served as a convenient *substitute* for wartime monetary expansion. Although moderate interest would be due on such borrowing, repayment could be delayed to dates that would both distribute the intergenerational burden of the war in a more

G

politically acceptable fashion and moderate the social costs of the anticipated postwar deflation. War finance in countries with mature gold standards was therefore typically marked by substantial issues of legislatively approved, long-term, governmental debt as well as by suspension-induced monetary expansions. The resulting *appearance* that the democratic legislatures of gold-standard countries were willing to support defensive warfare with substantial domestic issues of long-term debt has obscured, for even the most astute of contemporary economic observers, the fundamental problem that the gold standard was solving.

Without the gold standard, emergency finance would have doubtless remained in the hands of clubs of wealthy noblemen, bankers, and guild aristocrats, groups whose peacetime compensation for their extensive wartime sacrifices depended on the existence of highly elitist religions and philosophies, antimodern (although currently reemergent) value systems disserving their countries by exaggerating the personal wisdom and benevolence of appropriately educated aristocrats.

Indeed, before the nuclear age, no independent nation evolved from aristocracy to a surviving national democracy without the aid of a gold standard.

Mainstream Macroeconomics and the Gold Standard

Never recognized by mainstream economics, this major advantage of the gold standard has been obscured by an error in basic Keynesian theory, leading to the erroneous conclusion that a permanent increase in the supply of fiat money reduces interest rates. This theoretical error, the source of a major unresolved empirical paradox in Keynesian theory called the "Gibson Paradox," led Keynes and subsequent economists to the dangerously false belief that emergency expansions in the supply of an inconvertible paper money—correctly understood to be *permanent*—would be partially hoarded. According to Keynesian theory, such beneficial monetary hoarding would occur because of decreases in the foregone-interest cost of holding money. The increases in commodity prices during emergencies would then be proportionately *less than* the corresponding money-supply increases. If this *were* true, then the permanent money-supply increases would produce unambiguous increases in emergency governmental purchasing power, just as had occurred for the

temporary monetary expansions that had been induced by national emergencies under the classical gold standard. But a correction of this theoretical error leads to the opposite theoretical prediction. A permanent money-supply increase in a capital-theoretically correct macroeconomic model, by unambiguously increasing the marginal productivity of capital and leaving the rationally expected inflation rate constant, necessarily leads to an *increase* in the foregone-interest cost of holding money. Monetary dishoarding, not hoarding, is induced. A permanent increase in the money supply will increase prices *more* than in proportion to the increase in the money supply.

Besides resolving the Gibson paradox, this theoretical correction allows us to understand the uncharacteristic weakness of democratic Europe in responding to Fascist aggression in the late 1930s. It also enables us to understand why the United States, the only country that, at least in international transactions, did not abandon the gold standard, was able to generate uniquely large increases in emergency governmental purchasing power and, concomitantly, maintain exceptionally low interest rates throughout World War II. The intellectually fashionable abandonment of the gold standard in the early 1930s to combat the depression therefore appears to have been a serious error. The abandonment left democratic Europe wide open to the threat of all-out attack by military dictators, who then naturally emerged in the mid-1930s. The United States, the only country sufficiently resistant to intellectual fashion to remain on the gold standard, was therefore the only country able to finance a wartime defense effort adequate to the task of defending democracy.

Broad Price Trends Under the Gold Standard

It is helpful to temporarily assume a zero-transaction-costs, perfectly competitive equilibrium in all markets. Then, multiplying the government's fixed, intertemporally constant, money price of gold by the perfectly competitive equilibrium price of any other commodity relative to gold, we can immediately determine the *money* price of that commodity. Since this can be done for all commodities, and without reference to the passively determined money supply, equilibrium relative prices in a perfectly competitive money economy can be determined independently of the monetary sector. The resulting "classical dichotomy" between the real and the monetary sectors of an economy, which was implicit in most of classical and early neoclassical economics, greatly facilitates the quantitative analysis of the economy.

In a perfectly competitive economy with a gold standard, idle stocks of gold (called "monetary gold" when held by financial institutions), like any other currently nonproductive asset, must be expected to appreciate at a rate equal to the real rate of return to holding currently productive assets. Thus, issuers of gold-convertible paper money need not pay direct interest on their moneys. Indeed, convertible banknotes bore no direct interest while money prices in gold-standard economies generally fell slightly during peacetime, reflecting the slightly positive real interest rate on alternative investment goods.

In wartime, when gold-standard economies generated large increases in the money supply and suspensions of gold payments, there were typically substantial releases of monetary gold to the public, roughly constant money prices of gold, and therefore increases in the nominal prices of most other goods. Nevertheless, the rational expectation of postwar resumptions of gold payments, and corresponding postwar deflations implied higher-than-normal rates of return to holding paper money relative to goods during wartime emergencies. Substantial increases in the government's *real* wartime purchasing power therefore accompanied the substantial increases in the government's *nominal* issues of paper money. This powerful financial weapon provided a gold-standard government with a potential wartime increase in zero-interest purchasing power—limited only by the government's ability to repay the zero-interest loan after the war by suitably raising postwar taxes to finance future conversion payments. The increase in the rationally expected deflation also generated, after the brief learning period of 1695–1725, nominal interest rates that typically remained below 5 percent during major wars throughout the gold-standard era despite the obvious wartime increases in both real interest rates and default risks.

But this main advantage of the gold standard also implied postwar depressions as monetary gold was gradually reaccumulated by the central banks, which correspondingly increased the value of gold *relative to* other commodities. A long series of innovations economizing on gold conversion during these resumption periods—first by including silver as a conversion metal, then by limiting conversion to bullion, then by allowing conversion into another country's convertible currency, then by outlawing the private hoarding of gold, and finally by restricting gold conversion payments to a single country—beneficially served to mitigate these consistently depressionary resumption costs, producing a long-term trend of money prices that was roughly constant throughout the entire quarter-millennial epoch of the classical gold standard, 1694–1944.

The subsequent era of the international gold exchange standard, the quarter-century following World War II, analogously ended soon after the development of an *international* system of nuclear defense. As the underlying advantage of the gold standard to the European democracies was thus becoming obsolete, its main disadvantage in the form of potential cyclical instability obviously remained, most imminently in the form of a potential worldwide recession if the U.S. were to attempt a resumption of gold payments that had been war-suspended since 1968. So, by 1971, the enthusiasm of most practical politicians for maintaining the international gold exchange standard had eroded to insignificance.

Emergency Finance After the Gold Standard

Nevertheless, less-developed countries, while likely to be living under a larger nation's "nuclear umbrella," still have been facing substantial emergency financial demands to cover *domestic political uprisings*. The surviving governments of such countries, even after the 1971 abandonment of the Bretton Woods agreement, have typically had currencies that were convertible into the fiat currency of a foreign country, thereby maintaining the emergency financial advantages of the gold standard. However, repetitive domestic hyperinflations have proved that the legal systems of these countries do not treat their government's promise to convert a unit of its currency into a fixed amount of the inconvertible paper currency of a foreign country with nearly the same gravity as a promise to convert into gold. In response, these countries have enlisted the aid of international economic organizations set up at Bretton Woods and somehow survived the collapse of the original agreement to help commit themselves to more durably fixed exchange rates. These attempts, although arguably more successful in controlling the secular inflation rates in some of these countries, and in correspondingly promoting domestic political stability, have also backfired elsewhere, producing a number of third-world depressions quite analogous to the depressions occurring under the classical gold standard.

Nor has the problem of emergency finance in the more developed democracies *permanently* disappeared. Rather, while the continuing growth of governmental indebtedness is steadily diminishing the *ability* of governmental authorities to finance future emergencies with ordinary borrowing, the spread of sophisticated military weapons to the masses is steadily increasing the likelihood of future *domestic* emergencies. There is therefore an increasing need for developed democracies to provide mechanisms that will finance future emergencies. But modern democratic legislatures cannot be expected to adopt mechanisms that will burden their economies with postemergency depressions nearly as severe as those observed under the classical gold standard. It follows that if new, depression-resistant, mechanisms of emergency finance are not adopted, and if history and recent trends are any guide, the increasing emergency usefulness of small groups of wealthy individuals and companies relative to ordinary people will inevitably lead to a tortuous degeneration of our popular democracies back into elitist aristocracies such as those that dominated all of these governments prior to the adoption of the gold standard.

Earl A. Thompson

See also BANK OF ENGLAND; CENTRAL BANKING; GOLD STANDARD; GREAT DEPRESSION IN BRITAIN (1929–1932); GREAT DEPRESSION IN FRANCE (1929–1938); GREAT DEPRESSION IN THE UNITED STATES (1929–1938); HAWTREY, RALPH GEORGE; KEYNES, JOHN MAYNARD; MONETARY POLICY; PANIC OF 1893

Bibliography

Bloomfield, A. I. 1959. *Monetary Policy under the International Gold Standard.* New York: Federal Reserve Bank of New York.

Dell, S. 1981. *On Being Grandmotherly: The Evolution of IMF Conditionality.* Essays in International Finance, no. 144. Princeton: International Finance Section, Princeton Univ.

Edkins, J. 1901. *Chinese Currency.* Shanghai: Presbyterian Mission Press.

Eichengreen, B., ed. 1985. *The Gold Standard in History and Theory.* New York: Methuen.

Gilbert, M. 1968. *The Gold-Dollar System: Conditions of Equilibrium and the Price of Gold.* Essays in International Finance, no. 70. Princeton: International Finance Section, Princeton Univ.

Glasner, D. 1989. *Free Banking and Monetary Reform.* New York: Cambridge Univ. Press.

Hickson, C. and E. A. Thompson. 1991. "A New Theory of Guilds and European Economic Development." *Explorations in Economic History* 28:127–68.

Sherwood, S. 1893. *The History and Theory of Money.* Philadelphia: Lippincott.

Shyrock, J. K. 1932. *The Origin and Development of the State Cult of Confucius.* New York: Century.

Thompson, E. A. 1974. "The Theory of Money and Income Consistent with Orthodox Value Theory." In *Money, Trade, and Macroeconomics: Essays in Honor of Lloyd Metzler,* edited by G. Horwich and P. A. Samuelson, 427–54. New York: Academic Press.

———. 1979. "An Economic Basis for the National Defense Argument for Protecting Certain Industries." *Journal of Political Economy* 87:1–36.

Tracy, J. D. 1985. *A Financial Revolution in the Hapsburg Netherlands.* Berkeley: Univ. of California Press.

Goodwin, Richard Murphey (1913–)

The scholarly career of Richard Goodwin has had a single grand focus: to understand the causes of aggregate economic fluctuations. Early on, he recognized the limitations of linear models for the analysis of persistent fluctuations and began to explore nonlinear models in his influential paper, "The Non-Linear Accelerator and the Persistence of Business Cycles." In his best-known paper, "A Growth Cycle," he adapted the predator-prey, limit-cycle model of Volterra and Lotka to describe how wages and profits are determined dynamically as an economy fluctuates around its long-run growth path.

The rest of his work can best be understood in relation to the latter paper which he has called "the culmination of some thirty years preoccupation" (1983, viii). One line of development, collected in *Essays in Economic Dy-*

namics and *Essays in Non-Linear Economic Dynamics,* broadens the macrodynamic picture of the growth cycle by considering both shorter- and longer-run fluctuations generated by inventory behavior and waves of technological innovation. This body of work suggests that the observed complexity of macrodynamic processes may be explained in part by dynamic coupling of cycles of different phase. A second line of development, collected in *Essays in Linear Economic Structures,* explores economic dynamics at a sectoral level, disaggregating the growth cycle using the Leontief input-output framework. This work suggests that, even if the system as a whole is stable, complicated economic dynamics may occur simply through the interaction of multiple sectors in the economy. A condensed and simplified version of Goodwin's mature thought may be found in his revised lecture notes, published as *Elementary Economics from the Higher Standpoint* and *The Dynamics of a Capitalist Economy.*

Business Cycles

Following Schumpeter, Goodwin views an economy as a dynamic system that grows by fluctuating, constantly changing its form in the process. Like Schumpeter, he views technological change as the engine of growth and understands economic dynamics as the complex process of adjustment to technological change in particular sectors. Technological innovation in one sector upsets the equilibrium structure of relative prices and quantities, and adjustment proceeds according to specific sectoral evidence of economic disequilibrium—price unequal to cost, output unequal to demand. The process of real-time *tâtonnement* is conceived to be tending to establish new equilibrium prices and quantities. However, since technological change is always occurring in some sector, the economy as a whole is continually adjusting and never actually reaches the final equilibrium.

From this essentially Schumpeterian starting point, Goodwin builds on the insights of Keynes and Marx to argue that sectoral-adjustment processes have aggregate as well as sectoral effects. Following Keynes, he emphasizes that innovation is a source of new effective demand which spills over into other sectors, inducing additional investment in an unstable accelerator process. Following a suggestion from Marx's discussion of capitalist instability, he emphasizes that rapid economic growth tends eventually to exhaust supplies of labor,

bidding up real wages at the expense of profits which tends to slow investment. The combination of these demand and distribution effects causes the economy to adjust to sectoral technological change by means of aggregate fluctuation. Technological change stimulates investment and precipitates a cumulative upward spiral which is eventually choked off by labor scarcity and rising wages. The resulting investment slump then precipitates a cumulative downward spiral which is eventually reversed as the flow of new opportunities for innovative investment once again stimulates demand. In formal terms, Goodwin envisions the macroeconomy as an unstable nonlinear dynamical system confined between the ceiling of labor supply and the floor of innovative investment. The simplest mathematical construct which exhibits these features is a limit cycle, which Goodwin provides in his paper "A Growth Cycle."

Goodwin's growth-cycle model is a dynamical system which, though locally unstable, is subject to global auto-control. In a process of self-organization through fluctuation, wages are determined so that, on average, the rate of capital accumulation just equals the sum of the rates of growth of the labor force and of labor productivity. The limit cycle can thus be thought of as fluctuation around a steady-state growth path, so long as we keep in mind that the parameters of that growth path are themselves determined by the dynamic process of fluctuation.

Macrodynamic Irregularity

Macroeconomic fluctuations are of course highly irregular and do not resemble a regular limit cycle. Goodwin develops three complementary explanations for such irregularity. First, dynamic coupling of the major cycle with the shorter stock cycle changes the period of both, shortening the short period and lengthening the longer period. More important, unless the two cycles are exactly in phase, dynamic coupling induces constantly changing periods of macroeconomic fluctuation.

Second, because the rate of technological change is not constant but changes over time, the ceilings and floors of the dynamic autocontrol process change as well. For example, suppose the rate of technological change follows a logistic curve as the new technology diffuses through the economy. Then at the midpoint of the logistic, rapidly growing productivity allows wages to increase rapidly without choking off investment so that high levels of employment can be achieved in the peaks of booms. Similarly, the same rapid growth of productivity induces a large amount of innovative investment which helps moderate the downturn. Thus the interaction of the major cycle with the long cycle of technological change causes different cycles to reach different levels of activity at peaks and troughs.

Third, important lags in economic behavior may cause chaotic or aperiodic dynamics. Because firms adjust current output in light of past deviations between output and demand, and because they adjust capacity over time to provide for desired output, the equations describing the dynamics of the economy are nonlinear difference equations. The ceiling and floor on the motion determined by such a system will contain the evolution of the economy within a bounded area but will not necessarily induce a single well-defined limit cycle. Rather, there may well exist a "closed orbital region which will contain the limiting trajectories of all motions" (1989, 153).

Sectoral Dynamics

Economic fluctuations are obviously irregular at the sectoral as well as the aggregate level. In a complex interdependent system where each sector's output price is another's input cost, the dynamic adjustment of prices and quantities to new equilibrium values can be very complicated. Goodwin's strategy is to conceive of this adjustment as tending toward the von Neumann growth path implicit in the current state of technology. In this approach, sectoral adjustment is the mechanism through which events in one sector affect other sectors, i.e., the transmission mechanism for idiosyncratic technological shocks, but is not itself a source of macrodynamic fluctuations. With this simplification, Goodwin makes considerable headway in analyzing the problem.

Following von Neumann, Goodwin posits a simple bilinear dynamics for the sectoral system. If in any sector price is greater than cost, then price falls. And if in any sector output is greater than demand then output falls. Under these assumptions the system can be shown to be generically stable. But the problem remains how to characterize the path followed by any particular sector to the long-run equilibrium. Since output prices are input costs and expenditures on inputs are receipts on the sale of outputs, the adjustment process can be quite complicated.

Following Sraffa, Goodwin uses a variable transformation to isolate problems of sectoral interaction from the problems of value and distribution. By transforming from the n actual sectors of the economy to n artificial eigensectors (defined by the eigenvectors of the input-output matrix), Goodwin greatly simplifies the analysis. Since the input-output matrix for these eigensectors is diagonal, with each diagonal entry the eigenvalue for one of the eigensectors, the dynamics of the eigensectoral adjustment process are simple to understand and analyze. The adjustment path of actual sectors can then be reconstructed as a weighted sum of the paths of these eigensectors.

Conclusion

Goodwin's vision of the economy poses considerable challenges for the theorist. In his view, macroeconomic fluctuations are not real oscillations at all, but rather complicated adjustments to sectoral technological innovations. The problems of macroeconomic trend and cycle are thus inexorably intertwined: it is technological change which causes growth and it is adjustment to technological change which causes economic fluctuation. By contrast, the usual method of analyzing business cycles as fluctuations around a steady growth path abstracts from this interaction in order to avoid the difficulties of dynamic analysis. To his credit, Goodwin embraced those difficulties and, using the mathematical formalism of the limit cycle, built simple and robust models to illustrate the interrelation of trend and cycle.

Equally challenging, Goodwin's vision underscores the close relationship between problems of macrodynamics and microdynamics, since it is sectoral adjustment to idiosyncratic technological shocks which causes macroeconomic fluctuations. Goodwin's technique of conducting analysis in terms of the latent roots and vectors of the input-output matrix greatly clarifies those dynamics without losing the complexity of sectoral interaction. The resulting elegant models go a considerable distance toward illuminating the process through which idiosyncratic technological shocks are transmitted throughout the economy.

Goodwin sought to understand business fluctuations as a dynamic process of multisectoral disequilibrium adjustment to sectoral technological shocks. His strategy was first to understand macrodynamics on their own, and then to explore the decentralized sectoral adjustments that underlie them. The picture he paints is one of a rather simple dynamical system which nevertheless gives rise to complex aggregate fluctuations coupled with rich sectoral dynamics. Up close the painting appears impossibly complex, but, from a few steps back, the simple limit cycle, the Goodwin growth cycle, to which all the complex detail contributes becomes clearly visible.

Perry Mehrling

See also CHAOS AND BIFURCATIONS; CEILINGS AND FLOORS; NONLINEAR BUSINESS-CYCLE THEORIES; POST-KEYNESIAN BUSINESS CYCLE THEORY; PRICE-QUANTITY ADJUSTMENT; SCHUMPETER, JOSEPH ALOIS; TRENDS AND RANDOM WALKS

Bibliography
Goodwin, R. M. [1951] 1982. "The Non-Linear Accelerator and the Persistence of Business Cycles." Chap. 6 in *Essays in Economic Dynamics*. London: Macmillan.
———. [1967] 1982. "A Growth Cycle." Chap. 14 in *Essays in Economic Dynamics*. London: Macmillan.
———. 1970. *Elementary Economics from the Higher Standpoint*. Cambridge: Cambridge Univ. Press.
———. 1982. *Essays in Economic Dynamics*. London: Macmillan.
———. 1983. *Essays in Linear Economic Structures*. London: Macmillan.
———. 1985. "A Personal Perspective on Mathematical Economics." *Banca Nazionale del Lavoro Quarterly Review*, March, 3–13.
———. 1987. *The Dynamics of a Capitalist Economy*. Cambridge: Polity Press.
———. 1989. *Essays in Non-Linear Economic Dynamics*. New York: Peter Lang.
Velupillai, K., ed. 1990. *Nonlinear and Multisectoral Macrodynamics: Essays in Honour of Richard Goodwin*. New York: New York Univ. Press.

Great Depression in Britain (1929–1932)

In the late 1920s and early 1930s, the major industrial economies of the world and many primary producers suffered severe economic depression. However, the nature, extent, and timing of that experience varied greatly from country to country. The United States suffered probably the greatest fall in output and employment. That experience has been intensively researched and the results are frequently assumed to hold for the wider world experience. But, in fact, they do not—particularly not for Britain.

The British economy turned down in the summer of 1929. The bottom of the trough has been dated as the summer of 1932. The beginnings of the upturn therefore started earlier in Britain than almost anywhere else. The upswing that followed and that lasted until the next peak in 1937 was the strongest in British history. Indeed, the British economy grew faster between the peaks of 1929 and 1937 than it had in two generations.

There are various ways to measure the severity of depression. If we regard total output as the best indicator of activity, the 1929–32 downturn was not as severe as the depressions following either the first or second World Wars. Real GDP fell by less than 6 percent in 1930, much less than output fell in the United States. Industrial production fell more sharply than GDP as a whole, but that has been the case throughout the modern period.

It is sometimes argued that unemployment should be used as an indicator of the pace of activity. But unemployment can be affected by a number of factors (such as demographic patterns, migration, institutional arrangements) which may not reflect the health of the economy. Unemployment in Britain did soar between 1929 and 1931, but much of the increase can be accounted for by real-wage behavior.

Within British historical experience, 1929–32 was not a *great* depression. Moreover, the depression did not last as long in Britain as in most other countries, and was probably milder in Britain than in any countries except Sweden and Japan.

The depression in Britain has often simply been assumed to have been caused by the depression in the rest of the world, especially in the United States. The argument is that because of its openness, the British economy has always been vulnerable to the fluctuations in the world economy. This certainly seems to have been true of the nineteenth century, and even between the wars, British exports were still roughly 15 percent of total national product. A fall in exports, via an income multiplier, could therefore have a significant effect on the economy. The two critical issues are then whether the timing and the size of the fall in exports can account, given a multiplier of plausible size, for the observed decline in income. There seems to be almost universal agreement on timing. The lead of exports into this depression seems sufficient to account for the downturn. Of course, employment in export-based or related industries was low. The magnitude of the fall in British exports also supports this thesis, for exports of goods and services collapsed from £1444 million to £773 million in 1932, reflecting the general collapse in world trade.

Nothing else is available to explain the decline in economic activity in Britain in this period. Monetary policy was not tightened and the decline in money did not precede the decline in activity at this juncture. No one has provided any evidence of an autonomous fall in investment and certainly not in consumption expenditures. The stock market did collapse, but there is even less reason to believe that this reduced spending in Britain than there is to believe that the stock-market crash reduced spending in the United States. A wealth effect was less likely to have occurred in Britain, where a much smaller proportion of investors had direct holdings in the stock market than in America.

It seems therefore that the conventional wisdom about the period has not been seriously challenged. Whatever we accept as the cause of the downturn in the United States, it was the downturn there and its reverberations around the world that account for the British downturn. Moreover, since the declining relative size of Britain's external account was reducing its exposure to the world economy, the depression had a comparatively mild effect on Britain.

Three policies are widely credited with having stimulated an early recovery in Britain:

1. Exchange-rate policy—the break with gold in September 1931 and the subsequent exchange-rate management via the Exchange-Equalization Account.
2. Commercial policy—primarily the general tariff of 1931.
3. Monetary policy—sometimes thought of as "cheap money" during the 1930s.

It is difficult to measure the impact of these policies, but recent research suggests that none made any significant contribution to recovery.

An outstanding feature of the depression of the 1930s was the collapse of world trade. Valued in predevaluation 1934 gold dollars, total world exports had fallen from $56 billion in 1928 to $22 billion in 1932 and they were to fall slightly further to $20 billion in 1935. By 1938, there was the mildest recovery showing at $23 billion. World trade in manufactures largely mirrors this, even if the collapse is less dramatic and the recovery is more substantial. The same pattern holds in Britain even though British imports fell by substantially less than those of any other developed country.

The view that recovery derived from the export sector cannot be sustained. Many examinations of the role of exports on the British economy between the wars confirm their role in leading into and out of the cycle. However, there is no evidence that this was true in the upturn of 1932, when exports lagged rather than led the upturn, and no evidence that exports stimulated growth in the rest of the decade.

There is less reason to believe that Britain's abandonment of almost a century of free trade for a general tariff in 1931 contributed to the recovery. Calculation of effective rates of protection shows that the tariff actually harmed the two largest industries, construction and iron and steel, which casts serious doubt on the significance of the tariff.

Though formally a discretionary act of policy, the abandonment of gold in September 1931 was actually forced on the authorities. For eighteen months or so after September 1931, there was a large gap between the pound and the dollar and since this is when the upturn started, a frequent, and too hasty, conclusion has been that the exchange rate provided the required stimulus for the British economy. But it must be remembered that this was when the Sterling Area was formalized and when several countries, including almost all the Empire, tied their currencies to sterling. Over 50 percent of Britain's trade was with these countries (a share that had been growing since the beginning of the century and continued to grow in the 1930s).

Much of the exchange-rate explanation is thus removed. When we recall that world trade collapsed and did not even begin to recover before 1935, that Britain was among the earliest economies to recover, and that exports were hardly prominent in that recovery, the basis for invoking the exchange rate to explain the recovery is weakened further. But there is a case that abandoning gold allowed Britain to escape further deflation. A great deal of the literature suggests that demand (reflected in a great surge in both construction, especially residential construction, and in iron and steel production) was responsible for the recovery. This may be true, but it is difficult to pin down.

A cheap-money policy is also cited as a principal contributor to the recovery. "Cheap money" is sometimes related to the surge in residential building. However, it seems that interest rates came down not because of *policy* but because the demand for money fell in the depression. In summary, none of the policies that were adopted in 1931–32 appear to have promoted recovery in Britain.

The alternative seems to be that recovery came naturally—that is, out of the normal dynamics of the capitalist economy. Such a suggestion was anathema as long as government planning or control was said to be the way ahead. But after all, economies passed through downs and ups in the nineteenth century without deliberate intervention by governments.

One possible explanation for recovery comes from the supply side. It is that real-wage behavior can throw some light on the course of unemployment. Real wages soared in Britain between 1929 and 1931 in part because of the very favorable movement in the terms of trade. Real-wage growth was steady thereafter, and productivity gains can in good part account for the subsequent path of employment and unemployment. We have noted that output did not fall greatly in Britain, but the puzzle has been why unemployment rose so sharply in precisely the period of the Great Depression in the United States and the rest of the world.

The downturn and downphase of the depression of 1929–32 were not dramatic in Britain. Britain suffered a depression at roughly the same time as other countries which was undoubtedly imported from abroad. Many of the features present in other economies are also present in Britain, albeit in greatly diminished form. Recovery, which came early, was due to domestic factors, and was exceedingly strong. The only slightly paradoxical element is the great growth in unemployment. But if we accept that the unusual behavior of real wages accounts for this, the paradox disappears.

Forrest H. Capie
Geoffrey E. Wood

See also CREDIT-ANSTALT; GOLD STANDARD; GOLD STANDARD: CAUSES AND CONSEQUENCES; GREAT DEPRESSION IN FRANCE (1929–1938); GREAT DEPRESSION IN THE UNITED STATES (1929–1938); HAWTREY, RALPH GEORGE; KEYNES, JOHN MAYNARD

Bibliography

Beenstock, M., F. H. Capie, and B. Griffiths. 1984. "Economic Recovery in the United Kingdom in the 1930s." *Bank of England Panel Paper,* no. 23.

Beenstock, M. and P. Warburton. 1986. "Wages and Unemployment in Interwar Britain." *Explorations in Economic History* 23:153–72.

———. 1991. "The Market for Labor in Interwar Britain." *Explorations in Economic History* 28:287–308.

Benjamin, D. and L. Kochin. 1979. "Searching for an Explanation of Unemployment in Interwar Britain." *Journal of Political Economy* 87:441–78.

Capie, F. H. 1983. *Depression and Protectionism: Britain Between the Wars.* London: Allen and Unwin.

Dimsdale, N. 1981. "British Monetary Policy and the Exchange Rate, 1920–1938." *Oxford Economic Papers* 33 (Supplement):306–49.

G

Great Depression in France (1929–1938)

The Great Depression in France was unique: it began more slowly than in the other industrial countries, was less severe, but lasted longer. The main reasons for these special features are the evolution of the exchange rate (undervalued before and overvalued after 1931), policy errors, exposure to foreign competition, and dependence on foreign markets.

The French economy grew rapidly in the 1920s. The volume of industrial production, which had fallen to 55 in 1921 (indices are in constant prices, 1913 = 100), reached 140 in 1930. Exports had a great role in this growth, rising to 148 in 1928 and representing 30 percent of manufacturing output. The constant depreciation of the franc (falling 80 percent in terms of gold from 1914 until its de facto stabilization in 1926) favored exports, since it was always ahead of the price variations keeping the franc below the purchasing-power-parity level. After a small crisis in 1927, due to the stabilization, a recovery occurred in 1928–29, and even the Wall Street crash did not seriously dampen the optimism: on 8 November 1929, Prime Minister Tardieu said the time had come for a "prosperity policy." No one thought the country was entering a major depression.

Dating the downturn precisely is difficult. It is usually given as later than in the United

States (from where the depression is presumed to have been imported) (Néré 1973). Manufacturing production and the investment index reach their peak in the first half of 1930; there was no unemployment at the end of 1929, and even a year later only 190,000 were receiving unemployment assistance. The French economy was insulated from the deteriorating international situation by an undervalued franc until England left the gold standard in September 1931 (Sicsic 1992), by the repatriation of capital (and the consequent monetary expansion until 1931), and by the stimulative fiscal policy of the Tardieu government after the budget surpluses of the Poincaré period (Kindleberger 1986). Others cite the rise in the retail price index until the end of 1930 which indicates that domestic demand was growing as foreign demand was falling (Asselain 1984). Moreover, the growth of private investment until 1930 was promoted by the absence of public borrowing from the financial markets (Eichengreen and Wyplosz [1988] 1990).

However, some analysts (primarily the Regulation School) contest the thesis of an imported depression, arguing that the crisis started before 1930 (Marseille 1980, Boyer and Mistral 1978). They show that unemployment was underestimated, at least at the beginning of the depression, and that the official index of manufacturing production gave excessive weight to protected industries which were sheltered temporarily from the depression. Moreover, many indices (wholesale prices, stock prices and issues, production in various sectors) began falling in France before they did in the United States. These analysts maintain that the French depression was autonomous, resulting from underconsumption and overinvestment, caused by an increasingly unequal distribution of income, and from the corresponding gap between the growth of investment- and consumption-goods industries (50 vs. 10 percent from 1913 to 1929). Only continuous devaluation of the franc would have permitted enough export growth to have delayed the depression; the depression followed the stabilization of 1926 and the resulting end of exchange-rate speculation.

The Regulation approach contends that the depression began before 1930 (the high level of investment in 1930 only reflecting the completion of ongoing infrastructure projects) and casts doubt on the efficacy, in the long run, of growth excessively dependent on exports. But it does not explain the crisis itself: after a

small reconversion crisis in 1927, caused by the stabilization of the franc, growth was undoubtedly rapid in 1927–29, driven by a rise in wages (see Dubois's contribution in Levy-Leboyer and Casanova 1991) as well as by investment. So, if the internal economy was not in crisis, the role of international conditions in starting the depression cannot be contested. The depression, in fact, began with a sharp fall in exports (from 52 billion francs in 1929 to 20 billion in 1932, in current prices) concentrated in the industries most dependent on foreign trade (for traditional quality goods like textiles the contraction began in 1928) and spread from there to the whole economy (Braudel and Labrousse 1980).

The timing debate then raises substantial questions about the sources of the depression. The Regulation approach sees the depression as a structural crisis that caused the regulation of capitalism to change from a competitive regime to a monopolistic and Fordist regime (with state- or monopoly-determined prices, and high wages supporting domestic demand). Its opponents consider the 1929 downturn the beginning of an ordinary cyclical crisis that simultaneously affected many countries. The crisis turned into a great depression only because of policy errors such as the devaluation of the British pound and the triumph of protectionism.

The second characteristic of the Great Depression in France is its relative mildness. Maximum unemployment was not reached until winter 1934–35 and summer 1936 (one million people according to the broadest estimate, less than 5 percent of the workforce in 1930—far below levels in the United States or Germany).

The relatively limited unemployment is partly explained by the fall in the workforce caused by a change in its age structure (a consequence of a stagnant population and a result of the Great War), by the return to the home of 500,000 women between 1931 and 1936, and by the departure of 350,000 immigrant workers. On the other hand, the return to the countryside, which has often been suggested as a cause of lower unemployment, is a myth. The importance of agricultural activity (more than 30 percent of the workforce) limited the visibility, not the magnitude of unemployment. Increased employment in commerce and public administrations had more effect. But the most important reason that visible unemployment was understated was the great increase in part-time work, especially in traditional industries. In mid-1935, part-time work may have represented the equivalent of 1.3 million unemployed.

The fall in production was also relatively moderate, in commerce and manufactures, never exceeding 20 percent of the 1929 peak; and the fall in real GNP could not have exceeded 10 percent. Household consumption did not fall substantially, because nominal wages were maintained while prices fell sharply.

Conditions varied greatly among industries. Modern industries protected from international competition (paper, rubber, electricity, oil refining) soon restored production and even profits. Cartels supported by the government limited the recession in other industries (sugar refining, ship building, coal mining). But nonprotected industries, often widely scattered, like metallurgy and textiles, faced falling prices and sales in their export markets, and stable prices from their (protected) suppliers. Many such industries could not even cover the depreciation of their equipment, especially the most modern and capital-intensive ones that had invested heavily in the preceding years.

Finally, the relative mildness of the depression can be linked with the mildness of the banking crisis of 1931–33 in France, which was the consequence both of limited foreign financial commitments in 1931 and the traditional caution of the major banks in their relationships with manufacturers. Only one major bank failed, and a rescue operation organized by the Treasury, the Bank of France, and the other banks avoided a panic.

While the French depression was relatively mild, it was also unusually long. In many industries, production did not reach its lowest point until 1935 or later. The 1930 level of industrial production was not equalled before World War II, and unemployment was still near its maximum in spring 1939.

In the Regulation school's neo-Marxist approach, the long duration corresponds to important structural changes, particularly in the regulation of the labor force (Salais et al., 1986). But these changes were not more important in France than elsewhere. The persistence of the depression might then be explained by a succession of external events (devaluation of the pound and the dollar) and policy errors that blocked several incipient recoveries (in early 1931, mid-1932, mid-1933, and 1936).

Several explanations are probably necessary. The most important seems to be the overvaluation of the franc after the pound was devalued in 1931 (Sauvy 1984, Eichengreen and Sachs 1985), which blocked the recovery of exports until 1936. The difference between French and English prices fluctuated around 20 percent, a gap that no deflationary policy could overcome. It was psychologically impossible to devalue before 1934, because the French were proud of their stabilized currency and of the international speculation in its favor. But in 1934, after speculation changed direction when the dollar was devalued, hostility to devaluation remained universal (except for Paul Reynaud). The reasons invoked were national honor, honesty, and, mainly, fear of inflation, since inflation had resulted from depreciation of the franc in the 1920s (Mouré 1991). The franc was devalued in September 1936 only under the pressure of speculation and renewed inflation (a consequence of monetizing the budget deficit). It was too late, world prices were already rising, and the devaluation contributed mainly to accelerating inflation.

The great fall in investment (more than 30 percent from the 1930 level) also prolonged the depression. It was the macroeconomic corollary of the stability in consumption. In a microeconomic view, it was due to reduced confidence and profitability. New issues became impossible in a declining stock market, and rising real interest rates and public-sector borrowing displaced private bond issues (Saint-Etienne 1984).

Inconsistent government policies also deepened the depression. Several governments sustained depressed industries by setting prices or organizing cartels, forcing deeper price reductions in other markets. In 1935, the deflationary policy of Laval was inconsistent with the obligatory discounting of Treasury bills by the Bank of France (in order to finance the budget deficit without tax increases). Under the pressure of a growing trade deficit and the demands of many manufacturers, protectionist quotas and clearing agreements were imposed on 57 percent of French imports by 1935. Protection could have served as the condition for an internal demand-driven recovery, but even the Socialists refused to impose the exchange control necessary for such a policy to work, because it would have meant joining the dictatorships. As a consequence, protection simply increased inequalities among industries.

The rigid and sudden reduction of the work week to forty hours in 1936 seems to have caused bottlenecks in many industries, which

G

blocked the start of recovery (Sauvy 1984; Baverez and Villa in Boyer 1991). The great fall in investment in the early 1930s also held back the recovery, because the manufacturing industries had old equipment and insufficient capacity to meet a surge in demand (Braudel and Labrousse 1980). Nor did they have funds available to buy intermediate goods and rebuild stocks, because of the excessive caution of the banking system and increases in the Bank of France's discount rate (Levy-Leboyer, in Levy-Leboyer and Casanova 1991). The 45-percent rise in labor costs under the Popular Front and the need for a recovery in profits to finance investment together helped produce inflation after 1936.

Further, social cohesion collapsed after the Laval government's wage cuts in 1935 and the Popular Front in 1936 (Kindleberger 1986). An unstable political situation discouraged domestic investment and led to the export of capital that reduced the money supply.

France provides an example of a great depression with no violent domestic crisis. The length of the depression resulted from the coincidence of a great international crisis, rapid structural change in an economy that had preserved its traditional character too long, and governments with limited courage and no clear understanding of the appropriate policies. Thus in 1939, the country was divided and poorly prepared for war. But the depression also helped to achieve transformations in minds, social relations, and production methods that prepared the way for postwar growth.

Pierre-Cyrille Hautcoeur

See also BANK OF FRANCE; GOLD STANDARD; GOLD STANDARD: CAUSES AND CONSEQUENCES; GREAT DEPRESSION IN BRITAIN (1929–1932); GREAT DEPRESSION IN THE UNITED STATES (1929–1938); REGULATION SCHOOL

Bibliography
Asselain, J.-C. 1984. *Histoire économique de la France du XVIIIème siècle à nos jours.* Paris: Seuil.
Boyer, R., ed. 1991. *Paradoxes français de la crise des années 1930. Le Mouvement Social* no. 154 (special issue).
Boyer, R. and J. Mistral. 1978. *Accumulation, inflation, crises.* Paris: Presses Universitaires de France.
Braudel, F. and E. Labrousse, eds. 1980.
Histoire économique et sociale de la France. Vol. 2. Paris: Presses Universitaires de France.
Eichengreen, B. and J. D. Sachs. [1985] 1990. "Exchange Rates and Economic Recovery in the 1930s." Chap. 9 in B. Eichengreen, *Elusive Stability: Essays in the History of International Finance, 1919–1939.* Cambridge: Cambridge Univ. Press.
Eichengreen, B. and C. Wyplosz. [1988] 1990. "The Economic Consequences of the Franc Poincaré." Chap. 7 in B. Eichengreen, *Elusive Stability: Essays in the History of International Finance, 1919–1939.* Cambridge: Cambridge Univ. Press.
Kindleberger, C. P. 1986. *The World in Depression, 1929–1939.* Rev. and enl. ed. Berkeley: Univ. of California Press.
Levy-Leboyer, M. and J.-C. Casanova, eds. 1991. *Entre l'Etat et le marché.* Paris: Gallimard.
Marseille, J. 1980. "Les origines 'inopportunes' de la crise de 1929 en France." *Revue Economique* 31:648–84.
Mouré, K. 1991. *Managing the Franc Poincaré.* Cambridge: Cambridge Univ. Press.
Néré, J. 1973. *La crise de 1929.* Paris: Armand Colin.
Saint-Etienne, C. 1984. *The Great Depression, 1929–1938.* Stanford: Hoover Institution Press.
Salais, R. 1988. "Why Was Unemployment so Low in France during the 1930s?" In *Interwar Unemployment in International Perspective,* edited by B. Eichengreen and T. J. Hatton, 247–88. Boston: Kluwer.
Salais, R., N. Baverez, and Bénédicte Reynaud. 1986. *L'invention du chômage.* Paris: Presses Universitaires de France.
Sauvy, A. 1984. *Histoire Economique de la France entre les deux guerres.* 2d ed. Paris: Economica.
Sicsic, P. 1992. "Was the Franc Poincaré Deliberately Undervalued?" *Explorations in Economic History* 29:69–92.

Great Depression in the United States (1929–1938)
Between 1929 and 1938, the United States experienced the most serious depression in its history. During the contraction phase (1929–33),

real GNP declined by 30 percent; unemployment reached 24 percent of the labor force, and prices as measured by the GNP deflator fell by 23 percent. During the recovery phase, real GNP remained below the 1929 level until 1937; unemployment did not fall below 10 percent until 1941; and prices rose by 13 percent. The contraction phase lasted 43 months and the recovery phase 50 months. Of the two phases, the slow and erratic recovery may be the more puzzling. However, both the contraction and the recovery remain enigmatic. Milton Friedman and Anna Schwartz (1963) called the Great Depression idiosyncratic, and Robert Lucas (1987) said that it defies explanation.

Describing and interpreting what happened during the Great Depression is the task of the macroeconomic historian, and, at its best, is an exercise in applied macroeconomics. As an exercise in applied macroeconomics, our understanding of this event is necessarily constrained by the state of the art as reflected in recent interpretations of the episode. Primary consideration will be given to surveying the causes of the Great Depression including real and monetary, domestic and international. It will be useful to distinguish between the cause or causes of the initial downturn and the causes of the unusual severity and duration of the depression. The search for causal explanations may not be a search for a single event like the banking crisis of 1930 or the Smoot-Hawley tariff, but a series of interrelated events extending over the complete depression-recovery cycle.

The 1929 Downturn
Following World War I, the U.S. economy suffered a severe depression in 1920–21 and two mild recessions in 1923–24 and 1926–27. When the economy turned down in August 1929 and in the months immediately following, there were no tell-tale signs that something more ominous than an ordinary recession was in the cards. The stock-market crash in October did not by itself signal a major depression. Stock prices had regained at least one-half of their precrash levels by April 1930. Specific events in 1930 allegedly transformed what was then regarded as an ordinary contraction into a full-fledged depression.

Explanations for the initial phase of the recession included high nominal and real interest rates induced by the Federal Reserve policy in 1928–29 of attempting to control stock-market speculation, a decline in residential housing construction, and the operation of the recently reinstituted gold standard. A credit-stringency explanation is shared by Friedman and Schwartz (1963), Hamilton (1987), and Saint-Etienne (1984), though there are differences in emphasis regarding the channels through which credit stringency affected output and employment. Gordon and Wilcox (1981) and Hickman (1973) attributed the initial downturn to a decline in residential housing construction due to slowing population growth following the 1921 and 1924 legislation limiting immigration and due to overbuilding in the 1920s. Temin (1976) has questioned Hickman's interpretation on the grounds that the evidence was not sufficient to rule out reverse causation; that is, income causes housing rather than housing causes income.

Meltzer (1976) has suggested that the gold standard may have contributed to the start of the 1929 recession. Economic expansion triggered by Federal Reserve policies to moderate the 1926–27 recession was more rapid in the United States than in the rest of the world. Under the price-specie-flow mechanism, prices were expected to rise more in the United States than in the rest of the world, leading to a fall in exports, an outflow of gold, and a decrease in the money stock. Although prices did not rise in the United States, they fell less in the U.S. than in several leading countries. According to Meltzer, the 1929–30 recession resulted from a change in relative prices in 1928–29.

Banking Crises
Friedman and Schwartz identified the first banking crisis in November–December 1930 as the catalyst that converted the recession into a major depression. They maintained that a decline in the stock of money initiated by an accelerated rate of bank failures in late 1930 caused income to decline. Subsequent banking crises in 1931 and 1933 were attributed to prior changes in income and the inept responses of the Federal Reserve policymakers. According to Friedman and Schwartz, an autonomous disturbance in the currency-deposit ratio provoked a rash of bank suspensions that decreased the money stock, which, in turn, caused income to decline. A contagion of fear spread among depositors mainly in agricultural areas where the incidence of bank suspensions had been highest in the 1920s.

McFerrin (1939) supplied the missing clue, not otherwise identified specifically by

Friedman and Schwartz, concerning why the rate of bank failures accelerated in November 1930. The collapse of Caldwell and Company, a large investment-banking house in Nashville, Tennessee, spread panic during a two-week period engulfing at least 120 banks in Tennessee, Arkansas, Kentucky, and North Carolina. He showed how poor loans and investments in the 1920s were the principal factor contributing to the weakness of the suspended banks, an interpretation consistent with the view of Friedman and Schwartz that the bank suspensions in November 1930 were unrelated to movements in current income and interest rates. Temin (1976) rejected the Friedman and Schwartz explanation. He conjectured that declining prices of low-grade corporate bonds brought on by the depression were the principal cause of the bank failures in November and December 1930. However, Temin produced no evidence to support his hypothesis. Without data on the portfolios of suspended banks, he acknowledged that he could not show how the decline in bond prices had contributed to those failures.

Kindleberger (1988) attributed the bank failures to the decline in commodities prices following the 1929 stock-market crash. He maintained that the decline in stock prices spread to commodities when foreign goods shipped to New York and normally sold on consignment could not be financed because of the inability of New York banks to replace money withdrawn from the call-money market. The malaise in the commodities markets spread to B-grade bonds, leading to default on bank loans and bank failures and subsequently to a decline in the money stock. But Kindleberger had no explanation for the first banking crisis beginning at the end of 1930. Neither White (1983) nor Wicker (1980) was able to confirm any close relationship between deteriorating bond prices and the rate of bank failures.

One of the weaknesses of the Friedman and Schwartz hypothesis concerns their unsubstantiated claim that bank failures were independent of the prior changes in income. They made no effort to model the bank-failure rate or to test its implications. Anderson and Butkiewitz (1980) attempted to remedy this alleged defect in the Friedman and Schwartz argument by constructing a structural model in which both income and the bank-failure rate were endogenous variables. They found that the money-supply function was not significantly influenced by either interest rates or income, but was significantly affected by bank failures. Seventy-two percent of the decline in the money stock was accounted for by bank failures. They found no reason to reject the hypothesis that bank failures were an important cause of the decline in the money stock during the Great Depression.

Both Wicker (1982) and White (1983) showed that the 1930 banking crisis may have had some regional and local impact on economic activity, but had little or no national import.

Temin (1976) denied that monetary stringency accompanied the 1930 banking panic on the grounds that it conflicted with what we know about the behavior of interest rates and the real money stock. If the decline in output was caused by monetary stringency, then short-term interest rates should have risen, and we know that they did not. Moreover, he argued in 1976 that the monetary-stringency claim was inconsistent with the increase in real money stock. In response to criticism by Gordon and Wilcox (1981), Temin (1981) recanted, admitting that a rise in real balances could be consistent with the Friedman and Schwartz hypothesis. Temin now maintains that his interpretation is roughly the same as that of Gordon and Wilcox in attribution of ultimate effects. The only difference between them is about what initiated the downturn, an autonomous spending shock or a monetary shock.

Bernanke (1983) also assigned a key role to widespread bank failures, but, unlike Friedman and Schwartz who emphasized the relationship between money and output, he looked to the supply of bank credit as the nonmonetary channel through which financial distress exerted real effects. Bank failures increase the real costs of financial intermediation (information gathering and nontrivial market making), thereby making credit more expensive and more difficult to obtain. The resulting credit squeeze converted a recession into a serious downturn by contributing to its severity and duration. Adding credit proxies to a regression similar to one used by Barro (1977), Bernanke showed that the proxies improved the purely monetary explanation of short-run output movement. Nevertheless, evidence is still lacking about any direct relationship between bank credit and output. Although Bernanke agreed that the decrease in the money stock was important, he doubted whether it provided a complete explanation for the decline in output during the Great Depression.

Spending Hypothesis

After rejecting the purely monetary interpretation of the Great Depression advanced by Friedman and Schwartz, Temin proposed his own monocausal explanation. He conjectured that the behavior of interest rates and real money balances was consistent with a strong autonomous decrease in the *IS* schedule caused by an inexplicable decrease in consumption expenditures in 1930. He thought that the onset of the banking crisis in November–December 1930 was too late to have any explanatory value for the 9 percent decline in output. Temin fitted a life-cycle model of consumption to interwar data, and then interpreted the residuals and the change in the residuals as evidence for an autonomous increase in consumption expenditures. Both Mayer (1978) and Gandolfi and Lothian (1977) rejected Temin's hypothesis. Mayer denied that a change in residuals was the relevant variable; he fitted regressions to the levels of the data as well as to their differences, and the level regressions rejected Temin's hypothesis. Gandolfi and Lothian estimated a permanent-income consumption function for 1889–1941 and concluded that the average absolute value of the change in residuals demonstrated that 1930 was far from unique. The size of the negative residual for 1925, for example, was four times larger than the residual for 1930. Why, they asked, was there no deep recession in 1925?

Attempts to determine the direction of causality, that is, whether money causes income or income causes money, have been made by performing Granger-causality tests, but the results to date have been disappointing. Schwartz (1981) tested for Granger-causality during the Great Depression interval 1929–39 and concluded that money and income were mutually interdependent. Gordon and Wilcox (1981) performed similar tests using both quarterly and monthly data for three time periods, only one of which was 1929–41. Their results confirmed Schwartz's findings—simultaneity of movements in money and income, a conclusion that is consistent with either hypothesis about the direction of causality. There still remains the unanswered question whether the Granger tests are appropriate if both the money stock and income are endogenous variables.

Mishkin (1978), like Temin, assigned an important role to the behavior of real expenditures in contributing to the severity of the Great Depression. But his explanation resides in balance-sheet effects generated by declining commodities and stock prices which increased the real burden of household indebtedness and reduced the value of financial assets as well. Mishkin acknowledged that the balance-sheet effects must be viewed as endogenous; that is, as being equally compatible with either some exogenous monetary or real shock. Moreover, balance-sheet effects provide a richer description of the transmission mechanism. His regression estimates of consumer-durable and residential-housing expenditures track very closely the actual behavior of expenditures during the first year of the depression. But in order to generate these estimates, he assumed that the coefficients of his depression estimates were the same as the coefficients of his post-World War II estimates—an interesting conjecture, but one that requires a more explicit rationale than Mishkin provided.

New Classical Explanations of the Great Depression

The New Classical macroeconomics has stressed wage and price flexibility, strong self-corrective forces, and unanticipated monetary shocks. Lucas and Rapping (1972) modeled the labor market as though it were in continuous short-run equilibrium. They made labor supply a function of the real wage workers expected (the normal wage) relative to the actual average wage. Unemployment during the Great Depression was therefore mainly voluntary, a view so sharply at variance with the conventional Keynesian view that unemployment was involuntary that it may be rejected too hastily. Their model predicted a 17-percent rate of unemployment during the 1929–33 contraction, not too far from the actual 25-percent unemployment rate. But the model fared less well in predicting unemployment during the recovery phase. Darby (1976) reestimated the Lucas-Rapping model using unemployment estimates that excluded emergency workers (WPA) on the ground that the workers were no longer engaged in search activity and would not now be classified as unemployed by the Bureau of Labor Statistics. His results show a speedier return to normal levels of unemployment than is suggested by conventional data sources. But there is some evidence that emergency workers left WPA jobs as soon as new jobs became available. Baily (1983) rejected the Lucas-Rapping findings because the implied elasticity of labor supply was much too high. The implicit elasticity is 2.4 compared to standard microeconomic estimates of the response of labor supply to a change in the wage rate which are close to zero.

Explicit-contract theory is of little or no help in explaining either the behavior of wages or employment during the Great Depression, since explicit contracts played only a minimal role at the time in wage negotiations. Not much more can be said about implicit-contract theory which postulates that wage decisions are made in the context of long-term relationships between firms and their workers. Baily (1983) rejected the narrow risk-sharing version of implicit-contract theory as an explanation of wage rigidity between 1929 and 1941 on the grounds that the depression-recovery interval was too long to have been perceived as a temporary change in fundamental conditions. He preferred an eclectic account of wage rigidity. Price cutting was frowned upon, because the threat of retaliation might leave everyone worse off and because ensuing wage reduction might affect the morale of the workers and the reputation of the firm adversely. The importance firms attach to their reputation, Baily argued, is evidenced by labor-turnover data during the depression years. The layoff rate was 3.8 per hundred workers per month over the three-year period 1930–32. The 3.9 new hiring rate was equally high. Such an unexpected hiring rate provided the requisite incentives for firms to be especially attentive to their reputations.

Another implication of the New Classical models when combined with the rational-expectations hypothesis is the unimportance of anticipated money as a cause of output change. Rush (1986) repeated Barro-like tests for the significance of unexpected money using the monetary base instead of money as the dependent variable. He concluded that unexpected money shocks were incapable of explaining the Great Depression.

The natural-rate hypothesis seems to have fared no better. Deviations from the natural rate presumably generate self-correcting mechanisms that cause a reversion to the natural rate. When unemployment remains above the natural rate, deflation should accelerate. During the Great Depression the unemployment rate remained above 8.5 percent for 12 years (1930–

41) with no sign of accelerating deflation. Between 1934 and 1940, the GNP deflator remained relatively constant while unemployment remained above 14 percent, a fact difficult to reconcile with the natural-rate hypothesis.

New Deal measures like the National Industrial Recovery Act (NRA) and the Wagner Act may have shifted up the Phillips curve and effectively disguised its negative slope. Nevertheless, Gordon (1976) maintained that the NRA episode was too brief to have generated the observed price effects, and the Wagner Act could not have been responsible for downward inflexibility of wage rates. DeLong and Summers (1988) also rejected the natural rate as a plausible interpretation of what happened to output and employment during the Great Depression. They do not deny that there are tendencies for the economy to move back to trend levels after demand shocks, but they maintained that the self-regulating mechanisms are weak. The Great Depression is consistent with multiple-equilibrium models where the economy can fall into a low-activity state and remain there for a long period with no noticeable tendency to return to a high-employment equilibrium. Theoretical models of multiple equilibria rely on credit-market failures and asymmetric price adjustment to explain long delays in the reversion of the economy back to full resource utilization. The Great Depression is also consistent with the view that output shocks are transitory. They argue that real business-cycle models, in which the fall in output has strong effects on the natural rate of unemployment, are difficult to reconcile with evidence from the Great Depression. They concluded that this evidence, by itself, is sufficient to reject the claim that a shock to output was a permanent one.

International Considerations

We now turn to those interpretations of the Great Depression that stress international considerations. The Smoot-Hawley tariff was enacted in June 1930, increasing the effective duty on imports between 1929 and 1932 by as much as 50 percent. The market value of exports and imports in current prices fell by approximately 30 percent in 1930, due perhaps to the tariff increases and to worldwide deflation. Moreover, there was a 27 percent decline in the quantity of farm exports. Meltzer (1976) argued that the tariff was an important, though not the only, factor in turning the 1929 recession into the Great Depression. He recognized a link between the Smoot-Hawley tariff, the acceleration of bank suspensions at the end of 1930, and the decline in the stock of money. By increasing the price of U.S. imports and by inducing foreign retaliation, the tariff further reduced farm prices and weakened the banks in rural areas. Meltzer concluded that in the absence of Smoot-Hawley, subsequent tariff retaliation, and the policy errors of the Federal Reserve, there would not have been a depression of the same magnitude as the one we experienced.

Eichengreen (1989) concluded, contrary to Meltzer, that the macroeconomic effects of Smoot-Hawley, including the retaliation effects, were small compared with the output decline during the Great Depression. He simulated a Mundell-Fleming model with two symmetrical countries faced with a tariff increase in one and retaliation by the other and found no support for Meltzer's hypothesis that Smoot-Hawley worsened the depression.

Kindleberger (1988) maintained that competitive exchange-rate depreciation in the early 1930s added to the severity of the world depression since depreciation left prices unchanged in the initiating country and reduced them abroad, thereby aggravating deflationary pressures. But Eichengreen countered that competitive depreciation switched expenditures toward domestic goods and relaxed the exchange-rate constraint on monetary policy. These effects, he maintained, stimulated rather than impeded recovery in the initiating country.

Kindleberger's argument about the effects on the devaluing country is not relevant to the United States during the contractionary phase of the depression. The U.S. did not abandon gold until April 1933, and, hence, could not have been a factor in prolonging the downswing. Nevertheless, it could have restrained recovery, but Eichengreen and Sachs (1985) argued that devaluation was a powerful instrument of economic recovery. Their evidence, however, is confined to ten European countries.

Temin and Wigmore (1990) attributed a key role to dollar depreciation working through rational-expectations channels in explaining economic recovery in the U.S. According to the rational-expectations hypothesis, future rates of inflation are conditioned by agents' perceptions of long-term government monetary and fiscal policies. In other words, a change in policy regime that is correctly anticipated can terminate

deflation with favorable employment and output effects. Roosevelt, on this interpretation, established a new macroeconomic-policy regime, which brought the contraction to a halt and initiated economic recovery. Temin and Wigmore state that the change in regime was signalled by Roosevelt's abandonment of the gold standard and the deflationary expectations that it implied. Although the evidence is suggestive, it is also consistent with alternative explanations of the recovery. The main problem, however, is that the rational-expectations hypothesis does such a poor job in explaining the lethargic recovery. With market-clearing, one would predict that unexpected shocks would be followed by temporary, not prolonged, departures from the natural rate. Recent studies by Temin (1989) and Eichengreen (1992) attribute a major role to the gold standard in the causation and transmission of the Great Depression.

On the basis of the historical and econometric evidence, we cannot discriminate among the rival theories and explanations of the Great Depression, whether they be mono- or multicausal, monetary or real, domestic or international. Nevertheless, progress can be measured by the retreat from simplistic explanations and the gradual accumulation of a body of knowledge, perhaps more negative than positive, and not quite so decisive as we might desire, which augurs well for our future understanding of the worst economic catastrophe of the twentieth century.

Elmus Wicker

See also BANK OF ENGLAND; BANK OF FRANCE; BANK OF UNITED STATES; DEPRESSION OF 1920–1921; DEPRESSION OF 1937–1938; FEDERAL RESERVE SYSTEM: 1914–1941; FISHER, IRVING; FRIEDMAN, MILTON; GOLD STANDARD; GOLD STANDARD: CAUSES AND CONSEQUENCES; GREAT DEPRESSION IN BRITAIN (1929–1933); GREAT DEPRESSION IN FRANCE (1929–1938); HAWTREY, RALPH GEORGE; SMOOT-HAWLEY TARIFF; SNYDER, CARL; STOCK-MARKET CRASH OF 1929

Bibliography

Anderson, B. and J. Butkiewitz. 1980. "Money, Spending, and the Great Depression." *Southern Economic Journal* 47:388–403.
Baily, M. N. 1983. "The Labor Market in the 1930s." In *Macroeconomics, Prices, and Quantities,* edited by J. Tobin, 21–62. Washington, D.C.: Brookings Institution.

Barro, R. 1977. "Unanticipated Money Growth and Unemployment in the United States." *American Economic Review* 67:101–15.

Bernanke, B. S. 1983. "Nonmonetary Effects of the Financial Crisis in the Propagation of the Great Depression." *American Economic Review* 73:257–76.

Calomiris, C. W., R. A. Margo, C. D. Romer, and P. Temin. 1993. *The Great Depression. Symposium. Journal of Economic Perspectives,* Spring, 39–102.

Darby, M. R. 1976. "Three-and-a Half Million U.S. Employees Have Been Mislaid: Or, An Explanation of Unemployment, 1934–1941." *Journal of Political Economy* 84:1–16.

DeLong, B. and L. Summers. 1988. "How Does Macroeconomic Policy Affect Output?" *Brookings Papers on Economic Activity,* Number two, 439–80.

Eichengreen, B. 1989. "The Political Economy of the Smoot-Hawley Tariff." *Research in Economic History* 11:1–44.

———. 1992. *Golden Fetters.* New York: Oxford Univ. Press.

Eichengreen, B. and J. Sachs. 1985. "Exchange Rates and Economic Recovery in the 1930s." *Journal of Economic History* 45:925–46.

Friedman, M. and A. J. Schwartz. 1963. *A Monetary History of the United States, 1867–1960.* Princeton: Princeton Univ. Press.

Gandolfi, A. E. and J. R. Lothian. 1977. "Did Monetary Forces Cause the Great Depression?" *Journal of Money, Credit, and Banking* 9:679–91.

Gordon, R. J. 1976. "Recent Developments in the Theory of Inflation and Unemployment." *Journal of Monetary Economics* 2:185–219.

Gordon, R. J. and J. A. Wilcox. 1981. "Monetarist Interpretations of the Great Depression: An Evaluation and Critique." In *The Great Depression Revisited,* edited by K. Brunner, 49–107. Boston: Martinus Nijhoff.

Hamilton, J. D. 1987. "Monetary Factors in the Great Depression." *Journal of Monetary Economics* 19:145–69.

Hickman, B. G. 1973. "What Became of the Business Cycle." In *Nations and Households in Economic Growth: Essays in Honor of Moses Abramovitz,* edited by

P. David and M. Reder, 291–313. New York: Academic Press.

Kindleberger, C. P. 1988. "The Financial Crises of the 1930s and the 1980s: Similarities and Differences." *Kyklos* 41:171–86.

Lucas, R. E. 1987. *Models of Business Cycles.* Oxford: Basil Blackwell.

Lucas, R. E. and L. Rapping. 1972. "Unemployment in the Great Depression: Is There a Full Explanation?" *Journal of Political Economy* 80:186–91.

Mayer, T. 1978. "Money and the Great Depression: A Critique of Professor Temin's Thesis." *Explorations in Economic History* 15:127–45.

McFerrin, J. B. 1939. *Caldwell and Company.* Chapel Hill: Univ. of North Carolina Press.

Meltzer, A. H. 1976. "Monetary and Other Explanations of the Great Depression." *Journal of Monetary Economics* 2:456–71.

Mishkin, F. S. 1978. "The Household Balance Sheet and the Great Depression." *Journal of Economic History* 38:918–37.

Rush, M. 1986. "Unexpected Money and Unemployment: 1920 to 1983." *Journal of Money, Credit, and Banking* 18:259–74.

Saint-Etienne, C. 1984. *The Great Depression, 1929–1938: Lessons from the 1980s.* Stanford, Calif.: Hoover Institution Press.

Schwartz, A. J. 1981. "Understanding 1929–1933." In *The Great Depression Revisited,* edited by K. Brunner, 5–48. Boston: Martinus Nijhoff.

Temin, P. 1976. *Did Monetary Forces Cause the Great Depression?* New York: Norton.

———. 1981. "Notes on the Causes of the Great Depression." In *The Great Depression Revisited,* edited by K. Brunner, 108–24. Boston: Martinus Nijhoff.

———. 1989. *Lessons from the Great Depression.* Cambridge: MIT Press.

Temin, P. and B. A. Wigmore. 1990. "The End of One Big Deflation." *Explorations in Economic History* 27:483–502.

White, E. N. 1984. "A Reinterpretation of the Banking Crisis of 1930." *Journal of Economic History* 44:119–38.

Wicker, E. 1980. "A Reconsideration of the Causes of the Banking Panic of 1930." *Journal of Economic History* 40:571–83.

———. 1982. "Interest Rate and Expenditure Effects on the Banking Panic of 1930."

Explorations in Economic History
19:435–45.

Great Depression of 1873–1896

Opinion on the behavior of the British economy over the period 1873–96 has fluctuated. The period has at times been regarded as one of severe depression. But the consensus now is that while British agriculture was, indeed, depressed in this period—particularly in East Anglia—depression affected primarily nominal, not real, magnitudes.

Data Revisions

Part of the reappraisal of this period resulted simply from revisions in the data. Most important in shifting the interpretation have been Feinstein (1972) on output, and Crafts, Leybourne, and Mills (1989) on determining trend growth. There have also been major revisions to monetary data carried out by Capie and Webber (1985) which produced two significant types of change. They showed that existing measures of money differ from a series closer to the true one, and that they contain a spurious trend (of particular importance to the study of a long period of years). The spurious trend resulted because most series had been based on data in *The Economist* half-yearly "Banking Supplement." These data were compiled from the accounts published by banks. More and more banks published every year. Hence, even had the money stock in fact been constant, a larger and larger portion of it would have been reported. Although attempts were made to allow for this spurious trend, insufficient allowance was made.

Money and Output

These data revisions had two significant implications for the 1873–96 period: they reduced the variability of velocity of circulation, and they supported the view that falling prices between 1873 and 1896 were caused by a rate of money growth that did not match growth in the real economy. The money stock (on a broad definition including coin and bank deposits) grew by 1.3 percent a year in the years to 1896, and 2 percent a year from then to 1913. Over the downswing as a whole the money stock grew by 33 percent and real output rose by just over 53 percent. (In contrast, over 1896–1913, the money stock grew by 40 percent and output by 36 percent.) Money growth was deficient relative to output in the first half of the period, and excessive in the second.

This of course would be quite immaterial if the demand for money were not stable relative to income. In fact, it appears to have been. Despite some differences in data and statistical technique, numerous studies report the demand for money to be a stable function of a few variables; and, of particular importance, the income elasticity of demand is always in the neighborhood of unity.

This supports the view that falling prices over the period were caused by deficient money growth from 1873 to 1896 (and that the decline was reversed by excessive money growth).

A Real Decline?

Several accounts of Britain's economic performance point to the 1870s as the start of relative decline. But the data on which this conclusion is based seem not entirely reliable. Their unreliability is shown partly by the various dates when the climacteric occurred. It has been placed in both the 1870s and the 1890s, while Feinstein and his co-workers have shown slightly but steadily declining growth from the 1850s to the 1900s. Recent work finds only a slight fall in trend growth between 1899 and 1913, and no evidence whatsoever of a climacteric in the 1870s.

The evidence for a long-lasting depression, or even a slowing of growth, in the period 1873–96 is thus rather tenuous. However, there is clear evidence of a decline in prices. One of the various explanations of the decline may help explain how the idea that there was a nationwide depression emerged.

Price Behavior

Prices in Britain fell from 1873 to 1896. Here, too, there have been revisions. Wholesale prices (the indicator used at the time) fell by 39 percent; but Feinstein's GNP deflator fell by only 20 percent. (Prices were falling, it should be observed, in most of the developed and some of the developing world in this period.)

There have been two explanations for falling prices, one real and one monetary. The real explanation rests on the extension of arable farming in the New World and on the revolution in transport. These two combined to produce falling agricultural prices in Britain (and of course in the rest of Europe). This, it is said, reduced the general price level, because agricultural goods were significant in any index. But this explanation presumes that agricultural prices fell year after year for many years. After specifically investigating that question, Bordo and Schwartz (1981) conclude that agricultural prices did not fall steadily over a long period.

The alternative explanation accepts that agricultural prices fell, but contends that this affected *relative* prices. Prices in general fell, according to the alternative explanation, because, as noted above, money grew increasingly scarce relative to output. The increasing scarcity was caused by rapid economic development just as the main industrial countries were joining the gold standard, while, on the supply side, there were no new gold discoveries until the early and middle 1890s in Australia, South Africa, and the Klondike. The demand for gold was growing, but the supply of gold was not. In Britain (and also the United States) the trend growth rate of money depended closely on the trend growth rate of the monetary base—in this period gold (Cagan 1965).

Two Difficulties

At least two difficulties remain with this interpretation of 1873–96. First there is the Gibson Paradox. And second, if real output did not fall, why was there so much talk of depression?

Interest rates fell and rose with the price level—not, apparently, with its rate of change. It has been claimed that if prices were falling due to monetary tightness, then interest rates should have risen rather than, as they actually did, fall. In fact, as Irving Fisher showed, this paradox *can* be reconciled with a monetary explanation of prices. Expectations that price will continue to fall in the future reduce long-term nominal interest rates. Despite much subsequent attention to advancing alternative explanations, Fisher's theory stands, although certainly complemented by some new suggestions (Capie, Mills, and Wood 1991).

Why the anxiety about depression at the time? An explanation is that agriculture was depressed in Britain (and throughout Europe). Well represented in Parliament, agricultural interests were vocal and politically powerful in Britain. They promoted the idea that there was depression—indeed there was for them—and sought help, often through tariff protection.

Conclusion

The years from 1873 to 1896 in Britain were once viewed as years of continuous depression. The period lasted longer than a normal downswing, and it was thought to confirm the existence of the Kondratieff cycle. A new interpretation, bolstered by substantial revisions to data, has led to rejection of that belief.

Money growth in Britain was much slower than was thought even quite recently. This was the product of sluggish growth in the world supply of gold in combination with the new sources of demand for it. The result was a prolonged monetary stringency which reduced prices but did not reduce output. In Britain this produced a depression of nominal values but not of *aggregate* real variables. Depression there was, of course; agriculture was in difficulties. But this was the product of developments overseas, and technical progress in transport. There was no major real downswing in Britain from 1870 to 1896.

Forrest H. Capie
Geoffrey E. Wood

See also DEPRESSION OF 1873–1878; DEPRESSION OF 1882–1885; KONDRATIEFF CYCLES; PANIC OF 1873; PANIC OF 1893

Bibliography

Bordo, M. D. and A. J. Schwartz. 1981. "Money and Prices in the Nineteenth Century: Was Thomas Tooke Right?" *Explorations in Economic History* 18:97–127.

Cagan, P. 1965. *Determinants and Effects of Effects of Changes in the Stock of Money, 1875–1969.* New York: NBER.

Capie, F. H., T. C. Mills, and G. E. Wood. 1991. "Money, Interest Rates, and the Great Depression: Britain from 1870 to 1913." In *New Perspectives on the Late Victorian Economy,* edited by J. Foreman-Peck, 251–84. Cambridge: Cambridge Univ. Press.

Capie, F. H. and A. H. Webber. 1985. *A Monetary History of the United Kingdom, 1870–1982.* Vol. 1. *Data, Sources, and Methods.* London: Allen and Unwin.

Crafts, N., S. J. Leybourne, and T. C. Mills. 1989. "The Climacteric in Late Victorian Britain and France." *Journal of Applied Econometrics* 4:103–17.

Feinstein, C. H. 1972. *National Income, Expenditure and Output of the United Kingdom, 1855–1965.* Oxford: Clarendon Press.

Matthews, R. C. O., C. H. Feinstein, and J. Odling-Smee. 1982. *British Economic Growth, 1856–1973.* Oxford: Clarendon Press.

Saul, S. B. 1969. *The Myth of the Great Depression*. London: Macmillan.

Sked, A. 1987. *Britain's Decline*. Oxford: Basil Blackwell.

Growth Cycles

The term *growth cycle* has become common in the past twenty-five years and refers to cyclical fluctuations identified in kinds of aggregate economic activity that move alternately above and below their long-run trend rate. The first major study of growth cycles was Ilse Mintz's *Dating Postwar Business Cycles: Methods and Their Application to Western Germany, 1950–1967*. This was a period of very rapid growth in Western Germany, so that there were scarcely any conventional business cycles (now often referred to as *classical cycles* to distinguish them from growth cycles) as measured by the techniques developed and popularized by Wesley Clair Mitchell, Arthur Burns, and their associates at the National Bureau of Economic Research (NBER). The Burns-Mitchell emphasis was on recurring periods of absolute expansion and contraction in the levels of economic activity. Growth cycles were earlier called "deviation cycles" by Mintz and others to suggest that they were calculated as deviations from the long-run trend. Mintz found that many of the characteristic patterns found in business cycles were also present in her study of German growth cycles and that Germany did indeed suffer a number of "growth recessions" or "slowdowns" even though absolute declines were not visible in that period.

Growth cycles have become familiar as the type of instability monitored in many advanced market-oriented economies. In the United States they have been monitored chiefly at the Center for International Business Cycle Research (Columbia University), under the direction of Geoffrey H. Moore. Moore's Center has pioneered the development of techniques for measuring the underlying trend in a flexible (i.e., nonlinear) fashion and in developing growth-cycle chronologies for the major industrialized market-oriented economies (Boschan and Ebanks 1978).

In Paris, the Organization for Economic Cooperation and Development (OECD) has led in developing growth-cycle chronologies for member countries, based primarily on growth rates in "output—broadly defined" (usually the index of industrial production).

Even after it was determined that the NBER method of dating business cycles could be adapted to dating growth cycles, the question remained whether rough equivalents of the kinds of economic activity whose timing in relation to United States business cycles have typically been classified as leading, roughly coincident, or lagging would exhibit similar timing in relation to growth cycles both in the U.S. and in other market-oriented economies. A study by Klein and Moore (1985) answered both questions in the affirmative. Indeed in a number of cases an old charge, that the leading indicators give false signals, proved to be a measure of their cyclical sensitivity—they presaged slowdowns that did not become "classical" recessions as well as those that did.

A major question is whether we should monitor growth cycles, classical cycles, or both. The Department of Commerce in the U.S. continues to report monthly on changes in indicators relating to "classical cycles"; the Columbia Center reports on indicator changes relating to growth-cycle chronologies. In other countries the general preference is for monitoring growth cycles although events since the early 1980s in most countries suggest that classical business cycles must still be regarded as a threat.

Thus, for the foreseeable future there is much to be said for monitoring both kinds of instability, so that the development of growth-cycle analysis has enriched our forecasting and analytical tools considerably.

Philip A. Klein

See also ASYMMETRY; BUSINESS CYCLES; COMPOSITE AND DIFFUSION INDEXES; INDICATORS, QUALITATIVE; LEADING INDICATORS, HISTORICAL PERFORMANCE OF; MINTZ, ILSE SCHUELLER; MOORE, GEOFFREY HOYT; TRENDS AND RANDOM WALKS

Bibliography

Boschan, C. and W. W. Ebanks. 1978. "The Phase-Average Trend: A New Way of Measuring Economic Growth." *Proceedings of the Business and Economic Statistics Section, American Statistical Association* 24:332–35.

Klein, P. A. and G. H. Moore. 1985. *Monitoring Growth Cycles in Market-Oriented Countries, Developing and Using International Economic Indicators*. NBER Studies in Business Cycles, no. 26. Cambridge, Mass.: Ballinger.

Mintz, I. 1969. *Dating Postwar Business Cycles: Methods and Their Application to Western Germany, 1950–1967.* NBER, Occasional Paper no. 107. New York: NBER.

OECD. Department of Economics and Statistics. 1987. *OECD Leading Indicators and Business Cycles in Member Countries, 1960–1985.* Sources and Methods, No. 39. Paris: OECD.

H

Haavelmo, Trygve (1911–)

Trygve Haavelmo, the 1989 Nobel Memorial Prize winner in economics, was born on 13 December 1911 in Skedsmo, Norway. After the outbreak of World War II he left for the United States and worked for a period with the Norwegian Shipping and Trade Mission in New York City, while also working on his doctoral dissertation, *The Probability Approach in Econometrics,* which was submitted at Harvard in 1941. The far-reaching implications of the dissertation were immediately recognized by the leading econometricians of the time and a team of world-class economists and statisticians was gathered together at the Cowles Commission in Chicago to work out the details of the Haavelmo blueprint. The objective was to utilize and extend this Haavelmo blueprint to improve on the empirical modeling of the business cycle that had recently been developed by Tinbergen (1939). Haavelmo himself worked with the Cowles Commission until 1947 when he returned to Norway to become a professor of economics at the University of Oslo where he remained until retiring in 1979.

Published as a special supplement to *Econometrica* in 1944, Haavelmo's dissertation was instrumental in establishing econometrics as a separate discipline and marked a new era in empirical modeling. The two main contributions of his monograph were: (1) to introduce probability theory to econometric modeling, and (2) to offer a more coherent framework for bridging the gap between theory and data. It is interesting to note that several aspects of these contributions were published in two earlier papers on modeling business cycles (Haavelmo 1940, 1943).

Haavelmo's 1943 paper, "Statistical Testing of Business-Cycle Theories," can be viewed as a condensed version of the first six chapters in the 1944 monograph. It was written as a reply to Keynes's criticism of Tinbergen's monograph on empirical modeling of the business cycle. Haavelmo argued convincingly that the rejection of probability theory in empirical econometric modeling until then was based on a misunderstanding of the role and area of applicability of probability. Probability theory is appropriate not just when the data can be viewed as realizations of random samples (independent and identically distributed random variables) but even more so for time-series data where the independent and identically distributed assumptions are no longer appropriate. His argument was that the time-dependence in time-series data can best be modeled using *joint distributions.* At the same time, probability theory provides the framework for inductive inference beyond the data in hand. This is indeed what distinguishes statistical inference from descriptive statistics which had been the preferred framework in econometric modeling [described as historical curve fitting by Keynes (1939)]. He went on to argue that probability theory is also the best framework for the testing of theories, because it allows the risk of making the wrong decision to be evaluated.

Haavelmo's 1940 paper, "The Inadequacy of Testing Dynamic Theory by Comparing the Theoretical Solutions and Observed Cycles," concerned the important issue of linking the theory to the observed data. The apparent success of the Frisch model ([1933] 1965) of the business cycle encouraged modelers to concentrate exclusively on theoretical models whose final solutions (solving the dynamic equations as functions of time) gave rise to cyclic behavior paths. Haavelmo, using the results from a previous paper, suggested that this modeling strategy could be misleading because of the role of errors (or shocks). He used an example to show that a structural model whose (nonstochastic) homogeneous solutions did not yield any cycles had a general solution (with the errors attached) that exhibited cyclical path-like behavior. He therefore warned against building theories in order to account for the apparent behavior of time series. In modern terminology the issue is whether to estimate the final form or the structural form. Haavelmo warned against estimating a final form that is specifically built to account for the features of the time-series model.

In another short paper on the empirical modeling of business cycles by Tinbergen, Haavelmo (1941) warned against excluding the interest rate from the investment functions on the basis of their test of significance. He explained how a very significant variable can "appear" to be insignificant because of the presence of related variables in the same equation.

Haavelmo's most important contributions to business-cycle research were thus mainly related to the methodological issues of empirical modeling.

Aris Spanos

See also FRISCH, RAGNAR ANTON KITTEL; KOOPMANS, TJALLING CHARLES; MACRO-ECONOMETRIC MODELS: HISTORICAL DEVELOPMENT OF; TINBERGEN, JAN

Bibliography

Frisch, R. [1933] 1965. "Propagation Problems and Impulse Problems in Dynamic Economics." In *A.E.A. Readings in Business Cycles*, 155–85. Philadelphia: Blakiston.

Haavelmo, T. 1940. "The Inadequacy of Testing Dynamic Theory by Comparing the Theoretical Solutions and Observed Cycles." *Econometrica* 8:312–21.

———. 1941. "The Effect of the Rate of Interest on Investment: A Note." *Review of Economic Studies* 23:49–52.

———. 1943. "Statistical Testing of Business-Cycle Theories." *Review of Economic Studies* 25:13–18.

———. 1944. "The Probability Approach to Econometrics." *Econometrica* 12(Supplement):1–118.

———. 1960. *A Study in the Theory of Investment*. Chicago: Univ. of Chicago Press.

Keynes, J. M. 1939. "Professor Tinbergen's Method." *Economic Journal* 49:558–68.

Spanos, A. 1989. "On Rereading Haavelmo: A Retrospective View of Econometric Modeling." *Econometric Theory* 5:405–29.

Tinbergen, J. 1939. *Statistical Testing of Business-Cycle Theories*. 2 vols. Geneva: League of Nations.

Haberler, Gottfried [von] (1900–1994)

One of the great economists of the twentieth century, Gottfried Haberler made pathbreaking contributions in several fields of the discipline. After earning a doctorate in economics (and another in law) at the University of Vienna, he joined the faculty there in 1928.

In 1936 he accepted a professorship at Harvard and moved permanently to the United States. By that time he had produced pioneering work that revolutionized the theory of international trade. His subsequent contributions to international economics included breakthroughs in both trade theory and policy analysis.

In the 1930s, Haberler was also writing about business fluctuations (1932, 1936a, 1936b); his most outstanding work on cycles, *Prosperity and Depression,* appeared in 1937 and was recognized at once as a milestone in the field. Written for the League of Nations, which also sponsored Jan Tinbergen's groundbreaking statistical study of business cycles, *Prosperity and Depression* was intended to provide the theoretical backdrop for Tinbergen's study.

While Haberler's work in international economics is noted for brilliant theoretical innovations, the significance of his work in macroeconomics and business cycles lies primarily in his extraordinary ability to synthesize seemingly contradictory contributions and clarify their relationships, cutting through complicated theoretical material to identify core ideas and evaluate them with wisdom and common sense. A modern reader of *Prosperity and Depression* is likely to be struck by the number of basic macroeconomic issues that Haberler addressed with which we still grapple.

The great achievement of the book is its encyclopedic survey and synthesis of the major contending approaches to business-cycle theory. An excellent example is Haberler's extended treatment of Keynes's *General Theory* in the revised 1939 edition of *Prosperity and Depression*. This new chapter, relating the *General Theory* to the entire corpus of business-cycle theory, is still among the best analyses of many key aspects of Keynes's work. As was his hallmark, Haberler presents a reading that is both sympathetic and critical, restating convoluted arguments clearly.

Roughly equidistant from the Monetarist and Keynesian camps, Haberler stressed both the role of money and the institutional arrangements affecting the determination of wages and prices. He emphasized the search for both similarities *and* differences across business cycles, downplaying deterministic notions of the cycle. A reader of *Prosperity and Depression* would understand Haberler's observation (1991) that the German word *Konjunkturschwankungen* (meaning, roughly, business fluctuations) is a more descriptive term than "business cycles." He believed that external shocks frequently cause macroeconomic fluctuations, but nevertheless emphasized the role of various mechanisms that tend to limit upswings and downswings in the economy. In a 1962 article, Haberler ([1962] 1981) argued that depressions—though not fluctuations—are a thing of the past. He maintained that such depressions were caused by horrendous policy mistakes, no longer conceivable in leading industrial countries, but that milder fluctuations will continue.

Along with a chapter-by-chapter treatment of the cycle itself (definition, expansion, contraction, downturn, revival), Haberler's great book includes sections on all the major theories that had been developed to explain it (e.g., monetary, overinvestment, underconsumption, psychological) and on their combination to form a more comprehensive approach. Most of Haberler's analysis remains relevant today, in spite of the vast quantity of subsequent research. Macroeconomists trained during or after the rational-expectations revolution may be surprised by the considerable attention given to the role of expectations.

As Haberler (1985, 604) noted in a paper on rational and irrational expectations, "The view became widely popular in the 1920s that the business cycle would all but disappear if and when it was widely understood and correctly forecast." Such ideas were important precursors of modern rational-expectations analysis. But in contrast to rational-expectations theorists, Haberler underscores the roles played by uncertainty and by differences in expectations and in theoretical views. The evidence from the postwar period did not cause him to change the view expressed in *Prosperity and Depression* that "on the whole, it may be said that the differences and dissimilarities between different cycles are much greater than many cycle theories seem to assume" (1962, 275). Restating essentially the same point in reference to rational-expectations theorists, Haberler later observed "that the cyclical swings are too irregular and the government's policy reactions too uncertain to warrant the conclusion that all market participants, or the great majority, are likely to draw the same—correct—conclusions for the future. Thus, errors of optimism and pessimism continue to be made" (1985, 604).

One of the most influential international economists of this century, Haberler's chapter on international aspects of the business cycle in *Prosperity and Depression* is especially noteworthy. Particularly impressive is his clear discussion of how the degree of international capital mobility and the choice of exchange-rate system affect the international transmission of economic fluctuations—three decades before Mundell and Fleming pioneered the formal modeling of international capital movements in open-economy macroanalysis. He clearly explained, for example, how international capital mobility reduces the extent to which flexible exchange rates can insulate the domestic economy from foreign fluctuations, a proposition that was rediscovered in the international monetary literature of the 1960s and 1970s. Also of particular interest is Haberler's treatment of what is now called endogenous-policy theory, i.e., analysis not just of the effects of government policy on the economy but also of how the economy and other factors affect policy. Haberler observed that ". . . a certain cyclical movement [in commercial policy] is unmistakable. Every major depression brought a new outburst of protectionism, while prosperity periods have usually been marked by short steps back in the direction of freer trade" (1962, 414). Recent empirical research confirms the persistence of this tendency.

Prosperity and Depression exemplifies the powerful role of synthesis in the face of contending theories. It remains valuable to students of macroeconomic fluctuations as much for its substantive content as for its reminder of the intellectual shoulders on which we stand.

Patricia Dillon
Thomas D. Willett

See also EXPECTATIONS; PIGOU-HABERLER EFFECT; RATIONAL EXPECTATIONS; TINBERGEN, JAN

Bibliography

Baldwin, R. E. 1982. "Gottfried Haberler: Contributions to International Trade Theory and Policy." *Quarterly Journal of Economics* 97:141–48.

Gillis, M. 1982. "Gottfried Haberler: Contributions Upon Entering His Ninth Decade." *Quarterly Journal of Economics* 97:139–40.

Haberler, G. 1932. "Money and the Business Cycle." In *Gold and Monetary Stabilization*, edited by Q. Wright, 43–74. Chicago: Univ. of Chicago Press.

———. 1936a. "Mr. Keynes' Theory of the Multiplier: A Methodological Criticism." *Zeitschrift für Nationalökonomie* 7:299–305.

———. 1936b. "Some Reflections on the Present Situation of Business Cycle Theory." *Review of Economic Statistics* 18:1–7.

———. 1962. *Prosperity and Depression*. 4th rev. ed. Cambridge: Harvard Univ. Press.

———. [1962] 1981. "The Great Depression of the 1930s—Can It Happen Again?" American Enterprise Institute Reprint No. 118. Washington, D.C.: American Enterprise Institute.

———. 1985. *Selected Essays of Gottfried Haberler*. Edited by A. Y. C. Koo. Cambridge: MIT Press.

———. 1991. "What Happened to the Business Cycle?" In *Electronic Money Flows*, edited by E. Solomon, 81–88. Boston: Kluwer.

Officer, L. H. 1982. "Prosperity and Depression—and Beyond." *Quarterly Journal of Economics* 97:149–59.

Willett, T. D. 1982. "Gottfried Haberler on Inflation, Unemployment and International Monetary Economics: An Appreciation." *Quarterly Journal of Economics* 97:161–69.

Hahn, Lucian Albert (1889–1968)

L. Albert Hahn was a German banker and economist who taught at the New School for Social Research from 1939 to 1953. Though virtually unknown to economists today, Hahn's writings on banking and monetary theory were widely read in Germany and elsewhere in Europe in the 1920s.

His *Volkswirtschaftliche Theorie des Bankcredits* (Economic theory of bank credit), first published in 1920, contained a discussion of bank-money creation including a description of the deposit multiplier which, according to Schumpeter, was the most systematic of its day. Of still greater interest is Hahn's anticipation in the same book of ideas later developed by Keynes in *The General Theory*. Like Keynes, Hahn rejected Say's Law of the Markets, arguing that psychological factors could cause a "consumption deficit" before full employment was achieved. He also advanced a liquidity-preference theory of interest to explain why interest rates might remain too high for investment to absorb available savings. Finally, Hahn recommended credit expansion and increased government spending to eliminate the "reserve army of the unemployed" created by deficient private consumption. In so doing, he also offered an embryonic version of Keynes's multiplier theory, pointing out that a sufficiently large autonomous increase in spending would automatically stimulate enough added saving to finance the investment while also limiting the stimulative effects of the spending.

The similarity of these arguments to ones contained in the *General Theory* is unmistakable. Nevertheless, Hahn offered them only as a supplement to his theory of bank credit, not as part of a systematic theory of macroeconomics. For this and other reasons including their unfortunate timing at the onset of the world's most notorious episode of hyperinflation, Hahn's prescriptions were received harshly by German academic economists, who grudgingly consented to review the book only after it became a best-seller among the lay public.

Hahn left economics to pursue a career as a banker in Frankfurt during the late 1920s and 1930s. However, like many other German intellectuals, Hahn fled in 1939, taking an academic post at the New School where he resumed his scholarly writings. By then Hahn had abandoned his earlier views and the arguments of Keynes and his followers. This led to Hahn's publication of a series of critical articles, later collected in *The Economics of Illusion*, in which he anticipated anti-Keynesian arguments of the Monetarist and New Classical schools. Hahn was especially critical of the implicit assumption of static expectations in Keynesian theory. He instead distinguished between the impact of expansionary policies during a short-run "reaction-free period" and their impact following agents' "compensating reactions" induced by perceived changes in the purchasing power of money. This was quite similar to the short-run/long-run analysis of the Phillips curve developed by subsequent Monetarist writers. Hahn also adopted a rudimentary rational-expectations approach, insisting that entrepreneurs in the marketplace would generally outperform theorists in forecasting changes in demand, frustrating attempts to manipulate macroeconomic variables by monetary or fiscal means. Nevertheless, he dismissed theories in which the effects of effective-demand manipulation are entirely ignored as "hyper-classicism." This attitude suggests that Hahn would probably have been critical of the more extreme claims of the New Classical school.

Although Hahn's contributions are now chiefly of interest to historians of thought, his later writings especially can still be read with profit by students of macroeconomics and business-cycle theory, who are likely to find them more intuitively appealing than more recent writings with similar themes.

George A. Selgin

See also EXPECTATIONS; KEYNES, JOHN MAYNARD; NATURAL RATE OF UNEMPLOYMENT; PHILLIPS CURVE; RATIONAL EXPECTATIONS

Bibliography

Boudreaux, D. J. and G. A. Selgin. 1990. "L. Albert Hahn: A Precursor of Keynesianism and the Monetarist Counterrevolution." *History of Political Economy* 22:261–79.

Hahn, L. A. 1920. *Volkswirtschaftliche Theorie des Bankcredits*. Tubingen: J. C. B. Mohr.

———. 1949. *The Economics of Illusion*. New York: Squire Publishing Co.

Hansen, Alvin Harvey (1886–1975)

A student of business cycles throughout his professional life, Alvin Hansen based his broad view of cycles on theoretical, statistical, structural, and historical studies. He applied his findings to policy with such effect that, in Tobin's words, "no American economist was more important for the historic redirection of United States macroeconomic policy from 1935 to 1965" (1976, 32). Trained at the University of Wisconsin, he spent most of his professional life

at the University of Minnesota and at Harvard, where he achieved his greatest fame.

His first major monograph, *Business-Cycle Theory: Its Development and Present Status,* concluded that cycles were primarily initiated by such external forces as technological developments, territorial and population changes, and alterations in the accessibility of natural resources, all of which induced real investment by raising profit expectations relative to capital costs. This view placed Hansen with such theorists as Schumpeter, Cassel, Wicksell, Spiethoff, and Robertson who viewed investment fluctuations as the main determinant of business cycles.

These external initiating factors generated a cumulative process of induced spending (enhanced for capital goods by the accelerator) and expanded income that continued increasing, consistent with Say's Law, until constrained by such external factors as diminishing returns, factor-supply limitations, and shortages of credit (financial crises ordinarily terminated booms up to that time), which reduced demand for capital goods. A cumulative downward process would then start until reversed by some other external factor, and the game would begin again.

Hansen was not persuaded that the cycle was self-perpetuating, believing that external shocks were needed to sustain the attenuating fluctuations. Moreover, he suspected that the major disturbing forces of the previous 150 years—exploitation of new resources, revolutionary technical changes, agricultural fluctuations, uncontrolled credit, and wars—were moderating and would curb the business cycle's violence. This view was soothing in 1927, but agitating to some in the late 1930s when incorporated into his Keynes-like stagnation thesis.

Hansen's rather orthodox business-cycle views were severely shaken in the mid-1930s by Keynes's *General Theory of Employment, Income, and Money* (1936). His initial review of Keynes's work was unenthusiastic, concluding that it failed to provide "a foundation for a 'new economics'"(1936, 686). Precisely when his attitude changed is not recorded, but the incomplete recovery of 1934–37 played some role. By 1938 his introduction to *Full Recovery or Stagnation?* observed: "Few books in the whole history of economic literature have created such a stir among professional economists" (1938, 8). Hansen's embrace of the Keynesian system seemed complete in his 1938

American Economic Association presidential address. This change of heart was a remarkable feat for a man over fifty. It established him as the leading American advocate and expositor of Keynes's theory of income determination.

Hansen was stimulator and synthesizer, teacher and student. He and a brilliant group of Harvard students, most notably Paul A. Samuelson, clarified aspects of the Keynesian system and worked out its implications for business-cycle analysis, such as the multiplier-accelerator interaction and the balanced-budget theorem. Hansen's mature views on the business cycle, as found in *Business Cycles and National Income* (1951), were based on "three stepping stones": (1) the inducement to invest (the relationship between the marginal efficiency of capital and the rate of interest); (2) the investment multiplier; and (3) the acceleration principle. In this formulation, endogenous factors could halt an expansionary process without the previous reliance on exogenous limitations. Add timing response to this structure and the basis for much of the model building of the next two decades is essentially complete.

Hansen's interest in cycles was not limited to short-run phenomena; indeed, his close study of longer cycles added great richness to his short-run analysis. Short-run cyclical movements were imbedded in and affected by longer-run cyclical and structural movements. For instance, he used the building-construction cycle of 17–18 years to help explain the amplitude of short-run cyclical swings.

Hansen was profoundly disturbed when the economy in 1937 tumbled into one of the sharpest recessions in our business-cycle history after failing to reach the previous cyclical peak in either real output per capita or in employment. This failure, by itself, was not shocking to Hansen whose historical studies had found other incomplete recoveries. His search for an explanation, however, led him to conclude the United States economy might have entered a period of secular stagnation.

Hansen characterized the 1934–37 recovery as a "consumption" recovery fed by consumer installment credit, and by federal expenditures on recovery and relief and the veterans' bonus of 1936. The recovery ceased when these stimuli played out. Even worse, the new Social Security system started collecting revenues before paying benefits and sharp increases in wages and prices had reduced consumer purchasing power. New investment, tied closely to the short-run requirements of current consumption, could not offset these deflationary forces. Previous investment booms, in contrast, were propelled by the long-term profit expectations of entrepreneurs, not by short-run developments. The shortening of investment horizons seemed to confirm his earlier view that nineteenth-century investment booms might be a thing of the past.

Aggregate demand was also weakened by the halving of population growth in the 1930s with prospects for still further declines. The potential impact on capital formation of such a trend could be staggering. Hansen estimated that population growth in the last half of the nineteenth century might have accounted for up to 60 percent of the total capital formation of the United States. A loss of investment outlets so great would make achieving full employment far more difficult: the stimulus of new technologies would have to fill the gap, but that stimulus, Hansen believed, had weakened. Secular stagnation—an equilibrium at less than full employment—loomed ahead, with capital formation inadequate to absorb full-employment savings. To avoid that outcome, useful government expenditures were necessary to offset the secular deficiency of demand.

This thesis aroused a storm of controversy, but the preoccupations of World War II deferred it. The low population growth of the 1930s was supplanted by decades of high growth encompassing the baby boom of the 1950s; inflation seemed to be the major problem. Ironically, the strength of capital formation over this period, attributable in part to the baby boom, may actually have supported Hansen's concerns about falling population growth. On the other hand, we now also understand that the propensity to consume rises as the population ages, which partially offsets the weakening of capital formation.

Hansen created and—along with such disciples as Richard A. Musgrave and Walter Salant—was a major developer of the theory of fiscal policy as a stabilizing complement to monetary policy, completing a structure that was only implicit in Keynes's *General Theory*. Like Keynes and others, Hansen initially overemphasized reliance on government spending, especially when prescribing for a prospective secular stagnation. But his analysis broadened rapidly into the detailed and comprehensive classic, *Fiscal Policy and Business Cycles*. He examined many fiscal instruments, new and old, and their timing, and in this process rejected his earlier, orthodox view that compensatory action should be postponed until a depression's beneficial liquidation had taken place.

Though not directly involved in the legislative development of the Employment Act of 1946, viewed by many as the magna carta of government stabilization responsibilities, Hansen was the primary intellectual force behind it. His writings and his testimony before the Temporary National Economic Committee in 1939, set up to investigate the role of price policies in aborting the recent recovery, were major contributors to the public understanding of stabilization policies. But his personal involvement as governmental adviser in the early 1940s largely ended when the National Resources Planning Board was Congressionally eliminated in 1943 and he separated from the Federal Reserve Board in 1945. Nevertheless, Hansen continued into retirement as a powerful and influential voice, critic and commentator, on current governmental policies both in the professional journals and his many books.

An activist in pressing for full use of resources with stable prices, Hansen was ever in search of proposals to improve stabilizing instruments and governmental decision-making processes. His tireless and many-faceted attack on the business cycle, his prodigious productivity, his energy, enthusiasm, openness, and encouragement, so infectious to students and colleagues, made him the dominant figure in the midcentury taming of drastic business fluctuations.

E. Cary Brown

See also ACCELERATION PRINCIPLE; FISCAL POLICY; KEYNES, JOHN MAYNARD; SAMUELSON, PAUL ANTHONY

Bibliography

Hansen, A. H. 1927. *Business-Cycle Theory: Its Development and Present Status.* Boston: Ginn and Company.
———. 1932. *Economic Stabilization in an Unbalanced World.* New York: Harcourt, Brace and Company.
———. 1936. "Mr. Keynes on Underemployment Equilibrium." *Journal of Political Economy* 44:667–86.
———. 1938. *Full Recovery or Stagnation?* New York: Norton.
———. 1939. "Economic Progress and Declining Population Growth." *American Economic Review* 29:1–15.
———. 1941. *Fiscal Policy and Business Cycles.* New York: Norton.
———. 1951. *Business Cycles and National Income.* New York: Norton.
Hansen, A. H. and H. S. Perloff. 1944. *State and Local Finance in the National Economy.* New York: Norton.
Samuelson, P. A. [1959] 1966. "Alvin Hansen and the Interaction Between the Multiplier Analysis and the Principle of Acceleration." Chap. 84 in *The Collected Scientific Papers of Paul A. Samuelson,* vol. 2. Cambridge: MIT Press.
———. 1975. "The Balanced-Budget Multiplier: A Case Study in the Sociology and Psychology of Scientific Discovery." *History of Political Economy* 7:43–55.
Stein, H. 1969. *The Fiscal Revolution in America.* Chicago: Univ. of Chicago Press.
Tobin, J. 1976. "Hansen and Public Policy." *Quarterly Journal of Economics* 90:32–37.

Harrod, Roy Forbes (1900–1978)

Roy Forbes Harrod believed that the business cycle should be explained within a dynamic theory whose centerpiece is an equilibrium rate of growth. Booms and slumps should then be explained as deviations from this equilibrium rate, which he saw as giving rise to a line of steady advance. He first sketched this approach in *The Trade Cycle: An Essay,* and developed it further in "An Essay in Dynamic Theory," and *Towards a Dynamic Economics.* In these later writings the concept of an equilibrium rate of growth was made more definite. Cyclical deviations from the equilibrium rate of growth could be expected because the equilibrium was unstable. The instability of equilibrium, Harrod believed, is one of the ways that dynamic theory differs from static theory in which equilibrium is usually assumed to be stable. Unfortunately, Harrod's theory was often submerged in the economic literature in the "Harrod-Domar" model that excluded crucial elements in his theory.

Born in Norfolk, England, Harrod was educated at Westminster School and New College Oxford. His studies were in classics, philosophy, and modern history. At the age of twenty-two, he was appointed to a lectureship in modern history and economics at Christ

Church College, Oxford. In preparation for this post, Harrod spent a term at Cambridge under the tutelage of J. M. Keynes. Harrod was very prolific—making contributions to the theory of imperfect competition, international economics, to the understanding of Keynes's *General Theory* (he was Keynes's official biographer) as well as to the theory of macrodynamics that included his work on the trade cycle. He also published works on philosophy.

The first formal working out of Harrod's vision of business cycles as oscillations around a line of steady advance was contained in his 1936 book, *The Trade Cycle*. In this book, the line of steady advance is a notional or reference concept around which the actual values move. It was given more definite form in his subsequent writings where he set out an equation for the equilibrium rate of growth. According to Harrod, static theory is concerned with the values of the dependent variables at a point in time (he gave six months as an estimate of the length of this point), while dynamic theory is concerned with the rates of change in these values at that moment. A situation of short-period equilibrium can be represented by the equation:

$$I = S, \tag{1}$$

where I is net investment in the period (and it is equal to investment planned for the period), and S is desired net saving. This net saving equals the product of the economy's average propensity to save, s_d, whose value depends on the distribution of income between wages and profits, and the level of income Y. This equation can be used to determine, given I and s_d, the short-period equilibrium level of income. Harrod transformed equation (1) into a dynamic equation by multiplying both sides by different forms of $1/Y$. The left-hand side is multiplied by $(\Delta Y/Y)(1/\Delta Y)$, and the right-hand side by $1/Y$. The transformed equation can be written as

$$GC = s_d, \tag{2}$$

where G is the actual rate of growth of output $\Delta Y/Y$ over the period, and C is the capital coefficient $I/\Delta Y$, the net investment in the period divided by the increase in output over the period. In the special case where entrepreneurs judge the period's investment to have been justified by the increase in output, C is equal to C_r, the required capital coefficient, and the rate of growth of output is the entrepreneurial equilibrium or warranted rate of growth G_w. The equation for G_w can be written as

$$G_w = s_d/C_r. \tag{3}$$

The value for C_r depends on the state of technology, the nature of the goods that make up the increment of output, the phase of the business cycle, and the rate of interest. Since the values for both s_d and C_r depend on the phase of the cycle, it is clear that there is a large number of possible values for the warranted rate of growth. Harrod paid particular attention to the rate that corresponds to the normal utilization of productive capacity, which he called the "normal" warranted rate, referring to others as "special" warranted rates of growth. It was the normal warranted rate of growth that could potentially result in a line of steady advance. If this rate of growth occurred, then entrepreneurs would judge that the investment in the period had been justified, and "it will put them into a frame of mind which will cause them to give such orders as will maintain the same rate of growth" (Harrod 1939, 16). For entrepreneurial investment decisions to generate a steady rate of growth, in a world where the future cannot be known, the past must turn out to be a good guide to the future. In particular, the distribution of income must be constant (which is a requirement for an unchanging value of s_d), and technical progress must be natural, which ensures that with a constant rate of interest the required capital coefficient does not change. Harrod considered the line of output that would result from this warranted rate of growth as "a moving equilibrium, in the sense that it represents the one level of output at which producers will feel in the upshot that they have done the right thing, and which will induce them to continue in the same line of advance" (1939, 22).

Any deviation from this line of steady advance—and deviations could occur as a result of random disturbances—would bring the instability principle into operation. If, for example, the actual rate of growth G, exceeds G_w, then $C < C_r$, and the investment in the period is less than what would be justified by the period's increase in output. Harrod assumed that entrepreneurs would then be induced to step up the rate of investment, so that G would rise further above G_w. Conversely, if $G < G_d$, then $C > C_r$, and entrepreneurs would cut back on the planned rate of investment, causing G to fall further below G_w.

Harrod's explanation for the upswings and downswings of an economy thus relied on the deviation of its actual rate of growth from its normal warranted rate of growth. The special warranted rates of growth then become relevant in these cyclical phases. Harrod believed that the changes in the propensity to save due to changes in the profit share of the cycle dominate the changes in the warranted rate of growth. The warranted rate of growth would thus be dragged down by depression, and boosted in value by the increases in prices and profits during an expansion. These changes tend to pull the value of G_w in the same direction as G. The value of G is eventually subject to restraining forces. Its upward movements are limited by a "ceiling"—shortages of productive capacity and labor, concerns over the unsustainability of too rapid a rate of increase, etc.—and in a downward direction by a "floor" which is set by autonomous expenditures. (The equation for G_w can be readily adapted to allow for autonomous investment.) This restraint on the value for G and the cyclical changes in the value for G_w mean that their values will cross, setting the stage for cyclical movements in the opposite direction.

Harrod also defined a full-employment rate of growth G_n, which is the maximum rate of growth allowed for by the exogenously given growth of the labor force and the rate of technical progress. This natural rate of growth constrains the possible rate of growth over time, and its relation to the warranted rate of growth can indicate, according to Harrod's theory, whether the tendency towards inflationary booms or towards recessions is stronger. If $G_w > G_n$, then since G cannot exceed G_n for a long period of time, it often will be dragged below G_w, thus depressing economic activity. With $G_w < G_n$, this source of downward deviations will be removed, and inflationary booms will predominate.

In response to criticisms, Harrod blurred the sharp outlines of his theory in subsequent writings (1951, 1970, 1973). Alexander pointed out that Harrod, in defining the normal warranted rate of growth, made the unfounded assumption that achieving this rate would lead entrepreneurs to act so as to maintain it. Harrod could not justify the special assumption on which this assertion was based in a world in which the fortunes of entrepreneurs can change

unexpectedly, the world that he saw as the setting for his theory. This realization led Harrod to abandon a steady rate of growth as the equilibrium for a dynamic system. He also drew back from his early statements of the instability principle which led others to state that his dynamic equilibrium was poised on a "knife edge." Harrod later argued that a fairly large deviation was required to bring the instability principle into operation, and a "shallow dome" would be a more appropriate term to describe the character of his dynamic equilibrium.

Harrod's dynamic theory is important because of its attempt to integrate the trend and cycle, and its pioneering role in extending Keynes's *General Theory* to allow for the effects of investment on productive capacity as well as on effective demand.

Athanasios Asimakopulos

See also ASYMMETRY; CEILINGS AND FLOORS; KEYNES, JOHN MAYNARD; TRENDS AND RANDOM WALKS

Bibliography

Alexander, S. 1950. "Mr. Harrod's Dynamic Model." *Economic Journal* 60:724–39.

Asimakopulos, A. 1985. "Harrod on Harrod: the Evolution of 'a line of steady growth.'" *History of Political Economy* 17:619–35.

———. 1986. "Harrod and Domar on Dynamic Economics." *Banca Nazionale del Lavoro Quarterly Review,* September, 275–98.

Harrod, R. F. 1936. *The Trade Cycle: An Essay.* London: Macmillan.

———. 1939. "An Essay in Dynamic Theory." *Economic Journal* 49:14–33.

———. 1948. *Towards a Dynamic Economics.* London: Macmillan.

———. 1951. "Notes on Trade Cycle Theory." *Economic Journal* 61:261–75.

———. 1970. "Harrod After Twenty-One Years: A Comment." *Economic Journal* 80:737–41.

———. 1973. *Economic Dynamics.* London: Macmillan.

Kregel, J. A. 1980. "Economic Dynamics and the Theory of Steady Growth: An Historical Essay on Harrod's 'Knife-Edge.'" *History of Political Economy* 12:97–123.

Phelps-Brown, E. H. 1980. "Sir Roy Harrod: A Biographical Memoir." *Economic Journal* 90:1–33.

H

Young, W. 1989. *Harrod and his Trade Cycle Group: The Origins and Development of the Growth Research Programme.* London: Macmillan.

Hawtrey, Ralph George (1879–1975)

The work of R. G. Hawtrey has as one of its central themes the proposition that the trade cycle is "a purely monetary phenomenon." Hawtrey was educated at Eton and Cambridge, the same path followed a few years later by J. M. Keynes and D. H. Robertson. Unlike his two great rivals, Hawtrey was neither trained in nor a practitioner of Marshallian economics. The source of his economics was the practical wisdom of the City and the Treasury. He served in the British Treasury from 1904 to 1947, taking leave only in the 1928–29 academic year to teach at Harvard.

From the outset, economic fluctuations were Hawtrey's chief concern. *Good and Bad Trade,* his first published work in economics, is a study of the trade cycle. In this work he attributes economic fluctuations to variations in the money supply: nonmonetary shocks, involving changes in the supply of or demand for particular commodities or groups of commodities, are self-limiting. To affect total demand, nonmonetary shocks must be transmitted through the monetary mechanism. Monetary shocks, on the other hand, affect all sectors of the economy similarly and tend to generate cumulative processes of expansion or contraction.

Good and Bad Trade distinguishes between three interest-rate concepts: the natural rate, the profit rate, and the bank rate. The natural rate is the real rate of interest that would prevail in equilibrium with zero inflation. The profit rate equals the natural rate plus an allowance for expected price changes. The bank rate is the actual rate set by bankers, depending on whether they wish to encourage or discourage borrowing. Any difference between the bank rate and the profit rate, whatever its source, tends to widen until banks take corrective measures. Although Hawtrey later downplayed the distinction between natural, profit, and bank rates, the tendency of the profit rate and bank rate to diverge constituted one source of the "inherent instability of credit."

The other main elements of Hawtrey's theory of economic fluctuations are spelled out in *Currency and Credit.* With some modification, these ideas recurred throughout his later work.

The turning points of the Hawtreyan cycle are governed by bankers' decisions to expand or contract the supply of credit. A credit expansion is most likely to start near the trough of a downturn, fuelled by the reflux of reserves to the banking system from household cash balances. Consumers dissave out of cash balances in order to maintain consumption levels during the downturn. As reserves accumulate, banks begin to reduce lending rates. The important interest rates are short-term rates, and the main channel through which they operate is dealers' demand for inventories. Hawtrey consistently minimizes the role of the long-term interest rate. Not only does monetary policy have little influence over long-term rates, but fixed capital formation is less sensitive than the demand for inventories to interest-rate movements. Reduced short-term interest rates increase dealers' willingness to hold stocks and they increase their orders from producers who, in turn, raise output. Increased output, requiring a rebuilding of working capital, leads producers to increase borrowing from the banks. As employment recovers, the wage bill rises and workers gradually replenish their cash balances, drawing reserves from the banks. Rising employment expands consumers' income, and thus, consumers' outlay. Rising consumption spending prevents dealers from adding to stocks as rapidly as they wish, providing another impetus to increase orders and production. Hawtrey called this a benign circle of expansion.

The downturn is initiated by a tightening of credit. A credit contraction begins when banks, concerned about the adequacy of reserves, raise interest rates. The reserve drain temporarily continues, however, because of forward commitments and lags in the response of dealers to higher bank rates. As banks continue to lose reserves, they boost interest rates. Higher rates eventually take effect, and dealers try to reduce borrowing by running down their stocks of goods and cutting orders. Production and employment fall. In turn, the consequent reduction of consumers' income would curb consumers' outlay, further reducing desired stocks and production. This is the vicious circle of contraction. Because workers maintain consumption by running down cash balances, reserves gradually return to the banks, enabling them to expand credit anew.

Hawtrey attributes the periodicity of the cycle to the operation of the gold standard. The duration of credit expansions and contractions was governed by the gradualness of the drain and reflux of gold reserves. Before World War I, London was the world financial center and governed world financial conditions. The ebb and flow of reserves from the Bank of England guided the Bank's discount rate policy, a policy to which other gold-standard countries adapted. Correspondingly, Hawtrey believed that the international trade cycle, marked by regular periodicity, vanished along with the gold standard at the outset of World War I. After the war, economic fluctuations were disconnected national phenomena, depending on domestic monetary conditions.

Credit is inherently unstable. Any fortuitous change in the supply of or demand for credit can initiate a cumulative expansion or contraction that proceeds until reserve limits, deliberate monetary policy, or some other offsetting tendency takes hold. Hawtrey therefore advocated replacing the "pure" gold standard, under which the overriding objective of the central bank was to maintain convertibility, with a managed gold standard, under which the major central banks would cooperate to stabilize the "wealth-value" of gold.

Following the wartime and postwar inflation, Hawtrey warned that an uncoordinated return to the gold standard, accompanied by a competitive scramble for gold reserves, would result in deflation and unemployment. These concerns and his vision of international monetary cooperation were embodied in the Resolutions on Currency which he drafted for the 1922 Genoa Conference on international monetary reconstruction. Though adopted at the Conference, the Resolutions were never implemented, and despite Hawtrey's persistent advocacy, gradually fell into disregard.

Hawtrey attributed the onset of the Great Depression to a concatenation of policy errors, the underlying cause being the failure of the leading countries to agree to cooperate on monetary policy while independently seeking to reestablish a gold standard. Persistently high interest rates in Britain after the return to gold resulted in endemic high unemployment and the stultification of enterprise. French monetary measures in 1928–29 drained a significant amount of gold from the rest of the world to France. Finally, the Federal Reserve Board, overreacting to stock-market speculation, adopted an unduly tight monetary policy.

The persistence of unemployment in the early 1930s, despite low nominal interest rates, posed a serious problem for Hawtrey, who had previously acknowledged few limits to the power of interest-rate policy either to brake an expansion or spark an upturn. He responded by proposing the notion of a credit deadlock. A deadlock would exist when reducing the rate of interest would not induce further borrowing, rendering the standard tools of monetary stimulus ineffective. Such a deadlock arises after an unyieldingly restrictive credit policy has killed enterprise. Because not all prices and wages are equally flexible, the credit contraction also engenders "disparities" by distorting relative prices. The remedy for trade deadlock is monetary expansion. In his statement of the "Treasury View," public expenditure is stimulative only if it increases the flow of money expenditure in the economy. Deficit spending is useful only as a "piece of ritual," providing a cover for monetary expansion. Devaluation might help a country caught in a deadlock by mitigating a disparity between prices and wages. Nor would the effect on economies whose currencies have appreciated be fully offsetting, because the impulse toward a benign circle of expansion in the devaluing country would outweigh the diffuse restrictive impact on the rest of the world.

Hawtrey's analysis featured a fixed-price, quantity-adjustment mechanism with the dynamic behavior of the system governed by an aggregate-demand relationship (consumers' income and outlay supplemented by dealers' demand for stocks). These features of Hawtrey's work, along with his vision of the credit-using economy as inherently unstable in the absence of deliberate application of monetary policy, underlay Keynes's acknowledgment of Hawtrey as his "grandparent . . . in the paths of errancy" (1973, 132).

However, in the consolidation phase of the Keynesian Revolution, Hawtrey's work fell into neglect. His continued emphasis on money and interest rates isolated him from the dominant currents of economics. As a result, Hawtrey's contributions to economics in the interwar period did not receive the attention they warranted until after his death in 1975. Although few of his contemporaries endorsed Hawtrey's identification of short-term interest rates and stock holding as the key macroeconomic variables, many were influenced by his work, which was highly regarded in the interwar period, particularly in the 1920s before the Keynesian ascendancy. Hawtrey significantly advanced the analysis of monetary factors in economic fluctuations, convincing many economists and policymakers that money must be managed if prices and output are to be stabilized.

Patrick Deutscher

See also BANK OF FRANCE; CENTRAL BANKING; CREDIT CYCLE; FEDERAL RESERVE SYSTEM: 1914–1941; FISCAL POLICY; GOLD STANDARD; GOLD STANDARD: CAUSES AND CONSEQUENCES; GREAT DEPRESSION IN BRITAIN (1929–1932); GREAT DEPRESSION IN THE UNITED STATES (1929–1938); KEYNES, JOHN MAYNARD; MONETARY DISEQUILIBRIUM THEORIES OF THE BUSINESS CYCLE; MONETARY POLICY; RICARDO, DAVID; ROBERTSON, DENNIS HOLME

Bibliography

Davis, E. G. 1981. "R. G. Hawtrey, 1879–1975." In *Pioneers of Modern Economics in Britain,* edited by D. P. O'Brien and J. R. Presley, 203–33. London: Macmillan.

Deutscher, P. R. 1990. *R. G. Hawtrey and the Development of Macroeconomics.* London: Macmillan.

Hawtrey, R. G. 1913. *Good and Bad Trade: An Inquiry into the Causes of Trade Fluctuations.* London: Constable and Co.

———. 1919. *Currency and Credit.* London: Longmans, Green and Co.

———. 1928. *Trade and Credit.* London: Longmans, Green and Co.

———. 1931. *Trade Depression and the Way Out.* London: Longmans, Green and Co.

———. 1932. *The Art of Central Banking.* London: Longmans, Green and Co.

———. 1937. *Capital and Employment.* London: Longmans, Green and Co.

———. 1938. *A Century of Bank Rate.* London: Longmans, Green and Co.

Hicks, J. R. 1977. "Hawtrey." Chap. 5 in *Economic Perspectives: Further Essays on Money and Growth.* Oxford: Clarendon Press.

Howson, S. 1985. "Hawtrey and the Real World." In *Keynes and his Contemporaries,* edited by G. C. Harcourt, 105–24. London: Macmillan.

Keynes, J. M. [1936] 1973. *The General Theory and After. Part I: Preparation.* Vol. 13 of *The Collected Writings of John Maynard Keynes.* London: Macmillan.

Hayek, Friedrich August [von] (1899–1992)

F. A. Hayek was among the most prominent participants in the interwar debates on business cycles, capital theory, economic methodology, and monetary theory. His "Austrian" theory of the business cycle received a great deal of attention, especially in Britain, and for a while many economists regarded Hayek as the principal rival of John Maynard Keynes.

Hayek studied at the University of Vienna, receiving doctorates in politics and law. In 1923–24, he spent a year in New York studying business cycles, then returned to Vienna where he worked for the government, pursued economic research, and participated in the economic seminars led by Ludwig von Mises. In 1927, he became director of the Austrian Institute for Business Cycle Research, founded by von Mises. He was appointed lecturer at the University of Vienna in 1929. In 1931, at the invitation of Lionel Robbins, he gave a series of lectures on business-cycle theory at the London School of Economics. Their success was so great that he was offered a chair at the LSE which he occupied until 1950, when he moved to the University of Chicago. In 1962, he took an appointment at the University of Freiburg; from 1968 to 1977, he was Visiting Professor at the University of Salzburg. He returned to Freiburg in 1978. He was awarded the Nobel Memorial Prize in Economic Science in 1974.

A prolific and wide-ranging scholar, Hayek made important contributions to monetary theory and policy, business-cycle theory, capital theory, the theory of economic calculation under socialism, political philosophy, the philosophy of science and the methodology of economics, theoretical psychology, the history of ideas, and other subjects. His research on business was done mainly in the 1920s and 1930s. His first book, *Geldtheorie und Konjunkturtheorie* (Translated as *Monetary Theory and the Trade Cycle*), appeared in 1929. This was followed by *Prices and Production* (his LSE lectures), *Profits, Interest and Investment,* and "The Ricardo Effect."

Hayek's business-cycle theory owed a considerable debt to the capital theory of Eugen von Böhm-Bawerk and the monetary theory of Ludwig von Mises and Knut Wicksell. Its focus is on the "time structure" of production: if a society withdraws part of its resources from producing immediately consumable products, using them to produce tools and machinery instead, it will be rewarded with a larger consumable output in the future. How *roundabout* production becomes is governed by the rate of interest. An increase in people's willingness to postpone consumption causes the rate of interest to fall and the production of nonconsumables to rise, lengthening the *period of production*. A lengthening of the period of production might also result from a technological change that increases the volume of future consumables obtainable by savings (here the rate of interest will rise). The intertemporal coordination of economic activity is extremely complex—an investment decision made today will turn out to have been a correct one only if it is validated by the independent production and consumption decisions of others over a considerable period of time. And the monetary institutions which make it possible for the market rate of interest to differ from the *natural rate* (that which matches voluntary saving and desired investment) provide constant disruptions.

In his first two books, Hayek attributed the expansion to the market rate of interest being below the natural rate. This divergence might result either from an autonomous reduction in the market rate initiated by banks or the monetary authorities, or from a rise in the natural rate due to increased entrepreneurial optimism. In either case, the banks' ability to create money, and thus to accommodate entrepreneurs' demands for purchasing power in excess of voluntary savings provided by households, would lead to an unsustainable elongation of the production process. The ensuing investment-led boom would inevitably be followed by a recession.

The monetary injection works by altering relative prices. Entrepreneurs use the borrowed funds to increase their orders for the products of "higher stages" of the production process (which will yield consumable output only in the relatively distant future), raising the prices of those goods and drawing additional resources into their production. If the process begins at full employment, the output of "lower-stage" products (consumable immediately or in the near future) must decline. But this change in the composition of output frustrates consumers' desires for greater current consumption, and it can be maintained only so long as banks' provision of newly created money to entrepreneurs prevents consumers from making their demands effective.

In a first round, one might say, entrepreneurs bring about a reallocation of resources by shifting demand toward higher-stage products. But their expenditures become factor incomes, and in a second round factor owners spend their enlarged incomes. Prices of consumables, the output of which is less than consumers desire, are then driven up. *Forced saving* occurs as consumers find that their incomes do not permit them to consume as much as they had expected; but windfall profits accrue to suppliers of consumables, leading them to attempt to expand production. They will be prevented from doing so, and from bidding resources away from higher-stage production, so long as the banks, keeping the market interest rate below the natural rate, continue to issue credit to entrepreneurs for investment at the higher stages.

But their limited reserves constrain the banks from continuing monetary expansion indefinitely. Ultimately the market rate of interest must rise, the composition of demand must shift back toward lower-stage products, and the production process must become less roundabout. This shift marks the upper turning point, and recession ensues. Producers of higher-stage products suffer losses, some projects are abandoned, and the capital invested in many enterprises is consumed without replacement. Economic health is restored only when the structure of production again matches "the proportion between the demand for consumers' goods and the demand for producers' goods as determined by voluntary saving and spending" (Hayek 1931, 86–87). Expansionary policies should not be attempted: any policy that increases consumers' purchasing power would only aggravate the shortage of consumables, and expanding credit to entrepreneurs only prolongs the misallocation of resources.

In this account, increases in the quantity of money "falsify" relative prices and misdirect production. But Hayek differed from quantity theorists in focusing on relative prices rather than the general price level; and, since velocity could vary and money substitutes could be developed, he did not believe the quantity of money could or should be held fixed. Thus he recommended simply that central banks should exercise restraint in both good times and bad.

Although initially Hayek's cycle theory was very favorably received, the enthusiasm was short-lived. One of the reasons for this was surely Hayek's insistence that any expansionary action during a depression would only delay necessary readjustments and make matters worse. And his theory said little about the high unemployment in depressions; the structural changes that followed the boom might be expected to entail some dislocation, but it was not clear why this should be so extensive. And a theory that treated production of consumers' and producers' goods as strict substitutes, focusing on shifts in the allocation of given resources, became less and less tenable as economists were pressed to explain dramatic reductions in the total amount of resources utilized.

In 1939, Hayek startled his readers by presenting what seemed a quite different theory of the cycle in *Profit, Interest, and Investment*. In this account, the supply of money receives little mention and the rate of interest on loans remains fixed throughout the cycle. The boom begins from a position of less than full employment, nominal wage rates are fixed, and labor cannot be moved readily from one sector to another. Even under these assumptions (close to those of Keynes), Hayek argued, expansions cannot be sustained indefinitely if increases in investment expenditure outpace the growth of voluntary saving.

The central focus in this account is the level of real wages. During the expansion, while output and employment in the capital-goods industries are expanding, the output of consumer goods increases by less than consumers would like, causing the prices of consumables to rise. Whereas Hayek's earlier presentation had emphasized that this forced saving could be sustained only so long as the banks continued expanding credit, he now focused on the reduction in real wage rates caused by the price increases, given rigid nominal wages. Falling real wages induce producers to substitute labor for capital in what Hayek termed the "Ricardo Effect." As the desired capital-labor and capital-output ratios fall, the demand for machinery declines: total employment is reduced (due to labor immobility) and a recession begins. The recession can be a cumulative process, and expansionary action may be desirable.

Hayek had reshaped his argument in ways that he must have hoped his audience would find congenial. Consumption and investment moved together over the cycle, interest and wage rates were sticky, and changes in the level of output were as important as changes in its composition. Perhaps most significantly, Hayek had found a place for expansionary intervention. But the new ideas were poorly received (Moss and Vaughn 1986). After a prodigious effort to elaborate the capital-theoretic basis of his account of fluctuations—culminating in *The Pure Theory of Capital*—and a 1942 article on "The Ricardo Effect," Hayek gave up on trade-cycle theory (except for Hayek [1969] 1978) and moved on to other topics (Caldwell 1988). But he did not altogether abandon macroeconomics, remaining a lifelong critic of Keynesian economic theory and policy.

Janet A. Seiz

See also AUSTRIAN THEORY OF BUSINESS CYCLES; BÖHM-BAWERK, EUGEN RITTER VON; BURCHARDT, FRITZ (FRANK) ADOLPH; FORCED SAVING; FREE BANKING; KALDOR, NICHOLAS; KEYNES, JOHN MAYNARD; LACHMANN, LUDWIG MAURITS ; LINDAHL, ERIC ROBERT; LOWE, ADOLPH; MISES, LUDWIG EDLER VON; MONETARY DISEQUILIBRIUM THEORIES OF THE BUSINESS CYCLE; MONETARY EQUILIBRIUM THEORIES OF THE BUSINESS CYCLE; NATURAL RATE OF INTEREST; OVERINVESTMENT THEORIES OF BUSINESS CYCLES; PERIOD OF PRODUCTION; ROBBINS, LIONEL CHARLES; SHACKLE, GEORGE LENNOX SHARMAN; SRAFFA, PIERO; WICKSELL, JOHAN GUSTAV KNUT

Bibliography

Caldwell, B. J. 1988. "Hayek's Transformation." *History of Political Economy* 20:513–41.

Hayek, F. A. [1929] 1933. *Monetary Theory and the Trade Cycle*. Translation. London: Jonathan Cape.

———. 1931. *Prices and Production*. London: Routledge.

———. 1939. *Profits, Interest and Investment*. London: Routledge and Kegan Paul.

———. 1941. *The Pure Theory of Capital*. Chicago: Univ. of Chicago Press.

———. [1942] 1948. "The Ricardo Effect." Chap. 11 in *Individualism and Economic Order*. Chicago: Univ. of Chicago Press.

———. [1969] 1978. "Three Elucidations of the Ricardo Effect." Chap. 11 in *Further Studies in Philosophy, Politics, Economics and the History of Ideas*. Chicago: Univ. of Chicago Press.

———. 1984. *Money, Capital and Fluctuations: Early Essays*. Translated and edited by Roy McCloughry. Chicago: Univ. of Chicago Press.

———. 1991. *The Trend of Economic Thinking: Essays on Political Economists and Economic History.* Vol. 3 of *The Collected Works of F. A. Hayek.* Chicago: Univ. of Chicago Press.

———. 1994. *Hayek on Hayek,* edited by S. Kresge and L. Wenar. Chicago: Univ. of Chicago Press.

———. 1995. *Contra Keynes and Cambridge.* Vol. 9 of *The Collected Works of F. A. Hayek.* Chicago: Univ. of Chicago Press.

Hicks, J. R. 1967. "The Hayek Story." Chap. 12 in *Critical Essays in Monetary Theory.* Oxford: Clarendon Press.

Moss, L. S. and K. I. Vaughn. 1986. "Hayek's Ricardo Effect: A Second Look." *History of Political Economy* 18:545–65.

O'Driscoll, G. P. 1975. *Economics as a Coordination Problem: The Contributions of Friedrich A. Hayek.* Kansas City: Sheed Andrews and McMeel.

Hicks, John Richard (1904–1989)

Among the impressive number of his contributions, J. R. Hicks's work of 1950, *A Contribution to the Theory of the Trade Cycle,* is a classic. In fact, Hicks had been concerned with trade-cycle theories since the early 1930s, beginning with his article "Equilibrium and the Trade Cycle" first published in German in 1933. He continued to show interest in the trade cycle in *Value and Capital* and in "The Monetary Theory of D. H. Robertson." However, it was not until 1949, when Hicks reviewed Harrod's *Toward a Dynamic Economics* (1949) that he began working out a complete theory. For the first time, in *A Contribution to the Theory of the Trade Cycle,* Hicks provided a general theory of his own by integrating elements from already existing theories.

Although the combination was uniquely his, concepts of Keynes-Kahn, Clark, and Harrod were essential elements of his theory. Hicks's trade cycle was labelled Keynesian because of its fixprice theory of output and its use of the saving-investment multiplier mechanism. Hicks attributed the acceleration principle to J. M. Clark, although he admitted that Aftalion and Robertson had also made the point before Clark. From Harrod, Hicks obtained the idea of approaching the trade cycle as a "problem of an expanding economy." With these elements Hicks began to study "fluctuation about a rising trend."

Hicks's theory of the trade cycle describes the interaction between consumption, investment, and income expressed in real terms. By introducing lags for these three variables and by keeping other variables (prices, expectations, interest rate, and money) constant, Hicks showed that it is possible to generate fluctuations. The accelerator-multiplier interaction is the driving force behind the alternating expansion and contraction phases of the cycle. In the expansion, an increase in induced investment leads to an increase in income, which in turn induces more investment, then more income, and so on. In the contraction the process is reversed.

Hicks found the effects of a change in investment on income, the multiplier principle, to be stabilizing. He viewed the effect of changes in output on investment, the acceleration principle, as the main cause of fluctuations. The interaction between the multiplier and the accelerator determines the likelihood of fluctuations.

The Multiplier Principle

The multiplier in its simplest form can be computed by assuming (1) that for a given increment in income, some portion of it is consumed while the rest is saved, and (2) that income is identical to consumption plus investment. The portion of income saved is assumed to be invested and to generate additional income, of which again a portion is consumed and the rest saved, and so on.

In Hicks's view, Keynes's multiplier is a static principle, and although useful, it does not help to describe the "path" of a dynamic adjustment from one equilibrium to another (1950, 17). Hicks believed that a system's movement could be better described using Kahn's convergent series and an ensuing dynamic multiplier. The dynamic component was introduced simply by assuming that consumption depends on the income of the previous period. Hicks showed that however complex the lags, convergence would occur according to the amount of consumption lagged and the average length of the lags. "The marginal propensity to save outright" determines the position of equilibrium; "the characteristics of the transitory saving" or "deferred consumption" determine the rate at which equilibrium is approached (1950, 21).

The Acceleration Principle

To explain the accelerator principle, Hicks distinguished fixed from working capital. First, *fixed capital* requires the introduction of a depreciation factor, which implies a distinction between net and gross investment. Hicks supposed an economy in equilibrium: income is maintained at a constant level, with the capital stock fully adjusted to this constant level of income, net investment equal to zero, and gross investment equal to depreciation. He then argued that if for some reason income rose permanently to a higher level, additional equipment would be needed. Stocks would have to adjust to the new conditions, and the rate of depreciation would rise. According to Hicks, in a first period, net investment would increase by the value of induced investment. In the same period, gross investment would also increase by the same amount, while depreciation remained at its previous level. In the next period, when the capital good is completed, gross investment would decrease to its previous level, but the depreciation of the new equipment would be added to the previous investment, reducing actual net investment by this amount. In a following period, when capital must be replaced, net investment would increase by more than the previous gross investment in order to include the extra depreciation, and so on "indefinitely" (1950, 41).

Working capital or "goods in process," "minimum stocks of materials," and "half-finished goods" essential to the process of production, can be distinguished from *liquid capital,* or nonessential "reserve stocks," both "finished" and "unfinished" goods (1950, 47). Working capital and liquid capital move inversely. For example, when demand increases, it usually takes time for output to increase; in the meantime, stocks decrease. Thus, liquid capital is reduced, and working capital increased in response to the increase in demand. According to Hicks, the process of replacing working capital has no "determinate time shape." It can be fast or slow, depending on the state of the economy and on how enterprises react. A decrease in demand would trigger an opposite reaction.

Considering the multiplier and the accelerator principle together, Hicks then identified three phases in which their impact is felt: first, the period in which increased demand is met by withdrawing from stock (liquid capital); second, the period in which investment in fixed and working capital occurs; finally, the period in which equipment is replaced. These phases are clearly discernible in Hicks's one-sector model, where the change in demand is permanent. If, however, demand increases twice in succession, the model generates complicated results. Depending on specific cases, humps in investment might be intensified or offset altogether.

Equilibrium Conditions

The constant interaction of the multiplier and accelerator principles led Hicks to wonder if a "steady-equilibrium" trend could be defined as a benchmark in terms of which fluctuations could be measured. A regular progressive equilibrium is the trend in which output increases at a constant rate and induced investment and savings remain constant proportions of output. Hicks identified autonomous investment as that part of investment which does not occur in response to current changes in output. The appropriate equilibrium condition is then "Autonomous Investment + Induced Investment = Saving" (1950, 59).

Any economic trend corresponds to the growth of output which is determined by the growth rate of autonomous investment. In an equilibrium trend, saving and induced investment will grow at the same rate as autonomous investment. Furthermore, capital stocks will have adjusted to current output, and induced investment "must be such as to be consistent with steady development."

For Hicks the key question was not whether an economic system could be in equilibrium, but whether, as a dynamic system, it could remain in equilibrium, and if not what path it would follow. Hicks became quickly convinced that any deviation from the equilibrium path would move the system away from the trend. Further, he believed that if he could show that an economy, once disturbed, fails to return to its equilibrium path, but "would have a tendency to oscillate," he could well conclude that a cycle would be generated even without exogenous disturbances. Although Hicks insisted that endogenous forces generate the cycle, he also indicated that some exogenous forces could also cause fluctuations.

The Simultaneous-Equations Model

Using difference equations, Hicks constructed a model of cyclic systemic movement. To simplify his model, he assumed symmetrical increases and decreases in output, and ignored any remote effects of changes in output as well as the spending of depreciation allowances. He supposed that investment humps take the simplest form, that investment induced by a change in output occurs in a single period and consumption lags behind income by one period. The complete model is described by equations (1) through (3):

$$C_t = (1-s)Y_{t-1} \quad \text{Consumption Function,} \quad (1)$$

$$I_t = v(Y_{t-1} - Y_{t-2}) \quad \text{Investment Function,} \quad (2)$$

$$Y_t = C_t + I_t + \text{Aut} \quad \text{Income Function,} \quad (3)$$

where C is consumption, I is investment, Y is income, s is the propensity to consume, v is the capital coefficient, Aut is autonomous investment, and t is an index of the time period.

The model can be reduced to the following equation:

$$Y_t = (1-s+v)Y_{t-1} - vY_{t-2} + \text{Aut.} \quad (4)$$

If equilibrium income is $E_t = (1-s+v)E_{t-1} - vE_{t-2}$ and the absolute deviation from equilibrium is $y_t = Y_t - E_t$, then

$$y_t = (1-s+v)y_{t-1} - vy_{t-2}. \quad (5)$$

If the economy is growing at a constraint exogenously given rate g, i.e., $y_t = r_t E_0(1+g)^2$, then the relative deviations from equilibrium can be expressed as:

$$r_t = \frac{1-s+v}{1+g}r_{t-1} - \frac{v}{(1+g)^2}r_{t-2}. \quad (6)$$

Note that equation (5) is a special case of equation (6) when g equals zero and that the higher is g (and thus the smaller the value of the coefficient $v/(1+g)$ attached to the second-order variable y_{t-2}), the less likely are fluctuations. Depending on the value of the capital coefficient, four things may happen: a return to equilibrium, dampened oscillations, explosive oscillations, or relentless divergence (1950, 89). Hicks believed that the last possibility was the one which fit the facts.

The Economic Cycle

Hicks was convinced that any disturbance from the equilibrium path would make the system diverge from the trend. Together with the model as described by equation (6), he thus incorpo-

rated three conditions which would constrain the fluctuations: first, he assumed that any displacement from equilibrium, specifically in the investment and savings coefficients, would make the system diverge from the trend; second, he identified an upper-limit constraint, i.e., "scarcity of available resources"; and finally, supposing that the accelerator operates asymmetrically in the upswing and downswing, and that in the downswing the accelerator provides an indirect check, he concluded that no artificial lower limit is necessary.

The outlines of a typical cycle can be identified: an increase in output induces investment, which through the multiplier and accelerator, in turn generates extra output, hence more investment and so on, driving the system upward toward the upper limit of employable resources. Once that ceiling is reached, economic activity "creeps" along it, until bouncing off to move downward. As the expansion of output on the ceiling generates just enough investment to support the growth of output equivalent to that along its equilibrium path, output begins to decrease, generating ever smaller investment and so on. The system moves toward the equilibrium path. However, once investment reaches the equilibrium path, output still lags one period behind, and hence still exceeds the equilibrium amount. In the next period, output decreases again, while investment falls below its equilibrium value, which leads to falling output. The decline continues below the equilibrium path. The presence of fixed capital in the production slows the disinvestment as well as the accelerator process, and the growth of output eventually converges to "the Slump Equilibrium."

Just as fluctuations in the cycle have an upper limit, there is also a lower limit. There will always be some minimum investment without which an economy cannot survive. Once the growth of output reaches this lower equilibrium path, "geared to the autonomous investment," it will then follow the lower-limit equilibrium path causing the whole system to start rising and reactivate the accelerator-multiplier process. The path of output will keep bouncing between the upper and lower limits.

Hicks's theory of the trade cycle generated much interest as well as criticisms. Most of Hicks's responses to critics are found in his *Economic Perspectives*. Later, Hicks himself was very critical of his trade-cycle model: first, it was to his mind too mechanical, not taking into consideration expectations, money, or uncertainty; and second, it was ahistorical. He did not in fact produce any further trade-cycle theories, but continued to show interest in them in conjunction with all other aspects of his theoretical work. Although both Hicks and his readers were critical of his theory, all in all this single aspect of his work was regarded by the profession as an important conceptual device.

Omar F. Hamouda

See also ACCELERATION PRINCIPLE; AGGREGATE SUPPLY AND DEMAND; CEILINGS AND FLOORS; DEMAND FOR MONEY; LINDAHL, ERIK ROBERT; LOWE, ADOLPH; MULTIPLIER; NONLINEAR BUSINESS-CYCLE THEORIES; SAMUELSON, PAUL ANTHONY

Bibliography

Alexander, S. S. 1951. "Issues of Business Cycle Theory Raised by Mr. Hicks." *American Economic Review* 41:661–76.

Burns, A. F. 1952. "Hicks and the Real Cycle." *Journal of Political Economy* 60:1–24.

Duesenberry, J. 1950. "Hicks on the Trade Cycle." *Quarterly Journal of Economics* 64:464–76.

Dye, H. S. 1952. "Certain Questions Raised by Hicks's Theory of the Trade Cycle." *Southern Economic Journal* 19:200–210.

Hamouda, O. F. 1993. *J. R. Hicks: The Economist's Economist*. Oxford: Basil Blackwell.

Harrod, R. F. 1948. *Toward a Dynamic Economics*. London: Macmillan.

Hicks, J. R. [1933] 1982. "Equilibrium and the Trade Cycle." Chap. 3 in *Money, Interest Wages*. Vol. 2 of *Collected Essays on Economic Theory*. Cambridge: Harvard Univ. Press.

———. 1939. *Value and Capital*. Oxford: Clarendon Press.

———. 1942. "The Monetary Theory of D. H. Robertson." *Economica* n.s. 2:52–57.

———. 1949. "Mr. Harrod's Dynamic Theory." *Economica* 17:106–21.

———. 1950. *A Contribution to the Theory of the Trade Cycle*. Oxford: Clarendon Press.

———. 1977. *Economic Perspectives*. Oxford: Clarendon Press.

Kaldor, N. 1951. "Mr. Hicks on the Trade Cycle." *Economic Journal* 61:833–47.

Hilferding, Rudolf (1877–1941)

Rudolf Hilferding made two important but contradictory contributions to Marxian crisis theory. In his book *Finance Capital*, published in 1910, Hilferding offered a synthesis of several existing variants of the theory as part of an ambitious extension of Marx's *Capital*. In the mid-1920s, however, he proposed the concept of a new, stable "organised capitalism" which owed more to the prewar revisionists than to Hilferding's earlier, more orthodox, brand of Marxism.

Born in Vienna, of middle-class Jewish parents, Hilferding studied both economics and medicine at the University of Vienna. Qualifying as a doctor in 1901, he rarely practiced except during military service in World War I. After 1918, Hilferding moved to Germany, where he was a member of the Reichstag until 1933, serving twice as an impeccably orthodox finance minister. He spent the last eight years of his life in exile, and was apparently murdered by the Gestapo in occupied France.

As the title implies, *Finance Capital* was concerned primarily with the changes in capitalism associated with the growing power of banks and financiers in relation to industrialists. Only the five chapters of part 4 were devoted to economic crises. Hilferding began, in chapter 16, with a discussion of Marx's reproduction models in volume two of *Capital*. He concluded that equilibrium growth was possible so long as the correct proportions were maintained between the different departments of production, regarding crises as evidence of a failure of proportionality. This reflected the influence of Tugan-Baranovsky, but Hilferding did explicitly recognize that such disproportions might result from "the underconsumption of the masses," which is "inherent" in the capitalist mode of production. Or it "could just as well be brought about by a too rapid expansion of consumption, or by a static or declining production of capital goods" ([1910] 1981, 256). In chapter 17, Hilferding dealt with Marx's analysis of the falling rate of profit in volume three, treating this as evidence of a third type of disproportion (257–58) and cyclical fluctuations in the balance between supply and demand for labor power as a fourth (260). Finally, he argued that disproportions are connected with "disturbances in the price structure" of the economy, which involve "deviations of market prices from [long-run equilibrium] production prices" and "must eventually lead to a slump in sales" (266).

None of this amounted to a formal model of crises, nor did it successfully reconcile the quite different explanations suggested by the diverse types of "disproportion" which Hilferding had identified. (Indeed, the tension between them remains an important characteristic of Marxian crisis theory today.) Chapters 18 and 19 described events in the money markets over the course of the cycle. In the more significant chapter 20, Hilferding attacked the revisionist view that the growth of cartels and the expansion of credit had reduced the severity of crises. They had merely introduced a new type of disproportion: one between monopoly and competitive sectors, shifting the burden of the crisis from the former to the latter.

Here Hilferding refined and amplified the orthodox Marxist position already established by Karl Kautsky and Rosa Luxemburg. Like them, he also argued that imperialism and crises were intimately related. The export of capital helped to bring crises to an end (318), but the ensuing struggle for economic territory would intensify rivalry between the principal capitalist powers, and increase "the concentration of economic and political power in the hands of the capitalist oligarchy" (370). This, in turn, would incite the proletariat to socialist revolution. It was this final section of Finance Capital, rather than the more narrowly academic analysis of crisis theory, which proved most influential.

Although he never repudiated his earlier ideas, Hilferding had by the middle 1920s shifted his ground considerably. A new era of "organised capitalism" had begun, he now maintained. Developments in both the private and the public sectors had lessened the impact of disproportions, so that the capitalist economy was much less unstable than it had been before 1914. The trusts were now planning their investment expenditures, often in a deliberately countercyclical fashion. A further force for stability came from the collaboration of private banks and the monetary authorities. On the international plane, cooperation was replacing imperialist competition. In Hilferding's new, almost Fabian, vision, socialism would be introduced peacefully and gradually through a series of legislative reforms, as Bernstein and the revisionists had argued in the 1890s.

Finance Capital was both an impressive intellectual achievement and a major influence on many Marxian theorists, above all on Lenin. But its impact stemmed very largely from Hilferding's analysis of imperialism; the chapters on crises seem to have gone largely unread. His later vision of a crisis-free capitalism proved very attractive to anti-Communist socialists in Western Europe before it was shattered by the onset of the Great Depression.

M. C. Howard
J. E. King

See also BAUER, OTTO; BERNSTEIN, EDUARD; DISPROPORTIONALITY THEORY; FALLING RATE OF PROFIT; KAUTSKY, KARL; MARX, KARL HEINRICH; LUXEMBURG, ROSA; TUGAN-BARANOVSKY, MIKHAIL IVANOVICH

Bibiliography

Bauer, O. 1909–10. "Das Finanzkapital." *Der Kampf* 3:391–97.

Darity, W. and B. L. Horn. 1985. "Rudolf Hilferding: the Dominion of Capitalism and the Dominion of Gold." *American Economic Review Papers and Proceedings* 75:363–68.

Gottschalch, W. 1962. *Strukturveränderung der Gesellschaft und politisches Handeln in der Lehre von Rudolf Hilferding.* Berlin: Duncker und Humblot.

Hilferding, R. [1910] 1981. *Finance Capital.* London: Routledge and Kegan Paul.

———. 1924. "Probleme der Zeit." *Die Gesellschaft* 1:1–17.

———. 1926. "Politische Probleme." *Die Gesellschaft* 3:289–302.

Howard, M. C. and King, J. E. 1989. *A History of Marxian Economics.* Vol. 1. *1883–1929.* Princeton: Princeton Univ. Press.

James, H. 1981. "Rudolf Hilferding and the Application of the Political Economy of the Second International." *Historical Journal* 24:847–69.

Kautsky, K. 1910–11. "Finanzkapital und Krisen." *Die Neue Zeit* 29:764–72, 797–804, 838–46, 874–83.

Tugan-Baranovsky, M. I. 1901. *Studien zur Theorie und Geschichte der Handelskrisen in England.* Jena: G. Fischer.

Winkler, H. A. 1974. *Organisierter Kapitalismus: Voraussetzungen und Anfänge.* Göttingen: Vandenhöck und Ruprecht.

Hobson, John Atkinson (1858–1940)

The leading non-Marxian exponent of an underconsumptionist theory of business cycles in the late nineteenth and early twentieth century, John Atkinson Hobson is widely regarded (with questionable justification) as a forerunner of both the Keynesian theory of effective demand and the Leninist theory of imperialism. Educated at Oxford, Hobson's aspirations for an academic career in economics were frustrated by the opposition of F. Y. Edgeworth who, in Hobson's words, "had read my book and considered it as equivalent in rationality to an attempt to prove the flatness of the earth" ([1938] 1976, 30).

The book to which Hobson made reference was his first book, *The Physiology of Industry*, coauthored by A. F. Mummery. Hobson credited Mummery with having convinced him that the orthodox arguments that oversaving could not lead to unemployment and depression were wrong. The book presented the basic oversaving theory of depressions that Hobson was to espouse for the rest of his life.

According to Hobson, excessive saving constrains production. Without sufficient demand for consumption, production becomes excessive and trade depression and unemployment result. Denying Say's Law, Hobson argued that current production does not imply a corresponding current demand for goods since an individual could desire to store up purchasing power for the future just as well as desire immediate consumption. The problem could be rectified by redistribution of income from the wealthy to the poor, because the poor consume a higher proportion of their incomes than the wealthy.

Though undoubtedly Keynesian in spirit, Hobson's analysis cannot be considered Keynesian in substance. Whereas in Keynes savings can only be considered excessive relative to planned investment and any excess savings are not realized because output and income fall until excess savings disappear, in Hobson excess savings are realized and investment rises to match savings. Oversaving implies overinvestment, overaccumulation, and overproduction. Production is excessive, because demand is insufficient to allow producers to recover their costs.

Hobson later applied his analysis to an explanation of imperialism which he attributed to the effort of industrialists to avoid the impact of excessive savings on their profits in their home markets. Although superficially similar to the Leninist theory of imperialism, Hobson's theory differed from Lenin's inasmuch as Hobson did not regard imperialism as being structurally necessary to capitalism. Redistributive taxation that would counter the tendency toward oversaving would also eliminate the incentive for overseas investment.

An outcast from the economics profession for most of his career, Hobson found vindication at the end of his life when Keynes, who routed the Marshallian orthodoxy against which Hobson had railed, generously acknowledged ([1936] 1973, 364–71) Hobson's early contributions. Hobson had the good fortune to enjoy the last laugh over his orthodox foes in his *Confessions of an Economic Heretic*.

David Glasner

See also FOSTER, WILLIAM TRUFANT; INCOME DISTRIBUTION AND THE BUSINESS CYCLE; OVERSAVING THEORIES OF BUSINESS CYCLES

Bibliography

Hobson, J. A. 1894. *The Evolution of Modern Capitalism*. London: W. Scott.

———. 1896. The *Problem of the Unemployed*. London: Methuen.

———. 1902. *Imperialism: A Study*. London: Nisbet.

———. [1911] 1950. *The Science of Wealth*. 4th ed. with a preface by R. F. Harrod. Oxford: Home Univ. Library.

———. 1922. *The Economics of Unemployment*. London: Macmillan.

———. [1938] 1976. *Confessions of an Economic Heretic*. Brighton: Harvester Press.

Keynes, J. M. [1936] 1973. *The General Theory of Employment, Interest, and Money*. Vol. 7 of *The Collected Writings of John Maynard Keynes*. London: Macmillan.

Mummery, A. F. and J. A. Hobson. 1889. *The Physiology of Industry*. London: J. Murray.

Hong Kong Financial Crisis (1983)

The financial crisis that beset Hong Kong in 1983 had two features of particular interest. First, its genesis lay in political, not economic, uncertainties. Indeed, the economic fundamentals of the Hong Kong economy at the time were unquestionably sound. Second, the crisis was aggravated by the curious and unstable nature of the monetary regime that existed before October 1983, and was resolved when a new monetary regime was adopted on 17 October 1983.

Before 1982, there had been bouts of uncertainty about the future status of Hong Kong and its relationship with the People's Republic of China. But these had passed after causing only temporary disturbances. In 1982, however, the prospect of the termination of the lease on the New Territories in 1997 caused Prime Minister Thatcher to begin discussing the longer-term future of Hong Kong with leaders of the People's Republic while on a visit to Beijing. These discussions were reported and thought to have failed, apparently leaving the longer-term future of Hong Kong in jeopardy.

The result was a drop in the present value of long-lived assets, notably property, dwellings, and equities, and to cause capital flight as Hong Kong residents sought to diversify their assets against the political risk. The Hong Kong monetary regime was then unusual, perhaps even unique, in having a fiat currency operated not by a central bank, but by two note-issuing commercial banks, the Hong Kong and Shanghai Banking Corporation (HSBC) and the Standard Chartered Bank, though the HSBC was by far the bigger of the two. When HSBC needed notes to support its expansion, or to satisfy customers' needs, it purchased Certificates of Indebtedness, denominated in Hong Kong dollars, from the Hong Kong monetary authorities (the Exchange Fund), which authorized it to issue new Hong Kong dollar banknotes. The Exchange Fund captured all of the seignorage, and bore the costs of printing the banknotes of the two note-issuing banks. However, the quantity of notes issued was determined by market forces, as was the exchange rate which floated freely.

This regime had operated since November 1974, when the Hong Kong dollar was floated. Historically, the Hong Kong dollar had been pegged to sterling, but after sterling was itself floated in June 1972, the Hong Kong dollar was first pegged to the United States dollar, and then allowed to float in November 1974. What then determined the rate of monetary growth? In practice, the HSBC, acting as a quasi-central bank, led the Hong Kong Association of Banks (HKAB) in oligopolistically adjusting nominal interest rates as was thought best-suited (the HKAB was statutorily required to "consult" the Financial Secretary before such adjustments) to

the current conditions of Hong Kong. Demand for notes, bank borrowing, monetary expansion, exchange-rate adjustments, etc., then were influenced by the administered and cartelized choice of interest rates.

In 1982–83, however, the collapse in property prices and construction activity weakened many bank borrowers, so that the HKAB hesitated to raise local interest rates sharply, certainly not enough to offset the effect of political uncertainty on capital flows. Although the Hong Kong current account remained strong, the gathering capital flight depressed the exchange rate. The fall in the exchange rate then intensified the urge to transfer capital abroad, which, in turn, caused the exchange rate to drop even faster.

By the summer of 1983, the decline in the exchange rate was fueling domestic inflation, and the local population was expressing increasing concern about the prospects for economic, and more urgently, political stability. Meanwhile, the People's Republic was becoming concerned about the deteriorating conditions in Hong Kong, blaming capital flight on the desire of the British authorities to strip Hong Kong of assets before leaving (or on their attempt to encourage the currency disturbance to show the damage that control over Hong Kong by the People's Republic would cause). While both these assertions were completely untrue, the fact that three eminent American economists (Beers, Sargent, and Wallace [1983] 1986) could ascribe the decline in the Hong Kong dollar to a government-engineered devaluation shows how easily such errors could be made in the tense atmosphere of the time. When the People's Republic began to hint at immediate physical intervention in Hong Kong, bringing the specter of 1997 forward, the spiral of capital flight, depreciation, inflation, and political disturbance accelerated still further. The crisis came to a head on 24 September 1983.

Until then the government had done little to stay the deepening economic crisis, though, with a budget surplus and massive foreign-exchange reserves, it was in a strong position. The government, especially the Chief Secretary, Sir Philip Haddon-Cave, who played a major role in establishing the existing monetary regime, was deeply committed to laissez-faire. But the collapse of the exchange rate in September convinced the authorities that something had to be done. Indeed, public statements on 25 September that action would be taken to stabilize the foreign exchange rate helped to slow down the collapse.

However, the statements did not detail exactly what measures would be taken, nor was it clear that the authorities had any well-defined plans. Instead, the most significant suggestions for reform came from an economist with G.T. Management Plc, John Greenwood, who had helped found the *Asian Monetary Monitor.* Greenwood suggested several possible reforms, of which the most promising was to revert to a regime similar to the old British Currency Board system, which had operated earlier in Hong Kong from 1935 to 1972. Under such a system, any additional Hong Kong dollars were to be backed one-for-one by deposits in an international currency to which the Hong Kong dollar would be linked. However, Greenwood had antagonized some of those in authority with his earlier criticism of the existing monetary regime, and the authorities in any case wanted some outside advice. So Greenwood's basic proposals were reviewed for a few weeks before being introduced in mid-October.

The key requirement was to stabilize the exchange rate and to link the Hong Kong dollar to the United States dollar at a rate of 7.80 Hong Kong dollars to one U.S. dollar. The U.S. dollar, rather than the pound, the yen, or a basket of currencies, was chosen as the key currency for a combination of political and economic reasons. The proposed form of the link, whereby the banks could exchange U.S. dollars for Hong Kong banknotes, or retire Hong Kong notes and obtain U.S. dollars at a fixed rate, while the exchange market itself was left free, was expected to work via arbitrage. If the Hong Kong dollar depreciated, then the banks would find it worthwhile to take the Hong Kong dollar notes to the monetary authority to obtain U.S. dollars at the higher rate. The resulting reduction in the currency stock would then raise Hong Kong interest rates, leading to a restoration of the exchange-rate target.

In practice, the arbitrage points left more room for slippage than was comfortable in the highly charged atmosphere of the time. The HSBC (supported by the authorities acting via the Exchange Fund) brought about direct changes in interest rates to sustain the link. Although earlier concern over the fragility of bank borrowers had constrained the banks' interest-rate adjustments, the post-October 1983 movements in interest rates did *not* cause any significant domestic distress.

Indeed, once the link was firmly in place, and financial confidence was restored, the underlying strength of the Hong Kong economy soon reasserted itself, and its subsequent performance was extremely successful. Though the key importance of maintaining the link was widely appreciated, some concern persisted over the technicalities of the arbitrage mechanism, and over the extent to which it remained appropriate for the HSBC to maintain its central position in determining interest rates. Accordingly, in July 1988, a package of measures was introduced to give the monetary authorities in Hong Kong increased command over the interest-rate mechanism. The crucial feature of the 1988 measures was to transfer control over the ultimate liquidity of the banking system from HSBC to the authorities.

The link has managed, in practice, to maintain monetary stability in Hong Kong despite continuing political instability, as hopes for the protection of Hong Kong's long-term position as a special capitalist enclave within China (resulting from the negotiations over Hong Kong's future between China and the United Kingdom) were followed by dismay at the events of Tianenmen Square in mid-1989. Through all such vicissitudes, the value of the Hong Kong dollar has remained close to its parity with the U.S. dollar, and Hong Kong interest rates have remained close to U.S. rates. Indeed, events emanating from the United States, which have caused gyrations in the U.S. dollar exchange rate, rather than domestic Hong Kong developments, have been the source of monetary problems in Hong Kong. But the patent advantages of maintaining a regime that has demonstrated its capacity to withstand political shocks have reinforced the commitment of the authorities to maintain the link in the run-up to 1997.

C. A. E. Goodhart

Bibliography

Beers, D., T. J. Sargent, and N. Wallace. [1983] 1986. "Speculation about the Speculation against the Hong Kong Dollar." Chap. 6 in T. J. Sargent, *Rational Expectations and Inflation.* New York: Harper and Row.

Greenwood, J. 1981. "Time to Blow the Whistle." *Asian Monetary Monitor,* July/August, 15–34.

———. 1982. "Hong Kong's Financial Crisis: History, Analysis, Prescription." *Asian*

Monetary Monitor, November/December, 1–69.

———. 1983. "How to Rescue the Hong Kong Dollar: Three Practical Proposals." *Asian Monetary Monitor,* September/October, 11–39.

———. 1988a. "Hong Kong: Intervention Replaces Arbitrage—The July Package of Monetary Measures." *Asian Monetary Monitor,* July/August, 1–20.

———. 1988b. "Response to Dr. Jao." *Asian Monetary Monitor,* November/December, 7–12.

Jao, Y. C. 1988. "Hong Kong Intervention Replaces Arbitrage—The July Package of Monetary Measures: A Comment." *Asian Monetary Monitor,* November/December, 1–6.

Shah, P. 1988. "Hong Kong: The Decline of the Hong Kong Dollar in 1983: Devaluation or Depreciation?" *Asian Monetary Monitor,* November/December, 13–22.

Hume, David (1711–1776)

The contemporary student of philosophy knows of David Hume through his pathbreaking *A Treatise of Human Nature* published in 1739 which, at the time, attracted little attention. But over the next two decades, Hume published several collections of carefully crafted essays that earned him great praise in the literary circles of his day. These essays include Hume's important contributions to monetary theory, which have been incorporated into much of modern business-cycle theory.

In his *Political Discourses* (see Hume [1889] 1985), Hume opposed the Mercantilist idea that international trade is a zero-sum game. He called attention to the favorable impact trade has on both moral character and material well-being. In addition, Hume also combatted the Mercantilist fallacy that a "favorable balance of trade" is always advantageous to a nation. If exports exceed imports, the favorable balance implies an inflow of specie. An inflow of specie was considered to be an end in itself in Mercantilist discussions of economic policy. Thus, subsidizing exports and taxing imports, with the vigorous exploitation of colonies, and the associated discipline of low wages for city workers (producing high profit margins on exportables) were frequently recommended policies. A large hoard of specie would be available to help finance a war, and in peacetimes, the coins would permanently "circulate" and stimulate trade.

Hume's great contribution was to show that all policies to bolster specie holdings are ultimately self-defeating. Especially, if trade barriers between nations were insignificant, the world money supply (specie) would automatically distribute itself according to the "labour and industry" of each trading area regardless of the stimulative policies pursued by governments (1985, 315n).

If new specie flowed into England as a result of a favorable trade balance, the specie would ultimately raise local prices. The rise in prices would discourage foreign purchases and encourage domestic purchases of imports. By necessity, Hume argued, the favorable balance would gradually diminish until a new international equilibrium was established ([1889] 1985, 181–94). We may term this theory and variants of it Hume's *price-specie-flow mechanism.* The mechanism relies as much on alterations in the amount of cash held by individuals as it does on international price differences when exchange rates are fixed. The latter assumption has been criticized by advocates of the monetary approach to the balance of payments, because if all commodities were traded, then their international prices could not vary by more than transportation costs, thereby weakening Hume's specie-flow mechanism.

Historians have especially puzzled over Hume's assertion that an influx of gold can stimulate the national economy in the short run though not the long run. Was this a sudden concession to Mercantilist thought? Perlman (1987) has offered a gloss on these passages that brings Hume closer to the modern understanding of how changes in the money supply can have temporary output effects. The expansion in economic activity occurs when the specie enters the cash balances of prudent merchants who (unlike the prodigal landlords) invest those funds. Their investments bid up the money wage of labor and thereby encourage some workers to supply more labor effort—hence, the rise in real output.

The money eventually spreads throughout the economy, and commodity prices rise, which reduces *real* wages. In the long run the surge in output disappears, and the specie-enhanced economy returns to its old levels of output and employment, though at a higher price level.

Later, in the nineteenth and especially in the twentieth centuries, Hume's theory of the international payments mechanism became the cornerstone of the study of international business cycles. A business downturn in, for example, England would quickly be transmitted to its major trading partners. During the recession, English imports would fall off, depressing trade in other countries. Falling English incomes and prices also encourage exports. The resulting improvement in the English trade balance causes an inflow of specie which adds to the cash balances of English merchants and mitigates the downturn in England. Elsewhere, however, mercantile specie balances diminish because of the declining English demand, and economic conditions worsen. The business cycle is transmitted from one country to another through the cash-settlement mechanisms associated with the balance of payments (Haberler 1962).

One important objective of business-cycle theory is to derive a cyclical process from the microfoundations of rational behavior. It is probably fair to say that Hume's price-specie-flow approach, which links the balance of payments to international monetary conditions, is essential to providing those microfoundations (Mises [1924]1953). This approach can be traced back to the Spanish scholastic writers at Salamanca and was forcefully restated by Richard Cantillon in the 1730s. Perhaps, because of its greater accessibility in English and Hume's fame as a philosopher, most modern treatments credit Hume with originating the approach.

Laurence S. Moss

See also CANTILLON, RICHARD; LOYD, SAMUEL JONES

Bibliography

Cantillon, R. [1755] 1931. *Essai Sur La Nature du Commerce en General*. Edited by H. Higgs. London: Royal Economic Society.

Dornbusch, R. 1980. *Open Economy Macro-Economics*. New York: Basic Books.

Grice-Hutchinson, M. 1952. *The School of Salamanca*. Oxford: Clarendon Press.

Haberler, G. 1962. *Prosperity and Depression*. 4th rev. ed. Cambridge: Harvard Univ. Press.

Hume, D. [1889] 1985. *Essays Moral, Political and Literary*. Edited by E. Miller. Indianapolis: Liberty Classics Press.

Mises, L. von. [1924] 1953. *The Theory of Money and Credit*. 2d ed. New Haven: Yale Univ. Press.

Perlman, M. 1987. "Of a Controversial Passage in Hume." *Journal of Political Economy* 95:274–89.

Viner, J. 1937. *Studies in the Theory of International Trade*. New York: Harper.

Hutt, William Harold (1899–1988)

W. H. Hutt, a staunch upholder of neoclassical orthodoxy and an opponent of Keynesian theory and any form of interference with the price mechanism, was born and educated in London. He spent most of his career in South Africa where he was an outspoken critic of its racial policies, attributing them to the efforts of white trade unions to insulate themselves from the competition of nonwhite workers.

Hutt's most important theoretical contribution came in a short book, *The Theory of Idle Resources*, whose importance has yet to be fully acknowledged. The book challenged Keynes's contention that classical theory could not account for episodes of substantial unemployment. Hutt rejected Keynes's categorization of unemployment as either voluntary or involuntary and instead classified unemployment or idleness according to the motivation of the resource owner for not currently employing a resource. Expecting higher prices in the future, owners of resources might speculatively withhold resources, and expecting higher wages, workers might withhold their services. Withholding could be necessary to realize the expected higher prices or wages if employment now would preclude the anticipated future use or if workers could not efficiently search for the expected higher wages while employed. Expectations of higher future wages would also lead to additional current consumption of leisure, for investments in human capital, or for utilization of labor within the household.

Because resources or workers not employed for this reason are, given current expectations, actually being devoted to their most valuable uses, Hutt called such unemployment "pseudo-idleness." Thus, as early as 1939, Hutt anticipated the search and intertemporal-substitution explanations for unemployment that were, with only occasional acknowledgment of Hutt's priority, advanced decades later.

However, unlike many recent proponents of the search and intertemporal-substitution explanations of unemployment, Hutt did not believe in perpetual market clearing. In practice, he assigned more importance to restrictive practices by unions that frustrated wage and price adjustments than to search and intertemporal substitution. And in subsequent work, he argued that, by, in effect, justifying restrictions on wage and price flexibility, Keynesian policies left inflation as the only means of achieving adjustments in relative prices and wages.

In later years, Hutt extended his challenge to Keynesian doctrines, by offering *A Rehabilitation of Say's Law*. Keynes had rejected Say's Law, holding that it ruled out the very possibility of unemployment. In contrast, Hutt used Say's Law as a tool in the analysis of depressions. Hutt described a kind of multiplier process in which supply interruptions caused by the overpricing of resources have a cumulative effect. To explain this cumulative process, Hutt invoked Say's idea that supply creates its own demand to show that a withholding of supply in one sector could have repercussions in other sectors. One need not accept Hutt's argument in full to acknowledge its relevance to an understanding of how both supply and demand conditions can affect aggregate economic activity.

Despite the importance of many of Hutt's contributions, they received little recognition when first made and have not been fully appreciated subsequently. His career is one of the more unfortunate examples of the neglect by economists of important contributions to economic analysis.

David Glasner

See also DIVISIA MONETARY AGGREGATES; INTERTEMPORAL SUBSTITUTION; RICARDO, DAVID; SAY, JEAN-BAPTISTE; SAY'S LAW; SEARCH THEORY

Bibliography

Hutt, W. H. [1939] 1977. *The Theory of Idle Resources*. 2d ed. Indianapolis: Liberty Press.

———. 1963. *Keynesianism: Retrospect and Prospect*. Chicago: Regnery.

———. 1974. *A Rehabilitation of Say's Law*. Athens, Ohio: Univ. of Ohio Press.

———. 1975. *Individual Freedom: Selected Works of William H. Hutt*. Edited by S. Pejovich and D. Klingman. Westport, Conn.: Greenwood Press.

H

I

Implicit Contracts

The concept of implicit contracts helps account for the common observation that business cycles are marked by systematic movements in employment but not in wage rates. Employment and wage relationships are viewed as embodying enduring, long-term contractual elements between workers and firms. The employment contract is a mechanism for workers and employers to share consumption risks when risk-sharing opportunities outside the firm are limited. Thus observed wages embody elements of saving and dissaving that allow workers to smooth consumption over the cycle. These components must be netted out in ascertaining the pure productivity information content of wages for allocating labor supply.

Aggregate swings in employment over business cycles present problems for the standard impersonal-market model. In standard markets, prices adjust to allow buyers and sellers to transact under any conditions that arise. No transaction is involuntary, nor is anyone precluded from transacting on terms available to anyone else. Evidently, this is not so during recessions, which are marked by involuntary layoffs and unemployment. Furthermore, many laid-off workers are willing to work under the same conditions as those who retain their jobs, but cannot find the opportunity to do so. Why aren't wages in general bid down until all who seek work can find it?

Economists have considered wage rigidities essential for these observations, following Keynes, who made them central to his scheme in the *General Theory*. A well-known exposition of the Keynesian model by Modigliani ([1944] 1980) clearly identified wage rigidities as a key element of any macroeconomic model

of business cycles. Wage rigidities provide a workable, but uneasy, basis for theory, because they lack microeconomic foundation. Implicit-contract theory is one approach for providing that foundation.

Both theoretical and empirical work have contributed to a contractual view of labor markets. Search theory showed that transactions costs allow wage dispersion, making it optimal for a worker to accept only jobs that pay more than the reservation wage. Nor would firms fill jobs with the first applicant to come along. Thus, unfilled vacancies may coexist with unemployment. The search model further evolved to stress the matching or marriage aspects of employment. In most jobs the quality of the "match," or the degree of "fit" between worker and firm, is important for job performance and productivity. Consequently, it pays both the worker and firm to be choosy in filling a position. The cost of replicating these match-specific elements also make replacement costly. Thus, jobs should have substantial duration.

Enduring employment relationships suggest that "as-if" contracts can represent those implicit understandings between workers and firms that evolve over the course of their relationship. Empirical findings reinforce these views. First, the longest-lasting jobs held by the average worker are of long duration: twenty years is not uncommon. Most permanent job turnover occurs during the first year or two of employment, as information that match-specific attributes are unfavorable is acquired. The empirical frequency of job termination falls very rapidly with job duration: if a person has remained on a job for as long as two years, the job is likely to last for a very long time (Mincer and Jovanovic 1981). A parallel observation is that most layoffs are temporary, with laid-off workers ultimately returning to their original employer (Feldstein 1976). The forces that promote permanent attachments are strong enough to survive even lengthy lay-offs.

The elements of implicit-contract theory are generally attributed to Baily, Gordon, and Azariadis. This account is based on the economics of risk sharing and follows Rosen (1985), which can be consulted for details, background, and further references. Consider a risk-averse worker employed by a risk-neutral firm with production function $y = sx$, where y is output, x is effort and s is an identically distributed random variable with unit mean and known distribution $F(s)$. The worker has a convex utility function $u = u(c, z)$, where c is consumption and $z = 1 - x$ is leisure. The contract is an allocation of wages or consumption c and work effort x that is contingent on the value of s randomly drawn by nature. Gains from trade arise from the fact that the firm is risk-neutral and can offer consumption insurance to risk-averse workers, who could otherwise get it only on less favorable terms.

The competitively determined contract maximizes the expected utility of workers $Eu(c(s), z(s))$ subject to a zero-profit constraint for the firm: $Ec(s) - Esx(s) = 0$, where the expectation is taken over $F(s)$ in both expressions. The contract must be thought of as stating specific consumption (wages) and work hours in each state of nature s. This view is fundamentally different from the standard market model, where workers and firms are assumed to unilaterally choose hours at a single, competitively determined wage. Unilateral choice would create serious moral-hazard problems when there is consumption insurance, and contracts cannot be sustained unless both prices and quantities are fully agreed upon. In defining a work schedule to which all parties adhere, the contract model captures features of actual employment arrangements and clearly improves on the standard impersonal bourse model.

Two conditions characterize the optimal contract. One is familiar:

$$s \geq u_z(c(s),z(s))/u_c(c(s),z(s)),$$

so the marginal disutility of work is not greater than the marginal product of labor. A layoff may occur (x is set to zero) when the marginal product s is sufficiently small. Otherwise employment adjustments require marginal changes in hours of work. The second condition is less familiar and states that $u_c(c(s), z(s)) = k$, where k is a constant. This is the optimum insurance condition that the marginal utility of consumption should be equated in all states of the world.

Detailed analysis of these two conditions establishes essential features of the contract. For example, it can be shown that employment $x(s)$ in the contract is always increasing in s. The contract directs that more work be done when its marginal product increases. The effect of demand or productivity conditions on consumption is more complicated and depends on the cross derivative u_{cz}. In general, consumption can be shown to be decreasing or increasing in s as u_{cz} is positive or negative. However, the special case where u is fully separable in c and z illustrates contract theory to best advantage. In that case $c(s)$ in the contract is independent of s. The worker's consumption is constant and fully assured, whatever amount of work is required by contract. Dividing $c(s)$ by $x(s)$ in this case yields a kind of inverse wage flexibility in which the hourly wage rate is decreasing in s. This, of course, is required by full consumption insurance and is feasible because workers cannot freely choose hours *ex post* in the contract, but rather must supply whatever the contract stipulates. This helps explain why wages do not fall in recessions or rise in booms, but other utility functions lead to more complex wage behavior.

While the economics of implicit contracts has many attractive, empirically relevant features, it has a troublesome implication that is at odds with business-cycle data. For most commonly accepted forms of worker preferences, the optimal contract tends to "overinsure" in the sense of making workers absolutely better off when demand s is smaller and workers are less likely to be employed. This does not square with involuntary layoffs and unemployment and the general declines in living standards suffered by those laid off in recessions. This feature of the model can be repaired by introducing frictions and other restrictions on the amount of insurance feasible under a contract. However, such elements greatly complicate the model and reduce its utility. Nor do any generally accepted methods for imposing incompleteness on employment contracts exist. Hence implicit contracts are an interesting, but incomplete, solution to the intellectual problem that gave rise to them. The search for other solutions, two of which—efficiency wages and insider-outsider theory—are attracting much attention, is ongoing, but those solutions are also not without their problems.

Sherwin Rosen

See also EFFICIENCY WAGES; NEW KEYNESIAN ECONOMICS; OKUN, ARTHUR M.; SEARCH THEORY; WAGE RIGIDITY

Bibliography

Azariadis, C. 1975. "Implicit Contracts and Underemployment Equilibria." *Journal of Political Economy* 83:1183–1202.

Baily, M. N. 1974. "Wages and Employment under Uncertain Demand." *Review of Economic Studies* 41:37–50.

Feldstein, M. 1976. "Temporary Layoffs in the Theory of Unemployment." *Journal of Political Economy* 84:937–57.

Gordon, D. F. 1974. "A Neoclassical Theory of Keynesian Unemployment." *Economic Inquiry* 12:431–59.

Mincer, J. and B. Jovanovic. 1981. "Labor Mobility and Wages." In *Studies in Labor Markets,* edited by S. Rosen, 21–63. Chicago: Univ. of Chicago Press.

Modigliani, F. [1944] 1980. "Liquidity Preference and the Theory of Interest and Money." Chap. 2 of *The Collected Papers of Franco Modigliani.* Vol. 1. Cambridge: MIT Press.

Rosen, S. 1985. "Implicit Contracts: A Survey." *Journal of Economic Literature* 23:1144–75.

Impulse and Propagation
See FRISCH, RAGNAR ANTON KITTEL

Income Distribution and the Business Cycle

The business cycle can be explained by two distinct Marxian theories of change in income distribution between labor and property shares: the reserve-army theory, which implies a countercyclical labor share; and the underconsumption theory, which implies a procyclical share. By contrast, Kalecki's theory of the business cycle suggests that the labor share is countercyclical, though the wage share, which together with the salary component forms the labor share, stays constant.

Marx himself developed a theory of business cycles based on the industrial reserve army of labor. Profits stimulate accumulation which absorbs labor, though innovations tend to reduce absorption. When the reserve army of the unemployed—which includes disguised unemployment—diminishes, wages increase, reducing profits and discouraging further accumulation. Crisis ensues, and recovery becomes possible when wages fall after the reserve army has been replenished. To reduce it again requires a new and sufficient surge of accumulation to offset labor-saving innovations.

Goodwin's model encapsulates this theory in a Lotka-Volterra system of two nonlinear differential equations in two state-variables: the share of wages and the unemployment rate. The model assumes that all profits are saved and invested while wages are consumed, that real wages rise as full employment is approached, that labor productivity and labor supply grow at a constant rate, and that the capital/output ratio remains constant. The result is a persistent growth cycle of output and accumulation, whose trend is exogenously given by the growth rate of productivity and labor supply. A continuous stream of Harrod-neutral innovations determines productivity growth. As in Marx, if wages rise faster (slower) than productivity, the impact of costs on profits turns the cycle phase of the employment rate downwards (upwards). The labor share thus displays a countercyclical pattern.

Marx's sparse references to "realization failures of the full value of production," i.e., to conditions of selling at prices below costs inclusive of expected profit margin, prompted Sweezy (1942) to suggest an underconsumptionist explanation of crises. Sherman (1979) later built a full-blown underconsumptionist model of the business cycle. The core of the argument is that, first, labor productivity is procyclical and money wages change slowly because of lags in bargaining. Second, if wages increase faster (slower) than productivity, the demand-pull effect, through the propensity to consume and to invest, turns the cycle phase up (down). Thus, the labor share is procyclical.

In Kalecki's theory of the business cycle, changes in the wage share are determined rather than determining. His treatment of income distribution is based on the assumption that prices in the manufacturing sector are cost-determined, that short-run profit maximization is not pursued, and that constant unit prime costs prevail. Such costs include expenses for manual labor, i.e., wages, and for raw materials. The excess of price over unit prime cost, i.e., the degree of monopoly, includes profits and unit fixed costs, such as salaries. Thus, the wage share is a decreasing function of the degree of monopoly and of the ratio between raw-materials cost and manual-labor cost. Therefore, as output and value added fluctuate, the wage share remains constant insofar as the procyclical changes in the cost of raw materials, which are demand-determined, offset the countercyclical changes in the degree of monopoly, which includes salaries and other fixed costs that are spread over output. The wage-plus-salary share is thus moderately countercyclical, due to the fixed-cost spread. Kalecki attributes the paradoxical occurrence of downturns when full employment is reached and profits are high to the need to counteract the strength of labor to preserve political and social stability.

The neoclassical theory of distribution in income shares, which is a theory of long-run stable equilibrium at full employment, does not imply a theory of the business cycle. However, it does explain changes in income distribution when the economic system is in disequilibrium. On an upswing, for example, perfectly competitive firms move up the upward-sloping sections of their short-run marginal-cost curves, so that prices rise relative to wages (Hahn 1972). Thus, the wage share is countercyclical.

On the empirical side, Weisskopf (1979) has suggested a framework for testing different theories on changes in income distribution. For the United States nonfinancial corporate sector during the postwar period, he distinguishes two phases (A and B) in expansions; and a third phase (C) in contraction. During expansion the labor share at first declines (A) and then increases (B) and continues to increase even further during the contraction (C). No simple pro- or countercyclical pattern emerges, leaving room to argue about competing theories.

Adherents of the reserve-army theory (Boddy and Crotty 1975) stress that: (1) the labor-cost-push effect on profits can explain the cyclical upper turning point, since phase C lags behind the increase in the labor share (in phase B); (2) prices of raw materials do not have a significant role in stabilizing the labor share; (3) Kalecki's paradox of high profits during downturns does not arise.

By contrast, adherents of the cyclical version of the underconsumption theory (Sherman) stress that: (1) the labor-demand-pull effect on profits can explain the cyclical upper turning point, since phase C lags behind the reduction in the labor share (phase A); (2) larger changes

in productivity, rather than in real wages, account for changes in the labor share, since the effects of the fixed-cost spread, which includes fixed labor cost, seem to be substantial, while the pursuit of increased wages seems to be eroded by price inflation, as predicted by Kalecki.

Both theories are reflected in Weisskopf's eclectic conclusion drawn from accounting analysis. In fact, the upper turning point appears to be due to the rising labor-cost effect, while conditions under phases C and A appear to be due to, respectively, low and high utilization rates, which show the demand-pull effect.

On the whole, the safest conclusion is one that confirms the favorable effect of labor cost spread on profits, whereby the labor share tends to move countercyclically, as Kalecki argued. However, such an explanation for labor productivity behavior is at variance with standard neoclassical theory. Both the reserve-army theory and the underconsumption theory could explain the upper turning point of the cycle. Although they predict opposite cyclical behaviors of the labor share, the differences between them could be reconciled by different time lags. Finally, the constancy of the manual-labor share seems not to find significant empirical support. A more promising direction of research would therefore seem to be one that tests the two theories drawing a clear distinction between behavioral functions and accounting identities.

However, two difficult points remain to be explained: the lower turning point of the cycle and the endogenous trend of growth. These questions are evidenced in particular by the experience of the 1970s, when, moreover, the labor share became more countercyclical (Hahnel and Sherman 1982). The interpretation suggested by Gordon, Weisskopf and Bowles (1983) is that the standard cycle is a process for restoring profitability, thus allowing for growth; and that profitability can be restored only if a set of institutions, called the *social structure of accumulation,* provides economic stability and moderates political and social conflict. But the 1970s, like the 1930s, saw a break in the social structure, making it impossible to restore profitability.

Maurizio Pugno

See also GOODWIN, RICHARD MURPHEY; INFLATION; KALECKI, MICHAL; MARX, KARL HEINRICH; OVERSAVING THEORIES OF BUSINESS CYCLES; PARETO, VILFREDO; SOCIAL

Bibliography

Boddy, R. and J. Crotty. 1975. "Class Conflict and Macro-Policy: The Political Business Cycle." *Review of Radical Political Economics* 7:1–19.

Goodwin, R. M. [1967] 1982. "A Growth Cycle." Chap. 14 in *Essays in Economic Dynamics*. London: Macmillan.

Gordon, D., T. E. Weisskopf, and S. Bowles. 1983. "Long Swings and the Nonreproductive Cycle." *American Economic Review Papers and Proceedings* 73:152–57.

Hahn, F. H. 1972. *The Share of Wages in the National Income*. London: Weidenfeld and Nicolson.

Hahnel, R. and H. J. Sherman. 1982. "Income Distribution and the Business Cycle." *Journal of Economic Issues* 16:49–73.

Kalecki, M. 1971. *Selected Essays on the Dynamics of the Capitalist Economy 1933–1970*. Cambridge: Cambridge Univ. Press.

King, J. and P. Regan. 1976. *Relative Income Shares*. London: Macmillan.

Marx, K. H. [1867–94] 1967. *Capital*. Vols. 1, 3. New York: International Publishers.

Phelps-Brown, E. H. and P. E. Hart. 1952. "The Share of Wages in National Income." *Economic Journal* 62:253–77.

Sherman, H. J. 1979. "A Marxist Theory of the Business Cycle." *Review of Radical Political Economics* 11:1–23.

Sweezy, P. M. 1942. *The Theory of Capitalist Economic Development*. New York: Monthly Review Press.

Vercelli, A. 1977. "The Phillips Dilemma: A New Suggested Approach." *Economic Notes* 6:13–73.

Weisskopf, T. E. 1979. "Marxian Crisis Theory and the Rate of Profit in the Postwar U.S. Economy." *Cambridge Journal of Economics* 3:341–78.

Incomplete Markets

The theory of general equilibrium under incomplete markets is a natural extension of the older general-equilibrium theory under complete markets. The latter dates to the pioneering work of Arrow, Debreu, and others in the 1950s, and is the cornerstone of modern mathematical economics. More recently, much attention has been given to dynamic general-equilibrium theory. The static and dynamic models share a common theoretical framework. A brief review of the Arrow-Debreu model provides a useful reference point for examining models of equilibrium with incomplete markets and the role market incompleteness plays in some business-cycle models.

The Arrow-Debreu model of general equilibrium under complete markets is important for several reasons. It provides a rigorous axiomatic basis for proving the existence of a general equilibrium. It also provides an elegant and fairly general context in which general equilibrium implies Pareto-optimality (the "first welfare theorem"). Conversely, in the Arrow-Debreu model any conceivable Pareto-optimal allocation is a general equilibrium for some economy, namely an economy achieved by reallocating the initial endowments of commodities and shares of firm ownership (the "second welfare theorem"). In essence, these welfare results follow from the full flexibility in exchange—and thus reallocation—furnished by a complete set of markets. When the assumption of completeness is relaxed, these important results do not necessarily hold.

A system of markets is said to be *complete* when a market exists for every commodity. More specifically, completeness requires that every agent be able to exchange, either directly or indirectly, every Arrow-Debreu commodity with every other agent. A system of markets is *incomplete* when it is not complete. To be meaningful, however, these simple statements require a fuller definition of the terms "market" and "commodity." In the simplest benchmark case—the finite-dimensional, pure-exchange, complete-markets general-equilibrium model—a market is succinctly defined as a price, expressed in terms of the unit of account (strictly speaking, it is the relative prices of commodities that matter, rather than nominal prices in terms of the unit of account). All agents can either buy or sell each commodity at its corresponding price. A commodity is defined not only by its physical characteristics as a good, for example, the flavor of an apple or the fineness of a precious metal, but also by the time, location and, notably, the state of the world in which it is available. Time is treated as a finite sequence of discrete intervals, called *dates* (though there are extensions to infinite-dimensional spaces). Uncertainty is modeled as a finite collection of discrete states of the world, or simply *states*. A state is defined as a complete specification of the exogenous variables over all dates, including both exogenous fundamentals (e.g., a drought) and sunspot variables (e.g., hemlines). An *event* is a collection of states of the world. For example, the set of all states in which a recession occurs next year is an event.

Ultimately, the relevance of a distinction in commodity characteristics, timing, environment, and so on is determined by consumers' preferences. However, a key insight of the theory is that the mathematics of calculating equilibria is largely unaffected by the particular interpretation assigned to the term "commodity." Expressed mathematically, the important qualification is that each good be representable as a dimension in a linear space of date-state-goods, or Arrow-Debreu commodities. An important implication is that a market (i.e., price) for a commodity can exist without being expressed explicitly. That is, because commodities and markets are treated as elements of a problem in linear algebra, implicit markets for a commodity are equivalent to an explicit one. For example, if oranges are available only in bundles containing one apple and one orange for $5 per bundle, but apples trade separately for $3 per apple, then the solution of a simple system of two linear equations reveals that an orange is implicitly worth $2.

The problem of computing economic equilibria is thus susceptible to analytical techniques designed for vector spaces. A *pure-exchange economy* is defined as a combination of *endowments* and *preferences*. (This definition of an economy can be readily extended to accommodate the production technologies of firms.) A consumer's endowment is a commodity bundle, represented as a vector in the positive orthant of the space of Arrow-Debreu commodities. Preferences assign values to bundles of commodities, and are represented as functions mapping the possible Arrow-Debreu commodity bundles into the real line. Preferences are commonly represented as von Neumann-Morgenstern expected utilities, which are separable over time and across states. An *equilibrium* is then a vector of positive prices and an allocation of commodities satisfying three conditions: (1) given prices, each consumer obeys his budget constraint, so that the total value (price times quantity) of his consumption equals the total value of his endowment; (2) subject to the budget constraint, each consumer maximizes expected utility; and (3) the aggregate consumption of each commodity precisely ex-

hausts the aggregate endowment. In the case of complete markets, an equilibrium exists and satisfies the two welfare theorems.

Arrow demonstrated that a complete set of relative prices is not strictly necessary for an equilibrium to exist and be Pareto-optimal. An equivalent equilibrium can be achieved with a system of financial securities and spot markets for goods. Intuitively, agents need not be able to exchange individual goods across states, because goods from different date-events ultimately will not coexist. Securities provide flexibility for the *ex ante* reallocation of wealth across states, while spot markets provide flexibility for the *ex post* reallocation of endowments within states. A full array of spot markets is usually assumed to exist, and attention focuses on the number of linearly independent contingent-claim payoffs (or the *span* of the financial assets) relative to the number of future date-events.

The equilibrium and welfare theorems fail to hold when the system of markets is incomplete. Equilibria are generally not Pareto-optimal, although Arrow's result demonstrates that Pareto-inferiority does not necessarily follow from incompleteness. Under certain circumstances, equilibria may not even exist. It is significant, then, that even a conservative count of real-world goods, states, and dates is absurdly large. Moreover, market completeness requires some mechanism for exchange between generations that are not alive simultaneously. As a result, some additional relevance must be attached to the theoretical and political implications of incompleteness—for example, the possibility of nonneutral money or of a Pareto-improving role for government intervention in the market economy.

While the theory is general enough to include intertemporal dynamics, most general-equilibrium applications are concerned with the existence of equilibrium and are static in spirit. On the other hand, many business-cycle models implicitly or explicitly assume some form of market incompleteness. However, the incompleteness of a system of markets is neither necessary nor sufficient to induce fluctuations. Nothing about the Arrow-Debreu complete-markets model requires an equilibrium to be a steady state. Thus, although cyclical fluctuations can be symptomatic of a Pareto-inferior incomplete-markets equilibrium calling for government intervention, they can also occur in the Arrow-Debreu model, in which the first welfare theorem applies. Cycles can be achieved directly, for example, by assuming the requisite cyclical time dependence in preferences or production technology. Conversely, incompleteness is an insufficient condition for aggregate fluctuations: steady-state equilibria are clearly possible in models with incomplete markets. Thus, the significance of the theory of incomplete markets for modeling business cycles lies not in incompleteness per se, but in the particular ways in which incompleteness occurs. In certain cases, incompleteness can be shown to induce or facilitate cyclical fluctuations or other deviations from the steady state.

In this spirit, incomplete markets are a natural tactic for modeling dynamic general equilibria in which aggregate fluctuations arise endogenously. Such aggregate fluctuations can be cyclical and can even degenerate into chaos in certain cases. Incompleteness plays a significant role in many business-cycle models (Boldrin and Woodford 1990, especially sections 4 and 6, and the references therein). Incompleteness usually works in such models by constraining the ability of agents to smooth consumption or investment, or by restricting their ability to insure fully against uncertainty.

Some equilibrium models of endogenous fluctuations introduce incompleteness directly by imposing restrictions (a cash-in-advance constraint, for example) on the set of allowable transactions. For example, Woodford (1989) offers a model in which missing markets force entrepreneurs to rely on internal financing, because borrowing or lending between entrepreneurs and other agents is impossible. Entrepreneurs therefore cannot smooth capital accumulation completely over time. An increase in the capital stock raises the real wage, and can thus reduce profits and hence new investment. For certain parameter values, cyclical patterns in the capital stock unfold as increases in the capital stock induce subsequent decreases. Note that incompleteness can also play an indirect role in business-cycle models. *Sunspots,* for example, can be shown to induce cycles in some models, but they require some form of incompleteness to work. In an economy in which complete markets allow agents to insure against sunspot risk, sunspots do not affect the set of equilibria. Incompleteness has also entered business-cycle models as an *overlapping-generations* assumption. Grandmont (1985), for example, presents such a model. The overlapping generations approach implicitly involves incomplete markets,

because agents cannot trade with agents born in the distant future or past. People from non-overlapping generations never coexist, implying a restriction on the nature of intergenerational transactions.

Mark D. Flood

See also MONETARY EQUILIBRIUM THEORIES OF THE BUSINESS CYCLE; REAL BUSINESS-CYCLE THEORIES; SUNSPOT THEORIES OF FLUCTUATIONS

Bibliography
Arrow, K. J. 1964. "The Role of Securities in the Optimal Allocation of Risk Bearing." *Review of Economic Studies* 31:91–96.
Boldrin, M. and M. Woodford. 1990. "Equilibrium Models Displaying Endogenous Fluctuations and Chaos: A Survey." *Journal of Monetary Economics* 25:189–222.
Debreu, G. 1959. *Theory of Value: An Axiomatic Analysis of Economic Equilibrium.* New York: Wiley.
Geanakoplos, J. 1990. "An Introduction to General Equilibrium with Incomplete Asset Markets." *Journal of Mathematical Economics* 19:1–38.
Grandmont, J.-M. 1985. "On Endogenous Competitive Business Cycles." *Econometrica* 53:995–1046.
Magill, M. and W. Shafer. 1991. "Incomplete Markets." In *Handbook of Mathematical Economics.* Vol 4. Edited by W. Hildenbrand and H. Sonnenschein, 1523–1614. Amsterdam: North-Holland.
Woodford, M. 1989. "Imperfect Financial Intermediation and Complex Dynamics." In *Economic Complexity: Chaos, Sunspots, Bubbles and Nonlinearity,* edited by W. A. Barnett, J. Geweke, and K. Shell, 309–34. Cambridge: Cambridge Univ. Press.

Index Numbers

The subject of index numbers has been of great interest not only to academic economists and government officials but also to the general public. By summarizing information on price or quantity trends, indexes help people make comparisons over both time and space. The great importance of index numbers has led to the use of economic and statistical theory to increase the accuracy and relevance of the indexes.

There are two main approaches to index-number theory: (1) the microeconomic approach and (2) the statistical approach. The microeconomic approach to index-number theory is aggregation-theoretic in the sense that it considers unknown aggregator functions, which typically are utility functions, production functions, or cost functions. Once such functions are econometrically estimated, economic indexes are constructed. Such indexes, however, are estimator- and specification-dependent. Although the specification-dependency problem can be partially overcome by using a flexible functional form—an aggregator-function specification able to provide a second-order approximation to an arbitrary, twice-differentiable aggregator function—economic indexes are troublesome to governmental agencies, which therefore have always viewed the microeconomic approach to index-number theory as being solely a research tool, not useful for data-construction purposes. They have, instead, adopted the statistical approach to index-number theory.

By using parameter-free statistical indexes, statistical index-number theory eliminates the need to estimate the parameters of a parameterized econometric specification for the aggregator function. Well-known examples of statistical indexes are the Laspeyres, the Paasche, the Fisher ideal, and the Divisia index. Statistical indexes are mainly characterized by their statistical properties. These properties, studied in some detail by Wolfgang Eichhorn (1976), were first examined by Irving Fisher (1927) and serve as "tests" for assessing the quality of a particular index. Judged by these tests, it appears that the Fisher ideal index, followed by the Divisia index, is best.

Developments in microeconomic index-number theory and statistical index-number theory by and large followed separate paths until E. W. Diewert (1976, 1978) provided the link between the two approaches by attaching economic properties to statistical indexes. These properties are defined in terms of how closely the statistical indexes approximate a particular functional form for the aggregator function. In particular, Diewert showed that a number of well-known statistical indexes are equivalent to using a particular functional form. Such indexes are called *exact*. Diewert, however, advocated the use of statistical indexes that are exact to flexible functional forms—functional forms having the capacity to provide a second-order approximation to an arbitrary twice-differentiable aggregator function. He called such indexes *superlative* and showed that all known superlative indexes approximate each other to the second order. Hence, it does not matter very much which of these superlative indexes are used in applications.

Indexes, once properly constructed, are extremely useful in business-cycle research whose main objective is to explain the changes in different macroeconomic variables over time as well as the co-movement of many economic data series. Since macroeconometricians have abandoned the Burns and Mitchell approach to the study of business cycles, much of the recent work has focused on the time-series properties of the relevant macroeconomic variables.

The realization that many economic time series are characterized by a stochastic trend model opened up new avenues in the study of business cycles. In particular, Nelson and Plosser (1982) described this property as one of being *difference stationary* (DS)—stationary in first differences. An alternative *trend stationary* (TS) model, where a stationary component is added to a deterministic trend term, was found by Nelson and Plosser and others to be less appropriate.

The issue of nonstationarity also has several important implications for modeling procedures in business-cycle research. For example, there has been some controversy over the appropriate transformations to use when testing hypotheses. Whether standard inference procedures apply may depend on the degree of nonstationarity of the different variables (Engle and Granger 1987).

Apostolos Serletis

See also DIVISIA MONETARY AGGREGATES

Bibliography

Diewert, W. E. 1976. "Exact and Superlative Index Numbers." *Journal of Econometrics* 4:115–45.

———. 1978. "Superlative Index Numbers and Consistency in Aggregation." *Econometrica* 46:883–900.

Eichhorn, W. 1976. "Fisher's Tests Revisited." *Econometrica* 44:247–56.

Engle, R. F. and C. W. J. Granger, 1987. "Cointegration and Error Correction: Representation, Estimation, and Testing." *Econometrica* 55:251–76.

Fisher, I. 1927. *The Making of Index Numbers: A Study of the Varieties, Tests, and Reliability.* 3d ed. Boston: Houghton Mifflin.

Nelson, C. R. and C. I. Plosser, 1982. "Trends and Random Walks in Macroeconomic Time Series: Some Evidence and Implications." *Journal of Monetary Economics* 10:139–62.

Indicators, Qualitative

The term "qualitative indicators" has become popular in the past fifteen to twenty years, and is used to denote indicators of business-cycle turning points which are derived from survey data, in contrast to the well-known *quantitative indicators* developed in the United States at the National Bureau of Economic Research as a result of Wesley Mitchell's pioneering research into the causes of economic instability. While there are quite a few qualitative indicators for the United States, they have become particularly prominent in a number of European countries as well as in Japan since World War II. Initially this was partially the result of a shortage in many countries of reliable quantitative data. Such data shortages have increasingly been overcome and so qualitative indicators continue to be monitored because of their usefulness in enhancing economists' ability to analyze ongoing cyclical developments with quantitative indicators. Qualitative indicators thus enrich our forecasting arsenal.

In the U.S., the major qualitative indicators have emerged through the surveys undertaken over a long period by organizations such as the Survey Research Center at the University of Michigan, Dun and Bradstreet, Inc., McGraw-Hill Information Systems Company, and the Purchasing Management Association of Chicago. In Europe, a number of national organizations report monthly to the European Economic Commission, which publishes monthly the results of both a consumer- and a business-sentiment survey for member countries.

The areas covered by these surveys include production trends and expectations, trade or manufacturing sales, order-book levels (or new orders), export-order levels (or new export orders), stocks of various types (intermediate, finished goods, etc.), reports on order times ("vendor performance") reported, selling prices or expectations (retail or wholesale), profits and profit expectations, consumer expectations with respect to purchases and prices, and consumer or business "sentiment."

Often, as the listing suggests, the survey questions pertaining to these are phrased both retrospectively ("What has happened in the past *n* months?) and prospectively (What do you expect will happen in the next *n* months?). Often there is little difference in the results, the respondents tending to expect for the immediate future what has happened in the immediate past.

The results of these surveys are customarily presented in "net balance form"—that is, the percent of the respondents replying "up" or "increase" less the percent replying the opposite is reported (with the "no change" divided evenly between the optimistic and pessimistic responses (or simply left out altogether). A major difficulty with such results is that the month-to-month change in the net balances presents changes from one period to the next (and so are in "first-difference" form). The timing of turning points in such a series must be compared to the turning points in the first differences of the actual data, or else the survey results must be cumulated if they are to be compared to quantitative data in "level" form. Failure to make these adjustments makes survey results appear to lead when in fact they may not, or to exhibit longer leads than they really have. [Generally, the turning points in any series in change form (say, the monthly percent change in the index of industrial production) lead turning points in the same series in level form (the index of industrial production itself).]

Properly used, qualitative indicators, while no substitute for quantitative indicators, can be a valuable adjunct to the latter in the continuing efforts to better monitor cyclical instability in market-oriented economies.

Philip A. Klein

See also DE FOVILLE, ALFRED; LEADING INDICATORS: HISTORICAL RECORD; MARKET PRICE INDICATORS

Bibliography

Klein, P. A. and G. H. Moore. 1985. "Qualitative Indicators." Chap. 5 in *Monitoring Growth Cycles in Market-Oriented Countries: Developing and Using International Economic Indicators.* Cambridge, Mass.: Ballinger.

Oppenlander, K. H. and G. Poser, eds. 1983. *Leading Indicators and Business-Cycle Surveys.* Center for International

Research on Economic Tendency Surveys Biennial Conference Report. New York: St. Martin's Press.

———. 1985. *Business Cycle Surveys in the Assessment of Economic Activity.* Center for International Research on Economic Tendency Surveys (CIRET) Biennial Conference Report, no. 17 (also see other reports). Aldershot, England: Gower.

Strigel, W. H. 1977. *In Search of Economic Indicators: Essays in Business Surveys.* Berlin: Springer-Verlag.

Universities-National Bureau Conference Report. 1960. *The Economic Significance of Anticipations Data.* Princeton: Princeton Univ. Press.

Industrial Revolution (c. 1750–1850)

The revolution that launched modern economic growth began in England and soon spread to continental Europe and North America. Among the changes caused by the Industrial Revolution was the transformation of pre-modern business cycles and depressions into their modern forms.

The term "Industrial Revolution" is controversial and often misunderstood. It has meant, among other things, the rise of capitalism, the growth of the factory system, and the application of science to industry. Although all of these developments were features of the Industrial Revolution, none defines it. The Industrial Revolution was the beginning of modern economic growth. Other definitions describe aspects of the revolution, but do not indicate why it was important. As the start of modern economic growth, the Industrial Revolution must rank among the most important events in world history.

The long-run changes brought by modern economic growth were enormous, but before 1820, the year-to-year changes were relatively small. According to N. F. R. Crafts (1985), British income per capita (in 1970 U.S. dollars) rose from $333 in 1700 to $399 in 1800, but then jumped to $1130 in 1890. The changes that accompanied rising income included population growth, urbanization, increasing division of labor, and structural change. The most significant structural change—and the reason for the term "Industrial Revolution"—was the shift from agriculture to industry. The declining relative importance of agriculture was both a symptom and a cause of modern industrial growth.

Historians do not agree on the cause of the Industrial Revolution. Such disagreement makes it difficult to understand how the Industrial Revolution influenced modern business cycles, because different causal explanations imply different links between the two phenomena. Before we consider the cyclical effects of the Industrial Revolution, it is necessary to briefly survey the proposed causes. The many theories about the causes of the Industrial Revolution can be sorted into four groups:

1. *Capital accumulation.* Earlier historians thought that investment and capital accumulation led to the Industrial Revolution. Economic growth in this view is caused by an increase in the quality and quantity of machines, broadly defined. Modern economic growth does not really differ in kind from pre-modern growth; capital accumulation simply accelerated in the eighteenth century. Recent versions of the hypothesis also include human capital acquired through investments in education and training.

2. *Technological progress.* Invention and innovation increase the productivity of capital and labor. Measures of the contribution of growing capital and labor to overall economic growth show that growth is largely unexplained by the growth of inputs; the unexplained part of growth could be accounted for by technological progress. A variant of this theory identifies the entrepreneur who finds profitable uses for inventions and innovations, rather than on the invention itself, as the source of economic growth.

3. *Resources and geography.* Europe possessed a mix of raw materials, climate, and natural transportation conducive to modern economic growth. Another resource theory is that population growth increased the spread of the market and, by putting pressure on resources, induced innovation, technological progress, and ultimately the Industrial Revolution.

4. *Institutional factors.* Some historians identify cultural and religious variables as the cause of the Industrial Revolution. Others emphasize the growth of markets. According to others, the development of the money and credit economy played the key role. Another group stresses the spread of private property rights, arguing

that well-defined property rights create the proper incentives for innovation and investment and the consequent productivity growth. The rise of modern labor markets and wage labor is another possible institutional factor. Finally, some historians argue that the decline of absolutism and the acceptance of pluralism in politics and religion promoted the experimentation that led to the Industrial Revolution.

It is of course possible that a combination of causes brought about the great changes of the eighteenth and nineteenth centuries. The choice of a dominant cause will nonetheless influence interpretations of the relationship between the Industrial Revolution and business cycles. Although economic historians believe that the Industrial Revolution and modern business cycles are closely intertwined, the nature of the relationship is seldom explicitly specified. It is, however, possible to identify two views that link the secular and cyclical phenomena.

The first view holds that the Industrial Revolution created modern business cycles, in that the causes of modern economic growth necessarily led to modern business cycles. Suppose, for example, that capital accumulation caused the Industrial Revolution and modern economic growth. If the uneven pace of accumulation—called the investment cycle—causes the business cycle, then business cycles are a necessary consequence of modern economic growth. If technological progress caused the Industrial Revolution, growth and fluctuations may also be related. Many economic historians believe that technological progress is uneven, accelerating after a leading industry or an epochal innovation appears. The sporadic appearance of technological breakthroughs in turn causes economic growth to be uneven. The trough of the business cycle occurs with the playing out of a particular innovation, whereas the expansion occurs during its diffusion. The cyclical instability and uncertainty of modern industrial society may therefore be a necessary cost of those innovations and other changes that create and sustain an industrial economy. The idea that cycles are a by-product of growth also encompasses the various institutional theories on the origins of the Industrial Revolution. If, for example, the spread of markets led to both modern economic growth and business cycles, the two phenomena have a common cause.

The second view of the relationship between modern economic growth and cycles holds that the Industrial Revolution transformed business cycles but did not create them. A business cycle is simply the effect on the economy of some exogenous event, such as a monetary or real disturbance. The theory that outside forces created business cycles does not imply that the Industrial Revolution had no effect on business cycles. On the contrary, by altering the structure of the economy, by substituting a long-run trend of growth for long-run stagnation, and by increasing the rates of investment and technological progress, the Industrial Revolution profoundly altered the way exogenous shocks affected the economy.

The historical record provides little help in resolving whether the Industrial Revolution created business cycles or merely transformed them. In preindustrial societies, harvest cycles, wars, epidemics, civil disorders, and natural disasters all generated economic fluctuations. Were these fluctuations early versions of modern cycles or were they different in kind? The differences between modern and premodern cycles do not provide an obvious answer to that question, as can be seen from an examination of those differences.

One difference between modern and premodern cycles is that the modern cycle follows the familiar sequence of peak, recession, trough, expansion, whereas premodern business fluctuations displayed no such regularity. Another difference is that the modern cycle is characterized by swings in investment. A third difference is that in premodern economies, most workers were not hired in an open market. An economic downturn meant a reduction in output per person and in earnings, but it did not mean unemployment. By contrast, the most striking feature of modern cycles is the unemployment that accompanies the recession. Indeed, in the twentieth century, "depression" has come to mean mass unemployment. Another important difference between modern and premodern cycles is that modern cycles are applied to a long-run upward trend of output and income. Premodern growth was itself mostly the upswing of a long cycle. A final difference is that premodern cycles confined their effects to a particular region or industry. Modern business cycles are national and international in scope.

The relationship between the Industrial Revolution and the modern business cycle remains cloudy. None of the differences between modern and pre-modern cycles necessarily favors one of the two views of the relationship. Although it is difficult to believe that the simultaneous birth of the business cycle and the modern world was coincidental, the theories explaining that relationship—though plausible—are not entirely satisfactory. The difficulty in formulating a full explanation for the historical relationship between growth and cycles reflects the inadequacy of the general theories relating growth and cycles. The progress of such theories may be measured by the light they shed on the experience of Britain and other Western nations in the eighteenth and nineteenth centuries. Few economic historians will accept a theory of growth and fluctuations that fails to explain the Industrial Revolution.

Clark Nardinelli

Bibliography

Aldcroft, D. H. and P. Fearson. 1972. *British Economic Fluctuations 1790–1939.* London: Macmillan.

Ashton, T. S. 1948. *The Industrial Revolution: 1760–1830.* New York: Oxford Univ. Press.

Crafts, N. F. R. 1985. *British Economic Growth during the Industrial Revolution.* Oxford: Clarendon Press.

Gayer, A. D., W. W. Rostow, and A. J. Schwartz. 1953. *The Growth and Fluctuation of the British Economy 1790–1850: An Historical, Statistical, and Theoretical Study of Britain's Economic Development.* 2 vols. Oxford: Clarendon Press.

Hartwell, R. M. 1971. *The Industrial Revolution and Economic Growth.* London: Methuen.

Mantoux, P. [1927] 1983. *The Industrial Revolution in the Eighteenth Century.* Translation. Chicago: Univ. of Chicago Press.

Mirowski, P. 1985. *The Birth of the Business Cycle.* New York: Garland.

Mitchell, W. C. 1927. *Business Cycles: The Problem and Its Setting.* New York: NBER.

Mokyr, J. 1985. *The Economics of the Industrial Revolution.* Totowa, N.J.: Rowman and Allanheld.

Inflation

There are two types of inflation theories: monetary theories, based on variants of the quantity theory of money; and cost-based theories. As a good survey of the former is already available in Parkin (1987), this entry covers the cost-based theories of inflation, associated with Keynes ([1936] 1973), Weintraub (1961), Kaldor ([1959] 1964), Akerlof (1969), Davidson (1972), Tobin (1972) and other Keynesians, including New Keynesians (Blanchard 1986; Akhand 1992) and Post-Keynesians.

Let the wage bill $W \equiv wN$, where w is the money wage and N is employment. Let total output Z be some multiple of W, i.e., $Z = kW$. We also know that total output is price P times quantity, Q, i.e., $Z \equiv PQ$. Combining these relations we have

$$PQ = kwN, \qquad (1)$$

or,

$$P = kw/A, \qquad (1')$$

where $A \equiv Q/N$.

Expressing the above equation as proportions gives us

$$\dot{P}/P = \dot{k}/k + \dot{w}/w - \dot{A}/A \qquad (2)$$

where the left-hand side is the growth rate of the price level, or inflation. Thus inflation rises as the parameter k rises, or the money wage w increases, where the increases are uncompensated by increases in average productivity.

Note that $1/k = W/PQ$, or that $1/k$ is the wage share in total output or total income. If total income is divided between firms, which earn profits, and workers, then the firms' share is $1 - 1/k$.

Suppose now that unions and labor representatives attempt to set the money wage w at time t to achieve a target labor share α, based on their estimate of the price level $P^e(t)$:

$$w(t) = \alpha A P^e(t) \qquad (3)$$

Similarly let firms set prices $P(t)$, based on their estimate of the current wage level $w^e(t)$ and a target markup m over wages:

$$P(t) = (1/A)(1 + m)w^e(t) \qquad (4)$$

Both labor unions and firms attempt to appropriate productivity gains. Equations (3) and (4) are of course not independent, as the wage share plus the profit share must add up to total output. Hence both equations (3) and (4) must be consistent with equation (1). Consistency requires that $\alpha \leq 1/k$, and that $m \leq k - 1$. Alternatively, the consistency requirement can be expressed as:

$$\alpha(1 + m) \leq 1 \qquad (5)$$

When both parties' expectations are fulfilled, then equation (5) would be satisfied. Strict inequality implies that firms' profits are higher than expected (if the residual accrues to the firms) or that deflation occurs, or both. When expectations about wages and profits are fulfilled, there is no inflation, as increases in wages and profits just cover productivity gains.

However, when labor unions and firms set inconsistent targets, then $\alpha(1 + m) > 1$, in which case the conflict over income distribution causes inflation. The conflict may be avoided if both parties agree a priori that inflation is undesirable and make their income claims consistent with equation (5). Such an agreement amounts to a "social contract," or an "incomes policy." A decentralized economy, in which equations (3) and (4) hold, i.e., in which workers attempt to bargain or set wages and firms have the right to set prices, contains elements of the "prisoners' dilemma" (Maital and Benjamini 1980, Dalziel 1990). This is because neither party knows what productivity gains will be realized *ex post*. If workers make too low a bid, the residual accrues to profits. Similarly, if the markup is too low, workers would gain at the expense of profits. Consequently, both overstate their claims, which leads to inflation.

It is important to note that in the cost-based theory of inflation, the direction of causation is from wage increases to price increases, as labor cost is typically the largest component of cost. This, of course, does not exclude the possibility of one-time supply shocks (such as the oil-price shocks of 1973 and 1979) which contribute to inflation. However, such shocks are exceptional. Price increases result mainly from wage-cost increases that exceed productivity gains, as shown in equation (2).

The cost-based theory of inflation explains an important empirical regularity, namely that inflation tends to be procyclical: the bargaining power of labor tends to increase during expansions pushing up wage costs which in turn force up prices. It also means that wages, both nominal and real, are procyclical as well (Dore 1993).

Mohammed H. I. Dore

See also ECKSTEIN, OTTO; INCOME DISTRIBUTION AND THE BUSINESS CYCLE; MONETARY POLICY; MONETARY DISEQUILIBRIUM THEORIES OF THE BUSINESS CYCLE; PROFIT SQUEEZE; STYLIZED FACTS

Bibliography

Akerlof, G. 1969. "Relative Wages and the Rate of Inflation." *Quarterly Journal of Economics* 83:353–74.

Akhand, H. 1992. "Policy Credibility and Inflation in a Wage Setting Game." *Canadian Journal of Economics* 25:407–19.

Blanchard, O. 1986. "The Wage-Price Spiral." *Quarterly Journal of Economics* 101:543–65.

Dalziel, P. 1990. "Market Power, Inflation and Incomes Policies." *Journal of Post Keynesian Economics* 12:424–38.

Davidson, P. 1972. *Money and the Real World.* London: Macmillan.

Dore, M. H. I. 1993. *The Macrodynamics of Business Cycles: A Comparative Evaluation.* Oxford: Basil Blackwell.

Kaldor, N. [1959] 1964. "Economic Growth and the Problem of Inflation." Chap. 8 in *Essays on Economic Policy.* Vol. 1. London: Duckworth.

Keynes, J. M. [1933] 1972. *Essays in Persuasion.* Vol. 9 of *The Collected Writings of John Maynard Keynes.* London: Macmillan.

———. [1936] 1973. *The General Theory of Unemployment, Interest, and Money.* Vol. 7 of *The Collected Writings* of John Maynard Keynes. London: Macmillan.

Maital, S. and Y. Benjamini. 1980. "Inflation as Prisoner's Dilemma." *Journal of Post Keynesian Economics* 2:459–81.

Parkin, M. 1987. "Inflation." In *The New Palgrave: A Dictionary of Economics.* Vol. 2. Edited by J. Eatwell, M. Milgate and P. Newman. London: Macmillan.

Tobin, J. 1972. "Inflation and Unemployment." *American Economic Review* 62:1–18.

Weintraub, S. 1961. *Classical Keynesianism, Monetary Theory and the Price Level.* Westport, Conn.: Greenwood Press.

Interest Rates

Interest rates, particularly real interest rates, are among the most important economic variables affecting aggregate economic activity. They have been studied extensively and figure prominently in discussions of the transmission mechanisms of monetary policy, playing a prominent role in explanations of business cycles and individual business-cycle episodes. Real interest rates are a central element in savings-consumption and investment decisions and therefore are critical to debates about how to encourage investment and savings.

The interest rate of primary concern to economists is the real interest rate, which is adjusted for expected changes in the price level so that it accurately reflects the true cost of borrowing. The real interest rate (more precisely referred to as an *ex ante* real interest rate) on a one-period bond, for example, is defined as:

$$rr_t \equiv i_t - \pi_t^e \qquad (1)$$

where,

$rr_t \equiv$ the *ex ante* real interest rate on the one-period bond at time *t*: i.e., the *ex ante* real return from time *t* to *t+1*.

$i_t \equiv$ the nominal interest rate on the one-period bond at time *t*: i.e., the nominal return from time *t* to *t+1*.

$\pi_t^e \equiv$ the inflation rate from time *t* to *t+1* expected at time *t*.

The problem with measuring real interest rates is that neither expected inflation nor real interest rates are directly observable. Several approaches have been used to measure expected real interest rates. One approach uses survey data on inflation expectations, subtracting them from nominal interest rates to obtain measures of real interest rates. Because they question the reliability of survey measures of expected inflation, many economists prefer to measure real interest rates by adopting the rational-expectations assumption that forecast errors of expected inflation are uncorrelated with any past information. This allows researchers to infer the behavior of *ex ante* real interest rates from the relationship of the observable *ex post* real interest rates (the actual realized real return on bonds) to past data.

Although there is strong evidence that nominal interest rates are procyclical (i.e., rise in booms and decline during recessions), it is not clear that real interest rates move in tandem with the business cycle. In a study of the 1953–71 period, Fama (1975), for example, could not reject the hypothesis that real interest rates had been constant. Mishkin (1981), though strongly rejecting the constancy of real interest rates, found little evidence that real interest rates had a stable relationship with the business cycle.

[Although Hamilton (1985) found some countercyclical tendency of real interest rates in the postwar period (i.e., they rise in recessions), this result mainly reflects the behavior of real interest rates in the 1980s recessions.] Rather than moving with the business cycle, real interest rates seem to move with changes in expected inflation and changes in monetary regimes (Huizinga and Mishkin 1986) and with changes in the expected profitability of investment opportunities as reflected in stock-market returns (Barro and Sala-i-Martin 1990).

Although there is no clear relationship between real interest rates and the business cycle on average, movements in real interest rates have indeed played a prominent role in specific business-cycle episodes. Hamilton (1987) has argued that the tightening of monetary policy and raising of real interest rates by the Federal Reserve in 1928 and 1929 was an important cause of the initial economic downturn beginning in late 1929. Mishkin (1981) provided evidence that real interest rates were at extremely high levels during the contraction phase of the Great Depression, suggesting that monetary policy was extremely tight during this period and was a major cause of the economic contraction. Hamilton (1985) and Huizinga and Mishkin (1986) found that high real interest rates were also a prominent feature in the 1980 and 1981–82 recessions.

Sharp rises in interest rates have also been an important cause of several financial crises and panics in the United States. As defined in Mishkin (1992), a financial crisis is a disruption in financial markets that worsens adverse-selection and moral-hazard problems, so that financial markets cannot efficiently channel funds to those with the most productive investment opportunities. If market interest rates rise, because of increased demand for credit or because of a decline in the money supply, adverse selection in credit markets increases, because individuals and firms with the riskiest investment projects are precisely those who are willing to pay the highest interest rates. The rise in interest rates discourages good credit risks from borrowing, but not bad ones and the resulting increase in adverse selection discourages lenders from lending. Indeed, as Mankiw (1986) has demonstrated, because of this adverse-selection problem, a rise in the riskless interest rate can cause lending to drop sharply or even to collapse.

A common feature of financial crises is a sharp rise in interest rates. Mishkin (1991) has found that interest rates rose sharply before the financial panics of 1857, 1890, 1893, 1896, and 1907 and spiked contemporaneously with the other panics in the National Banking System era, 1873 and 1884. These sharp increases in interest rates aggravated adverse-selection problems for lenders, helping produce a steep decline in lending and hence a substantial decline in investment and aggregate economic activity. The most severe of these panic episodes (1857, 1873, 1893, and 1907) all accompanied the most severe economic contractions prior to the creation of the Federal Reserve System.

Frederic S. Mishkin

See also CRISIS OF 1857; CRISIS OF 1873; CRISIS OF 1907; PANIC OF 1893; TERM STRUCTURE OF INTEREST RATES

Bibliography

Barro, R. J. and X. Sala-i-Martin. 1990. "World Real Interest Rates." In *NBER Macroeconomics Annual 1990,* edited by O. J. Blanchard and S. Fischer, 15–61. Cambridge: MIT Press.

Fama, E. F. 1975. "Short Term Interest Rates as Predictors of Inflation." *American Economic Review* 65:269–82.

Hamilton, J. 1985. "Uncovering Financial Market Expectations of Inflation." *Journal of Political Economy* 93:1224–41.

———. 1987. "Monetary Factors in the Great Depression." *Journal of Monetary Economics* 19:145–70.

Homer, S. and R. Sylla. 1991. *A History of Interest Rates.* 3d ed. New Brunswick: Rutgers Univ. Press.

Huizinga, J. and F. S. Mishkin. 1986. "Monetary Policy Regime Shifts and the Unusual Behavior of Real Interest Rates." *Carnegie-Rochester Conference Series on Public Policy,* Spring, 231–74.

Mankiw, N. G. 1986. "The Allocation of Credit and Financial Collapse." *Quarterly Journal of Economics* 101:455–70.

Mishkin, F. S. 1981. "The Real Interest Rate: An Empirical Investigation." *Carnegie-Rochester Conference Series on Public Policy,* Autumn, 151–200.

———. 1991. "Asymmetric Information and Financial Crises: A Historical Perspective." In *Financial Markets and Financial Crises,* edited by R. G. Hubbard, 69–108. Chicago: Univ. of Chicago Press.

———. 1992. "Anatomy of a Financial Crisis." *Journal of Evolutionary Economics* 2:115–30.

International Lender of Last Resort

To avert international financial crises, an institution fulfilling the role of international lender of last resort would provide support to the international banking (and perhaps financial) system by lending directly to financial institutions or to countries with insufficient reserves of international currencies. Although the International Monetary Fund (IMF), which lends to member-country governments experiencing reserve currency shortages owing to trade deficits or capital flight, partially fulfills this role, such an institution does not now exist.

The internationalization of the banking system in the 1970s and the globalization of the financial system in the 1980s, which was accompanied by securitization, the expansion of the eurocurrency markets, and the creation of derivative financial instruments, may have increased the risk that the contagion effects of bank failures could reach beyond domestic financial systems. Risk of contagion occurs when banks are perceived by depositors and other creditors to hold portfolios containing risks similar to, or are known to be creditors of, banks with inadequate liquidity or capital. Additionally, international banks have appeared to display a "herd instinct," which has probably reinforced the belief that the risks in their portfolios are highly correlated.

The Mexican debt crisis in August 1982 revealed the importance of the federal institutions of the United States in supplying lender-of-last-resort support to the international banking system. Because the Mexican debt was almost entirely denominated in dollars, the United States Federal Reserve System and the Treasury had to act as first-line lenders of last resort since only they could supply large quantities of dollars at short notice. Subsequently, other central banks, via the Bank for International Settlements, supplied bridging finance while the IMF provided additional funds and helped put together a rescue package involving the major creditor banks, which were persuaded of their stake in the rescue operation.

Banking supervisors responded to the emergence of the Latin American debt problem by requiring banks to increase their capital-to-asset ratios and to set aside reserves against losses on loans to Latin American and other debtor countries. This process culminated in an international agreement on capital-adequacy requirements in July 1988, the Basle Agreement. The Committee on Bank Regulation and Supervisory Practices, known as the Basle Committee, whose work led to the conclusion of the Basle Agreement, had previously concentrated on allocating supervisory responsibilities among host and domestic supervisory authorities. This was achieved via the 1975 and 1983 Basle Concordats. The Basle Agreement marks a major step beyond supervisory coordination into the field of regulatory harmonization.

It was stressed in the 1983 concordat that the agreement entailed no commitment to provide lender-of-last-resort cover to the eurocurrency markets. However, the prompt, and seemingly coordinated, reaction by monetary authorities in the major financial centers to the October 1987 stock-market crashes revealed a desire to ensure that a crisis on the scale of that experienced in the 1930s not recur. They responded to the crashes by adding liquidity to their domestic financial systems and reducing interest rates. The unwillingness of the monetary authorities to specify the conditions under which lender-of-last-resort support would be provided derives from a moral-hazard problem. If support is known to be readily available, then financial institutions are likely to take greater risks. If it is unclear when, and under what conditions, support will be given, the uncertainty may deter risk taking. In his classic work on the lender-of-last-resort function, *Lombard Street,* Walter Bagehot stressed that support should be provided unstintingly, but at a cost. To the extent that the IMF functions as an international lender of last resort, it fulfills this requirement by applying "conditionality" which requires adoption of IMF-approved economic reforms to qualify for IMF loans.

Although the 1982 Mexican debt crisis and the October 1987 stock-market crashes passed without sparking a major international financial crisis, it remains possible that international cooperation and coordination might break down. Because the U.S. monetary authorities control the supply of dollars (still the major reserve currency), the international financial community must continue to rely heavily on them. However, the emergence of a more balanced multicurrency reserve system in the 1980s suggests an increasing need for cooperation. Without cooperation, the likelihood of international financial crises will increase. In the past, inter-national financial crises have been absent under international monetary arrangements in which there has been a de facto lender of last resort, such as the Bank of England in the nineteenth century, under the gold standard, and the U.S. monetary authorities and the IMF from the end of World War II until 1973, under the Bretton Woods agreement. Kindleberger has argued that the weak British position and the failure of U.S. institutions to fill the vacuum after World War I allowed the Great Depression of the 1930s to gather force. A similar vacuum may have been created following the collapse of the Bretton Woods system in 1973 and the subsequent decline in the importance of the dollar.

The creation of a fully effective international lender of last resort would require the creation of an international reserve currency controlled by an international institution. The alternative would be for an international institution, such as the IMF, to build up large, and normally idle, reserves of the major international reserve currencies. Holding reserves would be less efficient than developing a generally acceptable international reserve asset whose supply could be controlled by the international institution. The IMF first issued Special Drawing Rights (SDR), a weighted basket of major reserve currencies, in January 1970. The SDR has not yet become widely used as a reserve currency but, if its role can eventually be enhanced, the IMF might evolve into a full-fledged international lender of last resort. To manage the overall supply of international reserves, the international lender of last resort would have to have some control or influence over the national monetary authorities issuing other reserve currencies and, to reduce the moral-hazard problem, would have to have some regulatory and supervisory powers. Thus, it would be akin to a world central bank.

Internationalization and globalization in the 1970s and 1980s appear to have increased international financial fragility and thereby increased the need for an international lender of last resort to support the international financial system. To date, such support has been provided through cooperation by monetary authorities in the major financial centers and by international institutions such as the IMF and BIS. For an international institution to act as an international lender of last resort, it would have to control the supply of a generally acceptable international reserve asset. If the SDR became more widely acceptable, then the IMF could expand its current limited role as an international lender of last resort and evolve into a world central bank.

Andrew Mullineux

See also CENTRAL BANKING; KINDLEBERGER, CHARLES POOR; LDC CRISIS; LENDER OF LAST RESORT

Bibliography
Kindleberger, C. P. 1978. *Manias, Panics, and Crashes*. New York: Basic Books.
Kraft, J. 1984. *The Mexican Rescue*. New York: Group of Thirty.
Martin, W. M. 1970. *Toward a World Central Bank*. Washington: Per Jacobsson Foundation.
Portes, R. and K. S. Swoboda, eds. 1987. *Threats to International Financial Stability*. Cambridge: Cambridge Univ. Press.

Intertemporal Substitution

A typical postwar recession in the United States has lasted about a year during which real gross national product has dropped two to three percent, and the unemployment rate has increased three percentage points and nonfarm employment has declined three percent. The *intertemporal-substitution* hypothesis, developed by Robert Lucas and Leonard Rapping (1969), asserts that measured unemployment rises during a recession, because workers voluntarily reduce labor supplied. If workers engage in increased leisure or nonmarket work in recessions and engage in reduced leisure or nonmarket work during expansions, intertemporal substitution occurs in that people shift working time to periods when market work is relatively advantageous from periods when market work is relatively disadvantageous. Thus, the intertemporal-substitution hypothesis asserts that cyclical (un)employment and work-hours dynamics reflect increased leisure and nonmarket work during recessions, when pay is relatively low, and reduced leisure and nonmarket work during expansions, when pay is relatively high.

How to test the intertemporal-substitution hypothesis is best shown with an aggregate labor supply and demand diagram. Figure 1 illustrates the aggregate supply of labor, S_0, and the aggregate demand for labor, D_0, during a period of full employment. Because the labor market is a competitive auction under the intertemporal-substitution hypothesis, equilibrium point A, corresponding to real wage w_0 and total employment w_0, involves no cyclical unemployment, only normal or natural unemployment. If a recession reduces the aggregate demand for labor to D_1, the real wage falls to w_1, causing reductions in labor supplied and aggregate employment to E_1 as some workers withdraw labor (increase leisure and nonmarket work) to wait until the real wage returns to normal at w_0.

The intertemporal-substitution hypothesis interprets cyclical unemployment as a voluntary reduction in labor supplied during a recession when the real wage is low compared to the expected future real wage. Some of the reduced employment during a recession, $E_0 - E_1$ in Figure 1, is miscounted as unemployment because respondents misinterpret the question on the Current Population Survey used to measure unemployment. People questioned may believe that the Current Population Survey is asking if they are seeking work at the usual wage, w_0, rather than if they are seeking work at the current recessionary wage, w_1.

How elastic must aggregate labor supply be for intertemporal substitution to matter for (un)employment dynamics? As noted above, nonfarm employment falls about three percent during a typical U.S. recession. Real wages are less flexible, dropping at most one or two percent in recessions. So, if movements along the short-run (quarter-to-quarter) aggregate supply of labor cause most recession-induced unemployment, then the aggregate labor supply in Figure 1 must be wage-elastic.

Much econometric research has estimated the elasticity of labor supply in the United States

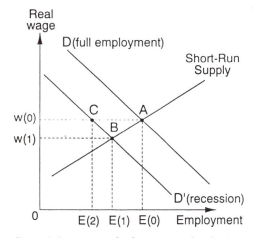

Figure 1. Intertemporal substitution and cyclical unemployment.

(Altonji 1982, 1986). However, little of the econometric research on U.S. labor supply is relevant to testing the intertemporal-substitution interpretation of cyclical (un)employment and hours-of-work dynamics (McCurdy 1990). Most labor-supply research has used annual data on hours of work per worker as the dependent variable, but the dominant cyclical adjustment in labor is a quarterly change in the number of employed workers. The percentage reduction in aggregate employment is about double the percentage reduction in the average workweek during a typical postwar U.S. recession. Nor can aggregate data pin down the short-run aggregate labor-supply curve. In particular, Kennan (1988) examined alternative specifications of an aggregate labor-supply-and-demand system and found that the U.S. macro data imply labor-supply elasticities spanning a wide range from positive to negative. Micro household data are needed to identify short-run labor-supply functions.

We now consider the results of estimated life-cycle labor-supply models in which the wage rate is taken as exogenous and represents the demand for an individual worker's labor. Workers are viewed as selecting hours of work at the competitive real wage. Richer microeconometric models of the demand for individual workers' labor are in their infancy (Card 1994). Labor-supply functions estimated separately for married men, married women, single men, and single women incorporating short-run movements into and out of the labor force can be aggregated to estimate the short-run elasticity of overall labor supply relevant to testing the intertemporal-substitution hypothesis (Heckman 1984).

The microeconometric labor-supply model normally used to examine the intertemporal-substitution hypothesis is contained in two structural equations from the so-called Frisch life-cycle labor-supply model developed in detail by McCurdy and Heckman (1980). In one equation, a person's lifetime real-wage profile W_{it} is a function of exogenous variables X_{it}, including education and family background of person i at time t, and a stochastic-error term e_{it}

$$W_{it} = f(X_{it}; e_{it}), \qquad (1)$$

and is used both to predict potential market wage rates for non-workers and to purge measurement errors in wage rates reported by workers. The second equation describes how a worker's optimal choice of hours to work, H_{it}, depends on the lifetime wealth constraint incorporating initial assets, lifetime wage-rate expectations in equation (1), and saving and investment opportunities

$$H_{it} = g(W_{it}, Z_{it}, F_i; m_{it}). \qquad (2)$$

The life-cycle labor-supply function in equation (2) contains exogenous variables affecting the labor-supply choice that reflect the lifetime evolution of a person's tastes for market work versus leisure and nonmarket work Z_{it} and a stochastic disturbance m_{it}. The focal point of the life-cycle labor-supply function is the difference between the effects of wage changes that are anticipated and wage changes that, for reasons such as recessions, are unanticipated.

In equation (2) F_i is a time-invariant individual-specific latent variable reflecting a person's lifetime wealth. When the labor-supply system in equations (1) and (2) is estimated with so-called panel or longitudinal data, which is a set of workers followed for several years, F_i is captured econometrically by a separate intercept for each person. Because the person-specific intercepts in equation (2) control for interpersonal wealth differences, the estimated direct labor-supply effect of a change in the real wage, $\partial g / \partial W_{it}$, is positive and reflects the marginal rate of intertemporal substitution between market work and leisure or nonmarket work. Testing the intertemporal-substitution hypothesis econometrically is complicated because recessionary wage changes are unanticipated and alter wealth. Examining the intertemporal-substitution hypothesis requires estimating the total labor-supply wage effects:

$$dH_t / dW_t = \partial g / \partial W_t + (\partial g / \partial F)(\partial F / \partial W_t), \quad (3)$$

for the decisions whether to seek employment and of many hours to work conditional on finding employment.

The best U.S. data to test the intertemporal-substitution hypothesis come from the Survey of Income and Program Participation, which questions approximately 20,000 households once every four months over three years (U.S. Bureau of the Census 1989, 301–436). One advantage of the Survey of Income and Program Participation data for examining the intertemporal-substitution hypothesis is the large sample size permitting separate labor supply functions by sex/marital-status groupings. Another advantage is the frequency of the interviews. Triannual data collection makes the Survey of Income and Program Participation more accurate than annual microsurveys, because respondents need only recall recent information, and triannual data are better than annual data for testing the intertemporal-substitution hypothesis, which involves short-run labor-force dynamics.

Kimmel and Kniesner (1995) used the Survey of Income and Program Participation data and the econometric techniques in McCurdy (1987) to estimate short-run wage elasticities of labor-force participation and hours of work. Kimmel and Kniesner found that the first term in the total labor-supply wage effect in equation (3) dominates the second term. Wealth effects are small and most of the labor-supply effect of a temporary unexpected wage change reflects intertemporal substitution. As noted above, the aggregate number of workers supplying labor must be wage-elastic, and the wage elasticity of hours of work supplied per worker must be about half the wage elasticity of labor-force participation if intertemporal substitution is responsible for aggregate U.S. labor-market dynamics. Evidence Kimmel and Kniesner found supporting the intertemporal-substitution hypothesis includes estimated elasticities of labor-force participation with respect to the real wage exceeding unity and estimated elasticities of hours of work with respect to the real wage of about one-half.

The intertemporal-substitution hypothesis emphasizing labor-supply behavior in aggregate cyclical (un)employment and average workweek dynamics has generated widespread discussion since its presentation by Lucas and Rapping. Much of the discussion centered on the normative issue of whether cyclical unemployment is involuntary from the perspective of workers. Here we have seen the positive aspect of the intertemporal-substitution hypothesis. Do estimates of labor-supply behavior produce wage elasticities that, when coupled with the typical cyclical variation in the real wage, imply variations in labor-force participation and hours of work mimicking the aggregate time-series outcomes for the United States? The intertemporal-substitution hypothesis has been subjected to complex, but irrelevant, econometric testing using annual data masking short-term variation in labor-force participation and hours of work. Econometric complexity is no substitute for proper data, and when the inter-temporal-substitution hypothesis is tested with household data capturing short-term variation in labor-supply variables, the results support the intertemporal-substitution hypothesis.

Thomas J. Kniesner

See also HUTT, WILLIAM HAROLD; MONETARY EQUILIBRIUM THEORIES OF THE BUSINESS CYCLE; REAL BUSINESS-CYCLE THEORIES; ROBERTSON, DENNIS HOLME; SEARCH THEORY

Bibliography

Altonji, J. G. 1982. "The Intertemporal Substitution Model of Labor Market Fluctuations: An Empirical Analysis." *Review of Economic Studies* 49(Supplement):783–824.

———. 1986. "Intertemporal Substitution in Labor Supply: Evidence from Micro Data." *Journal of Political Economy* 94(Part 2):S176–S215.

Card, D. 1994. "Intertemporal Labor Supply: An Assessment." In *Advances in Econometrics: Sixth World Congress*. Vol. 2. Edited by C. Sims, 49–80. New York: Cambridge Univ. Press.

Heckman, J. J. 1984. "Comments on the Ashenfelter and Kydland Papers." *Carnegie-Rochester Conference Series on Public Policy*, Autumn, 209–24.

Heckman, J. J. and T. E. McCurdy. 1980. "A Life Cycle Model of Female Labour Supply." *Review of Economic Studies* 47:47–74.

———. 1982. "Corrigendum on a Life Cycle Model of Female Labour Supply." *Review of Economic Studies* 49:659–60.

Kennan, J. A. 1988. "An Econometric Analysis of Fluctuations in Aggregate Labor Supply and Demand." *Econometrica* 56:317–33.

Kimmel, J. and T. J. Kniesner. 1995. "The First Test of the Intertemporal Substitution Hypothesis is Alive and Well (But Hiding in the Data)." Indiana University, Working Paper in Economics 93-014, Center for Econometric Model Research and the Department of Economics.

Kniesner, T. J. and A. H. Goldsmith. 1987. "A Survey of Alternative Models of the Aggregate U.S. Labor Market." *Journal of Economic Literature* 25:1241–80.

Lucas, R. E. and L. Rapping. 1969. "Real Wages, Employment, and Inflation." *Journal of Political Economy* 77:721–54.

McCurdy, T. E. 1987. "A Framework for Relating Microeconomic and Macroeconomic Evidence of Intertemporal Substitution." In *Advances in Econometrics— Fifth World Congress of the Econometric Society.* Vol. 2. Edited by T. Bewley, 149– 76. New York: Cambridge Univ. Press.

———. 1990. "Appraising Tests of the Intertemporal Substitution Hypothesis." In *Panel Data and Labor Market Studies,* edited by J. Hartog, G. Ridder, and J. Theeuwes, 215–30. Amsterdam: North-Holland.

U.S. Bureau of the Census. 1989. *Individuals and Families in Transition: Understanding Change Through Longitudinal Data.* Washington, D.C.: Government Printing Office.

Investment

Investment is the flow of current output devoted to accumulation of capital. As typically measured, nonresidential investment consists of fixed investment in plant and equipment and changes in the stock of business inventories. (In the United States national income accounts, private domestic investment also includes expenditure on new residential structures.) The total flow of investment spending in any period is called *gross* investment. *Net* investment measures gross investment less the depreciation of existing capital. This entry focuses on nonresidential fixed investment.

Business fixed investment is a volatile component of total output. In the United States, from 1971 to 1990, nonresidential fixed investment averaged 11.6 percent of gross national product, and the standard error of deviations of this share from its linear trend was 0.50 percentage points. By comparison, U.S. personal consumption averaged 63.7 percent of GNP over the same period, and the standard error of deviations of the consumption share from its trend was 0.82 percentage points. Thus, the coefficient of variation for the share of investment in total output (the standard error of deviations from trend divided by the mean) was 3.3 times greater than for the share of consumption. Largely because of its volatility, investment has received special attention in the study of aggregate economic fluctuations and the business cycle.

Theories of capital investment and its influence on the business cycle were put forward by various writers in the nineteenth and early twentieth centuries, but the modern analysis of the role of investment in initiating and propagating aggregate economic fluctuations began with Keynes's *General Theory.* In Keynes, investment is determined by the marginal efficiency of capital, which he defined as the discount rate that would equate the present value of prospective cash flows generated by a new capital asset with its purchase price. While prospective yields in part reflect the technical productivity of the investment project, Keynes emphasized how the marginal efficiency of capital depends crucially on entrepreneurial expectations. In chapter twelve of the *General Theory,* he argued that expectations of future market conditions can be volatile, as they are based on subjective opinions that may change rapidly and are influenced by fads and the herd-like behavior characteristic of agents in financial markets. Volatility of expectations induces volatility of investment itself, destabilizing aggregate demand and causing fluctuations in output and employment.

The emphasis on subjective expectations in determining investment was carried forward by what is often called the Post-Keynesian approach to macroeconomics. Joan Robinson (1962, 37) elaborated on Keynes's concept of "animal spirits" that determine the state of entrepreneurial expectations, defining animal spirits as the "historical, political, and psychological characteristics of an economy." The importance of financial conditions for investment was emphasized by Michal Kalecki, a contemporary of Keynes, who developed the "principle of increasing risk." Kalecki (1937) argued that as investment proceeds, the marginal compensation for risk required by an entrepreneur increases because borrowing increases relative to internal funds generated by the firm's operations. If internal cash flow increases, investment would rise as increasing liquidity offset increasing risk. Hyman Minsky (1975) further developed the links between finance, financial markets, and investment, focusing on the necessity of internal cash flows to "validate" debt commitments undertaken to finance historical investment, as a prerequisite for obtaining finance for new capital spending. As an expansion proceeds, the financing of new investment stretches the liquidity of firms to a greater and greater extent, increasing the chances that a downturn in profits and cash flow will create debt-repayment problems, thereby discouraging the financing of new investment and contributing to an economic downturn.

Many contributions to the investment literature that followed Keynes were based on the accelerator model which relates investment to output. More precisely, the accelerator links output to the level of the capital stock, so that investment, the change in the capital stock, follows the change in output. Paul Samuelson ([1939] 1966) wrote an early paper demonstrating mathematically how the accelerator together with the Keynesian consumption multiplier could generate cyclical dynamic paths for the aggregate economy. Robert Eisner (1978) later argued that the change in output entering the accelerator model should be the expected or permanent change, which he tied to a weighted average of past actual changes in output.

A major criticism of the accelerator theory is that by focusing exclusively on changes in output as the determinant of investment, the theory inappropriately ignores the role of relative prices in the choice of input mix. In a series of influential articles, Dale Jorgenson (1971) and his coauthors developed a neoclassical theory of investment based on dynamic optimization by a representative firm with a technology that allows substitution between capital and labor. With a Cobb-Douglas production technology, Jorgenson showed that the firm's desired capital stock K^* is proportional to the ratio of output Y to the implicit rental rate for capital c (adjusted for taxes) divided by the output price P:

$$K^* = \alpha Y/(c/P), \qquad (1)$$

where α is the exponent on capital in the Cobb-Douglas production function (the capital share under constant returns to scale). In a sense, the output term captures the accelerator effect, while the rental rate reflects relative-price effects.

Deriving the implicit rental rate was itself a significant contribution. The concept has been used to study how taxation affects investment by incorporating features of capital taxation, including, for example, the corporate tax rate, the investment tax credit, the structure of tax deductions for capital depreciation, and various aspects of the personal tax system, including the differential tax treatment of dividends and capital gains (Auerbach 1983).

While Jorgenson's neoclassical approach explains firms' demand for the capital stock, the rate of investment is not determined. To fill this

gap, many models were constructed assuming that firms face increasing marginal costs of installing new capital. Convex adjustment costs determine an optimal rate of investment that balances the marginal benefits of new capital against rising marginal costs of installation.

Empirical application of these models is hampered by their dependence on unobservable expectations of future output or prices. James Tobin (1969) addressed this shortcoming in what is now known as the q-theory of investment. The q variable is the ratio of the market value of incremental investment to its purchase price. If q exceeds one, firms can increase their market value by expanding their capital stock. Because q reflects market values, it is explicitly forward-looking. Several authors have since linked q-theory to other approaches in the investment literature by demonstrating that a q equation for investment can be derived directly from optimizing behavior of firms that face increasing marginal adjustment costs of investment (Hayashi 1982).

These largely neoclassical theories of investment, based on the assumption of optimizing firms operating in a market-clearing environment, have drifted away from the emphasis on the volatility of investment that was central to the Keynesian approach. Jorgenson's work, for example, treats investment primarily as a technological phenomenon; so it should be stable if the underlying technology itself is stable. In the new real business-cycle theories, however, output fluctuations are driven primarily by exogenous and permanent technology shocks that may alter the productivity of capital and change the desired capital stock. If adjustment costs are low, firms will adjust quickly to the new desired capital stock with changes in net investment. Because net investment is a small proportion of the capital stock, even a moderate change in desired capital can cause proportionately large changes in net investment, explaining the observed volatility of actual investment data.

Empirical work on investment has matched theoretical developments. The most robust finding has been the strength of current and lagged values of output or sales variables in investment regressions, estimated from both firm and aggregate data (Eisner 1978). This finding supports the traditional accelerator view. But these results are also consistent with some versions of the neoclassical investment model. With specific assumptions about the

I

form of the technology (parameterizations), the desired capital stock derived from neoclassical optimization depends on output, as well as on the cost of capital. Therefore, assuming that investment depends on current and lagged values of firms' desired capital stock, the neoclassical approach also predicts a link between investment and output.

Output also remains a significant determinant of investment in equations that include the q-ratio (Abel and Blanchard 1986, Fazzari, Hubbard, and Petersen 1988). This result is inconsistent with the simplest version of the q-theory which implies that q captures all relevant information for investment. Recent theoretical research, however, has shown that output can enter an empirical q-equation if firms have increasing returns to scale or operate in imperfectly competitive markets.

The empirical importance of the cost of capital for investment is more controversial. The emphasis on relative prices and tax effects in the neoclassical model of investment has stimulated much empirical research. If firms' technology is Cobb-Douglas, the desired capital stock, as presented in equation (1), depends on the ratio of output (or sales) to the implicit rental rate of capital, adjusted for various tax effects. To translate this theory into an operational specification for an empirical investment equation, many authors assume that investment is determined by a distributed lag of the ratio of output to the cost of capital. This variable usually performs well in investment regressions, but the specification does not allow one to distinguish the effect of the cost of capital from that of output.

More general specifications that allow output and various components of the cost of capital to have distinct empirical influences on investment lead to mixed results. There is some evidence that interest rates and tax effects may be significant in explaining investment fluctuations. But the economic importance of these effects has not been reliably established in the empirical literature (Bosworth 1985).

Two other issues complicate the empirical evaluation of the impact of relative prices on investment. First, the common assumption that firms' technology is Cobb-Douglas imposes a unitary elasticity of substitution between capital and other inputs (primarily labor). If the actual elasticity of substitution is less than one, the Cobb-Douglas parameterization overstates the sensitivity of investment to the cost of capital. Many studies have therefore adopted the more general constant-elasticity-of-substitution technology which implies that the desired capital stock is:

$$K^* = \alpha(c/p)^{-\sigma}Y, \qquad (2)$$

where, in addition to the variables defined above, σ denotes the elasticity of substitution. Some studies have estimated σ to be significantly less than one, implying less sensitivity of the desired capital stock, and therefore investment, to relative prices and the cost of capital. Second, many authors have argued that fixed capital investment is *putty-clay*. That is, prior to actual investment, firms may choose among different kinds of capital, each requiring a different amount of labor to operate it (the "putty" stage). But after a particular form of capital is chosen and installed, it can be operated with only a specific quantity of labor (the "clay" stage). Substitution possibilities *ex post* are limited. The operational significance of this point is that firms will delay responding to relative price changes that affect the optimal long-run mix between capital and other inputs until the old "clay" capital depreciates. But no such delay is necessary when output changes alter the desired capital stock. Therefore, investment may respond more quickly to output changes than to relative price changes.

Empirical results based on the q-approach have also been mixed. Most studies find a significant impact of q on investment. The q-variable alone, however, often leaves a large proportion of investment variance unexplained. Furthermore, the small regression coefficients on q in investment equations imply implausibly large adjustment costs. These problems have been addressed in several ways. Most empirical work measures q as the ratio of the market value of total capital to its replacement cost. This statistic measures *average q*, while the theoretical derivations identify the *marginal q* on new investment as the correct variable to explain investment fluctuations. The two measures may differ (Abel and Blanchard 1986), especially if firms operate in imperfectly competitive markets or they use technologies without constant returns to scale. Another problem arises if the stock-market prices that generate most of the variation in q are excessively volatile, that is, they fluctuate more than the true fundamental value of the underlying assets. Measured q would then be more volatile than the fundamental determinants of investment, and the regression coefficient on measured q would understate the effect of a theoretical q-variable that reflects fundamentals alone.

Most recent empirical studies do not emphasize financial constraints on firms' investment. However, the research in the Post-Keynesian tradition summarized above implies that access to finance may be an important independent determinant of investment. This prediction also follows from theoretical work on capital markets when borrowers and lenders do not have the same information about investment prospects (Gertler 1988). Empirical work on this topic has focused on how firms' internal cash flow affects investment spending. Many studies have found significant effects of cash flow or profits on investment. A key problem, however, is to separate the part of these effects that is due to the role of cash flow as a signal of future profits (and therefore as a proxy for investment demand), from its role in relaxing financial constraints. Using microeconomic data, Fazzari, Hubbard and Petersen (1988) attack this problem by dividing their sample into firms that are likely to face finance constraints and those that are not. They find that cash flow has a significantly greater impact on investment for low-dividend firms, which exhaust their internal funds, than for relatively mature, high-dividend firms which pay a substantial portion of their internal cash flow out to shareholders. This difference is consistent with the presence of financial constraints on investment. Such constraints may be important in explaining why investment fluctuates with the business cycle, and they link real investment to financial conditions in the economy.

Steven M. Fazzari

See also AUSTRIAN THEORY OF BUSINESS CYCLES; BUSINESS CYCLES; KALECKI, MICHAL; KEYNES, JOHN MAYNARD; MINSKY, HYMAN PHILLIP; OVERINVESTMENT THEORIES OF BUSINESS CYCLES; REAL BUSINESS-CYCLE THEORIES; TOBIN, JAMES

Bibliography
Abel, A. B. and O. J. Blanchard. 1986. "The Present Value of Profits and Cyclical Movements in Investment." *Econometrica* 54:249–73.

Auerbach, A. J. 1983. "Taxation, Corporate Financial Policy and the Cost of Capital." *Journal of Economic Literature* 21:905–40.

Bosworth, B. P. 1985. "Taxes and the Investment Recovery." *Brookings Papers on Economic Activity,* Number One, 1–38.

Eisner, R. 1978. *Factors in Business Investment.* Cambridge, Mass.: Ballinger.

Fazzari, S. M., R. G. Hubbard, and B. C. Petersen. 1988. "Financing Constraints and Corporate Investment." *Brookings Papers on Economic Activity,* Number One, 141–95.

Gertler, M. 1988. "Financial Structure and Aggregate Economic Activity: An Overview." *Journal of Money, Credit, and Banking* 20:559–88.

Hayashi, F. 1982. "Tobin's Marginal q and Average q: A Neoclassical Interpretation." *Econometrica* 50:213–24.

Jorgenson, D. W. 1971. "Econometric Studies of Investment Behavior: A Survey." *Journal of Economic Literature* 9:1111–47.

Kalecki, M. 1937. "The Principle of Increasing Risk." Chap. 4 in *The Theory of Economic Fluctuations.* London: Allen and Unwin.

Keynes, J. M. [1936] 1973. *The General Theory of Employment, Interest, and Money.* Vol. 7 of *The Collected Writings of John Maynard Keynes.* London: Macmillan.

Minsky, H. P. 1975. *John Maynard Keynes.* New York: Columbia Univ. Press.

Robinson, J. 1962. *Essays in the Theory of Economic Growth.* London: Macmillan.

Samuelson, P. A. [1939] 1966. "Interactions between the Multiplier Analysis and the Principle of Acceleration." Chap. 82 in *The Collected Scientific Papers of Paul A. Samuelson.* Vol. 2. Cambridge: MIT Press.

Tobin, J. 1969. "A General Equilibrium Approach to Monetary Theory." *Journal of Money, Credit, and Banking* 1:15–29.

I

Jevons, William Stanley (1835–1882)

William Stanley Jevons is now remembered as one of the progenitors of orthodox neoclassical economic theory due to his *Theory of Political Economy*. But in his lifetime, this work was less influential than his works on the logic and philosophy of science, or his 1865 book *The Coal Question* (which entertained the hypothesis that England was running out of coal), or a series of papers (collected posthumously as *Investigations in Currency and Finance*) which argued that business fluctuations could be caused ultimately by periodic fluctuations in sunspot activity.

While the sunspot activity is nowadays regarded as either an embarrassment or a joke, it had a modicum of legitimacy in late nineteenth-century scientific circles and within Jevons's own research program. That sunspot cycles might affect the earth's weather had been suggested by Jevons's Manchester colleague Arthur Schuster; and the further connection to crop cycles had been proposed by the physicists Balfour Steward and J. H. Poynting. Furthermore, most of Jevons's disparate writings—from the *Coal Question* to the comparison in the *Theory of Political Economy* of utility to the mathematical format of energy fields—were united by the theme that energy and energetic phenomena were vital to the understanding of the economy. In regarding the economy as governed by natural physical relationships, Jevons was challenged to explain the intermittent "unnatural" crises experienced by Britain throughout the nineteenth century. The resolution of this problem was ultimately to attribute the business cycle itself to natural physical disturbances, namely, energy fluctuations reaching the earth from the sun.

Jevons's early ideas on economic crises were shaped by his fellow member of the Manchester Statistical Society, John Mills. Mills thought the regular periodicity he observed in the occurrence of crises could be explained by periodic losses of confidence by investors, which resulted in credit contractions. Jevons was not satisfied that psychology could adequately explain the fixed periodicity, though he was to keep Mills's sequence of causes intact through his subsequent amendments; his task was to push the causes back to their natural origins.

Jevons's first article on this subject in 1875 attempted to establish that English grain prices from 1254 to 1400 cycled with a period of eleven years, in part because contemporary astronomers then believed that sunspots exhibited a cycle of 11.1 years. Subsequently, he shifted the basis of his argument to the eighteenth and nineteenth centuries, asserting without any time-series evidence the existence of a stable eleven-year pattern of English credit crises, and concluding that the periodicity was close enough to the sunspots to infer causality. When astronomers then revised their estimate of sunspot periodicity downwards to 10.45 years, he simply rearranged the dates of English crises to produce lower average duration.

However equivocal the empirical support, Jevons never wavered in his intent of finding a causal sequence that would link sunspots to British business cycles. When British crop statistics did not support a regular connection, he shifted the chain of causality to the colonies. Sunspots led to crop fluctuations in "India, China and other tropical or semi-tropical countries," which in turn led to fluctuations in British manufactures. British investment was then spurred, but just when "our manufacturers are prepared to turn out a greatly increased supply of goods famines in India and China cut off the demand" (Jevons 1972–81, 5:10–11). These alternations of euphoria and pessimism in turn triggered credit crises, preserving much of Mills's story. From Jevons's vantage point, market failures were exclusively *external* to the regular workings of the market: sunspots, foreigners, problems in long-distance communications. It was emphatically not an analysis of gluts or overproduction, for which he expressed contempt; and it was largely external to the theory of price which is now his main claim to fame.

After Jevons's death, weather explanations of business cycles went into decline, although a more sophisticated attempt to revive them was made by H. L. Moore in the early twentieth century.

Phillip Mirowski

See also AGRICULTURE AND BUSINESS CYCLES; MILLS, JOHN; MOORE, HENRY LUDWELL; PERIOD OF PRODUCTION; SEASONAL FLUCTUATIONS AND FINANCIAL CRISES; SUNSPOT THEORIES OF FLUCTUATIONS

Bibliography

Jevons, W. S. 1871. *The Theory of Political Economy.* London: Macmillan.
———. 1875. *Money and the Mechanism of Exchange.* London: H. S. King.
———. 1884. *Investigations in Currency and Finance.* London: Macmillan.
———. 1972–81. *Papers and Correspondence of William Stanley Jevons.* 7 vols. London: Macmillan.
Mirowski, P. 1988. *Against Mechanism.* Totowa, N.J.: Rowman and Littlefield.
Peart, S. 1991. "Sunspots and Expectations." *Journal of the History of Economic Thought* 13:243–65.

Johannsen, Nicholas August Ludwig Jacob (1844–1928)

The reception accorded to N. A. L. J. Johannsen's economic writings is one of the strangest episodes in the history of economics. Neglected by almost all of his contemporaries, he emerged from obscurity only after the Keynesian revolution had vindicated his early dissent from orthodoxy.

Johannsen described himself as an autodidact, a self-taught businessman with no academic degrees. Born in Berlin, he moved to New York City where he worked in the import-export business. Apparently, he was able to visit Germany regularly and maintained a keen interest in German political and economic affairs, as his economic writings appeared in both English and German. Research concerning his work has been hampered by his use of two pen names, "A. Merwin" and "J. J. O. Lahn," allegedly to avoid irritating one of his employers (Dorfman 1949).

Johannsen's theory of effective-demand failures has been recognized as one of the foremost anticipations of the Keynesian savings-investment nexus and the multiplier. Similar claims have been made about his contributions to monetary and trade-cycle theory, which, in the post-Keynesian era, have been distinguished from his depression theory (Hagemann and Rühl 1990).

By 1898, all of the essentials of Johannsen's reasoning had been developed in manuscripts which he circulated among German academic economists for comments. His analyses of the circular flow and of the depression theory were published shortly thereafter (Johannsen alias Lahn 1903a and 1903b). His books of 1908 (the most quoted, and the only one to appear in English) and 1913 represent further attempts to explain his depression theory to professional economists. Seeking recognition, he issued numerous articles, pamphlets, and leaflets, most of which were printed and circulated privately. Yet, while some of these earlier papers extend his monetary framework, they add little to his theory of effective-demand failures (Johannsen [A. Merwin] 1878, Johannsen 1906a, 1906b, 1926).

Johannsen's analytical framework relied heavily on the "income approach" to determine macroeconomic activity and on the circular flow of money to depict central economic relations. Production was limited by demand and decisions to save were clearly separate from decisions to invest. Johannsen's emphasis on aggregate income as "the genuine source of all demand" led directly to the question of how this aggregate is held or spent. As a result, Say's Law could no longer be upheld as a generally valid proposition.

Aggregate demand consisted of consumption and investment, while aggregate income should either have been spent on consumption or saved. With no guarantee that "saving funds" would be smoothly translated into productive investment, the act of saving per se was condemned as potentially harmful for the community as a whole, "tend(ing) to impoverish others to the amount of money saved" (Johannsen 1925, 4). Consumption and saving were both functions of current income and, in striking anticipation of the Keynesian consumption function, the marginal propensity to consume was assumed to be less than unity.

Full employment could be maintained only if all savings were invested in real capital formation. If savings were not so invested, due to a decrease in the rate of investment or an increase in the rate of savings, real income would shrink and the rate of saving would decline. Johannsen's decisive question was what happened to the "unused" excess of savings in such a case. Disregarding hoarding, he called any surplus of planned savings over planned investment *impair savings*. This was matched by *impair investment*, i.e., lending money to others, the purchase of existing assets, etc. Impair savings represented an excess of *ex ante* savings over *ex ante* investment. As Klein (1947) correctly observed, computing dissavings as negative savings would have led Johannsen to the algebraic result that aggregate net savings will always equal net investment.

The Keynesian consumption function and the denial that the rate of interest can coordinate macroeconomic activity are prerequisites for the view that income equilibrates saving and investment. Preoccupied by price level changes, Keynes brushed off Johannsen's idea of an underemployment equilibrium in his *Treatise on Money*, complaining that Johannsen had overlooked the impact of a fall in the rate of interest (Keynes [1930] 1973, 90).

However, Johannsen not only coined the expression "multiplying principle," he also tried to calculate numerically the secondary effects of an initial reduction in total expenditure. After a protracted struggle to find the correct formula, he at least presented the correct result: with a marginal propensity to consume of two-thirds, a decline in investment causes a decline in income three times as large (Johannsen 1913, 280–81). Whether anyone else came as close so early is doubtful, but Johannsen never explicitly stated Kahn's multiplier formula.

While not fully comprehending the independence of investment from prior savings, Johannsen clearly distinguished financing production through credit creation from financing it out of savings. Prior savings and the virtues of thriftiness were irrelevant to increasing the rate of accumulation, since "the financial means for an upswing will be raised during the upswing and not before" (Johannsen 1913, 250–51). As later reiterated by Keynes in defending his *General Theory*, investment could be constrained by a shortage of cash, but never by a lack of saving. Although the money market could become tight enough to bring about a crisis, such a crisis could be avoided by an accommodating increase in the money supply. More sensitive to inflationary dangers than some of Keynes's followers, Johannsen also proposed policies to guard against that threat (Johannsen 1906a, 1906b, 1926).

Johannsen's achievements were probably evaluated most honestly by Keynes himself in his tribute to his forerunners. Though by neglecting to include Johannsen in his commemorative list of "pioneers," Keynes unjustly prolonged the obscurity of his work. Even so, Johannsen surely "preferred to see the truth obscurely and imperfectly rather than to maintain error, reached indeed with clearness and consistency and by easy logic" (Keynes [1936] 1973, 371).

Christof Rühl

See also KEYNES, JOHN MAYNARD; MULTIPLIER; SAVING EQUALS INVESTMENT; SAY, JEAN-BAPTISTE; SAY'S LAW

Bibliography

Dorfman, J. 1949. *The Economic Mind in American Civilization*. Vol. 3. New York: Viking Press.

Hagemann, H. and C. Rühl. 1990. "Nicholas Johannsen and Keynes's 'Finance Motive.'" *Journal of Institutional and Theoretical Economics* 146:445–69.

Johannsen, N. [A. Merwin]. 1878. *Cheap Capital: New Light on an Old Subject*. New York: Edward Cuttle & Co.

Johannsen, N. [J. J. O. Lahn]. 1903a. *Der Kreislauf des Geldes und der Mechanismus des Social-Lebens*. Berlin: Puttkammer & Mühlbrecht.

———. 1903b. *Depressionsperioden und ihre einheitliche Ursache*. Brooklyn.

Johannsen, N. 1906a. *The Coming Crisis and How to Meet it: A Plan for Currency Reform*. New York.

———. 1906b. *A Guide for Determining the Proper Rate of Taxation*. New York.

———. 1908. *A Neglected Point in Connection with Crises*. New York: The Bankers Publishing Company.

———. 1909. *To the Economists of America: The New Depression Theory.* New York.

———. 1913. *Die Steuer der Zukunft und ihre Auswirkungen auf geschäftliche Depressionen und volkswirtschaftliche Verhältnisse.* Berlin: Puttkammer & Mühlbrecht.

———. 1925. *Business Depressions: Their Cause. A Discovery in Economics.* Rev. ed. Stapleton, N.Y.

———. 1926. *Two Depression Factors: The Minor One Known, not the Other.* Stapleton, N.Y.

Keynes, J. M. [1930] 1971. *A Treatise on Money.* 2 vols. Vols. 5–6 of *The Collected Economic Writings of John Maynard Keynes.* London: Macmillan.

———. [1936] 1973. *The General Theory of Employment, Interest, and Money.* Vol. 7 of *The Collected Economic Writings of John Maynard Keynes.* London: Macmillan.

Klein, L.R. 1947. *The Keynesian Revolution.* New York: Macmillan.

Joplin, Thomas (c. 1790–1847)

Thomas Joplin was born in Newcastle. He is significant in banking theory and practice for his advocacy of joint-stock banks at a time when the Bank of England monopoly interfered with their foundation in England and Wales, and for his work on behalf of the National Provincial Bank of Ireland and, subsequently, the National Provincial Bank of England. His most significant works are probably his *Essay on Banking,* which first appeared in 1822, his *Outlines* of 1823, his *Analysis* of 1832, and his *Currency Reform* of 1844. (Joplin was an extremely prolific writer although his works are now hard to obtain.)

As a native of Newcastle (and no doubt speaking with the very distinctive accent of that part of the Northeast of England), Joplin was, as he himself clearly recognized, an outsider in the world of classical writers on money and banking (1832, 184). Indeed, he claimed, with considerable *prima facie* justification in view of the chronology, that Ricardo's National Bank plan had been taken, without acknowledgment, from his own work. (This issue is not addressed in the Sraffa edition of Ricardo's works.) Joplin does indeed have significant claims to originality. His basic analysis presented possibly the earliest statements of the principle of metallic fluctuation (i.e., the idea that a mixed currency of paper and metal should fluctuate as an identically circumstanced metallic one would), and the desirability of separating issue (of notes) from banking. Much more famous names (Torrens, Norman, Overstone) have been credited with suggesting the separation of the departments in the Bank of England, but on the basic issue Joplin has priority. He also stressed the harmful macroeconomic effects of changes in the money supply (here borrowing from Attwood), and the lagged responsiveness of prices to money supply. Lagged response meant that last-resort activities were thus perfectly safe, as crisis lending by the central bank could be recalled before it had time to affect the price level. He advocated the establishment of joint-stock banks to reduce the vulnerability of the banking system to monetary fluctuations, and put forward a monetary theory of the cycle which has received, even now, very little recognition.

The cycle theory was linked to the idea of "metallic fluctuation." Joplin argued that with a metallic currency, the rate of interest would equate savings and investment. With a nonmetallic currency, the country banks could not tell what the equilibrium rate of interest should be because monetary changes, involving a return to them of their notes, might result either from an increase in saving or from banking overissue. Without this basic information, the country banks were forced to hold the rate of interest fixed. This meant that the country-bank money market, unlike that in London, did not clear through interest variation.

The money supply varied with saving. Saving itself was affected by exogenous factors, especially by changes from war to peace. An increase in saving resulted in a reduction in the money supply and a fall in the price level.

The country-bank circulation, Joplin believed, in direct opposition to the orthodoxy stretching from Thornton through the Bullion Report to the Currency School, not only had a far greater impact on the national price level than the issues of the Bank of England but was also not controlled by the issues of the Bank of England. A reduction in the country money supply was therefore the primary cause of a falling national price level. A fall in the price level would cause a favorable exchange. This raised the supply of bills on London, which were the basic reserve of the country banks, so that the country circulation would increase. The general rise in the price level would eventually be checked by a gold outflow leading to *multiple* contractions in the note issue. Associated with all this were (lagged) changes in the price level involving the harsh and harmful effects of both inflation (including *forced saving*) and deflation. In the process of contraction, the vulnerability of the banking system was all-important; and thus the introduction of joint-stock banks on the Scottish model was highly desirable as these had proved very much less vulnerable than banks on partnership basis. The fundamental need, however, was to control the note issue to prevent the whole cyclical process. This could be done by a system of bullion certificates as the basis for the note issue. The money supply would behave as if it were purely metallic, but without the expense and other inconveniences of using precious metal.

Joplin was undoubtedly a significant monetary writer, producing a large output, and it is difficult to escape the conclusion that it was only his position as an outsider, coupled possibly with an abrasiveness of character, which is evident both in some of his writings and in his relations with the National Provincial Bank, that prevented him from receiving the recognition that was his due.

D. P. O'Brien

See also BANK CHARTER ACT OF 1844; BANKING SCHOOL, CURRENCY SCHOOL, AND FREE BANKING SCHOOL; FORCED SAVING; LOYD, SAMUEL JONES; TORRENS, ROBERT

Bibliography

[Joplin, T.] 1822. *An Essay on the General Principles and Present Practice of Banking.* London: Baldwin, Craddock and Joy.
————. 1823. *Outlines of a System of Political Economy.* London: Baldwin and Craddock.
————. 1832. *An Analysis and History of the Currency Question.* London: Ridgway.
————. 1844. *Currency Reform: Improvement not Depreciation.* London: Richardson.
Mints, L. W. 1945. *A History of Banking Theory.* Chicago: Univ. of Chicago Press.
O'Brien, D. P. 1993. *Thomas Joplin and Classical Macroeconomics: A Reappraisal of Classical Monetary Thought.* Aldershot, U.K.: Elgar.
Viner, J. 1937. *Studies in the Theory of International Trade.* New York: Harper.
Wood, E. 1939. *English Theories of Central Banking Control.* Cambridge: Harvard Univ. Press.

J

Juglar, Clément (1819–1905)

The French economist Clément Juglar is one of the founders of modern business-cycle theory. His father was a physician, and he himself studied medicine. A brilliant student, while an intern in Paris, he wrote a noteworthy thesis on the effect of heart disease on the lungs. The recession of 1847 and the revolution of 1848 drew Juglar's attention to economic issues.

In 1851 and 1852, Juglar's first economic publications appeared on the subject of tariff reform. He also wrote several other articles on French population movements between 1772 and 1848, in which the germ of his cycle theory can be found. Like a doctor examining a patient for telltale symptoms of his state of health, Juglar studied the relations between demographic trends and the wealth of nations. In 1856 and 1857, he published several articles analyzing crises, showing how the economic state of health of both France and England could be gauged from the accounts of their central banks.

In 1860, the Academy of Moral and Political Sciences held a competition for an essay on the study of the causes and effects of commercial crises in Europe and North America in the nineteenth century. Juglar entered and won the prize for *Des crises commerciales et de leur retour périodique en France, en Angleterre et aux Etats-Unis*, which was published in 1862. In 1889, Juglar published an updated edition of this study, which also contained extracts from subsequent articles on commercial crises.

Juglar won a second contest sponsored by the Academy in 1868 on the theme of "currency and freedom of issue." Juglar showed that the private issue of banknotes played only a minor role in triggering crises.

Basing his work on the painstaking observation of economic data, Juglar produced a clear and accurate historical record of commercial crises in France, England and the United States. The crises he studied were general, affecting all aspects of a country's economic activities, and universal, affecting several countries almost simultaneously.

Juglar rejected all the principal causes suggested by contemporaries to explain crises: sunspots, poor harvests, wars, excessive note issue, and bank monopolies, showing that they neither stood up to reasoned criticism nor fitted the facts. According to Juglar, such crises result from excessive prosperity and speculation. Their origins can be explained in terms of human psychology, economic activity being exaggerated during periods of prosperity only to be abruptly halted thereafter. The excessive resort to credit instruments often accentuates the prosperous phase, rendering the subsequent crisis even more sudden and more disastrous. Extraneous factors, such as wars, revolutions, and famine may also worsen the crises, but cannot be considered their principal cause.

To identify and study the phases of the cycle, Juglar insisted on studying central-bank accounts, in particular discounted-bill portfolios and metal reserves. In parallel, he studied movements in prices.

In a period of prosperity, prices rise, but as the crisis looms, the quantity of discounted bills held by the banks increases while metallic reserves decline. When the crisis occurs, prices stop rising. To meet their repayment schedules, borrowers tend to discount all their bills, so that bank portfolios increase markedly and metallic reserves fall dramatically. Banks therefore must raise their lending rate. As credit becomes more expensive and more difficult to obtain, the liquidation phase begins. Fire sales are necessary to obtain financing. In a deflation, chain bankruptcies become increasingly common, confidence evaporates, and business grinds to a halt. The slowdown of the liquidation period is a reaction to the prior overheating. Stagnation is necessary for recuperation. The combination of low prices and reduced interest rates becomes the starting point for recovery.

Thus, Juglar explained crises in terms of the economic cycle he had highlighted. There are always three successive relatively regular phases: a period of prosperity followed by crises and then liquidation. Each phase follows from the preceding one and engenders the next. In this linkage, which Juglar saw as inevitable, crisis seemed to result from excessive prosperity and speculation. He therefore considered it a necessary purge of the economic system. The average time found for each complete cycle was between eight and ten years, depending on the country and the available periods of observation. Juglar identified ten crises in France between 1804 and 1882, which he dated as 1804, 1810, 1818, 1825, 1837–39, 1847, 1858, 1864, 1873, and 1882. The nine corresponding cycles averaged 8.7 years. For the same period in England, he found that crises occurred at practically the same dates. In England between 1696 and 1882, Juglar identified 23 crises, of which 22 were complete cycles averaging 8.4 years. For the United States, Juglar identified crises in 1814–18, 1825–26, 1836–39, 1848, 1857, 1864, 1873, and 1884. The average length of a complete cycle was 10 years.

Having examined many indicators of a country's economic wealth, Juglar concluded that the accounts of the official banks, and more especially, their portfolios and metallic reserves, were the most reliable gauge of the state of the economy. He even argued that by monitoring these variables, one could identify a country's current cycle phase and thus anticipate the inevitable crisis, or even delay and mitigate its effects.

Schumpeter linked Juglar's name to the cycle when he coined the term "Juglar cycle" to refer to cycles lasting between seven and eleven years. This was Schumpeter's homage to one of the first authors to use primitive statistical tools to isolate and describe the cycle. According to Schumpeter, the Juglar cycle is driven by medium-sized technological innovations and each cycle consists of four phases: prosperity, recession, depression, and recovery. The germ of the idea of a four-phase cycle, with two phases moving away from and two moving towards a state of equilibrium, can be found in Juglar's own theory. It is apparent in Juglar's distinction between two subperiods in the prosperity phase: a recovery phase induced by low prices and a period of overheating and undue speculation when prices rise above their "natural" level. The cause of Schumpeter's business cycle is strikingly different from the cause of Juglar's. For Juglar, the cause is speculation fuelled by easy credit, whereas for Schumpeter it is technological innovation. The crisis is a necessary constituent that sets limits to the cycle and gives it a certain irregularity, whereas for Schumpeter, the cycle does not require a crisis.

Though playing a marginal role in the doctrinal debate of the period, Juglar was nevertheless a precursor of later writers in the fields of business-cycle theory, economic indicators, and economic forecasting.

Gilbert Ducos

See also BUSINESS CYCLES; FREE BANKING; JUGLAR CYCLE; KITCHIN CYCLE; MITCHELL, WESLEY CLAIR; SCHUMPETER, JOSEPH ALOIS

Bibliography

Beauregard, P. 1909. "Notice sur la vie et les travaux de Clément Juglar." *Revue de l'Académie des Science Morales et Politiques* 171:153–79.

Juglar, C. 1856. "Des crises commerciales." *Annuaire de l'économie et de la statistique* 13:555–81.

———. 1857a. "Des crises commerciales et monétaires de 1800 à 1857." *Journal des économistes* 14:35–60, 15:255–67.

———. 1857b. "Situation comparée de la Banque d'Angleterre et de la Banque de France, d'après les comptes rendus officiels pendant les crises commerciales depuis 1799." *Journal des économistes* 16:262–63.

———. 1868. *Du change et de la liberté d'émission.* Paris: Guillaumin.

———. 1889a. "Les banque de dépôt, d'escompte et d'émission: résumé comparé de leur histoire et de leur organisation." *Dictionnaire des Finances.* Vol. 2. Edited by L. Say, 1348–55. Paris: Berger–Levrault.

———. 1889b. *Des crises commerciales et de leur retour périodique en France, en Angleterre et aux Etats-Unis.* 2d ed. Paris: Guillaumin. Partially translated as *A Brief History of Panics and Their Periodical Occurrence in the United States.* New York: Putnam, 1916.

———. 1898. "Le rôle de la statistique au point de vue historique et au point de vue économique." *Revue des travaux de l'Académie des Sciences Morales et Politiques* 150:672–90.

Levasseur, E. 1905. "Nécrologie de Clément Juglar." *Journal de la Societé de Statistique de Paris* 15:125–27.

Juglar Cycle

The Juglar cycle is a cycle in the level of economic activity with a period of nine to ten years. It is named after Clément Juglar, a French physician turned economist, who was a pioneer in recognizing cyclical movements in economic activity and in integrating theory, statistics, and history in the study of industrial fluctuations. Contemporary observers had viewed economic crises as isolated events, but Juglar recognized that periods of prosperity, crisis and liquidation follow each other in a wave-like fashion, helping to turn the theory of crises into the theory of business cycles.

Juglar developed statistical series on discount rates, bank balances, and commodity prices, which moved through cycles with an average life of nine to ten years. He did not claim that these cycles were regular, mentioning cycles ranging from two to ten years in the second edition of his treatise. He supported his findings with a history of crises from 1696, and evidence of cyclical patterns in marriage, death, and birth rates in France.

Juglar's explanation for cyclical movements in economic activity was monetary, emphasizing the role of bank credit in crises. Periods of inflation and expansion come to an end when pressures on specie reserve force the banking system to contract credit.

After Juglar, several authors found trade cycles with a periodicity of around nine to ten years. John Mills observed credit cycles of ten years duration. W. Stanley Jevons found British business activity to oscillate with periods of 10.45 or 11.1 years which he attributed to sunspots and prominences. M. Tugan-Baranovsky, M. Bouniatian, and G. Cassell observed cycles of seven to eleven, nine to eleven, and four to eleven years respectively.

Theorists as diverse as Karl Marx and W. W. Rostow attributed the Juglar cycles to fluctuations of fixed investment in machines and equipment. These cycles are generated through the Samuelson multiplier-accelerator mechanism. If consumption depends on last period's income, desired capital stock is proportional to output, and firms seek to acquire capital to diminish the gap between actual and desired capital, strong economic fluctuations may result.

Joseph Schumpeter integrated the Juglar cycle into his famous three-cycle schema. Fluctuations in economic activity were due to the short Kitchin cycles of some forty months duration, the intermediate-length Juglar cycles of nine to ten years duration, and the long Kondratieff cycles of forty-eight to sixty years duration. The different cycles were attributed to innovations of different magnitudes and periods of gestation. Actual economic fluctuations reflected the interaction and aggregation of all three cycles.

Mitchell and Burns could not find Juglar cycles of nine to ten years duration. Akerman suggested that Juglar cycles disappeared after 1896 with the completion of the railway system, and were supplanted by a four-year political business cycle. Mitchell found that two or three alternations of prosperity and depression frequently occurred between Juglar's crises. These shorter cycles contained no traditionally defined crises. Mitchell defined the business cycle as the shortest trough-to-trough interval exceeding a year, settling on one aggregate economic cycle with an average length of four years and a mode of three years.

Since Juglar originally identified a single aggregate economic cycle of irregular duration, we have now come full circle. The standard business cycle is the Juglar cycle, and thus most standard business-cycle theories are actually explanations of the Juglar cycle.

Linus Yamane

See also AKERMAN, JOHAN HENRIK; BUSINESS CYCLES; JUGLAR, CLÉMENT; KITCHIN CYCLE; KONDRATIEFF CYCLES; MITCHELL, WESLEY CLAIR; SAMUELSON, PAUL ANTHONY; SCHUMPETER, JOSEPH ALOIS

Bibliography

Akerman, J. 1947. "Political Economic Cycles." *Kyklos* 1:107–117.

Burns, A. F. and W. C. Mitchell. 1946. *Measuring Business Cycles.* New York: NBER.

Jevons, W. S. 1884. *Investigations in Currency and Finance.* London: Macmillan.

Juglar, C. 1889. *Des crises commerciales et leur retour periodique en France, en Anglettere, et aux Etats-Unis.* 2d ed. Paris: Guillaumin. Partially translated as *A Brief History of Panics and Their Periodical Occurrence in the United States.* New York: Putnam, 1916.

Mitchell, W. C. 1927. *Business Cycles: The Problem and its Setting.* New York: NBER.

Rostow, W. W. 1948. *The British Economy of the Nineteenth Century.* Oxford: Clarendon Press.

Schumpeter, J. A. 1939. *Business Cycles: A Theoretical, Historical, and Statistical Analysis of the Capitalist Process.* 2 vols. New York: McGraw-Hill.

Van Duijn, J. J. 1983. *The Long Wave in Economic Life.* London: Allen and Unwin.

K

Kaldor, Nicholas (1908–1986)

Professor Lord Nicholas Kaldor, one of the most original economists of the twentieth century, made lasting contributions in several fields of economics including the theory of the firm, welfare economics, Keynesian economics, public finance, and the theory of growth and distribution. His major contributions to trade-cycle theory were made from 1932 to 1947 while he was teaching at the London School of Economics (LSE). It was then that he escaped from the Austrian influence of Friedrich Hayek and Lionel Robbins, becoming an early convert to the Keynesian Revolution and a strong critic of Hayek. He was also critical of the (fixed) accelerator theory of investment and in 1940 produced an original nonlinear model of the trade cycle capable of generating self-sustaining (*limit*) cycles without the need for lags or shocks. From 1950 until his death, Kaldor taught at Cambridge University.

Hayek and the Austrian School propounded a monetary theory of the trade cycle, not dissimilar to the theory of the Swedish economist, Knut Wicksell. In 1929, Hayek published *Monetary Theory and the Trade Cycle*, which Kaldor (with H. Croome) translated into English in 1933. In 1931, Hayek published *Prices and Production* which elaborated on the changes in the real structure of production that follow from the initial monetary impulse. The theory was that credit expansion forces the market rate of interest below the *natural* rate of interest (at which the supply of and demand for real savings are equal) which leads to an increased capital intensity of production that can only remain profitable while the credit expansion continues. If credit is contracted and the rate of interest rises, the reversion to less capi-

tal-intensive methods of production causes problems of adjustment and unemployment.

Kaldor absorbed this theory while a student at the LSE from 1927 to 1932, and used it in his first published paper to explain the economic difficulties of Austria (Kaldor 1932). He then demolished it in a powerful paper, "Capital Intensity and the Trade Cycle" ([1939] 1960). Kaldor argued that *actual* capital intensity must fall during the boom, because the short-run fixity of capital means that output can be increased only by employing more labor. The long-run desired or "normal" capital intensity probably falls too, because real wages fall and interest rates rise. Now the lower the capital intensity of production, the greater the potential increase in output capacity for any given level of investment. Herein lies the problem, because consumption may lag behind the capacity to produce consumption goods, and investment cannot rise indefinitely because of a scarcity of labor. Hence, contrary to the Austrian theory, booms are doomed to failure, not because production techniques are too capital-intensive, but because they are not capital-intensive enough.

Hayek later changed his mind concerning the seeds of cyclical crisis during the upswing. In *Profits, Interest and Investment* (1939), he argued that employers would seek more labor-intensive methods of production as the price of consumption goods and the rate of profits rise and as real wages fall. This increases investment demand, but also encourages the adoption of less capital-intensive techniques (which Hayek labelled the "Ricardo Effect"). According to Hayek, the latter effect always dominates, causing the total demand for loanable funds to fall and a depression in the capital-goods industries. Kaldor also launched into this *volte face* in his paper "Professor Hayek and the Concertina Effect" ([1942] 1960). Objecting to Hayek's use of the term "Ricardo Effect" (because that referred to the relative price of labor and machinery), Kaldor argued that total investment could never be reduced by a rise in the rate of profit. Only if there were a rise in the rate of interest would there be a tendency for capital intensity to fall. But the rate of interest can rise only if investment increases. Hayek never answered Kaldor's critique.

Kaldor's own original contributions to trade-cycle theory date from his 1938 paper, "Stability and Full Employment." Here the focus was on why the boom should end. The model is Keynesian, but accepts Robertson's thesis that the trade cycle is the price to be paid for a high rate of economic progress. Full employment is bound to be unstable owing to the complementarity and specificity of the factors of production. In the short-run situation at full employment, there is a certain division of output between investment and consumption and a certain division of income between consumption and saving, but the divisions need not be equal. If saving exceeds investment, full employment in the investment-goods industries will not suffice to secure full employment in the consumption-goods industries. The demand for investment goods declines. If investment exceeds saving, prices rise and the natural rate of interest falls below the money rate of interest. If wages do not rise equiproportionately with prices, the share of profits in national income rises and excess investment must eventually turn itself into excess saving. (This is the germ of Kaldor's macrotheory of income distribution, not fully articulated until 1956.) In the long run, the boom is terminated by labor shortages, and investment demand declines unless there is sufficient labor-saving progress.

Kaldor's 1938 paper does not address the cyclical upturn. By 1940, Kaldor had in his mind a complete model of the cycle. He set out to explain oscillations between a low- and a high-level equilibrium, realizing that a simple linear accelerator, which makes investment an unlagged function of the rate of change of output, could not do so. However, a shifting nonlinear investment function could. Investment is likely to be unresponsive to changes in output at both high and low levels of output: in the former case because of the constraint of full employment; in the latter case because of excess capacity. Saving, by contrast, is probably more sensitive than normal at high and low levels of activity. (Kaldor anticipated Duesenberry's idea of a "customary" standard of living below which people dissave drastically and above which they save a lot.) These saving and investment functions (SS and II) are shown in Figure 1.

The economic system can reach stability at a low or a high level of economic activity (point A or B in Figure 1). But both the SS and II curves are short-run functions. Through time they will shift, which is the source of instability. For example, at a high level of activity, when the level of investment is high, the savings schedule will shift up but the investment schedule will tend to fall, because the accumulation of capital restricts the range of investment opportunities. Thus, point B gradually shifts leftwards and point C shifts rightwards, reducing the level of activity and ultimately bringing B and C together. Equilibrium becomes unstable in a downward direction and the level of activity falls to point A. At point A, the curves will tend to shift in the opposite direction and the reverse process takes place.

The *period* of the cycle depends on two time rates of movement: the rate at which the saving and investment curves shift, and the time required for the system to move from B = C to A or from A = C to B. The rate at which the SS and II curves shift depends on the construction period and the durability of capital goods. The shorter the construction period and the shorter the lifetime, the faster the rate of shift at any rate of investment and the shorter the cycle. The *amplitude* of the cycle depends on the shapes of the SS and II curves, which determine the distance between A and B at their normal position. A necessary condition to establish a limit cycle is that a movement along

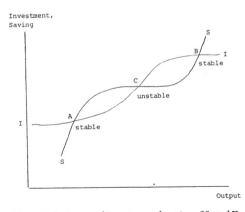

Figure 1. Savings and investment functions SS *and* II.

the *SS* or the *II* curve proceed more quickly than the rate of shift of the curves as a result of capital accumulation (Chang and Smyth 1971). In other words, adjusting output to a change in investment must take less time than changing investment (at a given level of output) on account of the change in the capital stock. This is implicit in the model, as it is in all Keynesian short-period equilibrium models which treat the capital stock as given. The beauty of Kaldor's 1940 model is that it can generate self-sustaining cycles without any time lags, shocks, or the rigid specification of parameters that characterize most other trade-cycle models. The model has close affinities to the later work of Goodwin.

Kaldor ([1951] 1960) was critical of the fixed-accelerator theories of investment used by, for example, Harrod and Hicks, but he agreed that a theory of the trade cycle must be built around a rising trend in output (Kaldor [1954] 1960). However, it is not the trend rate of growth of output that determines the strength and duration of the boom, but rather, by setting up forces and incentives to overcome physical limitations on capacity, the strength of the boom that determines the rate of growth. In particular, technical progress and labor-force growth are endogenous to an economic system—the product of social processes.

A. P. Thirlwall

See also ACCELERATION PRINCIPLE; AUSTRIAN THEORY OF BUSINESS CYCLES; ENDOGENOUS AND EXOGENOUS MONEY; GOODWIN, RICHARD MURPHEY; HARROD, ROY FORBES; HAYEK, FRIEDRICH AUGUST [VON]; HICKS, JOHN RICHARD; MONEY-INCOME CAUSALITY; NONLINEAR BUSINESS-CYCLE THEORIES; ROBINSON, JOAN VIOLET MAURICE; SUPPLY OF MONEY

Bibliography

Chang, W. W. and D. J. Smyth. 1971. "The Existence and Persistence of Cycles in a Non-linear Model: Kaldor's 1940 Model Re-Examined." *Review of Economic Studies* 38:40–44.

Goodwin, R. [1967] 1982. "A Growth Cycle." Chap. 14 in *Essays in Economic Dynamics*. London: Macmillan.

Harrod, R. 1936. *The Trade Cycle*. Oxford: Clarendon Press.

Hicks, J. R. 1950. *A Contribution to the Theory of the Trade Cycle*. Oxford: Clarendon Press.

Kaldor, N. 1932. "The Economic Situation of Austria." *Harvard Business Review*, October, 23–34.

———. [1938] 1960. "Stability and Full Employment." Chap. 5 in *Essays on Economic Stability and Growth*. Glencoe, Ill.: Free Press.

———. [1939] 1960. "Capital Intensity and the Trade Cycle." Chap. 6 in *Essays on Economic Stability and Growth*. Glencoe, Ill.: Free Press.

———. [1940] 1960. "A Model of the Trade Cycle." Chap. 8 in *Essays on Economic Stability and Growth*. Glencoe, Ill.: Free Press.

———. [1942] 1960. "Professor Hayek and the Concertina Effect." Chap. 7 in *Essays on Economic Stability and Growth*. Glencoe, Ill.: Free Press.

———. [1951] 1960. "Mr. Hicks on the Trade Cycle." Chap. 9 in *Essays on Economic Stability and Growth*. Glencoe, Ill.: Free Press.

———. [1954] 1960. "The Relation of Economic Growth and Cyclical Fluctuations." Chap. 10 in *Essays on Economic Stability and Growth*. Glencoe, Ill.: Free Press.

Thirlwall, A. P. 1987. *Nicholas Kaldor*. Brighton, U.K.: Wheatsheaf Books.

Kalecki, Michal (1899–1970)

Born in the Lodz, Poland, in 1899, Michal Kalecki studied engineering at the University of Danzig. Before graduating, he suffered one of the many hardships that were to plague his life. His father lost his job, and the young Kalecki permanently interrupted his formal studies. Kalecki tried his hand at economic journalism and produced a long series of painstakingly researched articles concerned with market analysis of particular commodities. He later cooperated in studies of national income and fluctuations in Poland and abroad. This training in producing detailed empirical studies, as well as his extraordinary theoretical insights, acute mathematical abilities, political astuteness, and social conscience, were all evident in his 1933 outline of business-cycle theory—*Próba Teorii Koniunktury*—one of the most original and fundamental (yet long-neglected) business-cycle studies of this century.

Kalecki independently discovered the essential ingredients of what later became the

Keynesian Revolution. But Kalecki's anticipation of Keynes is secondary to the fact that the Kaleckian construct surpasses the Keynesian one in several crucial respects. Besides integrating the theories of aggregate output, price, and distribution, Kalecki's theory of fluctuations in national income and its partition between wages and prices is more general than its Keynesian counterpart. Avoiding the distinction between macro and micro, Kalecki based his macroeconomic model on a realistic theory of the firm which incorporated imperfect competition and income distribution. And, unlike Keynes, he elucidated the dynamic properties of the economic process within an open economy.

Remarkably, Kalecki approached the theory of effective demand through a theory of the business cycle in which investment and its variability play a central role. While Keynes also identified the variability of investment as crucially affecting effective demand, Kalecki, even in his initial 1933 publication, probed deeper into the determinants of investment.

Keynes's approach to the determination of national income has become (or is criticized as) textbook orthodoxy. But Keynes did not offer a theory of the business cycle. Kalecki introduced an interpretation and analysis of the process by which a change in investment generates a matching change in savings very different from Keynes's. He did not develop the theory of effective demand by the Kahn-Keynes route of the multiplier, so that his version is somewhat less appealing than Keynes's, but no less forceful. He did, however, go straight to the pure (nonmonetary) theory of the business cycle (on which Keynes was weak) and his original treatment of the capital-stock-adjustment mechanism is now a basis for many business-cycle models. Kalecki's pioneering and distinct theory of cyclical fluctuations belongs to the family of maintained, macrodynamic, mathematical (econometric) models of the economic system. In some respects the architectonic contributions of these two scholars are complementary and not competitive. From the very beginning, one of the major strengths of Kalecki's business-cycle model (a rigorous, solvable mathematical model) was its deep roots in observable reality.

A theory of economic fluctuations must explain swings in the rate of economic activity, as reflected in economic time series. The fundamental issues are: why fluctuations recur, whether swings are generated from within the economic system or are externally precipitated, how their motion is kept alive, and how they are maintained or constrained.

Mathematical or econometric theories of business cycles tend to focus attention on systematic oscillations that spring from the internal structure of the economic mechanism and attempt to explain how the fluctuations are produced from the response of the economic mechanism to changes in exogenous variables. Cycle theory faces a fundamental difficulty in demonstrating that the oscillations are of a nondying and a nonexploding variety. The difficulty may be escaped by departing from a purely endogenous model and treating the actual process as a result of the operation of the self-generating mechanism and external impulses—as Kalecki does in his later work.

In Kalecki's original model (in a closed economy, without government demand), investment determines the level of economic activity. It is the volatile fluctuations in investment that generally dominate the ups and downs in economic activity. That is, aggregate output and consumption show smaller relative fluctuations than investment. Kalecki proposed basic relations concerning: (1) the impact of investment-induced effective demand on profits and national income, and (2) the determinants of investment. If fluctuations in investment cause fluctuations in economic activity, what determines investment? This thorny question preoccupied Kalecki most of his life. In his original presentation, he considered investment at time t to be an increasing function of national income at time t and a decreasing function of the stock of capital at time $t - 1$.

The early mechanism of business fluctuations involves the mutual interaction of the stimulating effect of higher income on investment and the depressing effect of growing productive capacity. "We see that the question, 'What causes periodical crises?' could be answered shortly: the fact that investment is not only produced but also producing." Investment viewed in its income-generating capacity creates prosperity, and every increase of it improves business and stimulates further investment. Simultaneously, however, new capital equipment adds to productive capacity and as soon as it is put into operation it competes with the equipment of older vintage. The tragedy of investment is that it causes crises because it is useful (Kalecki 1939, 148–49).

In his original model, Kalecki introduced fundamental and interesting dynamic features into his system, notably: (1) the time lag between investment decisions and realization, and (2) the determinants of investment decisions. Indeed, a distinctive and remarkable feature of Kalecki's model is the separation between the decision to invest and the actual implementation.

Investment decisions are necessarily forward-looking. Kalecki introduced uncertainty and expectations into his argument, although he did not provide a theory of how expectations are formed. In the Kaleckian system, national income lags behind investment, and investment behind decisions; past investment decisions determine the current national income, which influences current investment decisions, which, in turn, determine future national income.

The level of real national income delimits approximately its distribution among wage earners and profit earners, particularly the profits accruing to the capitalist sector. The prospective rate of profit, and, therefore, investment, is determined, *grosso modo*, by the level of national income and stock of capital, with an appropriate time lag. With a given stock of capital, the rate of profit that can be obtained under current conditions from a new investment is the greater, the larger the level of national income. But in an uncertain world, entrepreneurs often act as if they expected the existing situation to continue in the future. They tend to be optimistic when business prospers and pessimistic when it does not. Generally, the prospective rate of profit is a function of the actual rate of profit. Thus, with a given capital stock, the prospective rate of profit rises with the level of national income. For a given capital stock, profits will rise as effective demand grows, while a growing capital stock with constant aggregate demand implies a declining rate of profit. The larger the profit and the smaller the capital stock, the larger will be the prospective rate of profit on new investment.

Moreover, Kalecki emphasized that there are distinct limits to the financing of investment at a given rate of interest; i.e., the problem of availability of finance. The outside finance that a firm can secure is largely determined by the amount of capital owned by the firm. Kalecki viewed the limitation of the size of the firm by the availability of entrepreneurial capital as going to the very heart of the capitalist system—a limitation that cannot be ignored in the theory of investment decisions. An important determinant of such decisions is the accumulation of the firm's capital out of current profits (generated by prior investment). Profit influences the invest-

ment-demand function not only by providing a motive to invest, but also by providing the means of doing so. Investment decisions are related to the firm's "internal" accumulation of gross savings. These savings allow the firm to make new investments without facing the problems of the limited capital market or "increasing risk."

In later work, Kalecki (1971) attempted a theoretical integration of growth and cyclical processes. He advanced an original, provocative, but somewhat sketchy theory of long-run development trends, determining both trend and cycle. Innovation plays a cardinal role in transforming the static system subject to fluctuations (cyclical fluctuation around the zero level of capital accumulation) into one subject to a growth trend. Kalecki emphasized the relevance of the business-cycle approach to the study of economic development. He viewed the growth rate at any time as a phenomenon deeply rooted in past economic, social, and technological developments. He also believed that the two basic relations in the approach to business cycles: (1) the impact of investment-induced effective demand on profits and national income, and (2) the determination of the investment function by the level and the rate of change in income, could explain both the trend and the cycle. Such an approach is incomparably more exacting than the pure business-cycle model, but offers a truer insight and its results are closer to the reality of the process of development. For Kalecki, the difficulty of the task could not excuse disregarding an approach to a more realistic analysis of the dynamics of a capitalistic economy.

On his return to Poland in the mid-1950s, Kalecki retained a keen interest in the theory and practice of the dynamics of capitalism. However, his major preoccupation became the theory and practice of the dynamics of socialist and mixed economies. He summarized the theories of growth in different social systems in his last Cambridge lecture (Kalecki 1970). The successive versions of Kalecki's business-cycle theory are traced in Steindl (1981) and Feiwel (1975). The latter also provides an account of Kalecki's life and his contributions to the development of the theory of dynamics of socialist and mixed economies.

G. R. Feiwel

See also ACCELERATION PRINCIPLE; DISPROPORTIONALITY THEORY; INCOME DISTRIBUTION AND THE BUSINESS CYCLE; INVESTMENT;

KEYNES, JOHN MAYNARD; KOOPMANS, TJALLING CHARLES; LANGE, OSKAR; POLITICAL BUSINESS CYCLE; PREOBRAZHENSKY, EVGENII ALEXEYEVICH; ROBINSON, JOAN VIOLET MAURICE

Bibliography

Feiwel, G. R. 1975. *The Intellectual Capital of Michal Kalecki.* Knoxville: Univ. of Tennessee Press.

Kalecki, M. 1935. "A Macrodynamic Theory of Business Cycles." *Econometrica* 3:327–44.

———. [1936] 1982. Review of *The General Theory of Employment, Interest, and Money,* by J. M. Keynes. Translation. *Australian Economic Papers* 21:244–60.

———. 1937. "A Theory of the Business Cycle." Chap. 6 in *Essays in the Theory of Economic Fluctuations.* London: Allen and Unwin.

———. 1939. *Essays in the Theory of Economic Fluctuations.* London: Allen and Unwin.

———. [1954] 1965. *The Theory of Economic Dynamics.* London: Allen and Unwin.

———. 1966. *Studies in the Theory of Business Cycles 1933–1939.* Translation. Warsaw: Polish Scientific Publishers.

———. 1970. "Theories of Growth in Different Social Systems." *Scientia* 64:311–16.

———. 1971. *Selected Essays on the Dynamics of the Capitalist Economy.* Cambridge: Cambridge Univ. Press.

———. 1990–93. *The Collected Works of Michal Kalecki.* 5 vols. Edited by J. Osiatynski. Oxford: Clarendon Press.

Klein, L. R. 1964. "The Role of Econometrics in Socialist Economics." In *Problems of Economic Dynamics and Planning: Essays in Honour of Michal Kalecki,* 181–91. Warsaw: PWN.

Patinkin, D. 1982. *Anticipations of the General Theory and Other Essays on Keynes.* Chicago: Univ. of Chicago Press.

Robinson. J. 1952. *The Rate of Interest and Other Essays.* London: Macmillan.

———. 1976. "Michal Kalecki: A Neglected Prophet." *New York Review of Books,* March 4, 28–30.

Steindl, J. 1981. "Some Comments on the Three Versions of Kalecki's Theory of the Trade Cycle." In *Studies in Economic Theory and Practice: Essays in Honor of Edward Lipinski,* edited by N. Assorodobras-Kula et al., 125–33. Amsterdam: North-Holland.

Kautsky, Karl (1854–1938)

Sometimes called "the pope of Marxism," Karl Kautsky was the leading theoretician of German Social Democracy in its heyday, from the early 1880s to 1914. He laid down the catechism of orthodox Marxism, led the attack on revisionism, and countered the more radical elements in the movement. Kautsky's views on economic crisis were central to his political beliefs, and in turn molded the ideas of competing schools of thought within the Marxism of the Second International.

Kautsky was born in Prague; his mother was German, his father Czech. A socialist from his student days in Vienna, he founded *Die Neue Zeit* in 1881 and edited this most influential of Marxist journals until 1917. Kautsky returned to Austria in 1924, fleeing to Czechoslovakia after the Dollfuss coup and then to Holland, where he died. An astonishingly prolific writer, Kautsky's most substantial achievement was his *Die Materialistische Geschichtsauffassung.*

Together with the future revisionist Eduard Bernstein, Kautsky drafted the 1891 Erfurt program of German Social Democracy, which asserted baldly that economic crises were inevitable under capitalism, and were becoming more extensive and more severe. In his book *The Class Struggle,* Kautsky offered an underconsumptionist explanation of crises in which the driving force was the declining income share of both workers and small proprietors. In the process capitalism "begins to suffocate in its own surplus" ([1892] 1971, 85).

Towards the end of the 1890s Bernstein broke with Marxist orthodoxy, on this and many other questions. He denied the relevance of underconsumption when the living standards of both the proletariat and the middle classes were rising, arguing that the emergence of cartels and the growing use of credit had increased economic stability by confining any overproduction to the particular sector or sectors in which it had originated. Bernstein concluded that increasingly intense general crises were no longer unavoidable.

Kautsky defended the orthodox position in his *Bernstein und das Sozialdemokratische Program: eine Antikritik,* but he repudiated the so-called "breakdown theory" of inevitable economic collapse, which, he claimed, neither Marx nor his followers had ever advanced. However, Kautsky did reassert his underconsumptionist theory of crises and maintained that, in the face of chronic overproduction, the capitalist mode of production "tends to become impossible" (1899, 142).

In 1901, Kautsky criticized Tugan-Baranovsky's analysis of the trade cycle in similar terms, making underconsumption the ultimate cause of all crises. But there was now an important corollary: constraints on internal consumption forced capitalists to seek external markets, in noncapitalist areas. Kautsky argued that imperialist expansion was a necessary consequence of underconsumption, even though noncapitalist markets would prove inadequate to prevent continued crises. He had expressed the same view as early as 1884, in an article on the adventures of the French at Tongking; it was a line of reasoning that Rosa Luxemburg would follow in her *Accumulation of Capital*. Kautsky continued his critique of Tugan-Baranovsky by agreeing with the Russian writer that disproportionalities between the departments of production did operate as a cause (albeit a subsidiary one) of crises, and by endorsing Parvus's recent discovery of long waves in economic activity.

At the time of his review of Hilferding's *Finance Capital*, ten years later, Kautsky's ideas still had not greatly changed. The first signs of a rapprochement with revisionism appeared in 1914, when he raised the possibility of a cooperative and peaceful "ultra-imperialist" division of the world between the major capitalist powers. By the late 1920s, Kautsky had come to accept Hilferding's analysis of "organised capitalism." In his *Materialistische Geschichtsauffassung* (1929, 539–58), he argued that real wages were rising, while crises had become less acute, less threatening to the interests of capital, and less dangerous to the working class. Economic breakdown was unlikely, and there was no reason to suppose that capitalism faced insurmountable economic limits.

It is impossible to exaggerate the influence of Kautsky in the international socialist movement before the First World War. His writings on crises, as on every other major issue, were accepted as defining the position of orthodox Marxism. Thus Kautsky was responsible for the prominence of underconsumptionist ideas and of a rather ambivalent breakdown theory, as well as for the notion that imperialist expansion was inextricably linked to internal economic contradictions. After 1914, however, he was a much less significant figure.

M. C. Howard
J. E. King

See also BERNSTEIN, EDUARD; DISPROPORTIONALITY THEORY; HILFERDING, RUDOLF; LUXEMBURG, ROSA; MARX, KARL HEINRICH; OVERSAVING THEORIES OF BUSINESS CYCLES; TUGAN-BARANOVSKY, MIKHAIL IVANOVICH

Bibliography

Geary, D. 1987. *Karl Kautsky*. Manchester: Manchester Univ. Press.

Hansen, F. R. 1985. *The Breakdown of Capitalism: A History of the Idea in Western Marxism, 1883–1983*. London: Routledge and Kegan Paul.

[Kautsky, K.]. 1884. "Tongking." *Die Neue Zeit* 2:156–64.

———. [1892] 1971. *The Class Struggle*. Translation. New York: Norton.

———. 1899. *Bernstein und das sozialdemokratische Programm: eine Antikritik*. Stuttgart: J. H. W. Dietz.

———. 1901–1902. "Krisentheorien." *Die Neue Zeit* 20:37–47, 110–18, 133–43.

———. 1910–11. "Finanzkapital und Krisen." *Die Neue Zeit* 29:764–72, 797–804, 838–46, 874–83.

———. 1914. "Der Imperialismus." *Die Neue Zeit* 32:908–22.

———. 1929. *Die Materialistische Geschichtsauffassung*. Berlin: J. H. W. Dietz.

Salvadori, M. 1979. *Karl Kautsky and the Socialist Revolution 1880–1938*. Translation. London: New Left Books.

Steenson, G. P. 1978. *Karl Kautsky 1854–1938: Marxism in the Classical Years*. Pittsburgh: Univ. of Pittsburgh Press.

K

Keynes, John Maynard (1883–1946)

J. M. Keynes's *General Theory of Employment, Interest and Money* ([1936] 1973, JMK VII) shaped modern macroeconomics, setting the agenda for Monetarist and New Classical critics of Keynes as well as for economists who consider themselves Keynesian, Post-Keynesian, New Keynesian, or eclectic. The *General Theory* argued that the volume of output and employment depends on effective demand, and that without activist, stabilizing fiscal and monetary policy a monetary economy might not return to full employment after a shock. Keynes thus challenged those economists who, appealing to some version of Say's Law that the value of aggregate excess supply is zero, held that market forces would return the economy to full employment unless interfered with by destabilizing government intervention. He also challenged Marxists who denied that a capitalist society could reduce unemployment and dampen cyclical fluctuations.

Keynes graduated from Cambridge with first class honors in mathematics in 1905. His fellowship dissertation for King's College was on probability, and his only formal training in economics was preparing for the Civil Service examination in 1906. He was nonetheless steeped in Cambridge political economy, to which his father, John Neville Keynes, had contributed. He was particularly influenced by Alfred Marshall's testimony to official inquiries on monetary questions in the 1880s, which Keynes edited as Marshall's *Official Papers* (1926). Education as a mathematician did not keep Keynes from criticizing excessive mathematical formalism in probability and economics in his *Treatise on Probability* ([1921] 1971, JMK VIII) and the *General Theory*.

Keynes's first book, *Indian Currency and Finance* ([1913] 1971, JMK I), drew on his experience at the India Office (1906–08) before he returned to King's College, Cambridge, and led to his appointment to the Royal Commission on Indian Finance and Currency (1913–14). He advocated creating an Indian central bank to manage a gold-exchange standard resembling Ricardo's ingot plan. Paper rupees would circulate internally, economizing on mining gold, which would be used (along with sterling) only for external settlements to peg the value of the rupee.

Keynes became a celebrity with *The Economic Consequences of the Peace* ([1919] 1971, JMK II), the protest written after his resignation as Treasury representative at the Versailles peace conference. He argued that the reparations imposed on Germany were so large that they would create a festering grievance. Yet, since the victorious Allies would not tolerate the trade deficits required to balance the corresponding German export surpluses, they would never be collected.

A Tract on Monetary Reform ([1923] 1972, JMK IV) was based on articles Keynes had written for the Manchester Guardian Commercial's supplements on "Reconstruction in Europe." In this work aimed at a popular audience, Keynes analyzed the postwar inflations, deflations, and floating exchange rates that followed the collapse of the gold standard. The *Tract* discussed inflation as a tax on the holding of money, identified reduced holding of real money balances as a social cost of inflation and as a limit on the revenue

from the inflation tax, and related the interest-rate differential between two countries to the spread between spot and forward exchange rates. A more subtle danger of inflation that Keynes warned against was the search for scapegoats by those who misunderstood its complex sources. Also warning against deflation, he observed that the Czechoslovak deflation had caused unemployment and reduced output because of sticky wages and because nominal interest rates could not become negative. In *The Economic Consequences of Mr. Churchill* ([1925] 1973, in JMK IX), Keynes used a similar analysis to oppose Britain's return to the gold standard at the prewar parity. Keynes recommended that internal price-level stability be made the chief goal of monetary policy and underlined the conflict between this goal and adherence to the gold standard. Keynes reprinted three of the five chapters of the *Tract* in his *Essays in Persuasion* ([1931] 1971, JMK IX), indicating his continued interest in its approach.

The *General Theory* built on the analysis of investment and savings and of the demand for money as an asset in *A Treatise on Money* ([1930] 1971, JMK V–VI) while dropping the *Treatise's* "fundamental equations" for prices and its concept of Q, windfall profits, the difference between investment I and saving S. In their place was a theory of income as the variable equating saving to planned investment. The model of the *Treatise* produced cumulative deflation or inflation ($I > S$ would imply $Q > 0$ and a further increase in I) whenever the market rate of interest differed from the Wicksellian natural rate which would equate I to S. The dependence of saving on income in the *General Theory* would yield an equilibrium level of income Y determined by $I = S(Y)$. This followed the independent derivations by L. F. Giblin, R. G. Hawtrey, and R. F. Kahn of a finite multiplier relationship between changes in autonomous investment and changes in equilibrium income, and advanced beyond the crude multiplier analysis Keynes and Hubert Henderson used in *Can Lloyd George Do It?* ([1929] 1973, in JMK IX).

Keynes held that money wage rates would generally be slow to fall even with no irrational money illusion, because of overlapping contracts and the concern of workers with relative wages. Workers who would not resist price increases which proportionately reduced all real wages and incomes would nevertheless resist money wage cuts, which reduce their incomes relative to other workers whose contracts had not yet expired and to recipients of fixed nominal incomes. In chapter 19 of the *General Theory,* Keynes argued that even if money wages were flexible, deflation would not eliminate unemployment, since falling prices would prevent a reduction in real wages and increase liquidity preference and might induce expectations of further price declines.

Because of uncertainty about the future (which cannot be reduced to insurable risk), liquidity preference and the marginal efficiency of capital schedule are subject to shifts whenever long-period expectations are revised. The resulting fluctuations in investment induce fluctuations in consumption and income. Because of the volatility of private spending, Keynes advocated that government stabilize the economy by altering the level of public investment to offset fluctuations in private investment. Both public-choice theorists and Marxists have criticized Keynes for implicitly assuming that government policy is exogenously determined by a disinterested set of policymakers.

Keynes lumped economists from Ricardo to Pigou together as "classical" for accepting Say's Law of Markets, which Keynes characterized as "supply creates its own demand." Robert Clower and Axel Leijonhufvud have interpreted Keynes's rejection of Say's Law as a rejection of the applicability to effective demands of what Oskar Lange called Walras's Law (the value of excess demand sums to zero over all markets, including money). If there is excess supply of labor at a positive wage rate, the value of the labor that quantity-constrained workers are unable to sell should be counted in the budget constraint relevant to their demand for other commodities, so that the excess supply of labor may not be matched by an excess effective demand for anything else. There would then be no upward pressure on the output or price of any commodity, and the excess supply of labor would persist as long as the wage rate did not fall.

Keynes proposed a theory of the level of output and employment in his *General Theory,* in contrast to his focus on credit cycles and cumulative processes in the *Treatise.* In Book VI, "Short Notes Suggested by the General Theory," however, he included "Notes on the Trade Cycle" (JMK VII, chap. 22): "Since we claim to have shown in the preceding chapters what determines the volume of employment at any time, it follows, if we are right, that our theory must be capable of explaining the phenomena of the trade cycle" (313). He attributed regular fluctuations lasting three to five years to cyclical shifts in the marginal efficiency of capital schedule. Crises typically occur when volatile expectations about the future yields of capital assets are revised downward, rather than when interest rates rise. Liquidity preference increases after the onset of the crisis, due to "the dismay and uncertainty as to the future which accompanies a collapse in the marginal efficiency of capital" (316). The marginal efficiency of capital schedule would gradually shift up again as durable assets depreciate and stocks of durable goods are used up.

The main text of the *General Theory* had much more influence on the subsequent development of business-cycle theory and modeling than did Keynes's direct contribution in "Notes on the Trade Cycle." He redirected attention from price changes, such as the credit cycle analyzed in his *Treatise on Money,* to output fluctuations. Despite Keynes's concern about possible structural change in his skeptical review of Jan Tinbergen's *Statistical Testing of Business Cycle Theories* (1939), structural macroeconometric modeling drew inspiration from the *General Theory.* Proposals for countercyclical fiscal policy, such as Abba Lerner's functional finance, built on Keynes's preference for output stabilization over annually balanced budgets. Recent work in macroeconomics has examined overlapping contracts and relative wages as sources of money-wage stickiness without money illusion (see JMK VII, chap. 2) and the possibility that increased wage-and-price flexibility would be destabilizing (see JMK VII, chap. 19). Post-Keynesians have followed G. L. S. Shackle in stressing fundamental uncertainty, while fixprice or temporary-equilibrium macroeconomic theorists have taken up the rejection of Walras's Law for effective demands.

Robert W. Dimand

See also AGGREGATE SUPPLY AND DEMAND; BUSINESS CYCLES; CREDIT CYCLE; FISCAL POLICY; EXPECTATIONS; FUNCTIONAL FINANCE; GESELL, SILVIO; GOLD STANDARD; GOLD STANDARD: CAUSES AND CONSEQUENCES; HABERLER, GOTTFRIED [VON]; HAWTREY, RALPH GEORGE; HOBSON, JOHN ATKINSON; INVESTMENT; JOHANNSEN, NICHOLAS AUGUST LUDWIG JACOB; KALECKI, MICHAL; KOOPMANS, TJALLING CHARLES; LACHMANN, LUDWIG MAURITS; LALOR, JOHN; LERNER, ABBA; LIQUIDITY PREMIUM; MACROECONOMETRIC MODELS, HISTORICAL DEVELOPMENT; MARSHALL, ALFRED; MONETARY POLICY; MULTIPLIER; NATURAL RATE

K

OF INTEREST; NEW KEYNESIAN ECONOMICS;
PIGOU, ARTHUR CECIL; POST-KEYNESIAN
BUSINESS-CYCLE THEORY; ROBERTSON, DEN-
NIS HOLME; SAVING EQUALS INVESTMENT;
SAY, JEAN-BAPTISTE; SAY'S LAW; SHACKLE,
GEORGE LENNOX SHERMAN; TINBERGEN, JAN;
UNEMPLOYMENT; WALRAS'S LAW; WICKSELL,
JOHAN GUSTAV KNUT

Bibliography

Blaug, M., ed. 1992. *Pioneers in Economics:
John Maynard Keynes.* Aldershot, Hants,
England: Edward Elgar.

Dimand, R. W. 1988. *The Origins of the Keynesian Revolution.* Stanford: Stanford
Univ. Press.

Hamouda O. F. and J. N. Smithin, eds. 1988.
*Keynes and Public Policy After Fifty
Years.* 2 vols. New York: New York
Univ. Press.

Harrod, R. F. 1951. *The Life of John
Maynard Keynes.* London: Macmillan.

Kahn, R. F. 1984. *The Making of Keynes'
General Theory.* Cambridge: Cambridge
Univ. Press.

Keynes, J. M. 1971–89. *The Collected Writings of John Maynard Keynes.* Edited by
E. S. Johnson and D. E. Moggridge. 30
vols. London: Macmillan (cited by volume as JMK I, II, etc.).

Keynes, M., ed. 1975. *Essays on John
Maynard Keynes.* Cambridge: Cambridge Univ. Press.

Leijonhufvud, A. 1968. *On Keynesian Economics and the Economics of Keynes.*
New York: Oxford Univ. Press.

Meltzer, A. H. 1988. *Keynes's Monetary
Theory.* Cambridge: Cambridge Univ.
Press.

Minsky, H. 1975. *John Maynard Keynes.*
New York: Columbia Univ. Press.

Moggridge, D. E. 1992. *John Maynard
Keynes: An Economist's Biography.* London: Routledge.

Patinkin, D. 1976. *Keynes' Monetary
Thought: A Study of Its Development.*
Durham, N.C.: Duke Univ. Press.

Rymes, T. K., ed. 1990. *Keynes's Lectures,
1932–35.* Ann Arbor: Univ. of Michigan
Press.

Skidelsky, R. 1983–93. *John Maynard
Keynes.* 2 vols. London: Macmillan.

Wood J. C., ed. 1984. *John Maynard Keynes:
Critical Assessments.* 4 vols. Beckenham,
Kent: Croom-Helm.

Kindleberger, Charles Poor (1910–)

Charles P. Kindleberger's most prominent writings in the field of panics, financial crises, and
depressions are *The World in Depression,
1929–1939* and *Manias, Panics, and Crashes.*
Much of his writing in the 1980s, including his
A Financial History of Western Europe, extended these two works. All three books approach the study of bubbles, financial crises,
and depressions from a perspective valuable for
government policy and business practice, eschewing the misanthropic mathematics and
rigid ideologies that mark the work of many
modern writers on these subjects. His detailed
"literary" analysis of these subjects draws on
his strengths as a writer, which include a fond-
ness of irony, a wicked sense of humor, and the
use of colorful quotations found too rarely in
the writings of economists.

Spending his early career in government
during crucial times in international financial
history (at the Federal Reserve Bank of New
York in the late 1930s and the State Department during the Marshall Plan), Kindleberger
developed a practical understanding of the institutional characteristics and policy dilemmas
of international financial markets. Though
Kindleberger left government service permanently in 1948 for a long and distinguished
academic career, his preacademic experience
appears to have been the dominant influence on
his interpretation of financial history.

In *The World in Depression,* Kindleberger
sought to explain why the Great Depression in
the 1930s was so deep and so widespread. The
1929 depression, he maintains, was intimately
bound up in commodity prices and exchange
rates, factors which both Keynesians and Monetarists often ignore. Irreversible price declines,
for example, caused many bank failures in the
early 1930s. The deflationary impact on the
United States, Germany, and the gold bloc of
the sharp depreciation of the pound sterling
(causing appreciation of the dollar, the
Reichsmark, and the gold currencies) by 30
percent from September to December 1931 was
a major turning point of the Great Depression.

The difficulty in the 1930s was the considerable latent instability in the international financial system and the absence of a stabilizer
and international lender of last resort to halt the
financial liquidity squeeze and to prevent financial distress from rolling from one country to
another. Before World War I, Britain stabilized
the world economy, more or less, with the enor-

mous help of the gold-standard mythology, which promoted both stable exchange rates and coordinated macroeconomic policies. In 1929–31, Britain could not, and the United States would not, act as a stabilizer. When every country turned to protect its own national interest, the common international interest suffered disastrously, and with it the private interests of all.

Kindleberger concluded by listing five functions that must be assumed and executed by a single country that is responsible for the international economic system:

1. maintaining a relatively open market for distressed (temporarily oversupplied) goods;
2. providing countercyclical, or at least stable, long-term lending;
3. policing a relatively stable system of exchange rates;
4. ensuring the coordination of macroeconomic policies;
5. acting as a lender of last resort by discounting or otherwise providing liquidity in financial crisis.

Without a powerful leader and strong cooperation among nations to maintain stable international trade and finance, Kindleberger argued, the world-wide depression of the 1930s could occur again.

In his *Manias, Panics, and Crashes,* Kindleberger analyzed the long series of bubbles and financial crises that began with the Mississippi and South Sea Bubbles in 1719 and 1720 and that continue today. His research shows that although modern financial markets are efficient over the long run, they sometimes falter in the short run because of the unavoidable trade-off between liquidity and destabilizing speculation.

The central issue raised by these manias, according to Kindleberger, is whether markets are always rational. Kindleberger's view is that rational action in economics does not imply that all actors have the same information, the same intelligence, the same experience and purposes. Moreover, the fallacy of composition brings it about from time to time that individual actors all act rationally but in combination produce an irrational result, such as standing to get a better view as spectators of a sporting event.

The book uses a model of speculation, credit expansion, financial distress at the peak, and then crisis, ending in panic and crash. The model is drawn from early classical ideas of overtrading, followed by revulsion and discredit, as expressed by Adam Smith and John Stuart Mill, and subsequently by Irving Fisher, and, in our own day, by Hyman Minsky. Kindleberger applies this model to historical experience to illustrate the timelessness of the bubbles and financial crises and to indicate the range of policy implications for preventing bubbles and ameliorating financial crises.

These financial crises also have international components. International connections of these bubbles and crises run through many linkages: trade; capital markets; flows of hot money; changes in central bank reserves, reserves of gold, or foreign exchange; fluctuations in prices of commodities, securities, or national currencies; changes in interest rates; and direct contagion of speculation.

In coping with financial crises, both policymakers and transactors often rely on a lender of last resort to rescue markets from more permanent damage arising from asset deflation and bankruptcy. Kindleberger uses historical episodes to demonstrate the trade-off between having a lender of last resort ready and able to assist in any crisis and the moral hazard that arises from the knowledge that reckless speculative positions in a market will be rescued if markets are threatened with collapse during a financial crisis.

Eric S. Schubert

See also GREAT DEPRESSION IN BRITAIN (1929–1932); GREAT DEPRESSION IN FRANCE (1929–1938); GREAT DEPRESSION IN THE UNITED STATES (1929–1938); INTERNATIONAL LENDER OF LAST RESORT; MISSISSIPPI BUBBLE; SOUTH SEA BUBBLE

Bibliography
Feldstein, M., ed. 1991. *The Risk of Economic Crisis.* Chicago: Univ. of Chicago Press.
Kindleberger, C. P. 1993. 2d ed. *A Financial History of Western Europe.* New York: Oxford Univ. Press.
———. 1985. *Keynesianism vs. Monetarism and Other Essays in Economic History.* London: Allen and Unwin.
———. 1986. *The World in Depression, 1929–1939.* Rev. and enl. ed. Berkeley: Univ. of California Press.
———. 1988. *The International Economic Order.* Cambridge: MIT Press.

———. 1989. *Manias, Panics, and Crashes.* Rev. ed. New York: Basic Books.

Kindleberger, C. P. and J.-P. Laffargue, eds. 1982. *Financial Crises: Theory, History, and Policy.* Cambridge: Cambridge Univ. Press.

Kitchin Cycle

The Kitchin cycle is a cycle in the level of economic activity with a period of about 40 months or 3.5 years. It is named after Joseph Kitchin, a British statistician who identified both minor cycles of 40 months and major cycles of 7 to 10 years. The existence of major cycles had been well established, but the 40-month cycle was a new observation. Kitchin conjectured that major cycles were merely aggregates of two or three minor cycles.

Kitchin examined monthly statistics on bank clearings, commodity prices, and short-term interest rates in the United States and Great Britain from 1890 to 1922. All three series apparently moved together through 40-month cycles. Though the length of any particular cycle might deviate considerably from 40 months, he found that the average length changed little over time. The strong co-movement of the price level and short-term interest rates through the business cycle has come to be known as the "Kitchin Phenomenon."

Kitchin offered little theoretical explanation for the cyclical movements in economic activity. He thought that the capitalist process merely reflected rhythmical movements in mass psychology. The cycles were less than exact because of the nature of human behavior, and because factors like food production might fall out of step with the normal cycle.

In the same 1923 issue of the *Review of Economic Statistics* in which Kitchin published his findings, W. L. Crum examined interest rates on commercial paper and also found an average cycle of 40 months. His study, using periodogram analysis, was more careful and cautious than Kitchin's. He found 40-month cycles only when interest rates were fairly free of extreme deviations. He used monthly data from 1874 to 1913, a period beginning with the restoration of convertibility and ending with the founding of the Federal Reserve System. Panics were found to interrupt and delay the completion of a cycle, while severe panics could even obliterate cyclical movements. Crum also noted that upturns took longer than downturns. Though the data conformed moderately well to 40-month cycles, he hesitated to draw any strong generalizations about business cycles.

Even before Kitchin and Crum, H. S. Jevons (1909) had noted a tendency for British business activity to oscillate with a period of 3.5 years, attributing these cycles to sunspots and prominences. He suggested that fluctuations in the sun's heat affected economic activity primarily through agricultural production.

Joseph Schumpeter expanded on Kitchin's notion of two simultaneous cycles to include three cycles: Kondratieff cycles of 50 to 60 years, Juglar cycles of 9 to 11 years, and Kitchin cycles of about 40 months. Schumpeter attributed all three business cycles to the process of innovation. Differences in the magnitudes of various innovations along with their periods of gestation and absorption imply cycles of different frequencies. Kondratieff cycles are due to major innovations like steam power, railroads, electric power, and others. Juglar cycles are due to less revolutionary innovations. Kitchin cycles are due to innovations of sufficiently small magnitude to be adapted and put into effect relatively quickly.

Rostow attributed the Kitchin cycles in Great Britain during the nineteenth and early twentieth centuries to changing export conditions. But Schumpeter noted that the U.S. economy, which was much less integrated in the world economy at the time than was the British economy's, had much more pronounced cycles than did the British economy. Thus, integration into the world economy with policies of free trade appeared to smooth out or at least moderate economic fluctuations.

Mitchell and Burns found American business cycles to have an average length of four years and a mode of three years. However, they found no evidence of long cycles, which were multiples of the short cycles, as had been suggested by Kitchin and Schumpeter. Mitchell defined a business cycle as the shortest trough-to-trough intervals which exceed a year, a definition later adopted by the National Bureau of Economic Research. Thus, the Mitchell cycle was somewhat different from the Kitchin cycle of Schumpeter's system despite their similar durations. The Mitchell cycle is clearly discernible from the surface movements of time-series data; the Schumpeter-Kitchin cycle is apparent only after filtering the data of the longer cycles.

Modern theorists have attributed business cycles to fluctuating investment, and Kitchin cycles in particular to the accumulation and decumulation of inventories. Abramovitz found a strong relationship between inventory changes and cyclical movements in economic activity. Economic expansions are characterized by inventory buildup and contractions by inventory liquidation. Matthews drew a distinction between inventory investment as the generator of minor cycles and fixed investment as the generator of major cycles.

Inventory investment is the most volatile of all GDP aggregates. Turning points in inventory investment lead to turning points in the business cycle through the multiplier-accelerator mechanism. If actual inventory is below desired inventory holdings, firms respond by increasing their output or by increasing their orders to their suppliers. Thus, production increases, and income rises, creating additional demand. Firms then seek not only to replenish inventories, but to add to their stock of inventory to support increased sales. Initially, inventory investment accelerates, leading to even further growth in output. Eventually, inventories reach desired level, or sales growth slows due to the resource limits of the economy. Inventory investment then begins to contract, leading to a multiplied decline in output and sales. The decline in sales leads to additional inventory liquidation. This contraction continues until inventories are too small relative to sales. When the liquidation eventually slows down, output begins to rise and inventory investment spurs the economy through another cycle.

Linus Yamane

See also AKERMAN, JOHAN HENRIK; BUSINESS CYCLES; HAWTREY, RALPH GEORGE; JUGLAR CYCLE; KONDRATIEFF CYCLES; METZLER, LLOYD APPLETON; MILL, JOHN STUART MITCHELL, WESLEY CLAIR; SCHUMPETER, JOSEPH ALOIS

Bibliography

Abramovitz, M. 1948. "The Role of Inventories in Business Cycles." Occasional Paper, no. 26. New York: NBER.

Burns, A. F. and W. C. Mitchell. 1946. *Measuring Business Cycles.* New York: NBER.

Crum, W. L. 1923. "Cycles of Rate on Commercial Paper." *Review of Economic Statistics* 5:17–27.

Jevons, H. S. 1909. "The Causes of Unemployment. III. Trade Fluctuations and Solar Activity." *Contemporary Review,* August, 165–89.

Kitchin, J. 1923. "Cycles and Trends in Economic Factors." *Review of Economic Statistics* 5:10–16.

Matthews, R. C. O. 1959. *The Business Cycle.* Cambridge: Cambridge Univ. Press.

Metzler, L. A. 1941. "The Nature and Stability of Inventory Cycles." *Review of Economic Statistics* 23:113–20.

Mitchell, W. C. 1927. *Business Cycles: The Problem and its Setting.* New York: NBER.

Rostow, W. W. 1948. *The British Economy of the Nineteenth Century.* Oxford: Clarendon Press.

Schumpeter, J. A. 1939. *Business Cycles: A Theoretical, Historical, and Statistical Analysis of the Capitalist Process.* 2 vols. New York: McGraw-Hill.

Van Duijn, J. J. 1983. *The Long Wave in Economic Life.* London: Allen and Unwin.

Klein, Lawrence Robert (1920–)

Lawrence R. Klein, the 1980 Nobel Memorial Prize laureate and the 1959 recipient of the American Economic Association's John Bates Clark Award, has made profound and far-reaching contributions across a wide spectrum of topics in economic and econometric theory, methodology, and applied econometrics. Probably his most important contributions, however, were made in his pioneering work in the construction of national and international macroeconometric models. Under his leadership, large-scale macroeconometric models have been converted from statistical *curiosa* into powerful analytical instruments for studying fluctuations in business and economic activity. Indeed, the history of macroeconometric modeling is inseparable from the chronology of Klein's contributions.

Born in Omaha, Nebraska, Klein received his B.A. from the University of California in 1942 and his Ph.D. from MIT in 1944. He was the first Ph.D. in economics from that institution and Paul Samuelson's first doctoral student. He spent three years with the Cowles Commission, then at the University of Chicago, among a select and close-knit group which included T. W. Anderson, Kenneth J. Arrow, Trygve Haavelmo, Leonid Hurwicz, Tjalling C. Koopmans, Jacob Marschak, Don Patinkin, Herman Rubin, and Herbert A. Simon, four of whom later became Nobel laureates. Klein left the Cowles Commission in 1947 to spend a year in Norway, followed by a short stint at the National Bureau of Economic Research in New York. He was at the University of Michigan from 1949 to 1954 and at Oxford University from 1954 to 1958. Klein then moved to the University of Pennsylvania, becoming Benjamin Franklin Professor of Economics in 1968, where he remained until his retirement in 1991.

As Klein (1986) himself reports, it was the depression of the 1930s that impelled him to study intensely economics as well as mathematics and statistics at Berkeley. His subsequent work with Samuelson at MIT was intended to gain acceptance for mathematical methods and for Keynesian thinking and to establish its relevance to macroeconomic realities. His graduate research led to a series of important publications on theory and methodology, which brought him immediate recognition internationally. His 1946 article, "Macroeconomics and the Theory of Rational Behavior," was one of the first to introduce the word "macroeconomics" into professional usage. Moreover, it might surprise modern-day critics of macroeconomics to learn that, in this article, Klein addressed the problem of microfoundations of macroeconomics, through what Samuelson (1983) has termed "envelope aggregation." Klein's article, "Theories of Effective Demand and Employment," played an important role in the debate between the Keynesians and their critics, presenting an interpretation of the Keynesian model through a system of equations analogous to Hicks's *IS-LM* diagram. However, the full and best-known presentation of his interpretation of the Keynesian paradigm, along with its requisite microfoundations, appeared in his doctoral dissertation, *The Keynesian Revolution*. Here the Keynesian model was cast in the form of equations, which subsequently could be given a stochastic component and estimated econometrically. This was precisely what he accomplished at the Cowles Commission.

Klein focused there on statistical testing of this mathematically formulated Keynesian paradigm, using the best available statistical theory and empirical data. Indeed, new estimation techniques for systems of simultaneous equations were then being developed at the Cowles Commission. His work culminated in the publication, *Economic Fluctuations in the United States, 1921–1941*. This volume contained three econometric models of varying complexity, which were thought of as business-cycle models, as suggested by Jan Tinbergen's seminal contributions of the 1930s. Even though these early models showed that one could obtain credible empirical counterparts of Keynesian macroeconomic constructs, Klein and others stressed heavily the stability of the system, as implied by the magnitudes of the characteristic roots of the implicit fundamental difference equation of the system. If the characteristic roots were all less than unity in absolute value (modulus, for complex roots), then the solution path of all endogenous variables would describe either damped fluctuations (if there were complex roots) or monotonic convergence (if there were not). If there were two conjugate complex roots with modulus greater than unity, then the system would display *divergent* cycles, while the borderline case of neutral or maintained cycles was thought to be rare and highly improbable. It is worth noting that this analysis was carried out before high-powered computer technology was developed, so that it was the main technique available to study the *dynamic* properties of macroeconometric models.

The next step was the model that Klein constructed with Arthur S. Goldberger, at the University of Michigan. Although today this model, which has come to be known as the Klein-Goldberger model, is used as an expository ("classroom") model, the authors originally regarded it as a "working model." As Klein (1986, 27) wrote, "(i)t streamlined the models built at the Cowles Commission, used some of the survey findings and set about forecasting the economy on a regular basis." The model's first forecast, which applied to the years 1953 and 1954, was important for two reasons: first, it was reasonably accurate, and, second, it helped debunk some gloomy and frightening predictions being made by Colin Clark of a 1929-style collapse, due to the winding down of Korean War expenditures. Moreover, the model was used for rudimentary policy simulations, which can be interpreted either as generalizing the notion of multiplier calculations or alternatively as a type of conditional forecasting. Perhaps the most important use of the Klein-Goldberger model was the demonstration by the Adelmans (1959) that the facts of American business-cycle experience could be accounted for only by incorporating explicitly the stochastic nature of macroeconomic relations. [See Klein (1969) for an updated and slightly extended version of this model.]

After moving to the University of Pennsylvania, Klein shifted his interest to quarterly models to study precisely short-run fluctuations in business activity. Collaborating with a number of associates, he introduced the first generation of the series that has come to be known as the Wharton models. These models increasingly employed "expectations" variables generated from surveys of agents' anticipations; in addition, they went beyond the Klein-Goldberger model in specifying the national-income accounting identities in current values (as contrasted to approximate equalities relating to the price-deflated magnitudes). The model-building enterprise received a significant stimulus when the then current model accurately predicted a sharper than expected recovery from the 1960–61 recession. In 1963, Klein established the Wharton Econometric Forecasting Unit (later Wharton Econometric Forecasting Associates or WEFA), supported by five major business corporations, setting the stage for large-scale commercial forecasting. Backed by newer and more advanced computer technology, macroeconometric modeling was becoming a growth industry, and Klein became progressively more involved, either as a participant, consultant, or dissertation supervisor, in modeling other economies. Whether they were models of other industrialized, developing, or socialist countries, they were all structured to reveal some unique characteristics of the economy under study.

Klein's contributions in developing a *team* approach to macroeconometric model-building also deserve mention. During most of the 1960s, Klein codirected an ambitious team project initiated in 1959, under the sponsorship of the Committee on Economic Stability of the Social Science Research Council. Drawn from several universities and the Brookings Institution, the team successfully created the first large-scale (400 equations in the largest version), short-run forecasting model of the American economy, which came to be known as the SSRC-Brookings (or just Brookings) model. Aspects of the Brookings model, along with substantive results, were published over a decade in three major volumes co-edited by Klein: *The Brookings Quarterly Model of the United States* (1965), *The Brookings Model: Some Further Results* (1969), and *The Brookings Model: Perspective and Recent Developments* (1975). This project marks a milestone in the history of macroeconometric model-building.

Finally, we have Klein's monumental insight (with Bert G. Hickman and other collaborators) of representing the entire world economy as a system of *linked* macroeconometric models of individual countries (or, in some cases, groupings of countries). Of necessity, this was a team effort with many individual collaborators, especially given the presumption that individual model-builders would have a superior knowledge of their home economy's institutions. Project LINK (as it was termed) was launched in the late 1960s as a cooperative venture, with the coordination provided by LINK central, located at the University of Pennsylvania. Over more than two decades, the implicit model of the world economy has expanded from seven countries or large groupings (e.g., the developing countries, the socialist countries, etc.) to 79 macroeconometric models (in 1987) and over 20,000 equations. Moreover, Project LINK has engendered a large literature. An excellent starting point is Hickman's chapter in Bodkin, Klein, Marwah (1991). In recent years, other systems of linked macroeconometric models have appeared, but at a minimum, one can claim for Project LINK that it was the original stimulus or inspiration.

The notion of macroeconometric models is inseparably linked with the name of Lawrence R. Klein, exactly as input-output analysis is linked with that of Wassily Leontief or general-equilibrium models with Léon Walras. Despite ebbs and flows, this concept has been successfully applied to many types of economic questions over the past forty years. Indeed, it has met the market test, as indicated by the rise of consulting companies specializing in macroeconomic forecasts based on macroeconometric models; many would argue that the tools and their uses have also satisfied standards of academic rigor.

Ronald G. Bodkin
Kanta Marwah

See also DIFFERENTIAL AND DIFFERENCE EQUATIONS; DUESENBERRY, JAMES STEMBLE; HAAVELMO, TRYGVE; KOOPMANS, TJALLING CHARLES; MACROECONOMETRIC MODELS, HISTORICAL DEVELOPMENT; MACROECONOMETRIC MODELS, USE OF; TINBERGEN, JAN

Bibliography
Adelman, I. and F. L. Adelman. 1959. "The Dynamic Properties of the Klein-Goldberger Model." *Econometrica* 27:596–625.
Ball, R. J. 1981. "Lawrence R. Klein's Contri-

butions to Economics." *Scandinavian Journal of Economics* 83:81–103.

Bodkin, R. G., L. R. Klein, and K. Marwah. 1991. *A History of Macroeconometric Model-Building.* Aldershot, Hants, England: Edward Elgar.

Duesenberry, J. S., G. Fromm, L. R. Klein, and E. Kuh, eds. 1965. *The Brookings Quarterly Econometric Model of the United States.* Chicago: Rand McNally.

———. 1969. *The Brookings Model: Some Further Results.* Chicago: Rand McNally.

Fromm, G. and L. R. Klein. 1975. *The Brookings Model: Perspective and Recent Developments.* Amsterdam: North-Holland.

Klein, L. R. 1946. "Macroeconomics and the Theory of Rational Behavior." *Econometrica* 14:93–108.

———. 1947a. "Theories of Effective Demand and Employment." *Journal of Political Economy* 55:108–31.

———. 1947b. *The Keynesian Revolution.* New York: Macmillan.

———. 1950. *Economic Fluctuations in the United States: 1921–1941.* New York: Wiley.

———. 1969. "Estimation of Interdependent Systems in Macroeconometrics." *Econometrica* 37:171–92.

———. 1986. "Lawrence R. Klein." In *Lives of the Laureates,* edited by W. Breit and R. W. Spencer, 21–41. Cambridge: MIT Press.

Klein, L. R. and A. S. Goldberger. 1955. *An Econometric Model of the United States, 1929–1952.* Amsterdam: North-Holland.

Samuelson, P. A. 1983. "Rigorous Observational Positivism: Klein's Envelope Aggregation; Thermodynamics and Economic Isomorphisms." In *Global Econometrics: Essays in Honor of Lawrence R. Klein,* edited by F. G. Adams and B. G. Hickman, 1–38. Cambridge: MIT Press.

Kondratieff Cycles

Nikolai D. Kondratieff, a Soviet economist, wrote in the 1920s about the existence and character of pervasive fluctuations in economic activity lasting forty-five to sixty years; and offered a model emphasizing the self-perpetuating nature of these fluctuations. Depending on the context and on the convictions of the user, "Kondratieff Cycles" may refer to the cycles that Kondratieff claimed to have discovered, to his theoretical model of those cycles, or to other purported cycles and models of cycles of similar length. Also known as long cycles and long waves, they should not be confused with long *swings* lasting twenty to twenty-five years.

The behavior of commodity-price indexes in England, France, and the United States from the late eighteenth century through 1920 was the empirical basis for much of Kondratieff's work. These series suggested to him a trough in 1789, a peak in 1814, a trough in 1849, a peak in 1873, a trough in 1896, and a peak in 1920. Usually he located the peaks and troughs of his cycles within intervals of five to seven years encompassing these dates.

Kondratieff purported to show that a number of economic series, including some that measured the volume of real activity, followed a path congruent with the *long waves* in prices. He also alleged that various technological, industrial, sectoral and social phenomena fluctuated synchronously with the long waves.

Kondratieff identified two complete cycles with trough-to-trough durations of sixty years (1789–1849) and forty-seven years (1849–96). He noted that the three rising portions of long cycles revealed by his data, 1789–1814, 1849–73 and 1896–1920, each lasted twenty-four or twenty-five years. These regularities encouraged him to propose a model of periodic long cycles.

Much of Kondratieff's evidence that was not direct price series consisted of series that were functions of the price level: nominal wages, the nominal value of foreign trade, and the inverse of bond prices. For series incorporating a real component—production, consumption and foreign trade—Kondratieff divided his data by population. Then he calculated nine-year moving averages of deviations from linear or higher-order least-squares trend lines. Cycles were discerned from these moving averages of per capita, detrended movements. Kondratieff's methods were taken directly from articles by Warren M. Persons in the first two issues of *Review of Economic Statistics* in 1919.

Kondratieff's Soviet critics, among them Leon Trotsky, were ideologically unwilling to view the downswing after World War I as merely part of a repetitive cycle, rather than the final crisis of world capitalism. Soviet and some Western critics also found fault with Kondratieff's pioneering use of quantitative techniques. Among these critics, Eugen Slutsky was inspired to develop his famous proof that moving averages of random numbers will often exhibit wave-like behavior.

The most telling criticism from Soviet and Western economists, concisely advanced by George Garvy in 1943, was that Kondratieff had failed to establish his case for the series of physical quantities. Few of the production and consumption series he examined actually conformed to the hypothesized cycles. Several moved in exactly the wrong direction. Many, often not mentioned by Kondratieff, exhibited no long cycle at all.

Additional data reconstructed since the end of World War II suggest that real growth rates were the opposite of what Kondratieff supposed. Periods of falling prices in 1814–49 and 1873–96 coincided with unusually rapid growth of real output.

The subsequent course of history has also invalidated Kondratieff's schema. With a few brief and minor interruptions, the price level in every major industrial country rose continuously after reaching a trough in the early 1930s. The regular wave motion of the price level that Kondratieff had perceived for the 140 years from 1780 to 1920 was undone by an upswing that lasted longer than both portions of previous waves and reached levels far above the apparent previous bounds.

Kondratieff was one of the first scholars clearly to distinguish invention from innovation. He perceived a period of intense invention in response to economic pressures over the course of the downswing. He also believed that the downward phases were characterized by severe declines in the relative prices of agricultural goods and by growing concentrations of liquid capital. These phenomena created the conditions for a profitable, readily financed outbreak of innovations and the renewal of investments in long-lived infrastructure projects like transportation networks.

The rising phase was powered by a network of demand effects from these investments. The initiations of expansions in the 1840s and the 1890s had coincided with major gold discoveries and with the addition of new parts of the world to the domain of capitalist trade. Kondratieff viewed both the gold discoveries and the expanding orbit of trade as consequences of the downswing. Once underway, Kondratieff believed the expansion phases were characterized by increasing wars and social upheavals caused by stresses related to the growth of the new in-

novations. These stresses and the eventual saturation of profitable investment opportunities led to the crises that marked the peaks and initial periods of decline of the cycles.

Every item on Kondratieff's list of technical, sectoral, and political features of the long cycles has been subjected to plausible criticism. However, items on the same list have also provided the sources from which others have elaborated their own versions of a long cycle.

Joseph A. Schumpeter was the first to reformulate Kondratieff's ideas. He elaborated the notions of invention as the consequence of decline and innovation as the cause of expansion. Schumpeter repaired a theoretical gap in Kondratieff's work which had relied on questionable arguments about the availability of financing and the profitability of the business climate to explain the simultaneous emergence of spending on infrastructure and on innovation. Instead, Schumpeter argued that innovations naturally cluster around central technical concepts and that each cluster of innovations implies a new technology for long-lived investments. Infrastructure is replaced not because it wears out, but because it is made obsolete, "creatively destroyed," by the new innovations. In this view, the clusters of innovation and the waves of investment in infrastructure are bound together so that they must be simultaneous.

Thus, the upswing starting in 1789 involved canal transportation and factory organization of production. The 1849 upswing involved railroads and the application of related steam and metallurgical technologies to a spectrum of industrial production. After 1896, internal-combustion engines, the exploitation of petroleum, and the development of electricity produced vast, interrelated changes in transportation, communication, infrastructure, household location, and household life.

W. W. Rostow took up the notion that agriculture suffers a relative decline in the downswing and, by implication, relative prosperity in the upswing. In Rostow's version of the long cycle, upswings are characterized by shortages of various raw materials. Investment cycles are driven by efforts to obtain relatively scarce foods or fuels in new ways or from new sources. The relative price structure of raw materials and manufactured goods also has extensive ramifications for the allocation of investment, the domestic and international distributions of income, and the consequent intensity and character of political and military conflicts.

K

David M. Gordon and various coauthors developed models of periodic long cycles driven primarily by changes in the balance of forces struggling over the division of income between worker well-being and the surplus available for growth and investment. Upswings occur under conditions of securely established "social structures of accumulation" that assure high current and prospective levels of profitability. However, the prosperity brought by the upswing tends to undermine the social structure on which it depends. The economic crises of the downswing result from the collapse of that structure and the ensuing struggle to establish a new one.

Jay W. Forrester and his colleagues at the Massachusetts Institute of Technology in the 1970s and early 1980s developed mathematical systems of simultaneous equations that generated fifty-year cycles caused by the dynamics of replacement and obsolescence cycles and by the reinforcing interactions of cycles with different periodicities.

The historical evidence does not conclusively indicate regular, half-century cycles. It is not surprising that price levels exhibit high serial correlation or wave-like behavior. However, even price levels appear to have followed a repetitive wave pattern for only two cycles. Wars and gold discoveries, which decisively influenced the timing of peaks and troughs in price series, may have been endogenous to some cyclical process; but, it is equally probable that they influenced economic events without being caused by them. Although the literature on Kondratieff cycles has not established an unambiguously self-generating cycle, it has provided many rich insights into the processes of capitalist development.

Robert B. Zevin

See also INVESTMENT; JUGLAR CYCLE; KITCHIN CYCLE; KUZNETS, SIMON SMITH; LONG-WAVE THEORIES; REGULATION SCHOOL; ROSTOW, WALT WHITMAN; SCHUMPETER, JOSEPH ALOIS; SLUTSKY, EUGEN; SOCIAL STRUCTURE OF ACCUMULATION

BIBLIOGRAPHY

Barr, K. 1979. "Long Waves: A Selective, Annotated Bibliography." *Review* 2:675–718.
Forrester, J. W. 1971. *World Dynamics.* Cambridge, Mass.: Wright Allen Press.
Garvy, G. 1943. "Kondratieff's Theory of Long Cycles." *Review of Economic Statistics* 25:203–20.
Gordon, D. M. 1990. "Inside and Outside the Long Swing." *Review* 13:452–87.
Kondratieff, N. D. [1925] 1979. "Long Waves in Economic Life." Translation. *Review* 2:519–62.
Persons, Warren M. 1919a. "Indices of Business Conditions." *Review of Economic Statistics* 1:5–107.
———. 1919b. "An Index of General Business Conditions." *Review of Economic Statistics* 1:111–205.
Rosenberg, N. and C. R. Frischtak. 1983. "Long Waves and Economic Growth: A Critical Appraisal." *American Economic Review Papers and Proceedings* 73:146–51.
Rostow, W. W. 1978. *The World Economy: History and Prospect.* Austin: Univ. of Texas Press.
Schumpeter, J. A. 1939. *Business Cycles: A Theoretical, Historical, and Statistical Analysis of the Capitalist Process.* 2 vols. New York: McGraw-Hill.
Slutsky, E. [1927] 1937. "The Summation of Random Causes as the Cause of Cyclic Processes." Translation. *Econometrica* 5:105–46.

Kondratieff, Nikolai Dmitriyevich (1892–1938)

The Russian economist N. D. Kondratieff is known in the Western world for his work on long waves of economic growth. The son of a farmer, Kondratieff was the eldest of ten children. At age seventeen, he enrolled at the St. Petersburg faculty of law, at which M. Tugan-Baranovsky was teaching, to study economics.

After completing his studies, Kondratieff taught at the Faculty of Political Economics and Statistics at the University of St. Petersburg. In 1917, he became Deputy Minister for Food in the Kerensky government. After Kerensky's flight, Kondratieff was imprisoned for several months.

In 1920, he founded the Moscow Business Conditions Institute, which he directed until 1928. Beginning in 1923, he combined this job with a professorship at the agricultural academy. Much of Kondratieff's work at the Institute was devoted to agricultural topics. He tried to obtain accurate statistical information on farming and elaborated a set of price indices, the so-called "peasant indices." In the early

1920s, Kondratieff drafted the first five-year plan for agriculture and firmly opposed the nationalization of agriculture. In 1924, Kondratieff visited universities and institutions in Western Europe and the United States.

Kondratieff's first approximation of a long wave, based on price trends, appeared in his 1922 article "The world economy and its condition during and after the war." Still very cautious, he characterized the long cycles in the capitalist economy only as probable. Published in Russian, the article was not translated.

The idea that there could be a long wave of some forty-five to sixty years duration may have been inspired by Tugan-Baranovsky ([1894] 1913). The possible existence of long cycles was suggested by several other economists, such as Wicksell ([1898] 1936), the Russian Marxist Helphand writing under the name of Parvus, the Dutch Marxist Van Gelderen writing under the pseudonym J. Fedder (1913), Aftalion (1913), Lenoir (1913), and later De Wolff (1924).

Kondratieff's most famous article appeared in 1925 in the first issue of *Voprosy Conjunktury*, the journal of his Conjoncture Institute. This paper was subsequently published in German and an abridged translation in English was printed in 1935. A new complete English translation was published in 1979. At the end of this effort to test for the existence of price and output long waves, Kondratieff concluded they were "at least very probable." But he provided no theoretical explanation of the long cycle.

The reactions of Russian economists to Kondratieff's work were generally negative. The most violent criticisms were partly due to the prediction implied by his theory: the final disintegration of the capitalist system would not occur.

A new paper, presented to the Economic Institute in Moscow in 1926, offered a tentative explanation of the long waves. Kondratieff's theory referred to a long-lasting investment cycle similar to Marx's shorter investment cycle and also mentioned other factors such as wars and gold discoveries. In 1928, he published the most important critique of his work, by D. I. Oparin, along with his own rebuttal.

Shortly thereafter, Kondratieff was removed from his post as director of the Conjoncture Institute. In 1929, the Soviet Russian Encyclopedia declared his theory "wrong and reactionary." He was arrested in 1930 for alleged membership in the illegal "Working Peasants" party. Although no trial was held, Kondratieff was given a seven-year prison sentence. He was in a Moscow prison until 1932 and was subsequently transferred to Suzdal. While in detention, he wrote an unpublished manuscript on economic dynamics.

In 1938, Kondratieff was sentenced to a second term and taken back to Moscow. He died, probably by execution, on 17 September 1938.

Subsequent investigations proved that the "Working Peasants" party never existed. The Supreme Court of the USSR eventually rehabilitated all those (including Kondratieff notably) who had been arrested in 1930–32 for their suspected membership in the party.

Schumpeter linked Kondratieff's name to the long cycles by attaching it to the longest of the three he identified. The empirical evidence for Kondratieff cycles has been criticized by Garvy (1943) and more recently by Lewis (1978), Van Ewijk (1981), Beenstock (1983) and Solomou (1989). Van Duijn (1983) has found strong evidence for long cycles in the world economy, although the evidence is weak at the national level.

Gilbert Ducos
Jacob Van Duijn

See also GREAT DEPRESSION OF 1873–1896; KONDRATIEFF CYCLES; KUZNETS, SIMON SMITH; LONG-WAVE THEORIES; REGULATION SCHOOL; ROSTOW, WALT WHITMAN; SCHUMPETER, JOSEPH ALOIS; TUGAN-BARANOVSKY, MIKHAIL IVANOVICH

Bibliography

Aftalion, A. 1913. *Les crises périodiques de surproduction*. Paris: Rivière.

Beenstock, M. 1983. *The World Economy in Transition*. London: Allen and Unwin.

De Wolff, S. 1924. "Prosperitäts und Depressions perioden." In *Der Lebendige Marxismus: Festgabe zum 70 Geburtstage von Karl Kautsky*, edited by O. Jensen. Jena: Thünngerverlagsanastalt.

Garvy, G. 1943. "Kondratieff's Theory of Long Cycles." *Review of Economic Statistics* 25:203–20.

Kondratieff, N. D. 1922. *Mirovoe khoziaistvo i ego kon'iunktury vo vremia i posle voiny* (The world economy and its condition during and after the war). Vologda: Oblastnoe Otdelenie Gosudartsvennogo Izdatelstva.

———. [1924] 1925. "The Static and Dynamic View of Economics." *Quarterly Journal of Economics* 39:575–83. Translated and abridged from "On the Notion of Economic Statics, Dynamics, and Fluctuations." *Sotsialisticheskoe khoziastvo* 2:349–82.

———. [1925] 1979. "Long Waves in Economic Life." *Review* 2:519–62.

———. [1928] 1984. *The Long Wave Cycle*. Translation. New York: Richardson and Snyder.

Lenoir, M. 1913. *Etudes sur la formation et le mouvement des prix*. Paris: Giard.

Lewis, W. A. 1978. *Growth and Fluctuations 1870–1913*. London: Allen and Unwin.

Solomou, S. 1989. *Phases of Economic Growth, 1850–1973: Kondratieff Waves and Kuznets Swings*. Cambridge: Cambridge Univ. Press.

Tugan-Baranovsky, M. I. [1894] 1913. *Les crises industrielles en Angleterre*. Translation. 2d rev. ed. Paris: Giard & Brière.

Van Duijn, J. J. 1983. *The Long Wave in Economic Life*. London: Allen and Unwin.

Van Ewijk, C. 1981. "The Long Wave: A Real Phenomenon?" *De Economist* 129:324–72.

Van Gelderen, J. [J. Fedder] 1913. "Springvloed: beschouwingen over industrieele ontwikkeling en prijsbeweging" (Observations on industrial development and price fluctuations). *De Nieuwe Tijd*, April–June, 253–77, 369–84, 445–64.

Wicksell, K. [1898] 1936. *Interest and Prices*. Translation. London: Macmillan.

Koopmans, Tjalling Charles (1910–1985)

Tjalling C. Koopmans, winner of the 1975 Nobel Memorial Prize in economics, was born on 28 August 1910. He studied physics at the University of Utrecht and completed his Ph.D. in econometrics at the University of Leiden in 1936. He thereupon began working as an economist with the League of Nations. After the outbreak of World War II, he left the Netherlands for the United States and worked with British Merchant Mission in New York City from 1940 to 1944. From 1944 to 1954, Koopmans was one of the leading researchers of the Cowles Commission at the University of Chicago. The Commission's primary mission was to formalize and extend the approach to econometric modeling proposed by Trygve Haavelmo (1944) to improve upon the methods Jan Tinbergen (1939) had used in his study of the business cycle. When the Cowles Commission was relocated at Yale University (becoming the Cowles Foundation), Koopmans accompanied it to become professor of Economics at Yale. He was director of the Cowles Foundation from 1961 to 1967.

Koopmans's contributions to economics began with his dissertation entitled *Linear Regression Analysis of Economic Time Series*. The dissertation attempted to conflate Ragnar Frisch's confluence analysis with R. A. Fisher's linear-regression formulation using a probabilistic framework (the sampling approach). The "hybrid" formulation from this union was not very successful, but his book had a lasting effect on the then-developing discipline of econometrics by introducing Fisherian linear regression and related techniques into the newly established discipline. Estimation had previously been viewed as curve fitting in the least-squares sense with no probabilistic foundation. The emphasis on linear regression within an explicit probabilistic framework was reinforced by Haavelmo's *The Probability Approach in Econometrics,* whose probabilistic schema provided the foundation for the new discipline.

Koopmans was primarily a methodologist (in a sense, the leading methodologist of his time) of econometric modeling whose writings about the business cycle were a means of promoting a particular approach to empirical modeling. He saw himself as the champion of the econometric approach to the study of business-cycle fluctuations. The approach was founded by Tinbergen, but its sources can be traced back to Frisch ([1933] 1965), Kalecki (1935), and Lundberg ([1937] 1955).

In his first paper on business cycles, Koopmans (1941) responded to Keynes's 1939 critique of the logical foundations of Tinbergen's method. Koopmans conceived of the analysis of the business cycle primarily in terms of an econometric model, because in his view, "it [the business cycle] deals with short-run movements [something which] increases the possibilities of extracting from statistical observations information regarding the relations underlying those movements . . ." (Koopmans 1941, 158). His main objective in this paper was to provide a more coherent framework for the econometric approach to business-cycle research which he viewed as an interplay between statistical techniques and economic theory. The keystone of this approach was the "causal connection between several variables in the form of equations," whose estimated form provides the only sound basis for theory testing. His discussion of the question "when a theory is accepted or rejected on the basis of the empirical evidence" constitutes an early example of the *falsificationist* position with *verification* restricted to nebulous statements of "good fit" and "low standard errors." His attempt to integrate the Neyman-Pearson statistical hypothesis-testing framework into economic-theory testing did not advance beyond a vague formulation.

Koopmans ([1947] 1965) returned to the methodology of econometric modeling in his second important paper on business cycles, a caustic critique of the NBER method of measuring business cycles. One of the best-known papers in the literature, "Measurement Without Theory" was a scathing attack on the statistical techniques employed by Burns and Mitchell (1946). Koopmans criticized Burns and Mitchell and the NBER method on two fronts. The first was for ignoring what we now call *statistical inference* proper and, instead, relying only on *descriptive statistics* whose lack of any probabilistic foundations rendered them inappropriate for inductive inference. The second criticism was that Burns and Mitchell ignored economic theory in their business-cycle analysis. Koopmans characterized their analysis as "measurement without theory."

Vining ([1949] 1965) mounted an ardent reply to Koopmans's criticisms, but the perceived outcome of this well-known controversy was to have far-reaching implications for the development of the methodology of econometric modeling. The perceived outcome was that the probabilistic structure of the data had no real role to play in econometric modeling whose main objective is the quantification of such models. Proper empirical modeling begins with an economic-theoretic model and the only relevant information from the econometric viewpoint was theoretical information. The data could only be used to accept or reject a theoretical model and any use of information contained in the data beyond this was viewed as "data mining." This view was rather unfortunate for the later development of econometric modeling, because instead of an interplay between statistical analysis and economic theory (as originally envisioned by Koopmans), modeling became an exercise in the quantification of economic theory with no essential role attributed to the probabilistic structure of the data.

In his last paper on business cycles, Koopmans (1949) summarized the econometric approach to the business cycle in an attempt to place it in the context of the simultaneous-equation framework then being developed by the Cowles Commission (see Koopmans 1950). He also used the opportunity to discuss several unsolved problems in the latter framework, the most important being that of the "macroeconomic-model-construction process."

Aris Spanos

See also BURNS, ARTHUR FRANK; FRISCH, RAGNAR ANTON KITTEL; HAAVELMO, TRYGVE; KLEIN, LAWRENCE ROBERT; MACROECONOMETRIC MODELS, HISTORICAL DEVELOPMENT; MITCHELL, WESLEY CLAIR; TINBERGEN, JAN

Bibliography

Burns, A. F. and W. C. Mitchell. 1946. *Measuring Business Cycles.* New York: NBER.

Frisch, R. [1933] 1965. "Propagation Problems and Impulse Problems in Dynamic Economics." In *A.E.A. Readings in Business Cycles,* 155–85. Homewood, Ill.: Irwin.

Haavelmo, T. 1944. *The Probability Approach in Econometrics. Econometrica* 12 (Supplement):1–118.

Kalecki, M. 1935. "A Macrodynamic Theory of Business Cycles." *Econometrica* 3:327–44.

Keynes, J. M. 1939. "Professor Tinbergen's Method." *Economic Journal* 49:558–68.

Koopmans, T. C. 1937. *Linear Regression Analysis of Economic Time Series.* Haarlem: Netherlands Economic Institute.

———. 1941. "The Logic of Econometric Business Cycle Research." *Journal of Political Economy* 49:157–81.

———. [1947] 1965. "Measurement Without Theory." In *A.E.A. Readings in Business Cycles,* 186–203. Homewood, Ill.: Irwin.

———. 1949. "The Econometric Approach to Business Fluctuations." *American Economic Review Papers and Proceedings* 39:64–72.

———, ed. 1950. *Statistical Inference in Dynamic Economic Models.* Cowles Commission Monograph no. 10. New York: Wiley.

Lundberg, E. [1937] 1955. *Studies in the Theory of Economic Expansion.*

Reprinted with an additional preface by the author. Oxford: Basil Blackwell.

Morgan, M. S. 1990. *The History of Econometric Ideas.* Cambridge: Cambridge Univ. Press.

Spanos, A. 1989. "On Rereading Haavelmo: A Retrospective View of Econometric Modeling." *Econometric Theory* 5:405–29.

Tinbergen, J. 1939. *Statistical Testing of Business-Cycle Theories.* 2 vols. Geneva: League of Nations.

Vining, R. 1949. "Methodological Issues in Quantitative Economics." In *A.E.A. Readings in Business Cycles,* 204–17. Homewood, Ill.: Irwin.

Kuznets, Simon Smith (1901–1985)

Born in Kharkov, Russia, Simon Kuznets migrated to the United States in 1922. After receiving his B.A., M.A., and Ph.D. from Columbia University, he served on the research staff of the National Bureau of Economic Research (1927–60) and taught at the University of Pennsylvania (1930–54), Johns Hopkins (1954–60), and Harvard (1960–71). He was awarded the Nobel Memorial Prize in 1971 for his empirical research on the economic growth of nations.

Kuznets's interests progressed from business cycles to national income and then to economic growth. He believed that the overriding goal of economic research is to discover verities helpful in formulating welfare-enhancing policies. His adoption of empiricism as well as his distinctive practice of quantitative inquiry reflect his philosophical understanding of their role in research.

This view of economic inquiry as a guide to enlightened policy illuminates both his choice of subjects and his approach. Kuznets was particularly interested in the welfare implications of his research. Economic activity has validity only if it provides goods and services to the current and future residents of a nation. The frequency, volume, distribution, and certainty of provision of these goods and services were thus the objects of his lifetime study. Since these characteristics could not be ascertained through theoretical inquiry alone, empirical analysis was imperative.

Kuznets envisioned three roles for quantitative research: interpretive, generalizing, and predictive. Each was pursued under known assumptions about the goals of economic life and the economic relationships embodied in existing theory. This meant quantitative research must accord with accepted economic theory and the institutional realities within which economic events unfold. Although repeatedly affirming the necessity of theory for empirical research, he expressed a distrust of theory, which arose from unsuccessful attempts to employ theoretical constructs to guide his empiricism.

Although employing economic theory to describe reality, generalize results, and derive ideas for research, he was highly critical of theories based on empirically unsubstantiated assumptions. Thus, he found the Marshallian representative firm of limited use, since industrial firms differ markedly from those in agriculture or trade. Kuznets (1930) also criticized business-cycle theories for relying on equilibrium economics, finding the concept of equilibrium too rigidly static and deterministic to describe dynamic processes that characterize business cycles. By the 1960s, however, he had grown more tolerant, and clearly found some theory useful not only in suggesting relationships to be investigated, but also for categorizing data and classifying activities. Yet Kuznets was a theorist; his empirical efforts would have been much less valuable had he merely reported data without searching for explanations of the relationships discovered.

Kuznets began his work on business cycles by analyzing retail and wholesale trade in the United States during 1919–25. This study revealed that although all branches of trade fluctuated cyclically, wholesale sales and manufacturing output varied more widely than did retail sales. This observation inspired Kuznets to construct a partial explanation of the business cycle.

A useful theory of the business cycle, Kuznets felt, required the assumption that an initial change in prices, in order to trigger an expansion, must occur in conjunction with a series of favorable circumstances. This assumption permitted the expansion to be explained in terms of successive changes in output, business confidence, wage payments, and sales.

Kuznets's innovation was to ascribe the dampening of an expansion to differences in the increase of business activity at different stages of distribution. These caused retailers and wholesalers to accumulate inventory, and, thus, induced a slowing and eventual downturn. Thereafter, the factors that had reinforced the upward trend could also explain the ensuing depression.

Seasonal Variations in Industry and Trade extended this theme. Seasonal variations were related to cyclical fluctuations through stocks of commodities, idle equipment, and a seasonal labor surplus. Kuznets discovered that industries requiring large capital stocks tend to react to a cyclical increase in demand with even larger increases in demand for equipment than those employing small capital stocks. Thus, capital-goods industries show larger cyclical swings than consumer-goods industries. Industries subject to seasonal variations cannot easily adjust to unexpected changes in off-season demand and, therefore, maintain significant inventories. However, these stocks may fuel cyclical activity by compounding random shocks to initiate a cycle (Kuznets 1933, 355–61).

From this early concern with business cycles, Kuznets's interests began to shift. To analyze long-term trends, Kuznets separated time series into secular, seasonal, and cyclical elements. These are the subjects of *Cyclical Fluctuations: Retail and Wholesale Trade, Secular Movements in Production and Prices,* and *Seasonal Variations in Industry and Trade.* Although drawn to these subjects through his interest in business cycles, these studies led Kuznets to discover and describe certain variations in economic and demographic variables which now bear his name.

In fitting a trend curve to United States data from 1865 to 1925, Kuznets discovered the persistence of certain long-term phenomena he named secondary secular movements. Production and consumption data for a large number of commodities and several countries were characterized by extended periods of ebb and flow lasting 18–25 years (Kuznets 1930, 77–197). He hesitated to identify these movements as "cycles" since he had not determined the existence or identity of the forces endowing these swings with self-initiating and self-perpetuating characteristics. He devised a hypothesis relating secondary secular movements to each other and provisionally explaining the long-term continuation and eventual termination of an expansion.

Kuznets begins by assuming a prolonged period of price increases. These cause real wages to fall since money wages do not increase as much as prices in an inflationary period. With retail prices rising less rapidly than wholesale prices, the costs of production (mainly determined by money wages) rise less than the value of output. The resulting increase in profits accelerates business activity and raises output. The increased output and the aforementioned redistribution from wage earners to profit earners combine to cause the sales and output of consumer goods to increase while the proportion of earnings devoted to saving declines.

Concomitantly, employment increases with attempts to increase output and capitalize on improved profit opportunities. The lags in translating higher prices into increased profits and higher profits into increased production lead to temporary shortages which cause prices to rise further. These lags and the differential changes in the output of producer and consumer goods prolong the upswing in prices, profits, output, employment, etc. Two characteristics of this acceleration eventually slow down the expansion: the decrease in productivity following the increase in employment and the decline in the rate of growth of the money supply (Kuznets 1930, 207–58).

Thus, Kuznets provisionally explained the nature and dynamics of the relationship between a series of variables. He concluded that, while the data had not revealed the source of these long-term movements, they had indicated the forces prolonging an expansion, once begun, and others that eventually caused a contraction.

Kuznets extended his investigation of secondary secular movements by examining data on population, flows of goods and services to consumers, net capital formation and its components, immigration and foreign trade, and investment. These variables exhibited long swings which Kuznets explained by arguing that a sustained expansion in the per-capita availability of goods and services to consumers causes, after a lag, prolonged increases in immigration and, thereafter, in the rate of net population growth. Subsequently, this increase in population induces similar increases in residential and other construction as well as "population-sensitive" capital expenditures by railroads. These in turn cause inverted long swings in other forms of capital formation and, hence, in per-capita consumption. This development would then stimulate another long swing (Kuznets [1958] 1965, 348–49).

Curiously, Kuznets eschewed any attempt at weaving into this theory the characteristics he had focused on in his 1930 study—prices, profits, real and money wages, productivity, and income distribution. His later work centered on broad trends in demographic and economic variables. His examination of the nature of capital formation and financing led to the discovery that any self-perpetuating mechanism apparent in long swings before World War I had since disappeared (Kuznets 1961, 349). This was not to say that long swings no longer exist but merely that the aforementioned relationships between per-capita consumption and immigration and between per-capita consumption and population growth were no longer evident.

Moses Abramovitz (1959, 1961, 1968) and Brinley Thomas (1972, 1973) extended the analysis of secondary secular movements, now named "Kuznets cycles." Abramovitz linked long swings to changes in the rates of growth of labor and capital productivity while Thomas focused on the "push" elements causing migration from countries of the Old World. Meanwhile, Roger Bird et al. and Irma Adelman argued that long swings had never existed and had been generated by the smoothing techniques employed. However, others maintain that long swings do exist in the raw data.

Kuznets's major contributions lay in the pursuit and practice of careful empirical analysis of economic phenomena and in the construction of theories based on its results. Although his business-cycle analysis was rapidly overshadowed, "Kuznets cycles" continue to engage professional attention.

Vibha Kapuria-Foreman

See also ABRAMOVITZ, MOSES; KONDRATIEFF CYCLES; LONG-WAVE THEORIES; MITCHELL, WESLEY CLAIR; THOMAS, BRINLEY

Bibliography

Abramovitz, M. 1959. Statement in *Hearings on Employment, Growth and Price Levels,* 411–66. United States Congress, Joint Economic Committee. 86th Cong. 1st sess., part 2.

———. 1961. "The Nature and Significance of Kuznets Cycles." *Economic Development and Cultural Change* 9:225–48.

———. 1968. "The Passing of Kuznets Cycles." *Economica* 35:349–67.

Adelman, I. 1965. "Long Cycles—Fact or Artifact?" *American Economic Review* 55:444–63.

Bird, R. C., M. J. Desai, J. J. Enzler, and P. J. Taubman. 1965. "Kuznets Cycles in Growth Rates: The Meaning." *International Economic Review* 6:229–39.

Easterlin, R. A. 1966. "Economic-Demographic Interactions and Long Swings in Economic Growth." *American Economic Review* 56:1063–1104.

Harkness, J. P. 1968. "A Spectral-Analytic Test of the Long Swing Hypothesis in Canada." *Review of Economics and Statistics* 50:429–36

Kapuria-Foreman, V. 1992. "The Empiricism of Simon Kuznets." In *Perspectives on the History of Economic Thought,* edited by S. T. Lowry. Vol. 8, 51–60. Brookfield, Vt.: Edward Elgar.

Kuznets, S. S. 1926. *Cyclical Fluctuations: Retail and Wholesale Trade, United States, 1919–25.* New York: Adelphi.

———. 1930. *Secular Movements in Production and Prices.* Boston: Houghton Mifflin.

———. 1933. *Seasonal Variations in Industry and Trade.* New York: NBER.

———. 1946. *National Income: A Summary of Findings.* New York: NBER.

———. 1952. "Long Term Changes in the National Income of the United States since 1870." In *Income and Wealth of the United States: Trends and Structure,* edited by S. Kuznets, 29–241. Cambridge: Bowes and Bowes.

———. 1953. *Economic Change: Selected Essays in Business Cycles, National Income and Economic Growth.* New York: Norton.

———. [1958] 1965. "Long Swings in Population Growth and Related Economic Variables." In *Economic Growth and Structure: Selected Essays,* 328–78. New York: Norton.

———. 1961. *Capital in the American Economy: Its Formation and Financing.* Princeton: Princeton Univ. Press.

———. 1972. *Quantitative Economic Research: Trends and Problems.* New York: NBER.

Lewis, W. A. and P. J. O'Leary. 1955. "Secular Swings in Production and Trade, 1870–1913." *Manchester School of Economic and Social Studies* 23:113–52.

Thomas, B. 1972. *Migration and Urban Development: A Reappraisal of British and American Long Cycles.* London: Methuen.

———. 1973. *Migration and Economic Growth: A Study of Great Britain and the Atlantic Economy.* 2d ed. Cambridge: Cambridge Univ. Press.

L

Lachmann, Ludwig Maurits (1906–1992)

A most distinctive and unorthodox representative of the Austrian school of economics, Ludwig Lachmann combined elements of the Austrian business-cycle theory with certain Keynesian ideas in a manner calculated to unsettle both Austrians and Keynesians. Lachmann studied economics in his native Germany under Werner Sombart, a bitter opponent of the Austrian school. His interest in the Austrians led Lachmann to the London School of Economics, where F. A. Hayek had become a dominant figure. In 1948, Lachmann left England to accept a teaching post in South Africa, which became his permanent domicile, though in later life he lectured and taught extensively in the United States.

The central element of Lachmann's approach is an extreme subjectivism derived from, but going beyond, Hayek ([1937] 1948) and Mises (1966). Lachmann viewed the economic choices of individuals as inherently unpredictable and unamenable to functional representation. Economists are, thus, unable to predict, and can only hope to achieve a kind of understanding, or *Verstehen*, as Weber called it. Lachmann deprecated equilibrium models as artificial constructs which abstract from the essential conditions in which economic activity takes place: time, ignorance, and uncertainty.

This view of the world and of economics perhaps most closely resembles that of G. L. S. Shackle—another student of Hayek's in the 1930s—who accepted Keynes's message less equivocally than Lachmann, but without completely discarding Hayek's teaching either. In this synthesis of Keynes and Hayek, the important message of the *General Theory,* made fully explicit in Keynes's 1937 paper, is the radically uncertain nature of the economic environment.

In Lachmann's view, the Austrian theory of the business cycle explains only the boom and the upper turning point of the cycle. An artificial boom stimulated by credit expansion proves unsustainable when the expansion of credit can no longer make up the difference between planned investment and voluntary savings. Some investment projects must be abandoned and resources must be reallocated from investment- to consumption-goods industries. The reallocation entails a period of liquidation and recession.

However, some Austrians, including Hayek, recognized that the liquidation could create further financial distress which may induce what they called a *secondary deflation*. This phase Lachmann was willing to analyze using a Keynesian approach—the key point being that the fundamentally uncertain environment in which entrepreneurs must operate precludes the formation of a self-consistent pattern of expectations that would allow a full-employment equilibrium to be achieved.

While other Austrians were prepared to concede that a process of secondary deflation could justify antideflationary monetary and fiscal policies that they normally rejected, Lachmann went further in agreeing with Keynes that in a state of depression, market forces might be too weak to restore the economy to full employment. A full-employment equilibrium, as Hayek ([1937] 1948) observed, requires that individual expectations of future prices be in agreement. Otherwise the mutual consistency of plans necessary for a state of equilibrium is impossible. But there is no market mechanism to ensure such a mutual correspondence. If expectations are badly confused by a period of deflation and depression, the correspondence of expectations may never be restored spontaneously.

Another noteworthy contribution of Lachmann's was his refutation of Sraffa's famous critique of the concept of the natural rate of interest. Sraffa (1932) alleged that the natural rate of interest was itself a purely monetary concept since in a barter economy there would exist no unique rate of interest, but rather a multitude of own rates corresponding to the intertemporal rates of substitution between each commodity. However, Lachmann (1956, 76–77) pointed out that, in equilibrium, a unique rate of interest would exist even for a barter economy. The natural rate of interest is not, as Sraffa had asserted, merely an average of these "own rates," it is the result of intertemporal arbitrage that would, in equilibrium, equalize the expected rate of return from holding all durable assets. The defect in the concept of a natural rate of interest was therefore not, as Sraffa had argued, that it pertained to a monetary economy, but that it could be defined only in a state of equilibrium, a concept that Lachmann rejected as useless for dynamic economic analysis.

While originally advanced as a criticism of some Austrian economists, such as von Mises, who insisted that market forces were universally equilibrating, Lachmann's argument against equilibrium analysis is also an implicit criticism of the rational-expectations approach and New Classical business-cycle theories. However antithetical much of his methodological position may be to modern research techniques, those seeking an alternative to the rational-expectations approach to business-cycle analysis may well find in Lachmann's work insights that can be usefully deployed in a more rigorous modeling strategy than Lachmann was willing to countenance.

David Glasner

See also AUSTRIAN THEORY OF BUSINESS CYCLES; EXPECTATIONS; HAYEK, FRIEDRICH AUGUST [VON]; KEYNES, JOHN MAYNARD; MISES, LUDWIG EDLER VON; NATURAL RATE OF INTEREST; PUMP-PRIMING; RATIONAL EXPECTATIONS; RÖPKE, WILHELM; SHACKLE, GEORGE LENNOX SHARMAN; SRAFFA, PIERO

Bibliography
Hayek, F. A. [1937] 1948. "Economics and Knowledge." Chap. 2 in *Individualism and Economic Order*. Chicago: Univ. of Chicago Press.
Keynes, J. M. 1937. "The General Theory of Employment." *Quarterly Journal of Economics* 52:209–23.
Kirzner, I., ed. 1986. *Subjectivism, Intelligibility and Understanding: Essays in Honor of Ludwig Lachmann*. New York: New York Univ. Press.
Lachmann, L. M. 1956. *Capital and its Structure*. London: Bell and Sons.
———. 1976. "From Mises to Shackle: An Essay." *Journal of Economic Literature* 14:54–62.
———. 1977. *Capital, Expectations, and the Market Process: Essays on the Theory of the Market Economy*. Edited with an introduction by W. Grinder. Kansas City: Sheed Andrews and MacMeel.
Mises, L. von. 1966. *Human Action*. 3d ed. Chicago: Regnery.
Shackle, G. L. S. 1972. *Epistemics and Economics*. Cambridge: Cambridge Univ. Press.
Sraffa, P. 1932. "Dr. Hayek on Money and Capital." *Economic Journal* 42:42–53.

Lalor, John (1814–1856)

John Lalor was born in Dublin. After working in Ireland for the Poor Law Commission, he moved to England and became a journalist, writing on both religious and economic matters. His writings on religion were in connection with the Unitarian cause which he had embraced in place of Roman Catholicism (1852, 318) and he became editor of *The Inquirer*, a Unitarian newspaper. The bulk of his economic writings are likely to remain unidentified as they were published anonymously in the *Morning Chronicle*.

However, in 1852, Lalor published *Money and Morals*, which undoubtedly summarized his position not only on the central questions of macroeconomics but also on a number of religious issues. This remarkable book, which seems to have remained unknown to twentieth-century economists until its rediscovery by Bernard Corry (in the nineteenth century it had been noted by Torrens), draws together the influence of a large number of economic writers including Tooke, Blake, Senior, Mill, Sismondi, and even Carlyle (to whom the book is dedicated). Although the influence of each of these writers is discernible in his masterpiece, the key influence upon him was undoubtedly Chalmers—fittingly, since Chalmers combined macroeconomic with religious controversy.

Lalor attributed economic fluctuations, and effective-demand failure (which he regards as a perpetual problem), to excessive capital accumulation. He distinguished between the act of saving and the act of investment; and he believed that there is an optimal capital/GNP ratio, so that if capital is accumulated beyond this point the return will fall and large amounts of capital will lie idle. This not only reduces demand in commodity markets but makes recurrent economic crises inevitable.

Once excessive capital accumulation has depressed the return sufficiently, the money market is in an "electric" state awaiting a storm. Eventually some apparently new field of investment opportunity opens up, and money capital pours in. Expenditure of the capital which had been awaiting investment raises income, but because many of the projects will not be successful the capital thus expended is not returned to the national capital stock. (In other words, the earnings on the projects will be insufficient even to amortize the investment, let alone to yield a return.) The capital destruction involved thus lowers the capital/income ratio below its optimum level. The trough of the business cycle follows, but saving, especially by the professional classes and by fixed-income recipients, which is primarily a function of income (and such incomes are largely maintained despite the slump), continues in the trough and the national capital stock is restored. However, the capital-income ratio continues rising past its equilibrium level until only very small returns are obtainable. Entrepreneurial expectations once again become extremely susceptible to any suggestion of new investment outlets. In the event of these being perceived, the investment-demand schedule shifts to the right and a speculative boom again ensues, the boom breaking when entrepreneurial expectations are not realized.

To the twentieth-century reader, the parallels between Lalor's text and Keynes's *General Theory* are quite extraordinary. Both consumption and saving are functions of income and the investment-demand schedule shifts about with entrepreneurial expectations. Stability in the level of income can only be achieved when expectations are fulfilled. Saving is not interest-inelastic. The notion that investment expenditure raises the level of income, and thus of consumption out of that income, is central to the work. Moreover, both of Lalor's remedies for the economic illness have a decidedly Keynesian ring. The first is increased government expenditure (though in Lalor's case this is to be, in particular, military spending—to defend democracy against the new French emperor); the second is to reduce speculative activity to stabilize the investment-demand function. In this latter connection, Lalor's religious interests are evoked; he writes extensively about the need for a moral revival, believing that this can be based on ecumenism, rather than upon sectarian Christianity, which will have the beneficial effect of bringing out all that is vital to society in the Christian religion.

Lalor was influenced not only by Christianity but also by the events through which he had lived as an economic journalist, notably the railway boom of the 1840s and the vicissitudes of the cotton industry. However, the end result of his journalistic musings upon this historical era was a work which, as its rediscoverer Bernard Corry has noted, deserves to stand alongside the other great monetary contributions of the nineteenth century.

D. P. O'Brien

Bibliography
Corry, B. A. 1962. *Money, Saving and Investment in English Economics 1800–1850.* London: Macmillan.
Lalor, J. 1852. *Money and Morals: A Book for the Times.* London: John Chapman.

Lange, Oskar (1904–1965)

Born in Tomaszow in 1904, Lange pursued his studies at the University of Cracow, where in 1926 he became assistant professor of economics. In 1937, he left Poland to become professor at the University of Chicago. A militant socialist, he returned to Poland after the war, engaging actively in politics, teaching, and research. In 1956, he became deputy chairman of the Council of State of the Polish People's Republic—a largely ceremonial position.

All his works reflected his interest in socialist economic theory. His classic article in this field was published in 1936. While at Chicago, he worked on the theory of interest, price flexibility, and equilibrium, publishing a synthesis of his research, *Price Flexibility and Full Employment,* in 1944.

Throughout his career, Lange was interested in economic cycles. In 1928, he wrote a thesis on Polish economic cycles after World War I, and in 1931 he studied economic cycles in a work on general economic equilibrium. After analyzing the dynamic equilibrium of an economy, he considered disequilibrium situations, or, in his words, "deviations from the state of equilibrium," which was the context in which he analyzed crises and business cycles.

In 1941, he reviewed Schumpeter's work on business cycles. After outlining Schumpeter's view of the cycle as the result of waves of innovation, he agreed that Kondratieff's long cycles could be the historical result of such waves, but maintained that Kitchin's cycles were too short to result from such waves. Attributing the cycle rather to investment-rate variations (with reference to Kaldor and Kalecki), he supported the hypothesis that the latter may, to a large extent, be caused by fluctuations in the innovation rate, which, in turn, depends on the risk of failure. However, his main criticism of Schumpeter was the lack of an unemployment theory in his explanation of the cycle. For Lange, fluctuations in employment (reflecting fluctuations in production) are the primary indicator of business cycles. Thus, employment must rise in the prosperity phase. But in the Schumpeterian view there is "a fall of real income consumed during prosperity" due to bidding for resources by innovators, which implies that consumption and employment will fall. Since employment is observed to increase during the recovery and prosperity phases, the Schumpeterian view cannot explain the observed cyclical fluctuations in employment.

Lange's review of Kalecki was the starting point for his own later reflections on the cycle. Kalecki's initial model—based on the lagged adjustment of the capital stock—presupposes an economy without trend, in which periods of capital expansion are followed by periods of decumulation. Since the statistical data show no drop in the stock of capital, Lange suggested that the model be made more realistic by introducing technical progress and the growth of natural resources and population, which would moderate both the fall of profitability and the decline in investment.

All Lange's later work in this field concerned endogenous cycles with capital accumulation, ignoring monetary and financial factors. In a subsequent outline of Kalecki's cycle thory, which he often reproduced in later years, he underscored the importance of an upward trend

in the economy (which Kalecki himself had subsequently adopted) and showed that for statistically significant values in the coefficients of the model, the process must be cyclical. Referring to Marx's enlarged reproduction theory, he proposed a growth model embodying both the cycle and the trend.

Lange developed this idea in his "Model of Economic Growth," using Leontieff's model, which he identified with Marx's schemes of reproduction, as a starting point. He began with a dynamic, n-sector input-output model, introducing investment and capital coefficients. To eliminate consumption from the balance-sheet equations, Lange defined, for every branch, a gross investment rate (the difference between gross output and consumption). He did not distinguish between intermediate consumption and the creation of fixed capital, referring instead to Marx's notion of constant capital. Working with a continuous-time model, he supposed that production was an exponential function of time, each sector having its own gross-product growth rate. This leads to a system of n first-order homogeneous differential equations with n unknowns. The solution of this system gives n roots of which some can be real (corresponding to trends) and others complex (corresponding to cycles). The combination of those rates (a linear combination in fact), makes production in each sector follow a path that is a combination of a trend and a cycle. As time passes, the greatest absolute values of growth coefficients will dominate.

After establishing the theoretical relationship between trend and cycle, Lange refers to reality by invoking the fact that cycles of varying length coexist in capitalist economies.

This mathematical demonstration of the possibility of cycle-trend interaction is of interest because it disaggregates the overall movement of the economy into endogeneous sector-by-sector output paths.

Conscious of the mathematical difficulties that arise in analyzing and solving systems of differential equations, Lange returned to Marx's schemes of reproduction and reduced his model to two sectors: one producing capital goods, and the other consumer goods. Aggregating the economy into only two sectors, he did not find any trend-cycle combination because of the necessary existence, in the solution of such a two-equations system, of two conjugated roots if complex. In that situation he supposes that the capital-goods sector does not use consumption goods, which allows him to find two well-defined real roots. The solutions he obtained in this way represent the rates of production growth for every sector, both being a function of the gross investment rates of the two sectors. This was the basis of his argument that cycles exist under capitalism but not under socialism. He emphasized that in a planned economy the decision maker could ensure the stability of investment rates, while in a capitalist economy this rate fluctuates because of variations in profitability.

He retained to the end the conviction that only the market economy is subject to cycles. In one of his last articles (1967, 159), he wrote: "The iterative market processes do operate with significant delays and oscillations and do not necessarily converge. This produces for example the 'cobweb' type of cycle, stock cycles, re-investment cycles, as well as the general overall business cycle."

It was only in conjunction with capital renewal that Lange came close to admitting the possibility of cycles in a planned economy ([1959] 1961, 1969). He maintained, however, that such fluctuations would diminish if not amplified by business cycles.

The importance of Lange's work lies in the combination (rare in business-cycle models) of nonlinearities and a sectoral approach. The solution of this type of model is very complex. Recent progress in the treatment of nonlinearities in a disaggregated approach, building on the foundations laid by Lange, may lead to new insights in business-cycle analysis.

Alain Alcouffe
Andrzej Dudzinski

See also BUSINESS CYCLES IN SOCIALIST ECONOMIES; COBWEB CYCLE; GOODWIN, RICHARD MURPHY; KALECKI, MICHAL; NONLINEAR BUSINESS-CYCLE THEORIES; SCHUMPETER, JOSEPH ALOIS; TRENDS AND RANDOM WALKS

Bibliography

Lange, O. 1928. *Koniunktura w zyciu gospodarczym Polski 1923–27* (The business cycle in the economic life of Poland 1923–27). Doctoral Thesis. University of Cracow.
———. [1931] 1973. *Statystyczne badanie koniunktury gospodarczej* (Statistical investigation of the business cycle). In *Dziela* (Works). Vol. 1. Warsaw: PWN.
———. [1936–37] 1938. "On the Economic Theory of Socialism." In O. Lange and F. M. Taylor, *On the Economic Theory of Socialism*, 55–143. Minneapolis: Univ. of Minnesota Press.
———. 1941a. Review of *Business Cycles: A Theoretical, Historical and Statistical Analysis of the Capitalist Process*, by J. A. Schumpeter. *Review of Economic Statistics* 23:190–93.
———. 1941b. Review of *Essays in the Theory of Economic Fluctuations*, by M. Kalecki. *Journal of Political Economy* 49:279–85.
———. 1944. *Price Flexibility and Full Employment*. Bloomington, Ind.: Principia Press.
———. [1958] 1961. "Michal Kaleckiego model cyklu koniunturalnego." In *Pisma ekonomiczne i spoleczne* (Social and economic writings), 264–79. Warsaw: PWN.
———. 1959. *Introduction to Econometrics*. London: Pergamon Press.
———. [1959] 1961. "Model wzrostu gospodarczego" (A model of economic growth). In *Pisma ekonomiczne i spoleczne* (Social and economic writings), 287–312. Warsaw: PWN.
———. 1967. "The Computer and the Market." In *Socialism, Capitalism and Economic Growth: Essays Presented to Maurice Dobb*, edited by C. H. Feinstein, 158–61. Cambridge: Cambridge Univ. Press.
———. 1969. *Theory of Reproduction and Accumulation*. London: Pergamon Press.
———. 1970. *Introduction to Economic Cybernetics*. London: Pergamon Press.

Lavington, Frederick (1881–1927)

Frederick Lavington was perhaps the most orthodox and certainly the most self-effacing of Alfred Marshall's Cambridge disciples. His orthodoxy and self-effacement were typified by his statement, "It's all in Marshall if one only digs deeply enough" (W[ithers] 1927, 504).

Despite his extreme modesty, Lavington achieved considerable acclaim for his book, *The English Capital Market*. Lavington there presents a comprehensive view of how the English capital market allocated the savings of individuals to finance the most promising opportunities for investment by business. This account included a detailed analysis of the role of the British banking system in this process. It also entailed a careful presentation of the

Cambridge version of the quantity theory, including an almost unexceptionable statement of the marginal conditions to be satisfied by a holder of money in equilibrium and a recognition that the rate of interest was the price of *holding* money.

Besides his elegant formulation of the Marshallian quantity theory and the cash-balance approach to the demand for money, Lavington also offered numerous insights into the influence of the monetary system on the business cycle. He argued that the banking system, within the loose constraints of the gold standard, would always seek to expand its lending, thereby causing prices to rise and output and employment to expand. To counter this tendency of the banking system, Lavington proposed that the Bank of England restrain lending in boom periods by nudging interest rates upward to prevent the overexpansion from occurring to begin with.

Lavington followed up these comments on business cycles and countercyclical policy in *The English Capital Market* with a short book on the subject, *The Trade Cycle*. The latter book elaborated on the Marshallian theory that the business cycle is generated by alternating periods of excessive optimism, in which optimism breeds optimism, and excessive pessimism, in which pessimism breeds pessimism. He also explored the reasons why nominal disturbances caused real disturbances. Disturbances could be cumulative, as Lavington (1922, 23) put it, because "the inactivity of all is the cause of the inactivity of each. No entrepreneur can fully expand his output until others expand their output."

Despite his disclaimers of originality, Lavington made an important contribution in explicitly stating, while also refining and extending, the Cambridge oral tradition on the theory of money and business cycles that Marshall never set down in published form. Had he lived longer, Lavington might well have developed that tradition further, if only to defend Marshallian orthodoxy against the Keynesian uprising of the 1930s. Sadly, serious illness and premature death cut short Lavington's career before the faithful promise of his early work could be fully realized.

David Glasner

See also CENTRAL BANKING; EXPECTATIONS; MONETARY POLICY; MARSHALL, ALFRED; PIGOU, ARTHUR CECIL

Bibliography
Lavington, F. 1921. *The English Capital Market*. London: P. S. King.
———. 1922. *The Trade Cycle*. London: P. S. King.
W[ithers], H. 1927. "Frederick Lavington" [obit.] *Economic Journal* 37:503–05.

Law, John (1671–1729)

John Law, an outstanding monetary theorist, was the principal personality behind Europe's first major stock-market boom and collapse, that of the Mississippi Company, during the period 1718–20. In Britain, the South Sea Company, modeling its debt-management strategy on the Mississippi Company, produced a similar boom and collapse, known as the South Sea Bubble, in 1720.

1720 was the year of John Law. In early January 1720, he was appointed Controller General of Finances in France, a position akin to that of prime minister, by a grateful French crown. By December, Law was fortunate to escape with his life as he fled from France.

Because of the failure of the Mississippi System, Law has often been dismissed as a monetary "crank." Analysis of his writings and an examination of the Mississippi System show that he made a serious attempt to solve the two macroeconomic problems then facing France: underutilized resources and a staggering national debt.

Background

Law was born in Edinburgh, the son of a goldsmith. Goldsmiths then acted as rudimentary bankers, so that the young Law learned the basic elements of banking. During his early career he acquired a reputation as a rake and a brilliant gambler. He was sentenced to death in London for killing a rival, but escaped from prison to the Continent where he toured many of the major financial centers, building up his knowledge of the different banking techniques of the time.

On returning to Scotland, he proposed the establishment of a land bank, a proposal he made in his first major monetary work, *Money and Trade Consider'd with a Proposal for Supplying the Nation with Money* (1705). The Scottish Parliament, preoccupied with the impending union with England, rejected his proposal. Undeterred, Law then attempted to persuade other European governments of the merits of his money and banking proposals.

Ultimately, in 1716, the Regent, Philip Duke of Orleans, allowed him to establish the Bank Général in France. Eschewing his idea for a land bank, Law modeled the Bank Général on the Bank of England. Despite a small capital base, the Bank Général was successful in issuing banknotes that had a guarantee of specie convertibility. The success of Law's banking operations encouraged the Regent to allow Law to establish, in August 1717, the Compagnie d'Occident, one of whose objectives was to develop the trading privileges of French Louisiana—a land mass corresponding to roughly half of the United States (excluding Alaska). The capital of this company (100 million livres) was subscribed for in *billets d'état*, which were part of the French government's floating debt. The swapping of government debt for shares in the company shows that debt management had become an important element of Law's financial policies.

By a series of takeovers, Law turned his company into a huge conglomerate which controlled all the colonial trading companies, the tax farms, the mint, and the French national debt. Shares in the company rose from 350 livres in 1717 to 10,000 livres in 1720. In February 1729, the Bank Général, which had been renamed the Bank Royale, merged with the Compagnie des Indes (formerly the Compagnie d'Occident) and became known as the Mississippi Company.

What Law was attempting to achieve through the Mississippi System can only be understood by examining Law's economic theory.

Law's Economic Theory

When writing *Money and Trade*, Law attempted to show that the underutilization of resources in Scotland was due to a shortage of money and high interest rates. Money, in his view, drove trade (a synonym for economic activity). Law was the first economist to use the term "the demand for money," which was "proportion'd to people, land or product" (Law [1703–04] 1994, 76–77; 1934, 190: 100, 139, 158, 160). Expanding the money supply, which would reduce the interest rate, would stimulate trade, ultimately increasing the demand for money. In his view, increasing the money stock would not be inflationary until economic activity was sufficient to fully utilize a country's economic resources. In this respect Law's theory resembles Keynes's theory. However, Law's use of the term "the demand for money" along with his exposition of how international arbitrage entails "the law of one price" also links him with some aspects of modern Monetarism.

Law believed that, like Scotland, France between 1716 and 1720 suffered from underutilizing her resources due to a shortage of money and high interest rates. France also had the additional problem of a massive burden of national debt which had been built up owing to the long and costly War of the Spanish Succession (1702–13). Law recognized that monetary policy, while necessary, was not sufficient. Although monetary expansion could help solve France's monetary crisis, a policy of debt management was required to solve her financial crisis.

In response to the financial crisis, Law mopped up the huge overhang of government debt by swapping shares in his companies for debt. The rise in the price of shares encouraged holders of government debt to acquire the shares of the Mississippi Company which seemed to promise substantial capital gains. Law also introduced a series of measures, ranging from the demonetization of gold and a phased demonetization of silver to a ban on using specie for large transactions in order to raise the demand for paper money. Furthermore, for a period in 1720, Law used the note issue to support a floor price of 9000 livres a share, effectively monetizing the shares of the Mississippi Company, in accord with his view that such shares were a new type of money.

For a while, the system seemed to work. Economic activity boomed; there was frenzied activity in the stock market; money was plentiful; the rate of interest fell to two percent; and the national debt seemed to be under control. By this stage, Law was giving priority to management of the debt. "He sacrificed," Law later wrote of himself, "the reputation that he had acquired, by the establishment of the bank . . . to the extreme desire that he had to reestablish promptly the affairs of the state by the extinction of all its debts" (Law 1934, 3:372).

As long as transactors were prepared to stay within the financial circuit, trading banknotes for shares and vice versa, no significant strains appeared. However, once money started spilling out of the financial circuit into the real circuit of the economy, inflationary pressures emerged. Belatedly, Law realized that he had overmonetized the system and that it was necessary to reduce the overall value of shares and banknotes. This he attempted to achieve by the *arrêt* of 21 May 1720, which ordered a phased reduction in the price of shares and banknotes. The resulting panic led to the repeal of the *arrêt* a couple of days later. Nevertheless, the price of shares and banknotes, along with the French exchange rate, fell continuously through the summer and autumn of 1720. Law was forced to flee from France in December.

Law's failure also led to his dismissal from the ranks of front-line economic theorists of the eighteenth century. Yet, a close reading of his work shows that he was an outstanding monetary theorist; that his banking theory was considerably ahead of his time; and that his attempts to solve the twin problems of underutilized resources and a heavy national-debt burden have distinct modern parallels.

Antoin E. Murphy

See also MISSISSIPPI BUBBLE; SOUTH SEA BUBBLE

Bibliography

Hamilton, E. J. 1936. "Prices and Wages at Paris under John Law's System." *Quarterly Journal of Economics* 51:42–70.
———. 1968. "John Law." In *International Encyclopedia of the Social Sciences*. Vol. 9. New York: Free Press.
———. 1969. "The Political Economy of France at the time of John Law." *History of Political Economy* 1:123–49.
Law, J. 1934. *John Law, Oeuvres Complètes.* 3 vols. Edited by P. Harsin. Paris: Sirey.
———. [1703–04] 1994. John Law's Essay on a Land Bank. Edited by A. E. Murphy. Dublin: Aeon.
Rist, C. 1940. *A History of Monetary and Credit Theories from John Law to the Present Day.* London: Allen and Unwin.

LDC Crisis

A debt crisis arises when scheduled debt payments cannot be met. Although developing countries have experienced several debt crises over the last century, the 1982 crisis gained attention for several reasons. First, many less-developed countries (LDCs) experienced debt-servicing difficulties simultaneously. Second, the soundness of the financial system in the United States was at risk. Third, the income gains that developing countries achieved during the 1970s were threatened. Fourth, the role of international organizations in debt negotiations was crucial.

Analytical Framework

A country's current-account balance (CAB) equals

$$CAB = \Delta A + \Delta R - \Delta D - \Delta I, \qquad (1)$$

where ΔA is the change, within a time period, of the nominal value of the stock of external assets held by the country's private-sector residents; ΔR is the change in the nominal value of the stock of external assets held by the public sector; ΔD is the change in the nominal value of the stock of external debt (public and private), and ΔI is net foreign direct investment. The current-account balance also equals

$$CAB = [P_x X(Y_+^*, E_+) - P_m M(Y_+, E_-)] + i(A + R) - (i + s)D - DIV, \qquad (2)$$

where P_x is the export price; X is the volume of exports which is positively related to both foreign income, Y^*, and the real exchange rate, E; P_m is the import price; M is the volume of imports which is directly related to domestic real income, Y, and negatively related to E; i is the nominal interest rate; s is a spread over i; and DIV is net dividend payments.

Combining equations (1) and (2) gives

$$(i + s)D = TB - KF - OR + \Delta D + (DI - DIV), \qquad (3)$$

where $TB = [P_x X - P_m M]$ is the trade balance; $KF = (\Delta A - iA)$ is net portfolio investment ($KF > 0$ means capital flight); $OR = (\Delta R - iR)$ equals changes in official foreign reserves; and $(DI - DIV)$ measures net foreign direct investment [Helkie and Howard (1994) describe these terms in greater detail]. Equation (3) says that interest payments on external debt, $(i + s)D$ are financed by surpluses in trade balances, $TB > 0$, net portfolio inflows $KF < 0$, official reserve withdrawals, $OR < 0$, or new loans, $\Delta D > 0$. (Net foreign direct investment played, until recently, a minor role in LDC debtors' external accounts.)

Initial Conditions

The process of LDC debt accumulation began in 1973–75 when the trade deficits induced by higher oil prices were financed largely by commercial banks (Krueger 1987). Developing countries increased their indebtedness further for three reasons. First, they could borrow at negative real interest rates. Second, their export prices grew faster than their external debt which lowered the burden of debt servicing. For example, the debt-export ratio $D/(P_x X)$ for the largest debtors fell from 203 percent in 1978 to 166 percent in 1980 (Table 1). Third, their real exchange rates appreciated with the ensuing trade deficits being financed by commercial banks. These banks found the increased exposure worthwhile given the spreads on these loans and the declines in LDCs' debt-export ratio. Overall, the largest debtors increased their indebtedness from $178 billion in 1978 to $377 billion in 1982 (Table 1). Most of this debt was issued by LDC governments, contracted with floating interest rates, and denominated in U.S. dollars.

Debt Crisis

The genesis of the 1982 debt crisis began in 1979–80 when industrial countries allowed their interest rates to increase in response to higher oil prices. In addition to raising debt service for heavily indebted developing countries, higher interest rates lowered economic activity in industrial countries, Y^*, which reduced debtors' export volumes and prices. The resulting contraction in the value of exports worsened LDCs' trade balance, raised their debt-export ratio, and nearly doubled the share of their exports devoted to interest payments $((i + s)D/P_x X)$ (Table 1). As a result, commercial banks became increasingly reluctant to continue financing developing countries' interest payments and trade deficits.

If LDC debtors had failed to service their debt, commercial banks would have had to increase reserves against "nonperforming" loans. Given the exposure of the largest U.S. commercial banks to developing countries, a default by one or more highly indebted developing countries would have strained the U.S. financial system. For example, a one-year suspension of debt service by Argentina, Mexico, and Brazil to the nine largest U.S. banks in 1982 would have eliminated banks' profits, reduced their capital by $8 billion, and contracted their lending capacity by $160 billion (Cline 1984). In the absence of official intervention, the cutback in

TABLE 1. External Debt and Economic Performance:[1] Fifteen Heavily Indebted Countries

	External[2] Debt ($ Bill.) D	Per[3] Capita Growth (%)	Debt Export Ratio (%) $D/P_x X$	Trade Balance ($ Bill.) TB	Interest Payments– Export Ratio (%) $(i + s)D/P_x X$
1978	178.2	0.6	203.4	−7.9	12.3
1979	217.4	3.7	181.7	−1.2	14.5
1980	267.5	2.6	165.8	5.6	15.8
1981	328.3	−1.5	199.2	−5.3	22.5
1982	376.8	−2.8	263.4	4.7	30.2
1983	390.9	−5.6	286.3	29.0	29.5
1984	407.4	0.3	269.3	43.4	27.7
1985	418.4	1.7	283.8	40.7	28.3
1986	442.1	1.0	343.2	20.9	29.7
1987	484.9	0.5	332.9	26.1	20.7
1988	473.6	−0.6	288.3	29.5	23.3
1989	475.6	−1.0	260.2	35.7	18.1
1990	491.1	−2.4	239.3	34.8	14.1
1991	495.1	−1.4	253.0	18.2	17.1

1 The countries are Argentina, Bolivia, Brazil, Chile, Colombia, Cote d'Ivoire, Ecuador, Mexico, Morocco, Nigeria, Peru, Philippines, Uruguay, Venezuela, and Yugoslavia. Data for 1978 to 1983 come from the IMF's 1986 *World Economic Outlook,* tables A48, A6, A50, A38, and A51. Data for 1984 to 1991 come from the IMF's 1992 *World Economic Outlook,* tables A47, A6, A48, A39, A49.
2 Excludes debt owed to the IMF.
3 Average for 1968–77 is 3.9 percent.

loans would have raised domestic interest rates; *allowance* for such intervention would have induced an increase in inflationary expectations that would have raised interest rates (Cline 1984).

Policy Responses: Phase 1

The immediate policy response to this crisis emphasized continuity of debt servicing. Maintaining debt service involved case-by-case negotiations among commercial banks, creditor-countries' official agencies, and debtor-countries' governments. The case-by-case approach was justified by the diversity of situations faced by developing countries and the evolutionary nature of U.S. policy towards the debt problem (Truman 1989).

Since the adjustment process involved both short- and long-run considerations (Truman 1986, 1989), the strategy entailed (1) policy adjustments by debtor countries (positive real interest rates, depreciation of real exchange rates, reduction of government budget deficits); (2) continued lending by commercial banks *on a concerted basis* and rescheduling existing obligations with both longer maturities and grace periods; (3) official bridge financing; and (4) increased financing from the International Monetary Fund (IMF) with associated conditionality. The IMF played a central role in these negotiations, because many smaller commercial banks lacked the incentive to continue lending to LDCs but would have benefitted from the increased quality of their loans if larger banks increased their exposure. To avoid these free-rider problems, the IMF did not provide financing until all other parties agreed to supply their share of financing (Cline 1984, Truman 1989).

Debt rescheduling, official financing, and concerted lending could not, by themselves, solve the debt crisis. Debt forgiveness contradicted the overall debt strategy and the gains from adopting structural-policy changes carried unavoidable delays. Thus the brunt of the adjustment fell on debtors' trade balances, which improved substantially (Table 1). This improvement arose from a contraction of imports induced by the depreciation of real exchange rates and an 8-percent decline in per-capita income from 1982 to 1984 (Table 1).

Policy Responses: Phase 2

From the standpoint of the international financial system, the strategy used to avoid large-scale defaults worked. Disruptions have been minor and transitory; banks have reduced their exposure in developing countries while increasing reserves against outstanding loans. However, this strategy transferred substantial resources to creditors without improving debtors' living standards. For the largest debtors, per-capita income has declined 10 percent since 1982 (Table 1). Initial expectations that faster growth in industrial countries would accelerate LDC exports (Cline 1984) did not translate into faster LDC growth. Similarly, export prices of developing countries have not increased, and the debt-export ratio remains above 200 percent for the largest debtors (Table 1).

Several analysts argued that the LDC crisis would not be resolved while debtors' economies remained stagnant and that focusing exclusively on the immediacy of debt service would not promote LDC growth (Truman 1986, Krueger 1987, Fischer 1989). These analysts point out that having to generate both foreign exchange and fiscal surpluses for debt service thwarts the incentives to adjust further. Specifically, because their debt is denominated in foreign currency, LDC debtors need to generate foreign exchange by reallocating resources towards the tradable sector. But because most of the external debt is government owed, these countries must also increase their taxes. Why would the private sector, then, assume the risks of reallocating resources if the resulting gains are taxed at a higher rate? A failure to reallocate resources means that exports will not increase, debt-export ratios will not decrease, and the country will not gain creditworthiness.

Several proposals had been advanced and implemented to stop declines in LDCs' income and promote their reentry into the international finance market: first, allowing for voluntary debt and debt-service reduction where debt forgiveness could be structured to reward debtors for their adjustment efforts and, by creating incentives to adjust further, bypass the detrimental effects of a debt overhang (Krueger 1987); second, promoting foreign direct investment and return of capital flight (Truman 1989); third, changes in the nature of the existing debt instruments to reflect the time-profile of the underlying LDC assets (Fischer 1989); and fourth, provision of official assistance to countries implementing enough policy reforms (Krueger 1987). This aid would be used to finance investment in the tradable sector, thus ameliorating the conflict between fiscal affairs and foreign-exchange needs.

Is the crisis over? Under the definition given at the beginning of this article, the 1982 crisis is over. Debtor countries are servicing their scheduled interest payments; commercial banks have lowered significantly their exposure and are better prepared to handle an LDC default now than in 1982. However, debt crises are likely to remain a recurrent phenomenon in the evolution of the world economy (Truman 1989, Lindert and Morton 1989).

Jaime Marquez

See also INTERNATIONAL LENDER OF LAST RESORT; LEWIS, WILLIAM ARTHUR; MONETARY REFORM

Bibliography

Cline, W. 1984. *International Debt: Systemic Risk and Policy Response*. Cambridge: MIT Press.

Fischer, S. 1989. "Resolving the International Debt Crisis." In *Developing Country Debt and Economic Performance: The International Financial System*. Vol. 1. Edited by J. Sachs, 359–85. Chicago: Univ. of Chicago Press.

Helkie, W. and D. Howard. 1994. "External Adjustment in Selected Developing Countries in the 1990s." *Journal of Policy Modeling* 16:353–93.

Krueger, A. 1987. "Debt, Capital Flows, and LDC Growth." *American Economic Review Papers and Proceedings* 77:159–64.

Lindert, P. and P. Morton. 1989. "How Sovereign Debt Has Worked." In *Developing Country Debt and Economic Performance: The International Financial System*. Vol. 1. Edited by J. Sachs, 39–106. Chicago: Univ. of Chicago Press.

Truman, E. 1986. "The International Debt Situation." *International Finance Discussion Papers*. No. 298. Washington: Federal Reserve Board.

———. 1989. "U.S. Policy on the Problems of International Debt." *Federal Reserve Bulletin* 75:727–35.

Leading Indicators: Historical Record

The origin of the leading and lagging indicators which are now widely used to track business cycles in many countries can be traced back to a study published in 1938 by W. C. Mitchell and A. F. Burns at the National Bureau of Economic Research. Their report, which was limited to indicators of revivals or upturns in the United States economy, listed some seventy-one indicators, arrayed according to the length of their average lead or lag at business-cycle troughs. The periods covered by the selected indicators started in the mid-nineteenth or early twentieth centuries, depending on the availability of data, and ended with the business-cycle trough in 1933.

In a 1950 article, this indicator-selection process was extended to cover the behavior of indicators at business-cycle peaks as well as troughs, and classified the indicators into leading, coincident, and lagging groups. The historical record used in making the selection and classification again covered varying periods, all ending with the business-cycle trough in 1938.

Many further developments followed these early studies. They include:

1. Techniques for constructing composite indexes based on groups of leading, coincident, or lagging indicators.
2. Extension of the indicator system to many other countries or regions within a country.
3. Adaptation to cover growth cycles, inflation cycles, and cycles in particular industries or markets.
4. Classification of leading indicators into long-leading and short-leading groups.
5. Use of the leading indexes to make explicit forecasts of production, employment, inflation rates, etc.

Table 1 provides a summary picture of how the group of leading indicators selected in 1950 performed in the United States during the historical periods examined when they were selected. This record is then compared with two subsequent records for the same indicators, one pertaining solely to the United States, the other pertaining to ten other countries. Hence, the table provides an extensive postsample test of the reliability of the leading-indicators approach.

Each of the eight indicators showed an average lead at U.S. business-cycle peaks after 1948 as well as before 1938. At troughs there were two exceptions: commercial and industrial building contracts and the index of sensitive commodity prices showed short average lags after 1948, whereas before then they showed short average leads. The post-1948 record for the ten other countries is similar—at peaks, all the averages are leads, while at troughs the same two series exhibit the only exceptions to the rule. With the results for peaks and troughs combined, as in the last three columns of the table, the post-sample record shows that in every instance the leading tendency observed before 1938 has persisted since then. Indeed, even the tendency for some indicators to lead by longer intervals than others has persisted. The average leads in the U.S. since 1948 are closely correlated with those before 1938 ($R^2 = .82$). The averages for other countries since 1948 are less closely correlated with those for the U.S. before 1938 ($R^2 = .27$). The correlation is noticeably better when the other countries' results are compared with the U.S. since 1948 ($R^2 = .52$). In any case, leading indicators have been found to work in similar ways in different countries, as well as at different times in the same country.

One of the first procedures that was used to put leading indicators together in a single index was to compute the percentage of the indicators that were rising at any given time. This is known as a diffusion index, since it shows how widely diffused the upward movement is, and whether it is getting more or less widespread. Such indexes are used today in surveys of consumer confidence and of business enterprises, which report the percentage of consumers expecting to increase their purchases or the percentage of firms with rising sales, etc. In the case of leading indicators, one would expect the percent expanding to decline below 50 percent before a business-cycle peak is reached, and to rise above 50 percent before a business-cycle trough is reached. These points can be identified readily by subtracting 50 from the percent rising each month and then cumulating this series from the initial month. The peaks and

TABLE 1. Lead/Lag Record of Eight Leading Indicators Selected in 1950

Average Lead (–) or Lag (+), in Months

Leading indicator, and initial year of U.S. series	at Peaks			at Troughs			at Peaks and Troughs		
	U.S. before 1938	U.S. 1948 –82	10 Countries 1948–82	U.S. before 1938	U.S. 1948 –82	10 Countries 1948–82	U.S. before 1938	U.S. 1948 –82	10 Countries 1948–82
Avg. workweek, mfg., 1921	–4	–10	–4	–3	–2	–4	–3	–6	–3
New orders, 1921	–7	–10	–2	–2	–2	–9	–4	–6	–6
Housing starts, 1919	–8	–15	–5	–4	–6	–7	–6	–10	–6
Commer. and industrial bldg. contracts, 1919	–5	–10	–2	–1	+2	0	–3	–4	–1
New incorporations, 1870	–2	–11	–8	–4	–4	–8	–3	–7	–8
Business failure liabilities, 1879	–10	–20	n.a.	–8	–3	n.a.	–9	–12	n.a.
Stock Price Index, 1873	–5	–9	–6	–6	–5	–7	–6	–7	–6
Sens. Commodity Price Index, 1897	–2	–8	–2	–1	+1	+1	–2	–4	–2
Average, 7 indicators*	–5	–10	–4	–3	–2	–5	–4	–6	–5
Average, 8 indicators	–5	–12	n.a.	–4	–2	n.a.	–4	–7	n.a.

* Excluding business failure liabilities, which is not available for the 10 countries.

Source: Center for International Business Cycle Research, March 1992.
Note: The U.S. data before 1938 were used in selecting the indicators in 1950. The averages are arithmetic means based on leads and lags at business-cycle turns covering varying periods depending on availability of data, ranging from 1921–38 to 1870–1938. The ten-country averages are medians based on growth-cycle turns covering varying periods between 1948 and 1982. The ten countries, each weighted equally, are: Canada, United Kingdom, West Germany, France, Italy, Japan, Taiwan, South Korea, Australia, and New Zealand.

TABLE 2. Lead/Lag Record of Cumulated Diffusion Index of 75 Leading Indicators, 1887–1938

Business Cycle Chronology		Cumulated Diffusion Index		Lead(–) or Lag(+) in months,	
Trough	Peak	Trough	Peak	at Troughs	at Peaks
5/85		n.a.		n.a.	
	3/87		2/87		–1
4/88		12/87		–4	
	7/90		2/90		–5
5/91		1/91		–4	
	1/93		7/92		–6
6/94		2/94		–4	
	12/95		8/95		–4
6/97		9/96		–9	
	6/99		5/99		–1
12/00		7/00		–5	
	9/02		4/02		–5
8/04		11/03		–9	
	5/07		1/06		–16
6/08		12/07		–6	
	1/10		9/09		–4
1/12		1/11		–12	
	1/13		8/12		–5
12/14		11/14		–1	
	8/18		11/16		–21
3/19		11/18		–4	
	1/20		10/19		–3
7/21		3/21		–4	
	5/23		2/23		–3
7/24		10/23		–9	
	10/26		12/25		–10
11/27		6/27		–5	
	8/29		1/29		–7
3/33		11/32		–4	
	5/37		3/37		–2
6/38		2/38		–4	
Average, T, P				–6	–6
T & P				–6	
Percent Leads, T, P				100	100
T & P				100	

Note: The diffusion index, published in 1960, is based on the specific cycle expansions and contractions of 75 leading indicators selected on the basis of their historical record before 1938. The cumulated index is derived by subtracting 50 from the percent expanding in each month and cumulating this series from the initial month, January 1885. For further description, see G. H. Moore, *Business Cycle Indicators,* vol. 1, chaps. 7 and 8, and vol. 2.

TABLE 3. Lead/Lag Record of Cumulated Diffusion Index of Eleven Leading Indicators, 1949–91

Business Cycle Chronology		Cumulated Diffusion Index		Lead(–) or Lag(+) in months,	
Trough	Peak	Trough	Peak	at Troughs	at Peaks
	11/48				n.a.
10/49		7/49		–3	
	7/53		5/53		–2
5/54		3/54		–2	
	8/57		2/56		–16
4/58		4/58		0	
	4/60		8/59		–8
2/61		11/60		–3	
	12/69		5/69		–7
11/70		11/70		0	
	11/73		11/73		0
3/75		7/75		+4	
	1/80		4/79		–9
7/80		8/80		+1	
	7/81		6/81		–1
11/82		8/82		–3	
	7/90		7/90		0
3/91		6/91		+1	
Average, T, P				–1	–6
T & P				–3	
Percent Leads, T, P				44	75
T & P				59	
Extra Cycles		5/52	4/51		
		5/67	8/66		
		4/85	6/84		

Note: The diffusion index is based on the six-month smoothed growth rates in the eleven leading indicators included in the leading index compiled by the U.S. Department of Commerce. The cumulated index is derived by subtracting 50 from the percent of series with positive growth rates in each month and cumulating the series from the initial month, January 1949.

troughs in this cumulated diffusion index can then be matched against the business-cycle peaks and troughs.

This is done in Table 2, covering the period from 1887 to 1938, and in Table 3, covering 1949–91. We find that in the earlier period the index led at every business-cycle peak and trough, on the average by six months, whereas since 1949 the leads have not been as consistent and have averaged only three months. Before jumping to the conclusion that leading indicators are not as reliable as they used to be, one should take into account two major differences between the two periods in the treatment of the data. One is that the seventy-five indicators in the 1885–1938 period were selected on the basis of their behavior during that period, as reported in 1950. The eleven indicators covering the more recent period were selected at various times, starting with the original 1950 list and with various substitutions and additions until the latest revision in 1989. The present list still contains five of the eight indicators in the 1950 list or close equivalents (average workweek, new orders, housing starts, stock prices, and sensitive commodity prices). Another factor affecting the comparison is that since the recent diffusion index is based on growth rates computed by comparing the current monthly figure for each indicator with the average of the preceding twelve months, it may not identify peaks or troughs immediately. This reduces the lead time of the recent index, but of course makes it feasible to use it on a current basis.

Since the two diffusion indexes are not strictly comparable in these respects, they do not necessarily demonstrate any deterioration in the leading indicators. Table 1 is more conclusive on this point, and it does not suggest any general deterioration. In any event, the evidence demonstrates that the tendency for leading indicators to lead at business-cycle turns has survived for at least a hundred years and for more than twenty business cycles.

Geoffrey H. Moore

See also BURNS, ARTHUR FRANK; COMPOSITE AND DIFFUSION INDEXES; INDICATORS, QUALITATIVE; LEADS AND LAGS; MACROECONOMETRIC MODELS, USE OF; MARKET PRICE INDICATORS; MITCHELL, WESLEY CLAIR

Bibliography

Mitchell, W. C. and A. F. Burns. [1938] 1961. "Statistical Indicators of Cyclical Revivals." In *Business Cycle Indicators*. Vol. 1. Edited by G. H. Moore, 162–83. Princeton: Princeton Univ. Press.

Moore, G. H. [1950] 1961. "Statistical Indicators of Cyclical Revivals and Recessions." In *Business Cycle Indicators*. Vol. 1. Edited by G. H. Moore, 184–260. Princeton: Princeton Univ. Press.

———, ed. 1961. *Business Cycle Indicators*. 2 vols. Princeton: Princeton Univ. Press.

Leads and Lags

Knowing how long before one change brings about other changes is at the heart of understanding the dynamics of business cycles. Lags abound in economic activity. There are, for example, delays between decisions to invest and the completion of capital goods, between the application of inputs and the availability of an output, between receiving income and making expenditures, delays in revising expectations about future states of the economy, and in taking new actions based on those revisions.

The types of lags, particularly as they pertain to economic policy, can be classified into the *data lag*, the *recognition lag*, the *decision lag*, and the *impact lag*. The data lag is the time needed to collect and disseminate information. The recognition lag is how long it takes to realize that some sort of action is needed. The decision lag reflects the time needed, after a problem has been recognized, to formulate and implement a plan of action. Finally, after action, such as a change in taxes or a change in the monetary base, has been taken, the impact lag refers to how long before other economic variables—such as employment, output, and prices—are affected.

The length of these lags can have important effects on the cyclical properties of an economy. Generally the longer the lags, the more drawn out are the responses to new information and hence the lower is the frequency of the cyclical movements. If longer lags also allow more cumulative movements in one direction, then they also result in a greater amplitude of the cycles. To be any more precise about the possible effects of different lags requires a formal specification of the lagged relationships.

Postulated lags are integral to theories of business cycles. But in using any theory to make predictions, one needs to combine the theoretical formulations with reliable empirical estimates of the length of these lags. Econometric techniques can be utilized to estimate inherent technological, psychological, and institutional delays that may exist. However, invariant lags that can be used in a reliable theory of business cycles have not yet been found.

An alternative empirical approach was pioneered by W. C. Mitchell and the National Bureau of Economic Research (NBER). Mitchell's strategy was to collect as much data as possible about economic variables and to search for similar patterns in the series. He found that during economic expansions, most series expand, and during contractions, most series contract.

The NBER began dating the peaks and troughs of a "reference cycle" and classifying series as generally leading, coincident, or lagging. Those series with peaks and troughs that consistently preceded the peaks and troughs of the reference cycle were singled out for use in an index of leading economic indicators. Those which were concurrent went into an index of coincident indicators and lagging series were used for an index of lagging indicators.

The latest indexes of leading, coincident, and lagging indicators and the statistics that go into constructing them are published monthly by the U.S. Department of Commerce in *Business Conditions Digest* (originally started in 1961 as *Business Cycle Developments*). The index of coincident economic indicators includes growth rates in industrial production, personal income less transfer payments, manufacturing and trade sales, and employee-hours in nonagricultural payrolls. The index of leading indicators, which gets by far the greatest attention from the news media, is constructed from eleven variables. The composition of and weights on the variables in this index are revised periodically.

A currently fashionable approach to business cycles originally developed by Slutsky ([1927] 1937) and Frisch ([1933] 1965) is to view them as a statistical process. Various impulses or shocks occur, and the delayed propagation of those shocks results in cyclical processes. An economy consists of relationships among numerous economic variables, all subject to unexpected shocks and with a variety of lags linking the variables. These relationships must of course be consistent with the empirical observation that most economic variables tend to move up and down together.

With the development of increased computer power, this statistical approach can help improve the construction of coincident and leading indicators. In a notable effort along these lines, Stock and Watson (1989) estimate a statistical series representing a common component in the movements of the series that comprise the index of coincident economic indicators. Called a new index of coincident economic indicators, this statistical series moves closely with the index published by the Department of Commerce. Its advantage is that it can be interpreted as a measure of the level of economic activity, not just as an indicator of whether economic activity is rising, falling, or passing a turning point.

They also use statistical techniques to cull from a huge variety of time-series data those variables which jointly best predict movements in their new index of coincident economic indicators six months later. From those variables, they construct a new index of leading economic indicators. The old NBER approach looked for individual series that generally led the reference cycle and combined those that did into a single index. Stock and Watson exclude any series lacking explanatory power given the other series in their index even if it does tend to lead general economic activity.

Some variables in the new index of leading economic indicators are not in the old one. Although the general approach is still atheoretical since selection is guided primarily by goodness of statistical fit, the reported improvement in forecasting ability provides an impetus for further analyses of why these leads exist. The new index, if its estimated linkages stand up to theoretical and empirical scrutiny and if it continues to outperform the old one as more data accumulate, will no doubt eventually become the official index of leading economic indicators.

John A. Carlson

See also FRISCH, RAGNAR KITTEL; INDICATORS, QUALITATIVE; LEADING INDICATORS: HISTORICAL RECORD; MARKET PRICE INDICATORS; MITCHELL, WESLEY CLAIR; ROBERTSON, DENNIS HOLME

Bibliography
Blanchard, O. J. 1987. "Leads and Lags." In *The New Palgrave: A Dictionary of Economics*. Vol. 3. Edited by J. Eatwell, M. Milgate, and P. Newman. London: Macmillan.
Burns, A. F. and W. C. Mitchell. 1946. *Measuring Business Cycles*. New York: NBER.
Frisch, R. [1933] 1965. "Propagation and Impulse Problems in Dynamic Economics." In *A.E.A. Readings in Business Cycles*, 155–85. Philadelphia: Blakiston.
Slutsky, E. [1927] 1937. "The Summation of Random Causes as the Source of Cyclic Processes." Translation. *Econometrica* 5:105–46.
Stock, J. H. and M. W. Watson. 1989. "New Indexes of Coincident and Leading Economic Indicators." In *Macroeconomics Annual 1989*, edited by O. J. Blanchard and S. Fischer, 351–94. Cambridge: MIT Press.

L

Learning

The term "learning" can be used to refer to any form of adaptive behavior in economics, and therefore the phrase used by itself is often not specific enough to impart meaning across groups of economists. In recent work in business-cycle theory, however, learning has referred specifically to methods of expectations formation, or updating of beliefs, on the part of individual agents. An introduction to the ideas in this area of macroeconomics is provided by Frydman and Phelps (1983). This particular application of the notion of learning is at the frontier of recent research in dynamic macroeconomic theory.

Many researchers analyzing aggregate fluctuations emphasize the idea that, for an individual agent, productive activity today depends in part on the agent's beliefs about the future. An important example is that of an investment that takes time to mature, forcing investors to assess carefully the future economic circumstances that will govern profitability. Economists such as Pigou and Keynes stressed the idea that the volatility of such expectations—"waves of optimism and pessimism" or "animal spirits"—might be somehow self-fulfilling in the aggregate and therefore a fundamental driving force behind observed business cycles. However, explicit modeling of expectations formation has proved difficult.

With the advent of rational expectations, a consensus was forged among most economists that long-run equilibria in economic models, however else they might be defined, should not imply that individual agents make persistent and systematic forecast errors. Rational agents, it was successfully argued, would recognize patterns in their forecasting mistakes and would use the information implicit in those patterns to improve their predictions. Implicit in the rational-expectations idea is that all systematic forecast errors are eliminated over time—that is, agents do learn. However, the process by which learning occurs was left unspecified, as it was simply assumed that whatever learning takes place had already occurred.

Some recent research in macroeconomics explicitly models the learning process implicit in rational expectations, formalizing the concept that while agents indeed make forecast errors, they eventually eliminate any systematic inaccuracies if their environment is sufficiently repetitive. The seminal work on this idea is contained in a series of papers by Marcet and Sargent and is summarized in Marcet and Sargent (1988). They assume that agents assess their future prospects by applying standard statistical procedures to past data generated by the system in which they operate.

In the view of some economists, the purpose of explicitly modeling learning is to justify the rational-expectations assumption by showing that allowing for learning does not change the inferences drawn from standard rational-expectations macroeconomic models. One might hope, for instance, that, even when learning is explicitly introduced into a standard model, the system converges to one or another of the rational-expectations equilibria, which would imply that the common practice of simply assuming rational expectations and ignoring learning altogether is a reasonable procedure. The explicit inclusion of learning might mainly be helpful in selecting a single equilibrium from among a set of equilibria. On the other hand, some view learning as a virtual replacement for the rational-expectations assumption. The evidence, based mostly on theoretical research, is mixed.

A key question is whether the set of long-run equilibria is altered by explicitly introducing learning into a macromodel. Marcet and Sargent (1988) emphasize that the systems they study, when they converge, often converge to rational-expectations equilibria. Other authors, including Woodford (1990), Bullard (1994), and Grandmont and Laroque (1991), suggest that systems under learning may never converge to fundamental rational-expectations equilibria, and yet not follow explosive trajectories. In particular, Grandmont and Laroque (1991, 248) suggest that including learning "might generate endogenously complex nonlinear trajectories." But irrespective of the convergence question, many researchers seem to agree that the stability properties of a given rational-expectations equilibrium are altered when learning is introduced. In order to discuss these results in more detail, a more precise definition of what is meant by learning must be developed.

Marcet and Sargent (1988) conceptualize the problem as follows. The (possibly heterogeneous) agents in the model are assumed to believe that the current state vector is related to the future state vector in a certain way, perhaps by a vector of parameters. This implies that the actual law of motion for the system must be defined in terms of agents' perceptions. When the agents' perceived law of motion is equivalent to the actual law of motion, a rational-expectations equilibrium is said to exist. An important aspect of the Marcet and Sargent formulation is that it explicitly recognizes the recursive aspect of agent learning in macroeconomic systems: beliefs affect outcomes and outcomes affect beliefs. Such a recognition is the hallmark of recent research in this area.

How should the perceptions of agents be modeled? While there are many possibilities, Marcet and Sargent analyze systems culled from the engineering literature based on versions of least-squares regression. Many of these ideas are summarized by Ljung and Söderström (1983). Marcet and Sargent emphasize that using the least-squares techniques does not mean that agents incorporate fully rational learning, as the agents choose an inference technique based on constant coefficients when the actual system is in fact time-varying. A possible extension in future research would be to consider agents that base their choice of estimation techniques on the assumption that they must track a time-varying system.

Approaches to learning other than least squares could conceivably be made to fit into the Marcet and Sargent conceptualization. White (1989) has studied learning based on neural networks, systems which are brought to bear from models of brain architecture. White stresses the similarities between these models and those based on classical statistics, and finds that systems based on neural networks can have good convergence properties. Arthur (1991) has suggested a calibrated approach to learning, where an algorithm is developed based on data from actual experiments on learning with human subjects published in the psychology literature. One might also reasonably adopt Bayesian approaches, such as those analyzed by Nyarko (1991), or give a Bayesian interpretation to the least-squares approach, as in Ljung and Söderström (1983). Models of learning based on genetic algorithms are also a possibility, and are briefly surveyed by Holland and Miller (1991). The important element in all of these approaches is that there must be some representation of agent beliefs and there must be a means—an algorithm—for updating the beliefs, in order to model the idea that systematic forecast errors are eliminated over time.

These ideas can be made more concrete by considering a version of an example, studied by Marcet and Sargent, in which agents use least-squares techniques. An overlapping-generations model where agents live for two periods can be written as

$$H_t/P_t = 1 - \beta\lambda^{-1t} \qquad (1)$$

$$H_t = \theta H_{t-1} \qquad (2)$$

$$F_t P_{t+1} \equiv \beta_t P_t \qquad (3)$$

where H_t is currency, P_t is the price level, F_t is the forecast at time t, and β_t is the perceived gross rate of inflation at time t. The savings function given in equation (1) obeys the gross-substitutes assumption, and can be obtained from a log utility specification where $\lambda \in (0,1)$ represents the size of the agent's second-period endowment relative to the first-period endowment. Equation (2) is the law of motion for currency creation, where $\theta \in (1, \lambda^{-1})$. If the model is solved under perfect foresight by setting $\beta_{t+1} = P_{t+1}/P_t$, the steady states are the zeros of the difference equation

$$\beta_{t+1} = \theta + \lambda^{-1} - \theta\lambda^{-1}\beta^{-1t} \qquad (4)$$

which occur at $\beta_1 = \theta$ and $\beta_h = \lambda^{-1}$, where $\beta_1 < \beta_h$. The fixed point at β_1 is the low-inflation rational-expectations equilibrium, also known as the monetary steady state, while the fixed point at β_h is the high-inflation equilibrium. Simple iteration of equation (4) shows that, for most initial conditions, $\lim_{t\to\infty} \beta_t = \beta_h$. If perfect foresight is replaced with least–squares learning, the system can be represented by the difference equation

$$\beta_t = \beta_{t-1} + g_{t-1}\left[\theta\frac{1-\lambda\beta_{t-2}^{-1}}{1-\lambda\beta_{t-1}^{-1}} - \beta_{t-1}\right] \qquad (5)$$

where, $\quad g_{t-1} = P_{t-2}^2\left[\sum_{s=1}^{t-1} p_{t-1}^2\right]^{-1}.$

This difference equation also has fixed points at $\beta = \theta$ and $\beta = \lambda^{-1}$. For low values of θ, this system converges to the monetary steady state, but for high values of θ (keeping $\theta < \lambda^{-1}$), this system does not converge—agents cannot learn to have perfect foresight.

This simple example illustrates several ideas that play important roles in the current research. First, the steady states of the alternative systems given by equations (4) and (5) are identical, which is suggestive of the idea that the long-run equilibrium set is not altered by the introduction of learning.

Second, the stability properties of the two steady states are reversed in the system with learning compared to the system with perfect foresight: while β_h is the attractor under perfect foresight, β_1 is the attractor under learning. Finally, in this example, when the system under learning converges, it attains a steady state, suggesting that the idea of eliminating systematic forecast errors by itself implies steady-state-equilibrium outcomes. Some authors, however, have analyzed systems where agents can learn to believe in cycles (Bullard 1994, Evans and Honkapohja 1995, Nyarko 1991).

Some researchers have attempted to ascertain whether perfect foresight or some adaptive method of expectations formation describes real-world data. Marimon and Sunder (1993) have actually placed human subjects in the context of the overlapping-generations model outlined above to observe actual outcomes under human decision making. While they note a number of caveats, their key qualitative result is that they never observed convergence to the high-inflation stationary state. In fact, they suggest that least-squares learning may give a good approximation to the behavior of their subjects in some cases.

A few tentative conclusions can be gleaned from the recent research on learning in dynamic macroeconomic models. First, a clear-cut justification of the rational-expectations assumption, in the sense of a general theorem showing how plausible learning mechanisms always converge to fundamental rational expectations equilibria, now appears unlikely. While it is perhaps comforting, as Marcet and Sargent (1988) suggest, that it is not difficult to find cases where convergence does obtain, there are also cases of nonconvergence that need to be addressed more fully. Second, while a great deal of work remains to be done on alternative approaches to learning, some results are available for recursive systems where agents use vector autoregressions to update their beliefs. These results suggest that the stability properties of rational-expectations equilibria can be altered when learning is introduced. Finally, it seems doubtful that the rational-expectations hypothesis will in any sense be replaced, since it serves as an important benchmark in the learning literature. Research on learning is likely instead to simply lead to more sophisticated treatments of expectations formation in macroeconomic models.

James Bullard

See also EXPECTATIONS; RATIONAL EXPECTATIONS; SUNSPOT THEORIES OF FLUCTUATIONS

Bibliography
Arthur, W. 1991. "Designing Economic Agents that Act Like Human Agents: A Behavioral Approach to Bounded Rationality." *American Economic Review Papers and Proceedings* 81:353–59.
Bullard, J. 1994. "Learning Equilibria." *Journal of Economic Theory* 64:468–85.
Evans, G. and S. Honkapohja. 1995. "Local Convergence of Recursive Learning Mechanisms to Steady States and Cycles in Stochastic Nonlinear Models." *Econometrica* 63:195–206.
Frydman, R. and E. Phelps. 1983. *Individual Forecasting and Aggregate Outcomes: Rational Expectations Examined.* Cambridge: Cambridge Univ. Press.
Grandmont, J.-M. and G. Laroque. 1991. "Economic Dynamics with Learning: Some Instability Examples." In *Equilibrium Theory and Applications,* edited by W. A. Barnett, 247–73. Cambridge: Cambridge Univ. Press.
Holland, J. and J. Miller. 1991. "Artificial Adaptive Agents in Economic Theory." *American Economic Review Papers and Proceedings* 81:365–70.
Ljung, L. and T. Söderström. 1983. *Theory and Practice of Recursive Identification.* Cambridge: MIT Press.
Marcet, A. and T. J. Sargent. 1988. "The Fate of Systems With 'Adaptive' Expectations." *American Economic Review Papers and Proceedings* 78:168–72.
Marimon, R. and S. Sunder. 1993. "Indeterminacy of Equilibria in a Hyperinflationary World: Experimental Evidence." *Econometrica* 61:1073–1107.
Nyarko, Y. 1991. "Learning in Misspecified Models and the Possibility of Cycles." *Journal of Economic Theory* 55:416–27.
White, H. 1989. "Some Asymptotic Results for Learning in Single Hidden-Layer Feedforward Network Models." *Journal of the American Statistical Association* 84:1003–1013.
Woodford, M. 1990. "Learning to Believe in Sunspots." *Econometrica* 58:277–307.

Lender of Last Resort

The term "lender of last resort" (LLR) refers to the responsibility of a central bank to prevent panic-induced contractions of the money stock. According to traditional doctrine, a central bank discharges this responsibility by making emergency loans of high-powered money to solvent, but temporarily illiquid, banks at penalty rates on good collateral. Ideally, the mere announcement of its intention, by assuaging fears of a shortage of cash, would suffice to still panics without the need for making loans.

The LLR concept originates with Sir Francis Baring who, in his 1797 *Observations on the Establishment of the Bank of England,* called the bank "the dernier resort" from which all sound banks could borrow in a crisis. But the idea was most systematically and fully developed by Henry Thornton and Walter Bagehot who articulated it in essentially its present form. Both Thornton in his *Paper Credit of Great Britain* and Bagehot in his *Lombard Street* insisted that the LLR had a duty (1) to protect the aggregate money stock, not individual institutions, (2) to support central-banking policies of long-run stable money growth by eliminating temporary instabilities associated with panics and crises, and (3) to preannounce its policy well in advance of crises to minimize the chances of a panic. They also recommended that the LLR let insolvent institutions fail, lend to creditworthy institutions only, charge penalty rates, and require good collateral. Such rules, they thought, would limit bankers' incentives to take added risks in anticipation of LLR accommodation, thus avoiding moral-hazard problems. From their writings derive the following propositions which constitute the analytical core of the modern theory of the LLR.

1. *LLRs emerge in modern financial systems because of (a) fractional-reserve banking and (b) central-bank control over the issue of high-powered money.* Fractional-reserve banking, which allows unaccommodated increases in the demand for high-powered money to induce multiple contractions in the money stock, creates a need for an LLR. And the ability of a central bank to create high-powered money provides an inexhaustible means of satisfying that need.

2. *The LLR is primarily a monetary, not a banking or credit, function.* The LLR's overriding duty is preventing panic-induced monetary contractions, contractions that would depress real economic activity. By raising suspicions that commercial banks cannot redeem their liabilities in hard cash, panics trigger a double demand for high-powered money. For just when money holders are attempting to convert suspect bank liabilities into cash, bankers are seeking to augment their reserves of high-powered money, both to meet anticipated cash withdrawals and to allay public suspicion of financial weakness. The resulting rise in cash-deposit and reserve-deposit ratios reduces the multiplier coefficient connecting high-powered money to the aggregate money stock. The LLR must offset a reduced money multiplier by raising the monetary base enough to prevent the quantity of money (and thereby aggregate spending and real economic activity) from contracting. Forestalling bank runs and averting credit crises, though undeniably important functions, are nevertheless ancillary and incidental to the LLR's primary task of maintaining the money supply.

3. *The LLR function holds across alternative monetary regimes and supports central-bank objectives in those regimes.* For example, under a gold standard, the LLR helps protect the nation's gold reserve, thus ensuring the fixed-rate convertibility of paper into gold. It does so (a) by stopping panics that would trigger reserve-depleting internal specie drains, (b) by raising the discount (penalty) rate to attract gold from abroad, and (c) by accommodating emergency demands for high-powered money with its own note issue, thereby rendering gold unnecessary for that purpose. Under an inconvertible-paper, floating-exchange-rate regime, the LLR can stabilize the internal purchasing power of the monetary unit by preventing catastrophic collapses of the money stock.

4. *The LLR function in no way conflicts with the monetary-control responsibility of the central bank.* The monetary-control responsibility requires limiting the growth of the non-metallic component of the money stock sufficiently to prevent inflation. By contrast, the LLR function refers to temporary and relatively minor deviations from a noninflationary monetary-growth path. Three considerations ensure that these deviations will be small in size and duration. First, if LLR emergency issues of base money merely offset declines in the money multiplier, they do not increase the money stock. Second, decisive LLR action will stop panics before base money diverges far from its long-run path. Third, deviations will be self-correcting as the LLR's penalty rate, by encouraging the prompt repayment of last-resort

loans, ensures the quick retirement of emergency issues. By preventing the monetary instability associated with panics and crises, the LLR function complements the anti-inflationary duties of the central bank.

5. *The LLR's responsibility is to stabilize the entire economy, not to protect individual banks.* Its duty is to provide liquidity to the market during panics and to announce in advance its commitment to do so in all future panics. This commitment reduces public uncertainty and promotes stabilizing expectations, thereby enhancing its ability to discharge its responsibility. It has no duty to sustain unsound (insolvent) banks. Poorly managed banks should be allowed to fail, the LLR acting only to contain such failures so that the money stock does not contract. Besides reducing the moral-hazard problem, this prescription conforms to the idea that the LLR should not prevent shocks from occurring, only minimize their repercussions (contagion or spillover effects) on the financial system. In short, the LLR should distinguish between preventing monetary contraction and protecting bank owners and managers. The former is a macro responsibility; the latter is not.

6. *The LLR function can be accomplished through open-market operations as well as through loans made at a penalty rate.* Either method can accommodate emergency demands for high-powered money. Both possess the added advantage of using market rather than nonmarket mechanisms to allocate LLR liquidity among competing uses and users.

These propositions, though honored in the breach as much as in the observance, continue to inform LLR policy today. The main challenge to them comes from proponents of free competitive banking who argue that removing all legal restrictions on banking would obviate the need for an LLR. But this argument, based on the proposition that free banking is sufficiently stable to avoid any need for LLR assistance, neglects the crucial distinction between inside (or bank-created) and outside (or high-powered) money. Even under free banking, occasional shocks such as the threat of war or the failure of a large firm may induce moneyholders to seek to switch from inside to outside money. Competitive banks, however, are inherently unable to provide outside money. They can only make their moneys redeemable in terms of some asset whose value they do not control. Given a fiat monetary standard, only the central bank or LLR provides

outside money. Thus, even if banks were completely free to issue their own notes they could not satisfy their depositors' panic-induced desire to switch to outside money. The banks would still have to rely on the LLR for help.

In sum, LLRs provide crucial backstops for modern banking systems. The absence of LLRs, or their failure to function, can be disastrous. A case in point is the Great Depression of the 1930s. Contributing heavily to that episode was the Federal Reserve's failure to act as an LLR and to issue enough high-powered money to keep the money stock from shrinking in the face of rising cash-deposit and reserve-deposit ratios. The resulting contraction of output and employment dramatically demonstrates the need for a properly working LLR in a fractional-reserve banking system.

Thomas M. Humphrey

See also BAGEHOT, WALTER; BANK CHARTER ACT OF 1844; BANK OF ENGLAND; BANKING PANICS; BARING CRISIS; CENTRAL BANKING; CLEARINGHOUSES; CRISIS OF 1847; FEDERAL RESERVE SYSTEM: 1914–1941; FREE BANKING; INTERNATIONAL LENDER OF LAST RESORT; MONETARY POLICY; OPTION CLAUSE; THORNTON, HENRY

Bibliography

Bagehot, W. [1873] 1962. *Lombard Street: A Description of the Money Market.* Homewood, Ill.: Irwin.

Bordo, M. D. 1990. "The Lender of Last Resort: Alternative Views and Historical Experience." Federal Reserve Bank of Richmond *Economic Review,* January/February, 18–29.

Garcia, G. and E. Plautz. 1988. *The Federal Reserve: Lender of Last Resort.* Cambridge, Mass.: Ballinger.

Humphrey, T. M. 1989. "Lender of Last Resort: The Concept in History." Federal Reserve Bank of Richmond *Economic Review,* March/April, 8–16.

Solow, R. M. 1982. "On the Lender of Last Resort." In *Financial Crises: Theory, History, and Policy,* edited by C. P. Kindleberger and J. P. Laffargue, 237–48. Cambridge: Cambridge Univ. Press.

Thornton, H. [1802] 1939. *An Enquiry Into the Nature and Effects of the Paper Credit of Great Britain.* Edited with an introduction by F. A. von Hayek. London: Allen and Unwin.

Lerner, Abba (1903–1982)

Abba Lerner was born in 1902 in Poland. He emigrated to London at a young age and after stints as a capmaker and a rabbinical student, he entered the London School of Economics, where he won most of the school's major prizes. In 1934, he won a scholarship to do empirical work at Manchester, but he stopped at Cambridge on the way to clear up "some confused thinking." While there he was converted to Keynesian economics, and, thereafter, as one of its most important interpreters and expositors, Lerner was a key figure in both Keynesian economics and business-cycle theory. His interpretation of Keynes, which, unlike Alvin Hansen's stagnation approach, was a cyclical one, is best seen in his famous "steering-wheel" analogy (Lerner 1941) in which he compared the economy to a driverless car zig-zagging from one side of a highway to the other because it had no steering wheel.

He argued that the key Keynesian insight is that the aggregate economy has no fixed equilibrium, because aggregate supply and aggregate demand are interrelated, and that individuals ignore the effect of their spending decisions on other individuals. The question to ask about business cycles is not why business cycles exist; the reasons for their existence are self-evident. The question is, rather, what can be done about business cycles. Lerner (1960, 133–34) wrote:

> A small buyer may neglect the effects on income of his decisions to spend or not to spend. Although someone else's income must be reduced by a dollar when he spends a dollar less, he is not concerned with this. It will have no discernible effect on his own income. . . .
>
> It is the inability of many to pay attention to the repercussions that leads them to balk at the bridge from "micro" to "macro" and to insist on the "self-evidence" of the proposition that a cut in prices would cure a depression, because a cut in the price charged by a small seller increases his sales.

In modern terms, Lerner's argument would be restated as an argument that macroexternalities amplify the effect of an exogenous shift in aggregate demand into a larger than desired shift. Thus, Lerner's microfoundation for macrotheory was dependent on individuals' spending decisions not fully incorporating the complete consequences of those decisions, and this is quite compatible with individuals having rational expectations.

Lerner agreed that in a purely theoretical model, instantaneous wage-price and interest-rate flexibility would eliminate business cycles, but he ridiculed the idea of even thinking about such instantaneous flexibility as being preposterous for any model purporting to describe the real world. If instantaneous price flexibility were to maintain full employment in a model, that model would have to assume that individuals fully recognize all future outcomes of complicated interrelationships; that they would want to adjust their wage, price, or interest rate to that equilibrium level, and that such fluctuating wages and prices would have no effect on the economy. None of these assumptions, he argued, is appropriate to a model describing the real world. Because such assumptions are inappropriate, the aggregate economy may be expected to be in a type of fluctuating permanent disequilibrium as the macro-reverberations of individual decisions work their way through the system.

Thus, Lerner's argument is that the aggregate equilibrium of an economy is, in modern terms, path-dependent: the final equilibrium is not independent of the disequilibrium adjustment process. For Lerner, a comparative-static analysis of the aggregate economy is impossible. Each equilibrium depends on where the economy has been.

Lerner's interest was not merely in explaining how business cycles came about; he wanted to explain how to control them, or, in terms of his famous analogy, how to add the steering wheel to the economy. He contrasted his proposed policy, *functional finance,* with *sound finance,* the doctrine that the government should always balance the budget. Functional finance requires the government to vary its spending and taxes, its borrowing and repayment of loans, its control of the quantity of money, with an eye only to the impact of these actions on output and employment, and not on any traditional doctrine about what is "sound" or "unsound" (1944, 302).

The concept of functional finance played an important role in the early debates about Keynesian policy, because it went right to the heart of the political debates in the 1940s. It said that the deficit does not matter. Keynes, who had a stronger sense and concern about political acceptability than Lerner did, firmly disagreed with this view and said that if this is what Keynesian economics meant then he was not a Keynesian (Colander 1984). He later recanted that statement, but wrote, in private correspondence, that if Lerner's correct, but politically embarrassing, result were to be publicized, it would slow the acceptance of Keynesian economics.

Lerner's functional-finance policy later became associated with fine-tuning and was in large part repudiated for political reasons. However, his theoretical contributions were not repudiated, and his conception of Keynesian economics and its micro-foundations laid the groundwork for the New Keynesian revival in the late 1980s and early 1990s.

David Colander

See also FISCAL POLICY; FUNCTIONAL FINANCE; KEYNES, JOHN MAYNARD; NEW KEYNESIAN ECONOMICS

Bibliography
Colander, D. 1984. "Was Keynes a Keynesian or a Lernerian?" *Journal of Economic Literature* 22:1572–75.
Lerner, A. 1941. "The Economic Steering Wheel." *The University Review* 7:2–8.
———. 1944. *The Economics of Control.* New York: Macmillan.
———. 1960. "On Generalizing *The General Theory.*" *American Economic Review* 50:121–43.
———. 1983. *Selected Writings of Abba Lerner.* Edited by D. Colander. New York: New York Univ. Press.
Scitovsky, T. 1984. "Lerner's Contribution to Economics." *Journal of Economic Literature* 22:1547–71.

Lewis, William Arthur (1915–1991)

W. Arthur Lewis, born and raised in his youth on the Caribbean island of St. Lucia, received the Nobel Memorial Prize in economics in 1979. The prize was awarded primarily for his research contributions in the field of development economics. He is most famous for his elaboration in a widely cited paper, first published in the *Manchester School* in 1954, of the "Lewis Model," which identifies prospects of rapid economic expansion in numerous developing countries with the presence of an unlimited supply of labor for their capitalistic or "modern" sectors.

The Lewis model was self-consciously intended to echo the thematic emphases of the Classical school of political economy—especially the themes developed by Smith, Ricardo, and J. S. Mill—on economic growth spurred by savings-driven capital accumulation. Capital accumulation would accelerate with an increase in the savings rate at any given level of income. The savings rate would increase if a relative redistribution of income favoring profits against wages took place, since the average propensity to save out of profits is higher than the propensity to save out of wages. The existence of a pool of labor that can be drawn on indefinitely at a fixed real wage constituted a recipe for precisely the type of redistribution of income that would favor the share of national income going to profits. The potential Keynesian problem of nonmobilized savings was not considered by Lewis, an abstraction very much in the Classical spirit.

All of Lewis's research endeavors possessed a characteristic practicality. Never attracted to intellectual frivolity or to theory for theory's sake, his work consistently had direct policy implications and was intended for application among nations or peoples possessing the relevant characteristics. For example, in the famous 1954 paper, Lewis (140) indicated that his model of unlimited labor may not be "appropriate in some parts of Africa and Latin America" where "there is an acute shortage of labor." In contrast, Lewis observed that a condition of unlimited labor "is obviously the relevant assumption for the economies of Egypt, India, or Jamaica." In those and other similarly situated countries, until the condition of unlimited labor no longer existed, neoclassical economics was not pertinent. The classical framework, as Lewis conceived it, was applicable instead.

The aura of practicality pervading Lewis's work is unsurprising given his early ambition to study business administration in England and then return to the Caribbean to take up a municipal service post or a private trade. He also studied law as a backup option. Following graduation, he failed, despite his qualifications, to obtain a position as an accountant for the Port-of-Spain City Council that he learned about while in London, because of local political machinations and nepotism in Trinidad (King 1985, 13). As a consequence, Lewis was shunted off to his illustrious career in economics.

The practical bent also underlies Lewis's investigations of the international dimensions of the business cycle. Concerned with the transmission of growth from rich to poor nations via international trade, Lewis's central emphasis was on policy. The Lewis vision of the international business cycle was elaborated in his Wicksell lectures published as *Aspects of Tropical Trade 1883–1965*, in *Growth Fluctuations 1870–1913*, in his Janeway lectures published as *The Evolution of the International Economic Order*, and in his Nobel address, "The Slowing Down of the Engine of Growth."

The essentials of the Lewis vision can be summarized as follows. The global pattern of trade reflects the structure established in the nineteenth century. The more affluent nations (MDCs) tend to be specialized in the production of manufactures while the poorer nations (LDCs) tend to be specialized in the production of primary products. The MDCs as a region possess an internal engine of growth driven by their domestic investment activity. Hence their growth rates are determined independently of the performance of the LDCs. In contrast, the LDCs possess an external engine of growth, relying on demand from the MDCs for their exports of primary products to dictate their pace of expansion. Hence the LDCs are highly dependent on the MDCs for their economic performance.

This asymmetric dependence means, in turn via the MDCs' demand for LDC exports, that MDC cyclical swings are transmitted to LDCs. When the MDCs are prosperous, their imports of primary products will boom, leading to a parallel upturn in the LDCs. When the MDCs are in recession, their imports of primary products will lag, leading to a parallel slowdown in the South. MDC growth drives the rate of growth in the South via the trade connection.

Lewis explored the implications for international inequality, observing that during the upturn, LDC industrial production for the home market received a stimulus as well. Indeed, the more rapid growth of industrial production in LDCs than in MDCs during a global upswing compensated for the slightly lower rate of expansion of export production in LDCs than in MDC industrial production. Similarly, during a downturn, industrial production would fall more rapidly in LDCs than in MDCs, offsetting the lesser decline in LDC export growth relative to the drop in MDC industrial production. Thus, the growth rates of the two regions were both about 5 percent a year between 1948 and 1973. However, because the growth of population is higher in LDCs than MDCs, equal rates of GDP growth translate into a widening gap in per-capita output. Lewis's mechanism for the international transmission of growth from rich to poor nations leads to a growing disparity between rich and poor nations in per-capita income (Lewis 1980, 556).

Lewis's claim that during the upturn, LDC export growth consistently falls slightly behind MDC export growth is embodied in his discovery of a key "stylized fact"—that the rate of growth of world trade in primary products from 1873–1913 was 0.87 times the rate of growth of industrial production in the MDCs and the same relationship held for the interval 1953–73 (Lewis 1978, 175–76). Thus, a 6-percent growth rate in MDC industrial production during an expansion would translate into a 5.2 percent growth rate in exports from the LDCs, the latter variable adequately proxied, according to Lewis, by growth in world trade in primary products.

The Lewis vision has been subjected to its most severe criticisms from James Riedel. Riedel rejects Lewis's "0.87 rule," denying that it is a stylized fact of a century of world trade. Riedel finds that the slope coefficient in the Lewis equation was closer to 0.60 in the 1960s than in the 1950s and 1970s—so that the relationship lacks the consistent stability ascribed to it by Lewis. However, the relationship is still positive, still statistically significant, even if the MDCs did not function as quite as strong an engine of growth for the LDCs in the 1960s as they did in other decades.

Riedel also stresses the changing compositions of LDC exports, arguing that the growth of LDC exports of manufactures undercuts the accuracy of the Lewis vision. Only the African LDCs continue, for the most part, to fit the model of primary-product export specialists (Riedel 1984, 63–64). Lewis was not unaware of such developments, but apparently felt that the core nature of trade between rich and poor nations still fit the traditional pattern. By 1980, imports of manufactures from LDCs remained only 2 percent of OECD countries' consumption of manufactures (Lewis 1980, 564).

The weakness that Lewis acknowledged in his story was its neglect of the channels of reciprocal dependence of MDCs on LDC economic activity. Certain LDC exports have proven to be essential to industrial production in some sectors of MDCs—e.g., minerals like copper, tin, bauxite, and, of course, petroleum (Lewis 1980, 559). In addition, Lewis observed that LDCs purchased 20 percent of OECD exports and thereby exercised some influence over MDC performance (Lewis 1980, 564).

But the extreme version of the Lewis vision, with one-way dependence, leads to clear but difficult practical advice for leaders of poorer nations. Lewis's admonition, similar to that of Ragnar Nurkse, is for LDCs to develop their own internal engine of growth. In short, extend the trend toward industrialization for both domestic use and for export. Lewis (1980, 562) even speaks of the prospect of new entrants into a "new center," exiting from the "periphery," with an entirely new engine of growth. But he remains worried about "those LDCs whose best option has been to export raw materials to MDCs" and who are unable to move into the center. The crux of the matter for Lewis was whether the LDCs can grow at a steady high rate, independently of fluctuations in the MDCs. In short, can they break out of the path foreordained by the international business cycle?

William Darrity Jr.

See also LDC Crisis

Bibliography
King, C. W. 1985. *"Summamttingitur Nitendo": A Tribute to Sir Arthur Lewis.* St. Lucia: Government of St. Lucia.
Lewis, W. A. 1954. "Economic Development with Unlimited Supplies of Labour." *Manchester School* 22:139–91.
———. 1969. *Aspects of Tropical Trade 1883–1965.* Stockholm: Almqvist and Wiksell.
———. 1977. *The Evolution of International Economic Order.* Princeton: Princeton Univ. Press.
———. 1978. *Growth and Fluctuations 1870–1913.* London: Allen and Unwin.
———. 1980. "The Slowing Down of the Engine of Growth." *American Economic Review* 70:555–64.
Riedel, J. 1984. "Trade as the Engine of Growth in Developing Countries Revisited." *Economic Journal* 94:56–73.

Lindahl, Erik Robert (1891–1960)
A central figure (along with Gunnar Myrdal, Bertil Ohlin, and Erik Lundberg) of the Stockholm School, Erik Lindahl provided the first formal statement of the concept of temporary equilibrium which has become a primary method of dynamic macroeconomic analysis. Not as well known as Myrdal and Ohlin, Lindahl nevertheless made theoretical contributions in public finance, income accounting, dynamic analysis, macroeconomics, and monetary policy that are scarcely less important than those of his more celebrated colleagues.

In his early work on capital theory ([1929] 1939), Lindahl provided, independently of Hayek ([1928] 1984), one of the first two explicit formulations of the concept of an intertemporal equilibrium. But while Hayek defined intertemporal equilibrium in terms of continuous time with economic agents correctly anticipating future prices, Lindahl defined intertemporal equilibrium as a sequence of discrete time periods in which all prices and quantities were determined at the outset. Recognizing that the concept of an intertemporal equilibrium is merely a limiting case in which the correct anticipation of future prices by all agents implied the mutual consistency of their individual plans, both Hayek and Lindahl agreed that the aim of dynamic analysis must be to comprehend the implications of incorrect anticipations which require the revision of plans by some or all economic agents. But whereas Hayek believed that equilibrium analysis, though useful in its own sphere, could not cope with such problems except under the *ceteris paribus* assumptions of partial-equilibrium analysis, Lindahl ([1930] 1939) attempted to apply equilibrium analysis by introducing the concept of a temporary equilibrium.

A temporary equilibrium is achieved within a short time period t if all prices adjust to equate demands and supplies. But if, owing to some change not foreseen in period $t–1$, prices in period t differ from those expected in period $t–1$, the temporary equilibrium will not correspond to a full intertemporal equilibrium, because agents will not be able to execute the plans they had formulated for period t based on the prices they had expected in period $t–1$.

Lindahl's papers on intertemporal equilibrium and temporary equilibrium were not translated into English until 1939. But J. R. Hicks, who had already become familiar with the concept of intertemporal equilibrium through his association with Hayek at the London School of Economics, learned about the concept of temporary equilibrium from personal contact with Lindahl in 1934–35. Thus, it was through Hicks's *Value and Capital*, in which Hicks adopted, with some modification, the method of temporary equilibrium, that the concept was introduced to most non-Swedish economists.

In later work, Lindahl himself sought to go beyond temporary-equilibrium analysis and formulated what he called sequence analysis (1939, 21–69). Erik Lundberg ([1937] 1955) used this method in his well-known contribution to dynamic analysis, the last major contribution by the Stockholm School to dynamic analysis. Nevertheless, although Hicks (1965) also came to be dissatisfied with temporary equilibrium as a method of dynamic analysis, temporary equilibrium remains an undeniably useful and popular tool for dynamic analysis.

In addition to his work on dynamic economic analysis, Lindahl also made important contributions in the field of macroeconomic and monetary theory and policy. Even aside from his work in public finance and social accounting theory, Lindahl's position among the leading figures of the remarkably productive interwar period is entirely secure.

David Glasner

See also EXPECTATIONS; HAYEK, FRIEDRICH AUGUST [VON]; HICKS, JOHN RICHARD; LUNDBERG, ERIK FILIP; MYRDAL, GUNNAR; OHLIN, BERTIL GOTTHARD; RATIONAL EXPECTATIONS; STOCKHOLM SCHOOL

Bibliography

Hayek, F. A. [1928] 1984. "Intertemporal Price Equilibrium and Movements in the Value of Money." Translation. Chap. 4 in *Money, Capital and Fluctuations: Early Essays.* Chicago: Univ. of Chicago Press.
Hicks, J. R. 1939. *Value and Capital.* Oxford: Clarendon Press.
———. 1965. *Capital and Growth.* Oxford: Clarendon Press.
Lindahl, E. R. [1929] 1939. "The Formulation of the Theory of Prices from the Viewpoint of Capital Theory." Translation. Part 3 of *Studies in the Theory of Money and Capital.* London: Allen and Unwin.
———. [1930] 1939. "The Means of Monetary Policy." Translation. Part 2 of *Studies in the Theory of Money and Capital.* London: Allen and Unwin.
———. 1939. *Studies in the Theory of Money and Capital.* London: Allen and Unwin.
Lindahl, G. and O. Wallmén. 1960. "Erik Lindahl. Bibliografi 1919–1960."
Eknomisk Tidskrift 62:59–74.
Lundberg, E. F. [1937] 1955. *Studies in the Theory of Economic Expansion.* Reprinted with an additional preface by the author. Oxford: Basil Blackwell.
Steiger, O. 1987. "Erik Robert Lindahl." In *The New Palgrave: The Dictionary of Economics.* Vol. 3. Edited by J. Eatwell, M. Milgate, and P. Newman. London: Macmillan.

L

Liquidity Premium

Liquidity premium refers to the nonpecuniary or immaterial yield of security on private property that is neither lent as credit nor used for investment. This yield is greatest on money, the most liquid form of private property. Monetary analysis in the tradition of J. M. Keynes suggests that this *premium*, which is not even mentioned in the conventional discussions of liquidity *preference* and the rate of *interest* (Panico 1987a, 1987b), may be decisive in causing business cycles.

Keynes, drawing on Frederick Lavington (1921, 30), introduced the concept of liquidity premium in chapter seventeen of the *General Theory*, calling it the amount that people are "willing to pay for the potential convenience or security" given by money ([1936] 1973, 226). This nonpecuniary yield of security is, thus, what causes interest. However, interest materializes only after "parting with control over the money in exchange for a debt" ([1936] 1973, 167). Keynes called the wish of an individual to hold wealth in the form of money *liquidity preference* ([1936] 1973, 166), a concept first hinted at by A. C. Pigou (1912, 424) and refined by Keynes ([1930] 1971, 127–29).

Keynes's assertion that liquidity preference would be absent "in a static society" or in one in which "no one feels any uncertainty about the future rates of interest" ([1936] 1973, 208) betrays circular reasoning. Since uncertainty about future rates of interest stems from fluctuations in liquidity preference, it cannot also explain why liquidity preference exists in the first place.

Keynes's confusion betrays a more general failure to distinguish between the three distinctive types of economy known in history. The relatively static ones are (1) *custom* or *tribal* and (2) *command* or *feudal* societies (including state socialism) in which the phenomena of interest and money are notoriously absent, because resources like land and labor cannot be sold, mortgaged, rented, or hired (Heinsohn and Steiger 1989). In tribal, feudal, or socialist societies, therefore, there are no business operations, and no *creditor-debtor contracts*; individuals may use *possessions* according to custom or command but do not know *property* in the sense of an absolute title allowing them to dispose of material and immaterial things however they please.

Only in (3) *private-ownership*-based societies can *individuals* dispose of property. Freed from duties to help imposed by tribal and feudal societies, they have to identify a yield accruing from their property at every moment. The size of this yield is determined less by the magnitude of private assets than by the proprietor's (i.e., the potential creditor's) estimate of his existential uncertainty, which cannot be cushioned by the collective-security arrangements of modern capitalist societies. Therefore, liquidity preference, liquidity premium, and their materialization into the rate of interest follow directly from the institution of private property.

To *increase* his wealth without more work the tribesman must *increase* the number of relatives by marrying off his daughters (exogamy) while the feudal lord must *increase* the number of his serfs. To do the same, the private proprietor must *decrease* the most liquid form of his property, i.e., sacrifice the security gained by holding control over money in exchange for a claim to interest.

According to Keynes, the comparison of the rate of interest with the liquidity yield involves the *second* of two distinct sets of decisions required by an individual's "psychological time preferences" ([1936] 1973, 166). The first set of time preferences involves an *intertemporal* choice between current and future consumption of his income. In neoclassical theory, the rate of interest is derived from this time preference. Interest is regarded as the return for a sacrifice of consumption today, i.e., for saving. Given the expectation of rising overall output in the future, owing to positive capital productivity, future consumption is regarded in the present as less valuable than an equal amount of immediate consumption. Lending today's resources, therefore, entails a material loss which the debtor must compensate with interest.

Keynes rejected the neoclassical derivation of the rate of interest as a return to saving, because *after* the first decision, an individual must decide whether to hold his savings in monetary (non-interest-bearing) form or in nonmonetary

(interest-bearing) forms for a stated period of *time*, i.e., as debts. *Time preference* explains the emergence of interest in both theories except that in the neoclassical theory creditors and debtors interact with each other as individuals who dispose of their initial endowments, i.e., as possessors of *resources*, whereas in Keynes's theory they are related to each other as possessors of *money*. Keynes eventually could not help but invoke the mere lapse of time, because he did not recognize that *in a money debt contract only the debtor is a possessor whereas the creditor is a proprietor*. Only the latter can choose between liquidity premium—which is not due to the perennial and, therefore, trivial lapse of time, but to the *social* institution of private property—and its materialization into interest.

Unlike the neoclassical creditor, the private proprietor, by supplying credit, suffers no material loss; he simply forgoes the access to his security. His demand for interest is wholly independent of positive capital productivity, and would be made even if overall output stagnated or decreased. The demand is occasioned only by the loss of the nonpecuniary liquidity premium which exists already as a by-product of private property. The debtor has to compensate for this loss by paying interest and, therefore, accepts the obligation if he expects to make a profit of at least equal value. It was Hugh Townshend who at least sensed that the basic cause of interest is not bound up with time as such when he elaborated on the *General Theory*: "The reluctance to part with liquidity—the property of liquid money which gives it exchange value and enables people to obtain interest by parting with money under contract—has its origin in the doubts of wealth-owners as to what my happen to values *before the end of any interval, however short*" ([1938] 1973, 290).

Keynes's linkage of liquidity preference to uncertainty about future rates of interest led him in chapter seventeen to attribute *depressions* to uncertainty. Assuming that asset yields generally decline as their stocks increase, Keynes showed that the yield of money, i.e., the rate of interest, falls more slowly than the yields of capital assets. This inflexibility of the rate of interest stems from (1) the "liquidity-motive" (holding money for its "potential convenience or security") together with (2) money's low elasticities of both production (supply) and (3) substitution. Thus, when wealth owners are uncertain about future economic conditions, the demand to hold money may be unusually high.

However, an increasing demand for money cannot be met by employing labor to produce more money. Nor, with its exchange value rising, can money be replaced by another commodity whose production is more elastic than money's. Consequently, when uncertainty is great, the rate of interest falls more slowly than the marginal efficiency of capital, and output and employment stop growing.

In chapter twenty-two of the *General Theory*, Keynes, in explaining economic *crises*, stressed the inflexibility of the rate of interest less than he did "a sudden collapse in the marginal efficiency of capital" ([1936] 1973, 315), occasioned by disappointed expectations about the future yields of capital goods. This disappointment creates uncertainty about the future which "precipitates a sharp increase of liquidity-preference—and hence a rise in the rate of interest" ([1936] 1973, 316), aggravating the crisis. The disappointment may be so complete that even a reduced rate of interest cannot start a recovery.

Advancing a "monetary Keynesian theory of interest," H. Riese (1986, 1987, 1989) sees uncertainty as inherent in a monetary economy and, thus, independent of future interest rates. Moreover, money's low elasticity of production is a necessary condition for money to be accepted in contracts, while its low elasticity of substitution is a necessary consequence of a monetary economy, since money alone discharges debts. Money, therefore, cannot be replaced by assets not accepted by creditors. The triviality of Keynes's properties of money is attributed to an imperfect understanding—despite important insights—of the difference between the "*contrived scarcity*" of money and the "*scarcity*" of money (Riese 1986, 53). For Keynes, in chapter fifteen of the *General Theory*, the rate of interest is determined by the speculative demand for money and the supply of money fixed by the *monetary authority*, i.e., it is the price of scarce money. Riese, drawing on chapters thirteen and seventeen of the *General Theory*, interprets the speculative motive not as a *demand for money* determined by the *rate of interest* but as *the withholding of money* by wealth owners as a function of the *liquidity premium*. Therefore, the rate of interest is determined not by an *institutionally* limited scarcity of money but by the decisions of *individual wealth owners*—represented by private banks—not to part with liquidity. Thus, the rate of interest reflects a *choice-theoretical* scarcity of money. Monetary authorities can change the rate of interest, but can control the supply of money only insofar as the rate of interest conforms with the wishes of wealth owners to exchange money for debt, i.e., with the liquidity premium.

These insights are developed into a theory of business cycles similar to Keynes's. The latter focused on unexplained fluctuations in expected rates of profit, whereas Riese (1986, 137–39, 148–50) interprets them as a result of inverse movements of the liquidity premium and the expected rate of profit. Thus, a *boom* is characterized by expectations of rising profits which reduce the liquidity premium, because creditors believe that the "reflux" of liquidity from debtors has become less risky. To dampen a boom, monetary authorities cannot raise the liquidity premium, only the rate of interest. Such a policy, however, risks turning the boom into a recession by curbing profit expectations. A *recession*, therefore, is characterized by expectations of falling profits, which increase the liquidity premium, because the reflux of liquidity has become more risky. Such a state of depression cannot be combatted by decreasing the rate of interest, only by a reduced liquidity premium which, again, cannot be controlled by the monetary authorities.

Although Riese rightly distances himself from Keynes's belief that the liquidity premium and the rate of interest are attributable to uncertainty about future rates of interest, he also attributes the rate of interest to uncertainty caused by the passage of time. In his reasoning, a rate of interest would not exist, nor would business cycles occur, if debtors could always guarantee the future reflux of the creditors' liquidity. In fact, this uncertainty can only explain why debtors must provide collateral that reverts to creditors in case of default. However, since the rate of interest—like the liquidity premium—obviously is *not* identical with surety, Riese, too, fails to explain this phenomenon satisfactorily (Heinsohn and Steiger 1988, 346–47).

In fact, the liquidity premium is part and parcel of private property. The organization of economic activity forces everyone to avoid overindebtedness by accumulating his wealth through the sacrifice of liquidity for interest or profit and, simultaneously, discourages him from risking his property by carelessly parting with liquidity. These opposing forces, responsible for boom and contraction alike, will persist as long as private ownership remains the organizing principle of society.

Gunnar Heinsohn
Otto Steiger

See also DEMAND FOR MONEY; KEYNES, JOHN MAYNARD; LOANABLE-FUNDS DOCTRINE; MONETARY POLICY

Bibliography
Bridel, P. 1987. *Cambridge Monetary Thought: The Development of Saving-Investment Analysis from Marshall to Keynes.* London: Macmillan.
Heinsohn, G. and O. Steiger. 1988. "Warum Zins? Keynes und die Grundlagen einer monetären Werttheorie." In *Keynes' General Theory nach fünfzig Jahren,* edited by H. Hagemann and O. Steiger, 315–53. Berlin: Duncker and Humblot.
———. 1989. "The Veil of Barter: The Solution to 'The Task of Obtaining Representations of an Economy in which Money is Essential.'" In *Inflation and Income Distribution in Capitalist Crisis: Essays in Memory of Sidney Weintraub,* edited by J. A. Kregel, 175–201. London: Macmillan.
———. 1996. *Eigentum, Zing, und Geld: Ungelöste Rätsel der Wirtschaftswissenschaft.* Reinbek: Rowohlt.
———. 1997. "Liquidity Premium, Property and Collateral: Three Neglected Concepts in the Theory of a Monetary Economy." *Economies et Sociétes,* vol. 31, série *Monnaie et Production,* no. 11 (forthcoming).
Keynes, J. M. [1930] 1971. *A Treatise on Money,* vol. 1. Vol. 5 of *The Collected Writings of John Maynard Keynes.* London: Macmillan.
———. [1936] 1973. *The General Theory of Employment, Interest and Money.* Vol. 7 of *The Collected Writings of John Maynard Keynes.* London: Macmillan.
Lavington, F. 1921. *The English Capital Market.* London: P. S. King.
Panico, C. 1987a. "Liquidity Preference." In *The New Palgrave: A Dictionary of Economics.* Vol. 3. Edited by J. Eatwell, M. Milgate, and P. Newman. London: Macmillan.
———. 1987b. "Interest and Profit." In *The New Palgrave: A Dictionary of Economics.* Vol. 2. Edited by J. Eatwell, M. Milgate, and P. Newman. London: Macmillan.
Pigou, A. D. 1912. *Wealth and Welfare.* London: Macmillan.
Riese, H. 1986. *Theorie der Inflation.* Tübingen: J. C. B. Mohr.
———. 1987. "Aspekte eines monetären Keynesianismus. Kritik der postkeynesianischen Ökonomie und Gegenentwurf." In *Postkeynesianismus. Ökonomische Theorie in der Tradition von Keynes, Kalecki und Sraffa,* edited by K. Dietrich, 189–206. Marburg: Metropolis.
———. 1989. "Geld, Kredit und Vermögen." In *Internationale Geldwirtschaft,* edited by H. Riese and H.-P. Spahn, 1–59. Regensburg: Transfer.
Townshend, H. [1938] 1973. Letter of November 11 to John Maynard Keynes. In *The Collected Writings of John Maynard Keynes.* Vol. 29. Edited by D. E. Moggridge, 289–93. London: Macmillan.

Loanable-Funds Doctrine

The loanable-funds theory, in its post-Keynesian formulations, summarizes the major static and dynamic determinants of interest rates in both the short term and the long term. The theory also provides an internally consistent account of the transmission mechanism between money, expenditures, and economic activity. The following interpretation is based on Dennis Robertson's identification of the major components of loanable funds and their connecting links. The loanable-funds theory will be contrasted with the liquidity-preference doctrine of Keynes, which orders the movements of interest, expenditures, and income differently.

Robertson (1940) identified the sources of loanable funds as current saving, "disentanglings" (the liquidation of past savings from fixed or working capital), net dishoardings of cash balances, and net additional bank loans. The demand for loanable funds originates in outlays for net new capital investment, replacement investment, increases in cash balances, and consumption in excess of current income.

The functioning of the loanable-funds market is described, on a first approximation, by assuming that saving is directed wholly to the purchase of securities (assumed to be a bond indexed to the price level) and that investment, a downward function of the interest rate, r, is financed entirely by issuing securities. In the existing-asset market the supply of and demand for real money balances, M/P and L, are the wealth complements of the real capitalized value of the existing stock of securities, S_E, and of the stock demand for securities, D_E:

$$L - M/P = S_E - D_E, \qquad (1)$$

where $\partial L/\partial r$, $\partial S_E/\partial r$, and $\partial(S_E - D_E)/\partial r$ are all < 0. The existing securities are claims to the entire stock of capital, none of which is directly held by wealth holders. The simplest formulation of the model is drawn in Figure 1 where both stock and flow markets are in equilibrium at a common real rate of interest r_0. On the left are the flow schedules, real saving S_0 and investment I_0. On the right are the demand for real balances L_0 and the stock of real balances M_0/P_0. The stock demand for and the existing stock of securities, D_E and S_E, are not shown in the diagram, but by Walras's law for stocks, they intersect at the same interest rate as do L_0 and M_0/P_0. The analysis abstracts from the growth of real income and output, which are assumed constant.

In Figure 2(a), I_0 shifts spontaneously to I_1, reflecting an increased demand for loanable funds, which, by assumption, consists in an increased flow supply of securities. Since saving (the flow demand for securities) has not increased, $I_1 - S_0$ at r_0 is an excess flow supply of securities, which tend to fall in price and rise in yield. The increased yield induces holders of the existing stock of assets to hold more securities and fewer cash balances. At $r_1 > r_0$, they buy the excess supply of new securities, transferring balances to investing firms. For an initial brief interval, the stock-flow equilibrium is:

$$I_1(r_1) - S_0(r_1) = M_0/P_0 - L_0(r_1) = \\ D_{E0}(r_1) - S_{E0}(r_1) > 0. \qquad (2)$$

The first pair of equalities is drawn in Figure 2 and corresponds to the boldface horizontal segments.

Because the money market is completely aggregated, the transfer of balances from asset holders to firms is not shown. To highlight the transfer, the balances at r_1 are assumed to be held momentarily and willingly by the recipient firms, as reflected in Figure 2(b) at point A on an increased total demand schedule $L_0 + \theta$. But the balances are earmarked for expenditure on new investment goods, corresponding, at the close of the period, to a leftward shift of L to its original position L_0 (θ returns to zero). With total output fixed, the general price level rises to P_1 and real balances fall synchronously with

L to M_0/P_1. The new point of equilibrium in the money market is B, at which the interest rate remains r_1 as determined by the excess flow supply of securities.

The adjustment pictured in Figure 2 continues through a sequence of similar periods until the market rate of interest is r_2, the "natural" level determined by the intersection of S_0 and I_1. In the money market at r_2, the price level is P_2, where $M_0/P_2 = L_0(r_2)$.

The analysis is readily applied to other disturbances. An instantaneous increase in the stock of money from M_0 to M_1 through a central bank's open-market purchase of existing securities would reduce the market rate from r_0 to r_1. The ensuing adjustment would resemble that following increased investment, except that, in the final equilibrium, interest returns to r_0 and prices rise to P_1 at which $M_1/P_1 = M_0/P_0$. If the central bank were to maintain r at r_1 by buying all excess flow securities forthcoming at r_1 after the initial purchase, $I_0 - S_0$ would be financed directly by a continuous increase in cash balances.

An autonomous increase in saving creates $S_1 > I_0$, which is an excess flow demand for securities. The excess demand spills into the existing-asset market where, by bidding up the price and reducing the yield to, say, r_1, it is spent on an equal excess supply of existing securities. The reduced quantity of securities demanded by asset holders coincides with the increased amount of desired real balances:

$$S_1(r_1) - I_0(r_1) = S_{E0}(r_1) - D_{E0}(r_1) = \\ L_0(r_1) - M_0/P_0 > 0. \qquad (3)$$

The additional desired balances are obtained as asset holders at r_1 hoard the receipts from their sale of preexisting securities. In the aggregate, however, an increase in the quantity of real balances to meet the increased quantity demanded at r_1 materializes only when the price level falls. That occurs as saving, following the increase to S_1, channels current receipts of income, through the stock-flow interaction, into the purchase of existing securities and into increased holdings of money in asset portfolios.

Of the remaining loanable-funds components cited by Robertson, two are particularly important: direct hoarding and dishoarding of cash balances. They can be introduced as structural features of the model by assuming that saving is allocated both to security purchases

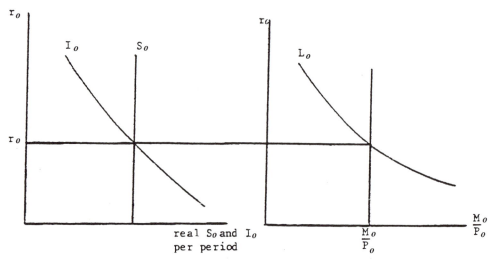

Figure 1. Stock-flow equilibrium in a loanable funds model.

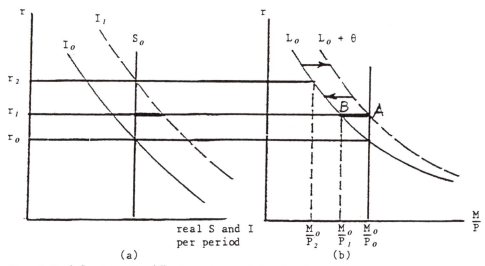

Figure 2. Stock-flow interaction following an increase in investment.

and to additional holdings of cash balances and that investment is financed both by issuing securities and by constantly drawing down cash balances. Saving is thus both a supply of and partially a demand for loanable funds, and investment is both a demand for and partially a supply of loanable funds. In this model, the equilibrium interest rate is determined by the intersection of the flow security components (Horwich 1964). Any excess of total saving over total investment demand at that rate is accompanied by a constantly increasing demand for real balances, $\dot{L} > 0$, and an equally increasing stock of real balances, $(\dot{M/P}) > 0$ owing to $\dot{P} < 0$. Alternatively, if $I > S$, then $\dot{L} > 0$, $(\dot{M/P}) < 0$, and $\dot{P} < 0$.

Keynes ([1936] 1973) advanced the liquidity-preference theory as a superior alternative to the loanable-funds doctrine of interest determination. As early as his *Treatise on Money*, he had argued that saving and investment in any relevant period are too small, relative to the accumulated stock of capital and financial assets, to affect the rate of interest directly. In the *General Theory*, Keynes hinted at and in a subsequent article (1937a) endorsed the view that all additions to expenditure raise the rate of interest indirectly by first raising income and then the demand for money, which raises the interest rate. Though widely accepted today, especially in modern textbooks (at the time, only Robertson questioned it), the analysis is inadequate because: (1) if the interest rate does not rise directly, dislodging portfolio balances, the desired expenditure may be unfinanced, and (2) an increase in income due to increased expenditures is an increase in money receipts which both motivates and, if $\partial L/\partial Y < 1$, provides the means for satisfying additional desired money holdings (Horwich 1957). Thus, acquiring cash balances by liquidating some existing securities (and thereby raising the rate of interest) is unnecessary when increased money income accrues as an increase in cash balances simultaneously received.

Writing after the publication of the *General Theory*, Keynes (1937b) introduced the notion of a "demand for finance," whereby firms planning new investment projects would first increase their demand for money and hence the rate of interest. Loanable-funds adherents, however, find it puzzling that changes in the demand for money and its wealth complement D_E, the stock demand for securities, could act directly on the rate of interest through the sale of existing securities while, because of alleged insufficient size, an equal increment in *flow* security supply originating in current investment could not (Horwich 1966).

In a second article on the subject, Keynes (1937c) extended the "finance" requirement to all expenditures, arguing that an increase in consumption would similarly be preceded by an increase in liquidity preference and the rate of interest (Tsiang 1956, Davidson 1965). But consumption need not be financed in this way (Horwich 1966). The most obvious funding source is the reduction in saving that accompanies increased consumption. At the same time, the resulting excess of I over S, in a loanable-funds context, raises the rate of interest directly and, in a stock-flow adjustment, maintains the funding of investment by dislodging cash balances from portfolios.

The claim that additional consumption raises the demand for money also ignores the fact that saving itself generally entails an expenditure—on securities. Like purchases of consumer goods, such expenditure must be supported by cash holdings. The shift between saving and consumption should therefore leave the total demand for money roughly unchanged.

The failure of Keynes and the Keynesians to define a consistent or meaningful role for liquidity preference in the dynamics of interest-rate determination does not imply that liquidity preference is unimportant. Its role, however,

can only be seen in the context of the stock-flow, loanable-funds process. At all times, the market rate lies at the intersection of the supply of and demand for money (assuming implicitly an infinite speed of adjustment in the existing-security market). But the equilibrating force moving the market rate is not a shift *of* the demand-for-money schedule, as Keynes argued. Rather, as illustrated in Figure 2, the stock-flow interaction moves the market rate *along* the liquidity-preference schedule. That movement coincides with a physical transfer of balances from asset holders to investing firms. For the economy as a whole, real balances fall when the excess investment raises the price level.

On this interpretation, loanable funds is clearly a more inclusive framework for the theory of interest determination than is liquidity preference. For the core flow components of loanable funds, saving and investment, not only drive the market rate in adjustment processes, but, reflecting the forces of thrift and productivity, determine the natural rate of interest toward which the money/existing-security market equilibrium is inexorably drawn.

In this light, the loanable-funds theory continues to be a powerful and valid underpinning of the standard macromonetary model in its dynamic applications.

George Horwich

See also AGGREGATE SUPPLY AND DEMAND; DEMAND FOR MONEY; LIQUIDITY PREMIUM; NATURAL RATE OF INTEREST; ROBERTSON, DENNIS HOLME

Bibliography
Davidson, P. 1965. "Keynes's Finance Motive." *Oxford Economic Papers* 17:47–65.
Horwich, G. 1957. "Money, Prices and the Theory of Interest Determination." *Economic Journal* 67:625–43.
———. 1964. *Money, Capital, and Prices.* Homewood, Ill.: Irwin.
———. 1966. "Keynes's Finance Motive: Comment." *Oxford Economic Papers* 18:242–51.
Keynes, J. M. [1930] 1971. *A Treatise on Money.* Vol. 1. *The Pure Theory of Money.* Vol. 5 of *The Collected Writings of John Maynard Keynes.* London: Macmillan.
———. [1936] 1973. *The General Theory of Employment, Interest and Money.* Vol. 7 of *The Collected Writings of John Maynard Keynes.* London: Macmillan.

———. 1937a. "The General Theory of Employment." *Quarterly Journal of Economics* 51:209–23.

———. 1937b. "Alternative Theories of the Rate of Interest." *Economic Journal* 47:241–52.

———. 1937c. "The 'Ex-Ante' Theory of the Rate of Interest." *Economic Journal* 47:663–69.

Robertson, D. H. 1940. "Mr. Keynes and the Rate of Interest." Chap. 1 in *Essays in Monetary Theory*. London: Staples Press.

Tsiang, S. C. 1956. "Liquidity Preference and Loanable Funds Theories, Multiplier and Velocity Analysis: A Synthesis." *American Economic Review* 46:539–64.

Long-Wave Theories

The expression *long wave* (or *long cycle*, or *major cycle*) describes a long-term fluctuation in the economy with a period of about 45–50 years, which is much longer than that of normal business cycles. This article does not discuss the problem of existence of long waves or specific statistical problems associated with them. It takes the existence of long waves for granted, without entering into the controversies about their existence.

Indeed if long waves do exist, business cycles are no longer a deviation from a linear trend, but must be related to the long-wave pattern. It seems clear that the analysis and forecast of business-cycle evolution cannot, in this case, abstract from long waves and, in particular, from the specific phase of the long wave within which it occurs.

The story of long waves begins at the end of the last century when some perceptive authors noticed empirical regularities in the behavior of the price level: prices rose from 1790 to 1815, from 1848 to 1873, and began to rise again from 1896; they fell from 1815 to 1848 and from 1873 to 1896. It is well known that monetary statistics were available before other real statistics and this was why the attention was concentrated on the price level. Moreover, many authors maintained that no fluctuations in real magnitudes had been associated with these movements in prices. This pattern therefore appeared to be consistent with the quantity theory of money, according to which the monetary and real variables of an economic system are separately determined. This interpretation was given among others by Cassel ([1918] 1932), Dupriez (1947), Simiand (1932) and shared by Oparin in his debate with Kondratieff.

However, Wicksell, in *Interest and Prices*, interpreted these price waves quite differently by elaborating his theory of the natural and market interest rates. His explanation was mathematically elaborated by Ragnar Frisch and has recently been supported by the work of the economic historian J. R. T. Hughes. Indeed fluctuations in the market rate of interest were amply recognized, among others, by Bresciani-Turroni [*Le Variazioni Cicliche dei Prezzi* (1913)].

After the gold standard was abandoned, such price-level fluctuations were no longer observed, and a clear upward trend dominated price-level movements. On the other hand, the simplistic view of a separation between real and monetary variables seemed to conflict with further empirical regularities that were being discovered.

An example of the latter is the behavior of the ratio of the prices of manufactured goods to those of agricultural and raw-material commodities. Rostow, in *The World Economy* (1978), reports that this ratio was decreasing in the following periods: 1790–1815, 1848–73, 1896–1920, 1936–51, 1973–78. Rostow (1975) argues that this pattern reflects the delayed response of the supply of primary products to changes in demand. The delay results from three main factors: (1) a substantial lag between the appearance of a profit possibility and the flow of new investments into the primary sector; (2) a lag between the start of an investment project and its completion; (3) a lag between the completion of the project and its full contribution to the actual flow of commodities. These lags induce a sort of cobweb phenomenon when demand changes with changes in income and production. In his explanation, Rostow considers both innovations that contribute to the growth of new industrial sectors and the population migration that induces investment in infrastructural capital.

Among the first authors who realized that long waves are a general phenomenon that include changes in the general price level, in relative prices, and in real magnitudes (particularly the rate of growth of output) was Kondratieff ([1925] 1979). Long waves are therefore often referred to as Kondratieff cycles, though such Dutch economists as Van Gelderen and De Wolff were among the forerunners (see Tinbergen's paper in Freeman

1983). Kondratieff underscored four major features of long waves (or major cycles as he called them): (1) before and after the lower turning point major changes occur in both adopted technology and gold production, and new countries enter the world market; (2) in the descending phase of the long wave there is widespread depression in the agriculture sector; (3) social revolutions and major wars accompany the final part of the ascending phase of the long wave; (4) during the upswing (downswing), trade cycles are characterized by short (long) recessions and long (short) expansions. Kondratieff argued that neither wars, gold production, nor even technical innovations are determining factors of the major cycle: on the contrary, they are wholly endogenously determined. He borrowed the main ingredients of his explanation from Tugan-Baranovsky's ([1894] 1913) theory of the business cycle. The explanation attributes long waves to the introduction or expansion of infrastructural capital (e.g., large-scale construction projects, big land-improvement projects, the construction of major railroads and canals, etc.) with very long periods of construction and requiring substantial inputs of resources. Financial conditions therefore play an important role in the realization of the investment. At the beginning of an upswing, a large amount of liquid capital is available for investment in replacing or expanding infrastructural capital: this engenders an upswing which is terminated precisely because the rate of increase of liquid capital falls short of the rate of increase in demand. During the ensuing downswing, the excess of liquid capital is restored, because deflation increases the real income of those with fixed nominal incomes (landlords, holders of consols and mortgages, civil and military servants, etc.) who typically belong to the saving classes. And a new long cycle can start again.

Though Kondratieff was not a (conventional) Marxist, and his theory was fiercely attacked in the 1920s as bourgeois theory, long-wave theory was cultivated in the USSR (Vasko 1987) and among contemporary Marxists at least in the 1970s. The most important representative is Mandel (1988). The mechanism he describes is rather traditional: at the beginning of the ascending phase, the rate of profit is high, stimulating expansion and technical innovations. The upper turning point is the result of the fall of the rate of profit due to the enormous development of fixed capital introduced to save labor. The lower turning point is really exogenous: every recession can be the last one in the history of capitalism if the working class takes power, whereas the political defeat of the workers permits a rise in the prospective rate of profit, favoring a new upswing.

A different application of long-wave theory was offered by Schumpeter (1939) who attributed the severity of the Great Crisis of 1929 to the coincidence of Juglar and Kondratieff cycles. His theory of the innovating entrepreneur probably fits the long-wave pattern better than the trade cycle. (For a beautiful formalization see Goodwin 1989.) Authors who follow the Schumpeterian hint include Mensch (1975) who insists that basic innovations grouping in the crisis are the main force in determining the lower turning point, and Freeman et al. (1982) who believe that each long wave is characterized by the adoption and diffusion across the whole economy of a techno-scientific paradigm (a concept elaborated by Giovanni Dosi) and that the downswing results from limits to the exploitation of economies of scale and to the increase in productivity. To restore economic expansion, a new paradigm must be adopted which involves changes in the institutional setup, the cultural framework of society, etc. Since such changes take time, the downswing continues for an extended period.

Finally there are authors who have a wider conception of the long wave: they believe that an integrated social-economic explanation of the phenomenon is needed. They include a group of American economists (see Gordon 1988) who hold that each long wave reflects the manifestation and dissolution of a specific form of the *social structure of accumulation*. They see the capitalist society as a whole and maintain that economic development needs a set of institutions to govern the conflicts and the distribution of power and wealth. When these interconnections no longer function properly due to the delegitimation of capitalistic power, a depression or recession sets in. The ensuing social conflict engenders a new set of rules and institutions, the new structure of social accumulation. In this interpretation, note that both the upper and the lower turning points are exogenous to the strict economic analysis.

In the context of interdependence between political and economic factors Pareto's (1916) analysis bears mention. Pareto viewed long waves as a process of creating savings (depressions) and dissipating them (prosperity) driven by the alternations of two types of agents: "speculators" and "rentiers" in the political and economic spheres.

By way of conclusion we remind the reader that at least since Kondratieff, via Hansen in *Economic Stabilization in an Unstable World* (1932), up to Goldstein (1988), wars and long waves have been regarded as closely related.

Massimo Di Matteo

See also FALLING RATE OF PROFIT; KON-DRATIEFF, NIKOLAI DMITRI-YEVICH; KON-DRATIEFF CYCLES; KUZNETS, SIMON SMITH; PARETO, VILFREDO; REGULATION SCHOOL; ROSTOW, WALT WHITMAN; SOCIAL STRUCTURE OF ACCUMULATION; TUGAN-BARANOVSKY, MIKHAIL IVANOVICH

Bibliography

Cassell, G. [1918] 1932. *The Theory of Social Economy.* Translation. 5th ed. New York: Harcourt Brace.

Di Matteo, M., R. M. Goodwin, and A. Vercelli, eds. 1989. *Technological and Social Factors in Long Term Fluctuations.* New York: Springer.

Dupriez, L. H. 1947. *Des Mouvements Économiques Généraux.* Louvain: Institut de recherches économiques et sociales.

Freeman, C., ed. 1983. *Long Waves in the World Economy.* London: Butterworths.

Freeman, C., J. Clark, and L. Soete. 1982. *Unemployment and Technical Innovation: A Study of Long Waves in Economic Development.* London: Pinter.

Goldstein, J. S. 1988. *Long Cycles: Prosperity and War in the Modern Age.* New Haven: Yale Univ. Press.

Goodwin, R. M. 1989. "Towards a Theory of Long Waves." In *Technological and Social Factors in Long Term Fluctuations,* edited by M. di Matteo, R. M. Goodwin, and A. Vercelli, 1–15. New York: Springer-Verlag.

Gordon, D. M. 1988. "Stages of Accumulation and Long Economic Cycles." In *Processes of the World System,* edited by T. K. Hopkins and I. Wallerstein, 9–45. Beverly Hills, Calif.: Sage Publications.

Kleinknecht, A., ed. 1991. *The Long Waves of the Economic Conjuncture: The Present State of the International Debate.* London: Macmillan.

Kondratieff, N. D. [1925] 1979. "The Long Waves in Economic Life." Translation. *Review* 2:519–62.

Mandel, E. 1988. *Long Waves of Capitalist Development: The Marxist Interpretation.* Cambridge: Cambridge Univ. Press.

Mensch, G. 1975. *Das technologische Patt: Innovationen uberwinden die Depression.* Frankfurt am Main: Umschau.

Pareto, V. [1916] 1935. *Trattato di sociologa generale.* Translated into English as *The Mind and Society: A Treatise on General Sociology* by A. Bongiurno and A. Livingston. New York: Dover.

Rostow, W. W. 1975. "Kondratieff, Schumpeter, and Kuznets: Trend Periods Revisited." *Journal of Economic History* 35:719–53.

———. 1978. *The World Economy: History and Prospect.* Austin: Univ. of Texas Press.

Schumpeter, J. A. 1939. *Business Cycles: A Theoretical, Historical, and Statistical Analysis of the Capitalist Process.* 2 vols. New York: McGraw-Hill.

Simiand, F. 1932. *Les fluctuations économiques à longue period et la crise mondiale.* Paris: Felix Alcan.

Tugan-Baranovsky, M. I. [1894] 1913. *Les crises industrielles en Angleterre.* Translation. 2d rev. ed. Paris: Giard & Briere.

Van Duijn, J. J. 1983. *The Long Wave in Economic Life.* London: Allen and Unwin.

Vasko, T., ed. 1987. *The Long-Wave Debate.* Berlin: Springer.

Wicksell, K. [1898] 1936. *Interest and Prices.* Translation. London: Macmillan.

Lowe, Adolph (1893–1995)

Adolph Lowe's contribution to the study of business cycles can hardly be overemphasized. His seminal works, especially his articles "The current state of research on business cycles in Germany" (1925) and "How is business cycle theory possible at all?" (1926) established him as the *spiritus rector* of the debates on business-cycle theory in Weimar Germany. (For a retrospective view, see Lowe 1989.) Lowe's leading role in these debates can also be seen by considering Hayek's *Monetary Theory and the Trade Cycle,* in which Hayek's dispute with Lowe plays an important and fruitful role. Lowe's contributions were also recognized outside Germany, as is shown by Kuznets (1930a, 1930b).

In contrast to economists like Hayek who attributed the cycle to monetary factors, Lowe emphasized technical progress. Indeed, he considered technical progress as the central determinant of both the cycle and the long-run growth trend, denying the possibility of distinguishing one from the other. His attempt to develop a theory of accumulation, technical progress, and structural change eventually culminated in his *The Path of Economic Growth* (1976). It shows Lowe to have been a pioneer along with J. R. Hicks in traverse analysis, i.e., in studying the conditions necessary for an economy to return to an equilibrium growth path after a change in a determinant of growth, such as the supply of labor or technical progress.

Born in Stuttgart, Germany, Lowe studied law, economics, and philosophy at the universities of Munich, Berlin, and Tübingen, receiving a doctorate from the latter in 1918. From 1919 to 1926 he worked in the Ministries of Labor and Economics, and in the Federal Bureau of Statistics in Berlin, cooperating with Ernst Wagemann who founded the Deutsches Institut für Konjunkturforschung, the first German institute for business-cycle research, in 1925. In 1926, Lowe became professor of economic theory and sociology at the University of Kiel as well as director of research at the Institute of World Economics where he founded the new department of statistical international economics and research on international trade cycles. He brought together a group of talented young economists, including Gerhard Colm, Frank Burchardt, Hans Neisser, Alfred Kähler and, briefly, Wassily Leontief and Jacob Marschak. The major research work of the Kiel School consisted in building a theoretical model of cyclical growth.

In 1933, Lowe was among the first professors fired by the Nazis. He emigrated immediately to England, where he was appointed special honorary lecturer in economics and political philosophy at the University of Manchester. In 1940, he joined the New School for Social Research in New York. After retiring in 1963, Lowe remained active as emeritus professor until his return to Germany in 1983.

In his brilliant 1926 paper, Lowe argued that a satisfactory business-cycle theory cannot simply model the consequences of an exogenous disturbance on an otherwise static economy. It must identify an endogenous causal factor that distorts the rigid interrelations implicit in a static general equilibrium.

Hayek ([1929] 1933, 33) accepted this methodological principle. Both also agreed on the importance of the underlying real structure of production and of changes in that structure over time. They differed in their identification of the distorting causal factor. Although he rejected oversimplified versions of the quantity theory and accepted most of Lowe's criticisms of monetary theories of the business cycle, Hayek nevertheless identified money and credit as the source of endogenous fluctuations. Real phenomena constitute the cycle, but monetary factors cause it.

Lowe (1928), however, denied that monetary fluctuations were in any way systematic. He assigned to monetary factors, at most, an intermediate causal role of intensifying any disequilibrium induced by nonmonetary causes. Lowe rather considered technological change in the era of progressive industrialization to be the decisive endogenous factor generating the trade cycle.

The Kiel School also studied the role of the industrial structure and of physical bottlenecks in production in the presence of structural change that may render the inherited stock of fixed capital goods inappropriate. The necessary adjustments are both costly and time-consuming. Economic investigation must therefore concentrate on the formation, allocation, and liquidation of real capital. Lowe (1952, 1955) later developed a structural model of production which he applied to his traverse analysis.

Two central ideas of his model originated in the research of the Kiel School which he revived and developed against the background of modern growth theory (Hagemann 1990). Lowe modified Marx's schemes of reproduction, whose division of the capital-goods sector into two parts, thereby extending the two-sector model into a three-sector model, he had always considered well suited to the study of real capital formation. A characteristic feature of Lowe's model is that a group of fixed capital goods classified as *machine tools* are capable of physical self-reproduction and therefore hold a strategic position in any industrial system analogous to that of seed corn in agricultural production. Moreover, the hierarchical order of the sectors implies a unique intertemporal complementarity which accommodates the

L

analysis of traverse processes in time. This intertemporal complementarity was reinforced by the Austrian flavor of Lowe's schema of industrial production (consisting of three sectors and four successive stages within each sector), which was based on the seminal synthesis of the sector model and the stage model of his colleague Frank Burchardt.

Unlike most contemporary economists, Lowe considers economics to be inseparable from social inquiry in general, a view permeating all his major works, especially his magnum opus, *On Economic Knowledge* (1977). [See also the contributions in Heilbroner (1969) and, more recently, Hagemann and Kurz (1990)]. He advocates a political economics whose central theoretical tool is instrumental analysis consisting not only of structural analysis but also of what Lowe calls force analysis.

Among the most challenging topics for instrumental analysis are structural change and technological unemployment. The main message of Lowe's traverse analysis is that capital formation is necessary for the reabsorption of displaced workers. The derivation of possible adjustment paths based on structural requirements is a necessary first step in Lowe's instrumental approach to political economy which seeks to formulate an economic policy for achieving balanced growth. Structural analysis must be supplemented by force analysis: the study of the behavioral and motivational patterns that will guide an economy along an appropriate traverse. Force analysis has a special significance for the analysis of adjustment processes in market systems. Lowe's force analysis underscores the crucial role of expectations and the significance of a functioning price mechanism.

In more than sixty years of research, Lowe has focused on technological change as the mainspring of destabilizing tendencies in industrial economies. One of the reasons for this is that innovations are a permanent feature of capitalist economies and are endogenously generated by the competitive process. In his latest work Lowe (1988, chap. 6) has been particularly concerned with the now dominant form of technological change, the microelectronic revolution, which is displacing labor not only from the production of goods but also from the provision of services. The specter of technological unemployment has reappeared. Although, in principle, compensation is possible, the main issue "is the question of whether the market system of late capitalism is endowed with a *self-regulating* mechanism capable of achieving compensation by the uncontrolled actions of private consumers and producers, or whether *public intervention* is necessary in order to counter destabilizing tendencies that an uncontrolled market is likely to create" (Lowe 1988, 99). Although Lowe, like Hayek, addressed the relevance of the time structure of production to economic fluctuations, the last statement highlights a major difference between them. Even without money, Lowe's model describes an adjustment process full of difficulties. Like the work of Hicks (1973), the other pioneer in traverse analysis, Lowe's work shows that the exclusion of money ensures neither a stationary equilibrium nor an equilibrium growth path.

Harald Hagemann

See also AUSTRIAN THEORY OF BUSINESS CYCLES; BURCHARDT, FRITZ (FRANK) ADOLPH; CAPITAL GOODS; HAYEK, FRIEDRICH AUGUST [VON]; REAL BUSINESS-CYCLE THEORIES

Bibliography

Hagemann, H. 1990. "The Structural Theory of Economic Growth." In *The Economic Theory of Structure and Change,* edited by M. Baranzini and R. Scazzieri, 144–71. Cambridge: Cambridge Univ. Press.

Hagemann, H. and H. D. Kurz. 1990. "Balancing Freedom and Order: On Adolph Lowe's Political Economics." *Social Research* 57:733–53.

Hayek, F. A. [1929] 1933. *Monetary Theory and the Trade Cycle.* Translation. London: Jonathan Cape.

Heilbroner, R. L. 1969. *Economic Means and Social Ends: Essays in Political Economics.* Englewood Cliffs, N.J.: Prentice-Hall.

Hicks, J. R. 1973. *Capital and Time: A Neo-Austrian Approach.* Oxford: Clarendon Press.

Kuznets, S. 1930a. "Equilibrium Economics and Business-Cycle Theory." *Quarterly Journal of Economics* 44:381–415.

———. 1930b. "Monetary Business Cycle Theory in Germany." *Journal of Political Economy* 38:125–63.

Löwe, A. 1925. "Der gegenwärtige Stand der Konjunkturforschung in Deutschland." In *Die Wirtschaftswissenschaft nach dem Kriege. Festgabe für Lujo Brentano zum 80 Geburtstag.* Vol. 2. Edited by M. J.

Bonn and M. Palyi, 329–77. Munich: Duncker und Humblot.

———. 1926. "Wie ist Konjunkturtheorie überhaupt möglich?" *Weltwirtschaftliches Archiv* 24:165–97.

———. 1928. "Über den Einfluß monetärer Faktoren auf den Konjunkturzyklus." In *Beiträge zur Wirtschaftstheorie. Zweiter Teil: Konjunkturforschung und Konjunkturtheorie,* edited by K. Diehl, 355–70. Schriften des Vereins für Sozialpolitik, 173/II. Munich: Duncker und Humblot.

Lowe, A. 1952. "A Structural Model of Production." *Social Research* 19:135–76.

———. 1955. "Structural Analysis of Real Capital Formation." In *Capital Formation and Economic Growth,* edited by M. Abramovitz, 581–634. Princeton: Princeton Univ. Press.

———. 1976. *The Path of Economic Growth.* Cambridge: Cambridge Univ. Press.

———. 1977. *On Economic Knowledge: Toward a Science of Political Economics.* Armonk, N.Y.: M. E. Sharpe.

———. 1987. *Essays in Political Economics: Public Control in a Democratic Society,* edited and introduced by A. Oakley. New York: New York Univ. Press.

———. 1988. *Has Freedom a Future?* New York: Praeger.

———. 1989. "Konjunkturtheorie in Deutschland in den Zwanziger Jahren." In *Studien zur Entwicklung der ökonomischen Theorie VIII,* edited by B. Schefold, 75–86. Berlin: Duncker und Humblot.

Loyd, Samuel Jones (1796–1883)

Samuel Jones Loyd was born on 25 September 1796 in Lothbury, England. Following in his father's footsteps, he became a distinguished country banker. Immersed in the practical economic issues of his day, he was an active member of London's Political Economy Club for nearly fifty-two years.

Loyd served on several Parliamentary committees such as the Commission of the Hand Loom Weavers (1837–40) and the Commission to Consider the Decimal Coinage (1855). In 1849, Lord Russell elevated Loyd to the House of Lords, conferring on him the title, "Lord Overstone," by which he is widely known. On Loyd's death in 1883, The *New York Times* called him the "greatest living authority on all matters connected with trade and finance."

Sometime in the 1830s, Loyd became a fervent advocate of the early Bullion Committee proposals (first presented in 1810) calling for the restoration of the gold standard at the old parity (Fetter 1965). By keeping 100-percent gold reserves behind each additional note issued above a statutory level, the Bank of England could maintain full convertibility of the currency at all times.

The worst catastrophe that Loyd imagined was the overissue of inconvertible paper money which could sap the foundations of a free society by undermining contractual relationships and engendering distrust among all social classes. Loyd's primary contribution to the study of the business cycle was to analyze the tendency of currency overissue to accentuate business instability.

Loyd took the novel view that business fluctuations are a true "cycle"—a recurring and unavoidable feature of a market economy. Periods of prosperity are followed by periods of crisis in business psychology or the "state of confidence." The cycle is tied to psychology and not to any structural feature of the capitalist economy.

Loyd's ([1857] 1972, 31) use of the metaphor "revolves . . . in an established cycle," and his references to business activity, "naturally" following a "circular course," were profoundly original. The prevailing view then was that "crises" were sporadic and not recurring. In his pamphlets and in his Parliamentary testimony, Loyd repeatedly explained that the overissue of paper money can accentuate the naturally recurring business cycle, thereby promoting economic instability.

Loyd spent most of his public life attacking the Bank of England for not adhering to the so-called "currency principle." In brief, the currency principle required that the bank vary the amount of its outstanding notes by exactly as much as its gold-coin or bullion reserves changed. If gold flowed in (out), then notes were to be issued (withdrawn). The currency principle was to be followed regardless of the state of the economy or what was actually causing the bank's reserves to fluctuate.

A number of economists such as Thomas Tooke, John Fullarton and, most notably, John Stuart Mill criticized the currency principle. They argued that the proper bank response to fluctuations in its reserves should not be automatic but should depend on the bank's assessment of the source of the disturbance.

Loyd was not the only economist of his day to advocate the currency principle. Other advocates included James Pennington, John McCulloch, George W. Norman, Robert Torrens and Mountifort Longfield. But it was Loyd who must be credited with recommending the celebrated, institutional reform of the Bank of England that was designed to ensure adherence to the currency principle.

Loyd argued that an issuer of convertible bank notes should be regarded as a special agent of the government, obligated to behave in a prescribed fashion. When printing paper money, the bank was to think of itself less as a bank and more as a special agent with a statutory duty to manage a portion of the nation's money supply in a particular way. Loyd, therefore, recommended splitting the Bank into two departments, of which one would be responsible for issuing banknotes and the other for all other banking operations.

The issue department was to be insulated from the pressures of the banking department, whose main function was to make profitable loans and, during times of financial crisis, to *accommodate* the needs of trade by lending to its customers. An experienced banker, Loyd knew full well the enormous pressures exerted on bank officers in times of financial distress. Favored customers ask for loans, and the officers are pressured to accommodate those requests. That is why it was critical to insulate the issue department from customer pressure. Peel's illustrious Bank Charter Act of 1844 institutionalized Loyd's proposal by mandating the creation of a separate note-issuing department within the four walls of the Bank of England.

In retrospect, the currency principle is the ancestor of all monetary reforms, both in the nineteenth and especially in the twentieth centuries, that are designed to substitute an automatic rule for the always varying and sometimes untrustworthy judgments of the central banker. Indeed, Loyd's work is firmly in the tradition of those who advocate requiring the money-issuing authorities to abide by a rule or limitation that would insulate the quantity of money from vicissitudes of local factions and party politics (Yeager 1976).

The significance of Loyd's work for the study of the business cycle lies in his clear statement of the advantages of rules over discretion in moderating the business cycle. Loyd's contribution was at the "constitutional" level of eco-

nomic organization. The codification of his ideas in Peel's Bank Reform Act of 1844 was a stunning victory for one important line of analysis of the classical school.

Laurence S. Moss

See also BANK CHARTER ACT OF 1844; BANKING SCHOOL, CURRENCY SCHOOL, AND FREE BANKING SCHOOL; BANK OF ENGLAND; CRISIS OF 1847; FULLARTON, JOHN; JOPLIN, THOMAS; MISES, LUDWIG EDLER VON; TOOKE, THOMAS; TORRENS, ROBERT

Bibliography

Fetter, F. W. 1965. *The Development of British Monetary Orthodoxy 1797–1873.* Cambridge: Harvard Univ. Press.

O'Brien, D. P. 1971. "Introduction." *The Correspondence of Lord Overstone.* Edited by D. P. O'Brien. Cambridge: Cambridge Univ. Press.

Overstone, Lord [S. J. Loyd]. [1857] 1972. *Tracts and Other Publications on Metallic and Paper Currency.* Edited by J. R. McCulloch. Englewood Cliffs, N.J.: A. M. Kelley.

Schwartz, A. J. 1987. "Banking School, Currency School, Free Banking School." In *The New Palgrave: A Dictionary of Economics.* Vol. 1. Edited by J. Eatwell, M. Milgate, and P. Newman. London: Macmillan.

Viner, J. 1937. "English Currency Controversies, 1825–1865." Chap. 5 in *Studies in the Theory of International Trade.* New York: Harper.

Yeager, L. 1976. "Proposals for Thoroughgoing Reform." Chap. 31 in *International Monetary Relations: Theory, History and Policy.* New York: Harper and Row.

Lucas Critique

Robert E. Lucas Jr. ([1976] 1981, 126) proposed an explanation for why coefficients in econometric equations might be nonconstant when policy rules change.

> [G]iven that the structure of an econometric model consists of optimal decision rules of economic agents, and that optimal decision rules vary systematically with changes in the structure of series relevant to the decision maker, it follows that any

change in policy will systematically alter the structure of econometric models.

Lucas's critique of econometric models focuses on how policy-rule parameters may enter parametrically into agents' optimization rules. Lucas considered examples where agents' *expectations* of policy behavior enter into their optimization problem, and so parameters relating to policymakers' rules appear in the agents' first-order conditions. In essence, the issue is whether an econometric model isolates "invariants" of the economic process, a topic with a lengthy and contentious history in the econometric literature (Haavelmo 1944, Frisch 1948, Aldrich 1989).

Lucas ([1976] 1981, 108–09) motivated his critique with four observations: "frequent and frequently important refitting of econometric relationships;" intercept adjustments in forecasting; the empirically superior forecasts by models with randomly varying coefficients; and the exclusion (in modeling) of data prior to 1947, even though such data should be informative. All four observations could arise from empirical model misspecification of the sort described by Lucas.

The general economic structure postulated by Lucas is considered below, and a simple expectations model provides an illustration. Further, the Lucas critique is refutable as well as confirmable, so tests of the Lucas critique are examined.

The Lucas Critique Confirmed

Following Lucas, consider an economy characterized by an agent decision rule $F(\cdot)$ derived from optimizing behavior and a policy reaction function $G(\cdot)$:

$$y_{t+1} = F(y_t, x_t, \theta, \varepsilon_t) \qquad (1)$$

$$x_t = G(y_t, x_{t-1}, \lambda, \eta_t), \qquad (2)$$

where y_t and x_t are the endogenous variables and exogenous (policy or forcing) variables at time t, θ and λ are the parameters of $F(\cdot)$ and $G(\cdot)$, and ε_t and η_t are the corresponding independent, identically distributed shocks. For instance, y_t and x_t might be consumer expenditure and a government-supplied income supplement, $F(\cdot)$ and $G(\cdot)$ the empirical consumption function and the rule for providing supplements, and θ and λ the respective parameters. Through agent optimization, θ might depend on λ, in

which case changes in the latter would alter the value of the former. Econometric models treating θ as a fixed parameter would then "break down" when policy changed λ, leading to the four confirmatory observations above. A *policy* is seen as "a specification of present and future values of some components of $\{x_t\}$" (Lucas [1976] 1981, 106–07), so policy can be interpreted quite broadly to include (e.g.) tax law, a meteor striking the earth, and the oil price set by OPEC.

Lucas has models with forward-looking expectations explicitly in mind, and the following example illustrates how such expectations create difficulty for conditional econometric models. Suppose equations (1) and (2) are:

$$y_{t+1} = \alpha E(x_{t+1} | I_t) + \varepsilon_t, \qquad (3)$$

$$x_t = \lambda x_{t-1} + \eta_t, \qquad (4)$$

where α is a "deep structural parameter" related to utility optimization, $E(\cdot)$ is the expectations operator, and I_t is the information available to agents at time t (when they decide on y_{t+1}). For $I_t = x_t$, then $E(x_{t+1} | I_t) = \lambda x_t$ from equation (4), so equation (3) becomes:

$$y_{t+1} = \theta x_t + \varepsilon_t, \qquad (5)$$

where $\theta = \theta(\lambda) = \alpha\lambda$. If the econometrician estimates θ via equation (5), ignoring the dependence of θ on λ, then policy simulations based on equation (5) for alternative paths of $\{x_t\}$ (and so for alternative values of λ) will give misleading results. The estimated value of θ, which is used in simulation of equation (5), need not be the value implied by the agents' rule, as represented in equation (3).

The Lucas Critique Refuted

Whether the Lucas critique applies for a specific model is thus an empirical issue. Specifically, two related properties of θ are of concern: its constancy (or lack thereof) as λ changes, and its dependence on (or invariance to) changes in λ. As suggested by Gordon (1976, 48–49) and developed by Hendry (1988), Favero and Hendry (1992), and Engle and Hendry (1993), these properties provide two approaches to testing the Lucas critique.

(i) Test for the constancy of θ in equation (1) and of λ in equation (2). If θ is constant but λ is not, θ is invariant to λ and so the Lucas critique could not apply. The three other combinations of constancy and nonconstancy for θ and λ could occur with the Lucas critique, but also could arise with other sorts of misspecification.

(ii) Develop equation (2) until it is empirically constant. For instance, by adding dummies or other variables, model the way in which λ varies over time. Then test for the significance of those dummies or other variables in equation (1). Insignificance in equation (1) demonstrates invariance of θ to the changes in λ, whereas significance shows the dependence of θ on λ.

The invariance of θ to changes in λ implies the super exogeneity of x_t, provided that the parameters of interest to the investigator can be retrieved from θ alone (Engle, Hendry, and Richard 1983). Hendry (1988), Hendry and Ericsson (1991), Favero and Hendry (1992), and Engle and Hendry (1993) provide evidence refuting the Lucas critique for money demand in the United States and the United Kingdom. Brodin and Nymoen (1992) and the papers in Ericsson (1992) provide evidence on other countries and other variables.

Remarks
Several remarks are in order. First, whether the Lucas critique applies depends on the class of changes to λ being considered. For instance, θ may be invariant to a temporary income supplement but not to a permanent one; and the cause and magnitude of the supplement may affect invariance. For tests (i) and (ii), the changes in λ occurring in-sample for the tests may or may not belong to the same class as do the policy simulations of interest to the economist. Second, and surprisingly, test (i) does not require a full specification of equation (2) to refute the Lucas critique. Details appear in Hendry (1988). Third, the observations motivating Lucas's critique could arise from more mundane causes, such as dynamic misspecification, omitted variables, and incorrect functional form; and those causes cannot be precluded a priori. Fourth, modeling of expectations does not necessarily resolve the Lucas critique. If expectations are improperly modeled, policy analysis with the corresponding misspecification of equations (1)–(2) may well result in inaccurate and biased simulations.

Summary
The Lucas critique provides one of several possible explanations for the less-than-satisfactory performance over the last two decades of many macroeconometric models. If the Lucas critique applies, it has ramifications for policy simulation with such models. If economic agents base their decisions on forward-looking expectations and empirical models fail to account for that, then those models will mispredict when policies change, generating misleading policy simulations. The Lucas critique is empirically testable, being both confirmable and refutable.

Neil R. Ericsson
David F. Hendry

See also EXPECTATIONS; MACROECONOMETRIC MODELS, HISTORICAL DEVELOPMENT; RATIONAL EXPECTATIONS; TINBERGEN, JAN

Bibliography
Aldrich, J. 1989. "Autonomy." *Oxford Economic Papers* 41:15–34.

Brodin, P. A. and R. Nymoen. 1992. "Wealth Effects and Exogeneity: The Norwegian Consumption Function 1966(1)–1989(4)." *Oxford Bulletin of Economics and Statistics* 54:431–54.

Engle, R. F. and D. F. Hendry. 1993. "Testing Super Exogeneity and Invariance in Regression Models." *Journal of Econometrics* 56:119–39.

Engle, R. F., D. F. Hendry, and J.-F. Richard. 1983. "Exogeneity." *Econometrica* 51:277–304.

Ericsson, N. R., ed. 1992. *Cointegration, Exogeneity, and Policy Analysis*. Special issues no. 3–4. *Journal of Policy Modeling*, vol. 14.

Favero, C. and D. F. Hendry. 1992. "Testing the Lucas Critique: A Review." *Econometric Reviews* 11:265–306.

Frisch, R. 1948. "Repercussion Studies at Oslo." *American Economic Review* 38:367–72.

Gordon, R. J. 1976. "Can Econometric Policy Evaluations Be Salvaged?—A Comment." In *The Phillips Curve and Labor Markets. Carnegie-Rochester Conference Series on Public Policy*, Spring, 47–61.

Haavelmo, T. 1944. "The Probability Approach in Econometrics." *Econometrica* 12 (Supplement):1–118.

Hendry, D. F. 1988. "The Encompassing Implications of Feedback versus Feedforward Mechanisms in Econometrics." *Oxford Economic Papers* 40:132–49.

Hendry, D. F. and N. R. Ericsson. 1991. "Modeling the Demand for Narrow Money in the United Kingdom and the United States." *European Economic Review* 35:833–81.

Lucas, R. E. Jr. [1976] 1981. "Econometric Policy Evaluation: A Critique." In *Studies in Business-Cycle Theory*, 104–30. Cambridge: MIT Press.

Lundberg, Erik Filip (1907–1987)

Erik Lundberg was the last surviving member of the Stockholm School, which, in the 1930s, made pioneering contributions to macroeconomics, transcending the static macroequilibrium approach of Keynes's *General Theory*. Lundberg's 1937 doctoral dissertation, *Studies in the Theory of Economic Expansion,* presenting the sequence approach, is the capstone work of the school on macroeconomic fluctuations.

As implied by the title of the study, the key feature of Lundberg's approach to the business cycle is his derivation of the cycle as inherent in a growing economy. This achievement marks Lundberg as a forerunner of Harrod's 1939 theory of economic growth (see Lindbeck's contribution in Jonung 1991). Lundberg's technically most notable contribution to business-cycle theory was to model the upper turning point in a Wicksellian setting in terms of an imbalance between aggregate investment and savings. However, while making explicit the behavior patterns governing the onset of the crisis and the ensuing downturn, Lundberg underscored their variability, and he did not model the bottom phase of the cycle. Anticipating Samuelson's ([1939] 1966) formalization of the multiplier-accelerator interaction, he developed a number of dynamic models (based on systems of difference equations) to illuminate these lags in the pattern of fluctuations.

A central feature of his models is a focus on the output lag (often termed the Lundberg lag) representing the lag between a change in demand and the realization of the output response to that change. The other lags in the pattern of macroeconomic fluctuations recognized by Lundberg were conceptually submerged in his models because of this emphasis on the supply response. In considering the various lengths of the latter, Lundberg introduced what he called the unit period, a methodological device that he

regarded as one of his most important accomplishments (see the preface to Lundberg [1937] 1955).

In discussing the lagged output response to changes in demand, Lundberg considered the inertia in the supply of both consumer goods and capital goods. His most noted model concerns investment in consumer-goods inventories which laid the groundwork for the later contribution by Metzler. Less noted is his treatment of capital goods through a model of long-run investment in building and structures analyzing the interactions between the financial and commodity markets during the upturn, which formalized the role of the rate of interest in so-called overinvestment crises.

A third type of model that Lundberg developed at some length concerns the medium run in which investment leads to increasing supply capacity. Here the issue is the possibility that the lag between current investment and increased production capacity may not match the corresponding lag on the demand side of the same process. In investigating the dynamics implied by these lags, Lundberg assumed that the cost of producing capital goods may fail to generate an equal amount of paid-out income (e.g., dividends may be withheld as retained earnings) and that there may be so-called Robertsonian lags between the receipts of disposable income and actual outlays. (One interesting version of this type of model concerned the implications of technical change when the resulting investment matures into capital goods yielding labor-saving productivity increases.)

Although Lundberg's study was well received when it appeared (see reviews listed in the bibliography), it seems, despite Metzler's later explicit acknowledgment, soon to have fallen from view. Both Hicks and Harrod subsequently claimed priority for contributions that should at least in part be attributed to Lundberg as well.

However, even with the resurgent interest in and now much improved understanding of his accomplishments, misconceptions about Lundberg's work persist. That it still stands "in the shadow of Keynes" suggests that the book has been read with insufficient attention to what Lundberg actually tried to do. Too much of the criticism of it has concerned its formal deficiencies. Although recent work (see Berg in Jonung 1991) has clarified the nature of some of the errors and deficiencies in the study, Lundberg's failure to solve the reduced forms of his systems of difference equations is still often attributed to an inability to do so. But the reason seems rather to have been methodological. Tracing an expansion as a disequilibrium sequence of temporary states was the essence of the *ex post/ex ante* method of the Stockholm School. This method permitted consideration of aspects of the process whose formal specification would have entailed nonlinearities requiring analysis in terms of chaos theory (Baumol 1990). Lundberg's sequence approach actually seems to have been the best way to cope with parametric variations that would now be recognized as instances of path dependence.

One reason why Lundberg's remarkable study was neglected might be that World War II interrupted the international exchange of ideas. The theoretical discussions about macroeconomic fluctuations became mainly an internal affair among Anglo-American economists. However, another reason is that the study that put Lundberg in the front row of Swedish business-cycle analysts also led to his becoming head of the Swedish National Institute for Economic Research or Konjunkturinstitutet (KI). The empirical and policy focus as well as the mere burden of work at KI kept Lundberg from participating in the further advance of business-cycle theory. He subsequently focused instead on applied business-cycle problems, making several contributions almost as interesting and important as his theoretical ones.

A major summary of Lundberg's applied work during his KI period is contained in his *Business Cycles and Economic Policy*. This book discusses and reports on, among other things, measurements of the inflationary gap and the forecasting activities and various types of policy analyses conducted by the KI. (Much of this work reflects not only the theoretical approach of his 1937 dissertation but also his early empirical research behind that study dealing in particular with the Great Depression.) The book also reports on empirical research on the cyclical robustness and sensitivity of the Swedish economy. In demonstrating its "inflation-proneness" as compared with, say, the United States' economy, Lundberg focused particularly on taxes as inflationary wedges. He worked out a formula for assessing their impact which he referred to as the "wage(-tax) multiplier."

Lundberg also used his dissertation models in later applied work, but as the postwar period seemed to indicate that the business cycle had disappeared, Lundberg's interests shifted toward the long run and the Schumpeterian aspects of economic change. Having resigned from KI in 1955 to resume full-time academic teaching, he began to study the causes of growth in productivity. However, his interest in business cycles continued, resulting in *Instability and Economic Growth*, a work that filled a notable void in the comparative literature on economic instability and stabilization policy.

Focusing mainly on Sweden, but always against the international background and in a comparative light, Lundberg in his applied work analyzed and evaluated the design and impact of economic policies in a small open economy. Here he drew on his own experience both as a policy adviser and as a participant in policy debates from the 1940s to the 1980s. His was an influential voice in the revival of monetary policy in Sweden that began in the 1950s. Lundberg's writings on economic policy contain quite modern public-choice views and anticipate many ideas that have been in the forefront of recent microbased supply-side analyses. However, despite his sophisticated eclecticism, Lundberg's basic policy stance has always remained closest to that of the old Keynesian.

Lundberg's last major applied work, "The Rise and Fall of the Swedish Model," is of interest as a synthesis of his previous work on Swedish stabilization policy during the postwar era. It also testifies to the importance he attached to the need to retain a historical perspective even when considering the short term. This particular feature in his methodological stance is also manifested in many of his other writings, such as in his economic-historical surveys of Sweden's performance over the last half century.

The leading Swedish representative in international professional circles, Lundberg served as a member of the board and finally also as the chairman of the International Economic Association, presiding over a number of its conferences devoted to macroeconomic themes (Lundberg 1955, 1977). It was therefore only natural that in his final years Lundberg emerged as the main trustee of the heritage of the Stockholm School, and wrote retrospectively on its thinking and its leading personalities, explaining also how his own early studies in business-cycle theory fit into that wider frame of reference. An English anthology of Lundberg's works (Lundberg 1995) will provide increased international access to his contributions.

Rolf G. H. Henriksson

See also DIFFERENTIAL AND DIFFERENCE
EQUATIONS; HARROD, ROY FORBES; KOOP-
MANS, TJALLING CHARLES; LEADS AND LAGS;
LINDAHL, ERIK ROBERT; METZLER, LLOYD
APPLETON; MYRDAL, GUNNAR; OHLIN,
BERTIL GOTTHARD; SAMUELSON, PAUL
ANTHONY; SAVING EQUALS INVESTMENT;
STOCKHOLM SCHOOL; WICKSELL, JOHAN
GUSTAV KNUT

Bibliography
Baumol, W. J. 1990. "Erik Lundberg, 1907–
   1987." *Scandinavian Journal of Eco-
   nomics* 92:1–9.
Bryce, R. B. 1938. Review of *Studies in the
   Theory of Economic Expansion* by E. F.
   Lundberg. *Canadian Journal of Econom-
   ics and Political Science* 4:118–22.
Harrod, R. F. 1937. Review of *Studies in
   the Theory of Economic Expansion*
   by E. F. Lundberg. *Zeitschrift für
   Nationalökonomie* 8:494–98.
Jonung, L., ed. 1991. *The Stockholm School
   of Economics Revisited*. Cambridge:
   Cambridge Univ. Press.
Kahn, R. F. 1938. Review of *Studies in the
   Theory of Economic Expansion* by E. F.
   Lundberg. *Economic Journal* 48:265–68.
Lange, O. 1938. Review of *Studies in the
   Theory of Economic Expansion* by E. F.
   Lundberg. *Economica*, n.s., 5:243–47.
Lundberg, E. [1937] 1955. *Studies in the
   Theory of Economic Expansion*. Re-
   printed with an additional preface by
   the author. Oxford: Basil Blackwell.
———. [1953] 1957. *Business Cycles and
   Economic Policy*. Translation. London:
   Allen and Unwin.
———, ed. 1955. *The Business Cycle in the
   Post-War World*. Proceedings of a Conference held by the International Economic Association in Oxford, September
   1952. London: Macmillan.
———. 1959. "The Profitability of Investment." *Economic Journal* 69:653–77.
———. 1968. *Instability and Economic
   Growth*. New Haven: Yale Univ. Press.
———, ed. 1977. *Inflation Theory and Anti-
   Inflation Policy*. London: Macmillan.
———. 1985. "The Rise and Fall of the
   Swedish Model." *Journal of Economic
   Literature* 33:1–36.
———. 1995. *Studies in Economic Instability
   and Change*. Edited with a postscript by R.
   G. H. Henriksson. Stockholm: SNS Förlag.
———. 1996. *The Development of Swedish
   and Keynesian Macroeconomic Policy*.
   Cambridge: Cambridge Univ. Press.
Metzler, L. A. 1941. "The Nature and Stability of Inventory Cycles." *Review of Eco-
   nomics and Statistics* 23:113–29.
Neisser, H. 1938. Review of *Studies in the
   Theory of Economic Expansion* by E. F.
   Lundberg. *Journal of Political Economy*
   46:253–56.

L

Lutz, Friedrich August (1901–1975)

F. A. Lutz was born in Sarrebourg (Lorraine), now
in France but then part of Germany, and studied
economics in Heidelberg, Berlin, and Tübingen.
After receiving his doctorate in 1925, and following a short detour into the world of practical affairs, Lutz became an assistant to his thesis supervisor, Walter Eucken, at the University of
Freiburg where he remained a lecturer until emigrating in 1938 as a result of Hitler's rise to
power. He commenced his academic career anew
at Princeton University, remaining there until
1953 when he accepted a chair at the University
of Zürich, which he held until retiring in 1972.

A variety of books and over 100 published
articles bear testimony to Lutz's exceptionally
productive career. His first major publication
was a splendid dissection of contemporary business-cycle theory—the last highlight in a German debate which, although cut short prematurely, did not lack distinguished participants or
controversial points of view. However, Lutz
soon turned to the field which would occupy his
research in the future: the neoclassical theory of
money, capital, and interest.

Lutz's first work on monetary theory appeared in 1936, and a number of important
papers followed his emigration. The most influential of these was his discussion of the term
structure of interest rates. These essays exhibit
a characteristic feature of Lutz's writings, an
ability to advance modern theory from the
firm ground of a profound knowledge of the
"classics." [Lutz (1962) is a collection of papers on monetary theory written before 1938
and after 1950.]

In 1951, Lutz coauthored (with his wife,
Vera Lutz) *The Theory of Investment of the
Firm*. Seminal in its merging of modern microeconomic theory with a treatment of "capital
and time" in the Austrian tradition, this work
greatly influenced modern capital theory and
would remain a major source of reference for

the next decade. However, Lutz's best-known work was published in 1956, in German. In 1967 the second, expanded, English edition, *The Theory of Interest*, appeared. Surveying interest rate theory from Böhm-Bawerk onwards and couching it in modern terms, it concluded with the author's own account of the state of the art. Now considered a classic, this work remains indispensable for those working in the field.

Equally noteworthy (and similar in its design), is Lutz's habilitation (1932), an early contribution to business-cycle theory. Written from the viewpoint of contemporary equilibrium theory, this work thoroughly reviews alternative theories of economic fluctuations, concluding that a systematic theory of the business cycle within the framework of equilibrium analysis is neither possible nor necessary. Though a "general glut" could be accounted for by properly incorporating money and credit into the analysis, the periodic recurrence of the cycle is depicted as inconsistent with the methodological "first principles" of general equilibrium theory. Instead, every cycle should be viewed as a unique historical event and explained as the consequence of an exogenous variation in the given set of data of the model. Regular periodicity therefore has to be derived from "outside" the system.

Lutz focused on the methodological principles of equilibrium theory on one hand, and exogenous versus endogenous explanations of the (observed) pattern of seemingly regular and periodic co-movements of aggregate time series on the other. Lutz rejected the "realistic" approaches of the interwar period for confusing inductive conclusions with pure theory. Although Marx and Schumpeter offered treatments that potentially represented endogenous explanations, Marx's theory was shown to be logically flawed and Schumpeter's was held to implicitly assume irrational behavior by entrepreneurs. A corrected version of Schumpeter's theory would have to rely on exogenous technological change, which amounts to a change in data and therefore does not necessarily imply periodicity. Similarly, he criticized monetary theories of the business cycle (e.g., those of Hawtrey and Hayek) for not providing a systematic account of the maladjustments of prices necessary to deduce periodicity.

This work has not attracted the attention it deserves, primarily because it has not been translated to English. Nonetheless, Lutz's discussion should be considered indispensable for any truly comprehensive account of the origins of contemporary equilibrium business-cycle theories.

Lutz, who appears never to have had any difficulty in reconciling his neoclassical perspective with his reading of the classics, later became also increasingly skeptical of the relevance of modern growth theory (1968). An outspoken opponent of totalitarian danger, he paid for his liberal views with expatriation. Described as a gentle man, combining "firmness in his convictions with respect for those of others" (Niehans 1987, 253), he is an outstanding example of the brain drain Germany suffered because of Hitler's rise to power.

Christof Rühl

See also MONETARY EQUILIBRIUM THEORIES OF THE BUSINESS CYCLE; REAL BUSINESS-CYCLE THEORIES; SCHUMPETER, JOSEPH ALOIS; TERM STRUCTURE OF INTEREST RATES

Bibliography
Lutz, F. A. 1932. *Das Konjunkturproblem in der Nationalökonomie*. Jena: G. Fischer.
———. [1936] 1962. "Das Grundproblem der Geldverfassung." In *Geld und Währung: Gesammelte Abhandlungen*, 28–102. Tübingen: J. C. B. Mohr.
———. [1938] 1951. "The Outcome of the Savings-Investment Discussion." In *Readings in Business Cycle Theory*, 131–57. Philadelphia: Blakiston.
———. 1940. "The Term Structure of Interest Rates." *Quarterly Journal of Economics* 52:588–614.
———. 1945. "The Interest Rate and Investment in a Dynamic Economy." *American Economic Review* 35:811–30.
———. 1962. *Geld und Währung: Gesammelte Abhandlungen*. Tübingen: J. C. B. Mohr.
———. 1967. *The Theory of Interest*. Dordrecht: D. Reidel.
———. 1968. "Probleme der Zinstheorie." *Weltwirtschaftliches Archiv* 101:1–18.
———. 1971. *Politische Überzeugung und nationalökonomische Theorie*. Tübingen: J. C. B. Mohr.
Niehans, J. 1987. "Lutz, Friedrich August." In *The New Palgrave: A Dictionary of Economics*. Vol. 3. Edited by J. Eatwell, M. Milgate, and P. Newman. London: Macmillan.

Luxemburg, Rosa (1871–1919)

Rosa Luxemburg's first contribution to the Marxian theory of crises came in her blistering attack on the revisionist ideas of Eduard Bernstein. Much more significant was the linking of imperialism and economic crises in her controversial *Accumulation of Capital*.

Luxemburg was born into a Jewish family in Russian Poland, grew up in Warsaw, and spent several years in exile in Switzerland. A resident of Germany after 1898, she worked for the Social-Democratic Party as a journalist and lecturer. Always prominent in the party's revolutionary left-wing, Luxemburg led the opposition to German involvement in World War I, was imprisoned, and then helped to set up the *Spartakusbund* in 1919. She was murdered by paramilitaries after the abortive German revolution.

Towards the end of the 1890s, Eduard Bernstein published a series of attacks on Marxist theory, which included claims that the emergence of cartels and the increasing use of credit had permanently ameliorated the impact of the trade cycle. The economic collapse of capitalism, Bernstein concluded, was no longer likely. In 1898, Luxemburg defended "socialist theory up to now" against the new revisionism. Marxism insisted that "the point of departure for a transformation to socialism would be a general and catastrophic crisis . . . [C]apitalism, as a result of its own inner contradictions, moves to a point when it will be unbalanced, when it will simply be impossible." For Luxemburg this proposition was one of the pillars of scientific socialism. If capitalism really were becoming more stable, as Bernstein maintained, proletarian revolution would be unnecessary. Luxemburg denied that this was so, since the factors cited by Bernstein actually worked in the opposite direction. The expansion of credit encouraged unsustainable and speculative increases in production, while cartels merely transferred profits from one industry to another, serving as an "instrument of greater anarchy" ([1899] 1970, 8–13).

There was no coherent theory of crises in this. However, *The Accumulation of Capital* did contain a very substantial discussion of crises in terms of the models of economic reproduction sketched by Marx in the second volume of *Capital*. Luxemburg's aim was to demonstrate that Marx had erred seriously in asserting that steady equilibrium growth was possible—at least in principle—in a closed capitalist economy. Against this, Luxemburg argued that customers must be available outside the system to purchase (in Marx's term, to "realize") the increasing amounts of surplus value which were produced within it.

Whether Luxemburg can be described as an underconsumptionist remains controversial. *The Accumulation of Capital* certainly addressed the underconsumptionist literature, surveying the writings of Sismondi, Malthus, Rodbertus, and the Russian populists in addition to those of Marx and the English Classical political economists. Luxemburg's problem was this: what generates the continuously growing demand which is needed to realize surplus value in an expanding capitalist economy? She examined, only to reject in turn, the possibility that a solution lies in the consumption of workers, of capitalists, or of Malthusian "third persons." Luxemburg denied, too, Tugan-Baranovsky's contention that it is capitalists' investment expenditures from which the increased demand originates. For Luxemburg, this made capitalists out to be "fanatical supporters of an expansion of production for production's sake. . . . [T]he upshot of all this is not accumulation of capital but an increasing production of producer goods to no purpose whatever" ([1913] 1951, 334–35).

Luxemburg concluded that capitalism was profoundly contradictory. It relied upon perpetually increasing consumer demand from noncapitalist producers, above all the peasants and artisans of colonial and semi-colonial territories. Hence the violent imperialist penetration of the precapitalist "hinterland." But, once contact had been made with noncapitalist societies, their disintegration and rapid assimilation into the capitalist world economy was inevitable. Eventually there would be no remaining noncapitalist customers. Either socialist revolution would intervene, or the entire system "must break down" (467). Meanwhile, periodic crises would result from "the deep and fundamental antagonism between the capacity to consume and the capacity to produce in a capitalist society" (347).

The fatal error in Luxemburg's reasoning had already been identified by Tugan-Baranovsky. The production of machines to produce machines for the production of yet more machines might well be profitable, both for individual capitalists and for the system as a whole, so long as the various types of machines (and consumption goods) were produced in the correct proportions. If so, stable accumulation was perfectly possible, no matter how absurd it might appear when judged by the standards of human well-being.

Luxemburg replied to her critics (the most important being the Austrian socialist Otto Bauer) in a polemical *Anti-Critique* which set out her argument more clearly than she had been able to do in *The Accumulation of Capital,* but added nothing to it. Her ideas have never commanded the support of even a significant minority of Marxian economists, yet they invariably attract attention whenever the relationship between imperialism and crisis is under discussion.

M. C. Howard
J. E. King

See also BAUER, OTTO; BERNSTEIN, EDUARD; DISPROPORTIONALITY THEORY; FALLING RATE OF PROFIT; KAUTSKY, KARL; MARX, KARL HEINRICH; OVERSAVING THEORIES OF BUSINESS CYCLES; TUGAN-BARANOVSKY, MIKHAIL IVANOVICH

Bibliography

Bauer, O. [1913] 1986. "Otto Bauer's 'Accumulation of Capital.'" Translated by J. E. King. *History of Political Economy* 19:87–110.

Bleaney, M. 1976. *Underconsumption Theories.* London: Lawrence and Wishart.

Geras, N. 1973. "Rosa Luxemburg: Barbarism and the Collapse of Capitalism." *New Left Review* 82:17–37.

Howard, M. C. and J. E. King. 1989. *A History of Marxian Economics.* Vol. 1. *1883–1929.* Princeton: Princeton Univ. Press.

Kalecki, M. 1971. "The Problem of Effective Demand in Tugan-Baranovski and Rosa Luxemburg." Chap. 13 in *Selected Essays on the Dynamics of the Capitalist Economy, 1933–1970.* Cambridge: Cambridge Univ. Press.

Luxemburg, R. [1899] 1970. *Reform Or Revolution.* New York: Pathfinder Press.

———. [1913] 1951. *The Accumulation of Capital.* London: Routledge and Kegan Paul.

———. 1972. "The Accumulation of Capital—an Anti-Critique." In *Imperialism and the Accumulation of Capital,* edited by K. Tarbuck, 47–150. London: Allen Lane.

Nettl, J. P. 1966. *Rosa Luxemburg.* Oxford: Oxford Univ. Press.

Robinson, J. 1951. "Introduction." In R. Luxemburg, *The Accumulation of Capital,* 13–28. London: Routledge and Kegan Paul.

M

Macroeconometric Models, Historical Development

Economists did not apply formal statistical techniques to empirical observations to estimate macroeconomic relationships or test macroeconomic theories until the twentieth century. The political arithmetic of Petty, Graunt, King, and Sussmilch was limited to demographic, tax, and balance-of-trade data, while Quesnay's pioneering representation of the circular flow of income and spending in his *Tableau Economique* (1758) used arbitrary numerical examples, rather than actual data. Economists ignored what Stephen Stigler (1986) terms "the first great synthesis" of nineteenth-century statistics, in which Laplace, Legendre, and Gauss related the principle of least squares to the normal distribution. But around the turn of the century they did take note of the correlation analysis of "the second great synthesis" of Galton, Karl Pearson, Edgeworth, and Yule.

Irving Fisher of Yale was a pioneer in efforts to empirically verify the quantity theory of money and the monetary theory of the trade cycle. In 1892 he constructed a hydraulic machine which used the actual flow of liquids to simulate monetary flows, with the level of liquid in a central reservoir indicating the price level. Fisher's contraption, which inspired a later hydraulic model by A. W. Phillips now on display at the London School of Economics, did not base rates of flow on empirical observations, but it allowed macroeconomic relationships to be simulated in the era before electronic computers. Fisher later calculated the correlation between the observed price level and the price level predicted by a constant-velocity version of the quantity theory, and the correlation between unemployment and a distributed lag of past changes in the price level (so that one of his articles was eventually reprinted as "I Discovered the Phillips Curve").

The availability of more plentiful data and increasing concern with aggregate fluctuations stimulated applications of correlation, and later regression, techniques to macroeconomic data in the 1920s and 1930s. Wesley Mitchell and his associates at the National Bureau of Economic Research and Warren Persons of the Harvard Economic Society correlated economic time series to find leading indicators and construct "business barometers," with little reliance on formal economic theory. Morris Copeland (1929) of the NBER correlated lead and lagged series to investigate the direction of causality among money, prices, and the volume of trade, anticipating later work by Granger and Sims. V. S. Dadayan (1981, Chap. 2) reports the beginnings of macroeconomic modeling of a centrally planned economy by Soviet economists in the 1920s (aborted by Stalin's purges of the economics institutes).

Other contributions were less useful: the attempts by R. M. Walsh to test the quantity theory's equation of exchange (without any assumption about velocity) against the "fundamental equations" of Keynes's *Treatise on Money,* and of Colin Clark to test Keynes's fundamental price equations against Hayek's theory, were vitiated by failure to notice that without further restrictions, these equations are untestable tautologies. Correlation studies of the effect of money on trade by the Industrial Institute and by R. G. Glenday, both published by the Royal Statistical Society in 1932, were shown by G. Udney Yule to owe their high correlation coefficients largely to the presence of time trends in the series being correlated.

Building on earlier regressions of demand and supply for single commodities, Ragnar Frisch and Jan Tinbergen applied multiple-regression analysis to macroeconomic systems of simultaneous equations. This work, for which Frisch and Tinbergen shared the first Nobel Memorial Prize in Economics, was carried on by two other Nobel laureates, Trygve Haavelmo, a student of Frisch, and Tjalling Koopmans, who studied with both Frisch and Tinbergen. Tinbergen estimated the first large macroeconometric model (of the Dutch economy) and then modeled the United States economy in the course of an ambitious League of Nations study testing macroeconomic theories. Such a project only became possible after the development of national income accounts by Simon Kuznets and others, Jerzy Neyman's and Egon Pearson's formulation of the classical theory of hypothesis testing, and the solution of the identification problem for simple cases by Frisch, Tinbergen, and Sewall Wright.

Tinbergen's study was sharply criticized in published reviews by J. M. Keynes and Milton Friedman, and by Frisch at a Cambridge conference in 1938. Some problems critics identified, such as biases due to omitted variables and neglect of simultaneity, created the agenda for Haavelmo and the contributors to Cowles Commission conference volumes. The issue of structural change proved more difficult to cope with than the others, and this criticism of Tinbergen has reappeared as the Lucas critique of using structural models to evaluate policy changes, which holds that a policy change may alter the structural coefficients.

Unlike the atheoretical time-series analysis of Mitchell and Persons, the Cowles Commission method, presented in Koopmans (1950) and Hood and Koopmans (1953), used a priori economic theory to impose coefficients of zero on enough variables to identify the structure of a system of simultaneous equations. Since the ordinary-least-squares (OLS) estimation of simultaneous equations used by Tinbergen is inconsistent because of the "Haavelmo bias" (bias due to simultaneity), Cowles researchers studied the asymptotic properties of systems estimators to find consistent alternatives to OLS. Limited-information maximum-likelihood estimation (LIML) was developed by T. W. Anderson of Cowles as a less efficient, but computationally-simpler, alternative to full-information maximum-likelihood (FIML) methods for consistent estimation. Theil's two-stage least squares and Theil and Zellner's three-stage least squares later provided even simpler consistent estimators for linear models.

While Frisch, Haavelmo, and Tinbergen withdrew from structural estimation to the degree that Frisch ignored it in a 1961 survey of forecasting methods, another Nobel laureate, Lawrence Klein, took a leading role in empirical macroeconometrics, from Klein Models I–III in his 1950 Cowles monograph through the Klein-Goldberger, Brookings and Wharton models of the United States economy, the Klein-Ball model of Britain, and finally Project LINK, a linking of national macroeconometric models to model the world economy. These structural models grew larger and less aggregated, from the fifteen equations of the Klein-Goldberger model in 1955 to the 2,094 equations of CANDIDE, the Canadian Inter-Departmental Econometric Model, fifteen years later. The gains from consistent systems estimators proved disappointing, so that while the Klein-Goldberger model was estimated with LIML, in 1979 the hundreds of equations of the Wharton model were estimated by OLS, without even correcting for serial correlation of errors. By the 1960s, structural models were widely used by governments and the private sector, both for forecasting and to evaluate policy changes.

Ta-Chung Liu (1960) sharply criticized identifying restrictions of structural models as frequently spurious, intended to avoid statistical difficulties rather than to incorporate economic theory or prior information. Exactly-identifying restrictions cannot be tested, while overidentifying restrictions, which can be tested, were often rejected in published tests. Liu suggested that the underlying structure might be too complex to capture with the available data (e.g., eighteen annual observations for the Klein-Goldberger model), while Lucas ([1976] 1981) reminded economists that policy changes can induce changes in behavior and hence in structure.

These concerns, reinforced by the unsuccessful out-of-sample prediction record of structural models, revived interest in forecasting methods that do not estimate underlying structure. One approach was to estimate small reduced-form models, such as the eight-equation Monetarist model of the Federal Reserve Bank of St. Louis. Another was the vector autoregression (VAR) of Sims, regressing each variable on its own lagged values and on current and lagged values of all variables, marking a return to the "measurement without theory" of Mitchell and the NBER. The forecasting success of these models has been uneven, and VAR models, lacking a priori exclusionary restrictions, easily grew to have more parameters per equation than observations, unless the number of variables and lag length were arbitrarily limited.

Another response to the Lucas critique, challenging to apply but ultimately more promising, has been to attempt to model "deep structure," that is, to estimate coefficients of objective functions that are invariant to policy changes. Computational advances have made possible FIML estimation of medium-sized nonlinear systems incorporating the cross-equation restrictions implied by rational expectations. Analysis of the properties of systems estimators in small samples, attempted but abandoned by Cowles staff in the 1940s and early 1950s, was resumed by R. L. Basmann in the 1960s and later by P. C. B. Phillips. Despite the difficulties of Cowles-style structural estimation, macroeconometrics may be reestablishing itself on a sounder footing.

Robert W. Dimand

See also FISHER, IRVING; FRISCH, RAGNAR ANTON KITTEL; FULL INFORMATION MAXIMUM LIKELIHOOD; HAAVELMO, TRYGVE; KLEIN, LAWRENCE ROBERT; LUCAS CRITIQUE; KOOPMANS, TJALLINGS CHARLES; MACROECONOMETRIC MODELS, USE OF; MITCHELL, WESLEY CLAIR; MODEL EVALUATION AND DESIGN; MOORE, HENRY LUDWELL; PERSONS, WARREN MILTON; RATIONAL EXPECTATIONS; TINBERGEN, JAN; VECTOR AUTOREGRESSIONS

Bibliography
Bodkin, R. G., L. R. Klein, and K. Marwah. 1991. *A History of Macroeconometric Model-Building*. Aldershot, Hants, England: Edward Elgar.
Copeland, M. A. 1929. "Money, Trade, and Prices—A Test of Causal Primacy." *Quarterly Journal of Economics* 43:648–66.
Dadayan, V. S. 1981. *Macroeconomic Models*. Moscow: Progress.
Dimand, R. W. 1994. *The Rise and Development of Macroeconomics*. Aldershot, U.K.: Edward Elgar.
Epstein, R. J. 1987. *A History of Econometrics*. Amsterdam: North-Holland.
Fisher, I. [1926] 1973. "A Statistical Relation Between Unemployment and Price Changes." Reprinted as "I Discovered the Phillips Curve." *Journal of Political Economy* 81:496–502.
Frisch, R. 1934. *Statistical Regression Analysis by Means of Complete Regression Systems*. Oslo: Univ. Economic Institute.
Haavelmo, T. 1944. *The Probability Approach in Econometrics. Econometrica* 12 (Supplement):1–118.
Hendry, D. [1980] 1993. "Econometrics: Alchemy or Science?" Chap. 1 in *Econometrics—Alchemy or Science? Essays in Econometric Methodology*. Oxford: Basil Blackwell.
Hood, W. C. and T. C. Koopmans, eds. 1953. *Studies in Econometric Method*. Cowles Monograph no. 14. New York: Wiley.
Klein, L. R. 1950. *Economic Fluctuations in the United States 1921–1941*. Cowles Monograph no. 11. New York: Wiley.
Koopmans, T. C. 1937. *Linear Regression Analysis of Economic Time Series*. Haarlem, Netherlands: De Erven F. Bohn.
———. [1947] 1965. "Measurement Without Theory." In *A.E.A. Readings in Business Cycles*, 186–203. Homewood, Ill.: Irwin.
———, ed. 1950. *Statistical Inference in Dynamic Economic Models*. Cowles Monograph no. 10. New York: Wiley.
Leamer, E. 1983. "Let's Take the Con Out of Econometrics." *American Economic Review* 73:31–43.
Liu, T. C. 1960. "Underidentification, Structural Estimation, and Forecasting." *Econometrica* 28:855–65.
Lucas, R. F. [1976] 1981. "Econometric Policy Evaluation: A Critique." In *Studies in Business-Cycle Theory*, 104–30. Cambridge: MIT Press.
de Marchi, N. and C. Gilbert, eds. 1989. *History and Methodology of Econometrics*. Special issue of *Oxford Economic Papers*. Vol. 41, Supplement.
Morgan, M. S. 1990. *A History of Econometric Ideas*. Cambridge: Cambridge Univ. Press.
Sims, C. 1980. "Macroeconomics and Reality." *Econometrica* 48:1–45.
Stigler, S. M. 1986. *A History of Statistics*. Cambridge: Harvard Univ. Press.
Tinbergen, J. 1939. *Statistical Testing of Business Cycle Theories*. 2 vols. Geneva: League of Nations.

M

Macroeconometric Models, Use of

Large-scale macreconometric models are now commonly used both to analyze and to forecast business cycles. A large-scale macroeconometric model utilizes large numbers and blocks of equations to represent such measures of economic activity as gross domestic product, total consumption, business investment, and the average price level. Parameter estimates for the equations are obtained by applying statistical-estimation and hypothesis-testing techniques to economic time series and using industry input-output data. The models are validated by computer simulations of historical behavior and macroeconomic response to changes in monetary and fiscal policies.

Large-scale macroeconometric models normally contain at least 100 stochastic equations for macroeconomic behavioral aggregates, with additional equations for definitions, exogenous inputs, and constraints. Large-scale models generally are nonlinear, time-dependent or dynamic, and involve many simultaneous interaction and feedback mechanisms. Most model-builders have focused on combinations of Keynesian-type (*IS-LM*-derivative) and neoclassical systems. Some have emphasized the financial aspects of macroeconomic behavior. And still others stress input-output relationships. The emphasis of a model and the detail of its specification depend on the purposes for which it is constructed and the questions it is supposed to address.

Large-scale macroeconometric models used in forecasting or business-cycle analysis usually are supplemented by additional complementary systems, with the model serving as the centerpiece. The model identifies and isolates the principal explanatory factors that affect major economic aggregates. The business-cycle analyst or forecaster can then focus on a limited number of main inputs with a high likelihood of having identified what is most important to macroeconomic activity. Adjustments to behavioral equations based on singular external events, errors of equations, and discrepancies relative to current data allow the incorporation of nonmodel information that can help improve forecast accuracy.

High-frequency, information-monitoring systems, using daily, weekly, or monthly instead of quarterly data help in assessing current economic and financial-market activity. Sensitivity and policy studies performed with the model assess responses to "what if" changes in exog-enous factors. Survey information and other monitoring methods can be used to identify the phase of the business cycle.

The development, use, and applications of large-scale macroeconometric models were originally undertaken in academia and government, with initial focus on the United States economy. The use of large-scale models to study business cycles began with Jan Tinbergen (1939) and was actively pursued over several decades by Lawrence Klein in collaboration with numerous colleagues and students. The pioneering work of Klein in the 1950s was followed by a burst of academic and research studies in the 1960s and 1970s: Duesenberry et al. (1965), the FRB-MIT-PENN model (De Leeuw and Gramlich 1968), which emphasized the role of financial markets and financial processes, and Fromm and Klein (1975). Modeling and forecasting have been performed with the University of Michigan Quantitative Research Seminar Model since 1953 (Suits 1962, Hymans and Shapiro 1974).

The cyclical characteristics of large-scale models were summarized in Hickman (1972). Findings of major large-scale model-builders were reprinted in Klein and Burmeister (1976) from a series of articles in the *International Economic Review,* where the structure, uses, and properties of then current large-scale models were described, compared, and contrasted.

Over the last three decades, important advances in macroeconometric modeling and applications have also occurred in a commercial setting. Large-scale macroeconometric models have been developed and used commercially as part of a systematic, quantitative approach to forecasting the economy and financial markets. Particularly noteworthy are models developed at Data Resources, Inc. [the DRI Model (Eckstein 1983)], Chase Econometrics, Wharton Econometric Forecasting Associates [the Wharton Model (Evans and Klein 1968, McCarthy 1972)], Lehman Brothers [Sinai-Boston Model (Sinai 1992)], and Lawrence Meyer and Associates (LHM&A Model).

Ray Fair (1974, 1976) has built a smaller model (approximately 30 equations), which runs without incorporating any outside information into model forecasts, and is mostly used for research and as a testing ground for applications of econometric methods to model estimation and simulation.

Macroeconometric models have been used to investigate the cyclicality and stability of the economy, effects of fiscal and monetary policies, open-economy interactions, and the mechanisms for propagating fluctuations. Analyses relating to damped or explosive cycles; impact, dynamic, and long-run policy multipliers; and the causes of the business cycle have been performed. Fromm and Taubman (1968), Fromm and Klein (1975), Klein and Burmeister (1976), and Adams and Klein (1991) report and discuss the performance of large-scale models on these topics. Eckstein and Sinai (1986) used the DRI Model to identify and examine impulse and propagation mechanisms in the American business cycle.

Policy studies have analyzed how monetary and fiscal policy work, their multiplier effects and patterns over time, the relative potency of monetary and fiscal policies, and the long-run effects of policies on the economy and financial markets. Crowding-out effects, time lags for the effects of policy changes, short- and long-run model properties, and the interactions of the financial system with the real economy have also been studied. Simulations of prospective Washington policies are regularly performed by macroeconometric-model builders, both to predict their effects and to assess the advisability of possible implementation. The effects of new macroeconomic policies are no longer guessed at blindly; they are now examined, both in and out of government, in simulations with the large-scale models.

The National Bureau of Economic Research-National Science Foundation (NBER-NSF) sponsored Model Comparison Seminar meets two or three times a year to discuss a variety of issues relating to the structure of macroeconometric models, the accuracy of model forecasts and of model proprietors, and the theory and practice of forecasting. Participants included representatives of the major academic, governmental, and commercial macroeconometric model builders and practitioners.

Large-scale macroeconometric models and their usefulness as forecasting tools have been extensively evaluated (Christ 1975, Wallis 1989, Zarnowitz and Braun 1992, McNees 1979, 1988, 1991). Forecasts based on large-scale econometric models, by and large, outperform forecasts based on other methods and measure up reasonably well against actual macroeconomic data. The greatest problems with forecasts based on macroeconometric models involve the prediction of turning points, the magnitude of business-cycle recessions and expansions, forecasting in periods just before or after external shocks, or during periods of change in the institutional backdrop. Whether the incremental benefits of forecasting with large-scale econometric models justify the high cost of maintaining large support staffs, of meeting huge data, computer, and software requirements, and of intensive high-frequency monitoring of the external setting remains an unanswered question.

International macroeconometric-model building has been extensive in recent years as open-economy macroeconomics has been absorbed into the thinking of model-builders and forecasters. The most prominent such effort is Project LINK. Begun in 1968, it has been an ambitious attempt to coordinate linkages of national large-scale macroeconometric models to better understand an increasingly integrated world economy and thus to improve the forecasts derived from those models.

Internationally, large-scale macroeconometric modeling and forecasts have been undertaken in the United Kingdom, Canada, and Japan. Dutch macreconometric modeling has been more concerned with structure and business-cycle analysis than with forecasting. Large-scale model analyses, to a much lesser degree, have been undertaken in France, Southeast Asia, and Latin America.

A major use of large-scale model outputs is as inputs to more disaggregated activities at the industry, company, or regional level, where the forecasts and analyses of fluctuations at the microlevel are made dependent on the macro backdrop and other more microfactors. Models of regional economies are widely used by commercial economic consultants and also in corporations and financial institutions. Corporations, financial institutions, and research institutions, with or without their own models, use forecasts from macroeconometric models for business and financial planning.

Some emerging activities with the large-scale models are to focus high-frequency computerized early-warning systems for coming changes in the economy and inflation for business planning, to develop satellite models that use macro-outputs in micro-decision-making with controls to determine strategies, and to more fully incorporate forward-looking expectations and nonlinearities into understanding the business cycle. New computer technologies and the increasing ability to process large masses of data are making these forays possible.

M

The use of large-scale macroeconometric models in business-cycle analysis and forecasting has come a long way from the initial work six decades ago. Having advanced the understanding of business cycles considerably, these models now routinely generate forecasts that are used widely in government, business, and financial decision making, and "what if" forecasts to assess the impact of alternative economic policies.

Allen Sinai

See also DUESENBERRY, JAMES STEMBLE; ECKSTEIN, OTTO; KLEIN, LAWRENCE ROBERT; LEADING INDICATORS: HISTORICAL RECORD; MACROECONOMETRIC MODELS, HISTORICAL DEVELOPMENT OF; RATIONAL EXPECTATIONS; TINBERGEN, JAN; VECTOR AUTOREGRESSIONS

Bibliography

Adams, F. G. and L. R. Klein. 1991. "Performance of Quarterly Econometric Models in the United States: A New Round of Model Comparisons." In *Comparative Performance of U.S. Econometric Models,* edited by L. R. Klein, 18–68. New York: Oxford Univ. Press.

Christ, C. F. 1975. "Judging the Performance of Econometric Models of the U.S. Economy." *International Economic Review* 16:54–74.

De Leeuw, F. and E. Gramlich. 1968. "The Federal Reserve-MIT Econometric Model." *Federal Reserve Bulletin* 54:11–40.

Duesenberry, J. S., G. Fromm, L. R. Klein, and E. Kuh, eds. 1965. *The Brookings Quarterly Econometric Model of the United States.* Chicago: Rand McNally.

Eckstein, O. 1983. *The DRI Model of the U.S. Economy.* New York: McGraw-Hill.

Eckstein, O. and A. Sinai. 1986. "The Mechanisms of the Business Cycle in the Postwar Era." In *The American Business Cycle: Continuity and Change,* edited by R. J. Gordon, 39–120. Chicago: Univ. of Chicago Press.

Evans, M. K. and L. R. Klein. 1968. *The Wharton Econometric Forecasting Model.* 2d ed. Philadelphia: Univ. of Pennsylvania Press.

Fair, R. C. 1974–76. *A Model of Macroeconomic Activity.* 2 vols. Cambridge, Mass.: Ballinger Press.

Fromm, G. and L. R. Klein, eds. 1975. *The Brookings Model: Perspective and Recent Developments.* Amsterdam: North-Holland.

Fromm, G. and P. Taubman. 1968. *Policy Simulations With An Econometric Model.* Amsterdam: North-Holland.

Hickman, B. G., ed. 1972. *Econometric Models of Cyclical Behavior: Studies of Income and Wealth.* No. 36, vols. 1–2. New York: NBER.

———. 1991. "Project LINK and Multi-Country Modeling." In *A History of Macroeconometric Model-Building,* edited by R. G. Bodkin, L. R. Klein, and K. Marwah, 482–508. Aldershot, Hants, England: Edward Elgar.

Hymans, S. H. and H. T. Shapiro. 1974. "The Structure and Properties of the Michigan Quarterly Econometric Model of the U.S. Economy." *International Economic Review* 15:632–53.

Klein, L. R. 1950. *Economic Fluctuations in the United States, 1921–1941.* New York: Wiley.

Klein, L. R. and E. Burmeister, eds. 1976. *Econometric Model Performance.* Philadelphia: Univ. of Pennsylvania Press.

Klein, L. R. and A. S. Goldberger. 1955. *An Econometric Model of the United States, 1929–1952.* Amsterdam: North-Holland.

McCarthy, M. D. 1972. *The Wharton Quarterly Econometric Forecasting Model: Mark III.* Philadelphia: Univ. of Pennsylvania Press.

McNees, S. K. 1979. "The Forecasting Record for the 1970s." *New England Economic Review,* September/October, 33–53.

———. 1988. "How Accurate are Macroeconomic Forecasts?" *New England Economic Review,* July/August, 15–36.

———. 1991. "Comparing Macroeconomic Model Forecasts Under Common Assumptions." In *Comparative Performance of U.S. Econometric Models,* edited by L. R. Klein, 69–85. New York: Oxford Univ. Press

Sinai, A. 1992. "Financial and Real Business Cycles." *Eastern Economic Journal* 18:1–54.

Suits, D. B. 1962. "Forecasting and Analysis with an Econometric Model." *American Economic Review* 52:104–32.

Tinbergen, J. 1939. *Business Cycles in the United States of America 1919–1932.* Vol. 2 of *Statistical Testing of Business-Cycle*

Theories. Geneva: League of Nations.

Wallis, K. F. 1989. "Macroeconomic Forecasting: A Survey." *Economic Journal* 99:28–61.

Zarnowitz, V. and P. Braun. 1992. "Twenty-Two Years of the NBER-ASA Quarterly Economic Outlook Series: Aspects and Comparisons of Forecasting Performance." In *Business Cycles, Indicators and Forecasting,* edited by J. H. Stock and M. W. Watson, 11–84. Chicago: Univ. of Chicago Press.

Malthus, Thomas Robert (1766–1834)

Thomas Malthus studied mathematics and also classics at Jesus College in the University of Cambridge, where he graduated in 1788. In 1789, Malthus became a Minister of the Church of England. In 1805, he was appointed to the East India College as professor of Political Economy and History. Malthus was one of the twenty original members of the Political Economy Club founded in London in 1821. He was elected a Royal Associate of the Royal Society of Literature in 1824. Malthus entered the public debate on various economic and social issues and was one of the most controversial authors of his time. Despite his many controversies with David Ricardo, the two remained close friends until Ricardo's untimely death in 1823.

Today, Malthus is primarily known as the author of *An Essay on the Principle of Population,* the first edition of which appeared anonymously in 1798. Five further editions of the book were published in his life. In the *Essay,* Malthus refuted the perfectibilist views of Godwin and Condorcet. Poverty and misery were, he maintained, caused by the tendency of population to increase faster than the supply of the means of subsistence. He criticized the Poor Laws, which were meant to alleviate poverty, but, in his view, had the opposite effect.

In 1811, Malthus contributed to the Bullionist controversy with two papers published in the *Edinburgh Review.* It was then that his contact and friendship with Ricardo began. On the one hand, Malthus seconded Ricardo's view that the recent rise in the price of bullion was preeminently the result of the increase in the circulation of Bank of England notes. On the other hand, he pointed out the role of a high demand for currency in explaining the rise in bullion. In three pamphlets published in 1814 and 1815, Malthus defended the Corn Laws, which led to the widespread opinion that he was an advocate of the interests of the landed gentry.

In 1820, Malthus published his *Principles of Political Economy Considered with a View to Their Practical Application.* In the introduction he pointed out that the book was particularly designed as a reply to Ricardo's *On the Principles of Political Economy and Taxation* (1817). Ricardo countered the criticisms of his doctrine with the *Notes on Malthus,* written in 1820. While the idea of publishing the *Notes* had been considered by Ricardo, he eventually refrained from doing so. In 1836, a second edition of Malthus's *Principles* appeared posthumously.

J. M. Keynes wrote a long biographical essay on Malthus full of praise for Malthus's achievements as an economist. While Ricardo was an a priori theorist, Keynes wrote, Malthus was an inductivist who tried not to depart from the actual facts. While Ricardo was mainly concerned with long-period tendencies of the economy, Malthus investigated what determines output as a whole in the short run. And while Ricardo started from the assumption of neutral money, Malthus dealt with the actual monetary economy in which we live. Keynes credited Malthus particularly for his criticism of Say's Law and the development of the principle of effective demand.

The core of Malthus's approach to an explanation of effective-demand failures and economic depressions is contained in chapter seven of the *Principles,* "On the Immediate Causes of the Progress of Wealth." The quarrel between Malthus and Ricardo concerned how accumulation affects the rate of profits and thereby the incentive to further accumulation. They both dissented from two propositions by Adam Smith, who had argued that a nation's wealth grows more rapidly the higher its proportion of productive to unproductive laborers and that, with the accumulation of capital, the rate of profit would fall. Ricardo accepted the first proposition and rejected the second, while Malthus took the opposite view.

Ricardo distinguished two cases in which the rate of profit tends to fall: (1) when, with unchanged technical conditions of production, the rate of accumulation exceeds the rate of growth of the labor supply, which drives up real wages; (2) when, with a given real wage rate, a larger quantity of means of subsistence can be produced only at higher unit costs, due to decreasing returns in the primary sector of the economy.

Smith had stated that capitals are increased by "parsimony" and that the growth of capital is a prerequisite to the growth of riches. To Malthus this view was only partly true, since "the principle of saving, pushed to excess, would destroy the motive to production" (1820, 8). Any accumulation of capital would be at the cost of "unproductive consumption," particularly of the propertied classes; at the same time, it would increase the ratio of productive to unproductive workers and thus expand the productive potential of the economy. With too great an accumulation, effective demand would fall short of potential output. This would cause a "general glut" with prices falling in relation to money wages, which can be taken as given in the short run. Increased real wages would, however, depress profitability and thus discourage further accumulation: "under a rapid accumulation of capital, or, more properly speaking, a rapid conversion of unproductive into productive labour, the demand, compared with the supply of material products, would prematurely fail, and the motive to further accumulation be checked, before it was checked by the exhaustion of the land." This led Malthus to the (in)famous conclusion that "it is absolutely necessary that a country with great powers of production should possess a body of unproductive consumers" (1820, 463).

Malthus thus confronted the "limiting principle" of the rate of profit, advocated by Ricardo, with his "regulating principle" of "demand and supply." He claimed that the latter "is producing effects which entirely overcome [the former], and often for twenty or thirty, or even 100 years together, make the rate of profits take a course absolutely different from what it ought to be according to the first cause" (313). A characteristic feature of the working of the regulating principle would be "that both capital and population may be at the same time, and for a period of great length, redundant, compared with the effective demand for produce" (469). Interestingly, Malthus believed that the "law of demand and supply" and Say's Law are incompatible (353). The idea that supply creates its own demand was considered by him a major fallacy, since in the short run, wants and desires may be practically taken as given and satiated. Consequently, there was no presumption that the growth of wants would keep pace with the growth in the productive powers of society. Hence, to expand effective demand it would not only be necessary to promote unproductive consumption but also to create new wants by way of product innovations.

Ricardo was strongly opposed to Malthus's doctrine. In his view, the criticism of Say's Law was entirely unsound. Since Malthus explicitly subscribed to Adam Smith's proposition "that the produce which is annually saved is as regularly consumed as that which is annually spent, but that it is consumed by a different set of people" (1820, 31), it is not at all clear how the alleged general glut could come about. In fact, both Malthus and Ricardo always identified decisions to save with decisions to invest; neither one raised the Keynesian problem of a possible discrepancy between savings and investment. [For a different assessment of Malthus, see Costabile and Rowthorn (1985).] Hence, Ricardo drew the logically consistent conclusion that demand could have no permanent impact on the rate of profit. Moreover, how can a redistribution of profits in favor of unproductive consumption increase the former? "[I]n the same way as a fire would" (1951, 425), reads Ricardo's dry answer.

Keynes summarized the debate between Ricardo and Malthus as follows: "since Malthus was unable to explain clearly (apart from an appeal to the facts of common observation) how and why effective demand could be deficient or excessive, he failed to furnish an alternative construction" ([1936] 1973, 32). However, Malthus deserves credit for having asked important questions and given valuable hints about where answers might be found.

Heinz D. Kurz

See also EFFECTIVE DEMAND; SAY, JEAN-BAPTISTE; SAY'S LAW; RICARDO, DAVID

Bibliography

Bonar, J. 1924. *Malthus and his Work.* 2d ed. London: Allen and Unwin.
Costabile, L. and B. Rowthorn. 1985. "Malthus's Theory of Wages and Growth." *Economic Journal* 95:418–37.
Garegnani, P. 1978. "Notes on Consumption, Investment and Effective Demand: I." *Cambridge Journal of Economics* 2:335–53.
Keynes, J. M. [1933] 1972. "Robert Malthus." Chap. 12 in *Essays in Biography.* Vol. 10 of *The Collected Writings of John Maynard Keynes.* London: Macmillan.

———. [1936] 1973. *The General Theory of Employment, Interest and Money.* Vol. 7 of *The Collected Writings of John Maynard Keynes.* London: Macmillan.

Malthus, T. R. 1798. *An Essay on the Principle of Population, as it affects the future improvement of society. With remarks on the speculations of Mr. Godwin, M. Condorcet, and other writers.* London: J. Johnson.

———. 1820. *Principles of Political Economy Considered with a View to Their Practical Application.* London: J. Murray.

———. 1823. *The Measure of Value Stated and Illustrated.* London: J. Murray.

———. 1827. *Definitions in Political Economy.* London: J. Murray.

Pullen, J. M. 1987. "Malthus, Thomas Robert." In *The New Palgrave: A Dictionary of Economics.* Vol. 3. Edited by J. Eatwell, M. Milgate, and P. Newman. London: Macmillan.

Rashid, S. 1987. "Malthus and Classical Economics." In *The New Palgrave: A Dictionary of Economics.* Vol. 3. Edited by J. Eatwell, M. Milgate, and P. Newman. London: Macmillan.

Ricardo, D. 1951. *Notes on Malthus's Principles of Political Economy.* Vol. 2 of *The Works and Correspondence of David Ricardo,* edited by P. Sraffa. Cambridge: Cambridge Univ. Press.

Market Price Indicators

Market price indicators—such as broad indices of commodity prices, foreign-exchange rates, and bond yields—may be useful in conducting monetary policy. Since monetary policy has an important impact on economic activity, these indicators may also be useful in monitoring the business cycle. Determined in centralized auction markets, these forward-looking indicators have a number of advantages over commonly used quantity data such as national-income-account statistics, employment or production statistics, or even data measuring monetary aggregates. Historically, the use of these indicators has found support from monetary theorists and has been supported by several types of empirical evidence.

Given current institutional arrangements (i.e., central banks and a flexible-exchange-rate regime), the goal of price stability involves a policy of stabilizing the exchange rate between money and goods, or stabilizing the value or price of money. Yet, attempting to control general prices directly is not desirable. Since policy lags remain long and variable in an uncertain world and general prices are sticky, such attempts could produce sizable swings in both economic activity and prices.

Because of these considerations, an intermediate-indicator approach to policymaking is essential. Intermediate indicators useful in stabilizing the value of money should possess a number of characteristics: they should be accurately measurable, flexible, readily available, and should be good proxies for the value of money. Accordingly, they should reliably respond to changes in monetary policy and reliably lead movements in the value of money (or general prices). Monetary theory suggests that nominal (rather than real) variables provide such reliable signals to monetary policymakers.

Since prices communicate knowledge about the relative scarcities of economic goods and services, the price system also communicates information and knowledge about the relative scarcity of money, i.e., about the exchange rate between money and goods. However, as Yeager (1968) has aptly shown, there is no formal market for money, yet money is traded in every market since it is the medium of exchange. That money is traded in every market suggests that the price system ought to yield useful information about the value of money.

Market prices from commodity, foreign-exchange, and bond markets seem to provide the best information for gauging movements in the value of money: these prices serve as useful proxies for the price of money from different perspectives. Market prices of this type reflect all relevant information, and embody a current consensus of knowledgeable opinion about prospective general price movements: they serve as useful leading indicators of movements in the value of money.

Commodity prices determined in competitive auction markets represent the (stock) price of money in terms of commodities. While specific commodities can be affected by supply and demand factors peculiar to their market, using broad indices of commodity prices minimizes the effect of such influences.

The price of foreign exchange represents the price of one money in terms of other monies. Given that money is neutral with respect to relative prices, monetary stimulation leads in the long run to proportionate changes in all prices including the price of foreign exchange. Since the exchange rate is flexible and sensitive, it can lead broader price movements, providing early signals of changes in the value of money.

The price of bonds is another proxy for the price of money from a different perspective. Since a bond constitutes a promise to pay a given quantity of money in the future, the price of a bond reflects the price of present money in terms of future money. Specifically, the prices of bonds provide information about how money is serving as a standard of deferred payments and how well money is maintaining its intertemporal stability.

Information from these three markets is particularly useful if they are judiciously considered simultaneously within a Wicksellian policy framework. Wicksell argued that information from commodity-price movements should be used to adjust the bank rate into equality with the (unobservable) natural rate to achieve price stability. Analogously, information from all three of these markets can be used to adjust the bank (Federal Funds) rate in order to achieve price stability.

More specifically, should joint assessments of these market prices indicate that the value of money is falling, the Federal Funds rate should be increased, whereas should evidence suggest the value of money is rising, the Federal Funds rate should be lowered. All else equal, stable market prices would indicate that the bank rate is close to the Wicksellian natural rate and need not be adjusted. The joint assessment of these three market prices within a Wicksellian policy framework allows more information to be processed than the assessment of any single market price or group of prices, so that the resulting decisions should be superior to those based on single indicators.

The advantages of employing market-price data in this fashion are best seen by recognizing many of the problems of commonly used quantity data. Data measuring quantities (such as income, production, employment, or monetary aggregates) are necessarily based on samples. Accordingly, such data are subject to substantial revisions. An inherent lag occurs in the reporting of quantity data, and they often reflect accounting concepts rather than economic principles. To be useful, these data must be seasonally adjusted. And should redefinitions (due to deregulation, institutional or technological change) occur, the altered measurements and changed behavior of particular variables can be substantial.

Market prices, on the other hand, are determined in centralized auction markets. These price data are easy to understand, timely and readily available, literally by the minute. They are accurate, less subject to sampling error, and are not affected by revisions, seasonal adjustments, or "shift-adjustments" that often plague quantity data.

The use of market-price data is based on the idea that prices are aggregators of information embodying the knowledge and expectations of large numbers of buyers and sellers who have incentives to make informed decisions in an uncertain world. Accordingly, these prices are inherently forward-looking, offering a distinct advantage over any form of quantity data and particularly pertinent for monetary policymakers who necessarily must also be forward-looking. Using such data takes advantage not of the knowledge of the monetary authority, but of the dispersed, decentralized knowledge that no single person or group of people possesses.

The use of market-price policy guides, however, is not foolproof. These market prices can be volatile, can reflect non-monetary influences, are not independent of one another, and are influenced by expectations of both policy action and inflation. While these properties present difficulties, they can be easily taken into account to preserve the efficacy of the market-price approach.

The above-described use of market prices as guides for monetary policy is not novel. Such an approach was employed by classical bullionist writers who indicated that (in a flexible-rate regime) it was the *duty* of the central bank to monitor bullion prices (the premium of bullion over the mint price) and exchange rates in conducting monetary policy. This prescription was restated by John Stuart Mill and refined by Knut Wicksell. The view was also prescribed by monetary theorists of many nationalities in the flexible-rate episode following World War I. And the view was very successfully implemented by the Swedish monetary authority (The Rikesbank) in the 1930s. Current proposals to employ market-price policy guides constitute the reemergence of this classical monetary-policy strategy.

Robert E. Keleher

See also BULLIONIST CONTROVERSIES; LEADING INDICATORS: HISTORICAL RECORD; LEADS AND LAGS; MONETARY POLICY

Bibliography

Keleher, R. E. 1991. "The Use of Market Prices in Implementing Monetary Policy: The Bullionist Contribution." *Southern Economic Journal* 58:144–53.

———. 1991. "The Swedish Market Price Approach to Monetary Policy of the 1930s." *Contemporary Policy Issues,* April, 1–12.

Yeager, L. B. 1968. "The Essential Properties of a Medium of Exchange." *Kyklos* 21:45–68.

Marshall, Alfred (1842–1924)

Alfred Marshall dominated British economics in the late nineteenth and early twentieth centuries. His influence was felt not only through his magisterial *Principles of Economics* from which two generations learned their economics, but also as a teacher whose students filled half the economics chairs in Britain, and as the source of the Cambridge oral tradition. The subject matter of the *Principles,* whose first edition announced it as volume one of a larger work, was the neoclassical theory of price, production, and distribution. Its companion volume on *Money, Credit and Commerce* did not appear until 1923, "when," in Keynes's words, "time had deprived his ideas of freshness and his exposition of sting and strength" ([1933] 1972, 161). "Fluctuations of Industry, Trade and Credit" were treated systematically only in the thirty pages of book four of *Money, Credit and Commerce,* but Marshall's interest in this subject went back at least to the short discussion of commercial crises in his and Mary Paley Marshall's *Economics of Industry* (154–55), which he paraphrased four decades later in *Money, Credit and Commerce.*

Marshall's monetary theory was presented primarily in his lectures and in his evidence to Royal Commissions, later edited by J. M. Keynes as Marshall's *Official Papers.* Marshall adhered to a traditional form of the quantity theory of money as the explanation of long-term movements in prices. Yet he made an important advance in the quantity theory in expressing the demand for money as the demand to hold an asset rather than as the demand for a flow. Moreover, Marshall clearly stated that the yield in convenience from holding money at the margin equals the foregone interest on alternative assets and the foregone utility on alternative consumption goods (1923, 38–39, 45; 1926, 267–68). The Cambridge "cash-balance" approach used by A. C. Pigou and by Keynes in his *Tract on Monetary Reform* (1923), from which both Keynesian liquidity-preference theory and the Monetarist reformulation of the quantity theory as a theory of a stable demand for money are direct descendants, was thus the invention of Marshall. However, Marshall's presentation of the quantity theory lacked an adequate stability analysis.

Marshall also clearly distinguished real and nominal interest rates in his *Principles* before Irving Fisher did in *Appreciation and Interest* (1896), though both had been anticipated by Henry Thornton. Marshall viewed the rate of interest as determined by the supply of and demand for capital, an approach later formalized in Dennis Robertson's loanable-funds theory.

Marshall attributed short-term fluctuations in prices to expansion and contraction of credit, rather than to fluctuations in the currency supply (1923, 19; 1926, 21, 23). His theory of a credit cycle, fueled by borrowers with optimistic expectations and accommodated by an elastic supply of credit, was not very different from that of J. S. Mill and other classical writers. Marshall tended to minimize the severity of unemployment associated with cyclical fluctuations, arguing that unemployment in industrial societies was more obvious, but probably less serious, than in preindustrial societies. Nonetheless, he regarded unemployment as the most serious consequence of the short-term fall in prices caused by the contraction of credit when expectations are disappointed. Marshall ([1890] 1961, 1:709–10) viewed the rigidity of money wages and the fact that prices may change in the interval between the incurring of production costs and the sale of output as the reasons why short-term price movements affect profits, output, and employment. Marshall followed Walter Bagehot in recognizing the cumulative process through which the contraction of one sector reduces demand for the output of the rest of the economy.

To minimize cyclical fluctuations, Marshall proposed minimizing the impact of fluctuations in the general price level. He wished to encourage voluntary adoption of a tabular standard to index monetary contracts to changes in an official price index, so that, *ex post,* the money rate of interest would not deviate from the real rate. He also proposed minimizing fluctuations in the price level itself by adopting a symmetalic monetary standard under which the pound would be convertible into a fixed quantity of gold *and* a fixed quantity of silver with the relative price of the two metals allowed to fluctuate. Keynes adopted this proposal in his *Indian Currency and Finance* (1913).

Because of the magnitude of his achievement in the *Principles,* and because *Money, Credit and Commerce* was not finished until he was over eighty years old, Marshall's contributions as a monetary theorist are often overlooked. The best measure of his achievement as a monetary and business-cycle theorist is perhaps the list of the Cambridge-educated economists who contributed to these fields under his influence. The list includes A. C. Pigou, Frederick Lavington, Dennis Robertson, and, even though he ultimately rebelled against his Marshallian upbringing, John Maynard Keynes.

Robert W. Dimand
David Glasner

See also CREDIT CYCLE; EXPECTATIONS; KEYNES, JOHN MAYNARD; LOANABLE-FUNDS DOCTRINE; LAVINGTON, FREDERICK; MONETARY DISEQUILIBRIUM THEORIES OF THE BUSINESS CYCLE; PIGOU, ARTHUR CECIL; ROBERTSON, DENNIS HOLME

Bibliography

Bridel, P. 1987. *Cambridge Monetary Thought: The Development of Saving-Investment Analysis from Marshall to Keynes.* London: Macmillan.

Eshag, E. 1963. *From Marshall to Keynes: An Essay on the Monetary Theory of the Cambridge School.* Oxford: Basil Blackwell.

Groenewegen, P. 1995. *A Soaring Eagle: Alfred Marshall 1842–1924.* Aldershot, Hants, England: Edward Elgar.

Keynes, J. M. [1933] 1972. "Alfred Marshall." In *Essays in Biography.* Vol. 10 of *The Collected Writings of John Maynard Keynes,* 125–217. London: Macmillan.

Lavington, F. 1922. *The Trade Cycle.* London: P. S. King.

Marshall, A. [1887] 1924. "Remedies for Fluctuations of General Prices." In *Memorials of Alfred Marshall,* edited by A. C. Pigou, 188–212. London: Macmillan.

———. [1890] 1961. *Principles of Economics.* 2 vols. 9th (variorum) ed. London: Macmillan.

———. 1923. *Money, Credit and Commerce.* London: Macmillan.

———. 1926. *Official Papers.* Edited by J. M. Keynes. London: Macmillan.

Marshall, A. and M. P. Marshall. 1879. *The Economics of Industry.* London: Macmillan.

Pigou, A. C., ed. 1924. *Memorials of Alfred Marshall.* London: Macmillan.

———. 1927. *Industrial Fluctuations.* London: Macmillan.

Robertson, D. H. 1915. *A Study in Industrial Fluctuations.* London: P. S. King.

Wolfe, J. N. 1956. "Marshall and the Trade Cycle." *Oxford Economic Papers* 8:90–101.

Marx, Karl Heinrich (1818–1883)

The general outline of Marx's life is well known and will not be reviewed here (see McLellan 1974, Seigel 1978). This article examines Marx's theory of economic crises and its role in Marx's overall thinking.

Crises and depressions became a central focus of Marx's economic theory and his political thinking in the aftermath of the revolutions of 1848. Marx initially expected another revolutionary outbreak soon thereafter, but further study and reflection (and the continued absence of a new outbreak), led Marx to the following important conclusions which guided his subsequent thinking: (1) the underlying cause of the revolutions of 1848 was the economic crisis of the late 1840s; (2) the return of prosperity in the early 1850s made a new revolution unlikely; and (3) "a new revolution is possible only in consequence of a new crisis" (Marx [1895] 1964, 132–35). Thenceforth, Marx's main intellectual goal was to discover the causes of recurring economic crises.

The long awaited "new crisis" finally arrived in 1857, and inspired Marx to begin writing *Capital.* In a burst of creative energy, Marx wrote the first draft of *Capital* (which eventually grew to over 800 printed pages) in less than six months. (The draft was eventually published in 1939 under the title *Grundrisse,* or "Outlines.") The new crisis was relatively short-lived and failed to ignite a new revolutionary outbreak, but one important legacy of the crisis of 1857 was the draft of *Capital.*

It was in the *Grundrisse* that Marx first

formulated his theory that the falling rate of profit is the main cause of economic crises (Marx 1973, 365–98; Seigel 1978, 304–16). Toward the end of the *Grundrisse,* Marx wrote that this theory "is in every respect the most important law of modern political economy" (Marx [1939] 1973, 748). This theory was further developed in Marx's later writings, especially in volume three of *Capital.*

According to Marx, the rate of profit declines because technological change causes the composition of capital (the ratio of constant to variable capital) to increase faster than the rate of surplus-value (the ratio of surplus-value to variable capital). The increased composition of capital implies a reduced ratio of labor employed to capital invested; less labor employed reduces the amount of value produced; and with a constant rate of surplus-value, less value produced results in less surplus-value produced per unit of capital invested; in other words, the rate of profit declines. This decline in the rate of profit might be offset by an increasing rate of surplus-value, which also results from technological change. However, Marx argued (but did not prove) that the composition of capital would increase faster than the rate of surplus-value, so that the rate of profit would tend to decline. "The rate of profit falls not because the worker is exploited less, but because altogether less labor is employed in relation to the capital employed" (Marx [1905–10] 1968–71, 439; see also Marx [1867] 1967, vol. 1, parts 4 and 7; vol. 3, part 3; and Marx [1939] 1973, 365–98, 745–58).

Marx argued further that a decline in the rate of profit would eventually reduce the rate of capital accumulation, which in turn would bring on a general crisis. One important element in the development of crises, which Marx discussed on occasion, but did not fully elaborate, is the increasing indebtedness of capitalist enterprises during the expansion. Capitalist enterprises can temporarily overcome the limits of a declining rate of profit by increased borrowing, but this temporary expedient increases their vulnerability to downturns and thereby intensifies the severity of the eventual depression (Crotty 1985).

The significance of this theory was that it identified an *inherent, endogenous cause* of capitalist crises and depressions: technological change which replaces labor with machinery. Thus, according to this theory, crises and depressions grow out of capitalism's internal dynamics. As Marx put it, "the *true barrier* to capital is *capital itself*" (Marx [1867–94] 1967, 3:250).

Marx also analyzed the causes of recovery from depressions, as well as the causes of depressions themselves. Since the main cause of depressions is a decline in the rate of profit, the main precondition for recovery is an increase in the rate of profit. According to Marx's theory, the rate of profit can increase in two ways: an increased rate of surplus-value or a reduced composition of capital. Marx argued that, although increasing the rate of surplus-value (through wage cuts, speed-up, etc.) would help raise the rate of profit, such an increase by itself would usually not increase the rate of profit enough to end the depression. Since the prior decline in the rate of profit was caused by an increased composition of capital (not a declining rate of surplus-value), restoring the rate of profit required a reduced composition of capital, or a significant "devaluation of capital." This devaluation is accomplished during depressions by means of widespread bankruptcies of capitalist enterprises. Eventually the devaluation of capital raises the rate of profit enough to make renewed capital accumulation and a return to prosperity possible (unless of course workers have succeeded in overthrowing capitalism during the depression). Thus, Marx provided at least the sketch of a complete theory of the alternating phases of prosperity and depression characteristic of capitalist economies (Mattick 1969, chaps. 5–10).

Marx's theory of the falling rate of profit has generated much controversy and debate over the years. The two main issues in this controversy have been: (1) whether Marx conclusively proved that technological change necessarily increases the composition of capital, and (2) even if the composition of capital does increase, whether Marx conclusively proved that it must necessarily increase faster than the rate of surplus-value. Almost everyone now seems to agree that the answer to both questions is no. On the other hand, many would argue that, although Marx did not provide conclusive proofs, he did offer plausible arguments that may be valid under certain historical circumstances. Whether Marx's theory is valid for a particular historical period is thus an empirical question.

It is also widely believed that Marx actually had *three* different (and perhaps contradictory) theories of crises: (1) the *falling-rate-of-profit* theory discussed above; (2) a *profit-squeeze* theory; and (3) an *underconsumption* theory (e.g., Wright 1975, Alcaly

1978). According to the profit-squeeze interpretation, the rate of profit declines because the rate of surplus-value declines, not because the composition of capital increases. It is argued that the rate of surplus-value declines (or wages increase faster than surplus-value), because the rate of unemployment declines during an expansion, which increases the bargaining power of workers. According to the underconsumption interpretation, a crisis occurs not because wages increase faster than surplus-value, but instead the opposite: because wages increase slower than surplus-value. It is argued that such an increase in the rate of surplus value results in turn in an insufficient demand for consumer goods, which precipitates a crisis.

Although a few quotations from Marx can be cited to support both of the other interpretations, the main cause of crises in Marx's theory (and in Marx's mind) seems to have been technological change that increases the composition of capital. Whether this theory is correct (or more correct than the other two interpretations of Marx's theory) is of course a separate question.

In conclusion, it should be emphasized that Marx was among the first to provide a systematic theory of crises and depressions in capitalist economies. The distinctive features of his theory are its focus on the rate of profit as the key variable and its conclusion that the rate of profit declines due to the inherent cause of labor-saving technological change. Marx's theory continues to be debated today and continues to inspire further investigations into why capitalist economies are vulnerable to crises and depressions.

Fred Moseley

See also BAUER, OTTO; DISPROPORTIONALITY THEORY; ENGELS, FRIEDRICH; FALLING RATE OF PROFIT; FALLING RATE OF PROFIT, EMPIRICAL TESTS; HILFERDING, RUDOLF; KAUTSKY, KARL; LUXEMBURG, ROSA; MATTICK, PAUL; OVERSAVING THEORIES OF BUSINESS CYCLES; PROFIT SQUEEZE; REGULATION SCHOOL; SAY'S LAW; SCHUMPETER, JOSEPH ALOIS; SOCIAL STRUCTURE OF ACCUMULATION; SWEEZY, PAUL MARLOR; STATE-MONOPOLY CAPITALISM; TUGAN-BARANOVSKY, MIKHAIL IVANOVICH

Bibliography

Alcaly, R. E. 1978. "An Introduction to Marxian Crisis Theory." In *U.S. Capitalism in Crisis,* prepared by the Crisis Reader Editorial Collective: B. Steinberg et al., 15–22. New York: Union for Radical Political Economics.

Crotty, J. 1985. "The Centrality of Money, Credit, and Financial Intermediation in Marx's Crisis Theory: An Interpretation of Marx's Methodology." In *Rethinking Marxism: Struggles in Marxist Theory,* edited by S. Resnick and R. Wolff, 45–81. New York: Autonomedia.

Marx, K. [1895] 1964. *Class Struggles in France, 1848–1850.* Translation. New York: International Publishers.

———. [1905–10] 1968–71. *Theories of Surplus-Value.* 3 vols. Translation. Moscow: Progress.

———. [1939] 1973. *Grundrisse: Foundations of the Critique of Political Economy.* Translated with a foreword by M. Nicolaus. Baltimore: Penguin Books.

———. [1867–94] 1967. *Capital.* Translation. 3 vols. New York: International Publishers.

Mattick, P. 1969. *Marx and Keynes: The Limits of the Mixed Economy.* Boston: Porter Sargent.

McLellan, D. 1974. *Karl Marx: His Life and Thought.* New York: Harper and Row.

Seigel, J. 1978. *Marx's Fate: The Shape of a Life.* Princeton: Princeton Univ. Press.

Wright, E. O. 1975. "Alternative Perspectives in the Marxist Theory of Accumulation and Crisis." *The Insurgent Sociologist* 6:5–40.

Mattick, Paul (1904–1981)

Paul Mattick was born in 1904 in German Pomerania (now Poland) and died in 1981 in Cambridge, Massachusetts. Mattick was not a professional academic, but was instead a rare "working-class theorist." As a young man, he was active in various Communist parties, wrote numerous articles for the left-wing press, and studied Marx's economic theory under Henryk Grossman. He emigrated to the United States in 1926, where he worked as a tool-and-die maker in Illinois and Michigan. In the 1930s and early 1940s, he participated in a number of working-class organizations (including the I.W.W.) and edited the journals *Living Marxism* and *New Essays.* After the war, he abandoned factory work, and wrote his major work, *Marx and Keynes: The Limits of the Mixed Economy.* His writings have been translated into eight European languages, his influence having been much greater in Europe than in the United States.

Mattick's greatest contribution to economic theory is his rigorous extension of Marx's theory of crises and depressions to analyze the effectiveness of Keynesian economic policies. The central question of this analysis is whether Keynesian policies can overcome the tendency of capitalism toward depressions. According to Marx's theory, the main cause of depressions is a falling rate of profit during periods of expansion and prosperity. The effectiveness of Keynesian policies to overcome depressions therefore depends on their ability to overcome the tendency of the rate of profit to fall. Mattick argued that Keynesian policies cannot in general increase profitability and thus cannot overcome depressions. On the contrary, the expansionary fiscal policy recommended by Keynes requires an increase in the portion of the total surplus-value produced that is borrowed by the government, which reduces the portion of surplus-value left over for capital accumulation. Thus, far from solving the problem of insufficient profitability, expansionary fiscal policies exacerbate it. Mattick acknowledged that Keynesian policies might temporarily increase output and employment. However, he insisted that a lasting recovery from a depression or crisis requires above all a significant increase in the rate of profit, and that Keynesian policies have the opposite effect.

Thus, as early as the 1950s, Mattick predicted (almost alone among economic theorists, including Marxist ones), that the postwar boom would sooner or later come to an end, and would be followed by yet another period of depression, as had all previous periods of prosperity. Furthermore, Mattick maintained, in the next depression, the Keynesian "solution" would have already been tried and abandoned, leaving the world capitalist economy even more vulnerable to a deep and lasting depression.

The events of the last twenty years provide support to Mattick's theory. Although another "great depression" has not yet occurred (except in the Third World), the economic crisis of the 1970s–80s has again raised fears among many that another great depression could occur. The long-run ineffectiveness of Keynesian policies is now accepted by almost all economists, and these policies have been largely abandoned by governments around the world. Thus, although generally overlooked, Mattick deserves to be ranked among the most prescient economic theorists of the post-World War II period. Mattick would have ascribed that prescience to Marx's theory of capitalism.

Fred Moseley

See also SWEEZY, PAUL MARLOR

Bibliography

Mattick, P. 1969. *Marx and Keynes: The Limits of the Mixed Economy.* Boston: Porter Sargent.
———. 1972. *Critique of Marcuse: One-Dimensional Man in Class Society.* London: Merlin.
———. 1978. *Anti-Bolshevik Communism.* White Plains, N.Y.: M. E. Sharpe.
———. 1981. *Economic Crisis and Crisis Theory.* White Plains, N.Y.: M. E. Sharpe.
———. 1983. *Marxism: The Last Refuge of the Bourgeoisie.* Armonk, N.Y.: M. E. Sharpe.

Metzler, Lloyd Appleton (1913–1980)

Lloyd Appleton Metzler made important contributions to several branches of economics, including business-cycle theory, in the 1940s and early 1950s. Trained at Harvard, Metzler spent most of his career at the University of Chicago. Although Metzler continued teaching at Chicago after removal of a brain tumor in 1952, unfortunately for the progress of economic theory, he published only infrequently thereafter.

Metzler's principal contribution to the study of business cycles was his 1941 paper on inventory cycles. The notion of an inventory cycle had been developed by Ralph G. Hawtrey who, unlike most other theorists, had emphasized the role of inventory accumulation and decumulation in his monetary theory of the cycle. Subsequently, Lundberg ([1937] 1955) had analyzed specific numerical cases of a dynamic model involving inventory investment without providing a general analytic solution. Samuelson ([1939] 1966), on the other hand, provided a general analytic solution to the problem of multiplier-accelerator interaction, but at a level of generality that left the role of inventories unspecified. Applying the analysis of multiplier-acceleration interaction that had just been developed by Samuelson, Metzler provided a general analytic solution, including stability conditions, to Lundberg's inventory model.

The economic mechanism used to generate cycles was the difference between forecast and realized sales. Businesses invest in inventories based on expectations of future sales, but if actual sales are less (greater) than expected sales, unplanned (dis)investment in inventories results. However, Metzler excluded the impact of interest rates on desired inventory investment from his model. Thus, the resulting cycle was a real cycle generated by firms' errors in forecasting future demand. Metzler's model was therefore a conceptual departure from Hawtrey's monetary theory of an inventory cycle, which had been the original stimulus of interest in inventory cycles. As a result, Haberler (1962, 472) expressed skepticism about the empirical relevance of Metzler's inventory model. Subsequent work by Lovell (1974) has attempted to incorporate a monetary element into the Metzler model by explicitly introducing the rate of interest as an explanatory variable affecting desired inventory holdings. (Also see Zarnowitz 1985, 541–42.)

Although not directly concerned with business cycles, Metzler's 1951 article "Wealth, Saving and the Rate of Interest" has become a classic in the literature on monetary and macroeconomic theory. Exploring the conditions under which monetary policy would not affect the real rate of interest, Metzler found that, contrary to the classical position, conventional open-market operations would affect the real rate of interest by altering the amount of securities held by the public and thus altering their desired savings. But the significance of the article transcended its substantive argument. The analytical approach Metzler employed and the masterful lucidity of his exposition of the neoclassical synthesis exerted an important influence on the subsequent development of monetary and macroeconomic theory.

David Glasner

See also HAWTREY, RALPH GEORGE; KITCHIN CYCLE; LUNDBERG, ERIK FILIP; SAMUELSON, PAUL ANTHONY

Bibliography

Haberler, G. 1962. *Prosperity and Depression*. 4th rev. ed. Cambridge: Harvard Univ. Press.

Horwich, G. and J. Pomery. 1987. "Lloyd Metzler." In *The New Palgrave: The Dictionary of Economics*. Edited by J. Eatwell, M. Milgate, and P. Newman. Vol. 3. London: Macmillan.

Horwich, G. and P. A. Samuelson, eds. 1974. *Trade, Stability, and Macroeconomics: Essays in Honor of Lloyd A. Metzler*. New York: Academic Press.

Lovell, M. C. 1974. "Monetary Policy and the Inventory Cycle." In *Trade, Stability, and Macroeconomics: Essays in Honor of Lloyd A. Metzler*, edited by G. Horwich and P. A. Samuelson, 355–71. New York: Academic Press.

Lundberg, E. F. [1937] 1955. *Studies in the Theory of Economic Expansion*. Reprinted with an additional preface by the author. Oxford: Basil Blackwell.

Metzler, L. A. 1941. "The Nature and Stability of Inventory Cycles." *Review of Economic Studies* 23:113–29.

———. 1946. "Business Cycles and the Theory of Employment." *American Economic Review* 36:278–91.

———. 1947. "Factors Governing the Length of Inventory Cycles." *Review of Economic Statistics* 29:1–15.

———. 1948. "Three Lags in the Circular Flow of Income." In *Income, Employment, and Public Policy: Essays in Honor of Alvin H. Hansen,* edited by L. A. Metzler et al., 11–32. New York: Norton.

———. 1951. "Wealth, Saving, and the Rate of Interest." *Journal of Political Economy* 59:93–116.

———. 1973. *Collected Papers*. Harvard Economic Studies, vol. 140. Cambridge: Harvard Univ. Press.

Niehans, J. 1978. "Metzler, Wealth, and Macroeconomics: A Review." *Journal of Economic Literature* 16:84–95.

Samuelson, P. A. [1939] 1966. "Interactions between the Multiplier Analysis and the Principle of Acceleration." Chap. 82 in *The Collected Scientific Writings of Paul A. Samuelson*. Cambridge: MIT Press.

Zarnowitz, V. 1985. "Recent Work on Business Cycles in Historical Perspective: A Review of Theories and Evidence." *Journal of Economic Literature* 23:523–80.

Mill, John Stuart (1806–1873)

John Stuart Mill, the preeminent British economist of the late classical period, first addressed the problems of business cycles in "Paper Currency and Commercial Distress," in which he articulated the analysis he would maintain throughout his life. Another paper on the subject, "Of the Influence of Consumption on Production," was written in 1830. *The Principles of Political Economy,* Mill's major contribution to economics, builds upon these essays and informs his later work on the topic. His analysis borrowed heavily from that of Thomas Tooke.

Unlike some of his contemporaries, Mill considered only an inventory cycle lasting eighteen to twenty-four months. Its most distinctive feature is the recognition that professional traders "who watch . . . the signs of future supply and demand," and rash speculators who gamble on "the immediate turn of the market" ([1826] 1967, 4:75), have different information sets, price expectations, and goals.

Cycles begin when professional traders observe rising market prices for their commodity due to an unanticipated shock such as "the opening of a new market" or simultaneous poor harvests. Each dealer, inferring from the price that there is an unsatisfied market demand, reacts by purchasing inventory with which to meet the demand before his competitors and thereby increase his market share ([1826] 1967, 4:76). Since each behaves similarly, prices rise even higher. In "The Currency Juggle," Mill acknowledged that an expected monetary expansion could initiate the upswing ([1833] 1967, 4:191; [1844b] 1967, 4:275), but he was careful to qualify the impact to avoid playing into the hands of the Currency School. The *Principles,* unlike the early essays, allowed for investment in fixed capital during an upswing, with subsequent unemployment ([1871] 1965, 741).

However, this error on the part of professional traders would not persist. Professionals use their contacts and agents to keep abreast of prospective demand and supply. Moreover, dealers in some commodities meet regularly to share information, and they may even have some degree of control over prices which they attempt (often unsuccessfully) to set over the course of the season ([1826] 1967, 4:75–77). But the original price increase attracts the attention of rash speculators, whose actions amplify price fluctuations and transmit the mania to other commodities.

Speculators, as outsiders to an industry, lack both the concrete sources of information available to professional traders and the motive to gather such information. The goal of the rash speculator is not to satisfy a stable or growing market share, but to purchase the commodity and turn it over at inflated prices to other dealers—behavior Mill considered both immoral and increasingly common ([1826] 1967, 4:77–78). As the normal rate of return in quiescent periods falls, ever larger numbers of merchants begin to gamble on the chance of higher returns in such projects ([1871] 1965, 742). Speculators amplify the price increase, and because their price expectations are not based on any solid data, related commodities may be affected. Speculators purchase stocks of (as yet) unaffected commodities, causing the price increases that they anticipated might occur simply because other prices were rising ([1826] 1967, 4:92).

The least satisfactory part of Mill's analysis concerns the recoil. For some reason, the optimism reverses itself and prices fall. Hollander suggests that this occurs because agents have some idea of "normal" prices, and attempt to realize their profits when market prices cross a customary threshold. The distinction between professional traders and speculators helps us to reconstruct Mill's logic. It is clear that professionals, who know "normal" prices, are aware of the activity of speculators who do not ([1871] 1965, 548). Professionals therefore refuse to purchase when prices are relatively high, and run down their inventories. This response slows the price increase, and, because rash speculators rely solely on market-price trends, induces a "panic as unreasoning as the previous over-confidence" ([1871] 1965, 542). Similarly, as dumping of commodities pushes prices below normal, the market is likely to recover, because professionals will eventually purchase.

The interaction between professional traders who have good information about market conditions, and rash speculators who do not, is sufficient to cause a cycle, which is worsened by monetary factors. Mill recognized that the velocity of circulation would increase during an upswing, allowing a general price increase even if the money supply remained constant ([1871] 1965, 451). Moreover, "book credit" extended to purchasers by suppliers would expand during an upswing and contract during the revulsion. During a panic, professional traders would be hard-pressed to gain even that customary credit which allowed them to meet normal demand ([1826] 1967, 4:96). Mill advocated an expansionary monetary policy in such circumstances, to avert the contraction of credit

M

during the recoil, so that professional traders could function ([1871] 1965, 671–72).

Mill's analysis of the business cycle was, he claimed, nothing more than was known to most "practical men." Its most interesting feature was the distinction Mill drew between professional traders and rash speculators, both of which were caricatures drawn from Victorian businesses. Anticipating theories of more than a century later, Mill recognized the role played by differing price expectations, and by differences in the information sets available to economic agents.

Evelyn L. Forget

See also BANK CHARTER ACT OF 1844; BANKING SCHOOL, CURRENCY SCHOOL, AND FREE BANKING SCHOOL; CREDIT CYCLE; EXPECTATIONS; KITCHIN CYCLES; SAY'S LAW; TOOKE, THOMAS

Bibliography

Forget, E. L. 1990. "John Stuart Mill's Business Cycle." *History of Political Economy* 22:629–42.

Hollander, S. 1985. *The Economics of John Stuart Mill.* Oxford: Basil Blackwell.

Mill, J. S. [1826] 1967. "Paper Currency and Commercial Distress." In *The Collected Works of John Stuart Mill.* Vol. 4. Edited by J. M. Robson, 71–123. Toronto: Univ. of Toronto Press.

———. [1833] 1967. "The Currency Juggle." In *The Collected Works of John Stuart Mill.* Vol. 4. Edited by J. M. Robson, 181–92. Toronto: Univ. of Toronto Press.

———. [1844a] 1967. "The Currency Question." In *The Collected Works of John Stuart Mill.* Vol. 4. Edited by J. M. Robson, 341–61. Toronto: Univ. of Toronto Press.

———. [1844b] 1967. "Of the Influence of Consumption on Production." In *The Collected Works of John Stuart Mill.* Vol. 4. Edited by J. M. Robson, 262–79. Toronto: Univ. of Toronto Press.

———. [1857] 1967. "The Bank Acts." In *The Collected Works of John Stuart Mill.* Vol. 5. Edited by J. M. Robson, 499–547. Toronto: Univ. of Toronto Press.

———. [1867] 1967. "Currency and Banking." In *The Collected Works of John Stuart Mill.* Vol. 5. Edited by J. M. Robson, 599–611. Toronto: Univ. of Toronto Press.

———. [1871] 1965. *The Principles of Political Economy.* 2 vols. 7th ed. Vols. 2 and 3 of *The Collected Works of John Stuart Mill.* Edited by J. M. Robson. Toronto: Univ. of Toronto Press.

Mills, Frederick Cecil (1892–1964)

Frederick C. Mills wrote extensively on the cyclical behavior of prices and production. His books, such as *Prices in Recession and Recovery* and *Price-Quantity Interactions in Business Cycles* used time-series techniques to examine movements in prices, but Mills was also interested in frequency distributions of prices, as is evident in his *The Behavior of Prices.* With *The Structure of Post-War Prices,* published in 1948, Mills became recognized as a leading authority on inflation in the United States.

His *Statistical Methods,* published originally in 1924 and revised in 1938, illustrated the use of moving averages, index numbers, and curve-fitting to measure, isolate, and correlate cyclical fluctuations. In his 1926 paper, "An Hypothesis Concerning the Duration of Business Cycles," Mills also made international comparisons of cyclical behavior.

Mills, reared in Oakland, California, received his B.A. (1914) and M.A. (1916) in economics from the University of California. He earned his Ph.D. from Columbia in 1917 and did postgraduate work at the London School of Economics in 1919.

Mills was a member of the faculty of Columbia University from 1919 until his death in 1964, serving as professor of economics and statistics. He was also on the research staff of the National Bureau of Economic Research from 1925 to 1953. He was president of the American Statistical Association in 1934, president of the American Economic Association in 1940, and vice-president of the American Association for the Advancement of Science in 1946. In 1948, he was director of a Congressional survey into the statistical agencies of the United States government.

Judy L. Klein

See also MOVING AVERAGES; PRICE RIGIDITY

Bibliography

Anonymous. 1948. "Mills, Frederick Cecil." *Current Biography,* 453–54. New York: H. W. Wilson.

Mills, F. C. 1926. "An Hypothesis Concerning the Duration of Business Cycles."

Journal of the American Statistical Association 21:447–57.

———. 1927. *The Behavior of Prices.* New York: NBER.

———. 1936. *Prices in Recession and Recovery.* New York: NBER.

———. 1938. *Statistical Methods.* 2d ed. New York: Henry Holt.

———. 1946. *Price-Quantity Interactions in Business Cycles.* New York: NBER.

———. 1948. *The Structure of Post-War Prices.* New York: NBER.

Mills, John (1821–1896)

John Mills published "On Credit Cycles and the Origin of Commercial Panics" in the 1867–68 *Transactions of the Manchester Statistical Society.* A London banker, Mills succeeded William Stanley Jevons as president of the Manchester Statistical Society in 1871, and corresponded frequently with Jevons. "On Credit Cycles" presented detailed diagrams showing the periodicity of bank reserves, bullion, prices, railway expenditures, pauperism, bankruptcy, and rates of discount in Britain since 1800. Briefly, Mills maintained that periodic commercial fluctuations were characterized and driven by alterations in commercial mood; throughout the commercial cycle a succession of commercial moods occurred in "the same relative order."

Research by William Langton, the founder of the Manchester Statistical Society, had revealed in 1857 that commercial fluctuations seemed to occur with a periodicity of about ten years. Mills insisted, in addition, that credit followed "normal and predictable phases" that were driven by fluctuations in commercial mood with a periodicity of ten years. He attempted to characterize these fluctuations in beliefs throughout the cycle, and to relate mood swings to credit formation and contraction. In "Credit Cycles," Mills defined the panic, or commercial crisis, as "the destruction, in the mind, of a bundle of beliefs" (1867, 19).

Speculative elements played a key role in causing the commercial collapse. "Over-trading," Mills observed, "is the common forerunner of Panic" (4). Expectations concerning the profitability of investment projects, Mills argued, are derived from prices that are used to make expected profit calculations. Investors project that current prices will prevail in future time periods, a projection that is decidedly in-

correct. Speculation also plays a role in creating cyclical pressures, since goods are placed on the market faster than they can be absorbed, and prices begin to fall. Eventually, loanable capital and "stable credit" (long-term sunk capital such as railways) are strained, and the collapse occurs.

Mills insisted that the speculative phase was partially held in check by convertibility. The role for monetary policy in the face of a commercial panic was limited. Mills did allow, however, that suspension of convertibility had on several occasions mitigated the worst features of the panic. More generally, he maintained that the "schoolmaster, rather than the legislator, is the magician who is to steady our rates of discount, and save Lombard Street from its decennial fits of terror" (40). This recommendation followed from Mills's conviction that "*ignorant* speculative excitement," as well as the "willingness to take *immoral* risks," caused the speculative "mania" (39).

Mills's characterization of the cycle, along with his careful empirical analysis of the features of fluctuations, earned him the respect of a subsequent influential business-cycle analyst, W. S. Jevons. Jevons relied on Mills's empirical analysis in his lectures delivered at Owens College (1875–76), and used Mills's diagrams revealing periodicity. Like Mills, Jevons insisted that expectations, or "commercial moods," were a key to understanding the cycle. Jevons's analysis of fluctuations continued to emphasize the importance of speculative elements throughout the cycle, and allowed, like Mills, that some *mistaken speculation* occurred throughout the upswing. But while Jevons accepted Mills's characterization of the cycle, as well as his insistence on the importance of moods, he maintained, in opposition to Mills, that an explanation of the cycle required an explanation of the periodic alteration in moods. The search for this explanation led Jevons to develop his renowned "sunspot" theory.

Sandra J. Peart

See also CREDIT CYCLE; EXPECTATIONS; JEVONS, WILLIAM STANLEY; SUNSPOT THEORIES OF FLUCTUATIONS

Bibliography
Jevons, W. S. [1875–76] 1977. *Lectures on Political Economy.* Vol. 6 of *Papers and Correspondence of William Stanley Jevons.* London: Macmillan.

M

Mills, J. 1866. "The Bank Charter Act and the Late Panic." Paper presented to the National Association for the Promotion of Social Science.

————. 1867. "On Credit Cycles and the Origin of Commercial Panics." *Transactions of the Manchester Statistical Society for the Session 1867–1868*, 5–40.

Peart, S. 1991. "Sunspots and Expectations: W. S. Jevons's Theory of Economic Fluctuations." *Journal of the History of Economic Thought* 13:243–65.

Minsky, Hyman Phillip (1919–   )

Following doctoral study at Harvard and teaching posts at Brown and the University of California at Berkeley, Hyman Minsky has spent most of his academic career at Washington University in St. Louis. Minsky's work is considered Post-Keynesian, stressing many themes developed in Keynes's *General Theory*: the inherent instability of market economies, the importance of aggregate demand, and the critical role of investment and fiscal policy. Minsky argues that conventional interpretations of Keynes insufficiently emphasize his view that the financial system is an important source of instability in an uncertain economy. He also builds on Irving Fisher's "debt-deflation" analysis of cumulative downswings.

In Minsky's view, during each phase of the business cycle, changes in financial conditions bring on the next phase. During boom periods, for example, "firms engage more heavily in debt financing, households and firms cut their cash and liquid-asset holdings relative to their debt, and 'banks' increase their loans at the expense of securities" (Minsky 1975, 123). Debts increase relative to assets, debt-servicing costs rise relative to revenues, and short-term debts become increasingly prevalent. These financial conditions make the system more vulnerable to shocks such as the stock-market crash and bank failures of 1929–33. Once a downswing is under way, declining prices and revenues increase the burden of debt service, leading to increased bankruptcy, forced liquidation, and serious curtailment of investment spending.

In his later writings, Minsky has argued that since the 1960s, increased debt, declining liquidity, and the failure of financial institutions have increased the fragility of the United States financial system. Incipient major crises in 1974–75 and 1982 were, in his view, averted in part because fiscal policy was stabilizing and in part because the Federal Reserve (and cooperating agencies) were effective lenders of last resort.

Minsky's analysis of fiscal policy goes beyond the conventional income-expenditure textbook discourse. An increase in the federal deficit enlarges the flow-surplus position of the private sector, and the attendant increase in the federal debt adds to the stock of low-risk financial assets and decreases the risk-exposure of private balance sheets. Further, Minsky argues, the government deficit and the level of business profits are, under certain conditions, positively correlated. Thus, "if the government deficit increases when investment and thus income declines, then profits will not fall as they would in the absence of the government deficit" (Minsky 1986, 148).

However, the bail-out orientation of government deficits and frequent reliance on a lender of last resort create an inflationary bias. Inflation is reinforced by the structure of costs and demand: "the emphasis upon growth through investment, the bias toward bigness in business, business styles that emphasize advertising and overheads, and the explosion of transfer payments are main causes of our current inflation" (Minsky 1982a, 112).

Minsky's work has not had a major influence in the macroeconomic discussions of the last thirty years. Contrary to prevailing research style, his presentation is largely verbal, with little use of mathematical models or econometric estimation. Nor does contemporary macroeconomics seem to have had much influence on Minsky. Much of his analysis seems to presuppose cyclical patterns more severe than those observed in the United States since 1945. Neither monetary policy nor international factors (including OPEC) figure significantly in his presentations. Probably his greatest contribution has been the continued insistence that financial institutions and practices are important to macroeconomic performance. He has kept asking the question "Can 'It' [the Great Depression] Happen Again?" and reminded us that debt burdens and thin margins of equity make the economy vulnerable to deflationary impulses.

The widespread concerns about the accumulation of public and private debt during the 1980s has drawn increased attention to Minsky's work. And in a measured yet sympathetic assessment, James Tobin (1989, 106) characterized Minsky as "the most sophisticated, analytical, and persuasive of those contemporary economists who believe that leverage is the Achilles heel of capitalism."

Paul S. Trescott

See also CREDIT CYCLE; DEBT-DEFLATION THEORY; FISHER, IRVING; INVESTMENT; POST-KEYNESIAN BUSINESS-CYCLE THEORY

Bibliography

Minsky, H. P. 1964. "Longer Waves in Financial Relations: Financial Factors in the More Severe Depressions." *American Economic Review: Papers and Proceedings* 54:324–35.

———. 1975. *John Maynard Keynes.* New York: Columbia Univ. Press.

———. 1982a. *Can "It" Happen Again?* Armonk, N.Y.: M. E. Sharpe.

———. 1982b. "The Financial-Instability Hypothesis: Capitalist Processes and the Behavior of the Economy." In *Financial Crises: Theory, History, and Policy,* edited by C. P. Kindleberger and J.-P. Laffargue, 13–39. Cambridge: Cambridge Univ. Press.

———. 1986. *Stabilizing an Unstable Economy.* New Haven: Yale Univ. Press.

Tobin, J. 1989. Review of *Stabilizing an Unstable Economy* by H. P. Minsky. *Journal of Economic Literature* 27:105–08.

Mintz, Ilse Schueller (1904–1978)

Ilse Mintz was born in Vienna, the oldest of the three daughters of Richard and Erna Schueller. Her father was also an economist who served the Austrian government for forty years both in the trade and foreign ministries.

Ilse Mintz studied economics at the University of Vienna, receiving her doctorate in 1927. She then worked for a year in the Austrian Institute of Business Cycle Research. Although she was not formally employed again until after emigrating to the United States, she was a member of the "Mises Seminar," a group of prominent economists including Hayek, Haberler, Machlup, and Morgenstern, which met regularly at Mises's invitation, to discuss economic questions.

Married in 1926 to Maximilian Mintz, a lawyer, she left Austria in March 1938 for Switzerland, but emigrated to New York in July 1938. Enrolling at Columbia in 1943, she received a Ph.D. in economics in 1951. Her doctoral dissertation, written under Arthur F. Burns

and entitled *Deterioration in the Quality of Foreign Bonds in the U.S., 1920–1930* was published by the National Bureau of Economic Research.

In 1948, Mintz began teaching at Columbia University and in the early 1950s she became a Senior Research Associate at the National Bureau of Economic Research, combining both positions until retiring in 1969.

Mintz published a number of studies at the National Bureau involving international trade and finance. These included *Trade Balances During Business Cycles: U.S. and Britain Since 1880; American Exports during Business Cycles, 1879–1958; Cyclical Fluctuations in the Exports of the United States Since 1879;* and *U.S. Import Quotas: Costs and Consequences* (1973).

While most of these studies involved the analysis of business cycles as well as international trade, her principal contribution to the former field was her pioneering study, *Dating Postwar Business Cycles: Methods and Their Application to Western Germany, 1950–67.* This study, appearing as it did at the end of what was then being billed as the "longest peacetime expansion in U.S. history" was very influential, because it developed the method, since widely emulated, for examining what she termed "growth cycles," a term many first construed as self-contradictory. In fact Mintz adapted a technique used first by Milton Friedman of taking the deviations of observations from an underlying trend. In effect, growth cycles become cycles in economic activity viewed as periods of greater and lesser growth than some long-term trend rate of growth. By looking at cycles in growth rates in the case of Germany, Mintz was able to find evidence of several cycles in the post-World War II period, whereas the rapid growth rate of the period produced no conventional (now called "classical") cycles at all.

Application of Mintz's basic approach has revealed measurable growth cycles in a number of other market-oriented economies, including the United States and the other major industrialized countries that have been studied. (While the United States Department of Commerce continues, for example, to monitor "classical cycles" through its monthly publication, *Business Conditions Digest* until 1990 and now in a selection of the *Survey of Current Business,* the OECD has chosen to monitor growth cycles in its monthly publication [see OECD, *Main Economic Indicators*].) In truth, the modern world continues to display evidence of both

<big>M</big>

types of instability. In this sense Mintz inaugurated a major addition to our tools for monitoring instability in the modern world.

Philip A. Klein

See also GROWTH CYCLES; MOORE, GEOFFREY HOYT

Bibliography
Mintz, I. 1959. *Trade Balances During Business Cycles: U.S. and Britain Since 1880.* New York: NBER.
———. 1961. *American Exports during Business Cycles, 1879–1958.* New York: NBER.
———. 1967. *Cyclical Fluctuations in the Exports of the United States Since 1879.* New York: NBER.
———. 1969. *Dating Postwar Business Cycles: Methods and Their Application to Western Germany, 1950–67.* New York: NBER.

Mises, Ludwig Edler von (1881–1973)

A central figure of the Austrian School of economics, Ludwig von Mises contributed broadly to both theoretical and applied economics. Dating from 1902, his writings developed into a comprehensive treatment of economic principles set forth in *Human Action,* a treatise which first appeared in German as *National-ökonomie* (1940). His economic thought is presented as an integral part of a *praxeological* system—a logic of action in the context of human purposes and the passage of time.

Though widely known for denying the possibility of rational central planning and as a life-long critic of interventionism, Mises also contributed importantly to monetary and business-cycle theory. In his *Theory of Money and Credit,* Mises demonstrated that the value of money, no less than that of other goods, is based on its marginal utility. Building on this early integration of value theory and monetary theory, Mises sought to explain how both market forces and bank policy affect the purchasing power of money. He also provided a clear account, in this first major work, of the credit-induced boom and subsequent bust. An extended treatment of what came to be known as the Austrian theory of the business cycle is provided in his "Monetary Stabilization and Cyclical Policy" and in *Human Action.* To formulate a theory of boom and bust, Mises drew insights from three sources: Eugen von Böhm-Bawerk of the early Austrian School, Knut Wicksell of the incipient Swedish School, and Lord Overstone and others of the British Currency School.

From Böhm-Bawerk, Mises adopted the conception of a production economy whose temporally sequenced stages of production employ capital goods and other resources. This capital-theoretic framework, in which some production processes are more time-consuming, or *roundabout,* than others, features a trade-off between the amount and the timeliness of economic output. In an economy unhampered by perverse bank policy, the economy's intertemporal structure of production is governed by the rate of interest, which reflects the "time preferences" of consumers. That is, the interest rate brings into balance the marginal productivity of roundaboutness with the relative marginal utilities of goods now and goods later. Mises's treatment of intertemporal resource allocation did not differ substantively from Böhm-Bawerk's. Original with Mises was his use of the Austrian theory of capital and interest as a basis for a theory of business cycles.

Mises borrowed from Wicksell the ideas that the bank rate of interest sometimes diverges from what Wicksell called the *natural* rate of interest. The natural rate, which excludes all monetary influences, was taken by Mises to be the interest rate consistent with consumers' time preferences; the bank rate, which is subject to monetary manipulation, was taken to be the focus of bank policy. Holding the bank rate below the natural rate requires a continuous expansion of bank credit. The divergence of the two rates of interest mattered to Wicksell primarily because it affected the general level of prices. Wicksell acknowledged that bank policy might also affect the allocation of resources, but any such allocational effects were reduced to "tendencies only" by his simplifying assumptions and thus were no part of his formal theory.

Mises, in effect, relaxed Wicksell's simplifying assumptions in order to investigate the allocational effects of bank policy. He specifically studied how credit expansion affected time-consuming, capital-using production processes. Tracing the effects of bank policy on production activity furthered the integration of monetary and value theory and identified the ultimate consequences of a cheap-credit policy. Since the natural rate is the rate of interest that reconciles intertemporal production activities with the time preferences of consumers, credit expansion, by keeping the bank rate below the natural rate, induces a fundamental inconsistency. A cheap-credit policy distorts business calculations causing the production of consumer goods to be reduced and production processes in general to be excessively roundabout. Mises described the policy-induced reduction in consumption as *forced savings* and the intertemporal misallocation of resources induced by artificially cheap credit as *malinvestment* (as distinguished from the more commonly used term, "overinvestment").

Mises transformed his insights about forced saving and malinvestment into a theory of the business cycle by recognizing the unsustainability of production activities based on a low bank rate. But the idea that the market's responses to credit expansion contain the seeds of their own undoing is older than either the Austrian or the Swedish Schools. A self-reversing process triggered by bank policy had been identified early in the nineteenth century by members of the Currency School. So similar in form was Mises's theory to the "Circulation Credit Theory of the Trade Cycle," as exposited by Lord Overstone and others, that Mises considered his own theory an extension of the Circulation Credit theory rather than a uniquely Austrian theory.

However, Mises found the formulation of the Currency School inadequate in two respects. First, it gauged bank policy too narrowly in terms of the quantity of banknotes, ignoring the equally if not more significant volume of demand deposits. Second, and more important, it failed to identify any domestic market forces that might counteract the initial effects of credit expansion. The unsustainability of the boom in the formulation of the Currency School derived exclusively from international repercussions. As an expansion of banknotes drove domestic prices upward, exports would fall while imports rose. The trade imbalance would drain gold, the redemption medium, from the expanding banks, eventually requiring the banks to contract. It is this specie-flow mechanism, in the Currency School's view, that limits the ability of any one country to maintain a cheap-credit policy.

Mises's formulation advanced the Circulation Credit theory by showing that credit expansion is unsustainable even in a closed economy—or in an open one in which banks of all countries expand together. In the early phase of a credit expansion, workers receive income from production activities undertaken on the basis of a low bank rate. But those same individuals, as consumers, spend their incomes at a rate corresponding to the higher natural rate of interest. This consumer spending eventually counteracts the initial effects of credit expansion. The rise of consumer-goods prices, which demonstrates the true strength of consumers' preferences for goods now over goods later, *dis*courages the relatively more roundabout production processes that cheap credit initially *en*couraged. Attempts by the central bank to reinforce the credit expansion also reinforce the market's "countermovements." As market forces continuously counteract bank policy, the artificial boom is eventually brought to an end. Some production processes that were initiated when credit was cheap can be completed only at a loss, while others must be liquidated. Even apart from international considerations, the credit expansion contains the seeds of its own undoing.

In sum, Mises saw the boom as a consequence of unenlightened bank policy, a period of artificial and unsustainable expansion, in which capital and other resources are committed to excessively roundabout production processes, and he saw the bust as the inevitable consequence of the credit-induced boom. In the end, the pattern of consumer spending wins out over the pattern of bank lending. Mises saw the recovery as the period during which malinvestments are liquidated and production activities are again reconciled with actual consumer preferences. Mises recognized, as did Wicksell, that enlightened bank policy would avoid credit expansion, thus minimizing the divergence between the bank rate and the natural rate. However, believing that central-bank policy as formulated by government officials would be ideologically biased towards cheap credit, Mises favored institutional reform in the direction of free banking.

Mises's theory underwent substantial development by F. A. Hayek, whose *Prices and Production* influenced many British and American theorists in the early 1930s, and retains an important place in the research agenda of the modern Austrian School. But the Austrian theory of the business cycle has not been incorporated into mainstream macroeconomic theory. Several factors inhibited a broader acceptance of Mises's views. First, mainstream macroeconomics since the Keynesian Revolution has developed with no grounding in capital theory of the sort underlying Austrian business-cycle theory. Thus, a capital-theoretic account of the unsustainability of a credit-induced boom, when grafted onto a macroeconomic theory that is otherwise free of such considerations, appears ad hoc and unduly complex. Second, because of fundamental difficulties in measuring capital and roundaboutness, especially in the context of artificial booms and consequent busts, the empirical—largely episodic—support for the Austrian theory does not conform well to the econometric procedures for model evaluation that now dominate modern empirical economics. And third, the implied policy of avoiding artificial booms as the only way of avoiding the otherwise inevitable bust is unattractive to policy activists committed to initiating and perpetuating economic booms.

Roger W. Garrison

See also AUSTRIAN THEORY OF BUSINESS CYCLES; BANKING SCHOOL, CURRENCY SCHOOL, AND FREE BANKING SCHOOL; BÖHM-BAWERK, EUGEN RITTER VON; CAPITAL GOODS; HAYEK, FRIEDRICH AUGUST [VON]; LACHMANN, LUDWIG MAURITS; LOYD, SAMUEL JONES; MONETARY DISEQUILIBRIUM THEORIES OF THE BUSINESS CYCLE; MONETARY POLICY; NATURAL RATE OF INTEREST; OVERINVESTMENT THEORIES OF BUSINESS CYCLES; PERIOD OF PRODUCTION; ROBBINS, LIONEL CHARLES; WICKSELL, JOHAN GUSTAV KNUT

Bibliography
Böhm-Bawerk, E. [1884–1909] 1959. *Capital and Interest.* 3 vols. South Holland, Ill.: Libertarian Press.
Hayek, F. A. 1931. *Prices and Production.* London: Routledge.
Mises, L. von. [1924] 1953. *The Theory of Money and Credit.* 2d ed. Translation. New Haven, Conn.: Yale Univ. Press.
———. [1928] 1978. "Monetary Stabilization and Cyclical Policy." In *Mises on the Manipulation of Money and Credit,* edited by P. L. Greaves, 57–107. Dobbs Ferry, N.Y.: Free Market Books.
———. 1966. *Human Action.* 3d rev. ed. Chicago: Regnery.
Mises, L. von, et al. 1978. *The Austrian Theory of the Trade Cycle and Other Essays.* New York: Center for Libertarian Studies.
Overstone, Lord [S. J. Loyd]. [1857] 1972. *Tracts and Other Publications on Metallic and Paper Currency.* Edited by J. R. McCulloch. Englewood Cliffs, N.J.: A. M. Kelley.
Wicksell, K. [1898] 1936. *Interest and Prices.* Translation. London: Macmillan.

Mississippi Bubble

The Mississippi Bubble refers to the first boom and bust on the Paris Bourse. It resulted from a complete transformation of the French financial, monetary, and fiscal structures executed on the initiative of John Law, an expatriate Scotsman who enjoyed the patronage of the Duc d'Orléans, regent for the future Louis XV. Law created what he called "le Système," in which foreign trade was monopolized by his Compagnie des Indes, while the money supply consisted of paper notes issued by his Banque Royale. The Compagnie des Indes had converted the outstanding government debt into its capital stock, imitating successful debt-equity swaps carried out previously in England by the South Sea Company (1711). But when Law tried to stabilize the value of the company's shares at 10,000 livres, by issuing paper notes from the Banque Royale upon presentation of a share, he monetized the entire government debt. This set off an uncontrollable inflation, brought to an end only by declaring the company bankrupt in July 1720. Law fled France in disgrace, leaving a legacy of revulsion against the financial innovations of the Dutch and English that retarded the development of French financial institutions well into the nineteenth century.

Law began his spectacular career by founding the Banque Générale in 1716, which tried to imitate on a very small scale the successes of the Bank of England and the Bank of Amsterdam by issuing paper notes fully backed by specie deposits. Due to their security and convenience, the notes rose to a premium over specie, which was then in a state of flux due to frequent recoinages. His success with this modest bank enabled him to take the next giant step, which was to create in 1717 a huge joint-stock company, the Compagnie d'Occident. This converted outstanding government debt up to 50 million *livres tournois* into equity in an enterprise granted the monopoly for exploiting the lands in the Mississippi drainage which had recently been won from Spain (the Louisiana Territory). The main tangible accomplishment of this company, popularly known as the Mississippi Company, was founding the city of New Orleans. Like the English South Sea Company, on which it was clearly modeled, the Mississippi Company's future lay in refinancing government debt rather than exploiting its trade privileges with the New World.

Meanwhile, in response to new revenue demands by Duc d'Orléans as he prepared to make war against Spain in 1718, Law's Banque Générale was enlarged in capital and expanded in function, becoming the Banque Royale beginning 1 January 1719. Its notes, denominated either in gold *ecus* or in silver livres, then became the media for tax payments. In May, the *louis d'or* was devalued against the livre, so the *billets-livre* became the preferred form of money for the public to hold. The next step was to merge the Compagnie d'Occident with the French East Indies Company and the China Company, forming the Compagnie des Indes in May 1719. Law then began a series of stock-market manipulations that drove the price of its shares above par by mid-June 1719 and double par by mid-July. Law's successful manipulation of the share prices had three key elements: (1) he gave favorable terms of purchase, with purchasers of new shares required to possess four old shares (ensuring capital gains to the original shareholders); (2) he constantly added new sources of revenue to the monopoly privileges of the company; (3) he enlarged the note-issue power of the Banque Royale greatly and repeatedly. These all led to a spectacular rise in the value of the shares from July 1719 onward, which led foreign speculators from all over Europe, especially Holland and England, to buy shares as well.

The decrees of 16–20 August 1719 completed the formation of the system with a bold step toward fiscal reform: the suppression and reimbursement of the *rentes* and many of the offices that had been sold in the previous two decades to raise money. The reimbursement took place in *billets de banque* at the offices of the company. Based on the increased revenues projected from the tax farm on indirect taxes that had been given to the company for the next seven years, as well as on revenues from the monopoly of the mint, these obligations, *actions rentières,* could have been very attractive investments. In effect, the elimination of direct taxes, offices, and the *rentes* could have been funded into the permanent capital stock of the company. As it was, Law proceeded with three successive new issues of capital stock (the fourth, fifth, and sixth issues) in the company on 2, 17, and 21 September 1719.

Those shares were issued at a face value of 5,000 livres each, with a promised dividend of 4 percent. Because the first three issues of shares had face values of 500, 550, and 1,000 livres, the possessors of these *mères, filles,* and *petites filles,* as they were popularly called, profited from enormous capital gains. Those who already held government debt, however, were accorded no priority in purchasing those new shares, but were forced to buy them at existing market value. This meant that they had to hope for further capital gains on their shares in the company if they were to offset any of the losses they had already suffered on government debts. The third step in Law's plan was to raise the market value of the shares to 10,000 livres—this in order to reduce the effective rate of interest to 2 percent.

To facilitate speculation, or, in his view, to mobilize the necessary capital, Law took the following steps:

1. He divided shares into fractions small enough so that modest investors could purchase them.
2. He provided for installment payments, 10 percent per month, and further provided that payments due the first two months could be deferred to the third. That meant that December and March were the months of reckoning.
3. He provided loans from the Banque Royale on the security of shares, even if only partially paid for.

To stabilize the price of Compagnie d'Occident stock after it had reached the desired level of 10,000 livres, Law took these additional steps:

4. Starting on 19 December (O.S.), he opened an office for the purchase and sale of shares in the company.
5. He later fixed the price of each share at 9,000 livres.

Law, in other words, manufactured the conditions necessary for a price bubble to occur in the stock of the Compagnie des Indes. At the top of the bubble in the middle of November, when the price per share had reached his target level of 10,000 livres, Law tried to lock-in the foreigners or to offset their exit from the

Paris market by bringing in a broader range of French participants. He issued 30 million livres worth of new shares during the next week to stabilize the price. At the end of that week, speculators left Paris for London.

Another exit of speculators' capital from Paris occurred in early February. On 12 February 1720, Law halted all dealings in France in stock, foreign exchange, and bank notes in an attempt to combat inflation and speculation. The price of Mississippi shares plummeted. At the same time, the English Parliament approved the South Sea Company's proposal for funding a large part of the national debt. So money left France and headed for England. Popular pressure forced Law to reopen the Paris stock market on 23 February, with the purchase and sale of unlimited quantities of shares priced at 9,000 livres, and to reopen the offices where the paper currency, *billets de banque,* could be converted to silver. That restored the stock-market boom, but speculation then took place in the *billets de banque.* Once the Paris Bourse reopened, the livre depreciated sharply, signaling the exodus of speculators.

The stock-market gyrations continued in France with mostly domestic speculators until the middle of May 1720. On 10 May, in desperation, Law announced a deflationary decree, again attempting to save his system. Convertibility of bank notes into specie was to end. The official price of shares of the Compagnie des Indes was dropped to 8,000 livres, with a target price of 5,000 livres by 1 December. The exchange rate fell again, indicating that the remaining speculators, French or foreign, transferred their money from France to put it in England for more profits or hid it in France in safer quarters.

From the deflationary decree in May (which Law lifted a week later, again under public pressure) onward, currency debasements and increased banknote issues caused a continued depreciation of the livre. The bankruptcy of 6 July (O.S.) of the Banque Royale shifted speculation in France from shares in the Compagnie des Indes to *billets de banque,* which depreciated until the exchange market in France closed in September 1720. In late September, the livre appreciated sharply as more traditional bankers regained power, causing a repatriation of gold and silver into France.

The net outcome was to reduce the government's debt service, but at the expense of stifling reforms in the tax system and entangling financial intermediaries in legal disputes for at least a decade, discouraging the rise of joint-stock companies, or modern financial institutions. With the restoration of a specie standard, however, the overseas trade of France flourished until the setbacks of the Seven Years War in India and Canada.

Larry Neal

See also LAW, JOHN; SOUTH SEA BUBBLE

Bibliography
Faure, E. 1977. *La Banqueroute de Law.* Paris: Gallimard.
Law, J. 1934. *John Law, Oeuvres Complètes.* 3 vols. Edited by P. Harsin. Paris: Sirey.
Murphy, A. E. 1986. *Richard Cantillon, Entrepreneur and Economist.* London: Oxford Univ. Press.
Neal, L. 1990. *The Rise of Financial Capitalism: International Capital Markets in the Age of Reason.* Cambridge: Cambridge Univ. Press.

Mitchell, Wesley Clair (1874–1948)

Wesley Mitchell spent most of his professional life studying "what happens during business cycles," and probably did more than any other economist to shape the thinking of Americans about business cycles. Although he presented a business-cycle theory in his first book on the subject, he is better known today for his subsequent work at the National Bureau of Economic Research (NBER) developing statistics on the behavior of hundreds of variables over the business cycle.

Mitchell studied economics at the University of Chicago, and was particularly influenced by Thorstein Veblen and J. Laurence Laughlin. His doctoral dissertation on money and prices during the Civil War was expanded into his first book, *A History of the Greenbacks* (1903). He taught at the University of California and Columbia University, was director of research at the NBER from 1920 to 1945, and was president of the American Economic Association in 1924. Mitchell also made contributions to the history of economic thought and methodology; the lecture notes for his history of economics course at Columbia, published as *Types of Economic Theory,* are still fascinating reading. And his "institutionalist" views on the importance of observation, induction, and a historical perspective appeared in many articles and particularly in *The Backward Art of Spending Money.*

In *Business Cycles,* his first book on the subject, Mitchell surveyed existing theories of fluctuations, examined the state of empirical knowledge about cycles, and presented his own "descriptive analysis." In this presentation, as Milton Friedman (1952) noted, theoretical arguments about the causation of cycles are "hidden" within an exposition of empirical material, so that description and theory are difficult to disentangle. (This analytical part of the book was reissued in 1941 as *Business Cycles and Their Causes.*) In his next book, *Business Cycles: The Problem and Its Setting,* Mitchell explicitly eschewed theorizing. "We must find out more about the facts," he wrote, "before we can choose among the old explanations or improve upon them" (1927, 2). He spent the rest of his life gathering and organizing information on business cycles, never managing to return to the question of causation. *Measuring Business Cycles,* coauthored with Arthur F. Burns, was published in 1946, and his last work, *What Happens During Business Cycles: A Progress Report,* was published posthumously in 1951.

Mitchell's work was guided by two hypotheses: the first was that business cycles are sufficiently alike to make describing a "typical" one possible. The second was that cycles are inherent in capitalist economies, and not just accidental consequences of occasional "external" disturbances.

Mitchell's 1913 account of the cycle focused on movements in profit margins due to lags between changes in selling prices and changes in costs, and on the relationship between production and the financial sector. His account begins in the recovery phase: spending is increasing, after having been depressed for some time, when conditions for expansion are favorable. Output, employment, inventories, prices, wages, indebtedness, interest rates, and profits are all low compared to their levels in the previous prosperity period. Thus, output and employment can increase for some time without driving up prices or wages. The expansion is a "cumulative process"—each increase in spending adds to incomes, builds confidence, and stimulates additional consumption and investment. Eventually, costs and prices begin to rise, and in late expansion, costs increase more rapidly than selling prices: wage rates are forced up, and "real costs" rise as production becomes less efficient. As their excess reserves run out,

banks must restrict credit, and both short- and long-term interest rates rise, discouraging investment and dampening spending in general. Because indebtedness mounts in the upswing, the financial crunch causes a panic and many bankruptcies, making producers pessimistic and cautious. The slackening of spending initiates a downward "cumulative process." Selling prices initially fall more rapidly than costs, shrinking profit margins. The depression can drag on for quite some time. During this phase, firms seek to cut costs, reduce their inventories and debt, and write down asset values. Lenders reduce interest rates on loans and bonds. These adjustments restore the conditions for profitable production; eventually a recovery begins when either consumers or firms increase their spending.

Mitchell believed that business cycles, though not entirely avoidable, could be moderated by government action, so the suffering accompanying recessions could be greatly reduced. He believed providing more information to the public about the phenomena of the cycle would itself be helpful. At various times he endorsed Irving Fisher's "compensated dollar" scheme to stabilize the price level, argued that the Federal Reserve should ease financial panics by acting as lender of last resort and should regulate credit policy to prevent booms from going too far, and suggested that public-works spending should be timed countercyclically. In the mid-1930s, he called for national planning, though without making clear just what that might mean.

Mitchell pictured the cycle not as a movement of a few aggregate variables, but as a complex of fluctuations in a vast array of interrelated prices and quantities. The empirical work of the NBER during Mitchell's tenure involved tracking the cyclical behavior of hundreds of variables and constructing measures with which to compare the amplitude and timing of movements in these variables within a cycle, across cycles, and across countries (Sherman 1991). This work was the foundation for indexes of leading, coincident, and lagging indicators which still guide much forecasting. Mitchell's work was at times unfairly ridiculed as "measurement without theory" (Koopmans [1947] 1965, see also Klein 1983), but today's business-cycle analysts are greatly indebted to Mitchell for the rich empirical legacy which he devoted his life to providing.

Janet A. Seiz

See also BURNS, ARTHUR FRANK; BUSINESS CYCLES; COMPOSITE AND DIFFUSION INDEXES; EXPECTATIONS; KOOPMANS, TJALLING CHARLES; LEADING INDICATORS: HISTORICAL RECORD; LEADS AND LAGS; MOORE, GEOFFREY HOYT; ZARNOWITZ, VICTOR

Bibliography

Burns, A. F., ed. 1952. *Wesley Clair Mitchell: The Economic Scientist.* New York: NBER.

Burns, A. F. and W. C. Mitchell. 1946. *Measuring Business Cycles.* New York: NBER.

Friedman, M. 1952. "The Economic Theorist." In *Wesley Clair Mitchell: The Economic Scientist,* edited by A. F. Burns, 237–82. New York: NBER.

Klein, P. A. 1983. "The Neglected Institutionalism of Wesley Clair Mitchell: The Theoretical Basis for Business Cycle Indicators." *Journal of Economic Issues* 17:867–99.

Koopmans, T. C. [1947] 1965. "Measurement without Theory." In *A.E.A. Readings in Business Cycles,* 186–203. Homewood, Ill.: Irwin.

Mitchell, W. C. 1913. *Business Cycles.* Berkeley: Univ. of Calif. Press.

———. 1927. *Business Cycles: The Problem and Its Setting.* New York: NBER.

———. 1937. *The Backward Art of Spending Money and Other Essays.* New York: McGraw-Hill.

———. 1941. *Business Cycles and Their Causes.* (Reprint of part 3 of *Business Cycles,* with a new preface.) Berkeley and Los Angeles: Univ. of Calif. Press.

———. 1951. *What Happens During Business Cycles: A Progress Report.* New York: NBER.

———. 1967–69. *Types of Economic Theory: From Mercantilism to Institutionalism.* 2 vols. Edited by J. Dorfman. New York: A. M. Kelley.

Sherman, H. J. 1991. *The Business Cycle: Growth and Crisis Under Capitalism.* Princeton: Princeton Univ. Press.

Model Evaluation and Design

Results from an empirical model need not be robust unless the model is well specified. Test statistics help assess the empirical adequacy of the model, and they may be categorized by principle and by information type. Additionally, test statistics may be applied in two contrasting manners: destructive via model evaluation, and constructive via model design. These issues are considered in turn.

Testing Principles

Test statistics are of three types: likelihood ratio (LR), Lagrange multiplier (LM), and Wald. For the LR statistic, the likelihood function is evaluated under both the maintained (unrestricted) and null (restricted) hypotheses, and the statistic is constructed as the negative of twice the difference of the log-likelihoods. For the LM statistic, the first derivative of the likelihood (the "score") under the maintained hypothesis is evaluated at the restricted parameter estimate. Deviations of that score from zero reflect the distance between the null hypothesis and the unrestricted estimate, which has a zero score. To measure the statistical importance of that distance, the LM statistic is constructed as a quadratic form in the score, with weightings from the covariance matrix of the score itself. By contrast, the Wald statistic uses only unrestricted parameter estimates. The degree to which these unrestricted estimates satisfy the parametric restrictions of the null hypothesis is evaluated, and the Wald statistic is constructed as a quadratic form of the (suitably weighted) discrepancies from the restrictions. Typically, the LM, LR, and Wald statistics are asymptotically equivalent (and asymptotically distributed as χ^2 under the null hypothesis), so computational convenience and finite sample properties determine which statistic to use. See Breusch and Pagan (1980) and Engle (1984) for comprehensive descriptions of the test procedures, and Buse (1982) for a graphical analysis of the relationship between the procedures.

Information Types: A Taxonomy

The main evaluation-design criteria in question concern goodness-of-fit, absence of residual autocorrelation and heteroscedasticity, valid exogeneity, predictive ability, parameter constancy, the statistical and economic interpretation of estimated coefficients, and the validity of a priori restrictions. Rather than discuss each criterion in an ad hoc manner, consider the taxonomy in Table 1, which was adapted from Hendry and Richard (1982) and Hendry ([1983] 1993, 1987), and in which criteria are related to particular types of information available to the researcher.

TABLE 1. A Taxonomy of Evaluation and Design Criteria

Information Set	Criteria
(A) own model's data	
(A1) relative past	white noise; innovation errors
(A2) relative present	weakly exogenous regressors
(A3) relative future	constant parameters, adequate forecasts
(B) measurement system: data ranges	data admissibility
(C) economic theory: theorists	theory consistency; cointegration
(D) alternative models' data	
(D1) relative past	parameter encompassing
(D2) relative present	exogeneity encompassing
(D3) relative future	forecast-model encompassing

Note: See Spanos (1986), Hendry (1987), and Ericsson (1992, Table 2) for details on alternative hypotheses and corresponding test statistics.

Specifically, the taxonomy partitions the information into:

(A) the data in one's own model;
(B) the structure of the measurement system (e.g., definitional constraints must not be violated);
(C) the subject-matter theory (so that the empirical model is consistent with the available theory); and
(D) the alternative models' data (which should contain no additional information relevant to explaining the variable of interest).

The data in (A) and (D) may be further partitioned into the relative past, present, and future. This two-tier partition of the information generates eight criteria. In statistical terms, each information set yields a criterion, which may be stated in terms of a corresponding null hypothesis (as in Table 1). Departures from each null could take many forms, generating a variety of test statistics.

As an example, the relative past of one's own data generates the criterion *innovation errors*. That is, lagged data provide no explanation of the variable of interest, beyond their explicit role in the empirical model. Improperly excluding lagged data induces non-innovation errors, which need not be white noise. Thus, one corresponding alternative hypothesis is autocorrelated errors, against which (e.g.) the Durbin-Watson statistic was designed to test.

Each criterion concerns whether the empirical model can ignore a certain set of information without loss of information. Equally,

each criterion in Table 1 matches some statistical "reduction" (or simplification) in deriving the empirical model from the underlying process generating the data. Conversely, each reduction corresponds to one or more criteria, depending on the particular information set being excluded.

Model Evaluation

In the context of model evaluation, the criteria are interpretable as null hypotheses and the associated statistics are used to test those hypotheses. Satisfying these criteria is a necessary condition for an empirical model to be congruent with the data and the chosen economic theory, so failing any of them is sufficient for rejecting the empirical model (at an appropriate significance level). Even so, meeting these criteria is only necessary (and not sufficient) to justify using a given model for inference, forecasting, or policy analysis.

Model Design

Test statistics also may be used as criteria to design models that satisfy the tests by construction. Such model design may be perfectly reasonable and desirable. Since the route chosen for obtaining the empirical model cannot affect the *validity* or *invalidity* of the finally selected model (because validity is intrinsic to a model), issues of model design only concern the *efficiency* of alternative model-building strategies. In presenting results, however, one ought to distinguish test statistics used as evaluation criteria from those used as (possibly implicit) design criteria. The role of the statistics does affect the *credibility* they give to a model (Leamer

1978). Genuine tests of a data-based formulation occur only if new data, new forms of tests, or new rival models accrue. "New" can also mean "unused" in this context.

For instance, modelers commonly neglect the usefulness of data from existing rival models, so tests based on (D) often can help *evaluate* a given model. That is, model adequacy requires evidence on the ability of a model to encompass rival hypotheses, demonstrating that the information in (D) is irrelevant, conditional on (A) and (C).

Encompassing

Encompassing can be understood intuitively from the following example illustrating *parameter* encompassing. Suppose Model 1 *predicts ã* as the value for the parameter *a* in Model 2, while Model 2 *actually* has the estimate *â*. Then test the closeness of *ã* to *â*, taking account of the uncertainty arising in estimation. Model 1 parameter-encompasses Model 2 if *ã* is "statistically close" to *â*, so that Model 1 explains why Model 2 obtained its results.

For single equations estimated by least squares, a necessary (but not sufficient) condition for parameter encompassing is *variance dominance,* where one equation variance-dominates another if the former has a smaller variance. Thus, encompassing defines a partial ordering over models, an ordering related to that based on goodness of fit; however, encompassing is more demanding than having the "best" goodness of fit. Encompassing is also consistent with the concept of a progressive research strategy, since an encompassing model is a kind of "sufficient representative" of previous empirical findings. White (1990) has shown that sufficiently thorough (model design) testing procedures will arrive at a well-specified characterization of the data generation process with confidence approaching certainty as the sample size grows without bound.

In general, an encompassing strategy suggests trying to anticipate problems in rival models of which their proponents may be unaware. For example, one model may correctly predict that the errors of another model are not innovations, or that the estimated parameters of the other model change over time. Corroborating such predictions adds credibility to the claim that the successful model reasonably represents the data process, whereas disconfirmation clarifies that it does not. For comprehensive accounts of tests for encompassing and of related non-nested hypothesis tests, see Mizon and Richard (1986) and Hendry and Richard (1989).

Illustrating the issues above, Hendry and Ericsson (1991) evaluate an empirical model of United Kingdom money demand from Friedman and Schwartz (1982). LM statistics for constancy, price homogeneity, and omitted variables reveal misspecification and imply the potential for an improved model. Hendry and Ericsson then design a new, better-fitting, constant money-demand equation that satisfies the earlier criteria (and others as well) and encompasses pre-existing models on the same data set. Key features of both Friedman and Schwartz's and Hendry and Ericsson's equations are their short-run (cyclical) and long-run properties; and reliable inference on those properties requires an adequate model specification.

Summary

The econometric use of test statistics in both design and evaluation is similar in spirit to the data-based aspect of Box and Jenkins's methods for univariate time-series modeling, but existing empirical models and available subject-matter theory play a larger role, while being subjected to a critical examination for their data coherency on (A)–(D). Further, given the Neyman-Pearson framework for hypothesis testing, it is natural first to estimate the most general model under consideration to establish the innovation variance. Then, given that most general model, it is of interest to ask what simplifications of that model are acceptable and how various simplifications affect the properties of the estimated model.

Neil R. Ericsson

See also COINTEGRATION; DISTRIBUTED LAGS; NONLINEAR STATISTICAL INFERENCE; PHASE AVERAGING

Bibliography

Breusch, T. S. and A. R. Pagan. 1980. "The Lagrange Multiplier Test and Its Applications to Model Specification in Econometrics." *Review of Economic Studies* 47:239–53.

Buse, A. 1982. "The Likelihood Ratio, Wald, and Lagrange Multiplier Tests: An Expository Note." *American Statistician* 36:153–57.

Engle, R. F. 1984. "Wald, Likelihood Ratio, and Lagrange Multiplier Tests in Econometrics." In *Handbook of Econometrics.*

Vol. 2. Edited by Z. Griliches and M. D. Intriligator, 775–826. Amsterdam: North-Holland.

Ericsson, N. R. 1992. "Parameter Constancy, Mean Square Forecast Errors, and Measuring Forecast Performance: An Exposition, Extensions, and Illustration." *Journal of Policy Modeling* 14:465–95.

Friedman, M. and A. J. Schwartz. 1982. *Monetary Trends in the United States and the United Kingdom: Their Relation to Income, Prices, and Interest Rates, 1867–1975.* Chicago: Univ. of Chicago Press.

Hendry, D. F. [1983] 1993. "Econometric Modelling: The 'Consumption Function' in Retrospect." Chap. 18 in *Econometrics—Alchemy or Science? Essays in Econometric Methodology.* Oxford: Basil Blackwell.

———. 1987. "Econometric Methodology: A Personal Perspective." In *Advances in Econometrics: Fifth World Congress.* Vol. 2. Edited by T. F. Bewley, 29–48. Cambridge: Cambridge Univ. Press.

Hendry, D. F. and N. R. Ericsson. 1991. "An Econometric Analysis of U.K. Money Demand in *Monetary Trends in the United States and the United Kingdom* by Milton Friedman and Anna J. Schwartz." *American Economic Review* 81:8–38.

Hendry, D. F. and J.-F. Richard. 1982. "On the Formulation of Empirical Models in Dynamic Econometrics." *Journal of Econometrics* 20:3–33.

———. 1989. "Recent Developments in the Theory of Encompassing." In *Contributions to Operations Research and Economics: The Twentieth Anniversary of CORE,* edited by B. Cornet and H. Tulkens, 393–440. Cambridge: MIT Press.

Leamer, E. E. 1978. *Specification Searches: Ad Hoc Inference with Nonexperimental Data.* New York: Wiley.

Mizon, G. E. and J.-F. Richard. 1986. "The Encompassing Principle and Its Application to Testing Non-nested Hypotheses." *Econometrica* 54:657–78.

Spanos, A. 1986. *Statistical Foundations of Econometric Modelling.* Cambridge: Cambridge Univ. Press.

White, H. 1990. "A Consistent Model Selection Procedure Based on *m*-testing." In *Modelling Economic Series: Readings in Econometric Methodology,* edited by C. W. J. Granger, 369–83. Oxford: Clarendon Press.

Modigliani, Franco (1918–)

Winner of the Nobel Memorial Prize in 1985, Franco Modigliani ranks as one of the preeminent economists of the second half of the twentieth century. He has contributed widely to the development of macroeconomic theory, especially the theory of the consumption function, and his work with Merton Miller on the theory of corporate finance revolutionized the entire field.

Among Modigliani's earliest contributions was his 1944 paper, "Liquidity Preference and the Theory of Interest and Money," in which he examined the roles of liquidity preference and wage rigidity in generating the Keynesian propositions about the possibility of an underemployment equilibrium and the dependence of the rate of interest on the quantity of money. Modigliani showed that these results were independent of the assumption of liquidity preference, except in the limiting "liquidity-trap" case in which the demand for money becomes infinitely elastic at some very low rate of interest. By clarifying the logical structure of the Keynesian model, Modigliani laid the groundwork for the neoclassical synthesis that defined macroeconomic orthodoxy for most of the second half of the twentieth century.

In the 1950s, in collaboration with Richard Brumberg and Albert Ando, Modigliani developed the "life-cycle" hypothesis of consumption behavior as an alternative to the Keynesian consumption function according to which consumption is a function of current income alone. The naive Keynesian consumption function was soon found to be empirically inadequate, and a variety of alternative hypotheses were advanced. However, only two of these hypotheses have proved theoretically persuasive and empirically robust: Milton Friedman's permanent-income hypothesis, and the life-cycle hypothesis of Modigliani and his associates.

According to the life-cycle hypothesis, households base their decisions about current consumption on the need to match income and consumption over their entire lifetimes, not over just one time period, as in the naive Keynesian consumption function, and not over an infinite time horizon, as in the permanent-income hypothesis. Early in their adult lives, consumers typically consume in excess of their current incomes in the expectation of rapidly rising future incomes. Later on, as incomes do increase, consumers pay off outstanding debts and accumulate assets to finance consumption during their retirement. Within such a long-term framework, variations in current consumption typically have little impact on current income, which implies a low marginal propensity to consume out of current income and thus a relatively low multiplier. The low multiplier suggests a more stable economic system than was implied by early estimates of the naive Keynesian consumption function. Moreover, the life-cycle hypothesis also suggests testable relationships between consumption and saving behavior and the age distribution of the population.

Modigliani was also a principal builder of the MIT macroeconometric model, a massive representation of the U.S. macroeconomy, which incorporated much of Modigliani's work on the consumption function, financial markets, and other macroeconomic relationships (Modigliani [1975a] 1980).

Despite the theoretical qualifications he added to the Keynesian system, Modigliani has remained an eloquent and outspoken supporter of activist Keynesian fiscal and monetary policies, and a trenchant critic of Monetarism, both as a theoretical alternative to the neoclassical synthesis and as a guide to macroeconomic policymaking.

David Glasner

See also CONSUMPTION EXPENDITURES; FRIEDMAN, MILTON; MACROECONOMETRIC MODELS, USE OF; WAGE RIGIDITY

Bibliography
Kouri, P. 1986. "Franco Modigliani's Contributions to Economics." *Scandinavian Journal of Economics* 88:311–34.
Modigliani, F. [1944] 1980. "Liquidity Preference and the Theory of Interest and Money." Chap. 2 of *The Collected Papers of Franco Modigliani*. Vol. 1. Cambridge: MIT Press.
———. [1969] 1980. "Liquidity Preference." Chap. 4 of *The Collected Papers of Franco Modigliani*. Vol. 1. Cambridge: MIT Press.
———. [1975a] 1980. "The Channels of Monetary Policy in the Federal Reserve-MIT-University of Pennsylvania Econometric Model of the United States."
Chap. 5 of *The Collected Papers of Franco Modigliani*. Vol. 1. Cambridge: MIT Press.
———. [1975b] 1980. "The Life Cycle Hypothesis of Saving Twenty Years Later." Chap. 2 of *The Collected Papers of Franco Modigliani*. Vol. 2. Cambridge: MIT Press.
———. [1977] 1982. "The Monetarist Controversy or, Should We Forsake Stabilization Policies?" Chap. 1 of *The Collected Papers of Franco Modigliani*. Vol. 1. Cambridge: MIT Press.
———. 1986. *The Debate over Stabilization Policy*. Cambridge: Cambridge Univ. Press.
Modigliani, F. and A. Ando. [1963] 1980. "The 'Life Cycle' Hypothesis of Saving: Aggregate Implications and Tests." Chap. 7 of *The Collected Papers of Franco Modigliani*. Vol. 2. Cambridge: MIT Press.
Modigliani, F. and R. Brumberg. [1954] 1980. "Utility Analysis and the Consumption Function: An Interpretation of Cross-Section Data." Chap. 3 of *The Collected Papers of Franco Modigliani*. Vol. 2. Cambridge: MIT Press.
———. [1979] 1980. "Utility Analysis and Aggregate Consumption Functions: An Attempt at Integration." Chap. 4 of *The Collected Papers of Franco Modigliani*. Vol. 2. Cambridge: MIT Press.

Monetary Disequilibrium Theories of the Business Cycle

It appears that it was Clark Warburton who introduced the term used here for the core of what is now called *Monetarism*. This theory addresses fluctuations—not, strictly speaking, cycles—in economic activity: it does not suppose that some internal dynamic drives phases of prosperity and depression. It attributes fluctuations mainly to divergences between the actual quantity of money and the quantity demanded at prevailing price and income levels. Such monetary disturbances are often external to any self-generating process and may result from policy blunders.

Elements of the theory trace at least as far back as David Hume and Pehr Niclas Christiernin, writing in Scotland and Sweden in the mid-eighteenth century. Even earlier in that century the theory must have been in the minds of policymakers in several American colonies, where new issues of paper money apparently did, as intended, relieve a "decay of trade" (Lester 1939, chaps. 3–5). Henry Thornton made a notable contribution in 1802. [Dorn (1987) reviews several other contributors of the nineteenth and early twentieth centuries.] Although such classical and neoclassical writers as Ricardo, J. S. Mill, and Marshall were usually concerned with long-run microeconomic questions and so legitimately abstracted from short-run monetary disequilibria, they recognized that such disequilibria do occur and sometimes paid explicit attention to them (Marshall [1887] 1924, Warburton 1981). A notable example is Mill's *Essays on Some Unsettled Questions of Political Economy* (especially essay 2). Although without using the term "monetary disequilibrium," Mill ([1844] 1967) clearly explains how the phenomenon can keep Say's Law from operating in the short run.

In 1913, both R. G. Hawtrey and H. J. Davenport presented clear monetary diagnoses of business fluctuations. Irving Fisher took a Monetarist line in a 1932 book and many earlier writings.

Warburton (1981) maintained that the monetary explanation of business fluctuations was dominant in early-twentieth-century America. Two developments, apparently, crowded it off the intellectual scene: first, the depth and persistence of the Great Depression, along with the supposed failure—as interpreted with mistaken theory—of an easy-money policy to cure it; and, second, the Keynesian Revolution.

During the years of its obscurity, Warburton labored almost alone compiling statistical and historical evidence bearing on the monetary theory of business fluctuations. Beginning in the 1950s, he was joined by Milton Friedman and other Monetarists.

Monetarists are sometimes accused, rather unfairly, of working with a "black box." The implication is that they announce mere statistical associations without adequately describing whatever causal processes they suppose to be at work. It is true that monetary-disequilibrium theory does not exist in a single canonical version. Some synthesis and interpretation is therefore in order here.

People (including business firms) specialize in producing particular goods and services to exchange them, sooner or later, for the specialized outputs of other people—Say's Law expresses a fundamental insight. One qualification is also fundamental: goods exchange for each other, not directly but through the intermediary of money. People hold cash balances as buffer stocks (Laidler 1987) through which their receipts and payments of money flow. They desire balances related, if loosely, to the sizes of flows through them. Anyone wanting to increase his cash balances can curtail his purchases and try harder to sell goods and services (and securities, too, although the story concerning them is more complicated).

If people should desire cash balances totaling more than the actual money supply, then quantities of goods and services demanded fall short, by and large, of quantities supplied at the old prices. Excess supplies exert downward pressure on prices. (The familiar story of the opposite disequilibrium—excess money inflating prices—needs no retelling here. An account of an apparently hybrid disorder, stagflation, would involve variability of money-supply growth.)

An excess demand to hold money, entailing excess supplies of goods and services, tends to remedy itself through price deflation. In real terms, the actual quantity of money rises to meet the demand for it—eventually. Meanwhile, since transactions are voluntary, the lesser of the quantities demanded and supplied is the quantity of each good and service actually exchanged. With transactions frustrated, the production of goods destined for exchange falls off, as do employment of labor and purchases of other inputs. The cutback of production and real income in each sector weakens its demands for the outputs of other sectors: the deterioration spreads.

The decline of income ends after going so far that people feel they cannot "afford" cash balances totaling more than the actual money supply. Any relief of this (suppressed) excess demand for money sets the stage for business recovery. Real money might grow either "automatically" through a further decline in prices and wages or, less painfully, through an increase in the nominal stock of money.

Sufficient price and wage flexibility could in principle prevent monetary disequilibrium in the first place by keeping the actual real quantity of money matched to the demand for it, whatever the nominal quantity might be. In practice, markets and prices cannot cope so quickly and smoothly with large monetary disturbances. Most prices, instead of being determined impersonally from minute to minute on an organized market, are deliberately set by someone and remain fixed until reset. For reasons that make excellent sense to individual business firms and labor negotiators, prices and wages are "sticky." Furthermore, the innumerable prices and wages, though interdependent, are set in a decentralized and piecemeal manner; hence the economy faces an immense task in groping its way to a new market-clearing pattern of prices and wages after a monetary shock. Market mechanisms work eventually, but not instantly.

Nor would rapid price and wage adjustments avoid the pains of a monetary shock. The shock confronts the economy with a catch-22; it is damned if adjustments do *not* occur sensitively and quickly and damned if they *do*. Price and wage cuts increase the real burden of existing debts, tipping some debtors into bankruptcy and so not benefiting their creditors (Fisher 1933, anticipated by Christiernin in 1761). If customers and business investors expect prices and wages to continue sagging, they postpone major purchases, meanwhile holding money and near-moneys. Depending on the structure of the banking system and on monetary policy, the nominal quantity of money may actually shrink, as happened in the United States from 1929 to 1933, worsening the excess demand for it.

An actual shrinkage of money is the most straightforward cause of a business downturn, but even a shortfall in monetary growth relative to the demand for cash balances in a growing economy could be the trigger. Through a price and wage downtrend, true enough, markets might cope with expected sluggishness of monetary growth, as happened in the United States in the closing decades of the nineteenth century. But major or unexpected monetary disturbances—even mere downward departures from a growth trend—have proved disruptive. Once a recession is under way, precautionary increases in cash balances desired relative to income and expenditure aggravate the deterioration.

Monetary-disequilibrium theory does not deny that relative prices and wages change as business declines and recovers. (Some formulations describe wages and other input costs as generally stickier than product prices, so that profit margins narrow and widen over the cycle.) Nor does the theory deny a role to interest rates. (An easy-money policy may temporarily lower them, stimulating business investment, just as a tight-money policy may do the reverse.) But unlike the Austrian theory of cycles, which blames unsustainable malinvestment of resources on falsification of market signals, monetary-disequilibrium theory does not stress relative-prices and interest-rate changes. It considers them less crucial than the imbalances between the actual quantity of money and the quantity that would be demanded at full employment and prevailing prices.

The theory recognizes that fixed and inventory investments by business typically fluctuate more widely over the cycle than do purchases of consumer goods (especially nondurable goods) and services. But it does not view this fact as evidence of causation. Quite understandably, firms and consumers may hasten or delay investments and purchases of durable goods when markets seem strong or weak.

What evidence supports the Monetarist interpretation over its rivals? First, it accords well with the circumstances and behavior of individual transactors and holders of money, including price setters and wage negotiators. Observers at widely separated times and places have seen reason to believe the theory. More specifically, we have the statistical evidence provided first by Warburton and later by Friedman and Schwartz and others. Their research reveals an association, typically a leading association, between monetary disturbances and business fluctuations. Reverse causation, running *from* business conditions *to* the quantity of money, is indeed conceivable; and two-way causation seems often to have occurred, with induced shrinkages of bank lending and bank-account money aggravating business declines. In numerous historical episodes, however, money has evidently been the active agent and no mere passive responder.

So-called "real" factors, such as inventions and natural disasters, undeniably do influence business conditions; but it is hard to believe that they alone, apart from monetary factors, account for pervasive prosperity or depression—ease or difficulty in finding customers and jobs throughout almost all sectors of an economy. A "real" theory should be able to identify the real factors at work and account for their intersectoral contagion. A purely real theory could not easily accommodate the near absence of cyclical phenomena when the U.S. economy reconverted massively and rapidly to a peacetime footing after World War II.

Monetary-disequilibrium theory does not go as far as New Classical or monetary equilibrium theories in attributing near perfection to markets. Unlike such approaches, disequilibrium theory does not view fluctuations in output and employment as responses of firms and workers, along their supply and demand curves, to fluctuations in perceived prices and wages and, notably, to misinterpretations of unexpectedly high or low levels or rates of change of prices and wages. Instead, it recognizes that activity may respond not only to price changes, but also more directly, to greater or lesser ease in finding customers and jobs.

Disequilibrium theory reaches much the same policy recommendations as the New Classical school, but by a more straightforward route (requiring less cleverness in ignoring or explaining away palpable facts of reality). Both schools recognize the futility, at least in the long run, of monetary tricks aimed at keeping output above and unemployment below their "natural" or general-equilibrium levels. Both are content merely to spare the economy from disruptive monetary surprises.

This means adopting a monetary policy or a set of institutions under which the quantity of money accommodates itself to the total of holdings demanded at full employment and a stable price level. One approach would firmly instruct the monetary authority to target overridingly on price stability. Various lags are widely thought to bedevil this approach. Perhaps they could be circumvented by a variant of Fisher's "compensated dollar" whereby the government would maintain continuous two-way convertibility between $1000, say, of its money and whatever variable physical quantity of gold is equal in value, at actual current market prices, to a specified bundle of goods. (The system would be a bundle standard, not a gold standard; and securities might serve better than gold as the medium of indirect redemption.)

A simpler alternative is the old Monetarist proposal to keep the money supply growing at a steady rate approximately equal to the long-run real growth rate of the economy. This idea incurs doubt, because financial innovation and other factors keep changing both the velocity of money and even the operational definition of money itself. More complicated rules have been suggested, such as one imposing feedbacks on an adjustable growth rate of the monetary base to keep total nominal income growing at approximately the long-run real growth rate of the economy (McCallum 1989, chap. 16). Such a rule does not presuppose any particular definition or measure of the quantity of money. If successfully implemented, it would maintain an approximately constant price level.

A radically different approach would abolish base money and, indeed, government money of any kind (Yeager and Greenfield 1989 and works cited therein). The government would define a new unit of account in terms of a comprehensive bundle of goods and services and would use the unit in its own transactions, pricing, and accounting; but otherwise it would shed any monetary role. Private banks and mutual funds would supply token coins, banknotes, and checking accounts. Competition would require issuing institutions to maintain two-way convertibility of their issues into and from commodity-bundles-worths of some redemption medium; this would be indirect convertibility reminiscent of Fisher's compensated dollar. Arbitrage would keep the total quantity of money always nearly equal to the demand for it at a stable price level corresponding to the commodity-bundle definition of the unit of account.

Here is not the place to urge any particular reform. Suffice it to say that considering reforms, especially radical ones, can provide further insight into the monetary diagnosis of business fluctuations.

Leland B. Yeager

See also AUSTRIAN THEORY OF BUSINESS CYCLES; BANKING SCHOOL, CURRENCY SCHOOL, AND FREE BANKING SCHOOL; BRUNNER, KARL; BULLIONIST CONTROVERSIES; CENTRAL BANKING; DEMAND FOR CURRENCY; DEMAND FOR MONEY; ENDOGENOUS AND EXOGENOUS MONEY; FREE BANKING; FISHER, IRVING; FRIEDMAN, MILTON; HAWTREY, RALPH GEORGE; HAYEK, FRIEDRICH AUGUST [VON]; HUME, DAVID; JONES, SAMUEL LOYD; KEYNES, JOHN MAYNARD; MARSHALL, ALFRED; MISES, LUDWIG EDLER VON; MONETARY EQUILIBRIUM THEORIES OF THE BUSINESS CYCLE; MONETARY POLICY; MONEY-INCOME CAUSALITY; NATURAL RATE OF INTEREST; NATURAL RATE OF UNEMPLOYMENT; REAL BUSINESS-CYCLE THEORIES; RICARDO, DAVID; ROBERTSON, DENNIS HOLME; SCHWARTZ, ANNA JACOBSON; SUPPLY OF MONEY; THORNTON, HENRY; WARBURTON, CLARK; WICKSELL, JOHAN GUSTAV KNUT

Bibliography
Davenport, H. J. 1913. *The Economics of Enterprise.* New York: Macmillan.
Dorn, J. A. 1987. "The Search for Stable Money: A Historical Perspective." In *The Search for Stable Money,* edited by

J. A. Dorn and A. J. Schwartz, 1–28. Chicago: Univ. of Chicago Press.

Fisher, I. 1920. *Stabilizing the Dollar.* New York: Macmillan.

———. 1932. *Booms and Depressions.* New York: Adelphi.

———. 1933. "The Debt-Deflation Theory of Great Depressions." *Econometrica* 1:337–57.

Friedman, M. and A. J. Schwartz. 1963. *A Monetary History of the United States, 1867–1960.* Princeton: Princeton Univ. Press.

Hawtrey, R. G. 1913. *Good and Bad Trade.* London: Constable.

Laidler, D. 1987. "Buffer-Stock Money and the Transmission Mechanism." Federal Reserve Bank of Atlanta *Economic Review,* March/April, 11–23.

Lester, R. A. 1939. *Monetary Experiments: Early American and Recent Scandinavian.* Princeton: Princeton Univ. Press.

Marshall, A. [1887] 1924. "Remedies for Fluctuations of General Prices." In *Memorials of Alfred Marshall,* edited by A. C. Pigou, 188–212. London: Macmillan.

McCallum, B. T. 1989. *Monetary Economics: Theory and Policy.* New York: Macmillan.

Mill, J. S. [1844] 1967. "Of the Influence of Consumption on Production." In *The Collected Works of John Stuart Mill.* Vol. 4. Edited by J. M. Robson, 262–79. Toronto: Univ. of Toronto Press.

Thornton, H. [1802] 1939. *An Enquiry into the Nature and Effects of the Paper Credit of Great Britain.* Edited with an introduction by F. A. von Hayek. London: Allen and Unwin.

Warburton, C. 1966. *Depression, Inflation, and Monetary Policy.* Baltimore: Johns Hopkins Univ. Press.

———. 1981. "Monetary Disequilibrium Theory in the First Half of the Twentieth Century." *History of Political Economy* 13:285–99.

Yeager, L. B. and R. L. Greenfield. 1989. "Can Monetary Disequilibrium Be Eliminated?" *Cato Journal* 9:51–67.

Monetary Equilibrium Theories of the Business Cycle

Monetary equilibrium theories of the business cycle are a species of the genus New Classical theories of the business cycle, in which the fundamental source of business-cycle fluctuations is the management (or mismanagement) of the supply of money. The theories are "equilibrium" in that all private agents are modeled as continuously optimizing, given their information. New Classicals believe that this implies that people have rational expectations, expectations that are correct up to a serially uncorrelated random error.

Some New Classicals see these theories as natural extensions of earlier work by F. A. Hayek and other Austrian economists. This connection is misleading at best (Hoover 1988, chap. 10). New Classicals and Austrians agree that equilibrium is a situation in which all agents are optimizing subject to their constraints, and that agents always seek to achieve such a situation. New Classical business-cycle models assume that agents are always successful in this quest. They are mathematically closed, predictive models. In contrast, Austrian models assume that agents are constantly adapting to pervasive ignorance, striving for, but rarely achieving equilibrium. Mathematically closed models are seen as incapable of predicting human action because rational behavior involves free choice.

The Elements of Monetary Business-Cycle Models

A business-cycle model comprises an original source of fluctuations and a propagation mechanism, which may amplify and transmit initial fluctuations to the rest of the economy. The term "equilibrium" in monetary equilibrium theories of the cycle refers principally to propagation mechanisms; while "monetary" refers mainly to the supposed source of fluctuations.

Monetary vs. Real Business-Cycle Theories

Monetary equilibrium theories have propagation mechanisms that are similar to those of real equilibrium business-cycle theories. Some commentators therefore seek to distinguish between them by calling a model real if money cannot affect real variables in any way. This, however, defines "real" too narrowly. Advocates of real business-cycle models typically find the major source of business-cycle fluctuations in shocks to technology, factor supplies or other real variables, but rarely deny possibility that monetary shocks could in principle also generate cycles. A more useful distinction would be that monetary theories assume that a benign monetary policy (or rule) could eliminate business-cycle fluctuations; while real theories assume that fluctuations are endemic whatever the stance of monetary policy.

Sources of Fluctuations

The original source of fluctuations in equilibrium monetary models may be either anticipated or unanticipated changes in the supply of money. Early monetary models concentrated on unanticipated changes and focused on two types of problems.

The first involves relative-price confusion. Robert Lucas ([1972] 1981) examined a model in which individual agents know the price in their own market immediately, but learn prices in other markets only after a delay. Thus, when an increase in the stock of money raises prices in general, suppliers cannot be certain whether it is only their price that has risen (a relative-price shift, which would encourage increased output or increased labor supply) or whether all prices have risen (inflation, which should not affect real variables). If inflation is widely mistaken for a relative-price increase, output increases, only to fall back again once agents learn the truth.

Agents must extract the signal (the change in relative prices) from the noise (the variability of inflation). Agents with rational expectations know, up to a serially uncorrelated error, the true variances of inflation and of relative prices. The higher the variance of inflation relative to the variance of relative prices, the smaller the proportion of any actual increase in his own price that an agent will ascribe to relative prices; and, hence, the less any increase in the money supply will raise output.

The second signal-extraction problem involves permanent-transitory confusion. Robert Barro (1976) studied a model in which agents may accurately know relative prices at any time, but, because they observe the money stock only with some delay, cannot be sure whether a current increase in prices is transitory or permanent. If prices are temporarily high today, then more output and more labor will be supplied today to take advantage of the economy's passing good fortune. If prices are permanently higher, there is no incentive to produce more today. So once again, agents face a signal-extraction problem.

Both relative-price confusion and permanent-transitory confusion depend on imperfect information about the money supply. Given other characteristic New Classical assumptions, any anticipated change in the stock of money is neutral. Only unanticipated changes can have real effects in this type of model.

Anticipated changes in the stock of money may cause business-cycle fluctuations in a different sort of New Classical model. Lucas (1987) considered a model in which, owing to informational uncertainty, some types of goods may be bought only with money, while other types may be bought on credit. The opportunity cost of buying a cash good rather than a credit good is measured by the nominal interest foregone on the cash spent. Anticipated (but not unanticipated) increases in the rate of inflation raise nominal interest rates and induce people to shift from cash to credit goods with concomitant real effects. Lucas and Stokey (1983) have developed the underlying monetary model in some detail, but have not fully integrated it into a model of business cycles.

Propagation Mechanisms

Signal-extraction problems were identified as sources of business cycles when New Classical economists first attempted to integrate the rational-expectations hypothesis into the expectations-augmented Phillips curve proposed by Milton Friedman and Edmund Phelps. It was quickly discovered that the data were serially correlated. Expectations-augmented Phillips curves with rational expectations fitted well only if this serial correlation was captured by using a lagged dependent variable (Lucas [1973] 1981). But if shocks to the money supply are not themselves serially correlated and are revealed after one period, then the lagged dependent variable is an ad hoc assumption inconsistent with the rational-expectations hypothesis.

Lucas ([1975] 1981) suggested two propagation mechanisms that would account for serial correlation in output (employment and unemployment). First, shocks to the money stock may be serially correlated (e.g., if the monetary authorities increase money in one period, they are likely to increase it also in the next period). Then information about the money supply helps agents to predict what happens next period; signal extraction improves gradually over time. Less and less of an inflationary shock is attributed falsely to relative-price shifts. The favorable effect of inflation on output continues past the first period, but the effect keeps diminishing.

Second, long-lived capital may produce serial correlation. The initial monetary shock induces additional investment. Once it is realized that the shock was inflation and not a relative-price shift, the capital stock will be seen to be greater than desired. The optimal path back to a steady-state in which actual and desired capital grow at the same rate is to let capital gradually depreciate and to let the growth of other factors of production and output steadily catch up with the larger amount of capital. As this process proceeds, the capital stock generates output above the steady-state trend, but the gap diminishes over time. Output (employment and unemployment) are thus serially correlated.

Evidence

If relative-price (or temporary-permanent) confusion under the rational-expectations hypothesis causes business cycles, then countries with more variable inflation should have steeper Phillips curves. Lucas ([1973] 1981) estimated the Phillips curves for sixteen countries and correlated their slopes with the variances of their inflation rates. His results supported the monetary-confusion hypothesis, but they were sensitive to the inclusion of Paraguay and Argentina—countries with extremely high rates and variances of inflation. Subsequent tests have been equivocal.

An essential premise of equilibrium monetary theories is that only unanticipated shocks to the money stock have real effects. Barro (1977, 1978) investigated this premise using a predictive model of the money supply. He interpreted the residuals of this model as unanticipated shocks and the predictions as anticipated shocks. Regressing output on the anticipated and unanticipated shocks, he found that, consistent with the hypothesis, only unanticipated shocks matter.

Barro and Zvi Hercowitz later devised a more direct test of the hypothesis that only unanticipated monetary shocks affect output. They reasoned that people rely on publicly announced data to estimate the stock of money. Revisions of the data reveal that former estimates must have been confused. One would therefore expect to find that revisions in the publicly announced data are correlated with changes in output as people act to correct mistakes based on their previous misperceptions. Barro and Hercowitz's failure to find any relationship undercuts the monetary-confusion story.

Subsequent research using more general methods than those of Barro has not convincingly supported the view that only unanticipated money matters. Frederic Mishkin (1983)

even found that anticipated money seems to affect output. This last result is consistent with recent research that rejects the superneutrality of money (that output is independent of the rate of inflation).

Conclusion

During the 1970s, equilibrium monetary theories of business cycles were the central item on the New Classical research agenda. Failing to find convincing evidence that monetary misperceptions are the principal source of cyclical fluctuations, New Classical attention has turned more and more to real equilibrium theories of the business cycle. While the latter models find the source of cyclical fluctuations in the real sector, they have nonetheless taken over much of the structure developed for monetary models—the rational-expectations hypothesis, signal-extraction mechanisms, intertemporal substitution, and propagation mechanisms based on serially correlated shocks and long-lived capital. Few are willing to say without qualification that money does not matter for business cycles, but what makes it matter is still an open question.

Kevin D. Hoover

See also EXPECTATIONS; FRISCH, RAGNAR ANTON KITTEL; INTERTEMPORAL SUBSTITUTION; MONETARY DISEQUILIBRIUM THEORIES OF THE BUSINESS CYCLE; MONETARY POLICY; NATURAL RATE OF UNEMPLOYMENT; NEUTRALITY OF MONEY; PHILLIPS CURVE; RATIONAL EXPECTATIONS; REAL BUSINESS-CYCLE THEORIES; SIGNAL EXTRACTION; SUPPLY OF MONEY

Bibliography

Barro, R. J. 1976. "Rational Expectations and the Role of Monetary Policy." *Journal of Monetary Economics* 2:1–32.
———. 1977. "Unanticipated Money Growth and Employment in the United States." *American Economic Review* 67:101–15.
———. 1978. "Unanticipated Money, Output and the Price Level in the United States." *Journal of Political Economy* 86:549–80.
Barro, R. J. and Z. Hercowitz. 1980. "Money Stock Revisions and Unanticipated Money Growth." *Journal of Monetary Economics* 6:257–67.
Friedman, M. [1968] 1969. "The Role of

Monetary Policy." Chap. 5 in *The Optimum Quantity of Money and Other Essays*. Chicago: Aldine.

Hoover, K. D. 1988. *The New Classical Macroeconomics: A Sceptical Inquiry*. Oxford: Basil Blackwell.

Lucas, R. E., Jr. [1972] 1981. "Expectations and the Neutrality of Money." In *Studies in Business-Cycle Theory*, 66–89. Cambridge: MIT Press.

———. [1973] 1981. "Some International Evidence on Output-Inflation Tradeoffs." In *Studies in Business-Cycle Theory*, 131–45. Cambridge: MIT Press.

———. [1975] 1981. "An Equilibrium Model of the Business Cycle." In *Studies in Business-Cycle Theory*, 179–214. Cambridge: MIT Press.

———. 1987. *Models of Business Cycles*. Oxford: Basil Blackwell.

Lucas, R. E., Jr. and N. L. Stokey. 1983. "Optimal Fiscal and Monetary Policy in an Economy without Capital." *Journal of Monetary Economics* 12:55–93.

Mishkin, F. 1983. *A Rational Expectations Approach to Macroeconomics: Testing, Policy Effectiveness and Efficient Market Models*. Chicago: Univ. of Chicago Press.

Monetary Policy

The term "monetary policy" has no unique meaning. Broadly speaking, it refers to the conscious manipulation by some official agency, usually a central bank, of such variables as the monetary base, the quantity of money, interest rates, or the exchange rate in order to attain goals for such variables as the level of output, the unemployment rate, the price level, or the balance of payments. In commonly used vocabulary, the latter variables are referred to as the *targets* of policy, and the former as its *instruments,* or if the authorities' control over them is indirect, as *intermediate targets*. Debates about monetary policy have been, and continue to be, about what targets monetary policy should be aimed at, and about what instruments should be controlled to achieve them. Modern analysis of monetary policy began in earnest in the nineteenth century, though it is worth noting that the Mississippi Bubble which culminated in the collapse of John Law's Banque Royale in 1721, and the Swedish inflation of the 1760s, generated debates earlier than that.

Conventional nineteenth-century wisdom about monetary policy, whose development is chronicled by Fetter, is enshrined in Walter Bagehot's *Lombard Street*. That wisdom took it for granted that maintaining convertibility of the currency into specie (gold, in the case of Britain) at a fixed price would achieve the target of long-run, price-level stability, and presumed that speculation fueled by commercial-bank lending played a major role in amplifying the credit cycle's upswing, a phase inevitably ending in financial crisis. Nevertheless, Bagehot did not suggest that the central bank attempt to stabilize the cycle. Rather, he saw its task as maintaining the country's gold reserves in the face of the balance-of-trade deficit that usually accompanied the crisis, while also ensuring that it did not provoke a collapse of the domestic banking system. To this end, Bagehot advised that, at the onset of a crisis, the Bank of England raise its interest rate enough to attract a short-term capital inflow, while simultaneously offering to lend freely to all solvent borrowers in the financial sector. The former measure would protect the gold reserves and hence maintain the convertibility of the currency; and the latter, which required the central bank to act as a "lender of last resort" to the banking system, would sustain public confidence in that system.

The deflation that began in the 1870s and the inflation that succeeded it in the mid-1890s, provoked much debate about monetary policy. There was discussion, both popular and professional, of instituting a bimetallic system, while such well-known economists as Jevons and Marshall advocated the use of indexed contracts, the latter in order to offset what he believed to be the tendency of price-level fluctuations to cause variations in income and employment; Irving Fisher advocated indexing money itself; while Knut Wicksell argued for abandoning gold convertibility and replacing it with an internationally coordinated paper-money regime in which the rate of interest at which banks made loans available would become the key instrument for achieving price-level stability. Such ideas had no immediate impact. The gold standard continued to spread throughout this period, and Bagehotian principles of central banking became internationally influential, not least in the foundation of the Federal Reserve System in the United States. However, they laid the groundwork for the discussions of monetary policy that accompanied the suspension of the gold standard during World War I and subsequent attempts to restore it.

M

Keynes's *Tract on Monetary Reform* of 1923 may be read as an attempt to apply the prewar monetary theory of Marshall to postwar problems. Still treating the domestic price level as monetary policy's principal target, Keynes argued that the quantity of money should become policy's main instrument (or at least an intermediate target), and that the gold standard be abandoned. In modern terminology, he advocated an adjustable exchange rate and controlling the money supply to stabilize the price level. To Ludwig von Mises and Friedrich A. Hayek, such quantity-theory-based analysis was superficial. Developing an essentially Wicksellian approach, they maintained that money creation by the banking system led to more investment in capital equipment than consumers' tastes for saving warranted. Money growth led to "forced saving," and a cumulative misallocation of resources towards investment which was the underlying cause of the cycle's crisis phase. Hence eliminating real fluctuations rather than stabilizing prices became the main target of monetary policy; and though its instrument was to be the quantity of money, this was to be held constant to avoid an unsustainable boom, not deliberately manipulated.

This Austrian view was not an inevitable implication of Wicksell's work. His Swedish successors (e.g., Myrdal and Lindahl) developed a theory of monetary policy in which stabilizing the cycle was to be accomplished by using an interest-rate instrument to achieve price-level stability. The analyses of Dennis Robertson, and of Keynes's *Treatise on Money* have much in common with Swedish work, but subsequent developments of the theory of monetary policy downgraded its importance. Keynes's *General Theory* seemed to most interpreters to cast grave doubts on the capacity of monetary policy, whether based on a money stock or an interest-rate instrument, to influence real variables. Furthermore, the idea that prices were proximately determined by money wages, which in turn were largely set by nonmarket forces, began to gain ground after 1930, so that the capacity of monetary policy to affect the price level was also called into question. This line of thought culminated in the 1959 publication of the *Report* of the British Committee on the Working of the Monetary System (*The Radcliffe Report*), which argued that, under a pegged (albeit in emergencies, adjustable) exchange-rate regime, interest rates should be manipulated to influence the economy's "liquid-ity," a concept which the *Report* left ill-defined. At best, such a monetary policy might promote an environment of long-term stability in which other devices, notably fiscal policy, could be deployed in a more active role.

The publication of the *Radcliffe Report* preceded by only one year that of Milton Friedman's *Program for Monetary Stability* which set out the policy implications of what Karl Brunner was to label *Monetarism*. The latter doctrine rests on the following propositions: a close empirical relationship exists between the rate of growth of the nominal quantity of money and money income in United States history; that this relationship can be attributed to causation running mainly from money to income; that within the cycle, money-income fluctuations involve both its real and its price-level components, but that price fluctuations dominate secular data. The Monetarist postulate about the transmission mechanism of monetary policy, namely that it worked through interest-rate effects, was qualitatively similar to that of Keynesian orthodoxy, but included a broader set of assets in the relationship—equity and consumer durables as well as bonds—and ascribed to it greater empirical significance than did the Keynesians. The conclusions for monetary policy that seemed to follow from these propositions were that the appropriate policy instrument was the quantity of money, that its rate of growth should be rigidly determined by some quasi-constitutional rule, and that such a policy would stabilize the price level in the long run, but also real variables in the short run because a major source of cyclical variations, namely fluctuations in money growth, would be eliminated.

An open-economy version of this essentially closed-economy doctrine was developed mainly by Robert Mundell, and by Jacob Frenkel and Harry Johnson. It noted that under a fixed exchange rate, the quantity of money was necessarily endogenous, but it also showed that controlling the domestic component of the asset side of the banking system's balance sheet would then be sufficient to control the size of its foreign component, the country's exchange reserves. Adapted to an open economy with fixed exchange rates, then, Monetarism identified domestic credit expansion as the appropriate policy instrument, and the overall balance of payments as its target. With flexible exchange rates, however, essentially closed-economy results were reestablished. In many respects, then, the "Monetary Approach to the Balance of Payments and the Exchange Rates" (as it came to be called) represented a refinement of ideas that had underpinned orthodox nineteenth-century thought about the gold standard.

The inflation of the 1970s led to the discrediting of Keynesian ideas about policy, and measures based on Monetarist ideas were widely adopted. These involved medium-term target ranges for the rate of growth of money, rather than a fixed rule, and with a view to restoring stability to a seriously inflationary economy, rather than maintaining stability in one that was already performing well, which had been the scenario implicit in Friedman's 1960 proposals. The general verdict on Monetarist policies has been one of disappointment. In particular, the work of Sargent and Wallace (1976), applying Lucas's ideas about rational expectations to monetary policy, had led to the belief (already implicit in Friedman's concept of the natural rate of unemployment) that changes in monetary policy that are anticipated by the private sector would affect only prices, so that only surprise measures have any real side effects. Because the adoption of Monetarist policies was widely announced and understood, their more zealous supporters predicted that they would reduce inflation with little loss in output, a prediction that was sadly disappointed in the early 1980s.

At the time of writing, there is no dominant doctrine about monetary policy. Some Monetarists take the view that their position is still fundamentally sound. Though recognizing that the tendency of institutional change to shift the money/money-income relationship over time renders constitutional rules for money growth unwise, they still argue that the quantity of money is a powerful instrument whose short-run real effects make it simultaneously unsuitable for achieving short-run real targets, but indispensable for achieving long-run price stability. On the other hand, Dow and Saville (1988) have found, in recent British history, material to support the case for reinstating interest-rate control as the key instrument of monetary policy, and to support an estimate of its overall importance very much in the Radcliffe tradition. And in an ironic twist, Monetarism has, by way of the New Classical economics, spawned a view of the business cycle which attributes it solely to supply-side disturbances. From such a viewpoint, the be-

havior of the price level is essentially irrelevant to the business cycle, and so, therefore, is money and monetary policy (King and Plosser, 1984).

Only time will reveal which school of thought is to become dominant, and how long its dominance will last.

David Laidler

See also AUSTRIAN THEORY OF BUSINESS CYCLES; BAGEHOT, WALTER; BRUNNER, KARL; CENTRAL BANKING; CREDIT CYCLE; EXPECTATIONS; FISHER, IRVING; FORCED SAVING; FRIEDMAN, MILTON; GOLD STANDARD; GOLD STANDARD: CAUSES AND CONSEQUENCES; HAWTREY, RALPH GEORGE; HAYEK, FRIEDRICH AUGUST VON; INTERNATIONAL LENDER OF LAST RESORT; KEYNES, JOHN MAYNARD; LENDER OF LAST RESORT; MARKET PRICE INDICATORS; MARSHALL, ALFRED; MISES, LUDWIG EDLER VON; MONETARY DISEQUILIBRIUM THEORIES OF THE BUSINESS CYCLE; MONETARY EQUILIBRIUM THEORIES OF THE BUSINESS CYCLE; NATURAL RATE OF INTEREST; NATURAL RATE OF UNEMPLOYMENT; RATIONAL EXPECTATIONS; REAL BUSINESS-CYCLE THEORIES; ROBBINS, LIONEL CHARLES; ROBERTSON, DENNIS HOLME; WICKSELL, JOHAN GUSTAV KNUT

Bibliography

Bagehot, W. [1873] 1962. *Lombard Street: A Description of the Money Market*. Homewood, Ill.: Irwin.

Brunner, K. 1968. "The Role of Money and Monetary Policy." Federal Reserve Bank of St. Louis *Review*, July, 8–24.

Brunner, K. and A. H. Meltzer. 1993. *Money and the Economy: Issues in Monetary Analysis*. Cambridge: Cambridge Univ. Press.

Committee on the Working of the Monetary System. 1959. *Report*. (The Radcliffe Report.) London: HMSO.

Dow, J. C. S. and I. Saville. 1988. *A Critique of Monetary Policy: Theory and British Experience*. Oxford: Clarendon Press.

Fetter, F. W. 1965. *The Development of British Monetary Orthodoxy*. Cambridge: Harvard Univ. Press.

Fisher, I. 1913. *The Purchasing Power of Money*. 2d ed. New York: Macmillan.

Frenkel, J. and H. G. Johnson, eds. 1976. *The Monetary Approach to Balance of Payments Theory*. London: Allen and Unwin.

Friedman, M. 1960. *A Program for Monetary*

Stability. New York: Fordham Univ. Press.

———. [1968] 1969. "The Role of Monetary Policy." Chap. 5 in *The Optimum Quantity of Money and Other Essays.* Chicago: Aldine.

Hayek, F. A. 1931. *Prices and Production.* London: Routledge and Kegan Paul.

Jevons, W. S. 1874. *Money and the Mechanism of Exchange.* London: Appleton.

Keynes, J. M. [1923] 1971. *A Tract on Monetary Reform.* Vol. 4 of *The Collected Writings of John Maynard Keynes.* London: Macmillan.

———. [1930] 1971. *A Treatise on Money.* 2 vols. Vols. 5 and 6 of *The Collected Writings of John Maynard Keynes.* London: Macmillan.

———. [1936] 1973. *The General Theory of Employment, Interest and Money.* Vol. 7 of *The Collected Writings of John Maynard Keynes.* London: Macmillan.

King, R. G. and C. I. Plosser. 1984. "Money Credit and Prices in a Real Business Cycle." *American Economic Review* 74:363–80.

Laidler, D. 1989. *Taking Money Seriously.* Oxford: Philip Allan.

Lindahl, E. 1939. *Studies in the Theory of Money and Capital.* London: Allen and Unwin.

Lucas, R. E., Jr. [1972] 1981. "Expectations and the Neutrality of Money." In *Studies in Business-Cycle Theory,* 66–89. Cambridge: MIT Press.

Marshall, A. [1887] 1924. "Remedies for Fluctuations in General Prices." In *Memorials of Alfred Marshall,* edited by A. C. Pigou, 188–212. London: Macmillan.

Mises, L. von. [1924] 1953. *The Theory of Money and Credit.* 2d ed. Translation. New Haven: Yale Univ. Press.

Mundell, R. 1971. *Monetary Theory.* Pacific Palisades, Calif.: Goodyear.

Myrdal, G. [1932] 1939. *Monetary Equilibrium.* Translation. London: William Hodge.

Robertson, D. H. 1926. *Banking Policy and the Price Level.* Westminster: P. S. King.

Sargent, T. J. and N. Wallace. 1976. "Rational Expectations and the Theory of Economic Policy." *Journal of Monetary Economics* 84:372–85.

Wicksell, K. [1898] 1936. *Interest and Prices.* Translation. London: Macmillan.

Monetary Reform

Monetary reform is the introduction of a new monetary policy accompanied by a new monetary unit. Reforms are instituted after crisis-induced expansionary monetary policies have caused high and unstable inflation rates. Through a monetary reform, the monetary authority seeks to attain at least two goals. First, since the new currency unit is worth hundreds of thousands of units of the old currency, the reform reduces the money values of exchanges, easing the bookkeeping burden on transactors. For instance, after Bolivia introduced the Boliviano, equal in value to one million pesos, a lunch that formerly cost ten million pesos cost only ten Bolivianos. A second (more elusive) goal is to signal a commitment to a new monetary policy. The introduction of a new currency is accompanied by official statements promising (and sometimes even legal or institutional changes requiring) a new low-inflation policy. The reform is intended to show that old monetary policies are being discarded with the old money. If the public regards the reform as a credible policy change, then the expected rate of inflation should fall. As expected inflation falls, interest rates and wage increases should also fall, increasing the chances that the reform will succeed.

Monetary reforms have a long history. Perhaps the best-known examples are the European reforms after World War I. The German reform followed the hyperinflation generated by wartime expenditures and a falling tax base. In 1923, a new Rentenmark was issued and the supply of new currency was limited by a decree that the gold held by the monetary authority had to equal 10 percent of the outstanding currency supply. Similarly, the 1928 French reform required the Bank of France to hold a gold reserve of not less than 35 percent of the outstanding currency. These legal restrictions on money creation provided the credibility needed to institute a successful reform and rapidly end the hyperinflation.

The modern era provides many additional episodes of monetary reform. Table 1 lists the countries, currencies involved, and dates and change introduced in the most recent reforms. The rate of exchange between old and new currencies ranges from ten to one for the Israeli pound/shekel in 1980 to one million to one for the Bolivian peso/Boliviano in 1987. The monetary reforms listed in Table 1 were responses to economic crises. In some cases (for example,

TABLE 1. Recent Monetary Reforms		
Country	*Old Currency/New Currency*	*Date and Change*
Argentina	peso/peso Argentino	1 June 1983
		1 peso Argentino = 10,000 pesos
	peso Argentino/Austral	14 June 1985
		1 Austral = 1,000 pesos Argentinos
Bolivia	peso/Boliviano	1 January 1987
		1 Boliviano = 1,000,000 pesos
Brazil	cruzeiros/cruzado	28 February 1986
		1 cruzado = 1,000 cruzeiros
Chile	escudo/peso	29 September 1975
		1 peso = 1,000 escudos
Israel	pound/shekel	22 February 1980
		1 shekel = 10 pounds
	old shekel/new shekel	4 September 1985
		1 new shekel = 1,000 old sheqalim
Peru	soles/inti	1 February 1985
		1 inti = 1,000 soles
Uruguay	old peso/new peso	1 July 1975
		1 new peso = 1,000 old pesos

Bolivia and Chile), the economic crisis produced a political crisis, so that a new government instituted the monetary reform.

In each case listed in Table 1, the monetary reform reduced nominal prices by moving the decimal point several places to the left for all prices. The table reveals that a one thousand to one rate of exchange of old money for new was the most popular reform. The reduction in nominal prices is not trivial since residents had to carry increasingly large quantities of currency to make transactions and the governments often responded by printing large-denomination currency notes. Maintaining accounts and performing transactions became increasingly difficult as the price level rose. By reducing the absolute level of prices, the reform, at least temporarily, remedied the difficulty.

However, the reduction in inflation following the reforms and accompanying new economic policies varied greatly across the countries. The reform policies reduced the rate of inflation significantly in Bolivia, Argentina (second reform), Brazil, Israel (second reform), and Uruguay. Yet even in these cases, the reduction varied considerably. In the others, the inflation rate actually rose after the reform. The differences across countries indicates that monetary reform is not sufficient to reduce inflation.

The underlying reason for the reform in each country was inflation caused by money growth used to finance the government budget deficit. The government's budget constraint indicates the link between monetary policy and fiscal policy. Government spending minus taxes must be financed by borrowing or money creation. A large fiscal deficit therefore implies a high rate of borrowing or a high rate of money growth. Those countries in which inflationary money growth led to monetary reforms relied on money creation to finance their fiscal deficits. In most cases, creditors would not extend sufficient loans to finance the budget deficits, so that money growth was the politically preferred method of deficit finance. The government budget constraint indicates that a successful monetary reform requires an accompanying fiscal reform. If the fiscal deficit is not reduced, or additional sources of loans not secured, then any benefits of a monetary reform will be temporary at best, as the monetary authority will have to create new money to finance the continuing budget deficit.

The association of monetary reforms with large fiscal deficits underscores the political difficulties besetting reforms. A monetary reform will be successful only if accompanied by a fiscal reform, but where does a government cut spending, and how can it raise taxes without losing political support? A successful monetary reform often requires the nation to endure a period of harsh adjustment as the fiscal deficit is cut by reducing subsidies and government employment, and by raising taxes. That monetary reforms have frequently yielded only short-term benefits indicates that governments often find the cost of permanent fiscal reforms too high. Ultimately, a permanent reduction in the fiscal deficit and monetary growth rate should allow a country to achieve steady growth with low inflation. But in the short run, too many beneficiaries of existing government programs are hurt for the incumbent government to retain power. Given the short-run perspective of the political process, many governments have been unwilling to risk the loss of power before the long-term benefits are achieved. The result is renewed inflation and large fiscal deficits, which may eventually culminate in a renewed attempt at monetary reform.

Michael Melvin
Jalal Uddin Ahmad

See also FISCAL POLICY; LDC CRISIS; MONETARY POLICY

Bibliography

Dornbusch, R. and S. Fischer. 1986. "Stopping Hyperinflations Past and Present." *Weltwirtschaftliches Archiv* 72:1–47.
Hawtrey, R. G. 1932. *The Art of Central Banking.* London: Longmans, Green and Co.
Melvin, M. 1988. "The Dollarization of Latin America as a Market-Enforced Monetary Reform: Evidence and Implications." *Economic Development and Cultural Change* 36:543–58.
Sargent, T. J. [1982] 1986. "The Ends of Four Big Inflations." Chap. 3 in *Rational Expectations and Inflation.* New York: Harper and Row.

Money-Income Causality

The high correlation between money and nominal income is one of the best attested facts in economics. Whether this relationship is causal and in which direction it runs are critical for the analysis of business cycles. If money causes income, then changes in the stock of money might be a source, even the most important source, of business-cycle fluctuations. If income causes money, then monetary models of business cycles must give way to models in which shocks to factor supplies, technology, other real variables, or nonmonetary elements of aggregate demand initiate fluctuations.

Implicit claims about the direction of causal influence between money and income are as old as the quantity theory of money. Assessing these claims—theoretically or empirically—is fraught with difficulty. The most fundamental problem is to decide exactly what it means to say that one variable "causes" another. Confusion among three possible definitions of causality pervades the literature.

Cause and Control

Money may be said to cause income if control over the stock of money yields control over income. Control requires a definite, exploitable relation between money and income. A correlation that disappeared as soon as policymakers attempted to use it would not qualify as a causal relation.

Control has been historically the most important notion of causality for the money-income debate. Irving Fisher (1913), for example, recognized that the quantity equation, $MV = PT$, which relates the stock of money, M, and its velocity of circulation, V, to the price level, P, and the level of real transactions, T, is a tautology lacking empirical content. He therefore devoted a crucial chapter to supporting the claim that, in the long run, money, velocity, and real transactions are independent of each other and of the price level. The independence of the other three variables implies that prices respond passively. Interestingly, Fisher's detailed statistical investigations suggest that, in the short run, money, velocity, and real transactions are not independent of each other, and may be influenced by prices.

Milton Friedman's and Anna J. Schwartz's monumental *Monetary History of the United States* aims to establish that money causes income. They ask, for example, whether a different Federal Reserve policy would have prevented the Great Depression. The implicit definition of causality is controllability. Friedman and Schwartz attempt to show not only that money and income are well correlated, but also that the correlation is stable across large changes in institutions and monetary policy.

The quantity equation with stable velocity suggests that money causes nominal income, without specifying how changes in nominal income are decomposed into changes in real income and the price level. Money can be a source of business-cycle fluctuations only if it affects real income. Monetarists such as Friedman and Schwartz typically hold that, in the long run, money is neutral and thus affects only prices.

Therefore, money causes real income only in the short run.

Philip Cagan's 1965 study on the determinants of the money stock complements the work of Friedman and Schwartz. Cagan follows Fisher in explicitly adopting the causal standard left implicit by Friedman and Schwartz. Cagan interprets the empirical evidence as supporting the view that, in the short run, income may cause money as well as money cause income, but not in the long run. Whether policymakers should ignore income-induced fluctuations in the stock of money or attempt to counteract them to ensure long-run stability of prices depends on the size and duration of such transitory effects.

In contrast, New Classical (rational-expectations) models question the long-run/short-run distinction. Some New Classical economists contend that anticipated changes in the stock of money are always neutral. Only unanticipated changes have real effects. Since policy cannot be systematically unanticipated, exploiting the causal connection between money and real output is impossible. The best policy is to minimize uncertainty by avoiding unanticipated shocks to the money supply. Evidence on whether only unanticipated changes in money affect output is mixed.

Some critics, agreeing that causality should be interpreted as control, nonetheless read Friedman and Schwartz as having defined cause as temporal priority and, therefore, as committing the fallacy *post hoc ergo propter hoc*. James Tobin (1970) offers a model in which money is temporally prior to income even though money reacts passively to income. However, Friedman and Schwartz ([1963] 1969) argue that timing relations between money and income are interesting only in the context of a well-supported theory that causally connects the two. Changes in the stock of dressmaker's pins might always precede changes in income. Yet no one would say that pins cause income. For neither camp, then, can causality be defined as temporal priority.

Robert King and Charles Plosser (1984) have proposed a real business-cycle model in which income causes money as in Tobin's model. Entirely based on correlations, their supporting evidence lacks the comparisons with different times, policy regimes, and institutions that gave the opposing Monetarist interpretation its persuasive force.

King and Plosser are largely in accord with the earlier Keynesian views of Britain's Radcliffe

Committee. The Radcliffe Committee concluded that monetary policy could not control income, because velocity could take on any value. In other words, the stable relation expressed in Fisher's quantity equation and its modern variants is chimerical. In response, Friedman and Schwartz (1982) argue that constant velocity is empirically a good first approximation for both the United States and the United Kingdom. David Hendry and Neil Ericsson (1991) have shown convincingly, however, that, for the United Kingdom at least, the opposite view, that velocity is a will-o'-the-wisp, statistically dominates the assumption of constant velocity.

Kevin Hoover (1991) has added new evidence that money does not cause nominal income in the control sense. Hoover revives Herbert Simon's characterization of causality as a relation of recursion in the true process that generates the data. He derives some typical econometric implications of prices causing money. For example, a regression of money on prices and other variables would be invariant to identifiable shocks in the price-determination process (e.g., the introduction of wage and price controls), while a regression of prices that excludes money would be invariant to shocks in the money-determination process (e.g., the legalization of interest-bearing checking accounts). Regressions of money on variables excluding prices would not be invariant to price shocks, while regressions of prices on money and other variables would not be invariant to money shocks. If money causes prices, similar implications follow *mutatis mutandis*. Using these implications as a guide to interpretation, Hoover finds that the balance of evidence supports the view that prices cause money in the postwar period. On this analysis, historical evidence for stable money-demand functions frequently cited to support Monetarism can be reinterpreted. A so-called money-demand regression typically regresses money on prices, income, and interest rates. If it remains stable across institutional changes, this suggests that the right-hand variables cause money.

Accommodation

On a second definition, income causes money if the monetary authorities accommodate independent increases in income. A popular view among some Keynesians (e.g., Nicholas Kaldor 1982) and Post-Keynesians (e.g., Basil J. Moore 1988) is that income may rise independently of

M

money, and the central bank must validate or accommodate this rise by increasing the money stock to avoid a recession or, worse, a collapse of the financial system.

Applying the definition of cause as control, Cagan effectively dismissed this argument. It implicitly concedes that the central bank can control the money stock and not accommodate if it so chooses. The central bank is forced to accommodate the increase in income only in the sense that, if it did not, something undesirable would occur. Causal direction then depends on policymakers' preferences, rather than being a stable property of the world that the policymakers can exploit or not exploit as they choose.

There is, however, a more subtle accommodationist argument. Kaldor concedes that, historically, velocity has been relatively stable; but this stability, he argues, depends on accommodation by central banks. If they failed to accommodate, velocity would rise, and new financial instruments would be created to substitute for money now in short supply. On this argument, money does not cause income, because it cannot be used to limit the growth of income; and income causes money so long as money includes the new instruments created through induced financial innovation.

Prediction
A third definition says that money causes income if money has predictive power for income. An econometrically precise definition of cause along these lines was developed in the 1960s by Clive Granger. In nontechnical terms, money Granger-causes income if income is better predicted from the past values of money in addition to its own past values than it is from its own past values alone. More technically, money in one period causes income in the next period if the probability distribution of the one-period-ahead prediction of income conditional on all past and present information is different from the probability distribution when information on past money is omitted from the information set.

Christopher Sims (1972) developed a practical test of Granger-causality. Sims noted that, if money Granger-causes income, then, in a regression of income on past, current, and future values of money, the future values would be statistically insignificant. Applying this test, Sims found that money Granger-causes income in the United States. Sims's later work shows that, if interest rates, money, and income are tested simultaneously, money does not Granger-

cause income, but interest rates do. But if the issue is whether the monetary authorities can affect income, and if interest rates are the *modus operandi* of monetary policy, this emendation may not matter. In attempting to reconcile conflicts in the voluminous literature on the Granger-causal relations among money, income, prices, and interest rates, James Stock and Mark Watson (1989) observe that minor technical differences in implementing the tests (e.g., differences in detrending) lead to strikingly different results.

It proved difficult to sort out the significance of Sims's and related work, since Granger-causality is tied up with issues of estimation, timing, and prediction. Two decades of discussion have produced a consensus that Granger-causality tests test incremental predictability, not whether one variable can control another, which, Granger says, is a "deeper" issue. Edward Leamer (1985) takes strong exception to Granger's use of the word "causality" for a concept unrelated to control. Granger, however, insists that his concept captures what economists often mean by causality. This is a matter on which economists can agree to differ, so long as questions of prediction are carefully distinguished from questions of control. Unfortunately, the two have often been confused in the debate over the causal direction between money and income.

Conclusion
The causal direction between money and income is critical in determining whether responsibility for business cycles may be laid at the feet of monetary policy. There are three central questions: First, how should "cause" be defined and investigated? Second, given a particular notion of cause, in which direction does empirical evidence suggest that causality runs? And third, are there sound economic theories that explain the observed causal direction? Through most of this century, economists have been unclear about the first question, but have usually answered the second and third questions by saying that money causes income. Recent efforts aim to clarify the first question, and the growing interest in real-business-cycle models suggests that the second and third questions are still open.

Kevin D. Hoover

See also BRUNNER, KARL; ENDOGENOUS AND EXOGENOUS MONEY; FISHER, IRVING; FRIED-

MAN, MILTON; KALDOR, NICHOLAS; MON-
ETARY DISEQUILIBRIUM THEORIES OF THE
BUSINESS CYCLE; MONETARY EQUILIBRIUM
THEORIES OF THE BUSINESS CYCLE; NEW
MONETARY ECONOMICS; REAL BUSINESS-
CYCLE THEORIES; ROSTOW, WALT WHITMAN;
SCHWARTZ, ANNA JACOBSON; TOBIN, JAMES;
VECTOR AUTOREGRESSIONS

Bibliography

Cagan, P. 1965. *Determinants and Effects of Changes in the Stock of Money 1875–1960.* New York: Columbia Univ. Press.

Fisher, I. 1913. *The Purchasing Power of Money: Its Determination and Relation to Credit, Interest and Crises.* 2d ed. New York: Macmillan.

Friedman, M. and A. J. Schwartz. 1963. *A Monetary History of the United States.* Princeton: Princeton Univ. Press.

———. [1963] 1969. "Money and Business Cycles." Chap. 10 in M. Friedman, *The Optimum Quantity of Money and Other Essays.* Chicago: Aldine.

———. 1982. *Monetary Trends in the United States and the United Kingdom: Their Relation to Income, Prices and Interest Rates, 1867–1975.* Chicago: Univ. of Chicago Press.

Granger, C. W. J. 1980. "Testing for Causality: A Personal Viewpoint." *Journal of Economic Dynamics and Control* 2:329–52.

Hendry, D. F. and N. R. Ericsson. 1991. "An Econometric Analysis of U.K. Money Demand in *Monetary Trends in the United States and the United Kingdom* by Milton Friedman and Anna J. Schwartz." *American Economic Review* 81:8–38.

Hoover, K. D. 1990. "The Logic of Causal Inference: Econometrics and the Conditional Analysis of Causation." *Economics and Philosophy* 6:207–234.

———. 1991. "The Causal Direction between Money and Prices: An Alternative Approach." *Journal of Monetary Economics* 27:381–423.

Kaldor, N. 1982. *The Scourge of Monetarism.* Oxford: Oxford Univ. Press.

King, R. G. and C. I. Plosser. 1984. "Money, Credit and Prices in a Real Business Cycle." *American Economic Review* 74:363–80.

Leamer, E. E. 1985. "Vector Autoregressions for Causal Inference?" In *Understanding Monetary Regimes. Carnegie-Rochester Conference Series on Public Policy,* Spring, 255–303.

Moore, B. J. 1988. "The Endogenous Money Supply." *Journal of Post Keynesian Economics* 10:372–85.

Sims, C. A. 1972. "Money, Income and Causality." *American Economic Review* 62:540–52.

Stock, J. H. and M. W. Watson. 1989. "Interpreting the Evidence on Money-Income Causality." *Journal of Econometrics* 40:161–81.

Tobin, J. 1970. "Money and Income: Post Hoc Ergo Propter Hoc?" *Quarterly Journal of Economics* 84:301–17.

United Kingdom. Parliament. Committee on the Working of the Monetary System (Radcliffe Committee). 1959. *Report.* Cmnd. 827. London: HMSO.

Zellner, A. [1979] 1984. "Causality and Econometrics." Chap. 4 in *Basic Issues in Econometrics.* Chicago: Univ. of Chicago Press.

M

Moore, Geoffrey Hoyt (1914–)

Geoffrey H. Moore, an economist who has specialized in the development of business-cycle indicators, attended Rutgers University, graduating with a B.S. in agricultural economics in 1933. He pursued doctoral studies at Harvard and was awarded the Ph.D. in 1947, writing his doctoral dissertation on harvest cycles.

Moore spent the bulk of his career at the National Bureau of Economic Research, which he joined in 1939, holding a variety of positions, including Director of Research (1965–68). He remained on the staff until his official retirement in 1979, taking a leave to be Commissioner of Labor Statistics (1969–73).

Brought to the National Bureau by Arthur F. Burns, Moore's approach to business-cycle analysis was influenced by Burns's perspective, and his work has, therefore, been in the Mitchell-Burns tradition. But he, himself, did much to shape the bureau's research program during his years with the bureau.

His interest in improving the statistical techniques with which business-cycle analysts examine basic data was evident in his first publication, *A Significance Test for Time Series and Other Ordered Observations,* written jointly with W. Allen Wallis. His concern that data accurately reflect the underlying economic activity that they supposedly represent surfaced in *Production of Industrial Materials in World Wars I and II,* which studied the then extant Index of Industrial Production and tested how closely it reflected movements in its components.

In his later work, Moore has sought to develop and refine business-cycle indicators in the United States and extend business-cycle indicator systems to other market-oriented economies. In this sense he has been explicitly advancing the Burns-Mitchell work, which had culminated with their *Measuring Business Cycles* (1946). One outgrowth of the technique of measuring business cycles developed by Burns and Mitchell was the creation of a National Bureau committee that would officially declare when the U.S. economy reached a business-cycle peak or trough. Along with maintaining an ongoing business-cycle chronology, the National Bureau began monitoring short lists of "most reliable indicators," classified as leading, roughly coincident, or lagging in relation to business-cycle turning points. The first such list appeared as the initial Burns-Mitchell work neared completion in 1938.

In 1950, Moore wrote *Statistical Indicators of Cyclical Revivals and Recessions,* an important monograph summarizing a renewed bureau analysis of about 800 time series and from which twenty-one series were newly chosen to constitute the first revised list of reliable indicators. The list contained eight leaders, eight roughly coincident series, and five laggers.

Moore revised the list of indicators again in 1960 (*Leading and Confirming Indicators of General Business Changes*), this time including twenty-six time series in the list. In 1967, Julius Shiskin joined Moore in yet a third revision of the indicator system. In addition to reassessing the performance of the list of indicators, they developed a scoring system to help evaluate the usefulness of proposed indicators. The system evaluates a number of statistical properties of each series, the coverage, and reliability of each series, as well as its ability to reflect cyclical changes. Much of the National Bureau's pre-1960 work on business cycles is included in a two-volume work edited by Moore, *Business Cycle Indicators.*

In the early 1960s, Bureau of Economic Analysis in the Department of Commerce took over from the National Bureau the task of presenting business-cycle indicators each month.

The monthly publication, originally called *Business Cycle Developments* but later known as *Business Conditions Digest,* continued to monitor business-cycle developments along the lines developed at the National Bureau with Moore's assistance. *Business Conditions Digest* was discontinued in March 1990, but the indicators are now published monthly in the *Survey of Current Business.* (The turning points continue to be selected by a National Bureau Committee on which Moore still sits.)

Following his retirement from the National Bureau in 1979, Moore started the Center for International Business Cycle Research, housed originally at Rutgers University in Newark and now located at Columbia University. At the center, Moore has continued his work in improving our methods for measuring business-cycle developments. Among the major accomplishments of recent years have been the creation of an indicator system for each of the major industrialized market-oriented countries, modeled on the U.S. system and comprised where possible of series that are roughly equivalent to the U.S. series included in each timing category. The principal results of the early work in this field are presented in *Monitoring Growth Cycles in Market Oriented Economies,* coauthored by Philip A. Klein and Moore and published by the National Bureau in 1985. This work demonstrates that business-cycle indicator systems can be developed for the major market-oriented economies with results that compare favorably with their historical record of behavior in the U.S.

The international work, pioneered by Ilse Mintz, has focused not on the traditional business cycles, which were the original focus of Burns and Mitchell, but on "growth cycles." After World War II, the focus in many countries abroad shifted to growth cycles, which are measured as deviations from trend. They have been shown to be detectable even in periods of rapid growth during which fluctuations in the level of economic activity (now often called "classical cycles") are absent. The recent historical record shows evidence of both growth cycles and conventional cycles, and both, therefore, are appropriately monitored. While many countries abroad now monitor only growth cycles, the United States Department of Commerce monitors "classical" cycles while Moore's CIBCR monitors growth cycles. The U.S. is thus the only country in the world with a fully developed indicator system kept up to date both for classical and for growth cycles.

A second publication emerging from the early analysis of growth cycles in market-oriented economies, *International Economic Indicators,* coauthored by Moore and his wife, Melita H. Moore, carefully describes the data underlying the international indicator system.

The ongoing assessment of growth cycles in eleven major market-oriented economies is published monthly in a CIBCR publication, *International Economic Indicators.* Many of Moore's early essays written at the CIBCR are available in *Business Cycles, Inflation, and Forecasting.*

Moore also pioneered in developing a variety of other techniques for monitoring cyclical developments. One CIBCR publication, *Recession-Recovery Watch,* presents a way of comparing recent changes in, for example, inflation, employment, or real GNP to their average behavior at comparable stages of earlier business cycles.

At the CIBCR, under Moore's leadership, growth cycles are continuously assessed in a variety of ways. One monthly publication, *The Leading Indicator Press Release,* summarizes recent changes for the U.S. in a special weekly leading index; in a long-leading index, which is composed of those series with historical records reflecting the longest lead times at cyclical turning points; a special leading employment index, sensitive to cyclical changes in that important measure; and a special leading inflation index. It also presents developments in the leading indexes of ten foreign market-oriented countries. More recently, the center has been working to develop indicators sensitive to cyclical changes in the burgeoning service sector of the U.S. economy.

Specialized business-cycle indicators which Moore and his colleagues have developed in recent years are now published regularly in *Business Week Magazine,* as well as by the Department of Commerce. Moore and his colleagues at the CIBCR continue to analyze business-cycle indicators, and their most recent assessment of the Commerce Department's present indicator system, along with suggestions for change, are offered in *Leading Indicators for the 1990s.*

Moore is widely consulted by economists in government, in business, in the media, and in academia—in short, by all those who concern themselves with evaluating current develop-ments pertinent to assessing the stability of the economy. Thus, Moore remains, after many years, a major figure in the analysis of ongoing business-cycle developments in the United States and abroad.

Philip A. Klein

See also BURNS, ARTHUR FRANK; COMPOSITE AND DIFFUSION INDEXES; GROWTH CYCLES; LEADING INDICATORS: HISTORICAL RECORD; LEADS AND LAGS; MARKET PRICE INDICATORS; MINTZ, ILSE SCHUELLER; MITCHELL, WESLEY CLAIR; ZARNOWITZ, VICTOR

Bibliography

Klein, P. A. and G. H. Moore. 1967. *The Quality of Consumer Installment Credit.* New York: Columbia Univ. Press.

———. 1985. *Monitoring Growth Cycles in Market Oriented Countries.* Cambridge, Mass.: Ballinger.

Moore, G. H. 1944. *Production of Industrial Materials During World Wars I and II.* National Bureau of Economic Research, Occasional Paper 18. New York: NBER.

———. 1950. *Statistical Indicators of Cyclical Revivals and Recessions.* National Bureau of Economic Research, Occasional Paper 31. New York: NBER.

———. 1958. *Measuring Recessions.* National Bureau of Economic Research, Occasional Paper 61. New York: NBER.

———, ed. 1961. *Business Cycle Indicators.* 2 vols. Princeton: Princeton Univ. Press.

———. 1983. *Business Cycles, Inflation, and Forecasting.* 2d ed. Cambridge, Mass.: Ballinger.

———. 1990. *Leading Indicators for the 1990s.* Homewood, Ill.: Dow Jones-Irwin.

Moore, G. H. and M. H. Moore. 1985. *International Economic Indicators: A Sourcebook.* Westport, Conn.: Greenwood.

Moore, G. H. and J. Shiskin. 1967. *Indicators of Business Expansions and Contractions.* National Bureau of Economic Research, Occasional Paper 103. New York: Columbia Univ. Press.

Moore, G. H. and W. A. Wallis. 1941. *A Significance Test for Time Series and Other Ordered Observations.* National Bureau of Economic Research, Technical Paper 1. New York: NBER.

Moore, Henry Ludwell (1869–1958)

Henry Ludwell Moore has often been called the father of modern econometrics in America, but during his lifetime he was best known for his weather theory of the business cycle and his subsequent attempt to construct what he deemed a "synthetic economics."

A student of Karl Pearson and J. B. Clark, he began his career by applying statistical and quantitative techniques to early neoclassical marginal-productivity wage theories. But upon encountering hostility to his correlation exercises from Marshall, Edgeworth, and others, he felt obliged to justify his use of stochastic techniques by studying the fluctuations of economic variables. His most controversial work, *Economic Cycles: Their Law and Cause* argued that the Marshallian approach was "barren" and that business cycles must be traced back to their natural causes. By applying such advanced techniques for that time as Fourier decompositions and Schuster periodograms, he claimed to have found an eight-year periodicity in rainfall. He then produced what was the first set of structural equations relating rainfall to crop yields to agricultural prices; augmented with a further notorious "upward-sloping demand curve" for pig iron, the tradeoff between "agricultural" and "industrial" purchases given an implicitly fixed trend in income was said to account for the business cycle. Subsequent books were devoted to fleshing out this sequence of causality in his theory of business cycles. *Forecasting the Yield and Price of Cotton* was intended to further document the effect of weather on crop output; whereas *Generating Economic Cycles* resorted to the physics and meteorology literature to show that the causes of the eight-year rainfall cycle might be traced back to the transit of Venus.

Moore's "mistakes" are often attributed by modern commentators such as Mary Morgan and George Stigler to his lack of appreciation for the identification problem in econometrics, but this explanation of his failure to convince his peers is not borne out by the historical record. What we find is perhaps the first macroeconometric model constructed along the lines of a block-recursive system. Instead, it was the rejection of orthodox Marshallian doctrines coupled with astronomical appeals, which bordered perilously on astrology, that accounted for the ridicule that his research program encountered in the 1920s. This rejection prompted the disappointed Moore to redouble his efforts to construct a dynamic quantitative and scientific economics. His final published book, *Scientific Economics,* presented the equations of his final macromodel. Fluctuations of any economic variable were to be decomposed into trend and periodic components, linked backwards to physical causes (such as weather cycles and nonperiodic components) due to displacements from a moving equilibrium determined by physical data (such as technology and population growth).

After brief stints at Johns Hopkins and Smith College, Moore spent most of his career at Columbia University, where he taught from 1902 to 1929. No school of econometrics coalesced around Moore, partly due to the forbidding character of his advanced mathematics, and partly from latent opposition from his Columbia colleague W. C. Mitchell. However, his most famous student, Henry Schultz, developed econometric practices contrary to the preferences of his mentor in fitting Marshallian demand curves, although it was Schultz who was responsible for proposing that Moore was the father of econometrics. From one point of view, Moore's work was premature, since the construction of macroeconometric models only took hold in the economics profession in the later 1930s; yet from an alternative point of view he was too late, since the heyday of weather-based explanations of the cycle occurred in the late nineteenth century. Nonetheless, Moore's influence was felt in the brief flowering of a Columbia school of statistical empiricism associated with the National Bureau of Economic Research from the late 1920s to the 1940s.

Philip Mirowski

See also AGRICULTURAL CYCLES; JEVONS, WILLIAM STANLEY; MACROECONOMETRIC MODELS, HISTORICAL DEVELOPMENT; SPECTRAL ANALYSIS; SUNSPOT THEORIES OF FLUCTUATIONS

Bibliography

Mirowski, P. 1990. "Problems in the Paternity of Econometrics: Henry Ludwell Moore." *History of Political Economy* 22:587–609.

Moore, H. L. 1911. *Laws of Wages.* New York: Macmillan.

———. 1914. *Economic Cycles: Their Law and Cause.* New York: Macmillan.

———. 1923. *Generating Economic Cycles.* New York: Macmillan.

———. 1929. *Synthetic Economics.* New York: Macmillan.

Morgan, M. 1990. *The History of Econometric Ideas.* Cambridge: Cambridge Univ. Press.

Stigler, G. J. [1962] 1965. "Henry L. Moore and Statistical Economics." Chap. 13 in *Essays in the History of Economics.* Chicago: Univ. of Chicago Press.

Moving Averages

The moving average is an empirical tool used to eliminate, highlight, or create cyclical variation in time-series data. Constructing a moving-average series is a process of smoothing, filtering, or graduating the original series by reducing the range, and often frequency, of fluctuations. What kind of new series and visual image results from this process depends on the correspondence between the period over which the average is calculated and the period of the cycles in the original time series.

The first extensive use of a moving average was in the Bank of England monthly reports of bullion holdings from 1833 to 1844. As James Wilson (founding editor of *The Economist*) noted in his 1840 tract, *Fluctuations of Currency, Commerce and Manufactures,* this method of reporting masked the extremes of bullion and deposit fluctuations and overestimated the value of bullion in times of persistent drains. Smoothing the data soothed people's reactions to changes, helping to prevent panics.

The monthly return reported by the Bank of England was the arithmetic mean of the three preceding months. It is now more common for a particular return to be the center of the averaging period, for example, the March value of a three-period moving average of monthly data would be the mean of the values for February, March, and April. The next value in the constructed moving-average series would be the April value, which would be the average of the original observations for March, April, and May. In some sophisticated applications, different weights are assigned to each observation in the averaging period, and for most purposes, the sum of the weights is equal to one. Moving-average weights can be estimated from polynomials fitted by least squares or from summation formulas.

By the latter half of the nineteenth century, economists were focusing on fluctuations that revealed a trade or business cycle. The moving average as an empirical tool of financiers was transformed into a statistical tool when correlations of deviations from moving averages were used to identify variables that moved together cyclically. In 1884, John Poynting first used this "method of averages" or "process of averaging" as a statistical, time-series tool in investigating the possibility that a common meteorological phenomenon was influencing the world-wide production of wheat, cotton, and silk. Poynting's choice of periods for calculating the "instantaneous average," as he called it, was somewhat arbitrary. In his 1901 study of the relationship between trade and the marriage rate, Reginald Hooker demonstrated that correlating deviations from a moving average, in order to highlight cyclical relationships, is only appropriate if the interval over which an average is taken is a multiple of the period of the trade cycle.

If the time series contains periodic cycles with equal amplitudes and if the period of averaging is equal to, or is a multiple of, the period of cycles in the time series, a plot of the moving average yields a straight line. For example, if observations of a variable showed cycles lasting seven years, a moving average that was computed over a seven- or fourteen-year span would eliminate the seven-year cycle and emphasize any long-term trend present. The moving-average series becomes an empirical approximation to the flow of the series and thus a useful tool for decomposing time series without recourse to freehand smoothing or fitting a curve to a mathematical function. For example, in the first step of Hooker's analysis, the transformation of the series into moving averages eliminated cyclical, seasonal, and random variation. Hooker then subtracted each annual observation from that year's moving-average value to reveal the cycle with the trend eliminated.

In the 1920s, Frederick Mills and Frederick Macaulay at the National Bureau of Economic Research made further strides by experimenting with weighted averages and systematically studying the effects of altering the span over which a moving average was calculated. Nowadays, moving averages calculated over short intervals are often used to eliminate random variation in order to highlight cyclical movements. In the *Business Conditions Digest* published by the United State Department of Commerce, the number of months over which a moving average is calculated for any variable (called MCD-months for cyclical dominance) is the minimum interval for which the average change in the value of the cyclical component is greater than that for random oscillations. Thus, the more erratic the series, the greater the MCD and the longer the period for the moving-average calculation.

This flexible tool for either eliminating or highlighting cycles can also create the illusion of cycles where none existed before. Simulations by Eugen Slutsky in 1927 and Udney Yule in 1926 demonstrated that a cyclical moving-average series could be constructed from a series displaying purely random variation. The Slutsky-Yule effect of misleading waves is one of the problems of flexibility. Others include biased estimation of the trend element if the latter is nonlinear, inability to represent discontinuities, and distortion in timing of turning points. The moving-average series can never be brought up-to-date, so the longer the period of averaging, the more lost coverage at the endpoints. These are serious problems for forecasting, and the alternative technique of exponential smoothing has become increasingly popular as a result.

The appropriateness of using moving averages to analyze cyclical change depends on the continuity and regularity of that change and the importance of precise dating of turning points. Constructing a moving-average series can be useful for tracking change when essentially uniform or harmonic motion is assumed and sought after. In such cases, the smoothed moving-average series can either represent a trend without cycles or, as is evident in each issue of *Business Conditions Digest,* represent undulating cycles without the noise.

Judy L. Klein

See also FILTERS; MILLS, FREDERICK CECIL; PHASE AVERAGING; SLUTSKY, EUGEN

Bibliography
Kohler, H. 1988. *Statistics for Business and Economics.* Glenview, Ill.: Scott, Foresman and Company.
Macaulay, F. R. 1931. *The Smoothing of Time Series.* New York: NBER.
Mills, F. C. 1938. *Statistical Methods.* 2d ed. New York: Henry Holt.
Slutsky, E. [1927] 1937. "The Summation of Random Causes as the Source of Cyclic Processes." Translation. *Econometrica* 5:105–46.

Multiplier

The concept of the multiplier is commonly attributed to Richard Kahn ([1931] 1972). However, it can already be discerned, at least in rudimentary form, in the writings of some earlier authors, most notably Nicholas Johannsen (Hagemann and Rühl 1987). The concept was adopted by Keynes in the *General Theory,* whose initial novelty, Keynes later wrote, "consists . . . in the proposition that it is, not the rate of interest, but the level of incomes which (in conjunction with certain other factors) ensures . . . equality" between saving and investment ([1937] 1973, 211). The multiplier analysis is concerned with the equilibrating mechanism referred to. It thus plays a central role in Keynes's attempt to demonstrate the principle of effective demand, according to which aggregate effective demand will generally fall short of the output produced from full employment of labor. The theory of effective demand, based on the multiplier, was developed independently of Keynes by Michal Kalecki (1971).

The (static) concept of the investment multiplier can be put as follows. In an economy with a sophisticated money and credit system, investment can be financed independently of previous or anticipated future saving. In the case contemplated by Keynes, with sufficient underutilized capacity and unemployment of labor, and on the assumption that prices remain constant in these circumstances, investment demand (as demand in general) can be realized in real terms. In a closed economy without a state, total aggregate demand D is equal to investment demand I plus consumption demand C, which, in the simplest case, is linearly dependent on actual (real) income Y. Hence,

$$D = I + cY, \tag{1}$$

where c represents the propensity to consume. In short-run equilibrium:

$$Y = D. \tag{2}$$

From equations (1) and (2) we get

$$Y = mI, \tag{3}$$

where m is the *income multiplier*, and is equal to $1/(1 - c)$. Taking into account the employment function, $N = f(Y)$, we obtain

$$N = f(mI) = nI, \qquad (4)$$

where n is the employment multiplier.

It goes without saying that essentially the same argument applies to other autonomous or quasi-autonomous components of aggregate demand, such as autonomous consumption demand, public expenditure and, in particular, foreign demand.

In the case discussed, with a given propensity to save, the volume of saving corresponding to the given volume of investment is generated via a change in the level of output as a whole. However, in a full-employment economy, with a given level of output, it is generated via a change in income distribution. The latter idea was advocated by Kaldor (1956) in his neo-Keynesian approach to the theory of distribution. However, it is doubtful that under conditions of full employment profit inflation can play a lasting role.

A detailed period analysis of multiplier processes, distinguishing between a temporary and a permanent change in the level of autonomous demand, was provided by Robertson (1937) and Machlup (1939). The multiplier was combined with the accelerator in models of cyclical growth by Harrod (1936, 1939) and Samuelson ([1939] 1966). Goodwin ([1949] 1983) and Chipman (1950) extended Keynes's concept of a marginal propensity to spend less than one to all sectors (or industries) of the economy. Their point of departure was the Leontief matrix of money quantities. Furthermore, they investigated the implications of assuming lags in the circulation of money by considering the conditions for dynamic stability. Multisectoral approaches to the theory of the multiplier were also elaborated by Schwartz (1961), Morishima (1976), and more recently by Kurz (1985), who have shown that there is no such thing as "the" multiplier. Rather, the multiplier effects depend on a variety of circumstances, such as the technical conditions of production, income distribution, consumption patterns, and the physical composition of investment demand, as well as on savings ratios and the aggregate volume of investment. The results derived within the framework of a one-commodity model generally do not carry over to the multi-commodity case, particularly if there is some jointness of production.

Heinz D. Kurz

See also Goodwin, Richard Murphey; Johannsen, Nicholas August Ludwig

Jacob; Keynes, John Maynard; Robertson, Dennis Holme; Samuelson, Paul Anthony

M

Bibliography

Chipman, J. S. 1950. "The Multi-Sector Multiplier." *Econometrica* 18:355–74.

Goodwin, R. M. [1949] 1983. "The Multiplier as Matrix." Chap. 1 in *Essays in Linear Economic Structures*. London: Macmillan.

Hagemann, H. and C. Rühl. 1987. "Nicholas Johannsen's Early Analysis of the Saving-Investment Process and the Multiplier." *Studi Economici* 42:99–143.

Harrod, R. F. 1936. *The Trade Cycle*. Oxford: Clarendon Press.

———. 1939. "An Essay in Dynamic Theory." *Economic Journal* 49:14–33.

Kahn, R. [1931] 1972. "The Relation of Home Investment to Unemployment." Chap. 1 in *Selected Essays on Employment and Growth*. Cambridge: Cambridge Univ. Press.

Kaldor, N. 1956. "Alternative Theories of Distribution." *Review of Economic Studies* 23:83–100.

Kalecki, M. 1971. *Selected Essays on the Dynamics of the Capitalist Economy*. Cambridge: Cambridge Univ. Press.

Keynes, J. M. [1936] 1973. *The General Theory of Employment, Interest, and Money*. Vol. 7 of *The Collected Writings of John Maynard Keynes*. London: Macmillan.

———. [1937] 1973. "Alternative Theories of the Rate of Interest." In *The General Theory and After: Part II, Defense and Development*. Vol. 14 of *The Collected Writings of John Maynard Keynes*, 201–15. London: Macmillan.

Kurz, H. D. 1985. "Effective Demand in a 'Classical' Model of Value and Distribution: The Multiplier in a Sraffian Framework." *The Manchester School* 53:121–37.

Machlup, F. 1939. "Period Analysis and Multiplier Theory." *Quarterly Journal of Economics* 54:1–27.

Morishima, M. 1976. *The Economic Theory of Modern Society*. Cambridge: Cambridge Univ. Press.

Robertson, D. H. 1937. "Some Notes on Mr. Keynes' General Theory of Employment." *Quarterly Journal of Economics* 51:168–91.

Samuelson, P. A. [1939] 1966. "Interactions between the Multiplier Analysis and the Principle of Acceleration." Chap. 82 in *The Collected Scientific Papers of Paul A. Samuelson*. Vol. 2. Cambridge: MIT Press.

Schwartz, J. T. 1961. *Lectures on the Mathematical Method in Analytical Economics*. New York: Gordon and Breach.

Mushet, Robert (1782–1828)

Robert Mushet was an important contributor to the development of the theory that monetary shocks from the central bank drive the business cycle. Following the crisis of 1825, Mushet (1826) gave an early and influential statement of the view that the Bank of England policy was to blame. In many ways, his was the most thorough exposition of that view during the classic British monetary debates among the Banking, Currency, and Free Banking Schools, which ran from the resumption of the gold standard in 1819 to the enactment of the Bank Charter Act of 1844.

Mushet was, from about 1804 onward, an employee of the royal mint, rising to the position of refiner. He participated in the Bullionist debates with an 1810 work on the depreciation of the pound, gave important testimony in 1819 before both the Commons' and the Lords' committees on resumption, and, in 1821, published tables on the fluctuations in the value of the pound.

Mushet (1826, 142–58, 203) attributed to "the power of the Bank of England of adding extensively to the currency," which swells the supply of loanable funds and creates an excess supply of money, "the whole of the speculations, now and heretofore, that have appeared to begin in prosperity, and to end in the distress and ruin of thousands" (142). He described a sequence of events that he believed fit the cycles ending in the crises of 1797, 1819, and 1825. In his theory, the Bank of England overexpands its discounts or security purchases, due to errors "of judgment rather than intention," reducing interest rates and encouraging speculation and "over-trading." The policy creates an "abundance of money," causing commodity and financial asset prices to rise in London. Interregional arbitrage spreads the increased commodity prices and more abundant money to the countryside. The country banks are not to blame for the expansion of the country circulation, as they cannot expand independently of the Bank of England. They are instead compelled to expand their nominal issues by the increase in prices.

The expansion of the Bank of England cannot be sustained in an open economy on an international gold standard. Increased prices for commodities and financial assets make it "in the end, profitable to export gold;" the Bank loses reserves, and "the safety of the Bank, sooner or later, requires a suspension of such [extended] accommodations, the currency is contracted," the rate of interest rises, "and stocks fall to their natural level" (158).

Mushet's account had its weaknesses. He suggested in some places (181) that the ability of the Bank of England to overissue hinged on the type of assets it acquired. This indicates a confusion characteristic of the real-bills doctrine, between the demand to hold money and the demand for loanable funds.

Later writers in the Free Banking School, particularly Henry Parnell and James W. Gilbart, cited Mushet and advanced similar views of the cycle. They elaborated much more fully the policy position Mushet sketched only in the last two pages of his work (206–207): "When the monopoly of the Bank expires, and the trade in money is perfectly free, a better order of things may arise," with steadier interest rates and prices, automatic checks against overissue, and lesser cyclical instability in output and employment. A similar cycle theory, though a different policy prescription, was advanced by those members of the Currency School who, like Robert Torrens, were most critical of the Bank of England.

Mushet clearly anticipated the monetary elements of Wicksellian business-cycle theory, particularly the Austrian variant developed in the twentieth century by von Mises, who associated his theory with that of the Currency School. In both accounts, the boom is caused by central-bank monetary expansion which lowers the market interest rate below its equilibrium level, and ends in crisis when the money stock and interest rate return to their natural levels. This sort of account survives in modern "natural-rate" monetary theories of the cycle.

Lawrence H. White

See also AUSTRIAN THEORY OF BUSINESS CYCLES; BANK CHARTER ACT OF 1844; BANKING SCHOOL, CURRENCY SCHOOL, AND FREE BANKING SCHOOL; FREE BANKING; MISES,

LUDWIG EDLER VON; RICARDO, DAVID; WICK-
SELL, JOHAN GUSTAV KNUT

Bibliography

Mushet, R. 1826. *An Attempt to Explain
from Facts the Effect of the Issues of the
Bank of England upon Its Own Inter-
ests, Public Credit, and the Country
Banks.* London: Baldwin, Cradock, and
Joy.

White, L. H. 1984. *Free Banking in Britain:
Theory, Experience, and Debate, 1800–
1845.* Cambridge: Cambridge Univ. Press.

Myrdal, Gunnar (1898–1987)

Swedish Nobel laureate Gunnar Myrdal is
known for his contributions to economic theory
and a number of other social sciences. His early
work on the theory of money and economic
fluctuations provided crucial components of
the methodological approach underlying the
Stockholm School of economics. Myrdal made
important contributions to the analysis of expectations, to the analysis of the relationship
between savings and investment, and to the
development of a method of dynamic analysis.
In many respects, Myrdal's monetary theory
was similar to the *General Theory* of John
Maynard Keynes, leading one commentator to
argue that "had the *General Theory* never been
written, Myrdal's work would have eventually
supplied almost the same theory" (Shackle
1967, 124).

Myrdal's doctoral dissertation, *The Problem of Price Formation and Change* (in Swedish only), tackled the problem of integrating
expectations into the microeconomic framework of his dissertation supervisor, Gustav
Cassel. Drawing on and criticizing the work of
Frank Knight, Myrdal analyzed how "conceptions of risks and valuations of risks affected
expected and realized profits as well as production and investment plans" of individual firms
(Lundberg 1974, 472). Expectations become
part of the data on which decisions are made,
thereby affecting price formation in the same
way as "objective" factors do. One of the most
important conclusions of Myrdal's dissertation
was that prices formed "dynamically" (anticipating the future) are not the same, in general,
as prices inferred from a static model. Although
the terms *ex ante* and *ex post* did not appear in
Myrdal's dissertation, the idea was already
there and was made explicit with the publication of *Monetary Equilibrium* in 1932 (English
edition, 1939).

Myrdal's best-known work on monetary
theory, *Monetary Equilibrium* presented an
"immanent criticism" of Wicksell's concept of
monetary equilibrium. That is, it accepted the
main conclusions of Wicksell's theory and attempted to determine the exact conditions
necessary for a monetary equilibrium to exist.
The book also integrated expectations into the
model through the *ex ante/ex post* distinction.

Wicksell meant by the term "monetary
equilibrium" the absence of a cumulative process. He thought that monetary equilibrium
entailed three conditions: (1) equality of the
monetary and real (natural) rates of interest;
(2) equality of the rates of saving and investment; and (3) stable prices. Myrdal attacked
Wicksell's notion of the natural rate of interest,
showing that it was not a purely physical or
technical phenomenon. Myrdal rejected any
strictly physical measure of productivity as the
measure of the natural rate of interest in favor
of the yield of planned investments, a concept
that corresponds to Keynes's marginal efficiency
of capital. He was able to show that equating
the (marginal) yield of planned investments to
the market rate of interest did not preclude the
existence of a cumulative process; that is, *ex
ante* savings do not necessarily equal *ex ante*
investment when this condition is met (Shackle
1967, 98–110).

Through his use of the concepts of *ex ante*
plans and *ex post* results, Myrdal was able to
clarify the relationship between savings and
investment. He considered the development of
this method to be the major contribution of
Monetary Equilibrium. Using the *ex ante/ex
post* method, Myrdal was able to demonstrate
clearly the mechanism bringing *ex post* savings
into equality with *ex post* investment—changes
in aggregate income. This analysis was very
similar to Keynes's in the *General Theory,* differing primarily in Myrdal's emphasis on price
(rather than output) changes and the absence
of any formal multiplier analysis in Myrdal's
theory.

Finally, Myrdal argued that Wicksell's
third condition, price stability, had nothing
to do with monetary equilibrium. Any rate of
stable inflation or deflation is compatible with
the absence of a cumulative process.

Not all of Myrdal's early work was devoted to monetary issues. He also helped develop the theory of fiscal policy. Myrdal rejected

M

the idea that an annually balanced government budget was beneficial, arguing that the budget instead should be balanced over longer periods. During depressions, the government should run deficits, which would be paid off when national income was growing strongly (Myrdal 1939). Myrdal's description of how government spending stimulates private spending shows that he understood the concept of the multiplier, although he was apparently unfamiliar with Kahn's famous article and never used a formal multiplier model (Dostaler 1990, 211–12).

In the late 1930s, Myrdal turned to broader social issues. He argued that economic problems could be addressed adequately only in their broader social context. For all intents and purposes, his career as a macroeconomic theorist ended in 1939.

Neil T. Skaggs

See also EXPECTATIONS; LINDAHL, ERIK ROBERT; LUNDBERG, ERIK FILIP; NATURAL RATE OF INTEREST; OHLIN, BERTIL GOTTHARD; SAVING EQUALS INVESTMENT; STOCKHOLM SCHOOL; WICKSELL, JOHAN GUSTAV KNUT

Bibliography

Dostaler, G. 1990. "An Assessment of Gunnar Myrdal's Early Work in Economics." *Journal of the History of Economic Thought* 12:196–221.

Hansen, B. 1981. "Unemployment, Keynes, and the Stockholm School." *History of Political Economy* 13:256–77.

Hansson, B. A. 1982. *The Stockholm School and the Development of Dynamic Method.* London: Croom Helm.

Jonung, L., ed. 1991. *The Stockholm School of Economics Revisited.* Cambridge: Cambridge Univ. Press.

Lundberg, E. 1974. "Gunnar Myrdal's Contribution to Economic Theory." *Swedish Journal of Economics* 76:472–78.

Myrdal, G. 1927. *Prisbildningsproblemet och foranderligheten* (The problem of price formation and change). Stockholm: Almqvist and Wiksell.

———. [1932] 1939. *Monetary Equilibrium.* Translation. London: William Hodge.

———. 1939. "Fiscal Policy in the Business Cycle." *American Economic Review Papers and Proceedings* 29:183–93.

Ohlin, B. 1981. "Stockholm and Cambridge: Four Papers on the Monetary and Employment Theory of the 1930s." Edited by O. Steiger. *History of Political Economy* 13:189–255.

Shackle, G. L. S. 1967. *The Years of High Theory: Invention and Tradition in Economic Thought, 1926–1939.* Cambridge: Cambridge Univ. Press.

N

Napoleonic Wars

The business cycles during the Napoleonic Wars have been analyzed only for Great Britain, the most advanced economy of the time and on its way to becoming the first industrial nation. Whether these were truly modern cycles is still in dispute, in part because it is not agreed whether Britain was yet an industrial nation, and in part because of the repeated disturbances caused by the war effort and the economic policies adopted by both sides. Nevertheless, the classic work of Gayer, Rostow, and Schwartz (1953) identified five distinct episodes in this period: the 1793–97 minor cycle, the 1797–1803 major cycle, the 1803–08 minor cycle, the 1808–11 major cycle, and the 1811–16 minor cycle, all measured trough to trough. These cycles reflect basically the fluctuations in textile exports. Cycles were classified major and minor depending on whether the cycle in textile exports was or was not accompanied by a cycle in domestic investment.

1793–97

The trough of this cycle followed the sudden collapse of the canal-building boom, itself a possible response to the influx of flight capital from revolutionary France, with the outbreak of war with France in February 1793. As was usual in the case of eighteenth-century wars, Britain engaged mercenary forces on the Continent and remitted large sums to pay and supply them. The real transfer of these subsidies to the First and Second Coalitions was achieved by a spectacular increase in exports, especially cotton textiles, to the Continent. Unfortunately, the mercenary forces engaged by the British faded away in the face of the French Revolutionary armies. Most serious was the fall of

Amsterdam in December 1794, which meant that British remittance operations had to be transferred north to Hamburg. Continued military losses led to reduced demand for exports, so that Continental subsidies eventually caused an external drain of specie. When the French Revolutionary government signaled its intention to return to a bimetallic standard in 1797, the return flow of specie to the Continent forced the Bank of England to suspend convertibility of its banknotes into silver or gold. This suspension of convertibility, known as the "paper pound," continued until the resumption of a gold standard in 1821.

1797–1803

As military effort slackened on the Continent and Napoleon stabilized political conditions, normal export relations began again (even with Holland) and a major building boom ensued in England, especially in the expansion of agricultural enclosures in response to the high grain prices at the turn of the century and the permissiveness of the Enclosure Act of 1800. Formal peace occurred with the Treaty of Amiens in 1802, but fighting with Napoleon's forces on land and at sea resumed. Good harvests in 1801–03 reduced quickly the high prices of foodstuffs that dominated the years 1799–1800. But the blockade of Continental ports to the import of British goods signaled the start of Napoleon's Continental Blockade strategy and brought a sudden drop in exports.

1803–08

The initial effects of the Continental Blockade were gradually circumvented and British shipping once again had free run of the open seas after Nelson's decisive destruction of the French and Spanish fleets at Trafalgar in October 1805. By spring 1806, however, Napoleon had defeated the Prussian army at Jena and tightened the enforcement of the blockade at Hamburg and along the Baltic coast of Germany. A mild stock-market boom occurred, however, on the London stock exchange in 1807, perhaps reflecting capital flight from northern Europe. The financial demands made by Wellington's Peninsular Army in the initial campaign of 1808 brought the stock-market boomlet to an end. Moreover, Jefferson's Embargo against the import of British goods became effective at the start of 1808. The combination of restricted export markets both in Europe and America brought this cycle to an end.

1808–11

This was an unusual cycle, completely dominated by the increased scale of military effort, now carried on directly by British forces on Iberian soil and supplied by British industry. Domestic iron production increased and new canals were constructed in South Wales and the iron districts of Staffordshire and Shropshire. A major trade crisis occurred in 1810 as Napoleon carried the Continental Blockade to its maximum effectiveness. Moreover, many exporters in Britain had anticipated a bonanza from the opening up of the markets of Spanish America and had invested heavily in inventories intended for the colonists now free to buy British goods directly and cut off from normal supplies from Spain. But these markets were not receptive to British goods and had been independent of the mother country for many decades. The paper pound depreciated sharply on the Hamburg exchange and a Parliamentary inquiry was launched into the responsibility of the Bank of England for the depreciation, presumably by excessive note issue unrestrained by convertibility. Or so claimed the famous *Bullion Report*, issued in 1811. The Peninsular Army, meanwhile, was achieving more and more military success.

1811–16

Recovery of the stock market was slow, partly because the Bank of England, chastened by the criticism of the Parliamentary committee and by the bankruptcies of a number of clients who had recently been admitted to its discounting facilities, restricted its domestic credit activities. But exports resumed as the needs of the new markets were identified and as the tide of mili-

tary results turned in favor of Britain and its Continental allies. Capital began to flow to the Continent after Napoleon's defeat in Russia, only to be interrupted by his Hundred Days return in early 1815, but resumed massively in 1816. The demobilization of British forces after the Battle of Waterloo was sudden, as was the cancellation of government orders for military and naval supplies. A classic deflation occurred as the Bank of England sought to stabilize the exchanges before resuming convertibility, and in so doing revealed the insolvency of a number of country banks which had proliferated during the period of the paper pound. Nevertheless, a major building boom occurred in London, revealing new opportunities for the output of the ironworks that had arisen to meet the military and naval demands of British forces during twenty-five years of intermittent, but intense, warfare. The Bank of England had prospered greatly as the fiscal agent for the government during this period, becoming a true central bank, responsible for regulating the nation's supply of money and credit. It failed to live up to its new responsibilities, however, in the stock-market panic of 1825. The resulting liquidity crisis forced widespread bankruptcies and dissolution of many country banks, which began to be replaced by joint-stock banks.

Larry Neal

See also BANK OF ENGLAND; BULLIONIST CONTROVERSIES; CRISIS OF 1819; PANIC OF 1825; RICARDO, DAVID; THORNTON, HENRY

Bibliography

Gayer, A. D., W. W. Rostow, and A. J. Schwartz. 1953. *The Growth and Fluctuation of the British Economy, 1790–1850: An Historical, Statistical, and Theoretical Study of Britain's Economic Development.* 2 vols. Oxford: Clarendon Press.

Neal, L. 1990. *The Rise of Financial Capitalism: International Capital Markets in the Age of Reason.* Cambridge: Cambridge Univ. Press.

Smart, W. [1910] 1964. *Economic Annals of the Nineteenth Century.* Vol. 1, *1801–1820.* Reprint. New York: A. M. Kelley.

Natural Rate of Interest

Prominent among older theories of inflation is the view that a rising price level reflects a discrepancy between two rates of interest. One, the *market* or *money* rate, is the observable rate that banks charge on loans; it clears the market for bank credit. The other is the unobservable *natural* or *equilibrium* rate that clears the goods market by equating saving with investment at full employment and that also corresponds to capital's marginal productivity or the expected yield on investment. First enunciated by Henry Thornton ([1802] 1939) and later developed by Knut Wicksell ([1898] 1936), the two-rate doctrine figured in the business-cycle theories of such leading twentieth-century economists as J. M. Keynes (before the *General Theory*), R. G. Hawtrey, D. H. Robertson, G. Cassel, B. Ohlin, G. Myrdal, L. von Mises, and F. A. Hayek. Moreover, it underlay the celebrated policy rule that the central bank should maintain price stability by adjusting the market rate in response to movements in the price level.

Basic Ideas

The two-rate doctrine describes what happens when real shocks to the natural rate or the interest-pegging policies of the central bank cause the market and natural rates to diverge. Suppose the expected yield on investment rises relative to rates charged on loans and paid to depositors, implying that the natural rate exceeds the market rate. Investors would then demand more funds from the banking system than are deposited by savers. If banks accommodate these extra loan demands by creating new demand deposits, the resulting monetary expansion would underwrite the excess demand for goods generated by the gap between investment and saving. A persistent and cumulative rise in prices would follow until the interest differential vanished. This would happen when banks raised their loan rates to prevent depletion of their cash reserves by drains into hand-to-hand circulation. Such drains arise from the price increases that necessitate additional cash for transactions settled in coin and currency. Conversely, a loan rate *above* the natural rate produces falling prices and a cash inflow. The inflow of cash reserves induces banks to reduce their rates in an effort to stimulate borrowing. These adjustments, however, may be too late to prevent substantial price-level movements. Here is the rationale for the central bank to keep the two rates in line by promptly moving its discount rate in the direction in which prices are changing, stopping only when price movements cease.

The Two-Rate Model

Henry Thornton and Knut Wicksell incorporated the foregoing ideas into a coherent analytical framework yielding strong policy conclusions. At the risk of oversimplifying what is in fact a complex and subtle theory, their schema can be represented by five equations relating the variables planned real investment at full employment, I, planned real full employment saving, S, the loan rate, i, the natural rate, r, excess aggregate demand, E, the change in the money stock, dM/dt, and the change in the price level change, dP/dt. The equations are as follows:

$$I - S = a(r - i), a > 0, \qquad (1)$$

which says that investment exceeds saving when the loan rate falls below the natural rate;

$$I - S \equiv dM/dt, \qquad (2)$$

which says that, because banks finance investment by creating money as well as by intermediating saving, the investment-saving gap identically equals the new money created to finance investment;

$$I - S \equiv E, \qquad (3)$$

which says that the investment-saving gap is identically equal to the excess aggregate demand for goods;

$$dP/dt = kE, k > 0, \qquad (4)$$

which says that prices rise in proportion to excess demand;

$$di/dt = b(dP/dt), b > 0, \qquad (5)$$

which says that bankers eventually raise loan rates in proportion to inflation to protect their reserves from cash drains into hand-to-hand circulation.

Substituting equations (3) and (1) into equation (4), and equation (1) into equation (2), yields the equations:

$$dP/dt = ka(r - i) \qquad (6)$$

and

$$dM/dt = a(r - i). \qquad (7)$$

Equations (6) and (7) state that inflation and the money growth that underlies it both stem from the discrepancy between the two interest rates. Here is the Thornton-Wicksell model's most famous prediction. Equation (5) implies that the market rate converges to the natural rate, as can be seen by substituting the equation (6) into equation (5) and solving the resulting differential equation $di/dt = bka(r - i)$ for the time path of the loan rate. When the market and natural rates coincide, saving equals investment, excess demand vanishes, money and prices stabilize, and banks lend only what savers deposit with them. These of course are the well-known Thornton-Wicksell conditions for monetary equilibrium.

Policy Applications

The Thornton-Wicksell two-rate model was designed to show what happens when banks, commercial or central, set market rates too low or too high for equilibrium. Thornton first used the model to explain the cause of the inflationary overissue of money by the Bank of England during the Napoleonic wars. He traced inflation to statutory usury ceilings which constrained the bank to a 5-percent maximum loan rate just when the natural rate, buoyed by the wartime boom, rose well above the ceiling. And in the 1920s, Mises, Haberler, Machlup, and Bresciani-Turroni all used the two-rate model to attribute the German hyperinflation to the Reichsbank's policy of pegging its discount rate at 12 percent (later raised to 90 percent) when the market rate of interest was more than 7000 percent per annum. This huge differential made it extremely profitable for the banks to borrow from the Reichsbank and relend to their customers, further expanding the money supply. In the 1960s and 1970s, Monetarists used the model to blame the Federal Reserve for causing inflation by pegging the federal funds rate at below-equilibrium levels.

Still other uses have been found for the model. Both Thornton and Wicksell employed it to refute the real-bills doctrine according to which monetary overissue is impossible if banks lend only on sound commercial paper arising from real transactions in goods and services. Thornton and Wicksell pointed out that loan demand becomes insatiable and the corresponding supply of commercial bills becomes inexhaustible when the loan rate of interest is below the expected rate of return on new capital investment. In such circumstances, the real-bills criterion fails to bar overissue.

Finally, Wicksell employed the two-rate model to resolve the famous Gibson paradox.

The paradox is that prices and market interest rates historically move together when theory suggests that they should move inversely. These direct co-movements Wicksell attributed to sluggish adjustment of market rates to prior changes in the natural rate. He noted that a rising natural rate, by creating a positive rate disparity, causes prices to rise. Market rates quickly begin rising to catch up with the natural rate, thus accounting for their observed co-movement with prices.

These examples attest to the model's lasting usefulness as a tool for monetary analysis. Many economists continue to gain insight from the two-rate distinction. Perhaps the main challenge to the model comes from New Classical proponents of rational expectations who deny that market rates can ever deviate systematically from their natural equilibrium values. Whether this criticism invalidates the two-rate model only further empirical research can determine.

Thomas M. Humphrey

See also Austrian Theory of Business Cycles; Hayek, Friedrich August [von]; Keynes, John Maynard; Lachmann, Ludwig Maurits ; Mises, Ludwig Edler von; Monetary Disequilibrium Theories of the Business Cycle; Monetary Policy; Real Bills Doctrine; Robertson, Dennis Holme; Savings and Investment; Sraffa, Piero; Stockholm School; Thornton, Henry; Wicksell, Johan Gustav Knut

Bibliography

Cassel, G. 1928. "The Rate of Interest, the Bank Rate, and the Stabilization of Prices." *Quarterly Journal of Economics* 42:511–29.

Humphrey, T. 1976. "Interest Rates, Expectations, and the Wicksellian Policy Rule." *Atlantic Economic Journal* 4:9–20.

———. 1986. "Cumulative Process Models From Thornton to Wicksell." Federal Reserve Bank of Richmond *Economic Review,* May/June, 18–24.

Laidler, D. [1972] 1975. "On Wicksell's Theory of Price Level Dynamics." Chap. 5 in *Essays on Money and Inflation.* Chicago: Univ. of Chicago Press.

Leijonhufvud, A. 1981. "The Wicksell Connection." Chap. 7 in *Information and Coordination: Essays in Macroeconomic Theory.* New York: Oxford Univ. Press.

Patinkin, D. 1965. *Money, Interest, and Prices*. 2d ed. New York: Harper and Row.

Thornton, H. [1802] 1939. *An Enquiry into the Nature and Effects of the Paper Credit of Great Britain*. Edited with an introduction by F. A. von Hayek. London: Allen and Unwin.

Uhr, C. 1960. *Economic Doctrines of Knut Wicksell*. Berkeley: Univ. of California Press.

Wicksell, K. [1898] 1936. *Interest and Prices*. Translation. London: Macmillan.

———. [1906] 1935. *Lectures on Political Economy*. Vol. 2, *Money*. Translation. London: Routledge.

———. 1907. "The Influence of the Rate of Interest on Commodity Prices." *Economic Journal* 17:213–20.

Natural Rate of Unemployment

Economists typically classify measured unemployment in one of three categories: frictional, structural, or cyclical. Workers are frictionally unemployed if they are between jobs, and structurally unemployed if their skills do not match existing vacancies or if vacancies and the unemployed are mismatched geographically. Cyclical unemployment refers to the fluctuations in the measured unemployment rate associated with changes in business conditions.

The notion of a natural rate of unemployment was introduced independently by Milton Friedman and Edmund Phelps, who were seeking to distinguish real from nominal influences on the unemployment rate. The natural rate of unemployment is said to include frictional and structural unemployment, both of which are assumed to depend solely on real factors. Frictional unemployment, which is an informational problem, depends on factors such as unemployment-compensation laws and the cost of job search. Structural unemployment depends on factors such as minimum-wage laws, the extent of unionization, and the skill and education level of workers.

The real factors affecting frictional and structural unemployment change over time, so the natural rate of unemployment is not necessarily constant. For example, the natural rate of unemployment in the United States rose during the 1970s, in part because of the large number of baby boomers who entered the labor force. Young and inexperienced, they took longer to find jobs than workers who had built up skills from previous work experience.

Cyclical unemployment is the amount by which the measured unemployment rate deviates from the natural rate. The natural-rate hypothesis contends that nominal influences, especially monetary growth, can affect cyclical unemployment, but not frictional and structural unemployment.

To illustrate, suppose that a sustained monetary stimulus is unexpectedly applied to an economy at the natural rate of unemployment. The inflation rate will rise, which will cause nominal wages to rise, but not as fast as prices. As a result, the real wage rate will fall, inducing firms to increase the quantity of labor demanded. Workers, however, base their labor-leisure decisions on the expected real wage, which is the nominal wage relative to the expected future price level. Workers observe nominal wages rising, but, because the monetary stimulus was unexpected, do not expect the price level to rise. The expected real wage therefore rises. As a result, the workers mistakenly supply the additional quantity of labor services that firms demand and measured unemployment falls below the natural rate. However, once inflation is fully anticipated, workers reduce their supply of labor services and real wages return to the previous level, restoring the unemployment rate to the original natural rate of unemployment. This adjustment is slow, because workers are assumed to form their expectations of the price level adaptively. The natural rate of unemployment is unaffected by this process, because the real factors determining frictional and structural unemployment are unaltered by nominal changes in aggregate demand.

The idea that the natural rate of unemployment depends on real factors, while nominal influences cause temporary deviations of actual unemployment from the natural rate, has at least two significant policy implications. First, any attempt by policymakers to permanently reduce unemployment below the natural rate is doomed to fail in the long run, but will succeed in permanently raising the rate of inflation. Second, in the long run, an economy can operate at the natural rate of unemployment with any stable inflation rate, which is why the natural rate is sometimes called the non-accelerating-inflation rate of unemployment (NAIRU). Thus, zero inflation, or price stability, is completely consistent with full employment.

This version of the natural-rate hypothesis implies that observed business cycles are persistent deviations of actual unemployment around a relatively stable natural rate resulting from unexpected changes in nominal aggregate demand. New Classical macroeconomics adopts the natural-rate hypothesis that the long-run rate of unemployment is independent of changes in nominal aggregate demand, but questions both the persistence of unemployment deviations and the stability of the natural rate. Lucas ([1972] 1981) developed one variant of New Classical macroeconomics by incorporating the notion that workers' expectations of the price level are formed rationally—that is, based on all currently available information, instead of just past information, as implied by the adaptive-expectations assumption. Since workers use all available information, including current levels of macroeconomic variables that influence the future price level, rational expectations implies that the expected price level adjusts quickly to changes in monetary growth. Thus, deviations of unemployment from the natural rate are assumed to be shorter than in the Friedman-Phelps version.

The second variant of New Classical macroeconomics is the real business-cycle model advanced by Kydland and Prescott (1982) and by Long and Plosser (1983). This version differs from the Friedman-Phelps view by arguing that observed business cycles largely reflect an unstable natural rate. Instability in the natural rate is assumed to be caused by random changes in real economic factors.

The natural-rate hypothesis has been an integral part of macroeconomics for two decades. However, it has been questioned by some economists attempting to explain the puzzle of persistently high unemployment in several European countries during the 1980s and 1990s. Early in the decade the unemployment rates rose in the United States and most European countries in response to falling inflation and a slowdown in economic growth. According to the natural-rate hypothesis, measured unemployment rates should have gradually fallen towards the rates that persisted before disinflation. The predicted reduction did occur in the United States, but not in Europe. France, West Germany, and the United Kingdom all reduced their inflation rates, but their rates of unemployment have apparently risen permanently.

Some attempts to explain the behavior of European unemployment rates utilize what has become known as the *hysteresis* hypothesis. Proponents of this view argue that changes in the actual unemployment rate can alter the natural rate of unemployment. Therefore, changes in nominal aggregate-demand growth that change measured unemployment rates can alter the natural rate of unemployment, contrary to the natural-rate hypothesis.

While views differ about why the natural rate of unemployment may lag the measured rate, discussions focus on three suspects. One is that a period of high unemployment can reduce productive capacity, for example if a decline in nominal aggregate demand reduces the rate of investment, the economy's capital stock may be permanently reduced. Conversely, a nominal-aggregate-demand stimulus can permanently increase the level of employment. Another view contends that high unemployment reduces the skill level of the labor force, making it harder for the unemployed to find new work. A nominal-demand-induced expansion could enable these workers to be reemployed and increase their skill levels through on-the-job training. A third explanation focuses on the difference between insiders (those who have jobs) and outsiders (those who do not). Insiders are assumed to have little incentive to allow the outsiders to reduce wages to obtain employment. Thus, the insiders use their market power to keep real wages, and therefore unemployment, high. Changes in measured unemployment cause changes in the natural rate of unemployment, because when unemployment rises, layoffs raise the number of outsiders who cannot get back in. During periods of falling unemployment some outsiders become insiders able to affect wages.

In summary, the natural-rate view of unemployment was important in pointing out the temporary nature of changes in economic output induced by nominal changes in aggregate demand. Under the natural-rate hypothesis, unemployment cycles are temporary, though persistent, fluctuations of measured unemployment around a stable natural rate. This view, however, has been challenged by both the New Classical macroeconomics and the hysteresis hypothesis. Which view is correct is an empirical issue which remains unsettled.

Thomas E. Hall

See also EXPECTATIONS; FRIEDMAN, MILTON; MONETARY POLICY; MONETARY DISEQUILIBRIUM THEORIES OF THE BUSINESS CYCLE;

MONETARY EQUILIBRIUM THEORIES OF THE BUSINESS CYCLE; MONETARY POLICY; NEUTRALITY OF MONEY; NEW KEYNESIAN ECONOMICS; PHILLIPS CURVE; RATIONAL EXPECTATIONS; SEARCH THEORY; UNEMPLOYMENT; WAGE RIGIDITY

Bibliography

Blanchard, O. J. and L. H. Summers. 1986. "Hysteresis and the European Unemployment Problem." In *NBER Macroeconomics Annual 1986,* edited by S. Fischer, 15–78. Cambridge: MIT Press.

Cross, R., ed. 1988. *Unemployment, Hysteresis and the Natural Rate Hypothesis.* Oxford: Basil Blackwell.

Friedman, M. [1968] 1969. "The Role of Monetary Policy." Chap. 5 in *The Optimum Quantity of Money and Other Essays.* Chicago: Aldine.

Kydland, F. E. and E. C. Prescott. 1982. "Time to Build and Aggregate Fluctuations." *Econometrica* 50:1345–70.

Lawrence, R. Z. and C. L. Schultze. 1987. *Barriers to European Growth: A Transatlantic View.* Washington, D.C.: Brookings Institution.

Long, J. B., Jr. and C. I. Plosser. 1983. "Real Business Cycles." *Journal of Political Economy* 91:39–69.

Lucas, R. E., Jr. [1972] 1981. "Expectations and the Neutrality of Money." In *Studies in Business Cycle Theory,* 66–89. Cambridge: MIT Press.

Phelps, E. S. 1967. "Phillips Curves, Expectations of Inflation, and Optimal Unemployment Over Time." *Economica* 34:254–81.

Phelps, E. S., et. al. 1970. *Microeconomic Foundations of Employment and Inflation Theory.* New York: Norton.

Neutrality of Money

The *neutrality* of money has had numerous meanings over the years. Patinkin (1987) traces the entire history of its use. Currently, the term is used in two specific ways. The first refers to the division of a static economic model into a real part, in which the quantity of output is determined, and a nominal part, in which nominal prices and wages are determined given the real quantities from the first part. In the second instance, the neutrality of money has come to mean that all anticipated monetary and fiscal policy—all aggregate-demand policy—has no effect on output and employment in either the short or the long run. The remainder of this article discusses the theoretical and empirical issues surrounding these two meanings.

Monetary neutrality in a static macroeconomic model is synonymous with the *classical dichotomy.* Standard models, such as Sargent (1986, chap. 1) exhibit this property, so that changes in the quantity of money cause proportional changes in all nominal variables, leaving real quantities unchanged. In other words, the model is homogeneous of degree zero in all nominal prices, nominal wages, and nominal money.

The following is a very simple version of such a model:

$$y = f(n) \text{ — Production function} \tag{1}$$

$$n^d = f'^{-1}(W/P) \text{ — Labor demand} \tag{2}$$

$$n^s = g(W/P) \text{ — Labor supply} \tag{3}$$

$$y \equiv c + i + \bar{g} \text{ — National income} \atop \text{accounts identity} \tag{4}$$

$$c = c(y) \text{ — Consumption function} \tag{5}$$

$$i = i(r) \text{ — Investment function} \tag{6}$$

$$M^d/P = L(y,r) \text{ — Money-demand function} \tag{7}$$

$$M^s/P = \bar{M}/P \text{ — Money-supply function} \tag{8}$$

where y is real output, n is the level of employment, W and P are nominal wages and prices, c and i are real consumption and investment, g is government expenditure on goods and services, r is the real interest rate, and M is the nominal money stock. The superscripts d and s refer to demand and supply, the overbar signifies that a variable is determined exogenously, and f'^{-1} is the inverse of the first derivative of the production function.

If we assume that the labor market clears, so $n^s = n^d$, equations (1), (2), and (3) determine the level of employment, output, and the real wage, without reference to either the level of government expenditure or the stock of nominal money. The real and nominal parts of this system are separate. Furthermore, changes in money have no impact on any real variables. Nominal prices and nominal wages adjust to keep the real wage and the level of real money balances constant.

Thus far, the discussion has proceeded in terms of a timeless, static model of the macro-economy. It is now useful to introduce time, and distinguish between short-run and long-run neutrality. Let us think of the short-run as several years and the long-run as a limiting concept. Until recently, there was consensus that money is neutral in the long run. That is to say, the impact of all monetary changes on output is eventually exhausted, so that the impact of changes in the quantity of money is limited to prices. Current developments in growth theory, primarily Romer's (1986) endogenous growth model, imply that short-run output declines (recessions) may cause decreases in (human) capital accumulation, which has permanent consequences. It may also be noted here that there is little consensus on whether money is *superneutral*. Superneutrality refers to the impact of changes in the rate of monetary growth on real variables. There are reasons to believe that, say, an increase in the rate of monetary growth can have real effects, as it increases the inflation tax on holding real balances and forces agents to use additional resources to change their prices.

The remainder of this article is devoted to the theoretical and empirical arguments for and against short-run neutrality. The work of Lucas ([1973] 1981), Barro (1978) and other New Classical macroeconomists has extended the concept of the neutrality of money to mean that an *anticipated* change in money, or any other aggregate-demand policy variable, does not change the level of real output in the short run. Their argument combines market clearing with rational expectations to yield the result that it is solely unanticipated policy, such as unexpected monetary shocks, that can affect output. Furthermore, by assuming that the markets for goods and labor are competitive, and clear each period, these researchers conclude that such shocks should be short-lived.

It is useful to phrase the issue in terms of the language of macroeconomics textbooks. The proposition that money is neutral in the long run is the statement that shifts in aggregate demand do not affect the *location* of the long-run aggregate-supply curve. Put another way, current changes in the quantity of money do not affect the natural rate of unemployment. Thus, the statement that money is neutral in the short run means that, following a disturbance, the short-run aggregate-supply curve shifts quickly to its long-run position.

The empirical case for short-run neutrality is extremely weak. Cecchetti (1986) derives a test under very general conditions that requires only that the econometrician choose the length of the maximum lag at which unanticipated money may influence output. The finding that money growth lagged is correlated with output movements contradicts the New Classical proposition that aggregate-demand policy is neutral in the short-run. It is worth noting that the evidence of long-horizon effects of money on output is prima-facie evidence in favor of the long-run nonneutralities emphasized in endogenous growth theory.

The New Keynesian Economics, surveyed in Ball, Mankiw, and Romer (1988), provides the main alternative to the New Classical proposition of short-run neutrality. While continuing to maintain the assumption that expectations are rational, New Keynesians examine the implication of a monopolistically competitive structure in which changing prices is costly, and prices change at different times. Nominal rigidities are important for two reasons. First, the cost of changing prices creates an *aggregate-demand externality;* and second, the assumption of staggered price setting yields a mechanism for monetary shocks to be propagated over time. We now discuss each of these nonneutralities in turn.

To understand the source of the aggregate-demand externality, assume that an individual firm's demand depends on its relative price and the level of aggregate real balances, which is a measure of aggregate demand. This can be written as:

$$y_i^D = \left(\frac{P_i}{P}\right)^{-\varepsilon}\left(\frac{M}{P}\right), \qquad (9)$$

where P_i is the individual firm's price level, P is the aggregate price level, and M is the stock of nominal money, and ε is the relative-price elasticity of demand. Now consider an experiment in which M drops. If the firm's price before the monetary contraction was set at the profit-maximizing level, then, as pointed out by Akerlof and Yellen (1985), according to the envelope theorem, the loss from not adjusting P_i is second order. This non-adjustment at the firm level implies rigidity of the aggregate price level, and generates a first-order fall in real balances, reducing the aggregate demand for goods. While this externality will generate first-order output fluctuations, Ball and Romer (1990) show that the welfare loss is also second-order. The aggregate-demand externality clearly implies monetary nonneutrality, but may not be important.

The second source of nonneutrality in New Keynesian models emphasizes the temporal propagation of monetary shocks. The issue here is to understand how a purely nominal disturbance could have long-lasting real effects that resemble business-cycle fluctuations. How is it that following a monetary contraction a recession can last for several years? Even if prices are changed frequently, asynchronous timing may cause shocks to affect output for a long time.

To understand how this works, assume the opposite—that firms' pricing decisions are perfectly synchronized. As noted by Ball and Cecchetti (1988), this is the only possibility under perfect competition, and so the results are analogous to those of the New Classical macroeconomics. If all firms change prices on the first day of every month, then adjustment to any monetary shock takes at most one month. While the shock can change real balances during the month, every firm adjusts at the beginning of the next month, knowing that all other firms are doing the same. This price adjustment will eliminate the real-balance effect of the shock. Lags for data collection in the real world may cause a one-month delay in this process. Nevertheless, the economy jumps quickly back to the optimal level and money is neutral in the short run.

Now consider the alternative in which firms adjust every month, but half change prices on the first of the month, while the other half change on the fifteenth. The reasons for this could be that firms receive idiosyncratic shocks at different times, as suggested by Ball and Romer (1989), or that firms stagger decisions in order to collect information, as described in Ball and Cecchetti (1988). Now consider a monetary shock that comes on the tenth of the month. Clearly this shock was unanticipated by the group that adjusted on the first of the month, and so their price will differ from those they would have set had they foreseen the shock. By contrast, the second group, the one adjusting on the fifteenth, has the opportunity to take the shock into account. The assumption of imperfect competition implies that there is some substitutability between the products of the firms adjusting prices at different times, which is why the relative price appears in equation (9). That

firms care about relative prices means that the firms adjusting on the fifteenth do not want their price to move too far from the prices of the firms that adjust on the first. Thus, the expectation error built into the first group's prices finds its way into the second group's prices as well. Similarly, when the first group's turn to change prices again arrives on the first of the month following the shock, they will take into account the prices of the firms that last set their prices, which now include the expectation errors of their original price set before the shock. In this way the impact of the shock dies out only asymptotically, with the effect peaking after all firms have adjusted prices once. The result is that nominal shocks have only short-run real effects.

Stephen G. Cecchetti

See also AGGREGATE SUPPLY AND DEMAND; EXPECTATIONS; MONETARY EQUILIBRIUM THEORIES OF THE BUSINESS CYCLE; MONETARY POLICY; NEW KEYNESIAN ECONOMICS; RATIONAL EXPECTATIONS

Bibliography

Akerlof, G. A. and J. L. Yellen. 1985. "Can Small Deviations from Rationality Make Significant Differences in Economic Equilibria?" *American Economic Review* 75:708–20.

Ball, L. and S. G. Cecchetti. 1988. "Imperfect Information and Staggered Price Setting." *American Economic Review* 78:999–1018.

Ball, L., N. G. Mankiw, and D. Romer. 1988. "The New Keynesian Economics and the Output-Inflation Trade-off." *Brookings Papers on Economic Activity*, Number One, 1–82.

Ball, L. and D. Romer. 1989. "The Equilibrium and Optimal Timing of Price Changes." *Review of Economic Studies* 56:179–98.

———. 1990. "Real Rigidities and the Non-Neutrality of Money." *Review of Economic Studies* 57:183–203.

Barro, R. J. 1978. "Unanticipated Money, Output and the Price Level." *Journal of Political Economy* 86:549–80.

Cecchetti, S. G. 1986. "Testing Short-Run Neutrality." *Journal of Monetary Economics* 17:409–23.

Lucas, R. E. Jr. [1973] 1981. Some International Evidence on the Output-Inflation

Tradeoff." In *Studies in Business-Cycle Theory,* 131–45. Cambridge: MIT Press.

Patinkin, D. 1987. "Neutrality of Money." In *The New Palgrave Dictionary of Economics.* Vol. 3. Edited by J. Eatwell, M. Milgate, and P. Newman. London: Macmillan.

Romer, P. M. 1986. "Increasing Returns and Long-Run Growth." *Journal of Political Economy* 94:1002–37.

Sargent, T. J. 1986. *Macroeconomic Theory.* 2d ed. New York: Academic Press.

New Keynesian Economics

Since the late 1970s, there has been much research on what has come to be known as the New Keynesian economics. Like the earlier Keynesian approach to business-cycle theory found in textbooks, this work emphasizes that the allocation of resources may not be efficient over the course of the business cycle, that money may not be neutral in the short run, and that activist monetary and fiscal policies can be welfare-improving. Unlike earlier Keynesian economics, the approach is grounded in rational-expectations models derived from individual utility and profit maximization. Also unlike the textbook Keynesian model, but perhaps in keeping with early Keynesian thinking, New Keynesian theorists question the existence of a unique long-run (*natural*) rate of unemployment. New Keynesian economics, however, is still more a collection of related ideas than a fully coherent and consistent paradigm (and some contributors would not even describe themselves or the literature as Keynesian).

This essay first briefly describes the main types of models, then evaluates their ability to explain the data, and finally considers their welfare and policy implications. Space limitations preclude the provision of a guide to the literature; the reader is referred to excellent and more detailed surveys by Mankiw and Romer (1991) and Gordon (1990) that contain extensive references.

Before the 1970s, Keynesian models generally assumed fixed (or sticky) prices and wages. New Classical economists criticized such models for their lack of microeconomic underpinnings. In response, some researchers considered models with maximizing agents and price rigidities, and showed how rationing in one market had spillover effects on behavior in other markets. But most subsequent Keynesian research focused directly on the microfoundations of price and wage determination, leading almost inevitably to models of imperfect or monopolistic competition to explain price setting in the goods market, and to contracting and other wage-setting models in the labor market.

Models of imperfect competition are of particular importance in the New Keynesian economics. Recent research emphasizes demand spillovers in general-equilibrium models of imperfect competition; the cyclical behavior of markups as a consequence of entry and exit or of sustainable collusion over the business cycle; and the staggering of pricing decisions. The key insight of this branch of the literature, though, is that nominal rigidities arising from small costs of changing prices (*menu costs*) can have effects on equilibrium quantities and welfare that are an order of magnitude larger than the costs: small changes in a firm's price have second-order effects on its profits, but first-order effects on welfare.

Work on *efficiency wages* considers the wage-setting decision when workers' productivity is positively related to their wage. Such models can explain rigid real wages in excess of market-clearing levels. Researchers have isolated a number of sources of such a wage-productivity link, such as firms' desires to reduce shirking or high worker turnover. *Implicit-contract* theories also explain real-wage rigidities: absent perfect insurance markets, risk-averse workers might accept a reduced average wage in return for the guarantee of a stable wage. Finally, New Keynesian work on credit markets focuses on the role of information imperfections in restricting bank loans and generating credit rationing.

Models of *thin-market* or *trading externalities* dispense with the Walrasian auctioneer and consider markets where buyers and sellers cannot be costlessly matched. If many traders are active in a market, it may be relatively easy to consummate trades and the incentive to participate may be correspondingly high, while if few participate, trade is costlier and the incentive to participate is low. There is then a *strategic complementarity:* increased activity by one agent causes increased activity by others. Sufficiently strong complementarities can generate social increasing returns and *coordination failures*—multiple, Pareto-ranked equilibria. The economy can get stuck in a low-activity equilibrium even if prices are flexible and even though everyone would be better off in an equilibrium with a higher level of economic activity. Expectations (and perhaps "animal spirits") then matter for equilibrium selection.

Models of coordination failure are related to work on *sunspots,* wherein extrinsic uncertainty influences equilibria, and also to the *new growth theory,* which suggests that physical- or human-capital accumulation may have significant external effects. As do writers on thick-market externalities, the new growth theorists emphasize increasing returns at a society-wide level, with a consequent possibility of multiple growth paths. Coordination failures arise also in models with technological externalities or imperfect competition, and price stickiness may itself result from coordination failures. Finally, a related idea is that of *hysteresis,* which suggests that the natural rate of unemployment is not unique; rather, the level of unemployment is history-dependent. For example, workers who are unemployed may lose some human capital, becoming less employable as a consequence.

Theoretical contributions must be evaluated in large measure by their ability to explain the data. New Keynesian economists have not, for the most part, taken the approach of theorists working in the competing *real business-cycle* paradigm, constructing and simulating stochastic general-equilibrium models of the economy. Rather, the empirical arguments in favor of New Keynesian theory are that the different contributions explain certain stylized facts of the macroeconomy better than do real business-cycle or other New Classical theories.

Imperfect competition and menu costs provide an explanation of observed nominal rigidities and, as an immediate corollary, monetary nonneutralities. One interpretation is that price stickiness gives rise to an upward-sloping aggregate supply curve, similar to the Lucas supply curve. In the presence of demand shocks, therefore, prices will be procyclical. A related point is that these models help explain why quantities move more than prices over the business cycle, although a combination of menu costs and real rigidities is probably required to explain fluctuations of the magnitude observed in the data. Imperfect competition also provides an explanation of the procyclicality of the *Solow residual* (that is, the change in output not explained by changes in inputs), since the residual as conventionally measured includes firms' monopoly profits. It should be noted that there is also direct evidence of significant imperfect competition and price stickiness in the U.S. economy.

New Keynesian models equally explain some of the stylized facts of the labor market. Since employment is procyclical, decreasing returns to labor imply that, other things equal, the marginal product of labor is countercyclical. But if prices are flexible and markets are competitive, the marginal product of labor equals the real wage, which is procyclical. (The real wage is also procyclical as a matter of theory if the labor market clears and leisure is a normal good.) Real business-cycle models explain the apparent paradox by assuming that the marginal product of labor is procyclical because of technology shocks. A New Keynesian explanation is countercyclical markups, which can reconcile the procyclicality of employment and the real wage and for which the data provide some support. New Keynesians also observe that wage and employment decisions may in any case be separated in an efficient labor contract.

New Classical theories suggest that employment falls in recessions, because workers choose to substitute leisure over the course of the cycle. This not only requires substantial intertemporal substitutability of labor, but is also hard to reconcile with the fact that most of the flow into unemployment arises from involuntary separations rather than quits, and the observations that quits are procyclical and layoffs countercyclical. Efficiency-wage models, by contrast, easily explain unemployment: if firms do not demand all the available labor at the efficiency wage, there will be unemployment; the real wage does not fall to eliminate this unemployment since a reduction in wages reduces productivity. Observed interindustry wage differentials, whereby essentially similar workers receive different wages, provide indirect support for the efficiency-wage hypothesis; more direct tests have also found efficiency-wage effects. Contracting models can, under some assumptions, generate layoffs and unemployment, but do not deliver robust conclusions: the implications of optimal contracting depend crucially on the information structure, the possibility of worksharing and severance pay, and the preferences of firms and workers.

Recent empirical work in macroeconomics reveals that shocks to the economy exhibit considerable persistence and may have permanent effects: the GNP time series may have a unit root. Real business-cycle theorists conclude that the GNP time series is dominated by technology shocks—shocks to supply rather than demand. New Keynesian theories offer other explanations: hysteresis or coordination failures can explain why demand shocks could have permanent effects. Wage and price staggering, and New Keynesian theories of the monetary transmission mechanism when credit markets are imperfect, can also explain the long-lasting effects of demand shocks.

Finally, New Keynesian models, like old Keynesian models, exhibit multiplier effects. Demand spillovers from imperfect competition can cause increased output in one sector to increase output in other sectors. Because of these strategic complementarities, small sector-specific shocks can generate correlated movements in other sectors. Such models explain relatively large fluctuations and comovements across sectors with small initial shocks. It is unclear to what extent demand spillovers are mitigated by life-cycle consumption smoothing, and thus whether or not they underlie substantial fluctuations at business-cycle frequencies.

New Keynesian theories share with recent New Classical theory an emphasis on microfoundations, but differ crucially in their welfare and policy implications. New Classical theories are often "Robinson Crusoe" models with flexible prices and competitive markets: the competitive equilibrium is Pareto-efficient, and there is no scope for active countercyclical policies. New Keynesian models, by contrast, generally contain distortions that occasion inefficiency. Even if all agents are identical, the economy need not necessarily behave as would the representative agent. There is no presumption that equilibrium is efficient, even in the long run, and government policies may be, at least in principle, welfare-improving.

Under imperfect competition, the equilibrium of the economy is generally suboptimal and characterized by insufficient production. Imperfect-competition models therefore have the appealing property that welfare rises in booms and falls in recessions, unlike the textbook model in which fluctuations on either side of the long-run equilibrium are equally bad. Given menu costs, expansionary monetary policies are thus welfare-improving, but stabilization is less obviously desirable since positive and negative shocks cancel each other out in welfare terms (to a first approximation).

If the economy exhibits multiple equilibria, government can be a coordinating agent by promoting sufficient economic activity to guide the economy to the best available equilibrium. One could argue that coordination failures provide a rationale for *indicative planning,* and even (though it is surely stretching a point) that government itself is a Coasian response to coordination failure. Other New Keynesian models suggest further inefficiencies: equilibria in efficiency-wage or credit-rationing models are not in general efficient. Finally, interactions between different distortions can imply multiplier effects in welfare terms and are important for understanding how inefficiencies are ultimately manifested in the economy. For example, inefficiently low demand for labor resulting from imperfect competition in the goods market may cause unemployment if firms pay efficiency wages; if the labor market is competitive and free from distortions, the consequence may instead (although need not) be underemployment.

There is thus far little formal work on appropriate macroeconomic policies in New Keynesian models, and not all the research to date necessarily supports traditional prescriptions. Even given a case in principle for government intervention, moreover, the well-known practical difficulties of policymaking still apply; it is perfectly reasonable to accept New Keynesian arguments, while opposing countercyclical macroeconomic policies. And there is an unavoidable tension in any Keynesian macroeconomics based on microeconomic principles. New Keynesian models identify particular microeconomic distortions as the source of inefficiencies. Standard welfare economics suggests that the best remedy is to correct such distortions directly. Any call for countercyclical policy appeals implicitly to an argument that such correction is impossible and that macroeconomic policies are a second-best response.

Andrew John

See also EFFICIENCY WAGES; FISCAL POLICY; IMPLICIT CONTRACTS; MONETARY EQUILIBRIUM THEORIES OF THE BUSINESS CYCLE; MONETARY POLICY; NEUTRALITY OF MONEY; OKUN, ARTHUR M.; PRICE-QUANTITY ADJUSTMENT; PRICE RIGIDITY; REAL BUSINESS-CYCLE THEORIES; SEARCH THEORY; WAGE RIGIDITY

Bibliography
Gordon, R. J. 1990. "What is New-Keynesian Economics?" *Journal of Economic Literature* 28:1115–71.

Mankiw, N. G. and D. Romer. 1991. "Introduction." In *New Keynesian Economics*, edited by N. G. Mankiw and D. Romer, 1–26. Cambridge: MIT Press.

New Monetary Economics

The new monetary economics focuses on financial innovations that would evolve in the absence of regulation, and contrasts these innovations to the operation of more regulated systems. Instruments bearing pecuniary returns would replace current forms of money, and there would be no well-defined money supply. Clear distinctions between banks and other financial intermediaries would diminish or disappear, and intermediaries would provide transactions services through checkable mutual funds instead of conventional deposits. Traders would use units of account separate from media of exchange. Furthermore, the legal restrictions that prevent such outcomes create microeconomic inefficiencies and increase the vulnerability of the economic system to monetary shocks.

While there are different strands within the new monetary economics (the name is taken from Hall 1982), these approaches are united in emphasizing the importance of the legal and regulatory setting on private financial intermediation. Wallace (1983), under the rubric of the legal-restrictions theory of money, argues that the demand for non-interest-bearing fiat money stems from legal barriers that prevent the use of other instruments for transactions and settlement purposes. If financial intermediaries were unrestricted, firms would "break up" large-denomination Treasury securities into small-denomination bearer instruments. Under laissez-faire, either nominal interest rates would be driven to the cost of denominational arbitrage, eliminating the wedge between the returns on bonds and noninterest-bearing money, or government currency would be replaced by pecuniary-return-bearing instruments.

Applying the logic of Wallace's analysis, the new monetary economics examines how an unregulated financial sector would evolve. Traditional banking structures would be unlikely to survive in a fully competitive environment. Transactions and savings accounts would be held with financial intermediaries offering diverse and diversified portfolios. The circulating (or electronically transferred) instruments would not have to be convertible into an outside money but would pay interest or fluctuate in capital value. The system could become strictly cashless through the use of an electronic funds-transfer system.

The institutions providing transactions services would resemble money market mutual funds more than today's banks (Glasner 1989, Cowen and Kroszner 1990). Structuring banks as mutual funds would eliminate the threat of bank panics to financial and macroeconomic stability. The first-come, first-served payment rules of a fractional reserve system lead individuals, who are not fully informed about the value of bank assets, to queue up to withdraw their deposits. Panic runs are precipitated, and these runs disrupt credit flows and the payments system.

Mutual-fund banking eliminates bank runs since the value of the "deposit," or shares, fluctuates with the market value of the underlying portfolio; the incentive to be first in line vanishes. Intermediaries could not become insolvent because the value of the liabilities would simply reflect the value of the assets. In addition, if the mutual-fund bank held a liquid portfolio, deposit insurance would have no role to play.

In an unregulated system, return-bearing media of exchange and settlement, such as shares in bond or equity mutual funds, would be distinct from the unit(s) of account. The accounting unit could be a commodity index or basket (Hall 1983) or abstract (Cowen and Kroszner 1987). Separating the unit of account from transactions media could mitigate monetary shocks to the economy. Changes in the supply of or demand for exchange media would be reflected in changes in the prices of those media rather than in pressures on the general price level. Monetary shocks would play no role in business cycles. White (1984), McCallum (1985), and Hoover (1988), however, have questioned the practicality of such arrangements.

Greenfield and Yeager (1983) have offered a concrete plan for a laissez-faire system which attempts to reduce monetary shocks to real activity. Their BFH proposal—so named for Black, Fama, and Hall—relies on an indirect convertibility mechanism in which privately-issued circulating media, denominated in terms of a comprehensive commodity basket, are redeemable not for the basket medium of account but for an intermediate asset such as gold. The government's role in the monetary and financial system would involve only the initial definition of the commodity-bundle index.

In the spirit of Irving Fisher's "compensated dollar" standard, Greenfield and Yeager argue that the BFH system would stabilize the purchasing power of the unit of account. BFH advocates argue that the disturbances due to poor government monetary policy would be eliminated, and that a stable unit of account would mitigate the problems of nominal rigidities. Cowen and Kroszner (1992) argue, however, that the BFH system exacerbates nominal rigidities in the face of real shocks requiring relative-price adjustments. Nor is it certain that the proposed structure of BFH banking operations would survive under laissez-faire.

Another version of the new monetary economics considers Wicksell's pure credit economy in which all transactions involve transfers of credit instruments through a sophisticated bookkeeping accounting system. Black, Fama, and such early twentieth-century German economists as Robert Liefmann (see Cowen and Kroszner 1992) emphasize the role of credit transactions in displacing monetary ones. Transactors' ability to shift from the traditional monetary sector into a credit or "giro" sector reduces the importance of monetary disturbances in business cycles. The provision of liquidity services would become demand-determined.

In a world in which the value of media of exchange and settlement float in terms of the unit of account, neither Keynesian nor Monetarist approaches are valid. The money supply is not well defined and "sophisticated barter" and credit transactions replace transactions involving a traditional medium of exchange. The quantity equation no longer holds under such conditions. For the Keynesians, with credit instruments substituting for money, the *IS* and *LM* curves cannot be defined independently of each other (Burstein 1990).

The separation of monetary functions allows multiple accounting, exchange, and settlement media to coexist. The unbundling of monetary functions may lead to optimum currency sectors, similar to optimum currency areas. Various sectors of the economy might use different media of account and exchange to insulate themselves from shocks to other sectors. Multiple media of account could allow the market to select and implement optimal indexation schemes that would insulate the economy from nominal and real disturbances.

Tyler Cowen
Randall Kroszner

See also Banking Panics; Endogenous and Exogenous Money; Financial Intermediation; Free Banking; Monetary Equilibrium Theories of the Business Cycle; Money-Income Causality; Real Business-Cycle Theories

Bibliography

Black, F. 1987. *Business Cycles and Equilibrium*. New York: Basil Blackwell.

Burstein, M. L. 1990. *The New Art of Central Banking*. New York: New York Univ. Press.

Cowen, T. and R. Kroszner. 1987. "The Development of the New Monetary Economics." *Journal of Political Economy* 95:567–90.

———. 1990. "Mutual Fund Banking: A Market Approach." *Cato Journal* 10:223–37.

———. 1992. *Explorations in the New Monetary Economics*. New York: Basil Blackwell.

Fama, E. F. 1980. "Banking in the Theory of Finance." *Journal of Monetary Economics* 6:39–57.

Glasner, D. 1989. *Free Banking and Monetary Reform*. New York: Cambridge Univ. Press.

Greenfield, R. L. and L. B. Yeager. 1983. "A Laissez-Faire Approach to Monetary Stability." *Journal of Money, Credit, and Banking* 15:302–15.

Hall, R. E. 1982. "Monetary Trends in the United States and the United Kingdom: A Review from the Perspective of New Developments in Monetary Economics." *Journal of Economic Literature* 20:1552–56.

———. 1983. "Explorations in the Gold Standard and Related Policies for Stabilizing the Dollar." In *Inflation: Causes and Effects,* edited by R. E. Hall, 111–22. Chicago: Univ. of Chicago Press.

Hoover, K. D. 1988. "The New Monetary Economics." Chap. 6 in *The New Classical Macroeconomics*. Oxford: Basil Blackwell.

McCallum, B. 1985. "Bank Deregulation, Accounting Systems of Exchange, and the Unit of Account: A Critical Review." *The New Monetary Economics, Fiscal Issues and Unemployment. Carnegie-Rochester Series on Public Policy,* Autumn, 13–45.

Wallace, N. 1983. "A Legal Restrictions Theory of the Demand for 'Money' and the Role of Monetary Policy." *Federal Reserve Bank of Minneapolis Quarterly Review*, Winter, 1–7.

White, L. H. 1984. "Competitive Payments Systems and the Unit of Account." *American Economic Review* 74:699–712.

Yeager, L. B. and R. L. Greenfield. 1989. "Can Monetary Disequilibrium be Eliminated?" *Cato Journal* 9:405–21.

Nonlinear Business-Cycle Theories

A *nonlinear business-cycle model* is characterized by nonlinear functional forms of the assumed dynamic relations. Depending on the specific nonlinearities, such a model can generate *endogenous oscillations* without resort to particular parameter values or exogenous shocks. Although these models became popular in conjunction with the interest in complex and chaotic behavior, nonlinear cycle models have a long tradition in economics. Early examples are the models of Kaldor ([1940] 1960) and Goodwin ([1951] 1982).

Nonlinear business-cycle models can be framed in sets of differential equations, difference equations, or delayed differential equations. The following sections concentrate on differential equations, discrete-time difference equations are mentioned only in passing.

Preliminaries

Consider the continuous-time dynamical system

$$\dot{x} = f(x), \ x \in \mathbb{R}^n, \ \dot{x} \equiv \frac{dx}{dt}. \tag{1}$$

An *attractor* for equation (1) is a bounded set $A \subset \mathbb{R}^n$ when there is a neighborhood U of A with the property that all trajectories starting in this set will remain there forever and converge toward A for t large enough.

When the set of A consists of a single point the attractor is called a *fixed-point attractor*. A nonlinear business-cycle model is an economic example of a dynamical system that possesses attractors differing from fixed points. Examples of these attractors are limit cycles, *tori* (i.e., the doughnut-like higher-dimensional equivalents of limit cycles), and *strange attractors* with chaotic motion.

Mathematical Tools

When nonlinearities are involved in equation (1), analytic expressions of the solutions, i.e., of functions like $x(t) = F(x(0),t)$, usually do not exist. It is therefore necessary to use other tools to identify the qualitative behavior of trajectories. The following two tools turned out to be particularly relevant for business-cycle theory.

Poincaré-Bendixson Theorem

In a rather untechnical way, the Poincaré-Bendixson theorem can be outlined as follows. Consider a two-dimensional dynamical system

$$\begin{aligned} \dot{x}_1 &= f_1(x_1, x_2) \\ \dot{x}_2 &= f_2(x_1, x_2). \end{aligned} \tag{2}$$

Assume that the fixed point of equation (2), i.e., $f_1(\cdot) = f_2(\cdot) = 0$, is unique and unstable. When it is possible to find an area $D \subset \mathbb{R}^2$ in the (x_1, x_2) plane such that the area encloses the fixed point and when all trajectories starting on the boundary of the set move into and remain in the interior of D, then there is at least one closed orbit in D (Hirsch and Smale 1974, 252).

In many cases, the boundedness of trajectories in an area D can be shown with relative ease. The Poincaré-Bendixson theorem is restricted to the two-dimensional case; extensions to higher dimensions ($n > 2$) are impossible.

Hopf Bifurcation Theorem

Bifurcation theory deals with the possible emergence of new dynamic patterns when a parameter is changed in a system of the form

$$\dot{x} = f(x, \mu), \ x \in \mathbb{R}^n, \ \mu \in \mathbb{R}. \tag{3}$$

The Hopf bifurcation theorem concerns the bifurcation of a single fixed point into a closed orbit and a fixed point. Assume that the Jacobian matrix of an n-dimensional ($n \geq 2$) dynamical system like equation (3), evaluated at a fixed point, has a pair of complex conjugate eigenvalues. Assume further that the real parts of the eigenvalues increase when the parameter μ increases. When (a) the real parts are negative for low values of μ, (b) when there is a value μ_0 such that the real parts become zero at μ_0, when (c) the real parts are positive for all $\mu > \mu_0$, and when (d) no other real eigenvalue equals zero, then closed orbits emerge in a neighborhood of a fixed point (Guckenheimer and Holmes 1983, 151–53).

Note that the Hopf bifurcation is a local phenomenon in a small neighborhood of a fixed point and that the orbits may have very small amplitudes. The advantage of the theorem is its

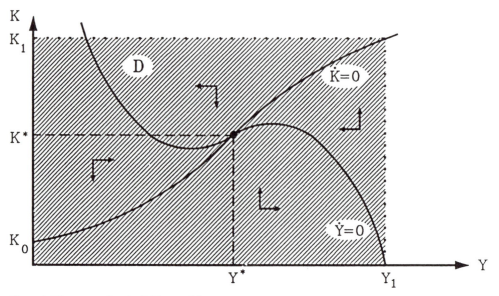

Figure 1. Phase space for the Kaldor model.

lack of restriction on the dimension of the system. The analogue of the theorem for discrete-time, difference equations is valid for $n = 2$ only.

Other Tools
Besides these two standard theorems, several other mathematical theorems are useful for establishing closed orbits in specific dynamical systems. For example, *predator-prey* models deal with the cyclic interaction of variables like the employment rate and the labor bill share (in some models closed orbits are not attractors!). The *Liénard* equation is a specific second-order differential equation that possesses a *unique* cycle. Models of *catastrophe theory* deal with abrupt changes in the value of a variable when a parameter (i.e., a very slowly changing variable) changes.

An Example: The Kaldor Model
The Kaldor model can be considered a proto-type model in nonlinear business-cycle theory, because it demonstrates all essential ingredients of more sophisticated nonlinear models. Consider the two-dimensional model

$$\dot{Y} = \alpha\big(I(Y, K) - S(Y)\big) \quad \alpha > 0$$
$$\dot{K} = I(Y, K) - \delta K, \quad \delta > 0, \tag{4}$$

with $Y, K, I, S, \alpha,$ and δ as income, capital stock, investment, savings, adjustment speed, and the depreciation rate, respectively. Let the savings function be linear with $S_Y > 0$ (subscripts denote partial derivatives). The investment function is nonlinear with $I_K < 0$, $I_Y > 0 \,\forall\, Y$, $I_{YY} > 0 \,\forall\, Y < Y^*$, and $I_{YY} \leq 0 \,\forall\, Y \geq Y^*$.

The sigmoid shape of the investment function allows for three partial equilibria in the goods market. Assume that $I_Y - S_Y$ is positive at (Y^*, K^*) and negative at two other partial equilibria. The phase space of the Kaldor model for that particular case is depicted in Figure 1 [the shape of the loci $\dot{Y} = 0$ and $\dot{K} = 0$ can easily be derived by totally differentiating both equations in equation (4)]. When the curves intersect at a point (Y^*, K^*) where the slope of the $\dot{Y} = 0$-curve is positive, the general equilibrium (Y^*, K^*) is unstable. The shaded region constitutes the set D required by the Poincaré-Bendixson theorem. On the boundary of D all vectors point into the interior of D. It follows that there is at least one closed orbit in D.

The Kaldor model can also be analyzed with the help of the Hopf bifurcation theorem. Let α be the parameter that can be changed exogenously. The determinant of the Jacobian matrix J of equation (4), evaluated at (Y^*, K^*), is

$$\det J = \alpha\big(I_Y - S_Y\big)\big(I_K - \delta\big) - \alpha I_Y I_K \gtreqless 0. \tag{5}$$

Assume that $\det J > 0$ in order to exclude a saddle point. The trace of J is

$$\operatorname{tr} J = \alpha\left(I_Y - S_Y\right) + \left(I_K - \delta\right). \qquad (6)$$

The trace is negative for low values of α, and positive for sufficiently high values of α. Let α_0 be the value that implies $\operatorname{tr} J = 0$. The eigenvalues are

$$\lambda_{1,2} = \frac{\operatorname{tr} J}{2} \pm \sqrt{\frac{\left(-\operatorname{tr} J\right)^2}{4} - \det J}. \qquad (7)$$

At α_0, the trace is zero, so that the eigenvalues $\lambda_{1,2}$ are purely imaginary. As there are no other eigenvalues $\lambda_{1,2}$, a Hopf bifurcation occurs at α_0.

The sigmoid shape of the investment function causes the presence of endogenous oscillations in this model. It is easy to construct other simple macroeconomic models that incorporate a similar nonlinearity in different functional expressions. The sigmoid shape of a single function like $I(Y,K)$ is not necessary, and other nonlinearities can also satisfy the requirements of the two theorems. However, closed orbits cannot emerge in the two-dimensional case unless the trace changes its sign in the domain of the system.

It should be stressed that the Kaldor model can be considered a didactical model because it demonstrates how easily endogenous oscillations can be generated in a simple nonlinear model. On the other hand, low-dimensional models that can be analyzed with the help of the Poincaré-Bendixson theorem or the Hopf bifurcation theorem are surely too simple to serve even as highly abstract explanations of cyclic motion in actual economies. The majority of more relevant nonlinear business-cycle models cannot be analyzed without using numerical techniques.

Irregular Oscillations

The above-mentioned tools are suited to establish regular types of dynamic behavior, i.e., abstract idealizations of empirically observable fluctuations. However, the real domain of nonlinear cycle theory consists of dynamic models that can endogenously generate bounded and irregular dynamic patterns resembling the motion known from stochastic models.

The relevant notion in this context is that of a *strange attractor*, i.e., an object that is neither a point nor a closed orbit. The presence of a strange attractor indicates that the trajectories generated by the dynamical system are *chaotic*. Several subtly different definitions of chaotic motion exist, but for the purpose of this outline it suffices to say that a chaotic dynamical sys-

tem possesses trajectories whose evolution appears to be stochastic though the system is completely deterministic.

Economic examples of chaotic nonlinear models exist in abundance (Gabisch and Lorenz 1989, Lorenz 1989). The list includes simple models framed in one-dimensional, nonlinear difference equations (equivalent to logistic equations), higher-dimensional difference equations, and differential equations (with a dimension $n \geq 3$). Except for low-dimensional discrete-time systems, mathematical theorems that permit an analytic investigation of chaotic motion usually do not exist. In most cases, numerical techniques are required to establish chaotic motion in a particular system.

The presence of chaotic motion in some nonlinear systems is relevant for business-cycle theory mainly for three reasons. First, when business-cycle theory aims to provide theoretical explanations of empirical fluctuations, chaotic motion allows us to avoid invoking exogenous factors to explain irregularities. Though exogenous influences cannot be completely ignored, they should not dominate an *economic* theory of the business cycle. Second, trajectories of a chaotic system may be extremely sensitive to the initial values of a variable. This can be relevant for forecasting business cycles. Since one usually does not know the true current values of an economic variable it may be impossible to forecast the business cycle using a chaotic model, regardless of how well the model describes real life and even if exogenous influences are absent in the future. Third, chaotic motion can indicate a misspecification of a business-cycle model when empirical irregularities appear as a kind of noise and when the model generates highly irregular trajectories. Thus, chaotic nonlinear models can be very useful for didactical purposes, because they allow for economic explanations of irregular oscillations. Empirically motivated theoretical studies should make use of the properties of chaotic systems only when there is strong evidence that actual time series are indeed chaotic.

Günter Gabisch
Hans-Walter Lorenz

See also CHAOS AND BIFURCATIONS; CHAOS, CONTINUOUS-TIME MODELS OF; DIFFERENTIAL AND DIFFERENCE EQUATIONS; GOODWIN, RICHARD MURPHEY; KALDOR, NICHOLAS; NONLINEAR STATISTICAL INFERENCE; POST-KEYNESIAN BUSINESS-CYCLE THEORY

N

Bibliography

Gabisch, G. and H.-W. Lorenz. 1989. *Business-Cycle Theory*. 2d ed. Berlin: Springer-Verlag.

Goodwin, R. M. [1951] 1982. "The Nonlinear Accelerator and the Persistence of Business Cycles." Chap. 6 in *Essays in Economic Dynamics*. London: Macmillan.

Guckenheimer, J. and P. Holmes. 1983. *Nonlinear Oscillations, Dynamical Systems, and Bifurcations of Vector Fields*. Berlin: Springer-Verlag.

Hirsch, M. W. and Smale, S. 1974. *Differential Equations, Dynamical Systems, and Linear Algebra*. New York: Academic Press.

Kaldor, N. [1940] 1960. "A Model of the Trade Cycle." Chap. 8 in *Essays in Economic Stability and Growth*. Glencoe, Ill.: Free Press.

Lorenz, H.-W. 1989. *Nonlinear Dynamical Economics and Chaotic Motion*. Berlin: Springer-Verlag.

Nonlinear Statistical Inference

Stylized facts concerning business cycles, such as a general pattern of asymmetry between long, slow expansions and short, quick contractions, have been well documented in the literature. Despite evidence of asymmetry in business-cycle data, macroeconomic models have tended to adopt log-linear specifications and to be driven by exogenous shocks that are symmetric in nature. As a consequence, macroeconomic models tend to yield unsatisfactory predictions and forecasts.

In an effort to better understand business cycles, researchers such as Grandmont (1985) have postulated deterministic models that display endogenous instability. Such models are characterized by deterministic chaos in the sense that they can generate seemingly random behavior.

Brock and Sayers (1988) applied a series of tests for chaos to United States business-cycle data. While finding little evidence to support the hypothesis that business-cycle data are generated by a chaotic mechanism, they developed the techniques used to search for determinism in time-series data into a statistical test that can detect hidden structure in putatively white time series. To test the hypothesis of nonlinear structure, the techniques were applied to residuals of low-order autoregressions fit to quarterly postwar employment, quarterly postwar unemployment, monthly postwar industrial production, and monthly pig-iron production from 1877 to 1937. Little evidence of nonlinear structure was found in quarterly postwar real gross national product or in quarterly postwar real gross private domestic investment.

Empirical Testing for Deterministic Chaos

Adopt the following definition of a deterministic explanation: a series $\{a_t\}$, $t = 1, ..., T$, has a deterministic explanation if there exists a system (h, F, X_0) such that $a_t = h(X_t)$ for all t, $X_t = F(X_{t-1})$, and X_0 is given. Here $\{a_t\}$ denotes the observed univariate time series which is known to the researcher at (or after) time t. The observation function, denoted by h, maps $\mathbb{R}^n$ to $\mathbb{R}$, is unknown to the researcher, and may scramble the signal from $\{X\}$ as it is mapped onto $\{a\}$. F denotes the unknown deterministic law of motion, where F maps $\mathbb{R}^n$ to $\mathbb{R}^n$, and X_0 is the unknown initial condition. Empirically, noise infects $\{a_t\}$. It is generally sufficient for the methods utilized that the variance of the noise be small relative to the variation in the data (Brock 1986, Brock and Dechert 1991).

The series $\{a_t\}$ is chaotic if it satisfies the deterministic definition and if nearby trajectories diverge from one another exponentially. Such trajectories demonstrate instability and sensitivity to initial conditions, which is formalized by the condition that the largest Lyapunov exponent, which measures the rate of spread of nearby trajectories in phase space, be positive.

In empirical studies, three main conditions must be satisfied to validate the claim of deterministic chaos. First, a researcher needs evidence of low correlation dimension. The correlation dimension allows the dimension, n, of $\mathbb{R}^n$ to be estimated and sets a lower bound to the number of variables necessary to model an observed time series. Second, a researcher needs evidence of sensitivity to initial conditions as demonstrated by positive Lyapunov exponents. Third, the underlying dynamics generating the series of observations must be reconstructed.

Because near-unit-root stochastic processes are pervasive in economic and financial data, these series often yield estimates of seemingly low correlation dimension and seemingly positive Lyapunov exponents. Since Brock and Sayers could not differentiate between Lyapunov exponent estimates obtained from pseudo-random numbers and those obtained from their short economic time series, the following discussion focuses on correlation dimension and methods of statistical inference based on the correlation integral.

The definition of dimension is familiar. For example, a line has dimension one, a plane has dimension two, and a cube has dimension three. In the limit, random numbers are of infinite dimension. An infinite series of random numbers will "fill" each space in which it is embedded. The estimated correlation dimension of a data set gives important information on the complexity of the model needed to reconstruct the dynamical process generating the observations.

The algorithm proposed by Grassberger and Procaccia (1983) is commonly utilized to estimate correlation dimension. To utilize the algorithm, the researcher forms m-histories, Y_t^m from a data set, $\{a_t\}$, $t = 1, ..., T$, such that $Y = (a_t, a_{t+1}, ..., a_{t+m-1})$, choosing the embedding dimension, m. For example, for $m = 1$, $Y_t^1 = (a_1), (a_2), ..., (a_T)$ and for $m = 2$, $Y_t^2 = (a_1, a_2), (a_2, a_3), ..., (a_{T-1}, a_T)$. The correlation integral is defined as

$$C(m, e) = \{ \#(i, j) \big| \| Y_i^m - Y_j^m \| < e, and\ i \neq j \} / N \tag{1}$$

where $\#(i, j)$ sums the number of (Y_i^m, Y_j^m) pairs such that

$$e > \| Y_i^m - Y_j^m \|,\ N = M^2 - M$$
$$\text{and } M = T - (m - 1)$$

is the number of m-histories that can be formed from a series of length T. The tolerance distance, e, is chosen by the researcher. The correlation integral may be interpreted as the probability that a given number of distances are within the tolerance distance e, out of all possible distances, N, for a given level of m.

Grassberger and Procaccia show that for small e, $C(m, e)$ grows as a power, $k \cdot e^\alpha$, where k is constant and α is the correlation dimension estimate. By taking natural logs of the power law, dividing by $\ln(e)$ and assuming $\ln(k)/\ln(e)$ to be small, one obtains the correlation dimension estimate

$$\alpha_m = \frac{\ln C(m, e)}{\ln(e)} \tag{2}$$

As the correlation dimension point estimate may be obtained by plotting $\ln C(m,e)$ versus $\ln(e)$ and searching for a zone of stability within

which the power law holds, an alternative estimate of correlation dimension is given by

$$SC_m = \frac{\{\ln C(m, e_i) - \ln C(m, e_j)\}}{\{\ln(e_i) - \ln(e_j)\}} \tag{3}$$

which measures the slope along the plot. Ramsey and Yuan (1989) discuss problems related to correlation dimension estimation.

Utilizing the above measures of dimension, Brock and Sayers obtained dimension estimates of between two and four for most time- and difference-stationary series, but their dimension estimates of the residuals obtained by fitting low-order regressions to the time-stationary data jumped to between six and ten. Since the Residual Diagnostic for Deterministic Chaos (Brock 1986, Brock and Sayers 1988) requires that the dimension of a deterministic time series equal the dimension of the residuals of a low-order, smooth, time-series model that is fit to that series, the hypothesis of determinism is rejected.

Historically, the major drawback to calculating dimension is that little distribution theory existed for the dimension estimate. The dimension estimates appear sensitive to the choice of embedding dimension and the number of observations in the data series. Furthermore, the dimension algorithms were developed for use in the natural sciences on experimentally generated data sets numbering in the tens of thousands, rather than on the small and noisy data sets common in economics. Brock and Baek (1991) have recently developed asymptotic distribution theory for the correlation dimension and other measures, including standard errors.

Statistical Inference Based on the Correlation Integral

The notion of the correlation integral was utilized by Brock, Dechert, Scheinkman, and LeBaron (BDSL) to develop a test which proves useful in detecting evidence of general structure in time-series data. The test is based on the null hypothesis of independent and identically distributed (IID) data series. Using the definition of the correlation integral in equation (1), for $m > 1$, define the BDS statistic,

$$BDS(m, e) = N^{1/2} \{ C(m, e) - [C(1, e)]^m \} / b_m \tag{4}$$

where b_m, the standard deviation of the BDS statistic, varies with m, the embedding dimension.

Under the null hypothesis of IID, for given levels of e and m, the quantity $\{C(m, e) - [C(1, e)]^m\}$

should equal zero. BDSL show that under the null the BDS statistic follows an asymptotic $N(0, 1)$ distribution as N goes to ∞. Thus, large values of the BDS statistic provide evidence that the data series of interest is not random but has an inherent structure.

The BDS test is free of nuisance parameter problems under reasonable conditions and has good power compared to a number of alternatives. Brock, Hsieh, and LeBaron (1991) provide a comprehensive reference on the topic of BDS and approximate finite-sample critical regions for the BDS statistic. In general, the BDS test has tolerable power for data sets containing between 250 and 500 observations and good power for data sets of 500 or more observations, when e is between 0.5 and 1.5 times the standard deviation of the data. BDSL discuss the size and power of the BDS statistic versus some specific alternatives. Baek and Brock (1992) provide multivariate extensions of the BDS test.

Brock and Sayers (1988) applied the BDS test to putatively white residuals of low-order autoregressive models fit to U.S. business-cycle data. Strong evidence against the null hypothesis of IID was found for employment from 1950–I to 1983–IV, unemployment from 1949–I to 1982–IV, monthly postwar industrial production, and monthly pig-iron production from 1877 to 1937. Since linear filters were utilized before applying the BDS test, it is reasonable to conclude that strong evidence against the null hypothesis is consistent with the existence of remaining nonlinear structures in these series. Little evidence of nonlinear structure was found in real gross national product from 1947–I to 1985–I or real gross private domestic investment from 1947–I to 1985–I.

The BDS test has been utilized to aid in model specification by researchers desiring a method of testing putatively white residuals of best-fitting models for hidden structures. Should evidence against the hypothesis of IID be indicated, additional model specifications may be attempted until the residuals are consistent with the IID hypothesis. Model specification is aided by providing the researcher with an additional tool for detecting data structures that may evade standard tests for linear specification.

Rejection of the null by the general BDS statistic may be interpreted as consistent with many alternative hypotheses such as linear and nonlinear structures, model misspecification, seasonalities, outliers, and nonstationarities remaining in the data under investigation. As the class of possibilities under rejection of the null is great, identification of the structure specification is a topic of ongoing research.

Conclusion

Research to date has tended to find that deterministic chaos is absent from economic data. While many series exhibit some instability and appear to be consistent with the low-dimensional hypothesis, dynamical reconstruction has not been successful. However, there appears to be abundant evidence of nonlinear stochastic components in economic and financial data.

In addition to the research discussed above, evidence of nonlinearity has been found in such series as monetary aggregates, work stoppages, exchange rates, stock and futures returns, and gold and silver rates of return. In contrast, Canadian business-cycle data show little evidence of nonlinearity. See Sayers (1990) for an introduction to many of the ideas discussed here.

Chera L. Sayers

See also CHAOS AND BIFURCATIONS; CHAOS, CONTINUOUS-TIME MODELS OF; NONLINEAR BUSINESS-CYCLE THEORIES

Bibliography

Baek, E. G. and W. A. Brock. 1992. "A Nonparametric Test for Independence of a Multivariate Time Series." *Statistica Sinica* 2:137–56.

Brock, W. A. 1986. "Distinguishing Random and Deterministic Systems: Abridged Version." *Journal of Economic Theory* 40:168–95.

Brock, W. A. and E. G. Baek. 1991. "Some Theory of Statistical Inference for Nonlinear Science." *Review of Economic Studies* 58:697–716.

Brock, W. A. and W. D. Dechert. 1991. "Nonlinear Dynamical Systems: Instability and Chaos in Economics." In *Handbook of Mathematical Economics*. Vol. 4. Edited by W. Hildenbrand and H. Sonnenschein, 2210–35. Amsterdam: North-Holland.

Brock, W. A., W. D. Dechert, J. A. Scheinkman, and B. LeBaron. 1990. "A Test for Independence Based on the Correlation Dimension." Dept. of Economics, Univ. of Wisconsin-Madison.

Brock, W. A., D. A. Hsieh, and B. LeBaron. 1991. *Nonlinear Dynamics, Chaos, and Instability.* Cambridge: MIT Press.

Brock, W. A. and C. L. Sayers. 1988. "Is the Business Cycle Characterized by Deterministic Chaos?" *Journal of Monetary Economics* 22:71–90.

Grandmont, J.-M. 1985. "On Endogenous Competitive Business Cycles." *Econometrica* 53:995–1045.

Grassberger, P. and I. Procaccia. 1983. "Measuring the Strangeness of Strange Attractors." *Physica D* 94:189–208.

Ramsey, J. B. and H.-J. Yuan. 1989. "Bias and Error Bars in Dimension Calculations and Their Evaluation in Some Simple Models." *Physics Letters A* 134:287–97.

Sayers, C. L. 1990. "Chaos and the Business Cycle." In *The Ubiquity of Chaos,* edited by S. Krasner, 115–25. Washington: American Association for the Advancement of Science Publications.

N

Ohlin, Bertil Gotthard (1899–1979)

Except perhaps for Gunnar Myrdal, Bertil Ohlin was the most influential Swedish economist after Knut Wicksell and Gustav Cassel departed the scene. One of the great economists of the interwar period, Ohlin earned his reputation in both international economics and macroeconomics.

In the former field, Ohlin, inspired by E. F. Heckscher's 1919 article in *Ekonomisk Tidskrift,* developed the famous Heckscher-Ohlin theorem which explains the direction of international and interregional trade in terms of differences in endowments of productive factors. For thus founding the modern theory of international trade, Ohlin was co-winner of the 1977 Nobel Memorial Prize in Economics. And in a celebrated exchange with J. M. Keynes on the German transfer problem in the *Economic Journal* in 1929, Ohlin also laid the foundations of the income theory of the balance of payments, anticipating all the main features of modern balance-of-payments theory.

In the second field, Ohlin contributed importantly to the macroeconomic theory of a group of Swedish economists, which in a 1937 article, he christened the "Stockholm School." Despite obvious parallels to Keynes's *General Theory*, the degree to which Ohlin and the Stockholm School anticipated the core of Keynes's main work is still controversial. And in his contribution to the Wicksell festschrift, Ohlin, in 1921, made a fundamental contribution to capital theory by solving the optimum rotation problem, later known as the Faustmann-Ohlin theorem.

Born in Klippan, Sweden, on 23 April 1899, Ohlin studied at Harvard in 1923 before receiving his Ph.D. from Stockholm University

in 1924. He was a professor of economics at Copenhagen University (1925–1930) and Handelshögskolan (1930–1965). As member of the Swedish parliament (1938–1970), Minister of Trade (1944–1945), and leader of the Liberal Party (1944–1967), Ohlin was one of the few economists to achieve both academic and political prominence. He died on 3 August 1979, in Valadalen, Sweden.

The macroeconomic approach of the Stockholm School can be characterized as an analysis of fluctuations through time in the price level and in aggregate output and employment, not, as in the *General Theory,* in the level of employment at a given time. The dynamic nature of the Stockholm theory made the analytical tools it used suitable for trade-cycle analysis, but not for determining macroeconomic equilibrium.

The analysis of the Stockholm School (Steiger 1987a, b) was based on Wicksell's notion of aggregate monetary demand and supply for commodities, which he used to refute Say's Law, and on its clarification and modification by Lindahl and Myrdal. In their "immanent criticism" of Wicksell's approach, Lindahl and Myrdal had originated two significant innovations: (1) the concept of a planned "savings ratio" (Lindahl), which related savings to income and which can be viewed as an alternative formulation of Keynes's propensity to consume, and (2) the concepts of *ex ante* and *ex post* (Myrdal) in a period analysis of flow-related macroeconomic variables. Lindahl's idea led to a division of aggregate income into savings and consumption demand and of aggregate output into investment and consumption supply, allowing for a definite distinction between savings and investment. Myrdal's notions implied a further distinction between the planned or expected values of these variables at the beginning of a period, referred to as *ex ante*, and their realized values at the end of the same period, referred to as *ex post*. These concepts were then transformed into an analysis in which discrepancies between the decisions to save and to invest, i.e., between savings and investment *ex ante*, which Lindahl and Myrdal regarded as the fundamental cause for macroeconomic processes, induced changes in aggregate income which caused savings and investment to be equal *ex post*.

In analyzing an economy in a state of depression, Ohlin ([1933] 1978, 1934, [1937] 1951) further elaborated these concepts. His approach, however, differed from that of Lindahl and Myrdal in two ways: (1) instead of their emphasis on discrepancies between savings and investment *ex ante*, Ohlin concentrated on differences between the aggregate monetary demand and the aggregate supply of commodities in a combined *ex post/ex ante* framework, in which events in the current period influence expectations of prices in the next one; (2) instead of their focus on variations in the price level, Ohlin explicitly analyzed changes in aggregate output. Aggregate monetary demand and supply in Ohlin's approach, therefore, involved quantities as well as the prices of consumption and investment goods.

In analyzing the relation between these four aggregates, thereby allowing for idle capacity so that changes in demand would affect quantities, Ohlin was mainly concerned with explaining the demand side ([1933] 1978, 354–59; 1934, 10–14; [1937] 1951, 61–64). He treated investment demand *ex ante* as a function of the expected return on investment (defined similarly to Keynes's marginal efficiency of capital) in relation to the rate of interest, where the latter, in contrast to Keynes's liquidity-preference approach, was determined in a loanable-funds framework ([1933] 1978, 381–83; 1934, 36–42; [1937] 1951, 107–14; 1937). Ohlin assumed that consumption demand *ex ante* was a function of expected income. A systematic treatment of variations in aggregate monetary demand as determined by these functions was the basis of Ohlin's contribution to the Stockholm theory of "*general* processes of expansion and contraction" ([1937] 1951, 118; see Ohlin [1933] 1978, 370–81; 1934, 24–36; 50–77; 1937[1951], 101–03, 127–28; Brems 1978; Steiger 1976, 1978). Ohlin treated the

quantity of money as an endogenous variable determined by the changes in aggregate monetary demand (1934, 45–48).

Ohlin characterized the processes of expansion and contraction as increases and decreases of aggregate *real* net income due to a rise and fall of aggregate output. A rise in aggregate output would occur "whenever aggregate demand is growing relative to supply" ([1933] 1978, 379), implying a simultaneous rise in employment and (depending on the elasticity of aggregate supply) of the price level. In analyzing a process of expansion, Ohlin assumed feedbacks between changes in output and consumption via generated income, i.e., multiplier effects implied by his hypothesis of a propensity to save less than unity, and via consumption-induced investments, i.e., accelerator effects. Thus, an increase in aggregate demand *ex ante* would increase not only consumption, savings, and aggregate income *ex post*, as in standard Keynesian analysis, but also investment *ex post*.

According to Ohlin, a process of contraction could be analyzed by the same reasoning, *mutatis mutandis*, as a process of expansion, i.e., as a fall of aggregate monetary demand relative to aggregate supply. However, he used different arguments to explain what stopped these processes and how they would be connected to form a business cycle. An expansion would come to an end and turn into a contraction through the interaction of the accelerator and multiplier effects mentioned above, while a contraction would be halted by multiplier effects alone and, due to liquidity preference, would not turn into an expansion automatically.

Ohlin argued that a process of expansion would increase capacity utilization and would induce an increased rate of investment output to widen capacities. Such a development could, however, only occur if the rate of consumption output rose—which would not occur, because the propensity to save relates savings not to the growth but to the level of output. As soon as entrepreneurs realized that consumption growth was unlikely, investments would be reduced and a process of general contraction would start. This process would proceed not to a complete collapse, but to a sort of unemployment equilibrium, because, with a propensity to save less than unity, consumption demand would fall less than aggregate income did. From this state of depression, endogenous forces could not be relied on to stimulate aggregate monetary demand. On the contrary, financial disturbances during a crisis would most certainly lead to a "preference for keeping money in liquid form . . . instead of investing it" (1931, 226; 1932, 139; 1934, 42, 49, 55, 69, 85).

In discussing alternative policies to generate an expansion in a deep and widespread depression, Ohlin (1934, 78–128), therefore, dismissed monetary policy as a means to increase investment demand, e.g., by reducing the long-term rate of interest through open-market operations of the central bank. Instead he proposed increasing public expenditures. The most important theoretical innovation in this analysis was, in contrast to his more descriptive discussion of multiplier effects in a process of expansion, an explicit calculation of the multiplier effect of public works. Ohlin's calculations demonstrate the different expansive effects of loan- and tax-financed public works, thereby providing an early formulation of the balanced-budget multiplier, as well as the leakages caused by savings and imports (Ohlin extended his analysis to an open economy).

Ohlin sought to perform a dynamic macroanalysis by giving as exact a description as possible of the cyclical changes of macroeconomic variables as processes in time. To some extent, this analysis resembled a dynamic version of Keynes's *General Theory*. However, his obvious disinterest in static equilibrium analysis together with a preference for casuistic reasoning—a common characteristic of the Stockholm School—led to an approach which lacked the theoretical rigor and precision of the *General Theory*. Ohlin's dynamic macroanalysis, therefore, presented the business cycle as a process in which—depending on assumptions about expectations, time lags, or speeds of reactions—anything could happen. This certainly was a main reason why Ohlin's approach never achieved an international recognition comparable to his contributions in international economics.

Otto Steiger

See also AGGREGATE SUPPLY AND DEMAND; EXPECTATIONS; KEYNES, JOHN MAYNARD; LINDAHL, ERIK ROBERT; LUNDBERG, ERIK FILIP; MULTIPLIER; MYRDAL, GUNNAR; SAVING EQUALS INVESTMENT; STOCKHOLM SCHOOL; WICKSELL, JOHAN GUSTAV KNUT

Bibliography

Brems, H. 1978. "What was New in Ohlin's 1933–34 Macroeconomics?" *History of Political Economy* 10:398–412.

Jonung, L., ed. 1991. *The Stockholm School of Economics Revisited*. Cambridge: Cambridge Univ. Press.

Ohlin, B. 1931. *The Course and Phases of the World Economic Depression: Report Presented to the Assembly of the League of Nations*. Geneva: League of Nations.

———. 1932. "Now or Never: Action to Combat the World Depression." *Svenska Handelsbankens Index* 7:127–57.

———. [1933] 1978. "On the Formulation of Monetary Theory." Translation. *History of Political Economy* 10:353–88.

———. 1934. *Penningpolitik, offentliga arbeten, subventioner och tullar som medel mot arbetslöshet. Bidrag till expansionens teori* (Monetary policy, public works, subsidies, and tariffs as remedies for unemployment: A contribution to the theory of expansion). Stockholm: Statens offentliga utredningar.

———. [1937] 1951. "Some Notes on the Stockholm Theory of Savings and Investment I–II." In *Readings in Business-Cycle Theory,* edited by H. S. Ellis and F. A. Lutz, 87–130. Philadelphia: Blakiston.

———. 1937. "Alternative Theories of the Rate of Interest. Three Rejoinders: I." *Economic Journal* 47:423–27.

———. 1981. "Stockholm and Cambridge: Four Papers on the Monetary and Employment Theory of the 1930s." Edited by O. Steiger. *History of Political Economy* 13:189–255.

Siven, C.-H. 1985. "The End of the Stockholm School." *Scandinavian Journal of Economics* 87:577–93.

Steiger, O. 1976. "Bertil Ohlin and the Origins of the Keynesian Revolution." *History of Political Economy* 8:341–66.

———. 1978. "Prelude to the Theory of a Monetary Economy: Origins and Significance of Ohlin's 1933 Approach to Monetary Theory." *History of Political Economy* 10:420–26.

———. 1987a. "Ex ante and Ex post." In *The New Palgrave: A Dictionary of Economics*. Vol. 2. Edited by J. Eatwell, M. Milgate, and P. Newman. London: Macmillan.

———. 1987b. "Monetary Equilibrium." In *The New Palgrave: A Dictionary of Economics*. Vol. 3. Edited by J. Eatwell, M. Milgate, and P. Newman. London: Macmillan.

O

Okun, Arthur M. (1928–1980)

Arthur Okun was a leading macroeconomist who made significant research contributions in the study of business cycles and other areas of economics. Among the highlights were his modeling of potential aggregate output and the relation between aggregate output and unemployment that came to be known as Okun's law, an analysis of the choices and conflicts between equity and efficiency that are endemic to market economies, and a comprehensive model of output and inflation based on realistic behavioral assumptions. His research was oriented toward policy and the real economic world, and he was an influential political adviser who served as Chairman of the President's Council of Economic Advisers.

Okun was born in Jersey City, New Jersey, on 28 November 1928, and died in Washington, D.C., on 23 March 1980. He graduated first in his class from Columbia University in 1949 and received his Ph.D. in Economics from Columbia in 1956. He became an instructor in the economics department at Yale in 1952 and a full professor there in 1963. For most of the period 1961–68, Okun was on leave at the President's Council of Economic Advisers in Washington, D.C., first as a senior staff member, then as a council member (1964–68) and finally as chairman (1968–69). From January 1969 until his death, he was a Senior Fellow at the Brookings Institution in Washington, D.C.

The work for which Okun first became widely known described and quantified the relation between real GNP and the unemployment rate over the business cycle. Okun showed that a one-percentage-point reduction in unemployment was associated with a three-percent gain in GNP, a relation that came to be known as Okun's Law. The concept has stood up remarkably well, needing only quantitative adjustments to allow for changing demographics and the like in order to apply to the economy a quarter-century after Okun devised it. As a byproduct, Okun estimated potential GNP as the output that would be produced with the economy operating steadily at full employment, and illuminated the difference between the trend and cyclical components of productivity and labor inputs. Okun's work laid the foundation for much of the subsequent analysis of cycles and trends as well as such related concepts as the difference between structural and actual budget deficits.

When Okun came to Brookings after serving as chairman of President Johnson's Council of Economic Advisers, he and his colleague, George L. Perry, started the Brookings Panel on Economic Activity and its journal, *Brookings Papers on Economic Activity*. It was Okun's vision to create this vehicle as a way of engaging top-flight macroeconomists from the research community to do policy-relevant applied research. His inspiration and energy were key in making the *Brookings Papers* an enormous success that continues to this day.

Okun was both a superb technical economist and a concerned political economist. His examination of the role of economic advice in the political arena, *The Political Economics of Prosperity*, combined his expertise as an analyst of business cycles and his experience as a presidential adviser.

During Okun's years at Brookings, after he left the government, inflation was a major concern of policymakers, and fighting it was a principal cause of business cycles. This period was also one of great ferment in macroeconomic theorizing about the inflation-output relation, the role of stabilization policy, and the behavioral underpinnings of macroeconomic models. Okun found that the predictions of the New Classical economics, which became popular in the 1970s, were at odds with important aspects of macroeconomic behavior. In his last published professional paper, he provided a telling critique of how the New Classical theory missed the central facts characterizing business cycles.

Okun's contributions to macroeconomic theory culminated in his *Prices and Quantities*, which was nearly completed at the time of his death and published posthumously. In place of the atomistic markets with fully flexible prices determined by "the invisible hand" that were assumed in many models of the time, Okun postulated markets in which reputation and long-run relationships were important and in which buyers and sellers took account of those long-run relations in their dealings with one another. Always an inspired phrase-maker, Okun coined the terms "customer markets" to describe this relation between buyers and sellers and the "invisible handshake" to characterize the long-term attachment between workers and firms. Okun's model provided an underpinning for business-cycle theory by showing that, in most markets, it was optimal for firms to vary quantities more than prices in response to fluctuations in demand. And he showed how these same institutions and arrangements could contribute to the problem of inflation coexisting with idle real resources, and to the difficulty of eliminating inflation.

When he delivered the Godkin Lectures at Harvard, published as *Equality and Efficiency: The Big Tradeoff,* Okun addressed what is perhaps the broadest issue of political economy—the fundamental choice between social equity and economic efficiency that confronts a market society, using the metaphor of a "leaky bucket" to describe the losses in aggregate wealth that may arise in the process of distributing that wealth more equitably. The book has become a classic and is used widely in university courses, in economics and in other disciplines.

George L. Perry

See also EFFICIENCY WAGES; IMPLICIT CONTRACTS; NEW KEYNESIAN ECONOMICS; PRICE RIGIDITY; UNEMPLOYMENT; WAGE RIGIDITY

Bibliography

Okun, A. M. [1962] 1983. "Potential GNP: Its Measurement and Significance." In *Economics for Policymaking: Selected Essays of Arthur M. Okun,* 145–58. Cambridge: MIT Press.
———. 1975. *Equality and Efficiency: The Big Tradeoff.* Washington, D.C.: Brookings Institution.
———. 1978. *The Political Economy of Prosperity.* Washington, D.C.: Brookings Institution.
———. [1980] 1983. "Rational-Expectations-with-Misperceptions as a Theory of the Business Cycle." In *Economics for Policymaking: Selected Essays of Arthur M. Okun,* 131–41. Cambridge: MIT Press.
———. 1981. *Prices and Quantities: A Macroeconomic Analysis.* Washington, D.C.: Brookings Institution.
———. 1983. *Economics for Policymaking: Selected Essays of Arthur M. Okun.* Cambridge: MIT Press.

Option Clause

An option clause is a clause in a banknote (or deposit) contract that gives the issuing bank the option to defer redemption of the note or deposit on the condition that it later compensate those whose demands for redemption are deferred. It thus allows a bank to protect its liquidity if demands for redemption increase unexpectedly and its reserves are insufficient to meet those demands. In turn, the knowledge that banks had this means of protection could reassure the public that banks were unlikely to become illiquid, thereby reducing the likelihood of a run occurring in the first place. Option clauses are thus a potentially important safeguard for banks that issue redeemable liabilities and operate with a fractional reserve.

The attraction of option clauses is that they avoid the disadvantages of convertibility on demand, on the one hand, and of meeting runs by government intervention to suspend convertibility, on the other. Convertibility on demand can be unattractive for several reasons: it can force banks to hold excessive reserves, and restrict lending; it can force banks to rely excessively on short term, marketable securities; it can lead banks to raise interest rates to very high levels in a panic; and the knowledge that banks do not have the reserves to meet a run creates the possibility of self-fulfilling panics in which the public's fear that the banks will default leads them to demand redemption, precipitating the very suspension they feared. Government intervention to suspend convertibility is also unattractive: it violates the contracts that banks made with their noteholders and depositors; it eliminates (at least temporarily) the "reflux mechanism" which otherwise ensures that excess issues of notes are returned to their issuers with relatively little effect on prices; there is little immediate incentive to resume convertibility after the crisis has subsided, and it usually takes political pressures to do so; and the expectation of legislated suspension can itself trigger a panic causing a suspension that would not otherwise have occurred.

The option clause provides a market-based means of suspension, and it can only be adopted if it is accepted by those who would be affected by it. A bank that introduced an option clause must persuade potential noteholders that they would be at least as well off with the clause as they would be without it—a bank that failed to do so would lose its market share to rivals that continued to offer notes that were fully redeemable on demand. A bank might persuade its noteholders to accept the clause by arguing that the greater security the clause offers the bank also benefits the noteholders. Noteholders would not need to worry so much about unexpectedly large demands for redemption because they would know that the bank could invoke the option to defend itself. The knowledge that the option exists would in turn discourage speculative runs, so a bank with the option-clause contract would be less prone to runs driven by self-fulfilling expectations that the bank would default (Dowd 1988, 1991).

A potential drawback is the fear that a bank with the option clause might abuse it—for example, an insolvent bank might use it to buy time to take further risks at noteholders' expense in order to salvage an otherwise bankrupt institution. More generally, the option clause could relax the discipline that convertibility imposes on the banker and thereby aggravate agency problems between the bank and its creditors (Calomiris and Kahn 1991). Noteholders would have to weigh these problems against the benefits of option clauses, and one cannot determine a priori that option clauses would always be adopted, or that they would never be. A possible solution to these problems would be a contract that specified certain other conditions that must be satisfied for the option to be exercised. The contract might, for example, require that the exercise of the option would trigger an automatic re-capitalization of the bank that would give the management some incentive to be prudent. Shareholder liability might automatically be extended, or the exercise of the option could trigger the conversion of subordinated debt into equity.

Instances of option clauses are extremely rare historically. The best documented case occurs in Scotland between 1730 and 1765. Option clauses were introduced by the Bank of Scotland in 1730 to protect itself from the attempts of its rival, the Royal Bank of Scotland, to drive it out of business by collecting its notes and presenting them unexpectedly for redemption (Meulen 1936, White 1984). The option gave it the right to defer redemption for six months on the condition that it pay compensation of one shilling on the pound (i.e., 5 percent). The Bank of Scotland announced the reason for the clause, and its notes continued to circulate at par afterwards. The Royal Bank refused for a long time to imitate it and advertised the fact that its notes were always redeemable on demand, but these attempts to win over the Bank of Scotland's market share proved futile, and the notes of the two banks circulated side-by-side at par. In the subsequent years other banks were set up in Scotland, and the pressure of high interest rates in London and the resulting drain of specie southwards apparently led all Scottish note-issuing banks to adopt the option clause by mid-1762. The Bank of Scotland and the Royal Bank both exercised the option clause at least once, in March 1764, and the use of the option clause by note-issuing banks was sometimes threatened on other occasions. The option clause gave rise to considerable controversy, however, and for reasons that are still not entirely clear, the Westminster Parliament responded in 1765 by banning the clause.

Kevin Dowd

See also Banking Panics; Free Banking; Lender of Last Resort

Bibliography

Calomiris, C. W. W. and C. M. Kahn. 1991. "The Role of Demandable Debt in Structuring Optimal Banking Arrangements." *American Economic Review* 81:497–513.

Dowd, K. 1988. "Option Clauses and the Stability of a Laisser Faire Monetary System." *Journal of Financial Services Research* 1:319–33.

———. 1991. "Option Clauses and Banknote Suspension." *Cato Journal* 10:761–74.

Meulen, H. 1936. *Free Banking: An Outline of a Policy of Individualism*. London: Macmillan.

White, L. H. 1984. *Free Banking in Britain: Theory, Experience, and Debate, 1800–1845*. Cambridge: Cambridge Univ. Press.

Overend, Gurney Crisis (1866)

The Overend, Gurney crisis was the third major crisis to wrack Britain's financial system in the quarter-century after the passage of the Bank Charter Act in 1844. The crisis, which erupted in May 1866, led to widespread commercial and financial failures and several months of dislocation in financial markets. The Overend episode was one of the last in a series of nineteenth-century British crises in which the Bank of England did not act as lender of last resort. A principal result of the Overend crisis was the recognition—hastened by Bagehot's *Lombard Street*—by the Bank of England of its responsibility to act as lender of last resort.

Like its predecessors of 1847 and 1857, the Overend, Gurney crisis followed on the heels of an investment boom. While speculation in the two previous episodes had focused on grain (1847) and railroads (1847 and 1857), the 1866 crisis was preceded by speculation in limited-liability companies. The speculative boom was fueled by an 1862 amendment to the company law that made it easier to create limited-liability companies. Because the London market had difficulty absorbing the huge volume of new shares, businessmen resorted to new methods of financing, including widespread use of accommodation bills. Unlike trade bills, which were collateralized by inventories of goods in transit, accommodation bills were issued against the security of shares in a new (and possibly not yet started) venture. Overend, Gurney and Co., which was itself floated as a limited-liability company in August 1865, took a leading role in discounting this type of potentially dubious paper.

The firm that eventually became Overend, Gurney and Company originated with the Gurney family of Norwich. Long established as wool merchants, and later as country bankers, members of the Gurney family moved to London in 1807 to enter the bill-broking business. The firm achieved such stature during the first half of the nineteenth century that, according to the *Times* (11 May 1866), it could "rightly claim to be the greatest instrument of credit in the Kingdom." When questioned about the extent of his firm's business before a House of Lords committee in 1848, Samuel Gurney conceded that it was about equal to that of all their competitors combined.

Members of the Gurney clan such as Hudson Gurney, Samuel Gurney, and David Barclay Chapman were widely credited with having raised Overend, Gurney to a position of supremacy among London bill brokers. These men were active in public debates over monetary policy and the Bank of England, and were as respected in the City for their prudence as for their commercial success. With the death of Samuel Gurney in 1856 and retirement of Barclay Chapman in 1857, the management of the firm fell into the hands of less able members of the Gurney and Chapman families.

In April 1860, the new management challenged the Bank's decision to limit brokers' access to its discount facilities by arranging a massive deposit withdrawal from the Bank of England. The Bank received an anonymous letter threatening that Overend and its friends were capable of withdrawing still more notes. The Bank quickly raised bank rate and the notes

were returned within a few days, but Overend's relations with the Bank and its reputation in the City suffered as a result.

The crisis was foreshadowed early in 1866 by the failure of the unfortunately named, and unrelated, Liverpool railroad contracting company of Watson, Overend, and Company. This failure was followed by the closure of the Joint Stock Discount Company which, like Overend, had held a large quantity of Watson, Overend paper. Discredit was heightened by news of the April collapse of Pinto, Perez and Company, to which Overend was known to be committed. On 9 May a court decision cast doubt on the value of Overend's holdings of acceptances of the Mid-Wales Railway, precipitating the firm's closure during the afternoon of Thursday, 10 May.

The failure of Overend, Gurney led to panic in the City which intensified the following day, "Black Friday." The panic soon spread to the provinces, and, while calm was restored within a few days, bank rate and money rates remained at record high levels until August.

By comparison with the crises of 1847 and 1857, in which the Bank of England raised its discount rate belatedly or not at all, the Overend, Gurney crisis was met with a swift rise in the bank rate. In response to the diminution of the bank's reserve and the growing state of market apprehension, the bank rate was raised to 7 percent (from 6 percent) on 3 May, 8 percent on 8 May, and 9 percent on 11 May, "Black Friday."

That Friday, Prime Minister Russell and Chancellor of the Exchequer Gladstone wrote to the Governors, recommending that the Bank of England increase its loans and discounts—after raising the bank rate to at least 10 percent—and, if necessary, exceed the fiduciary limit set by the Bank Charter Act. The letter was patterned on those issued during the crises of 1847 and 1857 in which the government promised to introduce a bill of indemnity into Parliament if the Bank of England exceeded the fiduciary limit. As in 1847 and 1857, publication of the government's letter calmed the more unreasoning fears although it by no means signaled the end of the emergency. Financial failures continued for several weeks, and the bank rate remained at 10 percent until August.

While the Bank of England rendered unprecedented levels of assistance to the market in the form of loans and discounts, it did not act as an effective lender of last resort. In the weeks that followed the crisis, several firms complained bitterly that the bank had not extended adequate assistance. Thus, while the Bank of England had made advances to the market on a scale unequaled in the post-Charter period, its failure to assist Overend, Gurney and its reluctance to provide assistance to other members of the financial community suggest that it did not fulfill the role of a lender of last resort.

The Overend, Gurney crisis, like the Baring crisis of 1890, was the result of speculative excess and culminated with the failure (or near failure) of one of the City's great firms. While the Bank of England rendered assistance to the market on both occasions, the crises had very different outcomes. The Overend, Gurney crisis was followed by three months of record high interest rates, waves of commercial and financial failures, and the disappearance of a firm which, according to tradition, had been second only to the Bank of England in the City of London. The Baring crisis, on the other hand, passed with only a brief rise in interest rates, while Baring Brothers was immediately reconstituted as a limited-liability company. The difference in outcomes can be traced to the evolution of the Bank of England as a lender of last resort.

Richard S. Grossman

See also BANK CHARTER ACT OF 1844; BANKING SCHOOL, CURRENCY SCHOOL, AND FREE BANKING SCHOOLS; BANK OF ENGLAND; BARING CRISIS; CENTRAL BANKING; CRISIS OF 1847; CRISIS OF 1857; LENDER OF LAST RESORT

Bibliography

Bagehot, W. [1873] 1962. *Lombard Street.* Homewood, Ill.: Irwin.
Batchelor, R. 1986. "The Avoidance of Catastrophe: Two Nineteenth-Century Banking Crises." In *Financial Crises and the World Banking System,* edited by F. Capie and G. Wood, 41–73. London: Macmillan.
Clapham, J. 1945. *The Bank of England: A History.* 2 vols. New York: Macmillan.
Fetter, F. W. 1965. *The Development of British Monetary Orthodoxy, 1797–1875.* Cambridge: Harvard Univ. Press.
Gregory, T. E., ed. 1929. *Select Statutes, Documents and Reports Relating to British Banking, 1832–1928.* 2 vols. London: Humphrey Milford.
Humphrey, T. 1975. "The Classical Concept of the Lender of Last Resort." Federal Reserve Bank of Richmond, *Economic Review,* January/February, 2–9.
Kindleberger, C. 1978. *Manias, Panics, and Crashes.* New York: Basic Books.
King, W. T. C. 1936. *History of the London Discount Market.* London: G. Routledge.
Pressnell, L. S. 1986. "Comment on Batchelor Paper." In *Financial Crises and the World Banking System,* edited by F. Capie and G. Wood, 74–76. London: Macmillan.
Sayers, R. S. 1957. *Central Banking After Bagehot.* Oxford: Clarendon Press.
Schwartz, A. J. 1986. "Real and Pseudo-Financial Crises." In *Financial Crises and the World Banking System,* edited by F. Capie and G. Wood, 11–31. London: Macmillan.
Thornton, H. [1802] 1939. *An Enquiry into the Nature and Effects of the Paper Credit of Great Britain.* Edited with an introduction by F. A. von Hayek. London: Allen and Unwin.

Overinvestment Theories of Business Cycles

The term "overinvestment" denotes an excess of investment expenditures over voluntary savings. Overinvestment arguments played an important role in pre-Keynesian business-cycle theories, but after the Keynesian Revolution, fell into neglect. The overinvestment approach to crises and depressions is basically different from, if not opposite to, that of *oversaving* theories. The latter emphasize decisions to save, especially in the context of an unequal income distribution, in restricting aggregate demand and triggering a *crisis.* The former, on the other hand, focus on the decisions to invest as the main cause of an upswing. Overinvestment theories contend that each crisis is the product of the preceding boom, which, as the consequence of overinvestment, is judged a pathological phenomenon.

Overinvestment must not be confused with overcapitalization, a situation in which the existing *stock* of capital exceeds the productive capacity justified by demand. Very often, overcapitalization arguments are used to account for the downturn of a business cycle, but not for the cycle itself. In fact, overcapitalization is usually considered a consequence of an overinvestment process that occurred during upswing, and only the latter is taken as the real cause of fluctuations.

One of the first overinvestment theories of the business cycle was advanced by M. I. Tugan-Baranovsky in his book *Les crises industrielles en Angleterre,* published in Russian in 1894. In Tugan's view, the cycle stems from the varying disproportions between the composition of aggregate demand and that of production. These disproportions depend on the relative movements of investment expenditures and current savings. Compared to the investment ratio, the saving ratio tends to be fairly stable through the various phases of the cycle. Investments fluctuate violently. Therefore, during depressions, the savings held as idle balances—termed "free capital" by Tugan—tend to grow. Then, at the beginning of the upswing, real capital accumulation can be sustained by the availability of cheap financial opportunities. The increasing demand for capital goods in the upswing stimulates both production and employment in the capital-goods sector. Furthermore, through a multiplier process similar to that envisaged by Kahn and Keynes, the increase in demand spreads to the consumer-goods sector, and the entire economy prospers. During the upswing, savings fall short of investment expenditures, but these can be financed through depleting idle balances and through credit expansion. However, liquid balances gradually dry up and credit facilities become increasingly scarce. The interest rate rises and investments become difficult to finance. This leads to the upper turning point of the business cycle. The downturn may also be triggered by the excess capacity built up during the upswing, but Tugan did not emphasize this point.

Tugan's book inspired several works in the German-speaking world. In particular, theories developed by Spiethoff (1902) and by Cassel ([1918] 1932) were built on Tugan's model.

The major weakness of Tugan's theory lay in the explanation of turning points. Though regarding the investment fluctuations as a real phenomenon, Tugan, to account for the cycle turning points, relied heavily on the movements of such supporting "financial" factors as the availability of free capital. But these do not adequately explain why the *incentive* to invest changes its sign at the turning points.

Spiethoff tried to fill this gap. Financial conditions, he argued, represent only a "push" factor in the fluctuations of investment activity. But "pull" factors are also necessary. These are represented by the appearance of new and relevant investment opportunities during the upturn, and by the "saturation" of the demand for capital goods during the downturn. The major sources of new investment opportunities are technical innovations and the opening of new markets. These stimuli do not occur evenly through time, but intermittently, in the form of external shocks. A strong enough shock can start the expansion. In a first stage, the existing plants rapidly reach full utilization; in a second one, new plants are built; and in a third one, they are completed. During these three stages, a sort of bandwagon process is set in motion. Demand for capital goods increases and raises their prices. Furthermore, as investments exceed savings, the demand for consumption goods exceeds supply and their prices also rise. Thus, profits increase in all sectors and investment is further stimulated. However, when all the new plants are completed, a fourth stage begins; capital is saturated, and investment slows down because of widespread excess capacity. The effects of the downswing are the opposite of those of the upswing: prices, profits, employment, wages, and consumption all decrease, and savings outstrip the outlets for them.

Cassel, writing several years after Tugan and Spiethoff, drew heavily on their ideas. Like Tugan, he stressed the influence of the supply of funds on investment decisions, and especially of changes in interest rates. During upswings, interest rates rise due to overinvestment. When they rise too high, the downturn begins. Then underinvestment allows interest rates to fall, so that, at the end of the crisis, the financial conditions of the upturn are restored. The cycle is damped, according to Cassel, but it does not disappear, because it is continuously revived by external shocks such as technical progress, the opening of new markets, and the growth of population. Cassel contributed two major advances to business-cycle theory: first, he brought to light the role played by time lags such as those between the completion of plants and the decision to invest and those between the latter and changes in interest rates; second, he had a clear intuition of the acceleration principle, recognizing that a given fall in consumption causes an even greater drop in the output of the capital-goods industries.

A particularly interesting business-cycle theory, one that combines overinvestment ar-

O

guments and the acceleration principle, is that of Aftalion ([1908–09] 1987, 1913). Fluctuations are triggered by changes in consumers' wants, and the consequent changes in capital formation necessary to modify productive capacity in the consumer-goods sector. But these changes cause overshooting, because capital construction requires a long "gestation period," during which consumption demand is incompletely satisfied, while investments outgrow voluntary savings. However, when the building up of plants is completed, the boom ends. Consumer goods are overproduced, and markets and consumers' wants are saturated. Consumer-goods prices fall due to the principle of diminishing marginal utility, while the substitution of capital for other factors is limited by the already high degree of capital intensity. Thus, prospective profitability falls, discouraging investments and triggering the crisis. The downswing can last for a long time, because capital goods are durable and the depleting of excess capacity is a slow process.

A particular emphasis on the role played by time as a major cause of economic fluctuations can be found in the Austrian theory of business cycles, developed mainly by Mises and Hayek. Hayek (1931) borrowed from Wicksell the idea of a cumulative process, and, on this ground, maintained that the principal source of economic fluctuations is a divergence between the market and the natural rates of interest. Credit expansion and cheap finance reduce market rates and encourage investments, thus increasing—in Austrian terminology—the *roundaboutness* of the overall economic process. However, the increased investment is not matched by additional *voluntary* saving. Overinvestment occurs. But since the production of consumer goods falls short of demand, their prices rise, so that *forced saving* by consumers during the upswing matches the overinvestment financed by credit expansion. The process cannot go on indefinitely. Eventually bank reserves dry up, while credit facilities shrink, and the market rates of interest rise. Investments are discouraged, and the process just described is reversed and the production process becomes less roundabout. The crisis brings about a process of disinvestment whose ultimate cause lies in the artificial and pathological overinvestment of the previous upswing.

In the interwar period, a number of other economists, like Hawtrey, Robertson, and even the Keynes of the *Treatise,* developed business-cycle theories in which Wicksell's cumulative process and forced saving play an important role. But in their arguments, monetary factors predominate over overinvestment problems as a cause of fluctuations. So their theories are better classified under the heading of monetary theories of the business cycle.

Ernesto Screpanti

See also ACCLERATION PRINCIPLE; AFTALION, ALBERT; AUSTRIAN THEORY OF BUSINESS CYCLES; CASSEL, CARL GUSTAV; FORCED SAVING; HAWTREY, RALPH GEORGE; HAYEK, FRIEDRICH AUGUST [VON]; MISES, LUDWIG EDLER VON; NATURAL RATE OF INTEREST; ROBERTSON, DENNIS HOLME; SPIETHOFF, ARTHUR; TUGAN-BARANOVSKY, MIKHAIL IVANOVICH; WICKSELL, JOHAN GUSTAV KNUT

Bibliography
Aftalion, A. [1908–09]1987. "La réalité des surproduction génerales: Essai d'une théorie des crises génerales et periodiques." *Revue d'économie politique* 97:745–66.
———. 1913. *Les crises périodiques de surproduction.* Paris: M. Rivière.
Cassel, G. [1918] 1932. *The Theory of Social Economy.* 5th ed. Translation. New York: Harcourt Brace.
Gordon, R. A. 1952. *Business Fluctuations.* New York: Harper and Row.
Haberler, G. 1962. *Prosperity and Depression.* 4th rev. ed. Cambridge: Harvard Univ. Press.
Hamberg, D. 1951. *Business Cycles.* New York: Macmillan.
Hansen, A. H. 1951. *Business Cycles and National Income.* London: Allen and Unwin.
Hansen, A. H. and H. Tout. 1933. "Investment and Saving in Business Cycle Theory." *Econometrica* 1:119–47.
Hayek, F. A. 1931. *Prices and Production.* London: Routledge.
Mises, L. von. [1924] 1953. *The Theory of Money and Credit.* Translation. 2d ed. New Haven: Yale Univ. Press.
Spiethoff, A. 1902. "Vorbemerkungen zu einer Theories der Überproduction." *Jarbuch für Gesetzgebung, Verwaltung, und Volkswirtschaft* 26:267–305.
Tugan-Baranovsky, M. I. [1894] 1913. *Les crises industrielles en Angleterre.* Translation. 2d rev. ed. Paris: Giard & Brière.

Oversaving Theories of Business Cycles

The term "oversaving" defines a situation in which planned savings exceeds investments. The same notion is sometimes characterized as *underconsumption*. The two notions are not synonymous, but, under certain assumptions, they are equivalent. In fact, given the composition of output in terms of both consumption and investment goods, an excess of planned savings over investment expenditures implies that consumption demand falls short of production; this is what is sometimes called "overproduction of consumption goods," or "underconsumption."

The first theories blaming oversaving for causing depressions were formulated early in the nineteenth century, and were immediately attacked by the classical economists, who disposed of them by invoking Say's Law. Afterwards, oversavings theories were long banned from orthodox economics. However, the Keynesian Revolution made it possible to understand the grain of truth they contained. It is now recognized that pre-Keynesian oversaving theories anticipated some aspects of Keynesian analysis. In particular, they identified the crucial role of income distribution in determining the aggregate saving ratio and, thus, the pace of growth of effective demand.

One of the first and most interesting oversaving theories of depression was put forward by James Maitland Lauderdale (1804). Lauderdale entered a debate stimulated by a debt-retirement program of his time, which he strongly opposed. The program was to increase taxes to set up a sinking fund, which would be used to buy bank government bonds. Lauderdale argued that this program was inimical to the growth of public wealth, because it would increase only the liquidity of bondholders, not necessarily their expenditure. Increased holdings of liquid assets would not find adequate investment outlets, because the level of consumption would have been curtailed by the tax increase. In fact, in Lauderdale's view, investment opportunities, under a given technology, depend on the level of consumption. This proposition rests on a basic hypothesis which Lauderdale did not formulate very clearly, i.e., that the aggregate propensity to consume depends on income distribution, with the well-off people displaying a higher "parsimony" than the poorer. Thus, the sinking-fund program, by reducing aggregate income (through taxes) and increasing the money holdings of the well-off

people (through debt repayment), could only have a deflationary effect.

During the French blockade of the British Islands, a debate developed about the role of foreign trade in sustaining growth. William Spence contributed to the discussion by advancing an oversaving theory in part similar to that of Lauderdale. Adopting a physiocratic approach, Spence supported the thesis that only the agricultural sector can produce a surplus, and that all the net incomes and expenses of the country are paid out of rent. Since all the incomes but rent are entirely spent either on consumption or on investment, the adequacy of effective demand rests on whether the landlords spend all their income on consumption goods. To rebut this thesis, James Mill formulated his own version of Say's Law: production creates purchasing power which is entirely and immediately spent on consumption or investments; therefore "the more you increase the annual produce, the more by that very act you extend the national market, the purchasing power and the actual purchase of the nation" (Mill [1808] 1966, 135). If landlords saved part of their income they could either invest it in agricultural production or lend it to the capitalists, who would invest it anyway.

Spence's rejoinder was twofold. First, investment opportunities in agriculture were limited, presumably because demand for agricultural products was growing very slowly. Second, investment opportunities in industry would be reduced by the very act of saving that financed it. The idea was that demand for consumer goods depends on the expenditures of the landlords. If savings reduce these expenditures, the inducement to invest would be reduced, so that savings would not be invested by the manufacturers. This is the central idea of any oversaving theory.

It was soon adopted by Malthus when he engaged in a debate with Ricardo very similar to the one between Spence and Mill. Malthus was mainly concerned with the post-Napoleonic Wars depression, which he attributed to an unusual stagnation of effective demand. In his theory, the lack of effective demand for consumer goods forced down market prices and thus squeezed profits. Reduced profits would discourage investment. The lack of effective demand was attributed to the "structure and habits of the society," i.e., to how the national income was distributed among the social classes and how each class was accustomed to spend it. Workers tend to consume the whole of their income, while capitalists tend to save the greatest part of their own. Due to the existence of profits and rents, the "labor commanded" by the national product necessarily exceeds that commanded by the wages fund or by the aggregate consumption expenditures of workers and capitalists. If profits are not entirely spent, effective demand will be lacking, unless it is supplemented by the expenditures of the landlords. The latter do not contribute to the production of material goods, but do contribute to the demand for them. An increase in the rent share of the national income or a decrease in the profit share would, therefore, accelerate the growth of effective demand.

The crux of Malthus's theory lay in explaining why capitalists' savings do not constitute effective demand. Malthus had an intuition of the possibility that the decisions to invest might diverge from the decisions to save. He even advanced a rough hypothesis of this kind in a letter to Ricardo in September 1814. But in his *Principles*, he seemed unaware of it when he assumed the equality of saving and investment, actually endorsing Say's Law.

Ricardo's criticism of Malthus, a criticism based on the assumption that saving always equals investment and therefore cannot affect aggregate demand, eventually succeeded in establishing the orthodoxy that dominated economic theory up to the Keynesian Revolution. After Ricardo, the oversaving approach was discredited among professional economists, and was cultivated only in the "underworld" of socialist economics. Among others, Sismondi and Rodbertus adopted it, but made no real analytical progress. When it reached Marx, who criticized it, it was discredited even among the socialists.

Oversaving theories of the crisis were revived after the Great Depression of the 1880s, and of course, after the Great Depression of the 1920s and 1930s. A leading figure in the "underworld" of oversaving theorists was J. A. Hobson, whose works inspired a series of other heterodox non-Marxist economists like C. H. Douglas, E. Lederer, W. T. Foster, and W. Catchings. But they also had a consistent influence on Marxist crisis theories of the early twentieth century. Actually, in the debates on the "breakdown" of capitalism that developed in the Second International, many Marxist economists, like Schmidt, Luxemburg, Boudin, and Bauer, expressed underconsumptionist views much reminiscent of Hobson's, even if his influence was rarely acknowledged in full.

Hobson's basic idea is that fast growth increases profits, because productivity increases and because wages lag behind prices. As profit earners have a propensity to save that is higher than that of wage earners, savings tend to increase and consumption to fall short of the production of consumer goods. If the increased saving ratio triggered an increase in investment, the glut would be mitigated. But it would do so only temporarily. In fact, investments will further increase the capacity available for producing consumer goods, which may eventually no longer be sold at profitable prices. A profit squeeze and a crisis will follow, which will only be resolved when, due to the wage lag, the wage share increases, the saving ratio shrinks, and inventories of consumer goods decline. However, there is a critical saving ratio, which, if attained, would sustain full-employment equilibrium. This ratio, termed the "right ratio" by Hobson, depends on the "state of industrial arts" and the "standards of consumption," but is nearly impossible to realize when the income distribution is as unequal as it is in modern economies.

The oversaving approach, especially Hobson's version of it, holds a twofold interest. First, it underscores, in a way reminiscent of the Post-Keynesian approach, and, especially, of the model used by Keynes in his *Treatise on Money*, the crucial role played by income distribution in determining the average saving propensity. Secondly, in emphasizing the difficulty of attaining the "right ratio" capable of preserving full-employment equilibrium, it anticipates some aspects of the modern "razor-edge" analysis of growth.

Ernesto Screpanti

See also BAUER, OTTO; DOUGLAS, CLIFFORD HUGH; FOSTER, WILLIAM TRUFANT; HOBSON, JOHN ATKINSON; INCOME DISTRIBUTION AND THE BUSINESS CYCLE; LUXEMBURG, ROSA; MALTHUS, THOMAS ROBERT; MARX, KARL HEINRICH; SAY, JEAN-BAPTISTE; SAY'S LAW; SISMONDI, JEAN CHARLES LEONARD SIMONDE DE; SWEEZY, PAUL MARLOR

Bibliography
Bleany, M. 1976. *Underconsumption Theories*. London: Lawrence and Wishart.
Haberler, G. 1962. *Prosperity and Depression*. 4th rev. ed. Cambridge: Harvard Univ. Press.

Hamberg, D. 1951. *Business Cycles.* New York: Macmillan.

Hansen, A. H. 1951. *Business Cycles and National Income.* London: Allen and Unwin.

Hansen, A. H. and H. Tout. 1933. "Investment and Saving in Business Cycle Theory." *Econometrica* 1:119–47.

Hobson, J. A. 1923. *The Economics of Unemployment.* New York: Macmillan.

Lauderdale, J. M. 1804. *An Inquiry into the Nature and Origin of Public Wealth.* Edinburgh: A. Constable.

Malthus, T. R. 1820. *Principles of Political Economy Considered with a View to Their Practical Application.* London: J. Murray.

Mill, J. [1808] 1966. *Commerce Defended.* In *James Mill: Selected Economic Writings,* edited by D. Winch, 85–159. Chicago: Univ. of Chicago Press.

Mummery, A. F. and J. A. Hobson. 1889. *Physiology of Industry.* London: John Murray.

Spence, W. 1807. *Britain Independent of Commerce.* 2d ed. London: T. Cedell and W. Davies.

Sweezy, P. M. 1942. *The Theory of Capitalist Development.* New York: Monthly Review Press.

O

P

Panic of 1825

The Panic of 1825 in England was a classic example of a speculation-fueled crisis. The panic did not spread to other European countries, though France suffered from a similar type of speculation-driven panic a few years later. At its height, the panic lasted one week in mid-December, during which several London banks ceased payment, causing scores of country banks to fail. The panic was stemmed by the discount policy of the Bank of England and two pieces of good luck: the timely arrival of a gold shipment from Paris, and the discovery of a forgotten box of banknotes. The panic itself was less memorable than the banking legislation that was enacted in response to it. This legislation was responsible for every major influence on banking evolution in England for the next twenty years.

Until 1825, England had a unit banking system which featured the Bank of England (which enjoyed a monopoly on joint-stock banking), approximately sixty other London-based private banks without note-issue privileges, and about 800 small private note-issuing country banks. The country banks were uncontrolled except for the limits on the note denominations they could issue and a prohibition against the ownership of a private bank by more than six partners.

Several factors contributed to a speculative fever which seems to have begun in late 1824. They included a widespread feeling of optimism at the time, a general shortage of investment vehicles resulting from the decrease in interest rates on bonds, an excess demand for several commodities, and the opening up of investment opportunities in South America.

There were several reasons for optimism in 1824–25. The feared war in Europe between Spain and France had been avoided, harvests had been good since 1822, the Bank was well stocked with bullion, interest rates were low, the government was opening new avenues of trade, and prospects for South American mining were favorable. In early 1825, the prosperity in the country was undoubted. In his speech in February, the King said, "there never was a period in the history of this country when all the great interests of the nation were at the same time in so thriving a condition, or when a feeling of content and satisfaction was more widely diffused through all classes of the British people."

South America became a focal point of the speculation when England formally recognized Mexico and the South American states in 1824 after they gained independence from Spain, creating opportunities for mining ventures in silver and gold and opening new markets for British goods. More than £150 million of British funds were invested in Mexico and South America during their first year of independence.

A few early purchasers, as is usual in speculation, were successful and attracted others into speculative ventures. Like the Bank of England, country bankers increased their issues with speculative advances on commodities when the speculative fever was raging. Speculation in the South American mines was fueled by a margin requirement of only 5 percent.

The April 1824 edition of *European Magazine* reported that "never since the South Sea Bubble has the mania been so endemic. There is not a capitalist nor moneylender all over the empire that is not infected with it, and, where it will end, no man can foresee" (Smart [1911] 1964, 2:188). Cotton was the first and most prominent good sought by speculators, followed by silk, wool, flax, and other goods. The price increases on some goods were justified by the shortness of supply, but the mania spread to other articles for which no such justification existed. The stock of coffee, for instance, was greater than in former years, yet its price rose 70 to 80 percent. Spice prices doubled and even quadrupled for no apparent reason.

Before the panic, the Bank of England contributed to the speculation by decreasing the interest on two of its bond issues, releasing the funds of those who refused to convert their issues to the new rate, and making current holders "restless" for higher returns in speculative investments.

In late November 1825, with the impending crisis evident, newspapers and public opinion called for the Bank of England to contract its issue, and cure the crisis by letting those bank houses with imprudent speculations fail. After having fueled the speculation with expansionary issues, the bank then reversed course.

The public clamored for notes or gold. However, neither could be made available fast enough, for gold was below the mint price and the mint was working furiously. In mid-December, the Bank of England temporarily ran out of five- and ten-pound notes, and had no smaller notes available (the issue of one- and two-pound notes had been suspended a few years earlier). Usury laws prevented interest rates from exceeding 5 percent, causing a shortage of loanable funds. Merchants who could not borrow had to sell goods at discounts up to 30 percent to obtain cash.

The first bank failure occurred on 29 November 1825. The London papers announced the failure of Sir William Eckford's, a large Plymouth bank, immediately followed by the failure of Wentworh & Co., a large Yorkshire bank. Pole, Thornton & Co. failed on 12 December, despite a £400,000 loan from the Bank of England, forcing sixty-three country banks into insolvency. The worst of the crisis followed. A run began on London banks, with six of them closing by mid-December, causing a general run on banks to convert notes. Pressure transferred to the Bank of England as country banks turned to it for reserves.

William Huskisson, president of the Board of Trade and governor of the Bank of England, reported to the House of Commons that on Monday and Tuesday, 12 and 13 December, even the best securities could not be converted into money. Even exchequer bills, bank stock, East India stock, and public funds could not be converted.

The merchants of London unsuccessfully petitioned the government for relief, claiming that the government had helped cause the panic by decreasing the interest rate on exchequer bills, and following a free-trade policy which diverted exports to India and South America. Further, they pleaded that since government action had been immediately successful in the 1793 panic, it would have the same results in the current crisis.

Lord Liverpool refused to grant any government aid. He insisted that the current panic was not like that of 1793, when war threw everything asunder. Now the cause was rash speculation, against which the government would not insure. He warned that he and his colleagues were determined to prevent passage of a bill for the relief of the sufferers of any losses from subscriptions in joint-stock companies.

On 14 December, the Bank of England once again reversed policy and eased credit, lending out £5 million. The issues were £35 million in the first two weeks of December, and £51 million in the last two. By 26 December, the panic was halted.

Help also arrived from abroad. By the end of 1825, runs on the Bank of England decreased its specie reserves to £1 million, nearly causing the bank to suspend payment. France provided the bank with gold in exchange for silver. Four million pounds in gold arrived from Paris on Monday, 19 December. Silver had been shipped to France as payment.

During that week, country demand for London credit was great. It was then that a forgotten box of one- and two-pound notes, previously unused, was accidentally discovered in a basement storeroom. The notes had been recalled a few years earlier. The Bank of England relieved the excess demand for credit from country banks by issuing as money approximately half a million of these notes. They were sent to the country banks, bringing immediate relief.

The speculative boom resulted in a dramatic increase in imports and domestic production, particularly in the cotton and iron industries, beginning in late 1824 and continuing until the financial market crashed. Investment funds were clamoring for a project in 1824 and 1825. At the beginning of 1824, there were 154 joint stock companies with capital of £48 million. An additional 624 such companies were either started or proposed during the next two years, 127 of which survived the crisis and were still in operation in 1827. The crash in the real sector followed that of the financial sector, with the bottom being reached in 1826. Indexes of textile, consumer goods, and total production all decreased, hitting their low points in 1826 after peaking in 1825. Labor strife reached its high water mark in 1826 when the slowdown in production caused a substantial increase in unemployment.

The country banks were widely blamed for their part in the panic, particularly the one- and two-pound notes that they circulated. It was argued that since these small notes circulated among the less educated and lower classes, they were especially subject to volatility. It was also argued that by driving gold out of circulation, small notes forced the country to carry on its transactions with a smaller stock of gold than would otherwise have been available.

Secretary Baring disagreed with the government policy of refusing aid. He did not believe that speculation was the problem. Rather, the Bank of England was at fault for first using its large accumulation of gold to fuel a monetary expansion, and then suddenly reversing its policy. Others argued that the monopoly of the bank was the root of the problem, and that if Britain had a banking system like Scotland's, the panic would have been avoided.

In Scotland, only three minor banks failed. The Scots maintained that Scottish banks failed less often than English banks because they were joint-stock companies while English banks, except the Bank of England, were private partnerships, consisting of at most six and usually only one or two partners.

In 1826, the government called for the credit system of the country to be placed on a firmer foundation. Lord Liverpool called for reforms including the replacement of one- and two-pound notes with coins, and the revocation of the monopoly of the Bank of England. He argued against continuing to allow any small tradesman to open a country bank, while prohibiting more than six persons with a fortune sufficient to carry on the concern with safety from doing so.

The crisis revealed the weakness of the English system of private banking and led to the passage of the joint-stock bank act in 1826. This act allowed joint-stock banks to be formed outside a sixty-five-mile radius of London. A compromise allowing the Bank of England to keep monopoly rights on joint-stock banking within sixty-five miles of London was necessary, because complete revocation of its monopoly violated the bank's charter. Although restrictions on forming joint-stock banks were removed in the 1826 act, partners were not granted limited liability until 1858. On 7 March 1826, a bill was passed calling for the gradual removal of one- and two-pound notes. This legislation also allowed the Bank of England to establish branches in the country.

Nearly two hundred banks either collapsed or stopped payment in the wake of the crisis. While recovery was slow—industry did not begin to revive until stimulated by increasing exports and loans to the United States in 1830—government reaction to the panic was swift, as is evidenced by the Act of 1826. It was this bank legislation following the crisis, rather than the crisis itself, which is the most memorable feature of the Panic of 1825.

Michael Haupert

See also BANKING PANICS; BANK OF ENGLAND; FREE BANKING; MUSHET, ROBERT; PARNELL, HENRY BROOKE

Bibliography

Anderson, B. L. and P. L. Cottrell. 1974. *Money and Banking in England: The Development of the Banking System, 1694–1914.* Newton Abbott: David and Charles.

Andreades, A. 1909. *History of the Bank of England.* London: P. S. King.

Ashton, T. S. 1953. "The Crisis of 1825— Letters from a Young Lady." In *Papers in English Monetary History,* edited by T. S. Ashton and R. S. Sayers, 96–108. Oxford: Clarendon Press.

Brock, W. R. 1941. *Lord Liverpool and Liberal Toryism, 1820–1827.* Cambridge: Cambridge Univ. Press.

Checkland, S. G. 1975. *Scottish Banking: A History, 1695–1973.* Glasgow: Collins.

Clapham, John. 1945. *The Bank of England: A History.* Vol. 2. Cambridge: Cambridge Univ. Press.

Del Mar, A. 1896. *History of Monetary Systems.* Orno, Maine: The National Poetry Foundation.

Gayer, A. D., W. W. Rostow, and A. J. Schwartz. 1953. *The Growth and Fluctuation of the British Economy, 1790–1850: An Historical, Statistical and Theoretical Study of Britain's Economic Develop-*

ment. Vol. 1. Oxford: Clarendon Press.

Levi, L. 1872. *History of British Commerce.* London: J. Murray.

MacLeod, H. D. 1896. *A History of Banking in Great Britain.* New York: *Journal of Commerce and Commercial Bulletin.*

Morgan, E. V. 1943. *The Theory and Practice of Central Banking, 1797–1913.* Cambridge: Cambridge Univ. Press.

Smart, W. [1911] 1964. *Economic Annals of the Nineteenth Century.* Vol. 2. *1821–1830.* New York: A. M. Kelley.

Wisely, W. 1977. *A Tool of Power, The Political History of Money.* New York: Wiley.

Wood, E. 1939. *English Theories of Central Banking Control, 1819–1858.* Cambridge: Harvard Univ. Press.

Panic of 1837

The panic of 1837 followed a series of unusual monetary and fiscal events. In chronological order, these events included, first, the controversy over rechartering the Second Bank of the United States (1830–34); second, devaluation of the gold dollar by almost 7 percent (1834); third, burgeoning land sales by the federal government, which temporarily doubled federal government revenues (1834–36); fourth, the distribution of the federal government's excess revenue to the states (1836–37); fifth, President Jackson's proclamation of a "Specie Circular" (1836); and, finally, the severe bank-credit contraction of 1837.

The Second Bank of the United States was chartered by the federal government, and government appointees served on its Board of Directors. Unlike other banks, it could have branches in all the states, its bank notes were legal tender for all payments to the federal government, and it was the federal government's bursar and depository. These characteristics gave the Second Bank some conventional central-bank powers that it had begun to use by the time its recharter became a political issue in the early 1830s.

Andrew Jackson, in opposition to the majorities of several Congresses, disapproved of the federal government's connection with the bank. He based his 1832 campaign for a second term on the opposition to the bank's recharter. He also vetoed two bills for the bank's recharter which Congress was unable to override. The state of Pennsylvania subsequently chartered the Second Bank in 1836.

To minimize the government's connection to the Second Bank, Jackson ordered his Secretaries of the Treasury to deposit government revenue received after 24 September 1833 in selected state bank depositories. Subsequently, these banks became known as "pet" banks, because their selection was allegedly based on political support of Jackson.

The Gold Coin Act of 1834 devalued the gold dollar by 6.6 percent without altering the silver dollar, so the mint values between the two metals changed from 15-to-1 to 16-to-1. The objective of the act was to get a gold-silver ratio that would overvalue gold slightly at the mint in order to attract the exports of gold from Mexico and South America.

The new mint value for gold, together with capital imports, significantly increased both silver and gold imports in 1834. These inflows continued through 1835 and 1836, lessened in 1837, and were again much above average in 1838. Between 1833 and 1837, the net inflow was slightly over $40 million, with silver accounting for about 68 percent of this increase (Hepburn 1924, 69). The result was a severe inflation. Between April 1834 and February 1837, the price level, as best as it can be measured, rose by 52 percent or by about 12 percent per year (Temin 1969, 69).

Between 1833 and 1836, the federal government also offered a large new supply of lands in several states bordering the Mississippi River and further west. The gradually declining real prices of public lands due to the inflation, together with the large increases in available supplies, generated an enormous increase in land sales that doubled the federal government's fiscal receipts in 1836. These revenues enabled the government to retire the entire national debt and have enough left for a substantial rebate to the states.

Congress saw to this "distribution" by passing an "Act to Regulate the Deposits of Public Money" on 23 June 1836. This act reflected the intention of Congress to provide for the safekeeping of the "public money" and for its equitable "deposit" in state governments' treasuries (Timberlake 1978, 52–53).

Jackson signed the distribution bill reluctantly. He objected generally to the existence of banks, and particularly to any connection of the federal government with banks. Therefore, in an effort to reduce the government's deposits in banks, he had his Secretary of the Treasury issue a restraining Executive Order on 11 July

1836 (after Congress had adjourned). This order, known as the Specie Circular, proclaimed that *after* 23 December 1836, and for parcels of land *over* 320 acres, the government would accept only specie.

The stated intent of the Specie Circular was to retard the sales of public lands, so that the government would have less deposits to keep in banks, and less surplus to distribute under the Deposit-Distribution Act. In fact, the proclamation had little effect. Land sales continued at a high volume even through the first quarter of 1837. Even if land sales had dropped to nothing, their absence would not have slowed total spending appreciably since the money stock had already burgeoned due to the inflow of specie. The only real "effect" of the Specie Circular was to confirm the deflationary policy preferences of the Jackson Administration (Timberlake 1978, 51).

The allocation of the surplus was in proportion to the total number of electors, and hence Congressmen, from each state. No state had fewer than two Senators and one Representative.

Three installments of the distribution were made on 1 January, 1 April, and 1 July 1837. The final installment, which was to have been made 1 September, had to be canceled when the fiscal balance of the Treasury fell to the point where the Treasury could hardly cover ordinary expenses. The total distribution was slightly more than $28 million, which exceeded by about 15 percent the federal government's ordinary annual expenditures at that time.

As the federal government paid out the first two installments of the distribution, some state governments simply redeposited the federal payments in their own accounts at the same banks that held the deposits for the federal government. In such cases, no withdrawals of specie occurred. Other state governments, however, demanded specie for the warrants that the federal government drew in their favor. One state (Arkansas) had no bank at all; and some state governments chose not to use banks for their fiscal necessities. When these states received their shares of the distribution, they transferred the specie from the federal depository bank to their own state treasuries (Timberlake 1978, 56).

Because the disposition of the monies from the distribution took time, significant lags occurred between the states' receipts of the money and subsequent disbursements that reinjected the specie into the normal channels of trade and into the banks. From the end of 1836 to mid-1837, bank-held specie fell from about $39 million to $30 million. The reduction in reserve balances was aggravated by a decline in the rate of increase of specie inflows, which were in 1837 only about half ($4.5 million) the average volume of the previous four years. This retardation resulted in part from Bank of England discount-rate policy that temporarily reduced gold flows from England (Temin 1969, 137; Matthews 1954, 5).

The Panic of 1837 began in early May when lack of specie forced banks to suspend specie redemption of their own notes and deposits. Banks in New York and New Orleans were the first to suspend.

Suspension was an admission of *illiquidity;* that is, of a bank's inability to redeem its own notes and deposits with specie (gold and silver). *Illiquidity,* however, does not imply *insolvency*—that is, a condition in which a bank's assets are worth less than the market value of its liabilities. Many banks that suspended because of illiquidity were undoubtedly solvent, with interest-earning assets that were generating plenty of income.

The suspension of specie payments spread throughout the banking system. Nevertheless, the disbursement of federal government deposits for the third installment of the distribution still required a transfer of banknotes or bank deposits to state government treasuries; but by this time the notes and deposits were not redeemable in specie. A corollary of this condition was a "premium on specie," meaning that a given quantity of gold or silver had a market value in bank notes or deposits greater than its legal or mint value. The premium on specie reached 10 percent in the summer of 1837, but generally was less than 5 percent. It disappeared altogether in May 1838 as the banks all resumed specie payments (Temin 1969, 118).

Prices and wages fell rapidly in 1837 after the suspension of specie payments, thereby ensuring that serious unemployment would not develop. Subsequently, specie inflows burgeoned to over $14 million ($11 million in gold) in 1838. Not only did banks resume specie payments, but prices rose almost to their high levels of early 1837. Thus, the Panic of 1837 was primarily monetary; it had little effect on employment and business activity. It resulted from distribution of the surplus and the associated bank-credit contraction, with Bank of England

P

policy and fluctuations in cotton sales also playing roles. As Temin (1969, 120) concluded, "The deflation of 1837 was mild and short-lived; it does not seem to have caused major distress in the economy."

Another conclusion of some academic importance is that the Panic of 1837 was not part of a long-term decline. Specie imports in 1838 restored business activity and the ability of the banks to redeem their demand obligations. Prosperity continued well into 1839 before a worldwide dearth of specie at prevailing price levels generated an ongoing deflation to the business-cycle trough of 1843.

Richard H. Timberlake Jr.

Bibliography

Bourne, E. G. 1885. *The History of the Surplus Revenue of 1837.* New York: G. P. Putnam's Sons.

Getell, F. O. 1964. "Spoils of the Bank War: Political Bias in the Selection of Pet Banks." *American Historical Review* 70:35–58.

Hammond, B. 1957. *Banks and Politics in America from the Revolution to the Civil War.* Princeton: Princeton Univ. Press.

Hepburn, A. B. 1924. *A History of Currency in the United States.* Rev. ed. New York: Macmillan.

Matthews, R. C. O. 1954. *A Study in Trade-Cycle History: Economic Fluctuations in Great Britain, 1833–1842.* Cambridge: Cambridge Univ. Press.

McGrane, R. C. 1924. *The Panic of 1837.* Chicago: Univ. of Chicago Press.

Scheiber, H. 1963. "The Pet Banks in Jacksonian Politics and Finance." *Journal of Economic History* 23:196–214.

Schweikart, L. 1987. *Banking in the American South from the Age of Jackson to Reconstruction.* Baton Rouge: Louisiana State Univ. Press.

Temin, P. 1969. *The Jacksonian Economy.* New York: Norton.

Timberlake, R. H. 1978. *Origins of Central Banking in the United States.* Cambridge: Harvard Univ. Press.

Panic of 1893

The Panic of 1893 was the culmination of an ongoing twenty-year political struggle between gold and silver advocates over the monetary standard. It emphasized the economic stresses that resulted from the government's attempt to maintain an official parity between two monetary metals. It also reflected the political pressures applied to the monetary system by special interests that had something to gain or lose from changes in the value of the monetary unit.

The postbellum period in the United States was full of monetary controversy. During the Civil War the federal government began issuing fiat paper currency—U.S. notes or "greenbacks." The resulting inflation raised the market prices of gold and silver coins well above their statutory mint prices. Postwar policy aimed to restore the self-regulating, bimetallic standard, which required bringing the mint and market prices of the two metals into congruence.

Government policy could accomplish this goal in three ways. First, Congress could raise the mint prices of the monetary metals to their postwar market values; second, it could shrink the stock of fiat paper money by providing for budget surpluses, thereby bringing down the general level of money prices including the market prices of the monetary metals; third, it could freeze the stock of fiat paper money and allow economic growth to produce a gradual decline in prices until the market and mint prices of gold and silver again coincided. A fourth possibility was an increase in the real output of the monetary metals sufficient to depress their inflated market prices to their original mint prices. In fact, the government did reduce the stock of fiat money through fiscal surpluses. Prices fell severely, activating political forces representing debtor classes which hoped to moderate the decline. Real output also increased markedly, which accelerated the decline in prices.

As it turned out, the mint prices of gold and silver were never changed, though the option was discussed. However, the decline in the cost of producing silver through new discoveries in the mid-1870s led to a dramatic increase in its output and a sharp decline in its relative value. Silver thereafter became a "cheap" money and replaced greenbacks as the favored vehicle for the political forces seeking a means to halt or reverse the ongoing decline.

The Bland-Allison Act of 1878 was the first success for the free-coinage-of-silver forces, but it was only a partial victory. It called for government silver purchases of $2 million to $4 million a month, the actual amount being left to the discretion of the Secretary of the Treasury. (While the act was in force, no Secretary bought more than the lower limit of $2 million per month.)

The production costs and market prices of silver steadily declined after 1875, so that the difference between the monetary value of a silver dollar—which was $1—and the cost of the silver in the silver dollar steadily widened. This difference, times the number of dollars coined, equalled the seignorage revenue accruing to the government.

Only a limited number of silver dollars would stay in circulation. The rest remained as an uncirculated stock in the Treasury. In 1886 Congress authorized the Secretary of the Treasury to issue paper silver certificates that represented the silver bullion in the Treasury. In this form, the silver currency circulated just as any other paper money, e.g., greenbacks.

Free-silver forces continued their efforts, and in July 1890, Congress enacted a new silver bill, the Treasury Note Act of 1890, popularly known as the Sherman Silver Purchase Act. (Senator John Sherman of Ohio was chairman of the House-Senate conference committee that reported out the successful compromise bill.)

The act called for the Treasury to purchase 4.5 million *ounces* of silver per month at market prices instead of the two to four million *dollars* per month required by the Bland-Allison Act. The two silver acts would have required the same *dollar* purchases of silver at a market price of $.444 per ounce. Since the average price of silver in the early 1890s was $.92 per ounce, the 1890 act more than doubled the federal government's dollar expenditures on silver and the amount of silver monetized.

The increased governmental demand for silver in the United States coincided with a declining demand for silver in the rest of the world. Many governments stopped the free coinage of silver and adopted a gold standard. Only Mexico, some South American countries, and China continued on a silver standard.

Exchange rates between gold and silver currencies fluctuated with the market values of the two metals. The relative value of gold to silver steadily increased. By 1893, the gold-silver price ratio was 26.5-to-1, and by 1896, it was 32-to-1. All through this period, free-silver forces in the United States argued for free coinage at a 16-to-1 ratio. Such free-silver policy, they thought, would significantly increase the U.S. price level.

As it was, limited monetization of silver in the United States had the same effect as a similar increase in the quantity of greenbacks. The new supply of currency raised prices in the United States relative to prices in countries not inflating their currencies, reduced the international value of the dollar, and by increasing imports while reducing exports, generated a constant outflow of gold. Coupled with these conventional economic forces was the common opinion that U.S. policy would lead to a monometallic silver standard. This expectation tended to be self-fulfilling. It encouraged foreigners who held fixed dollar claims payable in the United States to sell or redeem them for gold, thereby aggravating the gold outflow.

President Grover Cleveland, who was elected for a second term in 1892, opposed the movement to take the United States off the gold standard. This stance implied opposition to silver monetization, which also pitted him against the powerful silver forces in his own Democratic Party. His first major act as president was to call a special session of Congress in the summer of 1893 to repeal the Treasury Note Act of 1890. Despite a filibuster by free-silver elements in the Senate, his effort was successful. The silver-purchase clause in the Treasury Note Act was repealed on 1 November 1893.

Cleveland's principled effort to stop silver monetization led to a bitter schism in the Democratic Party, ending his role as party leader. From then on, Cleveland presided over a caretaker administration.

The silver controversy, combined with the outflows of gold and exacerbated by the anticipation that the gold standard would be abandoned, increased the demand for U.S. gold as well as for all U.S. currencies and securities redeemable in gold at a fixed price. Silver monetization thereby displaced more gold through capital exports than the quantitative increase in silver would have warranted. Silver policy, therefore, had a *deflationary* effect on the economy even though prices would certainly have risen if silver had replaced gold as the monetary standard.

The protracted Congressional debates over repeal of the silver-purchase clause during the summer and fall of 1893 caused a general uneasiness throughout the economy that particularly affected the financial sector. Foreign creditors redeemed American securities in gold. Much of this gold came from the U.S. Treasury, which held a gold reserve against outstanding

U.S. notes, national bank notes, and silver currency. In addition, interior banks tried to redeem their interbank deposits held in New York and other financial centers.

The external and internal drains of gold led to a currency "famine" centered in New York City. The "famine" was simply an extraordinary demand for gold or any obligations contractually redeemable in gold. Banks in financial centers called loans, and short-term interest rates rose to as much as 74 percent per annum. The premium on government currencies over other forms of money was as high as 4 percent.

Under these conditions, banks in Eastern financial centers—New York, Boston, and Philadelphia—began restricting cash redemptions by various means: for example, limiting the amount of cash withdrawals to $100 or $200 a day. The banks and their associated clearinghouses also issued clearinghouse loan certificates, as well as other clearinghouse currencies. These devices, although illegal or "extralegal" because of several earlier restrictive currency acts, proved beneficial to all concerned—financial center banks, small-town banks, and depositors. They provided additional currency to meet a manifest market demand for the same. The correspondence of the new supply of exchange media to the demand for it was so obvious that the federal government chose not to enforce its restrictive currency laws, confirming the inadvisability of such laws in the first place.

The Treasury's gold reserve fell from an average value of $118 million in 1891 to $65 million in 1894, and finally rose to slightly over $100 million by 1896. As the gold flowed out, the Treasury sold securities to replenish the gold, which could then flow out again. This "continuous cycle" could not be stopped until the U.S. money supply and U.S. prices receded to a level at which the real mint price of gold was high enough to discourage further gold outflows. This condition was not reached until mid-1896. While repeal of the silver-purchase clause started the movement toward equilibrium, ongoing agitation for further silver monetization caused the domestic money stock to decline until 1896. Total currency in circulation fell 12 percent while prices fell by about 10 percent.

After 1896, burgeoning world production of gold gave buoyancy to price levels everywhere, including the United States. No sooner did prices respond than the "question of the standard" faded from the political scene. On 14 March 1900, Congress passed the Gold Currency Act which made gold the single monetary standard in the United States. Thereafter, silver currency was officially subsidiary.

Richard H. Timberlake Jr.

See also BANKING PANICS; CLEARINGHOUSES; GOLD STANDARD; GOLD STANDARD: CAUSES AND CONSEQUENCES

Bibliography

Fels, R. 1959. *American Business Cycles*. Chapel Hill: Univ. of North Carolina Press.

Friedman, M. and A. J. Schwartz. 1963. *A Monetary History of the United States, 1867–1960*. Princeton: Princeton Univ. Press.

Hepburn, A. B. 1924. *A History of Currency in the United States*. Rev. ed. New York: Macmillan.

Hoffman, C. 1956. "The Depression of the Nineties." *Journal of Economic History* 16:164–87.

Hollingsworth, J. R. 1963. *The Whirligig of Politics*. Chicago: Univ. of Chicago Press.

Lauck, W. J. 1907. *The Causes of the Panic of 1893*. Boston: Houghton Mifflin.

Timberlake, R. H. 1978. *Origins of Central Banking in the United States*. Cambridge: Harvard Univ. Press.

Pareto, Vilfredo (1848–1923)

Vilfredo Pareto was graduated in 1869 with a doctor's degree in engineering from the Polytechnic Institute of Turin, Italy. In 1893, he succeeded Léon Walras in the chair of Political Economy at the University of Lausanne, Switzerland. In 1906, he retired and published his great work in economics, *Manuale d'economia politica,* and later his famous work in sociology, *Trattato di sociologia generale.* After the publication of the *Manuale,* Pareto devoted himself almost exclusively to research in sociology, which was published as the *Trattato.* The *Trattato* has generally been ignored by economists, although it is this work that contains Pareto's theories of cycles. His theories of cycles can be categorized as two distinctly different types: monetary and employment theories, which focus on business cycles, and theories of very long-term cycles, which account for the rise and fall of nation states, and are sociological in nature. This article is concerned with the former type.

Pareto's theory of business cycles joined sociological analysis with economic theory by analyzing the motivations of different socioeconomic classes and their role in the economic process. The analysis no longer focused on the behavior of individual elements, but instead, on the behavior of aggregates. The result was striking similarity between Keynes's later theory and Pareto's theory of consumption, savings, investment, and income. On the other hand, there were important differences between the two writers. Like Keynes, Pareto tended to discount the impact of interest rates on savings. But for Pareto, given psychological and institutional factors, aggregate consumption and savings were functions of the distribution of real income (as between rentiers, entrepreneurs, and workers) and of the aggregate level of output or real income. The three functional income groups were presumed to have different marginal propensities to consume (and save), so that a redistribution of income (say, due to inflation) from one group to another could increase spending and reduce savings if income was redistributed toward the group with the higher propensity to consume.

For Pareto, the components of savings are demand for bonds, D_b, demand for equities, D_e, and demand for money for non-transaction purposes, D_{m2}. The demand for bonds is a function of the interest rate, real wealth holdings of savers, and their real income. For Pareto, the demand for equities is "subjective" and involves speculative factors and is therefore excluded from his analysis. Finally, since holding nontransactions balances is an alternative to holding bonds, the demand for hoarded money depends on the same variables as does the demand for bonds.

The supply of bonds is derived from investment demand which in turn is a function of the interest rate. The equality of the demand for and the supply of bonds determines equilibrium in the bond market. The demand for money consists of transactions demand, D_{m1}, which is a function of the price level and the level of real output (i.e., the quantity theory) *plus* the demand for hoarded money balances, D_{m2}. The supply of money, M_0, is assumed fixed and the equilibrium price level is determined by $M_0 = D_{m1} + D_{m2}$.

Savings, S, and investment, I, are defined as follows:

$$S_t \equiv D_{bt} + D_{m2t},$$
$$D_{bt} \equiv I_t,$$
$$S_t - I_t \equiv D_{m2t}.$$

The final expression shows that for time period t the difference between savings and investment is the amount of hoarded money balances demanded for that period. If $D_{m2t} = 0$, then $S_t = I_t$, a result analogous to Keynes's condition. Pareto's definitions show that during periods of protracted hoarding (the contraction and depression phases of the cycle), the hoarded money balances permit "dishoarding" during the expansion phase to expand investment far beyond current savings.

The remainder of Pareto's theory, namely employment theory, is largely cast in the neoclassical mold. Prices are flexible, the demand for output depends on real income, and the interest rate and the supply of output depends on the real wage. One important departure from neoclassical doctrine is that, for Pareto, the supply of labor is more responsive to money wages than to real wages. Real-wage *shares* are equal to the level of employment times the real wage. Once the wage share of national income is accounted for, it remains to determine the other components of national income, rentier income, and entrepreneurial income. Rentiers are assumed to have more or less fixed *nominal* income, and entrepreneurial income is the residual after payments to labor (wages) and rentiers (interest) are made.

Pareto's system can be expressed as six simultaneous equations that determine the interest rate, r, the price level, P, the level of output, Q, the wage share, Y_w, the entrepreneurial share, Y_e, and the wage rate, W. The parameters are the money supply, the quantity of bonds held by rentiers, and rentier nominal income, Y_r.

In Pareto's theory of cycles, prices begin to rise during the ascending phase of the cycle, redistributing real income from rentier-savers (with a high propensity to save) to workers and entrepreneurs (with a low propensity to save). This can be shown by breaking aggregate real income into its share components.

$$\frac{Y_w}{P} + \frac{Y_e}{P} + \frac{Y_r}{P} = \frac{Y}{P} = Q$$

At a full-employment level of output, a doubling of the price level and money wages causes no change in the real-income share of workers. On the other hand, the real-income share of rentiers (with fixed nominal incomes) is reduced by half, and the entrepreneurs gain by exactly this amount. Aggregate real income does not change. If rentiers have a lower marginal propensity to consume than workers and entrepreneurs, the *aggregate average* propensity to consume will rise at the current level of real income.

As the ascending phase continues, consumption demand increases and savings fall due to the redistributional effects of rising prices. Declining savings reduces the demand for bonds, so that the interest rate rises. The rising interest rate reduces the nominal value of bond holdings, while the rising price level reduces the real value of bond holdings, inducing savers to hold current savings in the form of hoarded money balances, which further increases interest rates, and so on. The rise in the interest rate reduces investment demand, which brings on the crisis. Since investment demand is falling, the supply of bonds falls, so that interest rates stop rising or even decline. Later, in the descending phase, both the interest rate and the price level fall.

The falling price level redistributes real income toward rentiers, so that the aggregate propensity to consume decreases. Aggregate demand for output falls because of a decline in consumption demand. As the price level falls, because of declining demand for output, the real value of bond holding increases and together with a declining interest rate, increases the demand for bonds not only by the amount of current savings, but in addition, by the "dishoarded" money balances. This further reduces the interest rate, stimulating investment demand. Output increases, and the price level begins to rise. Eventually, hoarded balances are exhausted and the interest rate begins to rise as the ascending phase of the cycle continues. This completes the cycle.

Given perfectly competitive labor and product markets, an increase in prices induces employers to expand output, and raises nominal wages. Since, according to Pareto, workers are less sensitive to price changes than firms are, nominal-wage increases lag behind price increases during economic expansions, so that real wages fall. When prices are falling, money-wage decreases lag behind price decreases, because workers resist reduced nominal wages, so that real wages rise. Thus the supply of output and the level of employment are positively related to prices and negatively related to real wages.

Pareto's theory of business cycles anticipated some of the fundamental conceptions of later Keynesian theory, while also showing how price-level changes occur in and contribute to the cycle.

Vincent J. Tarascio

See also INCOME DISTRIBUTION AND THE BUSINESS CYCLE; LONG-WAVE THEORIES

Bibliography

Pareto, V. [1906] 1971. *Manual of Political Economy.* Translation. New York: A. M. Kelley.

———. [1916] 1935. *Trattato di sociologia general.* 4 vols. Translated into English as *The Mind and Society: A Treatise on General Sociology,* by A. Bongiorno and A. Livingston. 4 vols. New York: Dover.

Tarascio, V. J. 1969. "The Monetary and Employment Theories of Vilfredo Pareto." *History of Political Economy* 1:101–22.

Parnell, Henry Brooke (1776–1842)

Henry Parnell was the leading Parliamentary advocate of free banking in the British monetary debates of the 1820s and 1830s, and a key critic of what he saw as the cycle-amplifying policies of the Bank of England. His two contributions to the Free Banking School literature were *Observations on Paper Money, Banking, and Overtrading* and *A Plain Statement of the Power of the Bank of England and the Use It Has Made of It.* He had earlier published two pamphlets providing evidence of Bank of England overissues during the Restriction period, and had been a member of the Bullion Committee.

An Irish Protestant country gentleman, Parnell represented his native Queen's County in the House of Commons in 1802, the borough of Portarlington later in 1802, Queen's County again from 1806 to 1832, and Dundee, Scotland from 1833 to 1841. In 1841, he was created the first Baron Congleton, and became a member of the House of Lords until his suicide the following year. He was a radical liberal Whig M.P., well known for supporting Catholic emancipation, abolition of the Corn laws, electoral reform, tax reform, and reduction of military expenditures, among other causes. He belonged to the pro-free-trade Political Economy Club in London, where as early as 1825 he defended against J. R. McCulloch of the Currency School, and later against Thomas Tooke of the Banking School, the proposal to allow free note-issuing competition with the Bank of England. Parnell was appointed in 1832 to the Committee of Secrecy on the Bank of England Charter. Its only member opposed to renewing the Bank's charter, he complained with some justification in a Parliamentary speech (Hansard 1833, col. 1330–31) that the Committee's "inquiry and evidence was *ex parte* and one-sided" in favor of renewal.

Parnell's 1827 book was the first major work of advocacy by the Free Banking School. It sounded what would be the school's major themes, later elaborated by James W. Gilbart and others. He criticized the power of the Bank of England to control the currency stock, and, following Robert Mushet, attributed the crisis of 1825–26 to the Bank's overissues of 1824–25. He extolled a free-banking system, to be attained by eliminating the legal privileges of the Bank of England, under which money and credit would be regulated by competition among banks. He cited at length evidence that free banking worked successfully in Scotland, particularly the Scottish interbank note-exchange system, which promptly corrected overissues by any bank. His 1832 book returned to the same themes, and criticized McCulloch's anonymous 1831 defense of the privileges of the Bank of England.

Parnell was a highly skilled expositor of the Free Banking School's theories both in Parliamentary debates and in print. He was not highly original in developing a positive business-cycle theory, but he pioneered a major innovation in policy thought, identifying free banking as an antidote to the central bank's power to create monetary disturbances.

Lawrence H. White

See also BANKING SCHOOL, CURRENCY SCHOOL, AND FREE BANKING SCHOOL; FREE BANKING; MUSHET, ROBERT; PANIC OF 1825

Bibliography

Fetter, F. W. 1980. *The Economist in Parliament: 1780–1868.* Durham: Duke Univ. Press.

[McCulloch, J. R.] 1831. *Historical Sketch of the Bank of England: With an Examination of the Question as to the Prolongation of the Exclusive Privileges of that Establishment.* London: Longmans.

Parnell, H. 1827. *Observations on Paper Money, Banking, and Overtrading.* London: J. Ridgeway.

———. 1832. *A Plain Statement of the Power of the Bank of England and the Use It Has Made of It; with a Refutation of the Objections Made to the Scotch System of Banking; and a Reply to the "Historical Sketch of the Bank of England."* London: J. Ridgeway.

White, L. H. 1844. *Free Banking in Britain: Theory, Experience, and Debate, 1800–1845.* Cambridge: Cambridge Univ. Press.

Period of Production

The notion of a period of production was introduced to provide a scalar representation of the temporal circumstances under which commodities are produced. More specifically, it was meant to measure the *roundaboutness* or capital-intensity of production. It was thought that a collection of heterogeneous capital goods could thereby be reduced to homogeneous units of time. In this view, the production process was conceived as unidirectional rather than circular, extending from the initial expenditure of the services of "primary" factors of production, such as different kinds of labor and land, via one or several intermediary products to the completion of consumption goods. The idea was that the "quantity" of capital invested in a process of production could be increased either by using more of it, given the length of the process, or by lengthening the period of time for which it was invested.

The idea that all the differences in the processes of production "come under this one of time" can be traced back to Ricardo. It was further elaborated by John Rae. The first author to use time as a single measure of capital was perhaps Jevons (1871). He introduced a "production function" $y = f(T)$, where output per capita y is some continuous function of the absolute length of the production process T. Jevons showed that in equilibrium, the rate of interest is equal to $f'(T)/f(T)$. However, it was not until the development of the Austrian theory of capital and interest, with Böhm-Bawerk ([1889] 1959) as its main representative, that the concept gained fame. Böhm-Bawerk's concern was to explain why the rate of interest is positive. This he tried to answer in terms of "time preference" and the "average period of production," used to describe intertemporal consumer preferences and technical alternatives. As in Jevons, capital was conceived as a subsistence

P

fund that permitted more productive but also more time-consuming methods of production to be adopted. It was to the "average period of production" that the marginal productivity condition was applied in determining the rate of interest. From its very inception, Böhm-Bawerk's concept provoked controversies. The recent debate in capital theory has shown that it is impossible in general to measure aggregate capital using the period of production (Kurz 1987).

The concept under consideration was used not only in the theory of capital and distribution but attempts were made to integrate it and trade-cycle theory. The starting point was Wicksell's ([1898] 1936) distinction between the money or market rate of interest and what he called the *natural* rate of interest. The Austrian explanation of trade cycles, first put forward by Mises ([1924] 1952), maintained that changes in the money rate of interest attributable to central-bank policy affect the capital structure and thereby trigger economic fluctuations. This idea was further developed by Hayek (1931), who assumed that the allocation of resources among the different stages of production depends first and foremost on the market rate of interest. A fall in the interest rate, for example, would increase the relatively interest-elastic demand for resources in the early stages of production and thus lengthen the period of production. However, the price signals transmitted by the banking system through its creation of credit money lead to a misallocation of resources and to *forced saving*. An unduly low market rate of interest induces too many production projects to be started afresh. Not all of them can possibly be completed. The economic system ultimately runs into bottlenecks, which turn the interest-induced boom into a recession. A prerequisite for economic recovery is the annihilation of malinvestments and the reallocation of resources in accordance with consumers' time preferences, the available methods of production, and the existing productive resources.

Haberler (1962) grouped these approaches among the monetary overinvestment theories of business cycles. For a criticism of some of Hayek's propositions, see Sraffa (1932a,b). The concept of the period of production has been shown to be inadequate in steady-state capital theory, and there is strong evidence that it performs no better in an analysis of the trade cycle.

Heinz D. Kurz

See also AUSTRIAN THEORY OF BUSINESS CYCLES; BÖHM-BAWERK, EUGEN RITTER VON; BURCHARDT, FRITZ (FRANK) ADOLPH; CAPITAL GOODS; FORCED SAVING; HAYEK, FRIEDRICH AUGUST [VON]; MISES, LUDWIG EDLER VON; NATURAL RATE OF INTEREST; SRAFFA, PIERO; WICKSELL, JOHAN GUSTAV KNUT

Bibliography

Böhm-Bawerk, E. von. [1889] 1959. *Positive Theory of Capital*. Vol. 2 of *Capital and Interest*. South Holland, Ind.: Libertarian Press.

Haberler, G. 1962. *Prosperity and Depression*. 4th rev. ed. Cambridge: Harvard Univ. Press.

Hayek, F. A. 1931. *Prices and Production*. London: Routledge.

Jevons, W. S. 1871. *The Theory of Political Economy*. London: Macmillan.

Kurz, H. D. 1987. "Capital Theory: Debates." In *The New Palgrave: A Dictionary of Economics*. Vol. 1. Edited by J. Eatwell, M. Milgate, and P. Newman. London: Macmillan.

Mises, L. von. [1924] 1952. *The Theory of Money and Credit*. 2d ed. Translation. New Haven: Yale Univ. Press.

Sraffa, P. 1932a. "Dr. Hayek on Money and Capital." *Economic Journal* 42:42–53.

———. 1932b. "A Rejoinder." *Economic Journal* 42:249–51.

Wicksell, K. [1898] 1936. *Interest and Prices*. Translation. London: Macmillan.

Persons, Warren Milton (1878–1937)

Warren Milton Persons made important contributions in applying statistics to economic analysis and the measurement of business cycles. He played a major role in developing the Harvard Index of General Business Conditions. His most notable publications included *Indices of General Business Conditions* and *Forecasting Business Cycles*.

Persons earned his B.S. (1899) and his Ph.D. (1916) degrees from the University of Wisconsin. He taught mathematics at the University of Wisconsin (1901–06) and economics at Dartmouth, Colorado College, and Harvard. In 1928, he left Harvard to become a consulting economist in New York City.

He first applied statistics to economics when he used the coefficient of correlation to test various relationships between variables in the equation of exchange (1908). He concluded that available statistics could not answer the questions that the debate about the empirical validity of the quantity theory had raised. He also introduced into quantity-theory literature the first differencing method for removing trend influences from data (1910).

Persons's growing reputation as a mathematical economist led the Harvard Committee on Economic Research to hire him in 1917 as a visiting lecturer to develop further his "barometric" approach to forecasting. In 1919, Harvard hired him as Professor of Economics and as the first editor of *The Review of Economic Statistics*.

He published the initial version of the Harvard Index of General Business Conditions in 1919; subsequently, he and his colleagues refined, interpreted, and defended their techniques. Persons pioneered methods to eliminate seasonal (link-relative method) and secular-trend influences from time-series data. After correcting for these influences, Persons considered the resulting data to reflect cyclical fluctuations combined with an irregular (residual) element. Relying on the order of fluctuations for the 1903–14 period, he divided the resulting series into three groups (Harvard ABC curves).

Persons insisted that he was not guided in his empirical work by preconceived explanatory hypotheses; instead, the statistical homogeneity of each series determined the original grouping. Only later did he observe the economic relationship among the series in each group, finding that the A index represented speculative bond and stock prices, the B index represented business activity, and the C index represented short-term, money-market interest rates. Persons and his Harvard colleagues often protested that other writers misinterpreted their approach, especially their view of the periodicity of business cycles (Bullock, Persons, and Crum 1927). They stated that their evidence indicated that business cycles had been of varying lengths and did not exhibit periodicity, in the sense that they did not find an invariable succession of a business cycle of one fixed length followed by a business cycle of a second fixed length.

Persons argued that the best forecasting method supplemented statistical analysis (the index of general business conditions) with economic analysis that would identify any structural changes in the economy. His forecasts combined comparisons of current fluctuations to previous ones with adjustments for structural change. Although he insisted that forecasters needed to consider interactions among all variables, his own economic analysis stressed the importance of money-supply changes in initiating business cycles.

The 1930s severely tested Persons's forecasting techniques. In 1930, Persons asserted that, statistically, events of 1930 most closely resembled those of 1884–85, 1907–08, and 1921. He conjectured that if events followed these earlier episodes, recovery would begin early in 1931 and normal business conditions would be restored by the first quarter of 1932. Persons did not find any factors unique to the 1930 experience that would retard economic recovery. Moreover, he thought that responsible Federal Reserve behavior and already low interest rates could even expedite recovery.

As the depression deepened, Persons became actively involved in attempts to promote economic recovery. His proposals included monetary expansion, increased taxes, eliminating price-fixing policies, and retaining the gold standard. Although over fifty prominent economists and statisticians endorsed his program in 1932, Persons's ideas did not alter U.S. economic policy.

Warren Milton Persons was much honored for his work applying statistical analysis to economics; for example, he was elected president of the American Statistical Association in 1923. He pioneered techniques to remove trend and seasonal influences from data and to measure lags. Although Persons's three-curve, barometer-forecasting system did not survive the Great Depression, it was an early forerunner of modern indicator techniques and it influenced business-cycle forecasting, especially in Europe, during the 1920s. His reputation as an economic analyst ultimately suffered because he predicted an early end to the Great Depression and because he advocated policies that Keynesian economists rejected.

Robert Stanley Herren

See also BULLOCK, CHARLES JESSE; FILTERS; MITCHELL, WESLEY CLAIR; SPECTRAL ANALYSIS

Bibliography
Bullock, C. J., W. M. Persons, and W. L. Crum. 1927. "The Construction and Interpretation of the Harvard Index of Business Conditions." *Review of Economics and Statistics* 9:74–92.

Foster, W. T. 1939. "Warren Milton Persons." *Journal of the American Statistical Association* 34:411–15.

Morgan, M. S. 1990. *The History of Econometric Ideas*. Cambridge: Cambridge Univ. Press.

Persons, W. M. 1908. "The Quantity Theory as Tested by Kemmerer." *Quarterly Journal of Economics* 22:274–89.

———. 1910. "The Correlation of Economic Statistics." *Quarterly Publications of the American Statistical Association* 12:287–322.

———. 1919. *Indices of General Business Conditions*. Boston: Harvard Univ. Committee on Economics.

———. 1920. "A Non-Technical Explanation of the Index of General Business Conditions." *Review of Economics and Statistics* 2:39–48.

———. 1925. "Statistics and Economic Theory." *Review of Economics and Statistics* 7:179–97.

———. 1928. *The Construction of Index Numbers*. Boston: Houghton Mifflin.

———. 1931. *Forecasting Business Cycles*. New York: Wiley.

Pervushin, Sergei Alekseevich (1888–?)

The foremost Soviet historian of Russian business cycles, Pervushin published a monumental study, as yet unsurpassed, of fluctuations in Russian agriculture, industry, finance, and transportation from 1870 to the mid-1920s. After his dismissal from Gosplan in 1930, his works on economic cycles were disparaged or ignored by Soviet economists until the 1970s.

Pervushin's family background, education, and date of death remain obscure owing to the absence of information about him in Soviet reference works. His statistical studies on a variety of social and economic issues, such as the influence of crop fluctuations on the consumption of alcoholic beverages (1909) and the value of the ruble during the Russian Revolution (1922) earned him a professorial position at Moscow University, which he held until at least 1928. According to the database of Soviet officials compiled by Professor J. Arch Getty, Pervushin served from 1927 to 1929 as deputy head of the Domestic Cycles Branch (*sektor vnutrennikh kon"iunktur*) in the Economic Department of Gosplan, the State Planning Committee. For a multi-volume statistical study of Russian and Soviet economic trends edited by V. A. Bazarov, V. E. Varzar, and V. G. Groman (1929), he furnished various price and output indices. Although he did not stand trial with these Menshevik economists in March 1931, the deletion of his name from the list of permanent contributors to the journal *Planovoe khoziaistvo* (The planned economy) in June 1930 signaled the end of his career in historical statistics.

His immediate superior at Gosplan, Stanislav G. Strumilin (1877–1974), became the most prominent economic statistician of the Stalin era. However, Strumilin's articles (1939–40) on "industrial crises" in Russia from 1847 to 1907 lacked the precision and sophistication of the works that Pervushin completed before his dismissal: his major study of Russian economic cycles (1925); a discussion of his theory and method, in *Planovoe khoziaistvo* (1926, no. 12); and his article in *The Quarterly Journal of Economics* (1928) which summarized, in English, his book and earlier studies.

Pervushin's major achievement was to resolve the perennial debate between economists who considered the Russian Empire an integral part of the world economy and those who argued that peasant agriculture, mired in precapitalist stagnation, insulated Russia from international cycles. Having gathered a wealth of data on industry, commerce, finance, agriculture, transportation, and even social behavior (e.g., the marriage rate) from 1870 to the 1920s, Pervushin performed numerous statistical tests, including coefficients of correlation, with careful attention to distinctive patterns in various regions. He admitted that annual "changes in the purchasing power of the villages as determined by fluctuations in crops" had little direct effect on the Russian business cycle (1928, 586). However, by creating a "sliding coefficient of correlation" (agricultural indexes compared to industrial indexes two years later) he discovered significant relationships.

He observed, for example, a high sliding coefficient between movements of grain exports in 1890–1912 and changes in net incomes of corporations in 1892–1914. In his view, agriculture exerted a strong influence, especially after 1900, on the entire Russian economy through "changes in the amount of free capital accumulated in agriculture, resulting from fluctuations in crops, in grain prices and in salability. These changes are reflected in part in fluctuations in the value of grain exports. It is in this way that the influence of agriculture is felt in credit and money markets," although more as a "stimulus to expansion" than as a "factor of depression" in industry. He concluded that Russian business cycles corresponded to those in Western Europe in the 1870s and 1880s, anticipated those in the West in the 1890s, and responded more to fluctuations in Russian agriculture than to the European business cycle in 1900–14 (Pervushin 1928, 582, 586, 588).

Pervushin later wrote a survey of German mineral resources (1945) and co-edited a textbook on nonferrous metallurgy (1956). Scholarly recognition of the achievements of Pervushin, Kondratieff, and other statisticians whose careers were destroyed under Stalin did not occur until the 1970s, and then only briefly, as in the works of Aizinova, Broitman, Jasny, and Mironov. (Pervushin is not to be confused with Serafim Pavlovich Pervushin, a Soviet economist in the 1960s and 1970s, or Aleksandr Serafimovich Pervushin, a student of demography in the 1970s and 1980s.)

The pioneering statistical work of Pervushin and his fellow economists deserves renewed attention after decades of neglect. Although some of his conclusions will be modified in the light of new theoretical approaches and empirical findings, his magisterial synthesis remains the starting point for serious research on business cycles in Russia and the Soviet Union before 1930.

Thomas C. Owen

See also BUSINESS CYCLES IN RUSSIA

Bibliography

Aizinova, I. M. 1976. "Iz istorii izucheniia kratkosrochnykh ekonomicheskikh protsessov v sovetskoi statistike" (Aspects of the history of the study of short-term economic processes in Soviet statistics). In *Metodologicheskie voprosy v ekonomicheskoi statistike: aspekty istoricheskogo analiza* (Methodological issues in economic statistics: aspects of historical analysis), edited by T. V. Riabushkin, 46–61. Moscow: Nauka.

Broitman, R. Ia. 1970. "Kon"iunkturnye nabliudeniia v Gosplane SSSR i kon"iunktura sovetskogo narodnogo khoziaistva v 1922–1929 gg" (Cyclical controls of the USSR state planning committee and the economic cycle in the Soviet economy, 1922–1929). *Uchenye zapiski po statistike* (Scholarly notes on statistics) 17:9–61.

Jasny, N. 1972. *Soviet Economists of the Twenties: Names to be Remembered.* Cambridge: Cambridge Univ. Press.

Pervushin, S. A. 1914. *Teoriia krizisov Tugan-Baranovskogo* (Tugan-Baranovsky's theory of crises). Moscow.

———. 1917. "Novaia teoriia krizisov: po povodu knigi g. Bunitiana" (A new theory of economic crises: on Mr. Bounitian's book). *Vestnik Evropy* (The herald of Europe) 7–8:316–32.

———. 1925. *Khoziaistvennaia kon"iunktura: vvedenie v izuchenie dinamiki russkogo narodnogo khoziaistva za polveka* (The economic cycle: an introduction to the study of the dynamics of the Russian economy in the past fifty years). Moscow: Ekonomicheskaia zhizn'.

———. 1928. "Cyclical Fluctuations in Agriculture and Industry in Russia, 1869–1926." Translated by S. Kuznets. *Quarterly Journal of Economics* 42:564–92.

Strumilin, S. G. [1939–40] 1966. "Promyshlennye krizisy v Rossii (1847–1907)" (Industrial crises in Russia, 1847–1907). In *Ocherki ekonomicheskoi istorii Rossii i SSSR* (Outlines of the economic history of Russia and the USSR), 414–50. Moscow: Akademiia nauk.

Phase Averaging

Economic series sometimes are thought to be composed of several components, such as a trend, a cycle, a seasonal, and an irregular. In any given study, one of those components may be of primary interest. Burns and Mitchell (1946), for example, focused on the cycle, abstracting from noncyclical temporal differences. To do so, they established the NBER reference business cycles, dating the contraction and expansion phases of the cycles over the sample period, and then averaged the data across cycles for various points within the cycle. Conversely, Friedman and Schwartz (1982) focused on the longer-run features of the data. To filter out short-run (i.e., cyclical) properties of the data, they transformed (raw) annual series by averaging separately over contraction and expansion phases of the reference business cycles. This technique is phase averaging, and the resulting series are phase-average data.

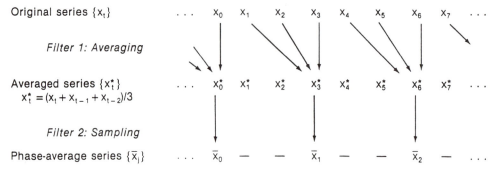

Figure 1. A schema for fixed 3-period phase-averaging.

Phase averaging is motivated by a simple, intuitive characterization of economic time series; and it has the additional appeal of computational ease. Its potential drawbacks include loss of information and irretrievability of some parameters of interest. To understand the economic, statistical, and econometric effects of phase averaging, it is helpful to view phase averaging as the application of two filters to the data.

Phase Averaging as Two Filters

Phase averaging sequentially applies two filters to the data: the first averages the data (as with a moving average), and the second selects moving-average data at non-overlapping intervals. The resulting series are the phase-average data. By analogy with seasonal adjustment of quarterly data, the first filter is like the X-11 procedure; the second filter discards all but the fourth-quarter data points. In statistical terms, the first filter re-parameterizes the data generation process and the second filter marginalizes that process with respect to the intermediate observations.

Algebraically, phase averaging may be expressed as follows, where, for analytical tractability, *fixed n-period phase averaging* is considered. Let the final period T of the series $(x_t; t = ...,1, 2,...,T)$ be a multiple of the phase length n; and let L be the lag operator, so $Lx_t = x_{t-1}$. Then the first filter is $(1 + L + L^2 + \cdots + L^{n-1})/n$, so the *averaged* series is:

$$x_t^* = \left(x_t + x_{t-1} + x_{t-2} + \cdots + x_{t-n+1}\right)/n \quad (1)$$
$$t = ...,1,2,...,T.$$

The second filter selects every nth observation of x_t^*, so the *phase-average* series is:

$$\bar{x}_j = x_{jn}^* \quad j = ...,1,2,...,T/n, \quad (2)$$

where an overbar denotes phase average. Figure 1 shows the steps going from $\{x_t\}$ to $\{x_t^*\}$ to $\{\bar{x}_j\}$ for fixed 3-period phase averaging.

Losses of Information

The averaging in equation (1) entails no loss of information except for end-points. Selection of phase-average data from the moving-average data via equation (2) causes a distinct loss of information, as is apparent in the reduction of the sample size from T to T/n. The loss of information is also apparent if phase averaging is viewed from the frequency domain. The second filter, sample selection, is analogous to observing discrete data from a continuous process, where the aliasing problem limits the range of identifiable frequencies. The importance or irrelevance of the loss of information depends on the process generating the data and the purposes for which the phase-average data are used.

The loss is unimportant if (a) all the parameters of interest can be recovered from the phase-average series and (b) there is no loss of power in testing the resulting model. However, concerning (a), many potential parameters of interest cannot be obtained from phase-average data, including parameters relevant to tests of Granger noncausality, short-run variability in the postulated relationships, and the dynamic mechanisms whereby the economy adjusts to "shocks." Additionally, variables weakly exogenous at the original observation frequency may no longer be exogenous when phase-averaged. Tests about parameters that *can* be retrieved from the phase-average data may be low in power relative to tests based on the unfiltered data.

Studies on the related issue of time aggregation indicate that sizable inefficiencies result from using least squares even if the regressors are strongly exogenous. If they are only weakly exogenous (e.g., include lagged dependent variables), least squares is generally inconsistent. Telser (1967) and Wei (1982) consider analytical effects of phase averaging on time series processes. Campos, Ericsson, and Hendry (1990) find analytically and empirically that phase averaging does not obtain two results important to Friedman and Schwartz's 1982 analysis, namely, reduction of serial correlation and reduction of the data variance. Additional discussion of phase averaging appears in Hendry and Ericsson (1991) and Friedman and Schwartz (1991).

While analytically convenient, the fixed-period model of phase averaging in equations (1)–(2) neglects two aspects of phase averaging in practice: (a) turning points may be included in both preceding and following phases, as in Friedman and Schwartz (1982); and (b) phases are dated by prior analysis of a data set related to the series being phase-averaged. The statistical effects of (a) appear minor in comparison to those from using phase-average rather than unadjusted data (Friedman and Schwartz 1982; 75, 81–85). Empirically, (b) also appears to be a second-order effect (Campos, Ericsson, and Hendry 1990). Even so, (b) raises several issues of general practical importance: the degrees of freedom lost by dating the phases, the exogeneity or endogeneity of the dates themselves, and (relatedly) the potential multivariate nature of the data.

Summary

Phase averaging has been proposed as a computationally convenient empirical method of separating cyclical and secular components. In general, phase averaging involves a loss of information, which can result in the inconsistency of previously consistent estimation procedures and in the endogeneity of previously exogenous variables. Given modern computational software and hardware, joint modeling of short- and long-run phenomena appears preferable to their sequential, separate modeling via phase averaging.

> *Julia Campos*
> *Neil R. Ericsson*
> *David F. Hendry*

See also BURNS, ARTHUR FRANK; COINTEGRATION; COMPOSITE TRENDS; DISTRIBUTED LAGS; FILTERS; MITCHELL, WESLEY CLAIR; MOVING AVERAGES; SERIAL CORRELATION; TRENDS AND RANDOM WALKS

Bibliography

Burns, A. F. and W. C. Mitchell. 1946. *Measuring Business Cycles*. New York: NBER.

Campos, J., N. R. Ericsson, and D. F. Hendry. 1990. "An Analogue Model of Phase-averaging Procedures." *Journal of Econometrics* 43:275–92.

Friedman, M. and A. J. Schwartz. 1982. *Monetary Trends in the United States and the United Kingdom: Their Relation to Income, Prices, and Interest Rates, 1867–1975*. Chicago: Univ. of Chicago Press.

———. 1991. "Alternative Approaches to Analyzing Economic Data." *American Economic Review* 81:39–49.

Hendry, D. F. and N. R. Ericsson. 1991. "An Econometric Analysis of U.K. Money Demand in *Monetary Trends in the United States and the United Kingdom* by Milton Friedman and Anna J. Schwartz." *American Economic Review* 81:8–38.

Telser, L. G. 1967. "Discrete Samples and Moving Sums in Stationary Stochastic Processes." *Journal of the American Statistical Association* 62:484–99.

Wei, W. W. S. 1982. "The Effects of Systematic Sampling and Temporal Aggregation on Causality—A Cautionary Note." *Journal of the American Statistical Association* 77:316–19.

Phillips, Alban William Housego (1914–1975)

The contributions to economics of Alban William Housego ("Bill") Phillips, of the Phillips curve, lay in the field of dynamic macroeconomic control, which he approached from the perspective of an electrical engineer, his original profession (1930–40). Phillips's output in economics consisted of twelve published papers (1950–67)—covering a gamut of problems connected with modeling, control, estimation, and political economy—and a hydraulic machine.

Studying for a B.A. in sociology at the London School of Economics, Phillips, prompted by Kenneth Boulding's 1948 picture of an hydraulic model of the interaction between a stock variable, its flow and price, built the hydraulic machine to represent such interaction at the macroeconomic level. The machine, which was sold as a teaching device in England and the

United States, contained a multiplier-accelerator mechanism which produced cyclical oscillations for plausible values of the system's parameters. Invited to present the machine at the Robbins research seminar, Phillips gave a brilliant demonstration that won him an assistant lectureship in economics at the LSE.

Using the hydraulic simulator to clarify his ideas, Phillips, in his Ph.D. thesis (1954), applied engineering control principles to the control of the macroeconomy. In engineering terminology, the economy was a negative-feedback system, in which an output of the system (for example, induced investment or price changes) fed back as an input to the system, in order to eliminate deviations between the system's actual and equilibrium states. In economics, the idea of adaptive expectations is based on the error-correction mechanism. Adaptive expectations appeared in a 1956 paper by Cagan on hyper-inflation. Cagan learned about adaptive expectations from Milton Friedman, who himself during a trip to England had learned about adaptive expectations from Phillips.

According to Phillips, the economy possessed three types of feedback mechanisms to correct deviations in output: a proportional control, P, which depended on the size; an integral control, I, dependent on the cumulative error; and a derivative control, D, related to the rate of change of the error. Phillips, following the Samuelson-Hansen microeconomic stability equation, made price flexibility a proportional stabilizer. A nonlinear curve later known as the Phillips curve showed the rate of change of the price-level, or the money-wage level, as a varying proportion of the difference between the actual and the equilibrium level of output.

Phillips saw that delays and lags in the price and other feedback mechanisms made the economy overshoot and oscillate around the equilibrium level of output. Moreover, price changes in certain circumstances induced expectations of further changes in the same direction, resulting in positive feedback which destabilized the system. Thus, Phillips thought that stabilization measures were needed to supplement the PID correction mechanisms of the private economy. Mainly as a consequence of his research on the stability properties of dynamic systems, the Economics Department in 1958 elected Phillips to the Tooke Chair of Economics and Statistics.

The election had little to do with the famous or infamous Phillips curve, to which he gave an empirical grounding during the mid-1950s national debate over the control of "creeping inflation." Using the Phelps-Brown/Hopkins money-wage series dating from 1860, Phillips (1958a) specified a relation between the proportionate change in the money-wage, $\Delta W/W$ (the dependent variable), and unemployment, U, and the proportionate change in unemployment, $\Delta U/U$. For each trade cycle during 1861–1957, this relation generated a loop that circled around a Phillips curve, a phenomenon that has been interpreted variously as due to expectations, time lags, or aggregation.

Given the computing technology available in the 1950s, Phillips was unable to estimate his preferred specification of the inflation-unemployment relation since it was nonlinear in parameters. Hence, Phillips omitted $\Delta U/U$ and estimated the relation between $\Delta W/W$ and U for 1861–1913 using a rule-of-thumb method, a crude method of curve fitting on grouped data (Wulwick 1989). He superimposed the result on scattergraphs for 1914–1957 and by the ad hoc lagging of unemployment by a few months, found a near perfect fit for the recent postwar years.

According to Phillips's policy pronouncements, his curve, incorporated within an eclectic growth-cycle model (1961, 1962), served as the basis for an inflation-unemployment tradeoff. Though subsequent econometric tests of the Phillips curve for other periods and regions have been mixed and the curve has lacked a coherent theoretical explanation, it nonetheless has remained an integral part of policy analysis and dynamic macroeconomic models (Wulwick 1987). Many economists, particularly Monetarists, have argued that the curve does not offer a practicable tradeoff.

Stressing that control of the economy required quantification, Phillips was one of the pioneers of time-series estimation. In 1956 he defined conditions that, if satisfied, permitted the consistent estimation of a distributed-lag equation in which the regressors figured as *causal* variables, in the sense later developed by Granger and Sims. Phillips (1978) later proposed a method of obtaining consistent and efficient estimates of the parameters of simultaneous-equation systems in which the disturbances are moving averages of random elements.

Phillips, the control engineer turned economist, approached economic control circumspectly. Having reproduced the time-forms of the lags of the response of production to changes in demand on the electronic simulator at the National Physical Laboratory, Phillips (1957, 1958b) stressed that *fine-tuning* could increase cyclical instability. To avoid such errors, he warned policymakers to limit the values of the proportional, integral, and derivative correction measures and reduce the delays in implementing them.

For Phillips (1968, also see Phillips and Quenouille 1960), controlling the economy meant modifying the structure of the system with the aim of reducing the variance of target variables. Yet, this definition implied that one could not predict the effects of a control from an econometric model without first identifying the changes in the underlying structural model that would be caused by the control. Pessimistic about solving this identification problem, which has reappeared in the Lucas critique, Phillips in 1967 accepted a chair in economics at the Australian National University where he devoted his attention to Chinese economic studies.

Obviously Phillips, as James Meade once remarked, "should not go down to history just as 'the Phillips curve' chap." The curve was a major event in the general progress of Phillips's studies on time-series modeling and classical economic control, which also is identified with his name.

Nancy J. Wulwick

See also EXPECTATIONS; FISHER, IRVING; FRIEDMAN, MILTON; LUCAS CRITIQUE; MACROECONOMETRIC MODELS, HISTORICAL DEVELOPMENT; NATURAL RATE OF UNEMPLOYMENT; PHILLIPS CURVE; UNEMPLOYMENT

Bibliography

Phillips, A. W. 1950. "Mechanical Models in Economic Dynamics." *Economica* 17:282–305.

——. 1954. "Stabilisation Policy in a Closed Economy." *Economic Journal* 54:290–323.

——. 1956. "Some Notes on the Estimation of Time-Forms of Reactions in Interdependent Dynamic Systems." *Economica* 23:99–113.

——. 1957. "Stabilisation Policy and the Time-Forms of Lagged Responses." *Economic Journal* 57:265–77.

——. 1958a. "The Relation between Unemployment and the Rate of Change of Money Wage Rates in the United Kingdom, 1861–1957." *Economica* 25:283–99.

——. 1958b. "La cybernetique et le contrôle des systèmes économiques." *Etudes sur la cybernétique et l'économie*, n.s., 21:41–50.

——. 1961. "A Simple Model of Employment, Money, and Prices in a Growing Economy." *Economica* 28:360–70.

——. 1962. "Employment, Inflation, and Growth." *Economica* 29:1–16.

——. 1968. "Models for the Control of Economic Fluctuations." In *Mathematical Model Building in Economics and Industry*, 159–65. New York: Hafner.

——. 1978. "Estimation of Systems of Difference Equations with Moving Average Disturbances." In *Stability and Inflation*, edited by A. R. Bergstrom, 181–99. New York: Wiley.

Phillips, A. W. and M. H. Quenouille. 1960. "Estimation, Regulation, and Prediction in Interdependent Dynamic Systems." *Bulletin de l'Institut Internationale de Statistique* 75:335–43.

Wulwick, N. J. 1987. "The Phillips Curve: Which? Whose? To Do What? How?" *Southern Economic Journal* 53:834–57.

——. 1989. "Phillips' Approximate Regression." *Oxford Economic Papers* 41:170–88.

Phillips Curve

In its original form (Phillips 1954, 1956), the Phillips curve related the output gap to the rate of price inflation. Letting Y and Y^* stand for actual and potential national income, and dP for the proportionate rate of price inflation (i.e., $(dP/dt)(1/P)$), we can write this as

$$dP = F_1 (Y-Y^*) \qquad (1)$$

In this form, the curve describes a trade-off between the output gap and the rate of inflation. The curve became famous, however, when transformed into a relation between the rate of change of money wages and the rate of unemployment (Phillips 1958). Letting U stand for the percentage of the labor force unemployed, and dW for the proportionate rate of change of an index of money wages (i.e., $(dW/dt)(1/W)$), we can write this as

$$dW = F_2 (U) \qquad (2)$$

In this form, the curve describes a trade-off between unemployment and wage inflation.

The curve described by equation (2) was assumed to have a negative slope that diminished in absolute value as U increased: $F_2' < 0$ and $F_2'' > 0$. The curve was important in providing a theoretical link, absent from early Keynesian models, between the goods market and the labor market. It also suggested an exploitable (policy-relevant) trade-off between unemployment and inflation. Although Phillips never said so, his contemporaries assumed that his relation held in the long as well as the short term. But a consensus later formed that it would hold (if at all) only over shorter periods such as characterize one business cycle.

In the early 1950s, Phillips was studying stabilization policy using dynamic Keynesian models. The models then available used a kinked, "ratcheting," aggregate supply curve. When aggregate demand was less than potential real income, the price level was constant while real income varied; when aggregate demand exceeded potential real income, real income was constant at its potential level, while the price level rose.

To provide a description of the simultaneous movements in real national income and the price level that are commonly observed over the cycle, Phillips closed his models with the curve shown in equation (1). He also provided a powerful, early, theoretical critique of fine tuning, which, he showed, could easily destabilize rather than stabilize a simple economy.

Phillips later transformed this part of his model from equation (1) into equation (2) and fitted it to British data from 1858 to 1957. Phillips (1958) found a remarkably stable relation between the two variables over the whole time period. Subsequently, R. G. Lipsey (1960) applied standard statistical techniques to the data. He later provided (1960, 1978) a theoretical explanation that linked unemployment to excess demand in labor markets and hence to the output gap on the one hand, and the rate of change of money wages to the rate of price inflation on the other.

In the 1960s, Phillips curves (as they soon came to be called) in the form of equation (2) were fitted to the data for many countries with apparent success. Economists and government officials spoke confidently about making choices between the level of unemployment and the rate of inflation—often choosing to increase inflation as the cost of reducing unemployment. (See, e.g., Samuelson and Solow [1960] 1966.)

The view that there is a permanent trade-off between unemployment and inflation was challenged theoretically by Phelps (1968) and Friedman ([1968] 1969). Then, as inflation accelerated in many countries towards the end of the 1960s, empirical Phillips curves began to break down. Given amounts of unemployment came to be associated with ever-higher rates of inflation.

It was soon accepted that the relation given in equation (2) would imply serious money illusion if it held as a long-term relation, because it implies that a given unemployment rate would cause a given rate of increase of money wages, whatever the rate of price inflation. An expectations term was therefore added to create what is now called an "expectations-augmented Phillips curve." According to this new relation, the rate of wage inflation is equal to the expected rate of price inflation (which keeps real wages constant) plus a demand component which is measured by the rate of unemployment (plus an error term to catch random shocks). The expectations term can be interpreted narrowly as just the expected change in the price level (Friedman 1975), or broadly as core inflation that incorporates expectations, lags, and inertias (Eckstein 1981). Letting dP^e and S stand respectively for the expected rate of change in the price level and random shocks, we can write this new relation as

$$dW = dP^e + F_2(U) + S \qquad (3)$$

Although written contemporaneously in equation (3), time lags are usually included in empirical fittings.

Letting the expected change in prices be zero and ignoring random shocks reduces equation (3) to equation (2). The pure Phillips curve in equation (2) may be interpreted as the demand component of wage inflation. Letting U^* be the rate of unemployment associated with potential income (and variously called the natural rate of unemployment or the non-accelerating-inflationary rate of unemployment (NAIRU)), $F_2(U^*) = 0$ and $F_2' < 0$. To handle productivity changes, dW can be interpreted as the rate of change of money wages *minus* the rate of change of labor productivity. This implies that when $U = U^*$ and $dP^e = 0$, wages are rising at the same rate as productivity. The influence of the demand component is thus to make money wages rise faster than productivity when $U < U^*$, and slower than productivity when $U > U^*$.

If this theory is correct, the Phillips curve of equation (2) should fit the data when expected inflation is low and fairly constant, as it was in the 1950s and early 1960s; but when the expected inflation rate is rising, the curve should drift upwards by an amount related to the P^e term, as it did in the late 1960s and 1970s.

Using equation (3), one can show that a stable inflation at an unemployment level below U^* is impossible. No matter how expectations are formed, the actual and expected rates of inflation must be equal in a stable situation. Thus a steady inflation, with $U < U^*$, implies that $dW > dP$. But an equilibrium inflation with all markets fully adjusted and no productivity change implies, inconsistently, that $dW = dP$, i.e., the real wage is constant.

According to equation (3), a steady-state inflation can occur only at U^*. In that case, F_2 is zero and inflation is fully expected and is passed directly onto wages, so that $dW = dP = dP^e$. (Monetary validation is required if the rise in the price level is not to eliminate the inflationary gap.)

The theory of accelerating inflation seems consistent with evidence from inflationary gaps, i.e., $U < U^*$. But it conflicts with the evidence from prolonged recessionary gaps with relatively constant inflation rates, since it predicts a continuous deceleration of the inflation rate. This embarrassing conflict has not attracted significant attention.

Important in Phillips's original analysis were loops around his stable curve. These loops were anticlockwise during the nineteenth century, with wages being above the value predicted by the stable curve on the upswing and below on the downswing. During the twentieth century, the loops changed direction and became predominantly, though not exclusively, clockwise. Lipsey (1960) tested for these loops by adding dU as an explanatory variable, finding it significant. He provided an explanation based on aggregation from microlabor markets. It is well known that lags in the adjustment of wages to unemployment can also produce loops. These tend to be clockwise, while aggregation tends to produce anticlockwise loops. This suggested a potential reconciliation with the data if the importance of lags and aggregation phenomena have changed over time. This matter was never resolved, and the loop phenomenon no longer attracts significant attention.

In the Keynesian model with a Phillips curve, the direction of causation is from demand, to income and unemployment, to wages, then to prices. This can be seen in either a Hicksian, *IS-LM* model or an aggregate-demand (*AD*)/aggregate-supply (*AS*) model. Starting from potential income, a demand shock, such as could be caused by reduced household saving, shifts the *IS* or the *AD* curve outward. This causes income to exceed potential, creating excess demand in goods and factor markets. As a first approximation, goods prices can be taken as cost-determined in mainly oligopolistic markets. (This can be justified by observing that, since markups cannot rise continually to cause any significant *trend* inflation, they can be taken as constant in an aggregate model of inflation.) As a result, factor prices rise under the pressure of excess demand, raising production costs and forcing goods prices to rise in turn. The rise in prices shifts the *LM* curve to the left and the short-run aggregate-supply (*SRAS*) curve upwards, causing income to revert to its potential level. In these Keynesian models, the role of the Phillips curve is to determine how fast the *LM* curve shifts leftward or, what amounts to the same thing, how fast the *SRAS* curve shifts upwards (Lipsey 1978, 1979).

In New Classical-type models, the causation is reversed, giving rise to the Lucas supply curve. The conceptual model is perfectly competitive and only unforeseen demand shocks affect real variables. If a shock is unforeseen, the price level rises unexpectedly and, mistakenly assuming that the rise in money prices is confined to his or her own output, each agent increases output. Output and unemployment appear on the left-hand side of equations (1) and (2), while both are a function of the difference between the actual and expected inflation rates.

The Phillips curve closes any standard macro-model in which variations in aggregate demand cause short-term variations in output. Output and the price level may vary simultaneously under the impact of inflationary and recessionary gaps. The nonlinearity of the curve implies that inflation may reach very high levels as excess demand rises, while deflation proceeds slowly even in major recessions. The curve embodies the relatively modest assumption that wages and prices tend to rise in booms and fall (relative to productivity) in slumps. Its strongest assumption is that the *larger* the deviation from potential income the *faster* the wage and price adjustments. In the absence of any standard dynamic theory based on maximizing behavior, this assumption must be ad hoc—but so must any other assumption about adjustment speeds. Although the curve was once the subject of passionate attack and defense, it is difficult to see what relation other than the expectations-augmented version of the curve might be used to close macro-models in which aggregate-demand fluctuations, foreseen or unforeseen, cause fluctuation in real output.

Richard G. Lipsey

See also AGGREGATE SUPPLY AND DEMAND; EXPECTATIONS; FISHER, IRVING; FRIEDMAN, MILTON; MONETARY POLICY; NATURAL RATE OF UNEMPLOYMENT; PHILLIPS, ALBAN WILLIAM HOUSEGO

Bibliography

Eckstein, O. 1981. *Core Inflation.* Englewood Cliffs, N.J.: Prentice-Hall.

Friedman, M. [1968] 1969. "The Role of Monetary Policy." Chap. 5 in *The Optimum Quantity of Money and Other Essays.* Chicago: Aldine.

———. 1975. *Unemployment versus Inflation?* London: Institute of Economic Affairs.

Lipsey, R. G. 1960. "The Relation between Unemployment and the Rate of Change of Money Wage Rates in the United Kingdom, 1862–1957: A Further Analysis." *Economica* 27:1–31.

———. 1978. "The Place of the Phillips Curve in Macro Economic Models." In *Stability and Inflation,* edited by A. R. Bergstrom et al., 49–75. New York: Wiley.

———. 1979. "The Micro Underpinnings of the Phillips Curve: A Reply to Holmes and Smyth." *Economica* 46:62–70.

Phelps, E. S. 1968. "Money Wage Dynamics and Labor-Market Equilibrium." *Journal of Political Economy* 76:678–711.

Phillips, A. W. 1954. "Stabilization Policy in a Closed Economy." *Economic Journal* 64:290–323.

———. 1956. "Some Notes on the Estimation of Time-Forms of Reactions in Interdependent Dynamic Systems." *Economica* 23:99–113.

———. 1958. "The Relation between Unemployment and the Rate of Change of Money Wage Rates in the United Kingdom, 1861–1957." *Economica* 25:283–99.

Samuelson, P. A. and R. M. Solow. [1960] 1966. "Analytical Aspects of Anti-Inflation Policy." Chap. 102 in P. A. Samuelson, *The Collected Scientific Papers of Paul A. Samuelson.* Vol. 2. Cambridge: MIT Press.

Pigou, Arthur Cecil (1877–1959)

Despite his important contributions to many branches of economic theory, Arthur Cecil Pigou is among the most underrated economists of the twentieth century. His pioneering work in welfare economics, *Wealth and Welfare* (later expanded under the title of *The Economics of Welfare*), was the first installment of a trilogy covering all of general economics. The subsequent volumes were *Industrial Fluctuations* and *A Study in Public Finance.* From 1933 onward, Pigou focused primarily on the specific problem of unemployment which had plagued England during the interwar period. It was Pigou's *Theory of Unemployment* that provided Keynes with a detailed exposition of what Keynes chose to call the classical view on the subject and became the focal point of Keynes's attacks. In its infancy the book bore the title *Unemployment* (1913), in its maturity that of *Equilibrium and Unemployment* (1941).

Born on 18 November 1877, Pigou entered Cambridge in 1896 from Harrow on a Minor Scholarship to King's College for History and Modern Languages. Having obtained a First in Part II of the Moral Sciences Tripos with distinction in advanced political economy, he became a lifelong Fellow of King's in 1902. This devoted disciple of Alfred Marshall was elected his successor as the Professor of Political Economy in 1908, when he was only thirty. Pigou retired from the chair in 1943, but not from writing. A stream of popular texts and articles flowed from his pen, the last of which was published only three years before his death on 7 March 1959.

Although decidedly Marshallian in his tools, Pigou produced theories complementary to his master's by emphasizing the importance of short-run fluctuations in economic activity and the resulting problem of unemployment. In his policy prescriptions, Pigou was much more Keynesian than Marshallian, for he focused on instances of market failure and proposed extensive measures to remedy them (Aslanbeigui 1987, 1990).

As a social reformer, Pigou sought to increase aggregate welfare. The mitigation of industrial fluctuations (business cycles) was a step toward that goal, because it would stabilize the employment, income, and consumption of the working classes. Since consumption and income both depended on employment, Pigou chose to focus on the changes in the volume of employment induced by cycles. It was Pigou's belief that such changes were only possible if the demand for and supply of labor changed disproportionately. Contrary to Keynes's misconceived characterization, Pigou held that the supply of labor does not shift in the short run. Any change in the volume of employment is therefore attributable to the demand side of the labor market (derived from the demand for products) which shifts whenever employers' expectations of future profits (yields) change. The general and wave-like swings in expectations affect the constructional industries (e.g., engineering, shipbuilding) most heavily.

In his *Industrial Fluctuations,* Pigou linked business expectations to real, psychological, and autonomous monetary factors. Changes in actual conditions such as crop size or technology constitute real causes that result in correct expectations. The most significant of autonomous monetary causes, which affect the level of borrowing and therefore prices, are the creation and destruction of bank credit in foreign countries (and therefore are exogenous to the system) which are large, recurrent, and long-lasting.

Psychological causes or changes in the "tone of mind" of business people arise spontaneously or as a consequence of real or monetary changes. Regardless of their origin, these causes are responsible for errors resulting from undue optimism or pessimism. Because the different sectors of the economy are related through the conducting rods of psychology, production linkages, and debt/credit, the errors, once created, are propagated to the rest of the economy; the interdependencies cause "action in droves."

Psychological factors explain both the existence and the rhythmic nature of fluctuations. Errors of optimism, for instance, generate errors of pessimism after a gestation period. The exaggerated expectations of future profits are put to the test of facts, engendering the realization that things are not as good as was expected. This checks the flow of business activity. Firms' overproduction leads to lower prices, losses, and the liquidation of loans, which generate pessimism. Bankruptcies do not destroy capital but do create fear; the more extensive they are, the more business confidence is shaken.

Depressions—Pigou's terminology for recessions—do not last forever. Reduced production and depletion of inventories eventually mean increased orders. Some bold entrepreneurs prepare for increased outputs or for adopting new techniques. As the first-comers make good profits, a new boom starts based on justified expectations, but, after a period, expansion creates new errors. The seeds of another bust are sown again.

Although the existence of industrial fluctuations can be taken for granted, their amplitudes cannot. The expanse of cycles depends on two factors: the elasticity of the supply of new capital, and price and wage rigidities. The elasticity of supply of capital depends on the monetary and banking arrangements of the economy: the more willing the banks are to let their reserve-liabilities ratios change, the more elastic the supply of capital would be.

The changed borrowing and expenditure, moreover, trigger price changes, which have two effects. First, because they are unforeseen and underestimated, they wrench "the real terms of contracts for loans and wages away from what was intended when these contracts were made" (Pigou 1929, 173). Changes in prices therefore imply windfall gains or losses (forced levies) for borrowers, financiers, or workers. Secondly, price changes cause further revisions in expectations, which alter the level of economic activity yet again.

Prices exhibit rigidity partly because producers and consumers find a certain degree of stickiness convenient—continuous price fluctuations make the future intolerably unforeseeable. During recessions, other factors breed rigidity. Firms make tacit agreements to reduce output to prevent markets from being spoiled in good times, price their products according to past not current market conditions, and hesitate to cut prices lest consumers expect further cuts. Wage rigidities are due to wage policy: workers' bargaining power, mutual employee-employer mistrust, and income-maintenance programs (unemployment insurance, Poor Law relief, charitable contributions).

Pigou also tried to estimate quantitatively the significance of factors causing business cycles and their amplitudes. Psychological and monetary causes are the most important ones: the elimination of each would cut down the amplitude of fluctuations by one-half. Removing crop variations would reduce the amplitude by one-quarter. Price rigidity contributes as much as one-sixteenth to the amplitude of cycles and wage rigidity as much as one-eighth. Other factors—technological change, strikes, labor mobility, etc.—are not significant.

Industrial fluctuations are intimately linked to unemployment. Contrary to common belief, Pigou did not hold that high real wages cause unemployment. In many cases, high real wages and high unemployment are both caused by other factors. The great slump of 1920–21, for example, was "a joint consequence of bursting of a gigantic bubble of unwarranted optimism, with a heavy fall in price." The same could be argued for the 1924–25 recession. Pigou concluded that the increased unemployment in both cases would have been "as large as it was, even though the rate of real wages had been prevented from rising in any degree" (Pigou 1929, 200–201).

Since industrial fluctuations are antisocial, their mitigation increases economic and social welfare. The remedies that Pigou proposed were indirect as well as direct. Indirectly, governments could help provide more and better information to reduce unwarranted errors or mistrusts. Since different factors, monetary or otherwise, work through monetary and banking institutions, the economy could be stabilized by stabilizing prices. Such stability could be achieved through a discount policy or a policy of rationing credit to control the swings of credit and, necessarily, expectations. Practical modifications in wage policy that enhance wage flexibility would not reduce the amplitudes substantially.

Industrial fluctuations could be directly counteracted by state intervention to increase the demand for commodities in bad times. To do so, the government could either increase its expenditure directly or provide incentives for private production through subsidies or by guaranteeing the payment of interest on loans received by the private sector.

Only recently have economic theoreticians again paid attention to Pigou's theory of business cycles (Shiller 1987). The prolonged neglect was due to the myth created by Keynes and propagated by some Keynesians that Pigou ignored the role of expectations in creating involuntary unemployment (Aslanbeigui 1992). Dispelling such myths would help rescue Pigou's valuable contributions to business-cycle theory from their unmerited oblivion.

Nahid Aslanbeigui

See also EXPECTATIONS; JEVONS, WILLIAM STANLEY; KEYNES, JOHN MAYNARD; MARSHALL, ALFRED; MILLS, JOHN; PIGOU-HABERLER EFFECT; SUNSPOT THEORIES OF FLUCTUATIONS; UNEMPLOYMENT; WAGE RIGIDITY

Bibliography

Aslanbeigui, N. 1987. "Marshall's and Pigou's Policy Prescriptions on Unemployment, Socialism, and Inequality." In *Perspectives on the History of Economic Thought,* edited by D. Walker, 191–204. London: Edward Elgar.

———. 1990. "On the Demise of Pigovian Economics." *Southern Economic Journal* 56:616–27.

———. 1992. "Pigou's Inconsistencies or Keynes's Misconceptions?" *History of Political Economy* 24:413–33.

Collard, D. A. 1981. "A. C. Pigou, 1877–1959." In *Pioneers of Modern Economics in Britain,* edited by D. P. O'Brien and J. R. Presley, 105–39. Totowa, N.J.: Barnes and Noble.

Pigou, A. C. 1912. *Wealth and Welfare.* London: Macmillan.

———. 1913. *Unemployment.* London: William and Norgate.

———. 1929. *Industrial Fluctuations.* 2d ed. London: Macmillan.

———. 1933. *The Theory of Unemployment.* London: Macmillan.

———. 1941. *Employment and Equilibrium.* London: Macmillan.

———. 1962. *A Study in Public Finance.* 3d ed. London: Macmillan.

Shiller, R. J. 1987. "Ultimate Sources of Aggregate Variability." *American Economic Review Papers and Proceedings* 77:87–92.

Pigou-Haberler Effect

The concept of a real-balance effect on aggregate consumption arose amid controversies of the 1930s and 1940s over the same orthodox presumption of a tendency toward full employment. It offered a new and distinctive mechanism for restoring full employment, through flexible wages and prices, if the Keynesian critique of the orthodox mechanism should hold. Economic theory before 1930 had generally held that if prices and wages were flexible, market forces would automatically propel the economy toward full employment. Falling prices and wages, coupled with low investment, were supposed to depress interest rates sufficiently to restore consumption and investment to full-employment levels. This proposition came under heavy attack from J. M. Keynes in his *General Theory*. Keynes argued that liquidity preference would prevent the interest rate from falling, and, even if not, saving and investment might not respond enough to low interest rates to restore full employment. In response to Keynes, Haberler (1941) (with an intervention by Scitovsky 1941) advanced the following arguments, the first of which was later made famous by Pigou (1943):

1. As the general price level falls and real cash balances rise, a price level will be reached at which the propensity to consume rises enough so that people stop saving.
2. If the above effect fails to restore full employment, the continuous fall of the price level will keep raising real balances, which people will regard as a continuous flow of income, out of which they will consume. At some rate of deflation, a dynamic equilibrium in which the extra consumption just suffices to maintain full employment will follow. (This has often been called the dynamic Pigou effect.)
3. However, the anticipation of further deflation could lead consumers and investors to defer spending; such deferral could prevent the mechanism from restoring full employment.

Although much has since been written about the real-balance effect, almost everything that has been said about its contribution, if any, to full employment appeared in Haberler's 1941 formulation. That formulation included the observation that prices and wages are in fact "sticky," so that the return to full employment from a deep depression, if there were no other mechanism to restore it, would be long delayed. He therefore concluded that monetary and fiscal policy should actively promote a high-employment, stable level of output. Price flexibility is desirable on other grounds, but so is a stable price level: for example, too much deflation would disturb the real values of contracts, fixed in units of money, and would cause wholesale bankruptcies. Except as noted below, these points in Haberler's exposition cover all that is relevant to full employment.

A new challenge to these effects of real balances came in a 1962 article by Harry G. Johnson, in which he observed that they require an asymmetry in household perceptions of assets and liabilities. Against households' private cash holdings, viewed as assets, must be set the government's non-interest-bearing debt in the form of currency and bank reserves. If households treat their pro-rata shares of government debts as liabilities, the real-balance effects described by Haberler will just cancel the corresponding effects on the liabilities side, with a net effect of zero. This argument parallels the concept of Ricardian equivalence in connection with the impact of fiscal policy and the burden of government debt.

A counterargument is that, since money bears no interest and has no maturity date, its discounted present value as a liability is zero. Money is held because it provides convenience for transactions and other related services (and costs the government only the expense of replacing worn-out currency). Hence it represents net wealth in the community, there being no offsetting liability; if so, the Haberler points appear, at first glance, to be sustained.

However, this counterargument itself undercuts the first, static real-balance effect. Their convenience value implies that real balances have a marginal product, either in measured production or in direct satisfaction, that justifies holding them. To see the impact of this consideration without confounding it with irrelevant effects, we must think in terms of partial derivatives—i.e., in terms of the effect of rising real balances at an unchanging interest rate. At a given interest rate, we do not generally observe that as households grow wealthier they increase consumption by more than their added incomes. Yet the static real-balance effect implies that they do, since it requires that they increase consumption by more than the yield of the incremental real balances. Unless consumption increases by more than the yield from incremental real balances, the gap between equilibrium income and full-employment income increases. Nothing in utility theory tells us that it happens; the issue is empirical.

There have been a number of attempts to measure the static real-balance effect. After some early, inconclusive results, several investigators found a statistically significant positive effect on consumption of real "liquid assets."

However, these results raise more questions than they answer. First, most liquid assets are liabilities of private-sector financial institutions, owned by households. Second, the regressions did not generally hold interest rates constant (did not include an interest-rate independent variable). For these and other reasons, one must doubt whether a positive effect of the kind discussed by Haberler and Pigou has reliably been found. A good review of most of three empirical studies is provided by Patinkin (1965).

In summary, the debates about the real-balance effects cannot be said to have resolved whether there is either a persistent tendency toward full employment, or a tendency toward secular stagnation and underemployment equilibrium.

The major conclusion to emerge from the debates was that the effects were principally of academic interest, while that interest lasted.

Martin J. Bailey

See also AGGREGATE SUPPLY AND DEMAND; HABERLER, GOTTFRIED [VON]; KEYNES, JOHN MAYNARD; MONETARY POLICY; RICARDIAN EQUIVALENCE; WAGE RIGIDITY

Bibliography

Bailey, M. J. 1971. *National Income and the Price Level*. 2d ed. New York: McGraw-Hill.

Haberler, G. 1941. *Prosperity and Depression*. 3d ed. Geneva: League of Nations.

Johnson, H. G. [1962] 1968. "Monetary Theory and Policy." Chap. 1 in *Essays in Monetary Economics*. London: Allen and Unwin.

Keynes, J. M. [1936] 1973. *The General Theory of Employment, Interest, and Money*. Vol. 7 of *The Collected Writings of John Maynard Keynes*. London: Macmillan.

Patinkin, D. [1948] 1951. "Price Flexibility and Full Employment." Reprinted in *Readings in Monetary Theory*, edited by F. A. Lutz and L. W. Mintz, 252–83. Homewood, Ill.: Irwin.

———. 1965. *Money, Interest, and Prices*. 2d ed. New York: Harper and Row.

Pigou, A. C. 1943. "The Classical Stationary State." *Economic Journal* 53:343–51.

Scitovsky, T. 1941. "Capital Accumulation, Employment and Price Rigidity." *Review of Economic Studies* 8:69–88.

Political Business Cycle

Business cycles have been recorded since at least Biblical times. Political business cycles are a product of the modern age of universal suffrage. They allegedly result from the attempts of politicians to affect the level of economic activity to obtain electoral advantage. The simplest and most widely held notion is that elected governments manipulate the economy to generate a boom in the run up to an election.

Several propositions follow from this view of politicians maximizing their chances of reelection. One is that democratic systems may, accordingly, have an inflationary bias—as politicians discount the long-run consequences of an inflationary boom. A related implication is that economic policymaking is socially suboptimal, because politicians seek their own advantage rather than that of the typical citizen. Fluctuations in the economy are greater than necessary for economic efficiency.

The literature on political business cycles dates back to the work of Kalecki in the interwar period. However, the modern literature was given academic status by the work of Nordhaus (1975) and Tufte (1978). The former, in particular, is often supposed to have proved both the existence of a cycle (preelection boom and postelection recession) resulting from the politicians' optimizing electoral advantage, and that democracy has an inflationary bias.

However, the naive boom-bust story was challenged on two fronts. First, the simple prediction of the theory, that economies would tend to exhibit booms before elections and downturns afterwards, could not be supported by the data. The 1972 presidential election in the United States was cited as an example, but hardly any other unambiguous cases can be found across all the major democracies. One observation is hardly enough to base a general theory on. Indeed, there is some evidence that the reverse pattern may dominate. Governments recently elected have pet projects they wish to introduce and supporters who have to be paid off, so they spend early on. Later they find that they have a big budget deficit or they have led the country into crisis, so they cut back before the next election.

The second problem with the conventional political-business-cycle story is that it requires an amazing degree of stupidity on the part of the electorate. The Nordhaus model, for example, requires voters to expect future inflation when bargaining for wages, but to ignore their own expectations when voting. Chrystal and Alt (1981) pointed out that it is one thing to assume that voters are stupid, but it is another to assume they are inconsistent. Indeed, Chrystal and Peel (1986) showed that the evidence is consistent with voters being very well informed and using their information efficiently.

If voters are "rational" and well informed, can there be anything left of the political business cycle? Surely this depends on the electorate being fooled by a temporary boom in the economy into believing that politicians have produced a lasting improvement in welfare. Rational electors would see through this strategy and reward only the politicians who delivered optimal long-term policies.

Remarkably, the existence of rational forward-looking voters does not preclude the possibility of an electoral cycle. However, it does change the character of what results. Chappell and Keech (1986) developed a model in which the alternative political parties offer radically different programs to be implemented should they be elected. Voters have both to choose between these parties and also to assess the probability of each being elected. Changing probabilities of either being elected will directly affect economic behavior, because they change expectations about the economy. Hence swings in popularity (especially in the run up to an election) will directly affect the economy.

A simple example may be helpful. Suppose a party in opposition proposes a policy of restricting overseas investment. An opinion poll showing that it has a lead over the government might cause rational investors to move funds out of the country right away. This in turn would depress the exchange rate and could force domestic interest rates to rise. Alesina and Sachs (1988) developed a test of this new way of thinking about political business cycles and found some support for it. However, it should be clear that the modern theory is far more subtle than the original and its implicit cycle pattern is far less obvious. The simple pattern of pre-election booms is no longer considered likely.

The early literature on political business cycles concentrated on the likelihood of a boom in the economy—as measured by GDP growth, falling unemployment, etc.—before an election. When it was found that such evidence was hard to find, an alternative strategy emerged, which was to look for changes in instruments of policy (rather than targets) before elections. This approach, associated with Frey and Schneider (1978), who elevated their approach to the status of a "Politico-Economic Model" of macro-policymaking, does not seem to have lived up to its early promise. Its lack of success is perhaps partly attributable to the increasing conservatism of most governments under the constraints of external conditions.

A final element of the political-business-cycle literature, which is central to the imposition of electoral goals on economic policy, is the popularity function. Study of this function has become an end in itself. The basic question is the existence of a stable statistical relationship between the state of the economy and the popularity of the government.

The literature on the popularity function has grown substantially over the last two decades. This suggests that it is a subject of ongoing interest, but also that a stable relationship has not been found. Virtually every time-series sample produces some plausible equation relating popularity or votes to economic indicators. However, different samples produce different results. The coefficients appear to lack temporal stability, which suggests that voter perception of the importance of issues may change. There are also, from time to time, special factors, like foreign wars or scandals, that disrupt attitudes. In principle, special factors can be accommodated, but there is now no reason to be very optimistic that a stable popularity function will be found.

A plausible explanation for the absence of a stable popularity function is that voters are not simply reacting to past events. When they choose a government they are looking forward and asking the question: which party is going to deliver the best economic conditions for me over the next incumbency? It may be that past events have been bad, but the current government could still be expected to deliver the best economic performance in the future. That is where the *rational-expectations* approach, so popular in recent economic models, comes in.

If voters are forward-looking, rational, and well informed, they will already have formed a view about which party they would support. This is based not just on past behavior, but also on expected future performance. What will cause the voter to change that set of expectations? The answer can only be: new information. New information is, by definition, unpredictable (if it were predicted, it would not be new). Since only new information changes voting intentions, and new information is random, the change in voting intentions must itself be random. It is this pattern for which Chrystal and Peel find statistical support. Although their results have been questioned on statistical grounds, the forward-looking approach to voter decision making seems to be widely accepted.

To conclude, there is no doubt that government behavior can create or aggravate cycles in the economy. Presumably, these actions are sometimes motivated by perceived electoral advantage. However, voters are not as naive as they were once thought to be. Nor do politicians quite have the economic power they were once supposed to wield. As a result, there is no simple pattern with robust empirical support that could be unambiguously ascribed to the political business cycle. Notwithstanding the academic evidence, the myth of the electoral cycle in economic policy remains firmly entrenched in the popular culture.

K. Alec Chrystal

See also AKERMAN, JOHAN HENRIK; ELECTORAL CYCLE IN MONETARY POLICY; FEDERAL RESERVE SYSTEM: 1941–1993

Bibliography

Alesina, A. and J. Sachs. 1988. "Political Parties and the Business Cycle in the United States, 1948–1984." *Journal of Money, Credit, and Banking* 20:63–82.

Chappell, H. W. and W. R. Keech. 1986. "Party Differences in Macroeconomic Policies and Outcomes." *American Economic Review Papers and Proceedings* 76:71–74.

Chrystal, K. A. and J. E. Alt. 1981. "Public Sector Behaviour: The Status of the Political Business Cycle." In *Macroeconomic Analysis,* edited by D. Currie, R. Nobay, and D. Peel, 353–76. London: Croom Helm.

Chrystal, K. A. and D. A. Peel. 1986. "What Can Economics Learn from Political Science and Vice Versa?" *American Economic Review, Papers and Proceedings* 76:62–65.

Frey, B. S. and F. Schneider. 1978. "A Politico-Economic Model of the United Kingdom." *Economic Journal* 88:243–53.

Nordhaus, W. 1975. "The Political Business Cycle." *Review of Economic Studies* 42:169–90.

Tufte, E. R. 1978. *The Political Control of the Economy.* Princeton: Princeton Univ. Press.

Post-Keynesian Business-Cycle Theory

A central proposition of all Post-Keynesian theory is that the conflict over income distribution is at the heart of the analysis of inflation, unemployment, and the business cycle (Eichner and Kregel 1975, 1308). Such a theory has been formulated by Richard Goodwin, a leading Post-Keynesian. His theory of business cycles also attempts to explain the most important empirical regularities of the history of observed business cycles. The most important of these regularities are the inverse relationship of wage inflation and unemployment, the co-movement of wage inflation with price inflation, the procyclical share of wages in total income, the nonseparability of the growth and the cyclical components of real GNP, the fluctuation of investment with profitability, and endogenously generated persistent cycles.

Persistence of cycles requires a nonlinear model. For example, in the linear multiplier-accelerator model (Samuelson [1939] 1966), the cycle depends on a particular value of the accelerator coefficient. For any other value of the coefficient, the cycle either dies away or becomes explosive. This dependence on a critical value of some coefficient makes all linear models unsatisfactory (Blatt 1983). In his 1950 model, Hicks retained the same basic multiplier-accelerator framework, but introduced a floor and a ceiling to sustain cyclical fluctuations. Mathematically, adding a floor and a ceiling made the cycle independent of the value of the accelerator coefficient, but it still did not incorporate growth into the cycle. Nor did it come close to explaining the other empirical regularities stated above. These shortcomings in business-cycle theory were remedied in a model developed and later extended by Goodwin ([1961] 1982; Goodwin, Kruger and Vercelli 1984; Goodwin and Punzo 1987, 1989).

The gist of Goodwin's model is grounded in the Lotka-Volterra, predator-prey equations, which model the conflict between labor and capital. The two crucial variables are the share of wages in GNP, and the fraction of the labor force currently employed, which will be called the employment ratio, λ. The pace of capital accumulation determines the demand for labor. If the rate of accumulation rises then so does λ. In the neighborhood of full employment, both the share of wages and the real wage rise. The rising wage share reduces both the share of capital and the rate of profit on capital. A reduced profit rate reduces new investment, and consequently depresses the employment ratio. Meanwhile, the labor force grows as a result of population growth as well as of technical displacement through labor-saving technology. The fall in employment reduces labor's bargaining power, so that the growth rate of real wages slows down, raising the share of capital and eventually restoring the profit rate. Investment now picks up, and the cycle is repeated.

Throughout, real wages continue to rise, as does output over the cycle. A simple numerical illustration of Goodwin's model confirms these results (Blatt 1983, 204–11). By using nonlinear equations, Goodwin made endogenous the fluctuation in inflation over the cycle which results from the conflict over income distribution. Goodwin was the first to formalize this conflict in a dynamic model of the growth cycle.

The assumptions of the model are:

A1. Labor productivity grows at a constant proportional rate: $a(t) = Y(t)/L(t) = a_0 e^{\alpha t}$ where Y is output and L is labor employed;

A2. The labor force grows at a steady rate: $N(t) = N_0 e^{\beta t}$;

A3. The employment ratio is $\lambda(t) = L(t)/N(t)$;

A4. The real wage is $W(t)$, and labor's share of output is $[W(t)L(t)]/Y(t) = w(t)$;

A5. The capital stock is $K(t) = vY(t)$;

A6. The proportionate growth rate of wages is a function of labor market tightness, i.e. $(dW/dt)/W = f(\lambda)$;

A7. Workers consume their wages and firms invest all profits.

From these minimal assumptions, Goodwin derives three fundamental coupled differential equations which determine cyclical growth:

$$\frac{dY}{dt} = \frac{1-w}{v} \cdot Y \qquad (1)$$

$$\frac{d\lambda}{dt} = \lambda \left(\frac{1-w}{v} - \alpha - \beta \right) \qquad (2)$$

$$\frac{dw}{dt} = w[f(\lambda) - \alpha] \qquad (3)$$

The derivations are straightforward. The first equation follows from A7, which implies investment is $[1 - w(t)]Y(t)$. Next, differentiate A5 and substitute into the former to get equation (1). To obtain equation (2), differentiate A3 and utilize A2 and A1, and equation (1) itself.

To obtain equation (3), differentiate A6 and note that from A4, $W(t) = \alpha w(t)$.

More recently, Goodwin (1989) has disaggregated his basic model and suggested an interesting possibility. Imagine now that both the wage share and the employment ratio are disaggregated, so that they become sectoral wage shares and sectoral employment ratios. Now each sector has its own cycle (called a limit cycle). The weighted sum of these sectoral oscillations produces an aggregate cycle that is highly irregular. Each sectoral cycle has a different periodicity; however, all sectors are interrelated through purchases and sales, and some sectors move together. Furthermore, if any one of the sectoral periodicities is an irrational ratio, then the aggregate cycle never repeats. Thus, each growth cycle is unique, but the irregularity in the time series of output does not make it chaotic in the mathematical sense; the series of output still resembles the actual GNP time series. The sectoral employment ratios, and hence the aggregate rate of unemployment, fluctuate, thus exhibiting Keynesian features. Borrowing from Schumpeter ([1912] 1934, 1939), Goodwin finds that the cycle emerges as a necessary condition for long-run growth. The cycles fluctuate around the von Neumann steady-state growth path, which becomes merely a reference point (Dore et al. 1989).

Mathematically, each sectoral cycle is a stable motion, a limit cycle that is independent of initial values. In contrast with linear models, Goodwin's model must be dynamically unstable to ensure that cycles persist, and the model is indeed dynamically unstable as required. The instability is assured by one essential nonlinearity, which is both necessary and sufficient: the proportional rate of change of the employment ratio changes from a positive to a negative value in the neighborhood of full employment. Unlike Hicks (1950), Goodwin derives the nonlinearity without artificial floors and ceilings. The stylized facts listed above are reflected in the Goodwin model. It integrates growth and cycles, in which the governing mechanism is the bargaining power of labor, which depends on the tightness of the labor market. It also displays a long "upswing," followed by a short downswing. If the inverse relationship between inflation and unemployment is characteristic of most free-market economies, then the Goodwin model best describes the governing mechanism of business cycles.

The Goodwin model also explains the technological superiority of capitalist economies. In such economies it is not price competition that is predominant, but competition for relative factor shares. Organized labor forces firms to reduce costs, to defend their profit margins. This is also a spur for labor-saving technological change, which happens to be a major consideration in implementing new technology. This spur was missing in Soviet-type command economies.

In a dynamic context, the merits of a competitive economy lie in its entrepreneurial adaptability and its long-run tendency towards labor-saving innovation, which have given capitalism a technological edge. If the price for this superiority is cyclical growth, then for Schumpeter at least, it was a price worth paying.

Mohammed H. I. Dore

See also ASYMMETRY; GOODWIN, RICHARD MURPHEY; HICKS, JOHN RICHARD; INFLATION; NONLINEAR BUSINESS-CYCLE THEORIES; SAMUELSON, PAUL ANTHONY; STYLIZED FACTS

Bibliography

Blatt, J. M. 1983. *Dynamic Economic Systems: A Post-Keynesian Approach.* Armonk, N.Y.: M. E. Sharpe.

Dore, M. H. I., S. Chakravarty, and R. M. Goodwin, eds. 1989. *Von Neumann and Modern Economics.* London: Oxford Univ. Press.

Eichner, A. S. and J. A. Kregel. 1975. "An Essay on Post-Keynesian Theory: A New Paradigm in Economics." *Journal of Economic Literature* 13:1293–1314.

Goodwin, R. M. [1967] 1982. "A Growth Cycle." Chap. 14 in *Essays in Economic Dynamics.* London: Macmillan.

———. 1989. "Swinging along the Autostrada." In *John Von Neumann and Modern Economics,* edited by M. H. I. Dore, S. Chakravarty, and R. M. Goodwin, 125–40. Oxford: Clarendon Press.

Goodwin, R. M., M. Kruger, and A. Vercelli, eds. 1984. *Nonlinear Models of Fluctuating Growth. Lecture Notes in Economics and Mathematical Systems.* No. 228. Berlin: Springer-Verlag.

Goodwin, R. M. and L. Punzo. 1987. *The Dynamics of the Capitalist Economy.* Oxford: Polity Press.

Hicks, J. R. 1950. *A Contribution to the Theory of the Trade Cycle.* Oxford: Clarendon Press.

Samuelson, P. A. [1939] 1966. "Interactions between the Multiplier Analysis and the Principle of Acceleration." Chap. 82 in *The Collected Scientific Papers of Paul A. Samuelson.* Cambridge: MIT Press.

Schumpeter, J. A. [1912] 1934. *The Theory of Economic Development.* Cambridge: Harvard Univ. Press.

———. 1939. *Business Cycles: A Theoretical, Historical, and Statistical Analysis of the Capitalist Process.* 2 vols. New York: McGraw-Hill.

Preobrazhensky, Evgenii Alexeyevich (1886–1937)

Evgenii Preobrazhensky is mostly known to economists and political scientists as a member of the left-wing faction of the leadership of the Soviet Communist Party. Expelled from the party in 1927, he broke with the opposition in 1929 and lent his support to Stalin. Arrested in 1935, he testified against Zinoviev only to be arrested again in 1936. He was shot without trial in 1937 (Ellman 1987).

Preobrazhensky contributed extensively to the debate about socialist industrialization, drawing heavily from Marx's notion of primitive accumulation. Yet, he was also a theorist of the capitalist economy, and he can be seen as the last of the advocates of the disproportionality theory of crises. His contribution to this brand of Marxian crisis theory is very little known because his book *Zakat Kapitalizma* (English title, *The Decline of Capitalism*), containing his main views, remained in almost complete obscurity from its publication in 1931 until it was unearthed and translated into English by Richard B. Day in 1985.

The Decline of Capitalism is certainly one of the most interesting works written in the classical tradition of Marxian economics in this century. As lucidly summarized by Sweezy (1942), the analytical structure of the debates about accumulation and crisis was centered on Marx's schemes of reproduction. The disproportionality school used those schemes to argue that crises would occur not because effective demand was lacking, but because the distribution of investment goods to the consumption and capital-goods sectors was imbalanced.

According to Preobrazhensky, crises are a necessary aspect of capital accumulation, given that the latter implies promoting the expansion of the productive apparatus ahead of consumption. At some stage, the system will endeavor to reconstitute the conditions of proportionality, since the interrelated sectors cannot grow apart forever. But the restoration of proportionality is achieved by cutting down on the expansion of fixed capital with negative effects on the effective demand for consumption goods. Preobrazhensky argued that under free competition crises are accompanied by falling prices and that it is this effect that allows the system to regenerate itself and to start a new phase of accumulation. The analysis is not always clear, because the schemes are presented in value terms while the adjustment process is discussed in price terms. Nevertheless, the essence of Preobrazhensky's position is that the variability of prices is a necessary condition for the economy to recover from the crisis.

In relation to earlier approaches to crisis theory, the truly novel element introduced by Preobrazhensky is the altogether different account of the dynamics of the crisis under monopolistic capitalism. Monopolism, he argued, "corrupts the mechanism of regulation through value, but it is obviously unable to achieve planned control of the production process" (Preobrazhensky [1931] 1985, 97). Under free competition, capitalists are always compelled to reduce costs, which leads to a reduction of prices. This process can be accomplished only by renewing the stock of capital and expanding production. By contrast, if monopolistic conditions prevail, prices will not be reduced, so that in a crisis production will be cut first. The rigidity of prices means that "the system loses an important lever for overcoming the crisis" (109).

Applying this set of ideas to Marx's schemes of reproduction, Preobrazhensky shows that under monopolistic conditions there is an immanent tendency to build up large reserves of productive capacity. As a consequence, the relations between the two sectors of production are constrained by the existence of unused capacity. The system therefore loses the stimuli for rapid expansion, preventing the utilization of the reserve army of labor. This last point is particularly innovative vis-à-vis traditional Marxian thought, since it envisages a form of (Keynesian) unemployment divorced from the functional link between the reserve army of labor and accumulation.

In his book, Preobrazhensky analyzed the world economic crisis of 1930–31 as well as the rise of fascism. Many of his ideas about the

macroeconomic role of monopolies can now be better understood by studying the work of Kalecki. Yet the credit for having developed a fully Marxian scheme of monopolistic accumulation and crisis, prior to Kalecki himself, undoubtedly goes to Preobrazhensky.

Joseph Halevi

See also DISPROPORTIONALITY THEORY; KALECKI, MICHAL

Bibliography
Ellman, M. 1987. "Evgenii Alexeyevich Preobrazhensky." In *The New Palgrave: A Dictionary of Economic Theory.* Vol. 4. Edited by J. Eatwell, M. Milgate, and P. Newman. London: Macmillan.

Kalecki, M. 1971. *Selected Essays on the Dynamics of the Capitalist Economy.* Cambridge: Cambridge Univ. Press.

Preobrazhensky, E. [1931] 1985. *The Decline of Capitalism.* Translated and edited with an introduction by R. B. Day. Armonk, N.Y.: Sharpe.

Sweezy, P. M. 1942. *The Theory of Capitalist Development.* New York: Oxford Univ. Press.

Price-Quantity Adjustment
Modern business-cycle theory is much concerned with microeconomic price-quantity dynamics. A fundamental issue of macrofluctuations has become the speed and stability of price and quantity adjustment in market economies (Tobin 1993). A common belief nowadays is that a sound theory of the business cycle requires a proper microdynamic foundation. However, there are many approaches to formulating "laws of motion" for prices and quantities, and they have different implications for macrofluctuations. This article reviews some alternative adjustment mechanisms and then integrates them into a composite dynamic mechanism which describes price and quantity adjustments more realistically than do one-sided mechanisms.

Price-Quantity Dynamics in Economic Theory
Extensive verbal formulations of price-quantity dynamics are contained in the work of such classical and early neoclassical economists as Smith, Ricardo, Walras, and Marshall. The dynamic price-quantity adjustment they described consists of a twofold mechanism:

1. the output of a commodity is expanded or reduced (through entry or exit of firms) whenever price is greater or less than cost (*law of excess returns*);
2. the price of a commodity is raised (reduced) whenever there is an excess demand (supply) on the market (*law of excess demand*).

In mathematical treatments, this classical view has been termed *cross-dual dynamics*. Goodwin ([1953] 1982) and Morishima (1960, 1977) have examined the stability properties of the classical view. More recently, Duménil and Lévy (1987) and Flaschel and Semmler (1987) have done so using the tools of modern stability analysis. Most of these studies show that the twofold law of motion is generally not stable.

Modern neoclassical theory since Hicks and Samuelson has used only the law of excess demand to characterize the law of motion of prices. This price-adjustment mechanism has been shown to be asymptotically stable under the assumption of gross substitutes or the weak axiom of revealed preference. However, later work showed that the law of excess demand proves to be unstable for a very general class of excess-demand functions.

Most of these studies assume that demand and supply adjust instantaneously to a change in the price vector. Although the approach to market-adjustment based on excess-demand functions alone is often attributed to Walras, Walras actually employed a classical "disequilibrium-production model" incorporating both the law of excess demand and the law of excess returns.

Both the classical and the neoclassical approaches to market adjustment postulate rapid adjustment of prices to achieve market equilibria. Those formulations of short-run market adjustment are unsatisfactory from a Keynesian perspective. The Keynesian adjustment process (*dual dynamics*) can be stylized as follows:

1. quantities increase (decrease) in response to excess demand (supply) (reaction of existing firms);
2. price changes are proportional to the difference between (marked-up) costs and prices.

In such "fixprice" economies, imbalances of supply and demand cause quantities to change and prices respond to differences be-tween marked-up costs and actual prices. Quantity adjustment has become an essential element in non-Walrasian models of quantity rationing and disequilibrium analysis (Benassy 1982). The price adjustment has been elaborated by earlier Keynesian theories as well as by the New Keynesians who base their price-adjustment mechanisms on the assumption of imperfect competition or imperfect information.

Jorgenson (1960) reformulated the earlier Keynesian dual-dynamics for Leontief systems in the form of a "dual-instability theorem" which assumes full utilization of capacity and a perfect-foresight path of prices. Later work, following Jorgenson, has mostly dropped the assumptions of full capacity utilization and perfect foresight when analyzing dynamic stability.

Since Jorgenson's contribution, dynamic models with saddle-point instability have become dominant in the rational-expectations approach, in which prices are assumed to change instantaneously to clear markets. Unbiased foresight of the future path of variables such as the money supply and the given transversality condition for the price path imply that, after any displacement from equilibrium, prices return quickly to the stable saddle path of the dynamics. Quantities, on the other hand, are unaffected even if prices diverge (Sargent and Wallace 1973).

This position appears inconsistent with empirical research. In particular, recent empirical studies on wage and price dynamics seem to suggest that prices generally respond sluggishly to quantity imbalances (Gordon 1990). Quantities appear to vary more than prices over the business cycle. Responding to the rational-expectations approach, many theorists, particularly the New Keynesians, have elaborated more plausible explanations than previously provided for price rigidities and quantity adjustments. They attempt to explain the sluggishness of price adjustments compared to output adjustments by invoking theories of imperfect competition and imperfect information. Strongly emphasizing the importance of nominal rigidities for macrodynamics and the business cycle, New Keynesians have suggested three types of explanations for nominal rigidities: (1) firms behave suboptimally; (2) changing prices is costly ("menu" costs); and (3) price changes create greater uncertainty for profit flows than quantity adjustments ("instrument uncertainty"). Though both the rationing approach and the New Keynesian approach support the earlier Keynesian emphasis on price rigidity, few studies have explored the stability properties of the implied price-quantity dynamics.

Composite Price-Quantity Dynamics

Given the different traditions of price-quantity dynamics, a natural way to overcome the deficiencies of each is to integrate the different adjustment mechanisms into a single approach. Empirically, it seems to be appropriate to maintain that price and quantity adjustments occur simultaneously, though at different speeds. There may also be differences across countries and industries and over time. A composite approach may add realism to the study of market dynamics and is consistent with microeconomic principles.

Integrating the dual and the cross-dual adjustment processes into a composite system suggests the following more complete dynamic adjustment mechanism (for purposes of illustration, specified for a constant-coefficient economy):

$$\dot{x} = D_{11}C(g)x - D_{12}C(r)'p' + q_1 \qquad (1)$$

$$\dot{p}' = D_{21}C(g)x + D_{22}C(r)'p' + q_2 \qquad (2)$$

Here D_{11}, D_{12}, D_{21}, D_{22} are diagonal matrices with positive diagonals, representing adjustment speeds. The $n \times n$ matrices $C(r)' = ((1 + r)A - I)'$, $C(g) = ((1 + g)A - I)$ contain I, the identity matrix, A, the usual intermediate-goods matrix, r, the rate of return on capital, g, the rate of growth, $q_1 = D_{11}c - D_{12}w$, $q_2 = D_{21}c + D_{22}w$, c, a (column) vector of final consumption goods, and w, a vector of wage payments per unit of output. The vectors x, p (corresponding to c, w) as usual stand for activity levels and prices, and $\dot{x}$, $\dot{p}$ denote their time derivatives. A limit case may arise when $g = r = r^*$, where r^* is the equilibrium profit rate. If we assume that $c \geq 0$ and $w > 0$, then $0 < r$ and $g < R^* - 1 = r^*$, derived from the scalar $1/R^* = \lambda_{max}(A) = \lambda_{max}(A') = 1/(1 + r^*)$, which is the maximum eigenvalue of the matrices A and A' (assumed for simplicity to be indecomposable).

The following microeconomic interpretation may be attached to this model. In the output-adjustment equation (1), firms are assumed to adjust output both in response to differences between demand and supply when revising production (and investment) decisions and in re-

sponse to differences between actual rates of return and a norm or target rate of return. However, compared with the (Keynesian) quantity reaction to quantity imbalances, the (classical) quantity reaction (mainly resulting from the entry and exit of firms) to profitability differences is assumed to be slow. This implies that $D_{12} < D_{11}$.

On the other hand, a price-adjustment model is made more realistic by positing a two-fold process. Accordingly, in equation (2) we suppose that when setting prices, firms follow two decision rules: (a) they provisionally set prices employing a mark-up (or target rate of return) calculation, and (b) using an error-correcting mechanism, they adjust prices in proportion to the imbalance between supply and demand in each market. The presumed mark-up procedure and price dynamics appear to be consistent with empirical studies (Hall 1988).

What are the dynamic properties of equations (1) and (2) in which different subsystems may interact? It can be shown that (for g, $r < r^*$) the Keynesian dual dynamics, captured by the diagonal of the above matrix, is asymptotically stable and that the classical cross-dual dynamics, portrayed in the off-diagonal terms of the matrix, is purely oscillatory (and thus marginally stable). One might therefore conjecture that the stability of this system is easy to demonstrate. Yet, even the simple case, with a constant coefficients (square) matrix and constant g and r, is not obviously stable. Traditional methods can demonstrate stability for such composite dynamic systems only under very restrictive assumptions about the reaction coefficients. New methods are needed to study the stability of composite systems. A method based on the tradition of Lyapunov's direct approach can be used to examine the dynamics of composite systems. This method works with vector Lyapunov functions and shows how conclusions may be drawn with respect to the composite systems (Flaschel and Semmler 1987, 1990). Computer studies can be added to strengthen conjectures concerning the stability of such composite systems, but generic proofs have not been provided. Counterexamples to stability can be constructed by employing eigenvalue studies for randomly generated matrices. Considering the unstable cases, one can suggest a sensible economic mechanism that, when introduced into composite dynamics, implies stability or at least bounded fluctuations. Additionally, introduced stabilizing terms (represented, for example, by derivative control terms), will stabilize such dynamics as portrayed in equations (1) and (2). The incorporated stabilizing terms are also of more general importance, for example, in stabilizing unstable excess-demand functions (Flaschel and Semmler 1987).

Some Conclusions

Most of the price-quantity adjustment mechanisms considered in the literature are one-sided. Stability theory can be made more realistic if different adjustment processes are synthesized and their dynamics studied jointly. If, indeed, product markets (and possibly factor markets) reflect a composite dynamics, then the volatility of macroaggregates will depend crucially on the speeds of adjustment of both prices and quantities.

Willi Semmler

See also NEW KEYNESIAN ECONOMICS; PRICE RIGIDITY; WAGE RIGIDITY

Bibliography

Beckmann, M. J. and H. E. Ryder. 1969. "Simultaneous Price and Quantity Adjustment in a Single Market." *Econometrica* 37:470–88.

Benassy, J. 1982. *The Economics of Market Disequilibrium.* New York: Academic Press.

Duménil, G. and D. Lévy. 1987. "The Dynamics of Competition: A Restoration of Classical Analysis." *Cambridge Journal of Economics* 11:133–64.

Flaschel, P. and W. Semmler. 1987. "Classical and Neoclassical Competitive Adjustment Processes." *The Manchester School* 55:13–37.

———. 1990. "On Competitive Classical and Keynesian Micro-Dynamical Processes." In *Dynamic Modelling and Control of National Economies,* edited by N. M. Christodoulakis, 271–79. Oxford: Pergamon Press.

Goodwin, R. M. [1953] 1982. "Static and Dynamic General Equilibrium Models." Chap. 5 in *Essays in Linear Economic Structures.* London: Macmillan.

Gordon, R. J. 1990. "What Is New-Keynesian Economics?" *Journal of Economic Literature* 27:1115–72.

Greenwald, B. and J. E. Stiglitz. 1989. "A Theory of Price Rigidities: Adjustment under Uncertainty." *American Economic Review Papers and Proceedings* 79:364–70.

Hall, R. E. 1988. "The Relationship between Price and Marginal Costs in U.S. Industry." *Journal of Political Economy* 96:920–47.

Jorgenson, D. W. 1960. "A Dual Stability Theorem." *Econometrica* 28:892–99.

Mas-Collel, A. 1986. "Notes on Price and Quantity Dynamics." In *Models of Economic Dynamics,* edited by H. Sonnenschein, 49–68. Berlin: Springer-Verlag.

Morishima, M. 1960. "A Reconsideration of the Walras-Cassel-Leontief Model of General Equilibrium." In *Mathematical Models in the Social Sciences, 1959,* edited by K. Arrow, S. Karlin, and P. Suppes, 63–76. Stanford: Stanford Univ. Press.

———. 1977. *Walras' Economics.* Cambridge: Cambridge Univ. Press.

Sargent, T. and N. Wallace. 1973. "The Stability of Models of Money and Growth with Perfect Foresight." *Econometrica* 41:1043–48.

Taylor, J. B. 1986. "Improvements in Macroeconomic Stability: The Role of Wages and Prices." In *The American Business Cycle: Continuity and Change,* edited by R. J. Gordon, 639–78. Chicago: Univ. of Chicago Press.

Tobin, J. 1993. "Price Flexibility and Output Stability: An Old Keynesian View." In *Journal of Economic Perspectives,* Winter, 45–65.

Price Rigidity

Prices, once set, often remain unchanged or rigid despite changes in the underlying conditions of supply and demand. Rigid prices can therefore prevent the equilibration of supply and demand and can lead to inefficiency. Macroeconomic models often rely on rigidity in prices or wages to show how inefficient unemployment can arise and can be combatted by macroeconomic policy.

The potential inefficiency associated with rigid prices is the reason for the great interest in the topic. This potential inefficiency would exist as long as prices fail to adjust fully to shifts in supply and demand. It is not their rigidity but rather their failure to equate supply and demand that is the key economic characteristic of rigid prices.

One of the earliest and most influential statements that prices do not equilibrate supply and demand was made by Gardiner Means (1935). Means asserted that some prices are "administered" and insensitive to the forces of supply and demand. Means attributed the severity of the Great Depression to administered prices that failed to adjust to a decrease in demand. Means's hypothesis has generated great controversy, partly because his work lacked a theoretical foundation (Beals 1975, Carlton 1989, Weiss 1977). Disagreements on the theoretical explanations for price rigidity and its consequences and on its empirical importance remain widespread.

Simple Theory and Consequences of Price Rigidity

The simplest explanation for why a price remains unchanged despite changes in underlying supply or demand is that changing prices is costly. The costs of changing prices are ignored in many economic models which assume that firms sell their product in a market and that somehow the "market" costlessly sets the price that equates supply and demand. If we drop the assumption that price formation is costless and assume instead that a transaction cost must be incurred every time a price is changed, then it is efficient for prices to change only occasionally. For example, changing price for items on a printed menu or in a catalogue is costly, since it costs money to print a new menu or catalogue. However, such explicit costs apply to relatively few commodities. More subtle types of transaction costs are likely to be relevant for other commodities. For example, when a firm decides what price to charge, its employees must usually gather and analyze some facts about the market. This decision takes time and consumes real resources.

Aside from the transaction cost that a firm incurs to change price, a price change can impose a cost on consumers. In some markets, consumers search over firms before purchasing and may expect observed prices to prevail for some time. Therefore, once they find a place to buy, they continue to return to the same firm unless prices change. Prices that remain constant for some time allow consumers to plan better and economize on search. A firm may therefore be reluctant to increase its price for fear of inducing its customers to search. A firm may also be reluctant to change price for fear that doing so will upset the oligopolistic discipline in the industry.

If prices do not adjust fully when supply or demand changes, the quantity supplied may not equal the quantity demanded. There could be either excess demand, manifested as a shortage, or excess supply, manifested as unemployed resources. Macroeconomics often relies on models with rigid prices to generate unemployment. It seems unlikely that the transaction costs of changing price can cause significant macroeconomic dislocations. However, several researchers (see, e.g., the studies in Mankiw and Romer [1991]) have shown that it is theoretically possible for "small" transaction costs to generate "large" efficiency losses. They show that in a world of monopolistic competition, a firm's private gain (i.e., increased profit) from changing price can be much smaller than the social gain (i.e., increased consumer plus producer surplus) and so, in the presence of transaction costs, price can remain unchanged even in the face of inefficient allocations. The reason for the disparity between the private and social gain is (roughly) that the private gain depends on the gap between marginal revenue and marginal cost, while the social gain depends on the larger gap between price and marginal cost. Despite this theoretical possibility, the small static efficiency loss that empirical studies attribute to monopoly would suggest that the efficiency loss under monopolistic competition in the incentive to change price is also small from the distortion.

More Sophisticated Explanations and Consequences of Price Rigidity

There are at least three reasons in addition to those already discussed for price rigidity or, more precisely, for a price that hardly changes in the face of changing conditions. Each of these explanations relies on more sophisticated theory than the earlier ones and each has significant implications for efficiency and market organization (Carlton 1989, Mankiw and Romer 1991).

First, price is only one of many dimensions of the terms on which goods are exchanged. The physical attributes and the delivery delay associated with a good matter a great deal to consumers. Since these other characteristics of the good can respond to changed supply and demand conditions, there may be no need for price to change significantly. For example, in response to an increase in demand, price may remain relatively unchanged, but consumers may have to wait a little longer for delivery.

Consumers may prefer to wait rather than pay a significantly higher price. Such an equilibrium can be efficient and should not be construed as inefficient just because customers are waiting for product delivery.

Second, sometimes a product's characteristics cannot be readily observed but are influenced by price. For example, all else equal, the average quality of job applicants rises with the wage offered since better workers apply for higher-wage jobs. In such a case, it may be impossible for price simultaneously to clear the market and to provide incentives for the efficient quality level. An imbalance of supply and demand may result, yet price will not change, because such a price change would adversely affect quality.

Third, because it is costly to let price *alone* clear markets (e.g., it is costly to set up the institutional structure necessary to have an exchange with brokers and traders whose function is to set market-clearing prices), firms use other mechanisms together with price to allocate goods to customers. One of the most common is for the firm's marketing department to choose which buyers should receive delivery first from among the buyers willing to pay the stated rigid price (the price may differ across buyers). Steady customers may be more likely to receive priority delivery when demand suddenly increases than transient customers (Carlton 1991).

Rigid prices can create an inefficiency when goods are allocated to buyers exclusively by price and the market-clearing price differs from the stated one. But if firms do not rely exclusively on price, but also use their discretion in allocating goods, then the inefficiency of a rigid price is not so obvious. In this circumstance, the firm takes over many of the allocative functions that economists usually attribute to the "market" in models with zero transaction costs and an exclusive reliance on price to allocate goods. If price alone does not allocate goods by equating supply and demand, then buyers will be concerned with the reliability of supply. Moreover, sellers will be concerned with the steadiness (or predictability) of a buyer's demand, because a steady customer is easier (less costly) to supply than one whose demands fluctuate widely. It then becomes natural for a buyer and a seller to stay together over long periods, so that they can get to know and rely on each other. Rationing will sometimes occur, but it would be a mistake to conclude that the rationing is necessarily inefficient since the cost of organizing a market that clears exclusively through price may be high (Carlton 1991).

Evidence

There is considerable evidence documenting the rigidity of prices. Early evidence comes from Mills (1927) who showed that prices tend to fall into two broad categories—highly flexible or highly inflexible. Means (1935) reported data on the flexibility of prices during the Great Depression and showed that while some (e.g., agricultural) prices fell precipitously, other prices (e.g., those of certain manufactured items) did not. Stigler and Kindahl (1970) criticized studies documenting price rigidity by showing that the price data (which were from the Bureau of Labor Statistics (BLS)) reflected list, rather than transaction, prices and so understated the degree of price fluctuations in actual transaction prices. Using data collected from surveys of buyers, they showed that transaction prices over the period 1956–66 were more flexible than the BLS price data.

Carlton (1986) reexamined the Stigler-Kindahl data and found the following:

1. Prices for many products (e.g., chemicals, steel, drugs) remained unchanged to buyers for more than one year. In several of these industries, there was concern about supply reliability.

2. The duration of price rigidity across products was positively related to the seller concentration of the market.

3. Buyers and sellers remained paired together for long periods even for what appear to be relatively homogeneous products.

4. There were many small price changes.

The main conclusions of the study are that price rigidity is indeed a significant phenomenon; it is likely that price alone does not allocate goods, so that sellers exercise discretion in deciding which buyers to supply. Because reliability of delivery is an important concern of buyers, buyers and sellers tend to remain together for several years, and the transaction cost of changing price is probably not uniformly high across all customers.

Several other empirical studies on price rigidity are listed in the bibliography. All the empirical studies confirm that price rigidity is widespread and significantly affects how firms operate.

Dennis W. Carlton

See also NEW KEYNESIAN ECONOMICS; PRICE-QUANTITY ADJUSTMENT; WAGE RIGIDITY

Bibliography

Beals, R. 1975. "Concentrated Industries, Administered Prices, and Inflation: A Survey of Empirical Research." Washington, D.C.: Council of Wage and Price Stability.

Blinder, A. S. 1991. "Why are Prices Sticky? Preliminary Results from an Interview Study." *American Economic Review Papers and Proceedings* 81:89–96.

Carlton, D. W. 1986. "The Rigidity of Prices." *American Economic Review* 76:637–58.

———. 1989. "The Theory and Facts of How Markets Clear: Is Industrial Organization Useful for Understanding Macroeconomics?" In *Handbook of Modern Industrial Organization.* Vol. 1. Edited by R. Schmalansee and R. D. Willig, 909–46. Amsterdam: North-Holland.

———. 1991. "The Theory of Allocation and Its Implications for Marketing and Industrial Structure: Why Rationing is Efficient." *Journal of Law and Economics* 34:231–62.

Cecchetti, S. G. 1986. "The Frequency of Price Adjustment: A Study of the Newsstand Prices of Magazines." *Journal of Econometrics* 31:255–74.

Gordon, R. J. 1983. "A Century of Evidence on Wage and Price Stickiness in the United States, the United Kingdom, and Japan." In *Macroeconomics, Prices, and Quantities: Essays in Memory of Arthur M. Okun,* edited by J. Tobin, 85–134. Washington, D.C.: Brookings Institution.

Kashyap, A. K. 1995. "Sticky Prices: New Evidence From Retail Catalogs." *Quarterly Journal of Economics* 110:245–74.

Lach, S. and D. Tsiddon. 1992. "The Behavior of Prices and Inflation: An Empirical Analysis of Disaggregated Price Data." *Journal of Political Economy* 100:349–89.

Mankiw, N. G. and D. Romer, eds. 1991. *New Keynesian Economics.* Cambridge: MIT Press.

Means, G. C. 1935. "Industrial Prices and Their Relative Inflexibility." Senate Document 13, 74th Congress, 1st session. Washington, D.C.: Government Printing Office.

Mills, F. C. 1927. *The Behavior of Prices.* New York: NBER.

Stigler, G. J. and J. K. Kindahl. 1970. *The Behavior of Industrial Prices.* New York: NBER.

Weiss, L. W. 1977. "Stigler, Kindahl, and Means on Administered Prices." *American Economic Review* 67:610–19.

Profit Squeeze

This strand of crisis theory argues that efforts by workers and others (e.g., third-world nationalist movements) to improve their economic position raises costs to firms and reduces profitability. Higher wages cut into profits; improved working conditions or alleviated work intensity constrain productivity, raising unit costs and squeezing profits. Improved terms of trade for primary commodities supplied by third-world countries redistribute profits from firms in the advanced countries. Declining profit rates trigger recessions and, if sufficient and sustained, long-run crises. While the basic argument was first advanced by Marx, interest was renewed in the 1960s, and it is currently one of the foremost neo-Marxian crisis theories.

Wage increases result from more frequent and more successful strikes due to economic circumstances or relatively autonomous increases in worker militancy, and from increased quit rates which pressure firms to raise pay to retain experienced employees. Critics note that average real wages change little over the cycle, rather than moving procyclically. But in an expansion, hiring of less skilled, less experienced, and younger workers (who typically earn less), increases, which should pull average wages down. Since we do not see countercyclical average wages, the underlying structure of wages must move upward in an expansion.

Productivity (hourly worker output) depends not only on efficiency, but on the quality of labor performance and the intensity of hourly effort. Collective or informal efforts by workers to improve the quality of worklife can lead to lower intensity—a reduced pace, or more time for breaks or safety checks—or can constrain the implementation of techniques which eliminate jobs or render them less interesting. Accelerated labor-management conflict impairs performance insofar as open lines of communication help to direct workers' effort productively and to avoid waste. While productivity growth tends to be procyclical, it slows before the economy turns down, leading the cycle. The secular productivity slowdown, which began in the late 1960s and early 1970s, also preceded the slow growth and deep recessions of the late 1970s and 1980s.

The profit-squeeze argument has several components and variants. The reserve-army theory attributes the profit squeeze in the latter part of business-cycle expansions to the benefits of sustained low unemployment for workers' collective-bargaining power and informal leverage on the job. The cyclical downturn then restores profitability by increasing the reserve pool of unemployed workers. Their competitive pressure on those retaining jobs leads to declining wage settlements and greater shop-floor discipline. While this process is endogenously generated, government fiscal and monetary authorities often intervene to expedite and manage both downturns and upturns. Social-welfare policies can mitigate the cyclical pattern by reducing or increasing the cost of job loss and therefore the effects of changes in unemployment.

A long-wave version of the reserve-army theory has also been developed. The postwar boom in most advanced capitalist countries reduced the threat of unemployment and the accumulated costs of economic insecurity (i.e., worker debt, defaults, and foreclosures). Consequently short-lived cyclical downturns had less and less effect in dampening accelerating wage demands. The logical counterpart of this argument is that only sustained high-unemployment policies could restore profitability; and in the 1980s, several advanced capitalist central banks and fiscal authorities did follow austerity policies aimed at such a result. These often succeeded in achieving a severe decline in wage growth or increased wage cuts, declining union representation, and increased job "flexibility" (elimination of work rules, the seniority principle for job placement, etc.). But they increased capitalists' relative income by sacrificing total income, and were therefore less successful in restoring profitability.

Another secular profit-squeeze argument attributes the wage boom of the 1960s in many advanced countries to increasingly combative working-class consciousness. A related view focuses on the delegitimation of postwar corporatist, social-welfare or collective-bargaining institutions (sometimes analyzed as part of an overarching Social Structure of Accumulation) which had been designed to contain wage demands and primary-commodity prices, and to manage negotiations without disrupting production. Such class consciousness has political as well as economic ramifications and cannot be restored to its previous status by anti-labor government policies; on the contrary, these further undermine the legitimacy of the state. Moreover, institutional breakdown is not remedied by extremes of behavior that test the limits of whatever conflict-channeling mechanisms remain available.

Profit-squeeze theories are closely related to conflict theories of inflation. Most analysts agree that rising wages and raw-material prices and falling productivity growth will in part be passed on in higher prices charged by core firms in healthy industries. However, there will also be a real-profits effect for several reasons. First, cost pressures affect firms unevenly within and across industries. Even given a single nationally negotiated wage contract, such issues as work rules and safety and health procedures or hiring and firing practices (which impinge on productivity) are commonly settled at the plant level. Moreover, national arrangements often allow for some wage flexibility for firms or plants situated in a tight regional labor market, leading to uneven "wage drift." Second, firms do not automatically pass on even common cost increases in the short run, given administered pricing arrangements and the value of price stability in reproducing firm-client relations. As Kalecki ([1971] 1991, 100–01) has argued, under such oligopolistic competition, trade unions can succeed in reducing mark-ups and squeezing profits. And in an increasingly global economy, import competition constrains mark-ups as well.

Critics of the profit-squeeze approach (including advocates of underconsumption theories) suggest that it focuses too narrowly on the supply-side, and fails to recognize the demand-augmenting effects of higher wages, which benefit sales and profits. The regulation school has emphasized that, rather than being restricted by wage increases, the postwar boom rested on wage-led growth and mass consumption. Kalecki, drawing on Marx's reproduction schemes in volume 2 of *Capital*, observed that if workers do not save, and capitalists do, income redistribution favoring workers will, in a slack economy, increase capacity utilization and the rate of profits. These benefits of wage increases for profitability are mitigated by an open economy, a progressive tax structure, or workers who save (or repay debts).

This critique of profit-squeeze theory abstracts from the cross-firm or cross-industry variation in cost increases discussed above; nothing guarantees that the firms hit hardest by rising costs will benefit most from increased demand. Until a recession or stagnation pushes such firms out of their industries, their low profitability drags down the average. Moreover, late in the cyclical expansion there is little room for capacity utilization to continue to rise, so increased demand due to higher wages must be met by new capital investment. As new fixed capital comes on line, capacity utilization and therefore profitability fall.

An alternative criticism of the profit-squeeze perspective interprets it as blaming workers for business cycles and long waves. This personalizes a structural conflict of interest between workers and capitalists. From managers' perspective, workers are lazy when they do not constantly strive to increase productivity, and greedy when they demand better wages. The profit-squeeze argument recognizes that managers' perceptions are grounded in the absolute priority that capitalism assigns profitability. To avoid or deny this is to fail to recognize a major source of capitalist crises, whether business cycles or depressions.

Michele I. Naples

See also FALLING RATE OF PROFIT; FALLING RATE OF PROFIT, EMPIRICAL TESTS; LONG-WAVE THEORIES; MARX, KARL HEINRICH; POST-KEYNESIAN THEORY; REGULATION SCHOOL; SOCIAL STRUCTURE OF ACCUMULATION

Bibliography

Boddy, R. and J. Crotty. 1975. "Class Conflict and Macro-Policy: The Political Business Cycle." *Review of Radical Political Economics* 7:1–19.

Crotty, J. R. and L. A. Rapping. 1975. "The 1975 Report of the President's Council of Economic Advisers: A Radical Critique." *American Economic Review* 65:791–811.

Crouch, C. and A. Pizzorno, eds. 1978. *The Resurgence of Class Conflict in Western Europe since 1968.* New York: Holmes and Meier.

Glyn, A. and B. Sutcliffe. 1972. *Capitalism in Crisis.* New York: Pantheon Books.

Gordon, D. M. 1981. "Labor-Capital Conflict and the Productivity Slowdown." *American Economic Review Papers and Proceedings* 71:30–35.

Kalecki, M. [1971] 1991. "Class Struggle and the Distribution of National Income." In *The Collected Works of Michal Kalecki,* vol. 2, 96–103. Oxford: Clarendon Press.

Marx, K. [1867] 1967. *Capital.* Vol. 1. New York: International Publishers.

Naples, M. I. 1976. "The Unraveling of the Union-Capital Truce and the U.S. Industrial Productivity Crisis." *Review of Radical Political Economics* 18:110–31.

Schor, J. B. 1985. "Wage Flexibility, Social Wage Expenditures and Monetary Restrictiveness." In *Money and Macro Policy,* edited by M. Jarsulic, 135–54. Boston: Kluwer-Nijhoff.

Weisskopf, T. E. 1979. "Marxian Crisis Theory and the Rate of Profit in the Postwar U.S. Economy." *Cambridge Journal of Economics* 3:341–78.

Weisskopf, T. E., S. Bowles, and D. M. Gordon. 1983. "Hearts and Minds: A Social Model of U.S. Productivity Growth." *Brookings Papers on Economic Activity,* Number Two, 381–450.

Pump-Priming

Research concerning the anti-depression policies actually proposed by academic economists in the 1930s has shown that Keynes was scarcely alone in calling for the activist monetary and (especially) fiscal policies that have become associated with his name. Davis (1971) for the United States and Hutchison (1978) for the United Kingdom have shown the broad consensus among academic economists on the necessity of such policies; the same can be said for many economists, particularly of the younger generation, in pre-Hitler Germany as the depression there deepened.

Yet it was possible to advocate such policies while still believing that there exists a set of self-correcting mechanisms that would, if a capitalist economy lapsed from high levels of output and employment, tend to restore it to those levels. Nor was the propensity of a capitalist economy to cyclical fluctuations necessarily to be deplored. After all, during the boom, overall investment is high, new techniques are being introduced, and the capital stock is being expanded rapidly. Similarly, the downswing and depression are vital in restoring the economy to "health" after the "excesses" of the boom: those parts of the productive structure that are economically unviable in the long run are purged, and the economy achieves a sounder state and permanently higher level of productivity.

But it was also recognized that the "primary deflation" through which the necessary "cleansing" was effected might degenerate, through a downward multiplier process, into a purely destructive "secondary deflation" that would wipe out completed, semi-completed, or even planned projects of long-run economic value. In the early 1930s, a large number of seemingly fortuitous events would be identified as causes of a secondary deflation: the destruction of world trade and capital flows first by Versailles' and later by Britain's abandonment of the gold standard; the enactment of the Smoot-Hawley tariffs by the United States; the currency chaos of the 1920s; the increasingly depressed state of world agricultural markets; population changes that depressed construction activity; and the general political disturbances of the late 1920s and early 1930s (Robbins 1934). The emergence of a secondary deflation could also be derived from more rigorous theoretical models, e.g. Fisher's debt-deflation theory of depressions or the model advanced by Röpke (1933).

In both approaches, one self-correcting mechanism in particular did not operate "normally": the stimulus supposedly provided to the output of investment goods by falling interest rates, wages, and raw-materials costs was counteracted by the general drying-up of entrepreneurial initiative. If reviving the investment-goods sector is crucial, and if entrepreneurial expectations were so pessimistic that reducing interest rates by monetary expansion would be ineffective, fiscal policy became the only alternative. If they were economically productive, the public works thereby financed would raise the demand for investment goods, both directly (by increasing the demand for equipment that would be required for their execution), and indirectly [by increasing the output of consumer goods and hence that sector's demand for equipment (Pribram 1931)]. Yet once the paralysis of the entrepreneur had been overcome, the system's automatic adjustment mechanisms would begin to work again, restoring high levels of output and employment. Indeed, the mere announcement that reflationary policies would be adopted could stimulate confidence and help to revive the economy (Fisher 1934). This hypothesis thus negates the main criticism of all such policies during the early 1930s: that unbalanced budgets would merely lead, via their effects on business confidence, to the "crowding-out" of private investment.

The reason for calling such a policy "pump-priming" is clear: if only the engine could be made to turn over, it would run again smoothly, and government intervention could then be tapered off—the choke could be pushed back in. Thus, pump-priming was seen as necessary only when the basically salutary primary deflation degenerated into a destructive secondary deflation. If pump-priming was intended to replace private by government expenditure in the crucial investment-goods sector, this was only in the short term, and only in the special, indeed abnormal, circumstances of the secondary deflation.

Although Keynes himself remained a pump-primer until the mid-1930s, many economists were already viewing the role of fiscal policy not as limited to special circumstances but as permanently necessary to stabilize the economy, by compensating for fluctuations in private spending. What became the classical Keynesian position on pump-priming was clearly stated by Samuelson in 1940 in similar terms. He analyzed the conditions necessary for pump-priming to work and characterized them as an "extreme case." He explicitly referred to the "volatile and capricious behavior" of net investment, and speculated that "in *any* community there exists a possibility of insufficient net investment" ([1940] 1966, 1126). The influence of the concept of pump-priming on actual *policy* was clearest in the United States in the early New Deal in 1933–34, but even there the idea that fiscal measures of assistance could be tapered off was abandoned by 1935–36.

Michael Hudson

See also FISCAL POLICY; FISHER, IRVING; HAWTREY, RALPH GEORGE; LACHMANN, LUDWIG MAURITS; RÖPKE, WILHELM; WOYTINSKY, WLADIMIR SAVELEIVICH

Bibliography

Davis, J. R. 1971. *The New Economics and the Old Economists.* Ames: Iowa State Univ. Press.

Fisher, I. 1933. "The Debt-Deflation Theory of Great Depressions." *Econometrica* 1:337–57.

———. 1934. *After Reflation, What?* New York: Adelphi.

Hudson, M. 1985. "German Economists and the Depression of 1929–1933." *History of Political Economy* 17:35–50.

Hutchison, T. W. 1978. "Demythologizing the Keynesian Revolution: Pigou, Wage-Cuts, and *The General Theory.*" Chap. 6 in *On Revolutions and Progress in Economic Knowledge.* Cambridge: Cambridge Univ. Press.

Pribram, K. 1931. "World-Unemployment and Its Problems." In *Unemployment as a World Problem,* edited by Q. Wright, 43–150. Chicago: Univ. of Chicago Press.

Robbins, L. 1934. *The Great Depression.* London: Macmillan.

Röpke, W. 1933. "Trends in German Business Cycle Policy." *Economic Journal* 43:427–41.

Samuelson, P. A. [1940] 1966. "The Theory of Pump-Priming Re-examined." Chap. 85 in *The Collected Scientific Writings of Paul A. Samuelson.* Vol. 2. Cambridge: MIT Press.

P

R

Rational Expectations

Almost all interesting macroeconomic models of the business cycle have equations that contain variables representing the expectations of economic agents. *Rational-expectations* models of business cycles have the further property that those expectations are consistent with the actual operation of the model. In particular, this implies that the predictions of variables by economic agents within the model must be the same as the predictions implied by the model itself.

By the early 1970s, all the major econometric models contained expectational variables in their key equations. Expectations of inflation entered equations determining wages, prices, and interest rates; investment equations often depended on expectations of future output; and consumption functions often depended on expected future labor income. To make these expectational variables endogenous within the econometric model, model builders included additional equations to generate these expectations. The most popular device was to assume adaptive expectations which, for example, implied modeling expectations of future inflation econometrically as a distributed lag on past inflation rates.

However, these procedures for modeling expectations allowed economic agents to have expectations that systematically diverged from the realized values for variables; for example, expectations of inflation could be systematically lower than actual inflation. In a series of important papers, R. E. Lucas (1981) developed a number of business-cycle models in which economic agents had rational expectations. In this work, he drew on and extended the methods developed by John Muth (1961) for analyzing models with rational expectations.

The early business-cycle models that Lucas developed had three important features: prices adjusted to clear all markets, economic agents lacked complete information, and expectations were rational given the information available. The principal idea of these models was that agents could not distinguish relative-price movements from movements in the general price level. They did, however, optimally forecast real relative prices of the products they supplied given the information available to them (see Hoover 1988). If inflation were higher than was rationally predicted, economic agents would all think that the real demand for their products had increased and a boom would ensue.

In these models, Lucas carefully spelled out the logic of rational expectations. Consider any model in which each agent forms expectations according to some rule. Given the stochastic processes for the exogenous variables, certain economic outcomes will result under each hypothetical rule. Different rules induce different outcomes. In general, for a given rule, the expectations will not be unbiased predictors of actual outcomes. Rational expectations are defined as the rule for which expectations are unbiased predictors of economic outcomes. They thus have a "fixed-point" structure in the sense that rational expectations are rules that induce outcomes that are then consistent with the rules.

If the stochastic processes for the exogenous variables change, perhaps because of a change in economic policy, then the rational-expectational rules will also change. A new rule will now be an unbiased predictor of economic outcomes. Insofar as expectations are embodied in the structural equations of an econometric model, these structural equations must also change. This phenomenon, termed the "Lucas critique," is a testable implication of rational-expectations models. If policy rules change, then any equation in the model involving expectations of related variables should also change.

The early rational-expectations models of business cycles developed by Lucas were unsatisfactory empirical descriptions of the economy in several respects. First, Lucas's earliest models lacked mechanisms to translate mistakes in predicting inflation into fluctuations in output lasting more than one period. However, Lucas and also Sargent (1979) soon developed models that featured *propagation mechanisms* such as capital or inventories in which mistakes in predicting inflation could lead to persistent movements in output. Second, many economists questioned whether models based on imperfect information about the money supply are a good description of modern economies. Finally, many economists questioned whether fluctuations in unemployment could really be explained by models in which labor markets are cleared.

It was soon recognized, however, that rational-expectations models of the business cycle need not depend on imperfect observation of the contemporaneous value of the money supply or require cleared labor markets. Fischer (1977) and Phelps and Taylor (1977) developed models that allowed for nominal-wage contracts and also a role for economic policy in moderating economic fluctuations. Taylor introduced overlapping nominal-wage contracts in an attempt to provide a better empirical description of the wage-price process within rational-expectations models of the business cycle. Blanchard (1981) demonstrated how to incorporate rational financial markets into an otherwise conventional *IS-LM* framework. All these models combine mixtures of such Keynesian features as nominal-wage contracts or sticky prices with rational expectations of either the actual course of inflation or of prices in asset markets. Such models have expanded the range of economists who find it valuable to work on rational-expectations models of business cycles. They also allow for policy analysis within rational-expectations models.

The "fixed-point" nature of rational-expectations models carries over to models with Keynesian features. This has led to the development of new tools for both theoretical analysis and for empirical work. In very simple macro-models, phase diagrams for differential equations can sometimes be used to describe the behavior under consideration. With rational expectations, the phase diagrams will exhibit "saddle-point" stability which, if there is a unique equilibrium, implies that from initial conditions all trajectories but one will diverge from a long-run stationary solution of the model. This fact determines the unique trajectory that converges to the steady state as the rational-expectations equilibrium path. Unfortunately, these techniques, described by Sheffrin (1983), only apply to very simple models.

In more complex models, it is necessary to find algorithms to calculate the rational-expectations equilibria or "fixed point" of the model. Fair and Taylor (1983) have developed general procedures to solve general nonlinear rational-expectations models. Their procedures are computer-intensive, because they must first solve the dynamic model for a given time path of expectations until the time paths for expectations are consistent with the actual evolution of the variables in the model. These methods have been applied in a number of applications including Fair's version of the Blanchard model.

Less complex rational-expectations models have been analyzed in *real business-cycle* models, which are essentially elaborations of optimal-growth models subject to technological shocks. Expectations in the models are rational and dynamics come from both capital accumulation and the desire to work more when times are relatively good, which has been termed intertemporal substitution. At this stage of their development, real business-cycle models have not been used as traditional econometric models for predictions or explanations of particular historical events. Instead, they have only been tested to determine if they can "mimic" the variances and covariances of macroeconomic variables.

While rational-expectations models of the business cycle are now commonplace in theoretical work and in simple empirical applications, they have not gained the acceptance that conventional macromodels did by the early 1970s. Indeed, the government and private sector continue to use conventional nonrational econometric models for both forecasting and policy analysis.

There are several reasons for the absence of large-scale rational-expectations models of the business cycle. First, the computational difficulties described above make it very difficult to use these models casually. Second, the econometric techniques and computer methods are relatively new. Moreover, other important issues concerning the nature of policy changes limit the use of rational-expectations econometric models of the business cycle.

In rational-expectations models, it is necessary to model policymakers as following rules so that the agents can calculate expectations. However, it is often difficult to determine what rules policymakers are actually following and whether proposed policy changes are viewed as "new" rules or applications of "old" rules. Economists must be able to make these difficult categorizations before using the models.

Finally, complications arise when rules change. Presumably economic agents take time to find the new "rational rules." But if they do, rational-expectations models may be of limited use when policy is changing.

In summary, rational-expectations models of business cycles are now commonplace and a staple of theoretical research. Keynesian features can be easily incorporated into this framework. However, computational difficulties and problems in interpreting economic policy have limited their usefulness for applied work

Steven M. Sheffrin

See also EXPECTATIONS; HAHN, LUCIAN ALBERT; LACHMANN, LUDWIG MAURITS; LEARNING; LUCAS CRITIQUE; MONETARY EQUILIBRIUM THEORIES OF THE BUSINESS CYCLE; MONETARY POLICY; NEUTRALITY OF MONEY; OKUN, ARTHUR M.; REAL BUSINESS-CYCLE THEORIES

Bibliography

Blanchard, O.J. 1981. "Output, the Stock Market and Interest Rates." *American Economic Review* 71:132–43.

Fair, R. C. 1979. "An Analysis of a Macro-Econometric Model with Rational Expectations in the Bond and Stock Markets." *American Economic Review* 69:539–52.

Fair, R. C. and J. B. Taylor. 1983. "Solution and Maximum Likelihood Estimation of Dynamic Nonlinear Rational Expectations Models." *Econometrica* 51:139–78.

Fischer, S. 1977. "Long Term Contracts, Rational Expectations, and the Optimal Money Supply Rule." *Journal of Political Economy* 85:191–205.

Hoover, K. D. 1988. *The New Classical Economics*. Oxford: Basil Blackwell.

Lucas, R. E. Jr. 1981. *Studies in Business-Cycle Theory*. Cambridge: MIT Press.

Muth, J. F. 1961. "Rational Expectations and the Theory of Price Movements." *Econometrica* 29:315–35.

Phelps, E. S. and J. B. Taylor. 1977. "Stabilizing Properties of Monetary Policy under Rational Expectations." *Journal of Political Economy* 85:163–90.

Sargent, T. J. 1979. *Macroeconomic Theory*. Orlando, Fla.: Academic Press.

Sheffrin, S. M. 1983. *Rational Expectations*. Cambridge: Cambridge Univ. Press.

Taylor, J. B. 1980. "Aggregate Dynamics and Staggered Contracts." *Journal of Political Economy* 88:1–23.

R

Real-Bills Doctrine

The real-bills doctrine states that the quantity of money can never be excessive or deficient if issued only against sound short-term commercial paper used to finance real goods in the process of production and distribution. More precisely, the doctrine contends that if banks lend only against short-term commercial bills of exchange, the money stock will be secured by and will automatically vary in step with real output, so that the latter will be matched by just enough money to purchase it at existing prices.

As a rule for stabilizing general prices, however, the real-bills doctrine is either unnecessary or fallacious. It is unnecessary for small open economies with fixed exchange rates. Price levels in such countries are exogenously determined in international markets, so a real-bills rule is not needed to anchor prices. And for predominantly closed economies or economies with floating exchange rates—countries in which domestic money stocks determine prices—the rule is fallacious and potentially destabilizing. It is fallacious, because it links the nominal money stock to the nominal volume of bills, a variable which moves in step with prices and thus the money stock itself. By linking the variables, it renders both indeterminate. It ensures that any random jump in money or prices will, by raising the nominal value of goods in process and hence the nominal quantity of bills presented as collateral for loans, cause further increases in money and prices ad infinitum in a self-perpetuating inflationary spiral. The doctrine's fatal flaw consists in the dynamically unstable price-money-price feedback loop that results when money is governed by the needs of trade.

The real-bills doctrine can be traced to Adam Smith. In his *Wealth of Nations,* Smith offered the doctrine as a prudent guide for bankers making loans in a convertible currency regime. The doctrine was later extended to an inconvertible currency regime by the Antibullionist defenders of the Bank of England during the Napoleonic Wars. Seeking to exonerate the bank from blame for the wartime inflation following the suspension of convertibility in 1797, the Antibullionists denied that the bank contributed to inflation since it had issued only against real bills of exchange and so had merely responded to the needs of trade.

Henry Thornton, in his *Paper Credit of Great Britain,* exposed the fallacy of this position by observing that rising prices would require an ever-growing volume of loans just to finance the same level of real transactions. Inflation would thereby induce the monetary expansion necessary to sustain it and the real-bills criterion would fail to limit the quantity of money. Thornton also enunciated a point later made famous by Knut Wicksell, namely that the demand for loans becomes insatiable when the loan rate of interest is below the expected rate of return on capital. In such circumstances, the supply of eligible bills seeking discount becomes limitless and the real-bills criterion does not bar overissue.

Despite these criticisms, the real-bills doctrine survived and prospered in nineteenth-century banking tradition. Renamed the *Law of Reflux* (according to which monetary overissue is impossible because any excess notes would be returned instantaneously to the banks for conversion into coin or for repayment of loans), the doctrine reappeared in the Currency School-Banking School controversy in the middle of the nineteenth century. In particular, the Banking School asserted that a convertible currency was regulated automatically by the needs of trade and required no mandatory specie-reserve requirements.

In this century, the doctrine was a key concept in the Federal Reserve Act of 1913. And during the German hyperinflation of 1922–23, the doctrine underlay the Reichsbank's policy of issuing astronomical sums of money to satisfy the needs of trade at ever-rising prices. The Reichsbank insisted on pegging its discount rate at twelve percent (later raised to ninety percent) when market rates of interest were well over 7000 percent per annum. This huge rate differential made it extremely profitable for commercial banks to rediscount bills with the Reichsbank and to lend the proceeds, thereby producing additional inflationary expansion of the money supply and further upward pressure on interest rates. The authorities showed no recognition of this inflationary sequence, repeatedly stating that their duty was to passively supply on demand the growing sums of money required to mediate real transactions at skyrocketing prices. Citing the real-bills doctrine, they refused to believe that issuing money on loan against genuine commercial bills could be inflationary.

Today the doctrine survives in the popular notion that the Federal Reserve should use expansionary monetary policy to lower interest rates to target levels consistent with full employment. For just as the real-bills rule calls for expanding the money stock when the needs of trade rise, the interest-targeting proposal calls for increasing the money stock when the market rate of interest rises above a target level. But this proposal produces the same price-money-price inflationary feedback mechanism that undermines the real-bills rule. For the more the Fed expands the money supply in a vain effort to reduce interest rates, the greater the inflationary pressure it puts on them. And the more those rates rise, the greater the monetary expansion required to temporarily reduce them again. Thus, attempts to peg interest rates generate a dynamically unstable process in which money and prices chase each other ad infinitum in a cumulative inflationary spiral. Herein lies the real-bills fallacy of linking the money stock to a nominal variable (the market-rate/target-rate differential) that varies in step with prices.

Thomas M. Humphrey

See also FULLARTON, JOHN; MONETARY POLICY; REICHSBANK; SMITH, ADAM; THORNTON, HENRY

Bibliography

Glasner, D. 1992. "The Real Bills Doctrine in the Light of the Law of Reflux." *History of Political Economy* 24:201–29.

Humphrey, T. M. 1982. "The Real Bills Doctrine." Federal Reserve Bank of Richmond *Economic Review,* September/October, 3–13.

Laidler, D. 1984. "Misconceptions About the Real-Bills Doctrine: A Comment on Sargent and Wallace." *Journal of Political Economy* 92:149–55.

Mints, L. W. 1945. *A History of Banking Theory*. Chicago: Univ. of Chicago Press.

Smith, A. [1776] 1976. *An Inquiry into the Nature and Causes of the Wealth of Nations*. Vol. 1. Oxford: Clarendon Press.

Thornton, H. [1802] 1939. *An Enquiry into the Nature and Effects of the Paper Credit of Great Britain*. Edited with an introduction by F. A. von Hayek. London: Allen and Unwin.

Real Business-Cycle Theories

Real business-cycle theories are those theories that attribute aggregate economic fluctuations to some periodic or randomly occurring real disturbance that can be propagated to the economy as a whole. The class of real disturbances includes changes in technology and changes in constraints, such as changes in fiscal policy, but usually not changes in tastes. Such theories are referred to as "real" to distinguish them from theories that attribute fluctuations to periodic or randomly occurring monetary disturbances.

Background

Historically, real theories have identified the source of disturbance as periodic fluctuations in weather conditions (e.g., the sunspot/weather theories of W. S. Jevons and H. L. Moore) or waves of investment resulting from uneven technological progress (e.g., the cycle theory of J. A. Schumpeter). Such theories typically have a monetary component, but changes in monetary conditions are thought to respond to real changes rather than the other way around.

In the 1920s and early 1930s, real business-cycle theories fell out of fashion as monetary business-cycle theories largely derived from Alfred Marshall or Knut Wicksell dominated the attention of economists. The Keynesian Revolution of the late 1930s for a time dampened interest in traditional business-cycle theories of all types. But Samuelson, among others, showed that the Keynesian multiplier combined with a simple accelerator mechanism could, depending on parameter values, generate a stable, damped, or explosive cycle following a shock to some component of autonomous spending. The potential for multiplier-accelerator interaction to generate cyclical time paths for real income and other aggregate variables was explored in the context of the early theories of economic growth which appeared at about the same time. Hicks's *The Trade Cycle* is perhaps the outstanding example of this genre of real business-cycle theories.

A further impetus for renewed interest in business-cycle theory came from an entirely different direction in the work of Milton Friedman and other Monetarists. Friedman and his principal collaborator Anna J. Schwartz endeavored to show the close relationship between business cycles and movements in the money stock over the course of American economic history. In particular, they argued that the Great Depression, which had created an intellectual environment receptive to Keynes's message in the *General Theory*, was itself the product of an enormous, and largely exogenous, shock to the money stock.

The monetary business-cycle theory developed by Friedman relied mainly on exogenous changes in the money stock resulting from misguided monetary policy to explain economic fluctuations. Subsequent attempts to restate Friedman's relatively informal model of business cycles within a more rigorous analytical framework led to the development first of the rational-expectations hypothesis and then to a combination of the rational-expectations hypothesis with the assumption of continuous market clearing that characterizes the New Classical macroeconomics.

Early New Classical models sought to show that monetary shocks would cause temporary departures from a hypothetical full equilibrium growth path. But it became evident that there were serious problems with a model that satisfied the a priori requirements of the New Classical approach (notably, rational expectations and continuous market clearing) while generating results consistent with the observed pattern of business-cycle fluctuations.

First, the rational-expectations assumption seems to preclude any real impact from an expected change in monetary policy. Only unexpected changes in monetary policy could affect real magnitudes. A New Classical monetary theory of the business cycle thus could be based only on randomly occurring monetary surprises. Even more problematic from the New Classical perspective were empirical studies that found only a weak and even doubtful relationship between monetary surprises and subsequent changes in output.

Monetary business-cycle theories in a New Classical framework had two further problems. First, how could one explain the persistence of

R

monetary shocks on real output? Once the monetary shock occurs, why shouldn't agents with rational expectations return to the optimal growth path in the period after the shock? To rationalize persistent deviations from the optimal growth path, New Classical theorists had to introduce durable capital assets or inventories into their models.

But conceptually there was a second, even more serious problem, which was to explain why a monetary surprise would have any impact on rational agents in the presence of full market clearing even in the period during which the surprise occurred. In Lucas's rendition of the theory there is an informational imperfection that prevents agents from perfectly distinguishing between relative price changes and absolute price changes. But, contrary to the underlying methodological prescriptions of New Classical theory, the informational imperfection is asserted rather than derived from basic assumptions.

The Basic Real Business-Cycle Model

Given the unsatisfactory reconciliation between monetary shocks and New Classical methodological principles, it is not surprising that some adherents of the New Classical paradigm would explore the possibility that business cycles are a purely equilibrium phenomenon that can be attributed to real disturbances.

The first significant attempt along these lines was made by Kydland and Prescott (1982), and they and others have since developed this approach in a number of directions. The basic approach is to simulate an equilibrium growth path derived from a neoclassical growth model subject to exogenous productivity shocks. The growth model has a single output which is produced, under the current technology, by inputs of labor and capital. Units of output can either be invested as replacements for, or additions to, the inherited capital stock, or consumed by households. Households choose how much labor services to offer and output to consume based on current and (rationally expected) future wages and prices. For specific functional forms of the utility (logarithmic) and production (Cobb-Douglas) functions, optimal solutions cannot generally be derived analytically and must instead be found by computational techniques. Parameters are chosen to correspond to their empirically observed or estimated values.

Once the optimal growth path has been specified, it remains to estimate the technology shocks to which the economy is subject.

Kydland and Prescott estimated exogenous productivity shocks to the United States economy by using the unexplained residuals found by Solow (1957) in his empirical study of the role of technical change in explaining aggregate productivity. They identified these deviations of aggregate output from the output implied by Solow's estimate of the aggregate production function of the U.S. economy as exogenous productivity shocks. Applying these productivity shocks to their simulation of the optimal growth path, they found that the implied fluctuations in output and investment could account for two-thirds of the fluctuations in output and investment in the observed time series for the United States.

Extensions

The basic real business-cycle model is characterized by three strong assumptions: (1) output consists of a single homogeneous good; (2) money does not exist; and, (3) households can vary as desired the amount of labor supplied in response to changes in the real wage, i.e., households are always on their labor-supply curve. The implications of relaxing these assumptions have been investigated in more recent work.

Single Homogeneous Output

The assumption of a single homogeneous output, which is hardly peculiar to real business-cycle models, implicitly assumes that the relevant disturbances for the purpose of business-cycle analysis are economy-wide shocks. Not only does this assumption preclude any inquiry into the reasons for temporal sequences in the observed co-movements between sectors, it precludes the possibility that sectoral interactions not only transmit disturbances from one sector to another, but that the disturbances may be amplified endogenously in the transmission process. If an endogenous intersectoral transmission process (in some sense analogous to the Keynesian multiplier process) amplifies sectoral disturbances, a one-sector business-cycle model abstracts an essential element of business cycles from the analysis.

Long and Plosser (1983) developed a multi-sectoral model in which technology shocks in one sector generate economy-wide fluctuations, but without suggesting a mechanism by which disturbances in one sector may be amplified by the intersectoral transmission mechanism. Moreover, as the number of sectors increases, positive shocks in one sector are likely to offset negative shocks in other sectors, so that sectoral shocks become unimportant in a model with many sectors. Lillien (1982) suggested that cyclically high rates of unemployment can be explained by high rates of intersectoral reallocation of labor, in which case sectoral shocks would not cancel each other out, but would be mutually reinforcing. But neither Lillien nor subsequent sectoral-shift models offer an intersectoral transmission mechanism for amplifying sectoral shocks.

Monetary Disturbances

Most real business-cycle theorists do not deny that monetary disturbances may, under some circumstances, cause business fluctuations. [However, see Black (1987) for such a denial.] But they do contend that real disturbances can account for most, if not all, of the observed fluctuations in output. On the other hand, the well-documented correlations between money and income require some theoretical explanation. King and Plosser (1984) provide such an explanation, arguing that the banking system supplies the amount of inside money demanded by the public. As income and prices rise, the nominal quantity of money demanded by the public also rises and is supplied by the banking system. The observed correlations between money, income, and prices can thus be reconciled with a real business-cycle theory in which monetary disturbances do not cause real fluctuations. Moreover, while different from the sort of disturbance usually considered by real business-cycle theorists, the disruption in the supply of credit by the banking system which Bernanke (1983) identified as an important factor in the Great Depression is viewed as a real disturbance by most real business-cycle theorists.

Variation in Labor Supply

The assumption that the labor market is cleared continuously remains one of the most controversial assumptions in real business-cycle theories. The proposition that intertemporal substitution can account for observed fluctuations in labor supply is generally viewed with skepticism, and most empirical studies have arrived at low estimates of supply elasticity. Hansen (1985) has shown that requiring that workers either work full-time or not at all (implying low estimated supply elasticities) does not change the fundamental properties of the model, even as the volatility of hours worked in response to productivity shocks increases. Another model-ing strategy adopted by King, Plosser and Rebello (1988b), among others, is to allow for heterogeneity in skill levels across workers.

Assessment

Despite their elegance, real business-cycle theories have not yet been widely accepted. Many critics dispute the assumption of continuous market clearing (particularly of the labor market), which it shares in common with New Classical monetary business-cycle theories. Others, including Lucas (1987, 71–72), find it implausible that technology shocks alone could account for cycles of the observed magnitude. Moreover, the success of real business-cycle theorists in building simple models which, when simulated, can account for a substantial portion of the observed fluctuations in output, has little empirical significance in the absence of a direct comparison of real business-cycle models with alternative models in accounting for those fluctuations.

However, disputes about continuous market clearing are more semantic than substantive. As a matter of positive economics, what counts is whether observed fluctuations in employment can be accounted for within some coherent theoretical framework. Neither real business-cycle theorists nor their critics have yet done so. Under a complete specification of all preferences and constraints, every rational agent must be in equilibrium at all times. But that does not mean that it is never useful to posit a less than complete specification, so that within the resulting model a given situation or phenomenon is viewed as a disequilibrium. Such questions cannot be settled by abstract methodological pronouncements about what constitutes good economics; they can only be settled by comparing the explanatory power of alternative theories.

Similarly, the a priori belief that technology shocks are or are not large enough to account for observed fluctuations is no argument against real business-cycle theories in general. Even if (in some sense) true, such a view would at most rule out one-sector real business-cycle models. But if there is an intersectoral transmission mechanism that amplifies technology shocks to one sector, the capacity of technology shocks to account for observed fluctuations does not depend solely on the magnitude of the shocks.

Such a mechanism was in fact postulated by classical adherents of Say's Law. If supply creates its own demand, then a negative technology shock in one sector reduces the demand for the output of other sectors. If the amount supplied within a sector immediately after a shock is, for whatever reason, less than the amount that would be supplied in the steady-state equilibrium following the shock, the demand for the output of all other sectors will be less than the demand for the output of those sectors would be in the new steady-state equilibrium.

Ironically, it is New Keynesians who, in seeking microeconomic explanations for rigid wages, now emphasize the role of reductions in supply as the source of effective-demand failures. Given Keynes's attack on Say's Law, such emphasis on the failure of wages to adjust sufficiently as the source of macroeconomic fluctuations is remarkably *un*-Keynesian.

All that is necessary to provide an intersectoral mechanism for amplifying sectoral shocks is that the short-run elasticity of labor supply to particular sectors be greater than the long-run elasticity. The resulting model would not differ, in its substantive implications about the behavior of the labor market, from New Keynesian disequilibrium rigid-wage models. Whether it would satisfy all the methodological prescriptions of the New Classical economics is perhaps another question.

David Glasner

See also CREATIVE DESTRUCTION; HICKS, JOHN RICHARD; HUTT, WILLIAM HAROLD; INTERTEMPORAL SUBSTITUTION; MONETARY EQUILIBRIUM THEORIES OF THE BUSINESS CYCLE; NEW KEYNESIAN ECONOMICS; OKUN, ARTHUR M.; RATIONAL EXPECTATIONS; SCHUMPETER, JOSEPH ALOIS; SEARCH THEORY; SECTORAL SHIFTS; RECESSIONS (SUPPLY-SIDE) IN THE 1970S; SUPPLY SHOCKS; WAGE RIGIDITY

Bibliography

Bernanke, B. 1983. "Nonmonetary Effects of the Financial Crisis in the Propagation of the Great Depression." *American Economic Review* 73:257–76.

Black, F. 1987. *Business Cycles and Equilibrium.* New York: Basil Blackwell.

Hansen, G. 1985. "Indivisible Labor and the Business Cycle." *Journal of Monetary Economics* 16:309–27.

Hicks, J. R. 1950. *The Trade Cycle.* Oxford: Clarendon Press.

Hoover, K. D. 1988. *The New Classical Economics.* Oxford: Basil Blackwell.

King, R. G. and C. I. Plosser. 1984. "Money, Credit and Prices in a Real Business Cycle." *American Economic Review* 74:363–80.

King, R. G., C. I. Plosser, and S. Rebello. 1988a. "Production, Growth and Business Cycles I. The Basic Neoclassical Model." *Journal of Monetary Economics* 21:195–232.

———. 1988b. "Production, Growth and Business Cycles II. New Directions." *Journal of Monetary Economics* 21:309–41.

Kydland, F. and E. C. Prescott. 1982. "Time to Build and Aggregate Fluctuations." *Econometrica* 50:1345–70.

Laidler, D. [1986] 1990. "The New-Classical Contributions to Macroeconomics." Chap. 4 in *Taking Money Seriously and Other Essays.* Cambridge: MIT Press.

Lillien, D. 1982. "Sectoral Shifts and Cyclical Unemployment." *Journal of Political Economy* 90:777–93.

Long, J. B. and C. I. Plosser. 1983. "Real Business Cycles." *Journal of Political Economy* 91:39–69.

Lucas, R. E. Jr. 1987. *Models of Business Cycles.* Oxford: Basil Blackwell.

Mankiw, N. G. 1989. "Real Business Cycles: A New Keynesian Perspective." *Journal of Economic Perspectives,* Summer, 79–90.

Plosser, C. I. 1989. "Understanding Real Business Cycles." *Journal of Economic Perspectives,* Summer, 51–77.

Schumpeter, J. A. 1939. *Business Cycles: A Theoretical, Historical and Statistical Analysis of the Capitalist Process.* 2 vols. New York: McGraw-Hill.

Solow, R. M. 1957. "Technical Change and the Aggregate Production Function." *Review of Economics and Statistics* 39:312–20.

Real Wages

No stable empirical relationship has emerged between cyclical movements in aggregate quantities (real GNP, employment, or unemployment) and real wages. This is not surprising. In projecting a price on a quantity, we should expect a positive relation when demand shifts dominate and a negative relation when supply shifts dominate. Nevertheless, it is very useful to know whether business cycles during any period reflect primarily shifts in labor demand or movements along a labor-demand schedule. Most theories of the cycle predict fluctuations to be of one type or the other. Real business cycles driven by shifts in technology or energy prices depend on procyclical shifts in labor demand. General-disequilibrium models (Barro and Grossman 1971) generate shifts in labor demand in response to tightening or relaxing a constraint on firms' sales. Most business-cycle theories involve no disturbances to labor demand; this includes explanations stressing sticky nominal wages, changes in government spending, shifts in consumption functions, or shifts in investment behavior (e.g., animal spirits). Therefore, fluctuations reflect movements along a labor demand schedule, with countercyclical real wages.

The debate about the cyclical behavior of real wages is fairly old. Pigou (1929) stressed the importance of real-wage movements in distinguishing sources of fluctuations. He reported that most business cycles in Britain from 1850 to 1910 displayed procyclical real product wages. Keynes ([1936] 1973) pointed out the strong prediction of his general theory for countercyclical real wages. Papers by Dunlop (1938) and Tarshis (1939) testing this prediction on United States and United Kingdom data soon followed. Both authors found a procyclical pattern.

Others have subsequently examined the correlation in post-World War II data, particularly for the United States. Results for aggregate time series can be summarized as follows. For the entire postwar period there has been a fairly weak positive correlation between the cycle and real wages. Real wages have become more procyclical in the latter half of the postwar period.

This is illustrated in Table 1, where the annual rate of growth in real annual hourly earnings is projected on the rate of growth in real GNP. Columns 1 through 3 correspond to deflation by the GNP deflator, the Consumer Price Index, and the Producer Price Index. For the period since World War II as a whole, real wages are procyclical regardless of choice of deflator; and the elasticity of real-wage growth with respect to real-GNP growth varies only from 0.143 to 0.193 across the three deflators. (Results are sensitive to choice of deflator within certain subperiods, particularly 1958 to 1968.) The results are very dependent on the choice of time period. The table breaks the period since World War II into four parts. Regardless of choice of deflator, real wages are much more procyclical in the second half of the period; and much of this procyclicality is concentrated between 1969 and 1979.

TABLE 1. Response of $\Delta \text{Ln}(W/P)$ to $\Delta \text{Ln}(Y)$ for Various Sample Periods and Price Deflators*

Sample Period	Series For Deflator		
	GNP Deflator	Consumer Price Index	Producer Price Index
1948–90	0.143	0.193	0.176
	(.056)	(.094)	(.152)
1948–57	–0.011	–0.125	–0.319
	(.131)	(.189)	(.265)
1958–68	0.040	0.327	0.195
	(.084)	(.090)	(.179)
1969–79	0.489	0.708	0.885
	(.112)	(.165)	(.375)
1980–90	0.082	0.175	0.332
	(.053)	(.215)	(.333)

* W denotes average hourly earnings for private, nonagricultural production workers; Y denotes GNP in constant (1982) dollars; P denotes the various price deflators listed at the top of the table. Standard errors are in parentheses. The regressions additionally include a linear time trend.

A number of researchers have employed panel data on individuals to examine the correlation between the cycle and real wages (Bodkin 1969, Geary and Kennan 1982, Barsky, Solon, and Parker 1994). Although these data sets cover a relatively short sample period, they can help address certain questions. One is whether there is an aggregation bias in measuring real-wage movements; a second is how real-wage movements vary across different types of workers.

Several papers (Stockman 1983, Bils 1985, Barsky, Solon, and Parker 1994) note that workers who exit the workforce in recessions have less experience and education, and relatively lower wages, than the typical worker. This creates a countercyclical bias in an aggregate real-wage rate. Using a sample drawn from the National Longitudinal Surveys, Bils finds that those entering and exiting the workforce have wage rates that are about 20 percent lower than the average for all workers. Barsky, Solon, and Parker, using a sample drawn from the Panel Studies of Income Dynamics (PSID), estimate a considerably higher differential. Bils and McLaughlin (1992), also using a sample from the PSID, find that workers who enter the workforce during expansions earn about 43 percent less than those already working; but those who depart the workforce during recessions were earning only about 15 percent less than other workers. Based on such evidence, suppose that workers who enter the workforce during an expansion have wages that are about 30 percent lower than those steadily employed. Then a 1-percent increase in employment, which would typically be associated with about a 2-percent surge in real GNP, causes a countercyclical bias of 0.30 percent in the aggregate wage. This is a fairly important bias. Correcting for it should approximately double the estimated procyclicality of the real wage for 1948 to 1990 reported in the first line of the table.

Cyclical expansions are associated not only with persons entering the workforce, but also systematically moving between industries. Much of this movement is into high-wage industries, for example durable manufacturing (Okun 1973). If workers move to higher-wage industries during expansions, then the aggregate average wage will be more cyclical than the typical industry average wage. Huizinga (1980) shows, at the one-digit industry level, that this is indeed what we observe. As an exercise, I confirmed this result for the period 1964 to 1987. In fact, the aggregate average wage is more procyclical than any one-digit industry wage rate.

These movements do not necessarily imply a bias in the aggregate wage rate. If relatively highly paid retailing workers move, with no significant change in wage, to become relatively low-paid workers in durable manufacturing, then the average wage falls in both retailing and durable manufacturing; but there is no impact on the average aggregate wage. By contrast, if workers moving to durable manufacturing obtain big wage increases, perhaps reflecting union bargaining in manufacturing, then it produces a procyclical bias in the aggregate real wage. Which is the correct interpretation? Durable manufacturing and construction are by far the most cyclical industries. Average wages in these industries averaged about 30 percent higher than in other industries over the past twenty-five years. Using the PSID, Bils and McLaughlin examine whether workers moving into durable manufacturing and construction receive wage gains. The answer is yes; but the increases are only on the order of 6–7 percent. So the shift of workers to high-wage industries in expansions creates only a small procyclical bias in the aggregate real wage.

Another issue is how wage cyclicality varies across workers. Raisian (1979) finds less procyclical wages for union workers. Blank (1989) finds that wages and annual hours are both more procyclical for workers with low income; on both counts, income inequality lessens in expansion. Bils (1985) finds that real wages are much more procyclical for workers who change jobs or who frequently enter and exit the workforce. This could reflect wage smoothing for workers with long-term job attachments; it could also reflect the movement of workers into higher-wage industries in expansions, as discussed in the previous paragraph.

If there are significant training costs, labor demand will depend not only on the current wage, but also on past and expected future wage rates (Oi 1962, Sargent 1978, Kennan 1988). Neftci (1978) and Sargent examine leads and lags in the relation between employment and real wages, and conclude that there is a negative relationship. But if their postwar samples are extended to include more recent observations, the non-contemporaneous correlations between real wages and measures of the business cycle appear to be very weak (Blanchard and Fischer 1989).

As explained by Oi, hiring and training costs should stabilize cyclical fluctuations in employment. By similar reasoning, Bils (1987) suggests that if employment is a quasi-fixed factor, then cyclical real-wage movements give a poor indication of cyclical movements in the marginal cost of labor. In expansions, the marginal cost of labor is to find, train, and pay a new hire; in contractions, in the midst of layoffs, the marginal labor cost is better represented by only the wage. Bils finds that even fairly minor costs of adjusting employment imply a real marginal labor cost that is far more procyclical than the real wage. This suggests that business cycles have been dominated by disturbances primarily affecting labor demand.

Mark Bils

See also REAL BUSINESS-CYCLE THEORIES; SECTORAL SHIFTS; STYLIZED FACTS; WORKER AND JOB TURNOVER

Bibliography

Barro, R. J. and H. I. Grossman. 1971. "A General Disequilibrium Model of Income and Employment." *American Economic Review* 61:82–93.

Barsky, R., G. Solon, and J. A. Parker. 1994.

"Measuring the Cyclicality of Real Wages: How Important is Composition Bias?" *Quarterly Journal of Economics* 109:1–25.

Blanchard, O. J. and S. Fischer. 1989. *Lectures on Macroeconomics*. Cambridge: MIT Press.

Bils, M. 1985. "Real Wages Over the Business Cycle: Evidence From Panel Data." *Journal of Political Economy* 93:666–89.

———. 1987. "The Cyclical Behavior of Marginal Cost and Price." *American Economic Review* 77:838–55.

Bils, M. and K. J. McLaughlin. 1992. "Inter-Industry Mobility and the Cyclical Upgrading of Labor." NBER Working Paper No. 4130, August.

Blank, R. 1989. "Disaggregating the Effect of the Business Cycle on the Distribution of Income." *Economica* 56:141–64.

Bodkin, R. G. 1969. "Real Wages and Cyclical Variations in Employment." *Canadian Journal of Economics* 2:353–74.

Geary, P. T. and J. Kennan. 1982. "The Employment-Real Wage Relationship: An International Study." *Journal of Political Economy* 90:854–71.

Huizinga, J. 1980. Real Wages, Employment, and Expectations. Ph.D. diss. Department of Economics, MIT.

Kennan, J. 1988. "An Econometric Analysis of Fluctuations in Aggregate Labor Supply and Demand." *Econometrica* 56:317–33.

Keynes, J. M. [1936] 1973. *The General Theory of Employment, Interest, and Money*. Vol. 7 of *The Collected Writings of John Maynard Keynes*. London: Macmillan.

Neftci, S. 1978. "A Time-Series Analysis of the Real Wages-Employment Relationship." *Journal of Political Economy* 86:281–91.

Oi, W. 1962. "Labor as a Quasi-Fixed Factor." *Journal of Political Economy* 70:538–55.

Okun, A. M. 1973. "Upward Mobility in a High-pressure Economy." *Brookings Papers on Economic Activity*. Number One, 207–52.

Pigou, A. C. 1929. *Industrial Fluctuations*. 2d ed. London: Macmillan.

Raisian, J. 1979. "Cyclic Patterns in Weeks and Wages." *Economic Inquiry* 17:475–95.

Sargent, T. J. 1978. "Estimation of Dynamic Labor Demand Schedules." *Journal of Political Economy* 86:1009–44.

Stockman, A. 1983. "Aggregation Bias and Cyclical Behavior of Real Wages." Manuscript, Dept. of Economics, Univ. of Rochester.

Tarshis, L. 1939. "Changes in Real and Money Wages." *Economic Journal* 49:150–54.

R

Recession of 1969–1970

The prosperity period which followed the recession of 1960–61 was the longest in the nation's history. The expansion lasted 106 months, and in its later stages was fueled by spending on the Vietnam War.

The expansion faltered only once. In 1965–66, the demand for credit from all sectors of the economy was strong and increasing, especially the demand for bank loans by business. Concerned about an increase in inflation, the Federal Reserve raised the discount rate in December 1965 and generally restricted the supply of money and credit. This resulted in what was then termed a "credit crunch" as interest rates climbed to the highest levels since the 1920s, causing a marked slowdown in residential construction during the summer of 1966.

Responding to indications late in 1966 that economic growth was slackening, the Federal Reserve reversed policy and began to accelerate monetary growth at year's end through the first half of 1967. Economic activity slowed in the first quarter of 1967, gross national product (GNP) showing no increase over the fourth quarter of 1966. However, economic expansion resumed in the second half of 1967 and rapid growth continued until late 1969. The rate of inflation began accelerating in 1967 primarily because of a high level of private spending and the expansive monetary and fiscal policies adopted by the federal government in the 1966–67 slowdown. Moreover, unemployment remained below 4 percent from 1966 to 1969, contributing to inflationary pressures.

The recession, beginning late in 1969, lasted through November 1970. The recession of 1969–70 was relatively mild compared to other recessions in the post-World War II period. (See Table 1.) While the measures of duration indicate that the recession of 1969–70 was of about average length, its impact on production and employment was clearly less severe than that of the typical postwar recession. For example, real GNP declined 1.1 percent during

TABLE 1. A Comparison of Selected Measures of Duration and Depth Between the Recession of 1969–70 and the Eight Post-World War II Recessions, 1948–82

Duration[a]	1969–70 Recession	Mean for the Eight Post-WW II Recessions
Business cycle	11	11.3
GNP, constant dollars	15	10.6
Coincident index	13	13.1
Industrial production	13	11.8
Nonfarm employment	8	11.1
Depth (%)[b]		
GNP, constant dollars	−1.1	−2.7
Coincident index	−6.3	−9.7
Industrial production	−6.8	−10.6
Nonfarm employment	−1.6	−2.9
Unemployment rate		
Maximum	6.1	7.8
Increase	+2.7	+3.3

Sources: U.S. Department of Commerce, U.S. Department of Labor, Board of Governors of Federal Reserve System, National Bureau of Economic Research.

[a]Months from peak (first date) to trough (second date).

[b]Percentage change from the peak month or quarter over the intervals shown above. For the unemployment rate, the maximum figure is the highest for any month associated with the contraction, and the increases are from the lowest month to the highest in percentage points.

the recession of 1969–70, compared to an average of 2.7 percent for eight postwar recessions from 1948–82.

The unemployment rate rose from 3.5 percent in November 1969 to 6 percent in December 1970. About 40 percent of the increase in unemployment was in manufacturing and two-thirds of this occurred in the durable-goods sector. The rise in unemployment was aggravated by a 1.1 million decline in defense employment during 1970, reflecting the reduced U.S. military role in the war in Vietnam.

While production and employment declines were relatively modest, the recession severely affected the financial markets. The average stock listed in Standard and Poor's index fell in value by approximately 30 percent from November 1969 to May 1970. The prices of common stocks declined somewhat more than in the early post-World War II recessions, but by less than the severe downturns of 1929–33 or 1937–38. Much of the decline in stock prices occurred in April–May 1970, after the failure of the Penn-Central Railroad. When Penn-Central defaulted on its short-term obligations, doubts arose about the solvency of other firms and fears of a liquidity crisis were widespread (Campagna 1987).

Causes of the Recession of 1969–70

The chief cause of the recession was the anti-inflationary monetary policy followed by the Federal Reserve for fifteen months in 1969 and early 1970, which raised interest rates to the highest levels since the Civil War. Credit stringencies in 1969 caused a substantial contraction in the housing industry. Total housing starts fell from a 1.68 million annual rate in the spring of 1969 to 1.21 million rate in January 1970.

Responding to the downturn, the Federal Reserve began to increase the supply of money and credit in early 1970. Thus, the money supply grew by 5.4 percent for the year after only a 1.2 percent increase in the second half of 1969.

With falling interest rates and increased credit availability, housing starts rebounded rapidly in the spring, reaching nearly 1.7 million units by November 1970. Moreover, by late summer, the fears of a liquidity crisis had abated, and stock prices rose substantially in the last four months of 1970.

Restrictive fiscal policy in 1969 also contributed to the economic downturn. However, fiscal policy became expansive in 1970. The budget, on a national-income-accounts basis, changed from a surplus of $9.3 billion in 1969 to a deficit of $10.8 billion in 1970, a difference of over twenty billion. The full-employment surplus fell from $11.7 billion in 1969 to $6.7 billion in 1970.

The recession of 1969–70 was not associated with inventory liquidation or a decline in business capital investment. In fact, firms continued to *accumulate* inventories in 1970 (although at a slower rate than in 1969), and capital outlays that year set a record.

International Considerations

Inflation and full employment in the U.S. from 1965 through 1969 while several other major industrial countries were operating at less than full employment caused the United States trade balance to deteriorate markedly during that period. However, in the second quarter of 1969, the U.S. merchandise trade surplus began to rise sharply, reaching $2.7 billion in 1970 compared to $1.3 billion in 1969. Reduced imports associated with the recession accounted for much of the increase in the trade surplus.

The recession of 1969–70 did not extend to Western Europe. Thus, as monetary policy eased during 1970 in the United States, the financial situation abroad continued to tighten in response to demand pressures. The shift in relative monetary conditions contributed to substantial net outflows of liquid capital from the U.S. during 1970.

Inflation and Price Controls

The consumer price index increased at a seasonally adjusted annual rate of 5.6 percent from the end of 1969 to November 1970. This was only slightly lower than the 6.1 percent increase during all of 1969, indicating that the recession had little impact on inflation.

The economy recovered quickly in early 1971. GNP in constant dollars grew by 8 percent in the first quarter of 1971 after a 4.1 percent decline in the fourth quarter of 1970. GNP growth was 4.8 percent in the second quarter of 1971, 3.9 percent in the third quarter, and 6.1 percent in the fourth quarter. During 1971 the economy received a major stimulus from a rapidly increased money supply, and price inflation continued at an annual rate of approximately 5 percent until mid-August.

On 15 August 1971, in order to combat inflation, President Nixon ordered a ninety-day freeze of prices and wages after which wage and price controls were to be established. The goal was to cut price increases to an average 2.5 percent per year, while wages were limited to an average gain of 5.5 percent. These targets assumed that productivity would increase at a rate of 3 percent per year.

At the same time, the Nixon Administration suspended the convertibility of the dollar into gold and other reserve assets. By closing the gold window, President Nixon unilaterally ended the international trading agreements reached at Bretton Woods some twenty-five years earlier.

The United States goal was to bring about an exchange-rate realignment that would devalue the dollar to improve the U.S. trade balance. Unable to secure international agreement to these changes, the United States acted unilaterally.

As pointed out by H. G. Johnson ([1972] 1975), the rise in the U.S. balance-of-payments deficit associated with domestic inflation (after 1965) and the Vietnam War put U.S. policymakers in a dilemma. They could choose to pursue domestic employment goals or to maintain their international obligations (fixed exchange rates) under the Bretton Woods system. The Nixon Administration chose the former.

It is still a matter of controversy whether the imposition of wage and price controls and the movement toward flexible exchange rates were the appropriate policies. However, it is clear that the movement to flexible exchange rates has done little to prevent a continuing deterioration in the U.S. balance of trade.

Economic activity continued to expand in 1972, and by the end of the year the economy was growing rapidly. Consumer prices rose only 3.5 percent in 1972, the lowest rate of inflation since 1967, reflecting the impact of wage and price controls. Federal Reserve monetary policy was expansive early in the year, but late in 1972, money growth was slowed due to renewed inflationary pressures.

The 1969–70 recession, in a sense, brought an end to the long post-World War II economic expansion. In addition, it contributed to the demise of the Keynesian consensus regarding macroeconomic policy management. Finally, it demonstrated, to the chagrin of many economists, that the business cycle was not obsolete.

Alan L. Sorkin

See also DISINTERMEDIATION; FEDERAL RESERVE SYSTEM: 1941–1993; GOLD STANDARD; GOLD STANDARD: CAUSES AND CONSEQUENCES

Bibliography

Campagna, A. S. 1987. *U.S. National Economic Policy, 1917–1985.* New York: Praeger.

Johnson, H. G. [1972] 1975. "Political Economy Aspects of International Monetary Reform." Chap. 17 in *Economics and Society.* Chicago: Univ. of Chicago Press.

U.S. Department of Commerce. 1971. *Economic Report of the President, 1971.*

Washington, D.C.: Government Printing Office.

Valentine, L. and D. Ellis. 1991. *Business Cycles and Forecasting.* 8th ed. Dallas: South Western Publishing Co.

Zarnowitz, V. 1985. "Recent Work on Business Cycles in Historical Perspective: A Review of Theories and Evidence." *Journal of Economic Literature* 23:523–80.

Recessions after World War II

This article is concerned with the economic fluctuations of the early postwar period (1945–61) when the accumulation and liquidation of inventories were important determinants of cyclical economic activity. The postwar reconversion period was viewed with trepidation by many economists and policymakers who felt that the economy would fall into a serious slump, reverting to prewar levels of employment and output. Production did decrease in 1946 and employment declined slightly as most firms responded to reduced production by eliminating overtime. However, in 1947, production and employment increased; the year was one of virtually full employment of labor and capital, and consumer demand remained at a high level. Prices rose during 1947 as consumer and producer demand increased more rapidly than supply.

As the world agricultural situation worsened, primarily because of poor crops in 1947, rising foreign demand for United States farm products created new upward pressure on prices. Subsequently, the Marshall Plan kept foreign demand at a high level, but below that reached during the second quarter of 1947.

The 1948–49 Recession

The economy continued to operate close to capacity levels during most of 1948. Wartime income tax rates were cut in spring 1948, and the additional disposable income was a stimulus to the economy. The price level increased more slowly in 1948 than in the previous years and the rate of increase in consumption expenditures began to slacken. Firms did not adjust immediately to the slower rate of increase in consumer spending, so that businesses found themselves with excessive inventories. Toward the end of 1948 and during the first quarter of 1949, firms reduced their purchases of goods and services, as they liquidated a substantial part of their inventories.

Primarily because of the decline in inventories, industrial production fell about 8 percent. Durable goods production fell 10 percent, but nondurable production dropped only 5 percent. Total employment declined slightly, and manufacturing employment was cut by 9 percent. Construction activity increased throughout 1949, and expenditures on producers' durable equipment was down by only 5 percent.

One reason that the business decline was not more severe was that personal consumption expenditures remained stable, even increasing slightly late in 1949. This was due in part to the payment of unemployment compensation to most of the laid-off workers and also to reductions in federal income taxes.

It became evident in the second half of 1949 that inventory liquidation had become excessive. Inventory accumulation resumed in early 1950, and economic activity concomitantly increased. A new boom began later in the year as the Korean War and large-scale rearmament sharply raised demand for goods and services.

The Korean War Period

The demand for goods arising out of the Korean War created new inflationary pressures. Consumers, remembering the shortages of World War II, spent heavily on various types of durable and semidurable goods as did business on inventories and capital equipment.

Despite these conditions, the Federal Reserve expanded the supply of money and credit considerably. Although the Board of Governors of the Federal Reserve wanted to raise interest rates to restrict expansion, they were committed to support the bond market by purchasing all government securities at or above par. Without this price-support policy, interest rates would have risen as the demand for loanable funds increased.

According to Valentine (1987), the controversy between the Treasury and the Fed developed into open conflict during the summer of 1950. The controversy intensified after the Fed had to engage in large-scale, open-market operations to aid in financing outstanding government debt.

The Treasury and the Fed reached an agreement on this matter in early 1951. This accord was designed to check credit expansion without the use of direct controls. Government bonds would no longer be purchased by the Fed to maintain a particular pattern and level of interest rates. However, the Fed continued to buy and sell some securities to maintain an orderly market.

The 1953–54 Recession
Business continued to advance in the first half of 1953, but by summer the rate of increase in business activity had slowed down, causing concern that a business decline might occur. The Fed eased credit in order to forestall the probability of a recession. Nevertheless, a downturn began in the third quarter of 1953 and continued through the second quarter of 1954. Industrial production dropped by about 10 percent from July 1953 to May 1954, and unemployment increased to about four million. Gross national product decreased by only about 2 percent, and personal income remained almost constant during the recession. After leveling off in the second half of 1953 and the first quarter of 1954, construction spending increased rapidly during the remainder of the year, partly in response to lower interest rates.

The 1953–54 downturn was largely caused by a drop in defense expenditures after the Korean War ended in August 1953. The reduction also led to some decline in business investment and a liquidation of inventories in late 1953 and 1954. Consumers, reflecting the increased uncertainty of the economic outlook, also cut back moderately on durable-goods expenditures, particularly for automobiles.

The readjustment to reduced government purchases and the resulting decline in investment expenditures and ultimately in inventories did not cause a severe recession. There were several moderating factors. Personal income held up fairly well during the business decline, because most sectors of the economy were not severely affected, and because personal taxes were cut by over $3 billion. Unemployment compensation also cushioned the decline in the personal income of the unemployed.

Economic activity increased rapidly in 1955 and personal consumption expenditures, especially on durable goods, increased. Automobile sales increased from about 5.5 million cars in 1954 to nearly eight million in 1955. Residential construction increased by over $3 billion from 1954 to 1955 and declined somewhat in 1956 and 1957. Inflationary pressures began to develop during this prosperity period. To prevent serious inflation, the Federal Reserve System followed a highly restrictive monetary policy, raising reserve requirements, and increasing the discount rate on several occasions.

The 1957–58 Recession and Recovery
In the late summer of 1957, the economy entered the third postwar recession. The recession was the most severe of the three postwar readjustments that had occurred up to that time, but the duration was the shortest. Industrial production dropped 13 percent between August 1957 and April 1958, compared with 10 percent in the two earlier recessions. By August 1958, unemployment had increased to 7.7 percent of the civilian labor force. Gross national product declined 2.5 percent, but disposable personal income changed little due to the automatic stabilizers.

A major cause of the decline in production and in gross national product was the liquidation of inventories. In the third quarter of 1957, inventories were being accumulated at a rate of more than $2 billion per year. During the first quarter of 1958, inventory liquidation was at an annual rate of $9.5 billion, and in the second quarter at $8 billion.

Other factors that helped cause the 1957–58 recession included a drop in capital expenditures, because plant and equipment had been expanded faster than the increase in demand for goods and services, and the changing composition of consumer expenditures. Less money was spent on durable goods and more on nondurables and services.

Shifts in foreign trade also affected the economy during the 1957 downturn. Exports of goods and services increased early in 1957 because of the Suez crisis that closed the Suez Canal and disrupted oil exports from that region. However, once the Canal was reopened in 1958, U.S. exports declined.

Economic activity reached a low point in April 1958. Subsequent gains in production came in part from the ending of inventory liquidation in the last quarter of 1958 and because of some increase of inventories during the first quarter of 1959. Another major impetus to recovery was the consumer sector as expenditures on nondurable goods and services increased. Residential construction also increased as interest rates declined and mortgage funds were made more readily available under FHA and VA programs.

Increased government expenditures also helped stimulate business activity. Federal government expenditures rose by almost $3 billion

TABLE 1. Selected Measures of Business

	Business cycle contractions 1948–61			
	Nov 1948– Oct 1949	July 1953– May 1954	Aug 1957– Apr 1958	Apr 1960– Feb 1961
Duration[a]	11	12	8	10
Depth[b]				
GNP, constant dollars	–1.4	–3.3	–3.2	–1.2
Industrial production	–10.1	–9.4	–13.5	–8.6
Nonfarm employment	–5.2	–3.4	–4.3	–2.2
Unemployment rate				
Maximum	7.9	6.1	7.5	7.1
Increase	+4.5	+3.6	+3.8	+2.3

Sources: U.S. Department of Commerce, U.S. Department of Labor, Board of Governors of the Federal Reserve System, National Bureau of Economic Research.

[a] In months from peak (first date) to trough (second date).

[b] Percentage change from the peak month or quarter in the series to the trough month or quarter over the intervals shown above. For the unemployment rate, the maximum figure is the highest for any month associated with the contraction, and the increases are from the lowest month to the highest, in percentage points.

from the third quarter of 1957 to the third quarter of 1958, and state and local government expenditures increased by almost $4 billion. By the spring of 1959, economic activity exceeded the prerecession levels in most sectors of the economy. However, unemployment remained a problem, remaining at 6 percent of the labor force during 1959, compared to about 4 percent in the 1955–57 prosperity period.

In the first half of 1959, a strong economic recovery occurred. However, the economy suffered a severe setback when the longest steel strike on record began during the summer. When the steel strike ended in November, economic activity increased again. Inventories were rebuilt through the first quarter of 1960, and production and GNP reached new highs by spring.

The 1960–61 Recession

The fourth postwar recession began in May 1960. Industrial production fell during the second half of the year and into early 1961. Gross national product declined somewhat during the last quarter of 1960 and continued falling in the first quarter of 1961. Although the 1960–61 recession was comparatively mild, unemployment almost reached the 1958 peak. One reason for the increased unemployment was a growing labor force due to a relatively high

birth rate after 1939. Another cause was accelerated automation resulting from new technological advances and rising labor costs. Finally, the relatively modest recovery in 1958–60 left unemployment at a high level.

The 1960–61 recession had several causes. As indicated above, inventories that had been depleted by the steel strike were rebuilt rapidly in the first quarter of 1960 and then more slowly in the second. This accumulation generated an increase in production that could not be sustained when inventory growth ceased in the third quarter. Residential construction also declined, as the backlog of deferred demand was satisfied. Moreover, mortgage money for residential financing was harder and more costly to obtain than it had been during the 1957–58 downturn and early recovery period. Consumer buying also weakened somewhat after midyear, especially for the purchase of durable goods. Rapid increases in the volume of consumer credit outstanding in 1959 and in the first half of 1960 caused consumers subsequently to slow down purchases in order to rebuild their equity position.

Table 1 compares selected economic statistics for the four postwar recessions discussed above. The four contractions from 1948–61 lasted an average of 10 months. They were mild to moderate in depth. As a generalization, these recessions can be characterized as "inventory recessions," that is, the business-cycle contractions were the result of excessive inventory accumulation and subsequent liquidation.

Tax cuts, particularly those that occurred in 1948 and 1953–54, helped to stabilize personal income and consumption spending, tending to moderate these recessions. The automatic stabilizers and accompanying federal budget deficits helped move the economy toward the recovery phase of the cycle.

Postwar Business Cycles in Western Europe and Japan

Western Europe moved from the period of postwar reconstruction into an unprecedented boom. By 1948 or 1949, industrial output in all countries already exceeded its prewar level. According to Van Der Wee (1987), combined Western European GNP between 1948 and 1973 rose in each succeeding year. It was only in some countries and in some years—for example Britain (1952), Belgium (1958), and Switzerland (1949 and 1958) that GNP actually declined. Nor did Japan experience a fall in GNP during any year in the 1948–73 period. Even when one considers industrial production, the period consists almost exclusively of yearly increases.

Thus, business contractions in Europe and Japan were replaced by variations in overall rates of growth. These latter fluctuations are termed *growth cycles* in which instability in economic activity was characterized by subsequent phases of slower and faster economic growth.

The 1951–52 slowdown in Western European economic growth was primarily the result of restrictive measures taken by governments to restore equilibrium in the balance of payments. This "growth recession" was also a reaction to the speculative fever that had broken out in 1950 as a result of the Korean War and the consequent fears of an expanding military conflict.

A second growth slowdown occurred in 1957–58. Its origin is to be found in the 1953–55 economic boom and concomitant fears of wage inflation. Wages increased considerably and higher imports of raw materials and semifinished goods put additional pressure on the balance of payments when demand for exported industrial finished products was declining. Restrictive monetary and fiscal policies, which were initiated in 1955 or 1956, helped cause the 1957–58 growth slowdown.

The Western European and Japanese economies moved out of this growth recession with the aid of specific government measures to stimulate the economy. Public works were expanded and installment-plan buying encouraged. The establishment of the European Economic Community in 1958 created a favorable climate for investment.

Alan L. Sorkin

See also FEDERAL RESERVE SYSTEM: 1941–1993; GROWTH CYCLES; KITCHIN CYCLES; METZLER, LLOYD APPLETON

Bibliography

Abramovitz, M. 1959. *Manufacturer's Inventories in the Study of Economic Growth.* New York: NBER.

Friedman, M. and A. J. Schwartz. 1963. *A Monetary History of the United States, 1867–1960.* Princeton: Princeton Univ. Press.

Lewis, W. 1965. *Federal Fiscal Policy in the Postwar Recessions.* Washington, D.C.: Brookings Institution.

Moore, G. H. 1983. *Business Cycles, Inflation and Forecasting.* Cambridge, Mass.: Ballinger.

Valentine, L. 1987. *Business Cycles and Forecasting.* 7th ed. Cincinnati: South-Western Publishing Company.

Van Der Wee, H. 1987. *Prosperity and Upheaval: The World Economy, 1945–80.* Berkeley and Los Angeles: Univ. of California Press.

Zarnowitz, V. 1985. "Recent Work on Business Cycles in Historical Perspective: A Review of Theories and Evidence." *Journal of Economic Literature* 23:523–80.

Recessions (Supply-Side) in the 1970s

In the 1970s, world oil prices twice rose sharply, and both times inflation accelerated while output declined, creating a condition referred to as "stagflation." The reduction in output was accompanied to a degree, and with a considerable lag, by a decline in employment. Indeed, both oil-price shocks were followed by unusual periods of output reduction and rising unemployment that, at least in the United States, were the worst since the depression in the 1930s.

Several features distinguish these episodes from stylized business-cycle recessions, hence the designation *supply-side recessions.* The principal differences are that the oil shocks were associated with temporary increases in inflation, permanent declines in output relative to labor employment (productivity losses), and permanent declines in the economy's capital-labor ratio. These features differ markedly from demand-side recessions, which, according to mainstream theoretical models, should result in reduced inflation and with only temporary declines in output. Nevertheless, since supply shocks in the 1970s also had features in common with demand-side recessions, such as a typical cyclical variation in employment, the episodes are appropriately referred to as recessions.

Another feature of the output losses associated with oil-price shocks is that they were permanent, in the sense that neither shock set in motion economic forces that would restore output to the level that available labor and capital resources and technology would have made possible in its absence. Some supply shocks, like a crop or production failure, are temporary since there are incentives, resources, and technology to restore output and employment relatively quickly. An additional distinguishing feature of these supply-side recessions is that their source was common to all countries. Thus, the cyclical experience internationally in these episodes showed more similarity in timing than is normally evident in other recessions.

The Oil Price Shocks in the 1970s

In October 1973, some members of the Organization of Petroleum Exporting Countries (OPEC) first imposed an oil embargo on the United States and other countries trading with Israel and then officially raised the benchmark price of crude oil. As a result, the world price of oil began to climb sharply for the next three quarters. The average price of oil paid by U.S. refiners rose from $4.15 per barrel in 1973 to $10.38 per barrel in 1974. The relative price of energy, measured by the producer price of fuel and power and related products deflated by the business-sector price deflator, rose about 40 percent from III/1973 (the third quarter of 1973) to III/1974. Oil and energy prices rose little relative to U.S. prices generally, from 1974 to early 1979.

Following strikes in Iranian oil fields, the fall of the Shah of Iran, and the outbreak of war between Iran and Iraq, OPEC doubled oil prices over the period from II/1979 to II/1980. The refiner's average cost of oil rose from $13.41 in

I/1979 to $27.91 in II/1980. The U.S. relative price of energy again rose about 40 percent over the same period. A further rise in U.S. oil prices in early 1981 put the quarterly average at its historical peak of $36.54. Thus, the two oil price shocks did not occur discretely, say within one month. Each shock extended over a four- (1973–74) to five-quarter (1979–80) period.

Energy Prices and Economic Capacity: The Permanent vs. Cyclical Confusion

The principal economic effects of an oil price hike are not transitory or cyclical. Instead, a rise in energy prices leads to a decline in output that, unlike the typical recession loss, cannot be reversed by market adjustments of nominal prices of other resources, goods, or services. A rise in the price of oil and energy resources reduces the capacity output of firms if capital and energy resources are substitutes, and raises the average and marginal cost of output (Rasche and Tatom 1977a, 1981). Capacity output is the output for which short- and long-run average (marginal) costs are equal. In effect, firms desire more capital for a given output, or demand the same capital to produce a smaller output. In the aggregate, the natural output rate declines and the minimum price level consistent with its production rises. Such a shift in the economy's aggregate supply arises from a relatively unchanged natural employment rate (unless the natural employment rate declines with the real wage), unchanged nominal wages and, in the short run, a given capital stock.

The primary changes in production associated with this loss are reduced use of energy resources, especially of oil, and changes in the optimal use of the existing capital stock. Also, since capital is not homogenous, prices do not instantaneously adjust to long-run equilibrium levels, nor does output adjust immediately to new capacity levels. As a result, some capital is scrapped or becomes obsolete, further reducing natural output. Some analysts focus on a "putty-clay" assumption, under which capital or labor cannot be substituted for energy in the short run. In these analyses, obsolescence is greater than under more conventional assumptions; relatively more of the capacity loss occurs over time instead of immediately. The decline in capacity occurs only as capital is scrapped and replaced with less energy-using capital goods. Finally, the decline in energy use reduces the marginal productivity of labor and capital resources, so that relative rental prices and quantities of resources demanded tend to fall. Given relatively inelastic labor supply and long-run relative rental prices of capital services that are unaffected by energy prices, the result is a decline in real wages in labor markets and a decline in the demand for capital services (and stocks). Thus, the capital-labor ratio falls, further reducing natural output.

In the short run, however, a shift in an economy's capacity to supply output is not accomplished with perfectly flexible prices. Nominal rigidities in prices can raise firms' marginal costs of production with little or no change in their product prices. Such firms will reduce output (and resource employment) by relatively more than the capacity loss. Also, if prices do not change initially, purchasers of output have little or no incentive to reduce their purchases. Thus, if productivity (output per hour or per worker) declines, an unchanged work force will produce less output, but, until prices rise, purchasers will desire unchanged quantities of output. Firms that choose to avoid undesired inventory reductions or stockouts could raise employment to offset some of their productivity decline. As cost rises relative to revenue, however, cyclical output losses can occur. Only when prices fully adjust to the capacity loss will the natural employment rate be restored.

Thus, supply-side recessions involve a subtle distinction between output and employment developments. Supply-side recessions tend to involve output reductions that are not inherently recessionary. Crop failures, for example, involve declines in output that are not associated, directly, with reduced employment. But supply shocks also can be amplified by typical economic forces like price rigidities that keep the economy from employing resources and producing output at the natural rates.

The economic capacity (or natural output) loss hypothesis is not universally accepted (Denison 1984). A variety of researchers have disputed its significance. Nevertheless, there is much econometric evidence supporting the hypothesis that past energy price shocks had these effects. These include production-function tests found in Rasche and Tatom (1977b, 1981), and in Helliwell et al. (1986). Hamilton (1983) provides evidence of the permanent output effect of oil price shocks. Hickman, Huntington, and Sweeney (1987) provide supporting evidence in a comparison of energy-price effects in fourteen econometric models of the U.S. economy.

The U.S. Recessionary Experience Following the 1970s Shocks

Like the rise in oil and energy prices, the effects of energy-price increases were spread over time as well. Productivity and output growth slowed relatively quickly in each instance. Inflation temporarily rose quite sharply with about a two-quarter lag for the GNP deflator and both shorter lags and larger impacts for consumer- and producer-price measures. The unemployment rate actually fell in the first quarter of each shock (IV/1973 and II/1979) and rose little in the first year. Civilian employment rose at a two-percent rate in the first year of the first shock (III/1973 to III/1974) and at a 1.6 percent rate in the first year of the second shock (I/1979 to I/1980). In the subsequent two quarters, employment fell; it declined at a 3.9 percent rate in the first case and at a 1.9 percent rate in the second case. A cyclical expansion in employment occurred in the next two-quarter period in each shock, with employment rising at a 1.8 percent rate from I/1975 to III/1975 and at a 2.7 percent rate from III/1980 to I/1981. Thus, the recessionary (employment) effects of the two oil-price shocks in the 1970s occurred more than a year after the initial oil-price rise. In each case, these recessionary developments were compounded by preceding sharp reductions in money growth which had matched in timing the adverse price effects of the oil-price shock. However, empirical studies find significant effects on the unemployment rate even when they control for the influence of money growth.

The Tax Analysis of Oil Price Shocks

Some analyses of oil price shocks do not focus on the loss in economic capacity. Instead, aggregate demand is the focus, especially net exports. In such an analysis, the significance of increased oil prices stems from the fact that oil is imported. A rise in oil prices is like a tax on purchasers of oil and oil-related products. The rise in the nation's import bill reduces its net exports and aggregate demand. In effect, the additional spending on oil imports reduces the income available for spending on domestic output. Like other aggregate-demand shocks, reductions in net exports due to oil-price shocks are expected to trigger a business cycle.

The aggregate-demand analysis of oil-price shocks suggests that the decline in output following an energy-price hike should be associated with downward pressure on the aggregate price level. It also suggests that oil-exporting countries, like Canada in 1973–74 or the United Kingdom in 1979–80, should have a cyclical expansion when oil prices rise. Net exports and aggregate demand rise in this case, putting upward pressure on output, employment and the aggregate level of prices. An oil-price hike simply redistributes aggregate output and employment from oil importers to oil exporters, according to this aggregate-demand channel. The evidence from these countries does not support this view, however. Nor are the effects of oil-price shocks across countries proportional to the share of oil imports in GNP, as the aggregate-demand view suggests. Finally, it is not clear that the net exports of an oil-importing country decline when oil prices rise. In both oil-price shocks in the 1970s, U.S. net exports rose sharply, even relative to GNP, as exports rose faster than imports.

A decline in investment provides another potential channel for a reduction in aggregate demand, since an aggregate-supply shock depresses the desired capital-labor ratio, temporarily lowering investment and the real rate of interest. For example, Helliwell et al. (1986) provide systematic evidence across countries showing declines in the capital-labor ratio and in investment. There is also evidence that the energy-price shocks reduced the real interest rate.

Energy Price Shocks, Sectoral Shifts, and Recessions

An alternative supply-side approach to energy price shocks relies on the sectoral-shift hypothesis. As in the real-business-cycle literature, the source of business-cycle movements in output and employment in the sectoral-shift analysis is a shock to the aggregate production function, called a technology shock. Positive shocks to output in one sector give rise to resource shifts in order to exploit new production opportunities. Relative price and wage movements provide incentives for the necessary movement of resources to expanding sectors. An increase in the dispersion of employment growth across sectors, a measure of sectoral shifts, subsequently raises the unemployment rate, but Loungani (1986) shows that the only sectoral shifts (labor dispersion) that are systematically related to unemployment are those associated with energy-price increases. Labor-growth dispersion, which is statistically independent of energy prices, has no significant effect on the unemployment rate. Loungani interprets these findings as supportive of the sectoral-shifts hy-

pothesis, despite the rejection of the significance of shifts that are unrelated to oil-price shocks. In any event, the Loungani findings point to the importance of sectoral differences in the cyclical process associated with energy-price shocks.

Conclusion

The cyclical experience associated with the 1970s' oil-price shocks was important for a variety of reasons. First, the recessions were the longest and, by a variety of measures, the deepest since the 1930s. Second, these recessions were unusual, because they were associated with supply shocks instead of demand shocks. Third, these recessions were associated with sharp declines in the trends in output per hour, real wages, and the capital-labor ratio, which were unique in modern business-cycle history. Economic developments related to a relatively large oil-price decline in 1986 and to the oil-price rise (and fall) due to Iraq's invasion of Kuwait also provide important examples of supply-side-related cyclical developments.

John A. Tatom

See also AGGREGATE SUPPLY AND DEMAND; REAL BUSINESS-CYCLE THEORIES; SECTORAL SHIFTS; SUPPLY SHOCKS

Bibliography

Denison, E. F. 1984. "Accounting for Slower Economic Growth: An Update." In *International Comparisons of Productivity and Causes of the Slowdown,* edited by J. W. Kendrick, 1–45. Washington: American Enterprise Institute.

Hamilton, J. D. 1983. "Oil and the Macroeconomy since World War II." *Journal of Political Economy* 91:228–48.

Helliwell, J., P. Sturm, P. Jarrett, and G. Salou. 1986. "The Supply Side in the OECD's Macroeconomic Model." *OECD Economic Studies* 8:75–131.

Hickman, B., H. G. Huntington, and J. L. Sweeney. 1987. *Macroeconomic Impacts of Energy Shocks.* Amsterdam: North-Holland.

Loungani, P. 1986. "Oil Price Shocks and the Dispersion Hypothesis." *Review of Economics and Statistics* 68:536–39.

Rasche, R. H. and J. A. Tatom. 1977a. "The Effects of the New Energy Price Regime on Economic Capacity, Production and Prices." Federal Reserve Bank of St. Louis *Review,* May, 2–12.

———. 1977b. "Energy Resources and Potential GNP." Federal Reserve Bank of St. Louis *Review,* June, 10–24.

———. 1981. "Energy Price Shocks, Aggregate Supply and Monetary Policy: The Theory and the International Evidence." In *Supply Shocks, Incentives and National Wealth. Carnegie-Rochester Conference Series on Public Policy,* Spring, 9–93.

Regulation School

The French Regulation School was originated in the late 1960s by Marxist economists who sought to overcome the philosophy of immiserization which dominated the thinking of both the Communist party and the trade-union organization COT. Its focus was the possible limits to the postwar stability of accumulation. In this context the term "regulation" encompasses both the notion of stability applicable to formal models, and the social conditions that allow accumulation to continue without major disruptions. Thus, while in traditional studies the stagflation of the 1970s is explained by exogenous shocks— as in the 1985 book *Economics of World Wide Stagflation* by Bruno and Sachs—for the Regulationists it expresses a crisis of the mode of regulation that sustained the postwar growth phase (Aglietta [1976] 1979, Lipietz 1979).

By the mid-1970s, three strands could be detected within the Regulation approach. The first is the State Monopoly Capitalism (SMC) strand (Boccara 1973), connected to the Communist party; the second is the Grenoble-based Research Group on the Regulation of Capitalist Economies, known as GRREC; the third is the Parisian CEPREMAP-located strand (Boyer 1987).

These three orientations all emphasize structural and sectoral relations, and distinguish short-term fluctuations from crises. Although none of the three has established a clear distinction between the former and the latter, the intuitive idea is that short-term fluctuations may actually restore the conditions of profitability and therefore belong to the normal working of a particular mode of regulation. By contrast, *great crises* signal the inadequacy of the mode of regulation itself. The latter comes to an end when the underlying *regime of accumulation* has either exhausted its potential, or is no longer compatible with the organizational forms that have hitherto sustained it. Broadly defined, a regime of accumulation constitutes a long period in which the conditions of consumption and of production are compatible and are, therefore, consistent with means of allocating the surplus. For example, relatively limited consumption per capita would be compatible with a regime of primitive accumulation.

For regulation theorists, major ruptures in the process of accumulation—for example, the Great Depression—play the role of identifying the phases of stability (Lorenzi et al. 1980). There is, therefore, no analytical procedure showing how instability arises from the period of stability.

Chronologically, the embryo of the regulation school started with the SMC approach whose position can be summarized in four points.

The first point extends Marx's theory of the falling rate of profit (FRP). According to Boccara, the economy does not adjust smoothly to a reduced profit rate brought about by a rising organic composition of capital. The FRP manifests itself in a tendency toward overaccumulation of capital leading to a crisis. The second step incorporates the Kondratieff cycle into the analysis. It is during the upswing of the long cycle that overaccumulation and a rising organic composition of capital become permanent features of the economy. The profitability of investment declines, and the cycle turns into a downswing. This is accompanied by structural changes, such as a preference for financial forms of investment. The third point relates to the role of the state, viewed as an essential instrument to secure the periodic loss in the value of constant capital previously caused by the competitive process. The devalorization of capital halts the fall in the rate of profit. The state, however, has more than a functionalist role. By expanding the public sector and by challenging, through its social policies, the supremacy of profit maximization, the state may damage the interests of large corporations. Consequently, the last point questions the ability of the state to overcome the difficulties engendered by the overaccumulation of capital.

The main problem with the SMC doctrine is that it does not integrate its Marxian analytical categories with the Kondratieff cycle—the former are tagged onto the latter. Furthermore, since Kondratieff is the exogenous explanation of both growth and cycles, the SMC approach says little about the uniqueness of the postwar growth decades.

Like the SMC, the Grenoble doctrine also adheres closely to Marxian concepts. It differs from the SMC in not focusing on overaccumulation. The basic stylized facts—warranting a theoretical explanation—are the instability of the international monetary system, the slowdown in accumulation, and the rise in unemployment—phenomena whose emergence is traced to the 1967–69 period (De Bernis 1990, GRREC 1983).

Accumulation is defined as structurally stable when a tendentially uniform rate of profit is maintained. If the forms of competition are compatible with that process, then the economy is said to be regulated. The history of modern capitalism is divided on this basis into three different regulations: the competitive nineteenth-century period based on small- and medium-sized firms; the stage of trusts and cartels, marked by antagonistic imperialisms, ending in 1919; the stage of monopoly capital and state intervention which arose after World War II. The Great Depression of the 1930s is interpreted as the crisis of the second stage and the gestation period of the third. Each mode of regulation has its own territorial dimension. During the phase of cartels and of antagonistic imperialisms, for instance, the space carved out by each power served the accumulation process of the industrial core.

While a tendency toward a uniform profit rate implies free mobility of capital and investment, the ability of a given mode of regulation to counteract the FRP tendency determines its capacity to control crises. Hence, the Grenoble school identifies the decline of profitability since 1967–69 as the main source of the crisis in the regime of accumulation and in the mode of accumulation as well. The role of the state in the third phase is to sustain the counteracting forces, yet the crisis also intensifies the difficulties the state has in performing its function. The world-wide nature of the problem is shown by the inability of the dollar-based monetary system to continue to impart coherence to capital accumulation, suggesting that the spatial dimensions of accumulation are being radically changed as well.

In the Grenoble approach, crises are not permanent, but usher in new forms of regulation. Yet the analytical reliance on the tendency toward a uniform and falling rate of profit actually narrows the breadth of the argument. Indeed, under monopolistic conditions there may be no such tendency. Moreover, profit rates may fall independently of Marx's organic composition of capital, say, because of oligopolistically induced unused capacity.

The Parisian CEPREMAP strand is the most complex one. Although its early contributions (Aglietta 1976, Boyer and Mistral 1978, Lipietz 1979) had a well-defined conceptual framework, this is no longer true of more recent works. Within the CEPREMAP approach, Aglietta's 1976 book is particularly significant, because it ties the theoretical framework to an analysis of the American economy, viewed as the cradle of the postwar regulation. Further studies by Boyer and Mistral (1978) on accumulation and the crisis in France, the work by Benassy, Boyer, and Gelpi (1979) on inflation, and by Bertrand (1983) on the sectoral transformation of the French economy constitute formal refinements as well as specific applications of the basic concepts of the Parisian school.

For the Parisian school, capitalist accumulation is spurred by the growth of the capital-goods sector. In contrast to the other two approaches, it views barriers to accumulation as coming from the *wage relation*. In the competitive phase of capitalism, surplus value and profits arose from the reorganization of the labor process, but without substantially changing traditional consumption patterns. This phase is called the period of extensive accumulation. The retarded structure of consumption hindered combining the expansion of the capital-goods and of the consumption-goods sectors. The rise of *Fordism*, that is of mass production of consumables, opened the way to a revolution in the wage relation and to the establishment of a regime of intensive accumulation based on oligopolistic firms.

Fordism, not the new form of competition, is what characterizes the mode of regulation prevailing from 1945 to the early 1970s. The American experience—exported to Europe after the war—started a historical phase in which mass consumption could be adapted to the productivity increases engendered by intensive accumulation. Generalized collective bargaining as well as elastic monetary and credit policies enabled wages to rise with productivity, thereby allowing for an integrated expansion of both sectors of production. Keynesianism is therefore a way by which the state promotes the adjustment to the Fordist mode of regulation. Income-transfer policies guarantee a steady flow of consumption demand, stabilizing aggregate demand. This allows firms to keep wages in line with productivity growth by means of mark-up pricing.

It is worth noting that the Parisian regulation school modifies, even as it relies heavily upon, the perspectives on oligopolies developed by American Institutionalists, by Marxists of the "Monopoly Capital" tradition, and by oligopoly theorists. For these economists oligopolistic pricing implies a tendency to excess capacity which depresses demand for investment. Hence, the severity of the Great Depression in the United States is ascribed to widespread monopolization. For the Parisian school, by contrast, the Great Depression is the final crisis of the competitive model of regulation, out of which sprang the Fordist one. In the latter, accumulation is driven by productivity gains, while income transfers and productivity-based wage increases secure the expansion of mass consumption.

The crisis of Fordism is primarily a productivity crisis, which is imputed to the vaguely defined technical and social limits to raising productivity (Coriat 1979, Lipietz 1987). Thus, any increase in purchasing power cuts into profitability, while any decline triggers a recession.

Here is where the coherence of the Parisian school ends. A survey prepared by one of its main representatives (Boyer 1986) observes that the authors who formed the Parisian school no longer share the same theoretical foundations. For some, the reference point is still Marxian, while others have shifted to an individualistic approach.

Certainly, all three Regulation schools have major weaknesses: an excessive reliance on overaccumulation *cum* devalorization in the SMC approach, a too strict adherence to the notion of a uniform rate of profit in the Grenoble approach, and perhaps an exaggerated emphasis on Fordism—often at the expense of other phenomena such as stagnation—in the Parisian school. Yet, the significance of the research programs of the Regulation schools lies in the formation of a new set of ideas directly related to the nature of modern capitalist accumulation.

Joseph Halevi

See also FALLING RATE OF PROFIT; GREAT DEPRESSION IN FRANCE (1929–1938); GREAT DEPRESSION IN THE UNITED STATES (1929–1938); KONDRATIEFF CYCLES; KONDRATIEFF, NIKIOLAI DIMITRIYEVICH; LONG-WAVE THEORIES; MARX, KARL HEINRICH; SOCIAL STRUCTURE OF ACCUMULATION; STATE-MONOPOLY CAPITALISM

Bibliography

Aglietta, M. [1976] 1979. *A Theory of Capitalist Regulation: The U.S. Experience.* London: NLB.

Benassy, J.-P., R. Boyer, and R.-M. Gelpi. 1979. "Régulation des économies capitalistes et inflation." *Revue économique* 30:397–441.

Bertrand, H. 1983. "Accumulation, régulation, crise: un modèle sectionnel théorique et appliqué." *Revue économique* 34:305–43.

Boccara, P. 1973. *Etudes sur le capitalisme monopoliste d'état, sa crise et son issue.* Paris: Editions Sociales.

Boyer, R. 1986. *La théorie de la régulation: une analyse critique.* Paris: La Découverte.

———. 1987. "Regulation." In *The New Palgrave: A Dictionary of Economics.* Vol. 4. Edited by J. Eatwell, M. Milgate, and P. Newman. London: Macmillan.

Boyer, R. and J. Mistral. 1978. *Accumulation, inflation, crises.* Paris: Presses Universitaires de France.

Coriat, B. 1979. *L'atelier et le chronomètre.* Paris: C. Bourgois.

De Bernis, G. D. 1990. "On a Marxist Theory of Regulation." *Monthly Review* 41:28–37.

GRREC. 1983. *Crises et régulation.* Grenoble: Presses Universitaires de Grenoble.

Lipietz, A. 1979. *Crise et inflation, pourquoi?* Paris: Maspero.

———. [1985] 1987. *Mirages and Miracles: The Crises of Global Fordism.* Translation. London: Verso.

Lorenzi, J.-H., O. Pastré, and J. Toledano. 1980. *La crise du XXe siècle.* Paris: Economica.

Reichsbank

The Reichsbank, the central bank of Imperial Germany, began functioning in 1875, after the German Empire adopted the gold standard. Its tasks were to issue high denomination notes (only notes over 100 marks) against a proportional reserve (one-third) of gold or gold convertible currency, to provide commercial credits, and to rediscount bills. Though its directors and president were appointed by the government, it was privately owned, and its policy could not be directly influenced by the Imperial government. Though other note-issue banks survived, the Reichsbank was awarded an overwhelming share of the German note issue.

As with other central banks on the prewar gold standard, the discount rate was the major policy instrument. In the classic view, reserves fell in boom periods, provoking a rise in rates, which tightened credit; and reserves rose in recessions, leading to a relaxation. In practice, as Bloomfield (1963) has demonstrated, reserve changes and alterations of the discount rate were poorly correlated. The Reichsbank altered rates much less frequently than did the Bank of England, employing instead a range of "devices" to insulate Germany from internationally caused movements (e.g., interest-free loans to gold importers, and interference with railway schedules to delay the transport of gold to ports). The rate reacted to changes in the domestic money market, and in 1908 the Reichsbank's president announced that its interest and discount policies were fundamentally passive.

Despite the Reichsbank's independence from the government, the passive monetary policy and the reluctant use of the discount rate tool were dictated by political considerations. Farmers, who had a great deal of political influence, viewed the Reichsbank with suspicion as an instrument of financial interests, and campaigned for cheaper credit and legal changes to the Reichsbank's statutes. At the same time, for investors, economic stability meant stable interest rates and bond yields. These considerations alone ruled out any possibility of adopting any broader definition of economic stability (or any notion of countercyclical policy).

The Reichsbank's discounts meant that it assumed the role of lender of last resort to a rapidly expanding commercial-bank sector. Its interventions were particularly important in the panics of 1900–01 and 1907, in the political and financial crises of 1911 (Morocco crisis), and following the outbreak of war in 1914. The United States National Monetary Commission considered this assistance the chief advantage of the Reichsbank system. The increased use by banks of the Reichsbank's facilities strained reserves, and in response the Reichsbank in 1906 obtained a new law permitting the issue of smaller-denomination (twenty and fifty mark) notes.

During and after World War I, the Reichsbank became highly controversial. Under its president, Rudolf Havenstein, it bore a major part of the responsibility for German inflation and hyperinflation (1914–23). It defended its actions by invoking the real-bills doctrine of discounting commercial and government bills presented to the bank, despite the suspension of the gold standard, which, before 1914, limited the Reichsbank's capacity to promote monetary expansion. The Reichsbank's conception of its role as lender of last resort provided one of the causes of inflation. However, as Holtfrerich (1986) has pointed out, an inflation whose origins lie in a massive public-sector deficit cannot simply be controlled by attacking private-sector liquidity. The Reichsbank's management had no doubt that the primary responsibility for inflation lay with the government.

After the end of the inflation (November 1923) and the introduction of a new currency (the Reichsmark) legally anchored to gold with a 40-percent proportional reserve requirement, the Reichsbank, under a new president, Hjalmar Schact, took a very different course from the passive accommodation of the past. Its management worried about the inflationary effects of bank lending and of the large capital inflows to Germany, which deprived discount rates of their effectiveness (because rate rises would encourage further inflows rather than restraining economic activity). Instead, the Reichsbank used the threat of credit rationing and a refusal to discount offered bills. The banks could no longer rely on the Reichsbank as a lender of last resort. A refusal to discount checked a potentially inflationary boom in April 1924; was used against a stock-market surge in May 1927; and contributed decisively to the illiquidity of German banks in the great bank crisis of June–July 1931, which was directly responsible for worsening the Great Depression in Germany.

In the aftermath of the inflation, the stated primary goal of the Reichsbank had been price stability, and this concern influenced the interventions of 1924 and 1927. The credit restriction of 1931, however, was a response to the loss of foreign exchange and the insistence of foreign central banks (chiefly the Federal Reserve Bank of New York and the Bank of England) that the Reichsbank use credit controls to stop speculation against the Reichsbank. During the interwar gold standard between 1924 and 1931, foreign linkages limited decisively the freedom of maneuver of the

Reichsbank, first during the credit boom and then during the world deflation.

After the crisis of 1931, exchange control, voluntary "standstill agreements" on foreign short-term debt service, effectively lifted the gold-standard constraint on Reichsbank policy, permitting a monetary expansion which allowed recovery from the depression and the financing of rearmament. By the later 1930s, as well as during World War II, the Reichsbank's policy became openly inflationary. The institution was dissolved by the Allied occupation authorities.

Harold James

See also CENTRAL BANKING; GERMAN BUNDESBANK; GOLD STANDARD; GOLD STANDARD: CAUSES AND CONSEQUENCES; MONETARY POLICY; REAL-BILLS DOCTRINE

Bibliography

Bloomfield, A. I. 1963. *Short-Term Capital Movements under the Pre-1914 Gold Standard*. Princeton Studies in International Finance, no. 11. Princeton: Dept. of Economics, Princeton Univ.

Borchardt, K. 1982. *Krisen, Handlungsspielräume der Wirtschaftspolitik: Studien zur Wirtschaftsgeschicte des 19. und 20. Jahrhunderts*. Göttingen: Vandenhoeck und Ruprecht.

Deutsche Bundesbank. 1976. *Währung und Wirtschaft in Deutschland 1876–1975*. Frankfurt: Deutsche Bundesbank.

Holtrerich, C.-L. 1986. *The German Inflation 1914–1923: Causes and Effects in International Perspective*. Berlin, New York: Walter de Gruyter.

James, H. 1985. *The Reichsbank and Public Finance in Germany 1924–1933*. Frankfurt: Fritz Knapp.

Lindert, P. 1969. *Currencies and Gold 1900–1913*. Princeton Studies in International Finance, no. 24. Princeton: Princeton Univ. Press.

Seeger, M. 1968. *Die Politik der Reichsbank von 1876–1914 im Lichte der Spielregeln der Goldwährund*. Berlin: Duncker und Humblot.

U.S. National Monetary Commission. 1910. *Interviews on the Banking and Currency Systems of England, Scotland, France, Germany, Switzerland, and Italy*. Washington: Government Printing Office.

Ricardian Equivalence

The *Ricardian equivalence* or *tax-discounting* hypothesis asserts that the path of government debt, given a path of government purchases, is irrelevant to the evolution of the economy. It is an extension of the permanent-income and life-cycle hypotheses to include government purchases, taxes, and debt.

To see the intuition behind Ricardian equivalence, suppose that the government, while keeping its path of purchases unchanged, decides to reduce current lump-sum taxes by B dollars per capita and issue B dollars of debt per capita instead. For simplicity, suppose the debt comprises perpetuities paying a coupon rate r. According to conventional theory, such a refinancing stimulates the economy and raises interest rates. Ricardian equivalence asserts that it has no such effects. The logic is simple. On the one hand, the representative individual gives up B dollars in the initial period to buy the new debt and expects to receive a stream of interest payments rB in all future periods. On the other hand, the individual's taxes fall in the initial period by B dollars but rise in subsequent periods by rB to finance the interest payments. Because every new inflow is matched by an equal outflow, the representative individual's net income and expenditure flows are unchanged; consequently, he perceives no change in his wealth. Because taxes are lump-sum, marginal rates of return are unchanged. The refinancing scheme therefore does not affect the representative individual's optimization and so has no important effects on the economy. The only effect it does have is to increase private saving. Recognizing that future taxes must rise to pay the interest on the debt, the individual uses his tax rebate to buy the new government bonds, whose interest earnings exactly enable him to meet the additional future tax obligations. Private demand for assets therefore moves one-to-one with the supply of public debt; so interest rates do not change and no "crowding out" occurs.

The restrictions required for Ricardian equivalence are many and unlikely to be met. The more important ones will be discussed here.

The preceding discussion tacitly assumed that people have infinite horizons. If they have finite horizons, Ricardian equivalence does not generally hold, because some of the future taxes arising from government debt will fall on future taxpayers. Thus, when debt is issued, the present value of taxes relevant to the representative individual is less than the value of tax reductions (that reduction equals the market value of the debt) and wealth effects arise from a debt-for-tax refinancing. Ricardian equivalence still can hold if individuals treat the utility of their children as extensions of their own and the population is constant. Although current taxpayers do not pay all the future taxes associated with government debt, whatever they do not pay is borne by their descendants. Altruistic parents offset this extra burden on future generations by bequeathing enough extra wealth to their children to cancel the future taxes they and their descendants will bear. Such altruistic behavior by parents converts a finite-horizon model into an infinite-horizon one, restoring Ricardian equivalence. However, if the population is growing, parental altruism guarantees Ricardian equivalence only if parents actually make bequests. They will do so only if the economy is sufficiently inside its efficient growth region. In particular, in the inefficient case, where there is too much capital, parents want to confer liabilities on their children (reduce the capital stock). Government debt helps them do that and so is not neutral. Even in the efficient case, parents may not love their children "enough" to make bequests.

Empirical evidence suggests that many economies are inside the efficient region. For Canada, England, France, Germany, Italy, Japan, and the United States, the return to capital (measured as the cash flows generated by production less wages) considerably exceeds the amount of investment, suggesting that these economies are well inside the efficient region. For the United States, the marginal product of capital is about 10 percent, much more than the economy's growth rate, consistent with the U.S. economy being inside the efficient region. However, there is no way to tell from this evidence whether these economies are far enough inside the efficient region for bequests to be large enough to establish Ricardian equivalence.

Altruism is not the only reason for bequests; other possible motives generally do not imply Ricardian equivalence. One possibility is that bequests are used to control the behavior of designated recipients. For example, parents might use bequests to coax attention from their children, threatening to disinherit insufficiently attentive children. In such cases, a debt-for-tax swap alters the threat point of the parents or the children and therefore has real effects, negating Ricardian equivalence. Another possibility is

that families act as incomplete annuities markets, insuring against the risk of low consumption due to unexpectedly long lives. Even if individuals were completely selfish, intra-family transfers including bequests would occur as a way of buying insurance services from the recipients. Ricardian equivalence fails because of the individuals' selfishness, even though deliberate bequests are the rule. Still another possibility is that bequests are accidental, arising only because people have uncertain lifespans and often die sooner than anticipated, making unintended bequests to their children with no altruism intended. People would recognize that some future taxes would be borne by people whose utility does not matter to them and so would prefer debt to current taxes. The empirical evidence suggests that some bequests are non-altruistic; whether any bequests are altruistic is unclear.

Even if families with children behave altruistically, some families are childless—about a fifth of all families in the United States. Having little or no concern for taxes levied on future generations, childless families alter their behavior when debt is substituted for taxes, invalidating Ricardian equivalence. Families with children may recognize that the existence of childless families implies more taxes for their own children and so may increase bequests to offset that extra future tax burden. The offset, however, is incomplete, for parents will give way on two margins, accepting part of the additional tax burden themselves but imposing the remainder on their children.

Uncertainty also can invalidate Ricardian equivalence. For example, if an individual is uncertain of his future income, he also is uncertain of the bequests he will want to make. As a result, he prefers an additional dollar now to a future payment to his children with a present value of a dollar. Ricardian equivalence therefore fails.

However, two of the most frequent objections to Ricardian equivalence are of dubious validity. One is that many households are liquidity-constrained and so would like current taxes reduced and future taxes raised by a debt-for-taxes swap. The empirical evidence does suggest that some households are liquidity-constrained. But the magnitude of the effects those constraints have on aggregate behavior often appears small. Furthermore, Ricardian equivalence is invalidated by liquidity constraints only if the government has some capability in the credit market that private agents lack. For example, if liquidity constraints arise because of transactions costs and if the government faces lower transactions costs than the private sector in lending to liquidity-constrained households, then issuing government debt relaxes the constraint and Ricardian equivalence fails. In contrast, if credit rationing occurs because all future incomes are uncertain (in which case the loan rate would be related to the size of the loan because of default risk), Ricardian equivalence continues to hold, because issuing government debt does not change the state of uncertainty and merely substitutes government loans for private loans. The little research done to date on the reasons for credit constraints does not illuminate whether they arise for reasons that would invalidate Ricardian equivalence.

The other dubious argument concerns marginal tax rates. Changes in government debt may be associated with changes in the path of marginal tax rates, leading to substitution effects and thus to violations of Ricardian equivalence. In fact, Ricardian equivalence does not fail, for the substitution effects and related behavioral changes arise from changes in the path of marginal tax rates, not from changes in the path of the debt. Although debt and marginal tax rates may change simultaneously, there is no necessity that they do so. A given change in the path of debt could be accompanied by a change in the path of tax revenue achieved by changing the path of marginal tax rates, which would have substitution effects, or by changing the path of the tax base (e.g., through lump-sum exemptions), which would have no substitution effects. It is the path of the marginal tax rate, not the debt, that determines whether real effects are present. Ricardian equivalence concerns only the effects of the path of the debt.

Finite horizons, nonaltruistic or insufficient bequest motives, childless families, liquidity constraints, and uncertainty can invalidate Ricardian equivalence. Although the evidence on the importance of these sources of nonequivalence is inconclusive, it seems improbable that all are absent, so that it appears unlikely that the world is strictly Ricardian. Nevertheless, Ricardian equivalence might provide a good approximation to reality. If so, it remains useful for empirical work and, because of its analytical simplicity, for theoretical work as well. We therefore turn to the evidence on Ricardian equivalence.

The early direct evidence on Ricardian equivalence was conflicting, but as time passed and researchers overcame problems of measurement, specification, differencing, simultaneity, and treatment of expectations, the results from a wide variety of tests converged on a conclusion. The most common tests examine the effect of government debt on consumption, usually in a life-cycle model, but sometimes in a permanent-income specification, in an Euler-equation framework, or with event studies. Perhaps the best consumption study is that of Kormendi (1983), because it nests essentially all other life-cycle studies and because it has elicited many comments and replies illuminating the important methodological issues involved (see Barth, Iden, and Russek 1986; Feldstein and Elmendorf 1990; Modigliani and Sterling 1986, 1990; and Kormendi and Meguire 1986, 1990). Most consumption tests have used U.S. data, but some have examined data from other countries. Besides consumption, researchers have tested the effect of government debt on current interest rates, steady-state interest rates, and holding-period yields, using data over long time spans and many countries; on international trade and finance variables, such as exchange rates and the trade balance; and on growth rates of various countries.

Almost all the tests that are not obviously methodologically unsound fail to reject Ricardian equivalence, with government debt having no significant effect on any of the dependent variables examined. The only rejections of Ricardian equivalence are occasional findings that government debt is negatively related to interest rates, a puzzling result inconsistent with any obvious theory of how government debt should affect economic activity. No tests support the traditional view that government debt stimulates the economy.

So do we conclude that Ricardian equivalence is true? Not necessarily. Another view of the effects of debt and deficits, based on less ideal assumptions than Ricardian equivalence, is consistent with the evidence and also is unaffected by such problems as large numbers of childless families or nonaltruistic bequests. Suppose that individuals can predict their own future tax liability reasonably well, but care little about the tax liability of future generations. Obviously, Ricardian equivalence does not hold. Nevertheless, at historical interest rates and average lifespans, most of the future tax

R

implied by a current bond issue will be borne by people currently alive, and individuals will see little increase in their net wealth from bond-financed tax cuts. Near-Ricardian equivalence then obtains if the permanent-income and life-cycle hypotheses are even approximately true, for under those hypotheses, the effects of changes in wealth are spread over the remaining lifetime and are small in any one period. A small change in wealth combined with a small response leads to a negligible effect, as simulation studies have confirmed. Obviously, the effects would be even smaller if any altruistic concern for future generations existed. Thus, for many purposes, this "approximate equivalence" model essentially reproduces Ricardian equivalence, and the distinction between pure Ricardian equivalence and approximate equivalence is inconsequential.

Just what, then, should we conclude? Theoretically, we can be almost certain that Ricardian equivalence is not strictly true, requiring too many stringent conditions to be believable. Nevertheless, Ricardian equivalence seems to be a good approximation empirically and also is analytically simple. It therefore is a useful theory of the economic effects of government debt.

John J. Seater

See also CONSUMPTION EXPENDITURES; FISCAL POLICY; PIGOU-HABERLER EFFECT

Bibliography

Barro, R. J. 1974. "Are Government Bonds Net Wealth?" *Journal of Political Economy* 82:1095–1117.

———. 1989. "The Ricardian Approach to Budget Deficits." *Journal of Economic Perspectives*, Spring, 37–54.

Barth, J. R., G. Iden, and F. S. Russek. 1986. "Government Debt, Government Spending, and Private Sector Behavior: Comment." *American Economic Review* 76:1158–67.

Bernheim, B. D. 1987. "Ricardian Equivalence: An Evaluation of Theory and Evidence." In *Macroeconomics Annual 1987,* edited by S. Fischer, 263–304. Cambridge: MIT Press.

Blanchard, O. J. 1985. "Debt, Deficits, and Finite Horizons." *Journal of Political Economy* 93:223–47.

Feldstein, M. and D. W. Elmendorf. 1990. "Taxes, Budget Deficits, and Consumer Spending: Some New Evidence." *American Economic Review* 80:589–99.

Hayashi, F. 1987. "Tests for Liquidity Constraints: A Critical Survey and Some New Observations." In *Advances in Econometrics, Fifth World Congress.* Vol. 2. Edited by T. Bewley, 91–120. Cambridge: Cambridge Univ. Press.

Kormendi, R. C. 1983. "Government Debt, Government Spending, and Private Sector Behavior." *American Economic Review* 73:994–1010.

Kormendi, R. C. and P. Meguire. 1986. "Government Debt, Government Spending, and Private Sector Behavior: Reply." *American Economic Review* 76:1180–87.

———. 1990. "Fiscal Policy and Private Sector Behavior Revisited." *American Economic Review* 80:604–17.

Modigliani, F. and A. Sterling. 1986. "Government Debt, Government Spending, and Private Sector Behavior: Comment." *American Economic Review* 76:1168–79.

———. 1990. "Government Debt, Government Spending, and Private Sector Behavior: A Further Comment." *American Economic Review* 80:600–603.

Plosser, C. I. 1987. "Fiscal Policy and the Term Structure." *Journal of Monetary Economics* 20:343–67.

Poterba, J. M. and L. H. Summers. 1987. "Finite Lifetimes and the Effects of Budget Deficits on National Savings." *Journal of Monetary Economics* 20:369–91.

Seater, J. J. 1993. "Ricardian Equivalence." *Journal of Economic Literature* 31:142–90.

Weil, P. 1987. "Love Thy Children: Reflections on the Barro Debt Neutrality Theorem." *Journal of Monetary Economics* 19:377–91.

Ricardo, David (1772–1823)

A towering figure in classical economics, David Ricardo did not advance a theory of business cycles. However, his contributions to the extended Bullionist controversies were later incorporated into monetary theories of crises and business cycles. Moreover, as a leading proponent of Say's Law, Ricardo helped crystalize the classical view that depressions or general gluts are fundamentally disequilibrium phenomena whose cure lies in market-clearing price adjustment.

Ricardo's first published writings in economics were his two letters to the *Morning Chronicle* in 1809 in which he attributed the inflation then occurring to monetary overissue by the Bank of England. Excess issue by the Bank of England was possible only because the Bank's legal obligation to convert its notes into gold at the legal parity had been suspended in 1797 to prevent a run on the Bank's dwindling reserves of gold. Ricardo's identification of the market premium on gold bullion as the sole indicator of overissue by the Bank of England followed directly from his definition of overissue as an issue of bank notes exceeding the amount that would circulate under convertibility.

So compelling was Ricardo's argument for a speedy restoration of convertibility that a Parliamentary Commission was appointed to study the policies of the Bank of England since the suspension of convertibility. The ensuing report of the Commission written in part by Henry Thornton endorsed Ricardo's proposal for a prompt restoration of convertibility, though it did not endorse Ricardo's theoretical position that only excess issue by the Bank of England could have caused a premium on bullion relative to the legal parity.

While Ricardo was critical of the Bank of England for having pursued an inflationary policy, he was not insensitive to the costs of restoring convertibility at the old parity once a substantial premium on gold had become effective. When a legal commitment to restore convertibility was made at the end of the Napoleonic Wars, Ricardo asserted that he would never recommend restoration of the old par if the premium on bullion exceeded 5 percent. Ricardo further sought to mitigate the impact of restoration with his "ingot plan" under which all gold coin would be replaced by tokens and paper notes convertible into gold bullion. Ricardo believed that, by reducing the monetary demand for gold, his plan would allow convertibility to be restored with little deflationary pressure.

The postwar deflation and depression that preceded the formal resumption of convertibility was deeply disturbing to Ricardo. Ricardo attributed the deflation to unnecessary accumulation of gold reserves despite the formal endorsement of his plan by the government and the Bank of England. Gold accumulation defeated the purpose of Ricardo's plan, which was to reduce the monetary demand for gold.

Frustration with the capacity of the Bank of England to undermine his ingot plan may have led Ricardo to propose depriving the Bank of England and all other private banks of the power to issue currency. Ricardo made this proposal in his final work, published posthumously, "A Proposal for a National Bank." Until that time, Ricardo had never questioned the right of private banks to issue convertible banknotes and had never attributed monetary disturbances to the competitive behavior of private banks. Subsequent authors, particularly those associated with the Currency School, influenced by Ricardo's rigid quantity theoretic analysis of an inconvertible currency and by his proposal for a national bank of issue, proposed to control the business cycle by the application of a rule rigidly constraining the quantity of money.

Failure to appreciate the evolution in Ricardo's monetary thought has caused misunderstanding not just of Ricardo, but of the entire development of classical monetary thought, because the existence of a classical theory of a competitive supply of money under convertibility was thereby obscured. Because of the affinity between the policy proposals of the Currency School and Ricardo's National Bank plan, subsequent commentators have tended to overlook the link between this theory (which the early Ricardo accepted and even the late Ricardo did not deny) and the later doctrines of the Banking School and Free Banking School.

Although Ricardo himself never did so, it was not difficult to combine his theory of the impact of monetary overissue with his theory of the impact of monetary contraction into a monetary theory of the business cycle. The cycle theories of such Currency School figures as Samuel Jones Loyd (Lord Overstone) and such Free Banking School figures as Robert Mushet can thus be regarded as within the Ricardian tradition.

Ricardo's explicit recognition that monetary contraction could cause commercial distress and unemployment shows that his espousal of Say's Law did not mean that he denied, as adherents of Say's Law supposedly did, that periods of economic depression or high unemployment could occur. What Ricardo meant to argue was that such situations would be self-correcting if market prices were allowed to adjust so that those seeking to supply goods and services could find buyers for what they wished to sell. It was the inability to sell that restricted their ability to buy. The cure for a depression was not to restrict production, which would only reduce demand even further, but to redirect it so that it would better correspond to demand. The point applies equally to a monetary or a barter economy. To make their demands effective, economic agents must succeed in finding buyers for what they are trying to sell. Nor did Ricardo and other supporters of Say's Law advocate deflation as a cure for unemployment, as shown by Ricardo's support, in principle, for devaluation as an alternative to restoring convertibility at the old sterling-gold parity and by his ingot plan.

The issue supporters of Say's Law were contesting was whether supply should be restricted to raise prices. Such policies have always been proposed in depressions as a cure for economic hardship. Ricardo and other advocates of Say's Law sought to show that restricting supply in one market could relieve economic distress for some only at the expense of creating even greater distress for others, because the restriction of supply would involve an equal reduction of demand for all other products.

Despite Ricardo's preeminence in classical economics, much of his work on monetary theory remains misunderstood or obscure. A serious reevaluation of Ricardo's work in this field is long overdue.

David Glasner

See also BANKING SCHOOL, CURRENCY SCHOOL, AND FREE BANKING SCHOOL; BULLIONIST CONTROVERSIES; HAWTREY, RALPH GEORGE; HUTT, WILLIAM HAROLD; MALTHUS, THOMAS ROBERT; NAPOLEONIC WARS; SAY, JEAN-BAPTISTE; SAY'S LAW; THORNTON, HENRY

Bibliography

Arnon, A. 1984. "The Transformation in Thomas Tooke's Monetary Thought." *History of Political Economy* 16:311–26.
———. 1990. *Thomas Tooke: Pioneer of Monetary Thought.* Ann Arbor: Univ. of Michigan Press.
Fetter, F. W. 1965. *The Evolution of British Monetary Orthodoxy, 1797–1875.* Cambridge: Harvard Univ. Press.
Glasner, D. 1985. "A Reinterpretation of Classical Monetary Theory." *Southern Economic Journal* 52:46–67.
———. 1989. "On Some Classical Monetary Controversies." *History of Political Economy* 21:201–29.
Hollander, J. 1979. *The Economics of David Ricardo.* Toronto: Univ. of Toronto Press.
Ricardo, D. [1810] 1952. *The High Price of Bullion: A Proof of the Depreciation of Bank Notes.* In *The Works and Correspondence of David Ricardo.* Vol. 3. Edited by P. Sraffa, 47–127. Cambridge: Cambridge Univ. Press.
———. [1816] 1952. *Proposals for an Economical and Secure Currency.* In *The Works and Correspondence of David Ricardo.* Vol. 4. Edited by P. Sraffa, 43–141. Cambridge: Cambridge Univ. Press.
———. [1824] 1952. *Plan for the Establishment of a National Bank.* In *Works and Correspondence of David Ricardo.* Vol. 4. Edited by P. Sraffa, 271–300. Cambridge: Cambridge Univ. Press.
St. Clair, O. 1957. *A Key to Ricardo.* London: Routledge and Kegan Paul.

Robbins, Lionel Charles (1898–1984)

Lionel Robbins was a major figure in British debates over macroeconomic theory and policy for more than a half-century. Robbins's macroeconomic thought before World War II was a blend of English, Swedish, and Austrian sources. English classical economics impressed upon him both the importance of the money supply and the necessity of studying it within the context of an open economy. The work of Wicksell provided him with the basic concepts of the natural and market rates of interest, and the importance for equilibrium of equality between the two. He was influenced by Austrian developments of Wicksell's work, especially those of Mises and Hayek. The result was a trade-cycle model which was put forward most notably in his *The Great Depression* (1934). But, because Robbins was blending together the work of different sources, he did not borrow wholesale the Austrian apparatus; in particular, he avoided the concept of the period of production.

He viewed the trade cycle as essentially a monetary phenomenon. Exogenously increased credit, reducing the market rate of interest, produced a rise in the demand for investment goods which did not reflect any change in *voluntary* saving habits. The investment-goods industries captured resources from consumption-goods industries, imposing *forced saving* on consumers. But the resources newly employed in the investment-goods industries, at increased rates of pay, demanded consumption goods with their incomes, increasing the demand for consumption goods and restoring the relative price level of consumption and investment goods that had existed before the monetary disturbance. The general rise in factor (primarily labor) costs upset the profit expectations of firms that had expanded on the basis of new credit, so that they required yet further credit to continue their operations. Eventually the increased demand for credit caused the market rate of interest to rise as banks ran up against reserve limits, which choked off the expansion of the investment goods industries and led to the unemployment of the extra resources that had been attracted into the investment-goods industries. In his 1934 book, Robbins was quite clear that this theoretical schema explained the interwar macroeconomic fluctuations very well.

Counterdepression monetary policy was ruled out. What was required in an open economy was a gold-standard regime with adherence to the Rules of the Game, so that discretionary monetary policy was avoided. The system should be allowed to return to (Austrian) general equilibrium through wage and price flexibility which would ultimately generate equilibrium relative prices of consumption and investment goods, reflecting, in turn, the demands of consumers for consumption goods and—through *voluntary* saving—investment goods. The most intervention that Robbins was prepared to countenance in the prewar period was a limited and cautious role for fiscal policy in concentrating public investment in a slump.

During the war, Robbins became convinced that government *should* act countercyclically. In the postwar era, he advocated a position which, while not Keynesian, had moved some way from the explicit Mises-Hayek development of Wicksell. It emphasized both monetary and fiscal policy as complementary tools for macroeconomic management. Wage demands themselves had little power to cause long-run disruption; their strength was crucially dependent upon the level of aggregate monetary demand. Robbins therefore had little use for prices and incomes policies to combat inflation except as a shock-absorbing device to help scale down expectations in *conjunction with* reductions in aggregate monetary demand growth. Indeed, Robbins's chief concern in the postwar years was inflation. It fostered corruption, social divisiveness, and an implicit repudiation of government debts. It distorted production planning, produced a cumulative shortfall of working capital, and disrupted labor and goods markets. In only the very shortest run—because expectations adapted quickly—was it stimulating to economic activity. Otherwise, it simply produced the phenomenon which was to become known as "stagflation."

The cause of inflation was excess monetary demand generated by governments. In the face of the ruling pseudo-Keynesian orthodoxy, Robbins stressed that fiscal policy *on its own* was totally inadequate for controlling aggregate demand. It was too clumsy and ineffective an instrument. Monetary policy was fast and flexible. The correct approach, in Robbins's view, was to control the "credit base" (by which he seems in general to have meant sterling M_3). This could be achieved through purchase of (highly liquid) Treasury bills by the monetary authorities who could replace them with longer-dated government securities. Another useful weapon lay in calls for special deposits. Financial innovation which weakened such control should simply be met by devising new methods of controlling credit innovations. Rising interest rates could not exercise sufficient control, without restraints on the growth of the monetary base and using appropriate fiscal weapons. Nonetheless, they had an important role to play—Robbins was highly skeptical of the idea that investment demand was interest-inelastic.

In the prewar years, Robbins's macroeconomic thought centered around the idea of a trade cycle produced by exogenous changes in the money supply leading to overinvestment in relation to plans to save, forced saving, relative price levels of investment and consumption goods that did not reflect the general-equilibrium preferences of society as a whole, and economic dislocation produced as rising interest rates choked off excess investment demand. After the war, the apparatus that Robbins used had largely shed the Mises-Hayek borrowings and relied instead upon a judicious mixture of English classical sources of monetary analysis although with the influence of Wicksell still discernible in some of Robbins's work.

D. P. O'Brien

See also AUSTRIAN THEORY OF BUSINESS CYCLES; FORCED SAVING; HAYEK, FRIEDRICH AUGUST [VON]; MISES, LUDWIG EDLER VON;

MONETARY POLICY; WICKSELL, JOHAN
GUSTAV KNUT

Bibliography
O'Brien, D. P. 1988. *Lionel Robbins.*
London: Macmillan.
Robbins, L. 1932. "Consumption and the
Trade Cycle." *Economica* 12:413–30.
———. 1934. *The Great Depression.*
London: Macmillan.
———. 1963. *Politics and Economics.*
London: Macmillan.
———. 1971. *Money, Trade and International Relations.* London: Macmillan.
———. 1979. *Against Inflation.* London:
Macmillan.

Robertson, Dennis Holme (1890–1963)

Dennis Holme Robertson, whose work is now almost wholly neglected, was regarded for almost half a century as a leading authority on the business cycle. It is no exaggeration to say that Robertson contributed substantially more to an understanding of the causes and the course of cyclical instability than did Keynes himself. It is true that in the 1920s it was hard to distinguish between their contributions, as both acknowledged. Although Robertson was in opposition and isolation by the time the *General Theory* had appeared, the theories of the cycle then evolved by Keynes's followers owed much to Robertson.

In his first book, *A Study of Industrial Fluctuations,* Robertson held that—foreign trade apart—the chief cause of instability was the changing demand for capital goods reflecting replacement and innovation. Even in a nonmonetary economy, these shifts in the return on investment could, by altering the reward for working, cause variations in output. If decisions to produce were made cooperatively, the variations so induced might be socially acceptable. But if management alone determined the outcome, a slackening of work effort could be concentrated on an unfortunate minority of the unemployed. In his later work, this nonmonetary model dropped out of sight, but it has some resemblance to the intertemporal-substitution hypothesis developed by Lucas and Rapping and others in the new literature on real business-cycle theories.

In a money economy, the amplitude of fluctuations is increased, because fluctuations in the return on investment, which are inadequately matched by changes in the market rate of interest, induce a cumulative process of expansion or contraction. Or, in Wicksell's well-established terminology, the *natural* and the *market* rates of interest diverge, and total expenditure changes. Robertson conceded that an alteration in monetary policy could be a contributory, or even the decisive, factor at a cyclical turning point. But he maintained—as did Wicksell—that changes in the natural rate, not in the market rate, were the principal initiating impulse.

In *Banking Policy and the Price Level,* Robertson meticulously analyzed the concept of *forced saving* during an expansion; but the special terminology he then employed was never adopted by his colleagues and he himself abandoned it in the 1930s. In more familiar language, *forced saving* occurs during an expansion, because prices rise faster than wages with consequential increases in profits and in savings. Both Robertson and the Austrians believed that, after a lag, wages would catch up, squeezing profits—although it was not clear why, with rising costs, prices should not also rise still higher, unless the supply of active money had been restricted. However, as Keynes pointed out, the words "natural" and "forced" suggest that, initially, both the rate of interest and the propensity to save are somehow uniquely appropriate, and obscure the fact that either may vary with changes in income. Robertson, for his part, had already accepted (1934) that there is an indefinite number of "quasi-natural" rates or "expenditure-stabilizing" rates. The meaning of "forced saving" is ambiguous for the same reason.

The similarities and contrasts between Robertson's views and those of modern Monetarists are illuminating. Like the Monetarists, Robertson did not doubt the importance of monetary policy. But he differed in emphasizing changes in the velocity of circulation, although he did not believe that velocity could fall indefinitely and render monetary policy incapable of alleviating the long-term deflation that Keynes had predicted. Money mattered, but changes in monetary policy were not the primary cause of instability. Monetarists view the economy as inherently stable, with any observed instability coming from a mishandling of the money supply. Robertson regarded the economy as basically unstable with its instability intensified both by changes in the money stock and in its velocity. It follows that different assumptions were made about the scope for a rise in real output when expenditure is increased. Monetarists have predicted no more than a small and temporary effect on output, or no effect at all if expectations are rational. Robertson, like Keynes himself, would have agreed that nothing could be achieved by spending more at full employment. But with slack resources, the rise in real income would not be a mere flash in the pan. On the contrary, history showed that it was in this uneven cyclical way that economic progress has taken place.

Unfortunately, Robertson's prolonged debate with Keynes and the Keynesians over savings, investment, and the rate of interest diverted attention from his work on cycles, particularly his use of period analysis and his emphasis on time-lags. The only lag normally associated with his name is that between the receipt of income and its expenditure, but he also stressed that the lag between a rise in expenditure and a rise in output could conceal an impending fall in the rate of return when new equipment comes on stream. Overinvestment would then be fostered. In Robertson's theory—as in the later models of Kalecki and Kaldor—the errors caused by this gestation period are one explanation of the downturn. He could have gone on to develop a lagged model of the interactions of multiplier and accelerator, but disliked the misleading suggestion of precision such models convey. He was also critical of a multiplier that assumed a constant marginal propensity to consume and stressed the effect on savings of cyclical changes in the share of profits. He observed that increased business savings during an expansion would encourage additional investment, not just offset independently determined investment as the theory of the multiplier implied. An expansion might then be explosive rather than damped, until the monetary authorities brought it to an end. Subsequently, the increasing obsolescence of the capital stock, together with some credit relaxation, would promote recovery.

Although Robertson emphasized that different trade cycles have common features, he did not seek to discern, or to impose, a sharply drawn pattern as did Schumpeter in his *Business Cycles* (1939). On the contrary, he stressed the unique features of each cycle. The recurring theme, however, was that innovational investment comes in uneven bursts. Although instability was the price of progress, the booms were more inflationary and the depressions far deeper than was necessary. Like Keynes, Robertson was appalled by the "obscene waste" of mass unemployment and by the hardships of the unemployed. A social evil requiring treatment, involuntary unemployment could not be explained away by semantic adroitness in interpreting what "involuntary" means. In his first book, he recommended countercyclical variations in public investment and, in the 1920s, he feared that Keynes was unduly emphasizing monetary policy to the neglect of fiscal policy. But after World War II, believing that the swing in the opposite direction had gone too far, he stressed the role of monetary policy, which was at that time vigorously denied by Keynesians.

Robertson became deeply concerned by the danger of prolonged and accelerating inflation. When booms with rising prices had been followed by slumps with falling prices, some stability over the cycle could be retained. In a high-employment economy with no periods of falling prices, how could inflation be checked? As an official government adviser, Robertson doubted that an effective incomes policy could be devised, but concluded that it would be prudent to accept a slightly higher rate of unemployment than had been customary in the 1950s and 1960s—that is to say, a rise to 2 or 3 percent. Although this was well below Keynes's own tentative 5 percent, it was regarded by his critics as evidence of a disregard for humane considerations. This was an unfair criticism of someone whose concern for the disadvantaged had been the stimulus to his lifelong work on economic analysis and policy.

Thomas Wilson

See also AUSTRIAN THEORY OF BUSINESS CYCLES; FORCED SAVING; FRIEDMAN, MILTON; INTERTEMPORAL SUBSTITUTION; KALDOR, NICHOLAS; KALECKI, MICHAL; KEYNES, JOHN MAYNARD; LEADS AND LAGS; LOANABLE FUNDS DOCTRINE; MARSHALL, ALFRED; MONETARY DISEQUILIBRIUM THEORIES OF THE BUSINESS CYCLE; MONETARY POLICY; NATURAL RATE OF INTEREST; REAL BUSINESS-CYCLE THEORIES; SAMUELSON, PAUL ANTHONY; WICKSELL, JOHAN GUSTAV KNUT

Bibliography

Presley, J. R. 1979. *Robertsonian Economics: An Examination of the Work of Sir D. H. Robertson on Industrial Fluctuations.* New York: Holmes and Meier.

Robertson, D. H. [1915] 1948. *A Study of Industrial Fluctuations, an Enquiry into the So-called Cyclical Movements of Trade.* Reprint, with a new introduction. London: London School of Economics.

———. 1922. *Banking Policy and the Price Level: An Essay in the Theory of the Trade Cycle.* London: Staples Press.

———. [1934] 1940. "Industrial Fluctuations and the Natural Rate of Interest." Chap. 5 in *Essays in Monetary Theory.* London: P. S. King.

———. 1940. *Essays in Monetary Theory.* London: P. S. King.

———. 1952. *Utility and All That.* London: Allen and Unwin.

———. 1957–59. *Lectures on Economic Principles.* 3 vols. London: Staples Press.

———. 1966. *Essays in Money and Interest: Selected with a Memoir by John Hicks.* London: Collins Fontana Library.

Wilson, T. 1953. "Professor Robertson on Effective Demand and the Trade Cycle." *Economic Journal* 63:553–78.

———. 1980. "Robertson, Money, and Monetarism." *Journal of Economic Literature* 18:522–38.

Robinson, Joan Violet Maurice (1903–1983)

Joan Robinson of Cambridge University was known internationally for her path-breaking contributions to modern economic theory of the Keynesian and Post-Keynesian tradition, and for challenges to American mainstream teaching and to general-equilibrium analysis.

She was a member of the Cambridge "circus" which J. M. Keynes used as a sounding board while he was developing the *General Theory.* While the circus worked with Keynes through his *Treatise on Money,* Robinson wrote an article on "A Parable of Saving and Investment." Her article, "The Theory of Money and Output," suggested that the circus did at times get ahead of Keynes (Turner 1989, 52–53). Keynes and the circus were groping for a new relationship between saving and investment. While Keynes's earlier work agreed with the prevailing belief that saving preceded investment in a capitalist economy, they concluded that, instead, it was spending on investment that caused savings to be accumulated, because the investment spending, through a multiplier effect, increased the national income. Given the propensity to consume, savings were generated out of these increases in income.

Keynes's *General Theory,* for a time, eclipsed other business-cycle theories. Robinson saw its contribution as demonstrating (1) that the economy could be at equilibrium at less than full employment, and (2) that the appropriate public policy was to arrange for a level of investment that would move the economy toward full employment. This contrasted with other theories of the 1920s and 1930s which assumed that there was no involuntary unemployment, that business cycles were temporary deviations from a full-employment equilibrium, and that monetary measures were the only state action required to counter the Great Depression of the 1930s.

Robinson ([1936] 1980) refined the Keynesian notion of involuntary unemployment, whereby a rise in expenditures provides additional jobs, by developing the concept of disguised unemployment. Disguised unemployment exists wherever dismissed workers take up employment that is less productive than their regular employment. Robinson further differentiated disguised unemployment from Marxian nonemployment or Third World unemployment, neither of which could be cured merely by an increase in effective demand (Robinson and Eatwell 1973, 327–28). She concluded that unemployment associated with trade cycles was of two sorts—the Keynesian insufficiency of effective demand where existing capital was not fully used and the Marxian nonemployment where workers would not find jobs even if all existing industrial capacity were fully utilized.

Robinson promoted the acceptance of Keynes's theory through her *Introduction to the Theory of Employment* and extended her analysis in her *Essays in the Theory of Employment.* Her "Concept of Hoarding" and her comments on R. G. Hawtrey's correspondence with Keynes (Keynes 1973, 13:612–13, 14:34–35) illustrate this early effort to explain and apply the *General Theory.*

While Robinson's seminal book, *The Economics of Imperfect Competition* (1934) was not worked into the *General Theory* by Keynes, it clearly challenged business-cycle models of any vintage that assume pure competition, market clearing, and that there is always some wage rate at which full employment is guaranteed. Instead, in her Post-Keynesian work, Robinson distinguished between the long- and short-period demand for labor. The amount of employment at any moment is a function of the number of machines in existence and their level of utilization (governed by the state of effective demand and not by bargaining over real wages). The long period, or rate of accumulation depends on investments by firms (and not the savings of households) (Robinson 1937b, 118–19). Robinson also adopted Michal Kalecki's application of the degree of monopoly and its effect on price mark-ups to remedy the Keynesian neglect of imperfect competition.

Robinson's other Post-Keynesian work involved her effort to introduce dynamics into Keynesian economics and is harmonious not only with the work of Kalecki, but also that of R. H. Kahn, N. Kaldor, and R. Harrod. Like Kalecki and Kaldor, she was concerned with the evolution of an economic system through time, disregarding any idea that the system would reach some equilibrium position. Her books *The Accumulation of Capital* and *Essays in the Theory of Economic Growth* substituted growth patterns for so-called equilibrium levels. For Robinson, business fluctuations would occur around the long-term trend of capital accumulation in a private-enterprise economy (1956, 208–18). She introduced two additional ideas valuable to cycle analysis: (1) that capital accumulation involves capital destruction, since in part it must be a substitution process (Goodwin 1982); and (2) that an "inflation barrier" to reaching full employment may be created by demands of workers for a certain standard of living (1956, 48–50, 356).

Robinson's mature view of business cycles, in which uncertainty and expectations account for turning points and fluctuations in trade, is summarized in a sophisticated textbook, *An Introduction to Modern Economics* (written with John Eatwell). In an appendix entitled "Instability" (119–26), Robinson and Eatwell present a Post-Keynesian "story" of the two-sided relation between investment and income in a private-enterprise society. Expectations determine the level of private investment and (with uncertainty) are the source of short-run instability and thus fluctuations. Some have labeled this a reliance on "animal spirits," but it is far more complex than that. A rise in the rate of investment initiates a Keynesian multiplier effect on employment and income and in turn an accelerator effect on investment, possibly generating a boom to be followed by a slump. Both uncertainty and expectations are thus introduced through the investment decisions made by entrepreneurs. This places

Robinson with those who rely on endogenous as well as exogenous shocks to explain business fluctuations in a private-enterprise society.

Robinson considered business cycles in historical as distinguished from equilibrium terms. For example, her analysis of "stagflation" (1980) includes a discussion of how prices are set in various types of markets, an approach pursued in the work of A. M. Okun.

Finally, Robinson insisted that theorists distinguish between calendar time in the ordinary sense and logical time employed in mathematical models. She became convinced that stringent mathematical models based on equilibrium analysis were inapplicable to the analysis of real-world business cycles (Robinson [1974] 1978).

Marjorie S. Turner

See also CAPITAL GOODS; HARROD, ROY FORBES; KALDOR, NICHOLAS; KALECKI, MICHAL; KEYNES, JOHN MAYNARD; POST-KEYNESIAN BUSINESS-CYCLE THEORY

Bibliography
Goodwin, R. M. 1982. *Essays in Economic Dynamics*. London: Macmillan.
Keynes, J. M. 1973. *The Collected Writings of John Maynard Keynes*. Vols. 13–14. *The General Theory and After. Parts 1 and 2*, edited by D. M. Moggeridge. London: Macmillan.
Rima, I., ed. 1991. *The Joan Robinson Legacy*. Armonk, N.Y.: M. E. Sharpe.
Robinson, J. 1933. "A Parable on Saving and Investment." *Economica* 39:75–84.
———. [1933] 1978. "The Theory of Money and Output." Chap. 3 in *Contributions to Modern Economics*. New York: Academic Press.
———. [1936] 1980. "Disguised Unemployment." Chap. 21 in *Collected Economic Papers*. Vol. 4. Cambridge: MIT Press.
———. 1937a. *Introduction to the Theory of Employment*. London: Macmillan.
———. 1937b. *Essays in the Theory of Employment*. Oxford: Basil Blackwell.
———. [1938] 1978. "The Concept of Hoarding." Chap. 12 in *Contributions to Modern Economics*. New York: Academic Press.
———. 1956. *The Accumulation of Capital*. Homewood, Ill.: Irwin.
———. 1963. *Essays in the Theory of Economic Growth*. London: Macmillan.

———. [1974] 1978. "History versus Equilibrium." Chap. 12 in *Contributions to Modern Economics*. New York: Academic Press.

———. 1980a. *Collected Economic Papers*. 5 vols. Cambridge: MIT Press.

———. 1980b. "Stagflation." Chap. 3 in *What are the Questions? and Other Essays*. Armonk, N.Y.: M. E. Sharpe.

Robinson, J. and J. Eatwell. 1973. *An Introduction to Modern Economics*. Maidenhead, England: McGraw-Hill.

Turner, M. S. 1989. *Joan Robinson and the Americans*. Armonk, N.Y.: M. E. Sharpe.

Röpke, Wilhelm (1899–1966)

Wilhelm Röpke, an extraordinarily prolific and multi-faceted scholar, established his reputation as a leading German business-cycle theorist when he published his first book on business cycles at the age of twenty-three. His reputation was such that in 1931, he was appointed to the Brauns Committee to investigate unemployment. His work on business cycles continued during the 1920s and 1930s. His opposition to Hitler led him into exile in 1934. He found refuge for a time in Turkey before settling in Switzerland in 1938. Although he remained in Switzerland after the war, he strongly influenced the policies of Ludwig Erhard, the West German finance minister and architect of the German "social market economy."

Röpke's theory of the cycle synthesized elements borrowed from a number of theories. Like many real-cycle theorists such as Spiethoff and Schumpeter, and monetary-cycle theorists such as Mises and Hayek, Röpke viewed the crisis and the ensuing depression as an inevitable reaction to, and corrective for, the preceding boom. The boom, in Röpke's view, was driven by a high level of investment that generated rapid increases in income and, via an accelerator mechanism, still more investment. The high levels of investment could generally not be financed by voluntary savings, so Röpke invoked a Mises-Hayek forced-savings mechanism operating through an expansion of bank credit. However, Röpke argued that the crisis was brought on by a rapid decline in investment caused by the operation of the accelerator mechanism rather than, as the Austrians maintained, by a sudden shortage of capital when the banking system ceased to generate further forced saving.

Röpke also differed with the Austrians on the appropriate policy to be followed in a depression. In the crisis of 1931, for example, Röpke broke with strict Austrian orthodoxy by opposing the deflationary policy adopted by Chancellor Brüning to protect the gold standard. Röpke distinguished between the crisis and initial contraction, which he felt were necessary to purge, as it were, the economy from the excesses of the preceding boom and a secondary deflation that could take hold and cause a cumulative contraction. Indeed in the section of the Brauns Commission's Report that was largely authored by Röpke, he employed a word (*initialzündung*) that may correctly be translated as "pump-priming" (Röpke 1931) and called for precisely the government activism that was advocated by those British and American economists known as "pump-primers."

Initially, Röpke conceded (1936b, 334–35) that the Keynesian theory was well suited to the analysis of the secondary deflation, but insisted that it was not helpful in understanding the onset of a crisis. However, after the war he came to regard Keynes's influence as baneful. Keynes, he believed, had not contented himself with calling for the extraordinary measures that Röpke agreed had been necessary in the desperate situation of the early 1930s, but had pushed the theory derived from that special situation into a "general theory" that rejected any but macroeconomic thinking (Röpke 1959, 172).

Röpke also made an interesting contribution (1936b) to the study of cycles under a socialist or centrally planned economy. He argued that the dislocations that manifested themselves in cycles in capitalist economies owing to high levels of investment were unlikely to be avoided in a socialist one. If *monetary forced savings* was necessary to achieve high investment in capitalist economies, then a form of *authoritarian forced savings* would be just as necessary in a socialist one. Nor was there any reason to believe the real effects of the accelerator mechanism would be absent in a socialist economy even if its direct manifestation was somewhat different from its manifestation in a capitalist economy.

While Röpke's theoretical contributions to business-cycle analysis may not have been as original or as technically impressive as those of some of his contemporaries, he still said a great deal that was courageous, correct, and wise.

David Glasner
Michael Hudson

See also ACCELERATION PRINCIPLE; AUSTRIAN THEORY OF BUSINESS CYCLES; BUSINESS CYCLES IN SOCIALIST ECONOMIES; FORCED SAVING; LACHMANN, LUDWIG MAURITS; PUMP-PRIMING

Bibliography

Boarman, P. T. 1966. "Wilhelm Röpke." *German Economic Review* 4:149–52.

Ellis, H. 1934. *German Monetary Theory.* Cambridge: Harvard Univ. Press.

Hudson, M. 1985. "German Economists and the Great Depression 1929–33." *History of Political Economy* 17:35–50.

Röpke, W. 1931. "Praktische Konjunkturpolitik: Die Arbeit der Brauns-Kommission." *Wetlwirtschaftliches Archiv* 34:423–64.

———. 1933. "Trends in German Business Cycle Policy." *Economic Journal* 43:427–41.

———. 1936a. *Crises and Cycles.* London: William Hodge.

———. 1936b. "Socialism, Planning, and the Business Cycle." *Journal of Political Economy* 44:318–38.

———. 1959. "Keynes and the Revolution in Economics." Chap. 11 in *Against the Tide.* Chicago: Regnery.

Rostow, Walt Whitman (1916–)

Born in New York City, Rostow attended Balliol College, Oxford, England, from 1936 to 1938 as a Rhodes Scholar and received his Ph.D. from Yale University in 1940. He has taught at Columbia University, Oxford University, Cambridge University, MIT, and is now professor emeritus at the University of Texas. Besides teaching, Rostow served in the State Department and was Special Assistant to the President for National Security Affairs for Presidents Kennedy and Johnson.

The genesis of Rostow's contribution to the theory of business cycles can be found in his *British Economy of the Nineteenth Century: Essays.* Here he identified the first modern business cycle as having occurred during the British economic expansion that began in 1783 and peaked in 1792. Business fluctuations had previously been caused by harvests and war. However, the latter part of the eighteenth century saw a major expansion in long-term capital investment—a prominent source of modern business cycles. Rostow defined a major cycle as one having full employment at its peak, with long-term investment commitments occurring in the latter stages. In minor cycles, a limited general expansion gives way to depression before full employment is reached. Using these classifications, Rostow identified and analyzed twenty-four cycles in the British economy over a period of 126 years. He provided further support for his theories with extensive data contained in *The Growth and Fluctuation of the British Economy, 1790–1850,* co-authored with Arthur Gayer and Anna Schwartz.

In later writings, Rostow emphasized the link between economic growth and business cycles, with the actual process of growth taking the form of a succession of cycles. In each cycle, investment exploits short-term profit opportunities in individual sectors caused by the long-run pressure of growth on resources. After exploiting those opportunities, investment drops, which then triggers a general downward movement in employment and income. He noted that the difference between his view of the business cycle and those of others lay in his characterization of the upper-turning point of the cycle. Rather than perceiving investment as strictly governed by the requirements of growth, Rostow argued that in the latter stages of a boom, investors simply revise their judgments about the appropriateness of capacity expansion in the particular sectors that led the boom. Investors in other sectors then respond accordingly. This could mean that downturns might be "unnecessary" since not all investments in all sectors require identical reassessments. Therefore, for such cycles to be controlled, an appropriate level of aggregate outlays and an appropriate composition of new investment must be maintained. Rostow emphasized the importance of rational long-run, rather than short-run, assessments of profitability to avoid follow-the-leader investment policies. Using his unbalanced growth and sectoral analyses, Rostow evaluated business cycles throughout the Western world from the 1700s through the 1970s in his book, *The World Economy: History and Prospect.*

Rostow also studied the role of money in business cycles, questioning whether the gradual tightening of money markets and rising interest rates late in an expansion actually played a decisive part in the downturn. Rising interest rates could affect both costs and entrepreneurial expectations, which would reduce expected returns and discourage investment. But he argued that if confidence is not badly

R

shaken, the credit supply in the short term is a weaker constraint on economic activity than are other factors of production. This is shown by the tendency of interest rates to fall in downswings, because of falling output, prices, and money wages. However, fluctuations of the short-term credit supply provide merely a necessary, not a sufficient, condition for business cycles to occur.

Relying on this theoretical framework and using data on business cycles from 1815 to 1914, Rostow advanced six propositions regarding the relationship between money and business cycles:

1. When neither the money stock nor money income is fixed, factors affecting costs and supply become directly relevant to price-level analysis.
2. Since the price level affects productivity, the rate of increase in output cannot be treated as exogenous with respect to the price level.
3. Changes in the money stock during business cycles originate from the demand for money, except during "deep" cyclical declines.
4. Historically, increased gold production and output occur along with an increase in the demand for money, thereby lessening its deflationary impact.
5. The concentration of large price increases in a relatively few years can make the analysis of broad price trends misleading unless it is related to what actually occurred during the periods encompassing those trends.
6. Because the monetary system interacts closely with real factors, monetary analysis cannot by itself explain price movements.

These propositions led Rostow to minimize the role of the quantity theory of money in business-cycle analysis, because it does not account for changes in technology, industrial capacity, infrastructure, and the supply of raw materials, all of which are critical to understanding long-term trends and business cycles.

Rostow extended the link between sectoral analysis and business cycles by using it as a basis for his stage theory of economic growth. While business cycles do not figure explicitly in Rostow's analysis of the stages of economic growth, the shift of investment between sectors also played a compelling role in his explanation of the growth process.

Dianne C. Betts

See also ENDOGENOUS AND EXOGENOUS MONEY; KONDRATIEFF, NIKOLAI DMITRIYEVICH; KONDRATIEFF CYCLES; LONG-WAVE THEORIES; MONEY-INCOME CAUSALITY; SCHWARTZ, ANNA JACOBSON

Bibliography

Gayer, A. D., W. W. Rostow, and A. J. Schwartz. 1953. *The Growth and Fluctuation of the British Economy 1790–1850: An Historical, Statistical and Theoretical Study of Britain's Economic Development.* 2 vols. Oxford: Clarendon Press.

Gustafsson, B. G. 1961. "Rostow, Marx and the Theory of Economic Growth." *Science and Society* 25:229–44.

Mason, E. S. 1982. "Stages of Economic Growth Revisited." In *Economics in the Long View: Essays in Honour of W. W. Rostow.* 3 vols. Edited by C. P. Kindleberger and G. Ditella, 1:116–40. London: Macmillan.

Rostow, W. W. [1941] 1948. "Business Cycles, Harvests, and Politics: 1790–1850." Chap. 5 in *British Economy of the Nineteenth Century.* Oxford: Clarendon Press.

———. [1940] 1948. "Explanations of the Great Depression 1873–96: An Historian's View of Modern Monetary Theory." Chap. 7 in *British Economy of the Nineteenth Century.* Oxford: Clarendon Press.

———. 1948. *British Economy of the Nineteenth Century: Essays.* Oxford: Clarendon Press.

———. 1952. *The Process of Economic Growth.* New York: Norton.

———. 1955. "Investment and the Great Depression." *Economic History Review* 8:136–38.

———. 1960a. "The Problem of Achieving and Maintaining a High Rate of Economic Growth: A Historian's View." *American Economic Review* 50:106–18.

———. 1960b. *The Stages of Economic Growth: A Non-Communist Manifesto.* Cambridge: Cambridge Univ. Press.

———. 1963. *The Economics of Take-off Into Sustained Growth.* London: Macmillan.

———. 1975. "Kondratieff, Schumpeter, and Kuznets: Trend Periods Revisited." *Journal of Economic History* 35:719–53.

———. 1978. *The World Economy: History and Prospect.* Austin: Univ. of Texas Press.

———. 1980. *Why the Poor Get Richer and the Rich Slow Down: Essays in the Marshallian Long Period.* Austin: Univ. of Texas Press.

———. 1990. *Theorists of Growth from David Hume to the Present.* London: Oxford Univ. Press.

Rostow, W. W. and M. Kennedy. 1979. "A Simple Model of the Kondratieff Cycle." In *Research in Economic History: A Research Annual.* Vol. 4. Edited by P. Udeling, 1–36. Greenwich, Conn.: JAI Press.

Turner, C. B. 1965. "The Soviet Economists on Rostow." *The South Atlantic Quarterly* 44:216–28.

Rueff, Jacques (1896–1978)

The French economist Jacques Rueff served in several government positions and was professor at the Institut de statistique at the University of Paris and at the Ecole libre de sciences politiques. He wrote extensively on monetary theory, methodology, and social philosophy. He was famous for his support of the gold standard and his oppositon to Keynes's theory of unemployment. His collected works have been reassembled and published in French.

The son of a physician who gave him a strong education in the sciences and ethics, Rueff studied at the Ecole Polytechnique. As a high civil servant, he served as a financial adviser at the French embassy in London (1930–33), a deputy director of the Treasury (1934–39), a member of the military mission for German and Austrian affairs (1944–52), a member of the European Court of Justice in Luxemburg (1952–62), and a personal adviser to President de Gaulle, designing the successful "stabilization program" of 1958.

Rueff gained recognition with two early articles (1925, 1931) in which he argued that there is a strong relation between the rate of unemployment and the real wage. Attributing high unemployment in Great Britain in the 1920s to excessive unemployment benefits, he initiated a vigorous public discussion of unemployment. Rueff's analysis was supported a half-century later by an important empirical study of British unemployment in the interwar period (Benjamin and Kochin 1979).

Accordingly, Rueff rejected Keynes's assertion that unemployment results from insufficient aggregate demand, and insisted that basic price theory be used to explain the workings of the labor market. If there is an excess supply of labor, a reduction in real wages would restore full employment. However, rigidities in the labor market, such as high unemployment benefits, and powerful trade unions, can prevent this adjustment from occurring.

According to Rueff, the notion of inadequate aggregate demand is meaningless, as is the concept of excessive savings. "Contrary to Keynes's view, [unemployment] does not result from an insufficiency of income. Income is never insufficient to absorb existing production, for, apart from special circumstances . . . it is engendered by this production and its amount at every period is identically equal to the value of this production" (Rueff 1947, 361). Specifically, he blamed Keynes for thinking that "saving is demanding nothing."

Rueff conceded that temporary situations of unemployment could exist, but he rejected the idea of permanent *equilibrium* unemployment. Consider the case in which the quantity of money is decreasing. "If there is really underemployment," Rueff (1947, 346) argued, "it is not that certain workers can do more work, but that, under the conditions offered by the market, they *wish* to do more work." And they want to work more only to be able to get "something." If they are not demanding consumption or investment goods, they are demanding money. To get money they offer goods and services or assets. The real-balance effect and the changes in the supply of money and in the rate of interest are the main adjustment mechanisms. Thus, an apparent excess supply of commodities (interpreted as a situation of insufficient aggregate demand) cannot last for long, except if there are obstacles to the working of the price mechanism or the mobility of productive factors. This is to say that unemployment is not due to a lack of aggregate demand, but to institutional rigidities that prevent the adjustment of the real wage rate and the quantity of money.

Rueff challenged Keynes's assumption of a fixed—or policy determined—quantity of money and, therefore, his emphasis on the variations of the interest rate in adjusting to an excess demand for or supply of money. Rueff argued that the quantity of money adjusts to the demand for money, both via the real-balance effect and via an endogenous change in the nominal money supply.

The solution to unemployment is therefore not found in creating additional monetary purchasing power, but in improving the working of the price mechanism. By manipulating the quantity of money, the monetary authorities simply bring about successive waves of inflation and deflation. To avoid such a discretionary process, Rueff advocated restoring the gold standard as a constraint on the power to create money. He described the self-correcting properties of such a system in detail (offering arguments on the role of arbitrage similar to those developed in the monetary approach to the balance of payments) and argued against the disequilibrating consequences of unconstrained money production whenever currencies are not convertible into gold.

One finds in the work of Rueff a deepening of the classical tradition, an explanation of the illusions of inflation (along lines which, in some sense, are close to those of the Austrian theory of the business cycle), and a thoughtful interpretation of the main economic events of the twentieth century.

Pascal Salin

Bibliography

Benjamin, D. K. and L. A. Kochin. 1979. "Searching for an Explanation of Unemployment in Interwar Britain." *Journal of Political Economy* 87:441–78.

Rueff, J. 1925. "Les Variations du chômage en Angleterre." *Revue politique et parliamentaire* 125:425–36.

———. 1931. "L'assurance-chômage: cause du chômage permanent." *Revue d'économie politique* 45:211–41.

———. 1947. "The Fallacies of Lord Keynes's General Theory." *Quarterly Journal of Economics* 62:343–67.

———. 1977–81. *Oeuvres complètes.* 6 vols. Paris: Plon.

Samuelson, Paul Anthony (1913–)

Widely noted for his contributions to a vast array of topics in both the public-policy and the technical literatures, and especially for his work in mathematical economics and international trade, Paul Sameulson received the Nobel Memorial Prize in 1970 for work that raised the level and rigor of scientific analysis in economic theory.

Through his extensive academic writings, and most especially his 1947 *Foundations of Economic Analysis*, Samuelson greatly influenced the character of later theorizing in the discipline, including theorizing about business cycles, shifting it towards more formal mathematical modeling and greater statistical precision.

Samuelson's primary contribution to the theoretical literature on business cycles is his celebrated 1939 article "Interactions Between the Multiplier Analysis and the Principle of Acceleration," which grew out of a model explored by Alvin Hansen. The article explored the theoretical characteristics of a highly simplified multiplier-accelerator model.

The model contains two variables. One is the slope of the aggregate consumption function, the marginal propensity to consume c, from which the multiplier k is derived via the formula

$$k = 1/(1 - c). \qquad (1)$$

The other variable is the marginal capital-output ratio, commonly called the accelerator. The principle of multiplier-accelerator interaction, in which an autonomous increase in spending increases income and consumption spending in subsequent periods (the multiplier effect), which in turn causes investment spending to grow (the accelerator effect), which in turn causes additional increases in consumption

spending and investment outlays, and so on, was a concept already well known to economists at the time of Samuelson's writing. Samuelson's contribution was to provide a formal model which was elegantly simple, produced useful conclusions, and was highly amenable to further enhancement and refinement.

Following Keynes's *General Theory*, Samuelson assumed consumption to be linearly related to income. But, following D. H. Robertson, instead of Keynes, he assumed that consumption lags income by one period. Samuelson further assumed that needed capital could, and would, be created without limit, while unneeded or surplus capital could, and would, be used up instantly.

Under these restrictive assumptions, Samuelson showed that the system collapses to a second-order difference equation of the form:

$$Y_t = c(1 + b)Y_{t-1} - bcY_{t-2} + G/(1 - c), \qquad (2)$$

where b is the accelerator, G is the level of government spending, and Y is income. Whether an economic system that is disturbed by a permanent shift in autonomous spending, (A) moves smoothly towards a new stable equilibrium, (B) undergoes gradually dampened oscillations leading to a new equilibrium, (B-C boundary) undergoes perpetual harmonic oscillation, (C) undergoes perpetual oscillation with growing cyclic amplitude, or (D) moves exponentially to zero or infinite output, depends on the assumed values of the marginal propensity to consume (α in his model) from which the multiplier is derived and the capital-output ratio (β in his model) from which the accelerator is derived. Schematically, the stability characteristics (Regions A, B, C and D) are as shown in Figure 1.

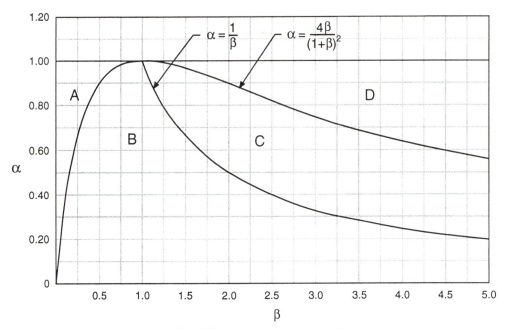

Figure 1. *Boundaries of regions yielding different qualitative behavior of national income.*

An interesting conclusion of the model, as Samuelson pointed out, is that if one assumes, for the United States, a reasonable real-world value for the multiplier of 2.5 to 3.0, and a reasonable real-world value for the accelerator of 1.0 to 2.0, then the U.S. economy would be on the boundary of stability. That is, its response to a shift in autonomous spending such as a change in the size of the federal deficit, would either be long-lasting economic oscillations that continued for a long period that only gradually diminished in intensity, or else perpetual oscillation with gradually increasing intensity. Thus, policymakers should be cautious about delaying a response to any major shock to the economic system, because it lacks a strong tendency towards stable equilibrium. The Samuelson model thus supported an activist monetary and fiscal policy.

Both the simplicity and the limitations of the Samuelson model have made its imitation with refinement a highly popular activity among business-cycle theorists. Among the more notable early intellectual descendants of the model, four may be mentioned.

John R. Hicks (1950) adjusted the model to reflect the inability of real economies either to expand to infinity or to collapse to zero, and their tendency to grow over time. In the Hicksian model, an economy's growth path has a ceiling reflecting bottlenecks of supply and resource constraints, and a floor resulting from the autonomous components (i.e., independent of the level of income) in government, investment, and private consumption spending. Both the ceiling and the floor rise over time due to economic growth. Hence a system that is inherently unstable (Samuelson's C or D regions) becomes stable because of the ceiling and floor. Hicks relied on an asymmetric accelerator [equations (3a) and (3b)] in which κ represents the stock of capital, δ the rate of physical depreciation of the capital stock, and I investment.

$$I_t = bc(Y_t - Y_{t-1}), \text{ for } Y_t > Y_{t-1} \qquad (3a)$$

$$I_t = -\delta \kappa_{t-1}, \text{ for } Y_t < Y_{t-1} \qquad (3b)$$

Thus, there is unidirectional convergence to the floor. In this model, a cumulative increase in economic activity is eventually halted by capacity constraints. Once growth is interrupted by capacity limits, the economy begins, with a lag, a cumulative contraction that is halted when the floor on economic activity is encountered.

Richard M. Goodwin ([1951] 1982) dealt with the explode-to-infinity/collapse-to-zero problem differently. Goodwin assumed a nonlinear multiplier and accelerator. Thus, if an economy were to expand (contract) greatly, and a turning point were approached, the value of the multiplier would begin to decline as would that of the accelerator. In this way, the economy's rate of growth (collapse) would begin to slow as economic turning points (ceiling and floors in the Hicksian model) were approached.

Nicholas Kaldor (1952) adopted a version of the accelerator derived from that of Hollis Chenery in which the actual and desired sizes of the capital stock might differ. In Kaldor, too, the accelerator becomes nonlinear at the turning points. But the nonlinearity results from changes in investment plans by business when the desired capital stock diverges from the actual.

The growth models of Roy Harrod (1939) and Evsey Domar (1947) represent still another application of the Samuelson Interaction Model. The assumptions of both models (which are often considered jointly as the Harrod-Domar growth model) about the conditions necessary for smooth economic growth reflect an implicit understanding of the cycle-inducing, growth-interrupting, properties of multiplier-accelerator interaction.

More recently, on Hansen's centennial, Samuelson (1988) gave a reprise of the exponential-growth and cycle dynamics of the accelerator-multiplier, while giving just credit to the Keynes-Hansen original innovations. Samuelson extended the model to incorporate Modigliani's life-cycle-saving model and synthesized the diverse cycle analyses of Harrod, Hicks, Goodwin, and Kaldor.

The Samuelson interaction model is fundamental to much of our theoretical and applied thinking about business cycles. The vast majority of all formal economic forecasting now incorporate a multiplier-accelerator relationship that owes a clear debt to Samuelson's work. The same could be said of most nonrational-expectations cycle models.

Charles E. Rockwood

See also ACCELERATION PRINCIPLE; CEILINGS AND FLOORS; GOODWIN, RICHARD MURPHEY; HANSEN, ALVIN HARVEY; HARROD, ROY FORBES; HICKS, JOHN RICHARD; KALDOR, NICHOLAS; LUNDBERG, ERIK FILIP; MULTIPLIER; NONLINEAR BUSINESS-CYCLE THEORIES; OKUN, ARTHUR M.; ROBERTSON, DENNIS HOLME; STOCKHOLM SCHOOL

Bibliography

Domar, E. D. 1947. "Expansion and Employment." *American Economic Review* 37:34–55.

Goodwin, R. M. [1951] 1982. "The Nonlinear Accelerator and the Persistence of Business Cycles." Chap. 6 in *Essays in Economic Dynamics*. London: Macmillan.

Harrod, R. F. 1939. "An Essay in Dynamic Theory." *Economic Journal* 49:14–33.

Hicks, J. R. 1950. *The Trade Cycle*. Oxford: Clarendon Press.

Kaldor, N. 1952. "A Model of the Trade Cycle." *Journal of Political Economy* 60:1–24.

Samuelson, P. A. [1939a] 1966. "Interactions Between the Multiplier Analysis and the Principle of Acceleration." Chap. 82 in *The Collected Scientific Papers of Paul A. Samuelson*. Vol. 2. Cambridge: MIT Press.

———. [1939b] 1966. "A Synthesis of the Principle of Acceleration and the Principle of the Multiplier." Chap. 83 in *The Collected Scientific Papers of Paul A. Samuelson*. Vol. 2. Cambridge: MIT Press.

———. 1947. *Foundations of Economic Analysis*. Cambridge: Harvard Univ. Press.

———. 1988. "The Keynes-Hansen-Samuelson Multiplier-Accelerator Model of Secular Stagnation." *Japan and the World Economy,* October, 3–19.

Saving Equals Investment

Saving is income not spent on current consumption. Investment is expenditure made today with the intention of increasing income in the future. Several theories of the business cycle have been couched in terms of the balance between saving and investment in the aggregate.

The balance between saving and investment is of interest only if the two are indeed distinct. Whether they are or not depends on the definition of income. In a barter economy—or in the "as if" barter economy of value theory—the income to be spent in a given period is taken to be the output of the same period. In this case, saving (income not spent on consumption) is identically equal to investment (output not consumed). However, in a monetary economy, saving and investment need not be equal. Monetary theories generally define the money income of a period as the sales receipts of the preceding period: in a monetary economy, goods must be sold for money before that money can be used to purchase other goods.

Money income received by households may either be spent, lent to others, or hoarded (held indefinitely). Thus, saving equals lending plus hoarding ($S = L + H$). This household lending is one source of finance for investment, but it is not the only source. Investment may be financed too by new bank credit created by monetary expansion. Investment expenditure, therefore, equals lending plus money creation ($I = L + DM$). Under this set of definitions, saving equals investment if and only if hoarding and money creation offset one another ($I = S - H + DM$); in the simplest case, both hoarding and money creation are zero.

Saving may exceed investment either because of hoarding—an increase in the quantity of money held as an asset—or because of monetary contraction. When saving exceeds investment, expenditure is less than money income (effective demand is deficient), exerting a deflationary pressure on the economy. If prices are flexible, they will fall. If they are not, output and employment will fall.

Investment may exceed saving either because of dishoarding—a decrease in the quantity of money held as an asset—or because of monetary expansion. When investment exceeds saving, expenditure is greater than money income (effective demand is excessive), exerting an inflationary pressure on the economy. If prices are flexible, they will rise. Rising prices cause *forced saving*: a decrease in households' purchasing power frees resources for investment beyond those freed by households' voluntary saving. If prices are not flexible, output and employment will increase (or there will be rationing).

If saving equals investment, then expenditure equals income. The economy is in equilibrium in the sense that there is no tendency for money income to rise or fall. This concept of equilibrium, distinct from an equilibrium of relative prices, has been called *monetary equilibrium*.

The Physiocrats were the first to suggest that excessive saving might be an obstacle to economic equilibrium. Classical economists dismissed these concerns, arguing that income not consumed must nonetheless be spent, because it must be lent to finance investment. They ruled out hoarding on the grounds that no rational man would hoard his money when he could lend it at interest.

The possible divergence of saving and investment reappeared in the work of Wicksell.

Wicksell distinguished between a *market rate of interest* and a *natural rate*. The market rate is the rate actually observed in the market for loanable funds: it is the rate at which the supply of loanable funds (lending by households, $S - H$, plus new bank credit, DM) equals the demand (planned investment, I). The natural rate is the interest rate that would make saving equal investment—the rate consistent with monetary equilibrium. The market rate need not equal the natural rate in the short run: rising prices are a sign the market rate is below the natural rate; falling prices, a sign the market rate is above the natural rate. Unnecessary economic fluctuations can be avoided if the central bank manipulates the market rate, through its power to control DM, to track the natural rate as closely as possible. That is, the central bank should cause the market rate to rise if prices are rising and to fall if prices are falling.

The equality or inequality of saving and investment played a prominent role too in the work of Keynes. In the *Treatise* ([1930] 1971), Keynes's treatment differed little from Wicksell's, or from those of contemporaries such as Robertson. Business fluctuations were seen as short-run deviations from equilibrium caused by an imbalance of saving and investment.

In the *General Theory* ([1936] 1973), however, Keynes departed radically from this view of fluctuations. Fluctuations were now seen as movements *of* an equilibrium rather than movements *about* an equilibrium. (The new notion of equilibrium no longer implied full employment: *unemployment equilibrium* was now possible.) In equilibrium, saving and investment are equal and it is their equality that determines the level of income. Investment, relatively insensitive to the interest rate, depends mainly on business expectations. Saving depends mainly on income. When desired investment changes, saving changes with it. The equality of saving and investment is maintained, not by changes in the interest rate, but by changes in the level of income through the multiplier process. Since this theory left the interest rate undetermined, Keynes suggested a new theory of the interest rate based on the idea of liquidity preference.

Recent work has resurrected the Wicksellian loanable funds theory and the notion that saving and investment can differ. A class of formal models, based on the finance or cash-in-advance constraint, gives expression to these ideas.

Meir Kohn

See also AUSTRIAN THEORY OF BUSINESS
CYCLES; FORCED SAVING; HAYEK, FRIEDRICH
AUGUST [VON]; KEYNES, JOHN MAYNARD;
MISES, LUDWIG EDLER VON; NATURAL RATE
OF INTEREST; OVERINVESTMENT THEORIES
OF BUSINESS CYCLES; ROBERTSON, DENNIS
HOLME; WICKSELL, JOHAN GUSTAV KNUT

Bibliography

Haberler, G. 1962. *Prosperity and Depression.* 4th rev. ed. Cambridge: Harvard Univ. Press.

Keynes, J. M. [1930] 1971. *A Treatise on Money.* Vols. 5 and 6 of *The Collected Writings of John Maynard Keynes.* London: Macmillan.

———. [1936] 1973. *The General Theory of Employment, Interest, and Money.* Vol. 7 of *The Collected Writings of John Maynard Keynes.* London: Macmillan.

Kohn, Meir. 1981. "A Loanable Funds Theory of Unemployment and Monetary Disequilibrium." *American Economic Review* 71:859–79.

———. 1986. "Monetary Analysis, the Equilibrium Method, and Keynes' 'General Theory.'" *Journal of Political Economy* 94:1191–1224.

———. 1988. "The Finance Constraint Theory of Money: A Progress Report." Dept. of Economics, Dartmouth College, October.

Leijonhufvud, A. 1981. "The Wicksell Connection: Variations on a Theme." Chap. 7 in *Information and Coordination.* New York: Oxford Univ. Press.

Lutz, F. A. [1938] 1951. "The Outcome of the Saving-Investment Discussion." In *Readings in Business Cycle Theory,* 131–57. Philadelphia: Blakiston.

Robertson, D. H. [1933] 1940. "Saving and Hoarding." Chap. 4 in *Essays in Monetary Theory.* London: Staples.

———. [1934] 1940. "Industrial Fluctuations and the Natural Rate of Interest." Chap. 5 in *Essays in Monetary Theory.* London: Staples.

Wicksell, K. [1906] 1935. *Lectures on Political Economy.* Vol. 2, *Money.* Translation. London: Routledge and Kegan Paul.

Say, Jean-Baptiste (1767–1832)

Jean-Baptiste Say was the son of a Lyons tradesman. Say's first publication, at age twenty-two, concerned freedom of the press. In 1799, Say

was nominated to Napoleon's *Tribunat* whose task was to ensure constitutionality of government actions. In 1803, the *Traité d'économie politique,* first edition, was published; Say was thirty-six.

By then, many previous supporters, Say among them, had been disillusioned with Napoleon. Say was dismissed from the *Tribunat,* and was only permitted to publish a revision of his treatise after Napoleon fell in 1814. In that year, the French government sent Say to England to study its vital economy, which he discussed in *De l'Angleterre et des Anglais.* Thereafter, Say dedicated himself to political economy—his avowed goal to make the subject accessible to everyone. He continued to rework the *Traité,* of which four more editions appeared.

In 1821, the government established a chair in industrial economics at the Conservatoire des Arts et Métiers, which Say held until his death. Say wrote one more major work, *Cours complet d'économie politique pratique* (1828–29) in which he tried, one last time, to ensure the accessibility of political economy to people in all walks of life.

Say and the Law of the Markets

Say was neither the originator of the Law of the Markets, nor one of its dogmatic adherents. Several discussions suggesting the essence of "Say's Law" appeared well before J. B. Say first wrote about it. Its origins have been traced to Francis Hutcheson (1694–1746) and to the Physiocrat Mercier de la Rivière (1720–1794). However, apparently Adam Smith ([1776] 1976, 1:438–39), a student of Hutcheson's at Glasgow University, first enunciated the principle explicitly, and described its logic more clearly than it was initially done by Say. James Mill is often credited for full and prior formulation of the principle, as well as recognition of its origins in the *Wealth of Nations.*

Though the second edition of the *Traité* contains a full statement of the principle and an extensive discussion of its logic, even here Say's position was a bit heterodox. For example, he argued that an excess demand for money will be cleared up, not by a reduction in prices, which raises the real value of the cash supply, but via merchants' creation of money substitutes such as bills of exchange. Later, particularly in an exchange of letters with Malthus, he made concessions which all but modified the law out of existence, to Ricardo's understandable displeasure.

The issue of priority between Say and James Mill as systematic formulators of the law has been clouded by incidental complications. Such careful scholars as Sowell and Thweatt have been left in disagreement, the former categorically awarding priority to Say, the latter to Mill.

The Various Meanings of Say's Law
Say's Identity
In Say's own work, and to some degree that of James Mill, the discussion of Say's Law encompassed a complex of ideas, only one of which is the proposition "supply creates its own demand" now generally associated with the term. Most immediately, its original proponents argued (1) that *only production creates the purchasing power that underlies demand,* and (2) that *business depressions cannot be caused by an impossible "general glut," though it may conceivably result from oversupply of some limited set of goods.*

Since Say's Law was incorporated into mathematical economics by Lange (1944) it is generally interpreted as what Becker and Baumol ([1952] 1960) labelled "Say's Identity." This is the strong requirement that the sum of the values of all goods and services *excluding money* demanded at any time be *identical* to the sum of the values supplied. The identity is required to hold regardless of whether the economy happens to be in equilibrium in some or all markets. If Say's Identity holds, it may be possible for the demand for and supply of one or several commodities to be unequal, but a total imbalance in aggregate supply and demand is impossible. This strong requirement is also equivalent to the assertion that the demand for and supply of *money* must always be equal. That follows from the accounting tautology that Lange labelled "Walras's Law"—the observation that if the demand for x dollars worth of some commodities is to be effective, the demander must be offering to supply in exchange either x dollars in money or x dollars in some other commodities. Hence, Walras's Law asserts, the values of all items, including money, supplied in any period is necessarily equal to the total value demanded. Equality of money supply and money demand then follows by subtraction of the value of all items demanded (excluding money) from the value of all items demanded (including money) and the corresponding subtraction on the supply side.

The logic of Say's Identity is straightforward, though few, if any, economists would be willing to accept it today. The argument is that no persons really desire cash for its own sake. They want it only to buy commodities or as a means to earn still more wealth. If so, individuals will never accumulate more cash than the amounts needed to conduct their affairs. If they happen to accumulate more, they will get rid of it (almost) immediately, either by purchasing goods, or by investing it, to avoid foregoing profit or interest through delay. Marx, and at one point, Say himself were among the first to recognize the main error in the argument. If market conditions make investment risky, or current expectations indicate that future investment will be more profitable than current investment, it may be rational to hold more cash than is desired for its own sake. If so, the foundation for Say's Identity crumbles.

Say's (Equilibrium) Equality
At times, the earlier writers appear to take a considerably weaker position. They suggest that while aggregate demand and supply can be unequal, this can only occur in disequilibrium, and that there exist strong economic forces which will rapidly move the economy toward equilibrium, with equality of aggregate supply and demand. The price level is usually taken as the equilibrating instrument. If, for example there is an excess demand for goods, prices must be pushed upward. The real purchasing power of the stock of cash will then fall, to the point at which the real money supply has been reduced to match the real demand for money. Then, the excess aggregate demand for goods that set the process in motion must also disappear.

Say himself did not always take so short-run a view of equilibration. Sometimes he emphasized only that demand will always catch up with supply *in the (very) long run.* Thus, he reiterated that the short-run unemployment created by new labor-saving technology will *ultimately* be eliminated by the enhanced demand for the affected products stimulated by the resulting fall in their costs. He also repeatedly observed that if demand could not be relied on ultimately to catch up with supply, the France of his day could not conceivably have absorbed the considerable multiplication of national output that had occurred since the miserable state of the country during the Hundred Years War (1337–1453).

Investment vs. Consumption as Stimulus for Production

Say, James Mill, and Adam Smith all had a broader purpose when they began their discussion of aggregate supply and demand. The Mercantilist literature, like the later writings of Malthus, had argued that an economy's production might be impeded by the inadequacy of effective demand. They defended consumption and, in particular, the wasteful consumption of the wealthy, as a means to avoid this. Savings, they suggested, constitutes a deduction from effective demand for commodities, thereby reducing the incentive for their production. Smith, Mill, and Say denied this emphatically, arguing that savings are generally devoted to investment, which constitutes as much a demand for output as any demand for ostentatious consumption. Thus, Say referred to investment as "productive consumption."

However, these authors emphasized, there is one basic difference between productive and unproductive consumption. The one contributes to the nation's wealth, while the other destroys it. To complete the logical foundation for this argument, they had to show why they believed savings were channeled automatically into investment, and this led them to argue that supply creates its own demand.

Keynes (incorrectly) took the law to imply that unemployment is impossible and, hence, was the bastion that had to be destroyed before one could build a theory of employment. This is ironic in light of the concern of both Say and Ricardo (that hard-line defender of Say's Law) over technological unemployment, which even led Say to advocate public works as an appropriate countermeasure.

William J. Baumol

See also FULLARTON, JOHN; HUTT, WILLIAM HAROLD; KEYNES, JOHN MAYNARD; MALTHUS, THOMAS ROBERT; RICARDO, DAVID; SAY'S LAW; SISMONDI, JEAN CHARLES LEONARD SIMONDE DE; WALRAS'S LAW; WICKSELL, JOHAN GUSTAV KNUT

Bibliography

Baumol, W. J. 1977. "Say's (at Least) Eight Laws, or What Say and James Mill May Really Have Meant." *Economica* 44:145–61.

Becker, G. and W. J. Baumol. [1952] 1960. "The Classical Monetary Theory: The Outcome of the Discussion." In *Essays in Economic Thought*, edited by J. J. Spengler and W. R. Allen, 753–71. Chicago: Rand McNally.

Lange, O. 1944. *Price Flexibility and Full Employment*. Bloomington, Ind.: Principia Press.

Marx, K. 1968. *Theories of Surplus Value*. Vol. 1. Moscow: Progress Publishers

Mill, J. [1808] 1966. *Commerce Defended*. In *James Mill: Selected Economic Writings*, edited by D. Winch, 85–159. Chicago: Univ. of Chicago Press.

Say, J. B. 1803. *Traité d'économie politique ou simple exposition de la manière dont se forment, se distribuent et se consumment les richesses*. Paris: Deterville. Translated under the title *A Treatise on Political Economy*. 4th ed. Philadelphia: G. R. Elliott, 1834.

Smith, A. [1776] 1976. *An Inquiry into the Nature and Causes of the Wealth of Nations*. 2 vols. Oxford: Clarendon Press.

Sowell, T. 1972. *Say's Law: An Historical Analysis*. Princeton: Princeton Univ. Press.

Thweatt, W. O. 1979. "Early Formulators of Say's Law." *Quarterly Review of Economics and Business* 19:79–94.

Say's Law

The history of economic theory from the classical period to Keynes can be regarded as a shift from a paradigm in which Say's Law holds to one in which it does not (Morishima and Catephores 1988, 23). But the meaning of Say's Law itself has changed as well. Keynes took Say's Law to imply that investment equals full-employment savings. By contrast, while Ricardo assumed that every act of saving implies a corresponding investment of equal magnitude and therefore denied the possibility of a "general glut" of commodities, he did not believe that this necessarily implied full employment. Hence Ricardo's finding that improved machinery may displace workers did not, in his view, contradict the "law of markets."

"[B]oth capital and population may be at the same time, and for a period of great length, redundant, compared with the effective demand for produce" (Ricardo 1951, 427). This statement, which could have been formulated by Keynes, comes from Malthus, Ricardo's adversary in the famous "general glut" controversy. The issue at stake was whether general overproduction of commodities was possible or whether money was neutral.

Keynes considered Malthus the most important precursor of his own theory of effective demand, arguing that the intellectual domination of Malthus's approach by Ricardo's for a whole century was a "disaster to the progress of economics" (Keynes 1978, 98). In Keynes's view, both the method and content of Malthus's analysis were superior to Ricardo's. Considering Ricardo an abstract and a priori theorist, Keynes praised Malthus for a realism that kept him from ignoring the facts. Keynes felt that Malthus understood the working of a monetary economy, whereas Ricardo was preoccupied with the abstraction of a neutral-money economy. In a monetary economy the crucial problem is equalizing savings and investment at full-employment income, and only in such an economy can effective demand limit production. Keynes praised Malthus for comprehending the effects of excessive saving on output via its effects on profits.

The dispute between Malthus and Ricardo concerned how capital accumulation affects the general rate of profits and, hence, the incentive to further accumulation. In particular, they disagreed about two propositions formulated by Adam Smith. The first one asserts that the growth of wealth depends on the ratio of productive to unproductive workers; the larger the ratio the more rapidly the economy expands. The second one asserts that capital accumulation reduces the general rate of profit, due to the merchants' intensified competition. Malthus accepted the second proposition and rejected the first, while Ricardo held the reverse view.

Ricardo denied any tendency of the profit rate to fall by observing that Smith's proposition erroneously analogized a single market to the entire economy, for which the rate of profit does not change unless the real wage rate or the technical conditions of production in the wage-goods industries change (Ricardo [1819] 1951, chap. 21). The rate of profit falls only (1) if with unchanged technical conditions of production the rate of capital accumulation exceeds the rate of growth of the work force, so that entrepreneurs bid up real wages; or (2) if with a constant real wage rate the output of means of subsistence for a growing population can be increased only at increasing labor costs due to decreasing returns in primary production.

Ricardo referred to the two cases in his *Notes on Malthus.* The first case is characterized by an "increase of the price of labour" due to a "scarcity of labour," while the second re-

sults from a "diminution in the productive powers of land" (Ricardo 1951, 321). In the first case, the money wage rate rises relative to the prices of the means of subsistence; in the second, it rises along with them. Ricardo subsumed both cases under the heading of high or low wages. Hence, Ricardo denied that demand would permanently affect profits. Discrepancies between supply and effective demand may affect individual commodities and cause differential profit rates. But intersectoral capital mobility tends to restore a uniform profit rate. Thus, Say's Law rules out a discrepancy between aggregate output and aggregate demand. Accelerated accumulation and an increased ratio of productive to unproductive laborers cannot cause a deficiency of effective demand: "there is no amount of capital which may not be employed in a country, because demand is only limited by production" (Ricardo [1819] 1951, 290). Notice that reference is to the employment of capital, not labor.

Malthus's disquisition began with the opinion shared by Smith and Ricardo that capital is increased by parsimony. According to Malthus, this proposition is true to a great extent, but not without limit: "the principle of saving, pushed to excess, would destroy the motive to production" (Ricardo 1951, 7–8). Too much capital accumulation reduces aggregate demand to a level too low to utilize productive capacity fully. General overproduction of commodities would result and prices would fall relative to money wages, reducing profitability.

Like Keynes, Malthus assumed workers are paid in money, not in kind. Hence the purchasing power of their wages depends on the level of prices for consumption goods. The level of prices depends on supply and demand in the goods markets. If the demand for goods is strong in relation to supply, prices are high and real wages low. The resulting high rate of profit encourages capitalists to accumulate, and the economy grows rapidly. Conversely, if demand is weak, the economy stagnates.

Malthus used what he called the *regulating principle* and the *limiting principle* to distinguish between his view and Ricardo's. While the limiting principle determines the maximum rate of profit compatible with a given state of labor productivity, the regulating principle determines the rate of profit given the prevailing level of effective demand. Ricardo dismissed Malthus's opinion on the grounds that Malthus shared the conventional view that by saving one either employs productive laborers, or lends to someone who does. Hence there is no distinction between productive capacity and aggregate demand, and none between the regulating and the limiting principle.

In the *General Theory*, Keynes unfortunately lumped together as classical economists both the classical economists and neoclassical economists like Marshall and Pigou. His failure to recognize the fundamental differences between the two groups regarding employment led him to criticize Say's Law only in its neoclassical formulation without considering the particular classical conception of the law.

In his attack on Say's Law in chapter two of the *General Theory*, Keynes did refer to one classical economist, J. S. Mill. In fact, Mill ([1871] 1965, 506) presenting himself as a devoted disciple of Ricardo, insisted that "[t]here cannot, in short, be intrinsically a more insignificant thing, in the economy of society, than money." Moreover, Mill emphasized that the supply of commodities cannot exceed the purchasing power of buyers. That is, sellers are inevitably buyers. However, there is another side to Mill. A series of credit crises in England, the first in 1825, two years after Ricardo's death, led Mill to reconsider the rigid adherence of classical economics to real analysis. First, Mill ([1871] 1965, 574) pointed out that in commercial crises "there is really an excess of all commodities above the money demand: in other words, there is an undersupply of money." This passage is particularly interesting, because it shows that a competent follower of Ricardo and adherent of Say's Law did not interpret the classical doctrine as denying the occurrence of "general gluts." At the same time, Mill explicitly treated this situation as a *temporary* phenomenon. Moreover, the quotation shows Mill to have been an early discoverer of Walras's Law. Second, Mill not only recognized that Say's Identity holds only for accounting money in a barter-type economy, but was the first explicitly to attribute the occurrence of crises to money's role as a *store of value*. In his essay "Of the Influence of Consumption on Production" he identified a decisive difference between a monetary economy and a barter economy. Under barter, selling and buying occur simultaneously in the same transaction, whereas it is money "that . . . enables this one act of interchange to be divided into two separate acts or operations; one of which may be performed now, and the other a year hence, or whenever

it shall be most convenient" (Mill [1844] 1967). As a consequence, the seller of one commodity may not necessarily demand another in the same period, and a temporary general glut may appear.

Although Mill, like most classical economists, spoke about full employment of capital whereas Keynes spoke about full employment of labor, there are similarities in their arguments. Mill's analysis of money as a store of value and the consequent separation of purchase from sale anticipated Marx's criticism of Say's Law. Although Marx (1968–71, chap. 17) criticized Mill by arguing that explaining the *possibility* of crises by no means explains their *actual occurrence*, his critique focused on the sale-purchase separation which leads to the realization problem and a breakdown in the circuit of money capital, $M - C \ldots P \ldots C' - M'$. While Mill admitted the possibility of temporary general gluts, Marx strove to show that capitalist economies are inevitably crisis-prone.

It is remarkable that Keynes, who was rather critical of Marx's doctrine, came close to Marx's argument in his attack on Say's Law. While Keynes (1983, 81) identified the theories of Ricardo, Mill, Marshall, and Pigou with the circulation formula $C - M - C'$ that corresponds to a real exchange (barter) or "cooperative" economy, he considered the Marxian formula $M - C - M'$ as "pregnant" for a monetary theory of production. Thus Keynes also took the potential separation of purchases from sales as an essential feature of an "entrepreneurial" or monetary economy.

A fundamental characteristic of a monetary economy is that full employment output may not be realized, because it is not profitable to produce that level of output. That is, M' may be smaller than M. A monetary theory of production, or theory of effective demand, is therefore necessary to determine the level of employment. To Keynes, Say's Law meant not only that the aggregate demand and supply functions coincide but it was also "equivalent to the proposition that there is no obstacle to full employment" (Keynes [1936] 1973, 26). While the neoclassical version of Say's Law implies that the economy achieves full employment and that changes in the interest rate ensure equality between saving and investment, Say's Law did not lead Ricardo to any such conclusion (Garegnani 1978, 338–41). Ricardo invoked Say's Law to show that there could be no *permanent* surplus of capital, so disproving the

Smith-Malthus argument. Marx, who otherwise was very critical of Ricardo's adherence to Say's Law, concurred. "Permanent crises do not exist" (Marx 1969, 2:497). Nor did Ricardo or Malthus believe that Say's Law implies the full employment of labor.

Say's Law holds when savings identically equal investment. For Keynes, an essential characteristic of a monetary economy is the independence of savings decisions and investment decisions. This is in remarkable contrast to the classical postulate that saving and investment are, in essence, identical. For Ricardo, the equality between investment and saving is assumed, not ensured by changes in the rate of interest. Like Smith, Ricardo associated savings with the capitalists and therefore identified savings with capital accumulation. Ricardo did not accept Say's Law because of an analysis of the saving-investment process, but rather, as Garegnani (1978, 340) has pointed out, because of "the lack of any such analysis."

Harald Hagemann
Heinz D. Kurz

See also FULLARTON, JOHN; HUTT, WILLIAM HAROLD; KEYNES, JOHN MAYNARD; MALTHUS, THOMAS ROBERT; MARX, KARL HEINRICH; OVERSAVING THEORIES OF BUSINESS CYCLES; RICARDO, DAVID; SAVING EQUALS INVESTMENT; SAY, JEAN-BAPTISTE; SISMONDI, JEAN CHARLES LEONARD SIMONDE DE; WALRAS'S LAW

Bibliography

Garegnani, P. 1978. "Notes on Consumption, Investment and Effective Demand I." *Cambridge Journal of Economics* 2:335–353.

Keynes, J. M. 1971–89. *The Collected Writings of John Maynard Keynes.* 30 vols. London: Macmillan.

Malthus, T. R. [1836] 1989. *Principles of Political Economy.* Variorum ed. Cambridge: Cambridge Univ. Press.

Marx, K. 1968–71. *Theories of Surplus Value.* 3 vols. Translation. Moscow: Progress.

Mill, J. S. [1844] 1967. "Of the Influence of Consumption on Production." In *The Collected Works of John Stuart Mill.* Vol. 4. Edited by J. M. Robson, 262–79. Toronto: Univ. of Toronto Press.

———. [1871] 1965. *The Principles of Political Economy.* 2 vols. 7th ed. Vols. 2 and 3 of *The Collected Works of John Stuart Mill.* Edited by J. M. Robson. Toronto: Univ. of Toronto Press.

Mongiovi, G. 1990. "Notes on Say's Law, Classical Economics and the Theory of Effective Demand." *Contributions to Political Economy* 9:69–82.

Morishima, M. and G. Catephores. 1988. "Anti-Say's Law versus Say's Law: A Change in Paradigm." In *Evolutionary Economics: Applications of Schumpeter's Ideas,* edited by H. Hanusch, 23–53. Cambridge: Cambridge Univ. Press.

Ricardo, D. [1819] 1951. *The Principles of Political Economy.* Vol. 1 of *The Works and Correspondence of David Ricardo.* Edited by P. Sraffa. Cambridge: Cambridge Univ. Press.

———. 1951. *Notes on Malthus.* Vol. 2 of *The Works and Correspondence of David Ricardo.* Edited by P. Sraffa. Cambridge: Cambridge Univ. Press.

Say, J.-B. [1821] 1834. *A Treatise on Political Economy.* 4th ed. Translation. Philadelphia: G. R. Elliott.

Schumpeter, Joseph Alois (1883–1950)

Born in Triesch (now Trest), Moravia in the Austro-Hungarian Monarchy, Schumpeter earned his doctorate in Vienna in 1906 and the Venia Legendi in 1909. In 1907–08, he practiced law in Cairo and acquired a considerable private fortune. In 1909, he became "Extraordinarius" in Czernovitz and a year later Professor in Graz. In 1913, he was the first Austrian Exchange Professor at Columbia University which conferred on him an honorary degree. During his "sacred third decade" he produced the *Wesen und Hauptinhalt der theoretischen Nationalökonomie, Die Theorie der wirtschaftlichen Entwicklung,* his first sketch of the history of thought, *Epochen der Dogmen- und Methodengeschichte* (1912) and numerous articles.

During the war, his major study on money ([1917/18] 1956) appeared, as well as *Die Krise des Steuerstaates* (1918) which analyzed in historical detail the rise and function of the modern state in an individualistic capitalistic society, arguing that only a private-enterprise capitalist economy could cope with the expected postwar problems.

In 1918, he became a member of the nonpartisan German Socialization Commission, and in 1919, Minister of Finance in the second postrevolutionary coalition cabinet under the socialist chancellor Karl Renner. His program for rehabilitating the exhausted Austrian economy followed his outline in the *Krise:* a "Great Capital Levy," conceived entirely as a measure to wipe out the monetary overhang before it could enter circulation; no attempt to raise the external value of the krone; freeing prices and the exchange rate; large-scale capital imports; and restructuring the tax system to promote savings. Such a program was successfully followed in Europe and Japan after World War II. Schumpeter failed because, domestically, no one was willing to face the magnitude of the task to be mastered and, internationally, because the Treaty of St. Germain was, in Schumpeter's words, a death sentence precluding any orderly fiscal and monetary policy.

Schumpeter lasted only seven months as minister. After a brief return to Graz and a disastrous venture into business as president of an investment bank, Schumpeter was in 1925 appointed to the chair for public finance at the University of Bonn, where he remained until moving to Harvard in 1932.

Schumpeter saw himself first as an economic theorist. But being an original sociologist and a trained historian, he viewed economic theory as the analysis of how capitalist institutions arose and worked, and how their internal logic changes them in time. For Schumpeter, the business cycle is the very essence of capitalist development which inevitably changes capitalism's nature.

Four of his major works display the successive enlargement of an intellectual horizon that is implicit in the first analysis.

Das Wesen und der Hauptinhalt der theoretischen Nationalökonomie has never been translated into English or reprinted in German. Schumpeter had planned to rewrite it completely under the title *The Theoretical Apparatus of Economics.* The central concern of the *Wesen* was the precise explanatory content of equilibrium theory. Schumpeter concluded that equilibrium theory could explain adaptive but never evolutionary processes. It presumed constancy of all basic data, particularly of production functions, and thus could not explain interest or growth. No psychological assumptions were needed to explain the working of a stationary economy.

Die Theorie der wirtschaftlichen Entwicklung appeared in 1911 (the title page says 1912). The revised second German edition appeared in 1926 without the long seventh chapter. The English edition, further shortened and amended by Schumpeter himself, appeared in 1934. The book works out the basic model of an evolutionary economy.

Schumpeter starts from a stable equilibrium in which all parameters stay constant or change only imperceptibly and all factors are "optimally" allocated. This starting point ensures that the explanation of evolution is not implicit in the assumptions. Schumpeter's aim was to identify the *economic* factors emanating from *within* the economy that destroy an existing equilibrium and lead to evolution. To start with, "optimization" of factor allocation refers only to the specific methods of production actually tried, not to all possible or even all known ones (a point later developed by Armen Alchian and other contributors to the New Institutional Economics and by Nelson and Winter). The methods themselves are infinitely improvable. "We are no nearer to the exhaustion of technical possibilities than at the stone age" (1912, 161). Schumpeter chided Keynes already in the 1920s for suggesting that technical change is itself subject to diminishing returns.

Equilibrium is destroyed by entrepreneurial action which requires special motivations and consists in changing production functions in the widest sense of the term. Resources (which in equilibrium are "optimally" allocated) must be redirected into new channels. While in a feudal or socialist economy, resources can be redeployed by fiat, they must be purchased or hired in a capitalist economy.

Innovations give rise to wave-like movements because after new processes are introduced, real time must elapse before they either reduce costs or generate new goods. When the results of innovations come on the market, a process of adaptation, which is the technical meaning of "recession," is necessitated. The economy reaches a new equilibrium that continues until something new happens to destroy it.

Walras had shown that money must exist in general equilibrium for reasons of internal logic, but there it serves only as a *numèraire.* In capitalist evolution, credit becomes a characteristic phenomenon which, as matter of fact ("though not by logical necessity") has to be created.

Thus the basic model has two phases: prosperity, which is a movement away from, and recession, which is a movement towards (a new) equilibrium. Credit is necessary to reallocate resources, a fact that is central to Schumpeter's definition of capitalism. The prosperity comes to an end when the new goods appear and trigger what Schumpeter originally called a process of integration (*Einordnungsprozess*), later, more dramatically, *creative destruction*. The process is discontinuous and necessarily takes real time.

Interest is payment for money. Schumpeter's is a monetary, not a real, interest theory. Productive interest arises with credits to finance innovations and disappears with the process of integration. Consumption loans, of course, also demand interest but present no theoretical problem. Consumption interest is paid out of a constant income; productive interest is paid out of profits, that is, out of increased income. Interest for productive purposes becomes a *social* phenomenon not inherent in all social systems.

Business Cycles appeared in 1939 but its ideas can be traced back to the 1920s. The work has three central features: (1) the four cyclical phases; (2) the three-cycle scheme; and (3) the "heroic" attempt to integrate theory and economic history.

1. Once evolution has started, savings appear, credit is created also for noninnovating industries and consumption. Avoidable speculative excesses like the Florida land boom of the 1920s also appear. This produces a secondary wave which is analyzed in terms of four phases: prosperity, which is a movement away from equilibrium; recession, a movement toward a new equilibrium; depression, defined as overshooting of the equilibrium caused by nonessential phenomena such as the Florida land boom which good policy could prevent without interference with evolution; and finally, recovery, which is a movement towards equilibrium. Thus the four phases have technical meanings and are not defined by severity or length.

2. Theorists have been greatly perplexed by Schumpeter's three-cycle schema. Schumpeter explicitly stated that it had no theoretical significance but was a method of interpreting observed reality. In principle, he admitted an indefinite number of wave-like movements that interacted in complicated ways. Among them was the reaction of an economy to *any* (including random) shocks from in-side or outside the system, powerfully developed by Ragnar Frisch. But Frisch's impulse-propagation scheme could explain only that there are cycles, not why there are growth cycles. Schumpeter thought that his theory of innovation explained more satisfactorily the impulse problem as well as growth cycles that arose from within the system itself. The long waves or "Kondratieffs" of 45–60 years—hardly a regular cycle any more than his "Juglars" of 8–11 years—are successive industrial revolutions in which particular innovations lead to others. The railroad Kondratieff ended only after the opportunities created by railroad investments were exploited.

3. Schumpeter's dating of the cycles did not depend only on the raw data. He carefully analyzed a particular situation, and when he found that, say, a downturn was explained by a particular historical event without which prosperity would have continued, he classified the particular year as a prosperity even if the economy in fact turned down.

Thus Schumpeter's is a truly historical theory of economics. "I strongly feel" he wrote to Mitchell (letter dated 6 May 1937, in the Harvard University Archive) "that we must thoroughly get rid of the prejudice that our phenomena are simple and can be directly handled by simple methods either theoretical or statistical." Only thorough historical analysis could come to grips with them. Nor could this be done "by counting from trough to trough or from peak to peak." But history is in principle unforeseeable and non-deterministic.

This leads to Schumpeter's popular success, *Capitalism, Socialism and Democracy*. In *Capitalism*, Schumpeter analyzes how the institutions of capitalism change out of their own logic. No system left to its own logic is permanent. The purely economic features of capitalism are stable—which is the major difference between Schumpeter and Marx, whose system is the first thoroughly analyzed and found wanting. But the economic features are imbedded in a social and political system with which they interact and which becomes hostile to capitalism. Capitalism will die of its success, not its failure.

Schumpeter defined capitalism as an economic system based on private property, in which decisions are made in principle in the private sphere, in which the services of factors of production must be purchased or hired, and in which factors of production are redirected in the course of evolution by means of credit.

Socialism, on the other hand, is defined as a system in which decisions are made in principle in the public sphere and factors of production are redirected by command of a central authority, even if property remains juridically private. Schumpeter "predicted" the coming of "socialism." But "prediction" means only what currently visible tendencies imply, not what will actually happen decades hence which is totally unforeseeable.

Note that the presence or absence of a market is not part of Schumpeter's definitions. Even markets for factor services may exist in socialism, and ever since slavery was abolished, no asset market for labor has existed in any modern capitalist country, while the market for land is severely controlled everywhere. However, gradually the content of private property changes, the economy becomes less atomistically organized, entrepreneurs become independent of borrowed money, and consumers' preferences are socialized. For Schumpeter, the real conflict is not between labor and capital but between the interests of the present and of the future. The end of capitalism will not be imperialism but laborism—the dominance of a class more interested in income distribution than in income creation.

It would be a serious misunderstanding to consider Schumpeter's analysis just another competing discussion of cyclical movements. They are an integrated analysis of social and economic forces, of continuities and discontinuities in history, including a discussion of the culture of capitalism, the increasing "rationalization" which capitalism has promoted through its necessity to calculate and by which it is ultimately undermined.

More than that, Schumpeter stressed that every historical period necessarily contains features of preceding periods and foreshadowings of the future. But while the future is in principle unforeseeable, it nevertheless has its own logic. Schumpeter never admitted that the Soviet Union had anything to do with socialism, regarding it simply as a system of brute force that would fail because it tried to skip necessary phases of development. It is no accident that Schumpeter's star is once again rising.

Wolfgang F. Stolper

See also BUSINESS CYCLES IN SOCIALIST ECONOMIES; CREATIVE DESTRUCTION; INVESTMENT; JUGLAR, CLÉMENT; JUGLAR CYCLE; KITCHIN CYCLE; KONDRATIEFF, NIKOLAI DMITRIYEVICH; KONDRATIEFF CYCLES; LONG-WAVE THEORIES; REAL BUSINESS-CYCLE THEORIES

Bibliography

Augello, M. 1990. *Joseph Alois Schumpeter: A Reference Guide.* Berlin: Springer-Verlag.

McCraw, T. K. 1991. "Schumpeter Ascending." *The American Scholar,* Summer, 371–92.

Schumpeter, J. A. 1908. *Das Wesen und der Hauptinhalt der theoretischen Nationalökonomie.* Munich and Berlin: Duncker und Humblot.

———. [1912] 1934. *Theorie der wirtschaftlichen Entwicklung.* Munich and Berlin: Duncker und Humblot. Translated by R. Opie, under the title *The Theory of Economic Development.* Cambridge: Harvard Univ. Press.

———. [1917/18] 1956. "Money and the Social Product." Translation. *International Economic Papers* 6:148–211.

———. [1918] 1954. "The Crisis of the Tax State." Translation. *International Economic Papers* 4:5–38.

———. 1928. "The Instability of Capitalism." *Economic Journal* 38:361–85.

———. 1939. *Business Cycles: A Theoretical, Historical and Statistical Analysis of the Capitalist Process.* 2 vols. New York: McGraw-Hill.

———. 1942. *Capitalism, Socialism and Democracy.* New York: Harper and Brothers.

———. [1951] 1991. *Essays of J. A. Schumpeter.* Edited by R. V. Clemence. Reprint with a new introduction by R. Swedberg. New Brunswick: Transactions Publishers.

———. 1952. *Aufsätze zur Oekonomischen Theorie.* Edited by E. Schneider and A. Spiethoff. Tübingen: J. C. B. Mohr (Paul Siebeck).

———. 1970. *Das Wesen des Geldes.* Göttingen: Vandenhoeck und Ruprecht.

S

———. 1985. *Aufsätze zur Wirtschaftspolitik.* Edited by W. F. Stolper and C. Seidl. Tübingen: J. C. B. Mohr (Paul Siebeck).

———. 1991. *The Economics and Sociology of Capitalism.* Edited by R. Swedberg. Princeton: Princeton Univ. Press.

Stolper, W. F. 1994. *Joseph A. Schumpeter, 1883–1950: The Public Life of a Private Man.* Princeton: Princeton Univ. Press.

Swedberg, R. 1991. *Schumpeter: A Biography.* Princeton: Princeton Univ. Press.

Schwartz, Anna Jacobson (1915–)

Anna Schwartz has contributed significantly to our understanding of the role of money in propagating and exacerbating business-cycle disturbances. Schwartz's collaboration with Milton Friedman in the highly acclaimed money and business-cycle project of the National Bureau of Economic Research (NBER) helped establish the modern quantity theory of money (or Monetarism) as a dominant explanation for macroeconomic instability. Her contributions lie in the four related areas of monetary statistics, monetary history, monetary theory and policy, and international arrangements.

Born in New York City, she received a B.A. from Barnard College in 1934, an M.A. from Columbia in 1936, and a Ph.D. from Columbia in 1964. Most of Schwartz's career has been spent in active research. After a year at the United States Department of Agriculture in 1936, she spent five years at Columbia University's Social Science Research Council. She joined the NBER in 1941, where she has remained ever since. In 1981–82, Schwartz served as staff director of the United States Gold Commission and was responsible for writing the Gold Commission Report.

Schwartz's early research was focused mainly on economic history and statistics. A collaboration with A. D. Gayer and W. W. Rostow from 1936 to 1941 produced a massive and important study of cycles and trends in the British economy during the Industrial Revolution, *The Growth and Fluctuation of the British Economy, 1790–1850.* The authors adopted NBER techniques to isolate cycles and trends in key time series of economic performance. Historical analysis was then interwoven with descriptive statistics to present an anatomy of the development of the British economy in this important period.

Schwartz collaborated with Milton Friedman on the NBER's money and business-cycle project over a period of thirty years. This research resulted in three volumes: *A Monetary History of the United States, 1867–1960, Monetary Statistics of the United States,* and *Monetary Trends in the United States and the United Kingdom, 1875–1975.*

The theoretical background to the project is the modern quantity theory of money. Based on the interaction of a stable demand for money with an independently determined money supply, the key proposition of the modern quantity theory is that changes in the rate of monetary growth produce corresponding but lagged changes in the growth of nominal income. At first, changes in money growth lead to changes in real output but in the long run, they are fully reflected in changes in the price level. Long-run historical evidence for the modern quantity theory is provided in *A Monetary History,* short-run cyclical evidence in "Money and Business Cycles," and long-run econometric evidence in *Monetary Trends.*

The overwhelming historical evidence gathered by Schwartz linking economic instability to erratic monetary behavior, in turn a product of discretionary monetary policy, has convinced her of the desirability of stable money brought about through a constant money-growth rule. The evidence of particular interest to the student of cyclical phenomena is the banking panics in the United States between 1873 and 1933, especially from 1930 to 1933. Banking panics were a key ingredient in virtually every severe cyclical downturn and were critical in converting a serious but not unusual downturn beginning in 1929 into the "Great Contraction." According to Schwartz's research, each of the panics could have been allayed by timely and appropriate lender-of-last-resort intervention by the monetary authorities. Moreover, the likelihood of panics ever occurring would be remote in a stable monetary environment.

Michael D. Bordo

See also CENTRAL BANKING; ENDOGENOUS AND EXOGENOUS MONEY; FRIEDMAN, MILTON; FEDERAL RESERVE SYSTEM: 1914–1941; GREAT DEPRESSION IN THE UNITED STATES (1929–1938); MONETARY DISEQUILIBRIUM THEORIES OF THE BUSINESS CYCLE; MONETARY POLICY; MONEY-INCOME CAUSALITY; ROSTOW, WALT WHITMAN; SNYDER, CARL; WARBURTON, CLARK

Bibliography

Bordo, M. D. and A. J. Schwartz. [1983] 1987. "The Importance of Stable Money: Theory and Evidence." Chap. 10 in A. J. Schwartz, *Money in Historical Perspective*. Chicago: Univ. of Chicago Press.

Friedman, M. and A. J. Schwartz. 1963. *A Monetary History of the United States, 1867–1960*. Princeton: Princeton Univ. Press.

———. [1963] 1987. "Money and Business Cycles." Chap. 2 in A. J. Schwartz, *Money in Historical Perspective*. Chicago: Univ. of Chicago Press.

———. 1970. *Monetary Statistics of the United States*. New York: Columbia Univ. Press.

———. 1982. *Monetary Trends in the United States and the United Kingdom: Their Relations to Income, Prices and Interest Rates, 1867–1975*. Chicago: Univ. of Chicago Press.

Gayer, A. D., W. W. Rostow, and A. J. Schwartz. 1953. *The Growth and Fluctuation of the British Economy, 1790–1850: An Historical, Statistical, and Theoretical Study of Britain's Economic Development*. 2 vols. Oxford: Clarendon Press.

Schwartz, A. J. [1986] 1987. "Real and Pseudo-Financial Crises." Chap. 11 in *Money in Historical Perspective*. Chicago: Univ. of Chicago Press.

———. 1987. *Money in Historical Perspective*. Chicago: Univ. of Chicago Press.

———. 1988. "Financial Stability and the Federal Safety Net." In *Restructuring Banking and Financial Services in America*, edited by S. Haraf and R. M. Kushmeider, 34–62. Washington: American Enterprise Institute.

Search Theory

Starting with Stigler's seminal contribution, search theory has been used extensively to analyze the economic consequences of informational imperfections and frictions. Much of that research has been directed toward understanding cyclical fluctuations in unemployment. Search theory attempts to explain more thoroughly than does conventional textbook Keynesian economics how labor markets are organized, the transaction costs imposed on market participants by imperfect information and costly communication, and how unemployment results from these considerations.

In the absence of movements into or out of the labor force, the increase in the number unemployed in any period must equal the number of job separations during the period minus job accessions. Walrasian general-equilibrium theory depicts a world in which a worker that leaves one job can find another immediately; separations always equal accessions and unemployment never arises. The theory is useless for understanding cyclical unemployment, because it abstracts from informational frictions and coordination problems. Conventional textbook Keynesian economics recognizes frictions and coordination problems, especially sticky wages, but assumes that both separations and accessions are controlled unilaterally by firms. It asserts that reductions in aggregate demand raise unemployment by inducing firms to increase layoffs and reduce hiring. Workers play no more than a passive role in the process.

The first phase of research in search theory following Stigler's seminal article also recognized frictions, but unlike Keynesian theory it imputed an active role to workers in the process determining unemployment. Most of the contributors to the famous 1970 Phelps volume used the reservation-wage approach to search theory. In this approach, unemployed workers visit firms and receive offers at a constant rate. After each offer a worker must either accept the offer or continue searching, but not both. Under quite general conditions, a worker's optimal strategy is to accept any offer above some unique wage, w^*, the reservation wage, and reject any below w^*. Sargent (1987, chap. 2) presents a rigorous derivation of w^*.

The reservation-wage approach offers a potential explanation of the propagation mechanism by which fluctuations in aggregate demand cause fluctuations in unemployment. Specifically, assume aggregate demand falls, inducing firms to cut wage offers. If workers see that wages are falling generally they will accept lower offers, knowing that the offers that could be obtained by searching elsewhere are also lower. In this case, unemployment need not increase. But if workers cannot see that wages are falling generally, many will reject the lower offers, choosing instead to continue searching or to quit their jobs in order to search. Thus accessions will fall, and separations will rise. Eventually, workers will correctly perceive their alternatives, and reduce their reservation wages accordingly. But meanwhile many of them will have mistakenly rejected offers, and unemployment will have risen, at least temporarily.

This explanation of cyclical unemployment has been challenged on three main grounds. First, it depends crucially on the assumption that searching is less costly while unemployed than while employed. Without this assumption, no one would reject an offer unless it were so low that leisure was preferable to working. The theory could then explain why changes in aggregate demand cause fluctuations in leisure, but not in unemployment. In fact there are good reasons to assume the contrary. Although job search admittedly takes time that could be spent working, it can usually be done during downtime or after-hours. In addition, there are bargaining, signaling, and other advantages to having a job when searching, which is probably why, in fact, most job changes occur with no intervening spell of unemployment.

A second criticism is that it is implausible to suppose that workers systematically misperceive changes in the state of the economy for long enough to account for rises in unemployment that last as long as in the typical business cycle. A third one is that the theory implies countercyclical quit rates (workers mistakenly quit when aggregate demand falls), whereas in fact quit rates are strongly procyclical.

Tobin (1972) advanced these criticisms in an influential article that helped discredit search theory as a tool for understanding unemployment fluctuations throughout much of the 1970s and 1980s. His basic point was simply that it is unrealistic to depict unemployment as resulting from voluntary search decisions of workers. Keynesian theory might have overstated the role of firms in dictating accessions and separations, but at least it recognized that from the workers' point of view much unemployment is involuntary.

In the 1980s, search theory entered a second phase, which improved upon the reservation-wage approach by recognizing some of the involuntary aspects of unemployment. Work by Diamond (1981) and Mortenson (1982) initiated this phase, using what may be called the search-externalities approach to search theory.

Instead of focusing exclusively on workers' search decisions, the search-externalities approach assumes that workers look for firms and firms look for workers. The resources devoted to search activities on each side of the market

enter as arguments in the economy's matching function. This function indicates how, given the organization of the market and the physical and logistical costs of contacting potential trading partners, the intensities of search and recruiting by workers and firms determine the rate at which contacts occur.

The matching function implies that there are externalities in the search process. For example, workers do not find offers at a constant rate as in the reservation-wage approach. Instead the rate depends, among other things, on firms' recruiting effort. This is an example of a *thin-market* externality, a common phenomenon in communication networks whereby an increase in contacting effort by some people benefits those being contacted. It is an externality because the party initiating the contact cannot propose the sort of agreement that might internalize the resulting benefits until the contact has already been made. Although some internalization can be accomplished by institutional arrangements such as labor-market exchanges, the costs of communicating match-specific information via third parties severely limits the scope of such arrangements. Similarly, there will be negative spillovers, or *congestion* externalities when additional workers looking for the same job interfere with the others, by increasing the length of queues, raising the probability that by the time a worker responds to an advertised vacancy it will already be filled, and so forth.

The theory of unemployment that emerges from the search-externalities approach has been thoroughly presented by Pissarides (1990). It differs from the one based on the reservation-wage approach in several important ways. It suggests an alternative channel through which changes in the demand for labor can cause changes in unemployment. When recruiting activity falls, job accessions can fall, not because wage offers fall below workers' reservation wages, but because it takes longer for workers to find offers. This nonprice interaction derives from the thin-market externality, and it is consistent with procyclical quits. That is, in a recession, workers are discouraged from quitting their jobs by the increased difficulty of finding another.

The search-externalities approach need not rule out on-the-job search. For even if workers accepted any offer that exceeded the value of leisure, cyclical fluctuations in accessions, driven by changes in aggregate demand or supply that affect firms' recruiting intensity, would still occur. Unemployment would rise when aggregate demand falls, because it takes workers longer to find acceptable offers, not because they reject more offers in order to commence or continue a search in which they can engage only while unemployed. Nor does the theory depend, as does the reservation-wage approach, on misperceptions of the state of the economy. The matching function implies directly that a fall in recruiting reduces both contacts and accessions. This need not be accompanied by any actual or perceived change in the distribution of offers.

Finally, if thin-market externalities are strong enough, the matching function can exhibit increasing returns to scale over some range, and multiple equilibria with multiple natural rates of unemployment are possible. As shown by Diamond (1982), there can be a high-level equilibrium in which people have a self-fulfilling expectation of a high level of search activity, and a low-level equilibrium in which people have a self-fulfilling expectation of very little search. Which equilibrium occurs can depend upon group psychology. But both equilibria are compatible with rational expectations. Thus, one possible explanation for cyclical fluctuations in unemployment is the old idea that alternating waves of optimism and pessimism make the economy oscillate between equilibria with different levels of search and unemployment.

Peter Howitt

See also HUTT, WILLIAM HAROLD; INTERTEMPORAL SUBSTITUTION; NEW KEYNESIAN ECONOMICS; SECTORAL SHIFTS; TOBIN, JAMES; UNEMPLOYMENT; WORKER AND JOB TURNOVER

Bibliography

Diamond, P. A. 1981. "Mobility Costs, Frictional Unemployment, and Efficiency." *Journal of Political Economy* 89:789–812.

———. 1982. "Aggregate Demand Management in Search Equilibrium." *Journal of Political Economy* 90:881–94.

Mortenson, D. T. 1982. "The Matching Process as a Noncooperative Bargaining Game." In *The Economics of Information and Uncertainty,* edited by J. J. McCall, 233–54. Chicago: Univ. of Chicago Press.

Phelps, E. S., et al. 1970. *Microeconomic Foundations of Employment and Inflation Theory.* New York: Norton.

Pissarides, C. A. 1990. *Equilibrium Unemployment Theory.* Oxford: Basil Blackwell.

Sargent, T. J. 1987. *Dynamic Macroeconomic Theory.* Cambridge: Harvard Univ. Press.

Stigler, G. J. [1961] 1968. "The Economics of Information." Chap. 16 in *The Organization of Industry.* Homewood, Ill.: Irwin.

Tobin, J. 1972. "Inflation and Unemployment." *American Economic Review* 62:1–18.

Seasonal Adjustment

Economic time-series data are often analyzed in seasonally adjusted form. The seasonal variation is removed from the data, so that the more interesting trend and business-cycle components can be better viewed. Taking exception to this general view, Barsky and Miron (1989) argue that the seasonal cycle displays the same characteristics as the business cycle for some macrovariables in the U.S. economy.

Different procedures are available for making seasonal adjustments. The success of a seasonal-adjustment procedure can affect the subsequent analysis of the time series, for example investigating the cyclical features of a particular series or studying the co-movements of macrovariables during the business cycle. Users of economic time-series data must therefore be aware of the possible consequences of using seasonally adjusted data.

Economists noted seasonal patterns in economic variables as early as 1841 when J. W. Gilbart found a seasonal pattern in the circulation of banknotes in the United Kingdom. Many other economic time series exhibit such recurring, though not necessarily regular, intra-year variation. This pattern is usually caused by exogenous non-economic factors such as the weather, institutional schedules, and religious festivals. For example, the unemployment rate usually goes up in spring when a large influx of students joins the labor force. Also, the national-income accounts fall to their yearly low in the first quarter of the year.

In general, a time series is seasonal if there are significant positive auto-correlations, r, at the k seasonal periods $k = s, 2s, 3s, ...$, where $s = 4$ for a quarterly series and $s = 12$ for a monthly series. In the frequency domain, seasonality is characterized by peaks in the spectrum of a series at or near the seasonal frequencies.

In many instances, seasonal fluctuations account for a significant part of the total variation of the series. Since the seasonality is generally caused by predictable non-economic factors, it is a nuisance for the data analyst who is interested in the variation due to trend or cyclical components. To identify these components, one must remove the seasonality or seasonally adjust the time series. Also, in multivariate analysis the analyst often seeks to relate the nonseasonal components of the economic series. For example, most business-cycle theories are concerned with the interrelationships among the nonseasonal components of the macroeconomic variables. Thus, by seasonally adjusting the data, the analyst removes the uncontrollable noneconomic seasonal influences before analyzing the economic forces affecting a time series.

Seasonal adjustment of a time series is based on the traditional unobserved-components model of time series. The simplest unobserved-components model assumes that a time series can be decomposed into two independent sub-components such that:

$$X_t = S_t + N_t, \qquad (1)$$

where X_t is the observed time series, and S_t and N_t are the unobserved seasonal and nonseasonal components. Defining the series in levels implies an additive model, while transforming it into logarithms defines a multiplicative model. In subsequent analysis the nonseasonal component can be further decomposed into cyclical, trend, and irregular components. Macroeconomists are primarily concerned with understanding and explaining the cyclical component or the business cycle, while growth theorists are primarily concerned with the (long-term) trend component. The irregular component is by definition unpredictable. The primary goal of seasonal adjustment is to estimate the nonseasonal component N_t. To accomplish this, the seasonal component must be estimated and removed from the original series. The estimated nonseasonal component or seasonally adjusted series is given by:

$$\hat{N}_t = \hat{X}_t - \hat{S}_t, \qquad (2)$$

where S_t is the estimated seasonal component. The difficulty is that there is no single best definition and estimator of the seasonal component. The seasonal component can be specified as deterministic or stochastic, additive or multiplicative, stationary or nonstationary. Furthermore, since the seasonal component is not pre-cisely defined, the adequacy of the seasonal adjustment is difficult to assess. Different estimates of the seasonal component yield different estimates for the nonseasonal component and, therefore, varying inferences about the trend, cyclical, or irregular components of the series. The differences can have dire consequences for the business-cycle analyst since they may imply significantly different estimates of the business-cycle component of a time series. This is true both for economic historians seeking to understand past business cycles and for forecasters seeking to predict turning points in the current cycle.

The task of seasonally adjusting time series has traditionally been left to institutional government agencies. The main advantage for users of economic data is that by using seasonally adjusted data they no longer need to consider seasonality. The disadvantage of seasonal adjustment is that it may reduce the quality of the data, thereby compromising the results of the empirical investigation. Recently, the use of officially seasonally adjusted data has been seriously questioned by the economics profession. The argument is that the disadvantages of official seasonal adjustment may be underestimated, because it is difficult to assess the resulting loss of information. The seriousness of the problem depends on what the data are used for. At a minimum, the data analyst should adjust for the loss in degrees of freedom in the seasonally adjusted data.

Ideally, practitioners should formulate explicitly the factors underlying the seasonality in their multivariate economic models, so that the source, transmission, and effects of the seasonal variation can be better understood in a particular situation. Granger (1978) has labeled this approach the causal-adjustment method of seasonal adjustment. Although this method is theoretically appealing, the lack of economic models of seasonality have caused most practitioners to avoid this modeling strategy.

The other main class of seasonal-adjustment methods is known as auto-adjustment. In this class, the current and past values of the series are used to estimate its seasonal component. Sometimes, predicted future values are also used in the adjustment. Most data analysts employ an auto-adjustment method since it is easier to use than the alternatives. Currently, the more mechanical moving-average-based techniques are the most frequently used. This approach has received much attention over the years, culminating in the complex Census X-11 program which was first developed for general use by Shiskin et al. (1967). The Census X-11 method is designed to handle a wide range of seasonal patterns and to adjust for extreme observations and other data anomalies. Its major drawback is that it is a black-box approach and there is no guarantee that it is optimal or even desirable when applied to a given time series.

An alternative method within the auto-adjustment class is the model-based approach. One such method is the optimal signal-extraction approach, advocated by Bell and Hillmer (1984). In this method, the time series are assumed to consist of signal (nonseasonal) and noise (seasonal) components. The mathematical solution of the optimal signal-extraction theory developed by Kolmogorov is applied to estimate the signal. Another member of this class is the multiplicative seasonal ARIMA (SARIMA) models introduced by Box and Jenkins (1970). This empirical approach specifies a parsimonious class of models that give a good approximation for many seasonal time series. The main advantage of the model-based methods is that they can be tailored to specific time series. However, these methods are more difficult to use than the mechanical methods and they sometimes overadjust the data for seasonality. Overadjustment means that the adjusted series has negative auto-correlations at the seasonal periods and dips in its spectrum at the seasonal frequencies.

Seasonal adjustment also has consequences for econometric modeling and statistical inference. Seasonally adjusted data can yield spurious dynamic relationships among economic variables as well as asymptotic biases in the parameter estimates of regression models. To avoid this possibility, Sims (1974) advocates using the same seasonal filter on all variables in a multivariate model. On the other hand, not seasonally adjusting can also have undesirable consequences. Relating unadjusted data may overstate the dependence among the variables. A strong common seasonal component caused by an exogenous factor like the weather may exaggerate and dominate the relation among the variables.

Without a precise definition of seasonality, any method of seasonal adjustment is somewhat arbitrary. Unfortunately, most current methods lack a clear theoretical foundation. Thus, applied practitioners are well advised to check important empirical results with both sea-sonally adjusted and unadjusted data. Institutions should facilitate this by making raw or unadjusted data more readily available. At the very least, applied practitioners must know precisely how the data are seasonally adjusted to ensure that important information about the purpose of the investigation has not been removed.

William Veloce

See also FILTERS; GILBART, JAMES WILLIAM; MOVING AVERAGES; PHASE AVERAGING; SEASONAL CYCLES; SEASONAL FLUCTUATIONS AND FINANCIAL CRISES; SPECTRAL ANALYSIS

Bibliography

Barsky, R. B. and J. A Miron. 1989. "The Seasonal Cycle and the Business Cycle." *Journal of Political Economy* 97:503–34.

Bell, W. R. and S. C. Hillmer. 1984. "Issues Involved with the Seasonal Adjustment of Economic Time Series." *Journal of Business and Economic Statistics* 2:291–320.

Box, G. E. P. and G. M. Jenkins. 1970. *Time Series Analysis: Forecasting and Control.* San Francisco: Holden-Day.

Cleveland, W. P. and G. C. Tiao. 1976. "Decomposition of Seasonal Time Series: A Model for the Census X-11 Program." *Journal of the American Statistical Association* 71:581–87.

Granger, C. W. J. 1978. "Seasonality: Causation, Interpretation, and Implications." In *Seasonal Analysis of Economic Time Series,* edited by A. Zellner, 33–46. Washington: U.S. Department of Commerce, Bureau of the Census.

Lovell, M. C. 1963. "Seasonal Adjustment of Economic Time Series and Multiple Regression Analysis." *Journal of the American Statistical Association* 58:993–1010.

Nerlove, M., D. M. Grether, and J. L. Carvalho. 1979. *Analysis of Economic Time Series: A Synthesis.* New York: Academic Press.

Newbold, P. and T. Bos. 1990. *Introductory Business Forecasting.* Cincinnati: South-Western.

Pierce, D. A. 1980. "A Survey of Recent Developments in Seasonal Adjustment." *The American Statistician* 34:125–34.

Shiskin, J., A. H. Young, and J. C. Musgrave. 1967. "The X-11 Variant of the Census Method II Seasonal Adjustment Program." Technical Paper No. 15. Washington: U.S. Department of Commerce, Bureau of Economic Analysis.

Sims, C. A. 1974. "Seasonality in Regression." *Journal of the American Statistical Association* 69:618–26.

Seasonal Cycles

Most research on macroeconomic fluctuations focuses on business-cycle fluctuations. However, a large fraction of the short-term variation in aggregate activity is accounted for by seasonal fluctuations. In addition, the characteristics of seasonal cycles are strikingly similar to those of business cycles. Since seasonal fluctuations are anticipated while business-cycle fluctuations are not, the similarity of the two kinds of fluctuations poses a strong challenge to many existing models of the business cycle.

Seasonal fluctuations are a dominant source of variation in every major type of economic activity, including consumption, investment, government purchases, industrial production, shipments, labor input, retail sales, unemployment, and the money stock. However, seasonal movements are not a quantitatively important feature of either real or nominal prices or interest rates.

The seasonal pattern in quarterly real GNP displays large increases in the second and fourth quarter, a large decrease in the first quarter, and a mild decrease in the third quarter. The seasonal patterns in consumption purchases and government purchases are similar to those in output, but fixed investment grows slightly in the third quarter and declines weakly in the fourth quarter. Monthly data show that industrial production falls strongly one to three months before Christmas, recovers in February, declines dramatically in July, and then rebounds strongly in August. Retail sales grow substantially in December but then decline tremendously in January. The money stock also exhibits a large positive growth rate in December and a large, negative growth rate in January. The movements in labor-market variables resemble those in output, although fluctuations are smaller. These seasonal patterns are characteristic of most developed countries, including Australia and New Zealand.

In addition to being quantitatively important, seasonal cycles display the key stylized facts that characterize business cycles. The most important such stylized fact is simply that there is an aggregate seasonal cycle: just as with business cycles, similarities in seasonal cycles across sectors are sufficient to generate a large seasonal cycle in *aggregate* output. The second stylized fact displayed by both business-cycle and seasonal fluctuations is an extreme absence of production smoothing (Miron and Zeldes 1988, Beaulieu and Miron 1991). A third important business-cycle stylized fact exhibited by the seasonal fluctuations is the procyclicality of labor productivity (Beaulieu and Miron 1991).

That business cycles and seasonal cycles have such similar properties suggests that a common propagation mechanism may be generating both the seasonal-cycle and the business-cycle variation in the economy. An additional fact about seasonal fluctuations reinforces the case for this conjecture: countries and industries that exhibit substantial seasonal variation are also ones that exhibit substantial business-cycle variation. This correlation holds across countries for industrial production, retail sales, the price level, the money stock, and nominal interest rates and across manufacturing industries, shipments, hours, employment, wages, and prices.

The cross-sectional correlation between seasonal and cyclical variation most likely occurs because a common propagation mechanism produces both seasonal and cyclical fluctuations. A large fraction of existing models of the business cycle distinguish between the effects of anticipated and unanticipated shocks. The results described above therefore suggest that this distinction may be substantially less important than existing work implies.

Jeffrey A. Miron

See also SEASONAL ADJUSTMENT; SEASONAL FLUCTUATIONS AND FINANCIAL CRISES; STYLIZED FACTS

Bibliography

Barsky, R. B. and J. A. Miron. 1989. "The Seasonal Cycle and the Business Cycle." *Journal of Political Economy* 97:503–34.

Beaulieu, J. J. and J. A. Miron. 1991. "The Seasonal Cycle in U.S. Manufacturing." *Economic Letters* 37:115–18.

———. 1992. "A Cross-Country Comparison of Seasonal Cycles and Business Cycles." *Economic Journal* 102:772–88.

Miron, J. A. and S. P. Zeldes. 1988. "Seasonality, Cost Shocks, and the Production Smoothing Models of Inventories." *Econometrica* 56:877–908.

Seasonal Fluctuations and Financial Crises

Before 1914, the distribution of financial panics in both the United States and Europe was highly seasonal. This phenomenon received considerable attention from economists and policymakers, most notably from W. S. Jevons in 1866. Jevons explained that the seasonal in panics occurred because shocks to the financial system were more likely to produce stress when banks held low reserves. The seasonal in reserves was in turn due to a seasonal in asset demands related to the harvest cycle. Jevons suggested that seasonal lending by the central bank would eliminate the seasonal in panics. Reducing the frequency of financial panics by accommodating seasonal asset demands was also a primary objective of the founders of the Federal Reserve System.

Table 1 lists the dates of financial panics in the United States during the 1873–1909 period. This is the period for which there is detailed information on the dating of panics, due to the work of the National Monetary Commission. The main sources are the parts of the Commission's *Report* written by E. S. Kemmerer and by O. M. W. Sprague. The two authors used different criteria to classify periods of financial stress and therefore identified different numbers of panics. However, the two authors agreed on the timing of the major panics, and Sprague's list is a subset of Kemmerer's more exhaustive one. In Sprague's terminology, a crisis is the most serious kind of financial distress involving a suspension of convertibility.

The information in Table 1 shows that the greatest numbers of panics occur in the spring and fall. Twelve of the twenty-nine panics identified by Kemmerer occurred in March, April, or May and ten occurred in September or December. A χ^2 goodness of fit test rejects (at the .001 percent confidence level) the hypothesis that the panics were uniformly distributed across seasons. Sprague emphasized that if severity is taken into account, the tendency for panics to occur in the autumn becomes more pronounced.

The limited evidence on the timing of financial panics before the Civil War also shows that panics occurred seasonally. Kindleberger dates the crises as beginning in November 1818, September 1837, and August 1857, consistent with Sprague's view that panics occurred predominantly in the fall harvest period.

TABLE 1. Dates of Financial Panics, United States, 1873–1909

Source	Classification	Year	Month
Sprague	Crisis	1873	September
	Panic	1884	May
	Financial stringency	1890	August
	Crisis	1893	May
	Crisis	1907	October
Kemmerer	Major panics	1873	September
		1884	May
		1890	November
		1893	May
		1899	December
		1901	May
		1903	March
		1907	October
	Minor panics	1876	April
		1879	November
		1880	May
		1882	March
		1887	June
		1888	March
		1893	February
		1895	September
		1896	June
		1896	December
		1898	March
		1899	September
		1901	July
		1901	September
		1902	September
		1904	December
		1905	April
		1906	April
		1907	March
		1908	September

Sources: Sprague (1910), pp. 33, 108–114, 124–52, 167, 246–56; Kemmerer (1910), pp. 222–23.

Financial crises before 1914 were seasonal in Europe as well as in the United States. Table 2 provides Kindleberger's evidence on the dates of panics in Europe. These data also show a strong tendency for financial difficulties to occur in the fall and spring; a χ^2 test again rejects (at the .001 percent level) the hypothesis that the panics were uniformly distributed across seasons. Commenting on this phenomenon, *The Economist* (2 December 1865, 1453) wrote, "Why was the pressure [in money markets] in

TABLE 2. Dates of Financial Panics, Europe,
1720–1914

Location	Year	Month
England	1720	September
France	1720	May
Amsterdam	1763	September
Britain	1773	January
England	1793	February
England	1797	February–June
Hamburg	1799	August–November
England	1811	January
England	1825	December
France	1827	December
England	1836	December
France	1837	June
England	1847	October
Continent	1848	March
England	1857	October
Continent	1857	November
France	1864	January
England	1866	May
Italy	1866	May
Germany	1873	May
Austria	1873	May
France	1882	January
England	1890	November
France	1907	August
Italy	1907	August

Source: Kindleberger (1978), pp. 253–59.

October 1847, in October 1857, in October last year, in October this year, and more or less in October every year?" (italics in original).

The generally accepted explanation for the seasonality of panics is the one offered by Jevons. Before 1914, asset demands were highly seasonal, leading in equilibrium to seasonal increases in nominal interest rates and seasonal decreases in reserve-deposit ratios. As a result, the reserve-deposit ratios of banks typically fell in the spring and fall when the demand for currency and credit rose. Thus, if a shock of some kind hit the financial system, it was more likely to precipitate a crisis in these seasons than if a similar shock hit in a season of high reserve-deposit ratios.

The seasonals in asset demands were mainly caused by the agricultural cycle. During the spring and fall, the demand for loans expanded as additional credit was required to finance the planting, harvesting, transporting, and warehousing of the crop. Currency demand also increased since the volume of transactions expanded in these periods. Other reasons for the seasonals in asset demands included quarterly dividend and interest settlements by businesses, increased rail and barge activity during warm weather, and holidays.

At least since Jevons, economists recognized that central banks could reduce the seasonal tendency toward financial crises by accommodating seasonals in asset demands. However, central banks were hesitant to accommodate increases in loan or currency demand because of their overriding commitment to the gold standard. Jevons insisted that central banks could accommodate *temporary* changes in demand without threatening their gold reserve. A fortiori, central banks could accommodate seasonal changes in asset demands, which not only are transitory but are known to reverse themselves within a short time.

In practice, central banks before 1914 hesitated to follow Jevons's advice, since no single central bank was powerful enough to sterilize the world's interest-rate seasonal. Cooperation among different central banks might have alleviated this problem, but the United States, already an important factor in world financial markets, had no central bank until 1914. In 1914, however, the desire to smooth interest-rate fluctuations and thereby eliminate financial panics led to the founding of the Federal Reserve System. Once the Fed was in place, all central banks began sterilizing interest-rate seasonals.

Since 1914, interest-rate seasonals have been largely absent in all countries, presumably due to deliberate sterilization by central banks. With the notable exception of the Great Depression in the United States, financial panics have also been largely absent. The timing of the panics that did occur during the Great Depression is consistent with the spring-fall pattern described above: three of the crises began in the fall, and two started in the spring (Friedman and Schwartz 1963, 305, 308, 313, 317, 324). As suggested by Miron, this evidence confirms the relation between panics and seasonal asset demands described above, because the Fed grew less accommodating of asset-market fluctuations beginning in late 1928. The absence of panics since 1933 is likely the result of the institution of deposit insurance in 1934. Insofar as deposit insurance has, by itself, eliminated the tendency of the economy toward financial panics, the necessity of seasonal loan accommodation is probably substantially reduced.

Jeffrey A. Miron

See also DEMAND FOR CURRENCY; FEDERAL RESERVE SYSTEM: 1914–1941; JEVONS, WILLIAM STANLEY; SEASONAL ADJUSTMENT; SEASONAL CYCLES; SPRAGUE, OLIVER MITCHELL WENTWORTH

Bibliography

Barsky, R. B., N. G. Mankiw, J. A. Miron, and D. N. Weil. 1988. "The Worldwide Change in the Behavior of Interest Rates and Prices in 1914." *European Economic Review* 32:1123–47.

Friedman, M. and A. J. Schwartz. 1963. *A Monetary History of the United States, 1867–1960.* Princeton: Princeton Univ. Press.

Jevons, W. S. [1866] 1884. "On the Frequent Autumnal Pressure in the Money Market, and the Action of the Bank of England." Chap. 5 in *Investigations in Currency and Finance.* London: Macmillan.

Kemmerer, E. W. 1910. *Seasonal Variations in the Relative Demand for Money and Capital in the United States.* National Monetary Commission. Washington, D.C.: Government Printing Office.

Kindleberger, C. P. 1978. *Manias, Panics, and Crashes.* New York: Basic Books.

Miron, J. A. 1986. "Financial Panics, the Seasonality of the Nominal Interest Rates, and the Founding of the Fed." *American Economic Review* 76:125–40.

Sprague, O. M. W. 1910. *History of Crises Under the National Banking System.* Washington, D.C.: Government Printing Office.

Sectoral Shifts

An enduring explanation of persistently positive unemployment rates is the frictional theory of unemployment elegantly formalized by Lucas and Prescott ([1974] 1981). In this theory, the economy consists of many spatially or institutionally distinct sectors, which may be thought of as geographical regions, firms, occupations, industries, or combinations thereof. The distribution of labor demand across sectors evolves stochastically, with demand rising in some sectors and falling in others. As an example, labor demand rose in Sun Belt states in the 1980s while demand simultaneously fell in the Northern states. Workers react to these *sectoral shifts* by migrating from sectors where demand is falling towards sectors where it is rising. Unemployment occurs because this mobility is time-consuming. If the variance of the cross-sector distribution of demand changes is constant over time, then the model implies a constant "natural" rate of unemployment. In this model, unemployment is both voluntary (since workers choose to move) and efficient (since workers move to where they are most productive).

While frictional theories have been widely accepted as important in any explanation of the natural rate of unemployment, economists have traditionally looked for other theories to explain cyclical fluctuations of unemployment. The sectoral-shifts hypothesis advanced by Lilien (1982) suggests that a unified explanation of both cyclical and natural-rate unemployment may be possible. The idea is that the variance in the distribution of cross-sector changes in labor demand is unlikely to be constant over time. Some periods may involve a great deal of sectoral reallocation of labor, and hence unemployment, while other periods may see little variance across sectors in demand growth, and hence little need for reallocative unemployment. The sectoral-shifts hypothesis has obvious appeal as an explanation of the rise in unemployment that occurred through the 1970s and early 1980s, as this period saw two large oil-price shocks and accelerated shifts from manufacturing into services.

In order to more formally test his hypothesis on the postwar unemployment experience of the United States, Lilien needed a measure of the variance of sectoral changes in labor demand. He chose the variance of employment growth rates across industries in the U.S. As it turns out, aggregate unemployment and this measure of the dispersion of sectoral demand are strongly correlated. Lilien interpreted this as evidence that sectoral shifts are an important determinant of fluctuations in aggregate unemployment.

Unfortunately, Lilien's findings are equally consistent with more traditional explanations. Abraham and Katz (1986) pointed out that a model with one aggregate disturbance can imply a positive correlation between aggregate unemployment and Lilien's dispersion index, provided that industries differ in their sensitivity to aggregate shocks. In comparison to employment in service industries, employment in manufacturing and construction declines precipitously in recessions, but increases quickly in recoveries. Therefore, the years immediately surrounding a business-cycle trough tend to exhibit a great deal of inter-industry dispersion in growth rates, even without a sectoral shift.

Abraham and Katz suggested a different method for empirically distinguishing sectoral shifts from aggregate shocks. They argued that the aggregate-shock hypothesis implies a negative correlation between help-wanted advertising and aggregate unemployment, whereas the sectoral-shifts hypothesis implies the opposite. They show that there is a strong negative correlation between help-wanted advertising and aggregate unemployment. While the help-wanted data are of somewhat suspect quality, this correlation suggests that aggregate shocks, rather than sectoral shifts, are the primary source of cyclical fluctuations in unemployment.

One appealing feature of the sectoral-shifts hypothesis in particular, and of frictional-unemployment theory in general, is that it makes predictions about who is unemployed. Unemployment occurs because workers make time-consuming transitions from low-demand to high-demand sectors. Therefore, the theory predicts that unemployment is concentrated among workers in the midst of moving from one sector to another. Unfortunately, these predictions are difficult to test with the aggregate data analyzed by Lilien and by Abraham and Katz. A second round of research on the sectoral-shifts hypothesis has, therefore, investigated the connection between sectoral mobility and unemployment.

Murphy and Topel (1987) used data from the Current Population Survey (CPS) for the 1968–85 period that included generally rising unemployment along with several cyclical episodes. They found that workers who change industries are more likely to be unemployed than similar workers who do not change industries. This finding supports one of the basic assumptions of the sectoral-shifts hypothesis. However, they also found that industry-movers account for only a small fraction of total unemployment. Moreover, they found that mobility is procyclical and that the rising trend in unemployment over this period was not accompanied by a rising trend in industrial mobility. In short, Murphy and Topel's findings do not support the sectoral-shifts hypothesis as an explanation for cyclical unemployment.

One drawback of the CPS data used by Murphy and Topel is that workers are not tracked over time. If a worker is unemployed through the survey date and subsequently becomes reemployed in a new industry, this industry change is unrecorded in the CPS. This is potentially an important problem since, as Murphy and Topel document, long unemployment spells (six months or longer) account for about half of all unemployment. To cope with this issue, Loungani and Rogerson (1989) examined true panel data in the Panel Study of Income Dynamics (PSID). The PSID follows workers for much longer periods than the CPS, so it is usually possible to learn whether long unemployment spells end with industry transitions. Loungani and Rogerson find that industry switchers account for roughly 25 percent of unemployment in normal years, but that this fraction increased to roughly 40 percent in the recessions of 1974–75 and 1980–82.

It should be clear from this discussion that there is no consensus yet on the importance of sectoral shifts as an explanation of cyclical unemployment. Among the aggregate analyses, Lilien finds support for the sectoral-shifts hypothesis while Abraham and Katz have offered conflicting evidence. Among the microanalyses, Murphy and Topel have argued against the hypothesis while Loungani and Rogerson argue that it is an important factor. This is not too surprising, since research on sectoral shifts is still in its early stages. Any future resolution of the controversy is likely to come from a careful examination of micro-data on unemployment and mobility. A potentially fruitful avenue is the use of matched CPS data that link individuals across years in the CPS. This data source has begun to be widely used in other applications and is a natural source of information on mobility and unemployment.

Sectoral shifts and aggregate shocks have generally been viewed as competing hypotheses. However, Davis (1987) has argued that the hypotheses can also be complementary mechanisms. Suppose there is a more or less continuous amount of sectoral reallocation called for by labor-demand fluctuations. If this reallocation entails some time out of work, then workers would be wise to time their sectoral migration with periods of slack aggregate demand, when the opportunity cost of migration is lowest. In this view, the effect of aggregate-demand fluctuations on unemployment is compounded by fluctuations in the pace of labor reallocation.

In essence, this view explains why workers might be willing to withdraw into unemployment in response to quite small changes in wages. Instead of the high elasticity of intertemporal substitution of leisure posited in some real-business-cycle models, this model posits a high elasticity of intertemporal substitution of job search.

William J. Carrington

See also REAL BUSINESS-CYCLE THEORIES; RECESSIONS (SUPPLY-SIDE) IN THE 1970S; SEARCH THEORY; WORKER AND JOB TURNOVER

Bibliography

Abraham, K. G. and L. F. Katz. 1986. "Cyclical Unemployment: Sectoral Shifts or Aggregate Disturbance?" *Journal of Political Economy* 94:507–22.

Davis, S. J. 1987. "Fluctuations in the Pace of Labor Reallocations." *Carnegie-Rochester Conference Series on Public Policy,* Autumn, 335–402.

Lilien, D. 1982. "Sectoral Shifts and Cyclical Unemployment." *Journal of Political Economy* 90:777–93.

Loungani, P. and R. Rogerson. 1989. "Cyclical Fluctuations and Sectoral Reallocation: Evidence from the PSID." *Journal of Monetary Economics* 23:259–73.

Lucas, R. E. Jr. and E.C. Prescott. [1974] 1981. "Equilibrium Search and Unemployment." In R. E. Lucas Jr., *Studies in Business-Cycle Theory,* 156–78. Cambridge: MIT Press.

Murphy, K. M. and R. Topel. 1987. "The Evolution of Unemployment in the United States: 1968–1985." In *NBER Macroeconomics Annual,* edited by S. Fischer, 7–58. Cambridge: MIT Press.

Serial Correlation

Any econometric exercise whose goal is inference about the underlying structure requires a correct specification of the model including specification of the stochastic assumptions. In their pioneering work, Yule, Slutsky, and Koopmans showed that serially correlated errors, common trends in time-series variables, and small samples of data cause Least Squares (LS) and Maximum Likelihood (ML) estimation procedures to produce spurious and inefficient estimates of the underlying economic model.

Aggregate macroeconomic time-series data are known to be highly serially correlated in raw-level form, where serial correlation is defined as a measure of the linear dependence between two separate points in a time-series variable. Variables such as GNP, real consumption expenditure, and real national income show nonstationary serial-correlation patterns characterized by a strong average upward trend component with shorter cycles around trend.

In developing early macrodynamic business-cycle models, Tinbergen acknowledged that high degrees of serial correlation in both regressand and regressors could cause spurious coefficient estimates, standard errors, and goodness-of-fit measures. Thus, he preferred to work with detrended data, using moving averages and other trend-removal techniques. Despite his attention to the spurious-correlation problem, most of his results had serially correlated residuals. This was because the dynamics in the dependent variables had been improperly modeled or because of the influence of noneconomic factors that cannot be incorporated into an economic model.

At about the same time, Koopmans showed that LS and ML estimation techniques required the errors in an econometric model to be serially uncorrelated. This tended to undermine the impact of Tinbergen's results. Modern texts teach that serially correlated errors render LS and ML estimators inefficient. Furthermore, Mann and Wald (1943) showed that LS and ML estimators are biased in any sized sample if the regression equation includes a lagged dependent variable and errors are autocorrelated. Lawrence Klein's 1950 business-cycle models also suffered from serially correlated residuals. His remedy (adopted by others as well) was either to add other variables such as lagged dependent and independent variables or abandon the specification altogether (Epstein 1987, 104–05). It was not until the late 1940s that the problem could be statistically remedied.

British statisticians believed that these errors in the Tinbergen and Klein equations reflected the omission of unobserved economic variables or of noneconomic variables that could not be modeled. Thus, adding variables to satisfy the statistical requirement that the errors be independent was to deliberately misspecify the model. This led Cochrane and Orcutt (1949) to propose the now famous Cochrane-Orcutt transformation and iterative estimation procedure as a way of restoring the optimal properties of LS in the face of serial cor-

S

relation (for details see Johnston 1984). However, the procedure only corrected for first-order serial correlation. Subsequently, many researchers extended the basic Cochrane-Orcutt method for higher-order autoregressive and moving-average errors (Harvey 1990). Generalized estimation methods that can handle very complicated autoregressive or moving-average errors are now common.

Diagnostic testing for serial correlation has become as sophisticated as estimation techniques. In the early years of large macrodynamic systems of Tinbergen and Klein, the von Neumann ratio was used to test for uncorrelated errors against first-order autoregressive errors. Unfortunately, since the residuals are not independent and identically distributed in finite samples (as assumed by the test), the exact distribution of the statistic is unknown and the normal approximation is valid only in large samples (a real problem in the early years).

Durbin and Watson (1950–51) remedied this problem by developing a similar statistic corrected for the number of degrees of freedom in the exogenous variables. The distribution of this statistic depended on the type of exogenous regressors used in the model. Fortunately, the variation in the percentiles was bounded, so that tables recorded the upper and lower boundary of the rejection region independent of the type of exogenous regressor. Rejection of the null hypothesis meant that serial correlation of at least first order existed in the residuals without precluding higher-order processes. The description and frequency tables of the Durbin-Watson (DW) test are included in almost every modern econometrics text. Tests against higher-order autoregressive and moving-average error structures were designed for cases where the DW test was invalid. For a thorough description of the diagnostic tests for serial correlation available to the practitioner, see Johnston (1984), Harvey (1990) and Judge et al. (1985).

By the late 1960s and the 1970s (if not earlier), the large simultaneous-equation systems used to estimate business-cycle models were losing favor with the profession. One reason was their consistently poor prediction record; another was the rise of single- and multiple-equation time-series models. Box and Jenkins developed and popularized a pure time-series modeling technique that, using simpler models, seemed to predict better than the macroeconometric models. The strategy is to allow a model of the serial-correlation pattern in the time series of the aggregate variables to dominate short-run and potentially long-run prediction and forecasting. The idea behind this approach is not new. Early hints at this kind of modeling can be found in Orcutt (1948) and Slutsky ([1927] 1937).

The most influential defense of this approach was made by Sims (1980), who advocates using complete multivariate time-series models for simulation and forecasting. The models, called *vector autoregressive* or VARs, are a system of autoregressive equations in which every variable, current and past, is a regressor in every other variable's equation. The coefficients, as in Box-Jenkins-type models, have no economic meaning—they are not structural coefficients. The approach seeks to avoid large models of economic behavior, and allowing the serial-correlation patterns in the data to dominate the forecasting exercise. The coefficients of these models, whether univariate or multivariate, are usually estimated by nonlinear LS or a modified ML routine. For a complete description of the Box-Jenkins method and VAR time-series modeling, see Box and Jenkins (1970) and Harvey (1990).

The major statistical feature of macroeconomic time-series data is their high degree of serial correlation. The identification, estimation, and testing of business-cycle hypotheses depend crucially on how we view the generation of the data. The early structural models attempted to characterize the underlying structure of this generation process. The presence of serial correlation in all major variables introduced spurious-correlation problems as well as technical estimation problems that had to be resolved before the estimates of structural coefficients could be credible. However, recent advances in time-series methods have allowed researchers to use the serially dependent nature of the data to build pure univariate and multivariate forecasting models without economic content.

Thomas A. Peters

See also FILTERS; KLEIN, LAWRENCE ROBERT; KOOPMANS, TJALLING CHARLES; MACRO-ECONOMETRIC MODELS, HISTORIAL DEVELOPMENT; MOVING AVERAGES; TINBERGEN, JAN; VECTOR AUTOREGRESSIONS

Bibliography

Box, G. E. P. and G. M. Jenkins. 1970. *Time Series Analysis: Forecasting and Control.* San Francisco: Holden Day.

Cochrane, W. and G. Orcutt. 1949. "Applications of Least Squares Regression to Relationships Containing Autocorrelated Error Terms." *Journal of the American Statistical Association* 44:32–61.

Durbin, J. and G. S. Watson. 1950–51. "Testing for Serial Correlation in Least Squares Regression." *Biometrika* 37:409–28, 38:159–78.

Epstein, R. J. 1987. *A History of Econometrics*. Amsterdam: North-Holland.

Harvey, A. C. 1990. *The Econometric Analysis of Time Series*. 2d ed. Oxford: Philip Alan.

Johnston, J. 1984. *Econometric Methods*. 3rd ed. New York: McGraw-Hill.

Judge, G. G., W. E. Griffiths, R. C. Hill, H. Lutkepohl, and T-C. Lee. 1985. *The Theory and Practice of Econometrics*. New York: Wiley.

Klein, L. R. 1950. *Economic Fluctuations in the United States 1921–1941*. New York: Wiley.

Koopmans, T. 1937. *Linear Regression Analysis of Economic Time Series*. Haarlem: De Erven F. Bohn.

Mann, H. B. and A. Wald. 1943. "On the Statistical Treatment of Linear Stochastic Difference Equations." *Econometrica* 11:173–220.

Orcutt, G. 1948. "A Study of the Autoregressive Nature of the Time Series Used in Tinbergen's Model of the Economic System of the United States 1919–1932." *Journal of the Royal Statistical Society,* series B, 10:1–45.

Sims, C. A. 1980. "Macroeconomics and Reality." *Econometrica* 48:1–45.

Slutsky, E. [1927] 1937. "The Summation of Random Causes as the Source of Cyclical Processes." Translation. *Econometrica* 5:105–46.

Stock, J. H. and M. W. Watson. 1988. "Variable Trends in Economic Time Series." *Journal of Economic Perspectives,* Summer, 147–74.

Tinbergen, J. 1939. *Statistical Testing of Business Cycle Theories*. 2 vols. Geneva: League of Nations.

Yule, G. 1927. "On a Method for Investigating Periodicities in Disturbed Series, with Special Reference to Wolfer's Sunspot Numbers." *Philosophical Transactions of the Royal Society* 226:267–98.

Shackle, George Lennox Sharman (1903–1993)

G. L. S. Shackle's contributions to business-cycle theory were originally made in the mid-1930s, as part of his doctoral dissertation, *Expectations, Investment, and Income,* published in 1938. He restated and evaluated the originality of these views thirty years later in the second edition of that book.

One starts with the twin reminders that in the 1930s, (1) the principal social and economic problem was unemployment (not economic growth), and (2) the key obsessive idea was to explain business cycles as an endogenous phenomenon. Even Mitchell, who concluded that the generative element likely changed for each cycle, saw the causes as internal. Trends may have been the product of exogenous forces, but cycles, as perceived, had to be understood in terms of self-generation (Shackle 1938, xix).

What Shackle suggested in his 1938 work was that the key to understanding the investment process was expectations, but that expectations could not be modeled as simple continuous functions. Expectations, once imagined and once the implementation efforts were underway, come to some sort of fruition, and at that point entrepreneurs assess what they had initially imagined and how the original concept has worked out. Perhaps drawing on an idea often associated with Kaldor's later repudiated emphasis on indivisibilities, Shackle stressed that a big dream requires not only a long time to implement, but that until the final stone is in place, the entrepreneur must live on his hopes. Shackle had written in 1936 how this waiting for results, particularly while others are also engaged in similar things, would greatly affect entrepreneurs' imaginations and what they would undertake immediately afterwards. A multiplier effect on these economic dreams cuts both ways. Initially an individual entrepreneur ought to feel buoyed by his awareness that others, too, share his confidence, but when all sorts of new things later emerge, the typical entrepreneur begins to worry that costs are rising too rapidly and that the market cannot absorb all there is for sale. Caution replaces confidence, hopes for profits are replaced with relative fears, and so forth.

What emerges most clearly in the 1938 book is Shackle's fascination with the fragility as well as the pliability of entrepreneurial expectations. Shackle's argument moves from a general statement of the asymmetry between the impact of the multiplier before, during, and after a downturn and its impact once the economy has passed a peak to a descriptive theory of the cycle itself. Shackle then turned to the question of interest-rate changes, stressing how the investment process, requiring different time stretches for the new equipment to come on line, provides an uneven flow of demand for borrowable funds. These fits and starts not only destabilize the bankers' and hoarders' preferences for orderliness, they reinforce the desire to hoard. For if one can hoard when all the others about him are doing otherwise, one is in place to make a killing.

Bearish hoarders are likely to keep hoarding, bullish ones to look for opportunities. But the expectations of the hoarders are matched by an independent set of entrepreneurial expectations. The latter, according to Shackle, divide into (1) foreseeable (discounted) changes over the time period during which the investment comes to fruition and (2) unforeseeable changes. Unforeseeable changes reflect von Thünian (or Knightian) uncertainty, and they are both subject to and creative of multiplier effects. Complicating the picture conceptually is the possibility that the entrepreneur may try to speed up (or slow down) the investment process in order to adjust changes in the time frame to his fears (or hopes) about the unknowable future. Lurking in the entrepreneurs' minds are thoughts about such unforeseeable things as political changes (remember Shackle was writing in the 1930s), natural events like droughts and earthquakes, to say nothing of a burst of Schumpeterian invention-innovation.

It is the combination of an Austrian subjectivism with a recognition of the impossibility of foreseeing the future that led Shackle to view entrepreneurial expectations as the critical factor in economic matters. Keynes called it animal spirits; Shackle came to call it the role of human imagination.

From the early 1940s until the 1980s, professional interest in business-cycle theory, particularly ideas relating to cycle causes, was generally overshadowed by a general interest in macroeconomic analysis. One product of this change was the development of national accounts, particularly as they were conceived within the framework of the Keynesian system. The ability to identify pockets of capital underutilization and to measure changes in gross and net income distribution seemed such powerful analytical aids that a priori theorizing was overwhelmed. This shift was no less the product of a long era of short and not very severe recessions than the result of a complete destruction of that intellectual "Berlin Wall" between economic theory and economic institutionalism. Just as the pragmatic test (ideas must not only be logical they must also pass the test of usefulness) had become part of the weltanschauung, so some form of empirical (quantitative) verification became a regular requirement. And in addition, one quite different factor was at work: economic growth displaced business cycles as the central concern of economic theory.

Shackle, inspired by his interest in the role of the imagination and his recognition of the unknowableness of the future, and utilizing his own method of schematically laying out a "probability-possibility" system for the imaginable, went on to develop a general theory of the way economies—themselves made up of entrepreneurs' fancies, schemes, plans, and dreams—work. Shackle once laid out what he thought was the kernel of his contribution as follows (G. L. S. Shackle, letter to author, 1980):

> I wished to escape from the logic that compels probabilities assigned to the members of a complete list of rival answers to some one question to add up to unity. The escape consists in saying that, in the most general context, the list of suggested answers cannot be deemed completable. Thus we need a measure of standing that need not, must not and cannot have its degrees respectively assigned to different answers, added together. The next step is to flesh-out these bones with some psychic content. My suggestion was potential surprise. It will be *zero* for answers (hypotheses) assigned the highest standing and an arbitrary maximum for lowest standing (entire rejection). . . . Standing is represented by degrees of *dis*belief. . . . It remains to seek some formally respectable or dissectible basis for potential surprise itself. Potential surprise will only be zero if the assessor knows of no principle or circumstance which is incompatible or incongruous with the truth of the hypothesis. It will attain its utmost degree if there is present to the assessor's thought some fatal obstacle to the truth of the hypothesis. . . . We may consider that "perfectly possible" and "perfectly impossible" are the only levels

which have meaning. To me it seems permissible to define intermediate levels, "imperfect possibility."

This scheme of ideas is what I would put in place of all meaning of "probability," including Keynes's "degree of rational belief." . . . In the end, [Keynes] . . . rejected probability as irrelevant, without however, suggesting anything in place of it. My endeavour to fill the vacuum is *not* another attempt to show that irremediable lack of knowledge (of time-to-come) can be remedied by some gimmick. It can, I think, be *exploited* (in the interest of a good state of mind) but not in any way which would satisfy men's notion of being master of their fate.

The Shackelian vision of business cycles combines the effect of individual entrepreneurs' imaginations, each playing with its own, possibly unique, perception of a firm's possibilities. These interact to cause specific (industrial) cycles, and, then the whole is identified, *ex post,* as the business cycle.

Mark Perlman

See also EXPECTATIONS; HAYEK, FRIEDRICH AUGUST [VON]; KEYNES, JOHN MAYNARD; LACHMANN, LUDWIG MAURITS; RATIONAL EXPECTATIONS

Bibliography
Boulding, K. 1973. Review of *Economics and Epistemics,* by G. L. S. Shackle. *Journal of Economic Literature* 11:1373–74.
Coddington, A. 1976. "Keynesian Economics: The Search for First Principles." *Journal of Economic Literature* 14:1258–73.
Earl, P. 1987. "Shackle, George Lennox Sharman." In *The New Palgrave: A Dictionary of Economics.* Vol. 4. Edited by J. Eatwell, M. Milgate, and P. Newman. London: Macmillan.
———. [1930] 1971. *A Treatise on Money.* 2 vols. Vols. 5 and 6 of *The Collected Writings of John Maynard Keynes.* London: Macmillan.
———. [1936] 1973. *The General Theory of Employment, Interest, and Money.* Vol. 7 of *The Collected Writings of John Maynard Keynes.* London: Macmillan.
———. 1937. "The General Theory of Employment." *Quarterly Journal of Economics* 51:209–25.
Meltzer, A. H. 1988. *Keynes's Monetary Theory: A Different Interpretation.* New York: Cambridge Univ. Press.
Patinkin, D. 1976. *Keynes' Monetary Thought: A Study of Its Development.* Durham: Duke Univ. Press.
Pigou, A. C. 1917. "The Value of Money." *Quarterly Journal of Economics* 32:38–65.
Shackle, G. L. S. 1936. "The Breakdown of the Boom: A Possible Mechanism." *Economica* n.s. 3:423–35.
———. [1938] 1968. *Expectations, Investment, and Income.* Oxford: Clarendon Press.
———. 1967. *The Years of High Theory.* Cambridge: Cambridge Univ. Press.
———. 1972. *Epistemics and Economics: A Critique of Economic Doctrines.* Cambridge: Cambridge Univ. Press.
———. 1973. *An Economic Querist.* Cambridge: Cambridge Univ. Press.
———. 1974. *Keynesian Kaleidics: The Evolution of a General Political Economy.* Edinburgh: Edinburgh Univ. Press.

S

Signal Extraction

The link between money and business cycles has long been a central concern of macroeconomic research. The rational-expectations hypothesis was first incorporated into an equilibrium framework that could examine this link in the seminal work of Robert Lucas ([1973] 1981). Subsequent equilibrium business-cycle models with rational expectations generally fall into two classes, which both attribute cyclical fluctuations to informational imperfections. One type adopts Lucas's hypothesis that agents cannot conclusively determine whether local price movements reflect changes in relative or absolute prices. Thus, output diverges from its full-information level due to purely nominal disturbances. The other type of model assumes that output fluctuations arise from confusion about whether a particular shock is nominal or real. Barro (1980), for example, argues that output deviates from its full-information level when agents misperceive money-supply shocks. Of course there is no reason that both types of confusion cannot occur simultaneously.

Since both types of models produce temporary Phillips Curve tradeoffs in the presence of long-run monetary neutrality, it is natural to ask whether monetary policy can exploit such tradeoffs. Sargent and Wallace (1975) initially answered this question by showing that systematic monetary policy is neutral. However, their analysis depends on the fairly restrictive information structure of their model. In a more general setting in which agents have both specific information and access to common information, their results do not hold. In one such generalization, the early rational-expectations models were extended to include a nominal interest rate. The interest rate is determined in an economy-wide asset market and is observed by all agents. Thus, agents observe an aggregate signal as well as prices in their local markets. The coupling of heterogeneous information with a common observable price allows systematic monetary policy to be non-neutral. In such circumstances, policy can clarify the information content of prices, allowing agents to better identify fundamental disturbances. Analysis along these lines was first performed by King (1982, 1983) and Weiss (1982) and was extended by Dotsey and King (1983, 1986) and by Canzoneri, Henderson, and Rogoff (1983).

Once it was understood that monetary policy can affect the information content of various market signals, the question arose whether similar effects could follow from changing the economic structure to expand or contract the information set available to agents. Papers by Kimbrough (1985), Boschen (1986), and Edwards and Hahm (1987) address this issue. Also, since monetary misperceptions are critical to the relationship between economic activity and unexpected price-level changes, the implications of including observable money have been explored by King (1981), Barro and Hercowitz (1980), and Boschen and Grossman (1982).

An overview of these types of analysis can be posed in the following general framework. Suppose economic agents seek to uncover the value of a variable (or vector of variables), x_t, that is not directly observable. In the Lucas framework, x_t corresponds to the aggregate price level, while in the Barro framework it corresponds to the money-supply disturbance. To make inferences about the value of x_t, agents use a vector of signals $s_t = (s_{1t} \ldots s_{nt})$ that contains information about x_t. These signals correspond to prices and quantities that are observable by agents. If x_t and s_t are jointly normally distributed, conditional on the information set I_{t-1}, then

$$Ex_t| s_t, I_{t-1} = Ex_t| I_{t-1} +$$
$$B_{xs}(s_t - Es_t| I_{t-1}),$$
$$\text{where } B_{xs} = \sigma_{xs}\Sigma_{ss}^{-1} \quad (1)$$
$$\text{and } \sigma_{xs} = Ex_t s_t|I_{t-1}, \Sigma_{ss} = Es_t s_t'|I_{t-1}.$$

That is, the forecast of x_t given the information contained in I_{t-1} and the signal s_t can be decomposed into a term involving only the information in I_{t-1} plus a term that incorporates the updating of expectations due to the signal s_t. The conditional variance of x_t given s_t is

$$\sigma_{xx} - \sigma_{xs}'\Sigma_{ss}^{-1}\sigma_{xs} \quad (2)$$

where $\sigma_{xx} = Ex_t^2|I_{t-1}$. A policy that reduces this conditional variance produces a better prediction or a better information state. In the Lucas framework, a policy improves the information state if it reduces $E(p_t - Ep_t|I_t)^2|I_t$. Since the variance of output around its full-information value is linearly related to the variance of this forecast error, such a policy also improves welfare. Similarly in Barro, a policy that reduces $E(m_t - Em_t|I_t)^2|I_t$ improves welfare.

Policy can alter the information state in two ways. One is to alter the list of signals without changing the covariance structure of the model. From elementary econometrics, we know that adding a signal (or independent variable) can only improve the forecast of x_t. The other is to alter the covariance structure of x_t, s_t (i.e., σ_{xs}). To determine how policy affects the conditional variance of x_t, the change in the covariance structure must be specified. In rational-expectations models nearly all policy interventions or changes in the structure of the economy affect the covariance structure of the model, while some also change the number of signals.

For example, consider the class of log-linear money-supply rules

$$M_t = M_0 + \sum_{j=1}^{n} f_j x_{j, t-1} + x_{1, t} \quad (3)$$

that involve feedback parameters on the past disturbances in the model. For simplicity, assume the disturbances, $x_{j,t}$, have mean zero and are independently normally distributed. The observation that is common to all individuals is the nominal interest rate R_t, which is composed of the real rate and expected inflation. The partially reduced-form expression for the nominal rate can be written as a combination of expected inflation, current unobserved disturbances, and past disturbances observable to everyone. The expected-inflation term represents an economy-wide average over all agents. Since agents have access to different information, this term is not known to any particular agent, because it reflects the uncertainty of others. In a sense, this unknown expectation contaminates the signal value of the nominal interest rate. However, since current disturbances will affect the future price level through the feedback rule, the monetary authority can suitably set the feedback parameters to increase the precision of the information that the nominal interest rate conveys about underlying disturbances. As King (1982) and Weiss (1982) have noted, this type of feedback is prospective in nature, since feedback on past disturbances does not affect output.

Besides direct policy, other changes in the informational structure of the economy can matter. For example, allowing agents to acquire information at some cost changes the behavior of those who obtain information directly and of those who get information solely from prices (Edwards and Hahm 1987). Because prices reflect the behavior of informed agents, prices provide more information to the relatively uninformed. The result is that unanticipated money generally has a smaller effect on output if agents can acquire information than if they cannot.

Instead of changing because individual agents acquire information, the informational structure could change if additional markets (such as a futures market or an indexed bond market) are introduced. For example, if a futures market generates a price reflecting a stochastic risk premium plus the average of the expected future price level, agents are provided additional information about the beliefs of others. If the risk premium were nonstochastic, then observing the future price would be equivalent to observing the average expected future price level. As Kimbrough (1985) points out, monetary feedback rules would no longer have any effects, although augmenting agents' information sets would move output toward its full-information value.

One potential source of information that we have neglected in examining how the information structure affects equilibrium in monetary business-cycle models with rational expectations is money itself. Since the interaction between nominal and real magnitudes results from monetary misperceptions, observability of the money supply destroys this linkage. King

(1981) has shown that in the presence of measurement errors, only revisions in monetary data should be correlated with real economic activity. Tests of this hypothesis generally do not support this conclusion. For example, Barro and Hercowitz (1980) fail to find correlations between output or unemployment and monetary revisions, while Boschen and Grossman (1982) found that contemporaneous monetary data are correlated with real activity. However, two implicit assumptions underlie these tests. One is that processing available information is costless, which seems unlikely. If processing costs are included in the costs of acquiring information, then information availability may still imply that only a fraction of agents actually make the effort that renders information useful.

Of greater importance is the assumption that money is exogenous. Boschen and Grossman are actually testing three joint hypotheses: that expectations are rational, that perceived money (initially reported data) is neutral, and that money is exogenous. King and Trehan (1984) find that relaxing the latter assumption can seriously bias the test results. If the monetary authority responds to contemporaneous shocks either directly or through some interest-rate smoothing scheme, then policy can induce correlations between perceived money and output even though money is neutral. Further, if monetary data convey information about fundamental disturbances, then money will not be neutral since agents' behavior depends on the signal-value of money. Tests taking account of the points raised by King and Trehan must be conducted before this class of models can be dismissed.

But even if this class of equilibrium monetary models of the business cycle, which explores how information affects macroeconomic equilibrium, turns out to be inconsistent with the data, these investigations are likely to be of permanent usefulness. Signal-extraction problems are not confined to a particular class of models, and knowledge gained from studying one class should be transferable to other approaches. However, one weakness of the entire analysis is that the accessibility and cost of processing information is generally not modeled in a fundamental way. Reducing the arbitrariness of assumptions about the availability of information should be an important goal of future applications of the signal-extraction problem in macroeconomic models.

Michael Dotsey

See also ENDOGENOUS AND EXOGENOUS MONEY; MONETARY EQUILIBRIUM THEORIES OF THE BUSINESS CYCLE; MONETARY POLICY; MONEY-INCOME CAUSALITY; NEUTRALITY OF MONEY; REAL BUSINESS-CYCLE THEORIES; SEASONAL ADJUSTMENT; SUNSPOT THEORIES OF FLUCTUATIONS

Bibliography

Barro, R. J. 1980. "A Capital Market in an Equilibrium Business Cycle Model." *Econometrica* 48:1393–1417.

Barro, R. J. and Z. Hercowitz. 1980. "Money Stock Revisions and Unanticipated Money Growth." *Journal of Monetary Economics* 6:257–67.

Boschen, J. 1986. "The Information Content of Indexed Bonds." *Journal of Money, Credit, and Banking* 18:76–87.

Boschen, J. and H. I. Grossman. 1982. "Tests of Equilibrium Macroeconomics Using Contemporaneous Monetary Data." *Journal of Monetary Economics* 10:309–34.

Canzoneri, M., D. Henderson, and K. Rogoff. 1983. "The Information Content of Interest Rates and the Effectiveness of Monetary Policy Rules." *Quarterly Journal of Economics* 98:545–66.

Dotsey, M. and R. G. King. 1983. "Monetary Instruments and Policy Rules in a Rational Expectations Environment." *Journal of Monetary Economics* 12:357–82.

———. 1986. "Informational Implications of Interest Rate Rules." *American Economic Review* 76:33–42.

Edwards, S. and S. Hahm. 1987. "Information Acquisition in an Incomplete Information Model of Business Cycle." *Journal of Monetary Economics* 20:123–40.

Kimbrough, K. 1985. "Futures Markets and Monetary Policy." *Journal of Monetary Economics* 15:69–79.

King, R. G. 1981. "Monetary Information and Monetary Neutrality." *Journal of Monetary Economics* 7:195–206.

———. 1982. "Monetary Policy and the Information Content of Prices." *Journal of Political Economy* 90:247–79.

———. 1983. "Interest Rates, Aggregate Information, and Monetary Policy." *Journal of Monetary Economics* 12:199–234.

King, R. G. and B. Trehan. 1984. "Money: Endogeneity and Neutrality." *Journal of Monetary Economics* 14:385–94.

Lucas, R. E. Jr. [1973] 1981. "Some International Evidence on Output-Inflation Tradeoffs." In *Studies in Business-Cycle Theory*, 131–45. Cambridge: MIT Press.

Sargent, T. J. and N. Wallace. 1975. "Rational Expectations, the Optimal Monetary Instrument and the Optimal Money Supply Rule." *Journal of Political Economy* 83:241–54.

Weiss, L. 1982. "Information Aggregation and Policy." *Review of Economic Studies* 49:31–42.

Sismondi, Jean Charles Leonard Simonde de (1773–1842)

Deeply disturbed by the consequences for the poor of the recurring depressions that followed the end of the Napoleonic Wars, Sismondi developed the argument that economic crises and depressions are due to underconsumption. He first advanced the theory that competition generates a chronic tendency towards underconsumption in his best-known work in the field of political economy, *Nouveau principes d'économie politique* ([1819] 1991). He defended and extended the theory in articles published between 1820 and 1835, and in the two-volume collection of some of his papers published under the title *Etudes sur l'économie politique*. However, some crucial elements of the theory appeared in earlier works, namely *De la richesse commerciale,* and the essay, "Political Economy" (reprinted in [1847] 1966). It is clear from the correspondence between Sismondi and Thomas Carlyle that the latter article, written in 1816–17, was translated by Carlyle.

Born in Geneva, where he was christened Jean Charles Leonard Simonde, Sismondi later changed his surname to Simonde de Sismondi in the belief that he was descended from a noble Italian family. French by citizenship (from 1798), English by marriage (to Jessie Allen), historian as well as political economist by profession, Sismondi acquired first-hand knowledge of economic conditions in England, France, and Italy. His awareness of panics, crises, and depressions in various European countries was no doubt enhanced by his services as secretary of the Geneva Chamber of Commerce.

While Sismondi's first major excursion into political economy, *De la richesse commerciale,* was intended to "explain and to apply to France the doctrine of Adam Smith" (1803, xxvi), an extended footnote that attempted to set out the determination of national income and production algebraically paved the way for departure from that doctrine. This algebraic model specified a one-year lag between production and income generated by expenditure. Such macroeconomic lag analysis, first developed by Sismondi, not only played a significant part in Sismondi's underconsumption theory, but also provided the basis for later business-cycle theories developed by Aftalion and Robertson (the former, at least, was directly influenced by Sismondi's ideas).

The importance of Sismondi's subsequent "Political Economy" article lies in its argument that imbalance between production and consumption leads to economic depression. Sismondi rejected Say's Law of Markets, advancing the then heretical theory that, in the aggregate, production could outstrip demand. Despite accepting the orthodox view that capital accumulation is a component of demand, he argued that a switch from consumption to capital accumulation could be too great for the increased flow of consumption goods which eventually resulted to be sold at cost-covering prices; in this case the aggregate cost of production of one period would not be covered by an equal income resulting from sales in the next. So great a switch to capital accumulation Sismondi at this time attributed to excessive manufacturing zeal on the part of governments, who "ordered stockings and hats beforehand, reckoning that legs and heads would be found afterwards" ([1847] 1966, 72).

At the time of writing his "Political Economy" article, Sismondi believed that market forces would normally maintain balance between production and consumption. By 1819, however, he had adopted the contrary view that free competition in the market typically causes production to outstrip consumption. He argued that excessive optimism about increasing their market shares leads firms to produce according to the supply of capital they can obtain, irrespective of the demand for their products. The resulting universal glut of goods causes the decline in prices and production and the rise in unemployment which characterize economic depression. In the light of this analysis, Sismondi by 1819 saw the government's role as being to moderate not only its own zeal but also that of private producers.

While in general optimistic that natural equilibrating forces would in time bring recovery, though not without great suffering in the interim, Sismondi did not believe that similar natural forces would prevent a recurrence. He therefore argued that governments should ameliorate, if not eliminate, economic depressions by passing inheritance levies and other laws that would reduce the inequality of income distribution. His argument was that rapid capital accumulation is normally accompanied by mass production of relatively coarse goods; these will not be purchased if the distribution of income is too unequal, for in that case luxury goods will be preferred, but there may be adequate demand for the coarser goods if a greater share of national income goes to the mass of the populace. Alternatively, governments could simply encourage less production; it was Sismondi's view that compared with the desire of the population as a whole, market forces created an imbalance between labor and leisure in favor of the former.

Unlike Keynes, Sismondi, in his analysis of economic depression in the *Nouveaux principes,* assigned no role to money. The closest he came to linking monetary factors with economic depression was in an 1810 article entitled "Du papier monnaie et des moyens de la supprimer," which argued that inflation, by interfering with rational economic calculation, causes an increase in nominal wealth to be followed (in his words) by panic, crisis, and real misery.

Although he anticipated a key element of the theories later developed by Aftalion and Robertson, Sismondi himself made no explicit contribution to business-cycle theory, except to argue (in the second edition of the *Nouveaux principes*) that economic fluctuations are more likely to emanate from government policy changes than from the private sector, where he believed individual changes tended to offset one another; and while he explicitly referred to panics, he did not attempt to analyze them. More important was his discussion of the causes of, and the remedies for, economic crises and depressions. His arguments failed to convince his contemporaries, but subsequently a number of economists have recognized their usefulness for understanding the complex phenomena of economic crises and depressions. This recognition was enhanced by the emergence of the Harrod-Domar growth theory, with which Sismondi's underconsumption theory has some affinity, notably because of their common emphasis on the capacity-creating effect of investment.

Michael Schneider

See also Income Distribution; Oversaving Theories of Business Cycles; Say, Jean-Baptiste; Say's Law

Bibliography

Bleaney, M. 1976. *Underconsumption Theories: A Historical and Critical Analysis.* London: Lawrence and Wishart.

Salis, J. [1932] 1973. *Sismondi, 1773–1842: la vie et l'oeuvre d'un cosmopolite philosophe.* Geneva: Slatkine.

Sismondi, J. C. L. S. de. 1803. *De la richesse commerciale.*

———. [1819] 1991. *New Principles of Political Economy: Of Wealth in its Relation to Population.* Translated and annotated by R. Hyse. New Brunswick, N.J.: Transaction.

———. [1820, 1824] 1957. "Two Papers on Demand." *International Economic Papers* 7:21–39.

———. 1837–38. *Etudes sur l'économie politique.* 2 vols. Paris: Treuttel et Wurz.

———. [1847] 1966. *Political Economy and the Philosophy of Government.* New York: A. M. Kelley.

Sowell, T. 1972a. "Sismondi: A Neglected Pioneer." *History of Political Economy* 4:62–88.

———. 1972b. *Say's Law: An Historical Analysis.* Princeton: Princeton Univ. Press.

Tuan, M.- L. [1927] 1968. *Simonde de Sismondi as an Economist.* New York: AMS Press.

Weiler, J., ed. 1976. *Histoire, socialisme et critique de l'économie politique.* Paris: Institut de Sciences Mathematiques et Economiques.

Slutsky, Eugen (1880–1948)

The Russian statistician and mathematical economist Eugen Slutsky is best known to economists for his 1915 paper on the theory of consumer choice, in which his analysis of the income and substitution effects of price changes anticipated the work of Hicks and Allen twenty years later. His principal scientific interest was in stochastic processes and time-series analysis, and most of his articles were in this field. This interest led him to an important contribution to business-cycle analysis, his 1927 paper on "The Summation of Random Causes as the Source of Cyclic Processes."

Using winning numbers in the Soviet government lottery loan to obtain three random series, Slutsky demonstrated that oscillatory series similar to many economic time series could be generated as moving sums or differences of random series. Apart from the impetus it provided to research in time-series analysis, Slutsky's paper demonstrated that shocks that were not themselves cyclical could generate oscillations in economic variables. Economists were thus freed from the belief that cycles in economic activity must be due to causes that were themselves periodic, such as sunspot cycles or cycles in rainfall.

Slutsky also pioneered the analysis of inflation as a method of taxation, in two articles in Russian in 1923 on "Calculation of State Revenue from the Issue of Paper Money" and "Mathematical Notes to the Theory of the Issue of Paper Money," the latter published by the Conjuncture Institute, Moscow. J. M. Keynes, presenting the theory of the inflation tax in a 1922 article reprinted in his *Tract on Monetary Reform* ([1923] 1971, 46–49), mentioned discussing the subject with Soviet financial experts at the Genoa conference in May 1922 and used data from the Conjuncture Institute, so he may have been influenced by the work leading up to Slutsky's 1923 publications.

Slutsky was born the son of a school teacher in Yaroslav province. After studying mathematics and physics at Kiev University, he was expelled in 1902 for taking part in student riots, and left Russia the next year to study engineering at the Munich Institute of Technology. Returning in 1905, Slutsky began teaching at the Kiev Institute of Commerce in 1913 and became a full professor in 1920. In 1926, he moved to Moscow as a member of the Conjuncture Institute directed by N. D. Kondratieff. After the Conjuncture Institute was purged and Kondratieff was arrested as the supposed leader of the Working Peasants Party, Slutsky survived by leaving economics for the safer field of meteorology. From 1931 to 1934, he was at the Central Institute of Meteorology, where, ironically given his work on business cycles, he studied the periodicity of sunspots. In 1934, Slutsky joined the Mathematical Institute of the University of Moscow, and, from 1936 until his death, was a member of the Mathematical Institute of the U.S.S.R. Academy of Sciences, where he worked on tables of the chi-square and other probability distributions.

Robert W. Dimand

See also FRISCH, RAGNAR ANTON KITTEL;
JEVONS, WILLIAM STANLEY; KONRATIEFF,
NIKOLAI DMITRIYEVICH; LEADS AND LAGS;
MACROECONOMETRIC MODELS, HISTORICAL
DEVELOPMENT; MOORE, HENRY LUDWELL;
MOVING AVERAGES; SERIAL CORRELATION;
SUNSPOT THEORIES OF FLUCTUATIONS

Bibliography
Allen, R. G. D. 1950. "The Work of Eugen
    Slutsky." *Econometrica* 18:209–16
    (including A. N. Kolomogorov's bibliog-
    raphy of Slutsky's writings).
Keynes, J. M. [1923] 1971. *A Tract on Mon-
    etary Reform*. Vol. 4 of *The Collected
    Writings of John Maynard Keynes*.
    London: Macmillan.
Koropeckyj, I. S., ed. 1984. *Selected Contri-
    butions of Ukrainian Scholars to Eco-
    nomics*. Cambridge: Harvard Univ. Press.
Slutsky, E. [1927] 1937. "The Summation of
    Random Causes as the Source of Cyclic
    Processes." Translation. *Econometrica*
    5:105–46.

Smith, Adam (1727–1790)

The generally acknowledged founder of the discipline of economics, Adam Smith has not been
rated very highly as a monetary economist.
Since the origins of business-cycle analysis are
to be found in classical monetary theory, Smith's
relevance to the study of business cycles depends on his contributions as a monetary theorist. His mediocre reputation stems partly from
his failure even to reproduce the exposition of
the quantity theory and the price-specie-flow
mechanism provided by his friend David Hume.
Another reason for a lackluster reputation is his
espousal of a form of the real-bills doctrine,
which was effectively criticized by Henry
Thornton. A third reason—perhaps most relevant in the present context—is his seeming
failure to take any note of the financial crises
that occurred about every ten years towards the
end of the eighteenth century, much less to recognize, as did Thornton, the role a lender of last
resort might play in countering them.

However, Smith's monetary theory was
both more coherent and more sensitive to the
problem of financial crises than these criticisms
imply. In fact, Smith was the first economist to
present a monetary theory that included a well-
worked-out theory of the banking system.
Hume did not do so and was ambivalent about,
if not hostile to, banks, which he viewed as inherently inflationary. In contrast, Smith argued
that as long as banks kept their notes convertible into gold or silver, overissue was not in a
bank's own self-interest. Instead, they would
substitute a low-cost paper currency for a high-
cost metallic one. The redundant metal could
then be exported for either consumption goods
or productive capital.

Under convertibility, the price level was
determined by the value of either gold or silver.
Those values depended on their relative costs of
production. Thus, in the case of a convertible
currency, Smith did not subscribe to the
Humean version of the quantity theory, since in
that case it was the quantity of money that adjusted to the price level, not the price level that
adjusted to the quantity of money. This fact
explains why Smith did not include the price-
specie-flow mechanism in his theory of international monetary adjustment—an omission that
Viner (1937, 87) considered one of the myster-
ies in the history of economics.

Moreover, since Smith assumed convertibility, he certainly never entertained the real-
bills doctrine in the form that Thornton criticized. Smith, unlike some later advocates of the
doctrine, did not assert that it would prevent
even an inconvertible currency from being over-
issued. Indeed, he explicitly denied that it
would. For Smith the doctrine was simply a
means by which banks could ensure their liquidity and their ability to shrink the size of
their portfolios if the public wished to reduce
the quantity of bank money it held (Glasner
1992). Although Smith devoted little attention
to financial crises, his espousal of the real-bills
doctrine was probably motivated in part by a
recognitition that banks unable to control the
volume of their outstanding liabilities should
avoid tying up their capital in unsecure and illiquid forms that would increase the likelihood
of insolvency in periods of declining demand for
bank liabilities such as a financial crisis. Smith's
advocacy of the real-bills doctrine makes good
sense in light of his implicit understanding of
what Fullarton later called the law of reflux.

His two proposals for restrictions on banks
also seem to have been motivated by a desire to
avoid financial crises and protect the public
from their ill effects. One was a restriction on
the option clause that many Scottish banks used
to postpone for six months their obligation to
redeem their liabilities for gold. Smith opposed
any attenuation of the obligation to convert,

fearing that unsafe banking practices and a tendency to overissue might result. Imperfect convertibility could lead first to expansion and then later to contraction. Here there is a hint of later Currency School doctrines. He also proposed the suppression of banknotes in denominations less than five pounds, because he feared that they would be held by the poorer classes who had little means of evaluating the solvency of the issuers.

Smith's defense of these proposals against the charge that such regulations infringed on natural liberty was to compare them to "the obligations of building party walls, in order to prevent the communication of fire" ([1776] 1976, 1:324). The comparison suggests that he perceived the potentially cumulative effects of financial crises and the need for taking policy steps to avoid or mitigate those effects.

But although Smith did show some appreciation of the problem of financial crises and the possibility that they would be contagious, he did not explicitly relate crises to output or employment. Nor did he perceive any cyclical pattern in their occurrence. However, considering his development of a theory of an endogenous money supply that adjusted to changes in the public's demand for money, Smith must be viewed as a forerunner of the Banking School and perhaps even of modern real business-cycle theory.

David Glasner

See also BANKING SCHOOL, CURRENCY SCHOOL, AND FREE BANKING SCHOOL; FREE BANKING; FULLARTON, JOHN; HUME, DAVID; MALTHUS, THOMAS ROBERT; OPTION CLAUSE; REAL-BILLS DOCTRINE; RICARDO, DAVID; SAY, JEAN-BAPTISTE; SAY'S LAW

Bibliography

Glasner, D. 1989. "On Some Classical Monetary Controversies." *History of Political Economy* 21:201–29.

———. 1992. "The Real-Bills Doctrine in the Light of the Law of Reflux." *History of Political Economy* 24:201–28.

Laidler, D. 1981. "Adam Smith as a Monetary Economist." *Canadian Journal of Economics* 14:185–200.

Mints, L. W. 1945. *A History of Banking Theory in Great Britain and the United States.* Chicago: Univ. of Chicago Press.

Smith, A. [1776] 1976. *An Inquiry into the Nature and Causes of the Wealth of Nations.* 2 vols. Oxford: Clarendon Press.

Vickers, D. 1975. "Adam Smith and the Status of the Theory of Money." In *The Market and the State: Essays on Adam Smith,* edited by A. S. Skinner and T. Wilson, 482–503. Oxford: Clarendon Press.

Viner, J. 1937. *Studies in the Theory of International Trade.* New York: Harper Bros.

Smithies, Arthur (1907–1981)

Arthur Smithies was a distinguished theorist who made important contributions in such areas as spatial economics, the budgeting process, and macroeconomic theory and policy. His important contribution to business-cycle theory was a detailed model of the interdependence between cycles and economic growth.

Born in Tasmania, Smithies earned a L.L.B. at the University of Tasmania (1929), a B.A. at Oxford (Rhodes Scholar, 1932) and a Ph.D. in Economics at Harvard (1934). After posts with the Australian Treasury Department (1935–38), the University of Michigan (1934–35, 1938–43) and the U.S. Bureau of the Budget (1943–48), Smithies returned to the Harvard economics department (1949–73).

Throughout his career, Smithies analyzed and extended Keynesian macroeconomic theory. He was most famous for his analysis of the interdependence between the federal budgetary process and fiscal policy in achieving both long-term objectives and improved stabilization policies. He contended that, by using automatic stabilizers and improved discretionary fiscal policies, governments could reduce the frequency and amplitude of business cycles.

Smithies devoted much effort to exploring the dynamic implications of Keynesian macroeconomics. In "Forecasting Postwar Demand: I," he attempted to reconcile a short-run nonproportional consumption function with a long-run proportional one. Smithies suggested that the short-run nonproportional function shifted up over time because of migration from farms to cities, increased equality of income, and rising living standards. Critics considered his arguments to be plausible but ad hoc, and later estimates for a different time period refuted his empirical hypothesis. Nevertheless, Smithies influenced James Duesenberry, a former student, whose relative-income hypothesis incorporated ratchet effects.

In several articles, Smithies constructed simple (few-equation) aggregative models to gain insights about the economy's dynamic properties. For example, his 1942 model of wartime inflation assumed that government expenditures are a constant percentage of GNP, wages lag prices, and consumption expenditures lag profits. Smithies demonstrated how the rate of inflation depends on the length of these lags.

His most significant contribution to business-cycle theory, "Economic Fluctuations and Growth," attempted to provide a "bridge" between business-cycle and growth theories by showing how growth could generate business fluctuations. He acknowledged particular writers for ideas that he incorporated into his model in a concise review of numerous business-cycle theories. He tried to synthesize Harrod-type growth theories with what he termed Tinbergen-type business-cycle theories, which used linear difference equations as a method of analysis and emphasized profits as a major determinant of investment.

His simplified model excluded the government, foreign, and monetary sectors. Consumption depended on current output and the previous peak output (ratchet effect). Investment depended on output in the previous period, the previous peak output, the difference between full-capacity output in the previous period and peak output, and a trend variable representing exogenous forces. Full-capacity output depended on investment expenditures, depreciation, obsolescence, and technical progress.

Smithies contended that the ratchet effects, which influence both consumption and investment expenditures, were the crucial factor that generate endogenous growth combined with fluctuations. The ratchet effects counteract decreases in demand when output declines and induce positive endogenous growth if output during an upswing exceeds its previous peak. Smithies argued that these ratchet effects provide a more realistic explanation for cyclical movements than the ceilings and floors that had been postulated by other economists. Smithies believed that his model explained the Great Depression of the 1930s and the sustained economic growth, but not the minor fluctuations, that had occurred since 1945.

Smithies later (1967) adapted his model to incorporate effects of monetary and fiscal policies. Moreover, the original aspects of his model attracted the interest of many other economists. Although some dispute that Smithies's model accomplished its objectives, all agree that it is an insightful, innovative effort.

After several decades of waning interest, economists during the 1980s renewed their investigation of endogenous growth and cycles—the question that intrigued Smithies. This revived interest was partly due to developments in statistical inference (unit roots) that allow researchers to distinguish a time series characterized by cyclical fluctuations about a deterministic linear trend from one characterized by a stochastic trend—that is, from one whose trend is itself stochastic. Moreover, macroeconomic theorists—particularly real business-cycle theorists—are investigating endogenous growth models to determine how supply-side shocks affect both growth and cycles. But unlike most current work, Smithies did not insist that all agents are optimizers, so that his was a non-equilibrium model of the business cycle.

Smithies's contributions extended over a wide range of theoretical and policy issues. He significantly advanced the study of macroeconomic dynamics with particular emphasis on providing an endogenous explanation of economic growth combined with cyclical fluctuations.

Robert Stanley Herren

See also ASYMMETRY; CONSUMPTION EXPENDITURES; DUESENBERRY, JAMES STEMBLE; FISCAL POLICY; TRENDS AND RANDOM WALKS

Bibliography
Gandolfo, G. 1980. *Economic Dynamics, Methods and Models*. Rev. ed. Amsterdam: North-Holland.
Kromphardt, J. and J. Dorfner. 1974. "The Capacity of the Smithies Model to Explain the Growth Trend by Endogenous Forces." *Econometrica* 42:667–77.
Smithies, A. 1942. "The Behavior of Money National Income Under Inflationary Conditions." *Quarterly Journal of Economics* 57:113–28.
———. 1945. "Forecasting Postwar Demand: I." *Econometrica* 13:1–14.
———. 1948. "Federal Budgeting and Fiscal Policy." In *A Survey of Contemporary Economics,* edited by H. S. Ellis, 174–209. Philadelphia: Blakiston.
———. 1955. *The Budgetary Process in the United States*. New York: McGraw-Hill.
———. 1957. "Economic Fluctuations and Growth." *Econometrica* 25:1–52.
———. 1967. "Fiscal and Monetary Policy: Uses and Limitations." In *Issues in*

S

Banking and Monetary Analysis, edited by G. Pontecorvo, R. P. Shay, and A. G. Hart, 147–64. New York: Holt, Rinehart and Winston.

Smoot-Hawley Tariff

The role of the Smoot-Hawley tariff in either causing or prolonging the Great Depression has been controversial ever since it was enacted in June 1930. At the time, the legislation elicited the almost unanimous opposition of economists, more than one thousand of whom signed an open letter to President Hoover asking him to veto the bill. The tariff, which raised duties on a broad range of industrial and agricultural products, has been blamed for precipitating a disastrous trade war that resulted in a downward spiral of international trade. The value of international trade measured in dollars fell by more than two-thirds between 1929 and 1933 (Kindelberger 1973, 172). In real terms the decline was over fifty percent.

During the Great Depression, many liberal economists and opponents of activist fiscal and monetary policies, while attributing its onset to other causes, blamed its severity, length, and the weakness of the subsequent recovery on the Smoot-Hawley tariff and the ensuing retaliatory tariffs imposed by other countries. However, consideration of the tariff as either a primary or contributing cause of the depression was cut short by the Keynesian Revolution with its focus on the inherent volatility of private spending and the need for activist fiscal and monetary policy to stabilize economic activity at a high level of output and employment.

Interest in the tariff remained largely dormant during the protracted debates over Keynesian theory that occupied the economics profession for decades after publication of the *General Theory* in 1936. It was only in the late 1970s, mainly as the result of an ideological tract on supply-side economics by a noneconomist Jude Wanniski (1978), that interest in the Smoot-Hawley tariff was revived. Assigning categorical blame to the tariff that even its early opponents had withheld, Wanniski argued that the tariff was itself the primary cause of the Great Depression, not that it had merely prolonged and exacerbated a depression that was the product of unrelated causes. Before Wanniski, such an argument had seemed too far-fetched to be tenable, because the initial downturn in the summer of 1929 and the stock-

market crash in October 1929 both preceded enactment of the Smoot-Hawley tariff by six to ten months. However, writing at the height of the rational-expectations revolution, Wanniski maintained that enactment of the tariff had already been anticipated in the fall of 1929, so that its contractionary impact preceded its enactment. Though seemingly far-fetched, Wanniski managed to lend considerable plausibility to his story by juxtaposing newspaper accounts of the progress of the legislation through congressional committees to final enactment with the volatile fluctuations of the stock market from the fall of 1929 through the spring of 1930.

Responding to Wanniski's provocative claim, Eichengreen (1989) and Kindelberger (1993) both offered a conventional Keynesian argument minimizing the role of the tariff. They argued that, for the United States, where the depression apparently started, the tariff, on balance, was probably expansionary, because its initial effect was to increase the U.S. export surplus. Even taking into account both the direct reduction in foreign demand for U.S. exports resulting from the tariff and the retaliatory tariff increases against U.S. exports, Eichengreen found the tariff to be a net stimulus for the U.S.

Although the conventional macroeconomic analysis on which Kindelberger and Eichengreen based their results may not capture the contractionary effect of the tariff on total world income and output and therefore probably understates its negative impact on the United States, it is still difficult to imagine that the distortionary impact of the trade war could have accounted for more than a fraction of the contraction in U.S. income and output in the Great Depression. And even if Kindelberger and Eichengreen failed to account fully for the global contraction caused by the tariff, their analysis still suggests that the contraction in the United States as a result of the tariff should have been less severe than elsewhere. In fact, the Great Depression was more severe in the United States than in almost any other country.

In a more traditional analysis, Meltzer (1976) considered the impact of the tariff and concluded, in line with the orthodox pre-Keynesian view, that the tariff did contribute to the length and severity of the depression, even though contractionary monetary policies were the primary cause for both the initial downturn and its unusual severity. According to Meltzer, the tariff was merely one of a series of misguided measures that, by interfering with market forces or adversely affecting business confidence, prolonged the downturn and weakened the recovery.

More recently Glasner (1989, 123–24) has suggested a link between the tariff and the monetary deflation that accompanied the Great Depression. Because of its massive war-time loans to the Allies, the United States emerged from World War I as the world's leading creditor nation. That position was further reinforced in the 1920s, when the U.S. provided short-term financing to enable Germany to make the reparations payments that had been imposed by the Treaty of Versailles. As a result, many U.S. financial institutions invested heavily in foreign, particularly German, debt during the 1920s.

For these obligations to be repaid, it was necessary for the United States to accept a balance-of-trade deficit of a corresponding magnitude. By making exports to the United States more difficult, the Smoot-Hawley tariff increased the likelihood that these obligations would not be repaid. Financial institutions in the United States and elsewhere that held foreign debt were weakened, which was a contributing factor to the international financial collapse that occurred in 1931.

Batchelder and Glasner (1995, 292) extended this line of reasoning by observing that faced with the tariff barriers the United States imposed against their exports, debtor countries had no choice but to accumulate gold with which to discharge their obligations under the newly reinstituted gold standard. Under the gold standard the increased worldwide demand for gold occasioned by the Smoot-Hawley tariff was inherently deflationary. And the deflationary pressure was most extreme in debtor countries, especially Germany, where the increased demand for gold was most pronounced.

Consistent with this analysis of the tariff, the Great Depression was most severe in Germany, the principal debtor country, which, until Hitler's rise to power, pursued a severely deflationary monetary policy, to accumulate enough gold to avoid default and in the United States, the leading creditor country, whose financial system was most vulnerable to default by foreign debtors.

Thus, if Wanniski is correct about the relationship between expectations about the enactment of the Smoot-Hawley tariff and the 1929 stock-market crash, the relationship probably depended more on its anticipated effect on the financial system and on its anticipated deflationary impact than on its distortionary impact on world trade.

David Glasner

See also GOLD STANDARD; GOLD STANDARD: CAUSES AND CONSEQUENCES; GREAT DEPRESSION IN THE UNITED STATES (1929–1938); SUPPLY SHOCKS

Bibliography

Batchelder, R. and D. Glasner. 1995. "Debt, Deflation, the Gold Standard, and the Great Depression." In *Money and Banking: The American Experience*, 277–310. Fairfax, Va.: George Mason Univ. Press.

Eichengreen, B. 1989. "The Political Economy of the Smoot-Hawley Tariff." *Research in Economic History* 11:1–44.

Glasner, D. 1989. *Free Banking and Monetary Reform*. New York: Cambridge Univ. Press.

Kindelberger, C. P. 1973. *The World in Depression*. Berkeley: Univ. of California Press.

———. 1993. *A Financial History of Western Europe*. 2d ed. New York: Oxford Univ. Press.

Meltzer, A. H. 1976. "Monetary and Other Explanations of the Start of the Great Depression." *Journal of Monetary Economics* 2:455–71.

Saint-Etienne, C. 1984. *The Great Depression, 1929–1938: Lessons for the 1980s*. Stanford, Calif.: Hoover Institution Press.

Temin, P. 1989. *Lessons from the Great Depression*. Cambridge: MIT Press.

Wanniski, J. 1978. *The Way the World Works*. New York: Basic Books.

Snyder, Carl (1869–1946)

Carl Snyder achieved prominence as a compiler and analyst of vast congeries of time-series data measuring business cycles and economic growth. His work gave great emphasis to economic growth when that topic was neglected by economists. He argued that the causes and potential prevention of disastrous economic fluctuations lay in money and monetary policy and supported the proposal that money/bank credit should grow at a constant rate reflecting the growth of productive potential.

Largely self-educated, Snyder was a voracious reader and prolific writer on many topics related to economic and social conditions. After a lengthy career as a journalist, he became at age fifty-one a member of the Statistics (soon to become Research) department of the Federal Reserve Bank of New York. He directed the collection of numerous monthly time-series data and subjected them to the then-conventional exercise of extracting long-run growth trends and seasonal movements to isolate the cyclical component. Nominal data were deflated to remove effects of price changes.

Much of Snyder's effort and enthusiasm went into developing aggregative index numbers, based chiefly on the equation of exchange $MV = PT$. He was particularly proud of his Index of the General Price Level and his Index of the Volume of Trade. Snyder also used the Federal Reserve Board's measures of the turnover (velocity) of bank deposits, which he extended backward in time with data on bank clearings. Snyder found a very high correlation between deposit velocity and the volume of trade, and he argued that there was a close logical connection between them. This relation implied that the V and T terms of the equation of exchange would move in proportion to each other. As a result, price changes would arise primarily from change in the money supply itself. Thus, Snyder became a strong supporter of the quantity theory of money in a very dogmatic form.

As early as 1923, Snyder strongly advocated an interventionist monetary policy aimed at stabilizing the price level, even if it meant significant changes in the existing gold standard. However, his book *Business Cycles and Business Measurements* did not develop these themes of policy and analysis. The book was devoted to presenting, describing, and comparing his many data series.

By 1929, Snyder was advocating a monetary policy in which the growth of bank credit and bank deposits (not always differentiated in his discussions) would grow at the same rate as national output. Snyder was one of the first American economists to propose such a rule.

In his memoranda and discussions inside the Federal Reserve, Snyder expressed alarm about the stock-market speculation of the late 1920s and favored vigorous credit restriction. As soon as the economy was headed downhill in 1930, he urged a sharp reversal, pressing repeatedly in 1930–31 for more aggressive Federal Reserve open-market purchases of securities. As early as December 1930, Snyder (1931, 173) perceptively characterized the downswing as "one of the most severe of which we have any definite measure." He also decisively rejected

the argument that the depression reflected "overproduction."

Snyder subsequently condemned the monetary contraction which occurred in 1930–33, arguing the depression could not have become so severe had money been stabilized. He also criticized much of the social experimentation and market intervention associated with the New Deal, chiefly on the grounds that by undermining business confidence such measures were discouraging private investment.

After retiring in 1935, Snyder published a lengthy book, *Capitalism the Creator*, which contains much material of interest to the modern reader. Primarily a study of economic growth and a defense of free-market institutions, it was marred by chaotic organization and annoying idiosyncracies of style. The book summed up Snyder's view of business-cycle analysis and policy and offered some valuable insights, but showed little advance over his earlier ideas or methods.

Although Snyder apparently exerted little influence inside the Federal Reserve System, his work was well known and well regarded by business men and economists in the 1920s. He was elected President of the American Statistical Association in 1928. But his work was largely ignored during the intellectual ferment of the 1930s. Despite his wide reading of and personal acquaintance with many leading economists, Snyder's work lacked a strong foundation in economic analysis. His statistical aggregates often betrayed a tinge of ad hoc improvisation. His index of the General Price Level, for instance, was a hodge-podge which included not only prices of products and services but also allotted 10 percent to security prices, another 10 percent to real-estate values and 15 percent to wages.

Snyder was only tangentially involved in the creation of such data series as the index of industrial production (developed at the Federal Reserve Board) and took no part in the creation of data on gross national product for the United States. Aside from the raw materials he furnished to these developments, his work was soon forgotten. However, his insights about the importance of monetary policy for economic stabilization were later extended by Clark Warburton, Milton Friedman, and others who displayed more patience and persistence than Snyder in the use of economic analysis and empirical data.

Paul B. Trescott

See also ANGELL, JAMES WATERHOUSE; FISHER, IRVING; FRIEDMAN, MILTON; GREAT DEPRESSION IN THE UNITED STATES (1929–1938); MONETARY DISEQUILIBRIUM THEORIES OF THE BUSINESS CYCLE; MONETARY POLICY; SCHWARTZ, ANNA JACOBSON; WARBURTON, CLARK

Bibliography

Garvy, G. 1978. "Carl Snyder, Pioneer Economic Statistician and Monetarist." *History of Political Economy* 10:454–90.

Humphrey, T. M. 1971. "The Role of Non-Chicago Economists in the Evolution of the Quantity Theory in America, 1930–1950." *Southern Economic Journal* 38:12–18.

———. 1973. "Empirical Tests of the Quantity Theory of Money in the United States, 1900–1930." *History of Political Economy* 5:285–316.

Reed, H. L. 1935. "The Stabilization Doctrines of Carl Snyder." *Quarterly Journal of Economics* 49:600–20.

Snyder, C. 1923. "The Stabilization of Gold: A Plan." *American Economic Review* 13:276–85.

———. 1924. "New Measures in the Equation of Exchange." *American Economic Review* 14:699–713.

———. 1927. *Business Cycles and Business Measurements*. New York: Macmillan.

———. 1929. "The Problem of Posterity: Presidential Address." *Journal of the American Statistical Association* 25:1–14.

———. 1931. "The World-Wide Depressions of 1930." *American Economic Review Paper and Proceedings* 21:172–78.

———. 1935. "The Problem of Monetary and Economic Stability." *Quarterly Journal of Economics* 49:173–205.

———. 1940. *Capitalism the Creator.* New York: Macmillan.

Social Structure of Accumulation

This framework for studying the sources of long-term crises and the conditions for their resolution emerged in the late 1970s. The Social Structure of Accumulation (SSA) refers to the set of institutions that order relations between and within classes in a given country at a given historical period. Because the institutional mechanisms and practices associated with the SSA reflect capitalism's class relations, they also embody its conflicts and contradictions (such as conflicts between employers and workers, unemployed and employed, industrial and finance capital). The SSA therefore is governed by a logic that shapes its development over time, and its own particular crisis tendencies. It also may become dysfunctional and break down as accumulation engenders new unanticipated class conflicts (e.g., the postwar recoveries of Germany and Japan, which undermined the oligopolistic structure of many basic industries).

While other strands of neo-Marxian crisis theory explain a profitability crisis as the result of conflict between or within classes, the SSA approach argues that the institutions that mediate conflict also mediate its impact on profits. Institutions provide mechanisms for expressing, and thereby regulating, conflict, and define legitimate points of contention, limiting discourse. When conflict is contained within these bounds, it reduces profitability less than when it takes less predictable and more disruptive forms. Similarly, conflicts over issues that are not conventionally "legitimate" can be more threatening to capitalist control or social stability than are conflicts over "legitimate" issues. Such institutional decay or breakdown in the SSA also slows the pace of accumulation, because it increases uncertainty, creating what Keynes called a poor state of confidence, which impedes investment. In such an uncertain environment, long-term investment is often misdirected or reoriented towards short-term, speculative gain, which reduces long-run profits.

As a crisis unfolds, the SSA tends to unravel further, partly because declining profits reduce the resources available to reproduce organizational arrangements. Individual sectors may temporarily benefit from a more laissez-faire environment, but the economy as a whole grows more fragile. Institutions that managed conflicts also insulated exterior sectors from those conflicts and their consequences. As an economy is deregulated or made more "flexible," it loses circuit breakers that prevent a crisis in one sector from rapidly spreading throughout.

While other crisis theories identify endogenous mechanisms that eventually countervail the initial source of crisis and restore profitability, the SSA analysis is less deterministic. A long-run crisis may also develop into a revolutionary conjuncture leading to an alternative, socialist economic organization; hence the SSA approach emphasizes the contingency of crisis resolution. Renewed accumulation requires a new social structure to contain class conflict and permit capitalism's reproduction. A vision of a new SSA may emerge as some sectors learn from the crisis how to attenuate or manage conflict while promoting class harmony and growth. To prevail, the advocates of this new world-view must win converts and suppress recalcitrants, which implies using force as well as building consensus. Once new paradigmatic "rules of the game" become ascendant, and a core of critical institutions is established, accumulation will accelerate. The remainder of the new SSA is then filled in over time.

SSA analysis has primarily been applied to the United States since World War II. Analysts have examined the development and unraveling of the SSA along several dimensions: the truce or accord between organized labor and capital; the social-wage and social-welfare system; the post-Jim Crow racial system; "populismo" in Puerto Rico; the patriarchal family-wage system; the Bretton Woods system of international trade and finance; the New Deal regulatory system for monetary policy and domestic banking; the international political system of Pax Americana and Cold War.

These various dimensions form a single SSA by virtue of their common world-view, sometimes called liberal capitalist democracy or social-welfare capitalism. It is distinguished from European corporatist and social-democratic systems by the centrality of anti-Communism for international policy and domestic politics, and by the limited role for worker representation in workplace negotiations and in national economic policy. Unlike earlier more laissez-faire SSA's in the United States, it features unionized basic industry, extensive national social-welfare policies, and U.S. international hegemony.

The SSA approach is similar in its sweep to European regulation theory, but the two differ. The social content of a *regulatory regime* is derived from the underlying paradigm for technological development; for instance, mass production made industrial unions and stable wage growth functional for capitalist demand management and profits. A crisis arose in the 1970s, because the benefits of the old technological paradigm (mass production) were exhausted, and no new paradigm had yet emerged. This analysis abstracts from the role of class actors and social movements; it focuses on structural logic and traces causation from production technology to social relations.

In SSA analysis, class struggles define the context for technical change and economic crisis. The structure of postwar labor relations emerged from and in reaction to the militant union-organizing efforts that had built the industrial unions; subsequent labor-saving technological developments reflected the high wages yet stable labor relations achieved under the truce. SSA analysis attributes crises to concrete behaviors and initiatives, and treats technology as shaped by social factors, rather than as an independent force.

Some have suggested that by forcing history into a single unifying framework, the SSA approach distorts the historical record. For example, it has been argued that it was not the union sector but nonunion manufacturing that was the postwar growth center for profits. But SSA analysts do not deny that factors beyond the arguments they emphasize affect macroeconomic performance. Rather, they systematically analyze how capitalist crises can be successfully resolved and accumulation renewed, and why the ensuing booms cannot be sustained.

Others maintain that SSA analysis merely applies the laws of motion of capitalism to historical events, adding little on the theoretical plane. Yet Marx emphasized that theory proceeds at different levels of abstraction. The SSA framework operates at an intermediate level, giving substance to the abstract categories of "capital" and "labor" in particular historical circumstances without moving to the most concrete level of detailed sectoral analysis. It retains a macroeconomic perspective, illustrating how capitalist dynamics unfold in a world that cannot be purely or entirely characterized by "wage-labor and capital."

Michele I. Naples

See also FALLING RATE OF PROFIT; REGULATION SCHOOL

Bibliography

Baron, H. M. 1985. "Racism Transformed: The Implications of the 1960s." *Review of Radical Political Economics* 17:10–33.

Block, F. L. 1977. *The Origins of International Economic Disorder: A Study of United States International Monetary Policy from World War II to the Present.* Berkeley: Univ. of California Press.

Bowles, S., D. M. Gordon, and T. E. Weiss-kopf. 1986. "Power and Profits: The Social Structure of Accumulation and the Profitability of the Postwar U.S. Economy." *Review of Radical Political Economics* 18:132–67.

Edwards, R. C. 1979. *Contested Terrain: The Transformation of the Workplace in the Twentieth Century.* New York: Basic Books.

Epstein, G. A. and J. B. Schor. 1989. "Macropolicy in the Rise and Fall of the Golden Age." In *The Rise and Fall of the Golden Age: Lessons for the 1990s,* edited by S. Marglin and J. Schor, 126–52. New York: Oxford Univ. Press.

Gordon, D. M. 1978. "Up and Down the Long Roller Coaster." In *U.S. Capitalism in Crisis,* edited by B. Steinberg et al., 22–35. New York: Union for Radical Political Economics.

Gordon, D. M., R. C. Edwards, and M. Reich. 1981. *Segmented Work, Divided Workers.* New York: Cambridge Univ. Press.

Kotz, D. 1987. "Long Waves and Social Structures of Accumulation: A Critique and Reinterpretation." *Review of Radical Political Economics* 19:16–38.

Naples, M. I. 1986. "The Unraveling of the Union-Capital Truce and the Industrial Productivity Crisis." *Review of Radical Political Economics* 18:110–31.

Reich, M. 1988. "Postwar Racial Income Differences: Trends and Theories." In *The Three Worlds of Labor Economics,* edited by G. Mangum and P. Philips, 144–67. Armonk, N.Y.: M. E. Sharpe.

Wolfson, M. H. 1986. *Financial Crises: Understanding the Postwar U.S. Experience.* Armonk, N.Y.: M. E. Sharpe.

Soddy, Frederick (1877–1956)

A trenchant critic of the money system, Frederick Soddy contributed to the analysis of the role of money in business cycles. His major works in economics are *Wealth, Virtual Wealth and Debt, Money versus Man,* and *The Role of Money.*

Soddy, Fellow of the Royal Society and Lee's Professor of Chemistry at Oxford, was the 1921 Nobel Laureate in Chemistry and a foreign member of the Swedish, Italian, and Russian Academies of Science. He worked with Rutherford on the theory of atomic disintegration and made basic contributions to the modern theory of atomic structure.

After 1918, Soddy turned to the study of refractory social problems in the modern scientific age, particularly those of depression and war. Soddy felt that the problem of producing wealth had been essentially solved. The egregious fault of modern economic society is that there is factitious poverty, because it fails to distribute the wealth that by scientific knowledge can be so abundantly produced.

Soddy thought that orthodox economists lacked a satisfactory explanation for why it was so difficult to maintain full employment and to realize the vast production made possible by the prodigal fruits of science. And he expressed scorn for the "conventions and half-truths that pass for economics" (1934, 3). The true answer, according to Soddy, lies with the money system and the role of fractional-reserve banks in creating money.

Soddy's theory may be described by explicating his views about wealth, virtual wealth, money and debt. The wealth of a nation consists of its goods and services. Wealth is desired because it yields direct utility. Money, however, gives no direct satisfaction. It is used in modern societies, because the barter system is insuperably inconvenient, and it is desired because it facilitates exchange. The fundamental principle of money is that its issuer, who first puts it into circulation, gets something for nothing. From the point of view of the holder "money now is the NOTHING you get for SOMETHING before you can get ANYTHING" (1934, 24). People who want money give up wealth to get it. They surrender their present command over goods and services for something that has no immediate and direct value. Issuers of money get something (current command over goods and services) for nothing.

The creation of money also gives holders of money a claim on society's future wealth. Soddy called the aggregate of these claims on society *virtual wealth.* Virtual wealth is the credit established by individuals with the nation; it consists of legal claims over and above the existing wealth already owned by others independently of these claims.

In an honest money system the state alone would create money. Borrowing and lending would not disturb the price level, because the expenditure on goods and services of the borrower would be matched by the abstinence of the lender. Things are very different in an economy with fractional-reserve banking. In such a fraudulent system, banks can expand the money supply by increasing their lending. For the borrower, this money is the something for nothing before anyone can get anything. This "banking le(d)gerdemain" (1931, 45) enables the borrower to get money without sacrificing the enjoyment of wealth and enables banks to create debts on which they earn interest. Soddy deemed private bank money to be even more reprehensible than counterfeit money and vituperated bankers for usurping the power of the state.

When banks create money, what the borrower gets to spend is given up by someone else. This must be the case, because nothing comes from nothing in accordance with the principle of conservation of matter and energy. Since there has been no genuine abstinence, what the borrower spends is not voluntarily given up by anyone else. Purchasing power, but not the supply of goods, is increased because time must elapse between initiation of the production process and its completion. The prices of consumer goods rise and it is because holders of money are deprived of a part of their purchasing power by the reduced value of their money balances that the borrowers from the banks can get something for nothing.

The profligate actions of private banks also cause business cycles. When banks expand loans they create purchasing power and prices increase, because it takes time for the output of goods to rise. When the supply of goods increases, more money is needed. But it is just then that banks contract loans and reduce the money supply because of the gold standard and other reasons. The fall in purchasing power causes a depression. Economic fluctuations are thus due to the wanton and capricious behavior of private fractional-reserve banks.

Under an ideal money system, those who initiate a new production process must be financed by others correspondingly abstaining from consumption over the period required for the new production to mature. More money is needed to complete and not to start the process and should be provided by the state to stabilize the price level.

Soddy's practical proposals were as follows. One-hundred-percent-reserve banking should replace fractional-reserve banking. Only the state should have the power to create money. The price level should be stabilized by appropriate changes in the quantity of money. Exchange rates should fluctuate freely to maintain external equilibrium.

Although Soddy held no academic appointment in economics, his views on money and business cycles have elements in common not only with plebeian writers such as Foster and Catchings, but with such orthodox economists as Wicksell, Fisher, Robertson, and Hayek. His views on policy are almost indistinguishable from those espoused by many eminent economists. That Soddy was primarily a chemist perhaps offended some orthodox economists who invidiously characterized him as an interloper or crank. However, as T. S. Kuhn has argued, paradigm shifts are often brought about by those who are either very young or very new to the field. Soddy's dissatisfaction with the orthodox theory of unemployment and his work on money and business cycles helped pave the way for the Keynesian Revolution. Unfortunately, his analysis was stultified by a tendency to blame bankers and fractional-reserve banking for all the evils of modern society.

Ghanshyam Mehta

See also FISHER, IRVING; FORCED SAVING; FOSTER, WILLIAM TRUFANT; HAYEK, FRIEDRICH AUGUST [VON]

Bibliography
Bradford, F. 1933. Review of *Wealth, Virtual Wealth and Debt* and *Money versus Man,* by F. Soddy. *American Economic Review* 23:760.
Cole, G. D. H., ed. 1933. *What Everybody Wants to Know about Money—A Planned Outline of Monetary Problems.* London: V. Gollancz.
Daly, H. 1980. "The Economic Thought of Frederick Soddy." *History of Political Economy* 12:469–88.
Fleck, A. 1971. "Frederick Soddy." In *The Dictionary of National Biography, 1951–1960,* edited by E. Williams and H. Palmer, 904–05. London: Oxford Univ. Press.
Mehta, G. 1979a. *The Structure of the Keynesian Revolution.* New York: St. Martin's Press.
———. 1979b. "The Keynesian Revolution." *International Journal of Social Economics* 6:151–63.

Shaw, E. S. 1935. Review of *The Role of Money*, by F. Soddy. *American Economic Review* 25:566–67.

Soddy, F. 1926. *Wealth, Virtual Wealth, and Debt: The Solution of the Economic Paradox.* London: Allen and Unwin.

———. 1931. *Money versus Man: A Statement of the World Problems from the Standpoint of the New Economics.* London: Elkin Mathews and Marrot.

———. 1934. *The Role of Money: What it Should Be Contrasted with What it Has Become.* London: George Routledge and Sons.

———. 1943. *The Arch Enemy of Economic Freedom: What Banking Is, What First it Was, and Again Should Be.* Oxon [i.e. Oxford]: Published by F. Soddy at Knapp, Enstone.

South Sea Bubble

The South Sea Bubble, lasting from February to October in 1720, was the first major speculative boom and bust on the London stock exchange. The price of a share in the South Sea Company rose from 128 percent of par at the beginning of the year to a peak of 950 percent in July. Beginning in late August, the price quickly collapsed to 300 percent and ended the year at 200 percent. Prices of shares in other joint-stock companies, especially the Bank of England and the East India Company, similarly rose and then fell. In addition, many new "bubble" companies were floated to exploit the buying mania that occurred in the months March through May. The Bubble Act, enacted in June at the urging of the South Sea Company, forbade any chartered joint-stock company from undertaking business activities beyond those expressly granted in its charter. Enforcement of this act against two waterworks companies that had begun a profitable business in underwriting insurance policies may have helped burst the speculative bubble for the market as a whole. It certainly restricted the formation of joint-stock corporations in banking and manufacturing for over a century afterwards.

The South Sea Bubble in England mimicked the Mississippi Bubble in France that began in 1719. Both bubbles resulted from an attempt by joint-stock companies with monopolies on overseas trading to refinance the immense debts accumulated by their governments during the War of the Spanish Succession (1702–13). The South Sea Company was created in 1711 by George Caswall and John Blunt to convert £9.47 million of the government's war debts into £10 million equity in the company, which would receive the future profits anticipated from a monopoly on English trade to the Spanish Empire and the cash flow on a perpetual annuity from the government paying 6 percent annually. The stockholders of the company thus exchanged their short-term government debentures, which were written in odd sums, deeply discounted, and difficult to transfer, for fungible and easily transferred shares in the company. These new shares were worth at least the annuity held by the company and promised further gains if the company profited from its trade monopoly.

The South Sea Company was successful as a long-term funding operation of the government debt—97 percent of the short-term debt was subscribed into its stock by the end of 1711. By contrast, the company's trade with the Spanish Main was not successful and the company failed to turn a profit on this monopoly. The directors subsequently turned their attention fully to the further conversion of government debt.

In 1719, the South Sea Company successfully converted a small issue of annuities from 1710 into new stock issued by the company. This was a trial run of the grandiose operations the company initiated in late 1719. All the government's remaining debt except that owed to the Bank of England and the East India Company, the other two chartered companies entrusted with administering the national debt, was to be subscribed into South Sea stock— provided the annuitants would accept the terms offered by the company. Holders of the £16,546,202 of redeemable government stock handled by the Bank of England had no choice but to subscribe or to be bought out by the government on worse terms. By contrast, the annuitants holding £15,034,688 worth of Irredeemables (divided into long annuities of ninety-nine years and short annuities of thirty years) had to be persuaded to exchange their annuities for the new South Sea Company stock, just as the annuitants in the conversion of 1719 had to be persuaded by the promise of higher returns and greater liquidity. The South Sea Company was authorized to issue new stock up to the nominal par value of the government debt they converted, which meant all

S

of the redeemable debt and whatever proportion of the irredeemable debt they managed to convert.

But, and this was the fatal attraction and duplicity of the scheme, the South Sea Company could set whatever conversion price it wished for the shares given to the debtholders in exchange for the old annuities. The higher the price the company could charge for its new shares without discouraging the holders of the Irredeemables from converting, the more of the new capital issue would be left to it to be used as it wished. If, for example, it set the conversion price of South Sea stock at the current market price of £135, £20 million of debt could be converted by issuing only £14,814,815 of new stock, leaving £5,185,185 for other uses. The Commons accepted the South Sea Company's proposal and it was enacted into law 7 April 1720.

The conversion operation formally began with the first subscription of stock on 14 April, which was quickly oversubscribed. The amount of new stock issued was small relative to the projected total issue, but it was large enough to pay the bribes that had been promised to Members of Parliament and officials in the government and to buy up enough Redeemables to satisfy the government's requirement, as well as to support the price of the existing stock. The new stock was not entered into the ledgers and available for transfer until December 1720, so only demand for the existing stock was increased, not the supply. Its price rose accordingly, from £288 on 13 April to £335 by 27 April. On 28 April, the company held the first registration of the Irredeemables. The company offered both the long and the short annuitants better terms than it was getting from the government but charged both classes of annuitants £375 for each £100 of new South Sea stock subscribed. (Existing shares were selling between £335 and £343.) It is not surprising that 63 percent of the Irredeemables were subscribed.

A second "money subscription" was held on 29 April, and it was quickly oversubscribed even though the price per £100 share was now raised to £400. The terms of purchase for the money subscriptions were very generous and amounted to buying on margin albeit with fixed margin calls at regular intervals. Only one-tenth to one-fifth of the sale price was paid at the time of subscription and the remaining payments were stretched up to three years. So these sub-scriptions were most attractive to speculators anticipating further rises in the price of South Sea stock and wanting to leverage their purchases as much as possible.

The price of South Sea stock continued to rise sharply during the month of May. The demand for South Sea stock was fueled by the increasing amounts of money the company lent on its stock beginning on 21 April. Nearly a million pounds was lent at the start. This had a double-barreled effect. It withdrew some £400,000 of stock from the supply available to the market and it pumped another £1 million of purchasing power into the demand for South Sea stock. On 19 May the South Sea Company announced the next conversions of debt and the very favorable terms being given to the long-term and short-term Irredeemables. They continued to grant more loans to aid buyers of additional stock.

This raised the bubble mania to its peak. The fresh loans were made at £400 for each £100 of shares. By 1 August the total that had been lent by the South Sea Company on its stock and on its subscription receipts amounted to over £11,200,000, or more than its original capital. The highest price quoted in Castaing's Course of the Exchange was £950 on 1 July. Meanwhile, new investment opportunities had arisen in competition with the South Sea Company, the so-called "bubble companies" that began to be promoted in the London stock market. The most important of these were two marine insurance companies which received their charters in June and began to be traded on 1 July. Moreover, payments on the First and Second subscriptions in South Sea stock—the equivalent of margin calls—came due as well.

The collapse of the bubble began in August when the transfer books of the South Sea Company were reopened and positions taken earlier by speculators could be unwound. A panic quickly ensued, produced unintentionally by the directors of the South Sea Company when they invoked a writ of *scire facias* on 18 August against two old chartered companies that had changed activities from building waterworks to underwriting insurance. They were attracting speculators from the South Sea Company which now charged them with violating the Bubble Act enacted in June. This prohibited any chartered joint-stock company from engaging in activities outside those authorized in its original charter.

The price of South Sea stock dropped sharply from the last half of August through the middle of October. The critical date in the collapse was 24 September, when the Sword-Blade Company, which had been acting as the banking agent for the South Sea Company, failed under pressure from the Bank of England asking that its notes be paid either in specie or in Bank of England notes. The result was a serious liquidity crunch in the London credit markets, eventually alleviated by the Bank of England. But this only occurred after the South Sea Company had been eliminated as a rival fiscal agent for the government. The bulk of the South Sea Company's new stock was redefined as a perpetual annuity yielding 3 percent and transferable on the same terms as the stock. This new financial instrument was the progenitor of the famed Three Per Cent Consol, created in 1752. The government gained its initial goal, reducing the annual burden of servicing its debt, and the holders of the irredeemable annuities who had converted gained in terms of liquidity. The losers were the directors of the South Sea Company who were forced to give up the bulk of their private fortunes by act of Parliament, the holders of the redeemable annuities who had been forced to convert on relatively unfavorable terms during the bubble, and, arguably, the foreign investors, mainly Dutch, whose speculative investments were now locked into the English capital market.

Larry Neal

See also LAW, JOHN; MISSISSIPPI BUBBLE

Bibliography

Dickson, P. G. M. 1967. *The Financial Revolution in England: A Study in the Development of Public Credit, 1688–1756.* London: Macmillan.

Neal, L. 1990. *The Rise of Financial Capitalism: International Capital Markets in the Age of Reason.* Cambridge: Cambridge Univ. Press.

Scott, W. R. 1910. *The Constitution and Finance of English, Scottish and Irish Joint-Stock Companies to 1720.* 3 vols. Cambridge: Cambridge Univ. Press.

Sperling, J. G. 1962. *The South Sea Company: An Historical Essay and Bibliographical Finding List.* Boston: Harvard Graduate School of Business Administration.

Spectral Analysis

Spectral analysis refers to a general class of time-series techniques designed to identify the systematic movements in a single time series and systematic co-movements between two or more time series. Spectral analysis is also referred to as *harmonic, Fourier,* and *periodogram* analysis and has found many applications in business and economics. Spectral analysis can best be understood by considering how it is used in measuring business cycles and how it evolved as a statistical technique.

A Method to Identify Business-Cycle Movements

In the statistical study of business cycles, spectral analysis has been used to identify the "hidden" periodic movements in an economic time series and to establish relationships between two or more economic variables at a given periodic movement. Economic time series consist of complex combinations of trends, business cycles, seasonal movements, nonbusiness/nonseasonal cyclical movements such as long swings, and irregular movements. Thus, the business-cycle component may be hidden by the other movements in the time series.

Spectral analysis is an obvious approach to the study of business cycles, because, unlike traditional time-domain methods, it is based on a periodic or frequency decomposition of a time series. Additionally, the spectral approach does not require the removal of non-business-cycle movements by moving averages which themselves can easily contaminate the time series. Rather, spectral analysis decomposes a time series into components each associated with a frequency or period. The period represents the time required for one complete cycle while frequency represents the fraction of a cycle completed in one time unit; for example, a period of ten years is associated with a frequency of 0.10 cycles per year.

Some mathematical sophistication is required to understand the underlying foundation of spectral analysis; however, the concept of the spectrum of a single time series can be illustrated with an analogy to a radio receiver suggested by C. W. J. Granger and M. Hatanaka (1964). The radio is assumed to emit a sound rather than words at every frequency. Nonbroadcasting frequencies emit a constant background or static sound of similar intensity; however, broadcasting frequencies emit a discernable sound and the stronger the signal at a given frequency, the more intense the sound. Thus, turning the dial on this radio from the low to the high frequency bands traces out a spectrum of sorts.

Similarly, the spectrum of an economic time series traces the power or variation of the series at each frequency. Sharp peaks in the spectrum at a given frequency (period) thus suggest that a major part of the variance of the time series occurs at that frequency or period.

The spectral approach to business-cycle measurement involves a visual examination of the estimated spectrum or spectral density function focused on the business-cycle frequency range of 12 quarters (0.08 cycles per quarter) to 20 quarters (0.05 cycles per quarter). A peak in the spectral density at the business-cycle frequency range then suggests that there is some important periodic movement in the time series. Tests are available to determine the statistical reliability of any peak in the spectral density function. Cross-spectral analysis can then be used to investigate the type of relationship between two or more time series at the business-cycle frequencies.

Evolution of Spectral Methods

The evolution of spectral analysis as a method for studying business cycles involved three stages.

First, the periodogram originally based on work of the mathematician J. Fourier was closely related to the modern spectral density function, but possessed undesirable statistical properties. It was first used to identify and measure sunspot periods by Sir Arthur Schuster and H. Turner in 1898. The periodogram was first used to study business cycles by Henry L. Moore in 1914. Moore developed an agricultural theory of the business cycle in which cycles in weather induced cycles in yields which in turn generated cycles in general economic activity. The periodogram was used to identify an eight-year cycle in rainfall, yields, and other related variables.

Several applications of periodogram analysis were made in the 1920s and 1930s; the last effort to establish periodogram analysis as a valid approach to the study of business cycles was made by H. T. Davis in 1941.

Although recognized by major business-cycle researchers such as W. C. Mitchell and J. A. Schumpeter, periodogram analysis was met with general skepticism. The technique required considerable computational effort in a pre-computer age and posed serious statistical problems that rendered the results, at best, difficult to interpret and, frequently, unreliable. The famous statistician M. Kendall regarded periodogram analysis as inappropriate for the analysis of economic time series.

The second development occurred in the 1950s when mathematicians such as J. Tukey found that certain transformations of the periodogram function, or more appropriately, the spectral density function, solved several serious statistical problems that plagued the periodogram. This rendered the spectral density function easy to interpret and more reliable for finding periodicities embedded in the time series. In addition, the availability of computers and new numerical algorithms facilitated estimation of the spectral density function.

The third and current development stage started in 1964 when Granger and Hatanaka's *Spectral Analysis of Economic Time Series* was published. They revived interest in spectral analysis, and the technique has subsequently been used to investigate a wide variety of cyclical phenomena such as seasonal movements, business cycles, long swings in economic and demographic variables, and building cycles. In addition, the technique has found useful applications in such areas as investigating the dynamic properties of structural models and estimating distributed-lag models.

Spectral analysis has now become part of the standard set of econometric tools used in business and economics. With the advent of econometric packages developed for microcomputers that permit spectral estimation, these methods are now readily accessible to business-cycle researchers.

Evaluation of Spectral Analysis

Spectral methods are generally accepted as a reliable method for isolating periodic movements in a time series and have been applied to other roles in statistical analysis. However, spectral analysis is not without its critics. Spectral analysis was developed primarily for the physical sciences, especially electrical engineering and communications, where large amounts of data are available and the systems generating data are largely deterministic. A number of researchers therefore question whether the spectral approach to economic time series is appropriate, since neither the quantity nor the quality of the data may be sufficient to permit effective use of the method.

Thomas F. Cargill

See also COMPOSITE TRENDS; DAVIS, HAROLD THAYER; FILTERS; MOORE, HENRY LUDWELL

Bibliography

Cargill, T. F. 1974. "Early Applications of Spectral Methods to Economic Time Series." *History of Political Economy* 6:1–16.

Davis, H. T. 1941. *The Analysis of Economic Time Series*. Bloomington, Ind.: Principia Press.

Granger, C. W. J. and M. Hatanaka. 1964. *Spectral Analysis of Economic Time Series*. Princeton: Princeton Univ. Press.

Moore, H. L. 1914. *Economic Cycles: Their Law and Cause*. New York: Macmillan.

Schuster, A. 1898. "On the Investigation of Hidden Periodicities with Application to a Supposed 26-Day Period of Meteorological Phenomena." *Terrestrial Magnetism and Atmospheric Electricity* 3:13–41.

Spiethoff, Arthur (1873–1957)

Arthur Spiethoff was a German economist well known for his research on business cycles and for his methodological studies. His brilliant idea that a parameter jointly determined by many persons influences each person and induces each of them to behave uniformly underlay both his notion of "economic style" (*Wirtschaftsstil*) and his concept that the investment climate may lead to a cumulative process. This idea seems to be rather modern and is essential for the new scientific field called synergetics.

In the first quarter of this century, beginning with an article on "overproduction" (*Überproduktion*) in 1902 and culminating in his famous article on "crises" (*Krisen*) in 1925, Spiethoff developed a profound and far-reaching theory of the business cycle. Relying on extensive and detailed empirical data, he gave, in his own words, an "explanatory description" (*Erläuternde Beschreibung*) of the upswings and downswings of a capitalist economy during the nineteenth century and generalized his findings to a "typical cycle" (*Musterkreislauf*). Spiethoff noticed a fundamental difference between the ups and downs of the economic development before and since the nineteenth century. Until the nineteenth century, ups and downs appeared to be caused by exogenous shocks such as wars, good or bad harvests, epidemics and so on, but in the nineteenth century, endogenous forces arose which cause, not only ups and downs, but more or less regular cyclical movements. These endogenous causes presuppose the emergence of the profit-seeking and speculating entrepreneur who, no longer bound by a diversity of individual, material, and institutional restraints, could channel huge masses of resources into the production of commodities. Thus, the modern, free entrepreneur as a risk-taking and venturesome investor is the creator of the business cycle.

To analyze the endogenous causes of the business cycle, Spiethoff divided the economy into an investment sector consisting of both the industries producing materials for investment goods and the investment-goods industries producing machinery, plant, and equipment, and a consumption sector consisting of plants for producing consumption goods. He assumed that materials and investment goods have to be financed on credit and that consumption goods are bought from earnings. In a depression, falling investment costs caused by underutilization of resources and the opening of new investment opportunities may eventually motivate some venturesome entrepreneurs to invest in producing investment goods. Demand for materials and investment goods rises; expected profitability improves, which causes other investors, attracted by the successes of the preceding investors, to invest. A cumulative process evolves because all investors together generate a positive investment climate which drives the expansion of the investment sector beyond its equilibrium value.

The investment boom and the upswing cease when investment opportunities are used up, when investment costs rise, and when, above all, the consumption sector, growing because of rising labor income, bids away resources and labor employed in the investment sector. Compared to a full-employment equilibrium, there is overproduction of investment goods and underproduction of consumption goods. This disproportion is due to the heterogeneity of the goods and the shortage of resources. Declining investment and stagnation ease the strains on capacity. But the reduction of demand and profitability causes the investment climate to deteriorate. A downward cumulative process of falling income and demand then begins. Eventually, new investment opportunities and low costs stimulate a revival of investment and a new upswing.

Spiethoff's typical cycle consists of two "stages" (*Wechsellagen*): an "upswing" and a "downswing." The upswing is subdivided into the "phases" (*Wechselstufen*) (1) of "second improvement," the phase of cumulative processes, (2) of "boom," the phase of increasing shortages, and (3) of "capital shortage," the phase of obvious disproportionality. The downswing is subdivided into the phases (1) of "recession," the phase of declining investment, and (2) of "first improvement," the phase in which investment stops declining.

According to Spiethoff, the fundamental causes of the business cycle are: the temporal structure of production; the durability of plants; convergence of investment plans by a multitude of individual investors creating an investment climate that evokes further investment; cumulative processes that lead to disproportionality; and finally the cessation of an upswing due to limitations of resources and the exhaustion of investment opportunities. In short, Spiethoff's business-cycle theory is an endogenous theory of the business cycle stressing heavily cumulative processes and disequilibrium.

Peter Weise
Manfred Kraft

See also OVERINVESTMENT THEORIES OF BUSINESS-CYCLES

Bibliography

Kraft, M. and P. Weise. 1987. "Eine Formalisierung von Spiethoff's Theorie der wirtschaftlichen Wechsellagen." *Schweizerische Zeitschrift für Volkswirtschaft und Statistik* 123:531–42.
Spiethoff, A. 1902. "Vorbemerkungen zu einer Theorie der Überproduktion." *Schmollers Jahrbuch* 26:267–305.
———. [1925] 1953. "Crises." *International Economic Papers* 3:75–171.
———. 1955. *Die wirtschaftlichen Wechsellagen.* 2 vols. Tübingen: J. C. B. Mohr.

Sprague, Oliver Mitchell Wentworth (1873–1953)

Oliver Mitchell Wentworth Sprague was a specialist in monetary policy and financial institutions; he extensively analyzed how various monetary and banking systems affected business cycles. His most notable works included *History of Crises Under the National Banking System, Banking Reform in the United States,* and *Theory and History of Banking.*

After receiving a doctorate from Harvard in 1897, Sprague taught there almost continuously from 1899 until his retirement in 1941, except for a three-year teaching stint at the Imperial University of Tokyo (1905–08). Between 1913 and 1941, he held the first endowed chair—the Edmund Cogswell Converse Professorship of Banking and Finance—at the Harvard Graduate School of Business Administration.

His *History of Crises Under the National Banking System* analyzed the crises of 1873, 1884, 1890, 1893, and 1907. He concluded that, while some crises had been initiated by monetary factors and some by real (nonmonetary) factors, the National Banking System had intensified all of them. Moreover, he believed the 1907 crisis was more serious and handled with less skill than previous crises. Sprague's research, commissioned by the National Monetary Commission, convinced Sprague to support a central reserve of lending power. Although he initially favored a central lending authority with only limited powers and strenuously argued against the creation of a powerful central bank, his views changed as he communicated with many leading participants in this reform movement. After the war, many organizations, including the Bank of England, the Reichsbank, the Bank of France, and the League of Nations as well as many private groups, recognized his expertise and sought Sprague's advice.

In 1922, Sprague returned to analyzing the role of monetary factors in business cycles. He stated that commercial-bank management practices intensified cyclical fluctuations because bank managers failed to realize that the quality of current assets deteriorated during the final portion of a business-cycle expansion. To ameliorate this problem, Sprague recommended that banks generally require an improving current ratio (ratio of current assets to current liabilities) as the expansion continues.

During the 1930s, Sprague attempted to explain why a business recession had deepened into a depression and to recommend policies to end the depression. In the early 1930s, he served as chief economic adviser to the Bank of England (1930–33) and as financial adviser and executive assistant to the U.S. Secretary of Treasury for six months in 1933. He resigned from the latter post because he disagreed with

President Roosevelt's decision to leave the gold standard and to devalue the dollar.

Sprague (1931) believed that economists had not explained well major trade fluctuations that occurred irregularly and resulted from disparate and unique forces. He observed that increased investment had been essential for recovery in all previous depressions and argued that monetary policy alone could not induce recovery from a deep economic slump. He contended that U.S. monetary policy had been easy during the 1930s and that a lower cost of capital, resulting from easy monetary policy, had not stimulated business investment during depressions (1934, 1938). Instead, he believed that major structural changes in the employment of labor and capital were needed before prosperity returned. To absorb unemployed labor and capital, Sprague advocated price cuts in industries having elastic demands; a general wage reduction for skilled workers and added competition in capital-goods industries were necessary for price reductions. He thought that construction of moderate-priced housing possessed the greatest potential for expansion, but that new business organizations to produce housing on a large scale were needed to take advantage of this potential.

As a widely respected economist (Sprague was elected president of the American Economic Association in 1937), Sprague's advice was sought by both policymakers and businesses. Sprague viewed trade fluctuations as a normal feature of the economic landscape though their frequency and severity could be reduced through improved government policy and commercial-bank management. His work on financial crises under the National Banking System is his most enduring work. However, the Keynesian Revolution diminished his reputation, because his insistence that general wage cuts and structural reforms were necessary for recovery was out of tune with the emerging Keynesian consensus.

Robert Stanley Herren

See also FEDERAL RESERVE SYSTEM: 1914–1941; OVERINVESTMENT THEORIES OF BUSINESS CYCLES; SEASONAL FLUCTUATIONS AND FINANCIAL CRISES

Bibliography

Cole, A. H., R. L. Masson, and J. H. Williams. 1954. "Memorial: O. M. W. Sprague, 1873–1953." *American Economic Review* 44:131–32.

Sprague, O. M. W. 1910. *History of Crises Under the National Banking System.* Washington, D.C.: Government Printing Office.

———. 1911. *Banking Reform in the United States.* Cambridge: Harvard Univ. Press.

———. 1922. "Bank Management and the Business Cycle." *Harvard Business Review,* October, 19–23.

———. 1929. *Theory and History of Banking.* 5th ed. New York: Putnam.

———. 1931. "Major and Minor Trade Fluctuations." *Journal of the Royal Statistical Society* 94:540–49.

———. 1934. *Recovery and Common Sense.* New York: Houghton Mifflin.

———. 1938. "The Recovery Problem in the United States." *American Economic Review* 28:1–7.

Sraffa, Piero (1898–1983)

Piero Sraffa's intellectual career presents a portrait of tantalizing mystery to the historian of ideas. Born in 1898 in Turin, educated at the University of Turin where he came under the influence of Umberto Cosmo and Luigi Einaudi, confidant and close friend of Antonio Gramsci, Sraffa began his career as a monetary analyst with strong socialist sympathies. This combination proved explosive enough to arouse the ire of Il Duce and the interest of Keynes. Eventually fleeing Fascist Italy, he spent the bulk of his career (from 1927 until his death in 1983) in Cambridge, England as a reclusive but influential figure. Widely credited for his critical faculty, he played a personal role in at least three major intellectual movements in Cambridge during the 1930s. Ludwig Wittgenstein claimed Sraffa as the decisive influence in his turn toward his later philosophical views, about which debate still rages. His teaching and his 1926 *Economic Journal* article on the Marshallian theory of the firm set Joan Robinson and Richard Kahn off on the road to the theory of imperfect competition. Less well known, but perhaps more important for developments in economic theory, Sraffa participated fully in the debates surrounding Keynes's *Treatise on Money* which eventually led to the *General Theory.* In each of these cases, it is characteristic that Sraffa's role was personal, unrecorded, and enigmatic. Additionally, Sraffa had a public persona in the profession at large through his scholarship. His scant output of published works includes the universally admired editorship of Ricardo's *Collected Works* and his slim 1960 tract on the foundations of value theory, whose meaning and significance are yet to be fully appreciated.

Sraffa's contribution to monetary and business-cycle theory reflects the intriguing combination of public obscurity, personal influence, and seminally influential thinking that marked his career in general. It is to Sraffa's activities in the crucial period of the 1930s, just when the *General Theory* was taking form in an atmosphere of collective critique (Sraffa was a member of the famous "Cambridge Circus"), that we turn for his influence on monetary matters.

From his early monetary work, Sraffa brought two themes that were to be borne out in the *General Theory*. First his attention to the distributional aspects of monetary *policy* gave him firm grounds for disputing the concept of neutrality in monetary *theory*. Secondly his analyses of the political aspects of monetary policy (Sraffa 1922a, 1922b), were marked by the conviction that monetary values (for example, the exchange rate) are highly conventional in nature (Panico 1988). Although there is little published correspondence, so far, by which to connect Sraffa and Keynes's monetary views, Keynes's collected works make it clear that Sraffa engaged him in long discussions over the propositions of the *Treatise* and the *General Theory* (Keynes 1973, 207–13, 229; Keynes 1979, 3, 12, 35, 62, 157–60). The only currently available direct evidence on this link concerns the relationship between Sraffa's critical review (1932a) of Hayek's *Prices and Production* and the culminating argument of chapter 17 of the *General Theory*.

Sraffa's review of Hayek is important in two regards. It began a critical onslaught on Hayek's argument that monetary policy is the source of business fluctuations that led to its eventual abandonment by the profession in the 1930s. Thus, it partly set the stage for the eventual dominance of Keynes's *General Theory*. Furthermore, it exhibits a crucial moment in the evolution of Keynes's (and the Circus's) viewpoint, from the dichotomized money-output relations of the *Treatise* to the integrated "Monetary Theory of Production" Keynes argued for in the *General Theory*.

In criticizing Hayek's business-cycle theory, Sraffa presents both an internal critique of Hayek's analysis and an external critique of the methodological tradition of money neutrality. Sraffa's internal critique questions the validity of Hayek's characterization of *forced saving* and the interpretation of the *natural rate of interest* as an identifiably unique outcome of a moneyless barter system. Forced savings cause cycles in Hayek's analysis due to the inevitable reversion of monetary induced expansions of investment to the unique natural structure of production. Sraffa, instead, argued that this example of temporary redistribution during the inflation could as easily result in a new equilibrium position as in reversion to the old. His point was driven home by noting that Hayek's argument in fact did not rest on monetary expansions, per se, but on the alleged nonproportional way in which new issues affect demand for consumption and investment goods. As Hayek (1932, 244–45) admitted in reply, if the monetary expansion were to somehow maintain the natural proportions between investment and consumer demand, monetarily induced price changes would not alter the structure of production. To Sraffa this meant that some influence other than the monetary expansion, in the supposed powers of the banks to settle the distribution of increased credits, is in fact responsible for Hayek's results.

Sraffa then turned to the conception fundamental to many neoclassical views of the business cycle, the natural rate of interest. Sraffa took issue with Hayek's implicit assumption that in a nonmonetary "real" system, which the natural rate was supposed to derive from, there would be a uniquely identifiable natural rate under conditions of accumulation. Sraffa simply stated that if no money existed, as this view requires, then interest rates would be defined as ratios of real quantities of goods traded over time. In times of expansion of the investment-goods industry, defined as characteristic of the upward side of the cycle by Hayek, these commodity-rates of interest would diverge between the sectors due to spot prices changing, relative to their expected long-run normal values. Thus, the disequilibrium of the real sector would be driven by the divergences of market and natural prices characteristic of the traditional view of the move toward the long period (in both the classical and neoclassical traditions). The damage of this insight is that it means that no identifiable *unique* natural rate is available to serve as a guide to policy or as a point of comparison between the natural and monetary systems. The relatively more expanding sectors' "natural" rates would be higher than the "natural" rates of other sectors. Unless one were willing (unlike Hayek) to consider the question of nonunique composite "natural" rates, the basis of the theoretical method falls to the ground.

Although suggesting various ways to correct Hayek's argument internally, Sraffa took this internal critique as evidence that the method of money neutrality was the real culprit in leading Hayek's analysis astray. To Sraffa, the illegitimacy of the method used by Hayek arises from an attempt to analyze monetary phenomena by reference to a theoretical system from which money had consciously been removed. Notably, he viewed the strict characterization of money as a neutral medium of exchange in Hayek's work as missing the essential manner in which a monetary and nonmonetary economy differ. To Sraffa, a truly monetary economy is distinguished by the fact that money is the social contrivance for fixing important social relations between people, not just by the existence of an efficient accounting scheme between things.

It is this last general theme of Sraffa's, the essentially social role of monetary relations, which is most forcefully expressed by Keynes in the *General Theory*. The move from a neutral view of money as affecting the price level only, to a "monetary theory of production" (Keynes [1933] 1973) in which "changing views about the future are capable of influencing the present situation" (Keynes [1936] 1973, 293) was one of the major breakthroughs made by Keynes and the Circus in the 1930s. In chapter 17 of the *General Theory*, which begins with an acknowledgement of Sraffa's review of Hayek, Keynes records his most developed conception of the role of monetary factors in the economy, a view described by Hugh Townshend (1937) as Keynes released from the debris of orthodoxy. Significantly, the argument is framed in terms of a general asset-market-equilibrium theory, where each asset is valued in terms of Sraffa's commodity rates (dubbed by Keynes "own rates") of interest. Yet now each of these assets, including money, is set in the context of a monetary economy where in addition to the real forces of yield and cost, liquidity governs relative value. Investment activity proceeds in pace and direction according to the divergences between these arbitraged equilibrium own rates for existing capital goods and the marginal efficiencies of producing new ones. Keynes's basic theme, whereby investment drives output

under the influence of financial-market behavior, is here brought under a unique equilibrium framework where Sraffa's conventional aspects of money are captured by the complex social psychology of Keynes's liquidity premium.

Michael Syron Lawlor

See also CAPITAL GOODS; FORCED SAVING; HAYEK, FRIEDRICH AUGUST [VON]; KEYNES, JOHN MAYNARD; LACHMANN, LUDWIG MAURITS; LIQUIDITY PREMIUM; NATURAL RATE OF INTEREST

Bibliography

Hayek, F. A. 1932. "Dr. Hayek on Money and Capital: A Reply." *Economic Journal* 42:237–49.

Keynes, J. M. [1930] 1971. *A Treatise on Money.* 2 vols. Vols. 5 and 6 of *The Collected Writings of John Maynard Keynes.* London: Macmillan.

———. [1933] 1973. "A Monetary Theory of Production." In vol. 13 of *The Collected Writings of John Maynard Keynes,* 408–11. London: Macmillan.

———. [1936] 1973. *The General Theory of Employment, Interest, and Money.* Vol. 7 of *The Collected Writings of John Maynard Keynes.* London: Macmillan.

———. 1973. *The General Theory and After: Part I, Preparation.* Vol. 13 of *The Collected Writings of John Maynard Keynes.* Edited by E. S. Johnson and D. E. Moggeridge. London: Macmillan.

———. 1979. *The General Theory and After: A Supplement.* Vol. 29 of *The Collected Writings of John Maynard Keynes.* Edited by D. E. Moggeridge. London: Macmillan.

Panico, C. 1988. "Sraffa on Money and Banking." *Cambridge Journal of Economics* 12:7–28.

Sraffa, P. 1922a. "The Bank Crisis in Italy." *Economic Journal* 32:178–97.

———. 1922b. "Italian Banking Today." *The Manchester Guardian.* Commercial Reconstruction in Europe, Supplement. 7 December.

———. 1932a. "Dr. Hayek on Money and Capital." *Economic Journal* 42:42–53.

———. 1932b. "A Rejoinder." *Economic Journal* 42:249–51.

———. 1960. *Production of Commodities by Means of Commodities.* Cambridge: Cambridge Univ. Press.

S

Townshend, H. 1937. "Liquidity Premium and the Theory of Value." *Economic Journal* 47:167–79.

Stable Paretian Distributions

The stable paretian family of distributions is the family that contains the limiting distributions of independently and identically distributed random variables with both finite and infinite variances. The stable paretian family generalizes the central limit theorem to distributions without finite moments. The family has been proposed as the relevant distribution for stock and commodity prices. While the distribution fits many price, or return, time series quite well, other models of the distributions of prices or returns seem to fit the observed data better.

Benoit Mandelbrot was the first to challenge the relevance of the normal distribution as a statistical model for economic and financial data. Eugene Fama also contributed substantially to the debate of this issue in a series of classic articles, and in two books.

Stock-market return data and the rates of change of commodity prices are inescapably nonnormally distributed. These series are far too leptokurtic (peaked) and the tails are too fat. The practical problem is, as always, what to do about nonstationarity and to find a suitable alternative distribution. Mandelbrot chose to generalize the class of distributions under consideration to the stable paretian. Mandelbrot's first argument was that the fat tails indicate an infinite variance. His second argument arose from his work in other disciplines, which suggested that many variables had the property that different levels of time aggregation, for example, daily, weekly, or monthly observations, have distributions that belong to the same class of distribution. Technically this property is known as *stability*.

The family must be defined in terms of its characteristic generating function, which is the Fourier transform of the distribution. The family is difficult to estimate except in a few special cases.

If $df(x)$ is any density function, the corresponding generating function is given by:

$$\phi(t) = \int_{-\infty}^{\infty} \exp^{itx} df(x).$$ (1)

For the stable paretian family the form of the characteristic generating function is:

$$\phi(t) = \exp\left\{i\delta t - |ct|^{\alpha}\left[1 + i\beta \operatorname{sgn}(t)\omega(t,\alpha)\right]\right\},$$

where $\operatorname{sgn}(t) = 1$, if $t > 0$
$\quad = 0$, if $t = 0$
$\quad = -1$, if $t < 0$ (2)
$$\omega(t,\alpha) = \left\{\tan(\pi\alpha/2), \quad \alpha \neq 1\right.$$
$$\left\{(2/\pi)\log|t|, \alpha = 1,\right.$$
$$0 < \alpha \leq 2 \quad -1 < \beta < 1 \quad 0 < c.$$

A useful synopsis of the main properties of the stable paretian distribution with references to the technical literature is in Granger and Orr (1972). δ is a location parameter and is therefore unimportant in this discussion. β measures the degree of asymmetry. All the early work assumed that the distributions were symmetric and so set β to zero. Koutrouvelis (1980) and others subsequently realized that while the asymmetry is not large, it exists and may affect the estimates of other parameters. c is the scale parameter and is proportional to the standard deviation when it exists.

The most important parameter is α, which determines the member of the class of distributions. If $\alpha = 2$, the distribution is normal and if $\alpha = 1$ the distribution is Cauchy, or t distribution with one degree of freedom; in both these cases β is zero. All absolute moments greater than or equal to α, $0 < \alpha < 2$ are infinite; only for $\alpha = 2$, the normal case, do all moments exist. Except for the normal, the stable paretian distributions have no variances and for members with α less than 1, they have no means either.

The normal distribution is well known as the limiting distribution for the sum of independently and identically distributed random variables with finite variances. The stable paretian distributions are correspondingly the limiting distributions for independently and identically distributed random variables without finite variances.

The stable paretian distribution is closed under convolution; that is, if X_1 and X_2 are each distributed as stable paretian with parameter $\alpha = \alpha_0$, then the convolution sum of the two is also stable paretian with parameter $\alpha = \alpha_0$. The stable paretian limit is relevant only if economic variables are the sum of independently and identically distributed random variables. But "fat tailed" distributions can be generated without assuming infinite variances. Granger and Orr noted that early attempts to check for the relevance of the stable paretian models were judgmental, rather than formal tests of hypotheses. These procedures included the use of normal probability plots, sample fractiles, plotting the log of tail probabilities against the log of the variable, and checking for the convergence of the variances as sample size is increased. Hsu, Miller, and Wichern (1974) provided one of the first formal tests of the stable paretian family. They demonstrated that a minimum χ^2 goodness of fit test could be used with the stable paretian family. Their results showed that for daily stock-price data the symmetric stable paretian family was not consistent with the observed sample. However, the use of monthly data suggested that the stable paretian family was consistent with the observations; the parameter α was estimated to be less than 2. This difference in result between the daily and monthly observations which has been confirmed by Fama (1976, 33, 38), provides some empirical evidence against Mandelbrot's hypothesis that financial data have the same distribution at most levels of time aggregation. The authors also considered the alternative hypothesis that the data were nonstationary with time varying variances. The authors concluded that nonstationary provides the better description; and that normality, or a mixture of normals, is the relevant distribution.

Koutrouvelis extended some previous theoretical work on the estimation of the characteristic function itself and extended the family of distributions to include the nonsymmetric members. Stock returns are well known to be nonsymmetric, even though the nonsymmetry is not large. The results confirmed earlier work; α was estimated to be approximately *1.8*. However, these results must be viewed cautiously since even if a model fits the observed data well, its acceptance as a useful model depends on comparisons with other plausible models. Madan and Seneta (1987) made such a comparison. They recognized that the parameters of a stable paretian distribution can be estimated from the moments of a simple cosine transformation of the original data. Maden and Seneta compared the stable paretian family to the "normal compound Poisson" distribution and to what they describe as the variance gamma distribution. The idea of the normal compound Poisson distribution is that each realization of a stochastic process is the sum of N_t normal deviates and the number N_t is itself a random variable with a Poisson distribution. The idea of the variance gamma distribution is that the stochastic process is the realization of an independent sum of gamma increments.

Using returns on nineteen stocks on the Sydney Exchange, Madan and Seneta compared the three alternative models. The symmetric stable paretian family was not preferred over the alternative models. However, what the result would have been if the nonsymmetric stable paretian family had been used is not known.

Clark (1973) has generalized this approach in an economically plausible way. Clark's idea is that information reaches a market at different rates. Thus, price evolution is slow when information is slow and is fast when information is fast. Clark tested the symmetric stable paretian family against a version of what is known as a subordinated stochastic process. Clark used daily cotton futures prices to conclude that the subordinated process model was preferable to the stable symmetric paretian family.

The stable paretian family is relevant in situations best characterized by the "constant" sum of independently and identically distributed random variables. Neither independence nor identical distributions can be assumed with any confidence with economic data. If this view is correct, the stable paretian family is not relevant. The alternatives that have been examined with persuasive results are that economic data are not stationary; that mixtures of distributions, or subordinated stochastic processes, or compound processes, are strong competitors to the stable paretian family. When the stable paretian family has been tested against, or at least compared to, these alternatives, the alternatives have been chosen.

James B. Ramsey

Bibliography

Clark, P. K. 1973. "A Subordinated Stochastic Process Model With Finite Variance for Speculative Prices." *Econometrica* 41:135–55.

Fama, E. F. 1963. "Mandelbrot and the Stable Paretian Hypothesis." *Journal of Business* 36:420–29.

———. 1976. *Foundations of Finance*. New York: Basic Books.

Fama, E. F. and M. H. Miller. 1972. *The Theory of Finance*. New York: Holt, Rinehart & Winston.

Fama, E. F. and R. Roll. 1968. "Some Properties of Symmetric Stable Distributions."

Journal of the American Statistical Association 63:817–36.

———. 1971. "Parameter Estimates for Symmetric Stable Distributions." *Journal of the American Statistical Association* 66:331–38.

Fielitz, B. D. and E. W. Smith. 1972. "Asymmetric Stable Distributions of Stock Price Changes." *Journal of the American Statistical Association* 67:813–14.

Gnedenko, B. V. and A. N. Kolmogrov. 1968. *Limit Distributions for Sums of Independent Random Variables*. Translation. Reading, Mass.: Addison Wesley.

Granger, C. W. J. and D. Orr. 1972. "'Infinite Variance' and Research Strategy in Time Series Analysis." *Journal of the American Statistical Association* 67:275–85.

Hsu, D.-A., R. B. Miller, and D. W. Wichern. 1974. "On the Stable Paretian Behavior of Stock-Market Prices." *Journal of the American Statistical Association* 69:108–13.

Koutrouvelis, I. A. 1980. "Regression-Type Estimation of the Parameters of Stable Laws." *Journal of the American Statistical Association* 75:918–28.

Lukacs, E. 1960. *Characteristic Functions*. New York: Hafner.

Madan, D. B. and E. Seneta. 1987. "Chebyshev Polynomial Approximations and Characteristic Function Estimation." *Journal of the Royal Statistical Society* B 49:163–69.

Mandelbrot, B. B. 1963. "The Variation of Certain Speculative Prices." *Journal of Business* 36:394–419.

———. 1967. "The Variation of Some Other Speculative Prices." *Journal of Business* 40:393–413.

———. 1969. "Long-Run Linearity, Locally Gaussian Process, H-Spectra and Infinite Variances." *International Economic Review* 10:82–111.

Officer, R. R. 1972. "The Distribution of Stock Returns." *Journal of the American Statistical Association* 67:807–12.

Press, S. J. 1967. "A Compound Events Model for Security Prices." *Journal of Business* 40:317–35.

Teichmoeller, J. 1971. "A Note on the Distribution of Stock Price Changes." *Journal of the American Statistical Association* 66:282–84.

State-Monopoly Capitalism

The notion of state-monopoly capitalism was in common use by orthodox Marxist-Leninist theorists from the 1950s to 1970s to describe and explain the distinctive features of postwar capitalism. It was invoked to explain the surprising failure to occur of the economic catastrophe and political upheavals that they had so confidently expected after the Second World War. Its exponents typically argued that the state and monopolies had been fused into a single mechanism of political domination and economic exploitation whose principal functions were to repress popular resistance and transfer resources from the proletariat, peasantry, petty bourgeoisie, and nonmonopoly capital to the monopolies. They also argued that the state's new economic role had changed the forms in which cyclical patterns and capitalist crisis tendencies appeared, but could not abolish them. They would reemerge at a later stage and precipitate the delayed socialist revolution. Thus, the theory was concerned with the overall periodization of capitalism into distinct stages rather than with explaining business cycles, and it sometimes seemed as if a defining feature of state-monopoly capitalism in its early postwar versions was the elimination of cyclical phenomena through state intervention.

Although the term state-monopoly capitalism was first used by Lenin in the First World War, he was referring to the specific form of state that emerged to direct the war economy in Germany and Russia. Whereas Lenin saw imperialism as a distinct stage of capitalism with its own laws and crisis-tendencies, he treated state-monopoly capitalism as a purely conjunctural phenomenon. But it was still important, according to Lenin, because the extension of state control over the economy would facilitate the building of socialism in war-torn Russia. However, the concept was little used for some thirty years thereafter and gained its current meaning only after the Second World War. One might argue that this was anticipated to some extent in concepts such as "state capitalism" (Bukharin), "finance capitalism" (Hilferding), or in some contemporary Communist analyses of Nazism and the New Deal. However, although early discussions noted how the state could help to compensate for the crisis tendencies and stagnation associated with monopoly capitalism, they did not draw the economic and political lessons of postwar state-monopoly-capitalism theory or address the specific mechanisms associated with the postwar Keynesian welfare state.

The postwar theory was developed in the 1950s to account for the continued existence of capitalism despite an (alleged) worsening of "the general crisis of capitalism." Initially its proponents regarded state-monopoly capitalism as a last-ditch attempt to shore up capitalism during this general crisis through the direct, personal subordination of the state to a financial oligarchy; this led to specific policies favoring monopoly capital as well as to a general militarization of the economy prompted by hostility to the Soviet bloc and worries about domestic class struggles. In its Stalinist variant, the theory argued that the basic law of modern capitalism was the global striving of monopolies for maximum profit and that the state was directly subjugated to the monopolies as they attempted to maintain their economic and political domination. It emphasized the moribund, reactionary character of state-monopoly capitalism and its desperate, doomed attempt to avoid the stagnationary effects of monopoly.

As the intellectual climate eased after Stalin's death in 1953, more sophisticated versions of the theory, more attuned to contemporary capitalist realities, were developed. State-monopoly capitalism was now seen as a new stage of capitalism, which was quite compatible with continued accumulation. By the 1960s, it was seen as consolidated rather than emergent, permanent rather than temporary, total rather than partial in scope, preemptive rather than reactive in its crisis-management activities, long- rather than short-term in outlook, and international rather than just national in its reach. By the same token the range of mechanisms cited to explain the state's capacities to avoid crisis and stagnation had multiplied.

A synthetic account of state-monopoly capitalism would run as follows: free competition leads to the concentration and centralization of capital and produces monopolies in industrial and banking capital; these typically enjoy surplus profits (i.e., profits that tend to remain above the average) which depend more on the monopolies' economic and political strength than on their economic efficiency. When allied with the state, monopoly capital can reinforce its economic domination through political transfers of income and wealth from small and medium capital, the petty bourgeoisie, peasants, and workers as well as through the use of state power to promote its own inter-

ests. Among the mechanisms it uses are the unequal distribution of the tax burden and tax concessions, state credit and monetary policies, public expenditure favorable to monopoly capital, the nationalization of key infrastructural branches, so that monopoly capital receives hidden subsidies for its inputs, the discriminatory setting of quotas and tariffs, and an arms race favoring the development of a monopolistic "military-industrial complex." It also helps to smooth out fluctuations in the business cycle through economic forecasting, programming, planning, Keynesian demand management, incomes policies, and so forth. However, while this tends to smooth out the cyclical fluctuations, it serves to reinforce stagnationary tendencies. These in turn are overcome through increased resort to deficit finance with long-run inflationary implications. Eventually this leads to problems manifested in the fiscal crisis of the state, tax resistance, and an overloading of the unproductive burden of state activities on accumulation.

While much state intervention in the period of state-monopoly capitalism reflects the power and greed of monopoly capital, it is also prompted by objective tendencies and imperatives in modern capitalism. In particular, it reflects a fundamental contradiction between the increasingly social character of the productive forces and the continued private appropriation of profit. As the scientific and technical revolution accelerates and ties deepen between material production and intellectual labor, the state intervenes to ensure continuity of production, match demand and productive capacities, underwrite investments in industries with high fixed costs, long gestation periods, long turnover times, and uncertain returns. Here there are strong similarities with Galbraith's account of the "new industrial state."

The intensifying crisis of Communist parties in the West and the demise of Communism in the East has prompted a decline of interest in state-monopoly capitalism. Other theories have emerged in the West to account for the dynamic of postwar capitalism and there has been a general move away from Marxist political economy to embrace market economics in the countries of the former Soviet bloc. Little original work has been done in this field since the 1970s. And the political appeal of state-monopoly capitalism—its justification for an antimonopoly popular front embracing small and medium capital as well as the petty bourgeoisie, peasants, and workers—long ago lost its political resonance. In short, this approach to capitalism is now as moribund as it once declared capitalism itself to be.

Bob Jessop

See also HILFERDING, RUDOLF; REGULATION SCHOOL

Bibliography

Boccara, P., et al. 1976. *Traité d'economie politique: le capitalisme monopoliste d'état.* 2d ed. Paris: Éditions sociales.

Cheprakov, V., ed. 1967. *State Monopoly Capitalism.* Moscow: Progress Publishers.

Fine, B. and L. Harris. 1975. *Rereading Capital.* London: Macmillan.

Galbraith, J. K. 1967. *The New Industrial State.* Boston: Houghton Mifflin.

Jessop, B. 1982. *The Capitalist State.* Oxford: Basil Blackwell.

Lenin, V. I. [1917] 1989. *Imperialism: The Highest Stage of Capitalism.* New York: International Publishers.

Steindl, Josef (1912–1993)

Josef Steindl's major contributions to the analysis of economic fluctuations are found in his *Maturity and Stagnation in American Capitalism,* which offers an explanation for the slowdown in the growth of the United States economy that culminated in the Great Depression. The reasoning proceeds from the theory of effective demand initiated by Michal Kalecki, focusing on income distribution and imperfect competition. Extending this reasoning to the question of long-term growth, Steindl made important contributions to the theory of the dynamics of competition. His relating economic stagnation to the emergence of oligopoly in an economy of "mature" industries also greatly influenced Marxian theorists, most notably Paul Baran and Paul Sweezy and their theory of "monopoly capital." Steindl's later work on growth and fluctuations revised and extended the argument of *Maturity and Stagnation* to consider the importance of innovations and to update the story in the light of the recent history of economic and political developments.

Steindl's early economic training was in Vienna under the Austrian School, which he quickly came to reject. After emigrating to En-gland in 1938 due to the Nazi takeover, he met and worked with Kalecki at the Oxford Institute of Statistics. He returned to Vienna in 1950, resuming his position at the Austrian Institute for Economic Research until his retirement in 1978.

In *Maturity and Stagnation,* Steindl took from Kalecki the idea that fluctuations in output and employment are due to the interrelations among profits, investment, and capacity when price-cost margins do not adjust properly. Increased investment spending increases profits, which in turn spurs more investment, but also adds to capacity. However, the added capacity discourages investment, depressing profits and further discouraging investment until investment becomes profitable again. If the mark-up of prices over costs (mostly money-wage costs) does not fall, real wages and hence consumption cannot rise to offset falling investment, and output and employment must fall as well.

Kalecki felt that without technological innovations the capitalist system would stop growing. Steindl sought, however, to apply a combination of Kaleckian reasoning about cycles and his own ideas about the dynamics of competition to the analysis of long-term growth. His theory of competition begins with a new version of Alfred Marshall's explanation of differences in profit margins among competitors in an industry as differential rents. In industries in which entry is easy, there may be both small producers earning zero, or "normal" profits and bigger firms earning positive or "excess" profits reflecting their cost advantages over the marginal firms. The more successful firms in an industry thus have the advantages of lower costs and greater internal financing over their rivals. Using internal financing to increase capacity enables these firms to reduce unit costs, which may make cutting prices an effective strategy for driving smaller, higher-cost rivals out of business.

Such competition leads to growth in which investment increases productive capacity, and prices drop with costs as larger firms drive out higher-cost, "marginal" producers. The process continues as long as falling prices and expanding output increase the utilization of capacity and maintain the profitability of investment. But as industries reach "maturity," the stimulus to investment of price competition is lost, since price-cutting to keep utilization rates high and to spur growth by driving rivals out of business is no longer attractive.

This treatment of competition was an advance over Kalecki's, which simply discussed the static determinants of the "degree of monopoly." Steindl turned the tables on the older theories of imperfect competition by arguing that above-normal profit margins (and the holding of excess capacity) do not result from exploiting a less than perfectly elastic demand, but rather that it is holding excess capacity that generates above-normal profit margins. Firms want to hold some excess capacity to be able to keep up with competitors and to be sure of prospects for expansion. However, too much excess capacity, which is most likely to emerge in the stage of maturity when price-cutting to increase utilization is not so effective, depresses investment, and leads to the macroeconomic slowdown discussed above.

Steindl estimated that in the 1890s the U.S. economy had reached the stage of maturity at which the rate of growth of capital began to decline. However, the increasing availability of share finance largely offset any effect on the economy until the 1930s by enabling firms to channel outside saving into their equity at progressively lower costs. This explains the prosperity of the 1920s. But the unusually low yields on shares in that decade were unsustainable and provoked a reaction that overwhelmed the economy in the 1930s. The concluding chapter of *Maturity and Stagnation*, entitled "Karl Marx and the Accumulation of Capital," sympathetically criticizes Marx's theory of a falling rate of profit and offers a reformulation based on the argument of the book plus Sweezy's recasting of the Marxian notion of "underconsumption."

Nina Shapiro has criticized Steindl's assumption that firms invest only in their own industries, arguing that the development of new products, which might overcome the stagnation associated with maturity, is implicit in the competitive process that Steindl describes. Steindl himself has said that deprecating the influence of innovations on investment was a mistake, brought on by his impression that a long time is usually necessary for business to exploit a new scientific invention. He was also concerned that relying on innovations to generate an exogenous trend would inaccurately exclude the possibility of the existence of an endogenous trend. More recently, his attempts to marry the exogenous innovation-driven trend with the endogenous growth process have led him to conclude that the basic argument of *Maturity and Stagnation* about how the emergence of oligopoly affects the rate of growth is still valid.

In other recent work, Steindl has written on the prosperity and decline in the advanced capitalist economies since World War II. He attributes that prosperity to the high rates of public spending and to spillovers from government-financed, war-related research and development. He attributes the slowdown to the weakening of technological stimuli, to environmental and energy problems, and to a political reaction against full employment and growth caused by inflation and by resentment of union power and of minority and foreign workers.

Steindl's importance for the theory of economic growth and fluctuations comes from the underpinning his long-run theory of competition and the emergence of oligopoly provided for the Kaleckian theory of the macroeconomy. He has also clarified the issues involved in integrating the cycle and the trend and contributed to the theoretical and historical analysis within a Kaleckian-Keynesian-Marxian perspective of the long-run growth of capitalist economies.

Tracy Mott

See also FALLING RATE OF PROFIT; KALECKI, MICHAL; SWEEZY, PAUL MARLOR

Bibliography

Baran, P. and P. M. Sweezy. 1966. *Monopoly Capital: An Essay on the American Economic and Social Order.* New York: Monthly Review Press.

Kalecki, M. 1971. *Selected Essays on the Dynamics of the Capitalist Economy, 1933–1970.* Cambridge: Cambridge Univ. Press.

Shapiro, N. 1988. "Market Structure and Economic Growth: Steindl's Contribution." *Social Concept* 4:72–83.

Steindl, J. 1976. *Maturity and Stagnation in American Capitalism.* 2d ed. with a new introduction. New York: Monthly Review Press.

———. 1980a. "Stagnation Theory and Stagnation Policy." *Cambridge Journal of Economics* 3:1–14.

———. 1980b. "Technical Progress and Evolution." In *Research, Development, and Technological Innovation,* edited by D. Sahal, 131–41. Lexington, Mass.: Lexington Books.

———. 1981. "Ideas and Concepts of Long Run Growth." *Banca Nazionale del*

Lavoro Quarterly Review, March, 35–48.

———. 1982a. "The Role of Household Saving in the Modern Economy." *Banca Nazionale del Lavoro Quarterly Review,* March, 69–88.

———. 1982b. "Technology and the Economy: The Case of Falling Productivity Growth in the 1970s." In *The Transfer and Utilization of Technical Knowledge,* edited by D. Sahal, 5–13. Lexington, Mass.: Lexington Books.

———. 1983. "The Control of the Economy." *Banca Nazionale del Lavoro Quarterly Review,* September, 235–48.

———. 1984. "Reflections on the Present State of Economics." *Banca Nazionale del Lavoro Quarterly Review,* March, 3–14.

———. 1985. "Structural Problems in the Crisis." *Banca Nazionale del Lavoro Quarterly Review,* September, 223–32.

Stockholm School

The Stockholm School consisted of a number of Swedish economists studying both unemployment and stabilization policy from the late 1920s to the late 1930s. The term "Stockholm School" was first used by a leading member of the group, Bertil Ohlin ([1937] 1951), who argued that a new approach to employment theory had been worked out by a number of Swedish economists independently of Keynes's *General Theory.* Ohlin listed the following as the key characteristics of the Stockholm School: (1) aggregate analysis; (2) the distinction between *ex ante* and *ex post;* (3) consistent use of period analysis; (4) stress on the plans and expectations of individual households and firms, but not so much on the influence of the quantity of money; and (5) reliance on analysis of well-specified cases to ensure precision.

Some of the Swedish economists doubted that they belonged to a well-defined school, because the Swedes shared no common analytical structure comparable to Keynes's income-expenditure theory. But one could still speak about a group of Swedish economists who, from common starting points and through lively internal discussion, significantly advanced economic theory.

The Swedish economists were all strongly influenced by Knut Wicksell, principally by his inflation analysis, but also to some extent by his capital theory. Wicksell's cumulative process inspired them to use aggregate analysis, to investigate economic development period by period, and to base their analysis on something other than the quantity theory of money (Ohlin's points 1, 3, and 4).

A second common source of inspiration was Gunnar Myrdal's 1927 dissertation, *Prisbildningen och föränderligheten* (Pricing and Change). The strength of the dissertation lay in its richness of ideas and in the new approach it introduced: the behavior of firms ought to be analyzed as an intertemporal planning problem under incomplete information. He also stressed that expectations, via their effects on plans, have important implications for future developments (Ohlin's points 2 and 4).

Three overlapping stages mark the development of the Stockholm School. The first comprised interpretations and clarifications of Wicksell's cumulative process by Erik Lindahl's *Penningpolitikens medel* (The means of monetary policy, 1930) and *Studies in the Theory of Money and Capital,* Myrdal's *Monetary Equilibrium* (preceded by articles in 1931 and 1933), and Ohlin's "Till frågen on penningteoriens uppläggning" (On the question of the formulation of the theory of money [1933] 1978). These works discussed the equilibrium concept in Wicksell's cumulative process and were much influenced by Myrdal's 1927 study. Though mainly concerned with inflation theory, the contributions of Myrdal and especially Ohlin took up questions concerning aggregate production and employment.

The next stage addressed unemployment problems under the auspices of the official unemployment committee which was instituted in 1927. The project resulted in a number of publications that discussed various aspects of employment theory and anti-unemployment policy.

In *Penningpolitik, offentliga arbeten, subventioner och tullar som medel mot arbetslöshet* (Monetary policy, public works, subsidies and customs duties as means against unemployment, 1934), Ohlin presented an important analysis of unemployment and how to reduce it with *inter alia* monetary policy. The report contains much of the same basic macroeconomics as did the standard Keynesian approach of the 1950s and 1960s. Ohlin presented a simple multiplier analysis for an open economy, but did not derive the static multiplier. Instead, he worked out its impact over several periods. Investment was determined by a simple accelerator mechanism and Ohlin discussed (but only verbally) how, in combination with the multiplier, it could generate cycles. Unlike Keynes, Ohlin based his analysis of interest determination on the loanable-funds theory.

In *Finanspolitikens ekonomisk verkningar* (Economic effects of fiscal policy, 1934) Myrdal investigated the role of fiscal policy in dampening the business cycle. Myrdal concluded that the government budget ought not to be balanced each year, but over the whole cycle. Two additional important contributions were published as supplements to the unemployment investigations. D. Hammerskjöld studied the international propagation of business cycles and A. Johansson the relationship between wages and unemployment.

The role of the Swedish economists in influencing economic policy attracted a certain interest elsewhere, because Sweden was only mildly affected by the Great Depression. It was thought that the impact of the depression had been cushioned by the expansionary employment policy of the Social Democratic government starting in 1933. The minister of finance, Ernst Wigforss, cooperated closely with several young economists including Myrdal who had written a supplement to the government budget proposal of 1933.

However, the primary reason that Sweden was able to avoid the crisis was probably not fiscal and monetary policy based on advice from economists of the Stockholm School, but rather that Sweden, without deep reflection, followed the lead of Great Britain in September 1931, and abandoned the gold standard, devaluing the krona by approximately 30 percent.

The unemployment investigation was completed in 1935. At the end of the 1930s, important theoretical advances by two young economists began the final stage of the development of the Stockholm School. In his 1937 dissertation, *Studies in the Theory of Economic Expansion,* Erik Lundberg presented a number of dynamic macroeconomic models of the upturn phase of the cycle. His first model was of a simple multiplier type worked out for several periods, which also showed that the process converged towards the static multiplier. Lundberg then introduced inventory variations and investments in fixed capital analytically determined by a simple accelerator mechanism. Using numerical examples, Lundberg studied its development over several periods to determine whether the upturn could be interrupted and replaced by a downturn.

Thus, Lundberg presented the first mathematical model of the cycle based on a multiplier-accelerator interaction. However, he only worked out numerical examples and did not derive the mathematical solution, which was published two years later in Samuelson's famous 1939 article.

Svennilson's dissertation *Ekonomisk planering* (Economic planning, 1938) threw light on the microfoundations of the period analysis of the Stockholm School. Svennilson studied intertemporal planning by firms with incomplete information and discussed the relationship of this problem to the rest of the analysis of the Stockholm School. Svennilson partly based his research on problems formulated in Myrdal's 1927 work. Unlike Myrdal, Svennilson was well read in mathematics and mathematical statistics, so that his dissertation was technically more advanced than Myrdal's. However, much of the discussion was devoted to concepts and the formulation of problems, and provided few mathematical solutions.

In 1939, the last two important contributions of the Stockholm School were published: Myrdal's *Monetary Equilibrium* and Lindahl's *Studies in the Theory of Money and Capital.* In the main the two books contained translations into English of earlier published articles. However, Lindahl's book contained a previously unpublished introductory chapter which outlined how dynamic theory should in principle be developed.

The dissertations of Svennilson and Lundberg showed that introductory steps had been taken to implement Lindahl's research program. But after 1939, the creative capacity of the Stockholm School was on the whole exhausted. With a few exceptions, the Stockholm School did not even serve as an important source of inspiration for later research in employment theory or in stabilization policy. The exceptions were Myrdal's *ex ante/ex post* terminology, Herman Wold's causal-chain methodology, and Bent Hansen's theory of repressed inflation. Moreover, Lundberg's analysis had some influence on Lloyd Metzler's theory of the inventory cycle and Lindahl influenced Hicks in developing the theory of temporary equilibrium.

There are several reasons why the Stockholm School did not have an impact comparable to that of Keynes. Many of its important contributions were published only in Swedish or were translated into English only after long delays. At first, this was an advantage, since communications between members could be intensive and informal. But when the important members of the school took various political or administrative assignments (only Lindahl fully remained in the academic world), the research program collapsed. Only Lindahl's pupil, Bent Hansen, continued the tradition.

However, one could imagine that the dynamic analysis of the Stockholm School might have complemented the (originally) static analysis of the Keynesian theory. The reason that this did not happen was the preference of the Stockholm School for studying special cases (Ohlin's point 5), which meant that the analysis rapidly became intractable. It also appears that the dynamic problems chosen for study by the Stockholm School (e.g., Lundberg could only solve difference equations of the first order) were not analytically accessible with the tools then at hand.

Claes-Henric Siven

See also EXPECTATIONS; KEYNES, JOHN MAYNARD; LINDAHL, ERIK ROBERT; LUNDBERG, ERIK FILIP; MULTIPLIER; MYRDAL, GUNNAR; OHLIN, BERTIL GOTTHARD; SAMUELSON, PAUL ANTHONY; WICKSELL, JOHAN GUSTAV KNUT

Bibliography
Hansen, B. 1951. *A Study in the Theory of Inflation.* London: Allen and Unwin.
Hansson, B. 1982. *The Stockholm School and the Development of the Dynamic Method.* London: Croom Helm.
Jonung, L., ed. 1991. *The Stockholm School of Economics Revisited.* Cambridge: Cambridge Univ. Press.
Lindahl, E. 1939. *Studies in the Theory of Money and Capital.* London: Allen and Unwin.
Lundberg, E. 1937. *Studies in the Theory of Economic Expansion.* London: P. S. King.
Myrdal, G. [1929] 1939. *Monetary Equilibrium.* Translation. London: William Hodge.
Ohlin, B. [1933] 1978. "On the Formulation of Monetary Theory." Translation. *History of Political Economy* 10:353–88.
———. [1937] 1951. "Some Notes on the Stockholm Theory of Saving and Investment, I–II." In *Readings in Business Cycle Theory,* 87–130. Homewood, Ill.: Irwin, 1950.
Palander, T. [1941] 1953. "On the Concepts and Methods of the Stockholm School." Translation. *International Economic Papers* 3:5–57.
Samuelson, P. A. [1939] 1966. "Interactions Between the Multiplier Analysis and the Principle of Acceleration." Chap. 82 in *The Collected Scientific Papers of Paul A. Samuelson,* vol. 2. Cambridge: MIT Press.
Siven, C.-H. 1985. "The End of the Stockholm School." *Scandinavian Journal of Economics* 87:577–93.
Wicksell, K. [1898] 1936. *Interest and Prices.* Translation. London: Macmillan.

Stock-Market Crash of 1929

The stock-market crash of 1929 ended one of history's most spectacular asset bubbles. In the bull market of the late 1920s, stock prices apparently rose much more rapidly than dividends or earnings as the public, swept up in a wave of optimism, frantically traded stocks.

The bull market had its origins in the rapid economic growth in the United States after World War I. Part of this growth may be attributed to technological innovation and industrial reorganization that improved the productivity of American enterprise. In this period, the market for industrial securities came of age, as firms issued stocks and bonds to finance vertical integration and the acquisition of new plant and equipment.

The bubble in the stock market is usually identified as beginning in March 1928. Although some historians have treated the bull market as a pure bubble, investors had good reason to be optimistic. Earnings and dividends for many stocks were increasing, and few contemporary analysts expected that the economy's boom would come to an abrupt halt. The performance of many stocks was excellent. General Motors' stock was a high flyer, but the company's sales boomed and its dividends were rapidly increased. High-technology firms, like RCA, RKO, Alcoa, United Aircraft, and the electric utilities, grew very rapidly. Their stock prices soared even though these young companies usually paid no dividends. At the same time, the prices of stock for small companies and railroads, whose earnings changed little, were flat. This uneven performance reflects the important role of fundamentals in the stock-market boom.

Historians have traditionally argued that one key to the stock-market boom was the availability of easy credit in the form of brokers' loans. Buyers of stock could purchase shares on margin, providing only a fraction of the needed funds and borrowing the rest to enjoy the full capital gain less interest. Although the volume of brokers' loans surged during the bull market, credit was not cheap. From the beginning of 1928, the Federal Reserve pursued a tight monetary policy, aimed at halting stock-market speculation. While the interest rate on broker's loans continued to increase, investors were not dissuaded, emphasizing that the stock-market bubble was independent of credit conditions.

Bubbles may emerge in an asset market when fundamentals become difficult to assess. During the 1920s, the transformation of industry and financial intermediation increased the difficulty of analyzing the future prospects of firms. Major shifts occurred in many industries, and numerous prominent firms had not yet paid dividends. Furthermore, the sophistication of investors was diluted by the influx of many new investors into the market. The role of commercial banks in financing industry had declined, and investment banks and the securities affiliates of commercial banks sold large quantities of new securities to the general public. By mid-1929, many well-informed participants in the market believed that prices were far too high. Presidents of some firms even declared that the prices of their stock had risen too high, and brokers raised margin requirements on their loans to historic levels.

The market continued to move up until September 1929 when the economy began to slow due to the Federal Reserve's policy. The high interest rates in the United States attracted funds from abroad, but this led other central banks to pursue restrictive monetary policies, pushing the world economy towards recession. The decline in economic indexes and rising real interest rates began to depress stock prices. The market drifted downwards in early October. As trading volume rose, the ticker fell behind. Once prompt reporting ceased, investors lost track of their positions and panic selling began. There were severe panics on Black Thursday, 24 October and Black Tuesday, 29 October, when price drops led to margin calls on impaired accounts and a liquidation of holdings. While the frenzied selling slowed at times, the market could not be talked up by bankers or big investors.

A more widespread financial crisis threatened when banks and other lenders withdrew their loans to brokers. With the encouragement and assistance of the Federal Reserve Bank of New York, the large New York banks stepped in and quickly supplied credit to brokers. The direct effects of the crash were confined to the stock market by this prompt action and did not spread to the rest of the financial system. The New York Fed had initiated this policy, but the Board of Governors disapproved and censured the bank, maintaining its tight monetary policy. Although it briefly recovered, the continued decline of the stock market reflected the economy's policy-aggravated slide into depression.

After the crash, congressional investigations discovered evidence of stock manipulation and securities fraud during the boom. These findings and public anger over the collapse of stock prices led to passage of the Glass-Steagall Act, the Securities Act of 1933, and the Securities Exchange Act of 1934. This New Deal legislation attempted to correct the problems of the stock-market by separating commercial and investment banking and by imposing an array of new regulations on the securities business.

Eugene N. White

See also EXCESS VOLATILITY; EXPECTATIONS; FEDERAL RESERVE SYSTEM: 1914–1941; GLASS-STEAGALL ACT; GREAT DEPRESSION IN THE UNITED STATES (1929–1938); STOCK-MARKET CRASHES OF 1987 AND 1989; STOCK-MARKET PRICES; TULIPMANIA

Bibliography

Galbraith, J. K. 1954. *The Great Crash 1929*. Boston: Houghton Mifflin.

White, E. N. 1990. "The Stock Market Boom and Crash of 1929 Revisited." *Journal of Economic Perspectives* 4:67–83.

Stock-Market Crashes of 1987 and 1989

Stock-market crashes evoke considerable attention, both public and professional, first because they have significant immediate effects on shareholders and the economy in general, and second because they are rare and difficult to explain within standard models of stock-market behavior. The crashes of October 1987 and October 1989 are no exceptions, and provide important new information about stock-price movements.

Standard Valuation Models and Market Crashes

Much of the difficulty of explaining crashes results from the sheer magnitude of price decline that defines a crash. On Monday, 19 October 1987, the Dow Jones Industrial Average (DJIA) dropped 508 points, or 22.6 percent. From the close of trading on Tuesday, 13 October (*four trading days*) the DJIA fell 769 points, or 31 percent, representing a drop in the value of outstanding equity of some $1 trillion. Only the 12.8 percent drop in the Dow on 28 October 1929, and the fall of 11.7 percent on the following day, which together constituted the crash of 1929, have approached the October 1987 decline in magnitude.

On Friday, 13 October 1989, the stock-market dropped 190 points (6.9 percent). Although this was the second largest absolute decline, it was only the twelfth largest percentage decline. On Monday, 16 October, the DJIA had recovered 88 points (3.43 percent), and closed the week with a gain of almost 120 points. For the week 13 October to 20 October, the loss was only about 70 points (2.5 percent).

Other comparisons between 1987 and 1989 are also instructive. In 1987, the decline was "market-wide" across all stocks, while by contrast in 1989, the major losers were largely confined to leverage buyouts (LBOs) and other takeover targets. Similarly, the decline across countries was much more uniform in 1987 than in 1989, and lasted longer in 1987; prices did not return to pre-crash levels until early 1989. Finally, there was greater disruption of usual linkages across related markets in 1987 (stock, options, and futures markets), which, as discussed below, stimulated particular regulatory responses.

The 1989 "mini-break" is relatively easy to explain in terms of standard market-valuation models. Prices were not historically unusual by the standards of dividend yields or price/earnings (P/E) ratios in 1989, and the decline was concentrated in LBOs and other potential takeover targets. Not surprisingly, the decline on the thirteenth began shortly after 2:40 p.m., when the failure of financing for a proposed takeover of United Airlines and the suspension of trading in its stock were announced (McMillan 1990, Securities and Exchange Commission [SEC] 1988). Accordingly, the subsequent discussion of 1989 focuses on the performance of "circuit breakers" adopted in response to the 1987 crash.

However, the 1987 crash is difficult to explain within standard models, although a partial reconciliation may be possible. The major difficulty is to identify a source of the negative information or the increased discount rates that could account for a 31 percent drop in value from 13 October to 19 October 1987. The SEC Report (1988) notes that some negative news items occurred on 14–16 October, and Mitchell and Netter (1989) point to anti-takeover legislation proposed on 13 October as the fundamental cause of the 10 percent price decline by 16 October. However, although they regard this initial price decline as consistent with rationality, they do not explain how this "normal" price movement could trigger the massive decline on 19 October.

Moreover, traditional measures of value suggest that the market was unusually high just before the 1987 crash. Dividend yields were very low compared with historical levels. From 1956 to 1986, the average dividend yield was 3.8 percent. In September 1987, the yield was only 2.8 percent, and was back to 3.71 percent by December 1987. Similarly, in August-September 1987, P/E ratios were at historical highs. A reasonable inference is that the crash reflected a fundamental shift in equilibrium values, with the market returning from an unusually high to a more normal price level. The obvious question is whether such a large price change over such a short period could be rational.

Market Irrationality?

Some observers conclude that crashes such as October 1987 are overwhelming evidence of irrationality in stock prices. Keynes's attack ([1936] 1973, 155–62) on liquid stock-markets as promoting "a game of Snap, of Old Maid, of Musical Chairs," and his emphasis on "animal spirits" and "waves of irrational psychology" followed the crash of 1929 and the subsequent depression. Shleifer and Summers (1990) regard the 1987 crash as conclusive evidence for the inadequacy of the efficient-markets hypothesis, and propose an alternative model based on investor irrationality.

This debate actually goes back at least to the seventeenth century and the Dutch "tulipmania," with a recent revival based on apparent excess volatility in the stock market (LeRoy and Porter 1981, Shiller 1981). The subject remains controversial, whether concerning the tulipmania (Garber 1989) or excess volatility (Flavin 1983, Kleidon 1986, Gilles and LeRoy 1991, Cochrane 1992). In the current context, Shleifer and Summers base their belief in irrationality on the inability of standard models to explain the crash. However, as discussed below, reasonable extensions of standard rational models may, in fact, be able to explain market crashes. Moreover, attributing the decline entirely to chance or irrationality is difficult to reconcile with two observations: the universal decline in stock prices and the failure of stock-price indexes in all countries to reach their previous peaks for months.

Regulatory Reaction to the 1987 Crash

Questions about market rationality were largely sidestepped in the regulatory reaction to October 1987, which addressed the causes of the crash and the consequent disruption of market mechanisms. The most influential official reaction came from the Presidential Task Force on Market Mechanisms, or the Brady Commission. Before the official report (1988), the head of the commission, Nicholas Brady, noted in a discussion of possible causes that pre-crash stock prices were "incredibly high" by usual standards ("Before the Fall," *Wall Street Journal,* 11 Dec. 1987). While this view implicitly views the crash as a return by the market to reasonable levels, it does not explain why it was "incredibly" high before the crash.

Most of the official report focused on market disruption during the crash itself. Indeed, in the words of the Brady Report (1988, vi): "To a large extent, the problems of mid-October can be traced to the failure of these market segments [stocks, stock index futures and stock options] to act as one." The regulatory changes advocated in the Brady Report were intended to prevent the disintegration of markets that are normally highly integrated, and included a single regulatory authority for stocks, futures, and options, coordination across markets of margin requirements, and circuit breakers designed to give the markets more time to assess new information.

The Brady Commission advocated one regulatory authority because of the well-documented breakdown between the cash markets (NYSE) regulated by the Securities and Exchange Commission (SEC) and the futures markets regulated by the Commodity Futures Trading Commission (CFTC). However, the argument for unified regulation is not supported by an examination of the options market, which is also regulated by the SEC. Kleidon and Whaley (1992) demonstrate that, during the 1987 crash, the cash market was de-linked from both the options and futures markets, while the latter markets retained much of their usual linkage despite being regulated by different agencies. Kleidon (1992) traces the major source of market breakdown to mechanical order-processing problems in the cash market, which have since been remedied. Some divergences between the cash and futures prices may also have resulted from differences in liquidity across markets, given the problems caused by the huge volume during the crash (Amihud, Mendelson, and Wood 1990, Blume, MacKinlay, and Terker 1989).

If the problems during 1987 addressed by the Brady Commission can be attributed to mechanical difficulties on the NYSE, it would not be surprising if remedies such as circuit breakers were not particularly helpful during the mini-crash of 1989. The first circuit breaker was activated in the S&P 500 futures market at about 3:00 p.m. on Friday, 13 October 1989, when the index fell 12 points. Trading in the contract was suspended for half an hour as required under the regulations, while computerized trades were segregated from the rest of the market and put into a "side car." When trading resumed, another circuit breaker was triggered at about 3:45 p.m., and trading was suspended for the day. That the market continued to fall was the first hard evidence that market collapses had little to do with computerized trading per se, and McMillan (1990) concludes that the circuit breakers have not fulfilled their advertised role of facilitating price discovery.

Recent Models of Crashes

Two recent papers propose extensions of standard rational-expectations models to explain the crash of 1987. A typical assumption in theoretical models is that market participants know both the strategies of other participants and the proportions of different types of agents in the market. Much attention was paid in 1987 to the possible role of portfolio insurance, which is a class of dynamic trading strategies that replicates a put on the market, thereby providing downside protection or insurance against a market decline. A feature of these dynamic strategies is that more stock is purchased after a rise in prices, and conversely. Gennotte and Leland (1990) and Jacklin, Kleidon, and Pfleiderer (1992) show that uncertainty about how widely such hedging strategies are followed can generate market crashes, even if investors rationally update their beliefs over time.

In particular, assume that a larger than initially expected subset of investors follows such a dynamic hedging strategy. Jacklin, Kleidon, and Pfleiderer show that on average the market price will initially rise above the price implied by market fundamentals had the proportion of traders following the dynamic strategy been known. If subsequent events reveal the true proportion of traders following these strategies, the price will fall to the level that would have prevailed initially had this information been known. The intuition of the model is that if the market underestimates the proportion of traders who follow mechanistic dynamic strategies, then their (uninformed) purchases following price rises may be incorrectly interpreted as information-containing purchases by informed traders. The "trigger" of price declines from Wednesday, 14 October, to Friday, 16 October 1987, is consistent with this model, since the consequent large sales by those with dynamic strategies reveals information about the proportion of traders following such strategies. This approach is consistent with arguments by Black (1988), Brennan and Schwartz (1989), Grossman (1988), and Miller (1990).

This explanation relies on the introduction of new investor strategies that are not fully assimilated by the market. Gennotte and Leland identify a 1929 counterpart to the 1987 portfolio insurance, namely stop-loss strategies coupled with increased borrowing on margin, and Jacklin, Kleidon, and Pfleiderer show that their explanation for the 1987 crash also applies to the crash of 1929. However, the 1929 crash was followed by the Great Depression, while the 1987 crash was not accompanied by a similar macroeconomic slump. One possibility is that lessons learned in 1929, particularly about liquidity, were applied in 1987. At a crucial time between the close of trading on 19 October and the opening on 20 October, the Federal Reserve staff in Washington released Chairman Alan Greenspan's pledge to supply liquidity during the crisis. Even with these assurances, the system came perilously close to financial gridlock on 20 October ("Terrible Tuesday," *Wall Street Journal*, 20 Nov. 1987).

Conclusions

Market crashes challenge traditional models of price behavior, but also provide new evidence that can increase our understanding. The crash of October 1987 led to regulatory changes that were tested during October 1989, with little evidence of success. However, since the rationale for these changes was largely to avoid the market breakdowns of the 1987 crash, this may not be surprising given the recent evidence that the breakdowns were caused by mechanical order-processing difficulties on the NYSE that have since been (internally) remedied.

Deeper questions are raised about the rationality of prices that change drastically over short time periods. Recent extensions of standard rational-expectations models to incorporate learning by traders about the strategies of others have dramatically increased our capacity to explain crashes without assuming investor irrationality. Success in accounting for crashes within rational models, simply by relaxing the unrealistic assumption of perfect knowledge about the strategies of others and allowing for learning over time (see also Marcet and Sargent 1989), suggests that an assumption of irrationality may not yet be dictated by the evidence.

Allan W. Kleidon
Rajnish Mehra

See also EXCESS VOLATILITY; EXPECTATIONS; LEARNING; RATIONAL EXPECTATIONS; STOCK-MARKET PRICES; STOCK-MARKET CRASH OF 1929; TIME REVERSIBILITY; TULIPMANIA

Bibliography

Amihud, Y., H. Mendelson, and R. A. Wood. 1990. "Liquidity and the 1987 Stock-Market Crash." *Journal of Portfolio Management* 16:65–69.

Black, F. 1988. "An Equilibrium Model of the Crash." In *NBER Macroeconomics Annual 1988,* edited by S. Fischer, 269–75. Cambridge: MIT Press.

Blume, M. E., A. C. MacKinlay, and B. Terker. 1989. "Order Imbalances and Stock-price Movements on October 19 and 20, 1987." *Journal of Finance* 44:827–48.

Brennan, M. J. and E. S. Schwartz. 1989. "Portfolio Insurance and Financial Market Equilibrium." *Journal of Business* 62:455–72.

Cochrane, J. H. 1992. "Explaining the Variance of Price-Dividend Ratios." *Review of Financial Studies* 5:243–80.

Flavin, M. A. 1983. "Excess Volatility in the Financial Markets: A Reassessment of the Empirical Evidence." *Journal of Political Economy* 91:929–56.

Garber, P. M. 1989. "Tulipmania." *Journal of Political Economy* 97:535–60.

Gennotte, G. and H. Leland. 1990. "Market Liquidity, Hedging and Crashes." *American Economic Review* 80:999–1021.

Gilles, C. and S. F. LeRoy. 1991. "Econometric Aspects of the Variance-Bounds Tests: A Survey." *Review of Financial Studies* 4:753–91.

Grossman, S. J. 1988. "Analysis of the Implications for Stock and Futures Price Volatility of Program Trading and Dynamic Hedging Strategies." *Journal of Business* 61:275–98.

Jacklin, C. J., A. W. Kleidon, and P. Pfleiderer. 1992. "Underestimation of Portfolio Insurance and the Crash of October 1987." *Review of Financial Studies* 5:35–63.

Keynes, J. M. [1936] 1973. *The General Theory of Employment, Interest, and Money.* Vol. 7 in *The Collected Writings of John Maynard Keynes.* London: Macmillan.

Kleidon, A. W. 1986. "Variance Bounds Tests and Stock Price Valuation Models." *Journal of Political Economy* 94:953–1001.

———. 1992. "Arbitrage, Nontrading, and Stale Prices: October 1987." *Journal of Business* 65:483–507.

Kleidon, A. W., and R. E. Whaley. 1992. "One Market? Stocks, Futures and Options During October 1987." *Journal of Finance* 47:851–77.

LeRoy, S. F. and R. D. Porter. 1981. "The Present-Value Relation: Tests Based on Implied Variance Bounds." *Econometrica* 49:555–74.

Marcet, A. and T. J. Sargent. 1989. "Convergence of Least Squares Learning Mechanisms in Self-Referential Linear Stochastic Models." *Journal of Economic Theory* 48:337–68.

McMillan, H. 1990. "Circuit Breakers in the S&P 500 Futures Market: Their Effect on Volatility and Price Discovery in October 1989." Manuscript, Transamerica Occidental Life, Los Angeles, California.

Miller, M. H. 1990. "Financial Markets: Some Current Problems and Future Prospects." Manuscript, Graduate School of Business, University of Chicago.

Mitchell, M. L. and J. M. Netter. 1989. "Triggering the 1987 Stock Market Crash: Antitakeover Provisions in the Proposed House Ways and Means Tax Bill?" *Journal of Financial Economics* 24:37–68.

Shiller, R. J. 1981. "Do Stock Prices Move Too Much to be Justified by Subsequent Changes in Dividends?" *American Economic Review* 71:236–37.

Shleifer, A. and L. H. Summers. 1990. "The Noise Trader Approach to Finance." *Journal of Economic Perspectives,* Spring, 19–33.

U. S. Presidential Task Force on Market Mechanisms. 1988. *Report of the Presidential Task Force on Market Mechanisms.* Washington, D.C.: Government Printing Office.

U. S. Securities and Exchange Commission. Division of Market Regulation. 1988. *The October 1987 Market Break: A Report.* Washington, D.C.: Government Printing Office.

Stock-Market Prices

Numerous studies of the National Bureau of Economic Research (e.g., Macaulay, Zarnowitz, and Boschan) have shown the general index of stock prices to be a leading indicator of the business cycle (i.e., the "40-month" economic-activity cycle). This well-known result indicates that major fluctuations in stock prices do not follow a random walk, although, since the duration of cycles varies greatly, they are nonperiodic. This justifies a search for structural relationships between stock prices and other macroeconomic variables.

Any such investigation requires a theoretical framework for explaining stock prices. If investors are rational, the price of a stock should equal the discounted value of the expected flow of income (earnings or dividends), i.e., the so-called present-value relation. Thus, aside from any possible aggregate bias, stock prices have two main components: expected income and the expected discount rate. Since both components are unobservable, the difficulty is to develop a model of how stockholders form their long-run expectations of income and the discount rate.

Shiller's pioneering work and ensuing empirical studies have shown that the present-value relation is inconsistent with perfect expectations. Of course, expectations may be imperfect but rational, and supporters of the rational-expectations hypothesis argue that stock prices have two components, a *fundamental* rational value (i.e., the present-value relation under certain assumptions) and a *rational bubble,* these two components being consistent with the efficient-market hypothesis. But studies by Shiller (1989) and West (1987) suggest that stock-market bubbles, and hence expectations, are most likely not rational.

In fact, other econometric studies (Keran 1971; Prat 1982, 1984) show that income expectations conform to a traditional limited-information model (involving past values of earnings or dividends per share), and this behavior may be economically rational if investors compare the additional cost with the additional utility of more accurate expectations. Such income expectations explain the secular trend of stock prices with a unit elasticity, as implied by the present-value relation (i.e., the dividend yield and price/earning ratio are stationary variables in the long run). However, cyclical fluctuations in earnings lag those of stock prices, while cyclical fluctuations in dividends are poorly correlated with those of stock prices. Thus, contrary to a currently held view, income cannot be primarily responsible for cyclical movements of stock prices; indeed, this view implies that movements in earnings are anticipated rationally, whereas the evidence suggests otherwise (as indicated above). These results have two implications. First, even though income expectations are wrong and systematically biased, they drive stockholder decisions: irrational income forecasts are imbedded in stock prices. Second, because dividends and earnings are price-indexed variables, stocks appear to be a good long-run hedge against inflation.

Many suggestions about how to measure the stockholders' discount rate have been proposed, including a constant value, market interest rates, and consumers' marginal rates of substitution between present and future consumption (which explicitly take into account risk aversion). In fact, none of those proxies leads to a good econometric explanation of stock-price fluctuations (Shiller 1989).

Thus, a more general framework for measuring the discount rate seems necessary. In this approach, the discount rate is decomposed into two components: the riskless rate, measuring the intensity of time preference, and the risk premium, reflecting uncertainty of future income (transaction costs and taxes are ne-

glected). Econometric models of stock prices show that a weighted average of past values of the yields of the highest-grade bonds gives a generally robust measure of the riskless discount rate, which then appears as a trend-value of the observed bond yields (Keran 1971, Rasche and Shapiro 1968, Prat 1982). But the risk premium embedded in the discount rate must be modeled separately, in particular by taking into account stockholders' opinions (Shiller 1989, Prat 1982). Concerning expectations of this discount rate, it is worth emphasizing that future income is commonly supposed to be discounted at a uniform rate, even though discount rates vary over time. This naive hypothesis leads to good econometric results, which are not improved by more sophisticated hypotheses about expectations.

Thus, neither expected earnings (or dividends), nor the riskless discount rate may be viewed as a primary cause of cyclical fluctuations in stock prices. Rather, the main cause appears to be the risk premium embedded in the discount rate. Macaulay's fundamental study highlighted the role of uncertainty in stock-market booms and collapses. Macaulay found an impressive negative correlation between major cyclical movements in stock prices and his so-called "economic drift," which corresponds to the spread between the yields of the lowest- and highest-grade bonds. Recent studies have confirmed this result.

Further evidence of the importance of uncertainty in cyclical fluctuations in stock prices is given by econometric studies showing that detrended stock-price movements may be adequately predicted by only two qualitative optimism indexes (Prat 1982):

1. A market-optimism index such as the Bearish Sentiment Index (constructed by the Boston Company), reflecting investors' expectations of stock-price changes in the near future. This index appears to be well explained by recent stock-price changes, which shows the naive character of stockholders' expectations about changes in the stock market itself [Livingston's survey microdata about stock-price expectations confirms this result, as shown by Pearce (1984)];

2. An economic-optimism index (similar to the Consumer Sentiment Index compiled from the surveys of the University of Michigan), reflecting households' percep-

tions and expectations about their personal economic and financial situation and consumption plans, and about the state of the national economy.

It should be noted that, if an economic-optimism index predicts cyclical fluctuations in stock prices, it does so only by reflecting the risk premium in the discount rate. We must therefore ask which economic variables can explain the risk premium. Following Ross's pioneering work, the modern theory of finance, as embodied in the Arbitrage Pricing Theory, estimates risk premia of individual stocks through the sensitivities of their yields to common economic variables. But this theory does not identify these variables, which must be discovered through factorial analysis. Although the empirical results appear highly sensitive to the period covered, they suggest that four variables may be related to cyclical movements in stock prices: real output, the general price level, interest rates, and the money stock. In fact, standard econometric methods based on stock-price indexes confirm these results perhaps in a more convincing way, as indicated below.

Cyclical fluctuations in stock prices lead those of real output by one to three quarters, but the rate of change of output leads the cyclical level of stock prices, so that past rates of change of output appear as an econometric factor of stock prices (Fama 1981, Macaulay 1938, Zarnowitz and Boschan 1977). Past rates of inflation are also a factor of stock prices. But, contrary to the long-run relationship, inflation appears to depress stock prices in a cyclical context (Fama 1981, Lintner 1973), at least above some level (around 3 to 5 percent a year in the United States). Furthermore, studies conducted at the University of Michigan have shown that consumer confidence is negatively related to past values of inflation and positively to those of the rate of change of output; thus, by explaining most of the variance of consumer confidence, inflation and the rate of change of output may explain the risk premium embedded in the discount rate and thereby the cyclical movements in stock prices.

According to the Monetarist view (Sprinkel 1971, Keran 1971), changes in the money stock are the primary cause of stock-price changes, because the money stock is the main determinant of corporate earnings, dividends, and, through the traditional liquidity, income, and price effects, the discount rate.

Moreover, these indirect influences are reinforced by a direct portfolio effect: when the money stock exceeds desired cash balances, households use undesired cash balances to purchase securities, bidding up stock prices (the so-called monetary portfolio theory). However, because the money stock operates through complex and conflicting channels such as income expectations and the discount rate, it appears to be econometrically dominated by nonmonetary variables in the present-value relation (Malkiel and Quandt 1972), this result being often confirmed by factorial analysis. In particular, although variations in the money stock are correlated with changes in consumer confidence, they contain no statistical information not contained in the rate of change of output and the rate of inflation, for explaining consumer confidence.

Finally, an old and still widely accepted theory asserts that changes in short-term interest rates negatively affect stock prices, because money-market rates represent the opportunity cost of the liquidity demanded by stock-market transactors (Owens and Hardy 1925). In fact, the data show that daily or weekly changes in short-term interest rates and stock prices are poorly correlated. However, the quarterly changes of the two variables are linked in a regular time sequence: an increase (decrease) of short rates is followed by a decrease (increase) of stock prices, which in turn is followed by a decrease (increase) in short rates and an increase (decrease) in stock prices, and so on. But the time lag of the first sequence (about nine months on average) is much too long to support the theory, and the second sequence is characterized by a positive correlation, which is inconsistent with the accepted theory. Moreover, although they are related to consumer confidence, short-term rates contain no information not contained in the rate of change in output and the rate of inflation.

Numerous macroeconomic variables are related to stock prices, and the relationships mentioned above hold in most advanced countries. But theoretical interpretation is tricky. First, while some variables seem to be economic determinants of stock prices, common phenomena may also explain observed correlations (see entry on Maurice Allais). A striking illustration of this possibility is the correlation between fluctuations in stock prices and short-term interest rates, since fluctuations in both are linked with the cycle of confidence. Second, as some economic variables are affected by stock prices, causation runs in both directions. Stock prices can affect investment via the cost of capital, consumption via the wealth effect, and money demand via the opportunity cost of holding money. But these effects do not appear econometrically very robust. Indeed, in a cyclical context, the cost of capital seems econometrically to be dominated by expected demand as a determinant of investment and the October 1987 crash apparently produced no wealth effect on consumption. Interest rates also appear to dominate the stock yield in empirical estimates of money demand. Finally, the increasing correlation between business cycles in various countries suggests that international factors affect stock prices. However, since expected exchange rates operate in international portfolio selections and because domestic factors remain dominant, the correlations between variations of most of the stock markets, though increasing, remain rather weak.

Georges Prat

See also EXCESS VOLATILITY; RATIONAL EXPECTATIONS; STOCK-MARKET CRASH OF 1929; STOCK-MARKET CRASHES OF 1987 AND 1989; TERM STRUCTURE OF INTEREST RATES; TIME REVERSIBILITY

Bibliography

Fama, E. F. 1981. "Stock Returns, Real Activity, Inflation and Money." *American Economic Review* 71:533–65.

Keran, M. W. 1971. "Expectations, Money and the Stock Market." Federal Bank of St. Louis *Review,* January, 16–31.

Lintner, J. 1973. "Inflation and Common Stock Prices in a Cyclical Context." In National Bureau of Economic Research *Annual Report,* 23–36.

Macaulay, F. R. 1938. *Some Theoretical Problems Suggested by the Movements of Interest Rates, Bond Yields and Stock Prices in the United States Since 1850.* New York: NBER.

Malkiel, B. G. and R. Quandt. 1972. "The Supply of Money and Common Stock Prices: Comment." *Journal of Finance* 27:921–26.

Owens, R. N. and C. O. Hardy. 1925. *Interest Rates and Stock Speculation: A Study of the Influence of the Money Market on the Stock Market.* London: Allen and Unwin.

Pearce, D. K. 1984. "An Empirical Analysis of Expected Stock Price Movements." *Journal of Money, Credit and Banking* 16:317–27.

Prat, G. 1982. *La Bourse et la Conjoncture Economique: Essai sur les Facteurs Déterminants du Cours Moyen des Actions.* Paris: Economica.

———. 1984. *Essai pour une Formulation Générale du Cours des Actions: Un Modèle d'Evaluation pour l'Ensemble du Marché.* Paris: Economica.

Rasche, R. H. and H. T. Shapiro. 1968. "The F.R.B.-M.I.T. Econometric Model: Its Special Features." *American Economic Review Papers and Proceedings* 58:134–37.

Roll, R. and S. A. Ross. 1984. "An Empirical Investigation of the Arbitrage Pricing Theory." *Journal of Finance* 39:1073–1103.

Shiller, R. J. 1989. *Market Volatility.* Cambridge: MIT Press.

Sprinkel, B. W. 1971. "Money and the Stock Market." Chap. 9 in *Money and Markets: A Monetarist View.* Homewood, Ill.: Irwin.

West, K. 1987. "A Specification Test For Speculative Bubbles." *Quarterly Journal of Economics* 102:553–80.

Zarnowitz, V. and C. Boschan. 1977. "Cyclical Indicators: An Evaluation and New Leading Indexes." *Business Conditions Digest* 17:170–84.

Stylized Facts

The stylized facts pertaining to a phenomenon are the enduring empirical regularities that are its defining characteristics. The stylized facts of business cycles have been the subject of empirical research since the last century and can be traced even to the classical economists. The sifting through the data for regularities is also in part driven by a priori theoretical considerations. For twentieth-century business cycles, empirical research has been carried out at a number of "business-cycle research centers," and in particular at the National Bureau of Economic Research (NBER), which has had an enduring interest in the subject, beginning with the work of Mitchell. Victor Zarnowitz (1985) has attempted to summarize this large and diverse body of empirical research, and before that G. H. Moore (1983) tried to identify the main characteristics of business cycles. No doubt more empirical work will be forthcoming as national-income data continue to improve.

However, for the purposes of theory choice, it is necessary to underscore the main characteristics or stylized facts that an adequate theory must explain. This is doubly necessary in economics, for unlike some physical sciences, there are no independent criteria for evaluating the validity of a particular economic model or theory. Without independent criteria with which to evaluate a theory, the stylized facts become the benchmark for judging a theory. Such a set of stylized facts is presented below. For twentieth-century cycles, especially those observed in free-market economies after World War II, the most striking stylized facts are the following:

1. An inverse relationship over time between wage inflation and unemployment (See Figure 1).
2. A co-movement between price inflation and wage inflation, with the latter usually leading the former except during very rapid inflations.
3. Procyclical wages, which indicate that the wage share out of national income is also procyclical. Consequently at cyclical peaks, the profit share, defined as one minus the wage share, is generally low.
4. A long-term positive trend rate of growth of real GNP. This implies each subsequent cyclical trough of GNP does not cancel out the "gains" made at the previous cyclical peak. This has led to the growing acceptance of the Schumpeterian view that growth and cycles are inextricably intertwined, and that the cycle is a necessary condition for growth and vice versa. This view is also associated with Harrod (1936) and Goodwin (1982).
5. Cycles are recurrent but nonperiodic. This suggests that while we can compute the average duration of a large number of cycles, as have researchers at the NBER, no two cycles ever appear to be of equal duration. Consequently, turning points cannot be predicted.
6. A procyclical relationship between labor productivity and output, which is apparently inconsistent with the standard neoclassical aggregate production function involving a declining marginal product of labor, as part of a business-cycle theory.

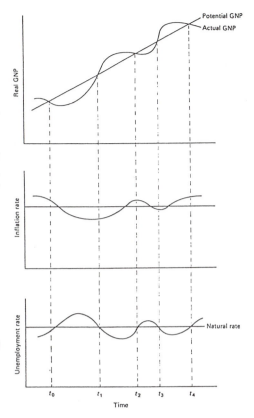

Figure 1. Real GNP, inflation, and unemployment.

7. Profits are generally procyclical. In particular, before sales decline, profits per unit of sales decline.
8. Investment in fixed capital and inventories is procyclical. While this is well established for the typical cycle, there are individual components that either lead or lag behind in the cycle.
9. The growth of credit and monetary aggregates is procyclical. Both narrowly and broadly defined monetary aggregates show reduced growth rates in contractions, but not absolute declines. This implies that the income velocity of money is also procyclical.
10. A tendency towards the synchronization of international cycles, especially over the last two decades. Institutional changes such as free capital mobility, floating exchange rates, and the increase in international arbitrage and speculative activities have increased interdependence among the major capitalist nations,

which is likely to lead to a further synchronization of cycles.

At least two of the above stylized facts are controversial and the subject of current research. The procyclical nature of wages has been debated since the 1930s (Dunlop 1938, Tarshis 1939). Keane, Moffitt, and Runkle (1988) correct for various biases and, using micro panel data, confirm that wages are procyclical over the cycle. The nonseparability of the growth and the cyclical component (stylized fact number 4 above) is also receiving increased attention (Stock and Watson 1988) as it casts doubt on the validity of neoclassical theories of equilibrium business cycles—both the (Lucas) misperceptions type and the so-called real business-cycle theories.

It is of course unlikely that any one model of business cycles would explain or reflect *all* the above stylized facts. Nevertheless, the task of a theory is to account for as many of these regularities as are considered central to the inquiry. In particular, a model must propose some governing mechanism of the typical cycle. In an ideal world, the hypothesis proposing a governing mechanism of the cycle would be falsifiable.

Mohammed H. I. Dore

See also ASYMMETRY; BUSINESS CYCLES; INCOME DISTRIBUTION; REAL WAGES; SEASONAL CYCLES; TRENDS AND RANDOM WALKS

Bibliography

Dunlop, J. 1938. "The Movement of Real and Money Wage Rates." *Economic Journal* 48:413–34.

Goodwin, R. M. 1982. *Essays in Economic Dynamics*. London: Macmillan.

Gordon, R. J., ed. 1986. *The American Business Cycle: Continuity and Change*. Chicago: Univ. of Chicago Press.

Harrod, R. F. 1936. *The Trade Cycle*. Oxford: Clarendon Press.

Keane, M., R. Moffitt, and D. Runkle. 1988. "Real Wages Over the Business Cycle: Estimating the Impact of Heterogeneity With Micro Data." *Journal of Political Economy* 96:1232–66.

Mitchell, W. C. 1913. *Business Cycles*. Berkeley: Univ. of California Press.

———. 1927. *The Business Cycle: The Problem and its Setting*. New York: NBER.

———. 1951. *What Happens During Business Cycles*. New York: NBER.

Moore, G. H. 1983. *Business Cycles, Inflation and Forecasting*. 2d ed. Cambridge, Mass.: Ballinger.

Stock, J. H. and M. W. Watson. 1988. "Variable Trends in Economic Time Series." *Journal of Economic Perspectives,* Summer, 147–74.

Tarshis, L. 1939. "Changes in Real and Money Wage Rates." *Economic Journal* 49:150–54.

Zarnowitz, V. 1985. "Recent Work on Business Cycles in Historical Perspective: A Review of Theories and Evidence." *Journal of Economic Literature* 23:523–80.

Sunspot Theories of Fluctuations

Early in the nineteenth century, analysts of fluctuations began to examine the role of "commercial moods" in the business cycle. By the second half of the century, economists sought the explanation for alterations in moods. William Stanley Jevons attributed such alterations to the periodic alteration in harvests due to sunspots. The "sunspot" cycle impinged on the economy both directly (as the harvest fluctuation altered aggregate demand), and indirectly (as the harvest fluctuation changed investors' expectations). By contrast, business-cycle theorists have recently developed theories of cycles in which "sunspots" refer to phenomena that, by themselves, do not affect the economy. However, as long as sunspots alter beliefs, cyclical economic effects result.

The early emphasis on the role of moods can be found in a work as well known as John Stuart Mill's *Principles of Political Economy.* Stressing the role of speculation and changes in investors' expectations in the cycle, Mill allowed that harvest fluctuations, among other things, might be the stimulating cause of the fluctuation. The *Principles* show little appreciation of ongoing fluctuations occurring with a decennial periodicity. By contrast, the London banker John Mills did recognize this regularity, which persuaded him that the decennial cycle must be explained by a single cause.

That single cause Mills found in commercial moods. Mills maintained that different commercial moods characterize different phases of the cycle. In turn, these moods determine the amount of loanable funds and investment activity forthcoming. Mills characterized the crisis or turning point as the "destruction, in the mind, of a bundle of beliefs" (1867, 19) regarding credit, that in turn causes a drain on capital.

Mills's characterization of the cycle, as well as his insistence on the importance of commercial moods, were accepted by an influential analyst of economic fluctuations late in the nineteenth century, W. S. Jevons. But, from as early as 1862, Jevons was more struck than Mills by *harvest* fluctuations. Also, even at this early date Jevons recognized that, as he later stressed, a theory of economic fluctuations requires an explanation for fluctuations in investors' moods.

In a series of papers written between 1875 and 1882, Jevons attributed periodic alterations in commercial moods to sunspots. Jevons explicitly related cycles to a common initiating cause (allowance being made always for disturbing causes that alter the course of the cycle)—namely, fluctuations in the corn harvest due to weather variations. He argued that merchants, bankers, and investors base their credit and investment decisions on observed data about the harvest. Like Mills, Jevons (1884, 215) attributed the cycle to "periodic variations" of "mental action," thus accepting Mills's characterization of a "commercial panic" as "the destruction of belief and hope in the minds of merchants and bankers."

In Jevons's view, the crisis, an "explosion of commercial folly followed by the national collapse," involved erroneous expectations, "bad trading and speculation" that produced inflated values which ultimately collapsed (Jevons 1973–81, 6:117). In a letter to *The Times,* Jevons reiterated this argument. Here he argued that expectations of economic performance are based on observed trade patterns, and lag behind economic potential. Economic agents incorrectly forecast profit-maximizing investment rates throughout the cycle. Thus, when "our manufacturers are prepared to turn out a greatly increased supply of goods," famines in India and China reduce the demand for British manufactured goods, and temporary excess capacity results (Jevons 1973–81, 5:10–11).

The point of Jevons's argument is that it is agricultural fluctuations that impinge on expectations, which in turn affect investment and speculative behavior, and amplify the effect of the initial shock. This is Jevons's major contribution to the understanding of economic fluctuations. His argument that cyclical variations in weather conditions cause alterations in commercial moods, via economic signals observed and interpreted by agents, as well as by direct changes in demand, added a dimension to Mills's purely psychological theory of economic cycles.

Jevons's emphasis on the role of expectations in the cycle, as well as the sunspot explanation for cyclical mood alteration, influenced twentieth-century analyses of cycles. Alfred C. Pigou explicitly acknowledged Jevons's work in *Unemployment,* in which he developed a theory of fluctuations strikingly similar to Jevons's. Like Jevons, Pigou (1913, 114) emphasized the role of expectations in creating fluctuations via changes in investment and credit decisions, and argued that cyclical weather patterns constitute a plausible explanation for mood alterations. Pigou maintained that when they are "prosperous," people tend to "look on the sunnier side of doubt." As a consequence, judgments are "biased" by people's "feelings." Since good harvests "directly and indirectly improve the fortunes of the business world," they tend to be "a spur to optimism," and thus indirectly affect aggregate output (115). Like Jevons, then, Pigou also concluded that the alteration in expectations itself affects aggregate output (115, 118).

More recently, analysts of business cycles have also focused on the role of expectations in the cycle. Contemporary studies acknowledge a longstanding tradition in the business-cycle literature whereby fluctuations involve agents "reacting to imperfect signals in a way which, after the fact, appears inappropriate" (Lucas [1980] 1983, 286). Indeed, Robert Lucas argues that this has been a "commonplace" in the verbal tradition of business-cycle theory at least since Mitchell. In fact, this tradition extends at least to John Mills, through Jevons and Pigou.

But some key theoretical shifts have occurred with the transition to modern sunspot theories. In contrast to the usage by Jevons and Pigou, theorists have now come to use the term "sunspot" to denote a variable that has no real effect on the economy. The similarity to the analysis by Jevons and Pigou, however, is that, in the modern accounts, sunspots do affect beliefs. The significance of sunspots is that this alteration in beliefs is enough to generate sunspot effects. Thus, while Jevons and Pigou maintained that the sunspot effect on beliefs reinforced the direct effect of harvest fluctuations on output, the modern treatment of sunspots relies only on the sunspot effect on beliefs.

Recent analyses have the further property, in contrast to the treatments by Mills, Jevons, and Pigou, that they presume fully rational and optimizing behavior. Thus, for instance, David Cass and Karl Shell have demonstrated that "extrinsic uncertainty" ("animal spirits" or "sunspots") can cause real effects in an overlapping-generations model in which agents have rational expectations. In this model, participation in a market is limited to those agents alive at the time the market opens.

An overlapping-generations model also forms the theoretical basis for a recent analysis of convergence to a stationary sunspot equilibrium. Here, agents initially do not believe that outcomes are different in different sunspot states, but they use an adaptive learning rule (Woodford 1990). Boldrin and Woodford (1990) survey dynamic general-equilibrium models in which endogenous fluctuations are possible. Optimizing behavior is shown to yield both perfect-foresight equilibria as well as sunspot equilibria.

Unlike the treatment by Mills, Jevons, and Pigou, modern sunspot research is highly theoretical and technical. Nor is there any consensus on whether (modern-day) sunspots actually play a key role in the business cycle.

Sandra J. Peart

See also EXPECTATIONS; JEVONS, WILLIAM STANLEY; MILLS, JOHN; MOORE, HENRY LUDWELL; PIGOU, ARTHUR CECIL; RATIONAL EXPECTATIONS; SIGNAL EXTRACTION; TULIPMANIA

Bibliography

Boldrin, M. and M. Woodford. 1990. "Equilibrium Models Displaying Endogenous Fluctuations and Chaos: A Survey." *Journal of Monetary Economics* 25:189–222.

Cass, D. and K. Shell. 1983. "Do Sunspots Matter?" *Journal of Political Economy* 91:193–227.

Jevons, W. S. 1884. *Investigations in Currency and Finance*. London: Macmillan.

———. 1973–81. *Papers and Correspondence of William Stanley Jevons*. 7 vols. Edited by R. D. C. Black. London: Macmillan.

Lucas, R. E. Jr. [1980] 1983. "Methods and Problems in Business Cycle Theory." In *Studies in Business-Cycle Theory*, 271–96. Cambridge: MIT Press.

Mill, J. S. [1848] 1965. *The Principles of Political Economy*. 2 vols. Vols. 2 and 3 of *The Collected Works of John Stuart Mill*. Edited by J. M. Robson. Toronto: Univ. of Toronto Press.

Mills, John. 1867. "On Credit Cycles and the Origin of Commercial Panics." *Transactions of the Manchester Statistical Society for the Session 1867–1868*, 5–40.

Peart, S. 1991. "Sunspots and Expectations: W. S. Jevons's Theory of Economic Fluctuations." *Journal of the History of Economic Thought* 13:243–65.

Pigou, A. C. 1913. *Unemployment*. London: Williams & Norgate.

Woodford, M. 1990. "Learning to Believe in Sunspots." *Econometrica* 58:277–307.

Supply of Money

A specification of the determinants of the money stock depends on how money is being defined. Viewing money as a medium of exchange permits only a narrow range of financial instruments to be included in the definition. Introducing the store-of-value function broadens considerably the range of eligible instruments. The chosen definition would reflect the transmission mechanism through which money is assumed to operate, and the controllability of the money stock would depend on the objectives of the policymaker and the openness of the economy.

It is best to consider the narrow definition of money before moving on to broader categories that include a richer array of liquid assets. Those instrumentsts that serve as a medium of exchange are currency and checkable accounts. The amount of currency in circulation is directly controlled by the monetary authority. The volume of checkable deposits depends on the behavior of the institutions that accept such deposits, on the willingness of individuals to hold such deposits, and on the monetary authority's control of financial institutions and markets. In this framework, the determination of the money stock is usually analyzed using a money-multiplier model that relates the total money stock held by the public M_s to the *monetary base, B*, created by the monetary authority.

Suppose that financial institutions issuing checkable deposits are called *banks*. Let D stand for the nonbank private sector's holding of checkable deposits. Let the nonbank private sector's holding of currency C_p be a fraction c

of their deposit holdings. In addition, assume that banks hold a fraction r of their deposits as *reserves*, R (claims to currency at the central bank). The monetary base consists of currency held by the public and reserves held by the banks. In this case the determination of the money stock can be characterized by the following equations:

$$C_p = cD \qquad (1)$$

$$R = rD \qquad (2)$$

$$B \equiv C_p + R \qquad (3)$$

Since $M_s \equiv C_p + D$,

$$M_s = (1 + c)D \qquad (4)$$

From equations (1)–(3) it is clear that

$$D = B/(c + r) \qquad (5)$$

Substituting equation (5) into equation (4) gives

$$M_s = B(1 + c)/(r + c). \qquad (6)$$

The expression $(1 + c)/(r + c)$ is the money multiplier, m, which was first discussed by C. A. Phillips and is a staple of undergraduate texts. If r and c are both small, then m is a relatively large number (e.g., if $r = .05$ and $c = .05$, then $m = 10.5$). If r and c are constant, then the stock of money depends solely on the monetary base. This simple model therefore illustrates the dependence of the money stock on the actions of the banks (or more generally of financial institutions and markets), the nonbank private sector, and the monetary authorities. However, this simplified version assumes that there are fixed coefficients. Under a legal reserve requirement, the assumption of a fixed r may be appropriate, although since banks normally hold excess reserves, even this is an insufficient reason to assume r is fixed rather than set it at a minimum. Whether c is fixed depends on the closeness of the substitutes available for checkable bank deposits and whether optimizing transactions behavior implies a simple relationship between deposits and currency.

Note that the Baumol theory of the transactions demand for money seems to contradict this very simple interpretation of the demand for the medium of exchange. In fact, short-run changes in monetary growth can be attributed to the variability of the money multiplier (although, as discussed below, the system of monetary control may be the major determinant of short-run volatility in the money stock). However, in the longer run, there is a clear role for variation in the monetary base and hence some form of the money-multiplier model has empirical relevance (Friedman and Schwartz 1982).

Although the money-multiplier model outlined above is quite simple, the analysis can be made more realistic. For example, financial institutions can create assets that are attractive to individuals as alternatives to the medium of exchange. Brunner and Meltzer (1968) considered a variety of different deposits, with different liquidities, which were demanded in varying amounts by economic agents. By assuming that the demand for these different types of deposits bears a fixed relationship to the size of the total deposit portfolio the individual wished to hold, Brunner and Meltzer developed an analysis of the money stock similar to that of the simple model, but with additional leakages resulting from the holding of nonmonetary assets which reduced the value of the money multiplier. Klein (1971) modeled the creation of bank deposits within a profit-maximizing framework. The importance of the banking firm for the provision of monetary instruments has recently been an active area of research and will be discussed later.

When the analysis is broadened to encompass all liquid assets and other nonbank financial intermediaries are introduced, it is interest-rate spreads that determine the demand for each type of asset. A general-equilibrium approach to analyzing the financial system is appropriate in this framework. Tobin (1963) specifically considered the role of banks in the financial system and Tobin and Brainard (1967) considered how nonbank financial intermediaries affected monetary control. Their approach was dubbed the "New View" in contrast to the "Old View" of a mechanistic multiplier. One implication of the New View is that the money stock should be defined broadly enough to encompass assets other than the medium of exchange, since narrow money has many close substitutes as a store of value. Thus, broader definitions of the money stock include interest-bearing deposits (both bank and nonbank) and even highly liquid money-market instruments.

The New View can also explain the mechanism by which interest rates can be used as an instrument of monetary control. If asset demands depend on interest-rate spreads rather than fixed coefficients, open-market operations change the level of interest rates and consequently change the demand for monetary assets. In these circumstances it is the interest rate, not the monetary base, that is the instrument of monetary policy, so that the monetary aggregates are demand-determined. Shocks to money demand mainly affect the money stock; if the monetary base is targeted, shocks to money demand mainly affect interest rates. The volatility of interest rates under monetary-base targeting is often cited as an argument against this method of monetary control (Bank for International Settlements 1980).

A further implication of the New View concerns whether the liability side (money stock) or asset side (credit) of banks and other financial institutions ought to be monitored. Brunner and Meltzer introduced the credit market directly into the standard *IS-LM* model and discussed how money and credit markets interacted. In particular, the real price of assets adjusts directly to changes in monetary conditions as well as through the conventional interest-rate channel. A further result of this analysis is that it may be better to target credit than the money stock if money-market shocks are greater than credit-market shocks (Bernanke and Blinder 1988).

The supposedly crucial importance of banks in the money-supply process is naturally challenged by the New View. However, more recent work by Diamond and Dybvig (1983) suggests that bank deposits provide a welfare-superior solution to other organizational structures such as financial markets, because of imperfect information about the liquidity requirements of individuals. An implication of the Diamond and Dybvig view of banks is that regulating deposit-creating activities and deposit-insurance schemes can be welfare-improving, particularly since they demonstrate that bank runs are equilibrium phenomena.

Such a result is confirmed by Bernanke (1983) who argues that a crisis of confidence in the financial system may appear through runs on banks, as economic agents switch from holding deposits to currency. In a simple money-multiplier model, this implies that c increases, which causes the money stock to contract. The contraction may be compounded if the monetary authorities do not provide liquidity to the banking system to prevent bank failures. Such a monetary squeeze is also a credit squeeze with

concomitant real effects, such as financial distress of firms and a collapse of investment. A recession may deteriorate into a depression. Hence the monetary process depends not only on how much control the central bank exerts on the financial system, but also on the strength of its commitment to act as lender of last resort. The Diamond-Dybvig analysis can thus serve as the basis for a model of financial distress and crisis.

Empirically, the money stock seems to conform with the business cycle, but to lead output. This pattern is consistent with a number of alternative views of the money-supply process. For example, the simple money-multiplier model is consistent with this pattern if banks reduce their holdings of excess reserves and individuals economize on their cash balances during economic expansions. Alternatively, it could be the result of monetary policy designed to reduce interest-rate variability, so that the central bank provides additional liquidity in response to the increase in economic activity. Williamson (1987) has shown that the Diamond-Dybvig analysis can help explain the behavior of the money supply over the course of the business cycle.

Two other issues that are relevant to a discussion of the money-supply process are the exchange-rate regime and the way in which the government financial deficit is covered. It is a well-established principle that if the monetary authority attempts to target the exchange rate it loses control over the money stock. In addition, if the government meets the difference between revenue and expenditure by selling government securities to the central bank, the monetary base must increase. However, this is a different policy from one in which the central bank initially buys all government securities and then sells them on the financial markets at times when the markets can absorb them. Such a policy is designed to reduce the destabilizing effects of large sales of government debt when the financial markets are short of liquidity. The short-run movements of the money stock may reflect this policy, but in the long run the money stock should not increase as a result.

David G. Dickinson

See also BRUNNER, KARL; CENTRAL BANKING; ENDOGENOUS AND EXOGENOUS MONEY; FINANCIAL INTERMEDIATION; FRIEDMAN, MILTON; MONETARY POLICY; MONEY-INCOME CAUSALITY; TOBIN, JAMES

Bibliography

Bank for International Settlements. 1980. *The Monetary Base Approach to Monetary Control.* Basle, Switzerland: BIS.

Baumol, W. J. 1952. "The Transactions Demand for Cash: An Inventory Theoretic Approach." *Quarterly Journal of Economics* 66:545–56.

Bernanke, B. S. 1983. "Nonmonetary Effects of the Financial Crisis in the Propagation of the Great Depression." *American Economic Review* 73:257–76.

Bernanke, B. S. and A. S. Blinder. 1988. "Credit, Money and Aggregate Demand." *American Economic Review Papers and Proceedings* 78:435–39.

Brunner, K. and A. H. Meltzer. 1968. "Liquidity Traps for Money, Bank Credit, and Interest Rates." *Journal of Political Economy* 76:1–37.

Diamond, D. W. and P. H. Dybvig. 1983. "Bank Runs, Deposit Insurance and Liquidity." *Journal of Political Economy* 91:401–19.

Friedman, M. and A. J. Schwartz. 1982. *Monetary Trends in the U.S. and the U.K.: Their Relation to Income, Prices and Interest Rates.* Chicago: Univ. of Chicago Press.

Klein, M. A. 1971. "A Theory of the Banking Firm." *Journal of Money, Credit, and Banking* 3:205–18.

Niehans, J. 1978. *The Theory of Money.* Baltimore: Johns Hopkins Univ. Press.

Phillips, C. A. 1920. *Bank Credit.* New York: Macmillan.

Pierce, J. L. and T. D. Thompson. 1972. "Some Issues in Controlling the Stock of Money." In *Controlling Monetary Aggregates II: The Implementation,* 115–36. Boston: Federal Reserve Bank of Boston.

Tobin, J. 1963. "Commercial Banks as Creators of Money." In *Banking and Monetary Studies,* edited by D. Carson, 408–19. Homewood, Ill.: Irwin.

Tobin, J. and Brainard, W. C. 1967. "Financial Intermediaries and the Effectiveness of Monetary Controls." *American Economic Review Papers and Proceedings* 57:383–400.

Williamson, S. D. 1987. "Financial Intermediation, Business Failures, and Real Business Cycles." *Journal of Political Economy* 95:1196–1216.

Supply Shocks

The term "aggregate supply curve" refers to a relationship between the average level of prices in the economy and the level of real output. If we plot a variable such as the consumer price index on the vertical axis and real GNP on the horizontal axis, then the aggregate supply curve appears as an upward-sloping or conceivably vertical relation. *Adverse supply shock* means a leftward shift of this relation. Macroeconomic models differ in how they characterize the aggregate supply curve and the forces that shift it. The frictionless neoclassical model assumes that buyers and sellers are fully informed and that wages and prices adjust instantly to any new developments. In such an economy, the level of output is determined by the preferences of households and by the technology available to firms. A vertical line drawn at this level of output constitutes the aggregate supply curve, since in this model the price level is unrelated to the factors that determine real activity.

A negative supply shock in such a model means a physical event such as a crop failure that depresses the productivity of labor at a given level of employment. In Keynesian models, a variety of factors may cause the price level and production to be positively related. Modigliani ([1944] 1980) proposed that nominal wages might be determined by prior arrangements and contracts. If so, increases in the price level reduce the real cost of labor and induce firms to hire additional workers and increase output. This positive comovement of output and prices is thought of as movement along the aggregate supply curve. This curve is also shifted left by adverse productivity shocks or by any increases in the nominal wage that are unaccompanied by increased productivity.

Friedman and Lucas stressed the potential misperceptions of workers as an explanation of why the aggregate supply curve is upward-sloping. If workers know the nominal wage they receive but are unsure about the prices of all the goods they buy, then an unanticipated increase in the price level reduces the real reward to labor. Firms do perceive the drop, which induces them to increase production. However, workers do not at first recognize that their paychecks have lost purchasing power, so they are willing to work longer hours for modest increases in the nominal wage. According to this view, unanticipated changes in the price level cause movement along the aggregate supply curve, whereas anticipated changes induce a leftward shift of the aggregate supply schedule.

The upward slope of the aggregate supply curve may also be derived from a disequilibrium interpretation of the output market. Firms may simply charge a price for their output that is a markup over costs, with the size of the markup a function of the strength of market conditions. As business improves, firms raise their markups, which suggests an alternative account of what it means for the economy to move along an aggregate supply curve. An exogenous increase in firms' costs of production is construed to cause a leftward shift of the aggregate supply curve. Thus the term "supply shock" is used to refer to a broad range of potential disturbances. Any exogenous development that increases the cost of labor or raw materials may be called a negative supply shock. The most obvious source of supply shocks would seem to be the weather, which potentially could cause big changes in agricultural productivity. However, Mitchell's studies suggest that agricultural production and prices have had very little impact on cyclical movements in aggregate output and prices over the last century. Crop failures may have contributed to the 1973–75 global recession, but cannot be considered a major factor in typical business downturns.

A more plausible source of cyclically important supply shocks is a disruption in world oil supplies precipitated by political instability. The Suez Crisis of 1956–57, the Arab-Israeli war and the oil production cutback by the Organization of Arab Petroleum Exporting Countries in 1973–74, the Iranian revolution of 1978–79, and the Iran-Iraq war begun in 1980 all led to sharp increases in the world price of oil, and each was followed by a global economic recession. Indeed, a dramatic increase in the price of crude petroleum has preceded (typically by about nine months) all but one of the recessions in the United States since World War II. While the statistical strength of this correlation may be persuasive, a satisfactory theoretical account has not yet been provided of how disruptions of the size seen historically could have moved the economy into recession.

Trade wars of escalating protectionist legislation, such as those seen in the Great Depression of 1929–39, would also shift the economy's production possibility frontier inward. The Smoot-Hawley Tariff of 1930 surely exacerbated that downturn, affecting, through a variety of channels, both aggregate supply and demand. Nevertheless, it is implausible to attribute the severity or duration of the depression to the effects of the tariff on aggregate supply.

Financial crises and panics were a very important part of pre-World War II economic downturns. While these are usually supposed to have affected the economy by reducing aggregate demand, they could also have affected aggregate supply. Bernanke and Gertler (1989) stress the role of the banking system in determining the creditworthiness of potential borrowers and providing funds for worthy projects. Financial panics greatly hinder the banking system in performing this vital role, frustrating the efficient allocation of the economy's capital and human resources.

An alternative to identifying specific causes of historical downturns is to see whether the broad characteristics of output fluctuations are more consistent with supply- or demand-based accounts. For example, if the Lucas misperceptions-based account of the aggregate-supply schedule is correct and if economic fluctuations are mainly caused by changes in aggregate demand, then during recessions inflation should be unexpectedly low (corresponding to movements down and to the left along a given aggregate supply curve). There is some basis for claiming that much of the deflation during the Great Depression of 1929–33 was unanticipated (Hamilton 1987). But there is little evidence that rational individuals made any more errors in forecasting inflation during postwar recessions than they did during expansions (Hamilton 1985, Litterman and Weiss 1985). Either aggregate-demand shocks were not a big factor in postwar U.S. recessions, or else Lucas's account of the nature of the aggregate supply relation is called into question.

Another way to measure the relative importance of supply and demand shocks is to define supply shocks as statistical events that permanently affect the level of real activity, whereas demand shocks are defined as events with purely transitory effects. Using this statistical decomposition, Shapiro and Watson (1988) concluded that demand factors account for less than 20 percent of the movements in real GNP at a two-year horizon.

James D. Hamilton

See also AGGREGATE SUPPLY AND DEMAND; GREAT DEPRESSION IN THE UNITED STATES (1929–1938); REAL BUSINESS-CYCLE THEO-

Bibliography

Bernanke, B. and M. Gertler. 1989. "Agency Costs, Net Worth, and Business Fluctuations." *American Economic Review* 79:14–31.

Blinder, A. S. 1979. *Economic Policy and the Great Stagflation.* New York: Academic Press.

Eichengreen, B. 1988. "Did International Economic Forces Cause the Great Depression?" *Contemporary Policy Issues* 6:90–114.

Friedman, M. [1968] 1969. "The Role of Monetary Policy." Chap. 5 in *The Optimum Quantity of Money and Other Essays.* Chicago: Aldine.

Hamilton, J. D. 1983. "Oil and the Macroeconomy Since World War II." *Journal of Political Economy* 91:228–48.

———. 1985. "Uncovering Financial Market Expectations of Inflation." *Journal of Political Economy* 93:1224–41.

———. 1987. "Monetary Factors in the Great Depression." *Journal of Monetary Economics* 19:145–69.

Litterman, R. B. and L. Weiss. 1985. "Money, Real Interest Rates, and Output: A Reinterpretation of Postwar U.S. Data." *Econometrica* 53:129–56.

Lucas, R. E. Jr. [1973] 1981. "Some International Evidence on Output-Inflation Trade-offs." In *Studies in Business-Cycle Theory,* 131–45. Cambridge: MIT Press.

Mitchell, W. C. 1951. *What Happens During Business Cycles?* New York: NBER.

Modigliani, F. [1944] 1980. "Liquidity Preference and the Theory of Interest and Money." In *The Collected Papers of F. Modigliani.* Vol. 1, 23–68. Cambridge: MIT Press.

Shapiro, M. D. and M. W. Watson. 1988. "Sources of Business Cycle Fluctuations." In *NBER Macroeconomics Annual,* edited by S. Fischer, 111–48. Cambridge: MIT Press.

Sweezy, Paul Marlor (1910–   )

Paul Sweezy was the first really significant Marxian economist in the United States, and remains the most important. His principal achievement, in collaboration with Paul Baran, was to formulate a distinctive theory of the monopoly stage of capitalism, based on a modified underconsumptionist theory of crises.

The son of a Wall Street banker, Sweezy studied at Harvard and the London School of Economics. He taught at Harvard from 1933 to 1942, worked for the Office of Strategic Services for the remainder of the war, and, anticipating a refusal of tenure, resigned from Harvard in 1946. Sweezy was co-founder in 1949 of the journal *Monthly Review,* which he has edited ever since.

Sweezy's *The Theory of Capitalist Development* is one of the best introductions to Marxian political economy ever written. It contains a lucid account of Marx's own crisis theory, concentrating on cyclical fluctuations in unemployment and their implications for real wages, profits, and the accumulation of capital. Sweezy's knowledge of German allowed him to draw on sources (including Marx's *Theories of Surplus Value,* then untranslated) which were inaccessible to most of his readers, and his masterly survey of the "breakdown controversy" introduced the ideas of Karl Kautsky, Rudolf Hilferding, Rosa Luxemburg, Otto Bauer, and Henryk Grossmann to the English-speaking world. The drift of Sweezy's own thinking was already apparent in his rejection of Marx's analysis in volume three of the falling rate of profit and his endorsement of Bauer's 1936 mathematical model of underconsumption. In the final part of the book, Sweezy outlined the alterations to the classical Marxian theory that he believed to be necessary in an era of monopoly, incorporating Keynesian elements in his analysis of capitalist stagnation.

The impact of the *Theory of Capitalist Development* was evident in the work of Sweezy's friend Paul Baran, whose *Political Economy of Growth* introduced the important new concept of the *economic surplus.* This was loosely defined as the difference between society's total output and the cost of producing it, and was intended as a generalization of the traditional Marxian notion of surplus value, allowing explicit attention to be paid to unproductive activities ("waste") in addition to profits, interest, and rent. In the jointly written *Monopoly Capital,* Baran and Sweezy argued that a "law of the rising surplus" could be inferred from the growing proportion of wasteful expenditures in the United States, and that the law itself reflected a deeply rooted tendency to stagnation. Giant corporations had suppressed price competition, but continued to reduce production costs. The gap between revenue and outlays was therefore constantly widening. The growing surplus had been absorbed, Baran and Sweezy maintained, only by the inexorable expansion of unproductive activities, most notably armaments expenditures and advertising. Major crises had for the moment been avoided, and stagnation deferred, but only at the cost of ever-increasing irrationality in economic life.

This was a heterodox Marxism of a recognizably North American type. European critics dismissed Sweezy as a "left Keynesian" who focused on the superficial phenomena of market exchange and ignored the deeper reality of capitalist production. Indeed, it was partly in reaction to *Monopoly Capital* that interest in the falling-rate-of-profit theory revived, since this seemed to offer a more conventional Marxian explanation of crises. Sweezy was unmoved by this new fundamentalism. However, by about 1980, it was possible to discern two subtle but important changes in his thinking. One was his recognition of strong theoretical affinities with Michal Kalecki, whose work was barely mentioned in *Monopoly Capital*. The other involved a growing emphasis on financial instability, especially that occasioned by the increasing burden of public and private debt, as the harbinger of a major future crisis.

As an expositor and propagator of a broadly Marxian approach to crisis theory, Sweezy has no peers. Outside the United States, however, his own idiosyncratic brand of underconsumptionism has always been rejected by the majority of Marxian economists.

M. C. Howard
J. E. King

See also BAUER, OTTO; FALLING RATE OF PROFIT; HILFERDING, RUDOLF; KALECKI, MICHAL; KAUTSKY, KARL; LUXEMBURG, ROSA; MARX, KARL HEINRICH; OVERSAVING THEORIES OF BUSINESS CYCLES; STEINDL, JOSEF

Bibliography

Baran, P. 1957. *Political Economy of Growth.* New York: Monthly Review Press.

Baran, P. and P. M. Sweezy. 1966. *Monopoly Capital.* New York: Monthly Review Press.

Foster, J. B. 1986. *The Theory of Monopoly Capitalism: An Elaboration of Marxian Political Economy.* New York: Monthly Review Press.

Georgescu-Roegen, N. 1960. "Mathematical Proofs of the Breakdown of Capitalism." *Econometrica* 28:225–43.

Hillard, M. 1985. "Harry Magdoff and Paul Sweezy: Biographical Notes." In *Rethinking Marxism,* edited by S. Resnick and R. Wolff, 397–404. Brooklyn, N.Y.: Autonomedia.

Howard, M. C. and J. E. King. 1991. *A History of Marxian Economics.* Volume 2, *1929–1990.* Princeton: Princeton Univ. Press.

King, J. E. 1988. *Economic Exiles.* London: Macmillan.

Magdoff, H. and P. M. Sweezy. 1981. *The Deepening Crisis of U.S. Capitalism.* New York: Monthly Review Press.

———. 1987. *Stagnation and the Financial Explosion.* New York: Monthly Review Press.

Steindl, J. [1952] 1976. *Maturity and Stagnation in American Capitalism.* New York: Monthly Review Press.

Sweezy, P. M. 1942. *The Theory of Capitalist Development.* New York: Oxford Univ. Press.

———. [1953] 1970. *The Present as History.* New York: Monthly Review Press.

———. 1972. *The Dynamics of U.S. Capitalism.* New York: Monthly Review Press.

———. 1981. *Four Lectures on Marxism.* New York: Monthly Review Press.

Wolff, E. N. 1987. *Growth, Accumulation and Unproductive Activity: An Analysis of the Post War U.S. Economy.* Cambridge: Cambridge Univ. Press.

T

Taste Shocks

The idea that taste shocks matter for business cycles and asset prices has been around some time. Black (1987) offers an example of a business-cycle model in which taste shocks matter. Black constructs a multisector stochastic growth model in which it is costly to move productive resources across sectors. In this model, taste shocks cause differences between demand and supply in output and labor across sectors. Since it is costly to shift resources across sectors, output and employment fluctuate over time.

Many economists have been critical of models that include taste shocks for at least two reasons. One is the effect on the welfare theorems. With preferences shifting over time, the welfare theorems may say nothing more than that people get what they want and that people want what they get. In this case, utility functions represent behavior rather than preference orderings (Pollak 1976, 1978).

The other misgiving economists have about models with taste shocks stems from an empirical critique. Since taste shocks come in an infinite variety of forms, models that use them to explain business-cycle facts lack economic content. That is, with no prior restrictions placed on them, taste shocks are free parameters that can be used to explain any set of puzzling empirical facts. To avoid this problem, Black makes taste shocks observable.

Among the taste-shock representations that have received the most attention are habit formation and home production. It is straightforward to base them on observables. However, responding to the empirical critique of taste shocks by using observables is not without its own pitfalls. Models of taste shocks may have more than one interpretation. With-out a bit of economic theory, simply making taste shocks observable does not allow them to be interpreted in an economically meaningful way.

Habit Formation

An early microeconomic theory of taste shocks is contained in the linear habit-formation models studied by Pollak (1970, 1976). Under linear habit formation, period household utility is written as

$$u\big(z(t)\big) = U\big(c(t), q(t)\big), z(t) = c(t) - gq(t) \tag{1}$$

where $c(t)$ is consumption expenditure, $q(t)$ is the taste shock, and $g > 0$. An interpretation of $q(t)$ is that it represents the subsistence level of consumption. To make $q(t)$ observable and habit forming, let it be determined by an infinite sequence of past consumption

$$q(t) = h(L)c(t); h(L) = h(1)L + h(2)L^2 + \ldots + h(p)L^p + \ldots, \tag{2}$$

where L is the lag operator, $h(i) \geq 0$, and $h(1) = 1$. An alternative to linear habit formation, nonaddictive habit formation where $z(t) = c(t)/q(t)$, is studied by Abel (1990), DeTemple and Zapatero (1991), and Campbell and Cochrane (1995).

Acting as a subsistence level of consumption, habit formation raises the value of the last unit of current consumption [the marginal utility of current consumption, $MU(t)$] to the household. For a given stochastic process generating consumption, habit formation reduces marginal utility and increases its sensitivity to a small change in current consumption.

$$MU(t) = \partial u\big(z(t)\big)/\partial c(t) -$$
$$gh\big(\beta L^{-1}\big)\partial u\big(z(t)\big)/\partial c(t);\ 0 < \beta < 1, \qquad (3)$$

where β is the household discount factor.

Sundaresan (1989), Constantinides (1990), DeTemple and Zapatero (1991), and Campbell and Cochrane (1995) study the implications for asset pricing of habit formation. Constantinides (1990) shows how a suitably parameterized asset-pricing model with linear habit formation can explain the equity-premium puzzle of Mehra and Prescott (1985). The puzzle concerns the small unconditional mean of the risk-free real interest rate, $r(t)$, in the United States for the last ninety years, given that the unconditional sample mean of consumption growth is less than 2 percent over the same period. Standard asset-pricing models predict that, on average, $r(t)$ should be large because of positive consumption growth rates.

The reason habit formation resolves the equity-premium puzzle is that it lowers the growth rate of consumption net of habits, $z(t)$. Since habit formation reduces the $MU(t)$ and increases its sensitivity to changes in $c(t)$, the expected marginal rate of substitution of consumption conditional on date-t information

$$MRS(t + 1) = \beta E_t\big\{MU(t + 1)/MU(t)\big\} \qquad (4)$$

is more volatile. The usual equilibrium relationship between $r(t)$ and $MRS(t+1)$ is

$$1 + r(t) = 1/E_t\big\{MRS(t + 1)\big\}. \qquad (5)$$

Hence with habit formation the price today of one unit of consumption tomorrow is higher on average and the average return on the asset trading this unit of consumption is lower than without habit formation.

A problem with habit formation is its economic interpretation. For example, linear habit formation can be reinterpreted as the service flow, $s(t)$, derived from consumption expenditures. Service flows, $s(t)$, depend on current and past $c(t)$

$$s(t) = d(L)c(t);\ d(L) =$$
$$d(0) + d(1)L + ... + d(p)L^p + ..., \qquad (6)$$

where $d(i) > 0$ and $d(1) = 1$. Current and past consumption expenditures matter for current utility, because the durability of $c(t)$ implies service flows from $c(t)$ that extend beyond date t. Ferson and

Constantinides (1991) assume that habits depend on $s(t)$ rather than $c(t)$. This yields restrictions on the habit- and service-flow parameters

$$z(t) = d(0)v(L)c(t);\ v(L) =$$
$$1 + v(1)L + ... + v(p)L^p + ..., \qquad (7)$$

where $v(j) = [d(j) - gh(d(j)L)]/d(0)$ and $h(d(j)L) = d(j - 1)h(1)L - ... - d(0)h(j)L^j$. If habits and durability exist at a given lag, then the relative sizes of the d's, g, and h's determine whether habits or durability dominate (Ferson and Constantinides 1991).

Whether habit formation or durability in consumption dominates is partly an empirical question. The empirical work in this area is not conclusive. Eichenbaum and Hansen (1990) and Heaton (1995) estimate models of durability of consumption and find some evidence for durability in consumption and little evidence for habits in consumption. However, the results of Ferson and Constantinides (1991) support habits mixed with durability in consumption. The difference in empirical results hinges on the frequency of the data and the conditioning information used in estimating instrumental variables. This suggests that claims made for or against habit formation as an explanation for asset-pricing puzzles remains tenuous and that the area remains open to further research.

Home Production

Benhabib, Rogerson, and Wright (1991), Greenwood and Hercowitz (1991), and Bencivenga (1992) construct real business-cycle (RBC) models that are in the spirit of the business cycle model of Black (1987). In these RBC models, taste shocks are represented as home-production technologies. Production in the home serves as the second productive sector of the economy.

By identifying the taste shock as the home-production technology, it is possible to make the taste shock observable. Benhabib, Rogerson, and Wright (BRW) construct the household period utility function

$$U\big(c(t),\ q(t)\big) = \Big[bc(t)^a + (1 - b)q(t)^a \Big]^{(1/a)};$$
$$b > 0,\ a > 0, \qquad (8)$$

where the impact of leisure on utility is suppressed. BRW discuss some of the theory underlying home production. A Cobb-Douglas technology is used by BRW for production in the home

$$q(t) = e(t)k(h, t)^\theta n(h, t)^{(1-\theta)};\ 0 < \theta < 1, \qquad (9)$$

where $e(t)$ denotes the home technology shock, $k(h,t)$, the part of the capital stock used in the home, and $n(h,t)$, labor input used in the home. Shocks to the home- and market-production technologies cause changes in the relative prices of $c(t)$ and $q(t)$. As in Black's model, taste shocks along with costly resource shifting cause business-cycle fluctuations because of their impact on the demand for and the supply of output and labor across the two sectors.

Although home production makes for an appealing story of the business cycle, the importance of home production for business-cycle research depends ultimately on empirical testing. Bencivenga (1992) estimates an RBC model with taste shocks and identifies them as shocks to a home-production technology. The fit of this model improves when these taste shocks are included.

The generality of these results is limited by the simplicity of the model Bencivenga studies. For example, the consumption taste shocks Bencivenga studies could be identified as service flows representing durability in consumption. The additional restrictions that the BRW model of home production imposes on the data could be used to resolve this quandary. This is an approach being pursued by McGrattan, Rogerson, and Wright (1997), but it remains open to further research.

Conclusion

Taste shocks are not necessarily catch-all expedients for explaining unresolved empirical puzzles. Taste shocks are useful devices when they can be given economic content. However, for taste shocks to have economically meaningful content, they must be grounded solidly in theory and tied to observable phenomena, which is not always easy. Even then, the efficacy of taste shocks is an open issue because of ambiguities in their interpretation.

James M. Nason

See also EQUITY PREMIUM; INTERTEMPORAL SUBSTITUTION; REAL BUSINESS-CYCLE THEORIES; TINTNER, GERHARD

Bibliography

Abel, A. B. 1990. "Asset Prices under Habit Formation and Catching up with the Joneses." *American Economic Review Papers and Proceedings* 80:38–42.

Bencivenga, V. R. 1992. "An Econometric Study of Hours and Output Variation with Preference Shocks." *International Economic Review* 33:449–71.

Benhabib, J., R. Rogerson, and R. Wright. 1991. "Homework in Macroeconomics: Household Production and Aggregate Fluctuations." *Journal of Political Economy* 99:1166–87.

Black, F. 1987. "General Equilibrium and Business Cycles." Chap. 1 in *Business Cycles and Equilibrium*. New York: Basil Blackwell.

Campbell, J. Y. and J. H. Cochrane. 1995. "A Consumption-Based Explanation of Aggregate Stock Market Behavior." NBER Working Paper no. 4995. Cambridge, MA.

Constantinides, G. M. 1990. "Habit Formation: A Resolution of the Equity Premium Puzzle." *Journal of Political Economy* 98:519–43.

DeTemple, J. B. and F. Zapatero. 1991. "Asset Prices in an Exchange Economy with Habit Formation." *Econometrica* 59:1633–57.

Eichenbaum, M. and L. P. Hansen. 1990. "Estimating Models with Intertemporal Substitution Using Aggregate Time Series Data." *Journal of Business and Economic Statistics* 8:53–69.

Ferson, W. E. and G. M. Constantinides. 1991. "Habit Persistence and Durability in Aggregate Consumption: Empirical Tests." *Journal of Financial Economics* 29:199–240.

Greenwood, J. and Z. Hercowitz. 1991. "The Allocation of Capital and Time Over the Business Cycle." *Journal of Political Economy* 99:1188–1214.

Heaton, J. 1995. "An Empirical Investigation of Asset Pricing with Temporally Dependent Preference Specifications." *Econometrica* 63:681–717.

McGrattan, E., R. Rogerson, and R. Wright. 1997. "An Equilibrium Model of the Business Cycle with Household Production and Fiscal Policy." *International Economic Review* vol. 38 (forthcoming).

Mehra, R. and E. C. Prescott, 1985. "The Equity Premium: A Puzzle." *Journal of Monetary Economics* 15:145–61.

Pollak, R. A. 1970. "Habit Formation and Dynamic Demand Functions." *Journal of Political Economy* 78:745–63.

———. 1976. "Habit Formation and Long Run Utility Functions." *Journal of Economic Theory* 13:272–97.

———. 1978. "Endogenous Tastes in Demand and Welfare Analysis." *American*

Economic Review Papers and Proceedings 68:374–79.

Sundaresan, S. M. 1989. "Intertemporally Dependent Preferences and the Volatility of Consumption and Wealth." *Review of Financial Studies* 2:73–89.

Term Structure of Interest Rates

The relation between the yields of default-free bonds differing only in time to maturity is called the *term structure of interest rates*. A plot of these yields as a function of time to maturity is popularly referred to as the *yield curve*. The shape of the yield curve and its informative content have been intensively analyzed by economists. Although the yield curve has historically taken a variety of shapes, a factor analysis reveals that most of the information in the yield curve is contained in two variables, the level of short rates and the spread between long and short rates (Litterman and Scheinkman 1991). Thus, humped shapes and other nonlinearities of the yield curve provide little information beyond that contained in these two factors. This article concentrates on the second factor, namely, the term-structure spread or *slope* of the yield curve.

The term-structure spread is, by its nature, a forward-looking variable. Suppose, for example, that the Federal Reserve announces that it will implement in three months a policy expected to decrease future short rates. Market transactors would then find that the pre-announcement bond yields offer attractively high returns compared to buying three-month bills and rolling them over every quarter. Investors would thus attempt to buy more bonds, driving bond prices up and yields down and, hence, reducing the term-structure spread. Later on, if the expectations of lower rates turn out to be correct and short rates decline, the earlier term-structure spread would be revealed as a good predictor of the change in short rates.

The term-structure spread, of course, contains information not only about the market's expectation of future interest rate movements, but also about the market's perceived risk from holding bonds. The reason is straightforward: if the perceived risk from holding long-term bonds increases, then, *ceteris paribus*, investors require an added premium for holding those bonds and thus offer reduced prices for the bonds. Bond yields rise and the term-structure spread increases.

Whether the historical variability of the term-structure spread reflects primarily the vari-ability of the risk premium or the variability of expected changes in future rates is an empirical question. The traditional *expectations hypothesis* of the term structure takes the extreme view that the risk premium is constant and that variations in the term-structure spread correspond to variations in expected future rates. Hypotheses such as the *liquidity-premium hypothesis* or the *preferred-habitat hypothesis* emphasize the other extreme, namely, fluctuations in the risk premium or other market imperfections. A review of these hypotheses and their empirical tests can be found in Shiller (1989).

Since World War II, the term-structure spread has been a good predictor of the subsequent cumulative change in short-term rates in the United States. Moreover, the interest-rate prediction is a composite prediction about both the real rate of interest and the rate of inflation (Fama 1990, Mishkin 1990). Over a horizon of about one year, the prediction is primarily about the real rate of interest. Over longer forecasting horizons, the prediction is primarily about future rates of inflation. At long forecasting horizons, the expectations hypothesis is also hard to reject: the term-structure spread moves almost one-for-one with the subsequent realized cumulative change in the short rate.

The predictive ability of the term-structure spread is closely related to the business cycle. Interest rates are procyclical, and long rates rise less than short rates during business expansions and fall less during recessions. Hence, the term-structure spread is countercyclical. It follows that changes in the spread are positively associated with *future* changes in both real GNP and the nominal rate of interest. The countercyclical pattern of the spread, however, does not exhaust its informative content. In multivariate regressions that include lagged real GNP growth, inflation, and other cyclical variables such as the index of leading indicators or the level of real interest rates, the term-structure spread continues to have extra explanatory power for future real GNP growth (Estrella and Hardouvelis 1991). Furthermore, the predictive power of the spread arises mainly from the market's correct anticipation of future real factors.

At short forecasting horizons, during which fluctuations in interest rates and real economic activity reflect temporary factors more than they do the business cycle, the term-structure spread continues to have predictive power, though the power is not as great as for longer horizons. At short horizons, monetary regimes seem to affect the predictive power of the term-structure spread. Specifically, whenever the Federal Reserve adopts nominal-interest-rate targets, changes in short-term interest rates become extremely unpredictable. The unpredictability results from the unpredictability of the targets themselves, which change in response to new information about the macroeconomy, and from the ability of the Federal Reserve to align the level of nominal short-term interest rates close to its targets over short periods of time.

From 1890 to 1979, the predictive power of the spread between a six- and a three-month rate varied with the degree to which the Fed adhered to its nominal-interest-rate targets. In particular, before the Federal Reserve was founded in 1913, short-term interest rates followed a strong and easily predictable seasonal pattern. After 1915, the Federal Reserve smoothed the seasonal component of interest rates and thus destroyed the short-run predictive power of the spread (Mankiw and Miron 1986). In the 1970s and 1980s, the predictive power at the short end of the yield curve also varied considerably over three subperiods characterized by different degrees of adherence to nominal-interest-rate targeting: pre-October 1979, October 1979 to October 1982, and post-October 1982. In the first subperiod, the Federal Reserve followed strict nominal-interest-rate targets; in the second subperiod, the Fed largely abandoned those targets; and in the third subperiod, it returned to a partial interest-rate targeting. The predictive power of the spread between yields with consecutive weekly maturities spanning a horizon of one to twenty-six weeks increased dramatically during the second subperiod. Nevertheless, the return to partial interest-rate targeting after October 1982 did not reduce the predictive power of the spread (Hardouvelis 1988).

To find whether the term-structure spread contains information about the risk premium, one can regress the *ex post* risk premium—the excess return over the nominal risk-free rate from buying the bond at the beginning of the holding period and selling it at the end of the holding period—on the term-structure spread. Under the hypothesis that investors in the market have rational expectations, the regression fit is an empirical proxy for the expected excess bond return or the *ex ante* risk premium. The empirical relation between the two variables is indeed positive, suggesting that part of the movement in the term-structure spread reflects

variation in the risk premium. However, the signal-to-noise ratio in the regression—the R^2—is very low in all the studies.

The type of risk reflected in the term-structure spread appears to be common to various financial assets. The term-structure spread predicts not only excess bond returns, but also excess stock returns (Campbell 1987). The common predictability of excess bond and stock returns reflects the variability of the risk premium over the business cycle: during business expansions the risk premium is low and during recessions it is high. However, the term-structure spread does not appear to capture all of the business-cycle risk but only that part of cyclical risk related to maturity: bonds with longer maturity are riskier because their prices are more sensitive to permanent changes in the discount rate (Fama and French 1989). A complementary measure of overall business-cycle risk is the default spread—the spread, say, between high- and low-grade corporate bonds of similar maturity. The default spread has also been a good predictor of crises and financial panics since 1857 (Mishkin 1991).

The presence of a time-varying risk premium in the composition of the term-structure spread contradicts the expectations hypothesis in a statistical sense. Similarly, in regressions of the change in the long rate on the earlier term-structure spread, the presence of a white-noise error component on long rates—the econometrician's measurement error, or perhaps a simple deviation from the theory—can result in a counterintuitive negative coefficient (Campbell and Shiller 1991). A negative coefficient can also arise from sluggishness in the long rate caused by a small amount of market irrationality (Froot 1989). However, short-run regressions such as the ones that uncover time-varying premia or find counterintuitive reactions of the long rate tend to emphasize tiny deviations from the expectations hypothesis and cloud its overall economic usefulness. This point can be illustrated by comparing the term-structure spread with its theoretical counterpart, namely, the spread that conforms exactly to the long-run predictions of the expectations hypothesis. Movements of the two variables are very similar, and their deviations are economically small (Campbell and Shiller 1991).

The view that the expectations hypothesis can closely describe the information of the term-structure spread is new in the literature and stands in sharp contrast with older studies that consistently rejected the expectations hypothesis in both a statistical and an economic sense. The old literature assumed that interest-rate levels are stationary and thus imposed a very strong mean-reversion requirement on the evolution of short rates. This requirement is absent from the new literature, which allows for the presence of time trends in short and long rates.

Recent theoretical work attempts to model the term structure of interest rates within a general-equilibrium framework. In finance studies, the aim is to derive closed-form price solutions that would be useful to a trader or a financial analyst. Thus, for tractability, these models assume that trading takes place in continuous time and that a single state variable—the instantaneous risk-free rate in Cox, Ingersoll, and Ross (1985) or the forward interest rate in Heath, Jarrow, and Morton (1992)—drives the dynamics of the economy. In macroeconomic studies, the link between the term structure of interest rates and the real sector of the economy is under sharper focus. For tractability, these models assume the existence of complete markets, stationary real economic output, and a representative agent that maximizes a time-separable utility function. So far, the models have had limited success in matching their theoretical predictions with the empirical properties of the yield curve over the business cycle (Backus, Gregory, and Zin 1990; Donaldson, Johnsen, and Mehra 1990). However, relaxing the stationarity assumption, thereby allowing for trends in output, appears to be a promising way to compare the theoretical properties of yield curves with their evolution over time.

Gikas A. Hardouvelis

See also EXPECTATIONS; INTEREST RATES; LUTZ, FRIEDRICH AUGUST; RATIONAL EXPECTATIONS; STOCK-MARKET PRICES

Bibliography

Backus, D. K., A. W. Gregory, and S. E. Zin. 1990. "Risk Premiums in the Term Structure: Evidence from Artificial Economies." *Journal of Monetary Economics* 24:371–99.

Campbell, J. Y. 1987. "Stock Returns and the Term Structure." *Journal of Financial Economics* 18:373–99.

Campbell, J. Y. and R. J. Shiller. 1991. "Yield Spreads and Interest Rate Movements: A Bird's Eye View." *Review of Economic Studies* 58:495–514.

Cox, J. C., J. E. Ingersoll, and S. A. Ross. 1985. "A Theory of the Term Structure of Interest Rates." *Econometrica* 53:385–407.

Donaldson, J. B., T. Johnsen, and R. Mehra. 1990. "On the Term Structure of Interest Rates." *Journal of Economic Dynamics and Control* 14:571–96.

Estrella, A. and G. A. Hardouvelis. 1991. "The Term Structure as a Predictor of Real Economic Activity." *Journal of Finance* 46:555–72.

Fama, E. F. 1990. "Term Structure Forecasts of Interest Rates, Inflation and Real Returns." *Journal of Monetary Economics* 25:59–76.

Fama, E. F. and K. French. 1989. "Business Conditions and Expected Returns on Stocks and Bonds." *Journal of Financial Economics* 25:23–49.

Froot, K. A. 1989. "New Hope for the Expectations Hypothesis of the Term Structure of Interest Rates." *Journal of Finance* 44:283–305.

Hardouvelis, G. A. 1988. "The Predictive Power of the Term Structure during Recent Monetary Regimes." *Journal of Finance* 43:339–56.

Heath, D., R. Jarrow, and A. Morton. 1992. "Bond Pricing and the Term Structure of Interest Rates: A New Methodology for Contingent Claims Valuation." *Econometrica* 60:77–105.

Litterman, R. and J. Scheinkman. 1991. "Common Factors Affecting Bond Returns." *Journal of Fixed Income* 1:54–61.

Mankiw, N. G. and J. A. Miron. 1986. "The Changing Behavior of the Term Structure of Interest Rates." *Quarterly Journal of Economics* 101:211–18.

Mishkin, F. S. 1990. "What Does the Term Structure Tell us about Future Inflation?" *Journal of Monetary Economics* 25:77–95.

———. 1991. "Asymmetric Information and Financial Crises: A Historical Perspective." In *Financial Markets and Financial Crises,* edited by R. G. Hubbard, 69–108. Chicago: Univ. of Chicago Press.

Shiller, R. J. 1989. "The Term Structure of Interest Rates." In *Handbook of Monetary Economics,* edited by B. Friedman and F. H. Hahn, 629–721. New York: North-Holland.

Thomas, Brinley (1906–)

Born in Port Talbot, Glamorgan, Wales, Brinley Thomas earned a B.A. from the University College of Wales and an M.A. and Ph.D. from the London School of Economics. The bulk of his work has been in the field of economic history and ranges over the Industrial Revolution, monetary policy during crises, and the relationship between migration and economic growth.

Thomas's *Monetary Policy and Crises* reviewed the course of monetary policy in Sweden from 1914 to 1935. It traced the causes of and policy responses to wartime inflation, the expansion of the 1920s, its culmination in depression and the subsequent recovery. These policies were analyzed in terms of their conjunction with developments in Swedish monetary theory.

Thomas ([1954] 1973) later conducted a series of studies on the relationship between the economies of Great Britain and the United States. He identified four major expulsions of population from Europe between 1844 and 1907 and confirmed that each wave led to an upsurge in the U.S. building cycle while coinciding with increased imports of capital and a transformation of production functions. Each massive inflow of labor into the United States stimulated an upswing in the long investment cycle in the United States coinciding with a downswing in the long investment cycle in the United Kingdom. Finally, swings in U.S. building cycles paralleled long swings in British home and foreign investment (Thomas [1954] 1973, 158–74).

Thomas took issue with those who regarded the U.S. economy as the source of these long swings in immigration. He argued that the "push" element was the major determinant of emigration from many countries of the Old World and that the timing of peaks in migration was determined by the cycle of births in European countries and by the occurrence of calamities and technological innovations. He maintained that swings in U.S. demand could not be the source of American long swings, because simultaneous swings occurred in Canada, Argentina, and Australia.

Thomas employed an interaction model of the Atlantic economy that explained simultaneous long swings in the New World countries and the corresponding inverse long swings in Great Britain in terms of a center-periphery relationship comprising real-resource flows and monetary factors. Flows of food and raw materials from periphery to center and of capital and labor from center to the periphery caused these alternating long cycles. The process was also affected by the gold standard and the Bank of England's reserve policy (Thomas [1954] 1973, 243). Thus, these swings were propelled by real factors but changes in the stock of money played a significant independent part in influencing the course of the economy, especially in the crucial phases when expansion gave way to contraction. Thomas (1972, 127–36) employed the same model to explain long swings in the period after the Second World War, with the United States taking over Great Britain's role as the source of funds (but not migrants) to the periphery while presiding over a worldwide dollar standard.

Thomas's later efforts dealt with domestic food consumption patterns and energy usage during the British Industrial Revolution, the possibility of an energy crisis in Great Britain in the seventeenth century, and issues related to the "brain drain." Although these efforts grow out of his interest in "long cycles," his work on migration and economic development continues to be his most influential.

Vibha Kapuria-Foreman

See also KONDRATIEFF, NIKOLAI DMITRIYEVICH; KONDRATIEFF CYCLES; KUZNETS, SIMON SMITH; LONG-WAVE THEORIES

Bibliography

Thomas, B. [1936] 1983. *Monetary Policy and Crises*. New York: Garland.
———. 1972. *Migration and Urban Development*. London: Methuen.
———. [1954] 1973. *Migration and Economic Growth: A Study of Great Britain and the Atlantic Economy*. Cambridge: Cambridge Univ. Press.

Thornton, Henry (1760–1815)

Henry Thornton, successful banker, philanthropist, respected Member of Parliament, author of a best-selling volume of *Family Prayers,* also wrote perhaps the finest treatise on monetary theory of the nineteenth century. A leading participant in the Bullionist controversies, Thornton was a member of the Select Committee of Parliament on the High Price of Bullion, and a principal author of its famous report (Cannan 1919).

Although Thornton wrote his great work, *An Inquiry into the Nature and Effects of the*

Paper Credit of Great Britain in 1802, well before a concept of business cycles had been formulated, episodes of financial distress or panic had already begun to occur with some frequency in the eighteenth century. The most recent had been in 1797, when the combination of a dwindling stock of gold and rumors of a French invasion incited a run on the Bank of England. To protect the Bank's gold reserves, the government suspended the convertibility of Bank of England notes. It was that suspension that set off the Bullionist controversies which continued intermittently for two decades. Thus, a major concern of Thornton was to analyze the causes of financial distress and to suggest appropriate policies to counter them.

The British banking system at the turn of the nineteenth century consisted of a multitude of country banks located outside London which issued a large portion of the total stock of banknotes. In London, however, the Bank of England had the exclusive right to issue notes. The country banks made their notes convertible into those of the Bank of England, so that convertibility into gold was maintained through the convertibility of Bank of England notes.

Thornton perceived that, under this arrangement, the Bank of England had a special responsibility to ensure the stability of the British financial system. Since he considered the public's confidence in the redeemability of the obligations of the country banks into those of the Bank of England to be highly volatile, Thornton contended that the Bank of England had to extend credit to the country banks to prevent a loss of public confidence from feeding on itself, even if this meant tolerating a loss of gold reserves. The appropriate response of the Bank of England to an internal drain was, therefore, not to restrict credit but to extend it. Assurance of the Bank of England's willingness to extend credit would itself reduce or eliminate the public's precautionary desire to convert the liabilities of the country banks into those of the Bank of England. Thornton was thus the first to recognize that the Bank of England was a "central bank" and to formulate the concept of a lender of last resort.

Thornton also recognized that drains on the Bank of England's gold reserves could arise from external causes as well as internal ones. In such cases, the Bank of England was confronted with a delicate judgment. The drain could be owing either to a domestic overissue or to a need to make exceptional overseas payments.

Such a need could arise if there was a poor harvest or if foreign remittances were needed to maintain armies overseas. If the drain was caused by overissue, then the bank ought to tighten its credit policy, though not so severely as to provoke a panic at home. If there was a need to make overseas payments, Thornton, unlike Ricardo and Wheatley, held that it would be a mistake to tighten monetary conditions. In these circumstances, Thornton preferred a temporary depreciation of the exchange rate to a restrictive policy aimed at maintaining exchange parity.

Thornton opposed any policy of deliberate restriction designed to counter exchange depreciation caused by external factors, because he recognized the link between deflation and the real economy. The link he saw was that wage rates were stickier than other prices, so that wages would not adjust promptly enough to allow profits and employment to stay at normal levels.

A further concern of Thornton's was to refute the real-bills doctrine as enunciated by the directors of the Bank of England. According to that doctrine, if the Bank of England only discounted real bills drawn to finance the production or distribution of real goods, no overissue of Bank of England liabilities was possible, even when the liabilities were not convertible into gold. Thornton observed that the demand for credit depended on the relationship between the expected rate of profit and the interest rate charged on loans. Thus, if the interest rate on loans were lower than the rate of profit borrowers expected, the demand for credit could increase without limit. Once freed from the constraint of convertibility, the Bank of England could create liabilities in unlimited amounts and drive prices ever higher unless it charged a sufficiently high interest rate or its lending was subject to some quantitative limit.

Thus, Thornton anticipated by almost a full century Wicksell's distinction between the market and the natural rates of interest. And just as he recognized that deflation would cause temporary reductions in output and employment, he understood that monetary expansion could increase output and employment. The reason he suggested for this short-run effect is that suppliers would confuse the increase in prices they were receiving as a result of inflation with a real increase in prices, anticipating the rationale used by many New Classical theorists for the nonneutrality of unanticipated changes in money. He also gave one of the first formulations of the forced-saving doctrine that figured prominently in business-cycle theory early in this century. Moreover, although he did not touch on the subject in *Paper Credit,* Thornton, in a Parliamentary speech, also anticipated—again by nearly a century—Irving Fisher's distinction between the real and nominal rates of interest.

While Thornton's influence on his contemporaries is undeniable, much of his analysis was gradually forgotten, as he was himself, later in the nineteenth century. Thornton's case is one of those instances in which ideas too far ahead of their time fail to take root, because the intellectual environment is not yet ready for them. Perhaps only after there was a greater appreciation of business cycles as a problem could Thornton's ideas be fully comprehended.

David Glasner

See also BANKING PANICS; BULLIONIST CONTROVERSIES; BANK OF ENGLAND; CENTRAL BANKING; FORCED SAVING; LENDER OF LAST RESORT; MONETARY POLICY; NATURAL RATE OF INTEREST; REAL-BILLS DOCTRINE; RICARDO, DAVID; WICKSELL, JOHAN GUSTAV KNUT

Bibliography

Cannan, E., ed. 1919. *The Paper Pound of 1797–1821: The Bullion Report.* London: P. S. King.

Fetter, F. W. 1965. *The Evolution of British Monetary Orthodoxy 1797–1875.* Cambridge: Harvard Univ. Press.

Forester, E. M. 1951. "Henry Thornton." In *Two Cheers for Democracy,* 192–96. London: E. Arnold.

Hicks, J. R. 1967. "Thornton's *Paper Credit.*" Chap. 10 in *Critical Essays in Monetary Theory.* Oxford: Clarendon Press.

Thornton, H. [1802] 1939. *An Inquiry into the Nature and Effects of the Paper Credit of Great Britain.* Edited with an introduction by F. A. von Hayek. London: Allen and Unwin.

Viner, J. 1937. *Studies in the Theory of International Trade.* New York: Harper Bros.

Thorp, Willard Long (1899–1992)

Willard Thorp's work on business cycles, depressions, and crises included both historical research and official posts during the Roosevelt, Truman, and Kennedy administrations.

Born on 24 May 1899, Thorp received his B.A. from Amherst in 1920, and his M.A. from the University of Michigan in 1921. He pursued further graduate studies at Columbia University under Wesley C. Mitchell, receiving his Ph.D. in 1924.

Thorp's chief work on cycles, *Business Annals,* was published in 1926 while he was on the research staff of the National Bureau of Economic Research. The *Annals* chronicled the annual status of business cycles in sixteen industrial countries from the beginning of the nineteenth century through 1925. After nearly seventy years, it remains an excellent reference, and is recognized as a classic study of sectoral and national cycles.

From 1933 to 1935, Thorp served the Roosevelt administration in four different posts. He was instrumental in securing the collection of detailed economic statistics, so that the government could effectively monitor cycles and make policies accordingly.

In 1935, Thorp became Head of Economic Research at Dun and Bradstreet and Editor of *Dun's Review.* In 1946, Thorp was appointed Assistant Secretary of State for Economic Affairs, and was referred to as the "leading obstetrician" of the Marshall Plan. During the postwar European crisis, Thorp worked closely with the West European countries, especially Germany, helping to create the climate for the "economic miracles" of the 1950s. Thorp was also head of Truman's Point IV plan, which marked a dramatic shift in U.S. strategy toward aid to less developed countries. Thorp was later appointed by President Kennedy to be Chairman of the Development Assistance Commission of the Organization of Economic Cooperation and Development.

Willard Thorp studied cycles and depressions both as a scholar and a policymaker. The author of a classic work in business-cycle literature, he was also one of the architects of the postwar European recovery.

Daniel Barbezat

Bibliography

Thorp, W. L. 1926. *Business Annals.* New York: NBER.

———, ed. 1939. *Economic Problems in a Changing World.* New York: Farrar and Rinehart.

Thorp, W. L. and R. Quandt. 1959. *The New Inflation.* New York: McGraw-Hill.

Thrift Crisis

Not since the Great Depression did the thrift industry undergo such turmoil and uncertainty as it did in the 1980s. The rate and cost of failures during this period with federal deposit insurance in existence were higher than during the 1930s without it. This situation has caused some to question not only the wisdom of federal deposit insurance, but also the need for specialized institutions to promote housing finance.

With relatively low and stable interest rates, the income of the thrift industry fluctuated within a narrow band from 1950 through 1980. Thrifts held long-term, fixed-rate mortgages funded with short-term deposits whose rates could not exceed a ceiling set by regulation. This mismatch in the maturities, or repricing periods, of assets and liabilities made thrifts susceptible to deposit outflows, or disintermediation, whenever market rates rose above the ceiling. Without the ceiling, thrifts could prevent disintermediation by raising deposit rates to match market rates, but would then incur losses because of the fixed rates on their mortgage assets.

After the Federal Reserve Board shifted to targeting monetary aggregates instead of interest rates in October 1979, the level and volatility of market interest rates increased sharply. The high and volatile interest rates caused record losses in the thrift industry in the early 1980s, eroding much of the industry's capital. The percentage of unprofitable institutions increased from only 7 percent in 1979 to 36 percent in 1980, and to a record 85 percent in 1981. Although the percentage of unprofitable institutions decreased to 68 percent in 1982 and to 35 percent in 1983, many thrift institutions never recovered from the high interest rates. The industry's poor profit performance was exacerbated by the subsequent downturn in real-estate markets in the Southwest.

The disparity among thrift institutions' performance and financial condition grew in the mid-1980s. Aggregate industry data were dominated by write-downs in the value of assets on the balance sheets at still open but insolvent institutions. Whereas solvent institutions reported net after-tax profits every year beginning in 1983, their profits were eventually more than offset by the losses incurred by insolvent institutions. However, due to a reduction in asset write-downs and, more important, to the liquidation or merger of insolvent institutions

by the Federal Savings and Loan Insurance Corporation (FSLIC) and subsequently by the Resolution Trust Corporation (RTC), total industry losses declined dramatically after 1988.

The thrift debacle of the 1980s led to a marked consolidation of institutions. The number of thrifts declined from four thousand in 1980 to just under three thousand at the end of 1988. Total assets, however, more than doubled over the same period, increasing from $604 billion to $1.4 trillion. By 1995, however, there were fewer than 1500 institutions with about $775 billion in total assets.

Most of the consolidation was due to actions taken by the FSLIC against more than 900 troubled institutions from 1980 through 1988, including 77 liquidations, 411 assisted mergers, 18 stabilizations, 333 supervisory mergers, and 77 management-consignment program cases. Nevertheless, hundreds of insolvent institutions remained open at year-end 1988, some having been insolvent for more than ten years. The Federal Home Loan Bank Board estimated in early 1989 that nearly 600 troubled institutions remained to be resolved at a cost of $38 billion, bringing the estimated total cost of the thrift crisis to at least $90 billion. By 1995, more than 1200 institutions had failed and were resolved at an estimated cost of $130 billion.

Numerous studies have attempted to explain the performance of individual thrift institutions (Barth et al. 1985), relying on financial ratios designed to measure capital adequacy, profitability, credit risk, interest-rate risk, and liquidity risk to explain performance. Some studies also include factors intended to measure the use of "new" asset powers by thrift institutions. These studies typically find that measures of capital and profitability are important in explaining performance. Other factors are not uniformly important across the different studies. The studies suggest that the causes of poor performance change over time, so that no single set of financial characteristics can be identified as the cause. Moreover, delay in closing troubled institutions, measured by the number of months between insolvency and closure, is found to increase FSLIC's eventual resolution costs.

One limitation of all these studies is that they examine the determinants of closure—when the FSLIC liquidates or merges an institution with regulatory assistance. One should also be interested in the determinants of economic insolvency. Before 1980, the distinction between closure and insolvency was unimportant—most institutions were closed when they became insolvent. Beginning in 1980, however, the number of closures was far less than the actual number of insolvencies. Another limitation is that the failure studies do not examine how supervisory or regulatory actions short of liquidation or merger affect performance.

Thus far, attempts to associate greater portfolio diversification with thrift failure have not been entirely successful. One reason is that most thrifts have remained committed to mortgage assets; relatively few institutions, solvent or insolvent, have extensively used the expanded asset powers they received in the early 1980s. For instance, in September 1988, only 9 percent of all insolvent institutions had nonresidential commercial loans exceeding 5 percent of their assets, and only 3 percent had consumer loans exceeding 20 percent of their assets—the statutory limits for federally chartered institutions prior to the passage of the Garn-St Germain Depository Institutions Act of 1982. Finally, less than 20 percent had commercial mortgage loans exceeding 25 percent of their assets despite the Garn-St Germain limit of 40 percent.

However, differences in the performance of solvent and insolvent institutions did reflect differences in their portfolio strategies. Solvent institutions remained heavily committed to the residential mortgage market, holding 64 percent of their assets in residential mortgage loans or mortgage-backed securities in September 1988. In contrast, insolvent institutions committed less than 50 percent of their assets to residential properties. Instead, they dramatically and rapidly increased their commercial mortgage lending. By September 1988, insolvent institutions had allocated nearly 14 percent of their assets to this category—almost half again more than their healthier counterparts. However, this shift into riskier activities appears to have occurred after these institutions became troubled, not before.

Although there is considerable debate about the causes of the thrift debacle, the structure of federal deposit insurance seems to have been a major factor (Barth 1991, Barth, Bartholomew, and Bradley 1991, Kane 1989, Brumbaugh 1988). Federal deposit insurance was established to prevent disruptions in the financial sector from generating or exacerbating a collapse in the entire economy such as occurred when thousands of financial institutions failed during the Great Depression. The Federal Deposit Insurance Corporation (FDIC) was created by the Banking Act of 1933 and the FSLIC was created by Title IV of the National Housing Act of 1934 and placed under the aegis of the Federal Home Loan Bank Board. However, in 1989 the FSLIC was abolished and replaced with the Savings Association Insurance Fund (SAIF), which is administered by the FDIC.

The major problem with federal deposit insurance is that it created a moral-hazard problem which induces insured depository institutions to hold riskier portfolios than they otherwise would have. Careful supervision of the activities of the insured by the insurer is essential whenever insurance creates a significant moral-hazard problem.

Yet, federal deposit insurers have always used practices different from those of private insurers. Unlike private insurers, both the FDIC and the FSLIC were intended to be guarantee funds providing deposit assurance (ultimately relying on government guarantees) rather than self-financing operational insurance funds. The FDIC and the FSLIC, moreover, were not designed to cover abnormal losses resulting from periods of economic crisis (Barth 1989b). Only in the early 1990s was the uniform flat-rate structure altered, although rates and coverage had changed since federal deposit insurance was established. These and other divergences between the practices of federal and private insurers allow one to identify federal deposit insurance as a major cause of the thrift debacle of the 1980s.

The thrift debacle has caused some to question the federal government's continued attempt to maintain a separate thrift industry, particularly after the Federal Home Loan Bank Board was abolished in 1989 and replaced with the Office of Thrift Supervision. Specialized thrifts may no longer be needed as a reliable source of credit for housing construction. Recent technological advances have permitted the mortgage product to be unbundled—the origination, servicing, and holding functions have been separated—thereby enabling funds to flow into housing from a variety of sources. Developments in the secondary mortgage markets, moreover, may have narrowed the spread between the rates earned on residential mortgages and thrifts' financing costs so much that thrifts specializing in such assets may no longer be profitable (Hendershott 1988). However, estimates of such spreads are highly sensitive to

T

numerous questionable assumptions. In addition, since many insolvent institutions have remained open and paid above-market interest rates, past estimates of thrifts' financing costs may be overstated and, therefore, may understate the spread.

Performance at thrifts, moreover, did improve as holdings of traditional mortgage assets increased. Institutions with greater holdings of traditional mortgage assets were better capitalized, enjoyed higher total returns on assets, and had fewer asset-quality problems in the late 1980s than those with relatively small holdings (Barth and Bradley 1989).

No matter how the debate over the continued viability of thrifts as portfolio mortgage lenders is resolved, housing and construction will likely remain among the most cyclically volatile sectors in the economy. Since housing starts are closely related to and lead gross national product, the role of thrifts in housing cycles remains an important issue. The extent to which the thrift debacle of the 1980s adversely affected mortgage rates and the real economy also remains a largely unexplored issue.

James R. Barth
Michael D. Bradley

See also DISINTERMEDIATION; FEDERAL DEPOSIT INSURANCE

Bibliography

Barth, J. R. 1991. *The Great Savings and Loan Debacle.* Washington, D.C.: American Enterprise Institute.

Barth, J. R., P. F. Bartholomew, and C. J. Labich. 1989a. "Moral Hazard and the Thrift Crisis: An Analysis of 1988 Resolutions." In *Bank Structure and Competition,* 344–84. Chicago: Federal Reserve Bank of Chicago.

Barth, J. R., P. F. Bartholomew, and M. G. Bradley. 1991. "Reforming Federal Deposit Insurance: What Can Be Learned from Private Insurance Practices?" *Consumer Finance Law Quarterly Report,* Spring,140–47.

Barth, J. R. and M. G. Bradley. 1989. "Thrift Deregulation and Federal Deposit Insurance." *Journal of Financial Services Research* 2:231–59.

Barth, J. R., M. D. Bradley, J. A. McKenzie, and G. S. Sirmans. 1988. "Stylized Facts About Housing and Construction Activity During The Post-World-War-II Period." In *Real Estate Market Analysis: Methods and Applications,* edited by J. M. Clapp and S. D. Messner, 215–37. New York: Praeger.

Barth, J. R., R. D. Brumbaugh, D. Sauerhaft, and G. H. K. Wang. 1985. "Thrift-Institution Failures: Causes and Policy Issues." In *Bank Structure and Competition,* 184–216. Chicago: Federal Reserve Bank of Chicago.

Barth, J. R., J. J. Feid, G. Riedel, and M. H. Tunis. 1989. "Alternative Federal Deposit Insurance Regimes." In *Problems of the Federal Savings and Loan Insurance Corporation (FSLIC).* Senate Committee on Banking, Housing, and Urban Affairs, part 2. 101st Cong., 1st sess.

Barth, J. R. and M. A. Regalia. 1988. "The Evolving Role of Regulation in the Savings and Loan Industry." In *The Financial Services Revolution: Policy Directions for the Future,* edited by C. England and T. Huertas, 113–61. Boston: Kluwer.

Brumbaugh, R. D. Jr. 1988. *Thrifts Under Siege: Restoring Order to American Banking.* Cambridge, Mass.: Ballinger.

Hendershott, P. H. 1988. "The Future of Thrifts as Home Mortgage Portfolio Lenders." In *Future of the Thrift Industry, Proceedings of the Fourteenth Annual Conference,* 153–63. San Francisco: Federal Home Loan Bank of San Francisco.

Kane, E. J. 1989. *The S&L Insurance Mess: How Did It Happen?* Washington, D.C.: Urban Institute.

Maisel, S. J. 1963. "Fluctuations in Residential Construction Starts." *American Economic Review* 53:359–83.

Time Reversibility

A stochastic process $\{X_t\}$ is *time-reversible* if it is invariant under the reversal of the time scale. The long debate about the symmetry of the business cycle is really a debate about its time-reversibility. In addition, most statistical time-series techniques applied to economic and financial models assume time reversibility. Consequently, evidence that some economic time series are time-irreversible would call into question the use of many conventional empirical and theoretical modeling strategies.

An unresolved issue in business-cycle analysis is whether the business cycle is symmetric. Claims that the business-cycle is asymmetric can be traced back at least to Mitchell and Keynes, who asserted that the business cycle is asymmetric in that upturns are longer, but less steep, than downturns. More recently, Blatt (1980) demonstrated that Frisch-type models, i.e., systems of low-order linear difference equations, subjected to a sequence of independently and identically distributed random shocks, cannot capture cyclical asymmetries. If cyclical asymmetries exist, then a research program based on Frisch-type models is misguided. Nonetheless, a very wide class of the business-cycle models currently used to analyze economic time series is of the Frisch type. Ramsey and Rothman (1996) applied the notion of time-reversibility to this problem and showed that the issue reduces to whether major macroeconomic time series are time-reversible.

Time-reversibility can be defined with respect to both deterministic and stochastic models. The deterministic definition is that the equations of motion are invariant to reversal of the time index. That is, the qualitative properties of the model are invariant; attractors remain attractors, repellors, repellors, and the number of fixed points and other dynamical properties do not change. Models in which entropy changes are time-irreversible.

Reichenbach was one of the first to distinguish between time irreversibility and concepts of causality. The equations of motion in mechanics are clearly causal, but are just as clearly time-reversible since the equations are invariant to the substitution of $-t$ for t. Mechanical equations of motion determine time order, a relationship between before and after that is symmetric in either direction. Time-irreversible systems imply a further property of time direction that is best illustrated by diffusive, or growth, processes. In time-irreversible systems, the equations are not invariant to time reversal, because the process involved can operate only in one direction. The unique direction of the process provides a unique direction to time; that is, time-irreversible processes define time and its direction.

It is to Georgescu-Roegen's great credit that he anticipated the importance of the distinction between time order and time direction for economics. "It is the essential difference between the temporal laws which are functions of [time order] and those which are functions of [time direction] that calls for a distinction between the two concepts" (Georgescu-Roegen 1966). Applying these ideas to economic con-

cepts he realized that: "the statement that an increase in price will bring about a decrease in the quantity demanded . . . is not a quantitative law in the usual sense of the word, for it does not imply a reversible relationship between prices and quantities" (Georgescu-Roegen 1950).

A classic model of business-cycle fluctuations is Samuelson's multiplier-accelerator model. Under certain conditions, the solution for national income (Y_t) is given by (Allen 1965, 214):

$Y_t = Ar^t \cos(\theta t)$,

where $r = \sqrt{w}$

$w = v - c_2$

v = value of the accelerator coefficient

c_2 = marginal propensity to consume out of Y_{t-2}

$\theta = \cos^{-1}\left((w - s + 1)/2\sqrt{w}\right)$

$s = c_1 + c_2$

c_1 = marginal propensity to consume out of Y_{t-1}

A is an arbitrary constant given by initial conditions.

For the case $r = 1$, the sequence (Y_t) is identical to the sequence (Y_{-t}), since $\cos(\theta t)$ is an even function of t. That is, for this parameter value the model is time-reversible. But the model is explosive for $r > 1$ and generates damped oscillations for $r < 1$, so that in either case it is time-irreversible.

Time reversibility was introduced into the statistical time-series literature by Brillinger and Rosenblatt (1967). A time series $\{X_t\}$ is time-reversible if for every positive integer n, and every $t_1, t_2, \ldots, t_n \equiv R$, the vectors $(X_{t1}, X_{t2}, \ldots, X_{tn})$ and $(X_{-t1}, X_{-t2}, \ldots, X_{-tn})$ have the same joint probability distributions. A time series that is not time-reversible is said to be time-irreversible.

Time reversibility should not be confused with stationarity. A stationary time series can be either reversible or irreversible. A nonstationary process can be time-reversible.

Linear models are generically time-irreversible. However, linear Gaussian models are time-reversible due to the special properties of Gaussian distribution. Time-irreversibility is also induced by most types of nonlinear models regardless of whether Gaussian innovations are used. For example, many bilinear models are time-irreversible; a bilinear model $B(x,y)$ is linear in either variable given the other.

Ramsey and Rothman (1996) propose a test for time-irreversibility for a stationary time series. Their test stems from a result on the equality between pairs of moments from the joint-probability distributions for a time-reversible stationary time series $\{X_t\}$. Provided the required moments are finite, $\{X_t\}$ is time-reversible only if:

$$E\left[X_t^i \cdot X_{t-k}^j\right] = E\left[X_t^j \cdot X_{t-k}^i\right], \qquad (1)$$

for all $i,j,k \in N$, where the expectation is taken with respect to each respective joint distribution.

Thus, if $\{X_t\}$ is time-reversible, functions of the form:

$$\gamma_{i,j}(k) = \left\{E\left[X_t^i \cdot X_{t-k}^j\right] - E\left[X_t^j \cdot X_{t-k}^i\right]\right\} \qquad (2)$$

are identically zero for all values of i, j, and k. A sufficient condition for time-irreversibility, therefore, is that $\gamma_{i,j}(k) \neq 0$ for some i, j, and k. In practice, most cases of interest can be handled with $i = 2$, $j = 1$ and k less than 10.

Most economic and financial models are time-reversible by assumption. For example, the Lucas ([1973] 1981) New Classical model of business cycles is log-linear with normal innovations and so is time-reversible. If $\{X_t\}$ is a sequence of independently distributed random variables, then the sequence is time-reversible. Many financial models of the stock market assume that the differences in stock prices are independently distributed random variables, so that implicitly these financial models assume that the process is reversible in the statistical sense.

Ramsey and Rothman found strong evidence of time irreversibility in annual macroeconomic time series for the United States as well as several other O.E.C.D. countries, confiming that business cycles are asymmetric in the largest industrialized economies.

James B. Ramsey
Philip Rothman

See also ASYMMETRY; CHAOS AND BIFURCATIONS; FRISCH, RAGNAR ANTON KITTEL; NONLINEAR STATISTICAL INFERENCE

Bibliography

Allen, R. G. D. 1965. *Mathematical Economics*. 2d ed. London: Macmillan.

Blatt, J. M. 1980. "On the Frisch Model of Business Cycles." *Oxford Economic Papers* 32:467–79.

Brillinger, D. and M. Rosenblatt. 1967. "Consumption and Interpretation of the *k-th* Order Spectra." In *Spectral Analysis of Time Series*, edited by B. Harris, 153–88. New York: Wiley.

Georgescu-Roegen, N. 1950. "The Theory of Choice and the Constancy of Economic Laws." *Quarterly Journal of Economics* 64:125–38.

———. 1966. *Analytical Economics*. Cambridge: Harvard Univ. Press.

Lucas, R. E. Jr. [1973] 1981. "Some International Evidence on Output-Inflation Tradeoffs." In *Studies in Business-Cycle Theory*, 131–45. Cambridge: MIT Press.

Ramsey, J. and P. Rothman. 1996. "Time Irreversibility and Business-Cycle Asymmetry." *Journal of Money, Credit and Banking* 28:1–21.

Reichenbach, H. 1956. *The Direction of Time*. Berkeley and Los Angeles: Univ. of California Press.

Tinbergen, Jan (1903–1994)

Jan Tinbergen shared, with Ragnar Frisch, the first Nobel Memorial Prize in Economics in 1969 in recognition of their role in the creation of econometrics, and of their subsequent work on development planning. In the decade before World War II, Tinbergen pioneered both the methods and use of multi-equation models for empirical macroeconomics and for testing alternative theories of business cycles.

After graduating from Leiden University, Tinbergen joined the Netherlands Central Bureau of Statistics in 1929, and also began teaching at the Netherlands School of Economics in Rotterdam from 1933. He edited *De Nederlansche Conjunctur*, a statistical business-cycle journal, and, with Irving Fisher, Ragnar Frisch, and Charles F. Roos, founded the Econometric Society in 1930. In 1931, Tinbergen showed that the lagged response of shipbuilding to freight rates could generate cyclical oscillations in shipbuilding even if the exogenous shocks were not oscillatory. Tinbergen used a 22-equation regression model of the Dutch economy to compare the effects of six policy options in a paper to the Dutch Economic Association in October 1936, and in a short book the following February. This model followed

Frisch's 1933 proposal for modeling a cyclical economic mechanism subject to external shocks. After estimating the structural relationships, Tinbergen derived the final equation of the model which implied a damped cyclical path for the economy.

From 1936 to 1938, Tinbergen worked for the League of Nations on econometric testing of the business-cycle theories surveyed in Haberler's *Prosperity and Depression* (1937). The first volume of Tinbergen's *Statistical Testing of Business Cycle Theories* discussed the methodology of statistical tests of economic theories, in contrast to his earlier work which had focused on explaining past data and on predicting the effects of policy choices rather than on choosing between alternative theories. The second volume presented an ambitious model of the United States economy estimated with annual data from 1919 to 1932, involving 71 variables and 48 equations. Highly controversial, the work drew sharply critical reviews from Keynes (volume one), to whom Tinbergen responded vigorously, and from Milton Friedman (volume two).

Tinbergen made several pioneering technical contributions. In 1932, he published a model with explicitly rational expectations, and in 1936 he performed the first regression estimation of the Phillips curve relation between inflation and unemployment (ten years after Irving Fisher calculated the correlation between the two series). Tinbergen (1930) gave one of the first two correct solutions of the identification problem for the simple supply-demand case. Robert Lucas ([1976] 1981) credited Tinbergen (1956, 149–85) with anticipating his critique of econometric policy evaluation.

Tinbergen greatly influenced macroeconometric modeling, both through his writings and through his training of such notable Dutch econometricians as Tjalling Koopmans and Henri Theil. Cowles Commission studies such as Lawrence Klein's *Economic Fluctuations in the United States, 1921–1941* (1950) combined Tinbergen's approach to modeling with advanced statistical methods that permitted simultaneous estimation of the equations.

In 1951, Tinbergen published *Business Cycles in the United Kingdom, 1870–1914*. Although the work had been done in 1939 and 1940, publication was delayed by the war. After the war, while serving as director of the Netherlands Central Planning Bureau (1945–55), Tinbergen shifted his research activity from business cycles to optimal short-term economic policy. He later turned to international economic cooperation and to long-term development planning for less developed countries, particularly after his appointment in 1966 as chairman of the United Nations Committee for Development Planning. Besides formulating and estimating the first large macroeconometric models, Tinbergen was a pioneer in recasting verbal theories of business cycles in econometrically testable form.

Robert W. Dimand

See also FRISCH, RAGNAR ANTON KITTEL; HAAVELMO, TRYGVE; KEYNES, JOHN MAYNARD; KLEIN, LAWRENCE ROBERT; KOOPMANS, TJALLING CHARLES; LUCAS CRITIQUE; MACROECONOMETRIC MODELS, HISTORICAL DEVELOPMENT; SERIAL CORRELATION

Bibliography
Epstein, R. J. 1987. *A History of Econometrics*. Amsterdam: North-Holland.

Friedman, M. 1940. Review of *Statistical Testing of Business-Cycle Theories,* vol. 2, by J. Tinbergen. *American Economic Review* 30:657–61.

Hansen, B. 1969. "Jan Tinbergen: An Appraisal of His Contributions to Economics." *Swedish Journal of Economics* 71:325–36.

Hughes-Hallett, A. J. 1989. "Econometrics and the Theory of Economic Policy: The Tinbergen-Theil Contributions 40 Years On." *Oxford Economic Papers* 41:189–216.

Keuzenkamp, H. A. 1991. "A Precursor to Muth: Tinbergen's 1932 Model of Rational Expectations." *Economic Journal* 101:1245–53.

Keynes, J. M. 1939–40. Review of *Statistical Testing of Business-Cycle Theories,* vol. 1, by J. Tinbergen. *Economic Journal* 49:558–68. Reply by Tinbergen and comment by Keynes in *Economic Journal* 50:141–56.

Klein, L. R. 1988. "Carrying Forward the Tinbergen Initiative in Macroeconometrics." *Review of Social Economy* 46:231–51.

Linden, J. T. J. M. van der. 1988. "Economic Thought in the Netherlands: The Contribution of Professor Jan Tinbergen." *Review of Social Economy* 46:270–82.

Lucas, R. E. Jr. [1976] 1981. "Econometric Policy Evaluation: A Critique." In *Stud-*

ies in *Business-Cycle Theory,* 104–30. Cambridge: MIT Press.

Magnus, J. R. and M. S. Morgan. 1987. "The ET Interview: Professor J. Tinbergen." *Econometric Theory* 3:117–42.

Morgan, M. S. 1989. *The History of Econometric Ideas.* Cambridge: Cambridge Univ. Press.

Passell, P. 1994. "Jan Tinbergen, Dutch Economist and Nobel Laureate, Dies at 91." *New York Times,* 14 June, D20.

Tinbergen, J. 1930. "Bestimmung und Deutung von Angebotskurven: Ein Beispiel." *Zeitschrift für Nationalökonomie* 1:669–79.

———. [1931] 1959. "A Shipbuilding Cycle?" In *Selected Papers,* 1–14. Translation. Amsterdam: North-Holland.

———. 1932. "Ein Problem der Dynamik." *Zeitscrhift für Nationalökonomie* 3:169–84.

———. [1936] 1959. "An Economic Policy for 1936." In *Selected Papers,* 37–84. Amsterdam: North-Holland.

———. 1937. *An Econometric Approach to Business Cycle Problems.* Actualités scientifiques et industrielles no. 525. Paris: Hermann & Cie.

———. 1938. *Les Fondements Mathematiques de la Stabilisation du Mouvement des Affaires.* Actualités scientifiques et industrielles no. 632 Paris: Hermann & Cie.

———. 1939. *Statistical Testing of Business Cycle Theories.* 2 vols. Geneva: League of Nations.

———. 1951. *Business Cycles in the United Kingdom, 1870–1914.* Amsterdam: North-Holland.

———. 1956. *Economic Policy: Principles and Design.* Amsterdam: North-Holland.

———. 1959. *Selected Papers.* Edited by L. H. Klaasen, L. M. Koyck, and H. J. Witteveen. Amsterdam: North-Holland.

Wolff, P. de and J. T. J. M. van der Linden. 1988. "Jan Tinbergen: A Quantitative Economist." *Review of Social Economy* 46:312–25.

Tintner, Gerhard (1907–1983)

A distinguished scholar in economics, mathematics, and statistics, Gerhard Tintner made fundamental contributions to economic theory, econometrics, and operations research. His work is intimately tied to the study of economic fluctuations, centering on expectations, uncertainty, and dynamics, the essence of business cycles. In the late 1930s, inspired by the works of Roos and Evans, he began a research program to extend static consumer and production theory into the time dimension and incorporate stochastic elements into economic theory.

Tintner received his doctorate in economics, statistics, and law at the University of Vienna in 1929. Most of his career was spent at Iowa State University (1937–62) and the University of Southern California (1963–73). From 1973 until shortly before his death in 1983, he was professor of econometrics at the Technische Universität in Vienna.

In his early work, between 1936 and the late 1940s, Tintner anticipated some important results in modern business-cycle and growth theory and the nonstatic theories of production, choice, and technological risk and uncertainty which were independently discovered by others a decade or two later (Fox 1988, 42). Tintner's later contributions broadened the scope of the stochastic approach in economics to discrete probability models, stochastic processes, stochastic-programming models, and control-theoretic models, many of them with applications to business cycles and economic planning. A complete bibliography of Tintner's publications is included in a volume of articles dedicated to his memory (Sengupta and Kadekodi 1988). An evaluation of Tintner's scientific work in all fields is given by Kadekodi et al. (1988) while Fox (1988) discusses the incorporation of the works of the early mathematical economists such as Roos, Evans, Davis, and Tintner into the later economic literature.

Tintner's first major economic contribution was *Prices in the Trade Cycle,* begun under the guidance of F. A. Hayek at the Institute for Trade Cycle Research in Vienna, which investigated the behavior of a large number of prices in European countries and in the United States before World War I. Finding that the cyclical movements differed greatly across industries (as other researchers have found for later periods), he concluded that the cyclical price movements were not uniform enough to be captured by a general index number.

In 1942 he published "A 'Simple' Theory of Business Fluctuations," a methodological article whose emphasis on market clearing and the importance of relative prices and substitution effects is quite modern. It may be considered as the simplest possible dynamic generalization of the Walrasian system of general equilibrium that derives business fluctuations from the existence of interrelated speculative markets. It can encompass a great variety of economic structures, such as those found in some recent real-business-cycle models. The buyers and sellers in these markets react not to actual prices but to anticipated prices (which depend on prevailing prices and the rate of change of prices in time). If the anticipations of buyers and sellers are asymmetrical, periodic fluctuations in prices and quantities may arise. All prices and quantities affected by the cycle will show the same period but may have different amplitudes and leads and lags, the essential characteristics of the business cycle. Thus, unanticipated changes in tastes and technology may cause shocks that will be propagated throughout the economy and can be responsible for recurrent sequences of expansions and contractions in aggregate economic activity.

Given the great variety in the movement of prices (and indeed also of wages), this simple business-cycle model, with its disaggregated structure and the explicit consideration of price-change effects on supply and demand, seems to be better suited than an aggregate model for investigating the controversy surrounding the Pigou effect: can a capitalist market economy be trapped in a depression, or is the depression just one point along a cyclical path? Tintner applied the model empirically in "The 'Simple' Theory of Business Fluctuations: A Tentative Verification," involving three price indexes (stock prices, wholesale prices of farm products, and prices of non-farm products) for the United States in the interwar period.

A discrete version of the simple business-cycle model (Tintner 1974) in the form of a Leontief model also explains both a long-term trend and the business cycle (again with strong similarities to more recent business-cycle models, e.g., Kydland and Prescott [1982]). The cyclical fluctuations coincide with the period of production in Böhm-Bawerk's theory.

Tintner's work throughout emphasized a broad view of probability in the behavioral sciences and economics and the need to understand the dynamics of individual and social behavior underlying most time series. Tintner sought to adapt the methods of cybernetics and systems theory to social modeling, emphasizing their potential for policy applications in economics and applying stochastic control theory

before most economists could visualize these connections.

Wolfgang Pollan

See also REAL BUSINESS-CYCLE THEORIES; TASTE SHOCKS

Bibliography

Fox, K. A. 1988. "Econometrics Needs a History: Two Cases of Conspicuous Neglect." In *The Econometrics of Planning and Efficiency,* edited by J. K. Sengupta and G. K. Gopal, 23–47. Boston: Kluwer.

Fox, K. A., J. K. Sengupta, and G. V. L. Narasimham, eds. 1969. *Economic Models, Estimation and Risk Programming: Essays in Honor of Gerhard Tintner.* Berlin: Springer.

Kadekodi, G. K., T. K. Kumar, and J. K. Sengupta. 1988. "The Scientific Work of Gerhard Tintner." In *The Econometrics of Planning and Efficiency,* edited by J. K. Sengupta and G. K. Gopal, 3–22. Boston: Kluwer.

Kydland, E. and E. C. Prescott. 1982. "Time to Build and Aggregate Fluctuations." *Econometrica* 50:1345–70.

Sengupta, J. K. and G. K. Kadekodi, eds. 1988. *The Econometrics of Planning and Efficiency.* Boston: Kluwer.

Tintner, G. 1935. *Prices in the Trade Cycle.* Vienna: Julius Springer.

———. 1942. "A 'Simple' Theory of Business Fluctuations." *Econometrica* 10:317–20.

———. 1944. The 'Simple' Theory of Business Fluctuations: A Tentative Verification." *Review of Economic Statistics* 26:148–57.

———. 1974. "Linear Economics and the Böhm-Bawerk Period of Production." *Quarterly Journal of Economics* 88:127–32.

Tintner, G. and J. K. Sengupta. 1972. *Stochastic Economics: Stochastic Processes, Control, and Programming.* New York: Academic Press.

Tobin, James (1918 –)

James Tobin's contributions range over the entire spectrum of economics. This essay reviews his contributions to monetary and macroeconomic theory, and finally considers his contributions to the debate on stabilization policy.

Financial Theory and the Demand for Money
Theoretical work on the demand for money concerns the transactions motives and risk-related, speculative, and precautionary motives for holding money. Tobin's early work helped dispel the notion that these motives could legitimately be treated separately.

The pre-Keynesian model of the demand for money, embodied in the equation of exchange, stressed the technology of transactions, attributing rather mechanical behavior to agents. In particular, it failed to explain why agents would *hold* cash balances; even if they were required to *use* cash in transactions, it would pay to *hold* interest-bearing assets and convert to cash when transactions occurred. In a 1956 paper, Tobin filled this gap by introducing transactions costs so that interest-bearing assets would not dominate money; households face a nontrivial choice between earning interest and incurring "brokerage" costs when cash is needed for transactions. The key proposition is that even with exogenous transactions, economizing on cash balances is possible and the demand for cash is interest-elastic.

In a fundamental 1958 paper, Tobin explained why individuals hold fiat money instead of other assets that bear positive interest, and why there is a negative relationship between the quantity of cash demanded and the yield on interest-bearing alternatives. Tobin also demonstrated the "separation" or "mutual fund" theorem, which has since become a centerpiece of the theory of finance. The breakthrough was to specify interest-rate expectations as a probability distribution rather than as a scalar. Liquidity preference results from the risk associated with the dispersion of the probability distribution, answering the objection that Keynes's liquidity preference presumes biased (i.e., irrational) expectations. Tobin showed that risk averters would diversify their portfolios between money, postulated to be a safe asset with a zero nominal yield, and a risky (basket of) asset(s) bearing a positive expected net return. He also showed that under plausible assumptions, the share of money in the portfolio would fall if the yield on the risky assets rose.

Macroeconomic Theory
The major issues in macroeconomic theory may be divided into two distinct categories, and Tobin has made important contributions to both. The first is how a given change in nominal income is divided between price-level changes and output changes (i.e., the analysis of aggregate supply). The second concerns how various exogenous and policy-induced disturbances cause national income to change (i.e., analysis of the transmission mechanism and the linkages between the monetary and real sectors of the economy).

Aggregate Supply
Tobin's first published paper (1941) discussed whether a cut in money wages would affect aggregate employment independently (i.e., other than via an effect on interest rates). This issue, of course, was central to the debate then raging about Keynes's *General Theory*. In 1955, Tobin published a three-installment paper with Challis Hall presenting a complete macroeconomic system and a full taxonomy of "special cases" on both the demand and supply sides. Explicitly derived, illustrated, and applied were the aggregate demand and supply curves that were considered an innovation many years later. The "missing equation," widely regarded as one of Milton Friedman's major contributions, was anticipated by fifteen years. The paper also anticipated "supply-side economics" by carefully analyzing the impact of taxes on labor supply in a neoclassical setting wherein factor supplies constrain output.

In his 1971 Presidential address to the American Economic Association, Tobin (1972) returned to the analysis of wages and aggregate supply, responding in particular to the influential Phelps-Friedman natural-rate hypothesis (Friedman [1968] 1969, Phelps 1967). Tobin argued that the zero-inflation unemployment rate is neither optimal, efficient, nor even "natural." Tobin also discussed search theory and the natural rate, arguing persuasively that there is no reason to believe that the natural rate gives rise to optimal search.

A related contribution of his Presidential address is an eloquent restatement of Keynes's hypothesis that workers' concerns about relative wages cause nominal-wage rigidities. This "wage-wage" model led Tobin to view inflation as "inertial" in nature, so that changes in aggregate demand primarily affect output rather than prices. This is true even if expectations are rational, since the inertial forces create a distinction between the ability to form expectations and the ability to act on them immediately.

Aggregate Demand
Tobin's contributions here are in two areas: the relationship between wealth and consumption

and the relationship between asset equilibrium and investment demand. Focusing on the wealth-consumption relationship within the life-cycle model, Tobin often rejected the convenient assumption of "perfect capital markets," which reduces the consumption-income relationship to a straightforward intertemporal-choice problem. Tobin argued that capital-market imperfections impose liquidity constraints on many households, so that current consumption is closely tied to current income. If households are liquidity-constrained, monetary policy can influence demand both directly by altering liquidity constraints and indirectly via conventional wealth/interest-rate channels.

The basic framework central to most macroeconomic inquiries on investment stems from Tobin, who relied extensively on Keynes's notion of the supply price of capital. Tobin first formally stated this key stock-flow relationship in a 1955 paper, "A Dynamic Aggregative Model," in which he linked the ideas central to Keynesian short-run macroeconomic models with the growth literature associated with Harrod, Hicks, Goodwin, and others. In retrospect, this paper seems far ahead of its time, foreshadowing the literature of the 1960s and 1970s on money and economic growth. This strand of his work illustrates the attention he has given to the relationship between short-run fluctuations and long-term growth.

In 1969, Tobin presented a formal summary of the framework which he had been using for over a decade. Of particular historical interest was the substitution of the relative price of capital goods (Tobin's q) for Keynes's rate of return (the supply price of capital). The two, of course, are monotonically related. Besides being observable in principle, q perhaps conveys the spirit of the model better than does the supply price of capital. The basic model contains demand for a stock of capital and the supply of a flow of investment; the relative price and the equilibrium rates of return are determined in asset markets, and the level of investment is that flow offered by suppliers at that relative price.

Stabilization Policy and the Monetarist Controversy

Tobin has contributed enormously to the theory of stabilization policy and has been actively involved in policy debates. His views on how to achieve given policy objectives reflect his analysis of the monetary mechanism and the determination of consumption and investment.

However, in controversies over policy he has often argued about what policy objectives should be pursued. These positions largely reflect his analysis of wage formation and aggregate supply.

Tobin has consistently advocated active demand management; he has also stressed the need to complement these policies with wage-price guideposts, incomes policies, negative income taxes, labor-market policies, etc. In the 1970s, the phenomenon of supply-shock-induced stagflation caused disagreement not only on "whether to use demand policy," but also on the *direction* in which to adjust policy. In these debates, Tobin has steadfastly advocated expansionary policy.

Worse still, in his view, is the policy of deliberately engineering recessions to combat inflation. In his 1980 address to the Royal Economic Society he argued that this is precisely what happened in each of the three recessions in the United States during the 1970s.

Tobin has often taken up the Keynesian banner in both public and professional debates on Monetarism. His participation in the debate probably starts with his review of Friedman's 1963 work with Anna Schwartz, (henceforth F-S). He distinguished two parts in their analysis: one concerning the determination of the stock of money and one concerning the determination of velocity. On the first, Tobin carefully discussed the research strategies F-S used in choosing a definition, and sought to compensate for the lack of consideration of alternative definitions by outlining a case for these alternatives.

Tobin's discussion of the F-S analysis of velocity, particularly of their explanation of the secular decline in velocity as indicating that money is a luxury whose income elasticity of demand exceeds unity, was more critical. He rejected the analogy both on empirical (firms hold most of the money) and theoretical (it is the services of money that are desired) grounds, and suggested an alternative explanation in terms of liquidity-preference theory. The sharp disagreement about the stability and independence of velocity mirrors a recurring point—the ambiguity of the causal inference to be drawn from the correlation between money and income. In 1970, Tobin offered an example of how an extreme Keynesian model could generate the timing relationships that Friedman interpreted as supporting the Monetarist view. Tobin did not suggest that these models were serious models of the economy; his point was methodological, concerning "the dangers of accepting timing evidence as empirical proof of propositions about causation" (1970, 303).

Ironically, the recent rational-expectations revolution *within* the Monetarist camp has provided additional arguments undermining any causal interpretation of timing relations. A further irony is the recent development of real-business-cycle theory, which jettisons any role for monetary factors and focuses on a stochastic Arrow-Debreu general-equilibrium model to explain business cycles. Much of the focus is on supply disturbances, in contradistinction to the traditional emphasis on demand disturbances. Another central distinction is whether business cycles are best interpreted as temporary, disequilibrium departures from trend growth, or as equilibrium phenomena. The modern real-business-cycle view is the latter, while Tobin and Friedman are both associated with the former. Thus, since both Tobin and Friedman essentially subscribe to a Phillips-curve-augmented *IS-LM* paradigm, the differences between them are minimal compared to the differences both of them have with the real-business-cycle view.

Conclusion

Tobin's work clearly demonstrates a theme common in the work of all important scientists—a persistent challenge to orthodox ideas and opinion, and an unwillingness to accept superficial answers to substantial questions. Thus, Tobin refused to accept the mechanical nature of traditional formulations of the demand for money; he reformulated Keynes's liquidity-preference theory to resolve certain anomalies in that theory, giving new life to its basic implications. Similarly he challenged the widely accepted properties of the so-called "natural" rate of unemployment. Such examples of Tobin's challenges to orthodoxy followed by the development of original and plausible alternatives are instances of what his teacher Joseph Schumpeter might have called the "process of creative destruction."

Douglas D. Purvis

See also AGGREGATE SUPPLY AND DEMAND; DEMAND FOR MONEY; FINANCIAL INTERMEDIATION; FISCAL POLICY; FRIEDMAN, MILTON; INVESTMENT; MONETARY POLICY; MONETARY DISEQUILIBRIUM THEORIES OF THE BUSINESS CYCLE; MONEY-INCOME CAUSALITY; NATURAL RATE OF UNEMPLOYMENT; REAL BUSINESS-CYCLE THEORIES; SEARCH THEORY; SUPPLY OF MONEY

Bibliography

Brainard, W. C., W. Nordhaus, and H. W. Watts, eds. 1991. *Money, Macroeconomics, and Economic Policy: Essays in Honor of James Tobin.* Cambridge: MIT Press.

Friedman, M. [1968] 1969. "The Role of Monetary Policy." Chap. 5 in *The Optimum Quantity of Money and Other Essays.* Chicago: Aldine.

———. 1970. "A Theoretical Framework for Monetary Analysis." *Journal of Political Economy* 78:193–238.

Friedman, M. and A. J. Schwartz. 1963. *A Monetary History of the United States 1817–1960.* Princeton: Princeton Univ. Press.

Phelps, E. S. 1967. "Phillips Curves, Expectations of Inflation, Optimal Unemployment over Time." *Economica* 34:254–81.

Purvis, D. D. 1980. "Monetarism: A Review." *Canadian Journal of Economics* 13:96–122.

———. 1991. "James Tobin's Contributions to Economics." In *Money, Macroeconomics, and Economic Policy: Essays in Honor of James Tobin,* edited by W. C. Brainard, W. Nordhaus, and H. W. Watts, 1–42. Cambridge: MIT Press.

Tobin, J. 1941. "A Note on the Money Wage Problem." *Quarterly Journal of Economics* 55:508–16.

———. 1955. "A Dynamic Aggregative Model." *Journal of Political Economy* 63:103–15.

———. 1956. "The Interest Elasticity of the Transactions Demand for Cash." *Review of Economics and Statistics* 38:241–57.

———. 1958. "Liquidity Preference as Behavior Towards Risk." *Review of Economics Studies* 25:65–86.

———. 1969. "A General Equilibrium Approach to Monetary Theory." *The Journal of Money, Credit, and Banking* 1:15–29.

———. 1970. "Money and Income: Post Hoc Ergo Propter Hoc?" *Quarterly Journal of Economics* 84:301–17.

———. 1972. "Inflation and Unemployment." *American Economic Review* 62:1–18.

———. 1977. "How Dead Is Keynes?" *Economic Inquiry* 15:459–68.

———. 1981. "The Monetarist Counter-Revolution Today—An Appraisal." *Economic Journal* 91:29–42.

Tobin, J. and C. A. Hall Jr. 1955–56. "Income Taxation, Output, and Prices." *Economia Internazionale* 8:522–542, 742–761; 9:1–8.

———. 1987. *Essays in Economics.* 2 vols. Cambridge: MIT Press.

Tooke, Thomas (1774–1858)

Thomas Tooke was known among his contemporaries as a collector and interpreter of prices. The six volumes of *The History of Prices* contain unique data about prices, a historical treatment of their main trends as well as attempts to explain and theorize about them. While some commentators regarded Tooke as a poor theoretician (Schumpeter even described him as a "wooly thinker"), others considered him an important figure in the development of monetary economics and banking theories.

Tooke published his first book in 1823 when he was forty-nine years old. He continued publishing until 1857—a year before his death. In the interim he changed his views quite dramatically. Starting as a follower of Ricardo, albeit with some important differences, Tooke ended up as one of his better-known critics. Accepting the quantity theory of money and other Ricardian monetary doctrines until the late 1830s, he thereafter rejected them. His critique led to the emergence of the famous Banking School. In 1844, during the intensive debate about the Bank Charter Act, Tooke published a pamphlet, *An Inquiry into the Currency Principle,* expressing monetary views entirely different from those of his first period. Tooke now argued that there is no theoretical distinction between banknotes and other means of payment such as checks and bills of exchange. In addition, Tooke argued that the quantity theory, which asserts that prices depend on the quantity of the medium in circulation, is wrong. Instead Tooke, and the Banking School, thought that under convertibility the quantity of the medium in circulation is determined by prices. Prices, he now argued, are determined ultimately by the incomes of the consumers.

Tooke's break with conventional wisdom was gradual. To understand it fully, one must consider the complicated issue of applying free-trade principles to banking. This fundamental issue, more than any other, separated Tooke

from the Currency School. After opposing the application of free-trade principles to issuing notes in his early writings, Tooke changed his mind by 1844, and became a systematic advocate of competition in the supply of notes. In the background, one should recall, was the famous debate on the 1844–45 Bank Charter Act. Supporters of the Act, the Currency School, proposed monopolizing note issues, while Tooke wanted note issuing to remain in the hands of the many country banks as well as in those of the Bank of England.

However, even as his views were shifting towards the new, innovative, Banking School theory, Tooke was convinced of the utmost importance of credit in the economy. While he had originally ignored the role banks play in determining the quantity of credit, allowing this function of the banks too to be governed by free-market forces, he continued to grapple with this difficult issue in later years. Thus, while his new position on money initially led him to oppose any discretion on the part of the banks, and in particular the Bank of England, in conducting monetary policy, his view gradually changed between 1844 and 1858. In these years, Tooke published the fourth volume of *A History of Prices* in 1848, a pamphlet *On the Bank Charter Act of 1844* in 1856, and then, in collaboration with Newmarch, the last two volumes of his monumental work in 1857. In these writings, as well as in his last committee appearance in 1848, Tooke sought to clarify his position on free trade in banking. His views remained incomplete, since he never developed a theory of how credit should be controlled, leaving it entirely to the Bank Directors' discretion. If Tooke deserves criticism for being atheoretical, it is on this point.

Tooke had a unique theory about "waves" in the economy, which one is tempted to call a crisis or a cycle theory. However, Gregory (1928, 19) was probably correct in arguing that Tooke's theory "is not equivalent to a theory of cyclical fluctuation." His was not a theory of cycles in the usual sense of this term, since it did not attempt to explain the sources of crisis in capitalist production endogenously. His argument rested on exogenous changes, mainly, but not exclusively, changing seasons. The rise in prices, which is the outcome of either a bad season or "new sources of demand," encourages borrowers to increase borrowing and lenders to increase lending, since they feel secure in the future. This is often known as a "confidence" situation. Borrowers anticipate price rises and prefer to keep their product (stock) longer or to buy "beneficial investments," whereas the lenders' securities which increase in value leave room for further advances.

Tooke maintained that such "waves," whereby an increase in prices induces an increase in the quantity of the medium in circulation (composed of "money" and "credit") which is followed by further increases in prices, continues until real counter-tendencies appear. Such counter-tendencies could either be exogenous, such as a good season, or endogenous. In all events, the monetary system can, for considerable periods of time, be in what Ricardian theory would consider a state of disequilibrium. Thus, when one considers fairly long periods, variations in the quantity of notes do not occur independently of variations in the money base.

Tooke considered monetary phenomena to be subordinate to and induced by real phenomena. He explained changes in the cycle of commodities mainly in terms of natural changes. Nevertheless, the monetary cycle does have a certain quantitative influence on the "real" one. Thus, if a contraction begins because of natural causes, money and credit circulation can amplify the disturbance into a larger wave. However, beyond attributing contractions and expansions to changes in nature, Tooke did not analyze their causes, and thus never developed a theory that specifically addressed the problem of crises under capitalism.

The issues with which Tooke struggled are of utmost importance in any monetary economy and are still debated today. Thus, it is not surprising that his views influenced many later economists from various traditions. Both Marx and Wicksell, for example, read Tooke carefully and acknowledged his influence. His later Banking School positions, when Tooke defended the endogeneity of money, the "reverse" causality between money and prices (from P to M and not, as traditional theory assumes, from M to P), and the immense importance of credit, have resurfaced frequently since Tooke stated them. Echoes of similar views are now found in the writings of the New Classical macroeconomics, the New Monetary economics and the post-Keynesian tradition. The same modern flavor is manifested also in Tooke's more general position on free trade in banking. Related issues such as rules versus discretion or no intervention at all are still open questions in monetary theory.

In his earlier writings, Tooke, like many other quantity theorists from Ricardo to Friedman, preferred rules over discretionary policies by the central bank. However, with the transformation in his thought in his later years, Tooke, somewhat like Hayek, was drawn to the possibility of applying free-trade principles to banking, at least to note-issue if not to credit at large.

Arie Arnon

See also BANK CHARTER ACT OF 1844; BANKING SCHOOL, CURRENCY SCHOOL, AND FREE BANKING SCHOOL; ENDOGENOUS AND EXOGENOUS MONEY; FREE BANKING; FULLARTON, JOHN; MONEY-INCOME CAUSALITY; RICARDO, DAVID

Bibliography

Arnon, A. 1991. *Thomas Tooke: Pioneer of Monetary Theory.* Ann Arbor: Univ. of Michigan Press.

Gregory, T. E. 1928. "Introduction." In T. Tooke and W. Newmarch, *A History of Prices.* London: King and Sons.

Laidler, D. [1972] 1975. "Tooke on Monetary Reform." Chap. 11 in *Essays on Money and Inflation.* Chicago: Univ. of Chicago Press.

Rist, C. 1940. *History of Monetary and Credit Theory from John Law to the Present Day.* London: Allen and Unwin.

Tooke, T. 1823. *Thoughts and Details on the High and Low Prices of the Last Thirty Years.* 2 vols. London: John Murray.

———. 1826. *Considerations on the State of the Currency.* 2d ed. London: John Murray.

———. 1838. *A History of Prices and the State of the Circulation from 1793 to 1837.* Vols. 1–2. London: Longman, Brown, Green, Longmans.

———. 1840. *A History of Prices and the State of the Circulation from 1838, 1839.* Vol. 3. London: Longman, Brown, Green, Longmans.

———. 1844. *An Inquiry into the Currency Principle: The Connection of the Currency with Prices and the Expediency of a Separation of Issue from Banking.* London: Longman, Brown, Green, Longmans.

———. 1848. *A History of Prices and the State of the Circulation from 1839 to*

1847. Vol. 4. London: Longman, Brown, Green, Longmans.

———. 1856. *On the Bank Charter Act of 1844, its Principles and Operation.* London: Longman, Brown, Green, Longmans.

Tooke, T. and W. Newmarch. 1857. *A History of Prices and the State of the Circulation from 1848–1856.* Vols. 5–6. London: Longman, Brown, Green, Longmans.

Wicksell, K. [1906] 1935. *Lectures on Political Economy.* Vol. 2. *Money.* Translation. London: Routledge and Kegan Paul.

Torrens, Robert (1780–1864)

Robert Torrens, Royal Marine, South Australia Commissioner, and government contractor, was an important classical economist whose writings on money and trade constitute a vital part of the classical economic literature.

In his early work, produced while still an officer in the Royal Marines, Torrens was not only an adherent of the Anti-Bullionist position, but an inflationist. Inflation had many desirable characteristics in his view, especially its stimulative impact on economic activity. He had no qualms about the loss to fixed-income recipients, who were only a small part of the community and might themselves be moved to effort. He favored a paper currency, the supply of which could easily be increased in response to increased demand. Depreciation of the exchanges did not in itself indicate a depreciation of the currency, which could only be inferred from changes in the prices of nontraded goods.

As late as 1819, Torrens was arguing that Ricardo's bullion plan was faulty because it would make the currency fluctuate as a metallic currency would have done. By 1826, however, Torrens had adopted a more favorable attitude towards Ricardo's plan, though he still tried to avoid advocating that the currency should fluctuate as if it were purely metallic, suggesting a system of convertibility lagged by a delay of three months. At this stage he was still taking the view that depreciation of the exchanges did not necessarily require contraction of the currency.

By 1833, he was prepared to advocate a bullion standard similar to that of Ricardo, although based on silver rather than gold; and in the years 1837–44, Torrens emerged as a leading member of the Currency School, building his theoretical model and his policy recommendations on the Ricardian definition of excess issue of currency—if the exchange was depreciated, then, *by definition,* the note issue was too large to maintain equilibrium in an open economy.

Thus, after 1837, Torrens adhered to the principle that the money supply should fluctuate in amount exactly as if it had been purely metallic, so that a balance-of-payments deficit, involving metal export, should reduce the money supply *parri passu.* This required separating the Bank of England into Issue and Banking Departments. Gold for export could be obtained only by reducing the note issue, rather than merely by drawing down deposits as had previously been the case; for a deposit would be redeemed in Bank of England notes, which had then to be presented at the Issue Department—thus taken out of circulation—to obtain gold.

Regulating the money supply in this way would stabilize economic activity, automatically dampening upswings and downswings in activity. This rule for controlling the money supply came to be known as the *Currency Principle;* the alternative principle, which involved varying the money supply in response to changes in the demand for money, was the *Banking Principle.* This, in Torrens's view, would amplify rather than dampen economic fluctuations. It would also gravely endanger convertibility of the note issue into gold—an objective that was not an issue between the Currency and Banking Schools. Both agreed that the only alternative to convertibility was long-term inflation.

However, Torrens's views on monetary control involved a number of difficulties. First, there was the question of control of that part of the money supply originating with the country banks rather than the Bank of England. By 1844, he had come to accept Overstone's argument that the country banks had plenty of scope for disequilibration in the short term. The second problem related to bank deposits. Torrens in fact was one of the first writers (after James Pennington) to put forward the concept of the bank-deposit multiplier. But he emphasized, particularly under the influence of Overstone, that deposits themselves were not money as they could not be used in final settlement. Instead, he maintained they increased the velocity of circulation. Torrens thought that deposits could be controlled through reserve ratios, although experiences in the years after 1844 seem to have made him more pessimistic about this.

The third problem related to the role of the central bank as lender of last resort and the possible need for an overriding "Relaxing Power" which would permit note issue to increase when the gold reserve was falling owing to an exceptional *internal* demand for cash. Like the other members of the Currency School, Torrens both supported the exercise of such a function in practice (in 1847 and 1857) but opposed a creation of a statutory power (which would undermine the prudential limits which bankers would otherwise place on themselves within the monetary framework of the 1844 Bank Charter Act). The idea that a developed fractional-reserve banking system fundamentally requires a lender of last resort was one that Torrens, like his Currency School colleagues, was unwilling to recognize.

Torrens was an extremely able, and agile, monetary theorist and controversialist. There can be little doubt that his adoption in the 1830s of a theoretical structure and policy recommendations based closely on the Ricardian definition of an excess currency issue contributed fundamentally both to the strength of the Currency School and to the form, and indeed the subsequent survival, of the Bank Charter Act of 1844.

D. P. O'Brien

See also BANK CHARTER ACT OF 1844; BANKING SCHOOL, CURRENCY SCHOOL, AND FREE BANKING SCHOOL; BULLIONIST CONTROVERSIES; FULLARTON, JOHN; LOYD, SAMUEL JONES; RICARDO, DAVID; TOOKE, THOMAS

Bibliography

O'Brien, D. P. 1965. "The Transition in Torrens' Monetary Thought." *Economica* 22:269–301.

Robbins, L. 1958. *Robert Torrens and the Evolution of Classical Economics.* London: Macmillan.

Torrens, R. 1837. *A Letter to the Right Honourable Viscount Melbourne on the Causes of the Recent Derangement in the Money Market and on Bank Reform.* London: Longmans.

———. 1844. *An Inquiry into the Practical Working of the Proposed Arrangements for the Renewal of the Charter of the Bank of England and the Regulation of the Currency.* London: Smith, Elder.

———. 1858. *The Principles and Practical Operation of Sir Robert Peel's Act of 1844, Explained and Defended.* 3d ed. London: Longmans.

Trends and Random Walks

Folk wisdom holds that choice of war strategies is far too important to be left to the generals. And the policy implications of the trend-cycle decomposition are far too important to relegate to a technical problem for econometricians. The problem is to decompose an observable series, say GNP, into its unobservable components, the trend and the cycle. The problem is similar to extracting the seasonal components of a series, but the policy implications are quite different. Weathermen only try to forecast the weather; they (at least, so far) don't try to control it. In contrast, the primary objective of macroeconomic policy in the United States, as codified in the Employment Act of 1946, is to moderate the business cycle. The decomposition of economic data into their trend and cycle components determines the measured amplitude of the cycle and hence the measured depth of the recession.

The more a decomposition smooths the trend component the more it amplifies the cyclical component, and vice-versa. It was, and still is, fairly standard practice to identify the historical average growth rate of real GNP as the constant trend, or potential, growth rate of output. Most macroeconomics texts illustrate the gap between potential output generated by a constant exponential trend and actual output. And, Federal Reserve officials frequently justify tighter monetary policy, e.g., 1988–89, as a response to an observed GNP growth that exceeds the "potential" growth. Measured average growth rates, however, are quite volatile. In the forty-five years after World War II, the real growth of GNP in the United States averaged 3 percent, but over the last half of the interval (since 1970), it averaged only 2.5 percent (see the pictures in Stock and Watson's excellent survey).

Beveridge and Nelson (1981) and Nelson and Plosser (1982) modified the traditional notion of a deterministic exponential trend by adding a stochastic error. This seemingly intuitive and harmless generalization launched hot and still unsettled debate. Nelson and Plosser found that a geometric random walk with drift explained most of the variation in GNP. The stochastic component of the trend absorbed almost all the variation previously assigned to the cycle, leaving little room (or need) for active countercyclical policy. The proponents of active policy attacked their results while the advocates of nonintervention used Nelson and Plosser's results to support their position.

The debate remains unsettled, because low frequency movements (the trend) are very hard to measure accurately (see the entry on unit root tests). Cyclical or seasonal components sum to zero after removing the trend or annual average. We observe annual data, so the seasonal extraction problem reduces to measuring systematic high-frequency deviations from the observable annual average. The trend, however, is unobservable. So extracting cyclical components requires joint estimation of the low-frequency trend and higher-frequency cycle. By definition, the trend is highly serially correlated, so each time-series observation carries little independent information. As a result, a precise estimate of the trend requires more data, or better econometric methods, than we have today. Nevertheless, this is a technical problem whose consequences are far too important for practical policymakers to ignore. Small changes in the trend lead to large changes in future output, and small changes in the trend, e.g., from 2.5 to 3 percent, change observed positive gaps from potential output into zero or negative gaps.

Roger Craine

See also ASYMMETRY; COMPOSITE TRENDS; FILTERS; GOODWIN, RICHARD MURPHEY; GROWTH CYCLES; SEASONAL ADJUSTMENT; UNIT ROOT TESTS

Bibliography

Beveridge, S. and C. R. Nelson. 1981. "A New Approach to Decomposition of Economic Time Series into Permanent and Transitory Components with Particular Attention to Measurement of the Business Cycle." *Journal of Monetary Economics* 7:151–74.

Cochrane, J. H. 1988. "How Big is the Random Walk in GNP?" *Journal of Political Economy* 96:893–920.

Nelson, C. R. and C. I. Plosser. 1982. "Trends and Random Walks in Macroeconomic Time Series: Some Evidence and Implications." *Journal of Monetary Economics* 10:139–62.

Stock, J. H. and M. W. Watson. 1988. "Variable Trends in Economic Time Series." *Journal of Economic Perspectives*, Summer, 147–74.

Tugan-Baranovsky, Mikhail Ivanovich (1865–1919)

Mikhail Tugan-Baranovsky was easily the most distinguished of the Russian revisionist Marxists in the quarter-century before 1914, his work being influential also in German-speaking Western Europe. Tugan-Baranovsky attacked the prevalent underconsumptionist interpretation of Marx's theory of crisis, and articulated a cogent and original critique of the analysis of the falling rate of profit in volume 3 of *Capital*. His own crisis theory centered on the role of disproportions between the various departments of production.

Half-Ukrainian and half-Tartar, Tugan-Baranovsky studied natural science, law, and economics, and taught economics at several Russian universities, including St. Petersburg. At first active in the socialist movement, he was a firm opponent of both populism and, increasingly, of orthodox Marxism. Tugan-Baranovsky returned to the Ukraine in 1917 and was appointed Finance Minister in the provisional government in Kiev shortly before his death.

Tugan-Baranovsky's views on economic crises were formed by his detailed analysis of the schemes of economic reproduction set out by Marx in the second volume of *Capital*. This led him to reject underconsumptionism. Capitalist production was undertaken for profit, not for the direct satisfaction of human needs. Tugan-Baranovsky concluded from this that there was in principle no limit to the extent to which capitalists might act as their own customers. With an increasing organic composition of capital, this implied that the realization of surplus value would become increasingly independent of consumption needs, so that the accumulation of capital involved producing means of production in order to produce yet more means of production. However irrational such accumulation might appear, Tugan-Baranovsky argued, there was no reason why it should not be viable indefinitely, so long as the correct proportions were maintained between the consumer-goods and investment-goods sectors. It was the absence in capitalism of any mechanism to ensure such proportionality which explained the occurrence of periodic economic crises.

These arguments were directed primarily against those populist economists who claimed that chronic deficiencies in effective demand blocked the full development of Russian capitalism. But they applied also to Marxian proponents of underconsumption theories, providing, for example, the basis for a critique of Rosa Luxemburg's later analysis of imperialism. Several Marxian theoreticians denounced Tugan-Baranovsky as a "harmonist" who believed that crises could be eliminated altogether. This was unfair; his own position was rather to reject any breakdown theory and to deny the prevailing dogma that crises would necessarily become increasingly severe. He believed that capitalism would undergo cyclical fluctuations, and provided a theory, which proved to be influential with non-Marxian economists, to explain them.

Tugan's theory of cyclical fluctuations hinges on the volatility of investment expenditure relative to the supply of loanable funds available to finance them. The level of savings, or, more generally, of idle money balances, is assumed to be roughly constant. When investment is low, this drives down the interest rate. In consequence, investment increases, inducing a cumulative expansion of the entire economy. Loanable funds become depleted, and interest rates rise. Ultimately, investment is choked off and the disproportionality between investment- and consumer-goods production engenders a contraction of economic activity. Conditions promoting a new cycle are thereby created.

This analysis proved influential among non-Marxian economists and, indeed, it had many strengths in comparison with the theories of Tugan's contemporaries. However, its limitations are now evident. Tugan conceived of demands and supplies in a neoclassical fashion, without realizing that deficiencies in aggregate demand then became impossible. In addition, by failing to distinguish between planned and realized saving and investment, he did not clearly establish the basis for an imbalance between loanable funds and accumulation.

In a further break with orthodox Marxism, Tugan-Baranovsky identified a logical error in Marx's account of the falling rate of profit. For Marx, technical progress increased the organic composition of capital more rapidly than the rate of exploitation, leading inexorably to a decline in the rate of profit. The argument can be summarized as follows.

Denote constant capital (the means of production: machinery, raw materials, and the like) by c; variable capital (representing the value of human labor power, or the amount of necessary labor performed) by v and surplus value (representing the remaining surplus labor which is carried out) by s. Then the rate of profit, r, can be written as:

$$r = \frac{s}{c + v} \qquad (1)$$

The organic composition of capital k is defined as the ratio of constant to variable capital, c/v, and the rate of exploitation e as the ratio of surplus value to variable capital, s/v. Dividing both the numerator and the denominator of equation (1) by v, we have:

$$r = \frac{\dfrac{s}{v}}{\dfrac{c + v}{v}} = \frac{e}{k + 1} \qquad (2)$$

so that r falls whenever k rises faster than e.

Tugan-Baranovsky's objection to Marx's analysis concerned the effect of technical progress on the productivity of labor. With a working day of constant length, rising labor productivity reduces necessary labor, since less time is needed to produce the workers' means of subsistence, and surplus labor increases. The rate of exploitation must therefore rise. Tugan-Baranovsky maintained that e would in fact rise at least as rapidly as k, so that the rate of profit cannot fall. In this he anticipated the modern Okishio Theorem on the effect of technical progress on the profit rate, which undermines one major strand in Marxian crisis theory.

The principal contribution of Tugan-Baranovsky was to focus attention on Marx's reproduction models as the basis for any serious study of the economic contradictions of capitalism. Although his own specific analysis of crises was heavily criticized, he had an enduring methodological influence on the development of Marxian political economy.

M. C. Howard
J. E. King

See also BAUER, OTTO; FALLING RATE OF PROFIT; LUXEMBURG, ROSA; MARX, KARL HEINRICH; OVERINVESTMENT THEORIES OF BUSINESS CYCLES

Bibliography

Amato, S. 1984. "Tugan-Baranovsky's Theories of Markets, Accumulation and Industrialisation: Their Influence on the Development of Economic Thought and Modern Historiographic Research." In *Selected Contributions of Ukrainian Scholars to Economics*, edited by I. S. Koropeckyj, 1–59. Cambridge: Harvard Univ. Press.

Howard, M. C. and J. E. King. 1989. *A History of Marxian Economics.* Vol. 1, *1883–1929*. Princeton: Princeton Univ. Press.

Kalecki, M. 1971. "The Problem of Effective Demand in Tugan-Baranovski and Rosa Luxemburg." Chap. 13 in M. Kalecki, *Selected Essays on the Dynamics of the Capitalist Economy, 1933–1970.* Cambridge: Cambridge Univ. Press.

Kowal, L. M. 1973. "The Market and Business Cycle Theories of M. I. Tugan-Baranovsky." *Rivista Internazionale di Scienze Economiche e Commerciale* 4:305–30.

Nove, A. 1970. "M. I. Tugan-Baranovsky (1856–1910)." *History of Political Economy* 2:246–62.

Tugan-Baranovsky, M. I. [1907] 1970. *The Russian Factory in the Nineteenth Century.* 3d ed. Translation. Homewood, Il.: Irwin.

———. 1901. *Studien Zur Theorie und Geschichte der Handelskrisen in England.* Jena: G. Fischer.

———. 1904. "Der Zusammenbruch der Kapitalistischen Wirtschaftsordnung im Lichte der Nationalökonomischen Theori." *Archiv Für Sozialismus und Sozialpolitik* 19:273–306. Reprinted in Tugan-Baranovsky (1905).

———. 1905. *Theoretische Grundlagen des Marxismus.* Leipzig: Duncker & Humblot.

———. 1954. "Periodic Industrial Crises." *Annals of the Ukrainian Academy of Arts and Sciences in the United States III* 3:745–802.

Tulipmania

When asset prices collapse for no obvious fundamental reason, educated observers and participants in asset markets often search for historical examples of bubbles and manias on which to base a crowd-psychology explanation of the collapse. First on this list of examples, the Dutch tulipmania of 1634–37, serves as a warning flag of how far asset prices may diverge from fundamentals. That prices of "intrinsically useless" bulbs could have risen so high and collapsed so rapidly seems to be a definitive example of the instability and irrationality that may infect asset markets.

In spite of regular invocation of this episode, our knowledge of the events of and the institutions surrounding the tulipmania is scanty. The source most often cited, Charles Mackay's *Extraordinary Popular Delusions and the Madness of Crowds,* contained only a seven-page history. The book so strongly influenced the beliefs of Bernard Baruch that he encouraged its reprinting in the 1920s, thereby cultivating it as folk-knowledge in the New York financial markets. Mackay plagiarized his description, with some literary embellishment, from Johann Beckmann's *History of Inventions, Discoveries, and Origins.* Beckmann's research included references to a sequence of commentators about the episode, but all sources ultimately emanate from three anonymously written dialogues between the fictional characters Waermondt (True Mouth) and Gaergoedt (Greedy Goods), published in 1637 after the collapse. These pamphlets were among dozens written just after the tulipmania by anti-speculative partisans attacking speculative markets and especially futures trading.

Most historians of the tulipmania were so intent on demonstrating the follies of speculative markets and, implicitly, on supporting the case for controlling market activities, that they failed to examine the fundamentals of bulb pricing. Yet, the pricing pattern of the valuable bulbs can be explained readily in terms of the fundamentals. Thus, like any large swing in asset prices, the tulipmania can be described in either idiom: that of speculative bubbles or that of market fundamentals.

Tulipmania as Bubble

The standard account of the tulipmania, based on Mackay's story, is the following. The tulip entered Europe from Turkey in the middle of the sixteenth century. It quickly spread to the Netherlands, which became a center of cultivation and development of new varieties. A market for rare varieties of bulbs, which arose among professional growers and wealthy flower fanciers, encouraged high prices. For example, a Semper Augustus bulb could fetch 2000 guilders in 1625, an amount of gold worth $16,000 at $400 an ounce. The high prices were received for rare varieties; bulbs of common varieties were sold for very low prices.

In 1634, nonprofessionals entered the bulb market. By 1636, prices were rising so rapidly that people from all classes liquidated their assets to invest in tulips. In the last frenzy of speculation, prices of all bulbs rose rapidly; for example, a single Semper Augustus bulb sold at the peak for 5500 guilders ($44,000). By way of comparison, Rembrandt was commissioned in 1638 to paint "The Night Watch" for 1200 guilders. In February 1637, the speculation suddenly terminated. Prices collapsed overnight, and bulbs could not be sold for even 5 percent of their peak values. Indeed, by 1639, the prices of all the most prized bulbs of the mania, even Semper Augustus, had fallen to no more than 0.1 guilder—just one-two-hundredth of one percent of the peak value of the Semper Augustus. The collapse led to economic distress in the Netherlands for years afterwards.

Mackay depicts the popular image of a bubble: a rapid increase in bulb prices followed by a sudden collapse to small fractions of the peak prices. The price increase was based on no obvious cause (except perhaps for rumors about the growing popularity of tulips in Paris). Yet, Mackay, before concluding that the episode was a mania, gave no consideration to what price for bulbs would have been dictated by market fundamentals. He provided no transaction prices for the rare bulbs immediately after the collapse. Rather, he reported the highest available tulip bulb prices from 60, 130, and 200 years after the collapse, as an indication of market fundamental prices. That these latter prices were far below prices during the tulipmania is interpreted as evidence of misalignment of prices during the mania.

In agreeing that the event was a mania, modern observers must have compared the reported prices with an implicit market fundamental price and found the divergence excessive. Tulip bulbs, after all, are intrinsically worthless agricultural commodities which can be rapidly reproduced. Any sharp rise in their prices should have been moderated or even precluded by a rational understanding that an immense supply response would quickly follow.

Tulipmania as Market Fundamentals

The tulip market involved only bulbs affected by a mosaic virus whose primary effect was to create strikingly beautiful feathered patterns in the flowers. Only diseased bulbs were prized by traders; the most beautiful patterns, such as Semper Augustus, commanded the highest prices. A particular pattern could not be reproduced through seed propagation. Only through budding of the mother bulb would a pattern breed true. In normal bulbs, asexual budding techniques produced an annual rate of increase

ranging from 100 to 150 percent, but diseased bulbs increased more slowly.

For new varieties of flowers, a standard pricing pattern results, even in modern markets. When a particularly prized variety is developed, its original bulb sells for a high price. As a stock of bulbs is accumulated and marketed, the variety's price declines so rapidly that after thirty years bulbs sell at about their reproduction and distribution cost. In modern markets, prices fall very rapidly. For example, a small quantity of a new variety of lily bulbs sold in 1986 for one million guilders ($480,000). Since these bulbs can be reproduced rapidly with tissue growth techniques, they were soon mass marketed at very low prices.

This pattern held in the eighteenth century, a period in which a sequence of market prices for bulbs can be observed from auction lists and bulb catalogues. Bulbs selling at high prices in 1707 (250–400 guilders) would command from 0.1 to 1 guilder by 1739, about the same prices as the outstanding bulbs still on the market from the tulipmania a century earlier. For prized new tulip varieties in the eighteenth century, the average annual rate of price depreciation over a fifteen-year period was 25 percent before bulb prices reached reproduction costs. A similar pattern emerged for prices of prized eighteenth-century hyacinth bulbs: the annual rate of price depreciation averaged 35 percent over decades.

For the bulbs of the tulipmania, hardly any postcollapse price data exist. While a price collapse for the more common varieties undoubtedly occurred in February 1637, accompanied by massive defaults on futures contracts, no prices for market transactions are available for the years immediately following the crash. The first observable prices of valuable bulbs emerge from a 1643 estate sale of an important bulb grower. Even then, the valuable bulbs of the tulipmania still carried high prices. For example, a bulb called English Admiral sold for 210 guilders in 1643; at the peak on 5 February 1637, a bulb of the same variety sold for 700 guilders. For the bulbs whose prices are available in 1643, the average annual price depreciation between the peak in February 1637 and the auction in 1643 was 30 percent, not greatly different from the eighteenth-century depreciation rate. Thus, the crash in February 1637, though associated in the folklore with the outlandishly high prices of the rare bulbs, had nothing to do with this market. The available evidence on rare bulb prices indicates that even at their peak, prices followed a market funda-mentals pricing pattern that has been observed for centuries.

The Market in Common Bulbs

The explanation presented above concerns the market for rare bulbs. Prices for these bulbs are those always cited when the apparently bizarre extent of the speculation is emphasized. The remarkable trading of nonprofessionals, how-ever, was largely confined to a futures market which began in the summer of 1636. The state had refused since 1609 to enforce futures con-tracts in which the holder of the short position did not currently possess the deliverable com-modity, a policy reinforced by further decree in 1636. Futures trading occurred in groups called "colleges," each of which would be located in a particular tavern. Each of the numerous trades would be accompanied by a round of drinks, so that it is hard to separate this aspect of the epi-sode from an outburst of general carousing. By late autumn 1636, as people without tangible wealth entered the trading, speculative trades shifted from the rarer bulbs toward the formerly disdained and inexpensive common bulbs. In January 1637 alone, the speculation in common bulb futures drove up prices as much as twenty-fold. This speculation was confined primarily to people in the lower social classes. Wealthier people confined their trades to the rare bulbs, whose prices only doubled or tripled from 1634 to 1637.

Since the futures contracts were unenforce-able, this facet of the speculation defies expla-nation. However, some commentators associate it with an outbreak of bubonic plague, a feature of the fundamental environment generally ig-nored in the folklore. This plague wiped out 15 percent of the population of Haarlem, the cen-ter of the bulb trade, from August to Novem-ber 1636, coincident with the advent of futures trading and the loss of morale evident in the rush to the taverns. The plague also wiped out a seventh of the population of Amsterdam in 1636 and a third of the population of Leiden in 1635.

Market Fundamentals vs. Crowd Psychology

The tulipmania has always supplied a rhetori-cal weapon in the enduring methodological debate over asset valuation between funda-mentalists and proponents of a fads or crowd-psychology view. Every observer of securities markets is influenced by histories of specula-tive excesses so extreme that any market-fun-damentals explanation would be implausible. Given a belief that manias drove these extreme events, it is prudent to believe that manias may occasionally figure importantly in less extreme events, such as recent stock-market history. Overt historical cases of crowd manias estab-lish prior beliefs about the existence of such events; in a new episode not readily explain-able in terms of current models of fundamen-tals, an observer may entertain a bubble expla-nation. However, even in an extreme case like tulipmania, a plausible market-fundamentals explanation is available. Of course, this does not preclude an explanation based on crowd psychology; it simply shifts the tulipmania from the "obvious bubble" column. The tulipmania is no longer a weapon, but, like all other remarkable speculative episodes, merely another battleground for two essentially ideo-logical views of how asset prices are deter-mined.

Peter M. Garber

See also EXCESS VOLATILITY; EXPECTATIONS; MISSISSIPPI BUBBLE; RATIONAL EXPECTA-TIONS; SOUTH-SEA BUBBLE; STOCK-MARKET CRASH OF 1929; STOCK-MARKET CRASHES OF 1987 AND 1989; STOCK-MARKET PRICES; SUNSPOT THEORIES OF FLUCTUATIONS

Bibliography

Anonymous. [1637] 1926. "Samen-spraeck tusschen Waermondt ende Gaergoedt: Flora." *Economisch-Historisch Jaarboek* 12:20–43.

Beckmann, J. 1846. *History of Inventions, Discoveries, and Origins.* Vol. 1. 4th ed. London: Harry G. Bohn.

Garber, P. M. 1989a. "Tulipmania." *Journal of Political Economy* 97:535–60.

———. 1989b. "Who Put the Mania in the Tulipmania?" *Journal of Portfolio Man-agement* 16:53–60.

———. 1990. "Famous First Bubbles." *Jour-nal of Economic Perspectives,* Spring, 35–54.

Mackay, C. 1852. *Extraordinary Popular Delusions and the Madness of Crowds.* Vol. 1. 2d ed. London: Office of the National Illustrated Library.

Posthumus, N. W. 1929. "The Tulip Mania in Holland in the years 1636 and 1637." *Journal of Economic and Business History* 1:434–55.

U

Unemployment

Although the terms *unemployment* and *under-employment* can apply to any resource, they usually refer to labor and, accordingly, signify a concept that is laden with controversies. One is whether unemployment is *voluntary* or *involuntary*. Because agents are assumed to be rational decision-makers, one is tempted to regard all unemployment as voluntary. But whether we call unemployment voluntary or involuntary is more a question of semantics than of substance. The more relevant question is whether, at current prices and wages, an agent wishes to supply more labor than he currently is supplying. If so, it is reasonable to call such a worker involuntarily unemployed or underemployed.

The controversy about whether unemployment is voluntary or involuntary also obscures a measurement problem that arises because measured unemployment generally includes several types of unemployment, frictional and structural, voluntary and involuntary. On the other hand, measured unemployment does not include the structural unemployment that arises from workers being overqualified for their jobs. A further dimension not captured by standard measures of unemployment is its duration. Duration is a key factor in the insider-outsider or hysteresis explanations of persistent unemployment.

There are many other theories of unemployment, including implicit-contract theory, search theory, and efficiency-wage theory, with which different definitions of unemployment and different possible remedies are associated. The focus here will be on so-called "disequilibrium theory" which excludes frictional unemployment to examine involuntary unemployment as defined above.

Still another controversy concerns precisely the equilibrium nature of unemployment. The simple demand-supply diagram underlying the classical view of unemployment associated with Pigou is clearly inadequate, because it suggests that unemployment can be eliminated by cutting nominal wages. A crucial step in the study of unemployment was to study it within a general-equilibrium, rather than a partial-equilibrium, framework. This, as later formalized by Clower and Leijonhufvud, was a primary message of Keynes in his *General Theory*. The distinction between equilibrium and disequilibrium is not really essential. Viewed from a short-run perspective, unemployment is basically a disequilibrium phenomenon, but one may also be interested in knowing whether unemployment is compatible with a long-run (stationary) equilibrium. Thus, recent equilibrium (real) business-cycle theories aim at explaining fluctuations in employment or in the "natural" rate of unemployment by focusing on cyclical unemployment and ignoring any involuntary unemployment that is not frictional or structural.

A less academic but more pressing issue concerns how unemployment can be cured in the short run, when a number of variables are exogenously fixed or constrained. This concern underlies the so-called *fix-price* method introduced by Hicks in *Capital and Growth* (1965) in which quantities are assumed to adjust infinitely faster than prices and wages. Time is divided into an infinite sequence of discrete periods. Prices and wages are fixed within a given period but are adjusted in between periods and the economy moves from one short-run (or temporary) equilibrium to another in response to the induced changes in the stocks, adjustments of prices and wages, and revisions of expectations.

In the tradition of Arrow-Debreu general-equilibrium theory, various concepts of equilibrium with price rigidities and quantity rationing were independently introduced in the early 1970s by Benassy, Drèze, and Younès. Rationing schemes are central in Benassy's definition; Younès is concerned with the role of money and emphasizes the condition of voluntary trading. Instead of fixed prices, Drèze considers the more general case of constraints on nominal or relative prices, such as downward wage rigidities, escalation clauses, and price controls. All these approaches are similar in spirit. In particular, they have in common the condition that the volume of trade is constrained by the short side of the market (orderly markets). Furthermore, when prices are partially flexible, quantity constraints are relevant only when the constraint on the price on the corresponding market is binding.

These concepts were later extended to cover monetary economies and have been applied to a simple macroeconomic model with three commodities (a consumption good, labor, and money) by Barro and Grossman, Benassy, Malinvaud, Younès, and others. In such a model, because the price level and the wage rate are fixed, there are four types of short-run equilibrium in which rationing is observed in both markets, namely classical unemployment, Keynesian unemployment, repressed inflation, or underconsumption. To these cases one must add the boundary cases which include the standard market-clearing Walrasian equilibrium. The most detailed study of these possibilities is contained in Malinvaud's Irjö Jahnsson Lectures (1977), which gave rise to a vast literature, especially in Western Europe where the problem of mass unemployment is most severe.

Among the features of the fix-price approach is that it provides a unified framework in which classical and Keynesian unemployment appear as particular cases, depending on the price-wage pair. Since observed unemployment cannot be uniquely characterized, some researchers have proposed disaggregated models in which production in any sector is constrained either by demand, by capacity, or by labor supply. An equilibrium is then defined in terms of the proportion of sectors in each of the three different types of regime. The econometric methods necessary to cope with markets in disequilibrium were developed in the early 1980s and applied to identify the kind of unemployment then prevailing in many Western European countries.

A further development of the fix-price approach is to study the dynamics of short-run equilibria. The first attempts relied exclusively on the dynamics generated by the endogenous evolution of the stock of money, while prices and wages remained constant. A natural way to introduce the adjustment of prices and wages is to assume that these adjustments reflect imbalances in the preceding period. However, whether there is convergence towards a Walrasian equilibrium, a long-lasting Keynesian depression, a Phillips curve, or transitory classical unemployment depends crucially on how the adjustment rules are specified. It also depends on the process by which agents revise their expectations about the future prices, wages, and constraints, the specification of the learning process being limited to simple revisions rules.

These approaches are all vulnerable to the criticism that they are perfectly competitive in nature and that the assumptions about price and wage rigidities and adjustment mechanisms are ad hoc. More recent studies have instead emphasized the role of imperfect competition in explaining unemployment, and the endogenous determination of prices and wages. Several imperfectly competitive models featuring unemployment have been proposed, some within a framework of monopolistic competition. However, the problem of incorporating imperfect competition in a general-equilibrium framework remains without a straightforward solution. Arrow's well-known demand for a general-equilibrium framework in which prices are set by agents in the economy has elicited many responses, but none is fully convincing.

Pierre Dehez

See also EFFICIENCY WAGES; IMPLICIT CONTRACTS; KEYNES, JOHN MAYNARD; NATURAL RATE OF UNEMPLOYMENT; NEW KEYNESIAN ECONOMICS; PHILLIPS CURVE; PIGOU, ARTHUR CECIL; SEARCH THEORY; SECTORAL SHIFTS; WAGE RIGIDITY; WORKER AND JOB TURNOVER

Bibliography

Barnett, W. A., et al. 1991. *Equilibrium Theory and Applications*. Cambridge: Cambridge Univ. Press.

Barro, R. J. and H. I. Grossman. 1976. *Money, Employment and Inflation*. Cambridge: Cambridge Univ. Press.

Beckerman, W., ed. 1986. *The Economics of Market Disequilibrium*. London: Duckworth.

Benassy, J.-P. 1982. *The Economics of Market Disequilibrium*. New York: Academic Press.

———. 1986. *Macroeconomics: An Introduction to the Non-Walrasian Approach*. Orlando, Fla.: Academic Press.

Drèze, J. H. 1991. *Underemployment Equilibria: Essays in Theory, Econometrics, and Policy*. Cambridge: Cambridge Univ. Press.

Drèze, J. H. and C. R. Bean. 1990. *Europe's Unemployment Problem*. Cambridge: MIT Press.

Gordon, R. J. 1990. "What is the New-Keynesian Economics?" *Journal of Economic Literature* 28:1115–71.

Lambert, J.-P. 1988. *Disequilibrium Macroeconomic Models*. Cambridge: Cambridge Univ. Press.

Lindbeck, A. and D. J. Snower. 1988. *The Insider-Outsider Theory of Employment and Unemployment*. Cambridge: MIT Press.

Malinvaud, E. 1977. *The Theory of Unemployment Reconsidered*. Oxford: Basil Blackwell.

———. 1980. *Profitability and Unemployment*. Cambridge: Cambridge Univ. Press.

Malinvaud, E. and J.-P. Fitoussi. 1980. *Unemployment in Western Countries*. London: Macmillan.

Nickell, S. 1990. "Unemployment: A Survey." *Economic Journal* 100:391–439.

Pissaredes, C. A. 1990. *Equilibrium Unemployment Theory*. Oxford: Basil Blackwell.

Sneessens, H. 1981. *Theory and Estimation of Macroeconomic Rationing Models*. Berlin: Springer-Verlag.

Younès, Y. 1975. "On the Role of Money in the Process of Exchange and the Existence of a Non-Walrasian Equilibrium." *Review of Economic Studies* 42:489–501.

Unit Root Tests

When the economy goes into a recession, how long is it before GNP returns to its prerecession trend line? Textbooks such as Robert J. Gordon's *Macroeconomics* (4th ed., 17) suggest that it does not take long, often requiring no more than a couple of years. In this view, GNP is *stationary*, or *mean-reverting*, around a trend line: shocks have transitory effects, with GNP reverting rapidly to a stable trend.

A contrary view, first proposed by Nelson and Plosser (1982), is that GNP is *nonstationary*, or has a *unit root*. To oversimplify somewhat, Nelson and Plosser argue that the current value of GNP is essentially the base for the future path of GNP. In this view, if we unexpectedly enter a recession, GNP even ten or twenty years from now is likely to be lower than had there been no recession.

Which of these contrasting views is correct has important implications for economic theory and policy. Nelson and Plosser argue that if the unit root model is appropriate, monetary theories of the business cycle are not very attractive, since monetary shocks are typically thought to have only transitory effects. Campbell and Mankiw (1987) argue that the concept of a stationary natural rate of unemployment is not very compelling if shocks are not routinely offset with a return to trend.

This article briefly outlines the Dickey-Fuller test, the most commonly used statistical technique for testing the null of a unit root in a time series against the alternative that the series is stationary around trend line. Additional discussion, as well as other tests, may be found in the references. Unfortunately, these references are for the most part fairly technical; a good textbook discussion may be found in Hamilton (1994).

The simplest example of a Dickey-Fuller test in a time series x_t involves the model:

$$x_t = m_0 + m_1 t + \phi x_{t-1} + \varepsilon_t, \tag{1}$$

where $-1 < \phi \leq 1$ and $m_1 = 0$ if $\phi = 1$ (these conditions rule out behavior that is rarely seen in economic data). If $\phi = 1$, the process has a unit root, this phrase deriving from the fact $z = 1$ is a root to the equation $1 - \phi z = 0$ if $\phi = 1$, but not otherwise. If $|\phi| < 1$, the process does not have a unit root but instead is stationary around the trend $m_0 + m_1 t$.

A Dickey-Fuller test for whether there is a unit root in the process (1) begins by rewriting the equation as:

$$x_t - x_{t-1} \equiv \Delta x_t = m_0 + m_1 t + (\phi - 1)x_{t-1} + \varepsilon_t$$
$$\equiv m_0 + m_1 t + \delta_0 x_{t-1} + \varepsilon_t. \tag{2}$$

Note that $\delta_0 = 0$ if and only if $\phi = 1$. So one estimates (2) by ordinary least squares, and calculates the usual t-statistic for $H_0: \delta_0 = 0$. The usual critical values for this t-statistic, however, should not be used, because under the null hypothesis of a unit root this statistic is *not* normally distributed, even if ε_t is normally distributed, and even in large samples. Instead, critical values tabulated in Fuller (1976, 373) may be used. At the 1-, 5- and 10-percent levels, the asymptotic critical values are −3.96, −3.66 and −3.41. Use of the usual asymptotic normal distribution, which would, for example, suggest rejecting at the 5-percent level in a one-tailed test if the t-statistic were less than −1.65, will, under the unit root null, lead to too many rejections; at this significance level one should instead reject the null only if the t-statistic is less than −3.66.

The reader familiar with standard macroeconomic data will recognize that most such data, including GNP, display behavior that is too complex to be captured by equation (1). One can test for unit roots in such series by adding additional lags of Δx_t as additional regressors:

$$x_t - x_{t-1} \equiv \Delta x_t = m_0 + m_1 t + \delta_0 x_{t-1}$$
$$+ \delta_1 \Delta x_{t-1} + \ldots + \delta_p \Delta x_{t-p} + \varepsilon_t. \quad (3)$$

Once again, x_t has a unit root if and only if $\delta_0 = 0$.

One can use equation (3) to test the unit root null exactly as before, by estimating equation (3) by OLS, computing the t-statistic for H_0: $\delta_0 = 0$, and using the same non-standard critical values that were used for equation (2). This is true even if in the population the disturbance to equation (2) is serially correlated, provided many lags of Δx_t are included. Somewhat more precisely, equation (3) can be used even if Δx_t has what time-series analysts call a moving-average component. In a Monte Carlo study, Schwert (1988) found that setting the number of lags equal to the integer part of $12 \times$ (sample size/100)$^{1/4}$ provides an adequate number of lags. Thus, if the sample size is 100, set $p = 12$ in equation (3); if the sample size is 200, set $p = 14$.

Some technical points: First, it is important to include the time trend (the $m_1 t$ term) in equations (2) and (3), if, as usual, the alternative is that the data are stationary around a time trend. Otherwise one is very likely to accept the unit root null even when the data are in fact stationary (West 1987). Second, Campbell and Mankiw (1987), Cochrane (1988), and Phillips and Perron (1988) among others have proposed alter-

natives or extensions to the Dickey-Fuller test. The Dickey-Fuller test is, however, the simplest, and is more reliable than some others in samples of the size usually used by economists (Schwert 1988). Finally, there are multivariate tests for the number of unit roots in vector time-series processes. The pioneering work here is by Engle and Granger (1987). Alternative, more general tests have been proposed by a number of authors. Some of these are presented in the June/September 1988 issue of the *Journal of Economic Dynamics and Control*. A consensus has yet to develop on which test is preferred.

For most macroeconomic data, tests for unit roots do not reject the null. See, for example, Nelson and Plosser (1982) for tests using annual United States data (including GNP). Taken at face value, these tests indicate that when GNP falls unexpectedly, one should expect a lower value for GNP indefinitely far into the future. Campbell and Mankiw (1987, 867), for example, suggest that if GNP falls unexpectedly by 1 percent, the forecast of GNP twenty years later falls by about 1.5 percent.

A much debated question is whether these results in fact *should* be taken at face value. Dickey and Fuller (1981) show that their tests are likely not to reject the null of a unit root if there is no unit root, but there still is considerable serial correlation in the series. (In the model (1), this is equivalent to ϕ being near but not quite equal to unity.) This has lead West (1988) and Christiano and Eichenbaum (1989) to argue that the tests do not establish the presence of a unit root, or even that mean reversion to a trend line is unlikely in, say, five years.

The debate over the presence of unit roots in economic time series is unsettled. Ongoing work on tests for unit roots may help a consensus emerge.

Kenneth D. West

See also COINTEGRATION; COMPOSITE TRENDS; TRENDS AND RANDOM WALKS

Bibliography

Campbell, J. Y. and N. G. Mankiw. 1987. "Are Output Fluctuations Transitory?" *Quarterly Journal of Economics* 102:857–80.

Christiano, L. J. and M. Eichenbaum. 1990. "Unit Roots in Real GNP—Do We Know and Do We Care?" *Carnegie-Rochester Conference Series on Public Policy,* Spring, 7–61.

Cochrane, J. H. 1988. "How Big is the Random Walk in GNP?" *Journal of Political Economy* 96:893–920.

Dickey, D. A. and W. A. Fuller. 1981. "Likelihood Ratio Statistics for Autoregressive Times Series with a Unit Root." *Econometrica* 49:1057–72.

Engle, R. F. and C. W. J. Granger. 1987. "Dynamic Model Specification with Equilibrium Constraints: Co-Integration and Error Correction." *Econometrica* 55:251–76.

Fuller, W. A. 1976. *Introduction to Statistical Time Series.* New York: Wiley.

Hamilton, J. D. 1994. *Time Series Analysis.* Princeton: Princeton Univ. Press.

Nelson, C. R. and C. I. Plosser. 1982. "Trends versus Random Walks in Macroeconomic Time Series: Some Evidence and Implications." *Journal of Monetary Economics* 10:139–62.

Phillips, P. C. B. and P. Perron. 1988. "Testing for a Unit Root in Time Series Regression." *Biometrika* 75:335–46.

Schwert, G. W. 1989. "Tests for Unit Roots: A Monte Carlo Investigation." *Journal of Business and Economic Statistics* 7:147–59.

Stock, J. H. and M. W. Watson. 1988. "Variable Trends in Economic Time Series." *Journal of Economic Perspectives,* Summer, 147–74.

West, K. D. 1987. "A Note on the Power of Least Squares Tests for a Unit Root." *Economics Letters* 24:249–52.

———. 1988. "On the Interpretation of Near Random Walk Behavior in GNP." *American Economic Review* 78:202–09.

U

V

Veblen, Thorstein (1857–1929)

Most of Veblen's analysis of the business cycle can be found in *The Theory of Business Enterprise*. Fundamental to his analysis is the distinction he made between business and industry. Within the more conventional view, an assumption is made that, while the two activities are not identical, in the pursuit of profits it is necessary to produce goods. In Veblen's fundamental distinction the two activities are distinguishable in such a fashion that it may actually be possible to make profits by "sabotaging" the industrial process. Capitalization is in no necessary way related to industrial activity, nor in any way proportional to it.

Pecuniary activity is centered on the capitalization of the expected rate of return from the employment of technological apparatus to produce a vendable product. The capitalization rests on nothing more robust than pecuniary anticipations.

A crisis has its beginnings in a rise in price in some particular large firm or industry. Thus, rising price encourages increased activity and serves as justification for enhanced capitalization and the enhanced extension of credit to support an enlarged output. The prosperity in the affected industry is spread to those industries both technologically and pecuniarily linked to it. A climate of opinion builds throughout the industrial economy that becomes conducive to a general expansion on the basis of optimistic expectations.

Prices of finished goods rise faster than costs of production. The differential between costs and price is what sustains the prosperity. However, the difference between costs and selling price is not sustainable, since it prevails because the costs of raw materials and labor, in particular, do not initially rise *parri passu* with selling price. But as real production increases, these lagged costs begin to rise faster than selling prices and snuff out the source of profit. When this occurs, real rates of return no longer sustain anticipated rates of return, provoking a financial crisis. During the crisis, the preceding capitalizations are liquidated through bankruptcy.

Veblen rejected any suggestion of a rhythmic cyclical movement in economic activity. He argued that depression of some type is the normal order of economic activity under capitalism. He also rejected any notion of equilibrium, although his position concerning the normal state of affairs is compatible with Keynes's notion that the economy could be in equilibrium for long periods at less than full employment.

Veblen, much like Keynes, did contend that the relation between the rate of interest and anticipated rates of return on capitalizations are critical to investment. But, unlike Keynes, Veblen contended that the technological process constantly threatens capitalized values. To Veblen, technology is a cultural process and innovation takes place even during periods of repressed economic activity. In fact, the nature of technology is such as to erode capitalized values at all times. Since capitalized values are based on some state of technology, new technology constantly threatens the capitalized values based on expectations that presume the now obsolete technology. Technological change constantly erodes pecuniary values.

Veblen contended that only two remedies exist under capitalism. One is increasing control over price by ever larger monopolists. This is socially undesirable, but very probable. Veblen saw a tendency in this direction as business countered the thrust of technology which, by creating abundance, could constantly undermine price and capitalizations. The other remedy is wasteful public expenditure in useless public enterprises or in wars and preparation for war. Veblen was not an advocate of such measures, but felt that these governmental sources of expenditure could sustain the economy. In his case, the word "wasteful" in reference to governmental expenditure must be interpreted in the manner he used the term in his *Theory of the Leisure Class*. Such expenditure is over and above what is necessary to achieve some end-in-view. In other words, government expenditure in and of itself is not necessarily wasteful.

To understand Veblen's approach to economic instability, one must keep clearly in mind that, as in all of his work, he made a cultural distinction between social behavior that is ceremonial and that which is instrumental or technological. These are behavioral terms. In *The Theory of Business Enterprise* the cultural dichotomy took the form of business and industry. These two cultural forces are antithetical to each other, as he insisted by his contention that the expansion of technology constantly erodes capitalized values.

Veblen's chief influence on business-cycle theory was through Wesley C. Mitchell, especially in his *Business Cycles and Their Causes*. Mitchell specifically acknowledged the influence of Veblen, although Mitchell did not make significant use of the Veblenian trademark, the cultural concepts of technology and institutions.

David H. Hamilton

Bibliography
Mitchell, W. C. 1941. *Business Cycles and Their Causes*. New York: NBER.
Veblen, T. [1899] 1934. *The Theory of the Leisure Class*. New York: Modern Library.
———. 1904. *The Theory of Business Enterprise*. New York: Scribner.

Vector Autoregressions

The vector-autoregression model is a statistical model that is easy to estimate and flexible enough to capture the variance, covariance, and autocovariance features of a wide range of time-series data. Christopher Sims (1980) presented the model as an alternative to large structural models of the macroeconomy, and vector autoregressions (VARs) have since become an important tool in analyzing macroeconomic fluctuations (Sims 1982, Sargent 1976) and in macroeconomic forecasting (Doan et al., 1984). See Lütkepohl (1991) for a survey of VAR modeling.

The VAR Model

The simplest VAR model is a first-order autoregression with one variable,

$$x_t = \phi x_{t-1} + \varepsilon_t \tag{1}$$

The kth-order model with n variables is a direct generalization,

$$X_t = \Phi_1 X_{t-1} + \Phi_2 X_{t-2} + \cdots + \Phi_k X_{t-k} + \varepsilon_t \tag{2}$$

where $X_t = (x_{1t}, x_{2t}, \ldots, x_{nt})'$ is a vector of n time-series variables at time t, ε_t is a vector of n random disturbances, and the Φs are fixed $(n \times n)$ matrices of coefficients. A VAR could also contain deterministic elements such as a constant term, seasonal dummy variables, or a time trend. The model is often written,

$$\Phi(L)X_t = \varepsilon_t \tag{3}$$

where $\Phi(L)$ is an $(n \times n)$ matrix, and each element, $\phi_{ij}(L)$, is a polynomial in the lag operator, L,

$$\phi_{ij}(L) = \sum_{m=0}^{k} \phi_{ijm} L^m \tag{4}$$

where $L^i X_t = X_{t-i}$.

The VAR model is a special case of the multivariate autoregressive moving-average model, which would include lagged values of both ε_t and X_t. Ruling out moving-average terms simplifies estimation and is justified by a result stating that any *stationary* and *invertible* time-series process can be well approximated by a VAR of some finite order. The demonstration of this result begins with the Wold (1938) decomposition theorem, which shows that any covariance stationary process can be represented by a vector moving-average process: $X_t = \Theta(L)\varepsilon_t$. When roots of the $\Theta(L)$ polynomial are outside the unit circle, $\Theta(L)$ is invertible, and the model can be written in autoregressive form $\Theta(L)^{-1}X_t = \varepsilon_t$. While this representation generally involves infinite lags of X_t, the coefficients decline as the lag length increases, and the process can be well approximated by considering only the first k terms of $\Theta(L)^{-1}$ for some finite k. Thus, the many economic models that generate stationary and invertible data are special cases of the VAR model.

Choosing the Order

While a VAR of some finite order can represent most time-series processes, each increase in k increases the number of parameters by n^2. Thus, the amount of data available provides an important constraint on the order of models that can be considered in practice.

There are two general approaches to limiting the order of the VAR. Under the sequential-testing approach (e.g., Hannan 1970), one begins with a maximum order, K, and tests whether the coefficient on the final lag, ΦK, is zero. If the hypothesis $\Phi K = 0$ is not rejected, one tests whether $\Phi_{K-1} = 0$ and so on. The second approach is based on information theory and suggests choosing k to minimize some function of minus the value of the likelihood function plus a penalty term for the number of parameters. For example, the Schwarz (1978) criterion selects the k that minimizes,

$$\ln\left(\left|\hat{\Sigma}\right|\right) + \frac{n^2 k \ln(T)}{T} \qquad (5)$$

where $\hat{\Sigma}$ is the variance-covariance matrix of the residuals of the estimated model, and T is the sample size. In a Monte Carlo study of several versions of the sequential testing and information-theoretic approaches, Lütkepohl (1985) concluded that the Schwarz criterion fared best in selecting the correct model order and in minimizing mean squared forecast errors from estimated models.

Estimation

Given the order of the model, the parameters of the VAR model can be consistently estimated by ordinary least squares. Each of the n variables in turn is taken as the dependent variable in a regression including k lags of all variables in the system. Under the assumption that the elements of the random disturbance term, ε_t, are jointly normal and not serially correlated, the ordinary least squares estimate coincides with the maximum-likelihood estimate, conditional on the first k observations. This simplicity is a major advantage of the pure autoregressive formulation—moving-average components are more difficult to estimate.

Bayesian VAR

The Bayesian VAR approach of Litterman (1982) is an alternative approach to estimating a VAR with a potentially large number of parameters. Instead of using some criterion to rule out certain higher-order lag coefficients, this approach uses a Bayesian prior distribution over the coefficients that tends to shrink the estimated coefficients toward zero. The prior is that the data series are independent random walks; lag coefficients beyond the first lag have prior mean zero and progressively smaller variance. This approach has been widely and successfully used for macroeconomic forecasting (McNees 1986).

Integration and Cointegration

Often in economic data, variables of interest appear to be integrated, implying that they are stationary only after being differenced one or more times. The standard response to this situation in univariate analysis is to difference each variable to induce stationarity before beginning the analysis. In the multivariate case, however, this can cause problems: if the data series are *cointegrated*, then there will be no VAR representation of process for differenced data.

A set of variables is cointegrated when each variable is integrated but some linear combination of variables is stationary (Engle and Granger 1987). The integrated variables each have infinite variance, but the linear combination has finite variance. In economics, such cointegrating relations are often implied by economic equilibrium arguments. While the price of steel in each of two countries may be integrated, the possibility of shipping steel from the low-cost country to the high-cost country—raising the price in the first country and lowering the price in the second—may cause the difference in the prices to be stationary.

The role of cointegration in VARs can be seen by transforming the standard model. Subtract X_{t-1} from both sides of equation (3) and rearrange terms to form

$$\Delta X_t = \Pi X_{t-1} + \Phi_1^* \Delta X_{t-1} + \dots$$
$$+ \Phi_{k-1}^* \Delta X_{t-k+1} + \varepsilon_t \qquad (6)$$

This is a VAR model of the differenced data with an additional term, ΠX_{t-1}. If there are cointegrating relations among the variables, then the matrix Π has less than full rank and equation (6) is called a vector error-correction model (VECM). The term ΠX_{t-1} captures the tendency of any *error* in the cointegrating relation among the levels of the variables to fall in subsequent periods. No VAR in the ΔX_t alone can capture this feature of the cointegrated data series.

Inference in models with integrated and cointegrated variables requires some special techniques. For example, standard test statistics, such as the regression t statistic, do not have their standard distributions when testing the cointegration features of the model. Thus, special critical values or tests are required. Test statistics for many questions not involving the cointegration features of the model—such as tests on the lag length in equation (6)—continue to have their standard distribution, however (Sims et al. 1990).

Identification and Interpretation

VAR models can involve quite complicated system dynamics. One widely used tool for interpreting those dynamics is a plot of the *impulse-response functions* for the model. The impulse-response function is obtained by inverting the estimated matrix polynomial, $\hat{\Phi}(L)$ in equation (3), to form the moving-average representation of the VAR:

$$X_t = \hat{\Theta}(L)\hat{\varepsilon}_t \qquad (7)$$

where $\hat{\Theta}(L) = \hat{\Phi}(L)^{-1}$. The i, j element of $\hat{\Theta}(L)$ is $\hat{\theta}_{ij}(L) = \Sigma_{m=0}^{\infty} \hat{\theta}_{ijm} L^m$. The coefficient $\hat{\theta}_{ijm}$ gives the time t response of the ith variable to an impulse at time $t{-}m$ in the jth shock. The sequence of $\hat{\theta}$ coefficients forms the impulse-response function. Standard errors for each coefficient in the impulse-response function can also be calculated. In practice, these standard errors are often quite large relative to the estimated coefficients, implying that individual coefficients of the impulse-response function are not very precisely estimated.

Interpretation of impulse-response functions is complicated by the observational equivalence of many representations of the VAR. These representations are equally consistent with the data, but may suggest much different interpretations of the structural relations among the variables. Given the moving-average representation, equation (7), one can generate observationally equivalent representations by taking any $(n \times n)$ full rank matrix, Γ_0, and forming,

$$X_t = \hat{\Gamma}(L)\hat{v}_t \qquad (8)$$

where $\hat{\Gamma}(L) = \hat{\Theta}(L)\Gamma_0$ and $\hat{v}_t = \Gamma_0^{-1}\hat{\varepsilon}_t$. (Since the lead matrix of $\Theta(L)$ is the identity matrix, the lead matrix of $\Gamma(L)$ will be Γ_0.)

The coefficients and disturbances in equation (8) are linear combinations of coefficients and disturbances in equation (7). To interpret impulse-response functions in an economically meaningful way, one must decide which of these representations is of most interest. Choosing a particular representation of the VAR is called *identifying* the VAR, and is a matter of choosing the n^2 elements of the matrix Γ_0.

Most identification schemes require that the identified disturbances, $\hat{v}_t$, be uncorrelated. This assumption is justified, for example, if the identified disturbances originate in behaviorally distinct sectors of the economy. If the estimated variance-covariance matrix of $\hat{\varepsilon}_t$ is $\hat{\Sigma}$, then the covariance matrix for the identified shocks is $\Gamma_0^{-1}\hat{\Sigma}\Gamma_0^{'-1}$. Requiring that the shocks be uncorrelated and, without loss of generality, normalizing the variance of the shocks to one provides $n(n + 1)/2$ restrictions on Γ_0, which can be written $\Gamma_0^{-1}\hat{\Sigma}\Gamma_0^{'-1} = I$.

There are three standard schemes for choosing the remaining $n(n{-}1)/2$ elements of Γ_0. First, Sims (1980) suggested imposing a recursive structure on the model, which implies that Γ_0 is lower triangular for the chosen ordering of the variables in the vector X_t. The economy is probably not recursive in this way, however, and the results of this approach are often sensitive to the recursive ordering of the variables.

The second approach uses economic reasoning about contemporaneous interactions among variables to justify zero restrictions on Γ_0 (Bernanke 1986, Blanchard and Watson 1986, Sims 1986). For example, suppose a VAR contained the growth rate of a monetary aggregate under control of the central bank and the unemployment rate. Tighter monetary policy this month may affect the unemployment rate. However, if the unemployment data are reported with a lag, then the unemployment rate this month cannot affect monetary policy until next month. This provides one zero restriction on the contemporaneous interactions in the VAR.

The third approach imposes restrictions on the long-run linkages among variables, rather than on the contemporaneous linkages (Shapiro and Watson 1988, Blanchard and Quah 1989, King et al., 1991). Blanchard and Quah, for example, identify aggregate-supply and aggregate-demand shocks in a bivariate model of output growth and the unemployment rate by assuming that demand shocks do not affect real output in the long run.

Conclusion

The VAR model is extremely flexible and easy to estimate. Effective use of VARs requires tools for dealing with problems such as the potentially large number of parameters in the model, integration and cointegration, and the many observationally equivalent representations of the model.

Jon Faust

See also COINTEGRATION; DISTRIBUTED LAGS; MACROECONOMETRIC MODELS, HISTORICAL DEVELOPMENT; MOVING AVERAGES; SERIAL CORRELATION

Bibliography

Bernanke, B. 1986. "Alternative Explorations of the Money-Income Correlation." *Carnegie-Rochester Conference Series on Public Policy,* Autumn, 49–99.

Blanchard, O. J. and M. W. Watson. 1986. "Are Business Cycles All Alike?" In *The American Business Cycle: Continuity and Change,* edited by R. J. Gordon, 123–56. Chicago: Univ. of Chicago Press.

Blanchard, O. J. and D. Quah. 1989. "The Dynamic Effects of Aggregate Supply and Demand Disturbances." *American Economic Review* 79:655–73.

Doan, T., R. Litterman, and C. A. Sims. 1984. "Forecasting and Conditional Projection Using Realistic Prior Distributions." *Econometric Review* 3:1–100.

Engle, R. F. and C. W. J. Granger. 1987. "Co-integration and Error Correction: Representation, Estimation, and Testing." *Econometrica* 55:251–72.

Hannan, E. J. 1970. *Multiple Time Series.* New York: Wiley.

King, R. G., C. I. Plosser, J. H. Stock, and M. W. Watson. 1991. "Stochastic Trends and Economic Fluctuations." *American Economic Review* 81:819–40.

Litterman, R. 1986. "Specifying Vector Autoregressions for Macroeconomic Forecasting." In *Bayesian Inference and Decision Techniques: Essays in Honor of Bruno de Finetti,* edited by P. K. Good and A. Zellner, 79–94. Amsterdam: North-Holland.

Lütkepohl, H. 1985. "Comparison of Criteria for Estimating the Order of a Vector Autoregressive Process." *Journal of Time Series Analysis* 6:35–52.

———. 1991. *Introduction to Multiple Time Series Analysis.* Berlin: Springer-Verlag.

McNees, S. 1986. "Forecasting Accuracy of Alternative Techniques: A Comparison of U.S. Macroeconomic Forecasts." *Journal of Business Economics and Statistics* 4:4–23.

Novales, A. 1990. "Solving Nonlinear Rational Expectations Models: A Stochastic Equilibrium Model of Interest Rates." *Econometrica* 58:93–112.

Sargent, T. 1976. "A Classical Macroeconometric Model for the United States." *Journal of Political Economy* 84:207–27.

Schwarz, G. 1978. "Estimating the Dimension of a Model." *The Annals of Statistics* 6:461–64.

Shapiro, M. D. and M. W. Watson. 1988. "Sources of Business Cycle Fluctuations." In *NBER Macroeconomics Annual 1988,* edited by S. Fischer 111–48, Cambridge: MIT Press.

Sims, C.A. 1980. "Macroeconomics and Reality." *Econometrica* 48:1–48.

———. 1982. "Policy Analysis with Econometric Models." *Brookings Papers on Economic Analysis,* Number One, 107–52.

Sims, C. A., J. H. Stock, and M. W. Watson. 1990. "Inference in Linear Time Series Models with Some Unit Roots." *Econometrica* 58:113–44.

Wold, H. 1938. *A Study in the Analysis of Stationary Time Series.* Stockholm: Almqvist and Wiksell.

V

Wage Rigidity

Wage rigidity has been among the most resilient explanations to be offered for the postwar business cycle in the United States. In its simplest and most common form, this explanation attributes economic recessions and expansions to the failure of nominal wage rates to adjust promptly to eliminate disequilibria in the labor market induced by fluctuations in aggregate demand. Thus, a decline in aggregate demand (due, perhaps, to a contractionary monetary policy) is supposed to cause prices to fall. If nominal wage rates are not free to adjust fully, falling prices raise real wage rates. Rising real wages cause firms to reduce employment and output, producing involuntary unemployment and a recession. The cause of an economic expansion is analogous to that of a recession. In either case, nominal-wage rigidity is the critical market failure that permits changes in aggregate demand to affect real variables and produce business cycles.

This simple story has attracted considerable attention over the past two decades. Numerous attempts have been made to discredit it and replace it with other explanations for the business cycle. At the same time, efforts to establish a link between wage rigidity and macroeconomic fluctuations have been persuasive enough to keep it on the menu of explanations. This article is concerned with the latter efforts. However, doubts about the optimality of contractual arrangements that specify a fixed nominal-wage schedule and leave employment decisions to the firm continue to concern researchers.

Efforts to improve our understanding of the relationship between wage rigidity and the business cycle may be categorized according to (1) how the inflexibility of wages is rationalized, (2) the hypothesized link between wage rigidity and macroeconomic fluctuations, and (3) the policies proposed.

Two classes of theory rationalizing the rigidity of wages surfaced during the 1970s. One class treats rigid wages as a contractual risk-sharing device through which firms insure risk-averse workers against fluctuations in their incomes. Such arrangements have become known as implicit contracts. However, models of risk-sharing behavior invariably imply that *real* wages are fixed; the models fail to explain the existence of nominal-wage rigidity. Accordingly (and contrary to the impression produced by a casual reading of the implicit-contract literature), they fail to shed any light on the relationship between nominal-wage rigidity and the business cycle. Nor, as it turns out, do they demonstrate any casual relationship between real-wage rigidity and the business cycle.

By contrast, contracting models of the sort developed by Gray (1978) and Canzoneri (1977) do explain the rigidity of *nominal* wage rates and a "neo-Keynesian" business cycle. The models attribute the inflexibility of wages to the transactions costs of adjusting wage rates in response to changing economic conditions. Doubts about whether these transactions costs are large enough to account for the substantial output losses associated with the business cycle have been addressed by Akerlof and Yellen (1985), Blanchard and Kiyotaki (1987), and others.

In this second class of contracting models, the degree of wage rigidity (as measured by the duration of contracts) is endogenously determined. It is a decreasing function of the amount of uncertainty facing firms and workers, and an increasing function of the cost of renegotiating wage contracts. The rigidity shows up in nominal wages if contracts do not allow for full indexation of wage rates to the price level. The degree of wage indexation, like contract length, is endogenously determined in these models and full indexation is generally not optimal. By rationalizing nominal wage rates that are incompletely responsive to price-level changes, they supply a Keynesian channel through which aggregate demand may affect real activity and generate business cycles.

We turn next to the relationship between wage rigidity and cyclical movements in real activity. The traditional view, as reflected in the first paragraph of this article, identifies wage rigidity as a primary cause of real economic fluctuations. This view has been called into question by recent prewar/postwar comparisons of United States macroeconomic performance. Among the stylized facts suggested by prewar/postwar studies is that while wages and prices have become less flexible in the postwar period, output has become more stable. Taylor (1986) documents the phenomenon and notes its paradoxical nature in view of standard Keynesian paradigms.

This apparent puzzle has prompted some economists to reconsider the relationship between wage and price rigidity on the one hand and macroeconomic stability on the other. Important work on the subject includes a paper by DeLong and Summers (1986) that extends Taylor's wage-setting model to include the effects of expected inflation and the real interest rate on aggregate demand. Their extended model shows that an exogenous increase in wage flexibility may actually destabilize output, increasing the amplitude of the business cycle. A shortcoming of the De Long and Summers analysis of the relationship between wage rigidity and the business cycle, and of more traditional analyses, is a failure to recognize the endogeneity of the flexibility of the price system. Alternatively stated, most work on this topic overlooks the question of what causes wage rigidity.

In models that investigate the source of wage rigidity, both the degree of wage flexibility and the amplitude of output fluctuations are endogenously determined, and the relationship between the two depends on what is affecting them. Thus, in contracting models of the sort developed by Gray and Canzoneri, increased wage rigidity (as reflected in increased contract

length) is accompanied by less stable output if the increased rigidity is caused by higher transactions costs. It is accompanied by *more* stable output, however, if the increased rigidity is caused by reduced economic uncertainty. And, in fact, aggregate demand has become considerably more stable in the postwar period. This feature of the postwar period can by itself explain both the increased wage rigidity and the reduced output variability characterizing the period.

Finally, we turn to the policy implications of wage rigidity. An important feature of nominal-wage-contracting models is an exploitable trade-off between output and unanticipated inflation. Unlike some of their well-known competitors, these models admit the possibility of effective countercyclical aggregate-demand policy. As Fischer (1977) demonstrates, countercyclical policies can stabilize output if policymakers can respond more quickly to changing economic conditions than wage setters. In the United States, where contracts last one to three years, this condition seems likely to be met. Thus, explanations of the business cycle that invoke wage inflexibility are a convenient analytical vehicle for advocates of countercyclical aggregate-demand policies.

An interesting twist on the policy debate is provided by proponents of profit-sharing compensation schemes. Weitzman (1985) has contrasted the macroeconomic implications of fixed nominal wages and profit-sharing and finds that profit-sharing better insulates the real sector from aggregate-demand disturbances and thus attenuates the business cycle. Observing that profit-sharing has not been widely adopted despite its apparent advantages, he suggests that externalities may explain the reluctance of individual firms to adopt this system of compensation and that policy should seek to encourage profit-sharing arrangements between firms and workers. Here, the policy prescription is, in effect, to increase the flexibility of the price system rather than to stabilize aggregate demand.

Jo Anna Gray

See also EFFICIENCY WAGES; IMPLICIT CONTRACTS; NEW KEYNESIAN ECONOMICS; PRICE RIGIDITY; UNEMPLOYMENT

Bibliography
Akerlof, G. and J. Yellen. 1985. "A Near-
    Rational Model of the Business Cycle,

With Wage and Price Inertia." *Quarterly Journal of Economics* 100:823–38.

Azariadis, C. 1987. "Implicit Contracts." In *The New Palgrave: A Dictionary of Economics*. Vol. 2. Edited by J. Eatwell, M. Milgate, and P. Newman. London: Macmillan.

Barro, R. 1977. "Long-Term Contracting, Sticky Prices, and Monetary Policy." *Journal of Monetary Economics* 3:305–16.

Blanchard, O. J. and N. Kiyotaki. 1987. "Monopolistic Competition and the Effects of Aggregate Demand." *American Economic Review* 77:647–66.

Canzoneri, M. 1977. "Labor Contracts and Monetary Policy." *Journal of Monetary Economics* 6:241–55.

DeLong, B. and L. Summers. 1986. "Is Increased Price Flexibility Stabilizing?" *American Economic Review* 76:1031–44.

Fischer, S. 1977. "Long-Term Contracts, Rational Expectations, and the Optimal Money Supply Rule." *Journal of Political Economy* 85:191–205.

Gray, J. A. 1978. "On Indexation and Contract Length." *Journal of Political Economy* 86:1–18.

Taylor, J. 1979. "Staggered Wage Setting in a Macro Model." *American Economic Review* 69:108–13.

———. 1986. "Improvements in Macroeconomic Stability: The Role of Wages and Prices." *The American Business Cycle: Continuity and Change*, edited by R. J. Gordon, 639–77. Chicago: Univ. of Chicago Press.

Weitzman, M. 1985. "The Simple Macroeconomics of Profit Sharing." *American Economic Review* 75:937–53.

Walras's Law

Since the excess-demand equations of a general-equilibrium system are subject to a common budget constraint, they are interdependent. Consequently, if $n - 1$ of the n markets are in equilibrium, the nth market must be in equilibrium, too. Lange named this proposition, first stated by Walras, *Walras's Law*.

Macroeconomic models often take the form of simple general-equilibrium models consisting of four markets: a market for goods, a market for labor, a market for loans, and a

market for money. Walras's Law is then used to "eliminate" one of the markets. That is, equilibrium is characterized in terms of three of the markets, with Walras's Law taking care of the fourth. While Walras's Law itself is unexceptionable, the utility of its application in macroeconomic theory has often been controversial.

The debate over Keynes's replacement of the loanable-funds theory of interest with the liquidity-preference theory focused on the use of Walras's Law. In the Keynesian system, the market for loans is the one eliminated and the interest rate is "determined" in the market for money. Opponents objected, arguing that the interest rate should be determined in the market for loans. This objection is, of course, mistaken. In general equilibrium, no variable is determined exclusively in any one market, but rather by the system as a whole.

The real issue here is not Walras's Law, but the use of a general-equilibrium model in the first place. Should business cycles be seen as movements *of* an equilibrium or movements *about* an equilibrium? If the latter, then the proper application of Walras's Law is considerably more complicated than simply "eliminating" a market.

The issues at stake have been thoroughly discussed by Clower (1965), Tsiang (1966), and Kohn (1981, 1986). Similar problems with Walras's Law as the basis for the monetary approach to the balance of payments have been discussed by Kohn and Karacaoglu (1989).

Meir Kohn

See also LOANABLE-FUNDS DOCTRINE; SAY, JEAN-BAPTISTE; SAY'S LAW

Bibliography

Clower, R. W. 1965. "The Keynesian Counter-Revolution: A Theoretical Appraisal." In *The Theory of Interest Rates*, edited by F. H. Hahn and F. P. R. Brechling, 103–25. London: Macmillan.

Kohn, M. 1981. "A Loanable Funds Theory of Unemployment and Monetary Disequilibrium." *American Economic Review* 71:859–79.

———. 1986. "Monetary Analysis, the Equilibrium Method, and Keynes' 'General Theory.'" *Journal of Political Economy* 94:1191–1224.

Kohn, M. and G. Karacaoglu. 1989. "Aggregation and the Microfoundations of the

Monetary Approach to the Balance of Payments." *Canadian Journal of Economics* 22:290–309.

Tsiang, S. C. 1966. "Walras' Law, Say's Law and Liquidity Preference in General Equilibrium Analysis." *International Economic Review* 7:329–45.

Warburton, Clark (1896–1979)

Clark Warburton received baccalaureate and master's degrees from Cornell University in 1921 and 1928, and a Ph.D. from Columbia University in 1932. After teaching in the United States and India and working on the national-income accounts at the Brookings Institution, Warburton joined the newly established Federal Deposit Insurance Corporation in 1934, where he worked until retiring in 1965. He remained active throughout his career and was working on a manuscript on disequilibrium monetary economics at the time of his death.

Warburton is widely acknowledged as a major forerunner of the Monetarist approach to business-cycle research. Warburton anticipated many of the major issues of the Monetarist-Keynesian debate in the 1960s and 1970s, as Milton Friedman and Anna J. Schwartz recognized in the preface to their *Monetary History of the United States*. They observed that time after time they found that Warburton had anticipated their findings.

Determining the deposit-insurance premium to be imposed by the newly established FDIC was one of Warburton's first responsibilities. It was in studying how bank failures had evolved during the early 1930s that Warburton began to formulate a monetary interpretation of Federal Reserve policy in the Great Depression. He argued that the Fed's policy had been one of tightness rather than of ease and that the Fed had been an ineffective lender of last resort. When the Monetarist view of the Great Depression was finally debated seriously in the 1960s, Warburton's views were largely vindicated.

Warburton published many papers between 1944 and 1953, a number of which appeared in major journals. Apparently, in 1953, Warburton's superiors pressured him to cease publishing and making presentations, bringing a sudden stop to his productivity. While a number of economists had questioned the nonmonetary version of the Keynesian system during the Keynesian Revolution, no other economist argued for a monetary approach as strongly as did

Warburton. In a 1948 paper, for example, Warburton challenged the profession to substantiate the nonmonetary interpretation of economic fluctuations with empirical evidence.

Warburton's work emphasized the following: (1) the need for detailed empirical research on how money and monetary policy influence the economy; (2) changes in the money supply are both sufficient and necessary to generate changes in economic activity; (3) money affects economic activity with a lag; (4) business cycles result from deviations of the money stock from a noninflationary growth path determined by the growth of potential income; (5) the Federal Reserve caused much of the instability in the U.S. economy after 1913 and, in particular, played a major role in prolonging the Great Depression; (6) economic stability could be most effectively promoted if the allocation of resources were left to the market, monetary policy were governed by steady monetary expansion, and the federal budget were balanced.

Despite the volume of work published by Warburton and the support that empirical research after 1960 provided to his views, Warburton was largely ignored by much of the profession. Certain characteristics of his work were partly responsible. Warburton continued to use the equation-of-exchange framework rather than the more widely accepted Cambridge version of the quantity theory, and his writing style was frequently argumentative and laden with strongly worded challenges that could easily have offended many readers. Additionally, Warburton had no graduate students and was not affiliated with a research institution concerned with macro issues.

More importantly, the Keynesian Revolution and the wide acceptance of its nonmonetary interpretation of the Great Depression discouraged a serious investigation of the role of money. The times were simply not receptive to the critical analyses Warburton offered.

By the early 1960s, when the Monetarist view was being seriously debated, Warburton's work was over a decade old and did not reflect the rising quantitative standards of the profession. Nevertheless, Warburton deserves to be called the first post-Great Depression Monetarist.

Thomas F. Cargill

See also ANGELL, JAMES WATERHOUSE; FRIEDMAN, MILTON; GREAT DEPRESSION IN THE UNITED STATES (1929–1938); MONETARY DISEQUILIBRIUM THEORIES OF THE BUSINESS

CYCLE; SCHWARTZ, ANNA JACOBSON; SNYDER, CARL

Bibliography

Bordo, M. D. and A. J. Schwartz. [1979] 1987. "Clark Warburton: Pioneer Monetarist." Chap. 9 in A. J. Schwartz, *Money in Historical Perspective*. Chicago: Univ. of Chicago Press.

Cargill, T. F. 1979. "Clark Warburton and the Development of Monetarism Since the Great Depression." *History of Political Economy* 11:425–49.

———. 1981. "A Tribute to Clark Warburton." *Journal of Money, Credit, and Banking* 13:89–93.

Friedman, M. and A. J. Schwartz. 1963. *A Monetary History of the United States, 1867–1960*. Princeton: Princeton Univ. Press.

Humphrey, T. M. 1971. "The Role of Non-Chicago Economists in the Evolution of the Quantity Theory of Money in America 1930–1950." *Southern Economic Journal* 39:12–18.

Warburton, C. 1948. "Hansen and Fellner on Full Employment Policies." *American Economic Review* 38:128–34.

———. 1966. *Depression, Inflation, and Monetary Policy: Selected Papers*. Baltimore: Johns Hopkins Univ. Press.

Wicksell, Johan Gustav Knut (1851–1926)

Knut Wicksell stands out as Sweden's most famous economist. He began his academic life studying mathematics at the University of Uppsala in the 1870s. While at Uppsala he discovered the writings of Malthus and became a lifelong proponent of Malthusianism.

In the late 1870s, he presented a public talk in which he attributed the major social ills in Swedish society to overpopulation. His message immediately triggered immense public debate and criticism. One critic, David Davidson, a professor of economics, suggested that Wicksell lacked knowledge of economics. Inspired by this critique, driven by a strong desire to improve social conditions, supported by generous grants, primarily from the Lorén foundation, and determinedly helped by the woman, Anna Bugge, with whom he had entered a contract of cohabitation, Wicksell began his study of economics.

From 1885 to 1890, he studied economics in Great Britain, Germany, Austria, and France.

In 1889, Wicksell became familiar with the work of the Austrian economist Eugen von Böhm-Bawerk, whose writings on capital theory profoundly affected Wicksell's work.

Returning to Sweden, Wicksell had difficulty finding a chair. His reputation as a radical pamphleteer made him an unattractive candidate. In 1901, he managed to obtain a temporary position as professor of economics at the University of Lund, and in 1904, he was appointed full professor despite strong resistance from conservative groups.

The 1890s were Wicksell's most productive period, when he published three books of lasting value. *Über Wert, Kapital und Rente (Value, Capital and Rent)* developed the marginal productivity theory of distribution and integrated Böhm-Bawerk's theory of capital with Walras's general-equilibrium theory. Like Böhm-Bawerk, but in contrast to Walras, Wicksell analyzed circulating capital, that is, stocks of raw materials, goods in process, and finished goods, while treating fixed capital like land ("rent goods"). Capital was not conceived of as a separate factor of production but was represented by dated inputs. The productivity of capital (the *natural* rate of interest) was then defined by the difference between marginal products of the inputs of the same factor of production at different times. Wicksell generalized Böhm-Bawerk's analysis by allowing dated inputs of both labor and land and by formulating a small neoclassical general-equilibrium model including time-consuming production processes. But unlike Böhm-Bawerk, Wicksell formulated his theory mathematically.

Finanztheoretische Untersuchungen nebst Darstellung und Kritik des Steuerwesens Schwedens (Studies in the theory of public finance) developed the theory of public finance based on marginal utility theory. Finally, in *Geldzins und Güterpreise (Interest and Prices)*, Wicksell reformulated the quantity theory of money.

While the classical quantity theory of money as developed in England in the eighteenth century by Richard Cantillon and David Hume assumed a system of pure outside money, Wicksell analyzed the other extreme—a system of pure inside money. This reflected the development of the banking system since the middle of the eighteenth century.

Wicksell sought to explain the observed positive correlation between bank lending and the rate of inflation. This correlation is contrary to Ricardo's analysis of inflation in England during the Napoleonic Wars, which maintained that monetary expansion temporarily reduces the rate of interest as prices are rising. In his analysis, Wicksell drew on Ricardo's (and indirectly Thornton's) view that the impact of monetary expansion can be analyzed in terms of the relationship between the loan rate and the natural rate of interest. The English classical economists regarded the rate of profit on the projects financed by the loans as a proxy for the latter.

In analyzing the natural rate of interest, Wicksell improved on the analysis by deriving the natural rate of interest from Austrian capital theory. But it must be stressed that Wicksell did not consider the natural rate of interest as simply the marginal productivity of the roundabout process, but rather an endogenous variable determined in a general-equilibrium solution of an economy without money.

Wicksell explained the paradoxical behavior of interest rates and price changes by attributing periods of inflation and deflation subsequent to the Napoleonic Wars to real disturbances affecting the natural rate of interest rather than to monetary shocks such as caused inflation during the Napoleonic Wars. The resulting gap between the natural and the loan rates of interest would increase the demand for bank loans and hence the demand for labor. Nominal wages and workers' incomes would rise, which would, in turn, increase the demand for goods and, finally, the price level.

In his discussion, Wicksell observed that his analysis was inconsistent with (the identity version) of Say's Law which rules out any overall excess demand for or supply of goods. But the gap between the natural and the loan rate of interest would only create excess demand for goods *ex ante,* and Wicksell assumed that the rise of the price level would restore equilibrium on the goods market. Wicksell did not analyze disequilibrium phenomena.

In an economy with a pure outside money, a change in the quantity of money changes the equilibrium price level via a real-balance effect. But in the pure inside-money case which Wicksell analyzed, the price level is indeterminate. Wicksell contrasted the stable equilibrium of relative prices to the meta-stable equilibrium of the price level. But there may nevertheless be an equilibrium rate of change of the price level. What accounts for this?

Wicksell assumed that economic agents expect a constant price level. An increased natural rate of interest implies increased demand for land and labor. To clear factor markets, nominal factor prices will increase. In the next period the increased purchasing power implies excess demand for goods. The goods market is cleared by an increase of the price level. The process goes on period by period as long as the gap between the natural and market rates of interest is positive.

The reason why inflation continues (price increases are cumulative) is that the normal price level always equals the price level of the previous period. If the price level increases in the current period, the normal price level in the next period will rise correspondingly. Although there is some inconsistency in this revision mechanism, the assumption may still describe fairly realistically how expectations are formed.

Wicksell's main assumption was that expectations are focused on a stable long-run price level. But he also considered the possibility that inflation could be expected. Wicksell was aware of Irving Fisher's analysis of inflation expectations and thought that inflation expectations could affect the rate of inflation. However, he was skeptical of a theory of inflation that relied only on inflationary expectations. There must be some independent reason for expectations of inflation to be formed.

Although Wicksell's *Lectures* ([1901–06] 1934–35) were mainly addressed to students, they contained further developments of his price theory and monetary theory. The concept of capital now included fixed capital. Wicksell replaced the concept of a natural rate of interest with the more operational concept of a *normal* rate of interest, defined to be the loan rate of interest that creates equilibrium in the goods market (i.e., equates investment with saving). Furthermore, Wicksell no longer believed that all excess demands for goods correspond to a gap between the normal and the loan rates of interest. For example, a gold discovery and the resulting excess demand for goods could directly increase the price level, with no gap between the two rates of interest.

There is a close correspondence between Wicksell's analysis of inflation and his analysis of business cycles. In both cases Wicksell identified real shocks as the impulse. He attributed the cycle to the uneven introduction of technical and commercial inventions. But the form of the cycle is not determined by the impulse mechanism, but by the reaction of the economy to the impulses.

In a 1918 review of *Ett bidrag till krisernas teori* by Karl Petander (*Ekonomisk Tidskrift* 20:66–75), Wicksell offered a famous analogy between business cycles and hitting a rocking horse. Even if the shocks are erratic, the motion will be regular. The problem of how the economy transforms erratic shocks into a regular cycle inspired Ragnar Frisch's famous 1933 paper "Propagation Problems and Impulse Problems in Dynamic Economics."

Wicksell did not present a systematic theory of the cycle or of unemployment. In both cases, the reason may be that Wicksell did not investigate disequilibrium phenomena. Nevertheless, he made the important observation that inventory changes play an important role in the cycle and that these changes to a great extent are involuntary. Concerning the problem of unemployment, he explicitly called it an enigma. However, when confronted with high and rising unemployment in Sweden in the early 1920s, Wicksell adopted a basically neo-Malthusian position, arguing that the major cause of high unemployment was too large a stock of workers.

Wicksell started his career with his talk in the 1870s. He remained active in public debate serving as journalist, public lecturer, and opinion maker, energetically propagating neo-Malthusianism until his death in 1926.

Wicksell exerted a significant influence on the development of Swedish monetary policy in the 1920s and 1930s. In 1931, when Sweden left the gold standard, the government and the Riksbank officially adopted price stability as the goal of monetary policy, thus becoming the first central bank to introduce Wicksell's norm as a guide for policy.

Wicksell's influence on the development of economic theory has been extraordinary. During the 1930s, almost all the important developments in business-cycle theory were traceable to Wicksell's influence. The development of employment theory by the Stockholm School was, to a large extent, inspired by Wicksell. One example is the elaboration of the cumulative process in the early 1930s by Erik Lindahl, Gunnar Myrdal, and Bertil Ohlin. F. A. Hayek was both directly and indirectly, via Ludwig von Mises, inspired by Wicksell in his development of business-cycle theory, as was D. H. Robertson. Wicksell's influence on John Maynard Keynes is especially strong in *Treatise on Money*. The natural rate/market rate distinction continues to be important in some theories of the business cycle and the savings-equals-investment paradigm remains dominant in most macroeconomic models. A small but telling example of Wicksell's enduring influence is Milton Friedman's choice of the term "natural rate of unemployment" in a conscious allusion to the natural rate of interest.

Lars Jonung
Claes-Henric Siven

See also AUSTRIAN THEORY OF BUSINESS CYCLES; BÖHM-BAWERK, EUGEN RITTER VON; EXPECTATIONS; FRISCH, RAGNAR ANTON KITTEL; HAYEK, FRIEDRICH AUGUST [VON]; KEYNES, JOHN MAYNARD; LINDAHL, ERIK ROBERT; LUNDBERG, ERIK FILIP; MISES, LUDWIG EDLER VON; MONETARY DISEQUILIBRIUM THEORIES OF THE BUSINESS CYCLE; MYRDAL, GUNNAR; NATURAL RATE OF INTEREST; OHLIN, BERTIL GOTTHARD; RICARDO, DAVID; ROBERTSON, DENNIS HOLME; SAVING EQUALS INVESTMENT; SAY, JEAN-BAPTISTE; SAY'S LAW; STOCKHOLM SCHOOL; THORNTON, HENRY

Bibliography

Gårdlund, T. 1958. *The Life of Knut Wicksell.* Stockholm: Almquist and Wicksell.

Jonung, L. 1979. "Knut Wicksell's Norm of Price Stabilization and Swedish Monetary Policy in the 1930's." *Journal of Monetary Economics* 5:459–96.

———. 1981. "Ricardo on Machinery and the Present Unemployment: An Unpublished Manuscript by Knut Wicksell." *Economic Journal* 91:195–205.

Patinkin, D. 1965. *Money, Interest, and Prices.* 2d ed. New York: Harper and Row.

Uhr, C. 1960. *Economic Doctrines of Knut Wicksell.* Berkeley and Los Angeles: Univ. of California Press.

Wicksell, K. [1893] 1954. *Value, Capital and Rent.* Translation. London: Allen and Unwin.

———. [1898] 1936. *Interest and Prices.* Translation. London: Macmillan.

———. [1901–06] 1934–35. *Lectures on Political Economy.* 2 Vols. Translation. London: George Routledge and Sons.

———. 1958. *Knut Wicksell: Selected Papers on Economic Theory.* Edited by E. Lindahl. London: Allen and Unwin.

Worker and Job Turnover

The fact that most unemployed workers have previously held a job raises a number of questions. Why did these workers leave a job with no new job immediately available? Were they fired or laid off, or did they quit? Is the separation of worker from job welfare-improving? The answers to these questions have important implications for our views on the causes and efficiency of cyclical fluctuations in employment.

Some basic facts on worker turnover in the United States economy are useful in addressing these questions. Recent data show that 15 percent of male household heads change jobs in an average year, with somewhat higher figures for women. However, aggregate figures mask enormous disparity in mobility rates among age groups. For example, Hall (1982) estimates that the average male worker will hold roughly eleven separate jobs during his career, but that six of these jobs will be held before the age of thirty. Similarly, Topel and Ward (1992) find that job mobility declines steadily as a worker accumulates labor-market experience.

Before interpreting these facts, one should note that a worker's first decade in the labor market is distinguished by relatively rapid wage growth. For example, Murphy and Welch (1990) show that more than half of all career wage growth occurs within the first ten years of a worker's career. (Topel and Ward provide an excellent analysis of the empirical connection between wage growth and job mobility.)

The concurrent timing of job mobility and wage growth is often interpreted in the context of job-matching models first formalized by Jovanovic (1979). In this view, workers and firms come to market with idiosyncratic skills, needs, tastes, etc. Each potential pairing of a worker and a firm has an associated "match" value that is a summary measure of the degree to which the worker and firm form a compatible pairing. Workers search across jobs for a good match, but the search is complicated by the fact that match quality reveals itself only gradually during an employment relationship. Workers may, therefore, take a job that looks promising only to find out several years later that it was really not the right job after all.

The fact that evaluating the quality of a match takes time means that workers typically will never find it optimal to search for the perfect job. Rather, they will sift through a number of jobs until they find one good enough to make further search and experimentation un-

profitable. Once such a job is found, job search is reduced and further job turnover becomes unlikely. If we associate movements to better matches with increased wages, then the model can also explain why most wage growth and most job mobility occur in the first decade of employment careers.

The aggregate rate of job separation is only weakly countercyclical. However, economists often think it useful to distinguish between employee-initiated *quits* and employer-initiated *layoffs*. The distinction is motivated by the fact that workers who quit are much less likely to be unemployed between jobs than are laid off workers. Quits and layoffs each account for roughly 50 percent of separations over the course of recent business cycles. But the composition of separations is highly cyclical, as quits are strongly procyclical and layoffs strongly countercyclical. Indeed, much of the increase in unemployment during recessions reflects the changing fraction of layoffs and quits among job separations (Lilien and Hall 1986).

A job separation is *efficient* if and only if a worker's productivity at the old firm is lower than at the best alternative. The cyclicality of quits and layoffs has led many observers to conclude that many separations are not efficient. In the simplest models, it is not obvious why inefficient separations should occur. For example, according to the theory of separations proposed by Becker, Landes, and Michael (1977), if firms and workers are free to bargain each period, then most reasonable bargaining games imply efficient separation rules. Similarly, McLaughlin (1991) has argued that the distinction between quits and layoffs is largely artificial and that separations are usually efficient. In his model, "quit" and "layoff" are simply labels attached to separations depending on whether separation was initiated by the worker or the firm. The labels have meaning only in indicating whether a separation is due to an increase in the worker's outside opportunities (a quit) or to a decrease in the worker's productivity at the firm (a layoff).

Many other observers reject the notion that separations are efficient. These models are too numerous to review here, but most are based on the assumptions that period-by-period bargaining is prohibitively expensive and that information is asymmetric. For example, Hall and Lazear (1984) argue that inexperienced bargainers are hesitant to enter into an employment relationship in which they must bargain over hours and wages each period. This leads to a contract that specifies work hours and wages in each period, perhaps conditioned on jointly observed factors.

However, the contract may be constrained by the inability of workers to observe the state of product demand and the inability of firms to observe workers' outside opportunities. This asymmetry of information may lead to opportunistic bargaining and misrepresentation of private information. For example, if a contract were to require more work (but no more pay) in high-demand periods, the firm would always have an incentive to claim that demand is unusually high. These considerations have led some observers to argue that relatively simple contracts are optimal in this second-best world. These simple (e.g., fixed-wage) contracts often lead to inefficient separation rules. In Hall and Lazear's model, inflexible wages lead to inefficiently frequent quits during booms (when firms won't match newly increased outside opportunities), and inefficiently frequent layoffs during recessions (when workers will not accept demand-necessitated wage reductions).

The model of Hall and Lazear is only one example from a lengthy literature (Rosen 1985, Hart and Holmstrom 1987). However, there are problems with models of aggregate unemployment fluctuations based on informational asymmetries. The most serious one is that information on aggregate economic activity is widely available and cheaply verified. It is easy for the average employee (employer) to verify the claims of his employer (employee) about aggregate output demand (outside opportunities). In that case, why isn't the contract conditioned on these aggregate outcomes? Several recent efforts to address this criticism have been reviewed by Hart and Holmstrom. But no consensus has yet emerged on whether these models adequately explain the observed pattern of quits and layoffs.

William J. Carrington

See also EFFICIENCY WAGES; IMPLICIT CONTRACTS; NEW KEYNESIAN ECONOMICS; SEARCH THEORY; SECTORAL SHIFTS; UNEMPLOYMENT

Bibliography

Becker, G. S., E. M. Landes, and R. T. Michael. 1977. "An Economic Analysis of Marital Instability." *Journal of Political Economy* 85:1141–87.

Hall, R. E. 1982. "The Importance of Lifetime Jobs in the U.S. Economy." *American Economic Review* 72:716–24.

Hall, R. E. and E. P. Lazear. 1984. "The Excess Sensitivity of Layoffs and Quits to Demand." *Journal of Labor Economics* 2:233–57.

Hart, O. D. and B. Holmstrom. 1987. "The Theory of Contracts." *Advances in Economic Theory: Fifth World Congress*, edited by T. F. Bewley, 71–155. Cambridge: Cambridge Univ. Press.

Jovanovic, B. 1979. "Job Matching and the Theory of Turnover." *Journal of Political Economy* 87:972–90.

Lilien, D. M. and R. E. Hall. 1986. "Cyclical Fluctuations in the Labor Market." In *Handbook of Labor Economics*, edited by O. Ashenfelter and R. Layard, 1001–35. Amsterdam: North-Holland.

McLaughlin, K. J. 1991. "A Theory of Quits and Layoffs with Efficient Turnover." *Journal of Political Economy* 99:1–29.

Murphy, K. M. and F. Welch. 1990. "Empirical Age Earnings Profiles." *Journal of Labor Economics* 8:202–29.

Rosen, S. 1985. "Implicit Contracts: A Survey." *Journal of Economic Literature* 23:1144–75.

Topel, R. and M. Ward. 1992. "Job Mobility and the Careers of Young Men." *Quarterly Journal of Economics* 107:439–79.

Woytinsky, Wladimir Savelievich (1885–1960)

A political activist and a highly respected scholar, Woytinsky devoted himself to the cause of social progress during some of the darkest episodes of this century. Both his academic and political activities were tools for supporting this cause. As a native of St. Petersburg, Woytinsky entered his hometown university in 1904. One year later, he joined the Bolshevist wing of Russia's Social Democratic Party. After a series of arrests, a four-year sentence of hard labor, and an exile to Siberia imposed on him for his activities in the revolutionary party, Woytinsky eventually broke his ties with the Bolsheviks and, while still in exile, married Emma Shadkan, his life-long companion and colleague.

The couple returned to St. Petersburg in 1917, once the Tsarist regime had been overthrown. Woytinsky resumed his political activities, though he now associated with the moderate reformers led by Tseretelli. After the usurpation of November 1917, Woytinsky was again imprisoned, but he and his wife managed to escape via Georgia to the West. They settled in Germany and began working on the seven-volume compendium, *Die Welt in Zahlen,* which established Woytinsky's international reputation as a statistician.

Woytinsky was appointed director of the German Federation of Trade Unions in 1929, in recognition of his success with *Die Welt* and other freelance publications. Yet he soon joined "another desperate fight for a lost cause" (Woytinsky 1961, 434), by actively promoting an expansive economic policy financed by deficit spending to rescue Germany's Weimar Republic from the misery of the Great Depression. Ironically, it was only after Hitler assumed power that these measures of demand management, designed to save the Republic, were actually implemented. Once the Trade Union had fallen under the spell of the Nazi regime, the Woytinskys left Germany, settling in the United States in 1935.

Woytinsky quickly made a name for himself in America. As a member of the Social Security Board, he developed the method for calculating unemployment benefits and contributions which was later adopted by the United States and Canada. His predictions of postwar prosperity in the U.S. (1943, 1945–46, 1947) made headlines in the press, while his related critique of the linear consumption function underlying most contemporary macromodels (which he held responsible for the failures of other forecasts) stirred controversy in academia as well (1946, 1948; Garvy 1962). In addition, the Woytinskys worked together on two significant statistical studies, comparable to their German predecessor in both size and craftsmanship (Woytinsky and Woytinsky 1953, 1955).

Woytinsky proved to be a prolific writer by any standards, leading to the claim that he had written more than "any other economist, living or dead" in his *New York Times* obituary. Only the years 1908 and 1909 are without entry in his bibliography (in E. Woytinsky 1962). Although his debut was a theoretical book (1906), it seems that over the years "his belief in good judgment and common sense grew, and his interest in abstraction faded" (Marschak 1962, 12). Later writings cover a broad range of issues, most of which concern questions of economic development and economic policy, including numerous economic and social case studies, forecasts of amazing scope and accuracy, and, of course, the assessment of statistical methods.

These voluminous statistical compendia, produced jointly with Mrs. Woytinsky, will probably remain the best remembered part of Woytinsky's work. They are more than an ephemeral agglomeration of numbers and tables, as we now recognize the presentation of "data." Rather, they provide what once had been understood by the term "statistics" (Colm 1962): the science of the state—an accounting assessment of the wealth, living conditions, and future prospects of a society. The Woytinskys produced those accounts on their own, but their compilation was far from complete. Although the data were available, their task was far from simple. However, given the state of modern information processing, these works will soon be considered a primitive step in the development of statistical methods.

Another visionary characteristic of Woytinsky's work, already evident when he was president of the St. Petersburg Council of the Unemployed in 1907, was his concern with economic fluctuations and the problem of unemployment. Troubled by the international "sound money" policy, and by the fate of the Weimar Republic, Woytinsky became a leader among those German economists who argued for an expansionary policy of public works (Woytinsky 1931). However, the Social Democrats refused to support any such proposal. Only the Nazis advocated public works in their platform for the crucial elections of 1932.

The results of this neglect are well known, and those modest proposals are no longer controversial. For contemporaries, however, Woytinsky's arguments implied disregarding the conventional account of the depression as part of a "regular" and unavoidable business cycle, and rejecting the prescription of austerity. Woytinsky never held the opinion that an economic upswing required prior savings. His persistent efforts to ameliorate economic conditions reflect his understanding that the uneven path of economic development creates situations in which trust in science does not suffice—situations calling for action, with or without the support of current mainstream theory.

Christof Rühl

See also CONSUMPTION EXPENDITURES; PUMP-PRIMING

Bibliography

Colm, G. 1962. "A Twentieth-Century Version of *Examen Rerum Publicarum Totius Orbis.*" In *So Much Alive: The Life and Work of Wladimir Woytinsky,* edited by E. Woytinsky, 156–59. New York: Vanguard Press.

Garvy, G. 1962. "Forecasting Trends in the American Economy." In *So Much Alive: The Life and Work of Wladimir Woytinsky,* edited by E. Woytinsky, 113–32. New York: Vanguard Press.

Marschak, J. 1962. "Wladimir Woytinsky and Economic Theory." In *So Much Alive: The Life and Work of Wladimir Woytinsky,* edited by E. Woytinsky, 11–20. New York: Vanguard Press.

Woytinsky, E., ed. 1962. *So Much Alive: The Life and Work of Wladimir Woytinsky.* New York: Vanguard Press.

Woytinsky, E. and Woytinsky, W. 1953. *World Population and Production: Trends and Outlook.* New York: Twentieth Century Fund.

———. 1955. *World Commerce and Governments: Trends and Outlook.* New York: Twentieth Century Fund.

Woytinsky, W. [1906] 1964. *Market and Prices: Theory of Consumption, Market and Market Prices.* Forewords by M. I. Tugan-Baranovsky and J. Marschak. New York: A. M. Kelley.

———. 1925–28. *Die Welt in Zahlen.* 7 vols. Berlin: Rudolf Mosse.

———. 1931. *Internationale Hebung der Preise als Ausweg aus der Krise.* Leipzig: Hans Buske.

———. 1943. *Economic Perspectives 1943–48.* Social Security Board Memorandum no. 52. Washington, D.C.: Social Security Board.

———. 1945–46. "Postwar Economic Perspectives." *Social Security Bulletin* Dec. 1945, Jan., Feb., March 1946.

———. 1946. "The Relationship between Consumers' Expenditures, Savings and Disposable Income." *Review of Economic Statistics* 28:1–12.

———. 1947. "What Was Wrong in Forecasts of Postwar Depression." *Journal of Political Economy* 55:142–51.

———. 1948. "The Consumption-Saving Function: Its Algebra and Philosophy." *Review of Economic Statistics* 30:45–55.

———. 1961. *Stormy Passage: A Personal History Through Two Russian Revolutions to Democracy and Freedom, 1905–1960.* New York: Vanguard Press.

Z

Zarnowitz, Victor (1919–   )

Victor Zarnowitz was born in Lancut, Poland in 1919. He received a Ph.D. in economics from the University of Heidelberg in 1951 and has resided in the United States since 1952. From 1959 until his retirement in 1989, he was a professor of economics and finance in the Graduate School of Business at the University of Chicago. He is currently co-director of the Center for International Business Cycle Research at Columbia University.

Zarnowitz's work has ranged across most categories of business-cycle research: theory, data construction, statistical analysis, business-cycle indicators, and forecasting. Most of his work has been carried out within the broad confines of the National Bureau of Economic Research business-cycle research program developed by Arthur Burns and Wesley Mitchell (1946). The NBER research program stressed the endogenous nature of cycles and devoted enormous time and effort to accumulating long data series and carefully plotting the average relationships among variables within cycles. Zarnowitz and Moore (1986) have provided an up-to-date example of the NBER approach. Based on Mitchell's pioneering work, the NBER approach focuses on the factors underlying movements in price-cost margins and on how the movements in price-cost margins affect inventory accumulation and business fixed investment. Skeptical that the relationships among economic variables across the cycle could be captured by any manageable system of equations, Burns and Mitchell and their followers did not seek to develop formal mathematical models of the underlying processes that might generate cycles.

Perhaps Zarnowitz's most important contribution to the assembly and analysis of business-cycle data is his 1973 book, *Orders, Production, and Investment*. In this book, Zarnowitz assembled data series back to 1870 which allowed him to trace out the cyclical relations between new orders, unfilled orders, production, shipments, and inventories. He found that new orders tend to lead production at both cyclical peaks and troughs. The cyclical amplitude of new orders is greater than the cyclical amplitude of production or shipments, in part, because firms make use of data on new orders to smooth production. Zarnowitz found that industries that produce mainly to stock attempt to use unfilled orders or order backlogs, rather than inventories of finished products, to stabilize production. Here, as elsewhere, Zarnowitz was impressed by the fact that the relationships among variables are generally nonlinear and often variable across cycles, which reduces their tractability to formal, mathematical analysis.

During its heyday, the main rival to the Burns and Mitchell research program was that associated with Ragnar Frisch ([1933] 1965) and Eugen Slutsky ([1927] 1937). Adherents of this view believe that business cycles can be well characterized by the effects of exogenous stochastic disturbances on a system of difference equations. While Zarnowitz is one of the few academic economists still working within the NBER research program, the Frisch and Slutsky approach has been adopted by modern real business-cycle theorists.

The dominance of real business-cycle models in current business-cycle research published in the leading economic journals clearly troubles Zarnowitz. He articulates his misgivings about the direction of current business-cycle research in several of the essays published in his 1992 collection, *Business Cycles: Theory, History, Indicators, and Forecasting*. He is particularly troubled that real business-cycle theorists have neglected the historical and statistical business-cycle research he and others have conducted. This neglect has led to the construction and acceptance of models that are inconsistent with the empirical evidence on business cycles.

Zarnowitz's long-standing interest in economic forecasting has also contributed to his skepticism of recent business-cycle models. In several papers reprinted in *Business Cycles* he shows that published forecasts often fail to satisfy the requirements of the rational-expectations hypothesis. He also finds that forecasts that include judgmental adjustments tend to perform at least as well as the forecasts of econometric models. The poor forecasting performance of econometric models reinforces Zarnowitz in his belief that the complex relationships among variables across business cycles are unlikely ever to be reduced to a set of equations.

Anthony Patrick O'Brien

See also BURNS, ARTHUR FRANK; FRISCH, RAGNAR ANTON KITTEL; MITCHELL, WESLEY CLAIR; MOORE, GEOFFREY HOYT; REAL BUSINESS-CYCLE THEORIES

Bibliography
Burns, A. F. and W. C. Mitchell. 1946. *Measuring Business Cycles.* New York: Columbia Univ. Press.
Frisch, R. [1933] 1965. "Propagation Problems and Impulse Problems in Dynamic Economics." In *A.E.A. Readings in Business Cycles,* 155–85. Homewood, Ill.: Irwin.
Slutsky, E. [1927] 1937. "The Summation of Random Causes as the Source of Cyclic Processes." Translation. *Econometrica* 5:105–46.
Zarnowitz, V. 1973. *Orders, Production, and Investment—a Cyclical and Structural Analysis.* New York: Columbia Univ. Press.
———. 1992. *Business Cycles: Theory, History, Indicators, and Forecasting.* Chicago: Univ. of Chicago Press.
Zarnowitz, V. and G. H. Moore. 1986. "Major Changes in Cyclical Behavior." In *The American Business Cycle Today: Continuity and Change,* edited by R. J. Gordon, 519–72. Chicago: Univ. of Chicago Press.

Appendix

The following four tables provide chronologies of classical business cycles in the United States, Great Britain, France, and Germany over various periods starting in the late eighteenth century, as well as a chronology of growth cycles in eleven countries since 1948. Readers may find it helpful to consult these tables as a ready reference, in conjunction with the various historical articles on business-cycle episodes in this volume, or with other articles concerning the definition or the dating of business cycles. The assistance of Victor Zarnowitz and his associates at the Center for International Business Cycle Research at Columbia University is gratefully acknowledged.

TABLE 1. Annual Reference Dates and Durations of Business Cycles in Great Britain and the United States

Dates of Peaks and Troughs by Years		Duration in Years			
Trough (T)	Peak (P)	Contraction P to T	Expansion T to P	Full Cycle T to T	P to P
Great Britain					
	1792				
1793	1796	1	3		4
1797	1802	1	5	4	6
1803	1806	1	3	6	4
1808	1810	2	2	5	4
1811	1815	1	4	3	5
1816	1818	1	2	5	3
1819	1825	1	6	3	7
1826	1828	1	2	7	3
1829	1831	1	2	3	3
1832	1836	1	4	3	5
1837	1839	1	2	5	3
1842	1845	3	3	5	6
1848	1854	3	6	6	9
1855	1857	1	2	7	3
1858					
Mean duration (years)		1.3	3.3	4.6	4.6
Standard deviation (years)		0.7	1.5	1.5	1.8
United States					
1790	1796		6		
1799	1802	3	3	9	6
1804	1807	2	3	5	5
1810	1812[a]	3	1.5	6	4.5
1812[a]	1815	0.5	3	2	3.5
1821	1822	6	1	9	7
1823	1825	1	2	2	3
1826	1828	1	2	3	3
1829	1833	1	4	3	5
1834	1836	1	2	5	3
1838	1839	2	1	4	3
1843	1845	4	2	5	6
1846	1847	1	1	3	2
1848	1853	1	5	2	6
1855		2			
Mean duration (years)		2	2.6	4.6	4.4
Standard deviation (years)		1.5	1.5	2.4	1.6

Source: Great Britain: Table 16 in A. F. Burns and W. C. Mitchell, *Measuring Business Cycles* (New York: NBER, 1946), p. 79; United States: 1790-1833, W. L. Thorp, *Business Annals* (New York: NBER, 1926), 113–26; 1834–55, and table 16, p. 78, in Burns and Mitchell (1946).
[a] In 1812 there is first a "brief recession," then a revival. The corresponding duration measures are based on the assumption that the recession occurred in the first half of the year, before the outbreak of the war with England [for evidence, see Thorp (1926), 42, 117].

TABLE 2. Business Cycles in the United States: 1790–1991

	Dates of Peaks and Troughs						Duration in Months*			
By Months		By Quarters		By Calendar Years			Contraction	Expansion	Full Cycle	
Trough (T)	Peak (P)	T	P	T	P		P to T	T to P	T to T	P to P
				1790	1796		—	72	—	—
				1799	1802		36	36	108	72
				1804	1807		24	36	60	60
				1810	1812		36	18	72	54
				1812	1815		6	36	24	42
				1821	1822		72	12	108	84
				1823	1825		12	24	24	36
				1826	1828		12	24	36	36
				1829	1833		12	48	36	60
				1834	1836		12	24	60	60
				1838	1839		24	12	48	36
				1843	1845		48	24	60	72
				1846	1847		12	12	36	29
				1848	1853		12	60	24	72
Dec. 1854	June 1857	4Q 1854	2Q 1857	1855	1856		24	30	84	36
Dec. 1858	Oct. 1860	4Q 1858	3Q 1860	1858	1860		18	22	48	40
June 1861	Apr. 1865	3Q 1861	1Q 1865	1861	1864		8	46	30	54
Dec. 1867	June 1869	1Q 1868	2Q 1869	1867	1869		32	18	78	50
Dec. 1873	Oct. 1873	4Q 1870	3Q 1873	1870	1873		18	34	36	52
Mar. 1879	Mar. 1882	1Q 1879	1Q 1882	1878	1882		65	36	99	101
May 1885	Mar. 1887	2Q 1885	2Q 1887	1885	1887		38	22	74	60
Apr. 1888	July 1890	1Q 1888	3Q 1890	1888	1890		13	27	35	40
May 1891	Jan. 1893	2Q 1891	1Q 1893	1891	1892		10	20	37	30
June 1894	Dec. 1895	2Q 1894	4Q 1895	1894	1895		17	18	37	35
June 1897	June 1899	2Q 1897	3Q 1899	1896	1899		18	24	36	42
Dec. 1900	Sept 1902	4Q 1900	4Q 1902	1900	1903		18	21	42	39
Aug. 1904	May 1907	3Q 1904	2Q 1907	1904	1907		23	33	44	56
June 1908	Jan. 1910	2Q 1908	1Q 1910	1908	1910		13	19	46	32
Jan. 1912	Jan. 1913	4Q 1911	1Q 1913	1911	1913		24	12	43	36
Dec. 1914	Aug. 1918	4Q 1914	3Q 1918	1914	1918		23	44	35	67
Mar. 1919	Jan. 1920	1Q 1919	1Q 1920	1919	1920		7	10	51	17
July 1921	May 1923	3Q 1921	2Q 1923	1921	1923		18	22	28	40
July 1924	Oct. 1926	3Q 1924	3Q 1926	1924	1926		14	27	36	41
Nov. 1927	Aug. 1929	4Q 1927	3Q 1929	1927	1929		13	21	40	34
Mar. 1933	May 1937	1Q 1933	2Q 1937	1932	1937		43	50	64	93
June 1938	Feb. 1945	2Q 1938	1Q 1945	1938	1944		13	80	63	93
Oct. 1945	Nov. 1948	4Q 1945	4Q 1948	1946	1948		8	37	88	45
Oct. 1949	July 1953	4Q 1949	2Q 1953	1949	1953		11	45	48	56
May 1954	Aug. 1957	2Q 1954	3Q 1957	1954	1957		10	39	55	49
Apr. 1958	Apr. 1960	2Q 1958	2Q 1960	1958	1960		8	24	47	32
Feb. 1961	Dec. 1969	1Q 1969	4Q 1969	1961	1969		10	106	34	116

Dates of Peaks and Troughs						Duration in Months*			
By Months		By Quarters		By Calendar Years		Contraction	Expansion	Full Cycle	
Trough (T)	Peak (P)	T	P	T	P	P to T	T to P	T to T	P to P
Nov. 1970	Nov. 1973	4Q 1970	4Q 1973	1970	1973	11	36	117	47
Mar. 1975	Jan. 1980	1Q 1975	1Q 1980	1975	1979	16	58	52	74
July 1980	July 1981	3Q 1980	3Q 1981	1980	1981	6	12	64	18
Nov. 1982	July 1990	4Q 1982	3Q 1990	1982	1990	16	92	28	108
Mar. 1991		1Q 1991		1991					
Averages									
14 cycles 1790–1864						24	31	56	55
14 cycles 1854–1913						23	25	49	47
8 cycles 1913–48						17	36	51	54
8 cycles 1948–90						11	52	56	63
44 cycles 1790–1990						20	34	53	53

Source: Center for International Business Cycle Research, Columbia University, New York, N.Y., November 1995.
*Entries from 1790 to 1855 are based on calendar year dates.

Note: For a basic statement of the method of determining business-cycle peaks and troughs, see chapter 4 in Burns and Mitchell (1946). Some of the dates shown there (p. 78) have since been revised. For a review of the chronology, including dates back to 1790, see G. H. Moore and V. Zarnowitz, "The Development and Role of the National Bureau of Economic Research's Business Cycle Chronologies," in R. J. Gordon, ed., *The American Business Cycle: Continuity and Change* (Chicago: Univ. of Chicago Press, 1986). For a description of how the National Bureau method has been applied more recently, see V. Zarnowitz and G. H. Moore, "The Timing and Severity of the 1980 Recession," in G. H. Moore, *Business Cycles, Inflation and Forecasting*, 2d ed. (Cambridge, Mass.: Ballinger, 1983).

TABLE 3. Business Cycle Chronologies and Durations to 1938

Dates of Peaks and Troughs				Duration in Months			
By Months and Quarters		By Calendar Years		Contraction	Expansion	Full Cycle	
Trough (T)	Peak (P)	T	P	P to T	T to P	T to T	P to P

United States, 1854–1938

Trough (T)	Peak (P)	T	P	P to T	T to P	T to T	P to P
December 1854:4	June 1857:2	1855	1856		30		
December 1858:4	October 1860:2	1858	1860	18	22	48	40
June 1861:3	April 1865:1	1861	1864	8	46	30	54
December 1867:1	June 1869:2	1867	1869	32	18	78	50
December 1870:4	October 1873:3	1870	1873	18	34	36	52
March 1879:1	March 1882:1	1878	1882	65	36	99	101
May 1885:2	March 1887:2	1885	1887	38	22	74	60
April 1888:1	July 1890:3	1888	1890	13	27	35	40
May 1891:2	January 1893:1	1891	1892	10	20	37	30
June 1894:2	December 1895:4	1894	1895	17	18	37	35
June 1897:2	June 1899:3	1896	1899	18	24	36	42
December 1900:4	September 1902:4	1900	1903	18	21	42	39
August 1904:3	May 1907:2	1904	1907	23	33	44	56
June 1908:2	January 1910:1	1908	1910	12	19	46	32
January 1912:4	January 1913:1	1911	1913	24	12	43	32
December 1914:4	August 1918:3	1914	1918	23	44	35	67
March 1919:1	January 1920:1	1919	1920	7	10	51	17
July 1921:3	May 1923:2	1921	1923	18	22	28	40
July 1924:3	October 1926:3	1924	1926	14	27	36	41
November 1927:4	August 1929:3	1927	1929	13	21	40	34
March 1933:1	May 1937:2	1932	1937	43	50	64	93
June 1938:2				13	63		

Averages

Twenty-one cycles, 1854–1938

				P to T	T to P	T to T	P to P
Mean duration (months)				21	26	48	48
Standard deviation (months)				14	11	18	20

Thirty-five cycles, 1790–1938[a]

				P to T	T to P	T to T	P to P
Mean duration (months)				23	28	50	50
Standard deviation (months)				16	14	24	20

Great Britain, 1854–1938

Trough (T)	Peak (P)	T	P	P to T	T to P	T to T	P to P
December 1854/55:1	September 1857:4	1855	1857		33		
March 1858:1	September 1860:4	1858	1860	6	30	39	36
December 1862:4	March 1866:2	1862	1866	27	39	57	66
March 1868:2	September 1872:4	1868	1873	24	54	63	78
June 1879:2	December 1882:1	1879	1883	81	42	135	123
June 1886:2	September 1890:3	1886	1890	42	51	84	93
February 1895:1	June 1900:3	1894	1900	53	64	104	117
September 1901:4	June 1903:2	1901	1903	15	21	79	36
November 1904:4	June 1907:2	1904	1907	17	31	38	48
November 1908:4	December 1912:1	1908	1913	17	49	48	66
September 1914:3	October 1918:2	1914	1917	21	49	70	70
April 1919:2	March 1920:2	1919	1920	6	11	55	17
June 1921:2	November 1924:4	1921	1924	15	41	26	56
July 1926:3	March 1927:2	1926	1927	20	8	61	28
September 1928:3	July 1929:3	1928	1929	18	10	26	28
August 1932:3	September 1937:3	1932	1937	37	61	47	98
September 1938:3		1938		12	73		

Dates of Peaks and Troughs				Duration in Months			
By Months and Quarters		By Calendar Years		Contraction	Expansion	Full Cycle	
Trough (T)	Peak (P)	T	P	P to T	T to P	T to T	P to P
Averages							
Sixteen cycles, 1854–1938							
Mean duration (months)				26	37	63	64
Standard deviation (months)				19	18	29	33
Twenty-nine cycles, 1790–1938[a]							
Mean duration (months)				22	39	60	62
Standard deviation (months)				16	18	24	28
France, 1865–1938							
December 1865	November 1867	1865	1866		23		
October 1868	August 1870	1868	1869	11	22	34	33
February 1872	September 1873	1871	1873	18	19	40	37
August 1876	April 1878	1876	1878	35	20	54	55
September 1879	December 1881	1879	1882	17	27	37	44
August 1887	January 1891	1887	1890	68	41	95	109
January 1895:1	March 1900:1	1894	1900	48	62	89	110
September 1902:3	May 1903:2	1902	1903	30	8	92	38
October 1904:3	July 1907:3	1904	1907	17	33	25	50
February 1909:1	June 1913:3	1908	1913	19	52	52	71
August 1914:3	June 1918:2	1914	1917	14	46	66	60
April 1919:2	September 1920:3	1918	1920	10	17	56	27
July 1921:3	October 1924:3	1921	1924	10	39	27	49
June 1925:3	October 1926:3	1925	1926	8	16	47	24
June 1927:3	March 1930:1	1927	1930	8	33	24	41
July 1932:3	July 1933:3	1932	1933	28	12	61	40
April 1935:1	June 1937:2	1935	1937	21	26	33	47
August 1938:3		1938		14		40	
Averages							
Mean Duration (months)				22	29	51	52
Standard deviation (months)				16	15	23	25
Germany, 1879–1932							
February 1879:1	January 1882:1	1878	1882		35		
August 1886:3	January 1890:1	1886	1890	55	41	90	96
February 1895:1	March 1900:2	1894	1900	61	61	102	122
March 1902:1	August 1903:3	1902	1903	24	17	85	41
February 1905:1	July 1907:2	1904	1907	18	29	35	47
December 1908:4	April 1913:1	1908	1913	17	52	46	69
August 1914:3	June 1918:2	1914	1917	16	46	68	62
June 1919:2	May 1922:2	1919	1922	12	35	58	47
November 1923:4	March 1925:2	1923	1925	18	16	53	34
March 1926:2	April 1929:2	1926	1929	12	37	28	49
August 1932:3		1932		40			77
Averages							
Mean duration (months)				27	37	64	63
Standard deviation (months)				18	14	24	29

Source: National Bureau of Economic Research.
Note: For a basic statement of the method of determining business-cycle peaks and troughs, see Burns and Mitchell (1946), chap. 4. Some of the dates shown there (p. 78) have since been revised.
[a] Combines the observations in Table 3 for 1790–1855 (converted from annual to monthly durations) with observations in this table for the subsequent cycles through 1938.

TABLE 4. Growth Cycle Peak and Trough Dates, Eleven Countries, 1948–1995 (Revised November 1995)

Period	Peak Or Trough	North America		Europe				Pacific Region					4 Countries Europe	5 Countries Pacific	10 Countries excl. U.S.	11 Countries
		United States	Canada	United Kingdom	West Germany	France	Italy	Japan	Australia	Taiwan, R.O.C.	South Korea	New Zealand				
1948–50	P	7/48														
	T	10/49	5/50													
1951–52	P	3/51	4/51	3/51	2/51				4/51							
	T	7/52	12/51	8/52					11/52							
1953–55	P	3/53	3/53					12/53								
	T	8/54	10/54	2/54				6/55								
1955–59	P	2/57	11/56	12/55	10/55	8/57	10/56	5/57	8/55				4/57		5/57	3/57
	T	4/58	8/58	11/58	4/59	8/59	7/59	1/59	1/58				3/59	3/59	2/59	5/58
1959–61	P	2/60	10/59						8/60							2/60
	T	2/61	3/61						9/61							2/61
1961–63	P	5/62	3/62	3/61	2/61			1/62					3/61	3/61	3/61	2/62
	T		5/63	2/63	2/63			1/63		6/63			2/63	1/63	2/63	2/63
1963–66	P					2/64	9/63	7/64	4/65					6/64	2/64	
	T	10/64			5/65	6/65	3/65	2/66		4/65				3/66		
1966–68	P	6/66	3/66	2/66		6/66						6/66	3/66			3/66
	T	10/67	2/68	8/67	8/67	5/68			1/68	8/67	9/66	4/68	5/68		5/68	10/67
1968–73	P	3/69	2/69	6/69	5/70	11/69	8/69	6/70	5/70	11/68	10/69	7/70	4/70	6/70	6/70	10/69
	T	11/70	12/70	2/72	12/71	11/71	9/72	1/72	3/72	1/71	3/72	11/72	2/72	1/72	2/72	11/71
1973–75	P	3/73	2/74	6/73	8/73	5/74	4/74	11/73	2/74	12/73	10/73	2/74	11/73	11/73	11/73	11/73
	T	3/75	10/75	6/75	5/75	6/75	5/75	3/75	10/75	2/75	6/75	3/75	11/75	2/75	11/75	5/75
1976–78	P		5/76				12/76		8/76	6/76		12/76		1/77		
	T		12/77				10/77		10/77	7/77		2/78		2/78		

1978–81	P	12/78	10/79	6/79	2/80	8/79	2/80	2/80	8/78	2/79	1/80	11/79	2/80	2/80	11/79
	T		5/80			9/81*				10/80	11/80		11/83		
1981–83	P		6/81	6/83	7/83	3/83*	5/83*		10/82						
	T	12/82	11/82			9/83*									2/83
1984–87	P	6/84*	1/86*	5/85*	7/86*		6/85*	5/85*	5/84*	2/84	8/84	11/85	5/85	5/85	5/85
	T	1/87*	11/86*	1/87*			8/87*	5/87*	8/85*	10/85	2/86*	3/87	5/87	5/87	1/87
1987–88	P				1/88*				9/87*						
	T														
1988–89	P	3/89*	2/89*			7/88*	11/89*			2/88*					
	T					5/89*				5/89*	8/89*				
1990–91	P			2/90*	2/91*	5/90*	5/91*			8/91*	8/90*	8/90	3/90	3/90	3/90
	T	12/91*							12/90*		6/91*				
1992–93	P		11/92*	12/92*		4/92*		12/92*		6/93*					
	T		12/92*			9/93*	12/93*	12/93*			8/93*			12/93	
1994–95	P					2/94*			2/94*			2/94			
	T														

Source: For the United States through 1982, National Bureau of Economic Research. For other countries, Center for International Business Cycle Research.
Note: The chronologies for groups of countries are based on composite indexes of output, income, employment and trade, weighted by each country's GNP in 1980, expressed in U.S. dollars. The chronologies begin at different dates, depending on when appropriate data became available. Since the chronologies are not frequently updated, the absence of a recent date does not necessarily mean that a turn has not occurred.
* Based on trend-adjusted coincident index.

Author Index

The main entry for each topic is listed in **boldface**.

Abel, A., 201, 338, 673
Abraham, K.G., 615–16
Abramovitz, Moses, **3–4**, 361, 372
Adams, F.G., 423
Adelman, Frank L., 251, 362
Adelman, Irma, 251, 362, 372
Aftalion, Albert, **6–7**, 65, 76, 217, 305, 367, 505–06, 625
Aglietta, M., 573
Aizonova, I.M., 525
Akerloff, G.A., 145, 190–91, 328, 482, 715
Akermann, Johann Hendrik, **12–13**, 250, 347
Akhand, H., 328
Alcaly, R.E., 431–32
Alchian, Armen, 603
Aldrich, J., 411
Alesina, A., 193, 537
Alexander, S.S., 109, 299
Allais, Maurice, **13–17**
Allen, R.G.D., 163, 626, 685
Allen, W.R., 239
Almon, S., 172
Alt, J.E., 537
Altonji, J.G., 334
Amemiya, T., 258
Amihud, Y., 657
Amoroso, Luigi, **17–18**
Anderson, B., 282
Anderson, L.C., 109
Anderson, M.D., 11
Anderson, T.W., 169, 258, 361, 420
Ando, Albert, 449
Andrew, A.P., 134
Angell, James Waterhouse, **19–20**, 217
Armstrong, P., 52
Arrow, K.D., 201, 321, 361, 704
Arthur, B., 389
Ashton, T.S., 63
Aslanbeigui, N., 532, 534
Asselain, J.-C., 278

Attwood, Matthias, 22, 57
Attwood, Thomas, **22–23**, 57, 344
Ayres, Clarence Edwin, **27–28**
Azariadis, C., 318

Backus, D.K., 678
Baek, E.G., 493, 494
Bagehot, Walter, **29–30**, 429, 457
    agriculture, cyclical role of, 30
    Bank Charter Act, 30, 32
    Bank of England, 29–30, 50–51
    banks, cyclical role of, 30
    central bank, responsibilities of, 29–30, 37, 47, 265
    depression, 30
    expectations, cyclical role of, 204
    Jevons's sunspot theory, 29
    lender of last resort, 30, 50–51, 332, 391, 502
    optimism and pessimism, shifts in, 30
    panic of 1825, 45
    panics, causes of, 30
    regularity of cycle, 30
    time in economic analysis, 30
Baily, M.N., 284, 318
Bajt, A., 76
Ball, L., 482, 483
Banerjee, A., 102
Bank for International Settlements, 668
Baran, Paul A., 650–51, 671–72
Baranzini, M., 60
Barman, R.L., 421
Barnett, W.A., 173–75
Barro, Robert J., 199, 282, 284, 330, 455, 482, 561, 621, 704
Barsky, R.B., 561, 609
Barth, J.R., 579, 683–84
Bartholomew, P.F., 683
Batchelder, R., 631
Bauer, Otto, **51–52**, 418, 508, 671
Bauer, T., 76–77
Baumol, W.J., 66, 87, 92, 145, 414, 598, 667
Beals, R., 545
Beaulieu, J.J., 612

Becker, G., 598, 722
Beckmann, Johann, 699
Beenstock, M., 367
Beers, D., 311
Bell, W.R., 228, 611
Belongia, M.T., 175
Benassy, J.-P., 542, 574, 704
Bencivenga, V.R., 674–75
Benhabib, J., 66, 87, 92, 95, 674
Benjamin, D., 591
Benjamini, Y., 329
Berg, Claes, 413
Bernanke, B.S., 69, 233, 266, 282, 559, 668, 712
Bernstein, Eduard, **53**, 200, 309, 354, 417
Bertola, G., 114
Bertrand, H., 574
Beveridge, S., 696
Beveridge, William, 28
Bewley, T., 181
Bills, M., 561–62
Bird, Roger, 372
Bizer, D., 182
Bjork, G., 124
Black, F., 253, 487–88, 559, 658, 673–75
Blake, Samuel Coleridge, 374
Blanchard, O.J., 328, 338, 554, 712, 715
Blank, R., 562
Blatt, J.M., 251, 538, 685
Blinder, A.S., 668
Bliss, C.J., 81
Bloomfield, A.I., 265, 576
Blume, M.E., 657
Boccara, P., 573
Boddy, R., 212, 320
Bodkin, R.G., 363, 561
Böhm-Bawerk, Eugen Ritter von, 23, 51, **53–54**
    capital theory of, 23, 54, 59–60, 82, 416, 440
    influence of, 23, 54, 302, 440, 719
    period of production, 521, 689
Boldrin, M., 92, 323, 666
Bolle, M., 241
Boot, H.M., 126
Bordo, M.D., 265, 288
Boschan, C., 289, 659, 661
Bosworth, B.P., 179, 338
Boudin, L., 508
Boulding, Kenneth E., 527
Bouniatian, M., 347
Bowles, S., 320
Bowley, A.L., 217
Box, G.E.P., 111, 448, 611, 618
Boyd, Walter, 56
Boyer, R., 278, 280, 573, 574, 575
Bradley, M.D., 683–84
Brainard, W.C., 232, 667
Braudel, F., 278, 280
Braun, P., 423
Brems, H., 498
Brennan, M.J., 658
Bresciani-Turoni, C., 404, 478
Breusch, T.S., 446

Brillinger, D., 685
Brock, W.A., 87, 180–82, 492–94
Brodin, P.A., 412
Broitman, R., 525
Brumbaugh, D., 683
Brumberg, Richard, 449
Brunner, Karl, **55**, 220, 458, 667–68
Bruno, M., 573
Bukharin, N.I., 648
Bulgakov, S., 166
Bullard, J., 388, 390
Bullock, Charles Jesse, **58–59**, 523
Burchardt, Fritz (Frank) Adolph, **59–60**, 407–08
Burmeister, E., 81, 422
Burns, Arthur Frank, **61–62**, 439, 445
    chairman of Federal Reserve, 61–62, 224–25
    definition of business cycles, 61, 63
    on diffusion, 109
    Juglar cycle, 347
    leading indicators, 383, 465
    measurement without theory, 61, 369
    and NBER, 61, 247–48, 289, 324, 360, 727
    reference cycle, 61, 248, 525
Burstein, M., 488
Buse, A., 446
Butkiewitz, J., 282

Caballero, R.J., 114
Cagan, Phillip, 68, 143, 146–47, 206, 248–49,
    288, 463–64, 528
Calomiris, Charles, 128, 502
Cameron, R., 39, 40
Campagna, A.S., 564
Campbell, J.Y., 204, 673–74, 677, 705–06
Campos, J., 527
Cannan, E., 34, 679
Cantillon, Richard, **79–80**, 314, 719
Canzoneri, M., 622, 715–16
Capie, F.H., 287–88
Card, D., 334
Carey, Henry Charles, 117, 245
Carlton, D.W., 70, 545–46
Carlyle, Thomas, 374, 624
Carmichael, H.L., 190
Carver, T.N., 4–5
Casanova, J.-C., 278, 280
Cass, D., 180, 666
Cassel, Carl Gustav, **83–85**, 196, 217, 473, 497
    accelerator model, 84, 505
    investment, cyclical role of, 295
    long cycles, 404
    natural rate of interest, 477
    overinvestment theory, 505
    periodicity, 347
Catchings, Waddill, **244**, 508, 636
Catephones, G., 599
Cecchetti, S.G., 482, 483
Chalfont, J., 175
Chalmers, Thomas, 375
Chang, W.W., 9, 351
Chappell, H.W., 537

Chavance, B., 77
Chen, P., 175, 177
Chenery, Hollis, 595
Chernoff, H., 258
Chevalier, Michel, 245
Chiang, A.C., 163
Chipman, J.S., 471
Christ, C., 423
Christiano, L.J., 706
Christiernin, Peter Niclas, 450, 452
Chrystal, K.A., 537
Clapham, J., 34
Clark, Colin, 362, 419
Clark, J.B., 468
Clark, J.M., 4–5, 11, 84, 217, 305
Clark, P., 229
Clark, P.K., 647
Cline, W., 381–82
Clower, Robert W., 188, 357, 703, 717
Cochrane, J.H., 657, 673–74, 706
Cochrane, W., 617
Cogley, T., 230
Colander, D., 259, 394
Cole, A.H., 130
Coleman, W.J., 182
Colm, G., 407, 724
Commons, John Rogers, **106–08**, 244
Constantinides, M., 201, 674
Cooper, J.R., 172
Copeland, Morris, 419
Coquelin, Charles, **117–18**, 245–46
Coriat, B., 575
Corry, Bernard, 374–75
Cosmo, Umberto, 643
Costabilo, L., 426
Courcelle-Seneuil, Jean Gustave, 245
Cowen, T., 487–88
Cox, J.C., 182, 678
Crafts, N.F.R., 229, 287, 326
Crotty, J.R., 212, 320, 431
Crum, W.L., 360, 523

Dadayan, V.S., 419
Danthine, J.P., 182
Darby, M.R., 283
Davenport, H.J., 451
David, P.A., 4
Davidson, David, 719
Davidson, J.E.H., 102, 104, 170
Davidson, P., 328, 403
Davis, Harold Thayer, **139**, 640, 688
Davis, J.R., 549
Davis, S.J., 616
Day, R.H., 574
Day, Richard B., 540
De Bernis, G.D., 574
Debreu, G, 181, 201, 321
Dechert, W.D., 492
De Foville, Alfred, **141–42**
de Leeuw, F., 108, 422
DeLong, B., 21, 284, 716

Denison, E.F., 571
De Temple, J.B., 673–74
De Wolff, S., 367, 404
Dhrymes, P.J., 168
Diamond, D.W., 231, 668
Diamond, P.A., 608–09
Dickey, D.A., 105
Diewert, W.E., 174, 324
Divisia, Francois, 174
Doan, T., 710
Dobb, Maurice, 52
Dolado, J.J., 102
Domar, Evsey, 217, 595
Donaldson, J.B., 181, 678
Dore, M.H.I., 329, 539
Dorfman, J., 342
Dorn, J.A., 451
Dornbusch, R., 9, 127
Dosi, G., 404
Dostaler, G., 474
Dotsey, M., 622
Douglas, Clifford Hugh, **178**, 508
Douglas, Paul A., 244
Dowd, K., 246, 502
Drèze, J., 13, 704
Duesenberry, James Stemble, **179–80**, 350, 422, 628
Duménil, G., 215, 542
Dunlop, J., 561, 664
Dupriez, L.H., 404
Durbin, E.F.M., 178, 244
Durbin, J., 618
Dutton, H.I., 178
Dybvig, P.H., 668

Eatwell, John, 586–87
Ebanks, W.W., 289
Eberly, J.C., 114
Eckstein, Otto, 67, **185–86**, 422–23, 530
Edgeworth, F.Y., 23, 310, 419, 468
Edwards, S., 662, 663
Eichenbaum, M., 674, 706
Eichengreen, B., 266, 279, 280, 285, 630
Eichner, A.S., 538
Eichorn, W., 324
Einaudi, Luigi, 643
Eisner, R., 337
Eliot, T.S., 178
Ellis, Howard Sylvester, **196–97**
Ellman, M., 540
Elmendorf, D.W., 579
Engels, Friedrich, **199–200**
Engle, R.F., 102, 103, 104, 105, 170, 171, 255, 324, 411–12, 446, 706, 711
Epstein, L.G., 201
Epstein, R., 617
Ericsson, Neil R., 102, 412, 448, 463, 527
Estrella, A., 676
Eucken, Walter, 415
Evans, G., 390
Evans, G.C., 688

Evans, M.K., 422
Ewis, N.A., 175
Ezekiel, M., 100

Fama, E.F., 330, 487–88, 646–47, 661, 676
Fanno, Marco, **216–17**
Favero, C., 411–12
Fazzari, S.M., 338, 339
Fedder, J. *See* Van Gelderen, J.
Feinstein, C.H., 287
Feiwel, G.R., 353
Feldstein, M., 11, 318, 579
Fellner, William John, 109, **226**
Fels, Rendigs, 148, 150
Ferson, W.E., 674
Ferri, P., 87
Fetter, F.W., 37, 253, 409, 457
Fischer, S., 9, 382, 554, 716
Fisher, D., 175
Fisher, Irving, 217, **238–39**, 244, 686
    compensated-dollar plan, 57, 239, 445, 453,
        457, 488
    debt-deflation theory, 66, 70, 121, 140, 238–
        39, 438, 452, 550
    econometric studies, 238–39
    expectations, 205–06, 238–39, 550, 720
    financial crises, 359
    functions of money, 145
    Gesell's stamped scrip, 261
    Gibson's Paradox, 288
    Great Depression, 239
    hydraulic simulation model, 419
    index number, 324
    influence on Commons, 107
    interest rates, 238–39, 429, 681
    monetary business-cycle theory, 55, 239, 451
    monetary control, 462
    100-percent-reserve banking, 144, 239
    Phillips curve, 239, 687
    quantity theory, 19, 239
    Roosevelt's devaluation of dollar, 140
    stock-market crash, 239
Fisher, R.A., 368
Fishman, G.S., 228, 230
Flaschel, P., 82, 542
Flavin, M.A., 657
Fleming, J.M., 293
Föhl, Carl, **240–41**
Ford, A.G., 265
Forrester, Jay, W., 366
Foster, J.B., 212
Foster, William Trufant, **244**, 508, 636
Fourier, Joseph, 12, 640
Fox, K.A., 688
Franker, J.A., 11
Fredman, G.T., 108
Freeman, C., 404
French, K.R., 203, 677
Frenkel, Jacob, 127, 146, 458
Frey, B.S., 537
Frickey, E, 148

Friedman, B.M., 68
Friedman, Milton, 20, 198, **247–49**, 439, 667,
        691
    adaptive expectations, 116, 205–06, 528
    aggregate supply curve, slope of, 669
    demand for money, 146, 448
    Federal Reserve policy 1914–41, 219–20
    free banking, 246
    gold standard, 150, 266
    Great Depression, 281–82, 557, 614
    and Keynes, 248
    on Mitchell, 445
    Monetarism, 55, 451–52
    monetary policy, 248, 458–59
    money-income causality, 248–49, 462–63
    money stock, cyclical variations in, 248
    NBER methods, use of, 247–48
    natural rate of unemployment, 479–80, 530,
        690, 721
    neutrality of money, 462–63
    permanent-income hypothesis, 115, 449
    phase averaging, 525, 527
    Phillips curve, 455, 530
    rules vs. discretion, 694
    and Schwartz, 606
    Snyder's influence on, 632
    Tinbergen's macroeconometric model, 420,
        687
    velocity, 145, 463
    wage and price adjustment, lags in, 68
    on Warburton, 718
Frisch, Ragnar Anton Kittel, 163, **250–52**, 686
    Akermann's theory, 12
    decomposition of time series, 250
    econometric modeling, 368, 411, 420
    impulse and propagation, 67, 250–52, 387,
        604, 687, 721
    influence of, 291
    long cycles, 404
    periodicity, 251
    stability of economic systems, 250
    stochastic disturbancs, 91
    stochastic linear models, 21
    Tinbergen's macroeconometric model, 420
    Wicksell's influence on, 721
Fromm, Gary, 422, 423
Froot, K.A., 677
Frydman, R., 388
Fullarton, John, 48, 117, **252–53**, 262, 627
Fuller, W.A., 105, 706

Gabisch, G., 491
Gaitskell, H.T.N., 178, 261
Galbraith, J.K., 649
Galbraith, J.W., 102
Galton, Francis, 419
Gandolfi, A.E., 283
Garber, P.M., 657
Garegnani, P., 81, 601, 602
Garvey, George, 365, 367, 724
Gauss, Carl Friedrich, 419

Gayer, A.D., 475, 589, 606
Geary, P.T., 561
Gelpi, R.-M., 574
Gennotte, G., 657
George, Henry, 261
Georgescu-Roegen, N., 685
Gertler, M., 339
Gesell, Silvio, **261**
Getty, J. Arch, 524
Giblin, L.F., 356
Gilbart, James William, 49, 117, **261**, 472, 521,
    609
Gill, P.E., 257
Gille, B., 39
Gillman, J., 214
Glasner, D., 252, 253, 487, 627, 631
Glendny, R.G., 419
Glick, M., 215
Glynn, A., 52
Goldberger, Arthur, S., 362
Goldman, J., 76
Goldsmith, R., 74
Goldstein, J.S., 406
Goodwin, Richard Murphey, **272–75**
    capital accumulation, 587
    growth cycles, 272–73, 538–39, 663, 691
    inflation, cyclical change in, 538
    Kaldor's 1940 cycle model, 351
    long-wave theory, 404
    nonlinear business-cycle models, 86, 272–74,
        489, 594–95
    predator-prey model, 272, 319, 538
    rate of profit, 211–12
    reproduction of capital, 82
    sectoral interactions, 273–75, 471, 539
    stability, 539, 542
    technological change, 273–74, 540
    threshholds, 87
    trend and cycle, 274, 539
Gordon, D.B., 199
Gordon, D.F., 318
Gordon, David M., 320, 366, 404
Gordon, Robert J., 281, 282, 283, 284, 411, 484,
    542, 705
Gramlich, E., 422
Gramsci, Antonio, 643
Grandmont, J.-M., 13, 95, 323, 388, 492
Granger, Clive W.J., 102, 103, 105, 170, 171, 324,
    419, 464, 610, 639–40, 646, 706,
    711
Grassberger, P., 493
Graunt, John, 419
Green, E.W., 185
Greenberg, E., 87
Greenfield, R.L., 453, 487–88
Greenwood, John, 312–13
Gregory, A.W., 678
Gregory, Paul R., 73–74
Grey, J.A., 715–16
Grossman, H.I., 561, 622, 704
Grossman, Henryk, 52, 432, 671

Grossman, S.J., 203, 658
Guckenheimer, J., 489

Haavelmo, Tygve, **291–92**, 361, 368, 411, 420
Haberler, Gottfried, 76, 217, **292–93**, 434, 439,
    478
    business-cycle theories, survey and synthesis
        of, 65, 292–93, 522, 687
    depressions, unlikelihood of recurrence, 293
    forced saving, 242
    full-employment policy, 535
    international transmission of cycles, 293, 314
    Keynes's *General Theory*, 292–93
    Pigou-Haberler effect, **534–36**
    price-level stability, 535
    rational expectations, 293
    sticky prices, 535
    Tinbergen's study, 292, 687
Hagemann, Harald, 342, 407, 470
Hahm, S., 622, 623
Hahn, F.H., 320
Hahn, H.-W., 240
Hahn, Lucien Albert, 196, **294–95**
Hahnel, P., 320
Hall, C., 690
Hall, G., 151
Hall, R.E., 116, 487–88, 543, 722, 723
Hamilton, J.D., 108, 281, 330, 571, 670, 705
Hammerskjöld, D., 653
Hanau, A., 100
Hancock, D., 175
Hannan, E.J., 711
Hansen, Alvin Harvey, 7, 28, 217, 244, **295–97**,
    528
    early orthodoxy of, 295, 297
    fiscal policy, 296–97
    forced saving, 242
    Keynesian economics, 295–96
    multiplier-accelerator interaction, 593, 595,
        296
    secular stagnation, 196, 296, 393
    wars and long waves, 406
Hansen, Bent, 653–54
Hansen, G., 559
Hansen, L.P., 674
Hansson, B.A., 242
Harcourt, G.C., 81
Hardouvelis, G.A., 676, 677
Hardy, C.O., 661
Harris, M., 181
Harrison, J., 52
Harrod, Roy Forbes, 217, **297–99**, 413, 587, 595,
    629, 663, 691
    fixed-accelerator model, 351
    growth and cycles, 297–99, 663
    growth theory, 297–99, 595, 629, 691
    Hicks, influence on, 305
    multiplier-accelerator interaction, 471, 595
Hart, A.G., 140
Hart, O.D., 723
Hartley, P.R., 732

Harvey, A.C., 227, 228–29, 230, 618, 639–40
Hausman, J.A., 257
Hautcoeur, P.-C., 41
Havenstein, R., 576
Havrilesky, T., 225
Hawtrey, Ralph George, 7, 196, 300–02
    aggregate demand, 301
    business-cycle theory, 187, 433, 451, 506
    credit deadlock, 301
    credit, instability of, 300–01
    gold standard, 301
    Great Depression, 301
    inventory investment, 121, 300, 433
    and Keynes, 300–01, 586
    multiplier, 356
    natural rate of interest, 300, 477
    periodicity, 301, 416
    public expenditure, 301
    real shocks, self-limiting nature of, 300
    Treasury view, 301
    wage-price rigidity, 301
Hayashi, F., 337
Hayek, Friedrich August, 196, 244, **302–04**, 439, 636
    Böhm-Bawerk's influence on, 54, 302
    business-cycle theory, 23, 54, 85, 117, 302–04, 349–50, 407, 506, 522
    capital theory, 302–04
    effective demand, 187
    equilibrium, limitations of, 396
    fixed capital, 60
    forced saving, 242, 303–04, 506, 644
    free banking, 246, 694
    and Hicks, 396
    and Kaldor, 349–50
    and Keynes, 302
    and Lachmann, 373
    and Lowe, 406–07
    and Mises, 302, 441
    monetary policy, 458
    natural rate of interst, 303, 349, 477, 506, 644–45
    periodicity, 416
    price expectations and intertemporal equilibrium, 54, 373, 396
    price level, unimportance of, 303
    Ricardo effect, 304, 349
    and Robbins, 302, 582–83
    and Röpke, 588
    and Shackle, 373
    and Sraffa, 644–45
    time structure of production, 302–03, 408
    and Tintner, 688
    upper turning point, 303, 506
    vertical maladjustment, 65
    Wicksell's influence on, 302, 506
Heath, D., 678
Heaton, J., 674
Heckman, J., 334
Heckscher, E.F., 497
Heilbroner, R., 408

Heinsohn, G., 398, 399
Helkie, W., 380
Helliwell, J., 571
Helphand, A. *See* Parvus
Hendershott, P.H., 683
Henderson, D., 622
Henderson, Hubert, 356
Hendry, David F., 102, 104, 168, 255, 257, 411–12, 446, 448, 463, 527
Hercowitz, Zvi, 456, 622
Hickman, Bert G., 67, 109, 281, 363, 422, 571
Hicks, John Richard, 217, **305–08**, 413, 542, 626
    accelerator, 5, 306, 351
    Austrian capital theory, 82
    business-cycle model, 306–07
    ceilings and floors, 66, **86–87**, 163, 307, 538–39, 594
    J.M. Clark's influence on, 305
    demand for money, 145
    equilibrium trend, 306–07
    fluctuations, causes of, 306
    fix-price method, 703
    growth theory, 691
    Harrod's influence on, 305
    Hayek's influence on, 396
    IS-LM model, 7–8, 362
    inconvertible money, 268
    Kahn's influence on, 305
    Keynes's influence on, 305
    Lindahl's influence on, 396, 653
    multiplier, 305
    multiplier-accelerator interaction, 91, 305–06, 557, 594
    price expectations and intertemporal equilibrium, 54
    price expectations and period analysis, 205
    self-criticism, 307–08
    slump equilibrium, 307
    temporary equilibrium method, 396–97
    traverse analysis, 82, 407–08
Hildreth, Richard, 245
Hilferding, Rudolf, 53, 166–68, **308–09**, 355, 648, 671
Hillmer, S.C., 611
Hinich, M.J., 175
Hirsch, M., 489
Hobson, John Atkinson, 27, 63, 244, **310**, 508
Holland, J., 389
Hollander, S., 435
Holmes, P., 489
Holmstrom, B., 723
Honkapohja, S., 390
Hood, W.C., 420
Hooker, Reginald, 469
Hoover, Kevin D., 454, 463, 487, 553
Hopkins, S., 528
Horn, E., 245
Horner, F., 57
Horwich, G., 9, 243, 402, 403
Hotelling, Harold, 247
Howard, D., 380

Hsieh, P.A., 494
Hsu, D.-A., 647
Hu, S.C., 9
Hubbard, R.G., 338
Huffman, W.E., 265
Hughes, J.R.T., 131, 404
Huizinga, J., 330, 562
Hume, David, **313–14**, 450, 627, 719
Huntington, H.G., 571
Hurwicz, Leonid, 361
Huskisson, William, 57, 512
Hutchison, Francis, 597
Hutchison, T.W., 549
Hutt, William Harold, 174, **314–15**
Hymans, S., 422

Iakovlev, A.F., 72
Ickes, B.W., 76
Iden, G., 579
Imai, H., 77
Ingersoll, J., 182, 678
Invernizzi, S., 96
Ishida, K., 175
Itoh, M., 211, 212

Jacklin, C.J., 657–58
Jaeger, A., 230
Jarrow, R., 678
Jasny, N., 525
Jenkins, G.M., 111, 611, 618
Jevons, H.S., 360
Jevons, William Stanley, **341–42**
    agricultural cycles, 10–11, 341
    capital and time, 82, 521
    indexed contracts, 457
    Mills's influence on, 341, 437, 665
    periodicity, 341
    seasonal fluctuations, 613
    signal extraction problem, recognition of, 665
    sunspot theory of cyles, 10–11, 29, 347, 557,
        664–66
Johannsen, Nicholas August Ludwig Jacob, **342–
    43**, 470
Johannson, A., 653
Johansen, S., 102, 105, 257
Johnsen, T., 678
Johnson, Harry G., 458, 535, 565
Johnston, J., 618
Jones, Harold, 266
Jonung, L., 413
Joplin, Thomas, 56, **344–45**
Jorgensen, D., 337, 542
Jovanovic, B., 146, 317, 722
Judd, K., 182
Judge, G.G., 618
Juglar, Clément, 63, **345–46**, 347–48
Juselius, K., 257

Kadekodi, G.K., 688
Kähler, Alfred, 60, 407
Kahn, C.M., 502

Kahn, Richard F., 217, 305, 352, 356, 470–71,
    474, 545, 587, 643
Kaldor, Nicholas, 241, **349–51**, 585, 587
    accelerator model, 349, 351
    central-bank accomodation, 463–64
    cobweb cycle, 101
    disproportionality, 167
    endogeneity of money, 178
    financial innovation, 464
    and Goodwin, 351
    growth and cycle, 350–51
    and Hayek, 349–50
    income distribution, 350–51, 471
    indivisibilities, 619
    inflation, 328
    investment, 376
    money-income causality, 463–64
    multiple equilibria, 350
    multiplier-accelerator interaction, 595
    1940 trade cycle model, 351, 489–91
    nonlinear business-cycle theory, 66, 349
    Ricardo/Concertina effect, 349–50
    and Robbins, 349
    saving, 350
Kalecki, Michal, 7, 241, **351–53**, 585
    capital-stock adjustment mechanism, 352
    cycle theory, 352
    development, 353
    econometric business-cycle model, 368
    effective demand, theory of, 352
    expectations and uncertainty, 353
    finance, availability of, 353
    income distribution, 353, 548–49
    increasing risk, 336, 353
    innovation, 650
    investment, 336, 352, 376, 650
    and Keynes, 352
    labor/wage share, cyclical changes in, 319–20
    Lange, influence on, 376
    monopoly, cyclical role of, 167, 541, 587,
        650
    multiplier, analysis of, 430
    Pigou-Haberler effect, 140–41
    political business cycle, 536
    profit squeeze and trade unions, 548
    Robinson, influence on, 587
    Steindl, influence on, 650
    Sweezy, influence on, 672
    trend and cycle, 353
Kane, E.J., 683
Kang, H., 110, 111, 229
Karacaoglu, G., 717
Katona, George, 205
Katz, L.F., 190, 615–16
Kautsky, Karl, 53, 309, **354–55**, 671
Keane, M., 664
Keech, W.R., 537
Kemmerer, E.S., 613
Kendall, M., 640
Kennan, J.A., 334, 561
Keran, M.W., 660–61

Keynes, John Maynard, 22, 29, 70, 154, 178, 196,
        207, 240, 243, 273, **355–57**, 432,
        519, 588, 591, 621, 625, 633
    animal spirits, 205, 336, 656
    anti-recession policy, 248
    asset-market equilibrium, 645
    classical economics, 357
    consumption function, 115, 593, 595
    credit cycle, 121, 357
    cumulative processes, 357
    cycle theory, 352, 357
    cyclical asymmetry, 685
    deflation, 140, 356
    effective demand, 187, 355
    expectations, 205, 336, 388, 399, 645, 709
    finance, demand for, 403
    fiscal policy, 235, 355, 357, 549
    influence on Föhl, 241
    forced saving, 584
    Friedman, compared to, 248
    full employment, restoration of, 355–56
    full-employment equilibrium, non-existence
        of, 535
    on Gesell, 261
    Gibson Paradox, 270
    gold standard, 268, 356, 458
    Haberler on General Theory, 292–93
    Hahn's anticipation of, 294
    Hansen, influence on, 295–96
    and Harrod, 298
    and Hawtrey, 300
    and Hayek, 302, 304
    Hicks, influence on, 305
    on Hobson, 310
    inconvertible money, analysis of, 268, 270
    inflation, 328, 356
    inflation tax, 356
    interest rate, 398–99, 402
    internal vs. external stability, 356
    investment, fluctuations in, 248, 336, 709
    involuntary unemployment, 314, 317
    and Johannsen, 343
    Kalecki, compared with, 352
    Lachmann, influence on, 373
    and Lalor, 375
    Law's theory, 379–80
    and Lerner, 393–94
    liquidity preference, 357, 397, 400, 690, 717
    liquidity premium, 397–98
    macrodynamic model, 85
    on Malthus, 425, 600
    marginal efficiency of capital, 336, 357, 473
    Marshall's influence on, 356, 429–30
    modern macroeconomics, influence on, 355
    monetary policy, 355, 357, 458, 549
    monetary theory of production, 644–45
    multiplier, 244, 305, 352, 356, **470–71**, 505,
        593, 595
    motives for holding money, 145–46
    natural rate of interest, 356, 477, 584
    and Ohlin, 497–99

    overinvestment theory in Treatise, 506
    and Pigou, 532–34
    Pigou-Haberler effect, 140–41
    price-level stabilization, 356, 458
    pump-priming, 550
    real wages, cyclical movements in, 561
    on Ricardo, 600
    and Robertson, 584
    and Robinson, 586
    savings and investment, 356, 586, 596
    Say's Law, 357, 599, 601
    and Sraffa, 643–45
    static equilibrium method, 188, 413
    stock prices, irrationality of, 656
    and Stockholm School, 652–53
    supply of money, elasticity of, 398
    supply price of capital, 691
    technical change, 603
    theory of output, 357
    time preference, 398
    Tinbergen and econometric modeling, 291,
        368, 420, 687
    uncertainty, 205, 357, 373, 398
    unemployment, 703
    unemployment equilibrium, 188
    wage-price flexibility, 357
    wage rigidity, 317, 356–57, 690
Keynes, John Neville, 356
Kimbrough, K., 622–23
Kimmel, J., 335
Kindelberger, Charles Poor, **358–59**
    crisis of 1873, 133
    financial fragility, 140
    financial panics, 613
    Great Depression, 278, 280, 282, 285, 332,
        358–59, 630
    international lender of last resort, 332, 359
    lender of last resort, 359
    Smoot-Hawley tariff, 630
King, Gregory, 419
King, J.E., 178
King, Lord Peter, 56
King, R.R., 207
King, Robert G., 197, 233, 253, 459, 463, 559,
        622
Kitchin, Joseph, 360
Kitson, Arthur, 178
Kiyotaki, N., 715
Kleidon, A.W., 657–58
Klein, B., 253
Klein, Lawrence Robert, 343, **361–63**, 420, 422–
        23, 617, 687
Klein, M.A., 667
Klein, Phillip A., 289, 445, 466
Kniesner, T.J., 335
Knight, Frank H., 205, 247, 473
Kochin, L., 591
Kohn, M., 717
Kolmogorov, A.N., 611
Kondratieff, Nikolai Dimitriyevich, 72, 364–66,
        366–67, 404–05, 525, 626

Koopmans, Tjalling Charles, 61, 255, 361, **368–69**, 420, 445, 617, 687
Kormendi, R.C., 579
Kornai, J., 77
Koutrouvelis, I.A., 646–47
Koyck, L.M., 5
Kregel, J.A., 538
Kroszner, R., 487, 488
Krueger, A., 380
Kruger, M., 538
Kuhn, T.S., 636
Kurz, Heinz, 81, 408, 471, 522
Kuznets, Simon Smith, 3, 73, 115, 217, 230, **370–72**, 407, 420
Kydland, F., 68, 230, 251, 480, 558, 689

Labrousse, E., 278, 280
Lachmann, Ludwig Maurits, **373–74**
Lahn, J.J.O. *See* Johannsen, Nicholas August Ludwig Jacob
Laibman, D., 212
Laidler, D., 147, 253, 451
Lalor, John, **374–75**
Landes, M., 722
Lange, Oskar, 357, **375–77**, 598, 717
Langston, W., 437
Laplace, Pierre Simon, 419
Laroque, G., 388
Lauderdale, James Maitland, 507
Laughlin, J. Laurence, 268, 444
Lavington, Frederick, **377–78**, 397, 430
Law, John, 40, **378–80**, 442–44, 457
Lazear, E., 722–23
Leamer, E.E., 447–48, 464
Le Baron, B., 493–94
Lederer, E., 417
Legendre, Adrien Marie, 419
Leggett, William, 245
Leifmann, Robert, 488
Leijonhufvud, Axel, 87, 357, 703
Leipnik, R.B., 255
Leland, H., 657
Lenin, V.I., 309, 648
Lenoir, M., 367
Leontief, Wassily W., 100, 273, 363, 376, 407
Lerner, Abba, 205, 258–59, 357, **393–94**
Leroy, S.F., 202, 656–57
Lester, R.A., 451
Lévy, D., 542
Levy-Leboyer, M., 39, 278, 280
Lewis, William Arthur, 367, **393–96**
Leybourne, S.J., 287
Lightner, O., 150, 151
Lillien, D., 559, 615–16, 722
Lindahl, Erik Robert, 187, **396–97**, 458, 497, 652–54
Lindbeck, A., 191, 413
Lindert, P., 266, 383
Lintner, J., 661
Lipietz, A., 573, 574, 575
Lipsey, R.G., 530–31

Litterman, R.B., 670, 676
Liu, Ta-Chung, 420
Ljung, L., 389
Lloyd, W.F., 117
Lombra, R., 198
Long, C., 148
Long, J.B., 480, 558
Longfield, Mountfort, 410
Lorenz, H.-W., 491
Lorenzi, J.-H., 573
Loria, Achille, 216
Lothian, J.R., 265, 283
Loungani, P., 572, 616
Lovell, M.C., 109, 434
Lowe, Adolph, 59, 82, **406–08**
Loyd, Samuel Jones, 48, 49, 117, **409–10**, 581
Lucas, R.E. Jr., 61–62, 68, 181–82, 206, 281, 283, 333, 335, 410–12, 420, 455–56, 459, 480, 482, 553, 558, 559, 584, 615, 621–22, 665, 669–70, 686, 687
Lundberg, Eric Phillip, 187, **413–14**, 368, 397, 433, 473, 653
Lütkepohl, H., 710, 711
Lutz, Friedrich August, **415–16**
Lutz, V.C., 415. *See also* Smith, V.C.
Luxembourg, Rosa, 51, 53, 166, 309, 355, **417–18**, 508, 671, 695

Macaulay, Frederick, 469, 659–61
Machlup, F., 439, 471, 478
Mackay, Charles, 699–700
MacKinlay, A.C., 657
Madan, D.B., 647
Madison, James, 124
Mage, S., 215–16
Maital, S., 329
Malinvaud, E., 188, 704
Malkiel, B.G., 661
Malthus, Thomas Robert, **425–26**
    Bagehot on, 29
    Bullionist controversies, 425
    capital accumulation, 425–26
    effective demand, 187–88, 425–26
    general gluts, 187, 426
    Keynes on, 22, 425, 600
    Luxemburg on, 417
    oversaving theory, 425–26, 507–08, 600
    population, 425
    real wages, 426
    regulating principle, 426, 600
    and Ricardo, 425–26
    saving and investment, 426, 508
    Say's Law, 63, 425–26, 508, 597
    short-run, focus on, 425
    unemployment, 599
Mandel, E., 405
Mandelbrot, Benoit, 646
Mankiw, N.G., 112, 113–14, 330, 482, 484, 545, 677, 705–06
Mann, H.B., 258, 617

Marcet, A., 388–90, 658
Marimon, R., 390
Marschak, Jacob, 8, 361, 407, 724
Marseille, J., 278
Marshal, Mary Paley, 429
Marshall, Alfred, 119, 217, **429–30**, 541–42, 601, 650
    credit cycle, 429
    demand for money, 429
    expectations, 429
    interest rates, 429
    and Keynes 356, 429–30
    and Lavington, 377–78
    loanable funds theory, 429
    monetary business-cycle theory, 429, 451, 557
    monetary theory, 378, 429
    and H.L. Moore, 468
    price-level stability, 429
    sectoral shocks, transmission of, 429
    symmetallic standard, 430
    tabular standard, 429–30, 457
    time in economic analysis, 30
    unemployment, 429
    wage rigidity, 429
Marwah, K., 363
Marx, Karl Heinrich, **199–200, 211–13, 213–16, 430–32**, 634
    capital, organic composition of, 52, 212, 214–15, 431
    capital accumulation, 166, 431
    capital theory, 59–60
    capitalism, collapse of, 64
    capitalism, instability of, 604
    crisis theory, 52, 212, 213, 431–32, 433, 601–02, 671
    disproportionalities, 166
    falling rate of profit, 51–52, 213–15, 308, 431–32, 573, 651, 697–98
    indebtedness, increase of, 431
    investment cycle, 367
    Juglar cycle, 347
    Luxemburg on, 417
    on Mill, 601
    oversaving, 508
    periodicity, 200
    predictions, 214–15
    profit squeeze, 431–32, 547
    real wages, 273
    reproduction schemes, 308, 376, 407, 540–41, 548, 697
    reserve army, 166, 212, 319
    Say's Law, 63, 598, 601
    Scottish banking system, 246
    surplus value, 214–15, 431
    Tooke's influence on, 694
    underconsumption, 200, 431–32
Matthews, R.C.O., 6, 37, 86, 87, 361, 515
Mattick, Paul, **432–33**
May, R.M., 93, 95
Mayer, T.J., 283
McCallum, B.T., 138, 453, 487

McCarthy, M.D., 422
McCartney, R.R., 132
McCloskey, D.N., 265
McCracken, H.C., 106
McCulloch, John R., 48, 49, 410, 520, 521
McCurdy, T., 334, 335
McFerrin, J.B., 281
McGrattan, E., 675
McLaughlin, K.J., 561–62, 722
McLellan, D., 430
McMillan, H., 656, 657
McNees, S.G., 423, 711
Means, Gardiner, 545–46
Medio, A., 96
Meguire, P., 579
Mehra, R., 181–82, 201–02, 674, 678
Meltzer, A.H., 55, 220, 281, 284–85, 630–31, 667
Mendelson, H., 657
Menger, Carl, 23
Mensch, G., 404
Merwin, A. *See* Johannsen, Nicholas August Ludwig Jacob
Metzler, Lloyd Appleton, 5, 65, 91, 243, 413, **433–34**, 653
Meulen, H., 502
Milbourne, R.M., 145
Michael, R.T., 722
Mill, James, 507, 597–99
Mill, John Stuart, **434–36**
    on Attwood, 23
    Banking School and law of reflux, 252
    credit cycle, 429
    crises, monetary explanation of, 601
    destabilizing speculation, 435
    expectations, 429, 435, 664
    financial crises, 359
    fixed investment, 435
    general gluts, 601
    information differences, 435
    inventory cycle, 435
    Lalor, influence on, 374
    monetary business-cycle theory, 451, 601
    monetary policy, 428, 435
    panic, 435–36
    saving and economic growth, 394
    Say's Law and Walras's Law, 601
    Tooke's influence on, 435
    velocity, cyclical variation in, 435
Miller, J., 389
Miller, Merton H., 146, 449, 658, 658
Miller, R.B., 647
Mills, Frederick Cecil, **436**, 469, 546
Mills, John, 121, 341–42, 347, **437**, 664–65
Mills, T.C., 287, 288
Mincer, J., 317
Minsky, Hyman Phillip, 69–70, 86, 140–41, 336–37, 359, **438–39**
Mintz, Ilse, 289, **439–40**
Mirman, L.J., 181
Miron, J.A., 220, 609, 612 614, 677
Mironov, Boris N., 72, 525

Mises, Ludwig Edler von, 314, 439, **440–42**
    Böhm-Bawerk's influence on, 440
    business-cycle theory, 23, 54, 117, 196, 373,
        472, 506, 522
    credit expansion, unsustainability of, 441
    Currency School's influence on, 441
    effective demand, 187
    forced saving, 441
    free banking, 246, 441
    and Hayek, 302, 441
    malinvestment, 441
    monetary policy, 458
    monetary theory, 440
    natural rate of interest, 440, 477–78
    Overstone's influence on, 441
    Robbins, influence on, 582–83
    Röpke, influence on, 588
    Wicksell's influence on, 440–41
Mishkin, Frederic S., 128, 283, 330–31, 456, 676,
        677
Mistral, J., 278, 574
Mitchell, Wesley Clair, 217, 238, 250, 324, **444–45**,
        465, 604, 652, 656, 662, 681
    agriculture, cyclical role of, 11, 670
    asymmetry, 685
    business-cycle theory, 445
    cost-price imbalances, 66, 445
    cumulative process, 445
    crisis of 1907, 134
    cycle-measurement techniques, 247–48, 289,
        727
    cycles, endogeneity of, 619
    definition of business cycle, 61, 63
    duration of cycles, 347–48, 360
    empirical legacy, 445
    expectations, 205, 445
    Fanno, influence on, 217
    indebtedness, 445
    indicators, 325, 383, 386, 419
    interest rates, 445
    Juglar cycle, 347
    Laughlin's influence on, 444
    measurement without theory, 61, 369
    and H.L. Moore, 468
    NBER, 247–48, 289, 444–45, 727
    optimism and pessimism, cycle between, 205
    panic, 445
    periodogram, 640
    policy proposals, 445
    reference cycle, 248, 387, 525
    Russian cycles, 73
    signal extraction problem, 665
    Veblen's influence on, 444, 710
Mizon, G.E., 171, 448
Modigliani, Franco, 9, 115, 317, **449–50**, 579, 595,
        669
Moffit, R., 664
Montgomery, J.D., 191
Moore, B.J., 463–64
Moore, Geoffrey Hoyt, 61–62, 289, 385, **465–67**,
        662, 727

Moore, Henry Ludwell, 11, 342, **468**, 557, 640
Moore, M.H., 467
Moran, M., 198
Morgan, M., 468
Morgenstern, O., 439
Morishima, M., 471, 542, 599
Mortenson, D.T., 608
Morton, A., 678
Morton, P., 383
Moseley, F., 215
Moulton, H., 28
Mouré, K., 279
Mumford, Lewis, 178
Mummery, A.F., 310
Mundell, Robert, 293, 458
Murphy, K.M., 616, 722
Murray, W., 257
Musgrave, Richard A., 296
Mushet, Robert, 48, 117, **472**, 521, 581
Muth, John F., 206, 553
Myrdal, Gunnar, 187, 396, 458, **473–74**, 477, 497,
        652–53

Nason, J.H., 230
Neftci, S., 21, 108–09, 562
Neisser, Hans, 407
Nell, E.J., 82
Nelson, C.R., 21, 102, 110, 111, 229, 324, 603,
        696–97, 705–06
de Nemours, Du Pont, 245
Néré, J., 277–78
Nerlove, M., 101
Netter, J.M., 656
von Neumann, J., 274, 539
Neumann-Spallart, F.X., von, 142
Newbold, P., 105
Newmarch, W., 693
Neyman, Jerzy, 420, 448
Nickell, S., 171
Niehans, J., 416
Niemira, M.P., 108
Norhaus, W., 193, 536
Norman, George Warde, 344, 410
Nove, A., 76
Nurkse, Ragnar, 60, 396
Nyomen, R., 412
Nyarko, Y., 389, 390

Offenbacher, E.K., 175
Officer, L.H., 265
Ohlin, Bertil Gotthard, 187, 396, **497–99**, 652–53
Oi, W., 562
Okishio, N., 213
Okun, Arthur M., **500–01**, 562, 587
Olivera, J.H.A., 76
Oparin, D.I., 367, 404
Orcutt, G., 617
Orosel, G.O., 82
Orr, D., 146, 646
Osterwald-Lenam, M., 105, 257
Overstone, Lord. *See* Loyd, Samuel Jones

Owen, Robert, 200
Owen, T.C., 74–75
Owens, R.N., 661

Pagan, A.R., 102, 104, 168–69, 446
Panico, C., 397, 644
Pantaleoni, Maffeo, 18
Pareto, Vilfredo, 405–06, **518–20**
Parker, J.A., 561
Parkin, M., 328
Parnell, Henry, 117, 472, **520–21**
Parvus, 355, 367
Pasinetti, L., 82
Patinkin, D., 243, 361, 481, 536
Pearson, Egon S., 420, 448
Pearson, Karl E., 419, 468
Peel, D.A., 537
Pennington, James, 410
Pereire, E., 39
Pereire, I., 39
Perlman, M., 313
Perron, P., 706
Persons, Warren Milton, 250, 364, 419–20,
    522–23
Pervushin, Segei Alekseevich, 73–74, **524–26**
Petander, Karl, 721
Peterson, B.C., 338, 339
Petty, William, 419
Pfleiderer, P., 657–58
Phelps, Edmund S., 388, 455, 479–80, 530, 554,
    608, 690
Phelps-Brown, E.H., 528
Phillips, Alban William Housego, 5, 9, 112, 170,
    419, **527–29**, 529–30
Phillips, C.A., 667
Phillips, P.C.B., 102, 105, 258, 421, 706
Pigou, Arthur Cecil, 66, **532–34**, 601
    Cambridge cash-balance approach, 429
    consumption and wealth, 243
    cyclical factors, relative importance, 533–34
    expectations, volatility of, 388, 533, 665
    Fanno, influence on, 217
    impulse and propagation, 67, 533
    and Keynes, 357, 532
    liquidity preference, 397
    Marshall's influence on, 429–30, 532
    monetary theory, 429
    optimism and pessimism, waves of, 66, 533
    Pigou effect, 243, 535
    policy prescriptions, 532, 534
    price-level stabilization, 534
    real wages, cyclical behavior of, 561
    signal-extraction problem, recognition of,
        665
    slump of 1920–21, 534
    unemployment, 532–33, 703
    wage-price rigidity, 533
    weather, as cause of fluctuations, 665
Pissarides, C.A., 608
Pittfield, R.A., 257
Plessis, A., 40

Plosser, Charles I., 21, 102, 110, 197, 233, 253,
    324, 459, 463, 480, 558, 559, 696–
    97, 705–06
Poincaré, Henri, 94
Pollak, R.A., 673
Pollard, S., 37
Poole, W., 198
Porter, R.D., 201, 656
Poterba, J.M., 203
Pound, Ezra, 178
Powell, M.J.D., 257
Poynting, John H., 341, 469
Prat, G., 660
Preobrazhensky, Evgenii Alexeyevich, 166, **540–41**
Prescott, Edward C., 68, 181–82, 201–02, 230,
    251, 480, 558, 615, 674, 689
Presnell, L., 38
Pribram, K., 550
Procaccia, I., 493
Punzo, L., 538

Quah, D., 712
Quandt, R., 661
Quenouille, M.H., 529
Quesnay, Francois, 419

Raasche, R.H., 571, 660
Rae, John, 521
Raisian, J., 562
Ramsey, J.B., 493, 685, 686
Rangel, J., 215
Rapping, Leonard, 283, 333, 335, 584
Rausser, G.C., 11
Rebello, S., 559
Reichenbach, H., 685
Reid, M., 37
Reinsel, G., 255
Rezneck, S., 150
Ricardo, David, 507, 541–42, **580–82**, 693
    on Adam Smith, 425
    aggregate demand, 187, 600
    banking panics, 45
    Banking School, link to, 581
    Bullionist controversies, 57, 580–81
    capital accumulation, 600
    Currency School, influence on, 581
    depreciation of sterling, 56, 720
    devaluation, preferred over deflation, 582
    external drain, 680
    Free Banking School, link to, 581
    freedom of note issue, 581
    general glut, 426, 580–81, 599
    ingot plan, 57, 356, 357, 581, 695
    Joplin, influence on, 344
    Keynes on, 425, 600
    limiting principle, 426, 600–01
    long-run tendencies, concern with, 425
    and Malthus, 425–26, 508, 600–01
    monetary business-cycle theory, 451
    natural rate of interest, 720
    overissue, 57, 581

postwar deflation, 57, 581
pre-Keynesian orthodoxy, 508
proposal for National Bank, 581
rate of profit, 600
real wages, 600
restoration of convertibility, 57, 581
rules vs. discretion, 694
saving and growth, 394
saving and investment, 426, 599, 602
Say's Law, 426, 580–82, 597, 599
technological unemployment, 599
time and production, 521
Rich, G., 265
Richard, J.-F., 104, 255, 446, 448
Riedel, James, 395
Riese, H., 399
Rietz, T.A., 207
de la Rivière, Mercier, 597
Robbins, Lionel Charles, 302, 528, 550, **582–83**
Robertson, Dennis Holme, 178, 196, 244, **584–86**, 596, 636
    accleration principle, 305
    Aftalion's influence on, 7
    disentanglings, 400
    effective demand, 187
    Fanno, influence on, 217
    forced saving, 584
    growth and cycle, 350
    Hawtrey and, 300
    inflation, 585
    intertemporal substitution, 584
    investment, cyclical role of, 295, 584–85
    and Keynes, 584–85
    lags, 413, 585, 593
    loanable funds doctrine, **400–03**, 429
    Marshall's influence on, 430
    Monetarists, compared to, 584–85
    monetary policy, 584–85
    monetary theory, 305
    multiplier, 471, 585
    multiplier-accelerator interaction, 585
    natural rate of interest, 477, 584
    overinvestment, 506, 585
    period analysis, 471
    public works, countercyclical role of, 585
    savings and investment, 585
    Sismondi's influence on, 625
    stability of economy, 584
    unemployment, 585
    velocity, 584
Robinson, Joan Violet Maurice, 81, 212, 336, **586–87**, 643
Rockoff, Hugh, 149, 265
Rodbertus, Johann Karl, 417, 508
Rogerson, R., 616, 674, 675
Rogoff, K., 622
Romer, D., 482, 483, 484, 545
Romer, P.M., 482
Rooke, John, 57
Roos, Charles F., 686, 688
Röpke, Wilhelm, 550, **588**

Rose, H., 66
Rosen, S., 318, 723
Rosenblatt, M., 685
Ross, S.A., 182, 661, 678
Rostow, Walt Whitman, 347, 360, 365, 404, 475, **589–90**, 606
Rotemberg, J., 174
Rothbard, M., 125
Rothman, P., 685–86
Rowe, D.A., 114
Rowthorn, B., 426
Rubin, Herman, 255, 258, 361
Rueff, Jacques, **591–92**
Rühl, C., 342, 470
Rush, M., 284
Runkle, D., 664
Russek, F.S., 579

Sabov, Z., 76
Sachs, J.D., 193–94, 266, 279, 285, 537, 573
Said, S.E., 110
Saint-Auben, Camille, 245
Saint Etienne, C., 279, 281
Salais, R., 279
Salant, Walter, 296
Salari-Martin, X., 330
Salmon, M., 102
Salop, S.C., 190
Samuelson, Paul Anthony, 528, 542, **593–95**
    consumption function, 593, 595
    expectations, 205
    and Hansen, 296
    inflation-unemployment tradeoff, 530
    and Klein, 361–62
    multiplier-accelerator model, 5, 20, 65, 86, 91, 337, 347, 413, 433, 538, 557, 593–95, 653, 685
    pump priming, 550
    Robertsonian income-consumption lag, 593
Sargan, J.D., 102, 104, 168, 169, 170, 171
Sargent, T.J., 108, 198, 311, 459, 481, 542, 554, 562, 607, 622, 658, 710
Sauvy, A., 279
Say, Jean Baptiste, 117, 187, **597–99**
Sayers, C.L., 492, 493, 494
Scazzieri, R., 60
Scheinkman, J.A., 493, 676
Schmidt, C., 508
Schneider, Erich, 240
Schneider, F., 537
Schultz, T.W., 11
Schumacher, E.F., 241
Schumpeter, Joseph Alois, 59, 585, **602–05**, 692
    business-cycle theory, 196, 557
    capitalism, instability of, 217, 604–05
    creative destruction, 118, 604
    credit creation, 603–04
    cycles and growth, 539–40, 663
    cyclical phases, 603–04
    development, wave-like character of, 118–19
    economic evolution, 603

economic integration, cyclical effect of, 360
entrepreneur, role of 118
entrepreneurial behavior, rationality of, 416
on equilibrium theory, 118, 603
Fanno, influence on, 217
and Föhl, 240–41
Goodwin, influence on, 273
Great Depression, severity of, 405
on Hahn, 294
identification of cycles, 360
impulse and propagation, 604
infrastructural investment, 365
innovations, cluster of, 365
interest, monetary theory of, 604
investment, cyclical role of, 295
Juglar's influence on, 346
on Juglar cycle, 346
on Kitchin cycles, 360
Kondratieff cycles, 367
Kondratieff's influence on, 365
periodogram, 640
Röpke, influence on, 588
socialism, trend toward, 605
Soviet economies, cyclicality of, 76
three-cycle schema, 347, 360, 604
on Tooke, 693
vertical maladjustments, 65
Schuster, Arthur, 341, 640
Schwartz, Anna Jacobson, 247, **606**, 667, 691
    agricultural prices in nineteenth century, 288
    banking panics, 606
    British cycles, 589, 606
    causality, meaning of, 462–63
    demand for money, 448
    Federal Reserve, 219–21
    free banking, 246
    gold standard, role in Great Depression, 266
    gold standard, uncertainty about adherence
        to, 150
    Great Depression, 281–83, 557, 614
    lender of last resort, 606
    Monetarism, empirical support for, 452
    money-income causality, 248–49, 283, 462
    Napoleonic Wars, cycles in, 475
    NBER techniques, use of, 606
    neutrality of money, 462–63
    phase averaging, 525, 527
    price-specie flow mechanism, 265
    quantity theory, 606
    real and pseudo financial crises, 135
    velocity, stability of, 145, 463
    wage-price adjustment, lags in, 68
    on Warburton, 718
Schwartz, E.S., 658
Schwartz, G., 711
Schwartz, J.T., 471
Schweikert, L., 128, 130
Schwert, G.W., 111, 706
Scitovsky, T., 535
Scott, W.R., 63
Seabourne, T., 136

Selgin, G.A., 246
Semmler, W., 82, 542
Seneta, E., 647
Sengapta, J.K., 688
Senior, Nassau, 374
Serletis, A., 175
Shackle, George, Lennox Sherman, 357, 373, 473,
    619–21
Shapiro, C., 190
Shapiro, H.T., 422, 660
Shapiro, M.D., 670
Shapiro, Nina, 651
Shell, K., 666
Sheplev, Leonid, E., 75
Sherman, H., 319, 320, 445
Shiller, R.J., 172, 202, 534, 656, 659–60, 676, 677
Shiskin, Julius, 466, 611
Shleifer, A., 656–57
Shohan, L.B., 109
Sicsic, P., 278
Siegel, J., 430
Simiand, F., 404
Simon, Herbert A., 361, 403
Simons, Henry C., 247
Sims, Christopher A., 108, 168, 198, 419, 420,
    464, 618, 621, 710, 712
Sinai, A., 67, 185–86, 422
Sismondi, Jean Charles Leonard Simonde de, 63,
    187, 374, 417, 508 **624–25**
Slutsky, Eugen, **626**
    consumer choice, theory of, 626
    impulse and propagation, 67, 91, 250, 387,
        727
    inflation tax on money, 626
    Kondratieff, criticism of, 364
    serial correlation, 617
    spurious cycles from moving averages, 365,
        420, 626
    time-series modeling, 618
Smale, W., 489
Smart, W., 511
Smith, Adam, 541–42, **627–28**
    banking theory, 627
    capital accumulation, 425, 600
    financial crises, 359, 627–28
    free banking, 245
    law of reflux, 627
    Malthus on, 425
    price-specie-flow mechanism, 627
    productive and unproductive workers, 500
    Ricardo on, 425
    real-bills doctrine, 556, 627
    restrictions on banks, 627–28
    savings and growth, 394
    savings and investment, 599, 602
    Say's Law, 597
    Sismondi, influence on, 625
    supply of money under gold standard, 268,
        627
Smith, V.C., 246. See also Lutz, V.C.
Smith, V.L., 207–08

Smith, W.B., 130
Smithies, Arthur, **628–29**
Smyth, D.J., 9, 351
Snower, D., 191
Snyder, Carl, **631–32**
Soddy, Frederick, **635–36**
Söderström, T., 389
Solomou, S., 367
Solon, G., 561
Solow, Robert M., 69, 205, 530, 558
Sombart, Werner, 373
Souza, R.C., 229
Sowell, T., 598
Spanos, A., 447
Spence, William, 507
Spiethoff, Arthur, 295, 505, 588, **641–42**
Spindt, P.A., 175
Sprague, Oliver Mitchell, 135, 148, 613, **642–43**
Sraffa, Piero, 81, 274, 344, 374, 522, **643–45**
Srba, F., 170
Steiger, O., 498
Steindl, Josef, 353, **650–51**
Sterling, A., 579
Steward, Balfour, 341
Stiflitz, J.E., 190
Stigler, George J., 247, 468, 546, 667
Stigler, Stephen, 419
Stock, James H., 108, 110, 387, 464, 664, 696
Stockman, A.C., 561
Stokey, N., 181, 455
Stone, R., 114
Strumlin, Stanislau G., 527
Stutzer, M.J., 95
Suchanek, G.L., 207–08
Suits, D., 422
Summers, L.F., 21, 203, 284, 656–57, 716
Sunder, S., 390
Sundareson, S.M., 678
Sussmilch, Johann Peter, 419
Svenilson, Ingvar, 653
Sweeney, J.L., 571
Sweezy, Paul Marlor, 52, 211–12, 319, 540, 650–51, **671–72**
Swofford, J.L., 175

Tarshis, L., 217, 561, 664
Tatom, J.A., 571
Taubman, P., 423
Taylor, J., 554, 716
Telser, L.G., 527
Temin, P., 116, 129, 248, 278, 281, 282–83, 285, 514
Temple, William, 178
Tenker, B., 657
Theil, H., 420, 687
Thomas, Brinley, 372, **679**
Thompson, E.A., 253
Thornton, Henry, **679–81**
    Bank of England, 32, 37, 680
    Bullion Report, 57, 581
    Bullionist controversies, 56–57, 581, 679

central banking, 680
country banks, 344
deflation, 680
depreciation of sterling and overissue, 56–57, 268, 478, 581, 680
expectations and interest rates, 204, 429, 681
forced saving, 681
lender of last resort, 391, 627, 680
monetary business-cycle theory, 55, 451
monetary equilibrium, 478
natural rate of interest, 477, 680, 720
non-neutrality of unanticipated money, 680
real-bills doctrine, 57, 478, 556, 627, 680
relative-absolute price confusion, 680
sticky wages, 680
Thorp, Willard Long, **681**
Thweatt, W.O., 598
Timberlake, R.H. Jr., 124, 135, 514
Tinbergen, Jan, 250, 368, 618, **686–87**
    British cycles, study of, 687
    Friedman, criticism by, 420
    Frisch, criticism by, 420
    Frisch's influence on, 686–87
    Haberler's survey of business-cycle theories, 292, 687
    identification problem, 420, 687
    Lucas critique, 687
    Keynes, criticism by, 291, 357, 420
    Klein influence on, 362, 687
    Koopmans, influence on, 687
    long-wave theories, 404
    macroeconometric business-cycle models, 291, 292, 419–20, 422, 629, 686–87
    optimal economic policy, 687
    Phillips curve, estimate of, 687
    rational expectations, 687
    serial correlation, 617
    Theil, influence on, 687
Tintner, Gerhard, **688–89**
Tobin, James, **690–92**
    aggregate demand, 690–91
    aggregate supply, 690
    debt-deflation effect, 141
    demand for money, models of, 145–46, 690
    depressions, role of money in, 248
    expectations, 205, 690
    financial intermediaries, 232
    on Fisher, 239
    and Friedman, 692
    growth and fluctuations, 691
    on Hansen, 295
    inflation, 328, 690
    liquidity constraints, 690–91
    liquidity preference, 690
    on Minsky, 438–39
    Monetarism, 691–92
    money-income causality, 463, 691–92
    natural rate of unemployment, 690
    Pigou-Haberler effect, 14
    portfolio diversification, 690

price-quantity adjustment, 541
q-theory of investment, 337, 691
rational expectations, 690, 692
search theory, 608, 690
separation theorem, 690
stabilization policy, 691
supply of money, 253, 667
wage rigidity, 690
Toma, M., 220
Tooke, Thomas, 48, 117, 252, 262, 374, 435, 520, **693–94**
Topel, R., 616, 722
Torrens, Robert, 48, 82, 117, 344, 374, 410, **695–96**
Tourgot, Jacques, 245
Townshend, Hugh, 398, 645
Trotsky, Leon, 364
Truman, E., 382–83
Trehan, B., 623
Trivedi, P.K., 172
Tsiang, S.C., 146, 403, 717
Tufte, E.R., 536
Tugan-Baranovsky, Mikhail Ivanovich, **697–98**
    on Bernstein, 53
    breakdown theory, 698
    Cassel, influence on, 505
    disproportionality theory, 166–67, 308, 697–98
    falling rate of profit, 52, 698
    Hilferding, influence on, 308
    investment, volatilty of, 698
    Kautsky's criticism of, 455
    and Kondratieff, 366–67, 405
    labor market, disregard of, 167
    Luxemburg's criticism of, 417
    multiplier process, 505
    non-Marxian economists, influence on, 698
    overinvestment theory, 505
    periodicity of cycles, 347
    saving and investment, 698
    Spiethoff, influence on, 505
    underconsumptionism, 697
    unlimited accumulation, 166
    vertical maladjustments, 65
Tukey, J., 640
Turner, H., 640

Valentine, L., 566
Van Boening, 207
Van Duijn, J.J., 367
Van Ewijk, C., 367
Van Geldern, J., 367, 404
Vasko, T., 405
Veblen, Thorstein, 27, 140, 444, **709–10**
Vercelli, A., 538
Viner, Jacob, 247, 253, 627
Vining, Rutledge, 364

Wagemann, Ernst, 407
Wald, A., 258, 617
Wallace, N., 198, 311, 459, 487, 542, 622

Wallis, K.F., 423
Wallis, W. Allen, 247, 465
Walras, Léon, 261, 363, 518, 541–42, 603, 717, 719
Walsh, R.M., 419
Walton, G., 149
Wanniski, Jude, 630–31
Warburton, Clark, 20, 450-52, 632, **718**
Ward, M., 722
Watson, G.S., 618
Watson, Mark W., 108, 110, 229, 387, 464, 664, 670, 696, 712
Watts, John, 200
Webber, A.H., 287
Weber, Max, 273
Weeks, J., 217
Wei, W.W.S., 527
Weil, V., 201
Weintraub, S., 328
Weiskopf, T.E., 211, 215, 320
Weiss, L.W., 545, 622, 670
Weitzman, M., 716
Weizsäker, C.C. von, 82
Welch, F., 722
Wesslau, D.E., 178
West, K.D., 706
Whaley, R.E., 657
Wheatley, John, 56–57, 680
Wheelock, David, 220
White, E.N., 282
White, H., 389, 448
White, L.H., 245–46, 487, 502
Whitney, G.A., 175
Whittle, P., 228
Wichern, D.W., 647
Wicker, E., 220, 282
Wicksell, Johan Gustav Knut, 196, 636, **719–21**
    aggregate monetary demand and supply, 497
    Austrian theory, influence on, 23, 54, 457
    Böhm-Bawerk's influence on, 719
    business-cycle theory, 59, 349, 557, 720
    capital theory, 719–20
    Commons, influence on, 106
    cumulative process, 506, 652
    effective demand, 187
    expectations and inflation, 720
    Fanno, influence on, 217
    Gibson Paradox, 478
    Hawtrey, influence on, 506
    Hayek, influence on, 54, 302, 506, 721
    impulse and propagation, 67, 250
    inflation, 720
    interest and scarcity of capital, 81–82
    investment, cyclical role of, 295
    Keynes, influence on, 457, 506, 721
    long cycles, 367, 404
    Mises, influence on, 440–41, 721
    monetary equilibrium, 473, 478
    monetary policy, 428, 441, 457, 721
    money, functions of, 145

Myrdal on, 473
natural rate of interest, 23, 56, 242, 428, 473, 477, 522, 584, 596, 680, 719–21
neo-Malthusianism of, 721
price level, focus on, 440
price-level stabilization, 458, 473, 721
public finance, theory of, 719
pure credit economy, model of, 488, 719–20
quantity theory, 719
real-bills doctrine, 478, 556
Robbins, influence on, 582–83
Robertson, influence on, 457, 506, 721
rocking-horse analogy, 12, 250, 721
savings and investment, 473, 596
Say's Law, 497, 720
Stockholm School, influence on, 457, 652, 721
technical progress, 59
Tooke's influence on, 694
valuation of capital, 81–82
vertical maladjustments, 65
Wigmore, B.A., 285
Wilcox, J.A., 281, 282, 283
Wiles, P., 76
Williams, A.W., 207–08
Williamson, S.D., 668
Wilson, James, 29, 117, 469
Winter, Sidney G., 603
Wittgenstein, Ludwig, 643
Wold, Herman, 653, 710

Wolff, E.N., 215
Wolowowski, Louis, 245
Wood, G.E., 288
Wood, R.A., 657
Woodford, Michael, 92, 323, 388, 666
Woytinsky, Emma Shadkan, 723–24
Woytinsky, Wladimir Savelievich, **723–24**
Wright, Carroll, 150
Wright, E.O., 431
Wright, R., 674, 675
Wright, Sewall, 420
Wulwick, N.J., 528
Wyplosz, C., 280

Yeager, Leland, 410, 427, 453, 487–88
Yellen, J.A., 482, 715
Yeo, S., 102, 104, 170
Younès, Y., 704
Yoo, B.S., 103
Yuan, H.-J., 493
Yue, P., 175
Yule, G. Udney, 250, 419, 470, 617

Zapatero, F., 673-74
Zarowitz, Victor, 70, 434, 659, 661, 662, **727–28**
Zecher, J.R., 265
Zeldes, S.P., 612
Zellner, Arnold, 420
Zeuch, W.E., 106
Zin, S.E., 201, 678

Subject Index

The main entry for each topic is listed in **boldface**.

acceleration principle, **4–6**, 65, 296, 505–06
    asymmetry of, 307
    cause of cycles, 4–6
    depreciation, 306
    derivation of, 4–5
    destabilizing effect of, 4–6, 305
    railroad investment and, 84
    rigidity of, 84
    shipping investment and, 84
    See also accelerator; flexible accelerator
accelerator, 4–6, 179, 226, 273, 349, 351, 653
    asymmetry of, 4–5
    coefficient, 5
    and durable-goods investment, 112
    and expectations, 5, 337
    flexible, 6, 65, 84
    investment boom, amplification of, 295
    and permanent output, 5
    relative prices and, 337
    simple, 6
accommodation, 463–64
accumulation. *See* capital accumulation
adaptive expectations, 116, 479
    in cobweb cycle, 101
    distributed lag and, 205–06
    in econometric models, 553
    and error correction, 528
    origins of, 528
    theoretical justification, lack of, 205–06
Adenauer, Konrad, 156
adjustment costs, 337
administered prices, 545
adverse selection, 189
    in deposit insurance, 44
    in financial crises, 330–31
    riskless real interest rate and, 330
    See also efficiency wages
aggregate demand, 301, 600, 690–691
    derivation of, 7–8
    dynamization of, 9
    extensions of, 8

    and price level, 8
    and unemployment, 607
    See also aggregate supply; aggregate supply
        and demand; effective demand
aggregate-demand externality, 482–83
aggregate supply, 690
    curve, slope of, 669–70
    derivation of, 7
    dynamization of, 9
    in early Keynesian models, 530
    and money illusion, 8
    and Phillips curve, 9
    and price level, 8
    See also aggregate demand; aggregate supply
        and demand
aggregate supply and demand, **7–10**, 497, 531,
    669
aggregation bias, 561–62
aggregation theory, 173–76
aggregator function, 324
agriculture, **10–11**
    cycle theories based on, 10–11, 341–42, 468,
        557, 664–66
    declining importance of, 10, 326
    depression in, 405
    in depression of 1873–79, 148–49
    in depression of 1882–85, 150
    general business conditions, relation to, 11
    in Great Depression of 1873–96, 287–88
    in nineteenth-century cycles, role in, 10, 30
    price flexibility in, effects of, 11
amplitude, cyclical, 61
animal spirits, 205, 336, 388, 587, 606, 656
arbitrage pricing theory, 661
Arrow-Debreu model, 321–22, 692, 704
asset liquidation, 140
asset-market equilibrium, 374, 645
asymmetry, 5, **21–22**, 492
    impulse and propagation, consistency with,
        251–52
    modeling cycles, implications for, 21
    and time reversibility, **684–86**
attractors, 489. *See also* strange attractors

attractors, chaotic, 92–94, 97. *See also* strange
     attractors
Austrian business-cycle theory, **23–26,** 302–03, 373,
     440–41, 472, 506
     cyclical unemployment, 26
     disequilibrium features of, 454
     fixed capital, role in, 60
     forced saving, 24, 303, 441, 584
     interest rates and fixed investment, 121, 452
     intertemporal misallocation of resources, 25
     labor-market adjustment in, 26
     and mainstream economists, 441–42
     malinvestment, 25, 441. *See also*
          overinvestment
     and monetary-disequilibrium theory, 452
     and monetary-equilibrium theory, 454
     natural rate of interest, 24, 374
     and period of production, 522
     policy recommendations, 26
     relative prices, role in, 452
     savings- and credit-induced expansions, 23–24
     secondary deflation, 26
     uncertainty and expectations, 205
     upper turning point, 373
Austrian capital theory, 23–26, 59–60, 82, 302–04,
     719–20
Austrian Institute for Business Cycle Research,
     302, 439
Austrian National Bank, 119–20
Austro-Marxists, 51
auto-adjustment method, 610. *See also* seasonal
     adjustment
autoregressions, 102
autoregressive and moving average(ARMA) pro-
     cesses, 110
autoregressive-integrated moving average (ARIMA)
     processes, 228
Ayr Bank, failure of, 122. *See also* bank failures

BDS statistic, 493–94
BFH plan, 487–88
Bagehot's rule, 265
balance of payments, 265
balance of trade, 313
balanced budget, 259, 653. *See also* fiscal policy
balanced-budget multiplier, 234, 296, 499
Bank Charter Act of 1844, 30, **31–32,** 117, 245,
     252, 262, 410, 472, 502, 693, 696
     Bank of England, role under, 32, 127
     country banks, effect on, 32
     debate over, 31–32, **47–49,** 252, 262, 693
     financial crises, role in, 32, 36–37, 50, 125–
          28, 131, 135, 503
     practical effect of, 32
     suspension of, 32, 36–37, 50, 126–28, 131,
          135, 136, 503
bank competition. *See* banking competition
bank credit, 65, 107, 217, 232, 282. *See also* credit
bank failures, 42, 44
     Ayr Bank, 122
     Bank of United States, **42–43**

City of Glasgow Bank, 50, 135
Credit-Anstalt, **119–20**
Credit Mobilier, 39
Danatbank, 120
Jay Cooke and Company, 133
Johnson-Matthey Bank, 38
Joint Stock Discount Company, 503
Knickerbocker Trust Co., 46, 134–35
Ohio Life Insurance and Trust Co., 128–29
Pole, Thornton and Co., 512
Sir William Eckford's, 512
Union Générale, 39, 151
Wentworth and Co., 512
Western Bank of Scotland, 131
Bank for International Settlements, 120, 331
bank holiday, 143
Bank Insurance Fund (BIF), 218
bank liabilities, 231–32
bank loans, 43–44
Bank of Amsterdam, 269, 442
Bank of England, **33–38,** 41, 151, 409–10, 442,
     469, 472–73, 642, 693
     Bank Charter Act, role under, 32, 127
     bank-rate policy of, 126–27
     banking and issue departments, 32, 36, 37,
          125, 410, 695
     in Baring crisis, 32, 38, 50–51, 135, 504
     central bank, role as, 88
     countercyclical policy of, 378
     and country banks, 344
     creation of, 31, 33, 88, 267–68
     Credit-Anstalt, assistance to, 120
     in crises of 1763 and 1772–73, 33, 122–23
     in crisis of 1836, 262
     in crisis of 1839, 262
     in crisis of 1847, 32, 37, 126–27
     in crisis of 1857, 32, 129, 131
     in crisis of 1914, 38, 136–37
     and cycles, 48
     debate about, 36, **47–49**
     deposit insurance, implicit provision of, 38
     depreciation of sterling, responsibility for, 56–
          57. *See also* Bullionist Controversies
     discount policy of, 40, 301
     foreign assistance to, 41, 50
     and gold standard, policy under, 37, 265–66,
          301
     and joint-stock banks, 36, 262
     as lender of last resort, 29–30, 33, 51, 131,
          457, 502–04
     long cycles, role in, 675
     monopoly of, 31, 33, 472, 511, 513
     Napoleonic Wars, 475–76
     in Overend Gurney crisis (1866), 32, 37, **502–
          04**
     overissue of notes, 49, 252, 520, 581
     owners and directors, incentives of, 34–37
     Palmer rule, adoption of, 31
     in panic of 1825, 23, 36, 262, 472, 476, **511–13**
     responsibilities of, 29–30, 31, 37, 51
     resumption of convertibility, 34, 36, 47, 476

rivalry with competitors, 37
and South Sea Bubble, **637–39**
suspension of convertibility, 22, 31, 34, 56,
    475, 520, 680
Treasury, reluctance to provide assistance to,
    34
wartime emergencies, role in, 269
See also Bank Charter Act; Banking School,
    central banking; Currency School and
    Free Banking School
Bank of France, **39–41**, 642
advances to state after 1918, 40
Bank of England, assistance to in crises, 41,
    50
Credit Mobilier, role in failure of, 39
in crisis of 1931, 39–40
Currency School principles, adherence to, 41
discount policy in nineteenth century, 40
founding of, 39
and gold standard, 40
Great Depression, role in, 40–41
inflationary practices after 1935, 40
international role of in nineteenth century, 41
as lender of last resort, 39
stabilization of franc in 1926, 41
Union Générale, role in failure of, 39, 151
Bank of Scotland, 502
Bank of the United States, 268. See also Second
    Bank of the United States
Bank of United States, **42–43**
bank portfolios, riskiness of, 44
bank rate, 89, 135, 300, 457. See also discount rate
bank reserves, 79, 221
bank runs, 42, 89, 119, 129, 134, 150, 487, 668
Banking Act of 1935, 222
banking and financial regulation, **43–45**, 47, 99,
    118, 331–32
banking assets, secondary market for, 45
banking competition, 48–49, 117–18. See also free
    banking
banking crisis of 1930, 281–83, 285
banking crisis of 1931, 281
banking crisis of 1933, 281
banking panics, 36, **45–47**, 89, 128, 133, 143–44
central banking and, 47
clearinghouses, role in, 47, 99, 133
in crisis of 1857, 128
in crisis of 1873, 133
in crisis of 1884, 150
in crisis of 1907, 134–35
and cyclical downturns, 606
debt contracts, role in, 46
in decentralized banking systems, 47, 130
deposit insurance and, 47
Monetarist explanation of, 69
and seasonal fluctuations, 46, **613–15**
in unregulated systems, absence of, 117–18,
    245–46, 487
Banking Principle, 695
Banking School, 39, **47–49**, 117, 246, 252, 262,
    581, 628, 693–94

bank deposits, importance of, 117
Bank of England, 36, 38
gold standard, 48, 695
law of reflux, 48–49, 252–53, 556
nonmonetary cycle theory of, 48–49, 253,
    693
banking theories of, 44, 55, 231–32, 252–53, 294,
    487–88, 627, 635–36, 667–68
bankruptcy, 77, 121, 124, 140
banks, 231–33, 487–88, 666–68
base money, effect on demand for, 231–32
commercial, 263–64
and deposit insurance, 44–45, 668. See also
    deposit insurance
investment, 263–64, 655
joint-stock, 36, 262
LDC crisis, 382
large, 44–45
medium of exchange, provision of, 231–33,
    487–88
monitoring function, 43
and other financial intermediaries, 231–33,
    487–88, 668
banks of issue. See Select Committee on Banks of
    Issue
Banque Générale, 379, 442–43. See also Banque
    Royale
Banque Royale, 442–44, 457
Baring, Alexander (Secretary), 513
Baring Brothers and Company, 50, 504
Baring Crisis, 32, 41, **50–51**, 135, 504
Baring, Sir Francis, 391
barometers, 18, 58–59, 142. See also Harvard ABC
    Curves
base money, 231–32. See also high-powered
    money; outside money
Basle Agreement, 44–45, 332
bifurcations, **91–92**. See also chaos
bimetallic standard, 142, 264, 516. See also
    symmetallic standard
bimetallism, 264, 457
Birmingham School, 22–23, 57
Bland-Allison Act, 516–17
Blumenthal, Michael, 224
Bonaparte, Napoleon, 22, 245
booms, 642
beginning of, 533
central-bank role in, 25, 440–41, 472
credit-induced, unsustainability of, 24–26,
    440–42
excesses of, 550
expectations of rising profits, 399
pre-election, 536–37
progress during, 550
psychological factors in, 205
stock-market, 476, 654–55
See also expansions; upswings
Box-Jenkins models, 101, 448, 618
Brady Commission Report, 657
branch banking, 130
Brauns Commission Report, 588

Bretton Woods system, 88–89, 264–65, 268, 271, 332, 565
Broderick, Joseph, 42
Brookings Model, 179, 363, 420
Bubble Act, 637
bubbles:
    informed insiders, effect on, 208
    short-selling, effect on, 208
    speculative, 43, 69, 699–701
    stock-market, 654, 660
    See also experimental price bubbles
budget deficit, 15, 20, 234–37, 301
    cyclical changes in, 234
    fiscal policy, measure of, 234
    inflation, effect on, 237
    and monetary reform, 461–62
    structural, 234
    total saving, relation to, 235–36
buffer-stock approach, 44, 147
Bugge, Anna, 719
building construction, 148–49, 281, 413, 684
building cycle, 296, 679
Bullion Committee, 409
Bullion Committee, Report of, 34, 57, 344, 476, 679
Bullionist Controversies, 47, **56–57**, 425, 472, 556, 580–81, 679, 695
Bundesbank. See Deutsche Bundesbank
Burns, Arthur Frank, 223–24
business confidence, 217
business cycles, **62–70**
business cycles in Russia, **72–75**, 524–25
business cycles in socialist economies, **75–78**, 377
busts, 25, 533, 536. See also downswings

Cambridge Circus, 644
Cambridge debate, 81
Cambridge oral tradition, 429
capital, 29
    circulating, 719
    confused meaning of, 27
    constant, empirical estimates of, 214–15
    fixed, 306
    fixed and working, distinction between, 60
    as fund, 82
    liquid, 306
    marginal product of, 528
    measurement of, 81–82, 521
    outside, 211–12
    and reproduction, 60
    and roundabout production processes, 54, 81
    and time, 81
    variable, 214–15
    working, 306
    See also capital goods
capital accumulation, 431, 573–74, 587, 625
    and crises, 540–41
    cyclical interaction with reserve army, 166
    and Industrial Revolution, 326–27
    and monopoly, 167–68
    and rate of profit, 52, 425–26, 600

    regime of, 573
    unlimited potential for, 167–68
capital goods, 59–60, **80–82**, 407–08, 506, 521–22.
    See also capital; machine tools
capital-goods industries, 371
capital-goods sector, 166
capital, organic composition of, 51–52, 212–13, 214–15, 431
    and falling rate of profit, 212, 573
    and technical progress, 697–98
capital replacement, 217
capital reversal, 81–82
capital shortage, 642
capital structure, 25
capital theory, 59–60, 80–82, 416. See also Austrian
    capital theory; Marxian capital theory
capitalism, breakdown of, 53, 64, 354–55, 568, 648–50, 698
cartels, 53, 167, 309
Carter, Jimmy, 195, 224–25
cash-in-advance constraint, 323, 596
catastrophe theory, 15, 163, 490
causal-adjustment method, 610. See also seasonal
    adjustment
causality. See Granger causality
ceilings and floors, 21, 66, **86–87**, 103, 273–74, 299, 307, 538–39, 594, 629
Center for International Business Cycle Research, 289, 406, 727
central authorities. See socialism
central-bank cooperation, 41
central banking, 47, **88–90**, 135, 457, 596, 642. See
    also central banks; lender of last resort
central banks:
    in banking crisis, 36–37, 42, 47
    in crisis of 1873, absence of, 148
    cyclical role of, 90
    discount policy of, 89
    discretionary authority of, 90
    and endogeneity of money, 198
    fiscal responsibilities of, 90
    under gold standard, 264–65
    independence of, 90
    as lender of last resort, 30, 89, **391–92**, 668.
        See also lender of last resort
    money supply, control over, 89
    monopoly over note issue, 88, 90
    regulatory responsibilities of, 90
    responsibilities of, 29–30, 265
    secrecy of, 90
    See also central banking
central limit theorem, 16, 646
centrally planned economies, **75–77**
chaos, 21, **91–92**, 274, 323, 489, 491, 492–94
chaos, continuous-time models of, **92–98**
chaos theory, 66, 87, 163
Chicago School, 247
China Company, 443
chronologies, growth-cycle, 289
circuit breakers, 656
circular flow, 187–88, 240

City of Glasgow Bank Crisis, 50, 135
classical cycles, 289, 439
classical dichotomy, 270–71, 481–82. *See also* neutrality of money
classical economists, 357, 596
clearinghouses, **99**
    banking panics, response to, 47
    in crisis of 1857, 131
    in crisis of 1873, 133
    currency, issue of, 99, 143, 518
    deposit insurance, provided by, 99
    as lender of last resort, 99
    in panic of 1893, 99, 518
    regulation of members, 47, 99
    See also New York City Clearing House
Cleveland, Grover C., 517
cobweb cycle, 5, **100–01**
Cochrane-Orcutt transformation, 617–18
Coinage Act of 1792, 264
coincident indicators, 387. *See also* leading indicators
cointegration, **101–06**, 257, 711–12
Columbia School, 468
Commerce Department, United States, 289
commercial moods, 664
Committee on Economic Research, Harvard University, 58
commodity theory of money, 264–65
common factors, 169, 171
Compagnie des Indes, 442–44
Compagnie d'Occident, 379, 442. *See also* Mississippi Company
compensated dollar, 57, 239, 445, 453, 457, 488
complementary function, 158, 162–63
complete markets, 181. *See also* incomplete markets
composite indexes, **108–09**
composite trends, **110–11**
concertina effect, 350. *See also* Ricardo effect
Congress, United States. *See* Federal Reserve System construction
construction. *See* building construction; building cycle
consumer confidence, 64, 661
consumer durables, **111–14**, 115–16, 283, 567
consumer-goods industries, 166, 371
consumption, 77, 426
    aging population, effect on, 296
    and fiscal policy, 235–36
    investment, effect on, 216
    liquidity constraints and, 690–91
    real wealth and, 243, 662, 690–91
    under socialism, cyclical role of, 77
    stability of, 85, 116
    stock market and, 662
    See also consumption expenditures; consumption function
consumption expenditures, **114–16**
    on durable goods, **111–14**, 115–16
    and expectations, 116
    in Great Depression, 116, 283

and liquidity constraints, 116, 235, 237, 690–91
models of, 115
See also consumption
consumption function, 115, 449–50, 497, 519, 593, 595, 628, 724. *See also* life-cycle hypothesis; permanent-income hypothesis; relative-income hypothesis
contagion effects, 46, 392
contingent claims, 187
convertibility, 40, 231, 271, 437, 457, 487, 556, 627. *See also* gold standard
convertibility, indirect. *See* indirect convertibility
convertibility, restorations of, 57, 265, 269, 516, 581
convertibility, suspensions of, 444, 581
    Bank of England in 1797, 34, 56, 475, 680
    banks outside New England in 1814, 125
    banks in panic of 1907, 46, 135
    clearinghouses, 99
    crisis of 1819, 125
    crisis of 1857, 128–30
    panic of 1837, 515
    wartime, 265, 269
convolution, 646
coordination failures, 484–86
copper standard, 267. *See also* metallic standard
Corn Laws, 425
correlation dimension, 492–94
correlation integral, 493–94
corridor, 87
cost-price imbalances, 65–66, 107, 445
countercyclical policy, 486. *See also* fiscal policy; functional finance; monetary policy; stabilization policy
country banks:
    Bank Charter Act, effect on, 32
    and Bank of England, 48–49, 344, 472, 680
    in crises, role of, 472
    in cycles, role of, 48–49
    destabilizing effect of, 344
    monetary disturbances in 1830s, role in, 31
    overissue by, 252
    in panic of 1825, 36, 472, **511–13**
coupling of cycles, 273
Cowles Commission, 291, 361–62, 368–69, 420, 687
creative destruction, **118–19**, 604. *See also* Schumpeter, Joseph Alois
credibility, 459, 450–62
credit, 113, 253
    cyclicality of, 65, 663
    direct vs. bank, 232
    disruptions in supply of, 69
    inherent instability of, 300–01
Credit-Anstalt, **119–20**
credit controls, 224
credit creation, 24, 603–04
credit crunch, 165, 563
credit cycle, **121**, 253, 357, 429
credit deadlock, 301
credit expansion, 24, 65, 107, 117, 441

credit market, 484, 668
Credit Mobilier, failure of, 39. *See also* bank failures
credit rationing, 484, 486
crises, 62–63, 601–02
    causes of, 63, 472, 504, 506
    and disappointed expectations, 664–65
    inevitability of, 601
    and Say's Law, 601
crisis of 1763, 33, **122–23**
crisis of 1772–73, 33, **122–23**
crisis of the 1780s, **123–24**
crisis of 1797, 472
crisis of 1810, 476
crisis of 1819, **124–25**, 472
crisis of 1825, 22–23, 48, 261, 472, 521, 601. *See also* panic of 1825
crisis of 1836, 262. *See also* panic of 1837
crisis of 1837, 36, 48. *See also* panic of 1837
crisis of 1839, 48, 262. *See also* panic of 1837
crisis of 1847, 32, 36, 50, **125–28**, 430, 502–03
crisis of 1857, 32, 37, 50, **128–31**, 430, 502–03. *See also* depression of 1857–58
crisis of 1866, 32, 37, 128. *See also* Overend Gurney crisis
crisis of 1873, **132–33**, 148. *See also* depression of 1873–79
crisis of 1878, 135. *See also* City of Glasgow Bank crisis
crisis of 1884, 642. *See also* depression of 1882–85
crisis of 1890, 642
crisis of 1893, 143, 642
crisis of 1907, 41, **134–35**, 143, 642. *See also* panic of 1907
crisis of 1911, 576
crisis of 1914, **135–37**, 576
crisis of 1920, 58. *See also* depression of 1920–21; recession of 1920–21
crisis of 1931, 39–40, 281, 588. *See also* Great Depression
crisis theory, Marxian. See Marxian crisis theory
crowd psychology, 699–701. *See also* mob psychology
crowding out, 550, 577. *See also* fiscal policy; investment
cumulative processes, 140–41, 295, 315, 357, 445, 473, 506, 641, 652
currency, 143, 176, 666, 668
currency, demand for, **143–44**, 232, 262, 614
Currency Principle, 31, 48–49, 126, 409–10, 695
Currency School, 23, 39, 41, **47–49,** 246, 252, 262, 435, 556, 695–96
    and Bank Charter Act, 36, 48
    on banknotes, uniqueness of, 31
    competitive note issue, opposition to, 49, 693
    country banks, 31, 49, 695
    cyclical theory of, 23, 48–49, 117, 440–41, 472, 581, 628
    gold standard, commitment to, 48, 695
    lender of last resort, 696
Current Population Survey, 334
customer markets, 500

DRI, 185–86
DRI model, 185, 422–23
Danatbank, failure of, 120
debt, 66, 69–70, 107, 140, 217, 438. *See also* indebtedness; overindebtedness
debt-deflation effect, 141
debt-deflation theory, 66, 70, 121, **140–41**, 238–39, 438, 452
    credit-cycle theory, extension of, 121
    cumulative process in, 140–41
    and great depressions, 239
    real-monetary interaction in, 238
    and secondary deflation, 550
debt-equity ratio, 212
debt, national, 237, 269–70
debt, return on, 201
default spread, 677. *See also* economic drift
deficit spending. *See* budget deficit
deflation, 57, 70, 515, 581, 680
    and convertibility, resumption of, 57, 516
    in depression of 1920–21, 152–53
    in Great Depression, 281–82
    and interest rates, 238–39
    and investment, 238–39
    tendency toward under capitalism, 27
    and unemployment, 356
    See also debt deflation theory; secondary deflation
demand for finance, 403
demand for money, **145–47**, 429, 448, 662
    buffer stocks and, 147, 451
    consumption vs. savings, effect on, 403
    interest-elasticity of, 662, 690
    legal restrictions and, 487
    risk aversion and, 690
    seasonality of, 133
    stability of, 287
demand shocks, 485–86, 670. *See also* shocks
deposit insurance, 44–45, 47, 69, 99, 668
deposit insurance, federal, **217–18**
    bank panics, elimination of, 47, 69, 217, 614
    business cycles, moderation of, 64
    flat-rate premium structure, 217–18, 683
    insolvency in 1980s, 217
    lender of last resort, alternative to, 89
    moral-hazard problem in, 44–45, 217–18, 683
    mutual-fund banks, unnecessary for, 487
    separation between commercial and investment banking, 264
    and thrift crisis, 683
deposit multiplier, 294
deposits, 117, 197–98, 232, 666–68, 696. *See also* inside money
depressions:
    gold standard and, 269–71
    policy mistakes and, 293
    postwar, 123, 269–71, 476
    psychological factors in, 205, 550
    secondary deflation and, 550
depression of 1841–42, 36
depression of 1857–58, 245–46. *See also* crisis of 1857

depression of 1873–79, **148–49**. *See also* crisis of 1873

depression of 1882–85, **149–51**. *See also* crisis of 1884

depression of 1920–21, 140, 143, **151–53**, 281, 534. *See also* crisis of 1920; recession of 1920–21

depression of 1937–38, 154–55, 296. *See also* Great Depression; recession of 1937–38

Deregulation and Monetary Control Act, 165

deterministic models, 87

detrended data, 21. *See also* time series

detrending, 110–11, 202–03, 227, 229–30, 617

Deutsche Bundesbank, **156–57**. *See also* Reichsbank

Deutsches Institut für Konjunkturforschung, 407

devalorization, 573, 575

devaluation, 301

development, 118–19

deviation cycles, 289

Dickey-Fuller test, 105, **705–06**

difference equations, **158–63**, 489

differential equations, **158–63**, 489, 491

diffusion indexes, **108–09**, 384–85

discount rate, 89, 203, 660. *See also* bank rate

disentanglings, 400

dishoarding, 242, 519

disintermediation, **164–65**, 682

disproportionalities, **166–68**, 308, 355, 505, 641–42. *See also* disproportionality theory

disproportionality theory, 53, **166–68**, 697. *See also* disproportionalities

distributed lags, 5, **168–72**, 205–06, 239

Divisia index, 173–76, 324. *See also* index numbers

Divisia monetary aggregates, **173–77**

dollar standard, 679

Douglas, Paul H., 222

downswings, 21, 505–06, 641–42. *See also* busts

downturn, 226. *See also* upper turning point

Dred Scott decision, 128

dual dynamics, 542

Durbin-Watson test, 447, 618

dynamic decentralization, **180–82**

East India Company, 637

Eccles, Mariner, 222

econometric modelling, 179–80

econometric models, 368, 411

econometrics, 238, 291

economic drift, 660. *See also* default spread

economic fluctuations, theory of, 352

economic surplus, 671

The *Economist*, 29, 613–14

effective demand, **187–88**, 295, 310, 352, 355, 425–26, 470, 600

effective-demand failure, 342, 560

efficiency wages, 70, **188–92**, 318–19, 484–86, 703

efficient growth region, 578

efficient-markets theory, 102, 202–04, 656

effort, 190

eigensectors, 274

Eisenhower, Dwight David, 223–24

elastic currency, 134

electoral cycle, **193–95**

emergency finance. *See* gold standard

employment, 3, 317, 333, 485, 690

Employment Act of 1946, 222, 297, 696

encompassing, 448

endogenous cycles, 538, 619, 721

endogenous fluctuations, 666

endogenous money, 178, **197–99**, 458, 498, 559, 591–92, 623, 693–94

endogenous theories, 65–66, 86, 93

English East India Company, 122–23

equilibrium, 416. *See also* general equilibrium

equilibrium models, 91–92. *See also* Walrasian general equilibrium model

equilibrium theory, 118

equity premium, **201–02**, 674

equity, return on, 201

Erhard, Ludwig, 588

error-correction models, 101–04, 169–71, 528

eurodollars, 164

ex ante/ex post, 205, 414, 473, 497–98, 652–53

excess demand, law of, 542

excess returns, law of, 542

excess volatility, **202–04**, 338–39, 656–57, 660

exchange rates, flexible, 148

exchange rates, fixed, 198, 264–65, 271–72

executive branch. *See* Federal Reserve System

exogeneity, temporal vs. theoretical, 197

exogenous factors, 65, 67

exogenous money, 55, **197–99**, 248–49, 452, 463–64

exogenous shocks, 86, 163, 248. *See also* shocks

exogenous theories, 86–87, 93

exogenous variables, 104–05, 526

expansions, 54, 445, 677, 709. *See also* booms; upswings

expectations, **204–06**, 207–08, 235, 294–95, 353, 399, 473, 619, 652, 690

in accelerator model, 5–6, 336

asymmetric, 689

in business-cycle literature of 1920 and 1930s, 205

in cobweb cycle, 100–01

convergence of, 207

in credit cycle, 429, 437

cyclical movements in, 107, 253, 435, 445, 533

cyclical role of, 204

of deflation after World War I, 151–52

and demand for money, 146–47, 690

and depression of 1873–79, 148

differences in, 293

disappointment of, 664

in expansions, 107, 399, 709

formation of, 388, 553, 720

endogenization of, 206

exogeneity of in economic models, 205

and harvests, 664

inconsistency of, 374

incorrect, 396, 665

indexes of, 660–61

and interest rates, 330, 681
and intertemporal equilibrium, 54, 374, 396–97
and inventory investment, 5, 434
and investment, 205, 240, 336, 587, 596
and involuntary unemployment, 534
in liquidity preference, 205, 690
in macroeconometric models, 363, 553
measurement of, 330
mistakes in, 238
modelling, difficulty of, 388
and multiple equilibria, 484–85, 609
in natural rate of unemployment, 479
and neutrality of money, 482
periodic changes in, 437, 664
of permanent income, 116
and Phillips curve, 530–31
of policy, 235, 411
in secondary deflation, 373, 550
in signal extraction, 622–23
and staggered price setting, 483
and stock prices, 659–60
and sunspots, 485
and term structure of interest rates, 676–78
and unemployment dynamics, 704
volatility of, 336, 388, 533, 665
of voters, 536–37
expectations, adaptive. *See* adaptive expectations
expectations hypothesis, 676–78
expectations, rational. *See* rational expectations
expenditure, global. *See* global expenditure
experimental price bubbles, **207–09**
exploitation, rate of, 52
external drain, 48, 50, 680

FRB-MIT-PENN model, 422
factorial analysis, 661
Fair model, 422
falling rate of profit, **211–13, 213–16**, 431–32, 433
and crises, 573–74
empirical tests of, **213–16**
Marx's theory of, 51–52, 308, 431, 573, 651, 697–98
rejection, 166, 671
revival, 672
Faustmann-Ohlin theorem, 497
federal deposit insurance. *See* deposit insurance federal
Federal Deposit Insurance Corporation (FDIC), 217–18, 682, 718
federal funds rate, 428
Federal Home Loan Bank Board, 683
Federal Open Market Committee (FOMC), 222–23
Federal Reserve Bank of New York, 41, 42, 222, 655
Federal Reserve Bank of St. Louis model, 420
Federal Reserve System, **219–21, 221–25**, 263, 457, 632, 682
and bank failures, 42–43, 156
in banking crises of 1931 and 1933, 281
banking panics, effect on, 46
Congress and, 222–25
creation of, 78, 134, 613–14

currency, demand for, 143–44
executive branch pressure on, 222–25
and fiscal policy, 233–34
in Great Depression, 217, 219–21, 248, 281–82, 301, 330, 392, 632, 655, 718
as international lender of last resort, 331
in Korean War, 222, 566
as lender of last resort, 217, 392, 718
monetary policy of, 198, 219–21, 677, 696
in 1920–21, 219
in 1920s, 219–20
in 1926–27, 281
in 1936–37, 154–55
in 1965–66, 563
in 1969–70, 564
in 1960s, 478
in 1970s, 478
in 1974–75, 438
in 1982, 438
and Regulation Q, 165
Treasury, relations with, 222, 566–67
after World War I, 151
in World War I, 219
in World War II, 221–22
Federal Savings and Loan Insurance Corporation (FSLIC), 217, 682–83
filters, **227–30**, 469, 526. *See also* detrending; Hodrick-Prescott filter; Kalman filter; moving averages; seasonal adjustment
finance constraint, 188, 336, 339, 403, 596. *See also* liquidity constraints
financial crises, 69–70, 345–46, 627–28
adverse-selection problem in, 330
causes of, 37, 69–70, 359
credit, disruptions in supply of, 69, 670
and deposit insurance, 69
disappointed expectations and, 399
high real interest rates in, 330–31
and investment booms, 205
moral-hazard problem in, 330
and speculative bubbles, 69
See also crises; banking panics; financial panics; panics
financial fragility, 43–45, 140, 438
financial innovation, 165, 464, 487
financial instability, 672
Financial Institutions, Reform, Recovery, and Enforcement Act, 218
financial intermediaries, 231–33, 487. *See also* banks; financial intermediation; New View
financial intermediation, **231–33**, 282
financial panics, 613. *See also* financial crises
financial sector, 43, 212
financial speculation, 70
fine-tuning, 180, 394, 529
fiscal policy, 20, **233–37**, 296–97, 355, 357, 473–74, 499, 628–29
automatic stabilizers, 64, 234
avoidance of crises in 1974–75 and 1982, 438
crowding out, 236

and depression of 1937–38, 154
expectations and, 235
functional finance, 258–259, 393–94
inflation and, 237
interest rates, effect on, 234–35
lags and effectiveness of, 235
limitations of, 180
liquidity constraints and, 235, 237
and monetary policy, 234–36
and monetary reform, 461–62
multiplier-accelerator interaction and, 594
and private-sector debt, 438
in recession of 1969–70, 564
stimulative French policy in Great Depression, 278
Stockholm School on, 414, 473–74, 499, 653
See also countercyclical policy; fine-tuning; functional finance; government spending; monetary policy; Ricardian equivalence; stabilization policy
Fisher ideal index. *See* index numbers
fix-price method, 301, 703
flexible accelerator. *See* accelerator
flow of funds, 179
fluctuations, short-term, 573
Föhl Theorem, 241
force analysis, 408
forced investment, 243
forced saving, **242–43**, 458, 596
    critique by Sraffa, 522, 644–45
    early formulations of, 22, 79, 345, 681
    natural and market rates of interest, 24, 242, 303, 440–41, 506, 522, 584, 644–45
    and overinvestment, 25, 65, 441, 506, 522, 584
    in twentieth-century cycle theories, 24–25, 242, 303–04, 440–41, 458, 506, 522, 583, 584, 588, 644
    under socialism, 588
    See also forced investment
Ford, Gerald, 193
Fordism, 574–75
forecasting, 362–63, 728
    and barometers, 58
    and composite indexes, 108
    cyclical turning points, 108
    Juglar, early attempts by, 346
    and Lucas critique, 411
    and macroeconometric models, 185–86, 362
Fordyce, Alexander, 122–23
foreign trade, 77
forgetfulness, rate of, 14, 16
forward looking theory of consumption, 115–16.
    See also life-cycle hypothesis; permanent-income hypothesis
Fourier decompositions, 468. *See also* spectral analysis
fractal dimension, 93
Franco-Prussian War, 132
free banking, 117, 144, **245–46**, 262, 441, 693–94
    credit expansion, unprofitability under, 246

historical experience of, 245–46
indirect convertibility under, 453
lender of last resort, lack of under, 392
in Scotland, 117–18, 245–46, 521
See also freedom of note issue
Free Banking School, **47–49**, 246, 262, 472, 520–21, 581. *See also* Banking School, Currency School
freedom of note issue, 144, 581, 694. *See also* free banking
French East Indies Company, 443
Fringe Banking Crisis, 37–38
Frisch-type models, 685. *See also* impulse and propagation
full information maximum likelihood, **254–58**
functional finance, **258–59**, 357, 393–94. *See also* fiscal policy
Fundamental Equation of Monetary Dynamics (FEMD), 14, 16

GRREC. *See* Grenoble School
Garn-St. Germain Depository Institutions Act, 165, 218, 603
general disequilibrium models, 561
general equilibrium, 68, 583. *See also* equilibrium
general gluts, 187, 416, 426, 580–81, 599–601, 625. *See also* Say's Law
Genoa Conference of 1922, 301
gestation period, 68, 506
Gibson Paradox, 270, 288, 478
gift-exchange models, 191
Gladstone, William Ewert, 29, 503
Glass, Carter, 263
Glass-Steagall Act, **263–64**, 655
global expenditure, 14–15, 16
gold, 271, 288, 301
Gold Commission, United States, 606
Gold Currency Act, 518
gold discoveries, 365–66
gold exchange standard, 264–66, 268, 271. *See also* gold standard
gold standard, 40, 150, 195, **264–66**, 458–59, 583, 591, 695
    Bank of England, role in, 265–66, 267, 269
    causes and consequences, **267–72**
    central banking under, 88–89
    criticsm of, 22, 57
    cyclical role of, 65
    demise in 1971, 265, 268
    emergency finance under, 267–72
    financial crises under, 265, 472
    financial institutions, failures of, 683
    Great Depression, breakdown in, 268, 276, 278, 279, 285, 301, 550, 576, 643, 653, 721
    and Great Depression of 1873–96, 288
    Great Depression, role in, 266, 269, 281, 285, 301, 631
    and long cycles in prices, 404, 679
    monetary policy under, 457
    periodic cycles under, 301

price level under, 270–71
rules of the game under, 264–65, 583
seasonal fluctuations under, 614
spread of in nineteenth century, 268, 288,
    517, 575
suspensions of, 34, 265, 269, 475
restoration after Civil War, 516
restoration after Napoleonic Wars, 472
restoration after World War I, 152, 220, 301,
    356, 576
uncertainty about U.S. adherence to, 150, 517
World War I, breakdown in, 264, 457, 576
See also convertibility; gold exchange stan-
    dard; metallic standard
Goodwin cycle, 212
Goschen, George, 50
government spending, 212, **233–37**. *See also* fiscal
    policy
Granger causality, 198, 283
Great Contraction, 606. *See also* Great Depression
great crises, 573
Great Depression, 140, 239, 405, 574–75, 682
    bank credit, restriction of, 282
    bank failures, 217, 281–82, 285
    Bank of France, role in, 41
    Bank of United States, failure of, **42–43**
    in Britain, 41, **275–77**
    commodity-price deflation, 358
    consumer-durables spending, effect on, 116
    consumption expenditures, 116, 283
    Credit-Anstalt, failure of, **119–20**
    deflation, 279, 281–82, 670
    demand for currency, 143
    Federal Reserve policy, 281, 330, 392, 557,
        632, 643, 718
    financial crises in, seasonal pattern of, 614
    in France, 41, **277–80**
    in Germany, 278, 576, 588, 631, 724
    gold standard, breakdown in, 268, 276, 278,
        279, 285, 301, 550, 576, 643, 653, 721
    gold standard, role of, 266, 269, 281, 285,
        301, 631
    indebtedness, 140, 631
    initial downturn, 275–76, 281
    international lender of last resort, lack of,
        332, 358–59
    international trade, collapse of, 275–76, 630
    New Deal, effects of, 283–84
    real interest rates in, 330
    real GNP, decline in, 281
    recovery from, 154, 275–76, 281, 284, 296
    Smoot-Hawley tariff, 281, 284–85, 550, **630–
        31**, 670
    stock-market crash. *See* stock-market crash of
        1929
    supply shocks in, 670
    in Sweden, mildness of, 653
    unemployment in, 275, 277, 278–79, 281,
        283–84
    in United States, 275, 278, **280–85**
    wages, 277, 279

See also crisis of 1931; depression of 1937–38
Great Depression of 1873–96, **287–88**
greenbacks, 195, 516–17
Greenspan, Alan, 225, 658
Grenoble School, 573–74. *See also* Parisian School;
    Regulation School; state monopoly
    capitalism
Gresham's Law, 142
growth, 538
growth cycles, 21, 272–73, **289**, 439, 538–39, 569,
    604, 663, 691. *See* classical cycles; trend
    and cycle
growth recessions, 289

Haavelmo bias, 420
habit formation, 201, 673–75
Haddon-Cave, Sir Phillip, 311
harmonic analysis, 12. *See also* spectral analysis
Harrod-Domar model, 297, 625
Harvard ABC Curves, 523. *See also* under
    barometers
Harvard Index of General Business Conditions,
    522–23
harvests, 664
Heckscher-Ohlin Theorem, 497
high-powered money, 89, 232. *See also* monetary
    base
hires. *See* job accessions; worker-job turnover
hoarding, 519, 596. *See also* dishoarding
Hodrick-Prescott filter, 230. *See also* filters
Hong Kong financial crisis, **310–12**
Hopf bifurcation theorem, 489–91
housing, residential, 283
Hungarian School, 76–77
hyperinflation, 153
hypothesis testing, 446
hysteresis, 480, 485–86, 703

IMF. *See* International Monetary Fund
IS-LM model, 67, 179, 240, 362, 692
    and aggregate demand, derivation of, 7–8
    credit market in, 668
    and new monetary economics, 488
    and Phillips curve, 531
    and rational expectations, 554
identification problem, 255, 420, 468, 529, 687
imbalances. *See* disproportionalities
immigration, 148, 150, 371–72
impair investment, 343
impair saving, 343
imperfect competition. *See* monopolistic
    competition
imperfect information, 231, 607
imperialism, 28, 51–52, 200, 309, 310
implicit contracts, **317–19**
    and involuntary unemployment, 317–18
    quits and layoffs, cyclical movements in, 484–85
    and wage rigidity, 70, 284, 703, 715
impulse and propagation, 66–67, 179, **250–51**,
        626, 720–21, 727
    asymmetry, consistency with, 251–52

deterministic nature of propagation mechanism, 251
econometric identification of, 423
inadequacy of, 604
stochastic nature of impulse, 250–51, 687
and time reversibility, 685
See also Frisch, Ragnar Anton Kittel
impulse and response, 387
impulses, 163. *See also under* shocks
income distribution, 278, **319–20**, 471, 562, 625
cyclical behavior of, 319–20, 562
cyclical effects of, 350–51, 519–20, 548–49.
   See also oversaving theories; underconsumption
growth, effect on, 298–99
labor share vs. wage share, 319–20
and long cycles, 366
theories of, 319–20
See also wealth distribution
incomplete markets, **321–23**. *See also* complete markets
increasing risk, principle of, 336, 353
indebtedness, 69–70, 121, 140, 431, 445, 631. *See also* debt; overindebtedenss
independent income, 27–28
index-number theory, 173, 323–24
index numbers, **323–24**
Divisia index, 173–76, 324
Fisher ideal index, 324
Laspyeres index, 142, 173, 324
Paache index, 142, 173, 324
Törnqvist index, 173–74
index numbers, superlative, 174–75
indexed contracts, 457. *See also* tabular standard
Indian Mutiny, 131
indicative planning, 486
indicators, intermediate, 427–28
indicators, lagging. *See* lagging indicators
indicators, leading. *See* leading indicators
indicators, qualitative, **325**
indirect convertibility, 453, 487
Industrial Revolution, 123, **326–28**, 679
industrialization, 64
inflation, 185, **328–29**, 690
and budget deficit, 237
and business cycles, 329, 500–01
causes of, 185, 328–29, 438
comovement of wages and prices, 538, 663
cyclicality of, 329, 538–39
and debt, 438
and demand for money, 146–47
effects of, 22, 236, 238–39, 356, 583
and energy prices, 186, 329
incomes policy and, 329, 583, 585
and natural rate of interest, 476–77
and natural rate of unemployment, 479
persistence after World War II, 70
and profit squeeze, 548
and stock prices, 660–61
in wartime, 139, 151, 270
inflation, expected, 9, 330, 720

inflation externality, 359
inflation tax, 237, 356, 482, 626
inflation-unemployment tradeoff, 528, 538–39, 663. *See also* Phillips curve
information, effects of differences in, 435–36
information, imperfect. *See* imperfect information
infrastructure 365, 405
initial conditions. *See* sensitive dependence on initial conditions
innovation, 65, 365, 404, 650
innovation errors, 447–48
input-output matrix, 274. *See also* Leontieff model
inside capital, 211–12
inside money, 197, 232. *See also* bank deposits
insider-outsider theory, 191, 318–19, 480, 703. *See also* efficiency wages
insolvency, 89
Institute for Trade Cycle Research, 688
institutional theory, 106. *See also* institutionalism
Institutionalism, 27, 168
institutions, cyclical role of, 179–80
integration, 101–02, 711. *See also* cointegration
interest, rate of, 397–99, 415, 429
and demand for money, 145
and intertemporal coordination, 24–25, 53, 303, 440–41
and inventory investment, 300, 434
and investment, 24–25, 240, 300, 303, 338, 440–41, 505–06, 596, 680
monetary phenomenon, 240, 604
as price of capital, 81
and roundaboutness, 24–25, 303, 440–41, 506, 522
in valuation of capital, 81
See also interest rates; natural rate of interest; real interest rates
interest-rate smoothing, 198
interest-rate targeting, 222, 556, 566–67, 667–68
interest rates, 258, **329–31**, 343
and business cycles, 330
cycle theories, role in, 452
cyclical changes in, 445
and inflation, 330, 429, 681
and monetary policy, 330, 556, 667–68
nominal, 238–39, 330, 429, 681
in panics, 330–31
real, 330–31, 429, 681
and saving-consumption decisions, 24–25, 330, 440–41
seasonal fluctuations in, 614
and stock-market prices, 661
See also interest rate of; term structure of interest rates
internal drain, 50, 477
international cooperation, 301, 332
international cycles, 663–64
international equilibrium, 7
international lender of last resort, 41, **331–33**, 358–59
International Monetary Fund, 331–33, 382
international propagation of business cycles, 293, 314, 653

intertemporal coordination, 303
intertemporal equilibrium, 25, 54, 158, 160–61, 396–97
intertemporal substitution, 314, **333–35**, 456, 485, 559, 584
inventories, 18
inventory cycle, 433. *See also* Kitchin cycle
inventory investment, 413, 653
    cyclicality of, 65, 663
    interest rates, effect on, 121, 300, 434
    and Kitchin cycles, 360–61
    lag behind change in output, 3
    and multiplier-accelerator interaction, 361, 413, 433–34
    in recession of 1969–70, 564
    in recessions after World War II, 566–69
    volatility of, 3, 361
    See also investment
investment, 244, 306, **336–39**, 367, 504–06, 629
    acceleration principle, 5, 84, 295, 505–06, 588
    in buildings, 413
    capacity, effect on, 352, 413
    cyclical role of, 295, 361, 584–85, 641, 650
    cyclicality of, 65, 84, 452, 663
    destabilizing effect of, 352
    expectations, dependence on, 240, 337, 587, 589, 596
    and financial sector, 232, 336, 339, 353, 505
    fiscal policy, effect on, 235–36
    forced investment, 243
    and forced saving, 242–43
    government investment, 236
    infrastructure, 365
    and innovation, 365, 376
    instability of, 4, 352, 698
    interest rates, effect on, 24–25, 240, 303, 440–41, 505–06, 596, 680
    loanable-funds doctrine, **400–03**
    and multiplier-accelerator interaction, 296, 337, 413, 498, **593–95**, 653
    optimum, 258
    and profits, 538, 629
    in recession of 1969–70, 564
    and stock-market prices, 662
    and technological change, 273
    theories of, 336–38, 415, **504–06**, 691
    wages, effect on, 273
investment, impair. *See* impair investment
investment climate, 641
involuntary unemployment. *See* unemployment

Jackson, Andrew, 514
Jay Cooke and Company, failure of, 133
job accessions, 607–09. *See also* hires, worker-job turnover
job separations, 607. See also layoffs, quits, worker-job turnover
job turnover, 317. *See* worker-job turnover
Johnson, Lyndon, B. 175, 224
Johnson-Matthey Bank crash, 38
joint-stock banking, 31, 513

joint-stock banks, 36, 262, 344–45
Joint Stock Discount Company, 503
Juglar cycles, 346, **347–48**, 360, 604
just price, 178

Kaldor model, 490–91
Kalman filter, 227, 229. *See also* filters
Kennedy, John F., 195, 224
Keynes effect, 140, 240
Keynesian-cross model, 8
Keynesian economics, 259
Keynesian macroeconomics, 628
Keynesian model:
    aggregate supply curve in, 530
    microeconomic foundations, lack of, 362, 484
    Phillips curve, role in, 530–32
    wage rigidity in, 449–50, 669
Keynesian policy, 259, 433, 450, 459
Keynesian price-quantity adjustment, 542–43
Keynesian Revolution, 508, 636, 643
    cycle theories, effect on, 451, 504, 557, 718
    and oversaving theories, 507
    Smoot-Hawley tariff, interest in, 630
Keynesian theory, 355–57, 588
Keynesian theory, anticipations of, 21, 244, 261, 294, 310, 342–43, 352–53, 356, 375, 425–26, 507, 519, 625
Keynesian theory of unemployment, 607–08
Keynesian theory, static expectations in, 294–95
Keynesianism, 488, 574–75
Kiel Institute of World Economics, 407
Kiel School, 467
Kitchin cycles, 13, 347, **360–61**
kiteflying, 122
Klein-Ball model, 420
Klein-Goldberger model, 251, 362–63, 420
Knickerbocker Trust Co., failure of, 46, 134–35
knife-edge, 52
Kondratieff cycles, 288, 347, 360, **364–66**, 367, 573, 604. *See also* long cycles; long waves
Konjunkturinstitutet, 414
Kuznets cycles, 3–4, 372. *See also* building cycles; long swings

LDC crisis, **380–83**. *See also* Mexican debt crisis
LHM&A model, 422
LINK, Project. *See* Project LINK
labor-force participation, 3
labor, marginal product of, 485
labor market, 167–68
labor-market adjustment, 26
labor/wage, 319–20
labor strikes, 149
labor supply, 519
    elasticity of, 284, 333–34. *See also* intertemporal substitution
    and inflation, 9, 479, 530
    and taxes, effect on, 690
lag structure, 95–97
lagging indicators, 61, 387
Lagrange multiplier statistic, 171

lags, 16, 216–17, 305, **386–87**, 413, 625
    between appearance of profit possibility and
        investment, 404
    between change in demand and output, 413
    between changes in money and money in-
        come, 606
    and chaotic dynamics, 274
    in cobweb model, 100
    between completion of investment and full
        contribution to output, 404
    in data collection, 386, 428, 483
    in decision-making, 386, 427–28
    and deviation from equilibrium, 528
    in difference equations, 161–62
    and fiscal policy, effectiveness of, 235
    gestation period, 506
    between income and consumption, 593
    in interest-rate adjustment, 239
    between invention and adoption of new pro-
        duction process, 118
    between inventory investment and output
        change, 3
    between investment decision and change in
        interest rates, 505
    between investment decision and realization,
        353, 505
    length of, 386
    Lundberg lag, 413
    Mitchell/NBER estimates of, 386–87
    and Phillips curve, 530
    between prices and costs, 709
    between prices and wages, 68, 584, 629
    between production and income, 625
    between profits and consumption, 629
    in recognition, 386
    Robertsonian lag, 413, 585, 593
    between start of investment and completion,
        404
    between unemployment and wage adjustment,
        531, 562
    in vector autoregressions, 710–12
Laval, Pierre, 279–80
Law, John, 40, **378–80**, 442–44, 457
law of reflux. See reflux, law of
Law of the Markets, 597. See also Say's Law
layoffs, 317, 485, 607
leading indicators, 169, **383–86**, 465
    composite indexes of, 383, 387
    diffusion index of, 384–85
    in forecasting, 383
    growth cycles, application to, 289, 383
    identification of 61
    statistically estimated index of, 387
League of Nations, 642
learning, **388–90**, 704
lender of last resort, 30, **391–92**, 445, 627
    Bank of England as, 33, 51, 122, 131, 457,
        502–04, 680
    Bank of France as, 39
    big banks, automatic access to, 45
    central banks as, 89, **391–92**, 668, 680

clearinghouses as, 99
in crisis of 1873, absence of, 148
and endogeneity of money, 198
in financial crises, 359, 391–92, 606
in Great Depression, absence of, 217
moral hazard, 359, 391–92
in Overend Gurney Crisis, absence of, 503–04
solvency as condition for assistance, 38, 89,
    332, 391–92
See also Bank of England; central banking;
    international lender of last resort
Leontief model, 273, 471, 689. See also input-out-
    put matrix
Lidderdale, William, 50–51
Liénard equation, 490
life-cycle hypothesis, 115, **449–50**, 577, 595, 691.
    See also consumption function; perma-
    nent-income hypothesis
likelihood functions, 254
likelihood ratio statistic, 171
limit cycles, 272–74, 489
limiting principle, 426, 600–01
linear models, 21, 86, 538
liquidation, 297
liquidation crisis, 212
liquidity, 140, 145
liquidity constraints, 116, 235, 237, 690–91. See
    also finance constraints
liquidity preference, 196, 294, 397–99, 498–99
    in crises, increase in, 399
    expectations and, 205, 357, 690
    and interest rate, determination of, 402–03,
        596, 717
    risk aversion and, 690
    See also liquidity premium
liquidity-preference theory, 400, 402–03, 429, 498.
    See also loanable-funds doctrine
liquidity premium, 261, **397–99**, 645. See also li-
    quidity preference
liquidity-premium hypothesis, 676–78. See also
    term-structure of interest rates
liquidity trap, 449
Liverpool, Lord, 23, 512–13
loanable funds doctrine, 23–24, **400–03**, 429, 498,
    596, 653, 717
London clearing banks, 38
London Stock Exchange, 637–38
long cycles, 274, 364, 367, 404, 679. See also Kon-
    dratieff cycles; long waves; major cycles
long swings, 3, 230, 364, 371–72, 679. See also
    building cycles; Kuznets cycles
long-wave theories, **404–06**, 548
long waves, 21, 355, 364, 367, 404–06, 604. See
    also Kondratieff cycles; long cycles; ma-
    jor cycles
lower turning point, 77, 320, 404, 505, 641. See
    also upswing
Lucas critique, **410–12**, 529, 554
Lucas supply curve, 485, 531
Lundberg lag, 413
Lyapunov characteristic exponents, 93, 97, 492

MIT model, 450
machine tools, 60, 82, 407
macroeconometric models, 361–63, 458, 710, 728
 estimation techniques, 420
 expectations in, 553
 forecasting with, 67, 185–86, 412, 422–24
 historical development of, 361–62, 368–69, **419–21**, 468, 686–87
 international models, 423
 Lucas critique of, **410–12**, 420–21
 policy analysis with, 186, 412, 422–24
 prediction record of, 618
 problems with, 420
 and rational expectations, 554–55
 regional models, 423
 use of, **422–24**
macroeconomic fluctuations, 273
major cycles, 589. *See also* Kondratieff cycles: long cycles; long waves
maladjustments, horizontal and vertical, 65
malinvestment, 25, 441. *See also* overinvestment
Marcus, Bernard K., 42
Marcus, Joseph S. 42
marginal efficiency of capital, 296, 473, 498
 in depressions, rapid fall in, 399
 expectations, dependence on, 205, 336
 instability of, 205
 money, relationship to, 20
marginal efficiency of investment, 3
marginal propensity to consume. *See* propensity to consume
marginal propensity to save. *See* propensity to save
market anti-inflation plan (MAP), 259
market clearing, continuous, 55, 68, 452, 553–54, 557–59
market-price indicators, **427–28**
markets experimental, **207–09**
markups, cyclical behavior of, 484–85, 670. *See also* profit margins
Martin, William McChesney, 222–24
Marxian capital theory, 59–60, 408. *See also* falling rate of profit
Marxian crisis theory, 51–52, 212–13, 308, 417, 431–32, 433, 601–02, 671–72. *See also* falling rate of profit
Marxian cycle theory, **211–13**. See also falling rate of profit
Marxian political economy, 671
matching function, 608–09
maturity, 657
May equation, 95–96
McCabe, Thomas, 222
measurement errors, 92–93
measurement without theory, 61, 369, 445
memory, 14
menu costs, 70, 484, 542, 545
metallic standard, 226. *See also* bimetallic standard; copper tandard; gold standard; silver standard; symmetallic standard
Mexican debt crisis, 44, 331. *See also* LDC crisis

Michigan Quantitative Research Seminar Model, 422
microelectronic revolution, 408
microfoundations, 70, 362, 484, 653
military expenditure, 27. *See also* government spending; publicexpenditure
Miller, G. William, 224
minor cycles, 589
Mississippi Bubble, 122, 359, 378, **442–44**, 637. *See also* Law, John; South Sea Bubble
Mississippi Company, 378–80, 442–43. *See also* Compagnie d'Occident
Mitchell cycle, 360
mob psychology, 46. *See also* crowd psychology
model evaluation and design, **446–48**
model misspecification, 411
Monetarism, 55, 247–49, 379, 450–53, 606, 718
 anticipations of, 20, 239, 294, 379, 632
 and Austrian theory, 452
 criticism of 450, 488, 691–92
 endogeneity vs. exogeneity of money, 198
 evidence for, 55, 68–69, 247–49, 280–83, 452, 459, 606, 691–92, 718
 interest rates, role in, 452
 investment volatility, 452
 lags in wage-price adjustment, 68
 money-income causality, 68, 247–49, 452, 459, 462–63, 691–92
 monetary policy, 248, 453, 458–59, 478, 718
 and New Classical theories, 452, 459, 692
 policy proposals, 248, 453, 458–59, 718
 real shocks, 452
 Robertson, compared to, 584–85
 wage and price flexibility, 451–52
monetary aggregates, 173–77
monetary analysis, 187
monetary approach to the balance of payments, 313, 458–59, 592, 717
monetary authorities, U.S., 332. *See also* Federal Reserve System; Treasury, United States Department of
monetary base, 89, 284, 391, 666–68. *See also* high-powered money; outside money
monetary business-cycle theories, 55, 121, 239, 451, 472, 557, 601, 705
 See also forced saving; monetary disequilibrium theories; monetary equilibrium theories
monetary control, 667–68
monetary disequilibrium theories, **450–53**, 459, 692
monetary equilibrium, 8, 473, 478, 596
monetary equilibrium theories, 452, **454–56**, 557–58. *See also* monetary business-cycle theories; monetary disequilibrium theories; New Classical economics
monetary expansion, 118
monetary nonneutrality, 485. *See also* neutrality of money
monetary policy, 15, 19–20, 22, 196, 355, **457–59**, **666–68**
 credibility of, 459

in crisis, 29–30, 36–37, 47, 265
in depression, 301, 479, 549–50, 584–85
disinflationary, effects of, 9
and disintermediation, 164–65
distributional aspects of, 644
and effective demand, 187
electoral cycle in, **193–95**
endogeneity of, 198–99
financial fragility and, 45, 438
financial intermediaries, role of, 232
and fiscal policy, 234–36, 585
in Great Depression, 217, 219–20, 276–77,
    281–83, 301
historical development of, 457–58
instruments and targets, 457, 583
interest-rate targeting, 222, 556, 566–67,
    667–68
internal vs. external stabilization, 156, 356
Keynesian ideas about, 458–59
limitations of, 18, 585
market-price indicators and, **427–28**
Monetarism and, 248, 453, 458–59, 632, 718
and natural rate of interest, 441, 458, 596
in a panic, 435, 437
political aspects of, 357, 644
rational expectations and, 459, 621–22
in recession of 1969–70, 564
stabilizing role of, 107, 357
in Sweden, 679, 721
tight, effects of, 7
See also price-level stabilization
monetary reform, 238–39, 312, 410, **460–62**
monetary services, 173–74
monetary shocks, 68, 221, 238, 248, 455, 487–88,
    557–58. *See also* shocks
monetary surprise, 459, 557–58
money, **145–47, 666–68**
assets classified as, 145–47, 666–67
in business cycles, causal role, 197, 248–49,
    450–52, 454–56, 462–64
creation, 55, 231–32, 596, 635–36, 666–67
existence of, reasons for, 55
formal market for, absence of, 427
functions of, 145, 666
illusion, 8, 356–57, 530
See also demand for money; endogenous
    money; exogenous money; high-powered
    money; inside money; neutrality of
    money; supply of money
money-income causality, 19, 68, 248–49, 283, 452,
    459, **462–64**, 691–92, 693–94
money multiplier, 19, 199, 232, 391, 666–68
money stock, 46, 130, 143, 661, 663, 668, 691.
    See also supply of money
monitoring costs, 231
monopolies, 154, 167–68, 541, 587, 659, 671, 709
monopolistic competition, 70, 482–83, 484–86
moral hazard:
    and deposit insurance, 44, 217, 683
    financial crises, exacerbation of, 330
    and implicit contracts, 318

and lender of last resort support, 332, 359,
    391
methods of reducing, 45
Morgan, J.P., 135
Morocco crisis, 576
moving averages, **469–70**
in detrending, 229–30, 611, 639
as filter in phase averaging, 526
problems with, 470
and serial correlation, 617
and spurious cycles, 365, 420, 470, 626
and vector autoregressions, 710–12
multiple equilibria, 284, 350, 484–85
multiplier, 234, 244, 275–76, 295–96, 352, **470–71**,
    585
and accelerator. See multiplier-accelerator
    interaction
early formulations of, 7, 20, 22, 294, 342–43,
    356, 470, 498–99, 505, 652
and effective demand, 471
and savings and investment, equality of, 596
sectoral multiplier, 471
stabilizing effect of, 305
static and dynamic versions, 305, 470–71
multiplier-accelerator interaction, 65, 91, 212, 296,
    413, 471, 498, 557, 585, 587, **593–95**
in ceilings and floors approach, 86–87, 306–
    07, 594
cyclicality of, 5, 538, 593–94
early formulations of, 20, 413, 498, 653
extensions of, 594–95
inventory-investment cycles, 361, 413, 433
investment cycles, 337, 413, 498, 593–94, 653
in Juglar cycle, 347
Robertsonian income-consumption lag, 593
Samuelson's formal model of, 593–94, 653
stability of, 87
time-irreversibility of, 685
See also Samuelson, Paul Anthony
multiplier effects, 486, 550
Mundell-Fleming model, 285, 293
mutual bank insurance, 130
mutual-fund banking, 487

NBER. *See* National Bureau of Economic Research
Napoleon I. *See* Bonaparte, Napoleon
Napoleonic Wars, 22, 34, **475–76,** 624
National Association of Purchasing Managers'
    index, 109
National Bank of Commerce, 134
National Banking System, 134, 642–43
National Bureau of Economic Research (NBER),
    61, 63, 148, 362, 383, 386–87, 439,
    444–45, 465–66, 468, 659, 662, 681,
    727
business-cycle analytical techniques of, 606,
    727
business-cycle chronology of, 130, 133
composite indexes of, 108
dating of business cycles, 152, 289, 386–87,
    466

macroeconometric models, comparison of, 423
qualitative indicators, developed by, 325, 386–87
reference-cycle approach of, 247–48, 386–87
national defense, 267–72
National Dividend, 178
National Industrial Recovery Act (NRA), 154, 284
National Monetary Commission, 134, 576, 613, 642
natural rate of interest, **476–78**
central bank policy and, 477, 596
critique of by Sraffa, 374, 644–45
in cumulative process, 473
equality with market rate and, 473, 582, 596
equilibrium character of, 374
Gibson Paradox, 478
inequality between market rate and, 24, 54, 65, 121, 242, 300, 303, 349, 356, 428, 440, 472, 476–78, 506, 522, 584, 596, 680, 720
loanable-funds framework, determined in, 401–03
long cycles in prices, 404
monetary equilibrium, 473, 478, 596, 720
nonuniqueness of, 584, 644–45
natural rate of unemployment, 453, **479–80**, 690, 692, 721
cyclical fluctuations in, 480
and cyclical unemployment, 479
empirical test of, 482
in expectations-augmented Phillips curve, 530
and Great Depression, 284
high European unemployment in 1980s and 1990s, 480
and hysteresis hypothesis, 480, 485
and neutrality of money, 482
in New Classical theory, 480
nonstationarity of, 705
and sectoral shifts, 615–17
See also nonaccelerating-inflation rate of un-employment (NAIRU)
needs of trade, 49, 268, 556
neoclassical growth model, 180
neoclassical synthesis, 449
neoclassical theory of investment, **337–38**
neo-Marxian crisis theory, 633. See also Marxian crisis theory
von Neumann-Morgenstern expected utility, 322
von Neumann ratio, 618
neutrality of money, 462–63, **481–83**, 621, 644, 680
New Classical economics, 253, 294–95, 300, 374, 452–53, 454–56, 486
anticipated changes in money, unimportance of, 284, 463, 482, 531, 557, 693–94
Great Depression, explanation of, 283
Keynesian models, microfoundations of, 484
market clearing, continuous, 55, 68, 452, 553–54, 557–58
methodological principles, 557–60
monetary surprises, role in, 459, 557–58
natural and market rates of interest, 478

natural rate of unemployment, 480
policy proposals of, 453, 486
rational expectations, 454, 456, 557
signal extraction, 455–56, 558, 621–22, 680
unemployment, explanation of, 283, 333–35, 456, 559
unrealism of, 55, 68
See also monetary equilibrium theories, real business-cycle theory
New Deal, 154, 263, 284, 632, 655
new growth theory, 485
New Keynesian economics, 482–83, **484–86**, 542, 560
new monetary economics, **487–88**, 694
New Institutional economics, 603
New View, 667–68. See also Yale School
New York City Clearing House, 42, 99, 129–30, 133–35, 150
New York Stock Exchange, 657–58
Newton, Sir Isaac, 264
Neyman-Pearson framework, 369
Nixon, Richard, M., 195, 224–25, 565
Nobel Memorial Prize, 13, 291, 302, 361, 368, 370, 394, 420, 449, 473, 497, 593, 686
Nobel Prize, 635
nominal rigidities, 239
nominal shocks, 378. See also shocks
nonaccelerating-inflation-rate of unemployment (NAIRU), 479, 530. See also natural rate of unemployment
nonlinear business cycle theories, 86–87, 272–74, 319, 377, **489–91**, 594–95
advantages of, 66
ceilings and floors, **86–87**, 273–74, 594–95
chaotic behavior, 489, 491
cyclical asymmetry, 21
cyclical persistence explained by, 538
Kaldor model, 350, 490–91
solution, difficulty of, 377, 491
See also nonlinearities
nonlinear statistical inference, **492–94**
nonlinearities, 86–87, 95, 163, 274, 377, 414
ceilings and floors, **86–87**, 163, 273–74
in chaotic models, 95, 163, 414
in cobweb model, 101
and cyclical asymmetry, 21
and time reversibility, 686
nonrenewable resources, 213
nonsense correlations, 101
nonstationarity, 102, 324, 705
normal distribution, 646
normal rate of interest, 720
North Pacific Railroad, 133
nutrition models, 190

OECD. See Organization for Economic Coopera-tion and Development
OPEC. See Organization of Petroleum Exporting Countries
Office of Thrift Supervision, 683
Ohio Insurance and Trust Co., 128–29

oil-price shocks, 8–9, 570–72, 615, 670. See also supply shocks; recessions (supply-side) of 1970s

Okishio Theorem, 698

Okun's law, 500

oligopoly, 650–51

100-percent-reserve banking, 19, 44, 144, 239, 636

open-market operations, 89, 144, 220, 243, 392, 401, 434, 668

optimism and pessimism, waves of, 30, 66, 205, 341, 378, 435, 437, 533–34, 553, 609, 664–66

optimum currency areas, 488

optimal growth model, 91–92, 554

option clause, **501–02**, 627

Organization for Economic Cooperation and Development (OECD), 44, 289

Organization of Petroleum Exporting Countries (OPEC), 570

output shocks, 284. See also shocks

outside money, 232. See also base money; high-powered money

overcapitalization, 505–06

Overend, Gurney and Company, 50, 503–04

Overend, Gurney Crisis, 37, 50, **502–04**. See also crisis of 1866

overindebtedness, 121, 239. See also debt; indebtedness

overinvestment, 24–25, 65, 413, 441, 504–06, 585. See also malinvestment

overinvestment theories, 242, **504–06**

overissue, 48–49, 56–57, 252–53, 478, 555–56, 581, 627, 680

overlapping generations model, 91–92, 323, 666

overproduction, 200, 625, 641

oversaving, 310, 507–08. See also underconsumption

oversaving theories, 310, 425–26, 504, **507–08**, 600. See also underconsumptionism; underconsumption theories

overtrading, 437, 472

Paache index. See index numbers

Palmer, J. Horsely, 31

Palmer rule, 31

panic of 1825, 36, 41, 45, 126, 476, **511–13**. See also crisis of 1825

panic of 1837, 126, **514–16**. See also crisis of 1837

panic of 1857, 331. See also crisis of 1857

panic of 1873, 74, 149, 331. See also crisis of 1873

panic of 1884, 331. See also crisis of 1884

panic of 1890, 331. See also crisis of 1890

panic of 1893, 99, 331, **516–18**. See also crisis of 1893

panic of 1896, 331. See also crisis of 1896

panic of 1900–01, 576

panic of 1907, 46, 99, 331, 576. See also crisis of 1907

paper money, inconvertible, 268, 270, 409

Paris Bourse, 442–44

Parisian School, 573–75. See also Grenoble School;

Regulation School; state monopoly capitalism

Patman, Wright, 223–24

Patterson, William, 33, 269

Peel, Sir Robert, 23, 31

Penn-Central Railroad, default of, 564

perfect foresight, 18

period analysis, 205, 240–41, 471, 471, 498, 652. See also sequence analysis

period of production, 6, 54, 82, 303, **521–22**, 582, 689. See also roundaboutness

periodicity, 30, 159–60, 200, 251, 301, 341, 523, 663

periodogram, 468, 640. See also spectral analysis

permanent-income hypothesis, 115, 283, 449, 577. See also consumption function; life-cycle hypothesis

permanent output, 5

phase averaging, **525–27**

Phillips curve, 284, 295, **529–32**, 704

breakdown of, 530

dynamic aggregate supply curve, derivation of, 9

early estimates of, 239, 419, 687

expectations-augmented, 455, 530–32

in Keynesian models, 530–32

loops around, 528, 531

and money illusion, 530

in New Classical models, 531–32

See also inflation-unemployment tradeoff

Physiocrats, 187, 576

Pigou effect, 243, 689. See also Pigou-Haberler effect

Pigou-Haberler effect. 140–41, **534–36**. See also Pigou effect

Pinto, Perez and Company, failure of, 503

Poincaré-Bendixson Theorem, 489–91

Poincaré map, 94, 98

Poincaré method, 94

Poincaré, Raymond, 41, 278

Pole, Thornton and Co., failure of, 512

policy, endogenization of, 68, 293

policy simulation, 362, 411, 422–24

political business cycle, 193, 347, **536–38**

Political/Income Redistribution Theory (PIT), 193–95

Political/Macroeconomic Outcomes Theory (POT), 193–95

Pollak Foundation for Economic Research, 244

Polo, Marco, 267

Popular Front, 280

population growth, 296, 326, 371–72

population migration, 404

popularity function, 537

portfolio insurance, 657–58

Post-Keynesian Theory, **538–40**, 586–87

disproportionality theory, 168

endogeneity of money, 198, 463–64

expectations, volatility of, 205, 336

income distribution, 538–40

investment and finance, 336, 339

uncertainty, 205, 357

postwar depressions. *See* depressions
predator-prey model, 211–12, 272, 319, 490, 538.
    See also Voltera-Lotka model
preferred-habitat hypothesis, 676
price adjustment. *See* price-quantity adjustment
price bubbles, experimental, **207–09**
price flexibility, 11, 70, 148, 187, 375, 451–52,
    528. *See also* price rigidity
price indexes, 139, 173, 688. *See also* Sauerbeck
    price index
price level, 238, 303, 440, 519–20
price-level stability 429, 473, 535
price-level stabilization, 57, 107, 238–39, 356,
    430, 453, 458, 534, 555, 632, 636, 721
price-quantity adjustment, 274, **541–44**
price rigidity, **544–47**, 716
    cyclical effect of, 533–34
    and employment, 704
    evidence for, 542, 546–47
    inflationary inmplications of, 315
    policy implications of, 535
    quantity adjustment, effect on, 301, 500–01
    reasons for 70, 484–85, 533, 542, 545–47
    spillover effects'of, 484
    supply shocks, amplification of, 571
    welfare effects of 484–85, 545
price-specie-flow mechanism, 48, 264–65, 281,
    313, 627
primary cycles, 12
primary deflation, 550. *See also* secondary deflation
probability theory, 291
productivity, labor, 611–12, 663
profit, falling rate of. *See* falling rate of profit
profit margins, 106–07, 213, 445. *See also* markups
profit, rate of, 425–26, 600. *See also* falling rate of
    profit
profit-sharing, 716
profit squeeze, 212, 431–32, **547–49**
profits, 65, 663
Project LINK, 363, 420, 423
propagation-mechanism, 251, 454–56, 483, 607–
    08, 612
propensity to consume, 20, 115, 584. *See also* con-
    sumption function
propensity to save, 85. *See also* saving
proportionality, 51. *See also* disproportionality
protection, trade, 279, 288, 293
Proxmire, William, 223
psychological rate of economic expansion, 14
psychological rate of interest, 16
psychology, 16, 205, 409, 533
public-choice theory, 194–95, 357
public expenditure, 301, 499, 585, 710
public works, 235, 244, 445, 585
pump priming, 180, **549–50**, 588
purchasing-power parity, 6
pure credit economy, 488. 719–20
putty-clay model, 338, 570

q-theory of investment, 337–38, 691
qualitative indicators, **325**

quantity adjustment. See price-quantity adjustment
quantity indexes, 173
quantity theory of money, 19, 239, 606, 632
    Cambridge version of, 378, 429
    exception to, 6, 458, 488, 590, 627, 652, 693,
      719
    and long cycles, 404
    money-income causality, 459
quits, 190–91, 485, 608. *See also* layoffs, worker-
    job turnover

random shocks, 21, 67, 86. *See also* shocks
random walks. *See* trend
ratchet effects, 628–29. *See also* consumption func-
    tion; relative-income hypothesis
Radcliffe Report, 458, 463
railroad construction, 126, 132, 148, 149
railroads, regulation of, 148–49
rational expectations, 54, 205–06, 207, **553–55**,
    687, 728
    anticipated policy, effects of, 68, 482, 554,
      622
    chaotic dynamics in, 91–92
    consumption expenditures, 116
    differences in expectations and, 293
    equilibrium character of, 374
    evidence, 68, 207
    expected inflation, measurement of, 330
    Great Depression, end of, 285
    and learning, **388–90**
    Lucas critique. *See* Lucas critique
    macroeconometric models, 554–55. *See also*
      Lucas critique
    market-clearing assumption. *See* market clear-
      ing, continuous
    monetary shocks, effect of, 68, 284
    in New Classical economics, 454, 456, 557
    in IS-LM model, 554
    policy rules, 555
    postwar depressions under gold standard, 269
    real business-cycle model, 554, 557. *See also*
      real business-cycle theory
    signal extraction, 621–22. *See also* signal ex-
      traction
    stability, 555
    sticky prices, 554
    stock-market crashes, 657–58
    sunspots, 666
    voter hehavior, 537
reaction time, 14, 16
Reagan, Ronald, 194–95, 224–25
real analysis, 187
real-balance effect, 7–8, 482–83, 534–36, 591–92.
    See also Pigou effect; Pigou-Haberler
    effect
real-bills doctrine, 49, 57, 252, 262, 263, 478, **555–**
    56, 627, 680
real business-cycle theory, 6, 15, 201, **557–60**, 628
    basic model and extensions, 558–59
    credit cycle, 121
    and Frisch-Slutsky approach, 727

growth and cycles, link between, 629, 664

investment, volatility of, 337

and monetary equilibrium theories, 456, 557–58

monetary policy, unimportance of, 459, 692

monetary shocks, possibility of, 454, 557

and natural rate of unemployment, 480, 703

in New Classical theory, 68–69, 459, 463, 480, 559

and oil-price shocks, 69, 572

optimal growth model, 554

real wages and employment, procyclicality of, 485

and sectoral shifts, 69, 572

Solow residual, interpretation of, 69, 485

taste shocks, 674. *See also* shocks

technology shocks in, 68–69, 485–86, 554, 558–60. *See also* shocks

technological progress theories, 557

stochastic disturbances in, 91

weather theories, 468, 557. *See also* sunspot theories

real-monetary interaction, 238

real shocks, 300, 452, 488. *See also* shocks

real wages, 273, 304, 426, 485, 534, **560–62**, 600. *See also* wages

recession of 1918–19, 151–52

recession of 1920–21, 219. *See also* depression of 1920–21

recession of 1923–24, 219–20, 281

recession of 1924–25, 534

recession of 1926–27, 219–20, 281

recession of 1937–38, 221. *See also* depression of 1937–38; Great Depression in United States

recession of 1969–70, **563–65**

recession of 1980, 330

recession of 1981–82, 224, 237, 330

recession of 1990–91, 225

recessions, 399, 642, 677

recessions, demand-side, 570

recessions (supply-side) in the 1970s, **569–72**

recessions after World War II, **566–69**

recursive competitive equilibrium, 181–82

redistribution, 194–95

reference cycles, 25, 61, 108, 247–48, 387, 525

reflux, law of, 48–49, 252–53, 269, 556, 627

regressions, spurious, 101

regulating principle, 426, 600–01

Regulation Q, 164

Regulation School, 278, 548, **573–75**, 634. *See also* Grenoble School; Parisian School; state monopoly capitalism

regulatory regime, 634

Reichsbank, 156, 478, 556, **575–77**, 642. *See also* Deutsche Bundesbank

relative-absolute price confusion, 68, 455–56, 553, 558, 621–22, 680. *See also* signal extraction

relative-income hypothesis, 628. *See also* consumption function

relative prices, 79–80, 452

rent-seeking, 194

representative agent, 180–81

reproduction, 60

reproduction schemes, 59–60, 166–68, 308, 376, 407, 540–41, 548, 697

reservation wage, 607

reserve army of unemployed, 52, 166, 212, 294, 319–20, 541, 548

reserve requirements, 45, 176, 197

reserves, bank, 89, 667–68

Residual Diagnostic for Deterministic Chaos, 493

returns to scale, increasing, 231

Reuss, Henry, 223

revisionism, 53, 354–55, 417, 697

Revolutionary War, 123

Reynaud, Paul, 279

Ricardian equivalence, 236–37, 535, **577–80**

Ricardo effect, 302, 304, 349–50

rigid wages. *See* wage rigidity

Riksbank, 88

risk, diversification of, 231

risk premium, 660–61, 676–77

Robertsonian lag, 413, 593

rocking-horse analogy, 12, 250, 721

Roosevelt, Franklin D., 140, 144, 154, 244, 285, 642–43

roundaboutness of production, 54, 81, 506. *See also* period of production

Royal Bank of Scotland, 502

rules of the game, 264–65, 583. *See* the gold standard

rules vs. discretion, 694

Russell, John, 503

Russia, business cycles in, **72–75**, 524–25

Russia, government of, 50

Sauerbeck price index, 85. *See also* price indexes

saving, 7, 65, 115, 242–43, 350, 394, 400–02

Saving Association Insurance Fund (SAIF), 218, 683

saving, impair. *See* impair saving

savings and investment, 187, 519

adjustment between, 9, 85, 242, 244, 294, 342–43, 356, 400–03, 413, 477, 497–98, 505–06, 507–08, 585, 586, 596

equality of, 8, 24, 85, 344, 400–03, 470, 473, **595–96**, 599, 635–36, 698, 720

identity between, 426, 602

savings equals investment, **595–96**

Say's Identity, 598, 720. *See also* Say's Law

Say's Law, 6, 63, 187, 295, 451, 507, 580–82, 597–99, **599–602**

and reflux, law of, 252

rejection of, 27, 294, 310, 315, 342, 355, 357, 425–26, 497, 625, 720

supply restrictions, cumulative effects of, 315, 559–60, 582

See also general gluts; Law of Markets; Say's Identity; Walras's Law

Schact, Hjalmar, 576

Scottish banks, 246, 345

search externalities, 608–09
search theory, 314, 317, **607–09**, 690, 703
seasonal adjustment, 227, 229–30, **609–11**, 696–97
seasonal cycles, 134, **612**
seasonal fluctuations, 12, **613–15**, 677. *See also*
    currency, demand for; demand for
    money
Second Bank of the United States, 125, 514. *See*
    also Bank of the United States
secondary cycles, 12
secondary deflation, 26, 373, 550, 588
secondary markets for bank loans, 45
secondary secular movements, 371–72
sectoral cycles, 539
sectoral fluctuations, 274
sectoral interaction, 179–80, 273–75, 429, 539,
    558–60
sectoral interrelationships, 186
sectoral multiplier, 471
sectoral shifts, 69, 572, **615–17**
secular stagnation, 196, 296, 393
Securities Exchange Commission Report, 656
Select Committee on Banks of Issue, 36
sensitive dependence on initial conditions, 86–87,
    92, 491–92. *See also* chaos
separation theorem, 690
sequence analysis, 397, 414. *See also* period analysis
serial correlation, **617–18**
service sector, 64
Seven Years' War, 122
Shah of Iran, 570
Shay's Rebellion, 124
Sherman, John, 517
Sherman Silver Purchase Act, 517
shipbuilding, 686
shirking, 190–91
shocks, 67, 387
    anticipated vs. unanticipated, 612
    demand, 485–86, 670
    exogenous, 86, 163, 248
    monetary, 68, 221, 284, 298, 300, 454–55,
        487–88, 557
    nominal, 378
    oil shocks, 8–9, 570–72, 615, 670
    output, 284
    persistent effects of, explanations for, 300,
        485–86
    random, 21,67, 86, 91
    real, 300, 452, 488
    supply, 9, 569–72, **669–70**
    taste, 674
    technology, 68–69, 181–82, 273–74, 485–86,
        554, 558–60
short-selling, 208
signal extraction, 228, **621–23**, 665
    nominal vs. real, 621
    permanent and transitory changes, 455–56
    relative and absolute prices 455–56, 553, 558,
        621–22
    seasonal adjustment, 611
Silver Purchase Act of 1878, 148, 195

silver standard, 516–17. *See also* bimetallic stan-
    dard; gold standard; metallic standard
simulations, econometric, 67, 179, 186
Sinai-Boston model, 422
Sir William Eckford's, failure of, 512
Slutsky-Yule effect. *See* Yule Slutsky effect
Snyder, John, 222
Smoot-Hawley tariff, 281, 284–85, 550, **630–31**,
    670
smoothing, data, 469
Social Credit Party, 178
social security, 296
social structure of accumulation, 320, 366, 404,
    548, **633–34**
social unrest, 148–49
socialism, 605
socialist economies, business cycles in, **75–78**, 119,
    588
Solow residual, 69, 485
South Sea Bubble, 122, 359, 511, **637–39**. *See also*
    Law, John; Mississippi Bubble
South Sea Company, 442–44, 637–39
Special Drawing Rights, 332
Specie Circular, 514–15
spectral analysis, 228–30, **639–40**
Sproul, Allen, 222
stability, dynamic, 528
stability, macroeconomic, 9, 250, 539, 542, 584
stabilization policy, 226, 529. *See also* counter-
    cyclical policy; fine-tuning; fiscal policy;
    functional finance; monetary policy
stable paretian distributions, **646–47**
stagflation, 451, 573, 583, 587
staggered price setting, 482–83, 486
Stalin, Joseph, 419, 525, 649
state monopoly capitalism, 573–74, **648–50**. See
    also Grenoble School; Parisian School;
    Regulation School
stationarity, 324, 685
sticky prices, 535
sticky wages, 607, 680. *See also* wage rigidity
stochastic disturbances, 91
stock-market booms, 443, 476, 654–655
stock-market crash of 1929, 220, 239, **654–55**,
    656, 658
    Bank of United States, effect on, 42
    in Britain, 276
    initial recovery from, 281–82
    securities of affiliates of commercial banks, 263
    Smoot-Hawley tariff, role in, 630
stock-market crash of 1987, 332, **655–58**, 662
stock-market crash of 1989, **655–58**
stock-market crashes, 133, 444
stock-market prices, 202, 656, **659–62**
    cyclical changes in, 661
    in depression of 1882–85, 150
    in depression of 1937–38, 154
    expectations and, 659–60
    leading indicator, 659
    macroeconomic variables, relationship to,
        661–62

time reversibility of, 686
See also excess volatility
Stockholm School, **396–97, 413–14, 497–99, 652–54.**
    See also Swedish School
strange attractors, 489, 491. *See also* attractors;
    attractors, chaotic
strategic complementarities, 484–85
Strong, Benjamin, 219–20
structural change, 408
structural time series models. *See* time series
stylized facts, 63, 612, **662–64**
Suez crisis, 567, 670
sunspot theories, 29, 341–42, 557, **664–66**. *See also*
    weather theories
sunspots, 11, 323, 341, 485, 664
superneutrality of money, 456, 482
supply of money, 64, 197–99, **666–68**
    banks, role in, 55, 231–32, 252–53, **487–88,**
        627, **666–68**
    central-bank control over, 55, 89, 176, 463–
        64, 667–68
    elasticity of, 398–99
    exchange-rate regime and, 198, 458, 668
    exogeneity of, 55, 197–99, 248–49, 452, 463,
        623
    under gold standard, 268
    government deficit, effect on, 15, 668
    informational content of, 623
    interest rates and 667–68
    lender of last resort role, 391–92, 668
    money multiplier and 19, 199, 232, 294, 391,
        666–68
    nonbank intermediaries, role in, 231–32, **487–
        88,** 667
    responsiveness to demand, 55, 252–53, 268,
        270, 627, 668
    See also money stock
supply shocks, 9, 569–72, **669–70**. *See also* shocks
supply-side economics, 414, 690
Supreme Court, United States, 154
surplus value, 214–15, 431, 671, 697
surprise, 620–21
Survey of Income and Program Participation, 334–
    35
Swedish National Institute for Economic Research,
    414
Swedish School, 440–41. *See also* Stockholm
    School
Sword-Blake Company, 639
symmetallic standard, 430. *See also* bimetallic stan-
    dard; metallic standard
symmetry. *See* asymmetry

Tardieu, André, 277–78
tariffs, 195, 276, 285, 288. *See also* Smoot-Hawley
    tariff
taste shocks, **673–75**. *See also* shocks
taxes, 215, 234–37. *See also* fiscal policy
technical change
    adjustment to, 273, 408
    under capitalism, 539–40

displacement of labor, 408
and falling rate of profit, 213, 431
technical progress, 698
    cyclical role of, 59, 557
    growth, effect on, 298
    in Industrial Revolution, 326–27
    organic composition of capital, effect on, 51
    proportionality, effect on, 51
technological change. *See* technical change
technological progress. *See* technical progress
technological unemployment, 408
technology shocks, 68–69, 181–82, 273–74, 485–
    86, 558–60. *See also* shocks
temporary equilibrium, 396–97, 653
Temporary National Economic Committee, 154,
    297
term structure of interest rates, 415, **676–78**. *See*
    also expectations hypothesis; liquidity-
    premium hypothesis; preferred habitat
    hypothesis
Thatcher, Margaret, 311
thin-market externalities, 484, 608–09
thrift crisis, 218, **682–84**. *See also* deposit insur-
    ance, federal
time, 82
time aggregation, 526–27
time, continuous vs. dicrete, 93–96
time preference, 25, 398
time, psychological, 16
time reversibility, **684–86**
time series:
    chaotic, 92
    components of, 229–30
    decomposition of, 21, 469
    detrending of, 110–11, 202–03, 229–30, 617
    filters, **227–30**, 469, 526
    nonstationarity of, 102, 324
    spectral analysis of, 228–30, **639–40**
    spectrum of, 228, 639
    structural models of, 228–29
Törnquist index, 173–74. *See also* index numbers
transactions costs, 715–16
transmission mechanism, intersectoral, 558–60
traverse, 59–60, 407
Treasury, United States, 150, 154
    in crisis of 1857, 129
    in crisis of 1907, 134–35
    Federal Reserve, relations with, 222, 566–67
    international lender of last resort, 331
    in panic of 1893, 518
Treasury view, 301
Treaty of Versailles, 631
trend, 110, 617
trend, ambiguity of, 21
trend, boom's effect on, 351
trend and cycle, 297–99, 306–07, 353, 376–77,
    404, 629, 651, 663–64, 689, **696–97**
trends and random walks, **696–97**
troughs, 61
Truman, Harry S., 222
tulipmania, 62, 656–57, **699–701**

turning points, 108, 423, 663
turnover costs, 190
turnover, worker-job. *See* worker-job turnover

uncertainty, 55, 205, 357, 373, 398, 587, 620, 666
underconsumption, 52, 200, 308, 310, 431–32, 507, 651
underconsumptionism, 6, 51, 178, 200, 319–20, 354–55, 417, 548. *See also* oversaving theories; underconsumptionist theories
underconsumptionist theories, 53, 624–25, 671, 697. *See also* oversaving theories; underconsumptionism
underemployment, 703
underemployment equilibrium, 449
unemployment, 619, **703–04**
    in Britain in 1920s, 591
    in crisis of 1819, 125
    in crisis of 1857, 131
    cyclical, 26, 333, 479, 607–09
    in depression of 1882–85, 149–50
    in depression of 1937–38, 154
    disguised, 586
    duration of, 703
    efficiency-wage theory. *See* efficiency wages
    and expectations of future wages, 314
    fiscal policy, 234
    frictional, 479, 703
    in Great Depression, 275, 277, 278, 279, 283–84, 532–33
    turnover costs, 190
    implicit-contract theory. *See* implicit contracts
    intertemporal-substitution hypothesis. *See* intertemporal substitution
    involuntary, 189–90, 217, 314, 317, 586, 608, 703
    Keynesian theory of, 607
    in Marxian theory, 212
    mismeasurement of, 333
    natural rate. *See* natural rate of unemployment
    Ohlin's analysis of, 652
    population growth, effect on, 3
    and Say's law, 599–602
    search theory. *See* search theory
    sectoral shifts and, 615–17
    structural, 26, 333, 479, 703
    technological, 408
    and unemployment benefits, 591
    wage rigidity, 429, 449, 533–34, 591–92, 680, **715–16**
    See also hysteresis; insider-outsider theory
unemployment equilibrium, 188–89, 596
union contracts, 70
Union Générale, failure of, 39, 151. *See also* bank failures
unions, 314–15, 328, 548
unobserved components model, 227–28, 610
unproductive expenditures, 213
unit of account, 487
unit period, 413

unit root tests, 105, 111, **705–06**. *See also* Dickey-Fuller test
unit roots, 101, 105, 485, 492, 629, 705
upper turning point, 54, 77, 320, 373, 404, 413, 505, 641
upswing, 21, 504–06, 539, 641
user cost, 173–74, 176

vacancies, 191
valuation equilibrium, 181
variance bound, 203
vector autoregressions (VAR), 67, 102,420–21, 618, **710–13**
velocity of money, 14, 19–20, 79
    cyclical variation in, 145, 435, 663
    stability of, 19, 463, 584, 691
    See also demand for money
Vietnam War, 564–65
virtual wealth, 635
Volcker, Paul, 224–25
Volterra-Lotka model, 211–12, 272, 319, 538. *See also* predator-prey model

wage and price controls, 224. *See also* incomes policy
wage and price flexibility, 141, 333, 357, 393, 451–52
wage rigidity, 284, 301, 426, 429, 535, 591, 704, **715–16**
    causes of, 357, 533, 715
    cyclical effect of, 534, 715–16
    efficiency wages and, 485
    increase in, reasons for, 70, 716
    and involuntary unemployment, 317
    in Keynesian model, 356–57, 449, 669
    policies to reduce, 534, 716
    quits and layoffs, cyclical behavior of, 485
    real vs. nominal rigidity, 715
    relative wages and, 690
    and unemployment equilibrium, 188–89
    unions and, 314–15
    See also sticky wages
wage share, 319–20
wages, 211–12, 317, 538, 547–48, 663–64. *See also* real wages
Wagner Act, 284
Wald statistic, 171
Walrasian general equilibrium model, 689
Walras's Law, 357, 401, 598, 601, **717**. *See also* Say's Identity; Say's Law
War of 1812, 124–25
War of the Grand Alliance, 33
warranted rate of growth, 29
wars, 139, 405–06
Wars of the French Revolution, crises of, 122. *See also* Napoleonic Wars
Watson, Overend and Company, failure of, 503
wealth, 242–43
wealth distribution, 635. *See also* income distribution
wealth effect, 276, 662
wealth, monetary, 175

wealth-saving relation, 8
weather theories, 468, 557, 665. *See also* Sunspot theories
Wentworth and Co., failure of, 512
Western Bank of Scotland, failure of, 131
Wharton Model, 363, 420, 422
Wicksell effects, 81–82
William of Orange, 31, 269
William III. See William of Orange
Wisconsin School, 106
wisselruiterij (kiteflying), 122

worker and job turnover, 284, 317, **722–23**
World War I, crisis at outset of, 38. *See also* crisis of 1914
World War II, 221

X-factor, 16
X-11 program, 526, 611

Yale School, 232. *See also* New View
yield curve, 676–78
Yule-Slutsky effect, 227, 470